The restaurants included in
The Good Food Guide
are the very best in the UK

Distributed by Combined Book Services Ltd
Unit D, Paddock Wood Distribution Centre, Paddock Wood, Tonbridge, Kent, TN12 6UU
Copyright © Waitrose Ltd, 2019. Waitrose Ltd, Doncastle Road, Bracknell, Berkshire, RG12 8YA

Data management and export by AMA DataSet Ltd, Preston
Printed and bound in Italy by LEGO SpA using paper from sustainable sources

A catalogue record for this book is available from the British Library
ISBN: 978 0 95379 838 4

Maps designed and produced by Cosmographics Ltd, cosmographics.co.uk
Mapping contains Ordnance Survey data © Crown copyright and database right 2019
UK digital database © Cosmographics Ltd, 2019. Greater London map and North and South London
maps © Cosmographics Ltd, 2019. West, Central and East London map data © Cosmographics Ltd,
2019 used with kind permission of VisitBritain.

Consultant Editor: Elizabeth Carter
Editor: Amber Dalton
Content Producer: Ria Martin

The Good Food Guide makes every effort to be as accurate and up to date as possible. All inspections
are anonymous, and main entries have been contacted separately for details. As we are an annual
publication, we have strict guidelines for fact checking information ahead of going to press, so some
restaurants were removed if they failed to provide the information we required. The editors' decision
on inclusion and scores in *The Good Food Guide* is final, and we will not enter into any discussion on the
matter with individual restaurants.

The publisher cannot be held responsible for any errors or omissions or for changes in the details given
in this guide. Restaurants may close, change chefs or adjust their opening times and prices during the
Guide's lifetime, and readers should always check with the restaurant at the time of booking.

We would like to extend special thanks to the following people: Iain Barker, Francesca Clarke,
Ruth Coombs, Alan Grimwade, Joanne Murray, Alan Rainford, Rochelle Venables, Ashleigh Vinall,
Lisa Whitehouse and Blanche Williams. And thanks in particular to all of our hard-working inspectors.

thegoodfoodguide.co.uk

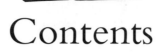

Contents

Introduction

Elizabeth Carter, Consultant Editor

For 69 years *The Good Food Guide* has been casting a critical eye over the UK's restaurants, pubs, bistros and cafés, longer than any other British guide to eating out. But why buy a printed guide book when we have ready access to instant, free information on the country's dining scene via digital media? To put it simply, the Guide's long-established, dependable voice is needed now more than ever. With such a wealth of information available, you need advice you can trust. Each year *The Good Food Guide* is fully researched and written from scratch. Entries are based on anonymous inspections, bolstered by feedback from readers to give a balanced view of what a restaurant is really like.

We all like a list

We compile an annual list of the top 50 restaurants in the country. Made up of the Guide's highest scorers, it is all about celebrating brilliant, innovative and consistent cooking and world-class service, wonderfully epitomised by L'Enclume and Core by Clare Smyth which are numbers one and two this year. It's been a delight to watch Mark Birchall of Moor Hall (our only new nine) making his way through the Guide's ratings at such an electric pace. And it says so much about the strength of British cooking that this year an extraordinary number of promising and dynamic chefs have scored seven in the Guide, making them all candidates for inclusion in

the Top 50. We've had to make some tough decisions, though. By summing up the cream of the UK's dining scene in just 50 places, it means some very good restaurants haven't made the cut. But we think it is crucially important to include the likes of Inver and Cail Bruich in Scotland, The Black Swan at Oldstead, Wilks in Bristol, Stockport's Where the Light Gets In, and London's Trinity – we are incredibly lucky to have such talent in the list for the first time and we believe these places have the promise to reach the very top.

Make do and mend

The Good Food Guide team has been impressed by the way so many chefs have adopted an eco outlook, reducing waste as a corrective to our disposable culture. 'My rule is that anything we can eat does not go in the bin,' says Chantelle Nicholson of Tredwells in London's Covent Garden and it's a view shared by lots of others who are exploring new uses for stale bread, spent coffee grounds, vegetable peelings, bruised fruit, offcuts from fish and meat, langoustine shells and much more. Many of these initiatives to reduce waste start with careful sourcing and ordering. Meat may be used sparingly and is often bought as whole organic carcasses, as at Brassica in Dorset where Berkshire pork and hogget is butchered on site with every part going in to the final dishes. And those chefs who aren't able to turn food scraps in to something delicious are handing

> 'The Guide is your opportunity to have a say in whether you have been surprised, delighted, let down or ripped-off by what you have eaten.'

them over to specialist companies which use anaerobic digesters to create biofertiliser. In recognition of his tremendous work in this field, we've named Douglas McMaster of Silo as our Sustainability Champion this year and can't wait for his move from Brighton to the Crate Brewery in east London.

Chain reaction

Once again, the Guide features a few small chains and we are happy to note that these distinctive and resolutely customer-focused restaurant groups continue to flourish, particularly in London. Some old stagers like the steak house group, Hawksmoor or Dishoom, a clever concept based on the Irani cafés of old Mumbai, have blossomed over the past few years and now have outposts in Manchester and Edinburgh. In the North West, Gary Usher's crowdfunding model means that many customers come ready to love his good-value, easygoing bistros (currently numbering six) including recent newcomers Pinion in Prescot and Manchester's Kala. After all, if you've helped to get a restaurant off the ground, you're more likely to eat there – especially if your name is on the founders' wall. At his Six by Nico chain which started in Glasgow, Nico Simeone's enterprising formula of a six-course tasting menu that changes every six weeks has recently spawned offshoots in Edinburgh, Belfast and, as we went to press, Manchester.

Calling time on no-shows

But it's not all rosy. If there's one issue that is likely to exercise chefs and owners, it's that curse of the moment, the no-show. The industry loses an estimated £16 billion of revenue every year because of diners who don't cancel a reservation in good time, thereby allowing their table to be offered up to other hopefuls. It's a problem that's at its worst on high-pressure days, the ones that a restaurant could book many times over such as Mother's Day, Valentine's Day and New Year's Eve and that are unlikely to be filled by walk-ins. These no-shows hit a restaurant's bottom line hard so it's no wonder some owners have taken to social media to vent their frustration.

A cultural shift

Once upon a time, you just picked up the phone and made a reservation directly with the restaurant – when it was open. Now we can do it online at any time of the day or night via third-party booking sites such as OpenTable or ResDiary, making it easier than ever to bag a reservation, perhaps at several places at once just to keep your options open. And while it is, theoretically, just as easy to cancel, it seems many customers don't bother.

Reminders, whether automated from a bookings system, or an actual call from the restaurant, are not failsafe. Ditto deposits: pitch them too low and they won't be a sufficient deterrent, too high and customers

> *'We were last here over 20 years ago and thought we'd revisit. We should have checked the GFG! Formulaic, uninspired, mass-produced, unloved cooking... and with a 14.5% service charge.'*

may book elsewhere; and in any case plenty of independents don't feel comfortable making these requests, preferring bookings to be based on mutual trust. 'I only want a meal, not a mortgage,' said one frustrated reader after grappling with a particularly awkward online booking system that required credit card details to secure a reservation. Some restaurants with a fixed-price menu use the Tock system of pre-paid tickets – Cambridge restaurant, Vanderlyle, The Fat Duck in Bray and London's Clove Club all require upfront payment, just as if you're going to the theatre or cinema. But watch out; policies vary and you may lose your money if you cancel less than 28 days before your reservation.

The human touch
Plenty of restaurant owners like the personal connection that comes from phone bookings which they feel instils a sense of responsibility in diners to honour their commitment, or cancel in a timely fashion. This doesn't just happen in small-scale neighbourhood spots either: Restaurant Sat Bains insists on phone bookings, Le Champignon Sauvage makes calling the easiest option, and Le Gavroche and Restaurant Gordon Ramsay are among a number of top-rated restaurants to give their customers a clear choice by displaying a telephone number (and office hours) on the bookings pages of their websites.

Whether it's effective for restaurateurs to use social media to rant about or even 'name and shame' offenders is a moot point, though it's easy to understand their anger and frustration. One thing is for certain, though; something has to change for the sake of the future health of the independent restaurants we love.

Send us your review
We need you to tell us about your experiences in UK restaurants. I say this every year, but the interest of the public in commenting on eating out continues unabated and the Guide is your opportunity to have a say in whether you have been surprised, delighted, let down or ripped-off by what you have eaten. To everyone who has used our online review system at thegoodfoodguide.co.uk over the last year, many thanks, and please keep the reports coming in – we read every piece of feedback and may well use some of your recommendations and quotes in next year's edition. By buying and using this guide you are helping to safeguard against a bad meal out for you and future readers.

Happy eating.

Elizabeth Carter
Consultant Editor

The Top 50
The UK's best restaurants

1   L'Enclume, Cumbria (10)
2   Core by Clare Smyth, London (10)
3   Restaurant Nathan Outlaw, Cornwall (10)
4   Ynyshir, Powys (9)
5   Moor Hall, Lancashire (9)
6   Claude Bosi at Bibendum, London (9)
7   Restaurant Gordon Ramsay, London (9)
8   Restaurant Sat Bains, Nottingham (9)
9   Casamia, Bristol (9)
10 Pollen Street Social, London (9)
11 Adam Reid at The French, Manchester (8)
12 Restaurant Story, London (8)
13 The Raby Hunt, County Durham (8)
14 Restaurant Andrew Fairlie, Tayside (8)
15 The Greenhouse, London (8)
16 The Ledbury, London (8)
17 Marcus, London (8)
18 The Fat Duck, Berkshire (8)
19 Roganic, London (8)
20 Fraiche, Merseyside (8)
21 Bohemia, Jersey (8)
22 Midsummer House, Cambridgeshire (8)
23 The Peat Inn, Fife (8)
24 Le Champignon Sauvage, Gloucestershire (8)

25 The Kitchin, Edinburgh (7)
26 Lake Road Kitchen, Cumbria (7)
27 Forest Side, Cumbria (7)
28 Orwells, Oxfordshire (7)
29 A. Wong, London (7)
30 Whatley Manor, The Dining Room, Wiltshire (7)
31 Trinity, London (7) *New*
32 Matt Worswick at the Latymer, Surrey (7)
33 Inver, Argyll & Bute (7) *New*
34 The Black Swan, Yorkshire (7) *New*
35 Restaurant James Sommerin, Glamorgan (7)
36 Winteringham Fields, Lincolnshire (7) *New*
37 The Sportsman, Kent (7)
38 The Whitebrook, Monmouthshire (7)
39 The Man Behind The Curtain, Leeds (7) *New*
40 Paul Ainsworth, Cornwall (7) *New*
41 Alchemilla, Nottingham (7) *New*
42 Wilks, Bristol (7) *New*
43 Cail Bruich, Glasgow (7) *New*
44 Where The Light Gets In, Greater Manchester (7) *New*
45 Sosban & The Old Butcher's, Anglesey (7) *New*
46 Restaurant Martin Wishart, Edinburgh (7)
47 Le Gavroche, London (7)
48 Artichoke, Buckinghamshire (7)
49 Adam's, Birmingham (7)
50 Castle Terrace, Edinburgh (7)

Restaurants marked '*New*' did not appear in the Top 50 in 2019

Editors' Awards

The editors of *The Good Food Guide* are delighted to recognise the following restaurants and chefs for their talent and commitment to excellence.

Chef of the Year
Pam Brunton
Inver, Strachur, Argyll & Bute

Chef to Watch
Will Devlin
The Small Holding, Kilndown, Kent

Restaurant of the Year
The Mash Inn
Radnage, Buckinghamshire

Best New Entry, UK
The Woodsman
Stratford-upon-Avon, Warwickshire

Best New Entry, London
Peg
Hackney

Sustainability Champion
Douglas McMaster

Best Local Restaurants

We asked our readers to nominate their favourite neighbourhood restaurants, places that give a warm welcome and share a passion for local produce, plus a commitment to the community. *The Good Food Guide* judges visited the finalists before selecting a winner in each region, plus an overall UK winner.

OVERALL WINNER
South East England
The Little Gloster
Gurnard, Isle of Wight

REGIONAL WINNERS
Wales
The Warren
Carmarthen, Carmarthenshire

Scotland
Number 16
Glasgow

North England
Route
Newcastle upon Tyne

Central & East England
Woolf & Social
Norwich, Norfolk

South West England
Brassica
Beaminster, Dorset

How to use
The Good Food Guide

In our opinion, the restaurants included in *The Good Food Guide*
are the very best in the UK; this means that simply getting
an entry is an accomplishment to be proud of, and a
Score 1 or above is a significant achievement.

T he *Good Food Guide* is completely
rewritten every year and compiled
from scratch. Our research list is
based on the huge volume of feedback we
receive from readers, which, together with
anonymous inspections by our experts,
ensures that every entry is assessed afresh.
Please keep the reports coming in: visit
thegoodfoodguide.co.uk for details.

Scoring

We add and reject many restaurants when we
compile each guide. There are always subjective
aspects to ratings systems, but our inspectors
are equipped with extensive scoring guidelines
to ensure that restaurant bench-marking
around the UK is accurate. As we take into
account reader feedback on each restaurant,
any given review is based on several meals.

'New chef' in place of a score indicates
that the restaurant has had a recent change
of chef and we have been unable to score it
reliably; we particularly welcome reports
on these restaurants.

Local Gem

These entries highlight a range of brilliant
neighbourhood venues, bringing you a wide
choice at great value for money. Simple cafés,
bistros and pubs, these are the places that sit
happily on your doorstep, delivering good,
freshly cooked food.

Readers Recommend

These are direct quotes from our reader
feedback and highlight places that have
caught the attention of our loyal followers.
Reports are particularly welcome on
these entries also.

Vegetarian and vegan

While many restaurants offer individual dishes
suitable for non-meat eaters, those marked
'V menu' (vegetarian) and 'Vg menu' (vegan)
in the 'Details' section of the entry offer
dedicated menus.

The Good Food Guide scoring system

1 Capable cooking with simple food combinations and clear flavours, but some inconsistencies.

2 Decent cooking, displaying good technical skills and interesting combinations and flavours. Occasional inconsistencies.

3 Good cooking, showing sound technical skills and using quality ingredients.

4 Dedicated, focused approach to cooking; good classical skills and high-quality ingredients.

5 Exact cooking techniques and a degree of ambition; showing balance and depth of flavour in dishes.

6 Exemplary cooking skills, innovative ideas, impeccable ingredients and an element of excitement.

7 High level of ambition and individuality, attention to the smallest detail, accurate and vibrant dishes.

8 A kitchen cooking close to or at the top of its game. Highly individual with impressive artistry. There is little room for disappointment here.

9 Cooking that has reached a pinnacle of achievement, making it a hugely memorable experience for the diner.

10 Just perfect dishes, showing faultless technique at every service; extremely rare, and the highest accolade the Guide can give.

Symbols

We contact restaurants that we're considering for inclusion ahead of publication to check key information about opening times and facilities. They are also invited to participate in the £5 voucher scheme. The symbols against each entry are based on the information given to us by each restaurant.

£XX The average price of a three-course dinner, excluding drinks.

£30 It is possible to have three courses, excluding drinks, at the restaurant for £30 or less.

£5 OFF The restaurant is participating in our £5 voucher scheme. See vouchers for terms and conditions.

The restaurant has a wine list that our experts consider to be outstanding, either for an in-depth focus on a particular region, attractive margins on fine wines, or strong selections by the glass.

Accommodation is available.

London explained

London is split into six regions. Restaurants within each region are listed alphabetically. Each main entry and Local Gem has a map reference. Here are the areas covered in each region.

CENTRAL
Aldwych, Bloomsbury, Covent Garden, Fitzrovia, Holborn, St James's, Marylebone, Mayfair, Pimlico, Soho, Victoria, Westminster

NORTH
Archway, Crouch End, Finsbury Park, Hampstead, Highbury, Islington, St John's Wood, Kensal Green, King's Cross, Maida Vale, Newington Green, Primrose Hill, Stoke Newington, Swiss Cottage, West Hampstead

EAST
Bethnal Green, Canary Wharf, City, Clerkenwell, Dalston, Farringdon, Hackney, Hackney Wick, Haggerston, Hoxton, Leytonstone, Moorgate, Old Street, Shoreditch, Spitalfields, Tower Hill, Whitechapel

SOUTH
Balham, Battersea, Bermondsey, Borough, Brixton, Clapham, Deptford, East Dulwich, Forest Hill, Greenwich, Herne Hill, Lambeth, Lewisham, Oval, Peckham, Putney, Wandsworth, Waterloo, Wimbledon

WEST
Belgravia, Chelsea, Chiswick, Earl's Court, Fulham, Hammersmith, Holland Park, Kensington, Knightsbridge, Notting Hill, Shepherd's Bush, South Kensington

GREATER
Barnes, East Sheen, Heathrow, Kew, Richmond, South Woodford, Southall, Surbiton, Twickenham, Walthamstow, Wanstead

LONDON

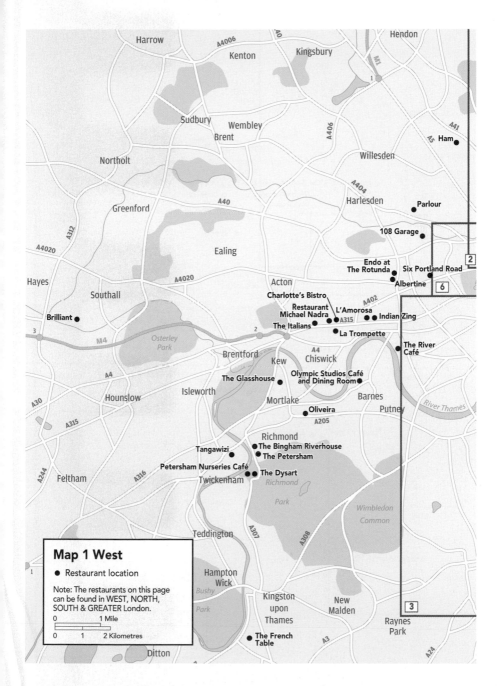

Map 1 West

● Restaurant location

Note: The restaurants on this page can be found in WEST, NORTH, SOUTH & GREATER London.

0   1 Mile

0   1   2 Kilometres

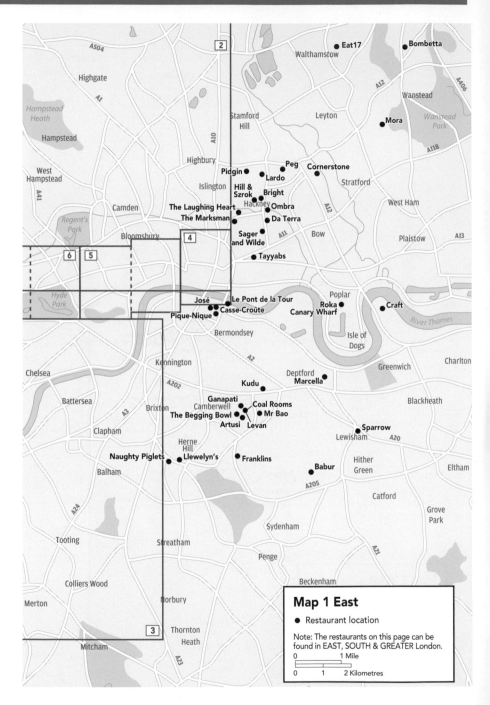

Map 1 East

● Restaurant location

Note: The restaurants on this page can be found in EAST, SOUTH & GREATER London.

0   1 Mile

0   1   2 Kilometres

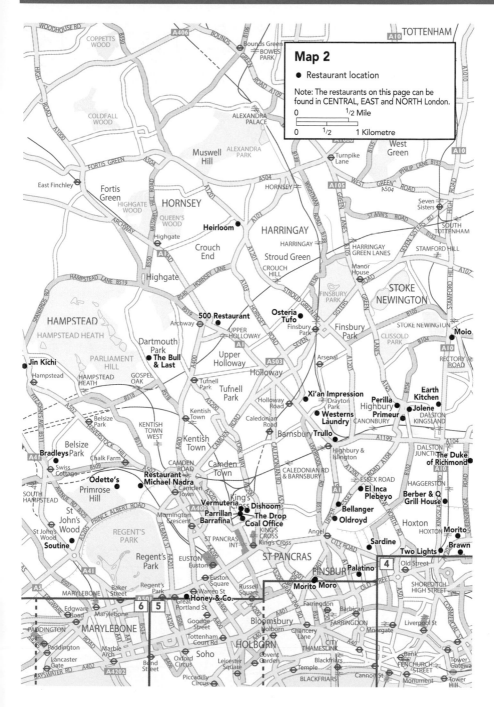

Map 2

● Restaurant location

Note: The restaurants on this page can be found in CENTRAL, EAST and NORTH London.

0   ¹/₂ Mile

0   ¹/₂   1 Kilometre

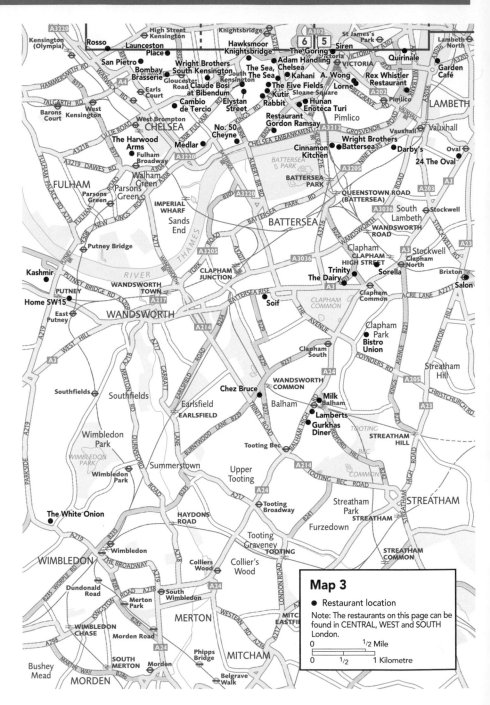

Map 3

● Restaurant location

Note: The restaurants on this page can be found in CENTRAL, WEST and SOUTH London.

0 _____ ½ Mile

0 ____ ½ ____ 1 Kilometre

Join us at thegoodfoodguide.co.uk

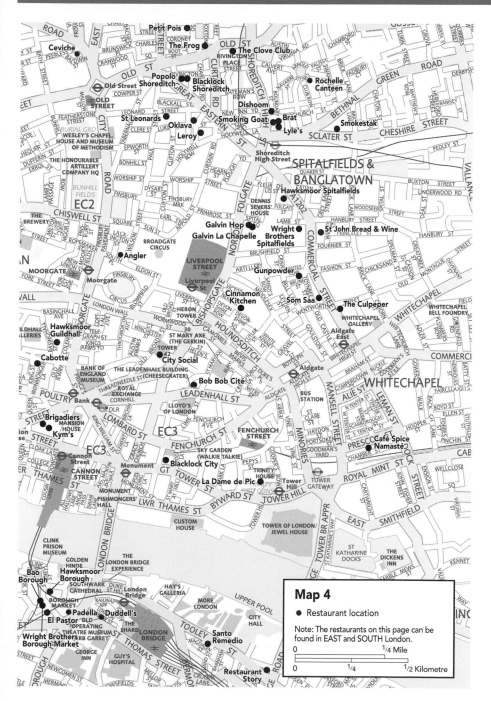

Petit Pois
Ceviche
The Frog
The Clove Club
OLD ST
Popolo
Old Street Shoreditch
Blacklock
Shoreditch
OLD
STREET
Dishoom
Rochelle
Canteen
St Leonards
Oklava
Smoking Goat
Brat
Smokestak
Leroy
Lyle's
Shoreditch
High Street
SPITALFIELDS &
BANGLATOWN
Hawksmoor Spitalfields
EC2
Galvin Hop
Wright
Galvin La Chapelle
Brothers
Spitalfields
St John Bread & Wine
THE
BREWERY
Angler
Moorgate
Liverpool
St
Gunpowder
Cinnamon
Kitchen
Som Saa
The Culpeper
Hawksmoor
Guildhall
Aldgate
East
Cabotte
City Social
Aldgate
Bob Bob Cité
WHITECHAPEL
Bank
Brigadiers
Kym's
Café Spice
Namasté
Cannon
Street
Blacklock City
La Dame de Pic
Bao
Borough
Hawksmoor
Borough
London
Bridge
Padella
Duddell's
El Pastor
Wright Brothers
Borough Market
Santo
Remedio
Restaurant
Story

Map 4

● Restaurant location

Note: The restaurants on this page can be
found in EAST and SOUTH London.

0   1/4 Mile

0   1/4   1/2 Kilometre

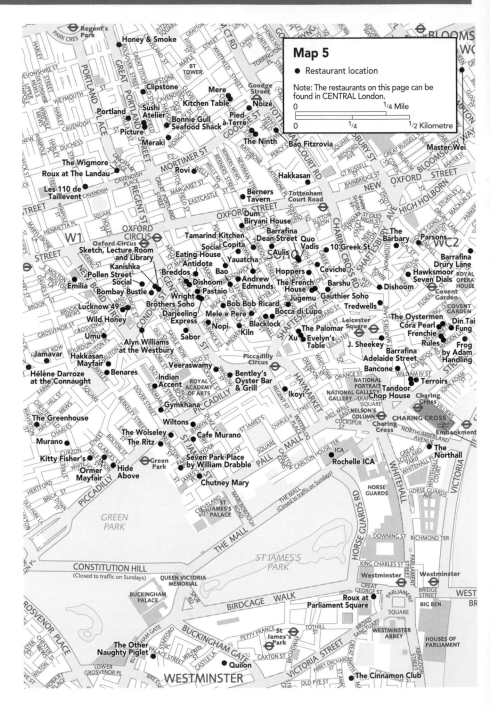

Map 5

● Restaurant location

Note: The restaurants on this page can be found in CENTRAL London.

0   1/4 Mile

0   1/4   1/2 Kilometre

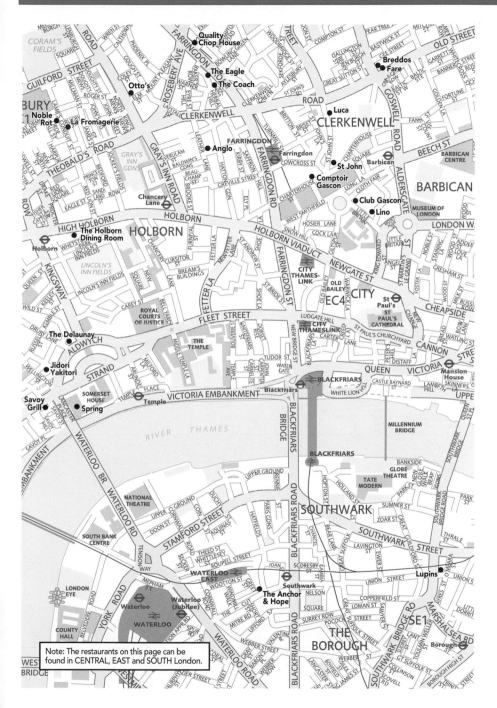

Note: The restaurants on this page can be found in CENTRAL, EAST and SOUTH London.

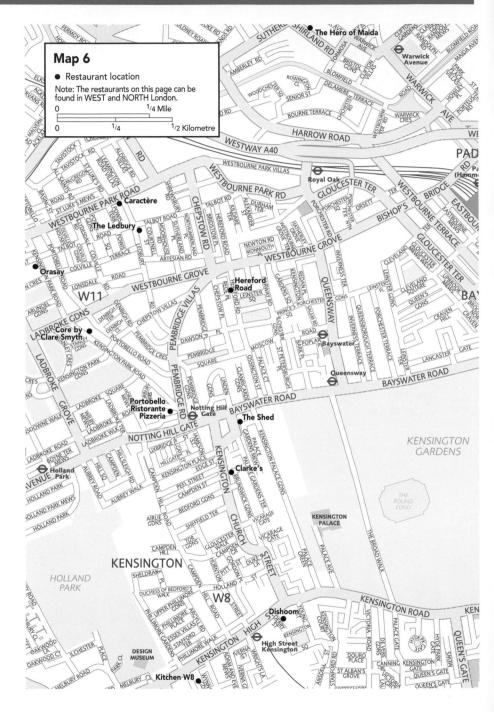

Map 6

● Restaurant location

Note: The restaurants on this page can be found in WEST and NORTH London.

0 .... ¼ Mile

0 .... ¼ .... ½ Kilometre

The Hero of Maida

Warwick Avenue

Royal Oak

Caractère

The Ledbury

Orasay

W11

Hereford Road

Core by Clare Smyth

Bayswater

Queensway

Portobello Ristorante Pizzeria

Notting Hill Gate

The Shed

NOTTING HILL GATE

Holland Park

Clarke's

KENSINGTON GARDENS

KENSINGTON PALACE

THE ROUND POND

HOLLAND PARK

KENSINGTON

W8

Dishoom

High Street Kensington

DESIGN MUSEUM

Kitchen W8

Join us at thegoodfoodguide.co.uk

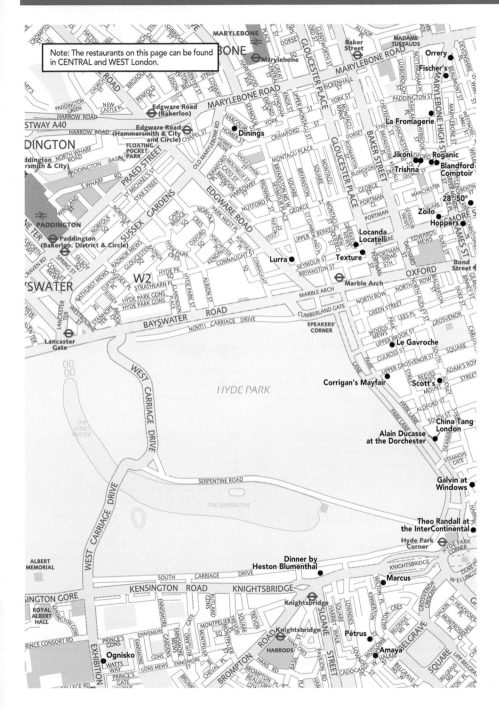

Note: The restaurants on this page can be found in CENTRAL and WEST London.

10 Greek Street

Cooking score: 3
⊖ Tottenham Court Road, map 5
Modern European | £42
10 Greek Street, Soho, W1D 4DH
Tel no: 020 7734 4677
10greekstreet.com

£5
OFF

The tiny dining room may be determinedly low key, with wooden floorboards, exposed brick walls, blackboards and bare tables, but it's the down-to-earth cooking and seasonal British produce that have diners clamouring for space (thankfully you can now book for lunch and dinner). The kitchen is scrupulously seasonal and deserves credit for its lack of ostentation: flavours are direct and enjoyable and there's no unnecessary garnish, whether in a classic potted pork with prunes, outstanding whole mackerel with blood orange, fennel, chilli and monk's beard, rich venison with celeriac, baby carrots and cavolo nero or a dish of Hereford beef with fried potatoes, kale and horseradish for two. Desserts will tempt, even if you didn't think you needed one. Rhubarb and almond tart and chocolate crème brûlée with pear and pistachio both come highly recommended. The reasonable prices extend to the stash of modern wines (from £18), with most available by the glass or carafe.
Chef/s: Marco Bianco. **Closed:** 24 to 26 Dec.
Meals: small plates £7 to £13. Large plates £18 to £26. **Details:** 35 seats. 2 seats outside. Bar. Music.

Les 110 de Taillevent

Cooking score: 5
⊖ Oxford Circus, map 5
French | £55
16 Cavendish Square, Marylebone, W1G 9DD
Tel no: 020 3141 6016
les-110-taillevent-london.com

A converted branch of Coutts Bank makes a suave home for the London outpost of august Parisian institution Taillevent. 'Les 110' is a diffusion line of sorts, offering a suggestion of the parent brand's food and wine minus the ruinous outlay. It's a clever concept, aimed at novices and 'noses' alike, that proposes four different wines by the glass (110 in total from a 1,500-bin cellar) for every dish available. Thus with steak tartare, a sophisticated take with smoked eel, mushroom jelly and a dusting of nori powder, one might drink Rhône Syrah at £8 or a premier cru red Burgundy at £43. With chalk stream trout, borlotti and caviar sauce, it might be a £12 Savennières or £45 Puligny-Montrachet. Chef Ross Bryans (ex-Corrigan's) applies his classical skills to some first-class ingredients. A dainty gariguette strawberry tart with various tuiles and twists points to strength in the pastry department, too. Service is formal and friendly enough, but too eager to up-sell (a £4 bottle of mineral water arrives unbidden). Overall, however, a good, business-friendly address.
Chef/s: Ross Bryans. **Closed:** Sun. **Meals:** main courses £28 to £36. Set L £28 (2 courses) to £32. Tasting menu £65 (6 courses). **Details:** 76 seats. 16 seats outside. Bar. Wheelchairs. Parking. Music.

28°-50°

Cooking score: 3
⊖ Bond Street, map 6
Modern European | £38
15-17 Marylebone Lane, Marylebone, W1U 2NE
Tel no: 020 7486 7922
2850.co.uk

🍾

It may be under new ownership since the last edition of the Guide, but don't worry – little has changed at this 'wine workshop and kitchen'. The menu has been slightly simplified but the dining room, with its big windows, zinc bar and marble tabletops, remains a relaxing place, the cheerful atmosphere helped along by brisk service. While wine steals the show – the outstanding list offers more than 30 bottles by the glass or carafe – the cooking is sound. Charcuterie, seafood platters, fish pie, steaks and burgers all feature, as well as Sunday roasts. A subtly gamey goose and mustard terrine with gribiche sauce got our inspection meal off to a solid start, although cod with saffron potatoes and samphire in a light shellfish bisque was underwhelming. A trio of chocolate madeleines dipped into crème anglaise got things back on track and cheeses from La Fromagerie allowed further exploration of the wide-ranging wine list – perhaps a foray into the rare collecters' bottles.

Chef/s: Julien Baris. **Closed:** Sun, 25 and 26 Dec, 1 Jan, 13 Apr. **Meals:** main courses £15 to £22. Set L and early D £19 (2 courses) to £22. Sun L £20 (1 course). **Details:** 50 seats. 14 seats outside. Bar. Wheelchairs. Music.

★ TOP 50 ★

A. Wong

Cooking score: 7
⊖ Victoria, map 3
Chinese | £60
70-71 Wilton Road, Victoria, SW1V 1DE
Tel no: 020 7828 8931
awong.co.uk

The dining room may have the feel of a traditional Chinese restaurant but the food is anything but, as diners making their way through the 12-or-so courses on Andrew Wong's revelatory Taste of China experience soon discover. What's in store is a memorable culinary trip across the country, a game-changing view of its food. Prime ingredients and nuanced cooking are key in a rich variety of dishes: Shanghai steamed pork dumplings with pickled tapioca, ginger vinegar and spring onion; Anhui province red-braised fermented wild sea bass served with a crunchy skin atop a smoked duck and fried kale 'bird's nest' with cod's roe; a Shaanxi pulled lamb burger (bao bun) with Xinjiang pomegranate salad 'providing a striking burst of freshness'; soy chicken in an oscietra caviar wrap with ginger oil, followed by an intriguing second chicken dish with roasted peanuts and sweet and spicy 'hotpot' essence. The tasting menu may be the best way to sample the sheer breadth of Wong's creativity, but à la carte options are equally remarkable, and immaculate dim sum keep things affordable at lunchtime. Indeed, readers have expressed delight at such good things as clear shrimp dumpling, scallop puff with dried scallop oil, wild mushroom and truffled steamed bun, wagyu tart with black beans, peas and crispy onion, and rabbit and carrot glutinous puff. Service is absolutely top-class. Food-friendly wines, mostly European but with a brief foray further afield, open at £30 for a Chilean Sauvignon Blanc.

Chef/s: Andrew Wong. **Closed:** Sun, 23 Dec to 8 Jan. **Meals:** main courses £10 to £25. Tasting menu £95 (12 courses). **Details:** 65 seats. 8 seats outside. Bar.

Alain Ducasse at The Dorchester

Cooking score: 7
⊖ Hyde Park Corner, map 6
Modern French | £110
The Dorchester Hotel, 53 Park Lane, Mayfair, W1K 1QA
Tel no: 020 7629 8866
alainducasse-dorchester.com

Accessed via The Dorchester's marble-columned Promenade, Alain Ducasse's London base makes a virtue of discretion, going about its business with gentle aplomb. The refined dining room looks the part: cream and white with well-spaced tables and extremely comfortable chairs, the sort of place in which there seems to be a waiter for every item – even the water. Jean-Philippe Blondet interprets the Ducasse style of contemporary French cooking with menus that allow you to chart paths of varying lengths, from three standard courses to seven tasting dishes. Combinations may be classic, as when Dorset crab appears with celeriac and caviar, or farmhouse veal medallion with sweetbread and carrots, but the presentations are spare and elegant and the flavours ring true. All of this and a generous budget (the prices are as gulp-inducing as ever) could make for a few hours' escape from the outside world but the cooking is still some way off challenging the best in the country. That said, the whole operation is very orderly and well behaved, the highlights for one diner being the legendary pile of cheese gougères, a delicate dish of raw sea scallop with bergamot and seaweed broth, and a fine fillet of John Dory with delicious confit turnip (but underwhelming sea urchin). The baba au rhum, like the Monte Carlo original, remains the pick of the desserts. From a strong base in France, the wine list turns up interesting bottles from all corners of the world and although prices are generally high, they start at £30.

Chef/s: Alain Ducasse and Jean-Philippe Blondet. **Closed:** Mon, Sun, 26 to 30 Dec, first week Jan, Easter, 3 weeks Aug. **Meals:** set L £70 Tue to Fri. Set D £110 to £130 (4 courses). Tasting menu £160 (7 courses). **Details:** 82 seats. V menu. Bar. Wheelchairs. Parking. Music. Children over 10 yrs.

Alyn Williams at the Westbury

Cooking score: 6

⊖ Oxford Circus, map 5
Modern European | £70
The Westbury Hotel, 37 Conduit Street, Mayfair, W1S 2YF
Tel no: 020 7183 6426
alynwilliams.com

£5 OFF

The principal dining space at the Westbury won't ruffle any style feathers when it comes to expectations of Mayfair dining. It's a comfortable, if faintly anonymous room decorated in wood and stone tones, with illuminated wine shelves and a brigade of discreetly attentive staff. The setting makes a productive contrast to Alyn Williams' culinary style, in which exquisitely presented dishes are founded on characterful combinations of expressive flavour and ingenious technique. Seafood is a leading suit, as in an appetiser of oyster and cucumber with dill granita; lobster tail in buttery sauce Jacqueline, or Cornish halibut in a truffled jus with celeriac and onion for the main event. Elsewhere, earthier notes surface in squab pigeon with beetroot and grapes, and a dressing of umami-rich 'ketchup', or a pairing of suckling pig and boudin blanc with kohlrabi and wild garlic. The tasting menus are the best way to hit the highlights. Desserts do deconstructive things with the likes of rhubarb and custard, or partner gooey salt caramel tart with the gentle sharpness of baked apple ice cream. A grand hotel wine list, opening at £40, has some reliable selections by the small glass.

Chef/s: Alyn Williams and Charlie Tayler. **Closed:** Mon, Sun, first 2 weeks Jan, last 2 weeks Aug. **Meals:** set L £35 to £45. Set L and D £70 Tue to Fri. Tasting menu £90 (7 courses). **Details:** 50 seats. V menu. Vg menu. Bar. Wheelchairs. Music.

Andrew Edmunds

Cooking score: 2

⊖ Oxford Circus, Piccadilly Circus, map 5
Modern European | £40
46 Lexington Street, Soho, W1F 0LP
Tel no: 020 7437 5708
andrewedmunds.com

One of the last of the Soho old guard, this atmospheric restaurant has been quietly going about its business in an 18th-century townhouse for 35 years. Its unpretentious attitude and full-flavoured bistro cooking seem no less relevant these days, with an authenticity that is hard to recreate. There's an energy and conviviality to the place as the two floors fill up (go for the ground floor if you can), helped along by a cracking wine list that embraces the world while steadfastly declaring its devotion to France. Whipped cod's roe on toast or a classic chicken and duck liver pâté with cornichons make a great start, but keep an eye on the blackboard for daily specials. Main-course roast pigeon arrives with lentils, broad beans and the warmth of mustard, while smoked haddock and mash is sheer comfort food. Finish with brown butter cherry tart. And of course there's a wine to match it all, with half bottles of premier cru Burgundy and Sauternes offering an affordable way in.

Chef/s: Chris Gillard. **Closed:** 24 to 30 Dec. **Meals:** main courses £15 to £27. Early D £19 (2 courses) to £22. **Details:** 60 seats.

Antidote

Cooking score: 3
⊖ Oxford Circus, map 5
French | £32
12a Newburgh Street, Soho, W1F 7RR
Tel no: 020 7287 8488
antidotewinebar.com
🍷

Food and wine share centre stage at this two-storey Georgian townhouse just off Carnaby Street. Those wines are organic and biodynamic, mostly French, with some excellent bins from the rest of Europe in support, and a goodly amount available by the glass. Sip away, perched at the bar or window counters in the bottle-lined ground-floor space, and tuck into plates of cheese and charcuterie or ham hock terrine with pickles. Upstairs, huge sash windows bathe the handsome dining room in light. Here, the kitchen turns out simple yet punchy plates such as mushrooms with parsley and confit egg yolk or slow-cooked pork belly with chickpeas and harissa. A hefty braised lamb shoulder (with green salsa and potato purée) is for two to share, fish options might be monkfish with capers and lemon or haddock brandade with chicory, while puds might stretch to a classic chocolate tart. Most of the wines are available to take away.
Chef/s: Sebastien Gagnete. **Closed:** Sun, bank hols. **Meals:** main courses £12 to £38. **Details:** 50 seats. 18 seats outside. Bar. Music.

Aulis

Cooking score: 6
⊖ Tottenham Court Road, map 5
Modern British | £195
16a St Annes Court, Soho, W1F 0BN
Tel no: 020 3948 9665
aulis.london

Opening subsidiary restaurants in different styles has long been a way for ambitious chefs to spread their wings, but with the Aulis concept, Simon Rogan introduced a new element to diversification. Beginning in the nerve centre of Cartmel, home to L'Enclume,

and subsequently extended to London and Hong Kong, this eight-seater chef's table format is founded on the idea of letting diners see and taste dishes at the development stage, while they are still being road-tested. 'Dining at Aulis involves complete surrender to the chef's creativity,' Rogan proclaims. Resistance is futile. The multi-course menus give next to nothing away, but there will be fulsome, technically specific guidance as you go, taking in perhaps a scallop with cavolo nero and seaweed, pork with intense concentrations of carrot and nasturtium, halibut with a razor clam, cabbage and dill, and rabbit with salsify and wild garlic. Each presentation is nothing less than a talking point, hardly flagging at desserts that might mobilise Jerusalem artichoke with malt and verjus, or the heavenly scents of gooseberry and woodruff. Wine matches are intriguing too, perhaps spanning an arc from English rosé via Portuguese Arinto to the Gaillac rarity Ondenc. The cost is high, but the experience undoubtedly something you'll be dining out on, albeit more mundanely, for years to come.
Chef/s: Simon Rogan and Tommaso Formica. **Closed:** Mon, Sun, Christmas, New Year, 1 week Jan. **Meals:** tasting menu £195. **Details:** 8 seats. Music. Children over 14 yrs.

★ NEW ENTRY ★

Bancone

Cooking score: 2
⊖ Charing Cross, Leicester Square, map 5
Italian | £28
39 William IV Street, Covent Garden, WC2N 4DD
Tel no: 020 7240 8786
bancone.co.uk
£5 OFF £30

'Pasta. Prosecco. Espresso' is the proposition emblazoned on the canopy of this stylish new venture within a pigeon's hop of Trafalgar Square. 'Bancone' refers to the sleek marble counter that forms the centrepiece, along which customers perch and beyond which chefs assiduously tend to bubbling pots. Imaginative antipasti hail from across the

Italian peninsula – golden Sicilian panelle fritters with smoked duck breast, lardo and whipped anchovies, or Veneto-style braised cuttlefish with saffron polenta. Pasta dishes are the true headliners, none more so than the signature dish of fazzoletti (silk handkerchiefs), walnut butter and confit egg yolk – or opt for St George mushroom, morel and ricotta ravioli. Round off with a simple, elemental dessert of wild strawberries, yoghurt foam, almond genoise, mint and Moscato. Our inspection showed some small inconsistencies in pasta textures – although prices are undeniably reasonable for these parts, with all-Italian wines from £21 a bottle. **Chef/s:** Louis Korouilas. **Closed:** 25 and 26 Dec. **Meals:** main courses £9 to £15. **Details:** 60 seats. Music.

Bao Fitzrovia

Cooking score: 2
● Tottenham Court Road, map 5
Taiwanese | £23
31 Windmill Street, Fitzrovia, W1T 2JN
Tel no: 020 3011 1632
baolondon.com
£30

Bao may have outposts in Soho and Borough (see entries), but it's in the first-floor bakery of this Fitzrovia townhouse that its trademark steamed buns are hatched. Many bao make the short trip downstairs to the horseshoe-shaped bar, while others might descend to the metallic basement dining room with its views of the open kitchen. The house special is a bao of battered cod with lemon mayo, or go for classic braised pork with peanut powder and fermented greens for a flavour of Taiwanese night markets. Supporting acts on the tick-box menu include grilled pork belly rice bowls and chilli chicken with aged white soy and kow choi. You might want to put your final tick against peanut ice cream roon bing with coriander. Few, however, would dispute that bao are the stars of the show here. The drinks menu includes an interesting line-up of sakes, both in and out of cocktails.

Chef/s: Shavkat Mamurov. **Closed:** Sun. **Meals:** bao £5 to £6. Small plates £5 to £8. Large plates £13 to £18. Set L £15. **Details:** 46 seats. 10 seats outside. Music.

Bao Soho

Cooking score: 2
● Oxford Circus, map 5
Taiwanese | £21
53 Lexington Street, Soho, W1F 9AS
baolondon.com
£30

Queues often snake out the door of this tiny – and original – outpost of the Bao empire. The formula is much the same as the somewhat bigger Fitzrovia branch (see entry), while the speciality here is the lamb shoulder bao with coriander sauce and garlic mayo. **Chef/s:** Shavkat Mamurov. **Meals:** bao £5 to £6. Small plates £4 to £7. Set L £15. **Details:** 33 seats. No reservations.

The Barbary

Cooking score: 4
● Covent Garden, map 5
North African | £35
16 Neal's Yard, Covent Garden, WC2H 9DP
thebarbary.co.uk

Regular queues around Neal's Yard testify to the success and pulling power of this spicy sibling of The Palomar (see entry). Taking its cue from North Africa's Barbary Coast, but casting its net across the Mediterranean and Middle East, it's dominated by a horseshoe-shaped bar where chefs and customers mingle and chat over plates of inspired food full of exotic nuances. Blistered, charred naans and ring-shaped sesame-coated Jerusalem bagels open the bidding, perhaps served with celeriac houmous or beetroot and labneh. After that, graze your way through potent, smokey dishes inspired by land, sea and earth, from seductively soft pata negra pork neck with sticky date syrup to monkfish with kumquats or black salmon dukkah. To conclude, there are ambrosial desserts such as the entirely legal 'hashcake' (made with ground pistachios) or 'funky monkey fro-yo' (banana and tahini ice cream with honey frozen yoghurt). Exotic fruity aperitifs are alternatives to the short (but pricey) multinational wine list. **Chef/s:** Daniel Alt. **Closed:** 24 to 26 Dec. **Meals:** main courses £13 to £26. **Details:** 24 seats. V menu. Music. No reservations. Counter bookings only at 12pm and 5pm. Children over 8 yrs.

Barrafina Adelaide Street

Cooking score: 4
Charing Cross, map 5
Spanish | £38
10 Adelaide Street, Covent Garden, WC2N 4HZ
barrafina.co.uk

Conveniently located in a light-filled corner site in Theatreland, this slick counter-only tapas bar has all the hallmarks of the Barrafina group – sherries, daily specials etc – with the advantage of a private dining room for parties of eight or more. For main entry, see King's Cross branch, north London. **Chef/s:** Angel Zapata Martin. **Closed:** 24 to 26 Dec, 1 Jan, 13 Apr. **Meals:** small plates £3 to £18. **Details:** 29 seats. No reservations. Maximum group size 4.

Barrafina Dean Street

Cooking score: 4
Tottenham Court Road, map 5
Spanish | £38
26-27 Dean Street, Soho, W1D 3LL
barrafina.co.uk

The original Soho Barrafina launched on Frith Street in 2006, relocating to its charming new home within Quo Vadis in 2016. It's a particularly popular branch, so go early to nab a seat. For main entry, see King's Cross branch, north London. **Chef/s:** Angel Zapata Martin. **Closed:** 24 to 26 Dec, 1 Jan, 13 Apr. **Meals:** small plates £3 to £20. **Details:** 28 seats. 12 seats outside. No reservations. Maximum group size 4.

Barrafina Drury Lane

Cooking score: 4
Covent Garden, map 5
Spanish | £38
43 Drury Lane, Covent Garden, WC2B 5AJ
barrafina.co.uk

Covent Garden's second Barrafina site is perfectly situated for pre- and post-theatre bites. This branch is notable for its covered terrace and creative specials such as stone bass tartare, and cecina rolls stuffed with duck liver pâté. For main entry, see King's Cross branch, north London. **Chef/s:** Angel Zapata Martin. **Closed:** 24 to 26 Dec, 1 Jan, 13 Apr. **Meals:** small plates £3 to £20. **Details:** 23 seats. 16 seats outside. No reservations. Maximum group size 4.

Barshu

Cooking score: 4
Leicester Square, map 5
Chinese | £35
28 Frith Street, Soho, W1D 5LF
Tel no: 020 7287 8822
barshurestaurant.co.uk

If you're in the mood for 'man and wife offal slices', 'pock-marked old woman beancurd', 'farmhouse fried rice' or slowly simmered sea cucumber in millet porridge, then make a beeline for this no-nonsense Szechuan firecracker on the fringes of Soho's Chinatown. Eating here is an 'interesting and unusual experience,' says one convert, but novices should be prepared for a sensory onslaught as the kitchen piles on the palate-numbing chilli heat and does wondrously scary things with anatomical offcuts. Ingredients are variously 'pounded', 'smacked', 'water-boiled' and stewed, although potent lip-tinglers such as 'mouthwatering' Szechuan chicken or 'fragrant and hot' lobster are tempered by the gentler tones of blanched spinach in sesame sauce or steamed scallops with bean thread noodles. Occasional misfires are not unknown ('undercooked' pig's trotter, for example), but the food is colourful, authentic, generous and uncompromisingly flavourful. Staff are extremely polite ('despite a few minor issues with communication'), and drinks include some 'unusual mocktails' alongside wines from £24.

Chef/s: Mr Zheng. **Closed:** 24 and 25 Dec. **Meals:** main courses £6 to £35. **Details:** 80 seats. Bar. Music.

Benares

Cooking score: 4
⊖ Green Park, map 5
Indian | £60
12a Berkeley Square, Mayfair, W1J 6BS
Tel no: 020 7629 8886
benaresrestaurant.com

The Berkeley Square location means expectations are raised, and first encounters of this Mayfair Indian do not disappoint, from the petal-strewn pond at the entrance to the richly decorated first-floor dining room. The menu combines careful sourcing with intriguing combinations, seen in prettily plated starters of crispy soft-shell crab with a quinoa and mixed bean jhalmuri – a riff on a street snack – and a tikka-style chargrilled and spiced saddle of rabbit with pickled baby carrot and plum. Accomplished cooking shines through in dishes such as meen dakshini (Deccan fish curry), cod (flaking perfectly), accompanied by cumin peas and a coconut-rich sauce, with kokum lending a welcome spicy sharpness and thinly shaved raw fennel a pleasing crunch. A lacklustre rogan josh, under-seasoned and tough-skinned aubergine side dish and disappointing breads threatened to undo the good work but a wonderfully perfumed alphonso mango dessert tipped the balance back in favour, as did the welcoming and attentive staff. Cocktails are a particular strength, and the wine list, carefully tailored to complement the spicing, is priced for the location, although by-the-glass selections start at a more modest £7.

Chef/s: Brinder Narula. **Closed:** 1 Jan. **Meals:** main courses £26 to £44. Set L £29 (2 courses) to £35. Tasting menu £98 (7 courses). **Details:** 85 seats. V menu. Bar. Wheelchairs. Music. Children over 7 yrs after 7pm.

Bentley's Oyster Bar & Grill

Cooking score: 4
⊖ Piccadilly Circus, map 5
Seafood | £60
11-15 Swallow Street, Mayfair, W1B 4DG
Tel no: 020 7734 4756
bentleys.org

It may have celebrated its 100th birthday in 2016, but this redoubtable seafood veteran is still full of vim and vigour – thanks largely to the efforts of ebullient chef-patron Richard Corrigan. Bentley's enchanting terrace is one of Mayfair's rare alfresco gems, while the marble-hued Oyster Bar exudes a bubbly metropolitan buzz as punters sip fizz and slurp expertly shucked briny bivalves. Dishes come with a weighty price tag, but the pay-off is top-quality fish cookery, from classic lobster thermidor to cleverly contrived modern ideas ranging from mackerel with kohlrabi and yuzu to sea trout with asparagus and rhubarb hollandaise. Meat eaters aren't ignored, and desserts such as Japanese cheesecake with orange and apricot show a surprisingly light touch. The upstairs Grill is a more sedate affair favoured by tourists. Varied Rieslings, Sauvignons and 'wines from maritime climes' are just some of the attractions on an expansive fish-friendly list with prices to match the Mayfair surrounds, although there are some excellent house selections from £26 a carafe.

Chef/s: Richard Corrigan and Michael Lynch. **Closed:** bank hols. **Meals:** main courses £21 to £33. Set early/late D £24 (2 courses) to £29. **Details:** 130 seats. 60 seats outside. Wheelchairs.

Berners Tavern

Cooking score: 5
⊖ Tottenham Court Road, map 5
Modern British | £60
10 Berners Street, Fitzrovia, W1T 3NP
Tel no: 020 7908 7979
bernerstavern.com

🛏

A tavern in the same sense that the venue's global restaurateur boss Jason Atherton is a cook. Appended to the Edition hotel, this is a room you know you are in: lively (rising to noisy), high-ceilinged, corniced to the nines and lined with gilt-framed artworks and the makings of multiple cocktails. Head chef Phil Carmichael has been in the saddle since 2013, offering an evolved take on European glam-café dishes plus – a new development – afternoon tea and weekend roasts. A Champagne trolley and tableside service of dishes such as pork pie with pickles allow the service team to shine, while the kitchen takes its turn with the odd inventive flourish. Good British ingredients are key to main courses, even on a set lunch dish that might combine Dingley Dell pork, Jersey Royals and Cropwell Bishop Stilton, while puds like chocolate and coffee choux with milk ice cream are unlikely to fail. Wines from £35 live up to the setting.

Chef/s: Phil Carmichael. **Meals:** main courses £20 to £35. Set L £25 (2 courses) to £30. **Details:** 140 seats. Bar. Wheelchairs. Music.

Blacklock

Cooking score: 2
⊖ **Piccadilly Circus, map 5**
British | £30
24 Great Windmill Street, Soho, W1D 7LG
Tel no: 020 3441 6996
theblacklock.com
£30

The original basement site of the Blacklock chophouse group has a discreet entrance that belies the buzz inside. Book well ahead for the Sunday roast. For main entry, see Shoreditch, east London.

Chef/s: Mirek Dawid. **Closed:** 24 to 26 Dec, 1 Jan. **Meals:** main courses £12 to £35. Sun L £20 (1 course). **Details:** 70 seats. Music. Lunch and early D bookings only.

Wheelchairs

We only indicate that a restaurant is wheelchair accessible if this includes access to toilets.

Blandford Comptoir

Cooking score: 3
⊖ **Baker Street, Bond Street, map 6**
Mediterranean | £38
1 Blandford Street, Marylebone, W1U 3DA
Tel no: 020 7935 4626
blandford-comptoir.co.uk
🍾

Xavier Rousset's little wine bar and diner is more *pichet* than magnum, but for all its modest dimensions, it has become quite the community hub in well-heeled Marylebone. Small plates and sharing platters find their natural home in the format, whether for fully loaded seafood options or polenta chips in truffle mayo. If you're three-coursing it, expect to progress from something like burrata with crushed peas and tarragon oil, through pork rump with grelot onions, apricot purée and spinach, to well-kept cheeses or a decadent chocolate délice with white chocolate macaron, and emerge happy. That last commodity is owing in no small measure to the wine list that constitutes the principal raison d'être of the place. France and its classic appellations are given star billing, gloriously so, but look further afield and find interesting varietals and obscure blends from all over. There are also excellent listings of sweet and fortified wines, from late harvest Banyuls to the legendary vin jaune of the Jura. Small glasses start at £6, but there is plenty of choice by the bottle below £40.

Chef/s: Ben Mellor. **Closed:** 24 to 26 Dec, 1 and 2 Jan. **Meals:** main courses £15 to £20. **Details:** 40 seats. 11 seats outside. Music.

Bob Bob Ricard

Cooking score: 3
⊖ **Piccadilly Circus, map 5**
Anglo-Russian | £55
1 Upper James Street, Soho, W1F 9DF
Tel no: 020 3145 1000
bobbobricard.com

Renowned for the 'press for Champagne' button at every marble-topped table, and styled after ornate Art Deco train carriages

with leather booths and plenty of bling, it's no wonder the kitchen takes a luxe approach to classic comfort food, in an Anglo-Russian kind of way. There's caviar and oysters, of course, as well as salmon or steak tartare (add caviar for an 'imperial' upgrade), beef wellington for two, lobster dumplings, upmarket chicken kiev or vegan-friendly pearl barley kasha with pickled forest mushrooms. Finish with the signature gilt 'chocolate glory' or a soufflé with a glass of honeyed Château d'Yquem. 'Off-peak' pricing (where dishes are about 20% cheaper) marks an innovative approach to luring in a lunch crowd that will surely catch on. Low margins and easy navigation make the vertiginously priced wine list more approachable than many. The Square Mile sibling, Bob Bob Cité, shares its swagger (see entry).
Chef/s: Eric Chavot. **Meals:** main courses £18 to £50. **Details:** 200 seats. Wheelchairs. Music. Children over 12 yrs.

Bocca di Lupo

Cooking score: 2
⊖ Piccadilly Circus, map 5
Italian | £50
12 Archer Street, Soho, W1D 7BB
Tel no: 020 7734 2223
boccadilupo.com

It's good to note that Jacob Kennedy and Victor Hugo's one-of-a-kind Italian eatery continues to be a crowd-puller. It broke the mould when it opened at the end of 2008 – with its clean, contemporary lines it barely shows its age – and the stunning line-up of sharply executed plates is based on a zealous enthusiasm for entirely fresh ingredients. The kitchen pulls in bright ideas from across Italy, ranging from simple raw salads (artichokes with pecorino and mint, say, or sea bream carpaccio with orange and rosemary) via spinach and ricotta malfatti with butter and sage (from Lombardy) or tortellini stuffed with pork and prosciutto (from Bologna), to a Tuscan grilled buristo (blood sausage) or a Roman dish of oxtail with celery and tomato. To finish, the Sicilian cannoli stuffed with sheep's ricotta,

chocolate and pistachio are a must. The regional theme runs through the deftly compiled wine list, with most available by the glass and carafe.
Chef/s: Giuseppe Ferreri. **Closed:** 25 Dec, 1 Jan. **Meals:** small plates £3 to £16. Main courses £10 to £29. **Details:** 68 seats. Wheelchairs.

Bombay Bustle

Cooking score: 3
⊖ Oxford Circus, map 5
Indian | £42
29 Maddox Street, Mayfair, W1S 2PA
Tel no: 020 7290 4470
bombaybustle.com
£5
OFF

Although this Mayfair street is a world away from the hubbub of Mumbai, there's stimulation enough in the Art Deco-style railway carriage design of this two-floor restaurant, and in the kitchen's desire to recreate the invigorating flavours of the bustling Indian city. If the tiffin tins of hungry workers are the proclaimed inspiration, what arrives on the plate is a mix of old and new ideas. Spiced scrambled egg with truffle naan is one of a dozen small plates (Malabar chicken wings, vegetarian samosa with mint chutney, battered squid), while the tandoor turns out Cornish lamb with pickled onion, as well as charred broccoli with tomato dust. Pungent curries include one rich with Devon crab, another with Hampshire mutton and dried red chillies. A brace of tasting menus includes a vegetarian version, while desserts such as cardamom panna cotta or jalebi cheesecake are no afterthought. Drink creative cocktails or wines from a global collection.
Chef/s: Surender Mohan. **Closed:** Sun, 25 and 26 Dec, 1 and 2 Jan. **Meals:** main courses £16 to £29. Set L and early D £28 to £33. Tasting menu £60 (5 courses) to £65. **Details:** 114 seats. V menu. Bar. Wheelchairs. Music. Children over 8 yrs at D.

Bonnie Gull Seafood Shack

Cooking score: 3
⊖ Oxford Circus, Goodge Street, map 5
Seafood | £50
21a Foley Street, Fitzrovia, W1W 6DS
Tel no: 020 7436 0921
bonniegull.com

This lively, tiny seafooder's winning formula takes in a suitably relaxed (if slightly cramped) dining room, welcoming and attentive service and spot-on fish cooking. There's no doubting the freshness of the raw materials on the concise and gently contemporary menu. The kitchen balances the odd fusion riff – Fowey mussels with coconut, chilli and coriander, say – with modern European influences such as Orkney scallops with clam beurre blanc or chargrilled Cornish sardines with ajo blanco and parsley oil. Plaice with anchovy butter and samphire is a straight-up main course, while cod arrives in the earthy company of wild mushroom purée, a herb crumb and bordelaise sauce. Don't miss out on sides of beef dripping chips or cauliflower with hoisin glaze and shallots. There's a brief list of fish-friendly wines (from £24) and a second branch on Bateman Street, Soho, W1D 3AN.
Chef/s: Max Shearer. **Meals:** main courses £18 to £30. **Details:** 26 seats. 24 seats outside. Music.

Breddos

Cooking score: 1
⊖ Oxford Circus, map 5
Mexican | £25
26 Kingly Street, Soho, W1B 5QD
Tel no: 020 3890 8545
breddostacos.com
£30

Short on elbow room, big on tacos, Breddos made the leap from Hackney shack to bricks and mortar in two central locations, first Clerkenwell (see entry) and then here in Soho. Fittingly, given both its origins and inspirations, the lively-looking Soho taquería doesn't stand on ceremony. Take a stool and rattle through a handful of handfuls made with tortillas pressed fresh every morning and

filled with lamb shoulder and árbol salsa, perhaps, or sweet potato with macadamia mole, whipped feta and sesame seeds. Eminently dippable starters include baked queso fundido and a choice of seven salsas with totopos. Drinks are wine on tap, Margaritas and pale ales.
Chef/s: Adrian Hernandez Farina. **Closed:** 25 Dec. **Meals:** main courses £8 to £11. **Details:** 70 seats. 6 seats outside. Bar. Wheelchairs. Music.

Café Murano

Cooking score: 4
⊖ Green Park, map 5
Italian | £37
33 St James's Street, Mayfair, SW1A 1HD
Tel no: 020 3371 5559
cafemurano.co.uk

There's a tad more informality here than at the mothership Murano on Queen Street (see entry), but it's a close-run thing. In a simple room with bistro furniture, the Italian doings are appreciably similar. Little cicchetti get you going nicely, as a prelude to classy antipasti dishes of creamy burrata or beetroot panzanella. Pasta is an object lesson in silky translucency, seen to great effect in the tagliatelle bulked with salsiccia ragù and radicchio, and the traditional mains that make the twin virtues of freshness and simplicity look all the more alluring: plaice in cockle butter fronded with sea herbs, or chicken milanese dressed in the eternal saladings of rocket, Parmesan and balsamic, perhaps supplemented by a side of spring greens pepped up with garlic and chilli. Expect to finish with something like buttermilk panna cotta, enriched with peaches and honeycomb. The quality-conscious list of Italian wines makes for much happy regional hunting, with glasses from £5.50 for a nutty Soave-like Veneto blend of Trebbiano and Garganega.
Chef/s: Adam Jay. **Closed:** 25 and 26 Dec. **Meals:** main courses £16 to £28. Set L and early D £19 (2 courses) to £23. Sun L £30 (4 courses). **Details:** 76 seats. 4 seats outside. Music.

Ceviche

⊖ **Tottenham Court Road, map 5**
Peruvian | £25
17 Frith Street, Soho, W1D 4RG
Tel no: 020 7292 2040
cevicheuk.com

£30

A lively and unpretentious Soho spot that brings Lima to London. The bang-for-buck menu covers some major touchpoints of this rich cuisine, from the Chinese-influenced chifa-style chicken wings to Japanese-Peruvian Nikkei ceviche, Andean home comforts and delicious beef heart anticuchos and picarones (pumpkin doughnuts) from the streets of the Peruvian capital. A quick lunch of quinoa croquettes and poke ceviche will set you back a tenner. Drink vibrant purple corn chicha morada, pisco sours or Cusqueña beer for the full experience. There's a second branch near Old Street in east London (see entry).

China Tang London

Cooking score: 2
⊖ **Hyde Park Corner, map 6**
Chinese | £70
The Dorchester Hotel, 53 Park Lane, Mayfair, W1K 1QA
Tel no: 020 7629 9988
chinatanglondon.co.uk

A vision of 1930s Shanghai whisks diners away to a world far removed from 21st-century Park Lane – at least for an hour or two. Sumptuous chinoiserie, carved woodwork, calligraphy and exotic pieces collected by late founder Sir David Tang help to sustain the illusion, while staff in smart uniforms attend to every detail. By contrast, the Cantonese menu is a surprisingly conventional run through the staples of the repertoire, with prices aimed squarely at very deep pockets (a bowl of fried rice is £8). Dim sum lunches keep things relatively affordable for those with a penchant for asparagus cheung fun, scallop dumplings and steamed beef balls. However, the evening carte is strictly for big spenders who are happy

to pay top dollar for lobster with noodles, chicken in lemon sauce and other precisely rendered classics. Drinkers will also shell out serious money for old-school cocktails and heavyweight wines.
Chef/s: Chong Choi Fong. **Closed:** 24 and 25 Dec.
Meals: main courses £16 to £55. Set L £45. Set D £82. **Details:** 120 seats. V menu. Bar. Wheelchairs. Music. Children over 10 yrs after 9pm.

Chutney Mary

Cooking score: 5
⊖ **Green Park, map 5**
Indian | £52
73 St James's Street, Mayfair, SW1A 1PH
Tel no: 020 7629 6688
chutneymary.com

Along with Amaya and Veeraswamy (see entries), Chutney Mary is one of a group of restaurants that has cast a glamorous glow over the business of Indian dining in the capital. This corner site in St James's is an expansive venue in every sense, with an elegant cocktail bar and palatial dining room full of gleaming surfaces and bold colours. Taking the entire diversity of Indian regional food as its template, the kitchen produces contemporary dishes from small plates to slow-cooked curries across a broad spectrum. From the former, expect golden fried prawns, griddled scallops in Mangalore spices and marinated bites of peppered ribeye, while the show-stopping principal dishes bring on Keralan fish curry, tandoori sea bass and chicken mappas cooked in coconut milk. A regional whistlestop is available in the form of a tasting platter. At dessert, things get distinctly cross cultural, as when gulab jamun appears in the guise of tiramisu. A wide-ranging wine list supplements those creative cocktails.
Chef/s: Achal Aggarwal. **Closed:** Sun. **Meals:** main courses £19 to £36. Set L £29 (2 courses) to £33. **Details:** 119 seats. V menu. No children after 8pm.

The Cinnamon Club

Cooking score: 5

⊖ Westminster, map 5

Indian | £75

30-32 Great Smith Street, Westminster,
SW1P 3BU

Tel no: 020 7222 2555

cinnamonclub.com

£5 OFF 🍶

'Immediately striking and huge, but handling the enormous number of covers with ease,' noted one reader after visiting this civilised Indian aristocrat – a demure dining room that lives up to its name with polished parquet flooring and wall-to-wall leather-bound books (this was the Old Westminster Library, after all). Everything is 'properly professional' here, from the 'confident interaction of the staff' to the conception of the menu, which is a tribute to the open-minded creativity of executive chef Vivek Singh. Expect a 'multiplicity of palate-tingling tastes' married to impressively sourced ingredients – from carpaccio of home-cured Shetland salmon with caramel jhal muri (puffed rice) or smoked herdwick lamb kebabs to 'luxurious fleshy prawns from Down Under' with an invigorating Keralan Alleppey sauce. Game is another highlight, judging by a dish of Anjou pigeon breast with 'brilliant' peanut and pumpkin chutney, while veggie options might include a banana chilli filled with fenugreek, raisins and bitter gourd on a green pea pilau. To finish, a delectable combination of cardamom shrikhand and tamarind-glazed berries has been deemed 'first class'. Numerous selections by the glass or carafe provide affordable access to the seriously impressive big-money wine list, which scours the globe in search of spice-tolerant bottles.

Chef/s: Vivek Singh and Rakesh Nair. **Meals:** main courses £21 to £38. Set L £28 (2 courses) to £32. Tasting menu £95 (6 courses). Sun L £45.
Details: 280 seats. Vg menu. Bar. Wheelchairs.

Clipstone

Cooking score: 5

⊖ Great Portland Street, map 5

Modern European | £40

5 Clipstone Street, Fitzrovia, W1W 6BB

Tel no: 020 7637 0871

clipstonerestaurant.co.uk

🍶

The third of Will Lander and Daniel Morgenthau's quartet of London restaurants (see entries for Emilia, Portland and Quality Chop House) has taken the classic neighbourhood bistro idiom and made it thoroughly modern. The corner spot's spartan look provides the perfect backdrop for the progressive culinary approach and bright, fresh flavours. The kitchen does clever things with stellar ingredients on two menus – a set lunch and evening carte – and the food is always poised. A little yuzu and sorrel peps up a starter of crudo of brill with raspberries (fruit features often in savoury dishes), and earthy girolles accompany a main course of Devon duck with burnt honey, almonds and grelot onion. Expect something light and creamy for dessert – herb ice cream with strawberries, maybe, or almond panna cotta with apricot and sablé. The well-chosen wines on the concise list are all available by the glass, carafe or bottle and come with helpful tasting notes. With a separate 'single bottle list' of noteworthy finds, there's plenty to encourage adventurous drinking.

Chef/s: Stuart Andrew. **Closed:** Sun, 2 weeks Dec to Jan. **Meals:** main courses £19 to £29. Set L £22 (2 courses) to £26. **Details:** 39 seats. 18 seats outside.

Wine list

🍶 Restaurants showing this symbol have a wine list that our experts consider to be outstanding, either for its in-depth focus on a particular region, attractive margins on fine wines, or strong selection by the glass.

Copita

Cooking score: 3
⊖ Oxford Circus, map 5
Spanish | £29
27 d'Arblay Street, Soho, W1F 8EP
Tel no: 020 7287 7797
copita.co.uk
£30

Context is everything. While many would balk at the idea of sitting on tall bentwood stools at window counters and shelves to eat traditional haute cuisine, bring on some classic and modern Spanish tapas and it's a different prospect altogether. Copita knows its business well, and is adept at feeding a ravenous Soho clientele, whether it's hurrying or hanging loose. There are Ibérico chorizo and jamón, garlic and chilli king prawns, bacalao fritters with lemon mayo, and beef onglet with shallots and chimichurri to please old-schoolers, but inveigled in among them are the more groundbreaking likes of burnt aubergine with labneh, pomegranate and nuts; monkfish with leeks and a tempura-battered yolk of duck egg, or pork crackling to dress a plate of smoked anchovies. Sticky orange polenta cake with green anise ice cream makes a properly indulgent finish. There is an infectious buzz and bustle to the place when it's in full spate, helped along by a go-ahead list of modern Spanish wines, served in small glasses and half-bottle carafes as well as bottles. The sherry listing is great, and there is a page of gins.
Chef/s: Ngamedy Khouma. **Closed:** Sun, 25 Dec, bank hols. **Meals:** small plates £4 to £18.
Details: 38 seats. 6 seats outside. Music.

Budget

£30 At restaurants showing this symbol, it is possible to eat three courses (excluding drinks) for £30 or less.

Cora Pearl

Cooking score: 4
⊖ Covent Garden, map 5
Modern British | £42
30 Henrietta Street, Covent Garden, WC2F 8NA
Tel no: 020 7324 7722
corapearl.co.uk

With plumply comfortable banquettes and tones of dark green, dark red and dark wood, Cora Pearl – named after a 19th-century courtesan – has stepped out of the shadow of its acclaimed sister, Kitty Fisher's (see entry), into its own decadent spotlight. Come for food with a flirty retro wink, such as ham and cheese toastie (cheffily done, but retaining all its essential soothing richness), or brown shrimp Ranhöfer, a lightly spiced prawn cocktail on toast. Follow these snacks with sea bream tartare of the freshest, lightest order, alive with the late spring notes of cucumber and elderflower; agnolotti that are butter-gold in their egginess, full with curd, fragrant with summer truffle, sweet with pea purée; or fillet of rose veal that is pinkly, givingly tender on a glossy bordelaise sauce studded with bone marrow. Flash back to childhood summers with a Neapolitan ice cream, but replace memories of lurid pink-brown-white confections with the sophistication of nubs of wild strawberries, pistachio and bitter chocolate. A short wine list opens at £28.
Chef/s: George Barson. **Closed:** 25 and 26 Dec, 1 Jan. **Meals:** main courses £18 to £27. **Details:** 52 seats. Bar.

Corrigan's Mayfair

Cooking score: 5
⊖ Marble Arch, map 6
British/Irish | £70
28 Upper Grosvenor Street, Mayfair, W1K 7EH
Tel no: 020 7499 9943
corrigansmayfair.co.uk

While some chefs and their restaurants evolve naturally from young buck to old guard, Corrigan's has always knowingly occupied

Asma Khan

Darjeeling Express, Soho, London

What do you enjoy most about being a chef?
I love seeing people eat the food I have cooked.

What is your favourite dish on your menu at the moment?
Paratha. It's my all-time favourite comfort food.

Name one ingredient you couldn't cook without.
Onions, but more specifically, perfectly thin caramelised onions. It takes time to get them right but they're essential in Indian Mughlai-style cooking.

Who are your greatest influences?
My mother and our family cook Haji Saheb. Sadly, Haji passed away last year but I still have his handwritten notes on how to combine masalas for certain dishes.

What's your favourite kitchen item?
In a corner of my kitchen I have dried wheat head spikes from my father's farm in India. When things get hard, they remind me why I am cooking: to present to my guests the gift of nature.

And finally... tell us something about yourself that will surprise your diners.
I have acute motion sickness. I can only commute to work by sucking mints and looking at a fixed point on the road.

clubby, nostalgic territory. The canopied frontage, abundance of leather and soft sheen of quality are the classic stuff of Mayfair. For diners willing to pay the price for some of the best produce from the British Isles, some grown at Corrigan's luxury estate in Cavan and an estimable cellar, it's the obvious choice. Head chef Aidan McGee presides over dishes that are on intimate terms with luxury: Dorset crab raviolo with caviar and shellfish sauce to start, perhaps, followed by Irish beef en croûte for two, and game aplenty. Outside influences – Vietnamese dressing on the Carlingford oysters, miso butter with the stuffed Dover sole – are there for those who want them. A final course might be steamed apple pudding, hazelnut choux bun or raw milk cheeses from Britain and Ireland. Wines, listed with a nod to style, require some serious outlay.
Chef/s: Aidan McGee. **Closed:** Sun, bank hols.
Meals: main courses £19 to £44. Set L £28 (2 courses) to £38. Tasting menu £120 (6 courses).
Details: 60 seats. Bar. Wheelchairs. Music.

★ NEW ENTRY ★

Darjeeling Express
Cooking score: 1
⊖ Oxford Circus, Piccadilly Circus, map 5
Indian | £32
Kingly Court, Carnaby Street, Soho, W1B 5PW
Tel no: 020 7287 2828
darjeeling-express.com
£5
OFF

Asma Khan grew up in Kolkata and her light, airy restaurant on the second floor of the Kingly Court development majors in street food and other dishes from home. In the kitchen an all-female team sends out bihari phulki (fried lentil fritters) with a fiery chilli and tamarind chutney, paneer in a creamy, chilli-infused sauce, and tender Bhopali chicken – bone-in thighs cooked with panch phoron (a fragrant blend of fennel seeds, fenugreek, nigella, mustard seeds and cumin) with yoghurt and chillies. Textbook paratha is worth a visit in its own right, and lassis and cocktails provide an alternative to mostly French wines on a brief list. Note: since Khan

featured on the Netflix documentary *Chef's Table*, it's nigh-on impossible to get a table without chancing a long wait, or booking a month in advance.
Chef/s: Asma Khan. **Closed:** Sun, 22 Dec to 1 Jan. **Meals:** main courses £12 to £16. **Details:** 55 seats. Music.

The Delaunay
Cooking score: 3
⊖ Temple, map 5
Modern European | £40
55 Aldwych, Covent Garden, WC2B 4BB
Tel no: 020 7499 8558
thedelaunay.com

Corbin and King are the go-to restaurateurs for all-day café dining in the central European style. Let's face it, there are days when the greasy spoon just doesn't cut it, when you will want to slip into one of the brass-railed banquettes and absorb the atmosphere, to which the plentiful, on-the-button staff contribute substantially. Warm breadsticks appeared as though by magic to a pair of languidly late lunchers (2.30pm? Not a problem), who went on to calf's liver on mash and salmon trout in light lemon cream. Daily specials rotate through the week – Thursday is braised pig's cheeks day – and there are dishes for two, such as whole roast monkfish tail with salsa verde. Early birds pop in for pre-office breakfasts, 3pm sees afternoon tea swing into action, and there are hot dogs and lobster rolls no matter the hour. This is very much how to cover all bases, which just leaves drinking. Start at £8 a glass, but spare a thought for the Lynch-Bages 1995 at £325, which is just coming to an agreeable pitch of maturity.
Chef/s: Malachi O'Gallagher. **Meals:** main courses £15 to £34. **Details:** 150 seats. 20 seats outside. V menu. Wheelchairs.

Din Tai Fung
Cooking score: 1
⊖ Covent Garden, Leicester Square, map 5
Taiwanese | £40
5-6 Henrietta Street, Covent Garden, WC2E 8PS
Tel no: 020 3034 3888
dintaifung-uk.com

The first London outpost of this legendary Taiwanese dumpling chain is set in a huge two-tiered modern dining room. Happily, stories about the difficulties of getting a table (no bookings are taken) are largely a product of the early months. The famed xiao long bao (aka soup dumplings) are at the heart of the menu; watch them being made in the glass-walled kitchen alongside dumplings every which way, including excellent pork and vegetable wontons with black vinegar and chilli oil. Expect, too, noodles, steamed chicken soup, prawn and egg fried rice and the salted yolk lava bun that is fast achieving cult status. Drink tea, beer or wine.
Meals: main courses £11 to £15. **Details:** 250 seats. No reservations.

Dinings
Cooking score: 3
⊖ Marylebone, map 6
Japanese | £40
22 Harcourt Street, Marylebone, W1H 4HH
Tel no: 020 7723 0666
dinings.co.uk

The two floors of an easy-to-miss townhouse on a Marylebone back street may be short on creature comforts but the take on Japanese cuisine is endlessly fascinating and full of vigour. Devotees of raw fish crowd the tiny ground-floor counter for reworked sushi, open rolls and inside-out rolls such as Scottish lobster with spicy sesame, while others decamp to the light but austere basement dining room for innovative ideas built around the crossover concept of hot and cold 'Japanese tapas'. 'Tar-tar chips' might include fatty toro tuna with jalapeño mayonnaise, but the

repertoire also extends to Mediterranean-inspired specialities such as sea bass carpaccio with fresh Umbrian truffle and ponzu jelly. There are luxuries, too, so expect liberal quantities of wagyu beef – perhaps in a char siu bun or seared with porcini salsa and ponzu sauce. Donburi rice bowls with miso soup are a popular shout at lunchtime, while sake is top of the drinks list.
Chef/s: Masaki Sugisaki. **Meals:** small plates £7 to £40. Sushi and sashimi £4 to £9. **Details:** 28 seats. Bar. Music.

Dishoom Carnaby
Cooking score: 2
⊖ Oxford Circus, map 5
Indian | £30
22 Kingly Street, Soho, W1B 5QP
Tel no: 020 7420 9322
dishoom.com
£30

This lively Indian chain celebrates the colour of the swinging 60s at its busy Carnaby Street site. Join the queue for the salli boti, a celebratory Parsi lamb curry with shoestring potatoes. For main entry, see Shoreditch branch, east London.
Chef/s: Naved Nasir. **Closed:** 25 and 26 Dec, 1 and 2 Jan. **Meals:** main courses £7 to £17. **Details:** 98 seats. 25 seats outside. Bar. Wheelchairs. Music.

Dishoom Covent Garden
Cooking score: 2
⊖ Leicester Square, Covent Garden, map 5
Indian | £30
12 Upper St Martin's Lane, Covent Garden, WC2H 9FB
Tel no: 020 7420 9320
dishoom.com
£30

The Mumbai-style Dishoom brand grew out of this original site in a retail development off Long Acre. Behold the bentwood chairs, sepia photos and whirring ceiling fans over a dish of the special mutton pepper fry. For main entry, see Shoreditch branch, east London.

Chef/s: Naved Nasir. **Closed:** 25 and 26 Dec, 1 and 2 Jan. **Meals:** main courses £7 to £18. **Details:** 98 seats. 25 seats outside. Bar. Wheelchairs. Music. No reservations. Bookings after 5.45pm only for groups of 6 or more.

LOCAL GEM
Dum Biryani House
⊖ Tottenham Court Road, map 5
Indian | £28
187b Wardour Street, Soho, W1F 8ZB
Tel no: 020 3638 0974
dumlondon.com
£30

Ordering the biryani at this colourful subterranean restaurant is a must. 'Dum' refers to the technique of steaming rice and meat or vegetables together under a lid, which translates here as a beautifully golden, crisp pastry topping. First, though, order from the plethora of south Indian snacks, perhaps masala paneer pav, Nizami chicken lollipops or fiery Andhra prawn fry with a flaky paratha. Kulfi or sugar-soaked doughnuts should hit the sweet spot. Keep your head straight with a refreshing lassi or chai, or dive into the fun list of aromatic cocktails. Sunday brunch is a compelling proposition. Lucknow 49 (see entry) is from the same owner.

★ NEW ENTRY ★
Emilia
Cooking score: 4
⊖ Bond Street, map 5
Italian | £45
7 Haunch of Venison Yard, Mayfair, W1K 5ES
Tel no: 020 7468 5868
emiliarestaurant.co.uk

The team behind Clipstone, Portland and Quality Chop House (see entries) have taken over the restaurant inside Bonhams auction house. With wood flooring, white table linen and walls dotted with modern art, there's a spare, minimal feel to the light-filled first-floor dining room, helped along by approachable, clued-up staff. It takes its name and inspiration from the region of Emilia-

Romagna, one of the main gastronomic centres of Italy, with a classically divided menu to match. Good ingredients form a solid foundation, as seen in a pasta course of delicate tortellini filled with smoked eel in a broth given a tart edge by tomatoes, and in a tender piece of rose veal saltimbocca with earthy accompaniments of carrot purée and rainbow chard. Start, perhaps, with regional classics such as mortadella di Bologna or vitello tonnato, and finish with almond cake served with apricots, honey and chamomile, or wild strawberry granita and fennel ice cream. If your budget won't stretch to the outstanding wines on the Auction List sourced via Bonhams, there's a concise global selection from £26, with small glasses from £5. **Chef/s:** Stuart Andrew. **Closed:** Sun. **Meals:** main courses £12 to £32. **Details:** 25 seats. Bar.

Evelyn's Table

Cooking score: 3
⊖ Piccadilly Circus, map 5
Modern European | £55
The Blue Posts, 28 Rupert Street, Soho, W1D 6DJ
Tel no: 07921 336010
theblueposts.co.uk

Surprising things happen behind closed doors in Soho. That's certainly true of this micro-restaurant hidden beneath The Blue Posts pub. This lilliputian spot by the folk behind The Palomar and The Barbary seats just 15 at a marble-topped kitchen counter, commanded by an engaging Luke Robinson. Since its launch, the concept has shifted towards something more Italianate, teeing off the daily menu that majors in fresh pasta and Cornish dayboat fish with the likes of pizzette fritte, focaccia and charcuterie. Beyond those anchor points, the menu is dictated more by the seasons than regional affiliation: dishes might include caciocavallo cheese arancini; black bream crudo, blood orange and fennel; seafood risotto, bouillabaisse and sea herbs; or strawberry pavlova. This being a pub, liquid pleasures are many. Consider wines from a short but good list, a pint in the pub, or a cocktail from the glamorous bar upstairs. **Chef/s:** Luke Robinson. **Closed:** Sun, 24 to 26 Dec. **Meals:** main courses £14 to £31. **Details:** 15 seats. Bar. Music.

Fischer's

Cooking score: 2
⊖ Baker Street, Regent's Park, map 6
Central European | £40
50 Marylebone High Street, Marylebone, W1U 5HN
Tel no: 020 7466 5501
fischers.co.uk

Messrs Corbin and King have the market in grand European café dining cornered, and the reassuring bustle here suggests it was worth cornering. The orientation is turn-of-the-century Vienna, somewhere you might drop in for a brötchen of herring and beetroot in between your morning consultation with Dr Freud and an afternoon spin on the Prater ferris wheel. The decor, with its railway station clock and dark banquettes, looks very sober, but the all-day menus are full of cheering things. Schnitzels, würstchen with potato salad and sauerkraut, and peppery goulash with buttered spätzle capture the Mittel-European spirit, and there would be no Viennese eating without strudels, gugelhupfs and sachertorte to finish, or perhaps a figure-conscious slice of apple and lingonberry poppy seed cake. Take up the cholesterol slack with a cup of coffee piled high with a beehive of whipped cream. The wine list, from £26.50, is interleaved with a healthy showing of Austrian bottles. **Chef/s:** Lauren Kerr. **Meals:** main courses £15 to £38. **Details:** 100 seats. V menu. Wheelchairs.

The French House

Cooking score: 3
⊖ Leicester Square, Piccadilly Circus, map 5
French | £38
49 Dean Street, Soho, W1D 5BG
Tel no: 020 3985 7603
frenchhousesoho.com

Le tout Soho rejoiced to hear Neil Borthwick (ex-Merchants Tavern) was taking over the first-floor dining room at The French House, a tiny boho boozer and relic of 'old Soho'. The consensus is – and our inspection lunch confirms it – that Borthwick is the francophile for the job. He has worked in some legendary kitchens (Michel Bras's among them) and has the skills to prove it. Witness such labour-intensive country classics as pig's head terrine, ox tongue and sauce gribiche, and roast cod with artichokes barigoule, alongside good rustic plates of pork rillettes or tardivo, pumpkin and pickled walnut salad. Pudding was a choice between Paris–Brest and the cheeseboard, which was left with us until we'd had our fill. Such largesse easily compensates for the limited menu and tight space. Choose from the pub's all-French wine list (with over a dozen under a fiver a glass) or upgrade to the restaurant selection, from £38.
Chef/s: Neil Borthwick. **Closed:** Sat, Sun.
Meals: main courses £18 to £26. **Details:** 25 seats. Bar.

Frenchie

Cooking score: 4
⊖ Leicester Square, Covent Garden, map 5
Modern French | £55
16 Henrietta Steet, Covent Garden, WC2E 8QH
Tel no: 020 7836 4422
frenchiecoventgarden.com

Stepping around the tourist hordes thronging Covent Garden, you come to the calming blue Parisian-style frontage of this *très branché* neo-bistro. The long, narrow street-level dining room, stylishly turned out with blush pink chairs, curved banquettes, black and white

tiled floor, marble bar and globe lights, has a gentle buzz and is much preferred by readers, despite the basement dining area offering a ringside seat to the kitchen action. Everyone orders the famous bacon scones, but the rest of the repertoire takes in thoroughly modern ideas such as a rich lamb ragù with silky pappardelle, Kalamata olives and preserved lemon, and a thick tranche of perfectly cooked stone bass with lots of brown shrimp, fried courgettes, stuffed courgette flower, borlotti beans and a foamy seafood bisque. However, reports of 'disappointingly leaden' agnoletti and 'heavy' clafoutis served with a sorbet that 'just didn't taste of cherries' indicate that a little more balance and consistency would be welcome. The pre- and post-theatre menu is a good bet, and the predominantly French wine list (with sections for skin-contact and wild wines) has good choice by the glass (from £5.50) and 375ml carafe.
Chef/s: Gregory Marchand. **Closed:** 25 Dec, 1 Jan. **Meals:** main courses £26 to £32. Set L and early/late D £27 (2 courses) to £30. Tasting menu £65 (5 courses). **Details:** 72 seats. V menu. Wheelchairs. Music.

Frog by Adam Handling

Cooking score: 4
⊖ Covent Garden, map 5
Modern British | £65
34-35 Southampton Street, Covent Garden, WC2E 7HF
Tel no: 020 7199 8370
frogbyadamhandling.com

It looks like a lot of contemporary London restaurants – on the stark side of comfortable, with bare tables, hard floor, an open kitchen with counter seating – and the food follows suit with à la carte and tasting menus that are all about vivid modern British combinations. There are occasional flashes of brilliance in dishes that fully exploit contrasting flavours and textures, whether an opening snack of crab and kimchi tartlet or a starter of mushroom agnolotti with bone marrow and black garlic, or even the sourdough bread with its famous chicken skin butter. Elsewhere, pigeon is teamed with puffed rice and spiced cauliflower, and halibut with smoked eel, brown shrimp and kohlrabi. Equally, a beguiling combination of rhubarb, juniper and crème fraîche dazzles, although some diners suggest dessert is not a strong suit. To drink, there are cocktails, beers, and wines from £25.

Chef/s: Adam Handling and Steven Kerr. **Closed:** Sun, 24 to 27 Dec. **Meals:** main courses £27 to £35. Tasting menu £65 (5 courses) to £95. **Details:** 40 seats. V menu. Bar. Wheelchairs. Music.

LOCAL GEM
La Fromagerie Bloomsbury
⊖ Russell Square, Holborn, map 5
Modern European | £40
52 Lamb's Conduit Street, Bloomsbury, WC1N 3LL
Tel no: 020 7242 1044
lafromagerie.co.uk

Unlike its cousins in Highbury and Marylebone (see entry), this branch of the cheese-focused emporium stays open until 10pm every day (apart from an early finish on Sundays) – so take full advantage of the 'kitchen menu' with its line-up of seasonal bistro-style dishes ranging from crab ravioli to roast chicken with wild mushrooms. Of course, fabulously ripe cheeses and cheese-based specialities are La Fromagerie's USP, although artisan charcuterie and small plates such as courgette fritters make a quick daytime nibble with something from the short all-European wine list.

LOCAL GEM
La Fromagerie Marylebone
⊖ Baker Street, Bond Street, map 6
Modern European | £25
2-6 Moxon Street, Marylebone, W1U 4EW
Tel no: 020 7935 0341
lafromagerie.co.uk

£5 OFF   £30

Considered by many to be *the* London cheese shop (and wholesaler), Patricia Michelson's long-established homage to fromage is also a well-stocked deli and café, open from breakfast to early evening (and later on Friday nights). Found just off Marylebone High Street, and with branches in Bloomsbury (see entry) and Highbury, the format is simple enough – tuck into plates of cheese and charcuterie, seasonal salads and more, surrounded by shelves of enticing ingredients. Whether melted raclette or rare breed pulled pork bap, it's all honest, simple stuff. Wine pairings help things along, with craft beer by the bottle as well.

Galvin at Windows
Cooking score: 4
⊖ Hyde Park Corner, Green Park, map 6
French | £82
Hilton Hotel, 22 Park Lane, Mayfair, W1K 1BE
Tel no: 020 7208 4021
galvinatwindows.com

The views from the 28th floor are impressive, with floor-to-ceiling windows and a cleverly tiered layout ensuring most tables get a glimpse over Hyde Park and beyond. Tables are white-clad and chairs reassuringly comfortable but nobody could describe the dining room, decked out in tones of buff and boardroom brown, as colourful. Still, a lively, happy bustle comes as standard. The kitchen remains in the capable hands of Joo Won, who brings a few European influences to a fairly classic French menu in dishes from a salad of smoked duck with its confit leg, crispy gizzard, gem lettuce and pepper, via ballotine of black pudding with chicken, caramelised apple and grelot onion to roasted hake with crushed Jersey Royals, datterini tomatoes and beurre blanc. A tonka bean custard tart with prunes, Armagnac and vanilla ripple ice cream is a subtle twist on a classic. Weekends bring the possibility of Saturday brunch or a Sunday roast. France leads the charge on a wine list that has interesting global appeal and decent choice by the glass. Markups are high but the informed sommelier gives good advice.

Chef/s: Joo Won. **Meals:** set L £31 (2 courses) to £37. Set D £82. Sun L £55. **Details:** 107 seats. Bar. Wheelchairs.

Gauthier Soho

Cooking score: 6
⊖ Leicester Square, map 5
Modern French | £60
21 Romilly Street, Soho, W1D 5AF
Tel no: 020 7494 3111
gauthiersoho.co.uk
£5
OFF

The air of exclusivity that pervades a West End restaurant where a doorbell must be rung, beyond which a warren of rooms furnished with double-layered linen and triple-layered service awaits, is thrown into pleasurable relief when it's tempered by a flawless blend of warmth and professionalism. Such is Alexis Gauthier's place on the fringes of Soho, the youthful French staff, including an excellent sommelier, an enduring credit to it. Gauthier has established a versatile reputation for cooking to today's dietary regimes, so that alongside a core repertoire of distinguished modern French cuisine – paprika-roasted scallop in crustacean velouté, stone bass with sea purslane and leeks, black Angus in thyme jus – there are also vegetarian and vegan offerings resplendent with technical panache and culinary imagination. The spring vegan tasting menu included Loire asparagus with lovage cream and heirloom tomatoes, spring truffle tortellini, then a whole round courgette filled with red pipérade and crumbled pecan on Kalamata tapenade, and a triple-layered gnocchi of Bintje potato, truffle and garlicky green chard under smoked potato espuma. Even the dessert of chocolate tart layered with ganache, and gariguette strawberry with strawberry sorbet lacked nothing for want of lactose. The wine pairings were mostly great, too. And wine is taken very seriously, to the extent of much earnest discussion and a classy list that invites exploration. Small glasses start at £9.
Chef/s: Alexis Gauthier and Gerrard Virolle. **Closed:** Mon, Sun. **Meals:** set L £35. Set D £60 to £70. Tasting menu L £50 (5 courses) and D £80 (8 courses). **Details:** 80 seats. Vg menu. Wheelchairs.

★ TOP 50 ★

Le Gavroche

Cooking score: 7
⊖ Marble Arch, map 6
French | £150
43 Upper Brook Street, Mayfair, W1K 7QR
Tel no: 020 7408 0881
le-gavroche.co.uk
🍷 🛏

'We've wanted to eat here for ages but chose not to while they retained their archaic "jackets required" policy,' admitted one couple who finally took the plunge and made the trip to this bastion of French haute cuisine in all its classique finery. The dress code may have been relaxed, but Le Gavroche is still a formal restaurant; a cocoon-like basement room in shades of green, where the service is 'entirely proper but full of hospitality' and your guests will be given unpriced menus. From the exquisite canapés to the mighty cheese trolley, it's a culinary journey full of master strokes – perhaps a single, perfectly cooked scallop with a slice of smoked Jerusalem artichoke, some artichoke purée and artichoke crisps or a raviolo of 'heftily flavoured' braised herdwick lamb shoulder with a little savoury sauce, some pumpkin purée and amaretti. Honourable mentions go to the cured trout ('almost the texture of jelly') with beetroot, black sesame purée and crunchy monk's beard, and a choux bun filled with new season's rhubarb, vanilla cheesecake and ginger. Each course 'flows into the next', nothing jars and the cumulative effect is one of unabashed pleasure. Prices are high, of course, although the 'business lunch' offers a more affordable way in. Wines are, *naturellement*, exceptional – peerless vintages costing a pretty penny but delivering top-quality drinking to accompany the kitchen's flights of fancy. French supremacy is evident from the off, with selections from £50.
Chef/s: Michel Roux Jr and Rachel Humphrey. **Closed:** Mon, Sun, bank hols, 20 Dec to 7 Jan, 10 to 13 Apr. **Meals:** main courses £27 to £69. Set L £74. Tasting menu £178 (8 courses). **Details:** 68 seats. Bar. Music.

★ TOP 50 ★

The Greenhouse

Cooking score: 8

⊖ Green Park, map 5

Modern French | £110

27a Hay's Mews, Mayfair, W1J 5NY

Tel no: 020 7499 3331

greenhouserestaurant.co.uk

This Mayfair stalwart has weathered the tidal waves of London restaurant fashion with impressive durability. It's still a sexy place to arrive at, especially after dark, when the decked walkway through an ornamental garden builds a sense of anticipation for the gently attired room, its pale green scheme offset by a display of tree branches behind a vitrine wall. Staff are on point, nimbly attentive and entirely devoid of hauteur. Alex Dilling arrived in August 2018 from Hélène Darroze (see entry), the bar set high by his predecessor. There is some outstanding cooking going on, probably the venue's best, presented in the form of a fixed-price dinner or two tasting menus. Our inspection meal opened with a stunning Cornish mackerel escabèche in intense vadouvan cream and apple-fennel dressing. Oeuf noir is so-called for the white-gloved shaving of black truffle it receives at the table, its golden yolk exploding into a rich Périgord reduction. Blanquette de veau is opulent too, a bowl of supremely creamy stock laden with gently textured veal, its sweetbread encrisped in puffed buckwheat. The fashionable robust approach to fish is forsworn in favour of a piece of turbot in elderflower beurre blanc with green almonds and daikon, while the main meat might be a crown of red-rare Breton pigeon roasted with lavender, served with petits pois and Alsace bacon. A coconut bavarois encased in white chocolate and laced with whole caramelised Piedmont hazelnuts maintains the standard. To say that all this comes at a price is to state the obvious, but whatever you thought it would cost will become a dwindling dot even with wines by the glass. It's one of the best lists in London, but markups take no prisoners.

Chef/s: Alex Dilling. **Closed:** Mon, Sun. **Meals:** set L £45. Set D £110 (4 courses). Tasting menu £125 (6 courses) to £155. **Details:** 60 seats. V menu. Wheelchairs.

Gymkhana

Cooking score: 5

⊖ Piccadilly Circus, Green Park, map 5

Indian | £65

42 Albemarle Street, Mayfair, W1S 4JH

Tel no: 020 3011 5900

gymkhanalondon.com

£5 OFF

Due to reopen before the end of 2019 after fire damage, this Indian thoroughbred is out of the same stable as Brigadiers, Trishna and Hoppers (see entries) – so diners can expect a convincing, classy package that ticks all the boxes. The interior speaks of colonial clubbiness with its whirring ceiling fans, rattan-trimmed booths and old photos of polo teams, while the stand-alone basement bar dispenses reinvented punches in medicine bottles alongside nibbles of venison keema naan or Amritsari shrimps with dill raita. The modern-accented food in the ground-floor dining room centres on grills, game and chops, from Bengali-style salmon with chilli and lime yoghurt to quail kebabs pointed up with mustard and mint chutney – although some of the most interesting things are the 'nashta' small plates, perhaps scrambled duck egg bhurji with lobster and a Malabar paratha or yam and Tellicherry pepper dosa with coconut chutney. Fans of chicken butter masala also have plenty to cheer about, while desserts (aka 'meetha') take inspiration from Indian tradition and Western techniques – as in a hibiscus and rasgulla (sponge) trifle with raspberry sorbet. Own-label Gymkhana lager and thoughtfully selected wines suit the food admirably.

Chef/s: Jitin Joshi and Sid Ahuja. **Closed:** Sun, 25 Dec, bank hols. **Meals:** main courses £17 to £38. Set L £28 (2 courses) to £33. Set D £30 (2 courses) to £35. Tasting menu £85 (7 courses). **Details:** 90 seats. V menu. Vg menu. Bar. Music. No children after 7pm.

Hakkasan

Cooking score: 5
⊖ Tottenham Court Road, map 5
Chinese | £80
8 Hanway Place, Fitzrovia, W1T 1HD
Tel no: 020 7927 7000
hakkasan.com

The entrance down a tiny narrow road is so anonymous you might feel you are being smuggled in, but down the black staircase is a sultrily lit shrine to contemporary Chinese cuisine, now running in London for nearly 20 years. Long-time chef Tong Chee Hwee has left the group, and a new executive chef, Andrew Yeo, has been drafted in to head things up both here and at the Mayfair branch (see entry). Otherwise, the menu approach remains unchanged, with popular dim sum options such as har gau, scallop shumai and chive-laced jade dumplings to ease you into a brave new world of retooled Cantonese and other specialities. Spicy prawns with lily bulbs and almonds, Mongolian-style lamb chop, and truffled duck with tea-plant mushrooms are among the more opulent possibilities, and the traditional paucity of Chinese dessert offerings is put to flight with enticements such as an ice cream bombe coated in puffed rice with warm chocolate sauce. Piquant cocktails add to the fun, and there is a seriously weighty list of pedigree wines and sakes.
Chef/s: Andrew Yeo and Eng Soon Yeo. **Closed:** 24 and 25 Dec. **Meals:** main courses £19 to £75. Set L and early D £32 (2 courses) to £38. Set D £60 to £120. Tasting menu £70 (9 courses) to £120. **Details:** 200 seats. V menu. Bar. Wheelchairs. Music.

Hakkasan Mayfair

Cooking score: 4
⊖ Green Park, Bond Street, map 5
Chinese | £80
17 Bruton Street, Mayfair, W1J 6QB
Tel no: 020 7907 1888
hakkasan.com

Part of a global group known for its aspirational take on Chinese – nominally Cantonese – cooking, the Mayfair branch of Hakkasan suits its upmarket location. Noise levels can be deafening, especially if punters are fuelling up at the lively cocktail bar before moving through to the ice-cool dining room. Impeccable ingredients form the basis of menus that are identical to those served at the original London venue in Hanway Place (see entry), which many readers prefer. The Taste of Hakkasan set lunch is a good bet for those looking to keep the size of their bill in check. Otherwise, the carte is broad in scope, taking in dim sum platters, Mongolian-style lamb chops, wok-seared spotted bass in ginger soy, sweet-and-sour Duke of Berkshire pork with pomegranate, and lashings of big-money luxury such as wok-fried lobster with black truffle sauce and asparagus, or grilled Australian wagyu ribeye with spring onion soy. There are some alluring cocktails, but the wine list means business, with prices to match.
Chef/s: Andrew Yeo and Tan Tee Wei. **Meals:** main courses £19 to £75. Set L and early D £32 (2 courses) to £38. Set D £60 to £120. Tasting menu £70 (9 courses) to £120. **Details:** 220 seats. V menu. Bar. Wheelchairs. Parking. Music.

Hawksmoor Seven Dials

Cooking score: 4
⊖ Covent Garden, map 5
British | £60
11 Langley Street, Covent Garden, WC2H 9JG
Tel no: 020 7420 9390
thehawksmoor.com

This atmospheric branch of the easy-going steakhouse group is in a plum spot off Covent Garden's main drag, ideal for groups and pre- or post-theatre dining. The full restaurant menu is available in the bar. For main entry, see Knightsbridge branch, west London.
Chef/s: Karol Poniewaz. **Closed:** 25 and 26 Dec. **Meals:** main courses £17 to £60. Set L and early/late D £26 (2 courses) to £29. **Details:** 142 seats. Bar. Wheelchairs. Music.

Hélène Darroze at The Connaught

Cooking score: 5
⊖ Bond Street, Green Park, map 5
Modern French | £95
16 Carlos Place, Mayfair, W1K 2AL
Tel no: 020 3147 7200
the-connaught.co.uk

🛏

As we went to press, Hélène Darroze's London base was closing for refurbishment, reopening in September 2019. We don't yet know if the two Damien Hirst butterfly murals will remain, but we expect the supremely cosseting experience and choreographed service to continue to set the standard. Darroze is known for her pinpoint contemporary cooking with flavours and ingredients referencing her beloved Landes, as well as influences from faraway cuisines. From a recent menu, a clever, briny amalgam of Amur river caviar with oyster, dashi and sea urchin earns a £70 supplement, while Welsh lamb from Rhug Estate is intelligently paired with puntarelle, spiny artichokes, anchovies and lemon. As for the wine list, expect pages of Champagnes and a knowledgeably curated treasure trove of peerless vintages (especially from France) at head-spinning prices.
Chef/s: Hélène Darroze. **Meals:** set L £60. Set D £95 (5 courses). Tasting menu £110 (5 courses) to £185. **Details:** 62 seats. V menu. Vg menu. Bar. Wheelchairs. Music. Children over 7 yrs.

Hide Above

Cooking score: 5
⊖ Green Park, map 5
Modern British | £115
85 Piccadilly, Mayfair, W1J 7NB
Tel no: 020 3146 8666
hide.co.uk

The Piccadilly setting is a distinct tonal shift from the boiler room ambience of Olly Dabbous's first London venture. A spiral staircase in burnished oak leads to the monochrome upper room where battalions of staff will bid you good day. The tasting menu of four courses at lunch, seven at dinner, attempts to span an arc from almost provocative simplicity through energising intensities of flavour, and certainly hits some peaks. A mouthful of cured duck and another of pastrami exhibit exemplary curing, both packed with fatty concentration, and are succeeded by a near-black mushroom consommé of startling depth. The signature Dabbous coddled egg served in its shell in a nest of hay is still going strong, and there are desserts to write home about, from a 'technically magnificent, gorgeous-tasting soufflé of apricot and sugared almonds' to a come-hither gooey pistachio cake with cleansing sorrel granita. At inspection, however, there were too many combinations that seemed wilfully dissonant: a roast scallop with crushed swede was overpowered by its additions of wood-sage honey and saffron buttermilk, while a lobe of glazed veal sweetbread hardly stood a chance against its glutinous chestnut purée and a sauce combining the jangling elements of fennel and coffee. If dishes were brought more reliably into their own internal harmony, this could be truly groundbreaking cooking. From a wine list of colossal scope and Piccadilly percentages, some relief comes in an impressive selection by the glass, from £9 a small measure.
Chef/s: Ollie Dabbous and James Goodyear. **Meals:** set L £48 (4 courses). Tasting menu £115 (7 courses). **Details:** 80 seats. V menu. Vg menu. Bar. Wheelchairs. Music.

The Holborn Dining Room

Cooking score: 3
⊖ Holborn, map 5
Modern British | £55
Rosewood London, 252 High Holborn, Holborn, WC1V 7EN
Tel no: 020 3747 8633
holborndiningroom.com

🛏

The impressive scale of this high-ceilinged brasserie within the Rosewood London hotel reminded one reader of La Coupole in Paris,

with its marble pillars, studded leather banquettes and antique mirrors – although the food stays much closer to home. Counters loaded with crustacea and charcuterie supplement a plucky menu that takes in everything from gin-cured salmon with pickled cucumber to roast Suffolk pork belly or smoked haddock with poached egg. However, eating here is really about the pies, which are handmade in a dedicated room attached to the restaurant: flavours vary, but you might find anything from curried mutton with mango salsa to a hand-raised porcine classic packed with meaty bits, smoked bacon, fennel seeds and sage. The 'very filling' steak and kidney pud has also been endorsed, and if you still have room there's pineapple upside-down cake for afters. A 50-strong line-up of gins is sure to impress, although wines plump up the bill by at least £24 for a 500ml carafe, or £10 a glass.
Chef/s: Calum Franklin. **Closed:** 10 days Jan. **Meals:** main courses £18 to £44. **Details:** 160 seats. 50 seats outside. Bar. Wheelchairs. Music.

Honey & Co.
Cooking score: 3
♻ Warren Street, map 2
Middle Eastern | £35
25a Warren Street, Fitzrovia, W1T 5LZ
Tel no: 020 7388 6175
honeyandco.co.uk

Anyone with a beating heart can't fail to be charmed by Sarit Packer and Itamar Srulovich's tiny Middle Eastern restaurant (booking is obligatory). Warmth and generosity at this, their original Fitzrovia venture, is never off the menu and it suffuses each and every abundant plate of food. Sit elbow to elbow and start with the popular mixed meze selection, a cornucopia of deliciousness in which Yemeni falafel with smooth as silk tahini always features. Every one of the couple's dishes involves a riot of flavours and superior British produce. Essaouira fish tagine made with Cornish sea bass, chickpeas and Swiss chard in a rich chermoula sauce begs to be mopped up with

homemade bread, and lamb is ever present, perhaps in a slow-cooked stifado. Vegetarian offerings, maybe roasted mauve aubergine with BBQ tahini crust, jewelled rice salad and lime, rightly vie for attention, too. Finish with one of Sarit's desserts from the counter. The European-led wine list keeps things brief and straightforward, and they do wonderful things with eggs at breakfast.
Chef/s: Sarit Packer and Itamar Srulovich. **Closed:** Sun, 24, 26 and 31 Dec, 1 Jan. **Meals:** main courses £17. Set L and D £31 (2 courses) to £35. **Details:** 28 seats. 9 seats outside. Music.

Honey & Smoke
Cooking score: 4
♻ Great Portland Street, Warren Street, map 5
Middle Eastern | £38
216 Great Portland Street, Fitzrovia, W1W 5QW
Tel no: 020 7388 6175
honeyandco.co.uk

Israeli husband-and-wife team Sarit Packer and Itamar Srulovich (both ex-Ottolenghi) followed up the success of their diminutive debut Honey & Co (see entry) with their colourful take on a Middle Eastern grill. The seasonal sharing menu, bristling with spice and promise, is the way to go here, beginning with meze for the table (which might be pea and feta fritters, aubergine and tomato salad and always, always, houmous and falafel) followed by a choice of mains grilled over the coals, such as whole Cornish sea bass with courgette, currant and pine nut salad or saffron-tinted chicken joojah. Feta and honey cheesecake – 'the one from Honey & Co', as they put it – is not to be missed. Start the day well over breakfast of sabich, boureka, red shakshuka or grilled bread with labneh and urfa chilli. The kindly priced wine list is short but interesting and selected for the season.
Chef/s: Sarit Packer and Itamar Srulovich. **Closed:** Sun, 24 to 26 Dec, 1 Jan. **Meals:** main courses £18 to £19. Set L and D £33 (2 courses) to £38. **Details:** 80 seats. Bar. Wheelchairs. Music.

Hoppers Soho

Cooking score: 3
⊖ Tottenham Court Road, map 5
Sri Lankan | £29
49 Frith Street, Soho, W1D 4SG
hopperslondon.com
£30

Since bringing the exotic flavours of Sri Lanka and Tamil Nadu to Soho, the Sethi family has opened a larger, more easily bookable Marylebone offshoot, but this original spot's popularity remains undiminished. The low-lit restaurant, with its rattan ceiling, terracotta tiles and ochre yellow walls, evokes the island's roadside taverns and fans brave Hopper's queuing system – they take your number so you don't have to line up – for the namesake savoury pancakes. Order those lacy bowls, made with a fermented rice and coconut batter, or a dosa; pick a pungent, fiery kari (curry), a chutney and a fresh sambol relish and tear it, or fill and roll it. 'Short eats' inspired by Sri Lanka's street-food hawkers include rotis, devilled squid and mutton rolls, and there are a good few meatless dishes. Expect heat to come from pepper, not chillies, and quench thirst with tropical cocktails or a cooling beer. **Chef/s:** Renjith Sarathchandran. **Closed:** Sun, bank hols, Christmas. **Meals:** main courses £8 to £23. Set L £19 (2 courses). Tasting menu £32 (5 courses). **Details:** 40 seats. V menu. Bar. Music. No reservations. L bookings only for groups of 4 or more Mon to Fri.

Hoppers St Christopher's Place

Cooking score: 3
⊖ Bond Street, map 6
Sri Lankan | £32
St Christopher's Place, 77 Wigmore Street, Marylebone, W1U 1QE
Tel no: 020 3319 8110
hopperslondon.com

Better known perhaps as an appam, a hopper is a pancake made from fermented rice and coconut milk, and it's the perfect foil for the

sambols, chutneys and curries (karis) up for grabs at this simple Sri Lankan eatery with its modern-meets-tropical aesthetic. Don't worry – there's a useful glossary of food terms for those unfamiliar with the cuisine. A giant cone of masala dosa arrives with pungent, aromatic accompaniments such as pol sambol and coriander chutney, while exuberant plates of black pork ribs (with cashew and fennel sambol) and fish 'buriani' with acharu pickle hit the spot. Confident spicing is evident in karis from pumpkin to lamb shank, and in the street snack-inspired kothus. Curiosity is reason enough to try the only dessert: love cake ice cream sandwich. Drink enticingly spiced cocktails, Sri Lankan or British beers, or wines from £30. Hoppers Soho is to be found in Frith Street (see entry). **Chef/s:** Renjith Sarathchandran. **Closed:** bank hols, 24 to 26 Dec, 1 Jan. **Meals:** main courses £8 to £21. Set L £20 (2 courses). Tasting menu £32 (5 courses). **Details:** 96 seats. V menu. Bar. Wheelchairs. Music. L bookings for groups of 2 or more. D bookings for groups of 4 or more.

Ikoyi

Cooking score: 4
⊖ Piccadilly Circus, map 5
Modern West African | £75
1 St James's Market, St James's, SW1Y 4AH
Tel no: 020 3583 4660
ikoyilondon.com
£5 OFF

'Some of the quirkiest, creative and downright unusual cooking in London' is to be found at this slick modernist dining room – an expensive mix of gleaming surfaces, terrazzo floors, abstract oil paintings and hand-crafted crockery. The kitchen takes its cue from West African cuisine, although this is merely the jumping-off point for a repertoire of precise produce-led Westernised dishes – not surprising given that chef Jeremy Chan is a veteran of some big-name UK kitchens. Prices are high, ingredients are obscure and the only option at dinner is a blind tasting menu, which makes the whole show even more exclusive. The signature plantain with smoked Scotch bonnet chilli and freeze-dried raspberries is an Insta favourite, while a plate of 'fried chicken' (actually a slice of poached breast wrapped in a skin-like crumb wrapper with pickled onion petals) shows off Chan's 'mesmerising technique'. To finish, try the 'malty' brown rice ice cream with a millet-like fonio cracker and honey-hydrated mango. Wines start at £32 and there are some oddball cocktails, too. **Chef/s:** Jeremy Chan. **Closed:** Sun, 24 Dec to 1 Jan. **Meals:** set L and early D £35. Tasting menu £75 (6 courses) to £100. **Details:** 42 seats. Bar. Music.

Indian Accent
Cooking score: 4
⊖ **Green Park, map 5**
Indian | £55
16 Albemarle Street, Mayfair, W1S 4HW
Tel no: 020 7629 9802
indianaccent.com

The original branches in Delhi and New York are both world-class destinations in their own right, and this swish offshoot also knows all about putting on the style. The dining room's striking green upholstery, gleaming parquet floors, mottled marble tables and smoky mirrors speak of money lavishly spent, while the food is likely to shake up most of your preconceived ideas about Indian cuisine. Chef Manish Mehrotra surprises and thrills diners with his freestyling approach and eclectic borrowings – just consider a fenugreek chicken 'cornet' with pickle cream or tiger prawns with sago fritters and Indian sorrel chutney. Vegetarians and vegans do exceedingly well here (try the spherical potato chaat with white pea mash or the tofu masala with shishito pepper and quinoa puffs), while the self-styled 'bread bar' goes way beyond the usual chapatis (don't miss the herb-flecked millet roti or the addictively moreish smoked bacon kulcha). Tuned-in young staff are also on hand to dispense fancy East-West cocktails and classy spice-friendly wines with top-end Mayfair price tags.

Chef/s: Manish Mehrotra. **Closed:** 25 Dec, 1 Jan. **Meals:** main courses £21 to £27. Set L £24 (2 courses). Tasting menu £85 (7 courses). **Details:** 70 seats. 6 seats outside. V menu. Vg menu. Bar. Music.

J. Sheekey
Cooking score: 4
⊖ **Leicester Square, map 5**
Seafood | £55
28-32 St Martin's Court, Covent Garden, WC2N 4AL
Tel no: 020 7240 2565
j-sheekey.co.uk

On this site off Charing Cross Road since 1896, Sheekey is wearing well. The appeal, in a nutshell, is fresh fish and shellfish served in a series of small, highly polished panelled rooms where the 'food, service and atmosphere are of a high standard'. You can look forward to classics such as oysters, shellfish platters, crab bisque, grilled Dover sole and the near-legendary fish pie. But worked into the mix are more modern ideas: whole Cornish lemon sole, say, with sea kale and blood orange, or fillet of hake teamed with roasted chicken broth, crispy wings and caramelised shallot purée. You'll also find a few meat dishes (perhaps chargrilled Bannockburn ribeye steak with béarnaise sauce), vegetarian and vegan choices, and for dessert, the irresistible banoffee profiteroles with caramelised banana ice cream – although the savoury Welsh rarebit has its devotees. The wine list is a French-led upmarket selection that's bedevilled by stiff markups.

Chef/s: Andrew McLay. **Meals:** main courses £19 to £44. Set L and late D £25 (2 courses) to £30. **Details:** 90 seats. 40 seats outside. V menu. Vg menu. Bar. Wheelchairs.

No reservations
If a restaurant doesn't take reservations, or only allows them for groups, this is indicated in the details at the end of the entry.

Jamavar

Cooking score: 5
⊖ Bond Street, Green Park, map 5
Indian | £60
8 Mount Street, Mayfair, W1K 3NF
Tel no: 020 7499 1800
jamavarrestaurants.com
£5
OFF

An atmosphere of dazzling opulence reigns, with shimmering gilt mirrors and ornate wall decorations reflecting the original in Bengaluru, southern India. Along with its central London partner, Bombay Bustle (see entry), Jamavar aims to bring a sense of ceremonial occasion to the cuisine of the Mughal and southern coast, as well as to the street foods of north and south. To that latter end, open with soft-shell crab dressed in Tellicherry black pepper and garlic, with mango chilli chutney and garlic chips, and perhaps a paratha topped with a shami of kid goat in bone marrow sauce. Following on are exemplary vegetable biryani or Hampshire lamb with crisp-fried onions and minty raita, the signature king prawn moilee in shallots, curry leaves and mustard, or a sumptuous version of corn-fed butter chicken, chargrilled and pulled, then garnished with tomato and fenugreek. Precise spicing is evident in a vegetable side of slow-cooked dhungar dhal (smoked yellow lentils with ginger and tomato). To finish, there is luxurious mango rasmalai or nougat chocolate mousse with cinnamon ice cream. A wine list to match the surroundings, as well as the postcode, doesn't stint on quality, with small glasses starting at £7.50.
Chef/s: Surender Mohan. **Closed:** 25 and 26 Dec, 1 and 2 Jan. **Meals:** main courses £12 to £32. Set L and early D £25 (2 courses) to £35. Tasting menu £80 (6 courses). **Details:** 100 seats. 8 seats outside. V menu. Bar. Music. No children after 6pm.

Jidori Yakitori

Cooking score: 3
⊖ Covent Garden, map 5
Japanese | £30
15 Catherine Street, Covent Garden, WC2B 5JZ
Tel no: 020 7836 3145
jidori.co.uk
£30

Japan's jidori chickens are no ordinary birds. Stringent breeding criteria and a free-roaming life make for exceptionally full-flavoured, succulent meat, perfect for skewering and grilling in Tokyo's casual yakitori-yas. This minimalist space is spread over two narrow floors, with a basement karaoke room, and almost no part of the premium bird escapes a skewering. Small plates – perhaps koji-fried chicken with nori salt or katsu curry Scotch egg – start things rolling, but the yakitori cooked on the custom-made charcoal grill are the main draw, perhaps tsukune (minced chicken) skewers with egg yolk lightly cured in umami tare (dipping sauce) or tender hearts impaled with bacon. Rice bowls and a katsu 'sando' satisfy lunchtime crowds, while ginger ice cream with miso caramel, sweet potato crisps and black sesame is a standout dessert. If the yakitori tasting menu (omakase) appeals, do book ahead. Beer or sake might seem the obvious match, but the few wines work well, too. Expect a similar menu at the original Dalston branch: 89 Kingsland High Street, London E8 2PB.
Chef/s: Shunta Matsubara. **Closed:** Sun. **Meals:** small plates £6 to £10. Tasting menu £33 (4 courses). **Details:** 50 seats.

Jikoni

Cooking score: 2
⊖ Baker Street, Bond Street, map 6
Pan-Asian | £30
19-21 Blandford Street, Marylebone,
W1U 3DH
Tel no: 020 7034 1988
jikonilondon.com
£30

Simple, unaffected charm and good-value food bring the crowds to this small, colourful Marylebone restaurant. The cooking draws on the mixed heritage and travels of the owner, chef and TV presenter Ravinder Bhogal, so expect the wide-ranging flavours of East Africa, the Middle East and Asia. Start with snacks of prawn toast Scotch eggs with banana ketchup or roasted scallop with avocado and yuzu purée, and small plates of, say, kimchi royals – new potatoes topped with salted and fermented vegetables, Japanese mayo and prawn crackers. Hard to resist is tiger prawn khichdi (a delicious, creamy coconut curry), which arrives with a little coconut sambal and lemon rice on the side. Tempura inari (rice ball) filled with moong dhal arrives with sweet-and-sour tomatoes and carrot kraut, while the signature banana cake with miso butterscotch, peanut brittle and Ovaltine kulfi makes a fitting finale. Drink spice-infused cocktails such as machungwa (orange) and chilli martini or wines that have been chosen to match the food.
Chef/s: Ravinder Bhogal. **Meals:** small plates £10 to £11. Large plates £15 to £26. **Details:** 50 seats.

Jugemu

Cooking score: 3
⊖ Piccadilly Circus, map 5
Japanese | £35
3 Winnett Street, Soho, W1D 6JY
Tel no: 020 7734 0518

Opposite the stage door of the Gielgud Theatre on the southern fringe of Soho, Jugemu rapidly fills up with Japanese business people in the after-work hour. It's not exactly a contemplative temple of cuisine, more a tiny café, although watching the sushi chefs from a counter seat is mesmerising in itself. With just a few tables and no decor to speak of, its back-to-basics approach gives no hint of the finely wrought Japanese food to come. The sashimi and tempura variations are light and delicious, and there are handmade rolls of salmon and avocado or scallop and cucumber, as well as the traditional likes of beef tataki, soba noodles with seafood, and crisp-fried pork fillet with ponzu. Omakase (chef's choice) is the obvious way to go for newcomers. Given the limited dimensions of the place, booking is strongly advised. Wines by the glass, sake and Japanese beer provide liquid refreshment.
Chef/s: Yuya Kikuchi. **Meals:** small plates £4 to £10. Sushi and sashimi £13 to £33. **Details:** 19 seats.

Kanishka

Cooking score: 4
⊖ Oxford Circus, Piccadilly Circus, map 6
Indian | £45
17-19 Maddox Street, Mayfair, W1S 2QH
Tel no: 020 3978 0978
kanishkarestaurant.co.uk

Atul Kochhar's new venture has a more casual feel than his previous venue, Benares (see entry). Modish black and white flooring and a palette of blue and aquamarine greet diners in the airy ground-floor dining room, while the muted shades of the basement draw attention to the 'living' ceiling and open kitchen. The cooking has also taken a new direction, focusing on the 'unexplored' (at least on these shores) cuisine of the north-eastern corner of India, with momos (dumplings) or Tibetan thukpa (noodle soup) popping up among the starters. A trio of fat hand-dived scallops paired with fried cauliflower pepped up with smoked chilli made a good opener on our visit, followed by a rich and spicy goat curry flavoured with cumin and black pepper, and best enjoyed with fluffy naans. Dessert was a beautifully crafted peanut butter pavé with salted caramel chikki (brittle) accompanied by caramelised banana. Service is attentive and responsive and there are bespoke flavoured cocktails, 30 wines by the glass and bottles from £25.

Chef/s: Atul Kochhar. **Meals:** main courses £20 to £38. Set L and early D £28 (2 courses) to £32. **Details:** 127 seats. V menu.

Kiln

Cooking score: 4
⊖ **Piccadilly Circus, map 5**
Thai | £24
58 Brewer Street, Soho, W1F 9TL
kilnsoho.com

£30

The heady scent of spice hits you as soon as you're through the door, once you've got in – bookings are taken only for four or more. Add your name to the waiting list and grab a drink nearby until you are called – it's worth the wait. There's dining space in the basement, but squeezing in at the stainless-steel counter on the ground floor is the preferred spot. Here, a masterful amalgamation of stellar British seasonal produce and the rich, diverse culinary culture of northern Thailand gives your senses a thorough workout. Cornish dayboat fish is stuffed with pungent spice pastes or baked in jungle curry, there are aromatic laabs (meat salads), more curries – beef neck, perhaps – and signature claypot-baked glass noodles with brown crabmeat and rare breed pork are a must. Expect heat, and if you're averse, let your waiter guide you. The short list of wines, each available by the glass, is challenging if you're unfamiliar with natural viticulture, but fully suited to the boisterous food. Cocktails, ferments and soft drinks are worthy of exploration.

Chef/s: Meedu Saad. **Closed:** 25 Dec. **Meals:** small plates £5 to £14. **Details:** 48 seats. Music. No reservations. Bookings only for groups of 4 or more.

Kitchen Table

Cooking score: 6
⊖ **Goodge Street, map 5**
Modern British | £150
70 Charlotte Street, Fitzrovia, W1T 4QG
Tel no: 020 7637 7770
kitchentablelondon.co.uk

For diners who like to get close to the action, James Knappett's particular brand of kitchen table is a huge draw. If it isn't the curtained entrance (you'll wait in Bubbledogs; fizz if you like, but stay off the hot dogs), it's the eat-over counter, the chef's tweezers, the meticulous plating – not to mention the chefs choreographed to produce at least 12 (16 on our visit) intricately realised courses under full customer glare, and still be nice about it. It's not a chatty, sleeves-up kind of an evening, but there's a surpassing thrill about dishes like an early 'ever so pretty' course of Porthilly oyster with a rich bavarois of oyster with smoked oil, icy-sweet elderflower granita and elderflower vinegar. Knappett has an eye for beauty, although some say they'd like more of the knack for texture that shows in a snacky sandwich of chicken skin with mascarpone and smoked bacon nuggets. Bigger dishes can be boldly simple – see crisp-skinned lamb breast with lamb jus and mint oil – or full of intrigue, as in an asparagus and hollandaise tartlet with last year's oranges: sour, sweet and salt all at once. Foraged London ingredients give the latter courses an offbeat twist, as in ice cream with beetroot and woodruff granita. As you'd expect with Bubbledogs next door, the wine list has oodles of fizz and some quirky treats. Prices start at £10 a glass (£39 a bottle), and great advice comes as standard.

Chef/s: James Knappett. **Closed:** Mon, Tue, Sun. **Meals:** tasting menu £150 (12 courses) to £195. **Details:** 20 seats. V menu. Vg menu. Bar. Children over 12 yrs.

Kitty Fisher's

Cooking score: 5
⊖ Green Park, map 5
Modern British | £50
10 Shepherd Market, Mayfair, W1J 7QF
Tel no: 020 3302 1661
kittyfishers.com

'Nothing here is different interior-wise,' noted a returning customer to this doll's house of a restaurant where 'two diminutive, dark, atmospheric dining rooms are stacked atop each other, connected by a wobbly staircase.' The basement can feel 'a bit like eating in a museum', so if you are inside, stay at ground level or grab one of the few outdoor tables. Undressed dark wood tables, coarse linen napkins and straightforward tableware are matched by a concise menu that tempts with earthy, rustic platefuls of seasonal British ingredients presented with no standing on ceremony by charming, chatty staff. Pig jowl croquettes with apricot ketchup make the perfect opener, then quail and cauliflower risotto before principal dishes of, say, lamb with carrots and mead. Add some 'decadent' crispy potatoes on the side ('bit like a posh hash brown'), and finish with spiced cake with rhubarb and evaporated milk ice cream. A succinct, mostly European wine list opens with house French by the carafe (from £13), rising to some limited-supply reserve bottles.
Chef/s: George Barson. **Closed:** Sun. **Meals:** main courses £24 to £30. **Details:** 34 seats. 8 seats outside. Music.

Locanda Locatelli

Cooking score: 4
⊖ Marble Arch, map 6
Italian | £65
8 Seymour Street, Marylebone, W1H 7JZ
Tel no: 020 7935 8390
locandalocatelli.com

Synonymous with understated glamour and well-upholstered comfort, Giorgio Locatelli's Marylebone stalwart soothes and reassures with help from domed mirrors, pale leather trim and cleverly designed semi-private booths. It's the backdrop for cooking that explores the byways of Italian regional cuisine, melding tradition with a full-on commitment to provenance as well as flavour: from gloriously fresh salad plates (marinated anchovies with smoked potato, radicchio and green sauce) to magnificent hand-crafted pastas (perhaps spaghetti with stewed octopus or buckwheat pizzoccheri with savoy cabbage, leeks and Bitto cheese). Bigger plates also shine – basil-crusted plaice fillet served simply with black olives and tomato sauce, for example, or pan-fried calf's kidneys with potato purée and stewed lentils. To finish, time-honoured Italian desserts (tiramisu, budino) sit alongside more intricate creations including bay leaf panna cotta with orange, basil and grapefruit compôte, lemon biscuit and green olives. High prices and big bills are a given, especially if you're tempted to explore the patrician wine list – although you'll be treated to some fabulous drinking from some of the masters of Italian regional viticulture.
Chef/s: Giorgio Locatelli and Rino Bono. **Closed:** 24 to 26 Dec, 1 Jan. **Meals:** main courses £16 to £37. **Details:** 75 seats. Bar. Wheelchairs.

Lorne

Cooking score: 6
⊖ Victoria, map 3
Modern European | £55
76 Wilton Road, Victoria, SW1V 1DE
Tel no: 020 3327 0210
lornerestaurant.co.uk
🍾

'Lucky Wilton Road' to have A. Wong (see entry) and this smart grey-fronted 'neo-bistro' within yards of each other, observed a reader who loved Lorne's inviting, grown-up vibe and spot-on noise levels. Set up by sommelier Katie Exton and chef Peter Hall (ex-River Café and The Square, respectively), this place shows its style with a street-facing marble counter, some adorable two-seater booths for tête-à-têtes and a clean-lined dining room with Scandi chairs and parquet floors. The kitchen works to an ever-changing menu with occasional global flourishes (soft-shell crab with katsu sauce, avocado and radish, say), although the biggest hits owe their allegiance to French and European cuisine. A dazzling starter of veal sweetbread with burnt apple purée and a disc of buckwheat praline is worth the price of admission alone, while harmonious flavours and spot-on technique also shine brightly in a dish of crisp-skinned hake with 'cauliflower mushroom', asparagus, mussels and buttery chive-flecked sauce. As for dessert, nothing outshines the tantalisingly savoury and 'perfectly wobbly' Brillat-Savarin panna cotta topped with a layer of red grape jelly and wonderfully sharp green apple sorbet. Katie Exton's knowledgeable and intelligently chosen wine list offers terrific drinking by the glass or carafe, while lifting the lid on some more obscure food-friendly bottles from £22.

Chef/s: Peter Hall. **Closed:** 23 Dec to 2 Jan. **Meals:** main courses £20 to £30. Set L £22 (2 courses) to £27. Set D £35 (2 courses) to £42. Sun L £35. **Details:** 42 seats. Music.

★ NEW ENTRY ★

Lucknow 49

Cooking score: 3
⊖ Oxford Circus, Bond Street, map 5
Indian | £32
49 Maddox Street, Mayfair, W1S 2PQ
Tel no: 020 7491 9191
lucknowldn.com

Following on from the success of his Soho venture, Dum Biryani (see entry), Dhruv Mittal has settled on Mayfair for his second opening. The brightly decorated restaurant – patterned walls, sumptuous cushions and simple wooden furniture – reels in passers-by with a takeaway lunch menu and good-value two-course deal, but the concise carte also offers kind prices for the area. The food is inspired by the Indian city that lends its name to the restaurant, which means plenty of meat and carbs. In a starter of dhal kachori bhalla chaat (a lentil-stuffed flatbread, rice and lentil dumplings, sweet yoghurt, tamarind and coriander chutney) sprinkled with pomegranate seeds, the balance of sweet and

sour is 'spot-on'. For mains, taar gosht – lamb slow-cooked in trotter stock for 12 hours with over 30 spices – appears with raita, basmati rice and gilafi kulcha, a layered and flaky bread cooked in the tandoor. Drink cocktails, beer or spice-friendly wines from a short list (from £29).

Chef/s: Dhruv Mittal and Irfan Khan. **Meals:** main courses £12 to £18. Set L and early D £20 (2 courses) to £25. **Details:** 40 seats.

Lurra

Cooking score: 2
⊖ Marble Arch, map 6
Spanish | £45
9 Seymour Place, Marylebone, W1H 5BA
Tel no: 020 7724 4545
lurra.co.uk

Its sibling and near-neighbour, Donostia, takes its name from the indigenous word for San Sebastián. Lurra, meanwhile, translates more generically as 'earth' or 'land'. Either way, these two eateries have turned Seymour Place into something of an enclave for proper Basque cooking, with Lurra specialising in the region's traditional *erretegias* – charcoal and wood grills. The dining room is tricked out with swathes of white marble, pale wood and close-set tables – although it's worth bagging a spot by the counter if you like being close to the action. The star attraction is dry-aged on-the-bone beef from Galicia's famous 'old cows' (14-year rubia Gallega, or Galician blond), along with other mighty sharing plates such as shoulder of suckling pig. To start, there are tapas nibbles such as Guernica peppers with sea salt or grilled octopus with piquillo sauce, while obscure but helpfully annotated wines from the Basque region and beyond suit the food perfectly.

Chef/s: Charlie Bourne. **Closed:** 22 Dec to 3 Jan. **Meals:** main courses £12 to £22. Set L £25 to £32. **Details:** 78 seats. 24 seats outside. Bar. Music.

Master Wei
⊖ Russell Square, map 5
Chinese | £20
13 Cosmo Place, Bloomsbury, WC1N 3AP
Tel no: 020 7209 6888
masterwei.co.uk

£30

In the same stable as Xi'an Impression in north London (see entry), this modest, tightly packed eatery is the place to come for the long, flat, hand-pulled noodles of Shaanxi province in north-west central China. It's fast-paced food, so busy diners drop in just for a bowl, say vegetarian or beef biang biang noodles in a deep paprika-coloured broth that's all salt, sour and hefty flavours. There's Xi'an street food too, perhaps fried chicken and mushroom potsticker dumplings, a pulled pork burger, and spicy pork dumplings in soup. Drink Tsingtao beer or tea.

Mele e Pere
⊖ Piccadilly Circus, map 5
Italian | £35
46 Brewer Street, Soho, W1F 9TF
Tel no: 020 7096 2096
meleepere.co.uk

£5
OFF

There are a few tables on the ground floor, but head down the *mele e pere* (apples and pears) to the basement to get the full impact of this much-loved trattoria and vermouth bar. The arrival of homemade focaccia sets the standard for the full-flavoured plates that follow: taglierini with Umbrian black truffle, grilled

octopus with harissa or a beefy Welsh black Angus T-bone steak. A list of 30 vermouths includes the house blend.

★ NEW ENTRY ★

Meraki
Cooking score: 3
⊖ Goodge Street, Oxford Circus, map 5
Greek | £40
80-82 Great Titchfield Street, Fitzrovia, W1W 7QT
Tel no: 020 7305 7686
meraki-restaurant.com

Midway between Oxford Street and Fitzrovia lies Meraki, a Greek-themed venue from the team behind Roka (see entries). It's an expansive split-level barn of a place, with distressed brick walls, elegant wine shelves and seating along the kitchen counter. A menu divided conventionally into hot and cold meze, salads and signature mains deals in briskly retooled Greek dishes that crucially retain a feel for the appeal of eastern Mediterranean food. That includes sea-fresh shrimp saganaki style, with melting Mastelo cheese in resonantly concentrated tomato and chilli; rich lamb croquettes on courgette tzatziki; and benchmark houmous, snappy with toasted buckwheat and topped with slivers of smoked eel. More speculative offerings are carpaccio of sea bream scattered with orange zest and diced green apple, a refreshing proposition that sadly lacked its grey mullet bottarga at inspection, and mains such as long-simmered veal cheek in miso, served with a cloud of mash and deep-fried sweet potato threads. Finish with a coffee-boosted chocolate crémeux topped with Metaxa gel, with salted butterscotch and pistachio-studded buckwheat pasteli. A wine list full of the glories of new Greek wine-making comes at rocket-fuelled markups. Drink by the glass from £7.
Chef/s: Athinagoras Kostakos. **Meals:** main courses £16 to £26. Small plates £5 to £16. Set L £22 (2 courses) to £26. **Details:** 130 seats. 20 seats outside. Bar.

Local Gem

These entries are brilliant neighbourhood venues, delivering good, freshly cooked food at great value for money.

Mere

Cooking score: 5
⊖ Goodge Street, map 5
Modern European | £60
74 Charlotte Street, Fitzrovia, W1T 4QH
Tel no: 020 7268 6565
mere-restaurant.com
£5 OFF 🍾

Followers of *Masterchef: The Professionals* won't need introducing to Monica Galetti, who has been a judge on the show for over a decade. Having worked in the kitchens of Le Gavroche (see entry), she brings a French accent to the modern European dishes on offer at this elegantly burnished dining room in lively Fitzrovia. Ballotine of stuffed quail with confit leg, crispy grapes, onion purée and hazelnuts is ineffably French, an opener full of contrasting textural elements, but there is equal assurance to a pasta dish such as pumpkin agnolotti with mushrooms in an emulsified Marmite dressing. The trend for bold treatments of fish is celebrated when Cornish cod comes with artichoke, confit fennel, black olives and dulse aioli sauce, and there is resonant depth to meats such as roast breast and braised leg of pigeon with lardo and salt-baked celeriac in a treacle-rich reduction of Pedro Ximénez. Finish with poached peaches layered with elderflower posset, strawberry schnapps gel and lemon shortbread. The set lunch menu is splendid value. Wines by the small glass from £6.50 are inspired choices from top to bottom, but there is quality in abundance all through the varietally classified list.

Chef/s: Monica Galetti. **Closed:** Sun, bank hols, 24 to 26 and 31 Dec, 1 Jan. **Meals:** main courses £24 to £39. Set L £29 (2 courses) to £35. Tasting menu £75 (6 courses). **Details:** 55 seats. V menu. Bar. Wheelchairs. Music.

Murano

Cooking score: 6
⊖ Green Park, map 5
Modern European | £70
20 Queen Street, Mayfair, W1J 5PP
Tel no: 020 7495 1127
muranolondon.com
🍾

Tucked discreetly in among the converted townhouse offices of Mayfair, Angela Hartnett's Murano is an island of West End Mediterranean sunshine. If there is actual sunshine, soak it up at one of the handful of tables outside under the awning. In January 2019, Em Brightman stepped up to the post of head chef and shows every sign of maintaining Murano's reputation for graceful, flavour-driven, Italian-oriented cooking. The *carta* offers a trio of choices in each section, perhaps moving from an enterprising double act of seared scallop and chicken wing with taramasalata and grapefruit to an intermediary carb fix of risotto, gnocchi or pasta. Mains might include monkfish with a mussel raviolo and braised fennel in divinely aromatic saffron velouté or loin and belly of pork with chou farci, mustard fruits and apple purée. Evidence of careful sourcing is what distinguishes these dishes, right through to peanut mousse with banana sorbet and Madagascar chocolate, or the signature caramelised lemon tart made with Amalfi's finest. Italy is the centre of gravity of the excellent wine list, but it's demonstratively strong in all departments, leading with a covetable glass selection, including Coravin offerings.

Chef/s: Angela Hartnett and Em Brightman. **Closed:** Sun, 5 days Christmas. **Meals:** set L £32 (2 courses) to £37. Set D £55 (2 courses) to £95. **Details:** 56 seats. 6 seats outside. Wheelchairs.

£5 voucher

£5 OFF Restaurants showing this symbol are participating in our £5 voucher scheme, redeemable against a meal for two or more. Vouchers can be found at the back of this book.

The Ninth

Cooking score: 5
⊖ Goodge Street, Tottenham Court Road, map 5
Mediterranean | £60
22 Charlotte Street, Fitzrovia, W1T 2NB
Tel no: 020 3019 0880
theninthlondon.com

Long associated with big-city cooking, chef Jun Tanaka has settled comfortably into this, the ninth restaurant with which he has been associated. Split across two floors with bare brick, dark wood, chocolate leather and dangling glass lights giving a sultry urban feel, it's a setting that suits the ambitious selection of sharing plates emanating from the kitchen. Dishes are ingeniously composed to bring out the best in prime ingredients in a cooking style that explores the Med, combining the flavours of southern France and Italy. From the moreish snacks of barbajuans (flaky ricotta- and chard-stuffed fritters) and crispy pork belly to dessert of tarte tatin with rosemary ice cream, the menu is full of things you want to order. Yellowtail carpaccio with salsa verde, pickled fennel and apple, venison tortellini with walnuts and bone marrow, or roe deer in salt crust with cavolo nero, hazelnut pesto and plums showcase precision and flair. Also look out for the good-value set lunch. The Europe-heavy wine list opens at £26, with a reasonable selection by the glass.
Chef/s: Jun Tanaka. **Closed:** Sun, bank hols, 25 Dec. **Meals:** main courses £19 to £32. Set L £22 (2 courses) to £28. **Details:** 82 seats. 8 seats outside. Wheelchairs. Music.

Noble Rot

Cooking score: 5
⊖ Holborn, Russell Square, map 5
Modern European | £45
51 Lamb's Conduit Street, Bloomsbury, WC1N 3NB
Tel no: 020 7242 8963
noblerot.co.uk
🍾★

The claret frontage looks distinctly Parisian, and indeed the twin propositions of bar food and modern bistro cooking could well transport you to some indeterminate spot on the Rive Gauche. Walk in and hope for the former and, space permitting, you'll be regaled with the likes of potted shrimp, rabbit rillettes and chocolate fondant. If you've nailed a booking for the restaurant, there are preliminary forays into tapas territory with Ibérico bellota or cecina de León and pickled walnuts, amid the equally seductive likes of Provençal white asparagus with almonds and hollandaise, and hot-smoked salmon with radish and dill. Main courses are robust and filling, whether you choose thornback ray with roast fennel and capers, or roast wood pigeon with lentils and beetroot, with careful timing and forthright seasoning making instant impressions on the palate. Fill the gaps with apple tarte fine, or hazelnut cake and coffee ice cream. The wine list is structured like a varietal primer, but one primed with stunning bottles from around the vinous globe. Pinot Noirs are an aficionado's delight, there are scads of quality German Rieslings, a luxuriant garden of minority grapes and a clutch of splendid late harvest and rotted sweeties. Small glasses start at £4.50; very small at £2.75.
Chef/s: Paul Weaver. **Closed:** Sun, 25 and 26 Dec, 1 Jan. **Meals:** main courses £18 to £30. Set L £16 (2 courses) to £20. **Details:** 57 seats. 8 seats outside. Bar. Music.

Hotel chefs

Notable chefs have worked in luxury hotels since Auguste Escoffier cooked at The Savoy back in the 19th century. It's a trend that continues today, with a number of recent and planned high-profile openings. Having a well-known chef can help hotels draw in new diners while chefs can reach a wider audience and drive business to their other establishments.

Nathan Outlaw is no stranger to splitting his time across multiple sites. This year, he brought the flavours of his Cornish restaurants to **Siren** at London's iconic Goring, the first new restaurant in the Belgravia hotel for a century.

Later this year, restaurateur Robin Gill of **The Dairy, Darby's** and **Sorella** – all in south London – will be overseeing the restaurant at new Whitehall hotel Great Scotland Yard, while Anthony Demetre has relocated his acclaimed **Wild Honey** restaurant to Sofitel London St James.

The owners of The Standard have secured the services of Bristol-based chef Peter Sánchez-Iglesias, owner of **Casamia** and **Paco Tapas** for the rooftop restaurant of their first UK hotel in King's Cross, due to open in early 2020.

Noizé

Cooking score: 4
⊖ Tottenham Court Road, Warren Street, map 5
Modern British | £45
39 Whitfield Street, Fitzrovia, W1T 2SF
Tel no: 020 7323 1310
noize-restaurant.co.uk
£5
OFF

Sitting on a quiet Fitzrovia corner, this venture from Mathieu Germond, former co-owner and sommelier at Pied à Terre, is a ray of welcoming sunshine. It takes its name from the tiny French village where Germond's grandparents owned a family farm, and the dining room and basement wine bar are casually kitted out with colourful velvet seating, soft lighting and trailing plants; there's warm, on-the-ball service, too. A compact menu delivers modern, seasonal dishes such as white bean houmous with creamy burrata, spicy curried cauliflower, roasted hazelnuts, plump raisins and chilli salsa, as well as a glossy wild garlic velouté dotted with nuggets of fried Stornoway black pudding and topped with a tangle of crispy shallots, and a perfectly executed suckling pork belly with pomme purée, roasted apple and Tokyo turnip. Finish with a 'blissful' crisp and buttery pear and hazelnut tart, or pineapple carpaccio matched with zingy coconut sorbet and kaffir lime. Markups on the considerable wine list aren't too greedy.
Chef/s: Daniel Mertl. **Closed:** last week Aug.
Meals: main courses £18 to £28. **Details:** 50 seats.
Bar. Wheelchairs. Music.

Nopi

Cooking score: 3
⊖ Piccadilly Circus, map 5
Middle Eastern/Mediterranean | £50
21-22 Warwick Street, Soho, W1B 5NE
Tel no: 020 7494 9584
nopi-restaurant.com

A perfect fit for trend-conscious new Soho, this grown-up restaurant from TV chef, columnist and global food crusader Yotam Ottolenghi is a tad more organised than his frantic namesake cafés – although fans will recognise the gleaming white surfaces and other trademark fittings. It can get 'excessively noisy', but the food remains true to the owner's credo – a clever hotchpotch of vibrant, colourful assemblages often founded on obscure ingredients with a bias towards unexpected flavours from faraway lands. Sharing plates show off the kitchen's freewheeling veg-friendly approach: cauliflower with celery, sour cherries and smoked almonds, for example, or asparagus with miso tahini and pickled chilli. There are also a few bigger dishes such as Persian 'love rice' or steamed sea bass with burnt butter, nori and ginger, while desserts always feature YO's chocolate brittle. To drink, sip a zesty cocktail or try a skin-contact wine from the invigorating global list. 'Downstairs' is a separate entity, with an open kitchen and big communal tables geared up for groups.
Chef/s: Spyros Koufalakis. **Meals:** main courses £20 to £26. Set early D £26 Mon to Fri. **Details:** 108 seats. Bar. Wheelchairs. Parking.

★ NEW ENTRY ★

The Northall

Cooking score: 5
⊖ Embankment, map 4
Modern European | £65
Corinthia Hotel, 10a Northumberland Avenue, Westminster, WC2N 5AE
Tel no: 020 7321 3100
corinthia.com

The Corinthia is one of those London hotels that strikes a deeply luxurious note. With its choice of bars and restaurants, it's a good place to escape the hustle and bustle. Lose yourself in The Northall, a comfortable double-height space with enormous windows that is proving an easy fit for André Garrett, who arrives here from Cliveden. It's a work in progress: refurbishment of the dining room is in the pipeline and the menu is evolving as Garrett settles in. The chef has always had an appreciation of simplicity, and the appeal of his cooking lies not in fashionable ingredients and in-your-face flavours, but rather in well-sourced ingredients that are intelligently handled. Clarity and freshness go hand in hand, perhaps in a classic lobster bisque with broad beans and tarragon, or a beautifully balanced dish of Limousin veal (pink loin and slow-cooked breast) with king oyster mushroom, carrot and a glossy spiced jus. The set lunch and pre- or post-theatre menus are something of a bargain, on our visit producing delicate mackerel escabèche with horseradish, yoghurt and dill, then spot-on fillets of plaice with white asparagus tips, tiny Jersey Royals, monk's beard and yuzu, before a final flourish of sweet gariguette strawberries with slivers of almond, dabs of vanilla cream and an intense strawberry sorbet. Service radiates confidence from start to finish. Prices on the global wine list are in line with the setting, starting at £10 for a small glass of Grüner Veltliner; bottles from £40, and soon reaching triple figures.
Chef/s: André Garrett. **Meals:** main courses £40 to £70. Set L and early D £24 (2 courses) to £28. **Details:** 86 seats. V menu. Bar.

Ormer

Cooking score: 6
⊖ Green Park, map 5
Modern British | £65
Flemings, 7-12 Half Moon Street, Mayfair,
W1J 7BH
Tel no: 020 7499 0000
ormermayfair.com

This basement rendezvous with an entrance
reached via the foyer of Flemings hotel
matches plush interiors, mirrors and panelling
with food of real quality and distinction – all
based on meticulously sourced raw materials.
A starter of Jersey crab with Granny Smith
apple, lime, vanilla and peanut harks back to
Shaun Rankin's time as a high-flying chef in
the Channel Islands, while meat cookery is
more far-reaching in its scope – as in Challans
duck with pomelo, côte de boeuf or Iberian
pork secreto with calamari, chorizo, tomato
and Asian pear. One reader who went down
the tasting menu route also found much to
applaud, from a 'brllliant' scallop ceviche with
avocado sorbet, tomato and Vietnamese
dressing to a flavoursome, aromatic dish of
rabbit loin wrapped in pancetta accompanied
by herb gnocchi, cocoa beans, girolles and
delicate truffle oil. After that, a delightful pre-
dessert of dehydrated strawberry crunch,
watermelon and a smear of creamy foam was
followed by an exotic coconut mousse encased
in white chocolate alongside coconut sorbet,
pineapple and mango. Wines (from £24) are
'up to Mayfair standard', with some excellent
by-the-glass selections and half bottles
encouraging exploration.

Chef/s: Shaun Rankin and Kerth Gumbs. **Closed:**
Mon, Sun, 25 and 26 Dec, 1 Jan. **Meals:** main
courses £29 to £39. Set L £28 (2 courses) to £32.
Tasting menu £79 (6 courses). **Details:** 85 seats. V
menu. Vg menu. Bar. Wheelchairs. Music.

Orrery

Cooking score: 4
⊖ Baker Street, Regent's Park, map 6
French | £60
55 Marylebone High Street, Marylebone,
W1U 5RB
Tel no: 020 7616 8000
orrery-restaurant.co.uk

This first-floor room with its views through
half-moon windows over St Marylebone
Parish Church is a long white space that began
life as the upper part of a stable block. Through
successive owners, it has maintained a focus on
modern French brasserie food presented with
elegance and understated flair. There may be
spins on gravadlax and chicken liver parfait to
start, but look closer and find lobster sharply
pointed with wasabi, mango and avocado to
add an extra dimension. Main courses accord
their principal ingredients the spotlight, so
that Jerusalem artichoke and apple make
discreet partners to a fillet of sea bass, while
Kentish lamb needs only caramelised onion,
peas and a deeply aromatic rosemary jus to
allow it to shine. Many are the diners who will
rightly find justification for adding a side of
truffled potato mousseline to a main dish;
others will be enticed by a finale of Manjari
chocolate crémeux and raspberry, or
blackberry bavarois and matching sorbet. The
wine list roams far and wide, opening with
glasses from £8, half-litre carafes £22.

Chef/s: Igor Tymchyshyn. **Meals:** set L £26 (2
courses) to £30. Set D £55 (2 courses) to £60. Tasting
menu £89 (7 courses). **Details:** 100 seats. 20 seats
outside. V menu. Bar.

Visit us online

For the most up-to-date information
about *The Good Food Guide*, go to
thegoodfoodguide.co.uk.

The Other Naughty Piglet

Cooking score: 4
♻ Victoria, map 5
Modern European | £30
The Other Palace, 12 Palace Street, Victoria,
SW1E 5JA
Tel no: 020 7592 0322
theothernaughtypiglet.co.uk
£30

Head up the marble staircase (dramatically if you wish) in Andrew Lloyd Webber's The Other Palace Theatre (near *that* palace) and you'll find this diverting restaurant, a sibling of Naughty Piglets in Brixton (see entry). An open-to-view kitchen and stripped-back interior (with some communal tables) set the tone for an array of small plates that are big on flavour. Creamy burrata with soy-pickled mushrooms and furikake seasoning or crisp ham croquettes might get the ball rolling. Asian influences are worked to good effect in the likes of BBQ pork belly with sesame and Korean spices, while there's more of a European flavour to roast beetroot with blackberries and smoked crème fraîche, and black pudding with grilled pear and hazelnuts. Sweet courses run to bouncy cinnamon doughnuts with quince and sour cream. The wine list focuses on natural wines and includes some expensive limited editions from Lord Lloyd Webber's private collection.
Chef/s: Joseph Knowlden. **Closed:** Sun, bank hols, 24 Dec to 3 Jan. **Meals:** main courses £12 to £16. Set L £18 (2 courses) to £22. **Details:** 60 seats. Wheelchairs. Music.

Otto's

Cooking score: 3
♻ Chancery Lane, map 5
French | £46
182 Gray's Inn Road, Bloomsbury, WC1X 8EW
Tel no: 020 7713 0107
ottos-restaurant.com

'Long may it all last,' says one reader for whom Otto's is an old and valued favourite. Styled (with the exception of the now-famous cushions bearing Marilyn Monroe's image) in the manner of a venerable French institution, it's a deliberate homage to the glory days of at-table service, elaborate silverware and nose-to-tail preparations. Readers have had successful vegetarian meals at Otto's, but it's really the place to scratch an itch for calf's brain with lemon, capers and parsley, quenelles lyonnaise and hand-carved smoked salmon, followed by stuffed pig's trotter in Madeira sauce or beef tartare with soufflé potatoes. The much-loved house party trick is the elaborate pre-booked ceremony of lobster or duck à la presse, squeezed to extract the precious juices and presented in two services. Desserts aren't really the point, but include Marsala zabaglione and Grand Marnier soufflé, and wines cleave closely to France, with lots of digestifs to help all that tradition go down.
Chef/s: Michael Bocquiren. **Closed:** Sun. **Meals:** main courses £23 to £45. Set L £26 (2 courses) to £32. **Details:** 35 seats. No children

The Oystermen

Cooking score: 4
♻ Leicester Square, Covent Garden, map 5
Seafood | £40
32 Henrietta Street, Covent Garden, WC2E 8NA
Tel no: 020 7240 4417
oystermen.co.uk

Rob Hampton and Matt Lovell can no longer claim to own the smallest loo in London now that expansion has added space to their convivial all-day eatery. The welcome increase in size has not changed the nature of the cooking and The Oystermen continues as a relaxed spot for very fresh seafood, prepared and presented in a simple, unfussy manner. Prime ingredients shine through in openers of whipped smoked cod's roe (served with pickled beetroot and horseradish) and a pair of fried tempura oysters with Champagne aïoli and smoked herring caviar. Whole Brixham plaice with blood orange, monk's beard and radicchio also made an impression on readers. There's been praise, too, for whole undressed brown crab, a triumph of fresh, lively flavours,

requiring nothing more than some garlic aïoli and lemon. Meals end with a couple of desserts (gariguette strawberry trifle, for example) and a trio of British cheeses. A brief, well-judged wine list delivers by the glass or bottle.
Chef/s: Alex Povall. **Closed:** 25 to 31 Dec. **Meals:** main courses £22 to £35. **Details:** 47 seats. Music.

The Palomar
Cooking score: 5
⊖ Piccadilly Circus, map 5
Middle Eastern | £35
34 Rupert Street, Soho, W1D 6DN
Tel no: 020 7439 8777
thepalomar.co.uk

Every night's a Saturday night at this co-production between Jerusalem's Machneyuda restaurant and London siblings Layo and Zoë Paskin (The Barbary, Evelyn's Table). Launched in 2014, this small-scale spot – just 16 stools at the counter and an intimate dining room beyond – has a reputation for music, madcap and modern Middle Eastern flavours that keep guests coming back for more. Reservations can be hard to come by, although the bar is largely available to walk-ins. Via a small plates approach, the menu covers a lot of ground, introducing Jewish, Arabic and Mediterranean references from contemporary Jerusalem. Don't miss the Yemeni kubaneh bread, warm and puffy from the oven, nor such signatures as 'octo-hummus' with chickpea masabacha, and the minced lamb shakshukit, spiked with preserved lemon and harissa. Vegetarian dishes are many, including Persian pappardelle with artichokes, and zaatar burrata (try saying it out loud). Interesting global wines from £31.
Chef/s: Omri McNabb. **Closed:** 25 and 26 Dec. **Meals:** small plates £5 to £19. **Details:** 50 seats. Wheelchairs. Children in dining room only.

Parsons
Cooking score: 4
⊖ Covent Garden, map 5
Seafood | £45
39 Endell Street, Covent Garden, WC2H 9BA
Tel no: 020 3422 0221
parsonslondon.co.uk
🍾

'What a lovely little place – little being the operative word. We squeezed in.' For many readers there's no doubt Ian Campbell and Will Palmer's 'exceptional fish restaurant' is a brilliant, upbeat addition to the Covent Garden dining scene. It looks the part with its white tiles, tightly packed marble-top tables and large mirrors listing the day's catch, and there's genuine warmth from capable staff. Like the decor, the food is confidently no-frills: simply grilled fish on the bone might include sweet buttery skate, John Dory, plaice, or lemon sole with salsa verde. Preface that with some handsome snacks of brown crab pissaladière, potted shrimp croquettes, or half a dozen oysters, and a satisfying plate of octopus with duck-fat potatoes, paprika and parsley oil, and round off with an apple tarte fine or a savoury Welsh rarebit. A wide-ranging selection of fish-friendly whites, plus a handful of reds and an excellent by-the-glass selection, reflect a relationship with the 10 Cases wine bar across the road.
Chef/s: Tom Clements. **Closed:** Sun, bank hols, 25 Dec to 1 Jan. **Meals:** main courses £17 to £35. **Details:** 30 seats. 12 seats outside.

Pastaio
Cooking score: 3
⊖ Oxford Circus, map 5
Italian | £25
19 Ganton Street, Soho, W1F 9BN
pastaio.london
£30

Setting out its stall in the progressively crowded field of pasta-focused dining, Stevie Parle's formula is a democratic one: fresh pasta, keenly priced and served at communal tables to those willing to wait (an inevitability at the weekend). The modern, canteen-style space with terrazzo tabletops, bright op-art mural and open kitchen provides a playful backdrop for the star of the show, the pasta made from scratch every morning. Wedded to what tastes good rather than to tradition, the short menu of around eight dishes covers plenty of ground. A silky carbonara comes with bucatini rather than spaghetti, and there's vongole pasta 'en bianco' or squid ink ravioli. Cacio e pepe, a former signature dish, might be off menu, but have a word with your server and the kitchen may conjure it up. Antipasti and Italian desserts, including a fine tiramisu, top and tail proceedings, and collaboration with top-drawer producers delivers seasonal ravioli specials and sharing pastas. Expect a boisterous soundtrack, Prosecco slushies and all-Italian wines by the glass.

Chef/s: Stevie Parle. **Meals:** main courses £7 to £12. **Details:** 72 seats. Music. No reservations.

Picture

Cooking score: 3
⊖ Oxford Circus, Goodge Street, map 5
Modern European | £40
110 Great Portland Street, Fitzrovia, W1W 6PQ
Tel no: 020 7637 7892
picturerestaurant.co.uk
£5
OFF

A narrow grey frontage makes the place look less of a picture than it might, but inside it extends back into a whitewashed space under two large skylights, with abstract artworks and a properly animated feel. While the vogue for small plates endures, this Fitzrovia venue (there's another branch on New Cavendish Street, Marylebone) has it covered. The orientation is French and southern European, with pumpkin and caramelised onion ravioli, cavolo nero and pecorino competing for attention with smoked haddock brandade, brown shrimps and hispi cabbage. The meat dishes offer the most robust substance with beef fillet, bone marrow crumb and heritage carrots in red wine sauce among the richer options. If you can't quite choose, go for the six-course taster (vegetarian and vegan

versions available), which might conclude silkily with dark chocolate mousse, milk jam and salt caramel crumble. The short wine list has something to electrify most palates, in a reasonable price arc from £23.50 to £100, with no corkage fees on Mondays if you bring your own.

Chef/s: Alan Christie. **Closed:** Sun, 23 Dec to 8 Jan, 3 to 10 Aug. **Meals:** main courses £18 to £24. Set L £18 (2 courses) to £22. Tasting menu L £35 (5 courses) and D £45 (6 courses). **Details:** 53 seats. 4 seats outside. V menu. Vg menu. Bar. Wheelchairs. Music.

Pied à Terre

Cooking score: 4
⊖ Goodge Street, map 5
Modern French | £80
34 Charlotte Street, Fitzrovia, W1T 2NH
Tel no: 020 7636 1178
pied-a-terre.co.uk
£5
OFF

Something of an old-stager amid the restaurant hubbub of Charlotte Street, Pied à Terre refuses to rest on its laurels. A recent interior update has ushered in a striking mural and boldly busy colour palette, complete with raspberry-red carpet. It's been a haven of refined contemporary French gastronomy for years, and the pace continues under Asimakis Chaniotis. Artfully composed dishes make an impact on the palate, as in an opener of sea bream ceviche in a welter of bottarga, smoked almonds, lime, basil and parsley, each element having its say. Mains sustain the theme with fallow deer in cocoa and juniper, which comes with an endearing take on a club sandwich fashioned from chicken liver and red onion marmalade or, from the vegetarian menu, perhaps celeriac in black garlic consommé with winter truffle, hazelnuts and confit egg yolk. At show's end, the baba is doused with no mere ordinary rum but Venezuelan Diplomático Reserva Exclusiva, to go with olive-oiled pineapple, Maldon salt caviar, clotted cream and coriander. The legendary wine list is a bullet train of cosmopolitan producers, hurtling from Oregon and

Washington State to China and Japan with excitement to be had along the way. Prices are high although small glasses start at £6. **Chef/s:** Asimakis Chaniotis. **Closed:** Sun, 2 weeks Christmas and New Year. **Meals:** set L £33 (2 courses) to £43. Early D £43 (2 courses). Set D £65 (2 courses) to £80. Tasting menu £75 (7 courses) to £145. **Details:** 42 seats. V menu. Vg menu. Bar. Parking. Music.

★ TOP 10 ★

Pollen Street Social

Cooking score: 9
⊖ Oxford Circus, map 5
Modern British | £90
8-10 Pollen Street, Mayfair, W1S 1NQ
Tel no: 020 7290 7606
pollenstreetsocial.com

The pedestrianisation of Pollen Street has added a further frisson of anticipation to Jason Atherton's Mayfair flagship, a restaurant that continues to surprise even its most ardent fans. From the moment a receptionist opens the door, this cosmopolitan big hitter exudes sheer, unadulterated class. Confident, approachable and professional staff take it all in their stride, while the kitchen teases out the essence of flavour in dishes that seem to have even more clarity and fewer components as the years roll by. Consider a combo of braised Dorset snails and roast celeriac risotto, or an Orkney scallop, caramelised to the utmost sweetness, with chopped leeks, potato and a few pearly dots of Petrossian caviar. Elsewhere, a pink lamb chop and a cylinder of oh-so-tender fillet need only some crunchy fennel and a few saline notes of seaweed – although the kitchen throws a curveball by presenting the dish with an instantly addictive shepherd's pie, topped with the most buttery mash imaginable. Atherton has a penchant for gizmos and clever crockery, but this is never mere window dressing: a mysterious 'hot box' placed on the table reveals itself as a steamer for the sweetest cockles (the final addition to a technically faultless dish of fleshy Cornish turbot with charred cauliflower and wild

garlic), while an intense Kalamansi sorbet sits on a plate concealing a bowl of tiny wild strawberries pointed up with lemon thyme yoghurt. The knowledgeably curated and insightful wine list cannily mixes iconic vintages with esoteric artisan discoveries; prices are top end, but you can also sip regally by the glass.
Chef/s: Jason Atherton and Dale Bainbridge. **Closed:** Sun, 25 and 26 Dec. **Meals:** main courses £38 to £49. Set L £40. Tasting menu £115 (10 courses). **Details:** 82 seats. V menu. Vg menu. Bar. Music.

Portland

Cooking score: 5
⊖ Great Portland St, Oxford Circus, map 5
Modern British | £57
113 Great Portland Street, Fitzrovia, W1W 6QQ
Tel no: 020 7436 3261
portlandrestaurant.co.uk

Restrained but hospitable since it opened in 2015, this is Will Lander and Daniel Morgenthau's temple to both pickles and pithivier. Here, an utterly contemporary sensibility comes with the confidence to acknowledge that sometimes only a sausage roll (albeit served with wild cherry ketchup) will do. Pre-game snacks such as the perennial crisped chicken skin with liver parfait and candied walnuts, spider crab bun or plain pickles are the kitchen's constant strength. Bigger dishes are ardently seasonal and based on British ingredients. To start, try Graceburn cow's curds with roasted carrots, bitter leaves and sherry caramel; follow with Cornish pollack with parsnips, sea leeks, black garlic and dashi. That pithivier might be stuffed with duck and pigeon, and served with truffle jus to share. 'Savoury' herbs – rosemary in a crémeux, lemon thyme in soft-serve ice cream with an apple terrine – keep puddings grounded. The wine list ventures well beyond the usual suspects; thoughtfully annotated and packed with global interest, it offers multiple entry points from £5 a glass. Knowledgeable staff are happy to chip in with suggestions. **Chef/s:** Zach Elliott-Crenn. **Closed:** Sun, 22 Dec to 3 Jan. **Meals:** main courses £24 to £34. Set L £30 (2 courses) to £35. Tasting menu L £59 (6 courses) and D £69 (6 courses). **Details:** 36 seats. Wheelchairs. Music.

Quilon

Cooking score: 4
⊖ St James's Park, Victoria, map 5
Indian | £70
41 Buckingham Gate, Westminster, SW1E 6AF
Tel no: 020 7821 1899
quilon.co.uk
£5 OFF 🛏

Built in 1902 and now part of the Taj Hotels group, St James's Court is also home to Quilon – a smartly attired Indian restaurant with its own entrance and its own 'division bell' alerting visiting MPs to business in the House. It may seem corporate, but the gleaming dining room has been given some vitality with tropical murals and specially commissioned Indian artworks. Chef Sriram Aylur's enduring culinary focus is on the coastal provinces of southern India and their sophisticated seafood specialities – from Karwari oysters with chilli and onion chutney to buttery lobster with pepper sauce or a take on black cod utilising molasses instead of miso. Meat, game and vegetarian options also abound (try the stuffed quail legs fired up with mustard), while desserts move into crossover mode with the likes of lentil, jaggery and cardamom cappuccino. World beers, sake and sherry chime with Quilon's international clientele, and the substantial wine list has been thoughtfully compiled to complement all those spicy flavours – although prices are aimed squarely at expense accounts. **Chef/s:** Sriram Aylur. **Closed:** 25 Dec. **Meals:** main courses £21 to £45. Set L £27 (2 courses) to £31. Tasting menu £70 (4 courses) to £85. **Details:** 83 seats. V menu. Bar. Music. No children after 6.30pm.

Quirinale

Cooking score: 3
⊖ Westminster, map 3
Italian | £45
North Court, 1 Great Peter Street, Westminster, SW1P 3LL
Tel no: 020 7222 7080
quirinale.co.uk
£5 OFF

Moments from the Palace of Westminster, glossy Quirinale remains a premium address for modern Italian dining, where a cream, white and blond wood setting creates a discreet destination for expense-account diners – who would probably hand over their own cash here. One can expect refined, modern dishes – an antipasto such as beef carpaccio with rocket, Parmesan and Cipriani dressing sets the tone – and the menu includes bestsellers of daily changing pasta and risotto (with a sprinkling of truffle if requested), and the likes of veal cutlet milanese with cherry tomato and basil, fillet of beef with potato rösti, spring onion and mustard, or a perfectly cooked fillet of turbot teamed with onions, oranges, olives and a pistachio dressing. Ricotta and blueberry tart is a classy way to finish. The set lunch and early dinner are considered good value, service may be formal but it is also efficient, and on the wine front, the all-Italian list opens at £27. **Chef/s:** Stefano Savio. **Closed:** Sun, 24 to 30 Dec, Aug. **Meals:** main courses £24 to £29. Set L and early D £19 (2 courses) to £23. **Details:** 50 seats. Music.

Quo Vadis

Cooking score: 4
⊖ Tottenham Court Road, map 5
Modern British | £50
26-29 Dean Street, Soho, W1D 3LL
Tel no: 020 7437 9585
quovadissoho.co.uk

At Quo Vadis, pudding – not 'dessert', you understand – often comes with custard, cream and ice cream. This speaks volumes about the big-hearted approach one can expect at Jeremy

Lee's 'warm and welcoming' Soho dining room where 'serving staff hit exactly the right note of friendliness without familiarity'. It's undeniably small, but somehow grand, too, with its pristine linen, gorgeous blooms and sparkling silverware. Lee's Franco-British food is comforting, familiar stuff encompassing the likes of kedgeree, smoked salmon pancake with 'sinus-clearing' horseradish and beetroot, 'today's pie and mash' and 'the best chips bar none'. More extravagant turns such as turbot, artichokes and gremolata or octopus and puntarelle salad have one reaching for the wine list: a classically minded collection of global greats. Save space for afters: St Emilion au chocolat is a favourite and readers speak highly of the prune, medlar and sloe tart.

Chef/s: Jeremy Lee and Doug Sims. **Closed:** Sun, 24 to 26 Dec, 1 Jan, 13 Apr. **Meals:** main courses £18 to £34. **Details:** 25 seats. 16 seats outside. Bar.

Rex Whistler Restaurant

Cooking score: 3
⊖ Pimlico, map 3
British | £36
Tate Britain, Millbank, Pimlico, SW1P 4RG
Tel no: 020 7887 8825
tate.org.uk
£5 OFF

In times past, good food and cultural institutions were seldom on the same page, but this basement dining room is a long-established exception. Named after the artist whose whimsical mural covers the room wall to wall, the space exudes a quiet elegance. White-linened tables reflect a sophisticated culinary approach, forward-thinking and global in scope, particularly in starters that explore British heritage dishes. Mock turtle soup, game terrine (the kitchen comes into its own in the shooting season) or confit salmon with cucumber vichyssoise might pave the way for chargrilled pork loin with 48-hour pork belly, apples, miso cabbage and a cider sauce spiked with brandy or – on Sunday – roast beef or lamb from the carving trolley. The trolley rumbles back for 'Cheese Please',

unless your sweet tooth wins out, in which case there's sherry-soaked 'tipsy cake'. From the celebrated ever-evolving wine cellar comes a 'good choice of half bottles', and suggested wine pairings with each course. Bottles open at £28.

Chef/s: Alfio Laudani. **Closed:** 24 to 26 Dec. **Meals:** main courses £18 to £25. **Details:** 80 seats. 40 seats outside. Wheelchairs. Music.

The Ritz

Cooking score: 6
⊖ Green Park, map 5
British | £90
150 Piccadilly, Mayfair, W1J 9BR
Tel no: 020 7300 2370
theritzlondon.com

It's one of London's more exclusive addresses, and the appeal here is not excitement, and certainly not novelty. Yet beneath the unchanging and stately surface of what is considered one of the most glamorous dining rooms in town lies cooking that moves, albeit gently, with the times. Luxuries remain the foundation and traditional treatments are the order of the day – langoustine à la nage, veal sweetbreads with roast garlic, almond and Madeira, beef wellington with celeriac and Périgord truffle – but there are also departures such as heritage potato with lovage and chicken skin, and Bresse duck with beetroot and pickled blackberry, a sign that John Williams' kitchen is aware of what the rest of the world is up to. Sourcing is impeccable – British cheeses, for example, are superb – and soufflés (chocolate or Seville orange, say) are the pick of desserts. Lunch is still considered good value for the setting, but service from a brigade of formally dressed waiters comes in for some stick, and visitors recommend avoiding Live at the Ritz when, on Friday and Saturday evenings, a vocalist and string quartet accompany your meal. Wines play their part in pumping up the bill.

Chef/s: John Williams. **Meals:** main courses £38 to £56. Tasting menu £125 (6 courses). Sun L £69. **Details:** 90 seats. 18 seats outside. V menu. Vg menu. Bar. Wheelchairs. Parking. Music.

Rochelle ICA

Cooking score: 2
⊖ Charing Cross, map 5
Modern British | £35
ICA, The Mall, St James's, SW1Y 5AH
Tel no: 020 7766 1424
arnoldandhenderson.com

The Rochelle operation that began in Shoreditch (see entry) has an arriviste cousin in the confines of the ICA, with ground floor views on to The Mall. Dismiss all thoughts of inappropriate poshing, though. A white counter dispenses superior all-day café food St John-style (owner Margot Henderson is married to St John's Fergus Henderson) to white tables in an ambience with more than a hint of post-modern irony to it. Pie and a pint before you take in that avant-garde film? Step this way. There's a veggie version as well as the chicken and tarragon. Baked haddock with chard in butter sauce is another main option, with the likes of pig's head terrine and gribiche, and then buttermilk panna cotta with rhubarb and almonds to bookend it. Snack on smoked cod's roe and crisps while you make up your mind. The St John Languedoc blends at £5 a glass front a short wine list that finds big flavours to match the rustic chow.
Chef/s: Ben Coombs. **Closed:** Mon. **Meals:** main courses £14 to £22. **Details:** 45 seats. Bar.

Send us your review

Your feedback informs the content of the *GFG* and will be used to compile next year's reviews. To register your opinion about any restaurant listed, or a restaurant that you wish to bring to our attention, visit our website.

★ TOP 50 ★

Roganic

Cooking score: 8
⊖ Baker Street, Bond Street, map 6
Modern British | £65
5-7 Blandford Street, Marylebone, W1U 3DB
Tel no: 020 3370 6260
roganic.uk

'Who knew cheese ice cream, cranberry and caviar could be a thing, but wow it was!' One diner, mind boggled by the edible ingenuity at Simon Rogan's London outpost, vowed to return quickly, no doubt to revisit the fresh sweet-savouriness of frozen Tunworth cheese with fruit syrup, toasted hazelnuts and a salty dash of caviar. For some, the restaurant errs on the spartan side, for others the absence of frills means that it is the inventive preparation of outstanding ingredients, plenty from Our Farm in Cartmel, that makes this place tick. And that is how Rogan and his team like it. From opening snacks such as an ethereally light tartlet with flavours of pumpkin, pear and bay, and a shot glass of juice, to petits fours that might include a slender stick of smoked juniper fudge, this is a menu that pulses with innovation, seasonality and flavour; it left one guest 'tingling, in a good way'. There's lusty praise for braised, dry-aged shoulder of Cumbrian beef served with pickled leek and onion, and luxuriously smooth wild garlic purée; ditto 'surprising' salt-baked celeriac with celeriac purée and crisps, whey cream and malt crumb. Desserts are restrained in their sweetness, so that a pretty composition of rhubarb, buttermilk custard, Earl Grey ice cream and barley crisps leaves you feeling fresh rather than sugar-laden. Dig deep, both in terms of time and pocket – it takes a while and costs a fair whack to deliver 11 courses of this calibre, although there is a shorter menu, and a brisk four-course lunch option. Wines are punchily priced, but £65 will buy a highly recommended paired flight.
Chef/s: Simon Rogan and Oliver Marlow. **Closed:** Mon, Sun, 22 Dec to 6 Jan. **Meals:** set L £35. Tasting menu £65 (6 courses) to £85. **Details:** 42 seats. V menu. Vg menu. Music.

Anonymous

At *The Good Food Guide*, our inspectors dine anonymously and pay their bill in full. These impartial review meals, along with feedback from thousands of our readers, are what informs the content of the *GFG*.

Roux at Parliament Square

Cooking score: 4
⊖ Westminster, St James's Park, map 5
Modern French | £59
11 Great George Street, Parliament Square, Westminster, SW1P 3AD
Tel no: 020 7334 3737
rouxatparliamentsquare.co.uk
£5
OFF

This Westminster branch of Michel Roux Jr's evolving empire is very much geared to the ministerial classes, with well-spaced tables meaning top-secret conversations are likely to stay that way. One diner, however, thought the 'atmosphere arising from others at lunch rather muted'. Steve Groves' cooking marries modern French technique with top-quality British ingredients, eschewing novelty in favour of simply putting together interesting and complementary flavours. In summary, the restaurant delivers a high standard of consistent cooking without excessively challenging the taste buds. Expect smoked salmon teamed with beetroot, blood orange and dill, cod with white beans, morteau sausage and three-cornered garlic or venison with savoy cabbage, kohlrabi and smoked bacon. Finish with mango rice pudding soufflé with white chocolate and passion fruit. As you would expect, there is a lengthy wine list with a strong emphasis on French wines, with bottles starting at £39.
Chef/s: Steve Groves. **Closed:** Sat, Sun, 1 week Dec to Jan, 2 weeks Aug. **Meals:** set L £42. Set D £59. Tasting menu £69 (5 courses) to £89. **Details:** 60 seats. Bar. Wheelchairs. Parking.

Roux at the Landau

Cooking score: 5
⊖ Oxford Circus, map 5
Modern French | £66
The Langham, 1c Portland Place, Marylebone, W1B 1JA
Tel no: 020 7965 0165
rouxatthelandau.com
🍷 🛏

'The room still feels grand and special, but there's a real buzz and informality,' mused a returning visitor to what is considered one of London's most impressive dining rooms. With huge dome-topped windows to the front, a vaulted ceiling and wood-panelled walls, it's an impressive setting for 'consistently delicious cooking with superb ingredients and a classical approach that's nonetheless clear and clean'. Nicolas Pasquier proves himself adept at translating Michel Roux's contemporary French style. Opening snacks are considered a not-to-be-missed high point, say smoked sea bream with cauliflower, citrus and dashi. Then langoustines, teamed with scialetti pasta and saffron emulsion, could arrive ahead of roast suckling pig with choucroute, caramelised apple and morteau sausage. As for dessert, it's a hard choice between Grand Marnier soufflé or a blackcurrant and chestnut Mont Blanc. The wine list is a whopper: chock full of big names at big prices, there's not a bottle under £36 and few bargains. But for anyone coming without a strict budget there's a serious number of Coravin wines by the glass listed alongside the bottle price.
Chef/s: Nicolas Pasquier. **Closed:** Mon, Sun. **Meals:** main courses £20 to £38. Set L and early/late D £35 (2 courses) to £39. Tasting menu £80 (6 courses). **Details:** 80 seats. Bar. Wheelchairs. Music.

★ NEW ENTRY ★

Rovi

Cooking score: 4
⊖ Oxford Circus, Goodge Street, map 5
Middle Eastern/Mediterranean | £35
59 Wells Street, Fitzrovia, W1A 3AE
Tel no: 020 3963 8270
ottolenghi.co.uk

With his delicacy of touch and vibrant, healthy-leaning menus, restaurateur and *The Guardian* writer Yotam Ottolenghi's dazzling blend of Middle Eastern and Mediterranean styles has long appealed. No surprise, then, that there's a warm and convivial buzz to his latest opening, which occupies a large, multi-faceted space with lots of blond wood, opaque glass, foliage and neutral tones. Based on a zealous enthusiasm for entirely fresh ingredients, the kitchen takes a flavour-first approach, belting out a stunning, regularly changing line-up of sharply executed snacks, small and large plates. The lobster crumpet is already famous, but at an inspection meal 'sheer enjoyment' was delivered by tempura stems and herbs, served with a jammy, sweet-and-sour mandarin and lime leaf 'vinegar', by crisp melt-in-the-middle parsnip and pecorino croquettes, by smokey celeriac shawarma, and by the incredible squid and lardo skewer with fennel and aïoli that is fast achieving cult status. This is food that packs a major punch right through to dessert of beetroot and chocolate fondant with chilli, crème fraîche and ice cream. The wine choices fully live up to the ethos of the cooking, an up-to-the-minute list of low-intervention wines mainly from European vineyards.
Chef/s: Yotam Ottolenghi and Neil Campbell. **Closed:** 25 and 26 Dec. **Meals:** small plates £7 to £14. Large plates £18 to £21. **Details:** 102 seats. 8 seats outside. Bar. Wheelchairs. Music.

Rules

Cooking score: 3
⊖ Covent Garden, Leicester Square, map 5
British | £50
35 Maiden Lane, Covent Garden, WC2E 7LB
Tel no: 020 7836 5314
rules.co.uk

'To be honest, it was just lovely,' noted one visitor to London's oldest restaurant – established 1798 – which maintains a congenial atmosphere in its intimate, clubby rooms, and its repertoire of well-practised dishes. Famed when it opened for its 'porter, pies and oysters', it now offers a menu that ploughs pretty much the same furrow. Game broth, rib of beef, jugged hare, steamed steak and kidney pudding and roast haunch of venison form the backbone, although there are forays into the modern world, as in pear, bacon and walnut salad or Keralan fish curry; there's even a vegetarian menu. But most are drawn here for the classics. One visitor was in 'seventh heaven' with his steak and kidney pudding, his companion delighted by her braised wild rabbit. Puddings mean puddings, whether steamed syrup with custard or hot ginger cake with fig jam and clotted cream. Anchored in France, the wine list gathers good labels from across the globe, opening at £30.
Chef/s: David Stafford. **Closed:** 3 days Christmas. **Meals:** main courses £21 to £42. **Details:** 90 seats. V menu. Bar.

Sabor

Cooking score: 6
⊖ Piccadilly Circus, map 5
Spanish | £35
35-37 Heddon Street, Mayfair, W1B 4BR
Tel no: 020 3319 8132
saborrestaurants.co.uk

Among Heddon Street's multifarious eating and drinking opportunities, Nieves Barragán's streamlined tapas bar is the most compelling. The contemporary space suits the casual vibe, with comfy seating at the long, curved counter, and a bar in case you have to wait (no bookings are taken). A sensibly short menu focuses on tapas favourites – the likes of croquetas de jamon, arroz negro and classic tortilla have broad appeal – but there's also milk-fed lamb sweetbreads, beautifully timed hake a la romana, grilled quail and Jerusalem artichoke, and herb-crusted rabbit shoulder with romesco sauce. It's all a happy marriage of seasonal British ingredients and quality Spanish imports, with the quality of the ingredients standing out, whether in a salad of tomatoes, confit artichokes and txistorra (a chorizo-style sausage from north-west Spain) or a delicate, well-made rhubarb and mascarpone tart. Service is personable and professional. Drinks do their best to keep up, with plenty of choice by the glass on the short Spanish wine list of. Or head upstairs to El Asador where the headline attraction is shared platters of wood-roasted suckling pig, Galician rib of beef or Iberian lamb ribs, and tables are bookable though communal.

Chef/s: Nieves Barragán Mohacho. **Meals:** tapas £5 to £17. **Details:** 56 seats. Bar. Music. No reservations. Maximum group size 4.

Savoy Grill

Cooking score: 2
⊖ Charing Cross, map 5
Anglo-French | £58
The Savoy, Strand, Covent Garden, WC2R 0EU
Tel no: 020 7592 1600
gordonramsay.com

Forever associated with impossible heights of glamour, there's a lustre about the Grill that never dulls. Step into the polished dining room, with its glittering mirrors and chandeliers, to be transported to another era, one of formal service, crisp linen and supremely classic food. Omelette Arnold Bennett, originally created in the hotel's kitchen for the writer, is a menu fixture, ditto steak tartare with its confit egg yolk, or lobster thermidor, or oysters by the six or dozen. Your Dover sole could be grilled or à la meunière, your chateaubriand could come with béarnaise or peppercorn sauce, or perhaps you're in the mood for a deeply satisfying steak and ale pie. How wonderful that crêpes

Suzette, loved by many, are prepared with tableside panache, although a rum baba with caramelised pineapple and crème chantilly is understandably tempting too. Guests preferring vegetarian, vegan or gluten-free dishes are looked after, as are those wanting a decent bottle of wine from a list that explores some serious domaines, rising steadily from an opening price of £30.

Chef/s: Ben Waugh. **Meals:** main courses £14 to £49. Set L and early D £31 (2 courses) to £35. **Details:** 100 seats. V menu. Vg menu. Bar. Wheelchairs. Parking. Music.

Scott's

Cooking score: 4
⊖ Green Park, map 6
Seafood | £52
20 Mount Street, Mayfair, W1K 2HE
Tel no: 020 7495 7309
scotts-restaurant.com

A table at Scott's is still a covetable booking, although the restaurant's prestigious reputation would count for nothing if it failed to deliver top-drawer food and hospitality. Glamour and sophistication are the watchwords, from the doorman to the glossy leather banquettes, polished oak-panelled walls hung with modern art and marble-topped crustacea bar piled with seafood on ice. Assured fish cookery is Scott's culinary forte and you can eat as simply or extravagantly as you wish from a menu that spans everything from goujons of sole with tartare sauce to blackened miso salmon or chargrilled yellowfin tuna with ratatouille and courgette flowers. There are oysters galore, pots of caviar and trendy tartares, too, plus a few token meat dishes in the shape of Bannockburn rib steaks or rump of lamb with roasted squash and confit garlic. Cheeses and savouries round off the show, along with desserts such as passion fruit pavlova. Wines (from £36) are tailored to a moneyed clientele.

Chef/s: David McCarthy. **Closed:** 25 and 26 Dec. **Meals:** main courses £20 to £56. **Details:** 150 seats. V menu. Wheelchairs. Music.

Seven Park Place by William Drabble

Cooking score: 6
⊖ Green Park, map 5
French | £75
St James's Hotel and Club, 7-8 Park Place, Mayfair, SW1A 1LS
Tel no: 020 7316 1600
stjameshotelandclub.com
£5 OFF 🛏

William Drabble's idiosyncratic dining space was being redesigned as we went to press, and while diners can temporarily enjoy the full Seven Park Place menu in the 'stunning' library until late 2019, first-timers will sadly never experience the visual bombardment of the old decorative scheme. Shimmering yellow upholstery against dancing organic motifs in a sort of rollicking Art Nouveau, with variant fabric textures echoed by sumptuous floral displays, was a sensory seduction to which the cooking did its distinguished best to match. Drabble's menu specifications sound straightforward enough, but secrete a wealth of discovery on the plate. Baked red mullet is given its full Mediterranean value with caramelised fennel and a resonant citrus butter, while a pairing of pork galette and poached langoustines with grainy apple chutney furnishes a richly savoury opener. For mains, the duck breast appears with a Polish-inspired pierogi of leg meat and braised turnips for a subtly satiating dish, or there may be poached brill fillet, its meringue-light flesh enhanced by a seafood medley of mussels and clams. Grand Marnier ice cream and dark chocolate sauce add heft to the featherlight orange soufflé, or go for the tropical composition of coconut bavarois with mango crémeux, passion fruit, lychee and lime. Wines are of formidable pedigree, but the financial centre of gravity – prices start at £37 – is high enough to induce light-headedness in mere mortals.
Chef/s: William Drabble. **Closed:** Mon, Sun.
Meals: set L £28 (2 courses) to £33. Set D £65 (2 courses) to £75. Tasting menu £95 (6 courses).
Details: 28 seats. Bar. Music. Children over 12 yrs.

Sketch, Lecture Room & Library

Cooking score: 7
⊖ Oxford Circus, map 5
Modern European | £120
9 Conduit Street, Mayfair, W1S 2XG
Tel no: 020 7659 4500
sketch.london

The flamboyant kitsch and Wonderland-esque madcappery of Sketch is on a scale unfathomable to mere mortals. Years on from its 2003 landing in Mayfair, it still feels as if it hails from a galaxy far, far away. To call this place 'quirky', 'iconic' or 'unique' is, feebly, like calling the universe 'infinite'. Leave convention at the door as you trip up the stairs to the Lecture Room & Library where you will find neither lectures nor library, but some of the most exuberant and agile cooking in the city. Don't try to understand; just let it happen and enjoy the sequence of 'meals within a meal' that form the menu. Start with 'langoustines' and find yourself before small plates of immeasurable delicacy, the crustacea poached in a wakame broth, pan-fried and glazed with sea buckthorn juice, raw with Champagne, or alongside grilled cuttlefish. Follow with 'Portuguese coast' and be transported to the Atlantic via a galette of salted cod, piquillo peppers, cod cheeks, grilled octopus, sardines and salsa verde; 'pork' keeps you closer to home with sage-marinated fillet, stuffed trotter, black pudding, pig's ears – and the rest. Chef Pierre Gagnaire's stellar 'grand dessert' will send taste buds into a pick-and-mix frenzy of blood oranges, marrons glacés, Turkish delight, mojito baba and rhubarb crumble. First-rate sommeliers will guide you through a wine list of such scope that it would take a lifetime to master it. None of this comes cheap, of course, but oh, the stories you'll tell...
Chef/s: Pierre Gagnaire and Johannes Nuding.
Closed: Mon, Sun. **Meals:** main courses £50 to £55. Tasting menu £120 (7 courses). **Details:** 50 seats. V menu. Bar. Music. Children over 6 yrs.

Social Eating House

Cooking score: 6
⊖ Oxford Circus, map 5
Modern British | £50
58 Poland Street, Soho, W1F 7NR
Tel no: 020 7993 3251
socialeatinghouse.com

The Soho arm of Jason Atherton's London operations has a pleasingly old-fashioned feel, with a mixture of bentwood chairs, buttoned orange banquettes and booth seating behind the rather forbidding industrial-looking exterior. Here, the cooking is in the experimental vein so that, although there are references to tradition in the shape of slow-cooked lamb rump in sauce niçoise with olive oil mash, elsewhere things take a walk on the wild side. Home-smoked Scottish salmon is escorted by pak choi and pickled cucumber, as well as crème fraîche beefed up with truffle and miso; a mushroom assembly teams raw fungi with pickled girolles and wickedly rich cep purée on toast. Roasted hake is offset by a medley of contrasting notes – aubergine with tamarind, vadouvan, baby onion and a lemon, caper and bone marrow butter. Vanilla rice pudding turns into something altogether glitzier when quince jam and crystallised almonds are applied to it, or look to pineapple carpaccio in lime and ginger syrup with coconut sorbet for something lighter. Vegetarian and vegan menus, palate-priming appetisers in jars, and a cocktail range to conjure with all feature, and the wine list leads with quality glasses from £5.50 before jetting off round the world's premier vineyards.
Chef/s: Paul Hood. **Closed:** Sun, bank hols. **Meals:** main courses £27 to £35. Tasting menu £65 (6 courses) to £85. **Details:** 82 seats. V menu. Vg menu. Bar. Wheelchairs. Music.

Spring

Cooking score: 5
⊖ Temple, Waterloo, map 5
Modern European | £64
Somerset House, Lancaster Place, Aldwych, WC2R 1LA
Tel no: 020 3011 0115
springrestaurant.co.uk

Skye Gyngell's restaurant within the institutional confines of Somerset House is a counterintuitive wager on Londoners' yearning for the soil. She brings a highly seasonal style of pastoral cooking to the capital whose warmth of heart is echoed in the sympathetic approach of staff. With white columns and chandeliers like posies, the dining room creates a light, bright impression, while the plates often look contrastingly weighty. Vegetables are not hewn down into dainty dice or machined into purées, but often sit defiantly whole. Grilled spring broccoli and fat white beans appear with lamb in its red wine bagna cauda, while a clump of roasted endive accompanies a tranche of halibut in blood orange butter. Before these, there could be a serving of grilled calçots and wild onions in romesco, garnished with primo sale soft cheese and Ibérico ham, or a burst of colour in the form of stracciatella with fennel, pink grapefruit, artichokes and dill. Good cheese trios to finish come with elderberry jelly and rye crackers, or look to bitter chocolate tart with candied ginger for a dessert that doesn't just hit the sweet spot. The anti-waste pre-theatre Scratch menu is a wonderfully inventive and low-cost way in. Herbal liqueurs are a notable feature of the drinks list (sweet cicely or fig leaf awaiting exploration), while wines are fine but headily priced. Small glasses start at £6.
Chef/s: Skye Gyngell and Rose Ashby. **Closed:** Sun, bank hols. **Meals:** main courses £25 to £36. Set L £29 (2 courses) to £32. Early D £20. **Details:** 102 seats. Bar. Wheelchairs.

Sushi Atelier

Cooking score: 4
⊖ Oxford Circus, map 5
Japanese | £37
114 Great Portland Street, Fitzrovia, W1W 6PH
Tel no: 020 7636 4455
sushiatelier.co.uk

Nothing decrees that Japanese food must be eaten in hushed rooms at prices that would buy a used car, and this place is the vibrant proof of it. Brick walls, blackboards, an up-tempo soundtrack and chefs who flaunt their skills with effervescent energy rather than Zen-like concentration are the hallmarks of this appealing package. The food is colourful, bracingly fresh and zippy with umami, starting with appetisers like sweet shiitake mushrooms and spicy burdock root, or sautéed fat tuna with truffle butter and wasabi, before hot dishes of clear eel soup with shimeji mushrooms, or the covetable wagyu beef slider with apple yakiniku sauce. The sushi is top drawer, there are piquant salads and a range of dressed carpaccio plates, including octopus with adzuki bean relish. Finish with a cleansing sorbet or a soy milk panna cotta in black sesame sauce. A good sake range, whizz-bang cocktails, and wines from £6.80 a glass contribute to the fun.
Chef/s: Robert Kemeny. **Closed:** Sun. **Meals:** main courses £4 to £34. **Details:** 40 seats. Music.

Tamarind Kitchen

Cooking score: 3
⊖ Tottenham Court Road, map 5
Indian | £40
167-169 Wardour Street, Soho, W1F 8WR
Tel no: 020 7287 4243
tamarindkitchen.co.uk

An offshoot of Mayfair's Tamarind, this Soho joint is more informal and (in our opinion) better value than its parent – presenting a spirited take on Subcontinental cuisine. The operation sprawls over two floors: all dusky wood, plush velvet banquettes and fashionably distressed surfaces, with a short, confident menu that hops between regional culinary traditions. The small plates might see you start in the far west with Gujurati raj kachori (filled puris) or Mumbai favourite pav bhaji. Grills take you south to Goa with the likes of wild tandoori prawn balchão – but the heartland of the menu is its curries: classic Delhi butter chicken with caramelised tomato sauce and dried fenugreek, or Kolkata-style bhuna gosht. Finish with an intriguing masala chai brûlée. Spice-friendly wines compete for attention with palate-cooling cocktails.
Chef/s: Karunesh Khanna. **Closed:** 25 and 26 Dec, 1 Jan. **Meals:** main courses £9 to £19. **Details:** 85 seats. Music.

Tandoor Chop House

Cooking score: 2
⊖ Charing Cross, map 5
Indian | £30
8 Adelaide Street, Covent Garden, WC2N 4HZ
Tel no: 020 3096 0359
tandoorchophouse.com
£30

Designed for mass appeal in London's Theatreland, this idiosyncratic restaurant conjures up the essence of a street canteen in old Bombay while giving a nod to the spirit of the English chophouse. Instead of an old-fashioned grill, however, the food is mostly fired up in three massive brass tandoors, which dominate the scene in the wood-panelled dining room – a noisy space with close-packed tables and tiled floors. The menu is all about snacks, small plates and sharing, from seekh kebab rolls with green chutney or deconstructed 'bhajia' onion rings with smoked aubergine raita to signature plates such as tandoori rabbit leg or peppered chicken tikka. Charcoal-blistered naans, black dhal and nimbu masala fries shouldn't be ignored, and chutney fans are in for a treat. To finish, order a cup of chai with some cardamom puffs or chill down with a tandoor hazelnut espresso martini. A dozen wines start at £25.
Chef/s: Kundan Singh. **Closed:** 25 and 26 Dec, 1 Jan. **Meals:** main courses £8 to £17. Set L £20 (2 courses) to £28. Set D £28. Sun L £25. Feast menu £28. **Details:** 48 seats. Wheelchairs. Music.

Terroirs

Cooking score: 1
⊖ Charing Cross, map 5
Modern European | £32
5 William IV Street, Covent Garden,
WC2N 4DW
Tel no: 020 7036 0660
terroirswinebar.com

🍾

A mixture of oddball pictures overlooks a
scene of bistro furniture and weathered
banquettes at this two-storey oenocentric
venue near Charing Cross. The formula is very
much of the moment: snack on charcuterie
and/or cheeses, or sign up for two or three
small plates – perhaps raw beef with onions
and beer, fried Jerusalem artichokes with leeks
and goat's curd, or burrata with melon and
elderflower – or maybe just one of the larger
offerings, say plaice with cornichons, capers
and leeks in red wine. The focus, though, is on
a wine list of astonishing breadth and value,
with small glasses from £4, full of the less
explored corners of France (Jasnières, Savoie
and the Arbois) and strong in central Europe
and Italy. There's a second branch at 36–38
Lordship Lane, East Dulwich SE22 8HJ.
Chef/s: Simon Barnett. **Closed:** Sun, bank hols, 25
and 26 Dec, 1 Jan. **Meals:** main courses £18 to £23.
Small plates £6 to £19. **Details:** 100 seats. 6 seats
outside. Bar. Music.

Texture

Cooking score: 5
⊖ Marble Arch, map 6
Modern French/Nordic | £75
34 Portman Street, Marylebone, W1H 7BY
Tel no: 020 7224 0028
texture-restaurant.co.uk

A painting of a volcanic eruption is the only
thing to disturb the serenity of this expansive
white-walled, wood-floored dining room,
where staff are 'friendly and engaging, always
around but never overbearing'. The
Scandinavian approach is tempered here in
counterintuitive but successful ways, from the
moment the fine sourdough and seeded rye

breads arrive, not with butter but with
volcanic salt and olive oils. Culinary traditions
are interwoven in ways that suggest they
always were, as when a bowl of thickened
dashi and bonito broth is plied with smoked
eel and pickled turnip. That could be followed
by best end and shoulder cuts of wondrous
Icelandic lamb with Jersey Royals, minted
broccoli, peas and a light lamb jus, or its
famous compatriot cod served with brandade,
but also with accompaniments from much
further south – tomatoes, avocado and
chorizo. Dessert is the moment to explore the
possibilities of skyr – an Icelandic dairy
product reminiscent of yoghurt – which
comes in vanilla-laced and ice cream versions
alongside slices of tacle (an orange and
mandarin cross) on rye biscuit crumbs. Even
the pre-dessert offers a little taster of skyr with
blood orange granita. A tome of a wine list
undertakes a sweeping global shuffle, with
varietal Rieslings an obvious pick for the
food. Small glasses of a Rheingau Trocken
are £8.
Chef/s: Agnar Sverrisson and Karl O'Dell. **Closed:**
Mon, Sun. **Meals:** main courses £37 to £49. Set L
£29 (2 courses) to £34. Tasting menu £99 (7
courses). **Details:** 50 seats. Vg menu. Music.

Theo Randall at the InterContinental

Cooking score: 6
⊖ Hyde Park Corner, map 6
Italian | £52
InterContinental London Hotel, 1 Hamilton
Place, Mayfair, W1J 7QY
Tel no: 020 7318 8747
theorandall.com

£5
OFF 🛏

Since arriving in 2006, chef Theo Randall has
carved out an unlikely Italian niche within the
muted surrounds of the InterContinental
Hotel – although his windowless dining
room does its best to counter any corporate
starchiness with its pale colour scheme, acres
of wood and unclothed tables. Randall
learned his trade at The River Café (see entry),
so it's no surprise that spirited seasonal flavours

and a wood-fired oven play a central role in proceedings, the latter working its smokey magic on everything from turbot to guinea fowl (stuffed and served on pagnotta bruschetta with Swiss chard and portobello mushrooms). Triumphant pasta dishes show a proper respect for ingredients and artisan skills (handmade taglierini with peas, prosciutto, mint and Parmesan, for example), while desserts always include a signature Amalfi lemon tart alongside the likes of ricotta cheesecake (served with pears marinated in Marsala). A predominantly Italian wine list (from £36) opens the door to many unsung heroes of regional viticulture, although serious money is required to explore its byways. Also note the intriguing line-up of vermouths (including bespoke 'flights').
Chef/s: Theo Randall and Luis Brendon Rodriguez. **Meals:** main courses £21 to £38. Set L and D £29 (2 courses) to £35. Tasting menu £70 (5 courses). **Details:** 92 seats. Vg menu. Bar. Wheelchairs. Parking. Music.

Tredwells

Cooking score: 2
⊖ Leicester Square, map 5
Modern British | £35
4a Upper St Martin's Lane, Covent Garden, WC2H 9NY
Tel no: 020 3764 0840
tredwells.com

Fans of Agatha Christie will know that Tredwell was the butler in her book *The Seven Dials Mystery* – a reminder that this easy-going eatery from Marcus Wareing resides in the heart of Covent Garden. Step inside and you'll discover a cavernous box of a place, spread over three levels (and popular with groups), tricked out in vintage style with mirrors, green and white tiling, leather banquettes and wall lights. As for the food, Chantelle Nicholson's brasserie-style menu likes to go walkabout when it comes to flavours and influences: cod cheeks are served with celeriac kimchi, sesame and BBQ sauce, Lake District venison is paired with carrot, lentil ragoût and pickled walnuts, steaks are

from the charcoal grill, and desserts might include a 'chouxnut' with lemon curd and clotted cream. Other trend-conscious touches include Vegwells (a five-course plant-based menu) and a special offer for 'culinary kids', complete with recipes to try at home. Cocktails, craft beers and global wines complete a user-friendly theatreland package.
Chef/s: Chantelle Nicholson. **Closed:** 24 to 26 Dec. **Meals:** main courses £18 to £33. Early D £25 (2 courses) to £30. Tasting menu £39 (5 courses) to £45. Sun L £30. **Details:** 150 seats. 12 seats outside. V menu. Vg menu. Bar. Wheelchairs. Music.

Trishna

Cooking score: 4
⊖ Baker Street, Bond Street, map 6
Indian | £60
15-17 Blandford Street, Marylebone, W1U 3DG
Tel no: 020 7935 5624
trishnalondon.com
£5 OFF 🍾

Mid-century furniture, statement lighting and whitewashed brickwork give the dining room a distinctly Westernised look, with only a few retro Air India posters reminding diners that the culinary compass here points east. Run by the go-getting Sethi family, this Marylebone eatery focuses on the distinctive coastal cuisines of Kochi, Kerala and Mangalore, with seafood playing a prominent role in delectable, subtly spiced dishes ranging from nandu varuval (soft-shell crab with green chilli, white crabmeat and tomato chutney) to John Dory pollichathu – a blend of wild garlic, beetroot, prawn pickle and masala uttapam. The kitchen also pleases with a tasty assortment of creative specialities such as duck seekh kebabs pointed up with tomato pickle and pineapple chutney or aubergine varuval (with urd dhal, dry red chilli, shallots and curry leaves). Dishes are flagged with intelligent wine pairings, and the full list (curated by sommelier and co-owner Sunaina Sethi) sets off on a knowledgeable jaunt, opening with around 20 by-the-glass

selections before picking up bottles from some of the world's most prestigious growers (prices start at £21).
Chef/s: Karam Sethi. **Closed:** bank hols. **Meals:** main courses £15 to £35. Set L £25 (2 courses) to £29. Set D £32. Tasting menu £65 (5 courses) to £75. **Details:** 60 seats. 8 seats outside. V menu. Vg menu. Music. No children after 7pm.

Umu

Cooking score: 6
⊖ Green Park, Bond Street, map 5
Japanese | £150
14-16 Bruton Place, Mayfair, W1J 6LX
Tel no: 020 7499 8881
umurestaurant.com

From the moment you press the security touchpad recessed into the wooden door, this ultra-discreet Japanese restaurant exudes an air of highly personal exclusivity, thanks largely to the efforts of chef proprietor Yoshinori Ishii. His touch is everywhere, from the exquisitely designed ceramic tableware and rigorous floral displays to the poems on woodblock prints that appear alongside various dishes. The chef also teaches his Cornish fishermen 'ike jime' (an ancient method of killing fish humanely) and buys much of his green produce from NamaYasai, a pioneering organic farm in Sussex. This 'born of nature' approach reaches its arcane apotheosis with a ceremonial Kyoto-style kaiseki menu showcasing the very best seasonal ingredients and traditional cooking styles, from kombu-cured shellfish with sakura leaf and kimizu (egg and rice vinegar dressing) to a shabu shabu hotpot of wagyu beef. Eat from the carte and you'll find similarly harmonious dishes ranging from sake-infused Scottish langoustine with tomato jelly to Irish wild eel with a fuwa fuwa soufflé pancake, mushrooms and mitsuba (Japanese parsley), while desserts might include 'charamisu Mayfair garden', a Japanese tiramisu with matcha green tea, ginjo cake and blood orange. Prices are sky high, but

lunchtime bento boxes offer an affordable way in – provided you can resist the premium sakes and flashy global wines.
Chef/s: Yoshinori Ishii. **Closed:** Sun, 21 Dec to 4 Jan. **Meals:** main courses £36 to £98. Kaiseki menu £165 (8 courses). **Details:** 40 seats. Wheelchairs. Music.

Veeraswamy

Cooking score: 5
⊖ Piccadilly Circus, Oxford Circus, map 5
Indian | £70
Victory House, 99 Regent Street, Mayfair, W1B 4RS
Tel no: 020 7734 1401
veeraswamy.com

On this site since 1926, the capital's oldest Indian restaurant delivers the comfortable luxury you would expect from a West End location at prices that will make you wish you could turn back time. It's a first-floor location overlooking Regent Street, with plenty of soft carpets, high-quality napery and smartly besuited staff to reinforce its reputation for top-quality food and great service. The kitchen delights with its elevated renditions of Indian regional cuisine. Order garlic-and-salt-flavoured naan fingers to mop up the rich, aromatic coconut and ginger sauce that covers a fine starter of Scottish king scallops. Or choose Keralan-style spicy quail, the meat pulled and tossed with madras shallots, fennel and Wayanad pepper and coconut flakes. To follow, a spectacular slow-cooked Welsh lamb shank served with marrow sauce, or lobster Malabar curry with fresh turmeric root, coconut and green mango. The biryanis are quite something – how about aged basmati rice with chicken thigh infused with mild spices? Sides such as fresh pineapple curry add to the allure and there's a luscious rose kulfi to finish. Spice-friendly wines and cocktails complete the picture.
Chef/s: Uday Salunkhe. **Meals:** main courses £22 to £32. Sun L £33 (2 courses) to £37. **Details:** 110 seats. V menu.

The Wigmore

Cooking score: 3
⊖ Oxford Circus, Bond Street, map 5
Modern British | £28
15 Langham Place, Marylebone, W1B 3DE
Tel no: 020 7965 0198
the-wigmore.co.uk

🛏 £30

It's the sort of concept that's easily sniffed at: high-spend hotel commissions top French chef to develop redundant bar space as a mock pub. But the reality is it works. While busy and buzzy, the rooms feel discreet and classy: parquet floors gleam, brass lamps dot marble and wood-topped tables, space is generous. If you are settling in for drinks and just want to snack, the XXL stovetop three cheese and mustard toastie (generous enough for two to share) comes highly recommended with, perhaps, a portion of chips seasoned with Bloody Mary salt. Otherwise, 'perfect pub food' – the menu is overseen by Michel Roux Jr – takes in chicken, bacon and mushroom pie, confit rabbit leg with braised pearl barley and violet mustard or a cheeseburger with grilled ox tongue and crispy shallots. Sticky toffee pudding with caramel sauce, and rhubarb and apple crumble are typical desserts. Beer and cocktails are taken seriously, and there's a short wine list that opens at £25. **Chef/s:** James Hawley. **Closed:** Sun. **Meals:** main courses £11 to £15. **Details:** 80 seats. Wheelchairs. Music. No children after 6pm.

Wild Honey

Cooking score: 6
⊖ Piccadilly Circus, map 5
Modern European | £50
8 Pall Mall, St James's, SW1Y 5NG
Tel no: 020 7968 2900
wildhoneystjames.co.uk

🛏

Quite an ace to have up your sleeve when you're out to impress, this dramatic double-height space houses a true urban eatery, like the all-day French brasseries to which it pays homage. Anthony Demetre's relocation of

Wild Honey from Mayfair to a corner site within the Sofitel St James Hotel has breathed new life into an already successful formula. Gallic influences meet British ingredients in cooking that is at once familiar and yet sufficiently aware of changes in taste to have popular appeal. Dishes can be as French as summer vegetable pistou soup or classic Marseille-style bouillabaisse, or as contemporary as grilled Galician octopus with smoked cod's roe and grelot onion, and Daphne's Welsh lamb – loin and sweetbreads – with courgettes, pearly barley and mint. There's also perfectly timed Cornish cod with a warm vinaigrette of cockles, fresh white beans, tomato and parsley, and to finish a very good custard tart with a heap of golden sultanas and pine nuts in salted butter served alongside. The surroundings are tailored to conversational get-togethers helped by on-the-ball service and a wine list that majors in France, whips quickly round the world and offers a good by-the-glass selection from £6. **Chef/s:** Anthony Demetre and Simon Woodrow. **Meals:** main courses £11 to £28. Set L and early D £23 (2 courses) to £27. **Details:** 110 seats. V menu. Bar. Wheelchairs.

Wiltons

Cooking score: 4
⊖ Green Park, map 5
British | £70
55 Jermyn Street, Mayfair, SW1Y 6LX
Tel no: 020 7629 9955
wiltons.co.uk

A venerable upholder of tradition, eschewing the cult of the new while unapologetically relishing the values of yesteryear, this is a dining room (velvety and panelled) where formal attire is *de rigueur*, electronic devices are strictly taboo and impeccably groomed staff attend to every detail. At first glance, Wiltons' food is quintessentially Bulldog British – freshly shucked oysters from native waters, smoked salmon sliced to order, gargantuan lunchtime roasts carved from the trolley, furred and feathered game, mixed grills, savouries and nursery puddings such as strawberry and sherry trifle that are straight out of Mrs Beeton. Elsewhere, dishes such as burrata with figs, truffle and honey, lobster thermidor, cod with bouillabaisse sauce and pomme purée or raspberry soufflé with white chocolate ice cream speak of a kitchen with strong European allegiances. Vintage clarets and Burgundies from the great years hold sway on the fearsomely priced upper-crust wine list, with bottles starting at £35. **Chef/s:** Daniel Kent. **Closed:** Sun, 22 Dec to 2 Jan, 10 to 13 Apr. **Meals:** main courses £19 to £70. Set L and D £35 (2 courses) to £43. **Details:** 100 seats. Bar.

The Wolseley

Cooking score: 2
⊖ Green Park, map 5
Modern European | £40
160 Piccadilly, Mayfair, W1J 9EB
Tel no: 020 7499 6996
thewolseley.com

Once dubbed 'Piccadilly's Shining Pearl', this one-time showroom for prestigious Wolseley automobiles still has the magic – just look at those marble pillars, high-vaulted ceilings, hand-painted Japanese murals and sparkling chandeliers. As a luxe take on the European grand café for today's Londoners, it's an unrivalled all-day classic that happily feeds a motley crew from breakfasting early birds to night owls, from power lunches to dinner dates. Any time and any dish will do, whether it's a crispy bacon roll, muesli or chickpea socca pancakes, a plate of oysters, a mighty schnitzel, coq au vin or goulash. If you're into the sweet side of things, The Wolseley's afternoon tea is the ultimate soothing treat, although other equally indulgent temptations beckon – from éclairs and Black Forest gâteau to banana splits, fruit crumbles and ice cream coupes. Liquid refreshment covers all bases too, with wines from £26.50. **Chef/s:** David Stevens. **Meals:** main courses £13 to £49. Sun L £25. **Details:** 165 seats. V menu. Bar. Wheelchairs.

Wright Brothers Soho

Cooking score: 2
⊖ Oxford Circus, map 5
Seafood | £40
13 Kingly Street, Soho, W1B 5PW
Tel no: 020 7324 7731
thewrightbrothers.co.uk

Sharing dishes of a pan-Asian persuasion are on the menu at the relaxed Soho site of Wright Bros' seafood mini-chain. Enjoy Korean-fried mussels or salt and pepper squid in the open-air courtyard (covered in winter), if the weather allows. For main entry, see Borough branch, south London. **Chef/s:** David Jones. **Closed:** 25 and 26 Dec, 1 Jan. **Meals:** main courses £10 to £25. **Details:** 77 seats. 44 seats outside. Bar. Wheelchairs. Music.

Xu

Cooking score: 4
⊖ Piccadilly Circus, map 5
Taiwanese | £35
30 Rupert Street, Soho, W1D 6DL
Tel no: 020 3319 8147
xulondon.com

Having introduced Londoners to the pillowy delights of Taiwanese steamed buns, the people behind Bao (see entries) decided to turn the spotlight on their native island's more esoteric regional specialities. The result: a handsome Soho tribute to 1930s Taipei complete with vintage styling, ceiling fans, leather booths and even a bookable private room for those who want to play mahjong. Despite a change of chef, the food remains innovative and thrilling as ever – from 'xiao tsai' snacks of cuttlefish toast with whipped cod's roe or steamed egg with roast turnip and chive oil to more dramatic ideas such as 'master stock' poached goose accompanied by Chinese olive greens and burnt spring onion. There are imaginative dumplings too, plus side orders of rich, sticky 'lardo lard' rice that are much more than mere ballast. Rare, fragrant Taiwanese teas are served in delicate ceramic cups and the leaves also find their way into some clever cocktails; otherwise, pick from the short but super-trendy wine list (bottles from £28). **Chef/s:** Kimberley Hernandez. **Meals:** main courses £15 to £25. Set L £20 (2 courses). Tasting menu £39 (4 courses). **Details:** 74 seats. Bar. Music.

Yauatcha

Cooking score: 4
⊖ Tottenham Court Road, map 5
Chinese | £40
15-17 Broadwick Street, Soho, W1F 0DL
Tel no: 020 7494 8888
yauatcha.com

Depending on your mood, choose between the ground floor (blue-hued, bright and cool with a stylish fish tank) or head down to the basement (dark and sultry with twinkling lights overhead). Yauatcha is still known for classy, sophisticated Chinese food in a fashionable environment. The dim sum consistently get the thumbs-up, perhaps 'super-flaky' venison puff followed by 'gossamer-like' prawn and crispy beancurd cheung fun. Other highlights include 'crystal-clear' dumpling of king crab. Larger plates are just as thrilling, note tender stir-fried ribeye beef in black bean sauce, as well as tofu coated with spinach and served with shimeji mushrooms and baby asparagus. Patisserie crosses boundaries with success – rum baba with coconut sorbet enlivened by pineapple infused with Szechuan pepper, for example. Staff are attentive and visitors' only grumble is 'the tables are too small for the dishes'. The sharp list of cocktails and wines (from £31) matches the food.
Chef/s: Andrew Yeo. **Meals:** main courses £8 to £48. Set L £28. **Details:** 190 seats. Wheelchairs. Music.

Zoilo

Cooking score: 3
⊖ Bond Street, map 6
Argentinian | £45
9 Duke Street, Marylebone, W1U 3EG
Tel no: 020 7486 9699
zoilo.co.uk

The main action at this bijou Marylebone Bistro is centred on the softly lit ground-floor bar that conjures up images of Buenos Aires with its chequered floor tiles and mix of counter seating and red leather banquettes. Share starters of provoleta – baked provolone cheese with almonds and oregano honey (order the house-baked breads to mop it up) or classic empanandas, which come in pairs, say spinach and goat's cheese, raisins and pine nuts, but you may want to keep the main course to yourself. Argentinian beef is the thing, say bife de chorizo, a 300g slab of chargrilled sirloin served with an intense herb-laden dressing (there's a bone-in version too), as well as a catch of the day or a generous serving of green pea, mint and ricotta ravioli with girolle butter and Parmesan. Finish with a velvety dulce de leche crème brûlée with banana split ice cream. Service is effortlessly calm and charming, and cocktails vie for attention against the good-value all-Argentinian wine list (from £25.95).
Chef/s: Diego Jacquet. **Closed:** Sun, bank hols, 1 week Christmas. **Meals:** main courses £17 to £33. Set L £16 (2 courses) to £19. **Details:** 49 seats. Wheelchairs. Music.

LOCAL GEM

500 Restaurant

Archway, map 2
Italian | £29
782 Holloway Road, Archway, N19 3JH
Tel no: 020 7272 3406
500restaurant.co.uk

£5 OFF **£30**

This personable neighbourhood Italian keeps chugging on as reliably as its namesake automobile – the iconic Fiat Cinquecento (500). Pictures and prints of the car dominate the walls of the plainly decorated bare-tabled dining room, where locals gather for honest-to-goodness regional staples ranging from gnocchi with white sausage ragù to saltimbocca alla romana or baked rabbit rolls stuffed with sun-dried tomatoes and wild garlic. For afters, consider tiramisu, panna cotta or the 'coupe 500' (caramelised rhubarb with a scoop of strawberry sorbet). Italian wines from £18.50.

READERS RECOMMEND

Antepliler

45-46 Grand Parade, Green Lanes, Haringay, N4 1AG
Tel no: 020 8802 5588
antepliler.com
'This Green Lanes Turkish stalwart has been serving tender kebabs and lahmacun for years. Don't leave without trying the künefe from their café next door.'

★ NEW ENTRY ★

Barrafina Coal Drops Yard

Cooking score: 4
King's Cross, map 2
Spanish | £35
Unit 27, Coal Drops Yard, King's Cross, N1C 4AB
barrafina.co.uk

On the upper tier of the Coal Drops Yard development, the fourth and largest of the Hart brothers' barnstorming Barrafina tapas bars continues the tradition of delivering an irresistible taste of Spain to London diners. It has the same laid-back, agreeably understated look, counter seating and no-reservations policy as its siblings; jovial, knowledgeable staff do their bit, too. It's this no-nonsense approach, along with a fun atmosphere and good food, that makes the whole group stand out. Things can kick off simply with pan con tomate, a classic tortilla (made to order), portobello mushroom croquetas, Pyrenean lamb chops with tumbet (a Mallorcan roasted vegetable dish) or with the more unusual cuttlefish a la bruta with burnt leeks and piparra (chilli) oil. The excellent timing of fish cookery is noteworthy, with praise for a special of whole stuffed wild bream, as well as for monkfish fritura with bergamot mayo. Sherries in all styles, cavas and Spanish wines seal the deal.
Chef/s: Angel Zapata Martin. **Closed:** 25 and 26 Dec, 1 Jan, 13 Apr. **Meals:** main courses £8 to £21. **Details:** 40 seats. Wheelchairs. No reservations. Maximum group size 4.

Bellanger

Cooking score: 2
Angel, map 2
Modern French | £40
9 Islington Green, Islington, N1 2XH
Tel no: 020 7226 2555
bellanger.co.uk

The blue awnings out front and the interior atmosphere of dark wood, booth seating and waistcoated staff testify to the enduring appeal of traditional French brasserie eating, the road-tested Corbin and King formula applied winningly here to the food of Alsace. Drop in for a sustaining breakfast of eggs Benedict, a lunch of tarte flambée topped with fromage blanc, smoked bacon and onion, or the full evening drill of immaculate steak tartare crowned with glistening yolk, poached cod with crispy bacon in sauce verte, and a coupe of nutty ice creams lashed with butterscotch. The classic choucroute à l'alsacienne is essentially a gigantic heap of pig, with hock, belly and sausages galore. There's a separate vegetarian menu, too. It's all served by alert staff with the right attitude. More Alsace wines would be welcome (the region's sparklers are often better than the gatecrashing Crémant de Loire on offer), but the French list is comprehensive and reasonably priced, from £22.50 for Gascon and Languedoc blends. **Chef/s:** Wojtek Szymczyszyn. **Closed:** Mon. **Meals:** main courses £14 to £37. Set L and early D £15 (2 courses) to £17. **Details:** 195 seats. V menu. Bar. Wheelchairs.

Bradleys

Cooking score: 2
Θ Swiss Cottage, map 2
French | £30
25 Winchester Road, Swiss Cottage, NW3 3NR
Tel no: 020 7722 3457
bradleysnw3.co.uk
£30

Over a quarter of a century since its launch, Simon and Jolanta Bradley's neighbourhood restaurant remains a steadying presence in Swiss Cottage. Not that it has stood still, as evidenced by its inventive vegan options – how about red cabbage steak with chimichurri and sweet potato chips? – and the introduction of some more relaxed seating options. Chef Simon's classical French training informs the menu without weighing it down. Twice-baked leek and Gruyère soufflé and rack of lamb with heritage carrots and a cromesqui of the shoulder should please the traditionalists, while mushroom flan, tempura cauliflower and miso-glazed celeriac will open their eyes. Desserts are of the 'proper' variety: steamed rhubarb and orange pudding, perhaps, or chocolate tart. Pre-theatre menus (the Hampstead Theatre is close by), as well as Sunday and set lunches, are geared towards local needs. Regarding the wine list, half bottles and classic French appellations feel like smart inclusions. **Chef/s:** Simon Bradley. **Closed:** bank hols. **Meals:** main courses £17 to £25. Set L and early D £20 (2 courses) to £24. Set D £30. Sun L £28 (2 courses) to £32. **Details:** 63 seats. V menu. Vg menu. Wheelchairs. Music.

The Bull & Last

no score
Θ Tufnell Park, Kentish Town, map 2
Modern British | £39
168 Highgate Road, Hampstead, NW5 1QS
Tel no: 020 7267 3641
thebullandlast.co.uk

Six new bedrooms, a state-of-the-art basement kitchen and a totally revamped interior are part of the new look of this long-serving Victorian hostelry close to Hampstead Heath, which is scheduled to reopen before Christmas 2019, following months of refurbishment. The owners have taken the time out to travel and pick up some new recipes, although no menus were available before the Guide went to press. Hopefully, the kitchen will continue to deliver superior pub food based on seasonal ingredients, with back-up from London-brewed craft beers and a terroir-led list of global wines. Reports please. **Chef/s:** Oliver Pudney. **Meals:** main courses £15 to £25. **Details:** 45 seats. Bar. Wheelchairs.

★ NEW ENTRY ★

Coal Office

Cooking score: 4
Θ King's Cross, map 2
Middle Eastern | £40
2 Bagley Walk, King's Cross, N1C 4PQ
Tel no: 020 3848 6085
coaloffice.com

Competition is fierce in N1C. The capital's newest quarter has a thriving restaurant scene, but this collaboration between British designer Tom Dixon and chef Assaf Granit more than holds its own. The redesigned mid-19th-century building overlooking Granary Square delivers hard-edged vibes (from marble, brick and wood) but is the place to share food bursting with the warm-hearted flavours of the Mediterranean, North Africa and the Middle East. Some say the best seats are at the counter looking straight on to the open-plan kitchen, but if high bar stools don't appeal, there is a more conventional dining area. The renowned kubalah, a soft white loaf served with reduced yoghurt and a fresh, intense tomato confit is as hard to bypass as the delicate Josperised aubergine served with green tahini and pistachio. Follow with generous plates of shikshukit (a lamb and beef kebab) and sea bass fillet in a spicy tomato and pepper stew. Tahini ice cream and strawberry and black pepper sorbet lead the charge on a short list of fragrant desserts. Service is prompt, informative and friendly, breakfast and brunch are popular, and as for liquid refreshment, inventive cocktails and gutsy wines suit the food admirably.

Chef/s: Assaf Granit and Uri Navon. **Meals:** small plates £5 to £12. Large plates £13 to £25. **Details:** 80 seats. 80 seats outside.

Dishoom

Cooking score: 2
⊖ King's Cross, map 2
Indian | £30
5 Stable Street, King's Cross, N1C 4AB
Tel no: 020 7420 9321
dishoom.com
£30

The competition is fierce in restaurant-packed King's Cross, but Mumbai-themed bar restaurant Dishoom stands out with its affordable eats and sheer size. Based in a former Victorian goods shed, it's atmospheric but loud. For main entry, see Shoreditch branch, east London.

Chef/s: Naved Nasir. **Closed:** 25 and 26 Dec, 1 and 2 Jan. **Meals:** main courses from £7 to £22. **Details:** 98 seats. 25 seats outside. Bar. Wheelchairs. Music. No reservations. Bookings after 5.45pm for groups of 6 or more only.

★ NEW ENTRY ★

The Drop

Cooking score: 3
⊖ King's Cross, map 2
British | £25
Unit 22-24, Bagley Walk Arches, Coal Drops Yard, King's Cross, N1C 4DH
thedropwinebar.co.uk
£30

Sometimes new openings hit that something-for-everyone note pitch perfect. This delightful little wine bar from Sam and James Hart of Barrafina fame is tucked under arches in a corner of Coal Drops Yard and the appeal is instantly apparent. The short, regularly changing menu is a zesty assortment of dishes with influences from all over – whether it's half a dozen native oysters, sharing plates of cheese and charcuterie, chicken liver pâté or roast squash with onions, pumpkin seeds and sage. Portions are as generous as the flavours are meaningful: a meaty, well-made pork pie gets the thumbs-up from one diner, as does a more substantial plate of confit duck leg with duck-fat-fried savoy cabbage and mash. The casual look has been nailed, too – convivial with close-packed tables, bar-counter seating and spot-on service. A concise modern wine list, plus blackboard specials, starts at £25.

Chef/s: Karan Ghosh. **Closed:** 25 Dec, 13 Apr. **Meals:** small plates £7 to £22. **Details:** 50 seats. 24 seats outside. Music.

READERS RECOMMEND

Escocesa

67 Stoke Newington Church Street, Stoke Newington, N16 0AR
Tel no: 020 7812 9189
escocesa.co.uk
'We love this buzzy new spot. They use Scottish ingredients to make Spanish tapas, hence the name. Don't miss the courgette flowers stuffed with goat's cheese and honey when they're in season. Great wine list, too.'

Ham

Cooking score: 3
⊖ West Hampstead, map 1
Modern British | £33
238 West End Lane, West Hampstead,
NW6 1LG
Tel no: 020 7813 0168
hamwesthampstead.com

£5
OFF

Named after the Old English word for 'home', pronounced something like 'harm', this contemporary restaurant makes a good fist of exploring the farms, meadows and coasts of the British Isles for pristine modern produce. Light woods and pale brickwork behind a sky blue frontage give the place an uplifting feel, with modern presentations very much to the fore in assertive, impactful dishes. Start with nibbles such as celeriac croquette with preserved lemon and cucumber, before barbecued calçots with piquillo peppers and grapes in almond sauce, or a bowl of spicy prawn and noodle broth and oyster mushrooms. Pedigree Lake District meats are a strong draw, perhaps shorthorn beef seasoned with black sesame and teamed with sprouting broccoli and salted turnip, while the fish is Cornwall's finest, maybe brill with artichoke and freekeh in kombu butter. Cheeses from Mons and Neal's Yard Dairy are the alternatives to sweetnesses such as macadamia parfait with blood orange, mandarin sorbet and lemon thyme. Florally fragrant cocktails lead the drinks line, with a small spread of well-chosen wines from £20.
Chef/s: Matt Osborne. **Closed:** Mon, 25 and 26 Dec. **Meals:** main courses £16 to £23. **Details:** 42 seats. 6 seats outside. Bar. Music.

Readers recommend

These entries are genuine quotes from a report sent in by one of our readers. Please get in touch via our website if you agree with their recommendation.

Heirloom

Cooking score: 3
⊖ Highgate, map 2
Modern British | £35
33-35 Park Road, Crouch End, N8 8TE
Tel no: 020 8348 3565
heirloomn8.co.uk

Considered regional sourcing helps to shape the modern British menu at this upmarket neighbourhood restaurant with a pub-like bar, chunky wooden tables and stylishly mismatched seating. It's a family affair, fronted by chef patron Ian Macintosh and his brother, David. Small bites are indulgent and might include Lords Burgh cheese fritters and fabulous fat chips fried in beef dripping. On our visit, catch of the day was creamy brown Cornish crabmeat, slathered on sourdough, its mineral flavour offset by sweet garden peas. Substantial mains also impressed with rosemary-scented lamb roasted to perfect pinkness, simply served with chargrilled aubergine and steamed pak choi. Puddings are resolutely old-school – top marks for the citrussy tartness of a lemon posset crowned with a blush of rhubarb and accompanied by buttery shortbread. Do explore the excellent list of classy cocktails, British craft beers and biodynamic wines. Sunday lunchtime roasts are a hit with young families.
Chef/s: Ian Macintosh. **Closed:** Mon, Tue.
Meals: main courses £14 to £27. **Details:** 35 seats. Bar.

The Hero of Maida

Cooking score: 2
⊖ Warwick Avenue, map 6
Anglo-French | £35
55 Shirland Road, Maida Vale, W9 2JD
Tel no: 020 3960 9109
theheromaidavale.co.uk

Perhaps best known to Guide readers as the chef behind the late Racine in Knightsbridge, Henry Harris is now in the business of revitalising a clutch of London pubs, including this much-loved hostelry (formerly the Truscott Arms). The beating heart of the place is still the blue-toned ground-floor bar where pints of Timothy Taylor, Adnams, Curious IPA and the like are supped with classic snacks and pickings from the full menu. You can also graduate to the elegantly appointed upstairs room for a more leisurely meal of grilled rabbit with Alsace bacon and mustard sauce, say, or Cotswolds lamb rump accompanied by white asparagus, peas and lovage. Seasonal produce underpins just about everything, and Harris's liking for robust Anglo-French alliances continues right through to desserts of crème caramel or chocolate tart with salted caramel ice cream. Brunch and Sunday roasts broaden the pub's all-round appeal, while the wine list offers a lively selection from France, Italy and 'the rest of the world'.

Chef/s: Henry Harris and Harry Milbourne. **Meals:** main courses £14 to £26. Set L £16 (2 courses) to £19. **Details:** 110 seats. 30 seats outside. Bar. Music.

★ NEW ENTRY ★

El Inca Plebeyo

Cooking score: 2
⊖ Highbury & Islington, map 2
Ecuadorian | £30
162 Essex Road, Islington, N1 8LY
Tel no: 020 7704 9393
elincaplebeyo.co.uk

Ecuadorian chef and owner Jorge Pacheco draws on his heritage to provide home cooking for nearby residents and local South Americans. The restaurant is an informal set-up with colourful artwork and an open kitchen at the rear. Affordable cocktails, notably the pisco sour, are a big draw and work especially well with ceviche. On our visit, top marks went to sea-fresh prawns, cured in lime juice and chilli-spiked tamarillo pulp, matched with a side order of fried green plantain. Other recommendations include meaty grills and hearty stews, and sharing is encouraged. Make one of your choices the richly flavoured pearl barley and spinach

risotto, simmered in nutty-tasting corn beer and studded with tender lamb, and look out for the surprisingly light hot potato griddle cakes (llapingachos) filled with fresh homemade cheese. Visit for – as one reader suggested – 'food like your mum would make if she came from Quito and not Gants Hill'. The short wine list looks mostly to South America and Spain with bottles from £22.

Chef/s: Jorge Pacheco. **Closed:** 25 Dec, 1 Jan. **Meals:** main courses £12 to £26. **Details:** 40 seats. 10 seats outside. Bar. Music.

Jin Kichi

Cooking score: 2
⊖ Hampstead, map 2
Japanese | £40
73 Heath Street, Hampstead, NW3 6UG
Tel no: 020 7794 6158
jinkichi.com
£5
OFF

Channelling the convivial spirit of an izakaya, this tiny family-run Hampstead operation has become a home-from-home for anyone seeking a true taste of Tokyo. The menu nimbly covers a lot of ground. Order several dishes to make a meal, but something raw is a must – when it comes to sushi, they are masters of their craft. Opt for the likes of butter-soft sea urchin, tuna or sea bass sashimi, nigiri or sushi rolls, bookended by a clutch of small dishes – edamame and grilled eel, perhaps – and some thrilling robatayaki from the charcoal grill. Skewered explosions of umami feature every part of the chicken, ox tongue and more besides. There are myriad tempura delights, too, and the one-plate lunch dishes, served with rice and miso soup, are a steal. Jin Kichi seems to be perpetually packed, so book ahead. Dessert's a simple affair: go for sweet red-bean pancake, ice cream or sorbet. Swerve the wine in favour of sake by the bottle, jug or glass.

Chef/s: Rei Shimazu. **Closed:** Mon, 25 and 26 Dec. **Meals:** small plates £2 to £19. Sushi £2 to £20. **Details:** 40 seats. V menu.

Jolene

Cooking score: 3
⊖ Canonbury, Dalston Kingsland, map 2
Modern European | £35
22 Newington Green, Newington Green,
N16 9PU
Tel no: 020 3887 2309
jolenen16.com

Very easy to miss on the ground floor of a
new-build block of flats, Jeremie Cometto-
Lingenheim and David Gingell's latest
neighbourhood eatery majors – like its
stablemates Primeur, a scant couple of minutes
away, and Westerns Laundry (see entries) – on
field-to-plate food and bold, straight-talking
flavours. Concrete surfaces and communal
tables are the style, with a blackboard menu
divided into 'small plates', 'pasta' and 'sharing'.
This could bring six perfect, fat spears of
asparagus, zigzagged with a rich caramel
butter sauce, then wide ribbons of pappardelle
in a thick tomato ragù topped with tiny diced
pancetta that is 'both sweet and salty and richly
delicious', and slices of pink lamb leg with
lovely crunchy piattone beans dressed in a
light vinaigrette and an assertive dollop of
anchovy cream. Chocolate tart shows real skill
in the pastry department – light-as-air dark
chocolate mousse on a sweet, buttery, crisp
pastry base testament to the fact Jolene
operates as a bakery and café during the day. To
drink, there's a short all-natural wine list.
Chef/s: David Gingell and Jack Williams. **Closed:**
Mon. **Meals:** main courses £10 to £25. **Details:** 55
seats. Bar.

Send us your review

Your feedback informs the content of
the *GFG* and will be used to compile
next year's reviews. To register your
opinion about any restaurant listed, or a
restaurant that you wish to bring to our
attention, visit our website.

Moio

Cooking score: 1
⊖ Stoke Newington, map 2
Modern European | £35
188 Stoke Newington High Street, Stoke
Newington, N16 7JD
Tel no: 020 7923 7119
moiorestaurant.com

This high street eatery leads a double life: at
weekends it's a place for lazy Stokey brunches,
where diners graze on poke cones with cured
salmon, or sourdough creaking under strata of
harissa, aged burrata and avo. Come evenings,
the lights dim and the Portuguese accent
becomes a little stronger. Start with peppery
morcela sausage with smoked plum, or lamb
tartare with oyster and Margherita onion
purée. Sunny mains might see seafood barley
with spicy bisque and seaweed or slow-
cooked short rib with charred aubergine
purée. Conclude with pineapple carpaccio
with sweet wine and pink peppercorn sauce.
Service sparkles whatever the occasion. Drink
cocktails, beers or Portuguese wines.
Chef/s: Joao Ferreira Pinto. **Closed:** Mon, Tue.
Meals: main courses £14 to £17. **Details:** 35 seats.

Odette's

Cooking score: 3
⊖ Chalk Farm, map 2
Modern British | £50
130 Regent's Park Road, Primrose Hill,
NW1 8XL
Tel no: 020 7586 8569
odettesprimrosehill.com

Furnished in shades of brown, with framed
line drawings and dark wood fixtures, this
well-established restaurant has the feel of an
elegant private club. A mix of business suits,
romancing couples and lively groups all
endorse Bryn Williams' finely tuned modern
British menu. Our delicate pastry tart was a
spring highlight for its inspired filling of
crème fraîche, crisp asparagus and gutsy wild
garlic pesto. Next up was a beer-battered
turbot skirt, fried to splinter crispness and

topped with deliciously bittersweet strips of candied lemon zest. Main courses offer subtle flavours – the tenderness of a simply roasted Goosnargh chicken leg, complemented by buttery mushroom relish, chargrilled baby onion and a light chicken jus. A mile-high banana soufflé provided a fitting finale – we struck gold as warm rum and caramel sauce trickled into its centre. Dining here isn't cheap but the set menu is great value, and a globally sourced wine listing covers all budgets.
Chef/s: Bryn Williams and Tom Dixon. **Closed:** Mon, 2 weeks Dec to Jan. **Meals:** main courses £19 to £29. Set L £15 (2 courses) to £18. Tasting menu £56 (6 courses). Sun L £33. **Details:** 60 seats. 20 seats outside. V menu. Music.

Oldroyd
Cooking score: 3
⊖ Angel, map 2
Modern European | £35
344 Upper Street, Islington, N1 0PD
Tel no: 020 8617 9010
oldroydlondon.com

It's easy to walk straight past Tom Oldroyd's tiny restaurant. Once inside, you have the choice of perching at a stool overlooking the cramped kitchen, or clambering upstairs to the narrow dining room. A commitment to seasonality on the short, daily changing menu might see winter dishes of Puy lentils, chanterelles and goat's curd, or braised wild rabbit with pappardelle and confit carrots. Spinach malfatti has been described as a 'revelation, rich and light with the sweetness of braised squash and earthy chestnuts, perfect January food'. Other plates offer simple assemblies of fabulous flavours, say torched smoked eel with blood orange and castelfranco. In spring there might be asparagus, Parmesan cream and toasted buckwheat or braised lamb shoulder, wild garlic pappardelle, broad beans and ricotta. Do save room for the likes of dark chocolate and pistachio tart or Yorkshire rhubarb and custard. Mondays are meat free. A lively selection of cocktails sits alongside a suitably concise wine list, all available by the glass.

Chef/s: Karl Doering. **Closed:** 25 Dec. **Meals:** main courses £8 to £22. Set L £19 (2 courses) to £24. **Details:** 36 seats. 6 seats outside. Music.

Osteria Tufo
Cooking score: 2
⊖ Finsbury Park, map 2
Italian | £28
67 Fonthill Road, Finsbury Park, N4 3HZ
Tel no: 020 7272 2911
osteriatufo.co.uk
£5 OFF | £30

It may take its name from a volcanic rock that dominates the Bay of Naples but don't expect tectonic shifts at this pretty little place on a residential street. On our visit, the classic, calming space of chequerboard floors, tightly clustered tables and high ceilings echoed only to the gentle cadences of a singing waiter. The menu radiates southern Italian sunshine: evident in Pugliese burrata and Sicilian caponata, while capesante grigliate – grilled scallops in sweet potato sauce – stood out. Pasta mains are hearty portions: homemade pappardelle with luganica pork sausage, and Neapolitan tagliatelle alle vongole. Tiramisus and gelatos reign among desserts – while the short wine list represents all corners of the peninsula, from Piedmont to Palermo.
Chef/s: Diego Monticelli-Cuggio. **Closed:** Mon, 23 Dec to 10 Jan. **Meals:** main courses £14 to £18. Sun L £22 (2 courses). **Details:** 32 seats. 22 seats outside. Wheelchairs. Music.

Parlour
Cooking score: 2
⊖ Kensal Green, map 1
Modern British | £35
5 Regent Street, Kensal Green, NW10 5LG
Tel no: 020 8969 2184
parlourkensal.com

'Make it fun, make it memorable' is the mantra at Jesse Dunford Wood's all-day foodie destination, a one-time Kensal Green drinking den, now with a big smile on its face. There's a tiled bar area for those who get their kicks from small-batch beers, gins, modern

cocktails and McTucky's popcorn chicken nuggets, while the smart dining room draws those looking for solid sustenance. All-day breakfasts and brunches are a big shout hereabouts and the tongue-in-cheek full menu promises even more possibilities, from fish soup with 'prawn(less)' crackers to chicken Kyiv [*sic*] with hash browns or 'Desperate Dan's cow pie'. Alternatively, trade up to a fiercely seasonal fixed-price lunch or supper – perhaps Mary's 'piggy fritters' with quince and chicory followed by steamed whiting with Jerusalem artichokes and hazelnuts, plus Arctic rolls 'with lots of funky flavours' to finish. Everything on the appetising global wine list is available by the glass.
Chef/s: Jesse Dunford Wood. **Closed:** Mon, Christmas to New Year. **Meals:** main courses £16 to £20. Set L and D £15 (2 courses) to £21. Sun L £32. **Details:** 120 seats. 60 seats outside. Bar. Wheelchairs. Music.

★ NEW ENTRY ★

Parrillan
Cooking score: 2
⊖ King's Cross, map 2
Spanish | £35
Coal Drops Yard, King's Cross, N1C 4AB
Tel no: 020 7018 3339
parrillan.co.uk
£5
OFF

If you fancy eating alfresco, it's worth considering the Hart Brothers' latest opening in the stylish Coal Drops Yard development – a large covered and heated terrace on the upper tier next door to Barrafina (see entry). Cook your own food on a tabletop grill, the parrillan. Staff give cooking times for the likes of red prawns, milk-fed lamb's kidneys, middle white pork collar, butifarra pintxo, lamb entrecôte or duck breast. Ingredients are of exceptional quality and while you wait for your grill to be fired up you can order pan con tomate, a delicious escalivada of roasted vegetables or plates of presa Ibérica de bellota. Dessert is limited to a tart of the day or ice cream. And to drink? There are good cocktails and an excellent selection of sherries and

Spanish wines. Booking is essential in fine weather and we are told that Parrillan will run as a covered (and heated) outdoor venue in cooler months.
Chef/s: Angel Zapata Martin. **Closed:** 25 Dec, 1 Jan. **Meals:** main courses £11 to £16. **Details:** 80 seats. 60 seats outside. Children over 10 yrs.

Perilla
Cooking score: 5
⊖ Canonbury, Dalston Kingsland, map 2
Modern European | £42
1-3 Green Lanes, Newington Green, N16 9BS
Tel no: 020 7359 0779
perilladining.co.uk

There's something exciting happening in this corner site on Newington Green. At the pass is ex-Square chef Ben Marks, who cooks with a verve and vigour one rarely associates with 'neighbourhood dining'. At inspection, the cosy dining room, its distressed wood tables set with candles and pots of herbs, is busy 'but never chaotic'. The menu is sensibly compact (six dishes à la carte or a six-course taster) and balances affordability with inventiveness. Snacks such as yesterday's bread soaked in moules marinière, and gurnard fried in beef fat with chip shop curry sauce set the bar high. Burnt onion soup in a charred onion 'bowl' is a dramatic-looking Perilla signature, although another of monk's beard 'spaghetti' with salt cod ragù is arguably 'a bit too clever'. Better is the technical wizardry behind grilled pluma Ibérica topped with three blistered Padrón peppers, each filled with a different purée (parsley, garlic, tomato and chorizo), tasting potently of itself. Desserts impress too, notably a 'textbook' pastel de nata with blood orange. The neat European-focused wine list is updated to suit the menu.
Chef/s: Ben Marks. **Meals:** main courses £9 to £14. Tasting menu £44 (6 courses). Sun L £30 (2 courses) to £35. **Details:** 38 seats. V menu. Vg menu. Bar. Wheelchairs. Music.

★ NEW ENTRY ★

Primeur

Cooking score: 3
⊖ Canonbury, map 2
Modern European | £30
116 Petherton Road, Stoke Newington,
N5 2RT
Tel no: 020 7226 5271
primeurn5.co.uk
£30

'Barnes Motors' reads the sign above the door, a reminder of the garage that predated Primeur (established 2014). As the name suggests, it's a wine-focused establishment, with a leaning towards fashionable natural juice that it shares with siblings Westerns Laundry and Jolene (see entries). A single blackboard proves both functional – it lists the day's food and drink – and decorative in this sparsely accoutred place with communal tables, monochrome but for pops of colour from ochre velvet chairs, yellow jugs and a few flowers. Small plates are rustic with French and Italian accents: creamed butter beans, wilted bitter greens and crunchy pangrattato, remarkably light and seasoned just so; while boulangère-like chard and potato gratin with pickled walnuts might have emerged from grand-mère's country kitchen. More substantial plates might include nicely al dente fregola with tomatoey mussels and clams, or pork shoulder with polenta and sprouting broccoli. Finish with a soft-centred meringue, creamy lemon curd and strawberries. The European wines are all offered by the glass, carafe and bottle.
Chef/s: Chris Woolard. **Closed:** Mon. **Meals:** small plates £4 to £21. **Details:** 53 seats. Wheelchairs.

Restaurant Michael Nadra

Cooking score: 3
⊖ Chalk Farm, map 2
Modern European | £43
42 Gloucester Avenue, Primrose Hill,
NW1 8JD
Tel no: 020 7722 2800
restaurant-michaelnadra.co.uk

This second iteration of Michael Nadra's London operations occupies a listed horse tunnel that was crying out for a restaurant conversion. An atmospheric brick-walled space, together with a martini bar and courtyard garden, contribute to the multi-faceted appeal. There is some menu overlap between here and the original Chiswick venue (see entry), but the deal is still modern European dishes full of colourful flavours and quality ingredients, all beginning with excellent homemade breads. Start with the likes of sautéed scallops and squid in smoked paprika dressing, served with broccoli and cauliflower couscous, before rolling on with cheeks and fillet of Welsh beef with truffled mash and spinach, or perhaps steamed sea bass in crab bisque sauce with gingered carrot purée, Chinese greens and a spin on shumai dumplings of prawns and chives. Simple desserts like vanilla cheesecake with Yorkshire rhubarb are hard to argue with. House French blends from the Languedoc, at £4.90 a small glass, head up a comprehensive wine list that offers value and quality in balanced measure.
Chef/s: Michael Nadra. **Closed:** Mon. **Meals:** main courses £21 to £29. Set L and early D £19 (2 courses) to £26. Tasting menu £65 (6 courses).
Details: 72 seats. 32 seats outside. V menu. Bar. Wheelchairs. Music.

★ NEW ENTRY ★

Soutine

Cooking score: 2
⊖ St John's Wood, map 2
French | £35
60 St John's Wood High Street, St John's
Wood, NW8 7SH
Tel no: 020 3926 8448
soutine.co.uk

If you've missed the last Eurostar from St
Pancras, Soutine is the closest you'll get to a
Parisian arrondissement in north London. A
new venture by star restaurateurs Corbin and
King, interiors here go the full Montmartre:
Arts and Crafts panelling, fin de siècle
flourishes, a mural of cricketers the only clue
that Lords is far closer than Lourdes. The
kitchen observes the all-day brasserie
tradition, offering breakfast and brunch
menus, croques and omelettes. Those of more
substantial appetites pick from hors d'oeuvres
such as cured herring with sweet mustard, Isle
of Skye queen scallops and escargots. Mains
are brasserie aristocrats: hearty daube de boeuf
with celeriac purée and carrots, goujons of
haddock and coq au Riesling among their
number. Round off with indulgent gâteau
Napoléon, before adjourning to the bar,
which, in a spirit of *égalité* for these parts,
serves French wines from under £5 a glass.
Chef/s: Maciej Banas. **Meals:** main courses £15 to
£28. **Details:** 107 seats. 15 seats outside. V menu.
Bar. Wheelchairs.

Trullo

Cooking score: 3
⊖ Highbury & Islington, map 2
Italian | £40
300-302 St Paul's Road, Islington, N1 2LH
Tel no: 020 7226 2733
trullorestaurant.com

The midnight blue frontage hides a storeyed
venue – the bare-boarded ground floor for
less formal eating and drinking, a first-floor
room with comfortable banquette seating and
extra linen. The drill is homely Italian food
cooked with vivacity and care, the pasta hand-
rolled not long before you set foot in the place,
the fish and meat cooked over coals. Antipasti
set the ball rolling, the ubiquitous burrata
glamourised with grilled white peach and
basil, before an utterly comforting pasta dish
such as pici with cheese and pepper. Look then
to the charcoal grill for enticements like black
Hampshire pork chop with borlotti beans in
salsa verde, or a whole mackerel with
panzanella. It's all cooked and served with
gusto, in a buzzy atmosphere that fits Islington
like a glove. A chocolate tart won't lack for
takers at the close. The Italian wine list is full of
interest, with reasonable markups and useful
notes, the small glasses starting at £4.50 for a
lemony Sicilian Catarratto.
Chef/s: Conor Gadd. **Meals:** main courses £15 to
£20. **Details:** 78 seats. Bar. Wheelchairs. Music.

★ NEW ENTRY ★

Vermuteria

Cooking score: 4
⊖ King's Cross, map 2
Modern European | £50
38-39 Coal Drops Yard, King's Cross,
N1C 4DQ
Tel no: 020 3479 1777
vermuteria.cc

Chef Anthony Demetre's take on the
vermouth bars popular in Spain, southern
France and Italy is proving an instant hit.
Located at one end of this bold new
development, two converted coal warehouses
connected by architect Thomas Heatherwick's
stunning curved roof, this all-day spot attracts
a mixed and appreciative bunch. The dressed-
down room suits the location with its painted
brickwork, vermouth-lined bar, vintage
posters and close-packed tables, including a
few outside. A free-roaming menu evokes
Mediterranean holidays with sharing plates of
cheese or charcuterie and moreish crab
croquettes with aïoli, then moves northwards
for a spectacular venison ragù and gnocchi,
confit duck leg and winter vegetables, or
rabbit in mustard sauce with potato and kale.
Finish with tiramisu or ice cream. As well as a
short, gutsy list of European wines (from

£23), there's a world of vermouth to explore (and some very good vermouth-based cocktails, too).

Chef/s: Anthony Demetre and Gergely Csaba. **Closed:** 25 Dec. **Meals:** small plates £6 to £15. **Details:** 42 seats. 50 seats outside. Wheelchairs. Music. No reservations.

Westerns Laundry

Cooking score: 4
⊖ Holloway Road, map 2
Modern British | £40
34 Drayton Park, Highbury, N5 1PB
Tel no: 020 7700 3700
westernslaundry.com

One of a trio of acclaimed north London wine bar restaurants, which includes Primeur and Jolene (see entries), Westerns is housed in a striking 1950s industrial building. The enticing small plates menu, viewable daily on the restaurant's Instagram feed, is scrawled across a blackboard, one half food, one half wine. Seafood is the stated focus, and the special baked fideo pasta, maybe with crab or cuttlefish, is not to be missed. That said, there's usually good variety from land and sea, opening with tapas-esque offerings of lobster croquettes with basil mayo, roast onions, red wine and ricotta, or jamón de Teruel, building up to confit duck with lentils and green sauce or turbot, asparagus and hollandaise. Round off with cheeses or crème brûlée. The cool crowd appreciates the Gallic-chic setting, whose hard edges are softened by olive velvet, painted brick and earthenware pitchers. They come for good drinking, too, following their low-intervention European wines (bottles from £27) with tots of Fernet or liqueur de noix.

Chef/s: James Mitchell. **Closed:** Mon. **Meals:** small plates £4 to £20. **Details:** 70 seats. Wheelchairs. Music.

LOCAL GEM

Xi'an Impression
⊖ Holloway Road, map 2
Chinese | £20
117 Benwell Road, Highbury, N7 7BW
Tel no: 020 3441 0191
xianimpression.co.uk

£30

Outside it's unpromising, inside it's tiny and functional, but the cooking from north central China's Shaanxi province is homely and authentic, with many dishes built around the region's famed hand-pulled noodles served in a rich, umami-laden broth. There's biang biang – flat hand-pulled and hand-torn noodles – in a chilli sauce with chunky beef; slippery, crunchy cold noodles in sesame sauce; or sweet potato noodles in hot-sour soup. Also recommended are wontons in chicken soup, and the chicken and mushroom pot stickers. Master Wei in Bloomsbury (see entry) is part of the same family.

Angler

Cooking score: 6
⊖ Moorgate, map 4
Modern European | £65
South Place Hotel, 3 South Place, Moorgate,
EC2M 2AF
Tel no: 020 3215 1260
anglerrestaurant.com

Take the lift to the seventh floor of this
contemporary hotel and you'll discover a
modern fine-dining venue that's a boon for a
seafood-loving City crowd. All the details are
just so: the light-bathed dining room,
complete with clean-lined contemporary
furnishings, well-spaced tables and a covered
terrace, is full of convivial buzz and the results
from the kitchen are confident, comforting
and classy in equal measure. Gary Foulkes'
menu embraces British eclectic (Dorset crab
piled with avocado, dabs of wasabi and draped
with pink grapefruit jelly) with French
classique (John Dory with English asparagus,
black garlic purée and girolles). There's always
a token meat dish, say 21-day aged herdwick
lamb with pressed shoulder, preserved tomato
and broad beans. For the final act, a delicate
strawberry mousse flavoured with rose and
basil is given an added dimension by lychee
sorbet. Customers here are unlikely to flinch
at the prices (at the more affordable end of the
scale, consider the set lunch). The wine list
trades as extensively across the world as the
futures markets do, with France in the
ascendancy. Bottles open at £28 with decent
choice under £50.
Chef/s: Gary Foulkes. **Closed:** Sun. **Meals:** main
courses £34 to £40. Set L £30 (2 courses) to £34.
Tasting menu £70 (6 courses) to £100. **Details:** 70
seats. 20 seats outside. V menu. Vg menu. Bar.
Wheelchairs. Parking. Music.

Anglo

Cooking score: 6
⊖ Farringdon, map 5
Modern British | £55
30 St Cross Street, Farringdon, EC1N 8UH
Tel no: 020 7430 1503
anglorestaurant.com
£5
OFF

Just about everything about this compact
eatery captures the prevailing mood:
confidently pared-back interior (look for the
discreet green neon sign in the window);
'spirited, affable' service; dynamic British
cooking from a chef with a pedigree CV.
Diners are left 'hugely impressed' by Mark
Jarvis's food. Six- and seven-course tasting
menus lead the way in the evening, and
vegetarians and vegans fare well (with advance
notice) – king oyster mushroom with
beetroot and Puy lentils is singled out for
praise. Maximum flavour is extracted from
superb ingredients, even in the series of tiny
snacks that open a meal, and fish is a strong
suit: eye-catching courses could include hay-
smoked salmon with horseradish buttermilk,
or brill with cauliflower and enoki
mushrooms. Meat cookery is no less
impressive, say aged venison with broccoli and
cranberry. Dark chocolate délice with ceps and
beer is a daring combination that makes
perfect sense at first bite. The concise wine list
roams from Slovenia to Sonoma county via
Hampshire for an award-winning fizz.
Chef/s: Mark Jarvis. **Closed:** Mon, Sun, 22 to 30
Dec. **Meals:** set L £25. Tasting menu L £50 (5
courses) and D £55 (6 courses) to £65. **Details:** 30
seats. V menu. Vg menu. Music.

£5 voucher

£5
OFF
Restaurants showing this symbol
are participating in our £5 voucher
scheme, redeemable against a meal for
two or more. Vouchers can be found at
the back of this book.

Local Gem

These entries are brilliant neighbourhood venues, delivering good, freshly cooked food at great value for money.

LOCAL GEM

Berber & Q Grill House

⊖ Haggerston, map 2
Middle Eastern | £35
338 Acton Mews, Haggerston, E8 4EA
Tel no: 020 7923 0829
berberandq.com

Casual, with a stripped-back, knocked round the edges look and the kind of hip, utilitarian vibe you might expect from a restaurant operating out of a railway arch, this high-decibel space is the place to come for Middle Eastern and North African dishes cooked over charcoal. Meze run to burnt baba ganoush or wood-roasted beets, while big plate grills include Tamworth pork chop with green harissa, smoked short-rib tagine with prunes and quince, and whole roasted sea bream with chraimeh sauce. Cocktails are very good; the wine list is short and modern. An offshoot, Shawarma Bar, is at 46 Exmouth Market, EC1R 4QE.

Blacklock City

Cooking score: 2
⊖ Monument, map 4
British | £30
13 Philpot Lane, City, EC3M 8AA
Tel no: 020 7998 7676
theblacklock.com
£30

The Square Mile follow-up to the original Blacklock chophouse in Soho. Reservations (not taken at dinner) are essential at lunch. Closed weekends. For main entry, see Shoreditch branch, east London.
Chef/s: Mirek Dawid. **Closed:** Sat, Sun, 21 to 30 Sept, 1 Jan. **Meals:** main courses £12 to £35. **Details:** 92 seats. Music.

★ NEW ENTRY ★

Blacklock Shoreditch

Cooking score: 3
⊖ Old Street, map 4
British | £30
28-30 Rivington Street, Shoreditch, EC2A 3DZ
Tel no: 020 7739 2148
theblacklock.com
 £30

'The Blacklock formula really works,' reports an inspector of this chophouse mini-chain, now with three locations: Soho, the City (see entries), and this latest in Shoreditch. If anything, they've fine-tuned the concept here, taking reservations at lunch and dinner, serving bar food and an express Worker's Lunch – expect pie and mash and a 'secret' off-menu burger. The faux-industrial interior is nothing new but is robust and leaves the focus on the grass-fed meat from Philip Warren. The All In at £20 per head makes life easy, but it's far more fun to pick and mix pre-chop bites, chops, sides and sauces. Skinny chops (beef, lamb cutlet, pork belly) are nicely charred with well-rendered fat; beef dripping chips are crunchy without, fluffy within; but the star is the hanger steak sarnie from the lunch menu, zhuzhed up with bone marrow, dripping, mustard mayo and watercress. There are only two puds, but they're not why you come here. Sunday roasts are a big thing. Wines on tap and cocktails from the trolley add to the fun.
Chef/s: Mirek Dawid. **Closed:** 24 to 26 Dec, 1 Jan. **Meals:** main courses £12 to £35. **Details:** 100 seats. Bar. Wheelchairs. Music.

Bob Bob Cité

Cooking score: 3
⊖ Liverpool Street, Bank, map 4
French | £75
The Leadenhall Building, 122 Leadenhall
Street, City, EC3V 4AB
Tel no: 020 3928 6600
bobbobcite.com

Glamorous and glittering, this long-awaited
City sibling for Soho's voluptuous Bob Bob
Ricard (see entry) has rippled on to the
London dining scene to applause.
Resplendent in velvety blue and gold,
reflective with mirrors and decadent with Art
Deco lighting, it is, said one diner, 'a jewellery
box of a restaurant'. And despite its lofty
location in The Leadenhall Building (and
dress code), it's all about having fun, whether
by pressing the Champagne button on repeat,
or diving into the menu of full-on Gallic
favourites. Glossy onion soup is 'simple and
satisfying', a thick slice of baguette bubbling
with Comté, and a chicken pie is an
Instagrammable creation of burnished pastry,
crimped edges and rich mushroomy filling.
Lobster macaroni aux quatres fromages
(Gruyère, Cheddar, mozzarella and Parmesan)
is as decadent and powerfully flavoured as
you'd expect. Finish with a classic île flottante,
its silky meringue and cool crème anglaise
topping a layer of rich caramel, or an
'unabashedly citrussy' deconstructed lemon
meringue pie. Prices are not for the faint-
hearted, either for food or wine: a £36 South
African Chenin Blanc is lonely at that end of
the list because the party is happening at three
figures and beyond.
Chef/s: Eric Chavot. **Meals:** main courses £22 to
£50. **Details:** 240 seats. Wheelchairs. Music.

Brat

Cooking score: 5
⊖ Shoreditch High Street, map 4
British | £45
First Floor, 4 Redchurch Street, Shoreditch,
E1 6JL
bratrestaurant.com

East London continues to fill up with good
eating, and this light-flooded dining room on
the first floor of a former boozer in
Shoreditch's Tea Building is a valuable
addition to the scene. It's laid out in that all-
purpose, no-frills style beloved of the area,
with rows of plain tables for two so closely
packed they're almost communal, and
panelled walls that only amplify the noise –
yet the casual vibe, helpful staff and cooking
delight. Tomos Parry sources prime
ingredients and treats them simply and with
respect. Flames are at the heart of his cooking
– the first thing you see as you enter (by the
side of the open kitchen) is the blazing wood
grill and oven – and his chargrilling and
wood-roasting set the gold standard for dishes
of herdwick mutton, beef rib, roast duck,
whole John Dory, lemon sole and the famed
turbot. Readers also love the oysters lightly
roasted with seaweed, the smoked cod's roe
and the grilled bread with chanterelles and
winter truffle. For afters, burnt cheesecake
with rhubarb beckons. The European wine list
has been expanded, with listings under Easy
Drinkers, The Classics and Off the Beaten
Track, with decent choice under £40.
Chef/s: Tomos Parry. **Meals:** main courses £19 to
£44. **Details:** 60 seats. Wheelchairs. Music.

Anonymous

At *The Good Food Guide*, our inspectors
dine anonymously and pay their bill in full.
These impartial review meals, along with
feedback from thousands of our readers,
are what informs the content of the *GFG*.
Only the best restaurants make the cut.

Brawn

Cooking score: 4
⊖ Hoxton, map 2
Modern European | £50
49 Columbia Road, Hoxton, E2 7RG
Tel no: 020 7729 5692
brawn.co

A decade old this year, Ed Wilson's rollicking neighbourhood restaurant grows ever more assured over time. Wilson's name is all but a guarantee of stonking produce, rigorous European country cooking and an unswerving commitment to the best modern winemakers. The daily changing menu is evidence of a kitchen attuned to the seasons: expect raw scallops, marinda tomatoes and capers, or oxtail ragù lasagnette in colder months; rabbit ravioli, tomato and marjoram, or pork chop, chickpeas and harissa on warmer days. Ingredients set the agenda at Brawn, including well-sourced cheeses (French, most often), charcuterie (generally Italian) and Cantabrian anchovies, whose slimline fillets aswim in a pool of golden olive oil, have become a signature. The drinks list is a primer in what to drink now, be it The Kernel Brewery's damson saison, sparkling Vouvray by the glass, small-production fruit liqueurs or natural wines from France, Italy and beyond.
Chef/s: Ed Wilson and Doug Rolle. **Closed:** Sun, bank hols, 24 Dec to 3 Jan. **Meals:** main courses £14 to £28. **Details:** 60 seats. Wheelchairs. Music.

Breddos

Cooking score: 1
⊖ Barbican, map 5
Mexican | £25
82 Goswell Road, Clerkenwell, EC1V 7DB
Tel no: 020 3535 8301
breddostacos.com
£30

Once a humble taco shack in a car park, this bright and breezy eatery is now firmly parked at its permanent Clerkenwell address, with a second branch in Soho (see entry). Mexican street flavours are still the focus – the menu revolves around tortillas, made from corn ground in-house using a volcanic-stone mill. Salsa and totopos provide a prelude while you choose – chile de árbol for spice fiends, nam jim for a detour to Thailand. Next, dive into the tacos: perhaps Baja fried fish with pickled cabbage and salsa molcajete, the Arab-Mexican tacos Arabes made with lamb shoulder, or a meat-free combo of black bean and (presumably un-Mexican) Wensleydale. Quesadillas and tostadas complete the line-up, while a range of mezcal and tequila cocktails, micheladas and aguas frescas should help cool the fiery flavours.
Chef/s: Adrian Hernandez Farina. **Closed:** 25 and 26 Dec, 1 Jan. **Meals:** main courses £8 to £11. **Details:** 48 seats. Bar. Wheelchairs. Music.

Brigadiers

Cooking score: 3
⊖ Bank, Mansion House, map 4
Indian | £50
1-5 Bloomberg Arcade, City, EC4N 8AR
Tel no: 020 3319 8140
brigadierslondon.com
£5
OFF

Inspired by the mess bars of the Indian Army, its rooms adorned with faux-leopard print carpets, ceremonial daggers and retro Subcontinental curios, this boisterous Indian barbecue joint is a magnet for off-duty City workers. The bling extends to pool tables, screens showing live cricket and even self-serve beer taps. Ordinary civilians can pick through a menu comprising posh biryanis, rotis and kebabs – plates of Konkan Coast masala scallops or guinea fowl patties are typical of the high-ranking snacks on offer. Those whose stomachs rumble loudest should make for the grill selection: bhuna ghee masala goat chops, for instance, or Nepali bhutwa lamb belly ribs. The wine list and cocktails play second fiddle to a global selection of whiskies, representing all points from Islay to India.

Chef/s: Karam Sethi. **Meals:** main courses £12 to £36. Set L £20 (2 courses) to £25. Tasting menu £60 (4 courses). **Details:** 140 seats. 40 seats outside. V menu. Bar. Wheelchairs. Music. No children after 7pm.

★ NEW ENTRY ★

Bright
Cooking score: 4
⊖ London Fields, map 2
Modern European | £40
1 Westgate Street, Hackney, E8 3RL
Tel no: 020 3095 9407
brightrestaurant.co.uk

🍾

Hackney natural wine emporium Noble Fine Liquor launched Bright, its first restaurant proper, in 2018, adding to a hospitality mini-empire that also includes wine bar P Franco and newcomer Peg (see entry). William Gleave and Giuseppe 'Pep' Belvedere run the kitchen – they're well-known names locally, and regulars have been following the pair since their respective P Franco and Brawn days. Menus are organised under appealing sub-heads – snacks, shellfish, pasta etc – to be shared or coursed out as desired. A good evening's eating might begin with deep-fried cheese puffs, squares of chicken katsu-sando, and buttery sweetcorn with yuzu kosho, ahead of larger plates of partridge ragù tagliatelle or whole grilled John Dory with nothing but lemon and salt. The room is boxy and bare, but there's something about a good wine list that will liven a place up. Come with deep pockets; lovingly made wines from Europe's low-intervention leaders don't come cheap.
Chef/s: William Gleave and Pep Belvedere. **Closed:** Mon, Tue, 25 and 26 Dec. **Meals:** main courses £14 to £29. **Details:** 50 seats. 20 seats outside. Bar. Wheelchairs. Music.

Adam Handling
The Frog, Hoxton; Adam Handling, Chelsea & Frog by Adam Handling, Covent Garden, London

What ingredient are you getting excited about at the moment?
Cauliflower is one of my favourites which surprises people who have horrible memories of it from school dinners! For amazing flavour, my tip would be to try charring it.

Name one ingredient you couldn't cook without.
Salt. People may be surprised by just how many varieties there are, with each one bringing unique characteristics and depth to a dish.

If you could ban one thing from your kitchen, what would it be?
Lateness.

When you get home at the end of a long day, what do you like to eat?
Anything with sausages, but they have to be proper sausages, none of these new fancy ones!

And finally... tell us something about yourself that will surprise your diners.
I'm almost militant when it comes to my coffee: I always have a latte, with a double espresso shot poured first, then stir in one teaspoon of brown sugar before adding the milk.

Cabotte

Cooking score: 3
⊖ Bank, map 4
French | £40
48 Gresham Street, City, EC2V 7AY
Tel no: 020 7600 1616
cabotte.co.uk
£5
OFF

If you get lost in a wine list the way others get lost in a novel, then it's worth downloading Cabotte's 1,000-bin tome in advance so you can peruse it at leisure. Master sommeliers Xavier Rousset and Gearoid Devaney's chosen focus here is on Burgundy, be that inexpensive Aligoté, famous appellations such as Meursault and Gevrey-Chambertin, or icons like La Tâche. If the rest of the world is given short shrift, that's still over 300 wines (an impressive selection by anybody's standards). Classic French bottles call for classic French food, which Cabotte delivers. Maldon rock oysters with Chardonnay vinegar and shallots or squab pigeon with spiced beetroot and game jus will find many a potential vinous mate. Chicken with Brie de Meaux sauce and Périgord truffle or veal sirloin on the bone with Diane sauce suggest another bottle might just be in order. The stylish set-up is pleasingly unstuffy by City standards.
Chef/s: Edward Boarland. **Closed:** Sat, Sun, bank hols, 21 Dec to 2 Jan. **Meals:** main courses £19 to £30. **Details:** 80 seats. Music.

Café Spice Namasté

Cooking score: 2
⊖ Tower Hill, map 4
Indian | £42
16 Prescot Street, Tower Hill, E1 8AZ
Tel no: 020 7488 9242
cafespice.co.uk

The rather forbidding red-brick entrance to what was once a Victorian courthouse makes a neat contrast to the vividly designed interior of Cyrus Todiwala's long-running venue, where Indian dishes with the subtlest of European twists continue to draw a loyal crowd. Get stuck in with a forthrightly spiced Goosnargh duck sausage and Keralan potato bhaji, or crumbed langoustines in chilli-hot and vinegar-sour pathia sauce. The tandoor oven turns out well-timed halibut on chilli risotto with Goan coconut curry, while showboating mains include painstakingly prepared beef xacuti with its 21 ingredients and three separate stages of cooking. Seasonal specials, sharing platters and tasting menus aim to maximise the appeal, and a good slate of vegetarian dishes includes vegetable kofta in tomato and cashew sauce with saffron rice. Hazelnut kulfi or a crème brûlée spiced with saffron, cardamom and ginger are fitting finales. A chilli-laced apple mojito to start is one way of showing you mean business. Wines by the glass open at £7.
Chef/s: Cyrus Todiwala. **Closed:** Sun, bank hols. **Meals:** main courses £18 to £25. Set L and D £30 (2 courses) to £40. Tasting menu £70. **Details:** 120 seats. Music.

LOCAL GEM

Ceviche

⊖ Old Street, map 4
Peruvian | £25
2 Baldwin Street, Old Street, EC1V 9NU
Tel no: 020 3327 9463
cevicheuk.com
£30

The crosstown cousin of Soho's Ceviche (see entry), this handsome property off Old Street has eating and seating for everyone from solo diners to group bookings. A Peruvian restaurant lives or dies by its pisco sour and this one passes with flying colours, as does the eponymous ceviche. The style is 'authentic Peruvian' (with all the Japanese, Spanish and Chinese influences that entails) combined with British ingredients. National dishes of ají chicken curry or beef heart anticuchos pair well with Cusqueña beer or global wines (from £19).

Cinnamon Kitchen

Cooking score: 3
⊖ Liverpool Street, map 4
Indian | £35
9 Devonshire Square, City, EC2M 4YL
Tel no: 020 7626 5000
cinnamon-kitchen.com

With a funky covered courtyard for year-round alfresco dining, a stand-alone bar (Anise) dispensing Asian-themed cocktails and an all-day menu trading on flexibility and value, this casual offshoot of Westminster's Cinnamon Club (see entry) is a custom-built playground for the City crowd. Clusters of intriguing 'muzzeh' (Indian meze), such as chicken tikka and cheese naans or breadfruit kebabs, are one of the highlights, along with assorted tandooris, grills, biryanis and curries, including a 'Keralan boatman's' version with haddock. Lunchtime visitors in a hurry can opt for the express deal (one dish plus a side), while those booking in for dinner might prefer hot shrimp pepper fry with curried yoghurt followed by Chettinad mutton curry. Desserts such as malai kulfi with honeycomb crumble add some East-West fusion to proceedings. Well-matched spice-friendly wines start at £25.50. There's a branch in Battersea and an offshoot in Oxford (see entries).

Chef/s: Vivek Singh and Rakesh Nair. **Closed:** Sun, 25 Dec. **Meals:** main courses £8 to £19. Set L £16 (2 courses) to £19. Set early D £24 (2 courses) to £29. Tasting menu £70 (7 courses). **Details:** 110 seats. 40 seats outside. V menu. Bar. Wheelchairs. Music.

Wine list

🍷 Restaurants showing this symbol have a wine list that our experts consider to be outstanding, either for its in-depth focus on a particular region, attractive margins on fine wines, or strong selection by the glass.

City Social

Cooking score: 6
⊖ Liverpool Street, map 4
Modern British | £65
Tower 42, 25 Old Broad Street, City, EC2N 1HQ
Tel no: 020 7877 7703
citysociallondon.com
🍷

Once swept up to the 24th floor, you'll find a lot to like about Jason Atherton's clubby, sumptuous bar and restaurant beyond those amazing views. It accommodates a City crowd, but nobody need feel hurried if lunch lengthens into the kind of afternoon when work is put on hold. Such an inviting, worldly prospect demands fine food, and Tomas Lidakevicius's kitchen obliges with a cultured take on modern British cooking. Given the location, there will always be chargrilled steaks with duck-fat chips, but Cornish sea bass with squid bolognese, basil vinaigrette and an unusual civet sauce makes for a more inventive main course. Pig's trotter and ham hock with a crispy Lancashire black pudding and apple Madeira, or roasted French quail with cep fregola, smoked pancetta, black garlic and quail's egg are bold openers. So good was one visitor's meal that 'in hindsight I wish we had added that extra course', so perhaps explore an intermediate dish of rabbit and truffle tortellini with horseradish velouté and sorrel. It all ends on a high with a rum baba teamed with chantilly cream, mango, pineapple carpaccio and rum punch. The formidable wine list is tempting and impressively deep – do take the sommelier's advice, equally helpful whether you want a simple glass of red or something colossally expensive; excellent cocktails, too.

Chef/s: Tomas Lidakevicius. **Closed:** Sun, 25 and 26 Dec. **Meals:** main courses £24 to £42. **Details:** 112 seats. Bar. Wheelchairs. Music.

The Clove Club

Cooking score: 6

⊖ Old Street, Shoreditch High Street, map 4

Modern British | £95

Shoreditch Town Hall, 380 Old Street,
Shoreditch, EC1V 9LT

Tel no: 020 7729 6496

thecloveclub.com

Shoreditch Town Hall combines heritage presence with a dark edge that makes a fascinating backdrop to the high-minded cooking of Isaac McHale. It's only been six years since his creation morphed from supper club to destination restaurant, during which time it's matured into a grown-up restaurant complete with clever sommeliers, elaborate tableware and 'ticketed' bookings. Even with the shorter six-course menu, our inspection meal is a near-three-hour commitment (a four-course lunch is also available). We receive very proper service from our suited and booted waiter; a neighbouring table gets the matey 'guys' treatment. Such inconsistency feels at odds with the cooking, where clarity and precision impress at every course. This is food of real character, with nods to McHale's Scottish roots in a haggis bun snack and post-dessert peated barley bun, and some stellar ingredients such as house charcuterie (slivers of coppa, ventrèche and loin), a pink saddleback pork with south Indian spices, and hot smoked Wiltshire trout with almond milk and pike roe. Cornish monkfish with Périgord truffle and bacon is the star turn. Drink options cover great wines, ancient and modern, plus sake, whisky and even ambient tea.

Chef/s: Isaac McHale. **Closed:** Sun. **Meals:** set L £65 (4 courses). Tasting menu £95 Mon to Thur (6 courses) to £145. **Details:** 60 seats. V menu. Bar. Music. No children at D. Pre-payment required.

Club Gascon

Cooking score: 5

⊖ Barbican, Farringdon, map 5

Modern French | £50

57 West Smithfield, City, EC1A 9DS

Tel no: 020 7600 6144

clubgascon.com

£5 OFF 🍾

This former Lyons Corner House has been home to Pascal Aussignac's Gascon outfit for more than 20 years now, a long residency for an approach that many might wrongly have thought a passing fancy. Reinterpretations of the culinary heritage of the gastronomically rich south-west corner of France, served in a room that feels like a marble-clad executive lounge, remain as energetic and as precisely composed as ever. Arturo Granato brings the formula to life on a seasonally changing carte that might open in spring with flamed cuttlefish en mouclade with freshly shelled peas and ink-dark sauce noire, before heading into the open country for a French rabbit, served with carrots and wild garlic. Vegetarian dishes are as replete with imaginative energy, perhaps for an aromatically seasoned courgette with green tulip and dill gel. Roquefort cheesecake with tipsy grapes and chocolate soil might precede a dessert of fragrant delicacy like lime calissons (lozenges of fruit paste) in a verbena pond with white beer sorbet. The wine list is an authoritative tour of the protean south-west, in all its varietal heterogeneity and versatility, through to the luscious dessert wines. Small glasses of Jurançon and Roussillon are £8.

Chef/s: Pascal Aussignac and Arturo Granato. **Closed:** Sun. **Meals:** main courses £16 to £35. Set L £35 (2 courses) to £40. Tasting menu £85 (5 courses) to £110. **Details:** 42 seats. V menu. Wheelchairs. Music.

The Coach

Cooking score: 2
Farringdon, map 5
Modern French | £35
26-28 Ray Street, Clerkenwell, EC1R 3DJ
Tel no: 020 3954 1595
thecoachclerkenwell.co.uk

Arguably, the biggest draw of this self-confident, upbeat and invariably crowded late 18th-century inn is the fact that it operates as a proper pub with real ales and a racy, authentic atmosphere, although the kitchen puts up a good fight. Visit with friends to put Henry Harris and Aurelien Durand's Anglo-French menu through its paces. There's nothing fancy about a dish of saucisson noir de Bigorre with celeriac rémoulade, or escarole, radish and Mimolette salad with mustard dressing – they're just good ingredients simply put together. Move on to a sharing plate of roasted guinea fowl with leg croustillant, morels and Madeira, or keep a dish of grilled rabbit leg with mustard sauce and Alsace bacon all to yourself. Crème caramel makes for a classic finish, as do French cheeses, but there's also apple and ginger crumble with crème anglaise. The wine list is predominantly European, with bottles from £19.75. In the same stable are The Hero of Maida (see entry) and The Crown in Chiswick.
Chef/s: Henry Harris and Aurelien Durand.
Meals: main courses £13 to £20. Sun L £18 (1 course). **Details:** 100 seats. 20 seats outside. Bar. Wheelchairs. Music.

Comptoir Gascon

Cooking score: 3
Farringdon, Barbican, map 5
French | £28
61-63 Charterhouse Street, Clerkenwell, EC1M 6HJ
Tel no: 020 7608 0851
comptoirgascon.com
£5 OFF £30

The cheaper, cheekier sibling of nearby Club Gascon (see entry), this Smithfield bistro deli is a place one longs to be a regular – where the plat du jour is under a tenner, there's always a burger when you want it and you can pick up some confit duck on the way home. At the same time, one senses the presence of an artisan at the pass, proudly presenting chicken ballotine and hare 'à la royale' tagliatelle alongside the moules marinière and duck rillettes that the francophile Brit demands. Proudly regional, it celebrates France's south-west in both vinous and culinary form, with a nod to London fashion (duck burger with duck-fat fries and 'crazy salt' being a case in point). The sub-£50 wine list motors through the AOCs (Fronton, Cahors, Gaillac...). It might just inspire a road trip. *Allons-y!*
Chef/s: Pascal Aussignac. **Closed:** Mon, Sat, Sun, 22 Dec to 7 Jan. **Meals:** main courses £13 to £28. **Details:** 40 seats. 8 seats outside. Wheelchairs. Music.

Cornerstone

Cooking score: 6
Hackney Wick, map 1
Modern British | £40
3 Prince Edward Road, Hackney Wick, E9 5LX
Tel no: 020 8986 3922
cornerstonehackney.com

'We are fortunate.' Thus speaks one Hackney Wick local, giving thanks for the gift of Cornerstone, Tom Brown's modern British seafood restaurant. Remarks on its debut year have been effusive: 'spectacularly good', 'top class', 'masterful'. The chef, in his open kitchen, an 'oasis of calm' in the semi-industrial room, deserves all the plaudits. Pickled oyster with

Symbols

🛏 Accommodation is available
£30 Three courses for £30 or less
£5 OFF £5 off voucher scheme
🍷 Notable wine list

celery, horseradish and dill is 'an excellent start' followed by a thoughtful, textural assembly of cured gurnard, toasted almonds and grapes that simply dances across the palate. Mackerel, cured and in a pâté, is 'supported brilliantly by seaweed broth' and treacle bread 'perfect for mopping up the juices'. The kitchen does meat, too: 'poor man's goose' (a *Great British Menu* banquet winner of duck and hog's pudding) is a special on our visit. To finish, chocolate fondant has the essential 'ooh' factor. But there are 'buts': noise levels (blame the concrete floors), overstretched service, the short, pricey natural wine list. It's possible to love, nay, adore Cornerstone in spite of such niggles. For one fan, it's 'the best local restaurant I can ever recall'.

Chef/s: Tom Brown and Christian Sharp. **Closed:** Mon, Sun, 22 Dec to 6 Jan. **Meals:** main courses £13 to £30. Tasting menu £48 (8 courses). **Details:** 46 seats. V menu. Vg menu. Bar. Wheelchairs. Music.

The Culpeper

Cooking score: 2
⊖ Aldgate East, map 4
Modern European | £35
40 Commercial Street, Whitechapel, E1 6LP
Tel no: 020 7247 5371
theculpeper.com

A pub that gracefully straddles high Victoriana and high hipsterdom takes its name from 17th-century botanist, astrologer and Spitalfields local Nicholas Culpeper. He would no doubt approve of the heavenward-facing roof garden and greenhouse, from which E1-grown produce percolates downstairs into dishes served in the first-floor restaurant. Starters show sharp flavours and considered constructions – evident in charred globe artichoke hearts with black aïoli, goat's curd, candied cashews and a kick of horseradish. Presumably not inbound from the roof garden is a main of Barbary duck breast with commendably crisp fat, alongside duck heart tarte fine, spiced orange and kale. Otherwise go for a creamy root vegetable and goat's cheese pithivier atop hispi cabbage. Finish

with rhubarb and almond tiramisu, before adjourning to the horseshoe bar downstairs to plunder the full assembly of ales, cocktails and even orange wines by the glass.

Chef/s: Pawel Ojdowski. **Closed:** 22 Dec to 1 Jan. **Meals:** main courses £14 to £22. **Details:** 38 seats. 20 seats outside. Bar. Music.

★ NEW ENTRY ★

Da Terra

Cooking score: 6
⊖ Bethnal Green, map 1
Modern European | £73
Town Hall Hotel, 8 Patriot Square, Bethnal Green, E2 9NF
Tel no: 020 7062 2052
daterra.co.uk
£5 OFF 🛏

The dining room hasn't changed a great deal since its Typing Room days, projecting a very modern minimalism that integrates well with the arches, fireplace, parquet floors and big sash windows of what was once the ground floor of Bethnal Green's town hall. There may have been a change of name and chef, but the restaurant continues as a venue for the gastronomically curious, offering a tasting menu that one visitor described as 'inventive, generous and delicious'. It's very much the product of Rafael Cagali, a chef who latterly ran Aulis in Soho (see entry). The tone is set immediately with creative bitesize snacks such as a carrot tart with 'pastry' made from dehydrated carrot juice. What follows is a succession of highly stylised, perfectly plated, textural dishes: perhaps mussels with white asparagus (raw and seared), almonds (puréed and roasted), trout roe and verbena foam; or a chicken dish that includes 'a fabulously intense, savoury and rich aerated parfait' as well as roasted wings with roasted onion petals and purée, a still runny yolk and shards of crisp chicken skin. Sweet and savoury are often played off in desserts that could open with a 'knockout' crossover – a custardy, salty goat's cheese cream topped with a flat layer of guava jam that resembles quince jelly. Service is 'chatty, informed and relaxed', and the wine selection focuses on Spain and Italy. **Chef/s:** Rafael Cagali. **Closed:** Mon, Tue, Sun. **Meals:** Tasting menu £73 (8 courses) to £90. **Details:** 30 seats. Bar. Wheelchairs. Music.

La Dame de Pic
Cooking score: 6
⊖ Tower Hill, map 4
Modern French | £80
Four Seasons Hotel London at Ten Trinity Square, Tower Hill, EC3N 4AJ
Tel no: 020 3297 3799
ladamedepiclondon.co.uk

'A fabulous gastronomic experience, and one that tempts me to break my "no return" rule,' noted a reader who was 'hugely impressed' by this imposing restaurant on the ground floor of the landmark Four Seasons Hotel. Occupying a palatial high-ceilinged space with mirrored pillars, carved plasterwork and stylish leather banquettes, this is a showcase for the talents of French star Anne-Sophie Pic – although day-to-day cooking is in the hands of her head chef, Luca Piscazzi. The menu speaks of fashionable modern cuisine with a Gallic accent, but Pic is always seeking out new flavours and culinary possibilities – an extraordinarily daring starter of cuttlefish with shiso, marigold, clementine jelly and sea urchin rouille, say, or an equally inspired pairing of Scottish scallop, smoked beetroot and grapefruit with black pepper and hibiscus emulsion. Meat dishes might feature 'meltingly soft' shoulder of Pyrenean milk-fed lamb with lovage and potato mousseline, a 'salty finger' and millésime pepper, while desserts have included an exquisite lemon chocolate mousse infused with Douglas fir. 'Lovely well-trained staff' are on hand to lighten the mood if it all becomes too hushed. Elegant wines from the Rhône Valley (home to the original Maison Pic) receive star billing on the sophisticated wine list – although prices (from £38) require deep pockets.

Chef/s: Anne-Sophie Pic and Luca Piscazzi. **Closed:** Sun. **Meals:** main courses £38 to £67. Set L £32 (2 courses) to £42. Tasting menu £115 (6 courses). **Details:** 54 seats. V menu. Bar. Wheelchairs. Music. Children over 4 yrs at D.

Dishoom
Cooking score: 2
⊖ Shoreditch High Street, Old Street, map 4
Indian | £30
7 Boundary Street, Shoreditch, E2 7JE
Tel no: 020 7420 9324
dishoom.com
£30

Dishoom is a delightfully idiosyncratic chain with, even after a decade, just seven sites split between London, Edinburgh and Manchester. Each one has its own character but all have queues in common (seats on the verandah at this east London outpost are searingly hot property) and a cult following for the signature breakfast naan (now available with double the bacon). The fun concept, first brought to life in 2010, pays homage to the Irani cafés of early 20th-century Mumbai, whose spirit lives on in Dishoom's signature archive photography, marble tables and ceiling fans. The all-day menu of Mumbai comfort food, be it traditional pav bhaji, bhel puri or chicken 'Ruby Murray', or an on-trend vegan akuri scramble, changes little from branch to branch, although Shoreditch has an exclusive on its overnight-braised lamb raan, served whole or piled in a sourdough bun. Drinks are on-theme: try a rose-scented lassi, Dishoom IPA or a Bollybellini.
Chef/s: Naved Nasir. **Closed:** 25 and 26 Dec, 1 and 2 Jan. **Meals:** main courses £7 to £23. **Details:** 98 seats. 25 seats outside. Bar. Wheelchairs. Music.

Visit us online
For the most up-to-date information about *The Good Food Guide*, go to thegoodfoodguide.co.uk.

The Duke of Richmond

Cooking score: 3
⊖ Dalston Junction, Dalston Kingsland, map 2
Modern British | £42
316 Queensbridge Road, Dalston, E8 3NH
Tel no: 020 7923 3990
thedukeofrichmond.com
£5 OFF

Playing its part as a rebooted neighbourhood hostelry where the very decent selection of real ales is overshadowed by some superior food, this 'lovely pub' represents a branching out for Tom Oldroyd, owner of a self-named Islington restaurant (see entry). The short, briefly worded menu combines pub favourites (steak and kidney steamed pudding) with witty retro ideas (Cornish crab chip butty) and ingredient-led bistro dishes (whole roast gilthead bream, pink fir potatoes, sauce vierge and oregano), and the kitchen delivers confident cooking. Our perfectly puffy, crisp vol-au-vent stuffed with lobster, asparagus, broad beans, pea shoots and almonds with a delicate but sharp butter sauce was followed by a standout beef-rib burger with Roquefort, confit shallots, béarnaise and fries. Pistachio and cherry trifle is a fitting finale. It's a lot of fun and they are serious about affordability and quality, which is a boon for locals. House wine starts at £22.
Chef/s: Tom Oldroyd and Rory Shannon.
Meals: main courses £16 to £22. **Details:** 70 seats. 30 seats outside. Wheelchairs. Music. No children after 8pm.

No reservations
If a restaurant doesn't take reservations, or only allows them for groups, this is indicated in the details at the end of the entry.

The Eagle

Cooking score: 2
⊖ Farringdon, map 5
Modern European | £20
159 Farringdon Road, Clerkenwell, EC1R 3AL
Tel no: 020 7837 1353
theeaglefarringdon.co.uk
£30

The Eagle landed in January 1991, making it roughly as old as *Baywatch*. No dodgy reboots are necessary here, though, as the original formula continues to shine. Daily menus are chalked up on blackboards, a loyal crowd jostles for mismatched chairs, and orders must be placed at the bar, lined with enough taps to prove this is still very much a pub. While there are a few 'tapas' dishes, the menu skips starters and beelines straight for plucky British mains: try tender Gloucester old spot T-bone chop with lentils and sweet red onion, or kedgeree with flakes of smoked haddock, peas and egg. Mediterranean influences might surface in, say, rigatoni and Napoli sausage ragù – but for many the definitive dish here is the signature Bife Ana steak sandwich. Almost as much of an institution are pasteis de nata – or opt for saffron panna cotta and plums. Wines start at £4.40 the glass, with Hackney Session IPA the pick of those taps.
Chef/s: Ed Mottershaw. **Closed:** bank hols, 10 days Dec to Jan. **Meals:** main courses £9 to £18. **Details:** 65 seats. 24 seats outside. Music. No reservations.

Fare

Cooking score: 2
⊖ Old Street, map 5
Modern European | £30
11 Old Street, Clerkenwell, EC1V 9HL
Tel no: 020 3034 0736
farelondon.com
£30

This breezy new launch from the folk behind east London wine bar Sager and Wilde (see entry) wouldn't look out of place in New York

or Melbourne. It's every inch the modern eatery: brick walls slapped with white paint, industrial steel windows hung with macramé planters. It is multi-functional too, incorporating coffee bar (with bespoke beans from Assembly), cocktails, clattery all-day canteen, pizzeria and wine-focused basement restaurant. Sampling from the all-day menu, we enjoyed a decent semolina-dusted pizza with courgettes and good-quality anchovies; also some small plates, including lamb sweetbreads on toast drenched in a deliciously sticky sauce charcutière, and confit fennel with smoked butter and Innes goat's curd. The kitchen knows when to buy in: Hackney Gelato, Provisioners charcuterie and Little Bread Pedlar croissants show off their sourcing credentials. The real draw's the wine cellar, however: 250-plus wines from smart house pours (from £4.50 a glass) to the heights of Jacques Selosse Champagnes and white Burgundy from Domaine Roulot.
Chef/s: Pate Santo. **Closed:** Sun. **Meals:** main courses £11 to £16. **Details:** 130 seats. 90 seats outside. Bar. Wheelchairs. Music.

★ NEW ENTRY ★

The Frog Hoxton

Cooking score: 2
⊖ Hoxton, Old Street, map 2
Modern British | £42
45-47 Hoxton Square, Hoxton, N1 6PD
Tel no: 020 3813 9832
thefroghoxton.com

Having trialled his Frog concept at the Old Truman Brewery, Adam Handling now has an established site in Covent Garden (see entry) and this even bigger offshoot in Hoxton. As before, the interior is an on-trend mix of graffiti and modern art, although the menu seems to suffer from 'a case of confused identity'. There's 'dude food' for local hipsters, while other ideas are pitched at a more rarefied fine-dining market, with the common denominator being an 'overly heavy hand with the salt cellar'. To start, cheese doughnuts filled with mornay sauce wouldn't be out of place on a street-food stall, although the kitchen can

also deliver clarity and sophistication – as in expertly timed Cornish hake sitting in a thick seafood bisque with poached fennel and studs of tomato, or an elegant, light and refreshing dessert of iced verbena cream with blobs of grape jelly, sugarwork and verbena foam. Perfunctory service is mostly from the chefs themselves, while wines are of the low-intervention variety, with prices from £25.
Chef/s: Adam Handling and Jamie Park. **Closed:** Mon, Sun. **Meals:** main courses £15 to £23. Tasting menu £60 (7 courses). **Details:** 50 seats. 16 seats outside. Bar. Wheelchairs. Music.

Galvin Hop

Cooking score: 2
⊖ Liverpool Street, map 4
Modern British | £28
35 Spital Square, Spitalfields, E1 6DY
Tel no: 020 7299 0404
galvinrestaurants.com
£30

It isn't exactly accurate to call Galvin Hop a pub, although there is real Pilsner Urquell waiting in copper tanks above the bar, and the name gives something of a clue to the orientation. The food offering majors on tapas bites and fine charcuterie to kick things off, motoring on to dressed-down plates of hefty nourishing sustenance. Spring might be celebrated with a bowl of compendious minestrone lit up with pesto and wild garlic, or with new season's asparagus and pea shoots showered with pecorino. Big-hearted bistro mains follow: a confit duck leg bedded on Puy lentils and accompanied by puréed carrot, the skrei cod wood-fired and served with pink firs and lemon-splashed rocket. Finish with a mousse of salt caramel and Valrhona, or crème brûlée tricked out with poached rhubarb and pistachios. As well as the Pilsner, there are wines on tap, starting at £5.50 for a small squirt of Spanish Verdejo.
Chef/s: Jeff Galvin and Jhavari Brade. **Closed:** 25 to 26 Dec, 1 Jan. **Meals:** main courses £14 to £28. Set L and early D £20 (2 courses) to £25. **Details:** 68 seats. 150 seats outside. Bar. Wheelchairs. Music.

Galvin La Chapelle

Cooking score: 5
⊖ Liverpool Street, map 4
French | £68
35 Spital Square, Spitalfields, E1 6DY
Tel no: 020 7299 0400
galvinrestaurants.com

The third of the Galvins' enterprises has all the marble-pilastered, soaring-roofed grandeur to make a visit here a proper occasion, and staff play their part too, with chatty affability and pinpoint efficiency. Since autumn 2018, the kitchen has been headed by Josh Barnes, who takes on the mantle of delivering highly polished, finely detailed French dining with masterful panache. All the effort is concentrated on the menu dishes, so expect nothing more than good sourdough and a couple of petits fours at the margins. The long-standing lasagne filled with Dorset crab mousse in a coruscating beurre nantais, topped with a ruff of pea shoots, is silken simplicity itself, and so in another way is the Jerusalem artichoke velouté served with mushroom brioche and truffle butter. A Gascon approach to duck offers pink breast and confit leg with red cabbage purée and duck-fat rösti, but our inspection dish of fine red mullet was let down by a bland apple dressing, a clunky spinach layer and celeriac purée seemingly missing its advertised wasabi. Desserts restore confidence, with a solid rendition of properly sticky tarte tatin, and blood orange cheesecake with delectable dark chocolate sorbet. A sensational wine list, opening with excellent selections by the glass and 475ml carafe, will send the bill soaring.
Chef/s: Josh Barnes. Closed: 24 to 26 Dec, 1 Jan. Meals: main courses £32 to £39. Set L and early D £34 (2 courses) to £38. Tasting menu £85 (7 courses). Sun L £40. Details: 110 seats. 20 seats outside. V menu. Vg menu. Bar. Wheelchairs. Music.

Gunpowder

Cooking score: 2
⊖ Liverpool Street, Aldgate East, map 4
Indian | £30
11 White's Row, Spitalfields, E1 7NF
Tel no: 020 7426 0542
gunpowderlondon.com
£30

Assertively spiced small plates are the main event at this pocket-sized Indian canteen on a back street behind Spitalfields Market. You can't book and space is tight, but the kitchen doles out a fascinating mix of flavours – although chilli levels can be too much for some palates. Melt-in-the-mouth Kashmiri lamb chops are one of the top calls on a succinct menu that takes in everything from homemade uttapams amply filled with Chettinad pulled duck to Kerala beef pepper fry and an impressive-looking venison and vermicelli doughnut with fennel and chilli chutney. Vegetarians might fancy perfectly cooked spinach with tandoori paneer or bhuna aubergine and crispy kale salad, while desserts usually include 'old monk' rum pudding (a boozy Asian twist on bread and butter pud). Drink London-brewed Forest Road beer or one of the spice-tolerant wines (from £28). There's a bigger, slicker offshoot near Tower Bridge at 4 Duchess Walk, London SE1 2SD.
Chef/s: Nirmal Save. Closed: Sun. Meals: small plates £3 to £16. Details: 28 seats. Wheelchairs. Music.

Hawksmoor Guildhall

Cooking score: 4
⊖ Bank, map 4
British | £60
10 Basinghall Street, City, EC2V 5BQ
Tel no: 020 7397 8120
thehawksmoor.com

Geared towards a City clientele, this dark wood and leather-clad steakhouse is revered for its gargantuan breakfast for two. There's a private dining room for 22. For main entry, see Knightsbridge branch, west London.

Join us at thegoodfoodguide.co.uk

Chef/s: Phillip Branch. **Closed:** Sat, Sun, bank hols, 24 Dec to 1 Jan. **Meals:** main courses £17 to £60. Set L and early/late D £26 (2 courses) to £29. **Details:** 160 seats. Bar. Wheelchairs. Music.

Hawksmoor Spitalfields
Cooking score: 3
⊖ Liverpool Street, Aldgate East, map 4
British | £60
157a Commercial Street, Spitalfields, E1 6BJ
Tel no: 020 7426 4850
thehawksmoor.com

The original Hawksmoor is found near Christ Church Spitalfields, after whose architect the steakhouse group was named. For cocktails and burgers, head downstairs to the basement bar. For main entry, see Knightsbridge branch, west London.
Chef/s: Pavlos Costa. **Closed:** 25 and 26 Dec. **Meals:** main courses £15 to £29. Set L and early/late D £26 (2 courses) to £29. **Details:** 118 seats. Bar. Wheelchairs. Music.

Hill & Szrok
Cooking score: 2
⊖ Hoxton, map 4
British | £35
60 Broadway Market, Hackney, E8 4QJ
Tel no: 020 7254 8805
hillandszrok.co.uk

A top-end butcher's shop by day, a self-proclaimed 'cook shop' by night, this 'unique proposition' has gained cult status among London foodies – not only for its high-quality meat, but for its 'remarkable' wine list. H&S buys whole carcasses from small herds and makes use of every anatomical offcut – a dedication that's carried through to the tiny open kitchen that comes to life when the shop morphs into a no-bookings bistro. The mighty butcher's block and marble counters do duty as tables, while the evening's menu promises an uncompromisingly meaty line-up of chops and steaks, including a thick-cut pork T-bone with top-notch seasoning and just-pink flesh. A few sides and sharing plates, such as excellent roasted asparagus spears with

thick bagna cauda and an egg yolk for dipping, complete the offer. The vibe is cosy, warm and personal, service follows suit and the wine list is stuffed with on-trend low-intervention obscurities, although a bigger by-the-glass selection would be welcome.
Chef/s: Luca Mathiszig-Lee. **Meals:** main courses £14 to £55. **Details:** 25 seats. No reservations.

★ NEW ENTRY ★

Kym's
Cooking score: 2
⊖ Cannon Street, map 4
Chinese | £36
19 Bloomberg Arcade, City, EC4N 8AR
Tel no: 020 3929 2774
kymsrestaurant.com

Andrew Wong's second London venue is set amid the nouveau architectural glitz of the City. On two levels, connected by a curving staircase overhung with a thick canopy of artificial cherry blossom, it hit the ground running in 2018, offering traditional Chinese roasts in the Hong Kong style at the heart of proceedings, with some cool cocktails and gentle innovation at the margins. The roasts themselves look the part, inevitably best experienced in the Three Treasure offering of crisped pork belly, Ibérico char siu and soy chicken, each with its respective dip. Fish arrives in the form of a majestic tranche of sea bass, easily enough for two, in a lake of soy, spring onion and ginger, and the pick of the sides is Szechuanese spiced aubergine in a deeply glossy caramelised dressing, although we found no evidence of Szechuan peppercorns. Appetisers are more humdrum, as in the pile of iceberg lettuce in Thai-style dressing, although the steamed buns filled with wild mushrooms are an umami triumph. Finish with a sweet pineapple bun. As well as those cocktails, there's a City-weighted wine list that includes a decent choice of glasses and 50cl carafes, the latter from £20.
Chef/s: Andrew Wong. **Closed:** Sun. **Meals:** main courses £16 to £29. Small plates £3 to £12. Large plates £12 to £18. **Details:** 120 seats. Bar.

Lardo

Cooking score: 2
⊖ London Fields, map 1
Italian | £35
197-205 Richmond Road, Hackney, E8 3NJ
Tel no: 020 8985 2683
lardo.co.uk
£5
OFF

As casual and comfortable as your favourite pair of jeans, this perennially popular Hackney hangout keeps its regulars happy with a vibrant menu of contemporary pizzeria-trattoria fare. Classic margherita and anise pepperoni aside, the Neapolitan-style pizzas that issue from the mirror-tiled wood-fired oven are in the 'designer' mould: fig, goat's curd, prosciutto and walnut pesto or courgette, prawn, mint and sesame are more glamorous than the average pie. For carbs in another form, take a peek at the pasta specials scrawled on the tiles by the open kitchen. Homemade casarecce with pumpkin, greens and chilli or linguine alle vongole are good shouts. Antipasti – more 'small plates' really – might involve classic zucchini fritti or octopus and prawn spiedino with Amalfi lemon slaw, while weekend brunch means breakfast flavours with a groovy Italo twist. The wine list favours 'gentle' winemaking from sunny climes (Italy, Australia and the like) and includes 15 by the glass.
Chef/s: Matthew Cranston. **Closed:** 23 to 28 Dec. **Meals:** main courses £8 to £23. **Details:** 50 seats. 70 seats outside. Bar. Music.

The Laughing Heart

Cooking score: 3
⊖ Bethnal Green, Hoxton, map 1
Modern British | £35
277 Hackney Road, Hackney, E2 8NA
Tel no: 020 7686 9535
thelaughingheartlondon.com
🍾

At a time when sensible people are in bed, The Laughing Heart calls siren-like to east London's night owls. But its signature late hours (kitchen open until 1am, bar until 2am)

aren't the only distinguishing aspect of Charlie Mellor's jovial-by-name establishment. There's also the attached off-licence, releasing artisan and small-estate wines into the wild, and the kitchen's globe-roaming approach. The house style is to go full throttle on texture and flavour, and although the balance could be finer in places, this is food you know you've eaten. Signatures include olives with a laab-style stuffing and, in season, tempura of purple sprouting broccoli; chef Tom Anglesea has no qualms about swapping ingredients out of their geographically allotted roles. Other plates might carry a saddleback pork chop with calçots and capers, Cornish squid with fermented red pepper and fennel or, when pudding rolls around, a crème brûlée spiked with Szechuan pepper – conjuring fewer laughs and more tingles. The extensive wine list starts at £25.
Chef/s: Tom Anglesea. **Closed:** Sun. **Meals:** small plates £4 to £21. **Details:** 40 seats. V menu. Bar. Music.

Leroy

Cooking score: 4
⊖ Shoreditch High Street, map 4
Modern European | £35
18 Phipp Street, Shoreditch, EC2A 4NU
Tel no: 020 7739 4443
leroyshoreditch.com

This cool Shoreditch restaurant and cave à vin takes up where Ellory, its earlier and more formal Hackney incarnation, left off. Leroy is a co-production between two sommeliers and a chef. As such, it's as much a celebration of wine as it is of food. A stool at the counter, tapping one's feet to the all-vinyl playlist over a glass of orange wine and some saucisson is as true a 'Leroy' experience as any. The good-value set lunch tempts with such seasonal modern European fare as skate with monk's beard and ratte potatoes, and blanquette de veau, while the full carte encourages the sharing of a selection of snacks, plates, cheese and charcuterie. The cooking is understated: consider a dish of whipped ricotta with anchovies, garnished with toasted buckwheat, or pollock with charred hispi and beurre blanc, glistening with trout roe. The wine list champions Europe's natural wine superstars. **Chef/s:** Sam Kamienko. **Closed:** Sun. **Meals:** small plates £9 to £24. Set L £19 (2 courses) to £22. **Details:** 50 seats. Bar. Music.

★ NEW ENTRY ★

Lino
Cooking score: 2
⊖ Barbican, map 5
Modern British | £30
90 Bartholomew Close, City, EC1A 7EB
Tel no: 020 8016 5199
linolondon.co.uk
£30

A former linoleum and carpet factory now houses the workplace of chef Richard Falk, once of The Ledbury and The Dairy (see entries), with a mission statement to 'reuse, relove and reimagine'. That translates to salvaged light fittings in the post-industrial dining room, with its tangled ducts and bare concrete floors. On the menu it means a predilection for pickling, fermenting, baking and curing. Ponder the stacked jars by the kitchen as you snack on moreish sauerkraut and Cheddar croquettes atop truffled mayo. Small plates follow the same pattern: rich and smokey mackerel with pickles and aïoli, or perhaps Lino charcuterie and gherkins. Fresher flavours prevail among the large plates: carnaroli risotto with wild garlic and roasted courgettes – or a gust of Nordic air in cod with Jersey Royals, samphire, Sandefjord sauce and roe. Conclude with a simple summery dish of white chocolate crémeux with English strawberries and caramelised hazelnuts. Wines start at £25, although mocktails and cocktails star alongside a wide selection of gins and whiskies.
Chef/s: Richard Falk and Jeremy Besson. **Closed:** Sun. **Meals:** small plates £5 to £13. Large plates £15 to £20. Set L £19 (2 courses). **Details:** 90 seats. 30 seats outside. Wheelchairs. Music.

Luca
Cooking score: 3
⊖ Farringdon, Barbican, map 5
Italian | £68
88 St John Street, Clerkenwell, EC1M 4EH
Tel no: 020 3859 3000
luca.restaurant

'Luca may be one of the best-looking restaurants I've ever been to,' exclaimed one reader after visiting this 'super-sexy' venue from the team behind The Clove Club (see entry). From the green-tiled façade and cool marble bar to the dining room with its secret courtyard garden, it's a stunning prospect. Meanwhile, the kitchen turns out self-styled 'Britalian' dishes marrying home-grown produce with influences from the Mediterranean – perhaps a crostino of seasonal mushrooms with duck egg and Grana Padano or firm-fleshed Cornish monkfish dressed with seaweed butter, turnips, sea beets and shards of crispy pancetta. Pasta is made on site, although options such as rigatoni with sausage ragù can seem rather run-of-the-mill. To finish, tiramisu is served as a 'huge rustic blob', while panna cotta comes adorned with shiny strawberry jelly, meringue and other adornments. You can eat at the bar, although service can suffer if there's a run on cocktails. All-Italian wines start at £26.
Chef/s: Robert Chambers. **Closed:** Sun, 22 Dec to 5 Jan. **Meals:** main courses £28 to £37. **Details:** 60 seats. 25 seats outside. Bar. Wheelchairs. Music.

Lyle's
Cooking score: 5
⊖ Shoreditch High Street, map 4
Modern British | £59
Tea Building, 56 Shoreditch High Street, Shoreditch, E1 6JJ
Tel no: 020 3011 5911
lyleslondon.com

The London answer to the hip Parisian 'neo-bistro', James Lowe's stark Shoreditch address, with its Ercol stick-back chairs and concrete floor, is modern British in feel and philosophy; popular with both locals and itinerant foodies. Save for the superb sourdough that unites them – find it at Flor, Lyle's new sister bar and bakery in Borough – lunch and dinner offerings are quite different. While lunch means sharing plates (devilled rabbit and chicory or potted goose and damsons, say), dinner is a four-course that changes daily. At inspection, ours centred on guinea fowl (breast, thigh and heart) with Tropea onions and spelt dressed with duck fat. Complimentary extras – brandade and fried artichokes; dainty financiers – bookended the experience. Peerless ingredients are Lyle's hallmark, both in the kitchen and behind the bar. The dynamic wine list involves such cult producers as Baden's Enderle & Moll and Greece's Ligas. **Chef/s:** James Lowe. **Closed:** Sun. **Meals:** small plates L £9 to £15. Large plates £26 to £28. Set D £59 (4 courses). **Details:** 48 seats. V menu. Wheelchairs. Music.

The Marksman

Cooking score: 3
⊖ Cambridge Heath, Hoxton, map 1
British | £38
254 Hackney Road, Hackney, E2 7SJ
Tel no: 020 7739 7393
marksmanpublichouse.com

A pub perfectly targeted at the Hackney Road crowds. On the ground floor, there's dusky wood panelling and a hefty bar that mutters of East End boozers of yore: on the first floor, a dining room with patterned lino floors that's pitched more at the hipster demographic. Everyone, however, can unite over the food: snack on a curried lamb bun before taking aim at starters like pressed pig's head, radish and mustard, or else cured mackerel with chopped tomato and lovage. Mains, too, see old-school classics rebooted: share a rabbit, bacon and wild garlic pie, or savour a whiff of Mitteleuropa with a dish of curd dumplings, braised spring vegetables and saffron. Buttermilk ice cream with rhubarb and rose provides a perfect parting shot, although it's hard to resist brown butter and honey tart.

Europe dominates the wine list, with a small roster of cocktails competing with the ales at the bar. **Chef/s:** Tom Harris and Jon Rotheram. **Meals:** main courses £18 to £30. Sun L £30 (2 courses) to £35. **Details:** 70 seats. Bar. Music. No children after 7pm.

READERS RECOMMEND

Marmelo Kitchen

169 Francis Road, Leyton, E10 6NT
Tel no: 020 3620 7580
marmelokitchen.com
'We stopped at this neighbourhood café for brunch and we're so glad we did. Try the Turkish eggs with chilli oil and dukkah from the blackboard menu. We're already planning to go back for lunch when they do amazing fresh salads.'

LOCAL GEM

Mora

⊖ Leytonstone High Road, map 1
Italian | £28
487 High Road, Leytonstone, E11 4PG
Tel no: 020 8539 1731
moraitalianrestaurant.co.uk
£5 OFF £30

Carlo Usai and Silvia Scibetta have brought a welcome taste of southern Italy to this stretch of Leytonstone's main drag, allowing the food to take centre stage in their sparse, white-painted dining room. Crisp carasau flatbread, artisan cured meats, fregola and seada (a traditional pastry filled with lemony sheep's cheese, orange zest and honey) nod to Carlo's native Sardinia, although handmade pasta is the headline act – try the spaghetti with clams and bottarga. Back-up comes from a lively list of regional wines and beers.

Morito Exmouth Market

Cooking score: 3
⊖ Farringdon, map 2
Spanish/North African | £30
32 Exmouth Market, Clerkenwell, EC1R 4QE
Tel no: 020 7278 7007
morito.co.uk
£30

This colourful and cramped little sibling to next-door Moro (see entry) runs a daily changing menu of tapas and meze. Influences from Spain, North Africa and the Middle East jostle together, bringing such flavours to the table as grilled asparagus with orange and almond mojo, salt cod croquetas, lamb chops and anchovy butter, labneh with broad bean and pickles, and Galician Tetilla cheese with walnuts and membrillo, all served in rustic glazed earthenware. Against a backdrop of bright, sunny 70s-style orange surfaces, nothing pops quite like the vivid purple house signature, beetroot borani with feta, dill and walnuts. Finish with chocolate mousse or rose water and cardamom ice cream. Brilliantly simple cocktails, many vermouth based, are evocative of sun-kissed holidays (try the fino, vermouth and orange, or the 'Fabuloso Sour' with fresh lemon, brandy and rosemary honey). Wines are exclusively Spanish and priced between £20 and £50. It's a small spot but they do take bookings, just not at peak times on Thursday to Saturday evenings.
Chef/s: Sam Clark. **Meals:** tapas £7 to £14.
Details: 27 seats. 6 seats outside. Wheelchairs. Music.

Morito Hackney

Cooking score: 3
⊖ Hoxton, map 2
Spanish/North African | £30
195 Hackney Road, Hackney, E2 8JL
Tel no: 020 7613 0754
moritohackneyroad.co.uk
£30

This sunny restaurant comes from noble stock, being the offspring of Clerkenwell's Moro and the sibling to the original Morito, both on

Exmouth Market (see entries). Even so, it's earned its own distinct reputation since opening in 2016, and is comfortably installed out east – its Hackneyfied dining room replete with concrete floors, metal chairs and a giant horseshoe bar. The menu stays true to the family formula: pan-Mediterranean flavours on small plates. Spanish influence goes without saying – opt for sweet pepper and spinach tortilla among the nibbles, or secreto Ibérico pork with chickpeas and piquillo pepper sauce. Eastern Mediterranean dishes provide the counterpoint – a Levantine manakish with labneh and winter tomatoes, perhaps, although nothing on our visit surpassed fried aubergines sticky with date molasses and topped with feta. Finish with Seville orange and filo cake, or a sherry from the succinct Iberian-dominated wine list.
Chef/s: Marianna Leivaditaki. **Meals:** tapas £3 to £15. **Details:** 72 seats.

Moro

Cooking score: 5
⊖ Farringdon, map 2
Spanish/North African | £40
34-36 Exmouth Market, Clerkenwell, EC1R 4QE
Tel no: 020 7833 8336
moro.co.uk

Can it really be more than 20 years since Sam and Samantha Clark opened on Exmouth Market, bringing the then virtually unknown flavours of the southern Mediterranean fringe to London? Yes it can, and it is testament to the couple's unwavering tenacity that the place remains as crazy busy as ever. Be prepared for a certain level of hubbub in the hard-surfaced interior, but be primed also for strongly seasoned regional dishes that have plenty to say for themselves. Harissa is virtually the house condiment, firing up an opening dish of braised cuttlefish with artichoke hearts and new season's garlic, and offered as a side dip for any of the main courses. These range from robustly treated fish such as charcoal-grilled mackerel or wood-roasted sea bass, the two preparations alternating through the meat options too, the latter perhaps extending to roast pork belly with oyster mushrooms from the plancha and patatas aliñadas (potato and onion salad in sherry vinegar). Beguiling aromatics continue to weave their spell in desserts such as the signature rose water and cardamom ice cream, or yoghurt cake with pistachios and pomegranate. The Spanish and Portuguese wines, from £24.50, suit the food to a tee.

Chef/s: Sam and Samantha Clark. **Closed:** 24 Dec to 1 Jan. **Meals:** main courses £19 to £27. **Details:** 110 seats. 14 seats outside. Wheelchairs.

Oklava

Cooking score: 3
⊖ Shoreditch High Street, map 4
Turkish | £35
74 Luke Street, Shoreditch, EC2A 4PY
Tel no: 020 7729 3032
oklava.co.uk

At her restaurant a few miles south of London's Turkish-Cypriot heartland, Selin Kiazim puts a fresh spin on the food she grew up with. Seasonal British ingredients such as Cornish crab, wild garlic, Hampshire trout and hogget come into play on a changing menu of creative meze, pide and kebabs. The obvious option, if all your party agrees to it, is to take the Oklava Menu at £35 a head. Alternatively, dig into a few snacks such as grilled hellim (halloumi) with oregano and London honey or the still-warm baharat bread with date butter, while you weigh up spiced lamb and loquat kebab with urfa chilli dressing versus Black Sea cheese pide with a soft egg and zaatar butter. The wine list (from £30) is predominantly Turkish, with some interesting bottles from Greece, Georgia and Armenia. Oklava's Fitzrovia sister restaurant Kyseri specialises in manti dumplings.

Chef/s: Selin Kiazim and Laurence Louie. **Closed:** Mon, Sun, bank hols, 23 to 26 and 30 Dec, 1 Jan. **Meals:** sharing plates £10 to £19. Tasting menu £35 (7 courses). **Details:** 40 seats. 8 seats outside. Wheelchairs. Music.

Ombra

Cooking score: 4
⊖ Bethnal Green, map 1
Italian | £40
1 Vyner Street, Hackney, E2 9DG
Tel no: 020 8981 5150
ombrabar.restaurant
£5 OFF

Though passing gondoliers may be few and far between, Hackney canalside restaurant and bar Ombra succeeds in capturing the energy of a Venetian 'bacaro'. Since it launched in 2011, it's quietly morphed from artists' Aperol-fuelled hangout to a neighbourhood Italian of considerable clout. British and Italian seasonal ingredients are the starting point for ex-Clove Club chef Mitshel Ibrahim's daily menus that centre around homemade fresh pasta. Choose between temptations such as linguine al nero with Cornish crab and datterini tomatoes or buffalo ricotta ravioli with Amalfi lemon, adding a few cicchetti – crispy fried tripe or river Teign oysters perhaps – and antipasti (the gnocchi fritti draped with salumi are always a hit). Secondi are limited to a couple of choices, along the lines of osso buco milanese or turbot with sea kale and girolles. Finish with perennial favourite tiramisu. Modern Italian wines from £25 round out the offering.

Chef/s: Mitshel Ibrahim. **Closed:** Mon, 22 Dec to 5 Jan. **Meals:** small plates £3 to £11. Large plates £13 to £19. **Details:** 35 seats. 40 seats outside. Wheelchairs. Music.

Palatino

Cooking score: 3
⊖ Old Street, map 2
Italian | £35
71 Central Street, Clerkenwell, EC1V 8AB
Tel no: 020 3481 5300
palatino.london

Named after the sunny imperial hill from which the Empire was run, Palatino raises the standard for a uniquely Roman-style of cooking. Not that there's the slightest whiff of the Eternal City in the dining room – with the exposed ducts and modish mustard-

yellow banquettes you'd expect from a canteen adjoining a shared workspace near Old Street. Fortunately, the kitchen does the talking. The domestic comfort food of the Italian capital shines in the antipasti: simple anchovy with stracciatella, lemon and toast, or perhaps fried sage with honey vinegar. Primi might nod to the Roman predilection for offal, classic bucatini all'amatriciana starring guanciale, or showcase radiant simplicity in tonnarelli pasta with Tellicherry pepper and pecorino cheese. Similarly, secondi might be as straightforward as whole roast sea bream with salsa verde, while dolci of tiramisu and grappa panna cotta play to their strength. A north Italian-leaning wine list starts from £22.
Chef/s: Stevie Parle and Richard Blackwell. **Closed:** Sun, 24 Dec to 3 Jan. **Meals:** main courses £9 to £24. Set L and early D £16 (2 courses) to £20. **Details:** 76 seats. Bar. Wheelchairs. Music.

★ BEST NEW ENTRY, LONDON ★

Peg
Cooking score: 4
⊖ Hackney Central, Homerton, map 1
Japanese | £25
120 Morning Lane, Hackney, E9 6LH
Tel no: 020 3441 8765
peglondon.co.uk
£30

From the team behind Bright (see entry), this cool Hackney newcomer looks like it's come straight from the pages of a style magazine. The tableware is pastel – sunny yellow, baby pink, vibrant coral – the menu's a retro pegboard and the counters are terrazzo, fashioned from recycled yoghurt pots. Contrary to appearances, the kitchen's key reference is Japanese yakitori. Chicken bits and pieces figure prominently, therefore – for example tender hearts on a skewer under a blizzard of fresh horseradish, and wings encrusted with shichimi togarashi. These are beautiful, low-budget dishes, prepared with a precision that the paper napkins and plastic plates belie. Of the more obviously seasonal preparations, asparagus and ramsons chawan mushi is subtly flavoured, while smoked eel

with sweet-tart blackcurrants cooked down in beef fat is a glorious new way with a luxury ingredient. The style is light and low carb; it wouldn't be hard, between two, to see off the entire menu (13 dishes or so). Wines are low-intervention, with plenty in the £20 to £40 bracket. An exciting little place.
Chef/s: Byron Fini. **Closed:** Mon, Tue. **Meals:** small plates £3 to £11. **Details:** 30 seats. No reservations.

Petit Pois
Cooking score: 2
⊖ Old Street, Hoxton, map 4
French | £30
9 Hoxton Square, Hoxton, N1 6NU
Tel no: 020 7613 3689
petitpoisbistro.com
£30

Shut your eyes and you could be in Paris: the awning, the tables out front, the simplicity of the interior, all ensure that this little Hoxton Square restaurant captures the essence of a *bistro de quartier*. The menu fits too, reassuringly laden as it is with homespun French classics. Steak frites comes with béarnaise sauce, *naturellement*, and plump sole meunière with brown butter, lemon, capers and parsley. Sharing is quite the thing, so try some of the smaller plates designed for just that – sweet roast beets with salty Bleu d'Auvergne cheese and little gem, perhaps, or a few spears of grilled asparagus with Bayonne ham, or steak tartare with a cured egg yolk and baguette slices to scoop up every last bit. Just two desserts mean it's a toss-up between the fêted chocolate mousse spooned at table from a big bowl, or a pretty serving of meringue with fraises des bois. A short and mainly French wine list opens at £24.
Chef/s: Charles Withers. **Meals:** small plates £5 to £10. Large plates £15 to £20. **Details:** 26 seats. 10 seats outside. Wheelchairs. Music.

Pidgin

Cooking score: 5
Hackney Central, map 1
Modern British | £49
52 Wilton Way, Hackney, E8 1BG
Tel no: 020 7254 8311
pidginlondon.com
£5 OFF

For such an unassuming little place, done out in sparse contemporary style with close-packed tables and 'quick, attentive' service, it is packing a major punch in a quiet street near London Fields. Top-notch seasonal ingredients are the kitchen's building blocks, the common thread running through is food that fully exploits contrasting flavours and textures. A weekly changing no-choice tasting menu, a mix of tiny snacks and small plates, could start with a sparky couple of mouthfuls of diced Jersey Royals zippy with umami from white truffle and slivers of crisp chicken skin, with tobiko (flying fish roe) adding mild smokey notes, and a puffily light, creamy tempura goat's cheese served atop edamame, iced radish and frisée. Look out for a sensational oblong of thinly sliced beef cheek layered with sheets of pasta topped with intense, lightly pickled mussels and spring onion, and lamb served two ways – a sweetbread nugget with punchy zaatar mayonnaise and mint, and loin, pink and tender, lined up with kelp, al dente baby courgettes and basil. Both pre and dessert incline to lightness, the latter perhaps a modern trifle of whey, maple, peach and tarragon. There are cocktails (of course), and much of the compact, modern wine list is offered by the glass, carafe or bottle.
Chef/s: Greg Clarke. **Closed:** Mon, 24 Dec to 3 Jan. **Meals:** tasting menu £49 (8 courses). **Details:** 27 seats. 4 seats outside. V menu. Music.

Popolo Shoreditch

Cooking score: 4
Old Street, map 4
Italian | £35
26 Rivington Street, Shoreditch, EC2A 3DU
Tel no: 020 7729 4299
popoloshoreditch.com

Jon Lawson's tiny backstreet Italian is probably best known for its pasta, hand-rolled daily and formed into the likes of neat delica pumpkin ravioli with sage and olive oil, or taglierini with clams, bottarga and agretti. Lawson learned from Theo Randall (see entry) so has serious chops. But there's much more to explore on the seasonally responsive menu of tapas-esque plates that tip their hat to the traditions of Spain and the Middle East. Seated at the counter, watching the chefs at work, it's easy to work one's way through quite a selection, from the moreish fried olives to luxurious Sicilian red prawns and fresh borlotti beans with salt cod. Groups of three or more may be more comfortable on the first floor, where conventional table seating compensates for missing out on the kitchen action and energetic vibe. Wines are poured from a brief but regularly changing list, majoring on low-intervention producers from Italy.
Chef/s: Jon Lawson. **Closed:** Sun, 23 Dec to 6 Jan. **Meals:** small plates £5 to £17. **Details:** 34 seats. Bar. Music.

Quality Chop House

Cooking score: 4
Farringdon, map 5
Modern British | £45
88-94 Farringdon Road, Clerkenwell, EC1R 3EA
Tel no: 020 7278 1452
thequalitychophouse.com

Since its debut as a demotic workers' canteen in the mid-Victorian era, the Chop House has been all about popular sustenance. Its black and white floor and dark wood booth seating situate the place in its architectural era, but the menus these days, especially since the relaunch in 2012, deal in a more up-to-date version of London dining. There are still chops of course – middle white pork or Swaledale lamb – and bone-in steaks of Belted Galloway, but in the interstices between the grilling of meat, there might crop up Brixham turbot in sauce vierge, or a tomato tart with Ticklemore cheese. That said, you're never very far from meat and its fat, not when snacks include a scallop in mangalitza pork fat, the starters a serving of brawn and pickle, and the sides a portion of broccoli coated in dripping breadcrumbs and Parmesan. Finish virtuously with strawberry frangipane tart and crème fraîche, or a yellow peach with mascarpone, mint and lemon. The wine list is a vast, impressive document, from its glass selections (starting at £5) to its treasurable list of single bottles. **Chef/s:** Shaun Searley. **Closed:** bank hols, 1 week Christmas. **Meals:** main courses £18 to £90. Set L £22 (2 courses) to £26. Sun L £30 to £35 (4 courses). **Details:** 86 seats. Music.

Rochelle Canteen
Cooking score: 2
⊖ Shoreditch High Street, Old Street, map 4
Modern British | £35
16 Playground Gardens, Shoreditch, E2 7FA
Tel no: 020 7729 5677
arnoldandhenderson.com

The converted bike shed of the former Rochelle School is the scene of some real culinary action these days. Inside, the open kitchen and canteen aesthetic suit the simplicity of the dishes, while the (non-bookable) tables in the hidden courtyard garden are a summer hit. The daily changing menu is devotedly seasonal and unfettered, delivering the likes of whole roast quail with aïoli, fresh asparagus with butter, or ham, pea and lovage soup – three starters that say it all. Braised cuttlefish with polenta and gremolata reveals a passion for the Mediterranean, likewise a vegetarian main course of white beans with wild garlic and goat's curd. Finish with marmalade steamed sponge with custard, or homemade ice cream. The concise

wine list sticks to France with a Languedoc rosé the perfect choice for long, lazy lunches. A second Rochelle can be found across town at the Institute of Contemporary Arts (see entry). **Chef/s:** Euan Farmer. **Closed:** 24 to 31 Dec, bank hols. **Meals:** main courses £15 to £20. **Details:** 36 seats. 20 seats outside. Wheelchairs.

Roka Canary Wharf
Cooking score: 3
⊖ Canary Wharf, map 1
Japanese | £60
4 Park Pavilion, Canary Wharf, E14 5FW
Tel no: 020 7636 5228
rokarestaurant.com

It's more than 15 years since Rainer Becker launched trendy Japanese group Roka (branches in Fitzrovia, Aldwych and Mayfair) but still it's one of the hottest tickets in Canary Wharf. There's nothing quite like the buzz in here when the first-floor restaurant, bar and terrace fills with sushi-loving, edamame-popping suits let loose at lunch. The concept is robatayaki, or Japanese barbecue, which might run to asparagus spears, scallop skewers or Korean-spiced lamb cutlets cooked over charcoal. The sheer choice can be overwhelming but there are useful compilations of greatest hits on the lunch, tasting and weekend brunch menus. There are money-no-object moments (wagyu maki tempura, beef tartare with truffle ponzu etc) but the vegetable cooking can be more impressive – for example fried aubergine with sesame miso and the intense, savoury broccoli with moromi miso. On the drinks side are sake, shochu and some pretty swish wines. **Chef/s:** Libor Dobis. **Meals:** dishes £7 to £84. Set L £35 (2 courses) to £42. Tasting menu £70 (12 courses) to £90. **Details:** 151 seats. 40 seats outside. Bar. Wheelchairs.

Sager and Wilde

Cooking score: 2
⊖ Bethnal Green, map 1
Modern European | £35
250 Paradise Row, Bethnal Green, E2 9LE
Tel no: 020 7613 0478
sagerandwilde.com
🍾

The local town planner may have overstated the case in naming this gritty corner of Bethnal Green Paradise Row, but for wine-lovers, informal Sager and Wilde, tucked away in its old railway arch, will seem like heaven on earth. There are hundreds of bottles on the list, from France, Italy and the US predominantly (but by no means exclusively) and from some of those countries' most exciting producers (think Hirsch, Occhipinti, Selosse). Markups are gentle, and every wine on the list earns its place, be it the £26 house or a 1971 Barolo at £251. That's not to overlook the kitchen, which turns out small plates such as lemon and Parmesan bigoli or pea arancini at lunch and brunch, and a fuller modern European carte at dinner. Smoked cod's roe, kohlrabi, apple and dill followed by halibut, peas, asparagus and verjus make suitably wine-friendly picks. For dessert, choose gelato or a cheese plate.
Chef/s: Attila Pinter. **Closed:** 24 to 26 Dec.
Meals: main courses £12 to £24. **Details:** 70 seats.
50 seats outside. Bar. Wheelchairs. Music.

St John

Cooking score: 5
⊖ Farringdon, map 5
Modern British | £47
26 St John Street, Clerkenwell, EC1M 4AY
Tel no: 020 7251 0848
stjohngroup.uk.com

Fergus Henderson can truly lay claim to having brought about one of the dining revolutions in London a quarter-century ago, and it has proved, moreover, a lasting phenomenon. The former Clerkenwell smokehouse is stripped down to white walls and scuffed floors, with the kind of food that

encourages voluble conviviality and makes no bones about itself. Here is where to get a braised kid shank in red wine with mash for your main, and feel properly stuffed to the gunwales after it. Roast woodcock in the season comes with what might be termed its accoutrements for deliciousness and thrift, while fish could be a lump of bream with purple sprouting broccoli and the salty whack of anchovy. Appetisers get you limbered up for this robustness by means of deep-frying (skate cheeks with aïoli) or long simmering (chunky lamb broth), and there's Welsh rarebit among the sides if you're determined no gap should be left unfilled. Desserts are less about delicate seasonal fruits than they are about carbs and the transformations of sugar: ginger loaf and butterscotch sauce, burnt malt cream, honey and brandy parfait. Nor does the wine list go swanning off to Macedonia in search of fascinating singularity, when France is teeming demonstrably with it from nose to tail. Glasses of the house Languedoc blends in all three colours are £6.75.
Chef/s: Steve Darou. **Closed:** 25 and 26 Dec, 1 Jan.
Meals: main courses £16 to £46. **Details:** 120 seats.
Bar. Wheelchairs.

St John Bread and Wine

Cooking score: 3
⊖ Liverpool Street, map 4
British | £35
94-96 Commercial Street, Spitalfields, E1 6LZ
Tel no: 020 7251 0848
stjohngroup.uk.com

The St John ethos of stark white walls, bare tables, and functional crockery and glassware translates to this venue amid the Spitalfields bustle, the kitchen approach faithfully mirroring the Clerkenwell original (see entry). Seasonal British chow without any extraneous frilling, but founded on impeccable raw materials, is the order of every day. Late June caught the end of the asparagus season, when grilled spears were seasoned pungently with anchovy, while a bowl of peas with creamy curds and mint stood sentinel between spring and summer. The menus don't beat around the bush, so expect to mainline on blood cake and fried egg bun, rabbit saddle with dandelions and radish, or saffroned smoked haddock and mash. It's all appropriately robust and sustaining, up to the likes of rhubarb sorbet lashed with Polish vodka to finish, or a nectarine pavlova that sounds positively foofy in the circumstances. The wine list undertakes a thorough yomp through the French regions, with Languedoc house blends at £6.75 a glass.

Chef/s: Farokh Talati. **Closed:** 25 and 26 Dec. **Meals:** small plates £4 to £11. Large plates £14 to £23. **Details:** 64 seats. Bar.

St Leonards
Cooking score: 3
⊖ Old Street, Shoreditch High Street, map 4
Modern European | £35
70 Leonard Street, Shoreditch, EC2A 4QX
Tel no: 020 7739 1291
stleonards.london

This stylish restaurant looks every inch the Shoreditch archetype, its spacious dining room a study in exposed concrete, mid-century furniture and strategically suspended light fittings. Step inside and the eye is drawn to the hearth – all hanging cuts and leaping flames – setting the tone for the elemental, ingredient-led cooking on offer here. Oysters and scallops reign at the ice bar, while smokey notes prevail among small plates: coal-roasted beetroot with black garlic and crème fraîche for instance, or burnt leek with almond cream and summer truffle. More substantial dishes from the hearth might include Tamworth chop with mojo rojo sauce, hake with baby artichoke and bottarga – or else recruit someone with whom to share a staunchly Gallic helping of whole Challans duck with green olives and mint. Round off with alphonso mango sorbet. The wine list inclines to the Old World, with bottles from £26, and there's a roster of cocktails and artisanal beers in support.

Chef/s: Jackson Boxer and Andrew Clarke. **Closed:** Mon, Sun. **Meals:** small plates £6 to £9. Large plates £16 to £26. Set L and early D £18 (2 courses) to £22. **Details:** 70 seats.

Sardine
Cooking score: 2
⊖ Old Street, map 2
French | £35
15 Micawber Street, Hoxton, N1 7TB
Tel no: 020 7490 0144
sardine.london

Nothing short of a chilled glass of rosé conveys southern French holiday vibes quite as effectively as Alex Jackson's petite bistro within the Parasol Unit Foundation for Contemporary Art. It's a Londoner's homage to the region: contemporary and cool, but with classic signifiers of bentwood chairs, a long zinc-topped table and glazed ceramics to set the scene. Jackson's cooking – much of it done over a wood fire – indulges our nostalgia for such time-honoured treasures as bourride with aïoli, pork cooked in milk and the *specialité de la maison* leg of lamb à la ficelle (Saturday evenings and Sunday lunch only). Vegetarian options might include seven-vegetable tagine with couscous or grilled romanesco with romesco. Book ahead for lavish family feasts (bouillabaisse, roast chicken etc), drop in midweek for a sandwich or prix fixe, or try the popular weekend brunch featuring 'breakfast cassoulet' and a fried Cantal sandwich. French and Italian wines from £24.

Chef/s: Alex Jackson. **Closed:** 25 Dec to 1 Jan. **Meals:** main courses £15 to £20. Set L and early D £16 (2 courses) to £20. **Details:** 48 seats. Wheelchairs. Music.

Set menus
If a set lunch (L) or dinner (D) is offered, this is indicated under 'Meals'. Prices are for a standard three-course meal unless otherwise specified.

Smokestak

Cooking score: 2
⊖ Shoreditch High Street, map 4
Modern British | £25
35 Sclater Street, Shoreditch, E1 6LB
Tel no: 020 3873 1733
smokestak.co.uk
£30

As a barbecue restaurant, anonymous exterior clad in oxidised iron, it might have been art-directed in Hollywood for a post-industrial moviescape. Inside, there's loud music, dark wood, a heavy grill and the smell of meat cooked low and slow on the fire. The food comes quickly, first the brisket buns and pickled chillies with which Smokestak earned its 'cue credentials in its street-food days. And they are magnificent, the coils of smoked meat standing proud before collapsing into the sweetish, squidgy buns as the juices soak into the bread. Food is served on chunky plates and bashed up tins for sharing (not that this was explained to us beforehand). Even with some lighter dishes (sea bass with lime and coriander; salt-baked beetroot and goat's cheese under an avalanche of toasty hazelnuts), salt and fat dominate the meal. The attention-grabbing likes of baked potato, its carapace thick and blackened by fire, is simply too tempting. Finish with a refreshing mandarin sorbet. Thirst quenchers include local beers, cool cocktails and global wines from £24.
Chef/s: David Waller. **Closed:** 25 and 26 Dec.
Meals: main courses £10 to £18. **Details:** 70 seats. 60 seats outside. Music.

Smoking Goat

Cooking score: 3
⊖ Shoreditch High Street, Old Street, map 4
Thai | £27
64 Shoreditch High Street, Shoreditch, E1 6JJ
smokinggoatbar.com
£30

Transplanted in a blaze of chilli fire from its original Soho billet to the traffic-throttled blare of Shoreditch, the Goat continues its assiduous recreation of late-night Bangkok eating and drinking without missing a beat. Cluster around the bar in an ambience of floorboard and brick for food that bears a passing resemblance to good Thai home cooking and lights up the palate with spice and umami. Northern-style duck laab is electrifying with unapologetic chilli frazzle, the grilled Tamworth chop in nam pla scarcely less so. Ease yourself into these fiery mains with stir-fried asparagus and a lard-fried egg, or simple greens tossed in soy. Fish dishes look the business, as when a whole grilled John Dory turns up in its livery of red nam jim. Accompany mains with one of the rice variations and round off with coconut ice cream and plantain, dressed in lime and condensed milk. Breakfast on curried saffron eggs at weekends. Cocktails, beers and a few wines, from £6 a glass, will keep things motoring through midnight.
Chef/s: Ali Borer. **Closed:** 25 and 26 Dec, 1 Jan.
Meals: small plates £2 to £10. Large plates £9 to £17. Sharing plates £28 to £36. **Details:** 95 seats. Wheelchairs. Music. No reservations. D bookings only for groups of 6 or more.

Som Saa

Cooking score: 2
⊖ Aldgate East, map 4
Thai | £25
43a Commercial Street, Spitalfields, E1 6BD
Tel no: 020 7324 7790
somsaa.com
£30

Northern Thai-inspired dishes, full of heat, fresh herbs and vibrant flavours, are combined with a Shoreditch aesthetic of hard edges and raw concrete, vintage shutters, screens and exotic foliage. The result? Small, powerfully flavoured dishes for sharing – choose at least two each, along with sticky or steamed jasmine rice. Don't miss the som tam thai, a salad of green papaya, snake beans, dried shrimp, cherry tomatoes and peanuts, serving up heat and sourness in abundance. Pak plang fie daeng is a moreish and fearsomely hot mix of Ceylon spinach and morning glory with pungent fish sauce, while a whole deep-fried sea bass heaped with fresh herbs and chilli needs picking clean. Energising cocktails supplement a wine list designed to stand up to the punchy flavours, including a range of skin-contact and natural wines.

Chef/s: Andy Oliver and Mark Dobbie. **Closed:** Sun, 25 Dec, 1 Jan. **Meals:** small plates £9 to £18. **Details:** 80 seats. V menu. Bar. Wheelchairs. Music.

Tayyabs

Cooking score: 1

⚪ **Whitechapel, Aldgate East, map 1**
Pakistani | £30
83-89 Fieldgate Street, Whitechapel, E1 1JU
Tel no: 020 7247 9543
tayyabs.co.uk
£30

The queues are interminable (be sure to book), the pace is frantic and decibel levels high at peak times, but this legendary Pakistani/ Punjabi canteen is still a winner. Founded in 1972, Tayyabs' original premises (a defunct East End boozer) have been extended and given some Whitechapel edge over the years, but the food remains blisteringly good — and unbeatable value, too. Sizzling spiced tandooris, kebabs and grills are the big hits (mutton tikka, masala fish and the unmissable lamb chops), but also dip into the various curries served in cast-iron karahi dishes — the signature 'dry meat', 'small prawn', lamb with okra and so on. Unlicensed, but you can BYO (no corkage).

Chef/s: Wasim Tayyab. **Meals:** main courses £10 to £21. **Details:** 350 seats. Wheelchairs. Parking.

★ NEW ENTRY ★

Two Lights

Cooking score: 3

⚪ **Shoreditch High Street, Hoxton, map 4**
American | £55
28 Kingsland Road, Shoreditch, E2 8DA
Tel no: 020 3976 0076
twolights.restaurant

Casual and with a hip utilitarian vibe that goes with the territory, Chase Lovecky's first venture may not be much to look at (white-painted brick walls, counter or plain tables, open kitchen) but its popularity is not surprising. Lovecky has impeccable credentials, working at Jean-Georges, then Momofuku in New York before becoming head chef at The Clove Club (see entry) and his down-to-earth modern American cooking receives an emphatic thumbs-up from reporters. Like the decor, the food is confidently no-frills, built around seasonal British ingredients and offered via a sequence of sharing plates. Crab on a beef-fat chip is fast achieving cult status, but there's plenty of support for chicken liver parfait with black garlic and pickled pumpkin, as well as grilled flatbread of mussels and lardo, and clams with preserved lemon, chilli and bone marrow — a delightful balance of sweet and sour. Larger plates could bring grilled Hereford rump cap with smoked Cheddar and calçots, while vanilla custard tart with bourbon caramel makes a perfect finish. Service is warmly welcoming. Drink imaginative house cocktails or something from the modern, wide-ranging wine list of small producers.

Chef/s: Chase Lovecky. **Closed:** Mon, 25 Dec, 1 Jan. **Meals:** small plates £4 to £14. Large plates £17 to £25. Set L £17 (2 courses) to £20. **Details:** 50 seats. Wheelchairs. Music.

Wright Brothers Spitalfields

Cooking score: 2

⚪ **Liverpool Street, map 4**
Seafood | £40
8a Lamb Street, Spitalfields, E1 6EA
Tel no: 020 7324 7730
thewrightbrothers.co.uk

The east London outpost of this smart seafood chain benefits from a newly jazzed-up terrace, covered and heated for year-round alfresco dining. Inside, there's a lovely marble-topped oyster bar. The choice is yours. For main entry, see Borough branch, south London.

Chef/s: Michal Heins. **Closed:** 25 and 26 Dec, 1 Jan. **Meals:** main courses £11 to £35. **Details:** 120 seats. 30 seats outside. Music.

★ NEW ENTRY ★

24 The Oval

Cooking score: 2
⊖ Oval, map 1
Modern British | £30
24 Clapham Road, Oval, SW9 0JG
Tel no: 020 7735 6111
24theoval.co.uk
£30

'It's a nice little spot in a useful location near The Oval,' noted one summer visitor who recommends bagging a table on the rear terrace where one can almost forget the gritty Clapham Road setting. Inside there are scrubbed pine tables, reclaimed chairs, wall-hung plants and a menu that deals in fresh seasonal produce. At its best, the cooking is vivid and precise: try poached Tilley's Farm egg, charred leeks and pickled mustard seeds, Cumbrian cob chicken teamed with chantenay carrots and summer greens with a glorious glossy jus, or crisp-skinned cod served with flavour-packed colourful heritage tomatoes and a salsa made from tiny dice of red, yellow and green peppers dotted with a few mussels. Visitors have praised an 'exemplary' lemon tart, the sourdough bread gets things off to 'a cracking start' and set lunches are considered good value. A single-page wine list starts at £24 and includes a trio of reserve reds – pretty much what you want from a good neighbourhood joint.
Chef/s: Simon Woodrow and George East. **Closed:** Mon, Tue. **Meals:** main courses £15 to £20. Set L £16 (2 courses) to £20. Tasting menu £39 (6 courses). **Details:** 40 seats. 20 seats outside. Music.

The Anchor & Hope

Cooking score: 4
⊖ Waterloo, Southwark, map 5
Modern European | £33
36 The Cut, Waterloo, SE1 8LP
Tel no: 020 7928 9898
anchorandhopepub.co.uk

It may seem like any other city pub, with its dressed-down, rough around the edges look, but consistently delicious food means that this workaday local, not far from Waterloo Station and The Old Vic, is as popular as ever. A lively atmosphere, efficient service, unfussy cooking and an excellent drinks list (with great beer and cocktail selections) make for a 'phenomenal experience'. A spirited and generous approach to cooking takes British ingredients and gives them deft European inflections, whether in a much-praised snail and bacon salad or 'perfect crispy fries with homemade béarnaise (could have happily eaten just that on its own!)'. Hits on our visit were spiced duck hearts on sesame flatbread with tzatziki, and braised duck and red wine with grilled polenta and green olive tapenade – a superlative mix of flavours – followed by an accomplished baked custard tart with forced Yorkshire rhubarb. The wine list is no less delightful with an interesting selection of European producers from £21. Note, bookings are taken for Sunday lunch only.
Chef/s: Alex Crofts. **Closed:** 24 Dec to 2 Jan, bank hols. **Meals:** main courses £11 to £26. Set L £16 (2 courses) to £18. **Details:** 65 seats. 28 seats outside. Bar. Music. No reservations.

Artusi

Cooking score: 3
⊖ Peckham Rye, map 1
Italian | £28
161 Bellenden Road, Peckham, SE15 4DH
Tel no: 020 3302 8200
artusi.co.uk
£5 OFF   £30

Since opening in 2014, and 'as good as ever' under chef Emily Sansom, Artusi continues to embody the capital's take on Italy – pared-back aesthetic, short changing menu, a light, contemporary touch. The menu's rhythm (3-2-3-3 choices for starter, pasta, main and dessert) never falters, thrumming with quality from start to finish. Handsome starter plates include salt beef, dill mustard and watercress or crab with chicory and brown bread mayonnaise, to be followed by that pasta, perhaps tagliatelle with peas, mint and chilli. There's lots of good veg about at main-course stage, perhaps courgette, purple kale and heritage carrots paired with onglet. Simple puddings might include apple cake with custard and almond crumble. Larger tables get a family-style feast and Sunday lunch is a satisfying deal to know about. The wine list offers a brief but worthwhile tour of the Italian regions, with more boutique options than big hitters.

Chef/s: Emily Sansom. **Closed:** 1 week Christmas. **Meals:** main courses £12 to £20. Sun L £20. **Details:** 40 seats. 6 seats outside. Wheelchairs. Music.

Babur

Cooking score: 2
⊖ Honor Oak Park, map 1
Indian | £33
119 Brockley Rise, Forest Hill, SE23 1JP
Tel no: 020 8291 2400
babur.info
£5 OFF

'A local institution and such a lovely place to have down the road,' notes a reader who has nothing but praise for this 'welcoming' neighbourhood Indian. But Babur isn't your average curry house: there's a life-size effigy of a tiger on the roof, a hand-painted kalamkari horoscope in the foyer and lots of artefacts amid the exposed brickwork and veneered timbers. Meanwhile, the kitchen delivers 'high-quality cooking without the pretentiousness or fuss of some upmarket restaurants'. There's plenty to tempt vegetarians and vegans – beetroot cutlet with papaya chutney, say, or a wild mushroom and pea dosa – as well as those on special diets. Elsewhere on the extensive menu you'll find the likes of crab 'bonda' dumplings with mint and coriander purée, steamed shoulder of lamb accompanied by beetroot rice, or seared Gressingham duck breast with braised cabbage, cloves and sweet-and-sour plum sauce. Intriguing sides might feature crispy fried potatoes dusted with mango powder, while desserts are clever crossover ideas. The wine list has been knowledgeably assembled with food in mind, but it would be remiss to ignore the zesty Asian-themed cocktails.

Chef/s: Jiwan Lal. **Closed:** 26 Dec. **Meals:** main courses £15 to £20. Sun L £17 (buffet). **Details:** 72 seats. V menu. Vg menu. Wheelchairs. Music.

★ NEW ENTRY ★

Bao Borough

Cooking score: 2
⊖ London Bridge, map 4
Taiwanese | £18
13 Stoney Street, Borough, SE1 9AD
Tel no: 020 3967 5407
baolondon.com
£30

Bao Borough is the latest in the Bao family – it has sisters in Fitzrovia and Soho (see entries) – and the only one with its own KTV, aka karaoke room. You don't have to sing for a supper of curry cheese bao with Szechuan oil, or your choice of the wide selection of xiao chi (small eats), but it's an option.

Chef/s: Tomasz Kus. **Meals:** bao £5 to £6. Small plates £3 to £8. **Details:** 48 seats. 4 seats outside. No reservations. Bookings only for groups of 5 or more.

The Begging Bowl

Cooking score: 2
⊖ Peckham Rye, map 1
Thai | £32
168 Bellenden Road, Peckham, SE15 4BW
Tel no: 020 7635 2627
thebeggingbowl.co.uk

High demand at this cheery Peckham favourite has seen a recent expansion and refurbishment, including new bar seating for diners. The menu, which specialises in sharing plates of Thai street food, hits all the right spots when it comes to hot, sour, salty and sweet. New Zealander Jane Alty worked under Thai food maestro David Thompson and she was clearly paying attention when it came to mastering flavour-packed dishes. Authentic Thai ingredients are often paired with seasonal British produce. A typical meal might include pork neck marinated in Mekhong 'whisky' (actually a Thai spirit) with nam pla prik chilli sauce, followed by guinea fowl teamed with black kale, pickled garlic, Thai peanuts and pennywort, or stir-fried turnip tops with fermented yellow bean and Thai garlic. End with banana fritters in coconut sesame batter with tamarind caramel, peanut brittle and turmeric custard. Drink cocktails, beer on tap or by the bottle, or spice-friendly wines from £21.

Chef/s: Jane Alty. **Meals:** sharing plates £5 to £16. **Details:** 74 seats. Bar. Music. No reservations. Bookings for groups of 6 to 12.

Bistro Union

Cooking score: 3
♻ Clapham South, map 3
Modern European | £35
40 Abbeville Road, Clapham, SW4 9NG
Tel no: 020 7042 6400
bistrounion.co.uk

Fireworks may occur at its sibling, Trinity (see entry), but Bistro Union, in perennially smart Abbeville 'village', is a steady sparkler – looking the part more than ever after a subtle revamp. Chef Joshua Hooper oversees a menu that must catch many neighbourhood moods, doing so with restrained treatments of lovely ingredients. There's an Italian sensibility at work in small plates of daily changing homemade pasta or burrata with blood orange, chilli and mint, with larger dishes moving across Europe to cassoulet of duck with white beans and smoked ham, or roast ray wing with capers and pipérade. Blow-outs might call for a sharing dish, perhaps slow-cooked shoulder of Colne Valley lamb with pommes Anna and purple sprouting broccoli. Dessert eschews fashionable deconstruction for slices of brown butter custard tart or a crème caramel. The overall effect, in the unfussy dining room, is hospitable indeed. Wine starts at an accessible £21.

Chef/s: Joshua Hooper. **Closed:** 23 to 27 Dec, 1 to 3 Jan. **Meals:** main courses £16 to £21. Sun L £30. **Details:** 39 seats. 10 seats outside. Music.

Casse-Croûte

Cooking score: 4
♻ London Bridge, Borough, map 1
French | £36
109 Bermondsey Street, Bermondsey, SE1 3XB
Tel no: 020 7407 2140
cassecroute.co.uk

Six years since its debut, this resolutely French bistro has turned into something of an institution. The intimate dining room with its Gallic decorative theme – black and white chequered floor, walls covered in advertising posters, paper sheets over gingham tablecloths – may appear clichéd, but the short, daily changing blackboard menu reassures with its run-through of classic dishes with noticeable provincial overtones. The food is always fresh and full of flavour, whether in starters of sardines à l'huile, salade niçoise or croustillant de pied de cochon, or mains of poulet au Riesling with spätzle, boeuf en croûte, and paupiette of sole with haricots blancs – all well received dishes this year. Mousse au chocolat, and rhubarb with sablé breton are considered fine desserts. Service is cheerful and so are the customers. The wine list sticks to France, of course, with every bottle (from £24) offered by the glass and carafe.

Chef/s: Sylvain Soulard. **Closed:** 22 to 28 Dec. **Meals:** main courses £20 to £23. **Details:** 30 seats. 2 seats outside.

Chez Bruce

Cooking score: 6
♻ Balham, map 3
Modern European | £58
2 Bellevue Road, Wandsworth, SW17 7EG
Tel no: 020 8672 0114
chezbruce.co.uk
🍷

Bruce Poole's immensely likeable restaurant is happy to dish up classy platefuls for casual lunchtime catch-ups while putting on the style as a fail-safe evening destination. At the heart of things is the food – a highly distinctive take on Anglo-European cuisine

founded on top-drawer ingredients, hard-won technique and harmoniously balanced flavours. The kitchen shows its respect for the old ways by offering deep-fried calf's brains with sauce gribiche and morteau sausage alongside more eclectic seasonal starters such as confit charlotte potatoes with Provençal mackerel pâté, Ortiz anchovies and basil. Mains also promise richly satisfying, earthy comfort shot through with flashes of sprightly invention – as in a luxe combo involving roast rump of veal with gnocchi, ragù bianco, morels and sage. Standards remain sky-high right to the end, whether you're enjoying the glorious Anglo-French cheeseboard or savouring the sweet delights of a coffee and hazelnut éclair. Chez Bruce has one more ace up its sleeve in the shape of a staggeringly good, all-embracing wine list that has quality, pedigree and diversity dripping from every page; house selections start at £15 a carafe.
Chef/s: Bruce Poole and Matt Christmas. **Closed:** 24 to 26 Dec, 1 Jan. **Meals:** set L £35 Mon to Fri (2 courses) to £40. Set D £48 (2 courses) to £58. Sat and Sun L £45. **Details:** 80 seats. Wheelchairs. No children at D.

Cinnamon Kitchen Battersea
Cooking score: 1
⊖ Battersea Park, map 3
Indian | £40
4 Arches Lane, Battersea, SW11 8AB
Tel no: 020 3955 5480
cinnamon-kitchen.com
£5
OFF

Nestled beneath the swoop of a railway arch beside Battersea Power Station, this outpost of Vivek Singh's Cinnamon empire lives something of a double life. From Monday to Friday, a daytime menu serves casual diners, perhaps with Padrón pakora with coriander chutney, followed by a bhuna lamb and naan roll with kachumber and lime. Come evening, formality creeps in, the dinner menu ramps up and so do the prices – think Ibérico pork presa in vindaloo sauce or a Bengali king prawn curry, although the sharing-style tasting menu is good value. Subcontinent-themed cocktails include the likes of Assam Manhattan.
Chef/s: Vivek Singh and Rakesh Nair. **Meals:** main courses £9 to £12. Set L £15 (2 courses) to £18. Tasting menu £33 (9 courses). **Details:** 250 seats. 20 seats outside. Vg menu. Bar. Wheelchairs. Music.

Coal Rooms
Cooking score: 4
⊖ Peckham Rye, map 1
International | £33
11a Station Way, Peckham, SE15 4RX
Tel no: 020 7635 6699
coalroomspeckham.com

The setting may be vintage – a Grade II-listed former ticket office at Peckham Rye station – but the concept is anything but. For a primer in what a new London restaurant looks like, visit at any time of day. In the morning, Coal Rooms plays airy café, serving jam doughnuts and Old Spike coffee; at weekends, it's all about brunch and the coffee-cured bacon sandwich; at other times, it's an ambitious dining room with a mead bar (whatever next?) on the first floor. Chef Debbie Nicholls upholds the 'anything goes' mentality with a dashing menu that pairs Gloucester old spot Thai yellow sausage with tiger's milk; carrot tacos with chimichurri; and cured brisket with blackcurrant ketchup. Much is cooked over charcoal, including 40-day aged Hereford steaks and the typically eclectic vegetarian main of cauliflower, miso bagna cauda and furikake. There's good drinking too: consider a Made of Girders cocktail, smoked porter, kombucha or a bottle from an inexpensive selection of global wines.
Chef/s: Debbie Nicholls. **Closed:** 23 to 27 Dec. **Meals:** main courses £13 to £21. **Details:** 65 seats. Bar. Wheelchairs. Music. No children after 8pm.

Craft

Cooking score: 3
e North Greenwich, map 1
Modern British | £38
Peninsula Square, Greenwich, SE10 0SQ
Tel no: 020 8465 5910
craft-london.co.uk
£5
OFF

Craft feels less like a restaurant, more like a culinary citadel: proudly doing its own curing and smoking, baking and fermenting, growing its own vegetables on a nearby jetty and even keeping its own bees. Two floors up, a buzzing rooftop bar keeps watch over the Greenwich skyline; at street level a café serves sourdough pizzas and on-site roasted coffee. Sandwiched between them is the restaurant: strikingly designed in Majorelle blue, copper and turquoise, with a menu built on artisanal produce. Snack on tandoor flatbreads with baba ganoush as you choose between starters like Brixham crab, datterini tomatoes and rocket, or steak tartare and sourdough toast, potato and anchovy mayo. Vast portions and mighty flavours define the mains: crispy whole bream in lemon and caper sauce beside a slab of BBQ hispi cabbage, or grilled polenta with borlotti beans and salsa rossa. Finish with a simple salted caramel tart. A cleverly curated drinks list has a few curiosities, from Welsh fizz to French orange wine, starting at £25. **Chef/s:** Stevie Parle. **Closed:** Mon, Sun, 23 Dec to 5 Jan. **Meals:** main courses £14 to £26. **Details:** 75 seats. Bar. Wheelchairs. Music.

The Dairy

Cooking score: 5
e Clapham Common, map 3
Modern British | £38
15 The Pavement, Clapham, SW4 0HY
Tel no: 020 7622 4165
the-dairy.co.uk

Loitering at the north-east corner of Clapham Common, Robin Gill's Dairy is one of the trailblazers of contemporary British food served in dressed-down surrounds. The clamorous press of business in these modest confines, presided over these days by Ben Rand, is testimony to the enduring popularity of a cooking style founded on robust flavours and potent seasoning that eschews undue presentational flair. Don't swerve the nibbles, or you'll miss out on umami bombs such as spiced pollock cheek gougères or rich chicken liver mousse with date and apple jam. From the seasonal menu, there might be cedar-smoked eel with parsnip and cod's roe as an intro to luscious middle white pork with swede purée and braised red cabbage or bone marrow agnolotti with Jerusalem artichokes and cavolo nero. Vegetables come from a Sussex farm that grows on food-waste soil. Puds aren't the kitchen's strongest suit, although the tasting menu always features a fascinating pre-dessert such as fermented apple sorbet with whey caramel. Cocktails might include a negroni made with beetroot gin, while the short wine list starts with a red Rhône blend at £6 a small glass. **Chef/s:** Ben Rand. **Closed:** Mon, 24 to 26 Dec, 1 Jan. **Meals:** small plates £13 to £15. Set L £28 (4 courses). Tasting menu £48 (7 courses). Sun L £32. **Details:** 60 seats. 24 seats outside. V menu. Vg menu. Bar. Music.

★ NEW ENTRY ★

Darby's

Cooking score: 3
e Vauxhall, Battersea Park, map 3
Modern British | £45
3 Viaduct Gardens, Nine Elms, Battersea, SW11 7AY
Tel no: 020 7537 3111
darbys-london.com

No expense has been spared on the fit-out of Robin Gill's latest venture in the shadow of the new American Embassy, taking in an on-site bakery, a huge central bar, gorgeous semi-circular banquettes and perfectly subdued lighting. And the food? The culinary compass points to Gill's native Ireland and west across the Atlantic to the USA, with oysters, amusing nibbles like the 'Gilda little perverts' – a cocktail stick skewering smoked eel, a green olive and a pickled chilli (perfect with a

martini) – and meat and fish cooked on the huge charcoal grill. Highland short rib, cooked low and slow overnight, is a particular showstopper. There's a Franco-Med feel to starters of, say, stracciatella cheese with stone fruit and olive oil, or a superb beef tartare packed with capers and enriched with bone marrow, anchovy and tiny, lightly pickled chestnut mushrooms. A dollop of dark chocolate mousse paired with Guinness gelato really hits the spot, too. Easy and harmonious house wines launch a list that's broken down by category, with glasses from £4.50.
Chef/s: Robin Gill and Dean Parker. **Meals:** main courses £21 to £30. **Details:** 120 seats. 30 seats outside. Bar. Wheelchairs. Music.

Duddell's
Cooking score: 2
⊖ London Bridge, map 4
Chinese | £60
9 St Thomas Street, Borough, SE1 9RY
Tel no: 020 3957 9932
duddells.co

The repurposing of St Thomas's church in Southwark as an upmarket Chinese restaurant has been one of the more eye-catching transformations of recent years; aficionados of ecclesiastical interiors will note the survival of the dark oak reredos at one end. Otherwise, it's all café tables and sea-green tiling, as well as complexified Cantonese dishes lacquered in modern glamour. Soft-shell crab with spicy almonds or a bowl of abalone broth with chicken and kale might lead in to traditional halibut done in a bamboo steamer with charred spring onion and soy, or one of the chef's recommendations, opulent creations such as smoked black Angus ribs with soy-based red wine sauce and Japanese baby peaches. The main carte is weightily priced, but the lunchtime dim sum listing offers more obvious value in the form of dried oyster and chive dumplings, lotus wraps of chicken and glutinous rice, and shrimp cheung fun. Drink wines by the glass from £7.50, double that for the handful of Coravin selections.

Chef/s: Chris Tan. **Closed:** 25 Dec. **Meals:** main courses £17 to £54. Set L £24 (2 courses). **Details:** 102 seats. Bar. Wheelchairs.

Franklins
Cooking score: 2
map 1
British | £30
157 Lordship Lane, East Dulwich, SE22 8HX
Tel no: 020 8299 9598
franklinsrestaurant.com
£5 OFF £30

A long-time East Dulwich favourite, this Victorian corner restaurant has the well-worn, comfortable look and atmosphere that only a trusted neighbourhood spot can supply. Drinkers are welcome at the bar, known for its 'fantastic cocktails, wines and beers', while diners head for the linen-covered tables where 'consistently great food' and 'lovely staff' are the lure. Big-hitting flavours and robust combinations reveal a kitchen with its finger firmly on the pulse. Traditional ingredients are reimagined and reinvigorated, so come for ox heart with chickpeas and paprika, or pickled pigeon with capers, radish and frisée. Mains might take in calf's liver and parsley root mash with sage and onion, or red-leg partridge with celeriac and bacon. For afters, Welsh rarebit, Scotch woodcock and black pudding on toast are savoury alternatives to baked marmalade sponge and custard, or prune and almond tart. Well-chosen mainly European wines start at £18.
Chef/s: Ralf Wittig. **Closed:** 25 and 26 Dec, 1 Jan. **Meals:** main courses £15 to £24. Set L £14 (2 courses) to £17. **Details:** 70 seats. 12 seats outside. Bar. Wheelchairs.

Closed
Where closures are listed, these are for full days only. Please check opening times with the restaurant before travelling.

Ganapati

Cooking score: 2
⊖ Peckham Rye, map 1
Indian | £30
38 Holly Grove, Peckham, SE15 5DF
Tel no: 020 7277 2928
ganapatirestaurant.com

Be prepared not only to share one of the communal wooden tables at this laid-back colourful eatery, but also to taste really authentic south Indian cooking. Brightly painted walls, school chairs and shelves of trinkets set the tone in the dining room, and there's an inviting covered courtyard out back. The menu deals in rebooted home-style cuisine and regional street food from Tamil Nadu, Kerala and Karnataka, with a strong showing of vegetarian and vegan dishes alongside, say, deboned chicken leg in beetroot masala, lamb mappas with fresh coconut milk or tuna spiced with chilli, curry leaves and kodampuli (smoked tamarind). Thalis and one-plate weekday lunches are terrific value, and the parathas are 'still fabulous' after all these years, according to one reader. Drink fruity lassi, Bermondsey-brewed Fourpure beer or something from the basic wine list.
Chef/s: Claire Fisher and Aboobacker Pallithodi Koya. **Closed:** Mon. **Meals:** main courses £9 to £15. **Details:** 38 seats. 14 seats outside. Music.

Garden Café

Cooking score: 2
⊖ Lambeth North, map 3
Modern European | £32
Garden Museum, 5 Lambeth Palace Road, Lambeth, SE1 7LB
Tel no: 020 7401 8865
gardenmuseum.org.uk

In the shadow of Lambeth Palace, in a glass and bronze-tiled cloistered extension to the church of St Mary-at-Lambeth, this stylish café restaurant is a delightful lunch spot and 'a real find in an area that's a little off the beaten track'. It's a simple space flooded with light from the courtyard garden, offering a daily changing menu that puts simple, seasonal ingredients centre stage. Dishes are self-assured, big on flavour but not overly fussy, delivering thoroughly modern combinations such as sweetbreads with broad beans, radishes and bacon or bean and herb fritter with lemon mayo, ahead of veal onglet with rosemary potatoes and anchovy, or hake with grilled gem lettuce and lovage. Finish with crème brûlée and cherries. Coffee and cake are available at other times and the café is open for dinner on Tuesdays and Fridays. The compact international wine list is kindly priced.
Chef/s: Harry Kaufman. **Meals:** main courses £14 to £20. **Details:** 30 seats.

LOCAL GEM

Gurkhas Diner

⊖ Balham, map 3
Nepalese | £20
1 The Boulevard, Balham High Road, Balham, SW17 7BW
Tel no: 020 8675 1188
gurkhasdiner.co.uk

£30

On a corner just beyond Balham station, this place may look very much like your average local curry house, but don't be fooled – it's a 'rare spot', a genial family-run restaurant offering genuine Nepalese flavours without short-cuts. Fresh ingredients and whole spices are the building blocks for a repertoire that runs from momo cha (juicy steamed dumplings with sweet-and-sour achar dipping sauce) or tareko farshi (deep-fried courgette fritters) to 'richly unctuous' slow-cooked mayur lamb – order this with their unmissable guliyo roti bread. Drink Kathmandu beer or house wine, from £16.75.

Hawksmoor Borough

Cooking score: 4
⊖ London Bridge, map 4
British | £60
16 Winchester Walk, Borough, SE1 9AQ
Tel no: 020 7234 9940
thehawksmoor.com

Located in a former hops warehouse near Borough Market, Hawksmoor's newest London branch has an 18-cover private dining room with its own kitchen. For main entry, see Knightsbridge branch, west London.
Chef/s: Simon Cotterill. **Closed:** 24 to 26 Dec.
Meals: main courses £17 to £60. Set L and early/late D £26 (2 courses) to £29. **Details:** 140 seats. Wheelchairs. Music.

LOCAL GEM

Home SW15

⊖ East Putney, Putney, map 3
Modern British | £30
146 Upper Richmond Road, Putney, SW15 2SW
Tel no: 020 8780 0592
homesw15.com
£30

Upbeat from the off, Home springs to life at 10am and keeps up the pace through the day. Get going with Cornish crab cakes or shakshuka – good for breakfast, brunch or lunch, depending on your time clock. Feisty flavours run through to dinner, where burrata is fired up with 'nduja vinaigrette and blood orange, and sesame-crusted chicken escalope comes with spicy Asian slaw. Globally inspired bar snacks and classic cocktails fill any gaps. Fresh juices and smoothies are alternatives to the well-chosen wines.

José Tapas Bar

Cooking score: 3
⊖ London Bridge, Borough, map 1
Spanish | £30
104 Bermondsey Street, Bermondsey, SE1 3UB
Tel no: 020 7403 4902
josepizarro.com
£30

No one seems to mind queuing, even if it's standing room only once you're in, although there is some counter seating. This tiny, convivial corner bar makes Bermondsey feel like balmy Andalucía and it's easy to lose an afternoon here. Tapas chalked on the board change daily and ingredients exude noble heritage: jamón from acorn-fed pigs, say, or Basque-inspired hake with clams and salsa verde or red prawn rice. They share the billing with the simplest traditionally Spanish morsels such as pan con tomate or croquetas. Chocolate pot with olive oil and salt is a revelatory pudding. This place is as much about drink, too, and there are few better places to explore the diversity of sherry and Spanish wine, from complex, nutty finos to Basque txakoli (a lightly sparking white), and much of the wine list is available by the glass.
Chef/s: José Pizarro. **Meals:** tapas £4 to £18. **Details:** 17 seats. Wheelchairs. Parking. Music. No reservations.

LOCAL GEM

Kashmir

⊖ Putney, map 3
Indian | £30
18-20 Lacy Road, Putney, SW15 1NL
Tel no: 07477 533888
kashmirrestaurants.co.uk
£5 OFF £30

Not far from Putney's main drag, this much-loved and simply styled restaurant celebrates the cooking of northern India. Vivid artworks and comfortably upholstered chairs provide pops of colour in imitation of the bursts of flavour evident on the plate. There are familiar names along the way – biryanis, lamb rogan josh, chicken tikka masala – but it's worth exploring the eye-catching alternatives including kabargah (tender lamb ribs cooked in milk with Kashmiri spices) or dum aloo (fried potatoes in a spicy red curry sauce). A concise wine list opens at £19, or go for bottles of the habitual lager brands.

Kudu

Cooking score: 4
⊖ Queens Road Peckham, map 1
Modern European | £40
119 Queens Road, Peckham, SE15 2EZ
Tel no: 020 3950 0226
kudu-restaurant.com

Patrick Williams and Amy Corbin's low-key restaurant wouldn't look out of place in central London. That it's yards from Queens Road Peckham station is almost unbelievable. The narrow dining room is hugely welcoming despite the barest of fittings, and the tersely written dinner menu promises a taste of Williams' native South Africa tempered with some modern European ideas – say braai onion squash with goat's curd, dandelion and cavolo nero. While the cooking can appear deceptively simple, it works because of the quality of the fiercely seasonal ingredients. Confit duck with girolles, salsify and minestra nera, for example, has an earthiness that echoes the surroundings, while the freshness of burrata is perfectly accented by pickled beetroot, raisins and pine oil. The house-baked bread is a must, served with a choice of flavoured butters (have both), and for dessert, look no further than malted chocolate ganache with sesame ice cream and chocolate crumble. Weekend brunch/lunch is hugely popular. Drink cocktails or look to the short, enterprising wine list with everything offered by the glass, carafe or bottle.
Chef/s: Patrick Williams. **Closed:** Mon, Tue, 25 and 26 Dec, 1 Jan. **Meals:** main courses £11 to £36. Set L £17 (2 courses) to £20. **Details:** 40 seats. 12 seats outside. V menu. Wheelchairs.

Lamberts

Cooking score: 1
⊖ Balham, map 3
Modern British | £30
2 Station Parade, Balham High Road, Balham, SW12 9AZ
Tel no: 020 8675 2233
lambertsrestaurant.com
£5 OFF £30

A few yards from Balham station is this simply furnished neighbourhood bistro with plum-coloured banquettes and unadorned tables. The cooking is all about straightforward flavours and presentations, starters often simple assembly jobs such as cured wood pigeon with rhubarb and hazelnuts, or heritage beetroot with sheep's curd, walnuts and honey. A generous serving of brill with mussels and spinach was let down at inspection by under-seasoning and an insipid broth, but much better was a vegetarian dish of seared oyster mushrooms with white bean purée, crispy kale and burnt shallots. Finish with sweet apple and rhubarb crumble and oat milk sorbet. The midweek market menu remains a steal. A creditable wine list, arranged by style, opens at £7 a glass.
Chef/s: Miro Dohnal. **Closed:** Mon, 24 and 25 Dec, 1 Jan. **Meals:** main courses £17 to £20. Set D £19 Tue to Thur (2 courses) to £22. **Details:** 53 seats. 8 seats outside. Bar. Music.

★ NEW ENTRY ★

Levan

Cooking score: 3
⊖ Peckham Rye, map 1
Modern European | £32
12-16 Blenheim Grove, Peckham, SE15 4QL
Tel no: 020 7732 2256
levanlondon.co.uk

Opening in late 2018, Levan is named after the legendary 1970s New York club DJ, Larry Levan, hence the block-rocking beats. It's an all-day dining space with café tables, counter seating and wine shelves against a deep blue

background, serving a menu of snacks and sharers, plenty of vegetarian stuff, all underpinned by masses of resonant flavour. Comté fries – gram flour logs blitzed with grated cheese and saffron aïoli – will get hoovered up, as will the juicy ripe tomatoes seasoned with ponzu and white miso. From the smaller plates, the bavette steak tartare with Jerusalem artichoke crisps, anchovy and plenty of capers really stood out at inspection, as did the stonking potato, wild mushroom and Vacherin pie with a golden pastry dome and satisfyingly firm, peppery filling – definitely one to share. Otherwise, there may be sea trout with smoked cod's roe in nori vinaigrette, or Hebridean lamb rump with labneh and broad beans. An elderflower and rhubarb version of îles flottantes was a textural blur on our visit, but a poached apricot with almond milk ice cream should do the trick. Low-intervention wines furnish a forward-thinking list, with small glasses from £5.50.
Chef/s: Nicholas Balfe. **Closed:** 22 Dec to 2 Jan. **Meals:** small plates £3 to £19. Tasting menu £41 (5 courses). **Details:** 40 seats. 12 seats outside. Wheelchairs. Music.

Llewelyn's

Cooking score: 3
⊖ Brixton, map 1
Modern European | £32
293-295 Railton Road, Herne Hill, SE24 0JP
Tel no: 020 7733 6676
llewelyns-restaurant.co.uk

Next door to Herne Hill station and a minute's walk from Brockwell Park, this is the kind of restaurant we'd all love to have at the end of our road. With its wide glass frontage, plain white and wood decor and relaxed café ambience, it's a typical modern-day eatery with a menu focused on extracting maximum flavour from (largely British) seasonal produce. The kitchen certainly knows what's what when it comes to feeding loyal locals: a warm salad of Jerusalem artichoke, salsify, quince and hazelnuts might kick things off, ahead of roast sea trout with Italian winter greens and crab beurre blanc or pot-roast

partridge with smoked sausage and choucroute, although, for some, it's hard to get past the steak pie for two. Finish with chocolate and hazelnut cake with vanilla ice cream or a Muscat caramel custard. Excellent cocktails supplement the reasonably priced modern wine list (from £23).
Chef/s: Warren Fleet. **Closed:** Mon. **Meals:** main courses £16 to £18. **Details:** 44 seats. 24 seats outside.

Lupins

Cooking score: 4
⊖ Borough, London Bridge, map 5
Modern European | £35
66 Union Street, Borough, SE1 1TD
Tel no: 020 3908 5888
lupinslondon.com

£5
OFF

'It's so fresh, modern, airy and pretty – with food to match.' Readers' enthusiasm for this first-floor restaurant on the edge of Flat Iron Square continues. The unpretentious setting and cheerful service fit the bill, while the perfectly formed small plates menu, with its focus firmly on the seasons, offers up some good contemporary cooking. Snack on grilled oysters with sriracha and lime butter, lamb kofta with tahini yoghurt, and braised chicken arancini with Lincolnshire Poacher cheese and tarragon, before considering the likes of stone bass with 'nduja and mussel velouté. Meat isn't ignored, so look out for, say, pork belly with corn taco and ancho chilli, blood orange salsa and red cabbage. Finish with a silky lemon posset with lemon curd and shortbread. Attractive cocktails include strawberry and sage gin fizz, there's London-brewed beer, and the short, mainly European wine list is modern and keenly priced with a good selection by the glass.
Chef/s: Natasha Cooke. **Closed:** Sun, bank hols, 23 Dec to 2 Jan. **Meals:** small plates £5 to £14. **Details:** 30 seats. Bar. Music.

Marcella

Cooking score: 2
map 1
Italian | £28
165a Deptford High Street, Deptford,
SE8 3NU
Tel no: 020 3903 6561
marcella.london
£5 OFF £30

Unwavering local support ensures that this unassuming space, done out in spare contemporary style, is nearly always full to bursting. That it is an offshoot of Peckham's Artusi (see entry) helps. It's a place with a mission, too – nourishing its regulars (and irregulars) with a frequently changing menu of simple Italian dishes at kind prices. Trademarks include snacks of Old Winchester and truffle arancini, starters of prawns, chickpeas and rainbow chard, plates of pasta such as tagliatelle with bone marrow and Ibérico tomatoes, and hearty mains along the lines of pork loin with lentils, fennel and spinach. Finish with panna cotta with strawberry compôte. The quality of the ingredients stands out, service is delightful and the Sunday set lunch a particular steal. It's all fuelled by Italian-influenced cocktails and a brief selection of Italian wines, offered by the glass, carafe or bottle from £18.
Chef/s: Jack Beer and Jessica Cinquerrui. **Closed:** 1 week Dec to Jan. **Meals:** main courses £12 to £20. Sun L £20. **Details:** 58 seats. 6 seats outside. Music.

LOCAL GEM
Milk
⊖ Balham, map 3
Modern European | £12
18-20 Bedford Hill, Balham, SW12 9RG
milk.london
£30

In Balham, brunch is a type of cuisine and Milk a leading all-day proponent of it. When the kitchen isn't busy sourcing great eggs, sausages and coffee, it's playing with influences from some of the world's greatest breakfasts. The results, served in simple (and

often busy) whitewashed surrounds, might be the house ricotta on grilled brioche with greengages, honey and cobnuts, or sweetcorn fritters with grilled halloumi, avocado, kasundi (an Asian mustard sauce) and lime. Drinks including horchata and kombucha are, of course, made in-house. Look out for supper evenings with natural wine.

LOCAL GEM
Mr Bao
⊖ Peckham Rye, map 1
Taiwanese | £20
293 Rye Lane, Peckham, SE15 4UA
Tel no: 020 7635 0325
mrbao.co.uk
£30

Picking up on the trend for pillowy Taiwanese bao buns, pint-sized Mr Bao strikes just the right pose as a jaunty neighbourhood drop-in. The paper menu offers half a dozen jokey variations on the theme ('Bao Diddley' features marinated chicken, wasabi mayo, kimchi and coriander) and there are some inviting small plates for sharing (smacked cucumber, sesame spinach etc) – simply tick off your selections and wait, preferably with a plum wine negroni, lychee pale ale or some Taiwanese tea. The original branch (Daddy Bao) is at 113 Mitcham Road, Tooting, SW17 9PE and a third family member (Master Bao) is now open in Westfield, London W12 7GE.

LOCAL GEM
Naughty Piglets
⊖ Brixton, map 1
Modern European | £29
28 Brixton Water Lane, Brixton, SW2 1PE
Tel no: 020 7274 7796
naughtypiglets.co.uk
£30

Naughty by name, nice by nature, this Brixton restaurant and cosy basement bar is everything a neighbourhood joint should be. It's somewhere to relax, somewhere to celebrate, with a modish small plates menu and serious wine list that tries to deliver something different. Try Devon crab, peanut and pickled cabbage, BBQ pork belly and Korean spices or burrata and datterini tomatoes, and see if you can't find a match among the wines from small producers across England, Jura, Georgia and beyond. Sister restaurant, the Other Naughty Piglet, is located at The Other Palace Theatre in Victoria (see entry).

Padella

Cooking score: 2
⊖ London Bridge, map 4
Italian | £20
6 Southwark Street, Borough, SE1 1TQ
padella.co
£30

A Borough favourite, Padella is a rare (and consequently still rather exciting) occupant of the hallowed ground where really decent prices meet really decent food. While even a blow-out bill – antipasti, pasta, pudding and wine on tap – may be reasonable, there is a price: long and almost constant queues for access to modishly plain and distinctly undersized premises. Accept this from the outset, as its many fans do, and a great time awaits. This might begin with the house sourdough, or burrata with new season olive oil and your choice of good-for-you greens, and continue with the pasta made daily by hand on-site. It's all boldly simple. Try neat, silky ricotta ravioli with sage butter, gnocchi with English peas and mint, or taglierini with anchovy butter and pangrattato. 'Outstanding' almond and fruit tarts, perhaps with cherry or rhubarb, have been a mainstay of the pudding section since the beginning, with tap wine from £18 for a carafe of Falanghina.
Chef/s: Ray O'Connor. **Meals:** main courses £4 to £13. **Details:** 75 seats. Wheelchairs. No reservations.

El Pastor

Cooking score: 2
⊖ London Bridge, map 4
Mexican | £25
7a Stoney Street, Borough, SE1 9AA
tacoselpastor.co.uk
£30

It's a simple set-up – a clutch of tables outside; inside, brick-lined curved tin-roofed dining space runs past the bar through various arches to a mezzanine at the back, which is where the chefs work. As in a traditional tapas bar, there's a mix of high stools and standard seating but although El Pastor is part of the Hart Group's mini empire, the focus here shifts from Spain to Mexico and more specifically to tacos. Determine the heat of your salsa (from very mild Mexicana to dialled-up El Diablo) and tuck into tacos filled with chargrilled stone bass and caramelised onions, prawn with garlic, lime, chilli and coriander, or the famed 24-hour-marinated pork shoulder with caramelised pineapple. Dessert offerings include cinnamon-chilli spiced choc pot, guava flan, or hibiscus and lime sorbet, while drinks fly the flag for Mexico, embracing everything from cooling aguas frescas, beers and wines, to tequila-based cocktails and an impressive list of mezcals by the shot, glass or carafe. There's an offshoot, Casa Pastor, at Coal Drops Yard, King's Cross.
Chef/s: Laura Alvarado. **Closed:** 24 to 26 Dec, 1 Jan, Easter Mon. **Meals:** small plates £4 to £9. **Details:** 70 seats. 18 seats outside. Bar. Music. No reservations.

Pique-Nique

Cooking score: 2
⊖ London Bridge, Bermondsey, map 1
French | £35
Tanner Street Park, Bermondsey, SE1 3LD
Tel no: 020 7403 9549
pique-nique.co.uk

'A lovely little place that feels like a hidden gem' is a typical view of this curious, half-timbered pavilion in a corner of Tanner Street Park, next to a playground and tennis court.

Like its older sibling Casse-Croûte around the corner (see entry), it's quintessentially French, and perfect for a relaxed breakfast or lunch (with or without kids). A chalked-up specials board includes dishes for two to share, say chateaubriand, plus the renowned quarter, half or whole rotisserie chicken with roast potatoes, while a printed menu offers vol-au-vent filled with chicken oyster and wild mushrooms, pâté en croûte (aka pork and chicken pie with pistachio) and beef short ribs with Jerusalem artichokes and cabbage. Elsewhere, reports have praised a generous serving of sliced chargrilled tender beef heart with slivers of Parmesan, toasted pine nuts and crisp little gem, flecked with salsa verde. Desserts run from green apple soufflé to chocolate moelleux, and the brief European wine list opens at £24.

Chef/s: Sylvain Soulard. **Closed:** 24 Dec to 2 Jan. **Meals:** main courses £11 to £22. **Details:** 40 seats. 12 seats outside. Wheelchairs. Music.

Le Pont de la Tour

Cooking score: 3
⊖ London Bridge, Tower Hill, map 1
French | £55
36a Shad Thames, Bermondsey, SE1 2YE
Tel no: 020 7403 8403
lepontdelatour.co.uk

With Tower Bridge itself laid out before you, this former tea warehouse on the south bank of the Thames shouts iconic London, for all that its cultural orientation is more obviously the south side of the Channel. From the lavishly glitzy dining room, which evokes the inter-war Paris of the smart set, to the menus themselves, now under the aegis of chef Thomas Piat, the Gallic nostalgic note is strong. There are still modernist touches but the style has become a little more straightforward, as in starters of rabbit terrine and lemon mayonnaise, or Devon crab with apple and celeriac rémoulade. Traditional seafood is still treated with due respect, while main courses tap into regional tradition for cod with ratatouille provençale and stuffed piquillo pepper, or chicken breast with

artichoke barigoule, peas and bacon. For dessert, it could be a traditional tarte tatin, or pistachio-studded rice pudding with cherry sorbet. As befits a restaurant with its own wine merchant, there is a lengthy, formidably classical list that opens with small glasses from £9 and is soon away over the distant horizon.
Chef/s: Thomas Piat. **Meals:** main courses £22 to £48. Set L and early/late D £25 (2 courses) to £30. **Details:** 110 seats. 70 seats outside. Bar. Wheelchairs. Music.

★ TOP 50 ★

Restaurant Story

Cooking score: 8
⊖ London Bridge, map 4
British | £145
199 Tooley Street, Bermondsey, SE1 2JX
Tel no: 020 7183 2117
restaurantstory.co.uk

Tom Sellers' highly conceptualised restaurant is perched on the unlikeliest of London corners, at a junction where buses wait to turn towards Tower Bridge. The kitchen team can lay claim to CVs that reference progressive Scandinavian cuisine and our own Fat Duck, but the vision here is an entirely personal one, as is clued by that slightly gauche name. Every menu tells a story, one that Sellers and his development chef, Tom Phillips, have loaded with moments of suspense, sudden reveals and breathtaking climactic flourishes. Staff are 'exceptionally efficient, working entirely in a clockwise direction,' noted one visitor, and are fluent in explicating dishes that menu specs only teasingly hint at. From the quartet of extraordinary canapés, the tasting menu glides into its polished repertoire. Buttermilk blinis loaded with platinum caviar and golden beetroot are only the start of it. Along the way, there may be stunning textured combinations of lobster, leek and horseradish, or umami-dripping turbot and squid, and even when caviar makes an unexpected second appearance – oscietra to garnish a lobe of veal sweetbread and turnip in white chocolate butter – it adds an extra grace note, rather than simply gilding the lily. Some feel that dishes lose something of their punch through over-complexity, but when they hit the heights, as in the coruscatingly intense lemon sherbet, or the famous almond ice cream with toasted nuts and dill snow, there is no argument. A comprehensive approach to drinking brings on cocktails made with boutique gins, wacky bitters and scented syrups, as well as forward-thinking wines – artisan Champagnes, American aristos and central European interlopers. Wines by the glass, from £8, are excellent.

Chef/s: Tom Sellers and Tom Phillips. **Closed:** Sun, 24 Dec to 3 Jan, 29 to 31 Aug. **Meals:** tasting menu L £100 (8 courses) and D £145 (10 courses). **Details:** 34 seats. V menu. Wheelchairs. Music. Children over 8 yrs.

Salon

Cooking score: 4
⊖ Brixton, map 3
Modern European | £36
18 Market Row, Coldharbour Lane, Brixton, SW9 8LD
Tel no: 020 7501 9152
salonbrixton.co.uk

Originating in a pop-up venture above the cheese shop in Brixton's market precinct, Salon has grown into a full-fledged neighbourhood fixture with a younger sibling, Levan, in Peckham (see entry). Some quality drinking is offered in the ground-floor bar, with inventive cocktails, craft beers and wines to take seriously. Upstairs is all about modern urban gastronomy, with fixed-price menus that are teeming with zestful innovation and arresting flavours. Mussels in cider butter with January king cabbage, or truffled Jerusalem artichoke ravioli with cavolo nero and walnuts might open proceedings with bold assertions, while the main business might be game-rich partridge with potato terrine, butternut squash and hibiscus. The closing note could be a medieval-sounding milk sponge with brown butter mead, or more contemporary blood orange doughnuts. With appetisers such as

'nduja croquettes and aïoli, and some crunchy sourdough crisps with Westcombe Cheddar for the cheese course, there is encouraging attention to detail throughout. Those wines open at £5.50 a glass for Spanish Macabeo and Languedoc Petite Sirah.

Chef/s: Nicholas Balfe. **Closed:** Mon, 22 Dec to 2 Jan. **Meals:** main courses £11 to £18. Tasting menu £36 (4 courses) to £49. **Details:** 40 seats. 12 seats outside. Bar. Music.

LOCAL GEM

Santo Remedio

⊖ London Bridge, map 4
Mexican | £27
152 Tooley Street, Borough, SE1 2TU
Tel no: 020 7403 3021
santoremedio.co.uk

£5 OFF £30

The name translates as 'holy remedy', and anyone in need of a restorative dose of Mexican street food is advised to head to this buzzing, brightly coloured joint. Start with chunky guacamole with (or without) bona fide grasshoppers, before choosing from a formidable line-up of quesadillas, tostadas and tacos – punchy pork belly taco with chicharrón and tomatillo salsa among them. More adventurous options might be octopus tikin xik – a Yucatec Mayan dish marinated in achiote and served with a pineapple pico de gallo sauce. Drink Mexican beers and wines or explore the mezcal and tequila collection at the newly refurbished bar.

Soif

Cooking score: 1
⊖ Clapham South, map 3
Modern European | £35
27 Battersea Rise, Battersea, SW11 1HG
Tel no: 020 7223 1112
soif.co

Un petit coin de la France in deepest Battersea, this bar bistro aims to slake Londoners' thirst for adventurous wines served with good food in snugly proportioned premises furnished with bentwood chairs and blackboard. Fine charcuterie includes finocchiona and coppa, and there are small plates that give the air of being large, bearing taste-laden cargo such as cuttlefish croquetas with allioli, courgettes with ricotta, bottarga and mint, or bresaola with Stilton, hazelnuts and rocket. Fill up with lemon posset and shortbread afterwards. It's the wine collection, though, that amazes and delights, with artisan productions of organic and biodynamic estates, starting with some of France's hidden gems and rolling on confidently across both hemispheres, starting at around £24.

Chef/s: Anthony Hodge. **Meals:** small plates £7 to £11. Large plates £17 to £20. **Details:** 56 seats. Bar. Music.

Sorella

Cooking score: 4
⊖ Clapham Common, Clapham North, map 3
Italian | £35
148 Clapham Manor Street, Clapham, SW4 6BX
Tel no: 020 7720 4662
sorellarestaurant.co.uk

The decor may be unpolished, bordering on basic, but Robin Gill's easy-going neighbourhood Italian is obviously popular, noted for its ferociously seasonal viewpoint and brilliant, engaged and helpful service. The menu bristles with down-to-earth ingredients, and cicchetti such as truffle arancini or carta da musica flatbread with aubergine and pecorino prove good snacking with a glass from the all-Italian wine list. Antipasti of pork and fennel salami, and Jersey milk ricotta with Parmesan, are a good way to start, perhaps ahead of rich, silky pappardelle with veal ragù, while larger plates might bring Suffolk lamb with Jerusalem artichoke or pollock served on the bone with barbecued sprouts. A selection of Neal's Yard Dairy cheeses is worth sharing, although you may want to keep malted barley affogato and vodka milk to yourself. The cocktail list is worth

getting stuck into, and house white and red come by the glass, carafe and bottle (from £28).

Chef/s: Dean Parker. **Closed:** Mon, 22 to 29 Dec, 1 and 2 Jan, Easter Sun. **Meals:** main courses £14 to £28. Tasting menu £45 (5 courses). Sun L £27 (4 courses). **Details:** 55 seats. V menu. Bar. Wheelchairs. Music.

Sparrow

Cooking score: 2
⊖ Lewisham, map 1
International | £28
2 Rennell Street, Lewisham, SE13 7HD
Tel no: 020 8318 6941
sparrowlondon.co.uk

£5 OFF £30 ▼

Perched on a busy thoroughfare a short hop from Lewisham station, this venture comes from alumni of St John and Pollen St Social, Terry Blake and Yohini Nandakumar. Inside, it's modishly minimal – tall windows, dark floor boards, pendant light shades – with a convivial atmosphere buoyed by loyal regulars. Based around sharing dishes, the menu takes a magpie approach to culinary styles – expect Mediterranean airs in fresh baked focaccia and burrata with romano peppers and vincotto, while Asian accents come in the form of massaman beef cheek curry with bone marrow and steamed rice, or crispy char siu pork belly. Desserts see flavours from closer to home: a granita of East London Gin and tonic, say, or steamed date pudding with toffee sauce and clotted cream. Craft beers, wines by the glass and a cocktail of the day provide liquid enjoyment, and brunch menus appeal to the weekend crowds.

Chef/s: Terry Blake. **Closed:** Mon, 22 Dec to 7 Jan. **Meals:** small plates £9 to £17. **Details:** 38 seats. Wheelchairs. Music.

Trinity

Cooking score: 7

⊖ Clapham Common, map 3

Modern European | £70

4 The Polygon, Clapham, SW4 0JG

Tel no: 020 7622 1199

trinityrestaurant.co.uk

🍶🟊

It's a measure of the touchstone significance of Adam Byatt's achievement that other London chefs are frequently to be found at his tables. Polished parquet and pressed white linen, together with deep-piled chairs that are the last word in classy comfort, create an upmarket atmosphere at this destination venue near Clapham Common. From distinguished nibbles that punch well above their weight to superb focaccia, peripherals are all of a high order, even before you set about the standard four-course menu. The signature starter is a soused and blowtorched Cornish mackerel in a white gazpacho not dissimilar to Spanish ajo blanco, garnished with slivered red grape and tarragon oil. Next up might be a trio of new season asparagus, lightly blanched and peppered, its polonaise crumb dressing formed into a quenelle, the accompanying beurre blanc flavoured with smoked eel. Meats are superlative, as in the Lakeland beef sirloin roasted on the bone and served ingeniously with new potato scooped out and filled with Vacherin, wrapped in shallot petals and strewn with garlic flowers, all unified by a textbook sauce bordelaise. To finish, look to the chocolate 'tart', which resembles 'the world's most geometrically perfect brownie', at its centre an oozing hazelnut praline filling. The wine list equals these masterful productions, representing the best in contemporary oenology. As our inspector put it, 'while you won't find a bottle below £26, what you will find is perhaps the best selection in London at £40 to £100.'

Chef/s: Adam Byatt. **Closed:** 23 to 27 Dec, 1 to 3 Jan. **Meals:** set L £30 (2 courses) to £50. Set D £60 to £70 (4 courses). **Details:** 48 seats. 20 seats outside. V menu. Wheelchairs. No children at D.

The White Onion

Cooking score: 3

⊖ Wimbledon, map 3

Modern French | £42

67 High Street, Wimbledon Village, Wimbledon, SW19 5EE

Tel no: 020 8947 8278

thewhiteonion.co.uk

Obviously you'll need to book well ahead for a table during Wimbledon fortnight, but this good-natured neighbourhood bistro is capable of serving up culinary aces right through the year. Done out in smart-casual style with lots of prints and artworks emblazoned on deep blue walls, it provides an agreeable setting for capably executed French cooking with eclectic overtones – as in a mushroom and miso velouté with Roscoff onions or wild halibut partnered by olive oil mash, seaweed and caper chutney, monk's beard and matelote sauce. The kitchen is also tuned in to the calendar, perhaps creating a vol-au-vent of winter vegetables with chestnuts and truffle mornay or matching braised ox cheek with celeriac purée and glazed turnips when the season allows. Desserts are in similar vein, from sablé breton to gingerbread Paris-Brest with pear sorbet and a spiced pear crust. The wide-ranging wine list includes plenty of classic names alongside more 'off the beaten track' tipples.

Chef/s: Frédéric Duval. **Closed:** Mon, 22 Dec to 9 Jan. **Meals:** main courses £15 to £28. Set L £20 (2 courses) to £24. Sun L £22 (2 courses) to £26. **Details:** 64 seats. Wheelchairs. Music.

Wright Brothers Battersea

Cooking score: 2

⊖ Battersea Park, map 3

Seafood | £40

26 Circus West Village, Battersea, SW8 4NN

Tel no: 020 7324 7734

thewrightbrothers.co.uk

This bright seafood restaurant – part of a successful mini-chain – within the new foodie hub by Battersea Power Station has river views and alfresco seating. Inside, top

ingredients such as octopus, English asparagus and Brixham turbot are given the Josper-oven treatment to good effect. For main entry, see Borough branch, south London.
Chef/s: Gjergj Krrashi. **Closed:** 25 and 26 Dec, 1 Jan. **Meals:** main courses £18 to £37. **Details:** 120 seats. 40 seats outside. Bar. Wheelchairs. Music.

Wright Brothers Borough Market

Cooking score: 2
⊖ London Bridge, map 4
Seafood | £40
11 Stoney Street, Borough, SE1 9AD
Tel no: 020 7403 9554
thewrightbrothers.co.uk

The first and, for many, the pick of Ben Wright and Robin Hancock's seafood group may feel hard-edged and cramped but scores with superb sourcing, honesty of cooking and really exceptional service. Very fresh fish is the thing, of course, trucked up from the South West daily. So whether you perch at the bar or squeeze around close-set tables, you can look forward to plates of oysters, baked Devon crab with toasted sourdough or crispy squid with spicy sriracha mayonnaise. When it comes to mains, the kitchen displays an enviable grasp of technique and a sensitive approach to flavours, as in a perfectly timed grilled gurnard fillet with horseradish, beetroot and cranberries or a bravura dish of hake fillet teamed with celeriac purée and green harissa. Pudding could be chocolate and caramel mousse, although you might prefer a plate of Neal's Yard Dairy cheeses. Wines start at £23, cocktails are good and there's a commendable list of London-brewed beers.
Chef/s: Rob Malyon. **Closed:** 25 and 26 Dec, 1 Jan. **Meals:** main courses £9 to £40. **Details:** 70 seats. 5 seats outside.

Walk right in

To queue or not to queue? That's the question facing diners at restaurants where no-bookings policies ask them to wait patiently in line, from **Riley's Fish Shack** in Tynemouth to **Padella** in London's Borough Market and the growing **Dishoom** chain. While the presence of a large crowd outside creates a buzz for these establishments, it can alienate and inconvenience diners. If time is on your side, you may be willing to wait your turn but if the meter is running for the babysitter, or you've got theatre tickets, you'll want to make sure your table is secured before you head out.

Soho favourite **Pastaio** operates a virtual queueing system so you don't have to stand outside in all weathers. Need to make curtain-up? The West End branch of London chophouse chain **Blacklock** allows bookings until 6pm and **The Barbary** takes them at its counter for 5pm sharp.

The tide could finally be turning, though, as a number of 'no bookings' places change their policies. Hip bistro **10 Greek Street** in Soho now takes reservations at lunch and dinner while holding back several tables for walk-ins. **Bao** in Soho was famous for its queues but its second outpost in Fitzrovia accepts online bookings. Perhaps the wait is over.

108 Garage

Cooking score: 4
⊖ Westbourne Park, map 1
Modern European | £45
108 Golborne Road, Notting Hill, W10 5PS
Tel no: 020 8969 3769
108garage.com

This compact, stripped-back restaurant may look stark but the contemporary cooking is bold and complex, full of surprising flavours. As with anything that tries hard to be different, dishes might not always work, but when they do, they do so with gusto. Dining here is great fun, especially if you grab one of the six kitchen-counter stools and chat to the chefs as they work. A test meal opened with chicken parfait served with a spoonful of Belazu grape mustard, and went on to beautifully cooked Cotswold hen – the breast crisp-skinned – served with blowtorched little gem, sorrel, wild garlic and a slice of lardo. In a very pretty dish of Thai monkfish with octopus, Tropea onion and white beans, thinly sliced raw beans added an enjoyable contrast. Desserts are a highlight, particularly a Jerusalem artichoke ice cream topped with toasted white chocolate. Drink cocktails, or wines from £28.
Chef/s: Chris Denney. **Closed:** Mon, Sun, 22 Dec to 2 Jan, 28 Aug to 3 Sept. **Meals:** main courses £8 to £24. Set L £35 (6 courses). Set D £60 (6 courses). **Details:** 45 seats. 6 seats outside. Bar. Wheelchairs. Music.

★ NEW ENTRY ★

No. Fifty Cheyne

Cooking score: 4
⊖ Sloane Square, map 3
Modern British | £55
50 Cheyne Walk, Chelsea, SW3 5LR
Tel no: 020 7376 8787
fiftycheyne.com

Although relatively new on the scene, this busy, well-groomed restaurant has the confidence and charm of a place that's been around forever. Start with cocktails in the first-floor bar or the rather lovely drawing room, before heading back down to the very comfortable, deceptively large dining room. The kitchen uses top-notch ingredients to produce interesting takes on classics and there's a grill menu if you want to keep things simple. At inspection, beef carpaccio, dressed with asparagus, pickled hazelnuts and Berkswell cheese, was beautifully presented, delicate and flavourful, while scallop, served in a bath of asparagus sauce, was given sweet saltiness by bacon jam. Fillet of hake in the lightest white wine sauce came topped with summery broad beans and peas. To finish, caramelised puff pastry with strawberries and cream was a twist on a millefeuille, rounded off with strawberry sorbet. There's an impressive selection of bottles on the far-reaching wine list, but the range by the glass and carafe is good too.
Chef/s: Iain Smith. **Meals:** main courses £22 to £33. Set L £29 Mon to Fri (2 courses) to £35. **Details:** 70 seats. Bar.

★ NEW ENTRY ★

Adam Handling Chelsea

Cooking score: 4
⊖ Sloane Square, map 3
British | £78
75 Sloane Street, Chelsea, SW1X 9SG
Tel no: 020 8089 7070
adamhandlingchelsea.co.uk

Now part of the deluxe group of hotels owned by LVMH, the completely renovated Cadogan reopened in February 2019 with Adam Handling (a 2013 finalist in *MasterChef: The Professionals*) overseeing culinary operations. With understated grey wood panelling, herringbone flooring, bare wooden tables and an open-view kitchen, there's an informal feel to the two dining rooms divided by a marble fireplace. Handling showcases prime British produce while aiming to minimise food waste. A signature snack of cheese and truffle doughnuts is not to be missed, and the kitchen teases contemporary tastes from a perfectly timed halibut teamed with pickled kohlrabi, brown shrimps and sea herbs, finished with a lobster bisque and caviar. Classical dishes worked better than more modern ones, in particular a large lobe of excellent veal sweetbread, perfectly matched by the freshest of peas, morels and wild garlic. As a finale, a palate-cleansing pre-dessert of yoghurt ice cream with mango foam and a sprig of fresh coriander impressed more than the main event – an overly sweet white chocolate ganache with compressed cucumber, burnt basil and dill meringue. Service provides just the right amount of attention, and wines (from £35) are a sound international selection.

Chef/s: Adam Handling. **Meals:** main courses £32 to £42. Set L £37 (2 courses) to £45. Tasting menu £65 (5 courses) to £95. **Details:** 44 seats. 14 seats outside. V menu. Bar. Wheelchairs. Music.

Albertine

Cooking score: 1
⊖ Shepherd's Bush Market, Shepherd's Bush, map 1
Modern British | £30
1 Wood Lane, Shepherd's Bush, W12 7DP
Tel no: 020 8743 9593
albertine.london

🍾 £30

It takes a lot to emerge from the hulking shadow of Westfield shopping centre opposite, but Allegra McEvedy's distinctively domestic-feeling venue manages it. Dining goes on upstairs under big purple light shades with library shelves for company, and the bill of fare extends from a bar menu of halloumi fries, houmous and flatbread, whipped chilli lardo on toast and the like to main dishes such as bream fillet with new potatoes in sauce vierge and Ibérico pork presa with chips and chimichurri. Desserts keep things light with mirabelle plum and Prosecco sorbet or rhubarb tiramisu. The wine list is a gasp-inducing roll call of the contemporary global scene, led by grape varieties, and with naturals and biodynamics in profusion. Bottles open at £25, but it's worth being adventurous with a list of this rarity.

Chef/s: Benjamin Bocquet. **Closed:** Sun, 23 Dec to 4 Jan, last week Aug. **Meals:** small plates £4 to £17. **Details:** 60 seats. Bar. Music.

Amaya

Cooking score: 4
⊖ Knightsbridge, map 6
Indian | £60
15 Halkin Arcade, Motcomb Street, Belgravia, SW1X 8JT
Tel no: 020 7823 1166
amaya.biz

Amid the capital's booming Indian food scene, with openings across the spectrum, from high-end to street-food operations, those that laid the foundations keep quietly going about their business. One of a triumvirate of upscale restaurants that includes Veeraswamy and Chutney Mary (see entries), Amaya is cloistered in Belgravia's Halkin Arcade, where plush upholstery, low lighting and opulent decor suit the well-heeled clientele. At its heart is an open kitchen, a dramatic stage for grill- and fire-focused cooking. Kick off with small plates (there are larger versions for sharing) – sea bream grilled on banana leaf, or fiery black pepper chicken tikka – then move on to majestic curries, biryanis and a compelling roster of imaginative vegetarian dishes, perhaps beetroot kasundi kebab, before dessert of blackberry and toffee kulfi. The good-value lunchtime set menu comprises six small plates. Spice-friendly global wines include plenty for those with deeper pockets, and a fair few by the glass.

Chef/s: Sanchit Kapoor. **Meals:** main courses £16 to £43. Set L £26. Tasting menu £55 (7 courses) to £85. **Details:** 98 seats. V menu. Bar. Music. No children after 8pm.

LOCAL GEM

L'Amorosa

⊖ Ravenscourt Park, Stamford Brook, map 1
Italian | £35
278 King Street, Hammersmith, W6 0SP
Tel no: 020 8563 0300
lamorosa.co.uk

£5 OFF

Andy Needham went from Z to A on leaving his role as head chef at Zafferano to open his own place, L'Amorosa. He's created the kind of neighbourhood joint everyone covets, where excellent ingredients are handled with respect. Whether it's burrata with caponata or sea trout carpaccio with iced fennel and mint, full-on flavours abound. Pasta is handmade every day (agnolotti with braised and cured pig's cheeks), and desserts include dark chocolate fondant. A carafe of Sicilian house red or white sets you back £18.

Bombay Brasserie
Cooking score: 2
⊖ Gloucester Road, map 3
Indian | £51
Courtfield Road, South Kensington, SW7 4QH
Tel no: 020 7370 4040
bombayb.co.uk

Slow-whirring fans in the bar, huge chandeliers in the formal dining room and leafy greenery in the conservatory lend grand atmospherics, and the cooking is old-school too. Homely staples score over complex masalas – a rough-textured chana dhal, seasoned with fried garlic and nutty cumin, for example, or a dish of Punjabi fried cauliflower florets, which satisfies with its cloak of russet-hued onion and ginger masala and scattering of peas. Another highlight on our visit was skewered monkfish morsels steeped in a perky blend of pounded coriander, ginger, spring onions, lime leaves and green chillies, and grilled to perfect tenderness. Sadly, a lacklustre biryani let the side down with overcooked chicken and a shortfall of aromatic spicing. However, with its upmarket feel, a bar that offers a creative selection of Indian-themed cocktails, and friendly, helpful service, the venue remains popular with corporate business groups and international tourists with deep pockets.
Chef/s: Prahlad Hegde. **Closed:** 25 Dec.
Meals: main courses £19 to £29. Set L £27 Mon to Fri. Set D £51. Tasting menus £58 to £64. **Details:** 85 seats. 10 seats outside. Bar. Wheelchairs. Music.

Cambio de Tercio
Cooking score: 5
⊖ Gloucester Road, map 3
Spanish | £50
163 Old Brompton Road, Earl's Court, SW5 0LJ
Tel no: 020 7244 8970
cambiodetercio.co.uk
£5 OFF 🍾

This long-running Spanish venue rejoices in an exuberant informality, its linened tables packed into a room done vividly in the national colours of red and yellow. Tapas here double as starters before a substantial main course, for those not content to nibble ad lib. Amid the ham croquetas and pan tumaca, innovative things pop up: Galician octopus with potato and cauliflower purée spiced with sweet paprika, Andalusian-style sea bass with kimchi and lime mayonnaise, and Ibérico pork with roasted pineapple and chard. When it comes to main dishes, make way for oxtail caramelised in red wine with Colombian tamarillo, or halibut cooked on the plancha with grilled lettuce and a salad of wild garlic and watercress. The vigorous seasonings and unabashed heftiness of it all will leave you feeling replete, although not so as to avoid a finishing flourish of white chocolate ganache with ginger ice cream, pistachios and passion fruit. A viticultural map on the first page of the wine list offers a simplified version of the regions, but the choices that follow, from £26, are compiled with an aficionado's eye for detail and quality, opening with a brigade of sherries.
Chef/s: Alberto Criado. **Closed:** 22 Dec to 2 Jan.
Meals: main courses £25 to £33. Tapas £4 to £28.
Details: 65 seats. 12 seats outside. V menu. Music.

★ NEW ENTRY ★

Caractère

Cooking score: 5
⊖ Westbourne Park, map 6
Modern European | £55
209 Westbourne Park Road, Notting Hill, W11 1EA
Tel no: 020 8181 3850
caractererestaurant.com

With its dim lighting and unclothed tables of wood and marble, this place may seem understated but look closer at the beautiful modern crockery and comfortable banquettes and it's clear a lot of thought – and, no doubt, money – has gone into the fit-out. This is the debut restaurant from husband-and-wife team Emily Roux and Diego Ferrari. The daughter of Michel Roux Jr oversees front of house, while ex-Le Gavroche (see entry) head chef Ferrari runs the kitchen. The shortish French-Italian menu whimsically divides the dishes by their characteristics. In the Curious and Subtle sections (aka starters) you'll find a clever modern version of chicken with morels and vin jaune – skilfully made with a wealth of classical French technique behind it – alongside an Acquerello saffron risotto, which counters with the brilliance of simple Italian cooking. Crossover dishes work less well, as when a main of veal shin ravioli with gremolata and slow-cooked onions is enriched beyond comfort by a deeply reduced, over-grand French veal jus. However, chocolate cake with mascarpone ice cream and salted caramel sauce sets a new standard for 'best chocolate dessert ever'. The wine list is full of treats from France and Italy, but a little thin at entry level.
Chef/s: Diego Ferrari. **Closed:** Sun, first week Sept, 25 and 26 Dec, 29 to 31 Aug. **Meals:** main courses £22 to £32. Set L £39 Tue to Thur. Tasting menu £78 (6 courses). **Details:** 62 seats. Wheelchairs. Music.

Charlotte's Bistro

Cooking score: 3
⊖ Turnham Green, map 1
Modern British | £35
6 Turnham Green Terrace, Chiswick, W4 1QP
Tel no: 020 8742 3590
charlottes.co.uk

This useful neighbourhood restaurant is popular with locals either taking advantage of the well-priced set menu or looking for a step above a pub in the evening. The front is dominated by a huge bar, particularly well stocked with gin and small-batch spirits; for the restaurant proper, head up a short flight of stairs to a comfortable, modern room full of natural light. Expect a menu that covers all the bistro bases – steak and salad, soup and risotto – with a peppering of more exotic dishes, say octopus carpaccio with tarragon mayonnaise or slow-cooked lamb shoulder with baked aubergine. A Caesar salad comes well dressed with a good balance of sweet, salt, soft and crunch; a nicely pan-fried fillet of sea bass on its bed of soft polenta is given colour by tomato confit. If portions seem a little small, remember that the set dinner price is low. A European-leaning wine list starts at £21.50.
Chef/s: Lee Cadden. **Meals:** set L £17 (2 courses) to £20. Set D £29 (2 courses) to £35. Early D £30. Sun L £30. **Details:** 80 seats. Bar. Music. Cards only.

Clarke's

Cooking score: 4
⊖ Notting Hill Gate, map 6
Modern European | £55
124 Kensington Church Street, Notting Hill, W8 4BH
Tel no: 020 7221 9225
sallyclarke.com

For more than a quarter of a century, Sally Clarke has been nourishing loyal regulars with her meticulous season-led cooking. Breaking bread over pristine linen in the serene dining room – goods from Clarke's celebrated artisan bakery are ever-present – marks a prelude to a daily changing cast of beautiful, considered dishes. Over the years the chef has pivoted away from the Californian cuisine that so inspired her, and now delivers a menu with an equally sunny, Mediterranean feel. Purple Sardinian artichokes with Parmesan, pea leaves, lemon and organic Luberon olive oil or hand-rolled tagliolini could lead the way, followed by roasted Cornish brill with a sprightly black olive tapenade, Florence fennel, cime di rapa and riso nero. Indulge in warm almond shortcake with baked apples, prunes and cinnamon cream to finish. Only prestige ingredients will do, so expect prices to match. Excellent Californian wines and a compelling Old World cohort mark out a thoughtful list.

Chef/s: Sally Clarke and Michele Lombardi. **Meals:** main courses £29 to £36. Set L £28 (2 courses) to £34. Set D £39. **Details:** 90 seats. Wheelchairs.

★ TOP 10 ★

Claude Bosi at Bibendum

Cooking score: 9
⊖ South Kensington, map 3
Modern French | £115
Michelin House, 81 Fulham Road, South Kensington, SW3 6RD
Tel no: 020 7581 5817
bibendum.co.uk

The rather grandiose Art Deco building was commissioned by the Michelin Tyre Company as their first permanent British headquarters in 1909 and now provides an apposite setting for some modern French cooking. The first-floor dining room is an awesome statement of light and space, with those famous stained-glass windows and well-spaced, white-clothed tables speaking of comfort and money. Claude Bosi has always forged his reputation where it matters – on the plate – and once again his cooking has taken a deep breath and marched steadily forward. The results, seen in a short à la carte and tasting menu, allow the chef to compete at the top level. Tremendous intensity is conjured from simple ingredients and classic technique, as in a clever three-layered opening dish featuring a

base of creamy brown crabmeat under a generous portion of perfectly picked white meat and topped with a limpid jelly singing with the flavours of gazpacho. A fondness for unusual combinations sees veal sweetbreads wrapped in hay, baked in coffee beans (displayed theatrically halfway through the cooking process) and served with macadamia nut purée, a pickled walnut for acidity and a rich, nutty veal sauce. And then there are the signatures: 'nosotto' is a splendid riff on risotto, made with finely diced Mona Lisa potato (still with plenty of bite) with umami heft from 24-month-old Comté cheese and Lancashire mead and textural contrast from chicken oysters, and as a perfect finale a boozy Black Forest soufflé served with a sweet-sour griottine ice cream. Front of house chats amiably, dismantling the formalities while staying vigilant. Magnificent vintages and rare bottles appear on a wine list that traverses the world and, thanks to the Coravin system, includes some fine vintages by the glass; make the most of the sommelier's impressive knowledge to choose the right drop.

Chef/s: Claude Bosi and Francesco Dibenedetto. **Closed:** Mon, Tue, 23 to 26 Dec, 1 to 7 Jan, 14 to 22 Apr. **Meals:** main courses L £34 to £52. Set L £65. Set D £115. Tasting menu £125 (6 courses) to £185. **Details:** 50 seats. V menu. Bar. Wheelchairs. Music.

★ TOP 10 ★

Core by Clare Smyth

Cooking score: 10
⊖ Notting Hill Gate, map 6
Modern British | £90
92 Kensington Park Road, Notting Hill, W11 2PN
Tel no: 020 3937 5086
corebyclaresmyth.com

That a restaurant of such brilliance should exist in a place other than our imaginations is remarkable. Clare Smyth takes unruffled perfection, choreographed precision and faultless pedigree to hitherto unexplored levels, leaving one diner 'gasping in wonder' at a meal that was 'impossible to overpraise'. In the beginning is a collection of amuse-bouches on pieces of mossy wood: expect fluffy gougères to burst with pea and mint in early summer, or Périgord truffle in winter; a smoked eel tartlet to be ethereally fragile; and for the whole fairy garden to be enveloped in wisping beer-honey-thyme smoke when a cloche covering nuggets of chicken wings is lifted. It's enchanting. Exquisite, too, is a girolle and toasted buckwheat tart, flirty with wild garlic flowers and the slenderest of mushroom slices, its accompanying velouté robustly umami-rich. The charlotte potato and roe dish has fast become a signature, but where ordinary people might boil or steam a spud, Smyth slow-cooks it in butter and seaweed before serving with a dulse beurre blanc of head-spinning butteriness, cutting the richness with salty pops of herring and trout roe, and slivers of fermented potato crisp. A dish of lamb, hogget and mutton celebrates all ages of the animal with tender respect, the same care being afforded a stunning piece of roast monkfish with brown butter, Swiss chard and Morecambe Bay shrimps. The 'Core apple' pre-dessert – cubes of caramelised apple surrounded by a vanishingly light mousse, the whole coated in an apple jelly – is no less delicious for having been so often Instagrammed, ditto the 'Core-teser', a triumphant concoction of chocolate, hazelnut, malt and flighty chocolate feathers. The meal comes full circle when the logs return, this time dotted with crystal-clear jellies that dissolve into mouthfuls of Banyuls and Sauternes, and a tiny tart, baked moments previously, that runs with liquid chocolate. The wine list takes off from £37 on a tour of France's domaines, with brisker selections elsewhere and while you can easily sink four figures on a bottle, you can also drink by the small glass from £8. Advice is delivered with the impeccable grace and knowledge that you would expect in a restaurant of such world-class calibre.

Chef/s: Clare Smyth and Jonny Bone. **Closed:** Mon, Sun, 24 to 26 Dec, 1 Jan. **Meals:** set L £70. Set D £90. Tasting menu £125 (7 courses) to £145. **Details:** 54 seats. V menu. Vg menu. Bar. Wheelchairs. Music. No children.

Dinner by Heston Blumenthal

Cooking score: 7

⊖ Knightsbridge, map 6

British | £85

Mandarin Oriental Hyde Park, 66 Knightsbridge, Knightsbridge, SW1X 7LA

Tel no: 020 7201 3833

dinnerbyheston.com

🛏

An evening meal looking out over Hyde Park and watching the lights come on as darkness falls is a magical experience. Heston Blumenthal has most things right at this generously proportioned restaurant in the Mandarin Oriental, yet customers must have deep pockets – one certainty is that the final bill will be high. Blumenthal's homage to British culinary history, as interpreted by his executive chef Ashley Palmer-Watts, is lavish with punctiliously cared-for ingredients, with each dish outfitted sparingly, although these days the menu seems to promise a little more than it delivers. But many dishes are well liked, among them a satisfying pairing of chicken and asparagus (c1660), enlivened with morels, peas, dabs of lemon gel and sorrel purée, plus a little pot of deliciously rich gravy left at table. Or a starter of buttered crab loaf (c1710) given punch with pickled cucumber and pickled lemon, a lovely amalgamation of sweet and tart, soft and crunch. As for dessert, tipsy cake (c1810) is a certified hit, but there's admiration, too, for sambocade (c1390), a goat's milk cheesecake served with elderflower and apple, pickled blackberry and smoked candied walnuts. Service (lots of it) may be grand hotel but fails to create a sense of occasion. The wine list is worth taking time over, if only to read the historical notes.

Chef/s: Ashley Palmer-Watts and Jonny Glass. **Meals:** main courses £39 to £52. Set L £45. Tasting menu £95 (5 courses). **Details:** 149 seats. Bar. Wheelchairs. Parking. Children over 4 yrs.

Dishoom

Cooking score: 2
⊖ High Street Kensington, map 6
Indian | £30
4 Derry Street, Kensington, W8 5SE
Tel no: 020 7420 9325
dishoom.com
£30

Perhaps the most glamorous of the seven Dishooms, this Kensington branch suits the Art Deco surrounds of the former Barkers department store. Don't miss the mutton pepper fry, a spicy house special served with paratha. For main entry, see Shoreditch branch, east London.
Chef/s: Naved Nasir. **Closed:** 25 and 26 Dec, 1 and 2 Jan. **Meals:** main courses £9 to £18. **Details:** 98 seats. 25 seats outside. V menu. Bar. Wheelchairs. Music. Bookings after 5.45pm for groups of 6 or more.

Elystan Street

Cooking score: 6
⊖ South Kensington, Sloane Square, map 3
Modern British | £70
43 Elystan Street, Chelsea, SW3 3NT
Tel no: 020 7628 5005
elystanstreet.com

For a masterclass in ingredient-led cooking, look no further than Phil Howard and Rebecca Mascarenhas' light, elegant restaurant, which has settled in well to its Chelsea home three years since opening. Howard's glossy pedigree combined with Mascarenhas' experience as a restaurateur mean that nothing jars. Dishes are ingeniously composed to bring out the best in prime, seasonal ingredients, and the kitchen has the confidence to leave well alone once the components are in striking harmony. Thus a light potato cake comes with warm buttered crabmeat, mild curry, spring onion and apple, while Jerusalem artichoke vinaigrette and truffled hazelnut pesto enhance a breast of chicken; and baked fennel, blood orange, butter bean, chilli and olive oil partner

chargrilled octopus and squid. Sensational desserts might include pear tarte tatin with peppered vanilla and bay leaf ice cream. Lunch is good value, and on the authoritative wine list there is a noticeable attempt to keep prices relatively restrained for the area.
Chef/s: Phil Howard and Toby Burrowes. **Closed:** 25 and 26 Dec, 1 Jan. **Meals:** main courses £24 to £42. Set L £35 (2 courses) to £43. Sun L £50. **Details:** 64 seats. Wheelchairs.

★ NEW ENTRY ★

Endo at The Rotunda

Cooking score: 6
⊖ Wood Lane, map 1
Japanese | £150
8th Floor, The Helios, Television Centre, 101 Wood Lane, Shepherd's Bush, W12 7FR
Tel no: 020 3972 9000
endoatrotunda.com

On the eighth floor of a cylindrical building in the recently transformed former BBC Television Centre, this 16-seater restaurant is the brainchild of ex-Zuma sushi chef, Endo Kazutoshi. With a centrepiece 200-year-old hinoki wood counter, views over west London and an eye-popping cloud-like light installation, it's a space that takes Japanese aesthetics to another level. Counter-style dining – known as kappo – enables interaction between chef and diner. The only options at dinner are a 15- or 18-course omakase menu with prices to match, although plans are afoot to introduce a cheaper six-courser at lunch. Raw ingredients are impeccable, especially fish, changing daily depending on availability. The profusion of intricate dishes is a triumph of flavours and textures, from sublime sushi to hotpot-cooked yellowtail and juniper-smoked clam given vibrancy by a dribble of kinome (Japanese herb) butter. Unusual pairings inject personality – perhaps spider crab with truffle and slow-cooked egg yolk in a dashi stock – while sushi rice soufflé with brown sugar is surprisingly good. Capping it all off is Endo-san, a most engaging host. Is it worth it? Given the quality of the ingredients, fantastic sushi and sense of theatre, it's a resounding yes. Drink interesting cocktails or big-name wines from a short international list from £35.

Chef/s: Endo Kazutoshi. **Closed:** Mon, Sun. **Meals:** tasting menu £150 (15 courses) to £180. **Details:** 16 seats. Pre-payment required.

Enoteca Turi

Cooking score: 4
⊖ Sloane Square, map 3
Italian | £55
87 Pimlico Road, Chelsea, SW1W 8PH
Tel no: 020 7730 3663
enotecaturi.com

£5 OFF 🍷

An inspired mix of decorative touches adds elegant wine shelves and outline maps of the Italian regions to a background of spare, lemon-painted brick at Giuseppe Turi's family-run Italian. The kitchen is under the vigilant eye of Massimo Tagliaferri, who cooks with verve and flair, each dish given its regional attribution on the menu. Sicilian stuffed sardines filled with pecorino served with Swiss chard, pine nuts and raisins, is a whirlwind of an antipasto, presaging dramatic things to come, perhaps sea bass with clams and fennel Parmigiana (Campania) or veal cutlet with casseroled beans and cavolo nero purée (Toscana). Pasta is exemplary too, as when orecchiette and cime di rapa are bombed with anchovy, garlic and chilli under a breadcrumb gratin (Puglia). Rum baba with strawberry and rhubarb compôte and ginger panna cotta inveigles its way among the more familiar dessert options of tiramisu, affogato and gelati. From its opening clutch of Franciacorta sparklers to the crown jewels of Recioto and Vin Santo, the wine list is a stunner, a justly defiant demonstration of the breadth and depth of modern Italian winemaking. Assuming you're not going straight for the old Barolo, prices can be manageable, starting at £23.50.

Chef/s: Massimo Tagliaferri. **Closed:** Sun, 25 and 26 Dec, 1 Jan. **Meals:** main courses £15 to £35. Set L £25 (2 courses) to £29. **Details:** 75 seats. 8 seats outside. Music.

The Five Fields

Cooking score: 6
⊖ Sloane Square, map 3
Modern British | £80
8-9 Blacklands Terrace, Chelsea, SW3 2SP
Tel no: 020 7838 1082
fivefieldsrestaurant.com

£5 OFF 🍷

Discreet premises in a tranquil Chelsea byway lend The Five Fields the thrilling feel of an undiscovered hideaway, although the dining room itself is got up in the elegant livery of a grand hotel restaurant in miniature. Well-upholstered chairs at double-linened tables attended by smartly attired staff look the part, and Taylor Bonnyman has undoubtedly stamped his own personality on the whole operation. His culinary style is vigorous and imaginative, with plates that can look like quite an intricate pile-up of heterogeneous elements, but that are strongly convincing in the eating. Moving to a gentle seasonal rhythm, menus might open in late winter with a curried rhubarb and onion treatment for sea bass, before gliding on to distinctly Nordic roe deer with white roots, sour cream and rye, or perhaps John Dory in an earthy setting of artichokes, mushrooms and leeks. The eight-course taster is a compendious tour of the territory, closing with the obligatory brace of desserts, the second possibly a densely rich chocolate creation with coffee and whisky accompaniments. The wine list has been compiled to hold its own in SW3, teeming with French aristos and Balkan parvenus, the Napa and Barossa gangs, and some distinctly clubbable fizz. Small glasses start at £7.

Chef/s: Taylor Bonnyman. **Closed:** Mon, Sun, 3 weeks Dec to Jan, first 2 weeks Aug. **Meals:** set L £55 (2 courses) to £65. Set D £70 (2 courses) to £80. Tasting menu £75 (6 courses) to £90. **Details:** 40 seats. V menu. Bar. Wheelchairs. Music. Children over 12 years.

Symbols

🛏 Accommodation is available
£30 Three courses for £30 or less
£5 £5 off voucher scheme
🍷 Notable wine list

The Goring Dining Room

Cooking score: 5
⊖ Victoria, map 3
Modern British | £64
15 Beeston Place, Belgravia, SW1W 0JW
Tel no: 020 7769 4475
thegoring.com

🛏

With interiors fitted out by David Linley's design company, The Dining Room is a worthy flagship for this family-run hotel (and much-publicised royal bolthole). Following executive chef Shay Cooper's departure, his long-serving head chef Richard Galli has stepped into the top job, although the food is still an enlightened marriage of reassuring British tradition and striking contemporary innovation – all underpinned by seasonal and regional ingredients. Eggs Drumkilbo, grilled Dover sole, beef wellington and a luxed-up Black Forest gâteau satisfy the old guard, while other dishes cater to more inquisitive palates – Cornish mackerel with horseradish, pickled radish and watercress soup, perhaps, or Cotswold duck partnered by poached rhubarb, Tokyo turnips, winter greens and lime. A glazed lobster omelette with duck-fat chips and lobster Caesar salad should satisfy both camps, likewise a dessert of macerated strawberries with Champagne granita and strawberry sorbet. Lunchtime roasts and British cheeses arrive on perambulating trolleys, while the expansive (and expensive) wine list is everything you might expect from such a regally minded establishment; house selections start at £36
Chef/s: Richard Galli. **Meals:** set L £52. Set D £64. Sun L £58. **Details:** 70 seats. V menu. Vg menu. Bar. Wheelchairs.

Harwood Arms

Cooking score: 5
⊖ Fulham Broadway, map 3
British | £50
Walham Grove, Fulham, SW6 1QP
Tel no: 020 7386 1847
harwoodarms.com

🍷

'Intelligent sourcing, highly skilled cooking, creative and flavourful combinations.' Many readers feel this large corner pub on a residential street is rarely bettered in London. The talent of owners Brett Graham of The Ledbury (see entry) and Mike Robinson is for giving people what they want – a relaxed neighbourhood hostelry with deeply satisfying cooking. The team has got it right from the start with positive, approachable service and a keen eye on seasonality. Sally Abé heads the kitchen and her menus are full of well-judged combinations and bold flavours. Crispy lamb sweetbreads with Wiltshire truffle cream, malt and barley or a fabulous whipped chicken liver with thyme hobnobs and onion jam could precede Cornish pollack with cauliflower and smoked kipper, or roast haunch of fallow deer with celeriac, kale and pickled pear, with marmalade ice cream sandwich a perfectly balanced ending. The wine list is broad in scope, including plenty of French classics, with a selection of half bottles and decent choice by the glass.
Chef/s: Sally Abé. **Closed:** 24 to 26 Dec. **Meals:** set L £30 (2 courses) to £33. Set D £50. Sun L £50. **Details:** 60 seats. Bar. Wheelchairs. Music.

Hawksmoor Knightsbridge

Cooking score: 3
⊖ Knightsbridge, South Kensington, map 3
British | £60
3 Yeoman's Row, Knightsbridge, SW3 2AL
Tel no: 020 7590 9290
thehawksmoor.com

If, in some quarters, Hawksmoor is viewed as a pricey proposition, that's not the case in affluent Knightsbridge, where £33 ribeyes and £24 house wines amount to a bona fide

bargain and the set lunch and early/late dinner (a cornerstone of the eight-strong chain) is a steal. Since its launch in Spitalfields in 2006, the group has grown from a beef-mad boîte into the modern British steakhouse it is today. Each site is tailored to the locale and this address is a particularly smart one, boasting four-figure fine wines and premium seafood, including Dover sole and whole lobsters alongside the signature classics. The look is understated Art Deco, where commodious booths and wood-panelled walls provide a fitting backdrop for marmalade cocktails, sticky toffee sundaes and chipper staff clad in jeans and trainers. It's encouraging to see a chain, albeit a small one, celebrate British ingredients. Here, the dry-aged beef is grass-fed, the chips triple-cooked and the mash laced with Tunworth cheese. One for all ages.
Chef/s: Flamur Zeka. **Closed:** 25 and 26 Dec. **Meals:** main courses £17 to £60. Set L and early/late D £26 (2 courses) to £29. **Details:** 130 seats. Bar. Wheelchairs. Music.

Hereford Road
Cooking score: 3
Ꝋ Bayswater, map 6
British | £29
3 Hereford Road, Notting Hill, W2 4AB
Tel no: 020 7727 1144
herefordroad.org
£5 OFF £30

'This must be one of the most agreeable restaurants in London, totally at ease in its own skin, confident, hospitable and uninterested in fads' was the verdict of one satisfied regular to Tom Pemberton's well-established split-level eatery, adding 'for such a wealthy area, it is astonishing value for money'. The short, regularly changing menu is a zesty, seasonal assortment of mainly meat-based dishes with the execution tending towards the simple, say duck livers and hearts with green beans and tarragon or a main course of braised lamb shank and carrots. Simplicity doesn't mean lack of imagination or skill, however. Pemberton's cooking builds on a bedrock of British dishes, adding some

contemporary notes while retaining his reputation for emphatic, no-nonsense flavours. Fish gets the same treatment, so expect classic potted crab or whole grilled mackerel served with cucumber, kohlrabi and chervil. Old-fashioned desserts include sticky date pudding, and warm rice pudding and jam. The European wine list blends modern and traditional styles, starting at £24.50.
Chef/s: Tom Pemberton. **Closed:** 23 Dec to 4 Jan. **Meals:** main courses £14 to £19. Set L £14 (2 courses) to £16. **Details:** 50 seats. 8 seats outside. Wheelchairs.

Hunan
Cooking score: 3
Ꝋ Sloane Square, map 3
Chinese | £70
51 Pimlico Road, Chelsea, SW1W 8NE
Tel no: 020 7730 5712
hunanlondon.com

Pursuing its own path since 1982, Michael Peng's restaurant has the elegant neutrality you might expect from that era, and when it comes to its small plate concept, you might well conclude the rest of the world has caught up. The idea is simple enough: state your personal preferences (what you like, what you don't, what chilli heat you can take) and the kitchen (run by Mr Peng, Michael's father) does the rest. The small plates arrive in groups of three, with the influences and ideas garnered from across China. Plump and steaming hot Shanghai dumplings are as good as you'll find hereabouts, Scottish mussels come with the seldom seen moss hair (a sort of algae), and slow-cooked pork shoulder is stuffed into steamed buns and served with preserved vegetables. It's evident you're in very safe hands, and Hunan remains one of the most distinctive Chinese restaurants in the capital. The wine list is an intelligent collection of indisputable good taste, arranged by style and including many gems.
Chef/s: Mr Peng. **Closed:** Sun, bank hols. **Meals:** set L £46 (12 courses). Set D £70 (18 courses). **Details:** 44 seats. V menu. Vg menu. Music.

Indian Zing

Cooking score: 2
⊖ Ravenscourt Park, map 1
Indian | £33
236 King Street, Hammersmith, W6 0RF
Tel no: 020 8748 5959
indian-zing.co.uk
£5
OFF

Designed according to the principles of vastu shastra (the harmony of earth, fire, sky, water and air), Manoj Vasaikar's purple-fronted Hammersmith Indian is a top local destination known for its cool vibes and hot cooking. Clever textures, thrilling contrasts and exact spicing inform every flavoursome plateful, and Vasaikar is also on the money when it comes to sourcing organic and free range produce. Dishes such as Goan-style mussels with green herbs in coconut broth or a luxurious take on chicken korma redolent of saffron are delivered with aplomb, but also look for more idiosyncratic ideas such as his vegetable bhanola (a Maharashtrian spin on the ubiquitous onion bhaji), banana flower and colocasia-leaf kofta in a delicate pumpkin gravy or an equally vivid veggie pairing of artichokes and paneer cheese with tomato relish. For afters, try bebinca (a multi-layered Goan gâteau with virgin coconut milk, Cointreau and vanilla). Well-chosen, spice-friendly wines start at £20.
Chef/s: Manoj Vasaikar. **Meals:** main courses £11 to £22. Set L £16 (2 courses) to £19. **Details:** 52 seats. 28 seats outside. Wheelchairs. Music.

LOCAL GEM

The Italians

⊖ Chiswick Park, map 1
Italian | £10
454-456 Chiswick High Road, Chiswick, W4 5TT
Tel no: 07903 135441
theitalians.co.uk
£30

Brought to Chiswick by a 'community of Italian fine food enthusiasts', this super-friendly shop and café features a vast glass deli counter and a few tables (inside and out) for those who want to linger. The produce can't be faulted, whether you're building your own feast from the bounty on display or sampling one of their hot dishes – don't miss the umami-laden aubergine Parmigiana. Order Italian coffee, desserts and pastries from a separate counter. Lunchtime brings ciabatta rolls, there's a pizza menu on Saturdays, and the large wine cellar is a tempting diversion.

★ NEW ENTRY ★

Kahani

Cooking score: 4
⊖ Sloane Square, map 3
Indian | £50
1 Wilbraham Place, Chelsea, SW1X 9AE
Tel no: 020 7730 7634
kahanidining.com

On this, his first solo venture, Peter Joseph (ex-Tamarind) has taken over a venue that has been through a few incarnations in recent years. The basement dining room has been cleverly designed to create an inviting space with armchair seating, dramatic lighting, plus open-view kitchen and wine storage. The menu is divided into small and large plates, and inspired by British ingredients combined with Indian spices: Somerset lamb chops with Kashmiri chillies, say, or Gressingham duck breast with coriander. Seafood is handled with precision: a golden brown soft shell-crab infused with Mangalore spices accompanied by a 'wonderful' tomato chutney, or smokey Malabar prawns with turmeric, coconut and curry leaves, and a 'heavenly' halibut fish curry simmered with shallots, turmeric and tamarind. Cheesecake with a raspberry coulis centre paired with yoghurt ice cream is a sweet way to end. Service is very willing to please. The extensive drinks list features cocktails and pricey wines, with only a handful of bottles below £60.
Chef/s: Peter Joseph. **Meals:** main courses £12 to £34. Set L and early D £20 (2 courses) to £25. Tasting menu £52 (4 courses) to £70. **Details:** 90 seats. V menu. Vg menu. Wheelchairs. Music.

Kitchen W8

Cooking score: 5
⊖ High Street Kensington, map 6
Modern European | £48
11-13 Abingdon Road, Kensington, W8 6AH
Tel no: 020 7937 0120
kitchenw8.com

With so many restaurants noisily staking their reputation on unusual ingredients, whizz-bang techniques and challenging combinations, how lovely to know that this impeccable little place on a Kensington side road exists. Serene, confident and fresh from a refurb, this is a draw for those lunching for business and pleasure, or for evenings when a relaxed 'relatively informal' meal is in order. Grilled mackerel with smoked eel could start things off with oomph, butterhead lettuce with crisp shallots and a peppy mustard dressing being a more restrained choice. Follow with cod, plump and white, with cauliflower caramelised to gentle nuttiness and a pep of minerality from mussels and sea kale, or scallops and crab that salute late spring alongside lightly crushed potatoes, samphire and lemon. Apricots poached in Sauternes could finish a meal fragrantly. A £25 spend will get you going on the wine list, which has a good selection by the glass and 375ml carafe. **Chef/s:** Mark Kempson. **Closed:** bank hols, 24 to 26 Dec. **Meals:** main courses £17 to £30. Set L £25 (2 courses) to £28. Set D £27 (2 courses) to £30. Tasting menu £75 (6 courses). Sun L £39. **Details:** 70 seats. Wheelchairs.

★ NEW ENTRY ★

Kutir

Cooking score: 4
⊖ Sloane Square, map 3
Indian | £45
10 Lincoln Street, Chelsea, SW3 2TS
Tel no: 020 7581 1144
kutir.co.uk

Although Rohit Ghai's first solo venture inhabits an elegant townhouse on a quiet street off the King's Road, the name means a cottage in Sanskrit. Rather quaintly, you ring a doorbell to gain entry. Inside, Zoffany wallcoverings, striking foliage and natural tones of mint green and copper have turned the two dining rooms into elegant and calm spaces. The ex-Gymkhana and Jamavar chef's distinctive modern cooking features intriguing dishes not found elsewhere – perhaps wild morels with white turmeric or hand-dived scallops with aubergine fritters and mustard. Start, perhaps, with moreish pink prawn masala made with coconut and sesame, follow with naan topped with scrambled quail's egg and truffle or jackfruit kofta partnered with sautéed spinach and a tomato sauce. Desserts showcase creative pastry work: traditional bhapa doi (steamed yoghurt pudding) is paired with pineapple fritters. Enthusiastic staff add to the appeal. To drink, there are Indian-inspired cocktails and wines from around the globe (from £29). **Chef/s:** Rohit Ghai. **Closed:** 25 to 27 Dec, 1 to 3 Jan. **Meals:** main courses £14 to £20. Set L and early D £20 (2 courses) to £25. Tasting menu £55 (5 courses) to £65. **Details:** 65 seats. V menu. Music. No children after 7pm.

Launceston Place

Cooking score: 5
⊖ Gloucester Road, map 3
Modern European | £65
1a Launceston Place, South Kensington, W8 5RL
Tel no: 020 7937 6912
launcestonplace-restaurant.co.uk
£5 OFF

For years, this much-loved establishment has been the go-to for civilised celebrations and demure date nights in this inarguably classy neighbourhood. It's divided into small rooms, each feeling rather private, but all of them draped in napery and dotted with interesting paintings to critique should the conversation falter. It's a formal backdrop, enhanced by charming staff, but any stuffiness is knocked out by the humorous menu and presentation, which may grate at first, but will win you over in the end. Portions are delicate: a first course of simply poached lobster, with a strong, clean, yuzu-led sauce offers three mouthfuls of the crustacean. A show-stopping main course of mushroom – a medium-sized portobello, stuffed with a plethora of other varieties and garnished with dried mushroom – is the work of possibly six bites. But given the number of little first courses and amuse-bouches that lead into the main meal, this is all to the good. Milk-fed lamb – beautifully cooked, with a tiny rack of lamb and several other cuts – was the best dish at inspection. Stick to familiar tarts and soufflés at dessert: the experimental-sounding dishes – pea mousse with basil oil, anyone? – may well be what they seem. The extensive wine list opens with an organic Grüner Veltliner at £29, soon rising to match the locale.

Chef/s: Ben Murphy. **Closed:** Mon. **Meals:** main courses L £22 to £34. Set L £25 (2 courses) to £29. Set D £55 (2 courses) to £65. Tasting menu £85 (8 courses). Sun L £35. **Details:** 52 seats. V menu. Bar. Wheelchairs. Music.

★ TOP 50 ★

The Ledbury
Cooking score: 8
⊖ Notting Hill Gate, Westbourne Park, map 6
Modern European | £125
127 Ledbury Road, Notting Hill, W11 2AQ
Tel no: 020 7792 9090
theledbury.com

In this bronzed, mirrored and draped dining room, an exceptional front of house team, under genial general manager Darren McHugh, glides about its business. Instinctive service looks after solo diners and absorbed lovers as graciously as it does corporate types and deeply pocketed locals, and the food is correspondingly luxurious. A guinea fowl puff topped with a cube of clear mead jelly is as light as its name suggests, although a dumpling of confit muntjac shoulder that bursts in one hot, savoury bite stands out among the canapés. Start the four-course dinner with clay-baked white beetroot and smoked eel, translucent slices of the vegetable lying over the fish, and spoonfuls of sake cream with char roe poured at table. It's sweet

and savoury, delicate and robust, and captures in one plate Brett Graham's ability to tease flavours from ingredients and combine them into coherently delicious, strikingly beautiful food. He does it again with a bantam egg whose free range, corn-fed yolk flows into celeriac, dried ham and shaved truffle to create a dish of eye-closing joy. The fat on herdwick lamb loins slips from tender flesh in a main that nods to the eastern Mediterranean, with aubergine dusted with dried olives and black tea and scattered with pine nuts, but you could choose native lobster wrapped in shiitake, or pork jowl with the much-lauded lardo-encased hen of the woods. Finish with crunchy-topped brown sugar tart, a triumph of a dessert that wobbles a little and resists a little but is ultimately heavenly to scoop through stem ginger ice cream and poached muscat grapes. The wine list gathers strength once north of £60, although there is a Sicilian bianco for £39.

Chef/s: Brett Graham and Jake Leach. **Closed:** 24 to 26 Dec, Aug bank hol. **Meals:** set L £80 Wed to Fri (4 courses) to £125. Set D £125 (4 courses). Tasting menu £150 (8 courses). **Details:** 58 seats. V menu. Wheelchairs. Children over 12 yrs.

★ TOP 50 ★

Marcus
Cooking score: 8
⊖ Hyde Park Corner, Knightsbridge, map 6
Modern British | £90
The Berkeley, Wilton Place, Belgravia, SW1X 7RL
Tel no: 020 7235 1200
marcusrestaurant.com

The dining room at The Berkeley is a redoubt of tranquillity, insulated from the searing heat and roadwork racket of July. Dark panelling, deep oxblood upholstery and a brigade of effortlessly professional staff ensure an air of calm refinement. Mark and Shauna Froydenlund continue to bring transcendent levels of technical ability, imaginative energy and bedazzlement to Marcus Wareing's version of modern British dining, which showcases prime ingredients in exciting guises. A starter of Dorset crab is partly encased in puffed rice, partly moussed into a cylinder, and dressed with contrasting satay and yoghurt, with a crab tartlet served alongside. The finest cuts of herdwick lamb – vivid pink noisette and loin accompanied by a deep-fried croquette of the confit belly and shoulder – are paired with fragrant pesto and sweet beetroot purée. Goosnargh duck is teamed with apricot, pistachios and wild nettle, while a double act of Cornish cod and octopus in sauce matelote comes with calçot onions, fennel and lovage. Presentations are exquisite, through to a box-like construction of little balls akin to an executive toy – bitter chocolate curd, crème diplomate and whole pickled cherries sandwiched between chocolate sheets, the bottom one filled with cardamom fudge. The cheese trolley, once seen, is hard to resist. With a multitude of extras, perhaps starting with honey-dressed Spanish bresaola, not forgetting a pre-dessert of meadowsweet custard, passion fruit sorbet and diced mango, it's hard to fault the sense of value for a restaurant at this level. The wine list is as full of the high and mighty as a high and mighty clientele expects. By-the-glass selections offer some relief.

Chef/s: Marcus Wareing and Mark and Shauna Froydenlund. **Closed:** Sun. **Meals:** set L £55 (5 courses) to £60. Set D £90. Tasting menu £115 (5 courses) to £135. **Details:** 80 seats. Bar. Wheelchairs. Parking. Music. Children over 8 yrs.

Medlar

Cooking score: 5
⊖ Sloane Square, Fulham Broadway, map 3
Modern European | £53
438 King's Road, Chelsea, SW10 0LJ
Tel no: 020 7349 1900
medlarrestaurant.co.uk
🍷

A refined but congenial neighbourhood favourite that really looks the part with its distinctive green banquettes, pretty lamps, mirrors and front windows opening on to a sunny terrace. Chef and co-owner Joe Mercer

Nairne earned his stripes at Chez Bruce (see entry) and it shows in his fondness for gutsy, full-blooded Franco-European flavours. His signature duck egg tart with red wine sauce, turnip purée, lardons and sautéed duck hearts is a rich delicacy worth savouring, likewise Gigha halibut with boneless chicken wings, Jerusalem artichoke purée, salsify and black truffle. The kitchen also likes to toss a few unexpected ingredients into the mix, although the results are always thoughtful and harmonious – as in roast guinea fowl with sautéed nasturtium roots, dragoncello sauce, oca de Peru (oxalis tubers) and baby leeks. Desserts continue the eclectic theme, from tarte tatin and buttermilk panna cotta to mango, lime and pineapple salad revved up with passion fruit and coconut sorbet. A mighty contingent of big-hitting French wines is matched by plenty of intelligently chosen stuff from across the globe (even China gets a name check). There's also an exemplary selection by the glass or carafe.

Chef/s: Joe Mercer Nairne. **Meals:** set L £30 (2 courses) to £35. Set D £45 (2 courses) to £53. Sun D £35. **Details:** 87 seats. 8 seats outside. Wheelchairs. Music.

Ognisko

Cooking score: 3
⊖ South Kensington, map 6
Polish | £30
55 Exhibition Road, South Kensington, SW7 2PG
Tel no: 020 7589 0101
ogniskorestaurant.co.uk
£30

In 1939, Poland's expatriate community founded a club in London to maintain the integrity of the overseas resistance. Here, in these grand premises on Prince's Gate, the club endures, with balconies overlooking Kensington's green spaces and a restaurant that provides the true taste of hearth (*ognisko*) and home. The white-walled ground-floor room is a civilised space where dishes such as zurek, sour rye soup with white sausage and egg, pelmeni dumplings of veal and pork, and golonka – ham hock glazed in honey and mustard with sauerkraut and carrot salad and horseradish cream – provide fortification against the northern chill. A side order of kasza (roasted buckwheat) is a must, as is a dessert of plums poached in vodka with toasted almonds and vanilla ice cream. The list of vodkas is vast and Ognisko produces its own infusions of chilli or horseradish and honey. Premium names include Wyborowa's satin-smooth Exquisite and Baczewski, a true potato vodka. Wines start at £19.50. **Chef/s:** Jarek Mlynarczyk. **Meals:** main courses £16 to £22. Set L and early D £19 (2 courses) to £22. Sun L £22. **Details:** 80 seats. 70 seats outside. Bar. Music.

★ NEW ENTRY ★

Orasay
Cooking score: 2
⊖ **Ladbroke Grove, map 6**
British | £40
31 Kensington Park Road, Notting Hill, W11 2EU
Tel no: 020 7043 1400
orasay.london
£5
OFF

Scotland is famous for its seafood, although precious little of it stays on these shores, but this small neighbourhood restaurant attempts to redress the balance in its own small way. On the shortish menu there's not only the obvious (oysters, prawns et al), but also some slightly left-field suggestions (crab butter, smoked cod's roe). Start with a scallop large enough to be cut into four, sautéed with shiitake and wine, or deep-fried shell-on prawns, a smooth spiced avocado dip on the side to plunge them into. Follow with a wood-grilled John Dory (for two) or a fillet of sea bass with a simple butter and white wine emulsion. In the mood for meat? Then you should be more than happy with slow-cooked, beautifully soft Tamworth collar chop with a deeply flavourful jus, or an enormous shorthorn rib chop for two or three; vegetarians are well looked after too. Puddings and cheese – simple and straightforward – are big enough to share. The largely European wine list starts with a house Italian at a modest £20. **Chef/s:** Jackson Boxer. **Closed:** Mon, 23 Dec to 2 Jan. **Meals:** main courses £16 to £33. Set L £16 (2 courses) to £20. **Details:** 48 seats. Music.

Pétrus
Cooking score: 6
⊖ **Knightsbridge, map 6**
Modern French | £95
1 Kinnerton Street, Knightsbridge, SW1X 8EA
Tel no: 020 7592 1609
gordonramsay.com

With its hushed tones, thick carpets, dim lighting and pulled-down window blinds, this long-serving outpost of Gordon Ramsay's empire emanates a 'gold-standard cruise ship vibe' – albeit with the considerable bonus of a glass-fronted circular wine store stacked with verticals of the titular Château Pétrus (and more besides). Head chef Russell Bateman's take on modern French cuisine is 'flawless and perfect in every way', although diners may yearn for more 'moments of amazement' from dishes such as super-fresh Dorset crab with Granny Smith apple, lovage, sorrel and radish, or sea bream with salsify, leeks and mussel cream. Meat options are also impeccably executed (think fillet of Dexter beef partnered by Roscoff onion, nasturtium and charcuterie sauce), while desserts might include an 'exceptional' praline soufflé with roasted hazelnut ice cream. Prices can sting, although the set lunch is deemed 'excellent value' for the likes of green asparagus with gnocchi and morels followed by turbot with Jersey Royals, coastal herbs and seaweed beurre blanc. 'Formal but very personable service' comes as standard, staff delight in demystifying the wonders of the cheese trolley, and the aristocratic French-focused wine list is an unashamedly traditional tome with small glasses starting at £8 and bottles jetting rapidly skywards from £35. **Chef/s:** Russell Bateman. **Closed:** 26 to 28 Dec. **Meals:** set L £55. Set D £95. Tasting menu £120 (6 courses). **Details:** 55 seats. Bar. Wheelchairs.

GFG scoring system

Score 1: Capable cooking with simple food combinations and clear flavours.

Score 2: Decent cooking, displaying good technical skills and interesting combinations and flavours.

Score 3: Good cooking, showing sound technical skills and using quality ingredients.

Score 4: Dedicated, focused approach to cooking; good classical skills and high-quality ingredients.

Score 5: Exact cooking techniques and a degree of ambition; showing balance and depth of flavour in dishes.

Score 6: Exemplary cooking skills, innovative ideas, impeccable ingredients and an element of excitement.

Score 7: High level of ambition and individuality, attention to the smallest detail, accurate and vibrant dishes.

Score 8: A kitchen cooking close to or at the top of its game. Highly individual with impressive artistry.

Score 9: Cooking that has reached a pinnacle of achievement, making it a hugely memorable experience.

Score 10: Just perfect dishes, showing faultless technique at every service; extremely rare and the highest accolade.

Portobello Ristorante Pizzeria

Cooking score: 2
⊖ Notting Hill Gate, map 6
Italian | £35
7 Ladbroke Road, Notting Hill, W11 3PA
Tel no: 020 7221 1373
portobellolondon.co.uk

£5 OFF

What could be lovelier than to sit on an outdoor (covered) terrace in Notting Hill with a bottle of something cold when work is behind you and spring evenings have arrived? Once the inevitable nip in the air sets in, the heaters come on, and then you can get bedded in under blankets. The Portobello is a neighbourhood spot and then some, with squads of enthusiastic West Eleveners cramming the tables outdoors and in for well-wrought Italian cooking of honesty and integrity. Clams sautéed in white wine with garlic and chilli, hearty pasta variations such as paccheri tubes stuffed with herby minced veal, and mains of baked fish or grilled sirloin on balsamic rocket with shaved Parmesan are the stock-in-trade, but it's the exemplary pizzas, served by the metre and half metre, that keep the crowds returning. Crispy bases bombed with passata, and most gooey with mozzarella, feature anchovies and capers, cherry tomatoes and speck, sausage and broccoli rabe. The wine list explores Italy, from spumanti to premiums, in conscientious detail, starting at £24.
Chef/s: Gazmir Tefa. **Closed:** Aug bank hol.
Meals: main courses £13 to £26. Set L £15 (2 courses). **Details:** 60 seats. 30 seats outside. Music.

Rabbit

Cooking score: 1
θ Sloane Square, map 3
Modern British | £35
172 King's Road, Chelsea, SW3 4UP
Tel no: 020 3750 0172
rabbit-restaurant.com
£5
OFF

The mood is casual and the decor rustic at Richard and Oliver Gladwin's hard-working King's Road asset. Provenance and seasonality are to the fore and the approachable menu adds some Mediterranean vibrancy to core British ingredients, so most people find something they like. Everyone in the area knows about it so it's essential to book. Little bites – say mushroom Marmite éclair – are 'exemplary', small dishes are 'simple ideas attractively presented', perhaps fried goat's cheese with honey, almonds and thyme, wild mushroom ragoût or beef skewers with Douglas fir yoghurt and fermented beetroot vinaigrette. Finish with crunchy honeycomb, sweet mascarpone and tarragon sugar. Start with a cocktail or look to the list of affordable wines.

Chef/s: Oliver Gladwin. **Closed:** 23 Dec to 2 Jan.
Meals: main courses £9 to £20. Tasting menu £42 (8 courses). **Details:** 54 seats. Bar. Music.

★ TOP 10 ★

Restaurant Gordon Ramsay

Cooking score: 9
θ Sloane Square, Map 3
French | £120
68 Royal Hospital Road, Chelsea, SW3 4HP
Tel no: 020 7352 4441
gordonramsayrestaurants.com

Here, in an almost provocatively understated small room, Matt Abé brings panache and sophistication to his interpretation of Gordon Ramsay's philosophy. Menus evolve slowly, retaining a strong seasonal note, with many preparations founded on the methodology and compositional structure of classic haute cuisine. From the arrival of nibbles – say sashimi-style kingfish wrapped in seaweed, a potato crisp dotted with salty-citrussy flavours, cheese gougères – it's clear that attention to detail is paramount. This dedication to sustaining fine ingredients continues with roast sweetbread served with a little heap of spring vegetables and Pommery mustard seed in an intense beurre noisette, a highlight of our visit. Abé's ability to combine indulgence and lightness is a particular strength: note a reworking of a Ramsay classic – a fat, silky raviolo packed with lobster, langoustine and salmon in a deep, buttery sorrel sauce. His clear understanding of flavours and textures is demonstrated in full-flavoured herdwick lamb chops with a tangle of courgettes, romesco, black olives and marjoram, its accompanying glossy jus poured at table, or in a lightly coated blanquette of guinea fowl breast, its delicacy offset by tiny charred onions, crunchy hazelnuts and thyme. More artistry is lavished on desserts of cherry parfait coated with white chocolate and served with fresh cherries, sweet cicely, oxalis flowers and leaves, and slivers of green almonds, or textbook raspberry soufflé with pistachio ice cream. This is a serious restaurant, no doubt, and the dining room, ably overseen by Jean-Claude Breton and sommelier James Lloyd, is a model of its kind. Although drinkers on a tight budget will find their choice somewhat restricted, there is no denying the quality and appeal of wines on the large list of thoroughbreds, from imperious French vintages to a fabulous bunch by the glass.

Chef/s: Matt Abé. **Closed:** Mon, Sun. **Meals:** set L £70. Set D £120. Tasting menu £155 (7 courses) to £185. **Details:** 44 seats. V menu. Wheelchairs.

Send us your review

Your feedback informs the content of the *GFG* and will be used to compile next year's entries. To register your opinion about any restaurant listed in the Guide, or a restaurant that you wish to bring to our attention, visit: thegoodfoodguide.co.uk/feedback.

Anonymous

At *The Good Food Guide*, our inspectors dine anonymously and pay their bill in full every time. These impartial review meals, along with feedback from thousands of our readers, are what informs the content of the *GFG*, the UK's number one selling restaurant guide. Only the best restaurants make the cut.

Restaurant Michael Nadra

Cooking score: 3
Ө **Turnham Green, map 1**
Modern European | £43
6-8 Elliott Road, Chiswick, W4 1PE
Tel no: 020 8742 0766
restaurant-michaelnadra.co.uk
£5
OFF

Marble-topped tables and porthole mirrors lend a classy feel to the Chiswick arm of Michael Nadra's London operations (see also Primrose Hill, north London). The menu takes in a six-course taster as well as a premium carte, with an express option for the time-pressed, available at lunch and early dinner. Modern European food full of bright ideas and pertinent combinations is the stock-in-trade, and allows for an opener full of Spanish panache, comprising Teruel lomo, Ibérico pig's cheeks, and morcilla with chickpeas and piquillo peppers in sherry. On the Italian flank, a fabulously rich lasagne of guinea fowl with truffled leeks and wild mushrooms makes quite an intro, too. Hints of the modern French idiom surface in a main course of lamb loin with a rolled 'cigar' of garlicky confit meat, or there could be grilled cod in lemon and herb dressing with monk's beard, salsify and a generous lot of brown shrimps. To finish, it is hard to bypass the treacle tart with clotted cream and raspberry sorbet. Wines start at £23.
Chef/s: Michael Nadra. **Closed:** Mon. **Meals:** main courses £21 to £29. Set L and early D £19 (2 courses) to £26. Tasting menu £65 (6 courses). **Details:** 55 seats. Wheelchairs. Music.

The River Café

Cooking score: 5
Ө **Hammersmith, map 1**
Italian | £90
Thames Wharf, Rainville Road, Hammersmith, W6 9HA
Tel no: 020 7386 4200
rivercafe.co.uk

Originally conceived as a workers' canteen for Sir Richard Rogers' architectural practice next door, this slick riverside restaurant has gone on to achieve international stardom as a glowing tribute to Italian regional cooking. Diligent sourcing and vigorous rustic flavours are at the heart of Ruth Rogers' kitchen, with seasonal salads, silky homemade pastas and wood-roasted specialities headlining the daily menus. In winter, you might find panzotti with Swiss chard, ricotta and fresh walnut sauce; in summer, thoughts might turn to a risotto of clams and courgette flowers, slow-cooked veal shin or a tranche of turbot served with anchovy, capers, flowering oregano and young beets. Fragrant herbs, green leaves and vegetable embellishments are strewn everywhere, while desserts might promise prune and almond tart, polenta cake and, of course, the never-bettered chocolate nemesis. Prices are notoriously high, although set lunches are a relatively pain-free way of enjoying The River Café's many attributes – especially its views and covetable terrace. You'll also pay top lire (from £36) if you want to plunder the patrician wine list with its treasure trove of Italian regional tipples.
Chef/s: Ruth Rogers, Joseph Trivelli and Sian Wyn Owen. **Closed:** 24 Dec to 2 Jan. **Meals:** main courses £18 to £40. Set L £28 (2 courses) to £42. **Details:** 120 seats. 100 seats outside. Bar. Wheelchairs. Parking. Music.

Rosso

⊖ High Street Kensington, map 6
Italian | £25
276-280 Kensington High Street, Kensington,
W8 6ND
Tel no: 07384 595191
enotecarosso.com

£30

The tall wine shelves that punctuate the space inside this modern Italian bistro indicate the chief focus of proceedings, which is not to say that the lively cooking is to be sniffed at. With many dishes available in three sizes it's flexible, too, from tagliatelle with venison stew, cod in black ravioli or sliced ribeye with roast potatoes and radicchio, as well as main-course salads and desserts such as torta della nonna or fig cheesecake. A cartographical approach to the Italian regions makes the wine list user friendly, and markups are reasonable, with bottles from £22.

San Pietro

Cooking score: 2
⊖ High Street Kensington, Earl's Court, map 3
Italian | £45
7 Stratford Road, Kensington, W8 6RF
Tel no: 020 7938 1805
san-pietro.co.uk

£5 OFF

This offshoot of Notting Hill's Portobello Ristorante Pizzeria (see entry) promises the same focus on pasta, pizza and very fresh fish. It comes with all the right credentials: the light, bright interior is wonderfully warm and welcoming, staff are friendly, and while the cooking may not surprise or intrigue, you're unlikely to be disappointed. The list of old favourites includes moreish deep-fried zucchini, Parmigiana di melanzane, spaghetti alle vongole, and chargrilled lamb cutlets with ratatouille di verdure. A perfectly cooked sea bass from the daily specials comes highly recommended, as do veal meatballs, and tagliatelle with 'nduja and broccoli.

Homemade honey semifreddo with almond flakes is a fine finish, but you could choose a dark chocolate and ground almond cake served with vanilla ice cream. On the wine front, the all-Italian list has a good selection by the glass and carafe, with bottles from £24.
Chef/s: Mattia Pellegrin. **Meals:** main courses £9 to £27. **Details:** 50 seats. Bar. Music.

The Sea, The Sea

Cooking score: 4
⊖ Sloane Square, map 3
Seafood | £40
174 Pavilion Road, Chelsea, SW1X 0AW
Tel no: 020 7824 8090
theseathesea.net

Conceived by Bonnie Gull Seafood Shack's co-founder Alex Hunter and named after a line in a Paul Valéry poem, this is a high-end, chef-led fishmonger and restaurant anchored in a spendy enclave off Sloane Square. By day, it's a sleek retail space with a lunchtime oyster bar, by night the fish displays and crushed ice are cleared away to make space for 20 diners to tuck into small seafood plates. The naturalistic rough-textured walls and gentle lighting make for a mellow mood in which to order oysters, before moving on to the cured and lightly cooked, say pickled, crunchy potato 'noodles' with cured cod and coriander, and a deeply savoury dish of slivered scallop with sweetcorn and black garlic. For one visitor, the highlight was a chilled bowl of vanilla-infused apricots with caramelised yoghurt. Chef Leandro Carreira's experimental style might not be for everyone – note, there are chopsticks alongside the cutlery, a sign that the Japanese influence is writ large. Grower Champagnes dominate the short wine list and ordering fizz is almost obligatory.
Chef/s: Leandro Carreira and Renato Costa.
Closed: Mon. **Meals:** small plates £10 to £20.
Details: 20 seats. 8 seats outside.

Get social

Follow us on social media for the latest news, chef interviews and more.
Twitter @GoodFoodGuideUK
Facebook TheGoodFoodGuide

The Shed

Cooking score: 3
⊖ Notting Hill Gate, map 6
Modern British | £35
122 Palace Gardens Terrace, Notting Hill, W8 4RT
Tel no: 020 7229 4024
theshed-restaurant.com
£5
OFF

Farm to fork, vine to glass, the Gladwin brothers are an entrepreneurial duo with farming, viniculture and restaurants in their impressive portfolio. West Sussex is home to the family farm and Nutbourne Vineyards, with produce from both enlivening menus in this gloriously free-spirited spot close to Notting Hill Gate. In addition, foraged and wild ingredients loom large among the small plates. Tempura pickled walnuts with whipped smoked cod's roe leads the way on a menu with creative ideas and intriguing combinations in abundance: venison 'cigars' with the house harissa and tarragon; truffled artichoke ravioli, fermented black garlic and truffle powder; torched monkfish with burnt butter emulsion. Daily specials ('once they're gone, they're gone') might run to whole roast pheasant and, among puds, a vegan chocolate and pumpkin mousse competes with the showpiece honeycomb crunchie. All that and British beers, cocktails and a wine list featuring their own Sussex fizz and wines.
Chef/s: Oliver Gladwin. **Closed:** Sun, 23 Dec to 2 Jan. **Meals:** small plates £5 to £22. Tasting menu £42 (8 courses). **Details:** 54 seats. 12 seats outside. Bar. Music.

★ NEW ENTRY ★

Siren

Cooking score: 4
⊖ Victoria, map 3
Seafood | £70
The Goring, 15 Beeston Place, Belgravia, SW1W 0JW
Tel no: 020 7769 4485
thegoring.com

There is something traditional, understated and very English about The Goring, from the bowler-hatted doormen to the country-house-style bar through which you pass to reach the newly built garden extension housing this latest venture from Nathan Outlaw. Head chef Andrew Sawyer follows the specific Outlaw agenda: show what the sea can yield. His cooking doesn't seek to astound or amaze; rather it focuses on the sheer whoosh of very fresh fish, simple treatments and generous plates of, say, red mullet with devilled shrimp butter and chicory or baked hake with fennel and seaweed. From this perspective the food is well-judged and precisely rendered, if pricey. Meat isn't ignored – this is a hotel in Victoria, not the seaside – so think dry-aged steak with tarragon and anchovy sauce or a crossover starter of cuttlefish black pudding teamed with a punchy apple chutney and kohlrabi. Desserts might include a delicate, perfectly ripe strawberry tart with yoghurt sorbet or a classic crème brûlée topped with poached gooseberries. The wine list is equally wallet denting, with bottles from £34 and choice by the glass rising steeply from £9.50.
Chef/s: Nathan Outlaw and Andrew Sawyer. **Meals:** main courses £24 to £56. **Details:** 60 seats. Bar.

Six Portland Road

Cooking score: 2
⊖ Holland Park, map 1
Modern European | £45
6 Portland Road, Holland Park, W11 4LA
Tel no: 020 7229 3130
sixportlandroad.com

'All is pared back, comfortable and in the best possible taste' at this bistro-style restaurant in a higgledy-piggledy Georgian terrace just off Holland Park. The interior style suggests a perfectly confident, low-key neighbourhood eatery that sets out to please – a simple, uncluttered backdrop for a menu of simple, uncluttered dishes. A starter of dressed crab and mayonnaise looks pretty in pink and orange, with 'super-fresh' flavours matching its colourful demeanour, or you can keep it even simpler with a plate of radishes and anchoïade. After that, expect satisfying mains such as plaice with cider butter and samphire, or expertly timed pork loin (cut into three huge slices) with a citrussy saffron sauce, smokey, nutty romesco and rough-cut hazelnuts on the side. To finish, a satisfying dollop of rich chocolate mousse with crème fraîche and crumbled biscuit hits the sweet spot. Around 120 wines from eco-minded growers start at £29.
Chef/s: Nye Smith. **Closed:** Sun. **Meals:** main courses £19 to £34. Set L £19 (2 courses) to £21. **Details:** 36 seats.

La Trompette

Cooking score: 5
⊖ Turnham Green, map 1
Modern European | £58
3-7 Devonshire Road, Chiswick, W4 2EU
Tel no: 020 8747 1836
latrompette.co.uk
🍾

This expansive, airy restaurant was in the vanguard of the culinary renaissance of Chiswick when it opened nearly two decades ago, and still feels like a benchmark for the area today. It runs to a comforting rhythm, with clued-up staff to explain the tasting

dishes and a sommelier outlining the rationale for each pairing. As to Rob Weston's modern European menus, 'the 3D flavours work so well, each item on the plate working with any other, making for some wonderful combinations'. That might mean cured bream with green clementine, radishes and hot togarashi spices, or a grilled Orkney scallop in yuzu butter with sea cress. The centrepiece of the seven-course tasting menu may be roast Berkshire venison with Jerusalem artichokes and quince or, if you're sticking with fish, turbot and crab with barley, blood orange and pine nuts. Round off with a show-stopping Bramley apple crumble soufflé and vanilla ice cream. A vegetarian version of equal imagination demonstrates the kitchen's versatility. The wine list starts with a broad selection by the small glass from £8, opening out into an inspiring conspectus of modern viticulture, with fine producers throughout.
Chef/s: Rob Weston. **Closed:** 25 to 27 Dec, 1 Jan. **Meals:** set L £35 (2 courses) to £40. Set D £48 (2 courses) to £58. Tasting menu £75 (7 courses). Sun L £45. **Details:** 88 seats. 12 seats outside. V menu. Wheelchairs. No children at D.

Wright Brothers South Kensington

Cooking score: 2
⊖ South Kensington, map 3
Seafood | £38
56 Old Brompton Road, South Kensington, SW7 3DY
Tel no: 020 7581 0131
thewrightbrothers.co.uk

Handy for the museums, the South Ken outpost of the popular seafood chain has a separate cocktail and oyster bar, The Mermaid, in the basement. For main entry, see Borough branch, south London.
Chef/s: Colin Pritchard. **Closed:** 25 and 26 Dec, 1 Jan. **Meals:** main courses £18 to £29. Set L £19 (2 courses) to £21. **Details:** 56 seats. 4 seats outside. Bar. Music.

The Bingham Riverhouse

Cooking score: 4
⊖ Richmond, map 1
Modern British | £45
61-63 Petersham Road, Richmond, TW10 6UT
Tel no: 020 8940 0902
binghamriverhouse.com

'Much lighter and brighter than it was,' enthused one regular, delighted that the former Bingham is now 'trendily casual rather than boutique hotel'. There are hints at the ambition here, but a casual glance might miss them – beautiful glassware on the bistro-style tables; decent cutlery and napkins; a good selection of modern art adorning the walls of an otherwise comfortable but uncluttered set of rooms. If the menu, peppered with on-trend ingredients, appears a little fussy, the cooking lives up to its promise. A vivid green watercress risotto garnished with broad beans and pickled shallots is given oomph with a horseradish cream. Roast hake with white pudding and a white bean cassoulet would grace the table of any grand central London restaurant – the fish beautifully cooked, the meaty beans giving contrasting texture and flavour. Accomplished desserts follow, perhaps well-balanced bitter chocolate tart with a tropical fruit base, served with a delicate coconut sorbet and frozen white chocolate 'snow'. Add to this an approachable wine list, friendly and enthusiastic staff and the river rolling by outside and it's a very happy picture indeed.
Chef/s: Andrew Cole. **Meals:** set L £26 (2 courses) to £28. Set D £37 (2 courses) to £45. Tasting menu £60 (6 courses). **Details:** 40 seats. 15 seats outside. V menu. Bar.

Local Gem

These entries are brilliant neighbourhood venues, delivering good, freshly cooked food at great value for money.

LOCAL GEM
Bombetta

⊖ Snaresbrook, map 1
Italian | £35
Units 1-5 Station Approach, Wanstead, E11 1QE
Tel no: 020 3871 0890
bombettalondon.com

£5 OFF

The Puglian pork speciality that gives this modern trat its name arrives hot off the charcoal grill, just one of many meaty treats on offer at this neighbourhood eatery hard by Snaresbrook tube. A 'big friendly welcome' leads the way before cheese and meat platters, deep-fried mussels with garlic and mayo dip or whole sea bass with Italian beans and tomato sauce. The 'well chosen and affordable wine list' is mostly Italian and there's an on-site deli to tempt you.

Brilliant

Cooking score: 2
⊖ Hounslow West, map 1
Indian | £30
72-76 Western Road, Southall, UB2 5DZ
Tel no: 020 8574 1928
brilliantrestaurant.com

£5 OFF £30

First opening its doors in Southall in 1975, this family-run venture has a history dating back to 1950s Kenya where the current owner's forebears ran a restaurant of the same name. No doubt 'Very Good' would not have proven half as catchy. The kitchen turns out a populist blend of Indian curry house favourites with a Punjabi influence with nods to those early Kenyan days. Get the ball rolling with tandoori chicken wings or plump samosas (lamb or vegetarian), before masala king prawns or palak chicken. Vegetarian dishes are equally on point: a classic tarka dhal, say, or creamy paneer makhani. Among desserts, gulab jamun is a joyously sweet and sticky bowlful. Healthy options, marked as such on the menu, are made with low-fat yoghurts and lighter oils. A short wine list supplements the choice of lagers.

Chef/s: Dipna Anand. **Closed:** Mon. **Meals:** main courses £9 to £14. **Details:** 265 seats. V menu. Wheelchairs. Parking. Music.

The Dysart Petersham

Cooking score: 5
⊖ Richmond, map 1
Modern British | £47
135 Petersham Road, Richmond, TW10 7AA
Tel no: 020 8940 8005
thedysartpetersham.co.uk
£5
OFF

With scrubbed wooden tables and a bar dominating the room, the DP may have the appearance of a pub, but there's serious ambition in the kitchen. The place has a loyal following of regulars who know a good thing on their doorstep, as well as a smattering of foodie tourists. The modern cooking combines British ingredients with French technique and occasional whimsical Asian flair. A beautiful dish of middle white pork – slow-cooked shoulder croquette, a sliver of belly with crackling, a touch of loin – on a bed of mashed lentils with a sharp gherkin jus shows the kitchen cooking at the top of its game, well-matched by a delicate piece of charred mullet on a daikon radish base, bathed in a Champagne and ginger liquor. Presentation is thoughtful and deeply appealing without being too fussy, and puddings – an exemplary crème brûlée, homemade sorbets and ice creams, and the occasional complicated showpiece, are worth saving a little space for. The wine list has something for all occasions, but the somewhat eccentric house carafes are good value, too.

Chef/s: Kenneth Culhane. **Closed:** Mon, Tue, Wed, 1 week Jan, 1 week Aug. **Meals:** main courses £25 to £35. Set L and D £26 (2 courses) to £30. Tasting menu £70 (6 courses). Sun L £38. **Details:** 45 seats. 25 seats outside. V menu. Wheelchairs. Parking. Music. No children after 8pm.

Eat 17

Cooking score: 1
⊖ Walthamstow Central, map 1
Global | £26
28-30 Orford Road, Walthamstow, E17 9NJ
Tel no: 020 8521 5279
eat17.co.uk
£30

Handy to have about the place (the place being Walthamstow village), Eat 17's comfortable dining room sprang from the same minds that created the now renowned bacon jam. A magpie menu approaches global cuisine with fitting relish, offering everything from classic fish and chips to Korean-style chicken wings, from pie and mash to dhal. It's not consistently successful, but regulars have their favourites, and hits at inspection included firm, satisfying orecchiette with 'nduja, Flourish Farm kalettes, pecorino and tomato, and good-value BBQ sole on the bone. Puddings are a pass, but the neat wine list (from £19.50) shows a lively interest in variety.

Chef/s: Rowen Babe. **Closed:** 26 to 30 Dec. **Meals:** main courses £14 to £21. **Details:** 60 seats. 20 seats outside. Bar. Wheelchairs. Music.

The French Table

Cooking score: 3
map 1
French | £45
85 Maple Road, Surbiton, KT6 4AW
Tel no: 020 8399 2365
thefrenchtable.co.uk

The only table in town when there's something to celebrate, Eric and Sarah Guignard's restaurant stands out in the suburbs with a dashing French navy exterior. Regulars say both food and service are 'a joy', reporting also that food allergies are sensitively catered for and 'nothing is too much trouble'. Dinner in the long grey and white dining room is an easily navigable fixed-price menu. Tradition is not the kitchen's only aim, so for every silky Jerusalem artichoke velouté or duck and ham terrine there's a taste of something different, perhaps Cornish mackerel with vegetable escabèche, passion fruit purée, green tea and dashi foam. Fish and meat with immaculate pedigree are given clever counterpoints: venison might be rolled in earthy gingerbread, while Cornish stone bass has a generous tangle of accompaniments including a bergamot beurre blanc. Readers rate the pastry, say blood orange tart with matching sorbet. Wines, from £19.95, are as classy as the cool interior, although not always quite so French.

Chef/s: Eric Guignard. **Closed:** Mon, Sun, 25 Dec to early Jan, 2 weeks Aug. **Meals:** set L £22 (2 courses) to £27. Set D £39 (2 courses) to £45. Tasting menu £52 (6 courses). **Details:** 60 seats. Music.

The Glasshouse

Cooking score: 5
⊖ Kew Gardens, map 1
Modern European | £58
14 Station Parade, Kew, TW9 3PZ
Tel no: 020 8940 6777
glasshouserestaurant.co.uk

This elegant, light and airy dining room continues to knock out some of the best classical cooking in south-west London, with flavours and style as fresh as when it opened more than 20 years ago. The menu, a set-price affair and tweaked for every service, focuses on modern Anglo-French cooking underscored by a solid technical base. A simple combination – fresh asparagus and crab – is exquisite, especially with the addition of a richly savoury taramasalata made from smoked turbot roe. Chicory provides a welcome bitter note to a confit duck leg, served southern French-style with turnips, a sour cherry purée bringing a luxurious tartness. The cheeseboard is hard to ignore, but desserts are worth a look too: a perfect individual pavlova topped with tropical fruit and set off with lime ice cream; crème caramel flavoured with Sauternes and served with a small pain aux raisins. The wine list would keep an oenophile intrigued for hours, although the sommelier is on hand to offer gentle guidance for those who want it, and markups aren't too greedy.

Chef/s: Greg Wellman. **Closed:** Mon, 24 to 26 Dec, 1 Jan. **Meals:** set L £35 (2 courses) to £40. Set D £48 (2 courses) to £58. Tasting menu D £80 (5 courses). Sun L £45. **Details:** 60 seats. Wheelchairs. Children at L only.

Grand Trunk Road

Cooking score: 3
⊖ South Woodford, map 1
Indian | £40
219 High Road, South Woodford, E18 2PB
Tel no: 020 8505 1965
gtrrestaurant.co.uk

£5
OFF

Named after the epic 16th-century trade route that is, in almost every sense, a long way from South Woodford, Grand Trunk Road was restaurateur Rajesh Suri's gift to the suburbs when it opened in 2016. The task of providing a tour of regional Indian flavours falls to head chef Dayashankar Sharma. His grateful customers are more than willing to pay full fare, helped by a smartly appointed room and willing service. Elegantly presented starters might be crab cakes with lemongrass, curry leaves and a roasted garlic and pepper chutney, or Delhi chaat with sweet yoghurt. Main courses don't stray far from the familiar, but when butter chicken and keema mattar are done well, there's no need for diversion. From the tandoor, try rabbit with long peppers or Peshawari lamb chops with fennel, star anise and raw papaya, and don't forget the rotis. The bar is big on mixed drinks and spirits, but wine starts at £24.

Chef/s: Dayashankar Sharma. **Closed:** Mon, 25 and 26 Dec, 1 Jan. **Meals:** main courses £15 to £36. Set L £17 (2 courses) to £20. Tasting menu £58 Tue to Thur (5 courses). Sun L £29. **Details:** 54 seats. 12 seats outside. V menu. Wheelchairs. Music. No children at D.

Madhu's Heathrow

Cooking score: 2
⊖ Heathrow Terminal 1, 2, 3
Indian | £40
Sheraton Skyline Hotel, Bath Road, Harlington,
Hayes, UB3 5BP
Tel no: 020 8564 3380
madhusheathrow.com

Madhu's remains one of the big players on the Southall scene, but Sanjay Anand's sleek brand now has a flashy younger sibling within Heathrow's Sheraton Skyline Hotel. Fans of the original will recognise the trademark 'M' logo and the stylish black and red interiors, as well as many of the Punjabi/Kenyan dishes on the menu – from pani puri to home-style chicken or tilapia braised with masala spices and carom seeds. This branch also has a centrepiece robata grill that not only handles traditional tikkas and kebabs but also delivers prime-cut lamb ribs, seared king scallops with asparagus, whole baby chicken and dill-marinated salmon wrapped in a banana leaf. Spicing is toned down a notch for the (mainly) corporate international clientele, although sides, breads and accompaniments are all present and correct. Wines (from £24) are tailored to the food – otherwise sip bubble tea or fresh 'green' coconut straight from the shell.
Chef/s: Poonam Ball. **Meals:** main courses £11 to £19. Set L £30. Set D £40. Sun L £30. **Details:** 130 seats.

LOCAL GEM

Olympic Studios Café & Dining Room

⊖ Hammersmith, map 1
Modern British | £30
Olympic Studios, 117-123 Church Road,
Barnes, SW13 9HL
Tel no: 020 8912 5170
olympicstudios.co.uk
£30

This historic venue, which once played host to the likes of Led Zeppelin and The Who, is now home to London's premier Dolby Atmos surround-sound cinema and a sociable neighbourhood café and dining room serving food for our times. The all-day menu takes in small plates such as grilled sardines with buttermilk and caper sauce, trendy salads and mains ranging from chicken and mushroom pie to lamb rump with polenta, caponata and anchovy aïoli. They also do breakfast and feed kids admirably. Carefully selected wines from £18.

The Petersham

Cooking score: 2
⊖ Richmond, map 1
Modern British | £55
Nightingale Lane, Richmond, TW10 6UZ
Tel no: 020 8939 1084
petershamhotel.co.uk
£5 OFF 🛏

With its heavy curtains, chandeliers, thick carpets and hushed tones, this hotel restaurant is a favourite of Richmond locals, who not only use the place as a lunchtime bolthole, but also as a destination for celebratory bashes. The dining room makes the most of its enviable location, with inviting pastoral views from every table – cows grazing in meadows, the Thames meandering in the near distance. The menu may cater to conservative tastes, with smoked salmon carved from the trolley, Dover sole, and slabs of Angus beef fillet accompanied by all the trimmings (even if these include beetroot purée and truffle jus), but other ideas are more on-trend – perhaps oyster tempura soup, pickled mushrooms with 'edible worms' or octopus 'mosaic' with seaweed mayo, lemon sponge and yuzu pearls? To finish, you can play safe with crème brûlée or try the smoked chocolate délice. Wines offer sound drinking from £35.
Chef/s: Jean-Didier Gouges. **Closed:** 25 and 26 Dec. **Meals:** main courses £19 to £45. Set L and D £26 (2 courses) to £30. Tasting menu £75 (7 courses). Sun L £40. **Details:** 90 seats. Bar. Wheelchairs. Parking. Music.

Food fashion

Our inspectors tell us what's trending this year

Kombu An edible kelp used as a flavouring or 'sea vegetable' accompaniment. Try brill with artichoke and freekeh in kombu butter at **Ham**, West Hampstead.

Burnt butter Cooked slowly over low heat to produce a sweet, nutty flavour, it's used to dress Brixham ray wing at **The Wellington Arms**, Baughurst, or transformed into ice cream to accompany tonka bean panna cotta at **Osso**, Peebles.

Savoury ice cream Alongside blue cheese ice cream with port and pear poached in red wine at **Kota**, Cornwall, we've eaten asparagus, potato, bay leaf, sorrel and horseradish flavours either as palate cleansers or to balance out sweetness in desserts.

Lovage This punchy perennial takes centre stage at **Restaurant Sat Bains**, Nottingham, in an exceptional velouté but it's also been spotted in sauces, soups, emulsions and creams elsewhere.

Crumpets From the famous lobster crumpet 'nibble' at **Rovi**, Fitzrovia, to the 'bouncy' garlic crumpet with Baron Bigod cheese, ramson oil and truffle at **Forest Side**, Cumbria, the traditional British favourite is no longer restricted to elevenses.

Petersham Nurseries Café

Cooking score: 3
⊖ Richmond, map 1
Modern European | £50
Church Lane, Petersham Road, Richmond, TW10 7AG
Tel no: 020 8940 5230
petershamnurseries.com

For some 15 years, this abundantly floral café in a (posh) garden centre has been keeping the well heeled of Richmond not just in pot plants, but burrata, bottarga and brill, too. The place is adored, prices notwithstanding, regulars lingering at tables under lush early-summer canopies of bougainvillea, wisteria and jasmine to feast on a broadly Italian menu. Many of the ingredients, treated with the lightest of touches by talented chefs, are harvested from the nursery itself or sent up from the organic farm in Devon that also supplies the café's central London outposts, La Goccia and The Petersham in Covent Garden. Start with a perfectly poached egg and asparagus with a tangle of pea shoots (plus said bottarga), or a creamy pea risotto with mint and Parmesan. Lamb, chargrilled and on a bed of Castelluccio lentils, comes with chard and a perky salsa verde; and mackerel with rainbow relish, fennel, watercress and an Amalfi lemon mayonnaise. Round the experience off with a tarocco orange tart and tangy goat's cheese ice cream. The wine list launches its thorough tour of Italian vineyards with a £24 Frascati.
Chef/s: Ambra Papa. **Closed:** Mon, 25 and 26 Dec. **Meals:** main courses £23 to £29. **Details:** 120 seats. 100 seats outside. Wheelchairs. Parking.

Tangawizi

Cooking score: 2
⊖ Richmond, map 1
Indian | £30
406 Richmond Road, Twickenham, TW1 2EB
Tel no: 020 8891 3737
tangawizi.co.uk
£5 £30
OFF

With deep-purple-hued interiors, stylish contemporary lighting, mirrored panels and abstract prints, it's all a cut above your average local curry house – a fact not lost on the legions of fans who regularly make a beeline for this long-serving Indian near the southern end of Richmond Bridge. The menu covers a lot of ground and offers much more than the predictable litany of tandooris, jalfrezis, kormas and biryanis – although many regulars never venture beyond these old faithfuls. Among the less familiar ideas, you might be tempted by chilli fish (strips of spiced-up stir-fried tilapia), duck samosas or creamy masala liptey chicken, and there's an impressive selection for those who eschew meat – perhaps fresh mint tikki (spiced potato cakes with tamarind chutney), stir-fried okra with cumin seeds or the deliciously named gobi mehboobi (cauliflower florets with green chilli and curry leaves). Drink lassi, Kenyan Tusker beer or something from the workmanlike wine list.
Chef/s: Surat Singh Rana. **Closed:** 25 and 26 Dec, 1 and 2 Jan. **Meals:** main courses £7 to £17. **Details:** 60 seats. Music.

The Victoria

Cooking score: 3
⊖ Richmond, map 1
Modern British | £35
10 West Temple Sheen, East Sheen, SW14 7RT
Tel no: 020 8876 4238
victoriasheen.co.uk
⇌

Snugly tucked into a residential stretch of East Sheen, and with a conservatory dining room leading out to an attractive walled garden, this elegantly modernised hostelry has been serving its local community since the 1880s, fulfilling the role of neighbourhood resource with gusto. Damian Ciolek is shrewd enough to pitch his culinary offerings between classic pub fare – those in the market for a pie of the day with a heap of mash, or ale-battered fish and chips won't go unfed – and the kind of forward-thinking dishes that suit today's mood. Expect whipped truffled goat's cheese with marcona almonds, radishes and honeycomb, and then perhaps chargrilled chicken on barley with sweet potato and aubergine salad topped off with garlicky tzatziki. Vegetarian and vegan options keep things democratic, and the finisher might be mascarpone syllabub with Yorkshire rhubarb and oat crunch. A short but wisely chosen wine list starts at £6.50 a glass.
Chef/s: Damian Ciolek. **Meals:** main courses £13 to £25. **Details:** 90 seats. 60 seats outside. Bar. Parking. Music.

ENGLAND

Bedfordshire, Berkshire, Bristol,
Buckinghamshire, Cambridgeshire,
Cheshire, Cornwall, Cumbria, Derbyshire,
Devon, Dorset, Durham, Essex,
Gloucestershire, Greater Manchester,
Hampshire & the Isle of Wight,
Herefordshire, Hertfordshire, Kent,
Lancashire, Leicestershire and Rutland,
Lincolnshire, Merseyside, Norfolk,
Northamptonshire, Northumberland,
Nottinghamshire, Oxfordshire, Shropshire,
Somerset, Staffordshire, Suffolk, Surrey,
Sussex, Tyne & Wear, Warwickshire,
West Midlands, Wiltshire, Worcestershire,
Yorkshire

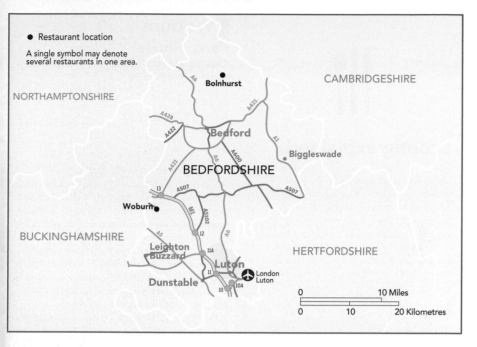

Bolnhurst

The Plough

Cooking score: 4
Modern British | £45
Kimbolton Road, Bolnhurst, MK44 2EX
Tel no: 01234 376274
bolnhurst.com

£5
OFF

In the northern reaches of the county, The Plough's location means it'll always be more destination than convenience. Co-owners Martin and Jayne Lee lay on enough temptation to keep readers coming back to the vaulted first-floor dining room of their pub restaurant; details are carefully attended to, from devils on horseback as a pre-dinner snack to homemade chocolate cookies with coffee. Top-notch British ingredients pervade the carte, which embraces the simplicity of grilled Cornish dayboat fish (a treat when you're this central) or Angus beef. More involved dishes include carpaccio of Balmoral venison with savoy cabbage, pickled

redcurrants and sour cream or Josper-grilled cauliflower with sesame and cauliflower purée and pickled radish, perhaps to be followed by Cornish lamb loin with shoulder hotpot and roast turnips. It's all thought through with the diner in mind, as are desserts of baked fine chocolate and salted caramel ganache, or blood orange posset. Wine starts at £19.95, but one of you is probably driving.
Chef/s: Martin Lee. **Closed:** Mon, 2 weeks Jan, 25, 31 Dec. **Meals:** main courses £18 to £34. Set L and D £21 (2 courses) to £26. **Details:** 80 seats. 30 seats outside. Wheelchairs. Parking.

Send us your review

Your feedback informs the content of the *GFG* and will be used to compile next year's entries. To register your opinion about any restaurant listed in the Guide, or a restaurant that you wish to bring to our attention, visit: thegoodfoodguide.co.uk/feedback.

Scoring explained

Local Gems, scores 1 and 2

Scoring a 1 or a 2 in *The Good Food Guide*, or being awarded Local Gem status, is a huge achievement. We list the very best restaurants in the UK; for the reader, this means that these restaurants are well worth visiting if you're in the area – and you're extremely lucky if they are on your doorstep.

Scores 3 to 6

Further up the scale, scores 3 to 6 range from up-and-coming restaurants to places to watch; there will be real talent in the kitchen. These are the places that are well worth seeking out.

Scores 7 to 9

A score of 7 and above means entering the big league, with high expectations of the chef. In other words, these are destination restaurants, the places you'll long to talk about – if you're lucky enough to get a booking.

Score 10

This score is extremely rare, with chefs expected to achieve faultless technique at every service. In total, only eight restaurants have achieved 10 out of 10 for cooking since the scoring system was introduced in 1998.

See page 13 for an in-depth breakdown of *The Good Food Guide*'s scoring system.

▎Woburn
Paris House
Cooking score: 6
Modern British | £70
London Road, Woburn Park, Woburn, MK17 9QP
Tel no: 01525 290692
parishouse.co.uk
£5 OFF

The name is no mere whim or fancy. The building that now stands amid the expanses of Woburn Estate was shipped, lock, stock and timbers, from the French capital in 1878 and reassembled on site. Of course, the interior is now bang-on contemporary (note the cheeky prints and zany modern sculptures in the dining room) and the food is of the moment too. Much of the kitchen's energy is focused on the six- and eight-course tasting menus peppered with European and Asian influences, and delivered with consummate panache and attention to detail. Risk-takers might relish adventurous combinations of, say, duck liver and ham, pomegranate and gingerbread, or silken tofu with charred plum soup and yuzu kosho, while those with more conservative palates will find pleasure in monkfish with curried mussels, Romano peppers and monk's beard. Mindful that the no-choice format is not to everyone's liking, Fanning has also introduced a 'Sentaku' menu (not Saturday evenings) – a selection of small and large plates lifted from the longer tasting menus and individually priced: hogget with escabèche carrots, peas and saffron, for example, or baked custard, spiced rhubarb and caramel pastry. Wine pairings come as standard across the board; alternatively, choose from the expertly assembled global list.
Chef/s: Phil Fanning and Dan Treadwell. **Closed:** Mon, Tue, Wed, 23 Dec to 2 Jan. **Meals:** main courses £28 to £36 Thur and Fri. Tasting menu L £52 (6 courses) and D £100 (8 courses). **Details:** 36 seats. V menu. Parking. Music.

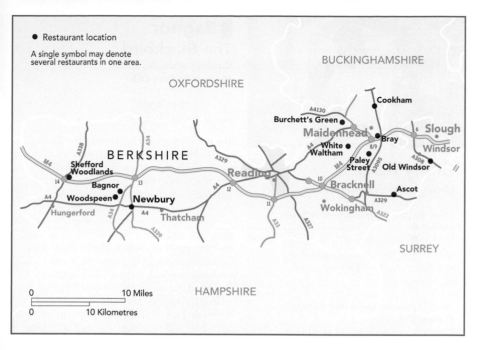

- Restaurant location

A single symbol may denote
several restaurants in one area.

BUCKINGHAMSHIRE

OXFORDSHIRE

Cookham

A4130
Burchett's Green
Maidenhead
Bray
6
Slough

White
Waltham
8/9
Windsor

BERKSHIRE
A329
Paley
Street
Old Windsor

Shefford
Woodlands
Reading
10

14
Bagnor
13
12
Bracknell
Ascot

A4
Woodspeen
Newbury
11
A329

Hungerford
A4
Thatcham
Wokingham
A322

SURREY

0   10 Miles   HAMPSHIRE
0   10 Kilometres

▌Ascot
Restaurant Coworth Park
Cooking score: 6
Modern British | £80
Blacknest Road, Ascot, SL5 7SE
Tel no: 01344 876600
dorchestercollection.com
£5 OFF

This extravagantly restored Georgian
mansion is a stunning prospect surrounded by
240 acres of manicured grounds, ancient
woodland and meadows. At the centre of
things is a smartly appointed dining room
complete with statement oak leaf chandelier
and views of the rose terrace – a special-
occasion backdrop for food with bags of
innovation, style and panache. Whether you
choose from the carte or the tasting menu, you
can expect thrilling food as well as a respectful
nod to seasonal British ingredients: marinated
scallops are paired with Yorkshire rhubarb and
hazelnut, while Waterford Farm lamb is
dressed with onion, shallots and turnips.

Luxuries abound, from 80-day salt-aged beef
short rib with lettuce and pickles to braised
turbot with truffles, morels and sea herbs,
while desserts include a high-end take on St
Honoré with salted caramel and Tahitian
vanilla ice cream. It's also worth spending
extra on a serving of cheese bread with
marinated figs. As expected, the wine list
features an extravagance of vintage
Champagne alongside top-ticket bottles at
top-ticket prices (from £35).
Chef/s: Adam Smith. **Closed:** Mon, Tue. **Meals:** set
L £35. Set D £50 to £80. Sun L £50. Tasting menu
£110 (7 courses). **Details:** 55 seats. V menu. Vg
menu. Bar. Wheelchairs. Parking. Music. Children
over 8 yrs after 7pm.

Vegetarian and vegan
While many restaurants offer dishes
suitable for non-meat eaters, those
marked 'V menu' (vegetarian) and
'Vg menu' (vegan) offer separate menus.

Issy Crocker

Emily Roux
Caractère, Notting Hill

What do you enjoy most about being a chef?
I love the whole dynamic of a restaurant and kitchen. The buzz you get during service is unique and the camaraderie is amazing.

What is your favourite dish on your current menu?
Celeriac cacio e pepe - it has become a 'signature' dish. Strands of celeriac, covered in a rich, peppery cheese sauce. What's not to love?

Name one ingredient you couldn't cook without.
Black pepper. It's definitely my number one go-to seasoning.

Who are your greatest influences?
There are many chefs I look up to; obviously a few family members as well. Alain Ducasse and Anne-Sophie Pic are both amazing entrepreneurs and chefs I admire.

What's your favourite kitchen item?
Our Japanese mandolin that creates the beautiful long strands of celeriac that go in the cacio e pepe dish.

When you get home at the end of a long day, what do you like to eat?
Normally something savoury. Toast with salted butter and some charcuterie or cheese.

▌Bagnor
The Blackbird
Cooking score: 5
Modern British | £45
Bagnor, RG20 8AQ
Tel no: 01635 40005
theblackbird.co.uk

Bagnor on the river Lambourn is a slice of affable Home Counties charm, into which this partly timbered and partly bricked 17th-century inn fits like a glove. The place feels agreeably unreconstructed inside, the contemporary designer's hand for once resisted in favour of bucolic simplicity, elderly furniture and display plates on shelves. That isn't the mode of Dom Robinson's culinary approach, though. The innovative country cooking in which he specialises has now branched out into a five-course Dégustation offering alongside the carte and midweek Menu du Jour. You might begin with tartare of aged beef and hazelnuts seasoned with lime and smoked chilli, and proceed via a reimagining of bonne femme mushroom sauce for a piece of brill, to roast lamb rump with its glazed sweetbreads and pommes Anna. A group eating in late autumn encountered a mixed bag – oddly flavourless partridge in its season – with some cheer arriving in the form of mature pork loin with confit root vegetables, choucroute and Cox's apple. The signature dessert is single-variety chocolate fondant with Baileys ice cream and coffee mousse. Wines have been chosen with an eye to variety and value within a relatively limited compass, starting at £26 for an organic Sicilian white.
Chef/s: Dom Robinson. **Closed:** Mon, Sun.
Meals: main courses £24 to £28. Set L £24 (2 courses) to £29. Tasting menu £65 (5 courses).
Details: 28 seats. 30 seats outside. Wheelchairs. Parking. Music.

Bray
The Crown at Bray
Cooking score: 2
British | £45
High Street, Bray, SL6 2AH
Tel no: 01628 621936
thecrownatbray.com

Aside from the chef's cookbooks on sale at the bar, there's no inkling that this 16th-century village boozer is part of Heston Blumenthal's mini empire in Bray. The Crown itself is a genuine local, with low beams, open fires and historic prints providing the backdrop for real ales and a menu with a British accent and heaps of vegetables on the side. The kitchen banishes fancy Heston-style wizardry in favour of expertly rendered classics – chicken and mushroom pie, whole roasted plaice with shrimps and burnt butter, a treacle-cured bacon burger or chargrilled Hereford sirloin steak with bone marrow sauce and fries. Kick off with lemon-cured salmon or a bowl of celeriac soup, finish with sticky toffee pudding, baked vanilla cheesecake or a trio of British cheeses with sultana bread. There's a snappy list of global wines (from £20) plus a vine-draped courtyard and sprawling garden for summer drinking.
Chef/s: Matt Larcombe. **Closed:** 25 Dec. **Meals:** main courses £13 to £29. **Details:** 55 seats. 80 seats outside. Bar. Wheelchairs. Parking.

★ TOP 50 ★

The Fat Duck
Cooking score: 8
Modern British | £325
1 High Street, Bray, SL6 2AQ
Tel no: 01628 367584
thefatduck.co.uk

The beamed room with its low ceilings and double-linened tables is one of the near-mythical locales for modern British cuisine. It seems extraordinary to recall that The Fat Duck is fast approaching its silver anniversary, a period in which its prime mover, Heston Blumenthal, has comprehensively rewritten the book on what restaurants at the rarefied end of the spectrum might offer. Two things need be said before one considers eating here: one is that the cost of it all is formidable, with wines helping to escalate the already sky-high price of the standard menu; the other is that the conceptual approach to individual dishes, present since the early days, has become a full-blown theme park experience, restauration's equivalent of the concept album. The narrative thread is a day's trip to the seaside, which has appropriated aspects of Lewis Carroll's Alice stories along the way. Staff are in character throughout, repeating their script from table to table. The menu remains a document of adamantine constancy, still incorporating the Campari and Prosecco ice lolly, the breakfast cereal variety pack, the whipped butter with coffee and tomato jam, the Sound of the Sea waves and seagull headphone experience, the 99 ice cream of crab and passion fruit, and so much more. The heart of the production comes with Are You Ready for Dinner?, an odd question after the multiplicity of courses that has already appeared, but which might turn on saddle of venison with celeriac, blackcurrant and smoked chestnuts, or caviar-dotted fish of the day in a green setting of cucumber and peppers. By the end, when whisky gums are followed by the famous levitating pillow of malt meringue, you may feel you have begun hallucinating, which would be entirely in keeping. There will always be the odd voice in the corner to say 'not much of it resembles real food', but as a once-in-a-lifetime event, all this adds up to something genuinely memorable, almost terrifyingly labour-intensive and replete with exhaustless technical imagination. With glass prices all in double figures, it's probably best to sign up for the flight, which is chosen with impressive sensitivity to the hugely demanding context.
Chef/s: Heston Blumenthal and Edward Cooke. **Closed:** Mon, Sun, 2 weeks Dec to Jan. **Meals:** tasting menu £325 (15 courses). **Details:** 42 seats. V menu. Vg menu. Wheelchairs. Music. Pre-payment required.

The Hind's Head

Cooking score: 3
British | £65
High Street, Bray, SL6 2AB
Tel no: 01628 626151
hindsheadbray.com
£5
OFF

As if there wasn't enough theatricality at its
sister restaurant down the road, The Hind's
Head adds its own flamboyant two pennies'
worth to Bray's food scene – or maybe that
should be two pounds' worth, for this is not a
'cheap pie and a pint' pub. Start with a cocktail
and substantial snacks – crab scones and mayo
perhaps, or a quail Scotch egg served in a
pewter cup – in The Royal Lounge where
tartan, velvet and dark walls suggest a clubby
intimacy and play to the historic setting. Then
dine on a menu fat with British classics dressed
afresh. Braised ox cheek with root vegetables,
champ mash and black truffle is rich fuel on a
chill spring day, warmer weather offering
roast plaice with girolles, pickled cucumber,
brown shrimps and mustard cream. Tick the
final Hind's Head box with the nutmeg- and
cinnamon-flecked panna cotta-cum-custard
tart that is the quaking pudding. An easy-
going Languedoc-Roussillon blend of Syrah
and Grenache opens the wine list at £32, but
it's best to know in advance that prices ramp up
quickly thereafter.
Chef/s: Peter Grey. **Closed:** 25 Dec, 1 Jan.
Meals: main courses £25 to £47. Set L £25 Mon to
Fri (2 courses) to £30. Sun L £47. **Details:** 72 seats.
Bar. Wheelchairs. Parking. Music.

The Waterside Inn

Cooking score: 7
French | £170
Ferry Road, Bray, SL6 2AT
Tel no: 01628 620691
waterside-inn.co.uk

It would be a stretch to say that The Waterside
invented Bray – Charles II and Nell Gwyn
had already discovered it during the
Restoration – but the riverbank retreat that

Michel Roux OBE opened here in 1972
certainly inaugurated a new era in its fortunes.
When the dining room is open to the birdsong
and weeping willows of a Berkshire summer's
day, it's an unalloyed treat, enhanced of course
by the magisterial French cooking that has
been in the hands of Michel's son Alain since
2002. The menus glide as sedately through the
times as do rowing boats on the Thames
outside, with quenelles de brochet and
langoustines to start, or Jerusalem artichoke
and leek pithivier and watercress salad in
truffle dressing. Main-course principals are of
unmistakable excellence, perhaps pearly-fresh
turbot glazed with seaweed, garnished with
crabmeat, razor clams and braised hispi in
horseradish beurre blanc, while meats look
fondly to the best Gallic traditions, as in a
daube combining oxtail and beef cheek
braised in Beaujolais with button onions,
mushrooms and lardons. An enterprising pair
might sign up for spit-roasted Challans duck
in mandarin jus with chestnut-stuffed
cabbage. Cheeses are in irresistible prime
condition, and desserts reliably include a
textbook soufflé, perhaps of banana, Valrhona
Caramélia chocolate and orange. As to the
wine list, its global reach and its prices you can
probably guess.
Chef/s: Alain Roux and Fabrice Uhryn. **Closed:**
Mon, Tue, 26 Dec to 30 Jan. **Meals:** main courses
£52 to £60. Set L £52 Wed to Fri (2 courses) to £64.
Set L £80 weekends. Tasting menu £170 (6 courses).
Details: 70 seats. Bar. Parking. Children over 9 yrs.

▉ Burchett's Green

The Crown

Cooking score: 6
French | £50
Burchett's Green, SL6 6QZ
Tel no: 01628 824079
thecrownburchettsgreen.com

The Bonwick family's reinvented village inn is
now firmly established as a serious but relaxed
dining destination: 'I noted Pierre Koffmann
at one table, and Stephen Harris and his staff at
another,' observed one eagle-eyed visitor.
Indeed, the food is leagues ahead of your

average pub offering. Chef Simon Bonwick has a high-end restaurant background and he knows how to use it – yet his food sits comfortably in this informal setting. While the menu descriptions are brief, there are spins and flourishes on the plate: a 'vibrant, clean-tasting' starter of Cromer crab with cashews, apple and passion fruit pleased one diner. The bar stays high for braised haunch of venison pie with a superb rowan sauce and Highland beef fillet 'steamed on string', its accompanying demi-glace deep and glossy. To finish, a textbook mango and coconut baba comes with two types of rum, ice cream, lime and freshly grated coconut. The meal is threaded through with careful details, say a pre-starter of limpid pheasant broth, warm bread rolls and a meaty beef dripping truffle as a finale. Son George heads front of house, aided by various siblings. Kind pricing extends to a concise wine list that opens at £21.

Chef/s: Simon Bonwick. **Closed:** Mon, Tue, 2 weeks Dec to Jan. **Meals:** main courses £13 to £24. **Details:** 20 seats. Bar. Wheelchairs. Parking. Music. Children over 12 yrs.

▌Cookham
The White Oak
Cooking score: 3
Modern British | £32
The Pound, Cookham, SL6 9QE
Tel no: 01628 523043
thewhiteoak.co.uk

£5
OFF

A pub for all seasons: a cosy bar after winter walks, a leafy garden for summer evenings, and a capable kitchen delivering a repertoire of modern dishes year round. Prime Highland steaks have long been at the vanguard of the menu (arriving with triple-cooked chips), although there are lighter dishes – torched Cornish mackerel with heritage tomato salad and lemon purée, or Wye Valley asparagus with hazelnut mayonnaise and crispy egg are among the starters. For mains, go for something as sprightly as crab linguine with lemon and chilli, or as gutsy as chargrilled

pork chop with sauce vierge and purple sprouting broccoli. Brioche doughnuts with custard and salted caramel sauce are a belt-slackening finale. There are handpumped ales and a succinct wine list starting at £20. Look out for good-value set lunches. The Three Oaks in Gerrards Cross, Buckinghamshire (see entry) is from the same owners.

Chef/s: Graham Kirk. **Meals:** main courses £14 to £23. Set L £16 (2 courses) to £19. Set D £19 (2 courses) to £21. **Details:** 75 seats. 35 seats outside. Bar. Wheelchairs. Parking. Music.

▌Newbury
★ NEW ENTRY ★
Henry & Joe's
Cooking score: 3
Modern British | £50
Cheap Street, Newbury, RG14 5DD
Tel no: 01635 581751
henryandjoes.co.uk

Squeezed into a row of catering outlets on what isn't exactly Newbury's prettiest street, this compact neighbourhood restaurant wears all its formidable charm on the inside. Airy and well lit, it basks in the radiant glow of Joe Byrne's front of house manner, for which 'obliging' is too small a word. He and chef Henry Ireson have put together a thoroughly enticing package, founded on deftly constructed modern British dishes that emerge from the open, tiled kitchen. Salt-baked kohlrabi is soft as butter, served on sweet white bean houmous with the bittering note of wild garlic. For main, a hefty tranche of pearly trout reclines across a whopping great calçot onion, with sweet potato purée, diced apple and smoked almonds adding support, or there might be lamb rump with sweetbread boudin in an inviting array of fresh curds, ale-braised clams and wild asparagus. For dessert, rhubarb crumble arrives wearing its topping like a hat, surrounded by a thin nutmegged anglaise. A useful list of wines by the glass starts at £6.

Chef/s: Henry Ireson. **Closed:** Mon, Tue, Sun. **Meals:** main courses £20 to £30. Set L and early D £23 (2 courses) to £26

The Vineyard

Cooking score: 5
Modern European | £69
Stockcross, Newbury, RG20 8JU
Tel no: 01635 528770
the-vineyard.co.uk

The walk-in glass wine cave at this secluded villa outside Newbury indicates the studious orientation of the place. The split-level dining room, with a Norma Desmond staircase descending into its lower reaches, is patrolled by staff who are 'incredibly poised and aware', displaying their assiduous wine training lightly. Tom Scade has taken over a kitchen that has seen several rounds of musical chairs in recent years, but indications from his tasting menu suggest no lack of confident application. Soy and treacle tuna with avocado purée and ginger jam is a successful reprise from Scade's predecessor. Deep caramelising sweetens a scallop that arrives with pickled and puréed celeriac, pressed apple and 'loads of truffle'. In the principal courses, the focus blurs a little. Loin and shoulder of lamb, the former bitterly herbed, the latter done in a compensating jammy braise, let the side down, but desserts have the flash of magic. Molten caramel is poured over a chocolate sphere to reveal the inner core of passion fruit mousse and mango ice cream. The wine list remains one of the best in the Guide, a Herculean labour of love with star billing going to wines from the owner's Sonoma County vineyards. With 300 by the small glass (from £6), there's ample opportunity to taste, in a range that sees young Burgundy growers rubbing shoulders with California dreamers, Greeks and Sicilians.

Chef/s: Tom Scade. **Meals:** set L £24 (2 courses) to £29. Set D £69. Tasting menus £89 (7 courses) to £99. Sun L £39. **Details:** 90 seats. V menu. Vg menu. Bar. Wheelchairs. Parking. Music. No children at D.

▌Old Windsor

The Oxford Blue

Cooking score: 5
Modern British | £50
10 Crimp Hill, Old Windsor, SL4 2QY
Tel no: 01753 861954
oxfordbluepub.co.uk

Seamlessly conjured out of a pair of Victorian cottages, with an extensive terrace out front and a spacious interior that contrasts tan banquettes with walls in – what else? – Oxford dark blue, this pub cuts quite a dash. Steven Ellis's food puts the emphasis firmly on assertive tastes and hearty proportions, beginning perhaps with trout cured in Treason IPA and served with pickled cucumber and dill mayonnaise, or savoury cheesecake made with goat's cheese, beetroot and walnuts. Venison from Windsor Great Park is a USP main course, served with a croquette of its braised shoulder and a tartlet of caramelised pear and chicory, while fish might be a boozy velouté of mussels to accompany Cornish cod. Don't expect the kitchen to take its foot off the gas at dessert stage, either, when chocolate soufflé with banana ice cream and toffee sauce is among the possibilities. Cask ales on tap herald a highly distinguished drinks list that moves on to wines arranged roughly by style. Quality and value reign supreme, opening with medium glasses from £6, or Coravin selections from £11.

Chef/s: Steven Ellis. **Closed:** Mon, Tue, 24 to 26 Dec. **Meals:** main courses £23 to £27. Set L £25 (2 courses) to £30. **Details:** 45 seats. 16 seats outside. Vg menu. Wheelchairs. Parking. Music.

Paley Street
The Royal Oak

Cooking score: 4
British | £45
Littlefield Green, Paley Street, SL6 3JN
Tel no: 01628 620541
theroyaloakpaleystreet.com

Nick Parkinson will be celebrating 19 years at The Royal Oak in 2020, and it says a great deal about his devotion to duty that he's managed a careful balance of pubby approachability, genuine civility, warmth and consistently good food. Devoted regulars and first-timers rub shoulders in the smart pair of beamed dining rooms, amid a setting of modern artworks, polished tables and comfortable chairs. Leon Smith's cooking is all about contrasting seasonal ingredients, be it a carpaccio of hare with pickled swede, leg ragoût and confit vegetables, a loin of 'very pink' venison with a little suet pudding of the shoulder, baby turnips, caramelised chicory and a well-reduced jus, or a dish of pork belly with Jerusalem artichokes, lentils, black pudding and apple purée. The cheese selection is well worth exploring, while desserts embrace traditional themes as in a treacle pudding with nutmeg custard and lime ice cream. The wide-ranging wine list will please extravagant diners wanting to push the boat out, but there are plenty of modest offerings and a decent range by the glass and carafe.

Chef/s: Leon Smith. **Meals:** main courses £18 to £26. **Details:** 80 seats. Bar. Wheelchairs. Parking. Music.

Shefford Woodlands
LOCAL GEM
The Pheasant Inn

Modern British | £30
Ermin Street, Shefford Woodlands, RG17 7AA
Tel no: 01488 648284
thepheasant-inn.co.uk

A new private dining room is just one of the features that attracts travellers and families to this cannily run 'free house and hotel' just off junction 14 of the M4. The menu is spot-on for its target audience, offering everything from sharing boards, sandwiches and reworked pub classics to more 'innovative' contemporary ideas such as tomato tartare with goat's cheese cream or sea bass in shellfish broth with seaweed butter sauce. Other plus points include a 'perfect pub interior', clued-up staff, a dedicated vegan menu and an affordable wine list.

White Waltham
The Beehive

Cooking score: 6
British | £38
Waltham Road, White Waltham, SL6 3SH
Tel no: 01628 822877
thebeehivewhitewaltham.com

'Roast beef and Yorkshire pudding sounds a mundane choice on a Sunday lunchtime, but not when the cooking is so good,' noted one visitor to Dominic Chapman's hugely enjoyable, hugely popular country pub overlooking the village cricket pitch. A boon for the area, it offers an agreeable blend of rusticity and well-heeled comfort, a place where you can settle in for drinks in the bar or head to the spacious adjoining dining room for produce-driven seasonal cooking. The starting point is high-quality – often local –

Anonymous

At *The Good Food Guide*, our inspectors dine anonymously and pay their bill in full every time. These impartial review meals, along with feedback from thousands of our readers, are what informs the content of the *GFG*, the UK's number one selling restaurant guide. Only the best restaurants make the cut.

raw ingredients, perhaps combined in a wild mushroom, goat's cheese, onion and red pepper tart, or a dish of fried Cornish squid with wild garlic mayonnaise. To follow, there could be a satisfying pie of Cotswold white chicken, ham, leek and mushroom or peppered haunch of venison with creamed spinach, celeriac purée and sauce poivrade. Desserts embrace buttermilk pot with caramelised blood oranges as well as soufflé of pineapple and coconut ice cream, while wines are an affordable, well-researched – and mainly European – selection, from £22.
Chef/s: Dominic Chapman. **Closed:** 25 and 26 Dec. **Meals:** main courses £17 to £29. Set L £20 (2 courses) to £25. Sun L £22. **Details:** 70 seats. 40 seats outside. Bar. Wheelchairs. Parking. Music.

sublime dipping – 'the best I've had in a long while,' enthused one diner. A thunderously good wine list makes for much happy exploration, with plenty of choice below £40, starting with small glasses of Veneto Soave and Merlot for £5.
Chef/s: John Campbell and Olly Rouse. **Meals:** main courses £18 to £36. Set L and early D £25 (2 courses) to £31. **Details:** 66 seats. 36 seats outside. Vg menu. Bar. Wheelchairs. Parking. Music.

◼ Woodspeen
The Woodspeen
Cooking score: 5
Modern British | £46
Lambourn Road, Woodspeen, RG20 8BN
Tel no: 01635 265070
thewoodspeen.com
£5 OFF 🍾

The dining room of this one-time red-brick pub is in a slick youthful extension of timber-clad ceilings and polished concrete floors. The open kitchen pours forth modern British constructions from an extensive menu. Among more successful combinations is a scallop starter, which comes with a pressed terrine of Jersey Royals, pickled mushrooms and hazelnuts in truffled mayonnaise, and another of Jerusalem artichoke and pear with crisped wild rice in a cashew sauce with wheatgrass oil. At inspection, a ribeye steak was over trimmed and inaccurately timed, its single batter-heavy onion ring hardly helping matters, but a breast of corn-fed chicken inspired more confidence, its flesh offset with buttery roasted hispi, asparagus and a punchy mushroom purée. Summer might bring gooseberry and elderflower fool with hazelnut sponge and sorrel sorbet, or crème brûlée topped with gariguette strawberries and black olives with olive shortbread for

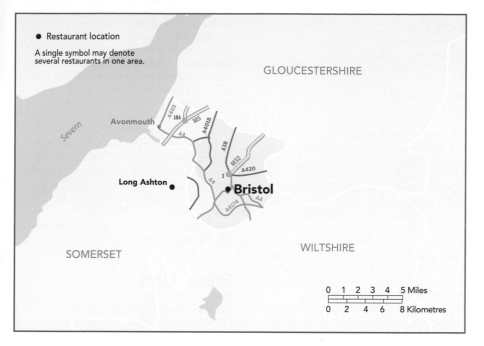

Restaurant location

A single symbol may denote
several restaurants in one area.

GLOUCESTERSHIRE

Avonmouth

Severn

Long Ashton

Bristol

SOMERSET

WILTSHIRE

0 1 2 3 4 5 Miles
0 2 4 6 8 Kilometres

◼ Bristol
Adelina Yard
Cooking score: 4
Modern European | £41
3 Queen Quay, Welsh Back, Bristol, BS1 4SL
Tel no: 0117 911 2112
adelinayard.com
£5
OFF

Jamie Randall and Olivia Barry's culinary
CVs read like a who's who of the London
restaurant scene, and they've put all that
experience to telling use in their thriving solo
venture down by Bristol's harbourside. With
its open kitchen and showpiece chef's table,
the dining room crams a great deal into a
narrow L-shaped space, while the cooking is
built around tasting menus and a brief carte
with modernist overtones. Dishes such as
fermented kale with gnocchi, goat's cheese
and slow-cooked egg have obvious Nordic
nuances, but the kitchen isn't a slave to the
zeitgeist – witness a sturdy plate of Cornish
beef with carrots, smoked potato, bone

marrow and onion; or cod, mussel and squid
agnolotti in a squid broth garlanded with
coastal herbs. In-vogue vegetables such as
turnips and calçots (green onions) are given
special treatment, and there are some suitably
modish pairings among the desserts – blood
orange, buttermilk and wild fennel, say. A
short, snappy wine list focuses on cherry-
picked European growers.
Chef/s: Jamie Randall and Olivia Barry. **Closed:**
Mon, Sun. **Meals:** main courses £19 to £26. Set L
£18. Tasting menu £45 (5 courses) to £65.
Details: 34 seats. 10 seats outside. Wheelchairs.
Music.

£5 voucher
£5
OFF
Restaurants showing this symbol
are participating in our £5 voucher
scheme, redeemable against a meal for
two or more. Vouchers can be found at
the back of this book.

Box-E

Cooking score: 4
Modern British | £29
Unit 10, Cargo 1, Wapping Wharf, Bristol,
BS1 6WP
boxebristol.com
£30

Take two shipping containers, add a stove called Sandra, and factor in two inspirational owners (Elliott and Tessa Lidstone), and you have the foundations of Box-E. With interior walls clad in plywood and an open kitchen (book a ringside seat to experience Elliott's cooking at close quarters), those two containers are full of life and noise during service. The format follows three-course convention and what arrives is intelligently judged and packed with flavour. Vegetables get starring roles in the likes of charred hispi cabbage with brown shrimps and lemon butter or roasted Jerusalem artichokes with White Lake goat's curd and black truffle. Elsewhere, guinea fowl might be teamed with crushed potatoes and kale, while hake and butter beans are enlivened by the feisty hit of sobrasada. Presentation is pleasingly rustic as in a dessert of chocolate mousse with blood orange and pistachio. Local beers add support to a multilingual wine list opening at £23.
Chef/s: Elliott Lidstone. **Closed:** Mon, Sun. **Meals:** main courses £14 to £18. Tasting menu £45 (7 courses). **Details:** 18 seats. 18 seats outside. Wheelchairs. Music.

Bravas

Cooking score: 2
Spanish | £20
7 Cotham Hill, Bristol, BS6 6LD
Tel no: 0117 329 6887
bravas.co.uk
£30

What started life as an under-the-radar supper club run from the owners' Bristol flat has grown into one of the city's favourite restaurants. Now Kieran and Imogen Waite's tapas bar is pretty much fully booked at peak times – in-the-know locals keep an eye on the 16 stools left unreserved at the bar and in the window. There's a real buzz as diners sit cheek by jowl at low tables (at the back) while higher ones closer to the bar give a ringside view of the small open kitchen and its sizzling plancha grill workhorse. The flavours of Spain permeate every inch of the menu, from chorizo cooked in cider or calçots with romesco sauce and almonds, right through to Cornish mussels with salsa verde and white wine or Newlyn mackerel with chilli and garlic and a dessert of arbequina olive oil and lemon cake with Moscatel cream. A well-curated all-Spanish wine list starts at £19 and there is an extensive sherry selection.
Chef/s: Mark Chapman. **Closed:** Sun. **Meals:** tapas £3 to £8. **Details:** 35 seats. Bar. Music.

Bristol Lido

Cooking score: 2
Mediterranean | £35
Oakfield Place, Bristol, BS8 2BJ
Tel no: 0117 332 3970
lidobristol.com

Visionary restaurateur Arne Ringner saved this Victorian lido from demolition 12 years ago. By restoring it to its original splendour, complete with a poolside restaurant, he created one of Bristol's more unique dining venues. From day one, the kitchen was run by chef Freddy Bird so his departure in early 2019 not only marked the end of an era but also the beginning of an exciting new chapter for his replacement, James Nathan. Although the chef's CV includes stints with Michael Caines, Michel Roux and Gordon Ramsay, the wood-fired oven remains the workhorse of the kitchen and influences from the Middle East and Spain still permeate the daily menu. River Fowey mussels and clams cooked in fino with sobrasada toast is one way to begin, before a Basque-style stew packed with monkfish, hake, mussels and prawns or wood-roast Devon beef with Sicilian tomatoes, spinach and horseradish. Finish with homemade chocolate and stout ice cream or Pedro Ximénez, date and custard tart. European-leaning wines from £19.50.

Chef/s: James Nathan. **Closed:** 25 Dec.
Meals: main courses £15 to £24. Set L and D £16 (2 courses) to £20. Sun L £16 (2 courses). **Details:** 120 seats. 30 seats outside. Bar. Wheelchairs. Music.

Bulrush

Cooking score: 5
Modern British | £68
21 Cotham Road South, Bristol, BS6 5TZ
Tel no: 0117 329 0990
bulrushrestaurant.co.uk

With the restaurant's slightly wonky frontage and lack of passing trade, received wisdom wouldn't have backed chef George Livesey when he opened in Cotham Road South. But the appeal of his cooking and the sheer inventiveness of tasting menus built of 'distinctly different' dishes offered at 'terrific value' have won diners over. 'Excellent service' keeps the atmosphere hanging together in an unusually proportioned, whitewashed space. There's enough crossover between à la carte and tasting menus for either to satisfy, although the tasting allows for more time spent with Livesey's little signatures, such as savoury macarons filled with goat's curd or duck liver. It's a carefully calibrated experience, with flavours balanced between subtle and punchy. Visitors' highlights include barbecued stone bass with king oyster mushrooms and monkfish liver, badger face lamb with sweetbread, whey and Roscoff onion, and a dessert of caramel chocolate, bay leaf and milk. In a move as bold as the food, the wine list tops out at a relatively modest £60.
Chef/s: George Livesey. **Closed:** Mon, Sun, 23 Dec for 3 weeks, 1 week May. **Meals:** main courses £18 to £24. Tasting menu £55 (8 courses) to £60. **Details:** 42 seats. V menu. Bar. Music.

★ TOP 10 ★

Casamia

Cooking score: 9
Modern British | £48
The General, Lower Guinea Street, Bristol, BS1 6SY
Tel no: 0117 959 2884
casamiarestaurant.co.uk

This is not a stuffy dining room: it is a smooth operation firing on all cylinders and there is no obligation to whisper. But while the food and service excel, the format can be confusing. The menu is understated, to say the least, with a single word describing each dish on the four- or eight-course tasting menu, only fleshed out verbally when one of the chefs brings the dish to table. But single-mindedness and a fiery determination to produce the best define Peter Sánchez-Iglesias's cooking. The chef is known for his instinct for building nuanced contrasts: from a tiny, delicate cream of Parmesan tart, through Galician beef with rendered fat and truffle spray, to the underscoring of sweet beetroot with Japanese pepper and ewe's curd, he knows his stuff and it shows. A triumphant standout is the rainbow trout with langoustine sauce and a trout mousse inflected with the zip of roe, trout skin wafer and lime zest that precedes an almost translucent hake, cured and steamed, with Champagne cream, and duck in two parts – firstly, in an intense sweet-sour broth with quail's egg, then tender pink breast with beautifully rendered crisp skin, salsify and greens. Passion fruit granita with passion fruit cream is the perfect curtain-raiser for a millefeuille with contrasting flavours of custard, tarragon and rhubarb creams, while madeleines make a fitting finale. Wine is a headline attraction, too; a wide-ranging list is stuffed with classy names, curious discoveries and instantly appealing by-the-glass selections.
Chef/s: Peter Sánchez-Iglesias and Jim Day. **Closed:** Mon, Tue, 25 to 28 Sept, 25 Dec to 7 Jan, 22 to 25 Apr, 24 to 27 Jun. **Meals:** tasting menu £48 (4 courses) to £118. **Details:** 30 seats. V menu. Bar. Wheelchairs. Music. Pre-payment required.

The Cauldron

Cooking score: 1
International | £26
98 Mina Road, Bristol, BS2 9XW
Tel no: 0117 914 1321
thecauldron.restaurant
£5 OFF £30

There is no gas supply to this lively neighbourhood restaurant, which means a kitchen fuelled on charcoal and kiln-dried logs. Locally reared meats are cooked over open fire, whether it's a flat iron steak or the minced pork kofta served with ginger, spring onions, tare (sweetened, thickened soy sauce), raw egg yolk and sticky rice. Elsewhere, chef Henry Eldon uses a heavy cast-iron cauldron for dishes such as smoked quinoa chilli with cornbread. A concise wine list is accompanied by a large choice of local beers, some brewed within walking distance of the restaurant. **Chef/s:** Henry Eldon. **Closed:** Mon. **Meals:** main courses £12 to £18. **Details:** 38 seats. 16 seats outside. Wheelchairs. Music.

Flour & Ash

Cooking score: 1
Italian | £20
203b Cheltenham Road, Bristol, BS6 5QX
Tel no: 0117 9083228
flourandash.co.uk
£30

This family-friendly pizza and ice cream venue in the shadows of railway arches towering over Cheltenham Road has been a go-to place for locals since former banker-turned-chef Steve Gale opened five years ago. Regulars are drawn by the good-value pizzas topped with high-end seasonal ingredients – perhaps marinated artichokes with

mozzarella, Cornish Gouda, broccoli tops and pesto, or Herefordshire snails with buffalo mozzarella, garlic butter, pancetta and spinach. You could start with smoked squirrel ravioli, wild mushrooms, hazelnut and tarragon butter, and to drink there are local ciders, Bristol-brewed beers and European wines from £17. **Chef/s:** Brendan Baker. **Closed:** 24 to 26 and 31 Dec, 1 Jan. **Meals:** main courses £9 to £15. **Details:** 41 seats. Music.

★ NEW ENTRY ★

Gambas

Cooking score: 2
Spanish | £20
Unit 12, Cargo2, Wapping Wharf, Bristol, BS1 6ZA
Tel no: 0117 934 9256
gambasbristol.co.uk
£30

Rather than clone their popular tapas bar, Bravas (see entry), Kieran and Imogen Waite have gone full-on seafood in this converted shipping container overlooking the harbour side. Tables on the suntrap terrace are in high demand at dusk, while inside, the compact restaurant and bar is dominated by an open kitchen with its plancha and huge paella pans. Although tapas staples – tortilla, patatas bravas, cod brandada tostada – are all present and correct, chef Gustavo Benet Fabra, formerly of Casamia (see entry), uses the daily specials to flex his culinary muscle in dishes such as whole gilthead bream with white wine and rosemary, cuttlefish stew, and in the choice of gambas – five types from soft-shell baby prawns to top-shelf Carabineros. Elsewhere, there could be rubia Gallega beef fillet and roasted bone marrow. Finish with a silky crema catalana or a couple of billowing, chewy meringues flavoured with orange and hazelnut and filled with whipped cream. Drink sherry, Spanish beers and wines from £19. **Chef/s:** Gustavo Benet Fabra. **Meals:** small plates £4 to £15. **Details:** 40 seats. 50 seats outside. Bar. Wheelchairs. Parking. Music. No reservations.

Greens

Cooking score: 3
Modern European | £32
25 Zetland Road, Bristol, BS6 7AH
Tel no: 0117 924 6437
greensbristol.co.uk

It's eight years since Martin Laurentowicz and Nick Wallace took over this neighbourhood restaurant from the family whose name remains above the door. Set back from the main drag, hidden down a quiet, leafy side street, this modern bistro is much loved by locals who appreciate no-frills, high-flavour European cooking. Crab and herb tart with hispi cabbage, parsley and Parmesan salad is a notable starter and could be followed by a classic bistro dish of rump of lamb with dauphinois potatoes, greens and mint salsa verde, or perhaps red lentil and pumpkin dhal with cumin rice, pistachios, pomegranate and raita. Panna cotta with rhubarb compôte and biscotti is one way to round things off. The set lunch and dinner menus remain a popular option, as do separate vegan and vegetarian menus. A compact wine list opens at £19.95 with plenty of choice by the glass and carafe.
Chef/s: Martin Laurentowicz. **Closed:** 24 to 28 Dec. **Meals:** main courses £16 to £29. Set L £13 (2 courses) to £17. Set D £18 (2 courses) to £24. Sun L £20. **Details:** 39 seats. 8 seats outside. V menu. Vg menu. Music.

The Kensington Arms

Cooking score: 1
Modern British | £27
35-37 Stanley Road, Bristol, BS6 6NP
Tel no: 0117 944 6444
thekensingtonarms.co.uk
£5 OFF   £30

Chef Josh Eggleton, owner of The Pony & Trap and Root (see entries), has raised the food credentials of this born-again Redland boozer, known locally as The Kenny, while maintaining its status as a laudable watering hole. Drinkers congregate in the bar with pints of ale from the Bristol Beer Factory; hungry diners head to the clubby dining room

in search of solid sustenance. The menu rolls with the seasons, offering a mix of pub staples (fishcakes, cheeseburgers, aged ribeye and chips) alongside more cosmopolitan ideas – perhaps pan-fried scallops with burnt blood orange and cardamom-pickled beets. Eclectic wines start at £20.
Chef/s: Luke Hawkins. **Closed:** 25 Dec. **Meals:** main courses £13 to £25. Set L £12 (2 courses) to £15. Sun L £26. **Details:** 96 seats. 20 seats outside. Bar. Music.

The Ox

Cooking score: 3
British | £45
The Basement, 43 Corn Street, Bristol, BS1 1HT
Tel no: 0117 922 1001
theoxbristol.com

This welcoming steakhouse and cocktail bar occupies what was once the subterranean Ocean Safe Deposit vaults in the heart of the city's old banking district. Frosted grape-cluster lamps, antique mirrors and distressed panelled walls add an Art Deco touch, and there's elegance to the flight of curving marble steps leading to the entrance. Often likened to London's Hawksmoor, The Ox attracts a cool crowd drawn to the locally sourced meat and fish cooked over charcoal. The range of steaks, from 170g D-rump to 850g T-bones to share, are the focal point of the menu, but there are plenty of other attractions, say farmhouse pork and pistachio terrine with tomato chutney to start, perhaps followed by pan-fried ray wing with brown shrimp butter. Vanilla and chocolate bread pudding with Kahlua custard is one way to finish. A concise wine list with a number of big-hitting reds opens at £20. There's a second branch on Whiteladies Road, BS8 2QX.
Chef/s: Todd Francis. **Meals:** main courses £15 to £31. Set L £12 (2 courses) to £15. Sun L £18 (2 courses). **Details:** 80 seats. Music.

Budget

£30 At restaurants showing this symbol, it is possible to eat three courses (excluding drinks) for £30 or less.

Paco Tapas

Cooking score: 5
Spanish | £40
3a The General, Lower Guinea Street, Bristol, BS1 6FU
Tel no: 0117 925 7021
pacotapas.co.uk
£5
OFF

'The thing that really struck me was the warmth of the welcome and the amazing service,' noted one visitor to this cosy Andalusian-inspired tapas bar from Peter Sánchez-Iglesias and the team behind neighbouring Casamia (see entry). On the water's edge in the rejuvenated General Hospital, head chef Kelvin Potter takes classic tapas to a higher plane, thanks in part to his precise skills, as well as to the quality of ingredients destined for the charcoal-fired grill in the open kitchen. Wafer-thin slices of smokey octopus 'a la Gallega' proved to be a standout dish for one diner, who commented that 'if money were no object, I'd go to Paco Tapas all the time... such fun and it really captures that neighbourhood-bar feel'. Other dishes to win praise include the meaty Duroc pork ribs, and lamb rump cooked in the coals. Wines start at £28, but there are also 14 sherries by the glass.
Chef/s: Peter Sánchez-Iglesias and Kelvin Potter.
Closed: Mon, Sun, 25 and 26 Dec, 1 Jan.
Meals: small plates £2 to £23. Tasting menu £50 (7 courses). **Details:** 32 seats. 32 seats outside. Music.

Pasta Loco

Cooking score: 3
Italian | £30
37a Cotham Hill, Bristol, BS6 6JY
Tel no: 0117 973 3000
pastaloco.co.uk
£5 **£30**
OFF

Judging by the crowds, the people of Bristol are indeed *loco* about pasta, so much so that a sibling (Pasta Ripiena, see entry) opened in the city centre in 2017. Dominic Borel and Ben Harvey offer the kind of easy-going contemporary space that suits their broad-minded take on modern Italian cooking, one where the kitchen turns out breezy openers such as punchy caponata with marinated artichokes, or an autumn salad enriched with pancetta and poached fruit. The pasta is handmade every day: look out for holey bucatini, dinky orzo, or pappardelle in a rich ragù of Lydney Park Estate wild boar. Taleggio with balsamic onions and biscuits is an alternative (or supplement) to chocolate délice with an intense espresso and grappa panna cotta. The astute wine list touches base with other great wine-producing nations, and the cocktails are well worth checking out.
Chef/s: Ben Harvey. **Closed:** Sun, 23 Dec to 3 Jan.
Meals: main courses £9 to £19. **Details:** 33 seats. Music.

Pasta Ripiena

Cooking score: 3
Italian | £28
33a St Stephen's Street, Bristol, BS1 1JX
Tel no: 0117 329 3131
pastaripiena.co.uk
£30

In a city brimming with quality independent restaurants, competition is beginning to be fierce, but this casual eatery more than holds its own. A lively chip off the old Bristolian block (Pasta Loco, see entry) right down to the same slatted wooden ceiling, paper bag lampshades, wood floor, black tables and open kitchen, Ripiena reflects its big brother's love affair with pasta, made in-house and teamed

with the pick of seasonal produce. You can eat very well here and at remarkable prices, whether ravioli of brown crab, mascarpone and chilli topped with Cornish shellfish, agretti and pangrattato or casoncelli of dry-aged salt marsh lamb with roast lamb belly, salsa verde and anchovy butter. Start with some red prawns cooked on the plancha with garlic butter, and finish with Tuscan chocolate and rum torte. The short European wine list is no less delightful, with a good selection by the glass and bottles from £19.
Chef/s: Joe Harvey. **Closed:** Sun. **Meals:** main courses £14 to £18. Set L £14 (2 courses) to £17. **Details:** 22 seats. Music.

Prego
Cooking score: 3
Italian | £30
7 North View, Bristol, BS6 7PT
Tel no: 0117 973 0496
pregobar.co.uk
£5 OFF £30

This neighbourhood bistro has been serving rustic Italian food to lucky locals for a decade now. The seasonal dishes are conjured from tiptop Italian and local ingredients and although the pizzas are a popular option, it's hard not to wander over to the specials board and carte, which might begin with Badminton Estate pigeon bruschetta with fig and red onion marmellata or a 'guazzetto' stew of baby octopus and squid braised in red wine with river Exe mussels. To follow, perhaps slow-cooked ox cheek ragù with pancetta, porcini, red wine, Grana Padano and pappardelle or roasted rump of lamb with potato al forno, heritage carrots, anchovy butter and salsa verde. All puddings are made on the premises, with marshmallow, hazelnut and chocolate ripple semifreddo one of the highlights. The wine list – supplemented by a range of vermouths and digestifs – rarely looks beyond Italy and opens at a commendable £16.50.

Chef/s: Danny Saville. **Closed:** Sun, 23 to 27 Dec, 1 and 2 Jan. **Meals:** main courses £10 to £17. Set L £13 (2 courses) to £18. **Details:** 50 seats. 30 seats outside. Wheelchairs. Music.

The Pump House
Cooking score: 2
Modern British | £33
Merchants Road, Bristol, BS8 4PZ
Tel no: 0117 927 2229
the-pumphouse.com
£5 OFF

A splendid location overlooking the historic docks makes this Victorian former pumping station particularly delightful in summer, when its harbourside garden springs to life. Inside, the busy ground-floor bar area is overlooked by a mezzanine that offers a quieter and more formal dining space. With everything made in-house, the seasonally changing menu is a mix of high-quality pub classics alongside more contemporary ideas, such as in an elegantly presented starter of Cornish squid, tomatoes, gooseberries and lovage. Chef proprietor Toby Gritten is a keen forager whose menu might feature locally picked wild garlic in a butter melting over onglet (and served with celeriac and fries), or wild mushrooms with braised spelt, onions and rarebit. Puddings are large and indulgent, perhaps a peanut parfait with banana, chocolate and dulce de leche. To drink, look to the awesome collection of gins and mixers – bar staff will happily advise – or choose something from the slightly pricey wine list.
Chef/s: Toby Gritten. **Closed:** 25 Dec. **Meals:** main courses £15 to £22. Tasting menu £45 (6 courses). **Details:** 100 seats. 100 seats outside. Bar. Wheelchairs. Parking. Music. Children over 14 yrs.

Root

Cooking score: 4
Modern British | £30
Cargo, Gaol Ferry Steps, Wapping Wharf,
Bristol, BS1 6WP
Tel no: 0117 930 0260
eatdrinkbristolfashion.co.uk
£30

'To be able to create something so intensely pleasurable to eat out of such humble ingredients is really my favourite kind of cooking' was the resounding endorsement of one visitor, wowed by this shipping container eatery on Bristol's waterfront. Since opening in 2017, Ex-Pony & Trap (see entry) chef Rob Howell has quickly established this Scandi-style operation as one of the city's must-visit restaurants. Most of the small plates are vegetable-based, with highlights including cauliflower pakora with blood orange and cashew milk, or roasted celeriac with almond curry and seaweed crisp. But that's not to say the meat and fish dishes aren't also standouts, as in cured sea bream, dill, cucumber and pickled chilli, or a Reuben-style flatbread layered with tongue, sauerkraut and Swiss cheese. The level of technical skill and creativity continues through to a chocolate ganache with passion fruit and coconut sorbet. Drink local ales, or wines from £25.
Chef/s: Rob Howell. **Closed:** Sun, 24 to 26 Dec.
Meals: small plates £4 to £10. **Details:** 32 seats. 48 seats outside. V menu. Wheelchairs. Parking. Music.

Tare

Cooking score: 3
Modern European | £40
Unit 14, Museum Street, Wapping Wharf,
Bristol, BS1 6ZA
Tel no: 0117 929 4328
tarerestaurant.co.uk
£5
OFF

Matt Hampshire's debut solo venture can be found in regenerated docklands, occupying two shipping containers within the Wapping Wharf Cargo development. Compact and contemporary, with just 24 seats (there are a few more on the suntrap terrace, weather permitting), Hampshire has to work within the confines of a galley kitchen, which means a no-choice four-course menu that changes frequently with the seasons. A meal might open with picked Dorset crab, apple, turnip, hazelnut and dill, move on to braised oxtail with pickled shallot, radish and parsley salad, then Beech Ridge Farm duck, which arrives with cranberry, salsify, savoy cabbage and five-spice sauce. Finish with chocolate délice with banana ice cream, honeycomb and pistachio or local cheese with quince chutney and sesame crackers. A separate vegetarian menu might include wild mushroom arancini, butternut squash, raisins and sage. To drink, there are local ales and a compact wine list, from £22.
Chef/s: Matt Hampshire. **Closed:** Mon, Tue, Sun.
Meals: tasting menu £40 (4 courses). **Details:** 24 seats. 14 seats outside. V menu. Wheelchairs. Parking. Music.

★ TOP 50 ★

Wilks

Cooking score: 7
Modern French | £64
1-3 Chandos Road, Bristol, BS6 6PG
Tel no: 0117 973 7999
wilksrestaurant.co.uk
£5
OFF

In the eight years since James Wilkins and Christine Vayssade launched Wilks on a quiet side street in one of the leafier suburbs, the city has seen a fair few high-profile openings – but for many readers, this smart neighbourhood restaurant has grown into one of Bristol's very best. The couple have worked in many notable restaurants around the world, with James spending time in the kitchens of Michel Bras and the Galvin brothers. The compact dining room has a calm, Zen-like feel, with muted shades offset by strikingly vibrant modern artwork. It's a serene backdrop for immaculate service and faultless modern French cooking with a strong reliance on prime raw materials. There are no cheap cuts or cutting corners here: note an ingenious dish of gravdlax of Brixham dayboat lobster tail (sweet and firm) with crunch from organic fennel and radish, sweet-sour from pink grapefruit and warmly spiced with timut pepper. Or a precisely cooked 28-day dry-aged Aberdeen Angus beef fillet teamed with white asparagus, sautéed fresh ceps, red chicory and a rich beef jus given a slightly spicy lift by Szechuan pepper leaf. Desserts are a strength, too, as illustrated by a light and crunchy pink praline meringue sphere served with fruity, jammy rhubarb compôte, jazz apple and blackcurrant sage sorbet. A French-heavy wine list opens at £28. **Chef/s:** James Wilkins. **Closed:** Mon, Tue, 3 weeks Christmas, 3 weeks Aug. **Meals:** set L £28 (2 courses) to £34. Set D £54 (2 courses) to £64. Tasting menu £64 (5 courses) to £88. Sun L £28 (2 courses) to £64. **Details:** 30 seats. V menu. Wheelchairs. Children over 6 yrs at D.

Wilson's

Cooking score: 6
Modern British | £50
22a Chandos Road, Bristol, BS6 6PF
Tel no: 0117 973 4157
wilsonsrestaurant.co.uk

Since opening four years ago, this pared-back modern bistro has established itself as one of the city's stars, with white walls and dark floorboards providing a stark backdrop to some dashing seasonal food. Chef Jan Ostle and his wife, Mary Wilson, continue to forge a reputation for their uncompromising plot-to-plate philosophy, and their urban smallholding now supplies the majority of produce for the kitchen. From the terse blackboard-only menu, a typical spring meal might open with warm courgettes, spider crab and nasturtiums, perhaps leading on to cod, turnips and broad beans or Wye Valley asparagus, morels and Somerset goat's curd. Chocolate tart enriched with Palestinian olive oil and served with sea buckthorn could be one of two desserts on offer, although you could end with a single artisan cheese – perhaps Oxfordshire's Rollright – drizzled with truffle honey. A concise but thoughtfully

designed wine list opens at £23 and offers interesting options by the glass, including whites from Slovenia and Greece. **Chef/s:** Jan Ostle. **Closed:** Mon, Sun. **Meals:** main courses £19 to £20. Tasting menu £50 (8 courses). **Details:** 26 seats. Music.

LOCAL GEM
Hart's Bakery
British | £8
Arch 35, Lower Approach Road, Bristol, BS1 6QS
Tel no: 0117 992 4488
hartsbakery.co.uk
£30

Rather than relying on the train buffet car, locals commuting to and from Bristol Temple Meads inevitably pre-plan and make a detour to Laura Hart's bakery café, hidden from view in an arch under the approach to the station. Here, excellent Bristol-roasted coffee and exemplary sweet and savoury pastries (to eat in or take away) are on offer from breakfast until lunchtime, when blackboard daily specials include the likes of roast pork shoulder, chilli, fennel salad and aïoli in a semolina bun or toasted orzo salad with feta, peas, asparagus, cherry tomatoes, broccoli and mint, with a honey and preserved lemon dressing.

LOCAL GEM
Sky Kong Kong
Korean | £13
Unit 2, Haymarket Walk, Bristol, BS1 3LN
Tel no: 0117 239 9528
skykongkong.co.uk
£30

Between the notorious Bearpit roundabout underpass and the city's bus station, this organic Korean café may not boast the most picturesque location but that hasn't stopped in-the-know locals flocking there to experience Wizzy Chung's food. Whether it's the lunchtime bento boxes or evening set, the good-value menu changes daily and often depends on what emerges from the owner's allotment or her trip to the local butchers and fishmongers. Typical dishes include roasted sea bream with prawn ceviche, and udon noodles with slow-cooked beef sirloin, nuts and pickled white garlic leaf. It's BYO booze and cash only.

LOCAL GEM
Spoke & Stringer
Spanish | £30
The Boathouse, Unit 1, Lime Kiln Road, Bristol, BS1 5AD
Tel no: 0117 925 9371
spokeandstringer.com
£30

What started out as an adjunct to a shop selling bicycles and surf clothing (hence the name, geddit?) has expanded into the adjacent harbourside bar with views across the water to the iconic *SS Great Britain*. By day, it's a hip hangout for brunch and lunch (think fish goujon sandwiches and slow-roasted pulled pork pittas), but it takes on a more Spanish accent in the evening with pintxos and tapas such as baked fillet of hake with piquillo pepper and olive stew and saffron allioli, or lamb albondigas with pistachios and apricots. Drink cocktails, wine or local beers.

READERS RECOMMEND
Cargo Cantina
Mexican
Unit 12, Cargo 2, Wapping Wharf, Bristol, BS1 6ZA
cargocantina.co.uk
'You feel as though you're in a backstreet joint in Mexico City and not a converted shipping container in Bristol. We love the tongue 'n' cheek taco but honestly they're all good. If you're not sure about trying neat tequila or mezcal, they do fab cocktails, including a chilli chocolate Margarita.'

∎ Long Ashton
The Bird in Hand
Cooking score: 2
Modern British | £30
17 Weston Road, Long Ashton, BS41 9LA
Tel no: 01275 395222
bird-in-hand.co.uk
£30

Having scored a palpable hit with The Pump House down by Bristol's harbourside (see entry), Toby Gritten has proved he's no one-hit wonder with this village boozer a few miles from the city. Drinkers still congregate for pints of local ale and cider in the bar, but most are here for the food. Scrubbed tables, prints and old advertising signs create just the right backdrop for muscular, rustic dishes with a modern British accent – as in ribeye steak with bone marrow and potato terrine, sprout tops and burnt onion. The kitchen also likes to inject some Mediterranean warmth, so expect anything from rabbit with white beans, pancetta and tarragon to glazed pork belly with crispy polenta and Jerusalem artichokes. Nibbles of crispy parsnips with curry sauce help to pique interest, while dessert might bring contentment in the shape of sticky toffee pudding with clotted cream or lemon leaf panna cotta dressed with Long Ashton honeycomb. Well-priced wines from £18.80.
Chef/s: Felix Rayment. Closed: 25 Dec. Meals: main courses £15 to £52. Details: 50 seats. 45 seats outside. Bar. Music.

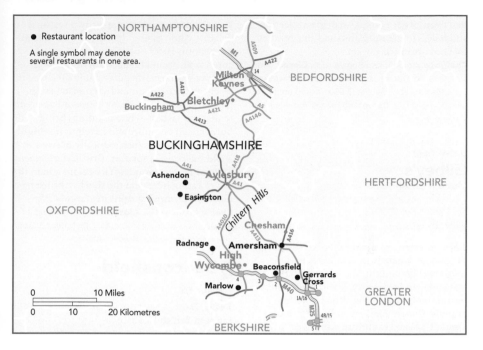

Amersham

Artichoke

Cooking score: 7
Modern European | £50
9 Market Square, Amersham, HP7 0DF
Tel no: 01494 726611
artichokerestaurant.co.uk

Amersham undoubtledly had its moments
before Laurie and Jacqueline Gear opened
Artichoke in 2002, but nothing could surely
compare to the golden age that their
supremely accomplished and vastly popular
restaurant has brought to the town. Bookings
well in advance are advisable. A creative touch
has been brought to the interior space, with
white banquettes adding the comfort note
against a backdrop of twigs, beams and globe
artichokes in relief. In this relaxing
environment, Ben Jenkins works alongside
Laurie Gear to produce dishes that sparkle and

dazzle, both visually and on the palate. Their
culinary style draws on modern European
currents, applying them to thoroughbred
regional British produce. The resulting
compositions are revelatory, as in roasted
Landes quail breast and shredded confit leg
with wild mushrooms and a quail 'tea' poured
from a thin-spouted teapot. There is no
shyness about treating fish in similarly
ebullient fashion, as when a tartare of hop-
smoked trout appears dressed with russet
apple, pickled mooli and a piercing beetroot
sorbet. Meats are top-drawer, perhaps
Scotsgrove Farm hogget crusted in mint and
parsley with a pastilla of the sweetbread and
kidney, all spiced in ras el hanout, or
Goosnargh duck glazed in maple syrup and
blood orange with a raviolo of the leg and
liver. Rhubarb is worth its journey from
Yorkshire, when it comes in two servings – a
rhubarb and ginger cocktail, and then
Cambridge burnt cream with rhubarb and
white chocolate. The personable front-of-
house approach makes this an unalloyed
pleasure, as does the expertly curated wine list

that opens with a useful small glass selection and builds to mature clarets and Burgundies for the bottomless pocket. **Chef/s:** Laurie Gear and Ben Jenkins. **Closed:** Mon, Sun, 2 weeks Dec to Jan, 1 week Easter, 2 weeks Aug. **Meals:** set L £30. Set D £50. Tasting menu £60 (6 courses) to £80. **Details:** 48 seats. 2 seats outside. V menu. Music.

LOCAL GEM
Gilbey's
Modern British | £38
1 Market Square, Amersham, HP7 0DF
Tel no: 01494 727242
gilbeygroup.com

The converted grammar school overlooking the market square is an invaluable local resource. Fish and chips, pork belly with crackling, and sirloin steak with Café de Paris butter show a kitchen willing to do the populist thing (and do it well). Dishes of almond-crusted sea bream with sweet potato bombas and romesco sauce or chargrilled rump of lamb with merguez sausage and potato, turnip and Gruyère gratin demonstrate more creative flair. Set lunches and dinners are good value and a house vin de France (£19.50) leads the charge on the well-annotated list.

▌Ashendon
The Hundred
Cooking score: 4
British | £30
Lower End, Ashendon, HP18 0HE
Tel no: 01296 651296
thehundred.co.uk

Once a traditional Chiltern watering hole, this centuries-old hostelry is now fitted out with deliberately distressed furniture, designer fabrics, modern artworks and polished floors. Its good looks are matched by bags of culinary ambition, thanks to chef owner Matthew Gill, who earned his stripes at London hot spots such as St John. Not surprisingly, his bold, uncompromising cooking revels in humble

British produce and home-grown seasonal delights while giving the nod to nose-to-tail gastronomy: beef mince on dripping toast, cured venison and horseradish or devilled kidneys with parsnip purée could give way to ox cheek with carrots and gremolata, lamb rack with turnips and mint sauce or hake with fennel and tartare, while puddings bring burnt cream or quince and hazelnut meringue. Considered details such as locally brewed ales, apple and rosehip spritzes, British cheeses and scoops of sweet woodruff ice cream add to the fun of eating here, and the short wine list has plenty of promising drinking from £23. **Chef/s:** Matthew Gill. **Closed:** Mon, 1 to 8 Jan. **Meals:** main courses £14 to £19. **Details:** 40 seats. 30 seats outside. Bar. Parking. Music.

▌Beaconsfield
LOCAL GEM
No. 5
Modern British | £35
London End, Beaconsfield, HP9 2HN
Tel no: 01494 355500
no5londonend.co.uk

The team behind a brace of foodie pubs, The White Oak in Cookham and The Three Oaks in Gerrards Cross (see entries), brought their ethos of relaxed contemporary dining to this restaurant in the centre of Beaconsfield in 2016. The period building has undergone a distinctly urban transformation while the menu keeps step, offering up the likes of a proper burger (with aged beef, tomato jam and smoked Cheddar) alongside lamb shoulder croquettes with black garlic and salsa verde, or grilled plaice with chorizo and caper sauce. Drink craft beer, or wines from £19.

Local Gem
These entries are brilliant neighbourhood venues, delivering good, freshly cooked food at great value for money.

Easington
The Mole & Chicken

Cooking score: 2
Modern British | £35
Easington Terrace, Easington, HP18 9EY
Tel no: 01844 208387
themoleandchicken.co.uk

It's a gift of a location. This ivy-clad pub with rooms is set high on a ridge overlooking the Buckinghamshire and Oxfordshire countryside where, on a sunny day, the 60-seater terrace comes into its own. Inside, it's darker and more atmospheric with real fires, oak beams and cosy corners. The culinary style is equally mixed, slipping between past and present. While the likes of beer-battered haddock and chips, and liver, bacon and kidneys with creamed potatoes, cabbage and onion gravy play the comfort card, there's much more besides. Wild mushroom risotto, for example, with fresh black truffle and whipped truffle cream, or a main course of oxtail ballotine served with veal pommes Anna, celeriac three ways and kale. Finish with apple tarte tatin with red apple sorbet and gingerbread. Liquid refreshment comes in the form of real ales and a well-annotated wine list (from £20).
Chef/s: Steve Bush. **Closed:** 25 Dec. **Meals:** main courses £13 to £29. Set L Mon to Fri and D Mon to Thur £15 (2 courses) to £20. **Details:** 62 seats. 60 seats outside. Bar. Wheelchairs. Parking. Music.

Gerrards Cross
The Three Oaks

Cooking score: 3
Modern British | £29
Austenwood Common, Gerrards Cross, SL9 8NL
Tel no: 01753 899016
thethreeoaksgx.co.uk
£30

Jason Biswell, promoted from sous-chef, now leads the kitchen at this substantial, genteel pub, sibling to The White Oak, Cookham and

No. 5 in Gerrards Cross (see entries). His cooking – good-looking and finely balanced – draws well-heeled regulars to the seemly dining rooms, where exquisitely mismatched furniture is carefully combined with designer wallpaper and weathered wooden floorboards. There's a decent-sized beer garden too, plus a bar with local ale on tap. At inspection, care was apparent in the good-value set lunch, which started with creamy chicken liver parfait followed by a flavour-packed fish (and shellfish) pie boosted by delectably smokey charred broccoli. A rice pudding teamed with pineapple sorbet and compôte was a luxurious finale. More intricate dishes might include torched plaice with spicy langoustine bisque or a texturally pleasing salt-baked kohlrabi with radish, halloumi, harissa and crunchy roast hazelnuts. Young, clued-up service and a Corney & Barrow-sourced wine list (from £19) with ample by-the-glass options complete this appealing prospect.
Chef/s: Jason Biswell. **Meals:** main courses £15 to £26. Set L £16 (2 courses) to £19. Set D £19 (2 courses) to £23. **Details:** 74 seats. 40 seats outside. Bar. Parking.

Marlow
The Coach

Cooking score: 4
Modern British | £30
3 West Street, Marlow, SL7 2LS
thecoachmarlow.co.uk
£30

Tom De Keyser has taken the reins here, but given his previous experience as sous-chef in Tom Kerridge's no-bookings town-centre hostelry, The Coach isn't about to crash. Its mock Tudor façade hides a pubby interior dominated by an L-shaped bar and open-kitchen rotisserie. TV screens (silent) and handpumps (including local Rebellion ales) are juxtaposed with classy monochrome photos and elaborate chandeliers. On the plate, pub classics are elevated to haute status, so Scotch egg arrives clothed in smoked haddock and black pudding, wearing a tiara of seared onion and paddling in fragrant moilee sauce.

The menu is confusingly split into 'meat' and 'no meat' dishes of varying sizes, but there's no denying the sublime, and elaborate, execution of the roast cod with Jerusalem artichokes and bacon (in the 'no meat' section), or shepherd's pie topped with mousse-like potato and Parmesan-flavoured puffs. Service can be too casual, but desserts are a highlight – perhaps whisky and rye pudding (a sticky toffee for grown-ups) – and the international wine list starts at £30.
Chef/s: Tom De Keyser. **Meals:** main courses £5 to £17. **Details:** 45 seats. Bar. No reservations.

The Hand & Flowers
Cooking score: 5
Modern British | £80
126 West Street, Marlow, SL7 2BP
Tel no: 01628 482277
thehandandflowers.co.uk

With a string of prime-time TV shows and bestselling cookbooks to his name, it's easy to forget that Tom Kerridge is also a working chef and restaurateur. Although he may be pulled in several directions these days, Marlow is still his home turf and this emblematic roadside pub with rooms his pride and joy. A couple of local ales, some cosy nooks and crooked beams are reminders that The Hand & Flowers was once a working boozer, but the jam-packed scrubbed tables and high-achieving menu tell a different story. At the stoves, Kerridge protégé Jamie May is tuned in to his master's voice, delivering cleverly reworked and highly pleasurable comfort food with a forthright British accent – from a pickled beetroot and Cheddar tart with lamb 'ham', haggis and horseradish cream to loin of Cotswold venison with carrot and Marmite purée, salt-baked carrot and spiced beef puff. Other dishes such as the near-legendary glazed smoked haddock omelette and the Essex lamb 'bun' with sweetbreads and salsa verde are immovable fixtures on the classics playlist, while desserts throw in a few surprises – a black cherry soufflé with salted almond

custard and dark chocolate sorbet, for example. A big, bold wine list opens with house selections from £28.
Chef/s: Tom Kerridge and Jamie May. **Meals:** main courses £40 to £47. Set L £25 (2 courses) to £30. **Details:** 52 seats. Parking. Music.

Sindhu
Cooking score: 5
Indian | £45
Compleat Angler, Marlow Bridge Lane, Marlow, SL7 1RG
Tel no: 01628 405405
sindhurestaurant.co.uk

With its polished mahogany tables, plush upholstery in citrus shades and colourful artworks, this impressive dining room overlooking Marlow weir and the Thames now exudes a contemporary vibe that chimes with its status as a gastronomic destination. Set up by chef Atul Kochhar and named after the Sanskrit word for the river Indus, Sindhu deals in the kind of food that gives modern Indian cuisine a good name – subtle, intricate and endlessly inventive, a cross-pollination of East and West founded on knowledgeably sourced British ingredients. Chargrilled organic salmon might appear with crab croquette and chilli-tinged asparagus, rabbit gets the tikka treatment with wild berry chutney, and roe deer steaks are daringly served with keema mattar (aka mince and peas) and chocolate curry. There's also plenty of convincingly creative stuff for vegetarians and vegans, from chukander kootu (beetroot with ginger, lentils and coconut) to soy kofta with a 'potato steak'. If you're looking for a surprising finale, seek out the rose bhapa doi (a traditional Bengali pudding) served alongside a caramelised banana tart. Wines include a fine selection by the glass or carafe, or you could opt for an Asian-themed cocktail.
Chef/s: Atul Kochhar. **Meals:** main courses £17 to £26. Set L £19 (2 courses) to £22. Tasting menu £49 (5 courses) to £69. Sun L £22 (2 courses) to £25. **Details:** 54 seats. V menu. Vg menu. Wheelchairs. Parking.

The Vanilla Pod

Cooking score: 3
Modern European | £45
31 West Street, Marlow, SL7 2LS
Tel no: 01628 898101
thevanillapod.co.uk
£5
OFF

A low-key but enviably consistent performer on Marlow's main thoroughfare, Michael Macdonald's narrow two-storey townhouse (once home to poet TS Eliot), is easy to walk past. Once inside, the compact bar and bland, white-clothed back dining room may not leap out as somewhere to eat well but be prepared to change your mind – it makes an unobtrusive setting for cooking that shows serious intent. The food is not about surprise or innovation, although there are some fairly modern dishes, but it is about comfort and indulgence: seen in seared scallops partnered by cauliflower purée and cep vinaigrette, in butter-roasted cod and vanilla-infused white beans, and in Cotswold white chicken with tartiflette and mushroom. If you still have room, round off with a helping of panna cotta with honey and cumin madeleines. The wine list leans towards France but offers satisfying scope elsewhere, with a good selection by the glass.
Chef/s: Michael Macdonald. **Closed:** Mon, Sun.
Meals: set L £16 (2 courses) to £20. Set D £40 (2 courses) to £45. Tasting menu L £30 (5 courses) and D £60 (7 courses). **Details:** 30 seats. V menu. Wheelchairs.

Send us your review

Your feedback informs the content of the GFG and will be used to compile next year's entries. To register your opinion about any restaurant listed in the Guide, or a restaurant that you wish to bring to our attention, visit: thegoodfoodguide.co.uk/feedback.

▌Radnage

★ RESTAURANT OF THE YEAR ★

The Mash Inn

Cooking score: 6
Modern British | £60
Horseshoe Road, Pornnett End, Radnage, HP14 4EB
Tel no: 01494 482440
themashinn.com

Having transposed a full smoke-and-sparks cooking range into the open corner of his quaint red-brick inn, owner Nick Mash might be suspected of some eccentricities. But as soon as diners cross the threshold, the fire (and, naturally, the foraging) make delicious, intuitive sense. Across a four-course daily menu or ten-course taster, 'pretty much everything is exposed to naked flames or burning charcoal', resulting in dishes that feel fresh but not slavishly fashionable. Highlights include darkly blistered chapa flatbread with clean, aerated romanesco and green apple soup, simple just-pulled radishes with hay mayo, and a memorable côte du boeuf with silky, umami-rich sesame miso sauce. A long, slender slice of milk chocolate and bergamot tart shows real pastry skill. This is a grown-up pub; understandably, under-16s aren't allowed, and the dining room is 'almost comically dark', so settle in to drink something from the 'mercifully short' wine list, from £29, by candlelight.
Chef/s: Jon Parry. **Closed:** Mon, Tue, 23 to 26 Dec, 1 and 2 Jan. **Meals:** set L £25 Wed to Fri. Set L and D £60 (4 courses). Tasting menu £95 (10 courses). Sun L £45. **Details:** 32 seats. Bar. Wheelchairs. Parking. Music. No children.

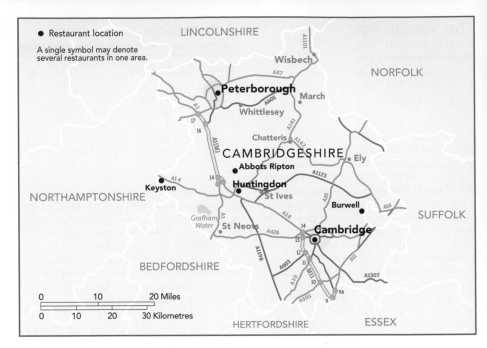

LINCOLNSHIRE

NORFOLK

Wisbech

A47

Peterborough
March

Whittlesey

17

16

Chatteris

CAMBRIDGESHIRE
Ely

Abbots Ripton

A1123

Keyston
14
Huntingdon

NORTHAMPTONSHIRE
St Ives

Burwell

SUFFOLK

Grafham
Water
St Neots
A428
14
Cambridge

13

12

BEDFORDSHIRE
11

A1307

10

9A

9

0   10   20 Miles

0   10   20   30 Kilometres

HERTFORDSHIRE
ESSEX

▮ Abbots Ripton
The Abbot's Elm
Cooking score: 2
Modern European | £32
Abbots Ripton, PE28 2PA
Tel no: 01487 773773
theabbotselm.co.uk

£5 OFF 🍴

Behind a picturesque thatched exterior is a
spacious modern pub with rooms – rebuilt
after a fire – where chef patron Julia Abbey
again heads the kitchen here after a spell of ill
health. The main bar incorporates a grand
piano, skylights and a snug front area, while
the separate restaurant features linen
tablecloths and wine racks. Slips aren't
unknown (a missing ingredient here,
uninformed service there), but staff are
friendly and a culinary lightness of touch is
evident: note the grape-like texture of a
fricassée of lamb's kidneys, or succulent roast
cod served over creamy broad bean and pea
risotto (pity about the accompanying sickly

sweet chilli jam). The best dish at inspection
was a perfect vanilla panna cotta: wobbly,
creamy and ideally matched with tart rhubarb
and crunchy almond granola. The set lunch is a
steal and a pair of draught ales supplement a
wine list that offers ample choice by the glass,
carafe and bottle (from £21).
Chef/s: Julia Abbey. **Meals:** main courses £13 to
£29. Set L £14 (2 courses) to £18. **Details:** 70 seats.
40 seats outside. Wheelchairs. Parking. Music.

▮ Burwell
LOCAL GEM
The Anchor
Modern British | £28
63 North Street, Burwell, CB25 0BA
Tel no: 01638 743970
theanchorburwell.net

£30

'It's got heart and soul,' said one diner, well fed
and happy after a meal at this family-run
village pub. It's a place to note in your little
black book of the Fens, because alongside the

warm welcome comes food that pleases and nourishes. Start with smoked mackerel and pickled cucumber, or ham hock terrine with a quail's egg and piccalilli, before a vast Barnsley lamb chop, a proper suet pudding, or a lighter dish of stone bass with a paella croqueta and squid ink allioli. To finish, you need to know just one word: doughnuts. Wine from £19.50.

▮ Cambridge

Midsummer House
Cooking score: 8
Modern British | £135
Midsummer Common, Cambridge, CB4 1HA
Tel no: 01223 369299
midsummerhouse.co.uk

In 2018, Daniel Clifford marked two decades at Midsummer House not only by publishing a book and overhauling his restaurant and kitchen, but also by ditching a tasting-menus-only approach in favour of à la carte. Then this giant of British cooking changed his mind, because tasting menus are, it turns out, what the legions of Midsummer fans prefer. Keep up, and head to this gloriously situated Victorian villa for an ambitious culinary adventure that can be eight courses of vegetarian, pescatarian or omnivorous dishes, according to taste. English asparagus is given stellar treatment on a spring menu, presented alongside pieces of aerated hollandaise, pickled and fresh onions, and a fine potato 'cannelloni' filled with chopped asparagus. Familiar, too, will be Clifford's obsessive championing of fleeting seasons: witness the wild garlic and morels in a stunning velouté on the vegetarian menu, the same ingredients giving oomph to a dish of turbot and cockles for pescatarians. Desserts are works of art and theatre, whether you have the lemon posset with olive oil cake, mint and black olive tuile (cue dry ice at table) or break into the refreshing flavours of a coriander and white chocolate dome with coconut, mango and puffed jasmine rice. The wine list (from £35) has all the heft you'd expect, but there's plenty of expertise willing and able to guide you.

Chef/s: Daniel Clifford. **Closed:** Mon, Tue, Sun, 21 Dec to 8 Jan. **Meals:** set L £50. Tasting menu £135 (8 courses). **Details:** 44 seats. V menu. Bar. Wheelchairs. Children over 10 yrs.

Parker's Tavern
Cooking score: 4
British | £40
Regent Street, Cambridge, CB2 1AD
Tel no: 01223 606266
parkerstavern.com

This is a grand place to eat, in a magnificent renovated hotel and dining room with its dark wood, leather and velvet, tall windows and even taller ceilings. It is uncompromisingly classical, a space where old-school club meets European turn of the (last) century brasserie. And the food fits the brief. Dive into the luxury of a truffle risotto, go simple with butterflied pilchards, roasted and served, tails fanned, under generous spoonfuls of salsa verde, a lemon wedge helping to counter their salty heft. Follow with buttered sole and brown shrimps, or slow-roast duck with greens and mash of a richness that makes you close your eyes to commit the moment to memory. Hay-smoked sea trout clamours for attention against plump shellfish, pancetta, a punchy sauce, slivers of cauliflower and watercress. Finish – of course – with a Cambridge burnt cream or channel your inner Snow White with a scarlet 'apple', the mirror glaze hiding nothing more sinister than apple and white chocolate mousse and compôte. Or you may well be tempted by a whole baked Tunworth brie with truffle. Cocktails are creative and wines on the European-focused list start at £20.

Chef/s: Tristan Welch. **Meals:** main courses £14 to £25. **Details:** 110 seats. Bar.

Restaurant Twenty-Two

Cooking score: 3
British | £45
22 Chesterton Road, Cambridge, CB4 3AX
Tel no: 01223 351880
restaurant22.co.uk

'This superb establishment has gone from strength to strength,' enthused a pair of returning visitors to Alex Olivier and Sam Carter's restored Victorian townhouse restaurant backing on to Jesus Green and the tranquil purlieus of the Cam. It's a distinctly classy operation run with the kind of sensitivity that everybody appreciates – service that's there when you need it, and not when you don't – and Carter's culinary style explores a range of innovative and modern flavours in the form of a carte, as well as tasting menus of five or seven courses. Canapés include a crisp pearl barley cracker topped with dots of spiced apple and black pudding, prior to Cornish cod in turnip dashi with whipped roe, then perhaps breast, wing and leg of Sutton Hoo chicken with charred cauliflower and puréed ceps in lustrous jus gras. At the end comes an irresistible dark chocolate délice with Jerusalem artichoke crisps and blood orange sorbet. A southern French Viognier with plenty of springtime florality (£21) opens an efficient list.
Chef/s: Sam Carter. **Closed:** Mon, Sun, 22 Sept to 1 Oct, 22 to 31 Dec. **Meals:** main courses £19 to £26. Set L £25 (2 courses) to £30. Tasting menu £45 (5 courses) to £55. **Details:** 22 seats. Music. Children over 12 yrs.

★ NEW ENTRY ★

Vanderlyle

Cooking score: 4
Modern European | £55
38-40 Mill Road, Cambridge, CB1 2AD
vanderlyle-restaurant.com

'Who knew you could extract so much flavour from strawberries?' wondered one diner, flummoxed – deliciously – by a mini sourdough crumpet topped with a savoury ragoût of strawberries and a tiny nasturtium

leaf. It's a highlight on the fixed-price menu at Alex Rushmer's relaxed, stylish Cambridge opening, which, although not officially vegetarian, delights on a summer visit with originality and vigour drawn entirely from fruit and vegetables. Salt-baked kohlrabi, cut carpaccio style with wafer-thin slices of striped chioggia beetroot, celtuce, soy and ultra-fresh leaves is summer on a plate. Not every dish convinces, but roasted hispi cabbage with smoked tea dashi and an onion reduction that's a dead ringer for a meat-based demi-glace, is a winner, especially with its accompanying kick of romesco and a neat, golden-topped potato and feta terrine. A 'pretty palate cleanser' of rhubarb and ginger semifreddo with sorrel granita precedes a sugar wallop that 'needs to be tamed' of malted caramel, cheesecake and blueberry ice cream. It's well worth opting for the matched drinks, although bottles on the short global wine list start at £24.
Chef/s: Alex Rushmer. **Closed:** Mon, Tue, Sun. **Meals:** tasting menu £55 (6 courses). **Details:** 25 seats. V menu. Pre-payment required.

LOCAL GEM

Amélie

French | £27
The Grafton Centre, Cambridge, CB1 1PS
Tel no: 01223 778898
amelierestaurants.co.uk

£5 £30
OFF

A sunflower-yellow Citroën van at the top of the escalators in the Grafton shopping centre marks the spot for cool, contemporary all-day eating at its brightest and freshest. On offer in this unexpected spot are crisp-edged flammekueche, or Alsatian flatbreads, made to order (they're adapted for vegan and gluten-free needs, as required) and topped with seasoned crème fraîche and onions, then the likes of smokey bacon and Gruyère (the Authentic), goat's cheese and beetroot, or spinach, ricotta and red pepper pesto. Apple and cinnamon with chocolate and rum-soaked raisins is pick of the sweet versions. It's great value, the coffee is strong and the brisk wine list has glasses from £3.70.

Fitzbillies

Modern British | £15
51-52 Trumpington Street, Cambridge, CB2 1RG
Tel no: 01223 352500
fitzbillies.com

£30

A café and coffee bar that has been serving the great and the good since the 1920s, Fitzbillies still looks the business (did the *Harry Potter* location scouts not see this place?). Things get started at 8am for breakfast and keep going through brunch, lunch and afternoon tea. They don't take bookings, and people are willing to queue for the famous Chelsea bun, the full breakfast, buck rarebit, hot-smoked salmon sandwiches and the like. Civilised aperitifs, wines and beers help things along.

■ Eye Green

READERS RECOMMEND

House of Feasts

Eastern European
41 Crowland Road, Eye Green, PE6 7TP
Tel no: 01733 221279
houseoffeasts.co.uk

'Steak tartare was really tasty and beautifully presented. Duck was perfectly cooked, the sauce was amazing. Traditional Polish faworki were delicious. Service was very, very good. The chef came out to check we had enjoyed our meal; that was a lovely touch.'

Readers recommend

These entries are genuine quotes from a report sent in by one of our readers. Please get in touch via our website if you agree with their recommendation.

■ Huntingdon

LOCAL GEM

The Old Bridge Hotel

Modern British | £38
1 High Street, Huntingdon, PE29 3TQ
Tel no: 01480 424300
huntsbridge.com

This showpiece ivy-clad hotel by the Great Ouse holds a stack of trump cards, including a conservatory-style restaurant with gardens running down to the river and a wine shop: 'I spent half an hour here before lunch,' remarked one distracted diner. The kitchen works to a monthly menu with British and Mediterranean overtones – rabbit tortellini with spinach and chargrilled oyster mushrooms or slow-cooked pork belly partnered by duck-fat potatoes, winter greens and spiced apple sauce. Neal's Yard Dairy cheeses encourage ordering another glass of something from an inspired global wine list featuring some brilliant house selections (courtesy of owner John Hoskins MW).

■ Keyston

The Pheasant

Cooking score: 2
Modern British | £32
Loop Road, Keyston, PE28 0RE
Tel no: 01832 710241
thepheasant-keyston.co.uk

£5 OFF

Out in the Cambridgeshire sticks, but easily accessible from the A14, this dapper thatched inn confirms its pubby credentials with rustic beams, open fires and real ales from local microbreweries – although most are here for the smart food and classy wines. The day's menu pulls in fashionable trends from far and wide, while respecting seasonal British ingredients, as in a twice-cooked asparagus and rosemary soufflé with broad beans or pan-fried mackerel with saffron potatoes, courgettes, spring greens, braised fennel and tomato salsa. There are also some 'traditional classics' for those who prefer the familiarity of spicy pan-fried fishcakes, steak and chips or maple-cured hot dogs with mash, while ripe Neal's Yard Dairy cheeses are alternatives to eclectic desserts such as carrot cake with cardamom yoghurt or lemongrass panna cotta with marinated pineapple. The global wine list (from £18.50) has pithy descriptions on every page, occasional half bottles and plenty of opportunities by the glass.

Chef/s: Simon Cadge. **Closed:** Mon, 2 to 12 Jan. **Meals:** main courses £12 to £26. Set L £15 (2 courses) to £20. Set D £25 (2 courses) to £30. Sun L £26. **Details:** 80 seats. 40 seats outside. Bar. Wheelchairs. Parking.

Chef/s: Lee Clarke. **Closed:** Mon, Sun, 1 to 15 Jan. **Meals:** set L £20. Set D £35. Tasting menu £50 (5 courses) to £75. **Details:** 40 seats. V menu. Vg menu. Bar. Music. Children over 8 yrs at D.

▌Peterborough

Prévost
Cooking score: 3
Modern British | £35
20 Priestgate, Peterborough, PE1 1JA
Tel no: 01733 313623
prevostpeterborough.co.uk

£5
OFF

Lee Clarke has been cooking in these parts for many a year, and his latest venture finds him creating thoroughly convincing 21st-century food in an historic street yards from the city centre. The dining room sets out its stall with a neutral colour scheme, snug lounge area and impeccably laid and well-spaced tables, while chefs in the black-tiled kitchen work to a series of fixed-price menus. Choose three, five or nine courses, and expect to be thrilled by the results: a courgette flower with Berkswell cheese and hazelnuts might open the show, ahead of chalk stream trout with cucumber, borage and chicory or a plate of Creedy Carver duck, monk's beard, three sorts of onion and foraged blackberries. To conclude, white chocolate custard with Yorkshire rhubarb and shortbread is one seasonal possibility. Meals always begin with snacks, and there are artisan British cheeses to round things off. Optional wine flights are gleaned from an impressive global list with bottles from £22.

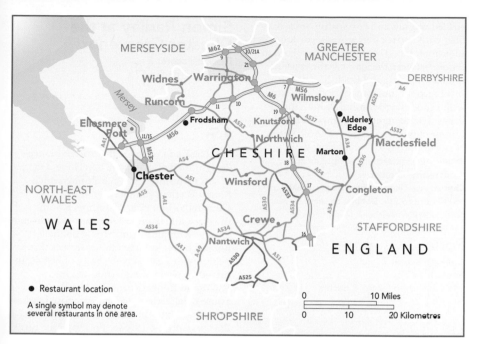

MERSEYSIDE

GREATER
MANCHESTER

DERBYSHIRE

Widnes / Warrington

Runcorn

Wilmslow

Ellesmere
Port

Frodsham

Knutsford

Alderley
Edge

Northwich

Macclesfield

C H E S H I R E

Marton

Chester

Winsford

Congleton

NORTH-EAST
WALES

W A L E S

Crewe

STAFFORDSHIRE

Nantwich

E N G L A N D

● Restaurant location

A single symbol may denote
several restaurants in one area.

SHROPSHIRE

0   10 Miles
0   10   20 Kilometres

▌Alderley Edge

LOCAL GEM
Yara
Lebanese/Syrian | £25
29 London Road, Alderley Edge, SK9 7JT
Tel no: 01625 584040
yara2eat.co.uk

£30

Enveloped within a shopping parade in smart
Alderley is one of a trio of family-run
restaurants specialising in the food of Lebanon
and Syria. Readers enjoy the smokey, savoury,
sweet-sharp baba ganoush, crunchy fatoush
salad, densely textured falafels with tahini and
yoghurt, and the abundant pitta. Mains such
as kabseh (rice topped with chicken and sweet
aubergine) and spice-soaked grilled lamb
chops are richly sustaining, with precisely
defined seasonings. Some dishes come with a
little chilli dip of the 'blow your head off'
variety. Wines from £14.50. The other
branches are at 23 Oxford Road, Altrincham,
and 7 Wilmslow Road, Cheadle.

▌Chester

Joseph Benjamin
Cooking score: 3
Modern European | £29
134-138 Northgate Street, Chester, CH1 2HT
Tel no: 01244 344295
josephbenjamin.co.uk

£30

Right by the ancient city walls and gate, a
previous regional winner of the Guide's Best
Local Restaurant continues to impress. Joe and
Ben Wright's lively operation is related to the
Porta tapas bar next door (see entry), the place
channelling a family-friendly community feel
with a passion for regional produce and a
fondness for ideas from around the world.
Lamb belly nuggets with roast garlic allioli,
courgette and mint salad is a typical opener,
while baked St Marcellin cheese with cured
chorizo, lomo Ibérico, chutney and
sourdough is a popular sharing dish to kick-
start a meal. Other satisfying options include
beer-braised ox cheek with parsley risotto,

pickled walnuts and horseradish or sea bass fillet with curried butter beans, coconut raita and coriander oil. As for dessert, it's hard to choose between the lemon verbena panna cotta with parkin and English strawberries or an affogato of muscovado ice cream served with a shot of espresso and Pedro Ximénez sherry. The thoughtfully compiled mostly European wine list starts at £18.50, with plenty of bottles to tempt below £35, including a smattering of organic and biodynamic choices.

Chef/s: Jose Garzón. **Closed:** Mon. **Meals:** main courses £13 to £19. **Details:** 36 seats. 20 seats outside. Bar. Wheelchairs. Music.

Porta
Cooking score: 2
Spanish | £22
140 Northgate Street, Chester, CH1 2HT
Tel no: 01244 344295
portatapas.co.uk

£30

The first of the Wright brothers' forays into tapas slots neatly in close to their bigger place, Joseph Benjamin, and shares the same top-notch local reputation. Behind a sunshine yellow frontage and spread over two small floors and a few outside tables, it offers a neat tapas workout from tomato bread to Andalusian-style fried squid with allioli. The standards, including potato and onion tortilla and croquetas of the day, are present and correct, although you may also meet an Italian interloper in the form of buffalo mozzarella with tomato and basil salad. Meatier dishes include seared Ibérico pork, served modishly pink, with mojo verde, and spiced lamb skewers with chimichurri. Dessert isn't a major event, but a pastel de nata with coffee is encouraged. Save for a couple of local beers, drinks are Spanish, and include a brace of vermouths at keen prices. There are branches in Salford and Altrincham (see entries).

Chef/s: Joe Wright and José Garzon. **Meals:** tapas £3 to £10. **Details:** 38 seats. 24 seats outside. Music. No reservations.

Simon Radley at the Chester Grosvenor
Cooking score: 7
Modern French | £75
Eastgate, Chester, CH1 1LT
Tel no: 01244 324024
chestergrosvenor.com

The black and white tiled portico entrance leads into a world of grand hotel luxe, a temple of soft furnishings and marble into which Simon Radley's dining room fits like Cinderella's foot in its glass slipper. Some feel the place still exudes a 1980s idea of high-end dining, with plush armchairs at double-linened tables, and the kind of service that begins with a gargantuan choice of breads. In this atmosphere of high expectation, Raymond Booker's hand on the tiller is assured, delivering precisely composed dishes that are complex in their construction and flavours, often wittily so. 'Bombay mix' turns out to be cod cheeks in light tandoori spicing with Menai mussels, the dish topped with the crunchy broken vermicelli of the Indian snack, while the croustillant of caramelised veal sweetbreads, deepened with wild mushrooms and spring truffle, shows a deep understanding of the sweetly earthy offal. A regular diner could have taken his autumn grouse – paired with crisped bacon, chervil root and elderberries – rarer but textural intricacy distinguishes a dish of turbot that comes with rice in three guises (fragrant, sticky and puffed) in miso with honey-charred octopus. Dessert could be as simple as a spin on crème caramel with rhubarb and ginger, or match a Valrhona Caramélia milk chocolate ganache with manuka wild honey. It's hard to take issue with a wine list with such lofty standards and global reach. Languedoc producer Gérard Bertrand features heavily and there are plenty of half bottles, with glasses starting at £9 for a Ventoux Viognier.

Chef/s: Simon Radley and Raymond Booker. **Closed:** Mon, Sun, 25 Dec. **Meals:** set D £75. Tasting menu £99 (8 courses). **Details:** 45 seats. V menu. Bar. Wheelchairs. Parking. Music. Children over 12 yrs.

Sticky Walnut
Cooking score: 4
Modern British | £30
11 Charles Street, Chester, CH2 3AZ
Tel no: 01244 400400
stickywalnut.net

£30

A short walk from the railway station, in a tucked away but busy shopping parade off Chester's main drag, the first in a growing chain set up by entrepreneurial chef Gary Usher certainly lives up to its 'neighbourhood bistro' tagline. It's set across two floors and visitors agree that the livelier dining option is a table downstairs in sight of the open kitchen and backed by homely shelves of well-thumbed cookbooks and bottles of wine. The kitchen keeps a close eye on the seasons with a concise menu of appealing dishes that pushes all the right buttons. A late spring meal started with plump and silky crab agnolotti teamed with pickled fennel, lovage and elderflower beurre blanc. To follow, a whole lemon sole was cooked on the bone with confident precision and zhuzhed up with crisp-crumbed mussels, samphire and lemon. A light steamed lemon sponge with milk ice cream and pistachios brought things to a comforting conclusion. The kindly priced and interesting wine list opens at £21.50.
Chef/s: Gary Usher and Jack Huxley. **Closed:** 25 and 26 Dec. **Meals:** main courses £15 to £66. Set L £17 (2 courses) to £20. Set D £18 (2 courses) to £21. Sun L £25. **Details:** 49 seats. Music.

Thwarting the 'no-shows'

With an industry-wide staff shortage, rising rates and uncertainty over food imports, many independent restaurants are under unprecedented pressure to balance their books. The last thing they need is no-shows – diners who make reservations and give little or no notice that they're not going to turn up. Which is why restaurants have begun to fight back.

At the vanguard of the struggle is full payment in advance. You'd cough up for tickets to the football or a gig, the argument goes, so why not pay for your dinner beforehand? Systems such as Tock allow prepaid reservations, usually for a fixed-price menu, leaving you to handle drinks and service on the day.

Many restaurants won't accept bookings without taking card details, either over the phone or via a booking site. Avoid reading out card numbers in public places by doing it online and always make sure you fully understand the cancellation policies, as they differ wildly and if you really can't make it, you may still be charged.

The middle ground is restaurants that take a deposit, again via online booking systems. Paying £10 or £20 per head in advance takes a nice chunk off the bill on the day, and means that errant customers think twice before a no-show.

▌Frodsham

Next Door

Cooking score: 4
British | £32
68 Main Street, Frodsham, WA6 7AU
Tel no: 01928 371053
restaurantnextdoor.co.uk

The Next Door narrative is as charming as the 17th-century cottage it occupies. Vicki and Richard Nuttall worked in high-end hospitality before opening their own place in the former premises of Vicki's family's butcher's shop. The couple live next door to the restaurant, a white and airy space dominated by pale beams and appreciated by regulars for its generous approach to good food and Vicki's relaxed, genuine welcome. The precision of dishes such as a starter of goat's cheese mousse with sweet raisins, a fragrant truffle confit and the slight bitterness of a dark-baked tuile, sets the kitchen apart. Dinner might continue with a thick piece of stone bass with samphire and punchy squid ink sauce, or a plateful of Cheshire pork with a red wine jelly that plays nicely against pink loin, crackling belly and a herby pressing of slow-cooked meat. A dessert of berry blackjack, which holds the flavours of liquorice, blackcurrant and apple in perfect balance across mousse, jelly, fudge and an exemplary sorbet, is absolutely spot-on. The neat wine list starts at £21.50.

Chef/s: Richard Nuttall and Warren Cohen. **Closed:** Mon, Sun. **Meals:** main courses £15 to £25. Set L £18 Thur to Sat (2 courses) to £22. **Details:** 50 seats. 20 seats outside.

▌Marton

La Popote

Cooking score: 1
French | £50
Church Farm, Manchester Road (A34), Marton, SK11 9HF
Tel no: 01260 224785
la-popote.co.uk
£5 OFF

A verdant orangery extension has added some light relief to this converted coach house with its sturdy old beams, exposed brickwork and 'proper tablecloths'. The kitchen, meanwhile, proves its worth with sound renditions of enduring French bistro classics: 'rich and warming' French onion soup, confit duck with red onion marmalade, entrecôte Café de Paris, sea bass bordelaise, tarte tatin – plus a host of popular specials including seared scallops with Champagne beurre blanc. Simpler and cheaper lunches also 'punch above their weight', perhaps a chunky game terrine with pear and plum chutney, long-cooked beef bourguignon, and a terrific croquette de poisson (aka a 'big fishcake') with frites. House wine is £19.75.

Chef/s: Victor Janssen. **Closed:** Mon, Tue, 25 Dec to 8 Jan. **Meals:** main courses £17 to £34. Set L £19 (2 courses) to £24. Sun L £27. **Details:** 56 seats. 36 seats outside. Bar. Wheelchairs. Parking. Music. No small children at D.

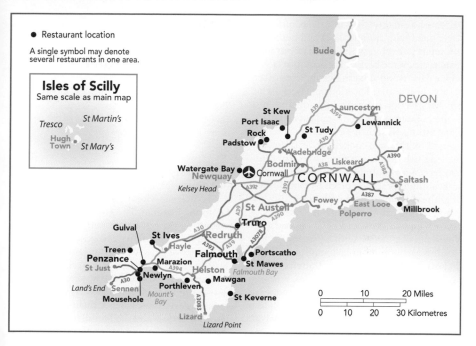

■ Falmouth

Oliver's

Cooking score: 2
Modern British | £33
33 High Street, Falmouth, TR11 2AD
Tel no: 01326 218138
oliversfalmouth.com

In a boho university town with a rapidly
changing and growing reputation for food,
Ken and Wendy Symons' compact bistro looks
positively old-school with its polished
floorboards, whitewashed walls and metal
seafood mobiles. Ken puts Cornish seafood
and locally reared meat to the forefront of his
menu, and dishes are delivered with good
humour by Wendy. To start, St Austell mussels
in a thyme-spiked heritage cider cream is well
executed and unapologetically retro, while
mains bring Cornish hake fillet with loaded
potatoes, courgettes and basil pesto or pig's
cheeks with buttered cabbage and spring
onion mash. Desserts are no afterthought,
with sound technical skill apparent in a

perfectly light chocolate espresso mousse with
caramel ice cream and honeycomb, although
the Cornish cheeseboard (which comes with
frozen grapes, chutney and biscuits) may
prove too distracting. Drink local beers or
pick from a serviceable wine list with decent
options by the glass.
Chef/s: Ken Symons. **Closed:** Mon, Sun.
Meals: main courses £14 to £24. Set L £17 (2
courses) to £23. Tasting menu £40 (7 courses).
Details: 28 seats. Children over 12 yrs at D.

Star & Garter

Cooking score: 2
British | £30
52 High Street, Falmouth, TR11 2AF
Tel no: 01326 316663
starandgarterfalmouth.co.uk

The date outside states 1892 but it was only
five years ago that visionary owners took over
this Victorian boozer and gave it a much-
needed new lease of life. Across the road from

Falmouth's old town hall in a steep, quirky street lined with antique shops and boutiques, this smart pub offers wonderful harbour views from tables at the back of the dining area where dark wood and candles are reminiscent of city chophouses. The kitchen has its own butchery section so expect high-quality meat – often underused nose-to-tail cuts – to get equal billing with the best local fish and seafood, with much cooked on the charcoal-fuelled grill. Crisp-crumbed lamb crubeens (trotters) with cooling cucumber chutney and labneh might precede a precisely timed fillet of gilthead bream served with cannellini beans, cockles, pancetta and wild garlic. If you're happy to share, order the smoked Moorland beef sirloin with asparagus, Cornish earlies and smoked bone marrow, but do leave room for the parkin, butterscotch, pear and ice cream. Drink local ales, well-crafted cocktails or look to the global wine list. **Chef/s:** Robert Bunny. **Meals:** main courses £15 to £18. Set L £18. Set D £24. Sun L £24. **Details:** 60 seats. Bar. Music.

LOCAL GEM
Rick Stein's Fish
Seafood | £30
Discovery Quay, Falmouth, TR11 3XA
Tel no: 01326 330050
rickstein.com

£5 £30
OFF

This Falmouth outpost of veteran TV chef Rick Stein's widespread empire might be more casual than his longstanding Seafood Restaurant (see entry) but there is no real difference when it comes to the quality of the raw ingredients or globetrotting flavours. Fish and chips from the takeaway counter might be the way to go if you are heading for the beach, or secure a table in the light and modern restaurant for pad thai noodles with prawns and egg followed, perhaps, by pan-fried Cornish hake, soy butter and spring onion mash. Wines from £19.95.

▌Gulval

LOCAL GEM
Tremenheere Kitchen
Modern British | £28
Tremenheere Sculpture Gardens, Gulval, TR20 8YL
Tel no: 01736 448089
tremenheerekitchen.com

£30

'What a surprise! What a spot!', exclaimed one first-timer, taking in the striking views across to St Michael's Mount from Tremenheere Sculpture Gardens. The gratifying aesthetic extends to the café and restaurant, with its Scandi-style neutrality and generous allowance of glass. Warm Puy lentil and walnut salad, 'bang-on' fish and chips, and croque monsieur show the way during the day. Tealights come out on Friday and Saturday evenings, when kimchi fires up tender Cornish pork belly, and local hake is dressed in parsley and lemon butter. A concise wine list opens at £24.

▌Helford

READERS RECOMMEND
Holy Mackerel Café
Helford Chapel, Helford, TR12 6JU
Tel no: 01326 231008
'This is a spectacularly good café in a delightfully converted chapel at the top of Helford village. Plenty of very pretty tables scattered outside and several in the warm interior. Everything is freshly prepared from excellent ingredients. Smoked mackerel salad a particular highlight.'

▌Lewannick
Coombeshead Farm
Cooking score: 6
British | £65
Lewannick, PL15 7QQ
Tel no: 01566 782009
coombesheadfarm.co.uk

🛏

Occupying 66 acres of tranquil Cornwall, this out-of-the-way farm is a hive of industry, from the pickling, curing and fermenting that underpin today's on-trend kitchens to pork butchery and the tending of a beehive. Have an amble round before you eat, and get a feel for the lie of the land. At dinner, it's hands-on with Oscar Holgado's collegiate team not only cooking but presenting the dishes before hurrying back to the stoves. You eat in the converted stone barn under hanging hops, and the seasonally changing menus are full of exploratory delights. The paper-thin mangalitza ham for appetiser is a creamy revelation, as is the benchmark sourdough bread. A spring visitor rejoiced in an extraordinary dish of uchiki kuri squash with its edible skin and smoked cream, but there was also venison tartare of uncommon tenderness, and an earthy dish of grilled leeks and sprouted buckwheat among the array of courses. The aged pork loin and onion that regularly features as a main is the last word in expressive, luxuriously fatted, full-flavoured meat, and things end on a rustic note, perhaps with sea buckthorn custard tart and bay leaf ice cream sweetened with the farm's honey. When it comes to wine, you could have a gander around the cellar and see for yourself, or look to owner Tom Adams' expertly curated list of modern gems. Small glasses are from £6.50 (£22 for 50cl carafes) for the fine Beaujolais of Domaine Saint-Cyr.
Chef/s: Oscar Holgado. **Closed:** Mon, Tue, Wed, early Jan to mid-Feb. **Meals:** set D £65 (5 courses). Sun L £35. **Details:** 18 seats. Bar. Wheelchairs. Parking. Music. Children at Sun L.

▌Marazion
Ben's Cornish Kitchen
Cooking score: 5
International | £28
West End, Marazion, TR17 0EL
Tel no: 01736 719200
benscornishkitchen.com
£5 OFF £30

Chef proprietor Ben Prior's appreciation of fine wines, especially those from South Africa, has resulted in his bistro on the town's main street doubling as a bottle shop. Shelves of wines now line one side of the white-painted dining room, with its polished wooden floor, rustic stone walls and enticing glimpses of St Michael's Mount. Ben's impeccable sourcing of tiptop raw materials, combined with kind pricing, means plenty of return custom as well as visits from holidaymakers. The produce may be proudly Cornish but the kitchen's creativity has a wider outlook, with a typical meal kicking off with smokey tandoori monkfish teamed with cauliflower, golden raisins, pine nuts and capers. It might lead on to a more modern European combination of lamb chump with gnocchi, early spring vegetables, hazelnut pesto and jus. Thai green curry sorbet with lemongrass granita and yuzu sake is one of the more outré desserts, but purists will delight in treacle tart and buttermilk ice cream. Well-chosen wines from £20.
Chef/s: Ben Prior. **Closed:** Mon, Sun, 22 Dec to 20 Jan. **Meals:** set L £17 (2 courses) to £21. Set D £28 (2 courses) to £34. Tasting menu £45 (5 courses). **Details:** 20 seats. Bar. Wheelchairs. Music.

Symbols

🛏 Accommodation is available
£30 Three courses for £30 or less
£5 OFF £5 off voucher scheme
🍷 Notable wine list

▌Mawgan
New Yard
Cooking score: 4
British | £25
Trelowarren Estate, Mawgan, TR12 6AF
Tel no: 01326 221595
newyardrestaurant.co.uk
£5 OFF ▐ £30

'A good evening with good food,' sums up many readers' views on Jeffrey Robinson's cooking. In a beautiful converted stable block on Sir Ferrers Vyvyan's historic Trelowarren Estate – which welcomes visitors to the gardens, art and craft galleries, and holiday cottages – the dining room makes for a warm and welcoming space with its arched windows, mismatched furniture and a wood-burning stove at each end. Here you can enjoy a three-course set menu or nine-course taster along with a predominantly Old World wine list (from £16.50). Robinson celebrates the abundant Cornish larder and foraged ingredients from Trelowarren's 1,000 lush acres with the strapline 'Simple food cooked to perfection'. Not all that simple when it's barbecued hogget with wild garlic and ewe's curd gnocchi or cured monkfish with a dressing of sea buckthorn caramel. 'I almost didn't have the cherry tomato gazpacho,' noted one enthusiastic reader, 'but it was probably the best thing I've eaten this year, possibly this decade.' Enough said.
Chef/s: Jeffrey Robinson. **Closed:** Mon, Jan, Tue (Oct to Dec, Feb to Apr). **Meals:** main courses £13 to £25. Tasting menu £35 (5 courses) to £58. Sun L £20 (2 courses). **Details:** 30 seats. 20 seats outside. V menu. Bar. Wheelchairs. Parking. Music.

▌Millbrook
The View Restaurant
Cooking score: 3
Modern British | £38
Treninnow Cliff, Millbrook, PL10 1JY
Tel no: 01752 822345
theview-restaurant.co.uk
£5 OFF ▐

There's a gloriously isolated feel to Matt and Rachel Corner's clifftop restaurant in the south-eastern corner of Cornwall. On a summer evening, watching the marine skies change colour by the minute, from a brightly designed room run by reassuringly friendly staff, is what it's all about. Matt's regionally informed cooking keeps things simple for dishes that major on seafood, starting perhaps with seared scallops and chorizo, or haddock ceviche with crab and pink grapefruit, before moving on to grilled monkfish, tiger prawns and cockles lashed with lemon and garlic. The alternative route might be via pigeon and poached grapes with crispy ham, and then a roast Spanish onion with gnocchi and Cornish camembert, while meat alternatives could be lamb rump or corn-fed chicken breast. Clotted cream ice cream is a must, especially when served with a satisfying blueberry clafoutis dessert, or try the impeccable West Country cheeses. Wines show restraint as to both range and price, with Spanish house at £20.
Chef/s: Matt Corner. **Closed:** Mon, Tue, 1 week Christmas, 2 weeks Feb. **Meals:** main courses £19 to £24. Set L £16 (2 courses) to £20. Sun L £16 (2 courses) to £20. **Details:** 45 seats. 20 seats outside. Bar. Wheelchairs. Parking. Music.

▌Mousehole

2 Fore Street

Cooking score: 3
Modern British | £34
2 Fore Street, Mousehole, TR19 6PF
Tel no: 01736 731164
2forestreet.co.uk

On the edge of the harbour, Joe Wardell's unassuming little restaurant is cordial and lively, with many regulars returning again and again to reclaim their favourite table in the window. The kitchen continues with its robust attitude to provenance and seasonality. As you'd hope, the local catch makes appearances in dishes such as crab soup with saffron rouille and Parmesan toast, or seafood and shellfish curry fragrant with lemongrass, chilli and coconut – Asian and Middle Eastern notes are deftly handled. But there's meat, too. Pressed eight-hour-roasted pork belly with sticky barbecue sauce and pickled chilli, and corn-fed chicken kiev. Lunch is simpler: well-filled sandwiches, comforting dishes such as beef burger, moules marinière and West Country cheese ploughman's. There are great alfresco possibilities, and appreciable efforts have been made with the global wine list (from £18.50). **Chef/s:** Joe Wardell. **Closed:** 3 Jan to 10 Feb. **Meals:** main courses £15 to £23. Sun L £16 (2 courses) to £19. **Details:** 36 seats. 36 seats outside. Music.

▌Newlyn

The Tolcarne Inn

Cooking score: 3
Seafood | £35
Newlyn, TR18 5PR
Tel no: 01736 363074
tolcarneinn.co.uk

This whitewashed pub near the harbour edge is a bustling local resource that fairly packs them in. Low white beams, a blackboard menu and one of those handy charts for identifying fish species form the backdrop for some bracing seafood cookery. A pair of

spring diners thoroughly enjoyed their lunch of salt cod fritters followed by John Dory, while in the evening things get more elaborate. Red mullet poached in coconut milk with dhal, curried cauliflower and green chutney makes an appetising prelude to one of the compendious main dishes, say cod fillet with chillied cavolo nero, lemon-glazed salsify, salt cod croquette and dates, all sauced with red wine. There's usually one meat dish and desserts such as caramelised banana rice pudding parfait with candied pecans and chocolate sorbet aim to tickle your fancy. The well-considered wine list has been compiled with seafood in mind. **Chef/s:** Ben Tunnicliffe. **Closed:** 25 and 26 Dec. **Meals:** main courses £18 to £21. **Details:** 40 seats. 24 seats outside. V menu. Parking.

READERS RECOMMEND

Mackerel Sky Seafood Bar

Seafood
The Bridge, New Road, Newlyn, TR18 5PZ
mackerelskycafe.co.uk
'There's nothing fancy about this little place but the seafood is super fresh. We ordered several tapas-style dishes to share – our favourites were salt & pepper squid with aïoli and crab nachos, lime sour cream and jalapeños. They don't take bookings.'

▌Padstow

★ TOP 50 ★

Paul Ainsworth at No. 6

Cooking score: 7
Modern British | £75
6 Middle Street, Padstow, PL28 8AP
Tel no: 01841 532093
paul-ainsworth.co.uk

Sometimes a restaurant's vibe is so clearly a true expression of its owner that you know in a heartbeat who is conducting matters. So it is with No. 6, where Paul Ainsworth's vigour sings, from welcome to farewell, via lusty dishes composed by his talented team. Simple homages are paid to North Cornwall. A single panko-coated Porthilly oyster pulses with the taste of the sea, slipping from its shell with a dot of smoked roe and a pinch of nori seaweed; spears of St Enodoc asparagus, picked and prepped that morning, lightly cooked and deftly seasoned with Cornish sea salt and Ligurian olive oil. This is a kitchen that knows when to stop: firm-fleshed monkfish, cooked skilfully on the bone, needs nothing more than an intense crab sauce; a bowl of white crabmeat, leek royale and crisped fish skin is served separately. Other dishes bring punchy layers of flavour and texture – perhaps a pig's head fritter with cubes of smoked eel brushed with soy, the sweetness balanced by the sharpness of Bramley apple, gherkin, capers and mustard; or translucent ribbons of raw bass, curled like a rose, pink-tinged and beautiful, on a sand shrimp slaw with katsuobushi mayo. Playfulness ramps up come dessert, no more so than in the Fairground Tale, still a rollicking, lip-smacking, barnstormer of a pudding: a bitter chocolate soufflé towers over a diminutive coconut-rum custard tartlet; a brown butter choc ice rides on the carousel in its paper wrapping alongside a bar of aerated chocolate whose sweetness and texture is sharpened by mandarin gel, the lightest pinch of sea salt and honeycomb. It disappears on the tongue like the slickest magic trick before the finale – fluffy, doughnutty 'monkey bread' so richly irresistible that even if your belly advises otherwise, you'll dive in. The wine list romps around the world (although it's most at home in France) with bottles from £35 and expert, sunny advice.

Chef/s: Paul Ainsworth and Chris McClurg. **Closed:** Mon, Sun, 24 to 26 Dec, 11 Jan to 6 Feb. **Meals:** main courses £35 to £46. Set L £30 (2 courses) to £34. **Details:** 44 seats. V menu. Vg menu. Bar. Music. Children over 4 yrs.

The Seafood Restaurant

Cooking score: 4
Seafood | £69
Riverside, Padstow, PL28 8BY
Tel no: 01841 532700
rickstein.com

Even with the rise of a fresh batch of local chefs with media clout to rival Rick Stein's, this harbourside spot still casts its spell. A long menu (there's a shorter lunchtime set) is rooted in Stein's beloved North Cornwall, and celebrates the region's oceanic bounty in, say, a fruits de mer platter that heaves with mussels, oysters, crab claws and the rest, magnificent lobster, or an exquisite piece of hake with palourde clams that delivers sufficient flavour as to render the fathomless pool of sauce superfluous. The menu jets off on lively culinary adventures, reflecting Stein's own, dropping in on Indonesia for an ever-popular curry that brims with bass, cod and prawns, and Japan for spring-in-your-step sashimi. Non-fish eaters might enjoy a grilled bavette steak or risotto primavera, and you could finish with a crisp-based walnut tart, although you may well be tempted by a waiter's swooning suggestion of the 'volcanic' hot chocolate fondant. 'It's all very pleasant,' concluded one diner who – like others – would have relished being wowed by an 'outstanding or surprising' dish. Some punchy food prices filter into the wine list (bottles from £35) but the range by the glass certainly deserves applause.

Chef/s: Stephane Delourme. **Closed:** 25 and 26 Dec. **Meals:** main courses £22 to £65. Set L £35 to £43. **Details:** 120 seats. V menu. Vg menu. Bar. Wheelchairs. Music. Children over 3 yrs.

Vegetarian and vegan

While many restaurants offer dishes suitable for non-meat eaters, those marked 'V menu' (vegetarian) and 'Vg menu' (vegan) offer separate menus.

Rick Stein's Café
Seafood | £25
10 Middle Street, Padstow, PL28 8AP
Tel no: 01841 532700
rickstein.com

🛏 £30

The appeal of this Stein enterprise, with its fresh, light atmosphere and fresh, light seafood menu, is a given. Start with a perky Vietnamese pho, or smoked mackerel salad with green mango and papaya, before a fragrant south Indian-inspired cod curry, or a bowl of linguine with tomatoes, capers and a pep of chilli from the separate vegetarian offer. Meat eaters should be satisfied by a rump steak with peppery leaves and chips, while the sticky toffee pudding with Cornish clotted cream will – surely – tick everyone's boxes. A compact wine list opens at £19.50.

▌Penzance
The Shore
Cooking score: 5
Seafood | £59
13-14 Alverton Street, Penzance, TR18 2QP
Tel no: 01736 362444
theshorerestaurant.uk

A five-minute walk from the sea, Bruce Rennie's compact restaurant is firmly established as a rising star of the Cornwall scene. Before going it alone in 2015, Rennie worked under Martin Wishart and Rick Stein, and although his cooking is grounded in classic technique, the flavours are more Asian than European, with a strong Japanese bias. The inspiration for the no-choice set menu is that day's catch at Newlyn fish market. The cooking is precise and everything on the plate is there for a reason. A typical meal could open with a Porthilly oyster topped with the clean crunch of apple and green chilli, then move on to mackerel sashimi teamed with sesame purée and a spicy wasabi sorbet that quickly melts into sweet, earthy beetroot. Equally fresh hake is balanced by a creamy, soy-seasoned purée of

garlic and pine nuts and the crunch of kohlrabi, but the real star of our inspection meal was monkfish coated with spicy red char siu sauce and served atop a tangle of fermented cabbage and amaranth. As a finale, pink rhubarb, white chocolate and meringue work in glorious harmony. The carefully matched wine and sake flight is optional but all part of the journey.
Chef/s: Bruce Rennie. **Closed:** Mon, Sun.
Meals: tasting menu £59 (6 courses). **Details:** 26 seats.

▌Port Isaac
Outlaw's Fish Kitchen
Cooking score: 5
Seafood | £50
1 Middle Street, Port Isaac, PL29 3RH
Tel no: 01208 881183
outlaws.co.uk

With ingredients as good as these and a commitment to local, seasonal and sustainable produce that has filtered down from parent Restaurant Nathan Outlaw at the top of the village (see entry), who needs fanfare? Outlaw's Fish Kitchen is a tiny, wonky, whitewashed box of wonders, a place where T-shirted front of house staff weave expertly between the crammed tables to bring small plates of seafood – as and when ready – in waves of easy-going deliciousness. Order bouncy wholegrain sourdough bread to deal with every drop of olive oil on a plate of cured brill that is sweet, smooth and sharp with spring onions, ginger and yoghurt. Enjoy the delicate freshness of gurnard ceviche with green chilli and mango, the no-pretension nuggets of fleshy cod coated in the crispest batter, or whole lemon sole with a green sauce butter. Leave room for dessert, and if you're lucky it'll be a coconut and raspberry baked Alaska that is simple perfection. A civilised wine list leans towards white, with bottles from £28 and plenty of choice by the glass and carafe.
Chef/s: Tim Barnes. **Closed:** Mon, Sun, 1 week Christmas, 1 Jan. **Meals:** small plates £8 to £15. **Details:** 24 seats. Music.

Restaurant Nathan Outlaw

Cooking score: 10
Seafood | £140
6 New Road, Port Isaac, PL29 3SB
Tel no: 01208 880896
nathan-outlaw.com

There is something magnificently unadulterated about Nathan Outlaw's cooking and the modest elegance of his restaurant at the top of pretty Port Isaac. Here, there is neither pomp nor circumstance, there's no swagger nor showmanship, nothing gratingly theatrical – although the view does deserve a standing ovation. What brings diners back time and again ('this is our nth visit,' said one fan) is the way Outlaw and his team take superlative ingredients, and handle them with respectful lightness and a touch of ingenuity to create plates of seafood in a four-course set menu that diners won't forget. A trio of amuse-bouches includes a shatteringly light filo pastry tartlet with pieces of lobster and slivers of revered St Enodoc asparagus, and an airy choux bun that bursts with briny, creamy, smoked mackerel mousse. A suggestion of chilli picks up the flavour of translucent sliced raw scallops, with cucumber and radish giving freshness and sharpness in a combination that dances on the palate. There's dancing, too, between delicate cured brill partnered with the first peas of the season as if they were made for each other. Weightier flavours follow: an impeccable piece of red mullet has been flashed in the pan and comes with sensational soused vegetables and a green sauce whose herbiness points up the sweetness of the fish; a plate of plump cod, basil and kohlrabi is a masterclass in apparent restraint – apparent, because the behind-the-scenes skill required to select and prep ingredients for dishes of this calibre is of course oceanic. Early dishes act as a prelude to the arrival of the 'immaculate' king of fish – turbot – unadorned and stately on a few spoonfuls of tartare hollandaise and spears of salt-flecked asparagus. Finish with nostalgia wrapped up in a strawberry ice cream sandwich, or a just-set egg custard with poached rhubarb, and an embracing waft of nutmeg and ginger ice cream. There are strokes of genius on the wine flight (£75), most notably the outstanding Rabbitsfoot Sauvignon Blanc from a tiny Stellenbosch vineyard, served with the turbot. Alternatively, allow the brilliant Damon Little to guide you through the treasure trove of a list, which opens, but doesn't linger, at £28.
Chef/s: Nathan Outlaw. **Closed:** Mon, Tue, Sun, 22 Dec to 1 Feb. **Meals:** set L and D £140 (4 courses). **Details:** 30 seats. V menu. Music. Children over 10 yrs.

LOCAL GEM

Fresh from the Sea

Seafood | £20
18 New Road, Port Isaac, PL29 3SB
Tel no: 01208 880849
freshfromthesea.co.uk
£30

'Last year Calum was struggling to catch brown crab and we explored using alternative sustainable shellfish such as spider crabs and velvet crabs, which taste fantastic.' Tracey Greenhalgh's proud claim outlines the core values of her unassuming daytime café (with the catch from her husband's boat, the *Mary D*, centre stage). The menu extends beyond the hugely popular crab sandwiches and whole lobsters to Porthilly oysters, smoked salmon and Davidstow Cheddar. To drink there's Camel Valley Bacchus (£25), Prosecco or local beers.

Readers recommend

These entries are genuine quotes from a report sent in by one of our readers. Please get in touch via our website if you agree with their recommendation.

CORNWALL

Chef/s: Jude Kereama. **Closed:** Mon, Sun, Jan.
Meals: main courses £15 to £26. Set D £23 (2 courses) to £28. Tasting menu £55 (7 courses).
Details: 32 seats. V menu. Wheelchairs. Music. Children over 10 yrs after 7pm.

READERS RECOMMEND
Pilchards at Port Gaverne
Port Gaverne, Port Isaac, PL29 3SQ
Tel no: 01208 880244
portgavernehotel.co.uk
'I thought this might be just another beach shack but it's not. I walked down from Port Isaac and stumbled on this gorgeous spot in the bay. I had amazing oysters and an incredible octopus dish. Lots of spicy, interesting flavours; really different and tasty.'

▌Porthleven
Kota
Cooking score: 4
Fusion | £45
Harbour Head, Porthleven, TR13 9JA
Tel no: 01326 562407
kotarestaurant.co.uk
£5 OFF ▭

'From the amuse-bouche of a cauliflower velouté to the desserts, everything was imaginative and excellent,' noted a returning couple to the Kereamas' former corn mill on Porthleven's harbour. The interior is simple and understated – tiled floors, off-white walls, exposed ceiling beams – putting the focus on Jude Kereama's cooking, which draws on the chef's Malay and Maori roots combined with a ready supply of local seafood. Menus run from hand-dived scallop crudo with apple, ginger, soy and avocado through to a 'superb' duck curry or a more traditional beef sirloin with ox cheek, carrots, oyster mushrooms, onion and truffle – dishes bursting with flavour and personality. Compositions on the tasting menu are well considered, right through to the closing notes of blue cheese ice cream with port and red wine poached pear, digestive biscuit and candied walnuts. Service is friendly and the wine list includes plenty from the New World; other drink options include classic cocktails, Cornish gins, beers and spirits.

▌Portscatho
Driftwood
new chef/no score
Modern European | £70
Rosevine, Portscatho, TR2 5EW
Tel no: 01872 580644
driftwoodhotel.co.uk
▭

In 2019, it was announced that Chris Eden, who has been at Driftwood since 2006, had been appointed head chef at Gidleigh Park near Chagford in Devon (see entry). We await developments here, but what won't of course change is the glorious location of the boutique hotel on the Roseland Peninsula overlooking sparkling Gerrans Bay. Venture down the woodland path to the hotel's own strip of beach, then when you have clambered back up, a regal welcome awaits in the refurbished dining room, where a light tone prevails and a decked terrace makes the most of the bay views. Seafood will doubtless continue to play a major part on the menus, which have featured the likes of rock oysters in white soy with frozen crème fraîche, caviar and sea purslane, perhaps followed by roast cod with toasted rye spätzle, crown prince pumpkin, Jerusalem artichoke and chanterelles. Aged beef cooked over coals is likely to remain a fixture, and the cheeses are excellent. Glasses from £10 lead off a well-written wine list that quickly gets into its economic stride, but there is reasonable choice below £40.
Chef/s: Oliver Pierrepont. **Meals:** set D £55 (2 courses) to £70. Tasting menu £85 (5 courses) to £100. **Details:** 34 seats. V menu. Bar. Wheelchairs. Parking. Music. Children over 5 yrs.

Rock
The Mariners

Cooking score: 3
Modern British | £30
Slipway, Rock, PL27 6LD
Tel no: 01208 863679
themarinersrock.com

£30

At the western extremity of little Rock, with the sweeping vista of the Camel estuary before it, The Mariners was acquired from Nathan Outlaw in 2019 by Paul Ainsworth of Padstow's No. 6 (see entry). The orientation of the place remains firmly on seaside bistro food on a long menu of favourites, with burgers and bangers inveigling their way among the more exploratory options. Breaded buttermilk chicken seasoned with garam masala and a dip of chipotle mayonnaise makes an assertive opener. Fish main courses on a glowing summer day make the most of the setting, especially when they're as sensitively wrought as a hefty wing of thornback ray doused in acerbic lemony dressing with capers and a multitude of tiny brown shrimps, with which a pot of unpeeled salty matchstick chips is the business. Properly matured steaks and homemade pies provide a roaring trade, and the desserts make all the right noises for profiteroles, spotted dick made with aged suet, and a take on pain perdu topped with apple, walnuts and clotted cream ice cream. The short wine list (glasses from £4.95) is boosted by a selection of bottled and draught ales.
Chef/s: Paul Ainsworth, Joe Rozier and Tom Dawes. **Meals:** main courses £12 to £22. **Details:** 96 seats. 54 seats outside. Music.

St Ives
Porthgwidden Beach Café

Cooking score: 1
Seafood | £30
Porthgwidden Beach, The Island, St Ives, TR26 1PL
Tel no: 01736 796791
porthgwiddencafe.co.uk

£30

More tucked away than the older Porthminster Café (see entry), this relaxed Antipodean-style seaside café overlooks St Ives Bay with views towards Godrevy Lighthouse. The simple whitewashed room and recently refurbished sea-facing terrace reflect the no-frills approach of the kitchen, which champions only the best local seafood and meat. St Ives mackerel fillet, celeriac rémoulade and tempura samphire might precede Thai fish curry or slow-braised beef cheek ragoût, potato gnocchi and Parmesan. Laid-back breakfasts and simple lunches such as fish and chips and burgers are also served. Drink Cornish cider and ale, or tuck into the modest wine list from £15.95.
Chef/s: Robert Michael. **Meals:** main courses £14 to £20. **Details:** 34 seats. 48 seats outside. V menu. Music.

Porthmeor Beach Café

Cooking score: 1
Modern European | £30
Porthmeor, St Ives, TR26 1JZ
Tel no: 01736 793366
porthmeor-beach.co.uk

£30

This sociable hangout below the Tate is known for its 'intoxicating' vibes and stunning views. Inside, diners sit on lime-green chairs and pick their cutlery from pink plastic buckets, while the kitchen serves up free-spirited food with a global slant – perhaps chermoula-crusted aubergine with Israeli couscous salad or confit duck with green-tea noodles, sake-infused cherry tomatoes and Asian broth. Lunch is a one-plate affair, and 'outstanding' tapas are available right through the day – from Padrón peppers to fennel sausage with chickpea dhal and coriander oil. Wine options start at £18.30 and 'unusual' cocktails might include a King's gin mojito.

Chef/s: Louis Wardman. **Closed:** 25 and 26 Dec, 19 Jan to 14 Feb. **Meals:** main courses D £15 to £18. Small plates £4 to £10. **Details:** 32 seats. 60 seats outside. Wheelchairs. Music.

Porthminster Café

Cooking score: 3
Seafood | £45
Porthminster Beach, St Ives, TR26 2EB
Tel no: 01736 795352
porthminstercafe.co.uk

Breezy Porthminster Point isn't exactly Bondi Beach, but Australian chef Mick Smith makes the most of this bracing beachside location with its fabulous panoramic views, surfing waves and photogenic sunsets (if you're lucky). His stark-white, Art Deco haunt still exudes a funky café vibe, although the cooking is a cut above with its telling mix of fusion and savvy crossover ideas – all underpinned by regular supplies of fresh Cornish seafood. Crispy fried squid is dressed with an Asian salad, lime and white citrus miso dressing, whole plaice turns up in company with tempura prawns, and Porthminster seafood curry comes spiked with tamarind. Elsewhere, beer-battered fish and chips, fillet steaks and fried halloumi salad with Padrón peppers are spot-on for their target audience. For afters, consider the likes of Cornish apple and filo crumble with Pedro Ximénez purée and crab apple plus a blackberry and yoghurt sorbet. Hand-picked global wines start at £17.50.

Chef/s: Mick Smith. **Meals:** main courses £15 to £30. **Details:** 48 seats. 56 seats outside. V menu. Music.

Blas Burgerworks

Burgers | £19
The Warren, St Ives, TR26 2EA
Tel no: 01736 797272
blasburgerworks.co.uk
£30

This small granite building just behind the harbour started life as a fishermen's net loft, but for the past 14 years has been a noteworthy, if compact, eco-friendly burger bar popular with all-comers. From the open kitchen facing the handful of reclaimed wood tables, Lisa Taylor and her team serve up chargrilled patties showcasing Cornish free range beef and chicken, local dayboat fish and innovative vegetarian options. Drink local beers and ciders or one of the five wines.

■ St Keverne
The Greenhouse

Cooking score: 4
Modern British | £35
6 High Street, St Keverne, TR12 6NN
Tel no: 01326 280800
tgor.co.uk
£5 OFF

'Very much liked this,' is the straightforward response from a first-time visitor to this unassuming restaurant just off the village square. Billed as a modern bistro, it matches a warm, conversational mood with precise cooking that hits all the right accents. Chef proprietors Leonie and Neil Woodward look to the locality for ingredients but mix in wider influences in the modern British way: pheasant and pistachio terrine with quince jelly rubs shoulders with lemongrass sugar-cured salmon with ponzu dressing, avocado and pickled turnip, say. There could be hake with curry sauce and mussels, corn and kale cakes with cucumber raita or a bavette steak with slow-cooked short-rib croquette, corn purée and beef sauce. Portions are generous and the homemade bread irresistible, so perhaps share a fresh cream pavlova with passion fruit curd or a plate of Cornish cheeses. Local beers and a brief, well-annotated list of organic wines suit any occasion. **Chef/s:** Neil and Leonie Woodward. **Closed:** Mon, Tue, Sun, Jan, first week Feb. **Meals:** main courses £13 to £19. **Details:** 28 seats. Music.

■ St Kew
St Kew Inn
Cooking score: 3
British | £30
St Kew, PL30 3HB
Tel no: 01208 841259
stkewinn.co.uk

£30

If North Cornwall's coastal crowds or relentless celeb-seekers grind you down, take some winding, wooded turns inland to St Kew. There, you'll find not much more than a substantial church and, in time-honoured tradition, a substantial pub next door where a confident kitchen team feeds those in the know (it's a popular chefs-day-off haunt judging by overheard conversations). The menu roams the region, scooping up Coombeshead sourdough, St Enodoc asparagus, Newlyn-landed fish, Porthilly mussels and oysters, to populate a menu that's bright with seasonality but that doesn't undermine the inn's essential pubbiness – you could have local ham, village eggs and chips, or burger with mustard mayo. A spring salad of pub-grown radishes is a playful riot of crimson and white varieties, a ruby-red orb with its leaves intact the hero of the dish, the pepperiness tempered by sweet potato 'butter' and a garlicky herb pesto. Monkfish, precisely roasted on the bone, is in robust partnership with griddled whole spring onions, asparagus and red gem, a fiery ribbon of 'nduja wrapping the flavour parcel up beautifully. Finish with pavlova, because the pleasure of first-rate meringue, early strawberries and Cornish clotted cream is peerless. Wine from £17.50.
Chef/s: Andi Tuck. **Closed:** 25 and 26 Dec. **Meals:** main courses £14 to £21. **Details:** 70 seats. 80 seats outside. Bar. Parking.

■ St Mawes
Hotel Tresanton
Cooking score: 2
Seafood | £48
27 Lower Castle Road, St Mawes, TR2 5DR
Tel no: 01326 270055
tresanton.com

£5 OFF 🛏

Olga Polizzi certainly injected a dash of Mediterranean glamour when she transformed this 1940s yachtsmen's club into a smart seaside bolthole in 1997. The hotel cuts a real dash in summer, when the gorgeous terrace overlooking the Fal estuary comes into its own, but the cream and blue restaurant with mosaic floors and shell-shaped lights has an elegant look all year round. The modern brasserie-style menu is of a similarly sunny disposition with local seafood a strong suit. A starter of perfectly al dente risotto nero with squid, clams and scallop might precede monkfish, asparagus and wild mushroom croquette, but meat dishes are handled well too – perhaps Cusgarne Farm beef, roast artichoke, carrots, parsnip and horseradish. Satisfying desserts have included a vanilla cheesecake paired with Yorkshire rhubarb. Well-made cocktails, served in the lounge or on the terrace, are a good way to warm up before diving into the Italian-heavy wine list.
Chef/s: Paul Wadham. **Meals:** main courses £18 to £48. Set L £25 (2 courses) to £29. **Details:** 70 seats. 90 seats outside. Bar. Wheelchairs. Parking. Children over 6 yrs at D.

■ St Tudy
St Tudy Inn
Cooking score: 2
Modern British | £30
Churchtown, St Tudy, PL30 3NN
Tel no: 01208 850656
sttudyinn.com

£5 OFF 🛏 £30

It may be 'a lovely pub' with its log fires and locally brewed ale, but this is no ordinary village inn. The food is 'a reason to return', stretching well beyond the usual pub standard – even the fish and chips are a cut above the norm. Emily Scott's menus are well considered and built around good, often local ingredients, perhaps air-dried charcuterie from nearby Deli Farm, Padstow crab or Cornish brie. Her cooking focuses on care and skill rather than convoluted complexity, as demonstrated by a straightforward starter of scallops with butter, thyme and garlic. The same goes for main courses, say a fish stew of gurnard, haddock, mussels and prawns served with crostini and saffron aïoli, and a simple lamb curry with spinach, yoghurt, coriander and rustic chips. Desserts stay dependably in the comfort zone of chocolate mousse and vanilla ice cream or banoffee pie. To drink, there are cocktails, as well as a concise, modern wine list starting at £20.

Chef/s: Emily Scott. **Closed:** 26 Dec. **Meals:** main courses £10 to £22. **Details:** 80 seats. 20 seats outside. Bar. Wheelchairs. Parking. Music.

▌Treen
The Gurnard's Head

Cooking score: 3
Modern British | £34
Treen, TR26 3DE
Tel no: 01736 796928
gurnardshead.co.uk
£5 OFF 🚗

On the winding road from St Ives to St Just, this remote mustard-coloured pub is steered in all things by its spectacular clifftop location. It is named after the rocky promontory visible from the coastal path at the back, and is run by the Inkin brothers along similar lines to The Felin Fach Griffin near Brecon (see entry). It's popular with city dwellers as a weekend haunt, but pretension is kept at bay by locals and muddy-booted walkers refuelling with real ale and cider in the bar. In keeping with its name, local fish and seafood dominates the menu. Warm fillets of mackerel with rhubarb, ginger and soy, and stone bass, celeriac, chicken butter, brown shrimp and kale are typical of the kitchen's straightforward style. Meat dishes can include rump of beef with

Marmite butter, celery, Stilton, hazelnuts and capers, while desserts such as buttermilk panna cotta, mango, cardamom and mint chocolate sorbet are spot-on. There's plenty by the glass and carafe on the well-researched wine list.

Chef/s: Max Wilson. **Closed:** 1 to 5 and 25 Dec. **Meals:** main courses £19 to £22. Set L £20 (2 courses) to £24. Set D £22 (2 courses) to £28. Sun L £20. **Details:** 50 seats. 50 seats outside. V menu. Vg menu. Bar. Parking. Music.

▌Truro
Tabb's

Cooking score: 3
Modern British | £35
85 Kenwyn Street, Truro, TR1 3BZ
Tel no: 01872 262110
tabbs.co.uk

Nigel Tabb's intimate neighbourhood restaurant has been well supported by locals since it opened in a former backstreet pub 15 years ago. The pale lilac walls and cream leather high-backed dining chairs may now look a touch dated but the food remains contemporary, with dishes underpinned by a solid grasp of classic techniques. Tabb has long trumpeted the quality of local producers and it's not just Cornish seafood that gets star billing. Flavours are robust, as in a starter of black linguine, smoked Cornish duck breast, goat's cheese, deep-fried egg, mustard mayo and truffle oil. A grilled fillet of ray wing, soy and pak choi, seafood sesame broth and chilli oil has become something of a menu staple, although seared fillet of beef, braised shin with green peppercorns, parsnip mash and brandy cream demonstrates a skilful approach to meat options. A perfectly molten chocolate fondant with black treacle ice cream is one satisfying conclusion. A global wine list plays it fairly safe with bottles from £18.50.

Chef/s: Nigel Tabb. **Closed:** Mon, Sun. **Meals:** main courses £16 to £21. Set L and D £22 (2 courses) to £28. **Details:** 28 seats. Bar. Music.

▌Watergate Bay
Fifteen Cornwall

Cooking score: 3
Italian | £39
On The Beach, Watergate Bay, TR8 4AA
Tel no: 01637 861000
fifteencornwall.co.uk

If ever a location should be devoured, it's here. Whether you've caught the flat calm of a summer's evening on Watergate Bay and a lazy sun slipping below the horizon, or the energy of surf-spitting oceanic rollers, it's a magnificent spot. There's enormous affection for Fifteen Cornwall, not least for its commitment under Jamie Oliver's Cornwall Food Foundation to opening employment doors for young people, so forgive some inconsistencies in the food. Apprentices deliver (under supervision) a broadly Italian menu, perhaps a 'superb' ribollita rich with winter root vegetables, or a bowl of vignole, a spring version of the stew packed with peas, broad beans, artichokes and prosciutto. Lighter dishes include Cornish crab with agretti, tomato and almonds, but you may be tempted by homemade tortelli that burst with mild buffalo ricotta and sharp sorrel, or a substantial piece of hake with St Austell Bay mussels. A strawberry mousse or rhubarb ice cream with rhubarb, lemon cake and herb granita round things up pleasantly, and something from the Italian-leaning wine list (from £22.50) might encourage you to linger and absorb yet more of the setting.

Chef/s: Adam Banks. **Meals:** main courses £19 to £33. Small plates £9 to £14. Tasting menu £68 (6 courses). **Details:** 100 seats. V menu. Bar. Wheelchairs. Parking. Music. Children over 4 yrs at D.

LOCAL GEM
The Beach Hut

British | £28
On The Beach, Watergate Bay, TR8 4AA
Tel no: 01637 860543
the-beach-hut.co.uk

🛏 £30

Part of the Watergate Bay Hotel, this easy, breezy, nautically styled spot with wide-screen views of the sea (which all but laps at the door at high tide) is perfect for anyone fresh from the surf or just keen to unwind. The menu has something for everyone, say Cornish mussels marinière, a local beef burger topped with Emmental, and chocolate pecan brownie with crème fraîche. Wines play it safe, too, with plenty of familiar favourites, most for less than £30.

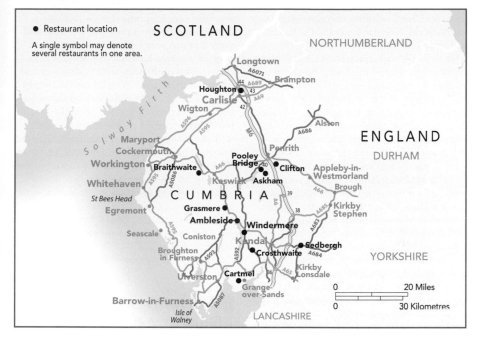

Restaurant location
A single symbol may denote several restaurants in one area.

▌Ambleside
The Drunken Duck Inn
Cooking score: 3
Modern British | £42
Barngates, Ambleside, LA22 0NG
Tel: 015394 36347
drunkenduckinn.co.uk

Recent renovations have done nothing to diminish the charm of this perennially popular pub, which counts a microbrewery among its many winning attributes. The food, of course, is another. Walkers welcome the addition of a brunch menu (served until noon), offering the chance to refuel on a bacon roll or a muffin topped with mushrooms and wild garlic pesto. Lunch brings doorstop sandwiches (maybe roast ham and piccalilli) and curry (a sharing bowl of chana masala, onion bhajia and aloo paratha), while more considered evening options run from artichoke ravioli with pine nut cream and sage to guinea fowl breast and thigh with morteau

sausage and cassoulet. For dessert, there could be rhubarb doughnut, buckwheat and miso caramel or lemon cake with blood orange sorbet and sesame. Besides that own-brewed beer, there's a decent global wine list with a good selection by the glass.
Chef/s: Jonny Watson. **Closed:** 25 Dec.
Meals: main courses £23. Sun L £16. **Details:** 60 seats. 40 seats outside. Bar. Wheelchairs. Parking.

★ TOP 50 ★

Lake Road Kitchen
Cooking score: 7
Modern European | £65
3 Sussex House, Lake Road, Ambleside, LA22 0AD
Tel no: 015394 22012
lakeroadkitchen.co.uk

Tucked away behind an unassuming grey exterior on a narrow street in the town centre at the northern end of Lake Windermere, the kitchen has become, in a few short years, one of the area's outstanding go-to destinations.

It's James Cross's intensity of commitment that has made this singular operation the success it is. The place itself looks like a Finnish sauna, with its plank walls and benches, but for the window opening on to a busily productive kitchen. Local pedigree meats, Norwegian and Scottish seafood, and foraged greenery form the backbone of tasting dishes that are described to you rather than written down. A winter night opened with a mini chicken kebab as a prelude to roasted mussels with 'last year's tomatoes' and kelp, and then a sustaining broth of herdwick lamb garnished with nettle pasta. An Iberian note wavers through a stew of razor clams, pine nuts and parsley, before steamed halibut arrives with trout roe in a butter sauce based on fermented white asparagus. Meat might be the celebrated Cumbrian blue grey ribeye, dry-aged and given resonant depth with a black truffle sauce. Impossibly aromatic woodruff ice cream marks a pause before a dessert such as cheesecake flavoured with koji, the Japanese fungus used in umami-laden fermented foods. Wine pairings are available; otherwise, there's 'a good list with modest mark ups and carefully chosen regions and grape varieties'. Drinking starts at £7.50 a glass or £30 a bottle.

Chef/s: James Cross. **Closed:** Mon, Tue. **Meals:** tasting menu £65 (5 courses) to £145. **Details:** 21 seats. Music. Children over 14 yrs.

Old Stamp House

Cooking score: 5
Modern British | £50
Church Street, Ambleside, LA22 0BU
Tel no: 015394 32775
oldstamphouse.com

'Excellent lunchtime experience. Could not fault it.' So writes one of Ryan Blackburn's growing army of fans. The surrounds may lack zest – a whitewashed stone-walled cellar, slate floors, plain wooden furniture, noisy when busy – but it hardly matters, as the cooking is triumphant. Blackburn's version of modern British is imaginative and well executed – joyously and seasonally rooted in Cumbrian

soil. One couple's guinea hen with parsnip, broccoli and truffle jus is a case in point, and there is praise, too, for roasted cod with celeriac, mussels, kale and dill, and the ever-popular potted shrimps with cauliflower and curry and mead sauce. Staples such as roasted scallop and the chef's variations on herdwick hogget 'always give pleasure', as do the puddings, perhaps Cumbrian gingerbread with ginger panna cotta and rhubarb. Friendly pricing at lunch also goes down well. The wine choices fully live up to the ethos of the cooking, an up-to-the-minute list (from £22) of low-intervention wines from mainly European vineyards.

Chef/s: Ryan Blackburn. **Closed:** Mon, Sun, 2 weeks Jan, 24 to 26 Dec. **Meals:** main courses £19 to £28. Set L £23 (2 courses) to £28. Tasting menu L £40 (4 courses) and D £55 (4 courses) to £70. **Details:** 30 seats. Music.

▌Askham
Allium at Askham Hall

Cooking score: 5
Modern British | £55
Askham, CA10 2PF
Tel no: 01931 712350
askhamhall.co.uk
£5 OFF

If you fancy living like a lord, this stunning 12th-century manor house, the former home of the Earls of Lonsdale, may just fit the bill. Considered too big for the family, the ancestral home has been turned into a sumptuous restaurant with rooms by Charles Lowther, owner of the George & Dragon at Clifton (see entry). It's grand but not intimidating, thanks to the charm of front-of-house manager and sommelier Nico Chieze, who serves pre-dinner drinks and impressive amuse-gueules in the vast drawing room, where traditional country house furnishings sit comfortably alongside contemporary art. Dinner is three or six courses, served in the conservatory by chef Richard Swale, who champions outstanding local produce and proves to have an instinct for putting ingredients together – say cured scallops paired with smoked cod's roe, hazelnuts and nasturtium leaves. Similarly he pairs loin of lamb with goat's curd, then adds a garnish of lightly pickled daylily shoots, all to wondrous effect. Desserts shine equally brightly, in particular a caramel tart with candied pecans and rosehip jelly, the sweetness balanced by a delicately flavoured sorrel ice cream. The bountiful and descriptive wine list curated by Chieze has bottles to suit all tastes and pockets.

Chef/s: Richard Swale. **Closed:** Mon, Sun.
Meals: set D £55. Tasting menu £70 (7 courses).
Details: 54 seats. Bar. Wheelchairs. Parking. Music. Children over 10 yrs.

▌Braithwaite
The Cottage in the Wood
Cooking score: 5
Modern British | £50
Magic Hill, Whinlatter Forest, Braithwaite, CA12 5TW
Tel no: 01768 778409
thecottageinthewood.co.uk
£5 OFF 🛏

Seen from a certain angle of approach, this white cottage really does hide amid the woods and hedgerows to the south west of Bassenthwaite Lake. The 17th-century house has been elegantly modernised within, centring on a light-filled conservatory dining space looking out on the terrain from which much of Ben Wilkinson's stock-in-trade is sourced. Fells and forest yield pedigree meats and distinctive foragings, while seafood comes from west coast waters, in cooking founded on classical technique allied to a forward-thinking approach to combinations and seasoning. Grilled mackerel is matched with a pig's cheek fritter in the sharpest setting of apple, pickled veg and capers, prior to aged Goosnargh duck with a sausage of the leg, roast parsnip and chestnut crumble in red wine sauce, or maybe turbot and baby leeks with a giant oyster mushroom and a dot of Exmoor caviar, all regally sauced in Champagne. The same confident layering of flavours applies to dessert, when a poached pear might appear with spiced rice pudding,

honeycomb and an intense pear sorbet. Artisan cheeses and water from the cottage's own spring on Magic Hill add to the allure. The wine list covers a fair amount of ground within a limited compass, from £23 for a Romanian Pinot Noir.

Chef/s: Ben Wilkinson. **Closed:** Mon, Sun, Jan.
Meals: set L £30. Set D £50. Tasting menu £70 (7 courses). **Details:** 36 seats. V menu. Vg menu. Bar. Wheelchairs. Parking. Children over 10 yrs at D.

▌Cartmel
★ NUMBER ONE RESTAURANT ★

L'Enclume
Cooking score: 10
Modern British | £155
Cavendish Street, Cartmel, LA11 6PZ
Tel no: 015395 36362
lenclume.co.uk
🍷 🛏

L'Enclume dazzles; not with glitter-ball ritz and razzmatazz, but with the understated glow that comes from being indisputably world-class. It is forged from Cumbria, rough-hewn in the image of the region, so that stones decorate tables, crockery is as irregular as the walls, and uncompromisingly seasonal produce is harvested from Our Farm. But for all its rural rootedness, from the hands of its talented chefs proceed 15 dishes that are breathtakingly skilful, memorably delicious. From the opening sip of a pitch perfect crémant de Bordeaux to the surely heaven-cast 'anvil' of caramel mousse, diced apple and miso, via the staggeringly delicious pork fat and crackling 'butter', dinner bewitches. Dots of pear vinegar and ramson oil create playful patterns in a fairy-light soup of peppery kohlrabi. Eccentric fritters of pork, eel and fermented sweetcorn capture salty-sweet-fatty-umami-sharp flavours in one textured mouthful. A tea-steamed scallop sits, plump and pearly, in a velouté dotted with smoked pike-perch roe; under its motherly softness hide tiny nuggets of nutty roasted cauliflower and in its wake come hints of grassy oolong. Earthy morels are stuffed with duck hearts and amplified by preserved wild cherry and red mustard, the dish elevated by a masterly pairing with Ikekame Turtle Red sake. Greens, butter-glossed but crystal clear in their minerally flavours, include sea aster, samphire picked from the Silverdale foreshore and chard from Our Farm, a spoon of caviar taking dinner as close to bling as it ever gets. A slice of milk-white Goosnargh guinea hen breast is given a genius savoury layer from the bird's crispy skin and yeast; and how on point that the subsequent ragoût uses the offcuts from this and the morels to create a bowl of no-waste comfort food. Diners are nudged towards dessert with nitro-frozen Tunworth, crumbs of the cheese mixed with sweet pear, malt and verbena, before beetroot and rhubarb (meringue shards, sorbet and juice) close the meal with technicolour flourish. A wine flight roams thrillingly from Kent to Japan by way of Portugal, Hungary and the Veneto, and a pairing of exotic teas is put together just as carefully. Instinctive service contributes hugely to the feeling that, after nigh on four hours, you don't want this to end. As one diner reported, 'This is the best meal I've ever eaten; I'm 62; we have eaten well all over the world, but not as well as this.'

Chef/s: Simon Rogan and Paul Burgalieres. **Closed:** Mon, first week Jan. **Meals:** tasting menu L £59 (8 courses) to £155 and D £155 (15 courses). **Details:** 45 seats. V menu. Wheelchairs. Parking. Children over 10 yrs.

Rogan & Co

Cooking score: 6
Modern British | £45
Devonshire Square, Cartmel, LA11 6QD
Tel no: 015395 35917
roganandco.co.uk
£5 OFF 🛏

The low-slung stone building in the centre of winsome Cartmel is the support act to nearby superstar L'Enclume. More than a mere understrapper, though, Rogan & Co has serious ambitions of its own, readily apparent in the appointment in 2018 of Tom Barnes, former head chef of L'Enclume. The place is

consequently firing on all cylinders, as was appreciated by a pair of summer visitors who enjoyed pork terrine with caper jam and pork fat, and duck leg with Jerusalem artichoke crisps, prior to a pair of dazzling fish main courses – butter-poached cod with cuttlefish and toasted yeast, and hake fillet with cockles and asparagus. Dishes are impressive for their willingness to court complexity, and the combinations of elements feel intuitive rather than grating. Traditionalists won't balk at a serving of aged short rib with creamed potato and bone marrow, its thoroughbred components all lusciously present and correct, nor at a more new-fangled rhubarb and marigold cheesecake, while the dark chocolate fondant is strewn with sea salt and garnished with mandarin. Service from youthful, friendly staff seals the deal. A short wine slate starts at £25, and stops just as three figures heave into view.

Chef/s: Tom Barnes. **Closed:** Tue, Wed (Nov to Apr), first week Jan. **Meals:** main courses £20 to £25. **Details:** 40 seats. Wheelchairs. Music.

▌Clifton
George & Dragon

Cooking score: 2
Modern British | £40
Clifton, CA10 2ER
Tel no: 01768 865381
georgeanddragonclifton.co.uk
£5 OFF 🛏

Given that it belongs to estate owner Charles Lowther, who runs nearby Askham Hall (see entry), it's hardly surprising that this sympathetically updated Lakeland coaching inn has bags of heritage chic – with the trappings to match (note the Champagne breakfasts, the high-walled courtyard and the boutique accommodation). The kitchen's activities are fuelled by supplies of home-grown and home-reared produce, especially shorthorn beef, saddleback pork, rough fell lamb and boer goat meat (some of it dry-aged at Askham Hall itself). 'Really excellent' steaks with chunky chips stand out on the seasonal menu, alongside other Cumbrian delicacies ranging from a pressing of free range goose with scratchings and rhubarb to red deer from the Lowther Estate served with a blue cheese steamed pudding, mash and red cabbage. Fish might be represented by grilled cod with a stew of butter beans, chorizo, mussels and roasted peppers, while desserts are mostly crumbles, tarts and old-fashioned puds. The 80-bin wine list is peppered with well-chosen bottles from family-run vineyards.

Chef/s: Gareth Webster. **Meals:** main courses £14 to £21. **Details:** 126 seats. Vg menu. Bar. Wheelchairs. Parking. Music.

▌Crosthwaite
The Punch Bowl Inn

Cooking score: 2
Modern British | £35
Lyth Valley, Crosthwaite, LA8 8HR
Tel no: 015395 68237
the-punchbowl.co.uk
£5 OFF 🍽

There is a genuine feeling of affection radiating from the readers' reports we receive for this Cumbrian institution. To be sure, it's a smart place; visitors appreciate its attractive interior (a mix of beams, slate floors, polished wood and leather) and the stunning location beside a church with glorious views over the Lyth Valley. The kitchen continues 'to go from strength to strength' with the food leagues ahead of your average pub offering. From twice-baked Lancashire cheese soufflé to Cartmel Valley venison loin with a beetroot choucroute, hispi cabbage and green peppercorn sauce, this is cooking that pleases and soothes in equal measure. Desserts are just as captivating, especially an avidly praised lemon tart with damson sorbet. Lunchtime sandwiches, steak or fish and chips, obliging service and well-chosen wines (arranged by grape variety) also repay the journey.

Chef/s: Oliver Mather and Stuart Green. **Closed:** 14 Jan. **Meals:** main courses £16 to £27. **Details:** 94 seats. 40 seats outside. V menu. Vg menu. Bar. Wheelchairs. Parking. Music.

▌Grasmere
★ TOP 50 ★

Forest Side

Cooking score: 7
Modern British | £75
Keswick Road, Grasmere, LA22 9RN
Tel no: 015394 35250
theforestside.com
£5 OFF 🍽

How reassuring in this pacy world to feel that the Lakeland fells and becks, heavenly views and rufty-tufty herdwick sheep around Grasmere are the same as those that inspired Victorian romantics to wonder and wander. How thrilling, then, that by contrast, the Cumbrian food revolution continues to move on apace. This is the narrative at Forest Side, where local-born Kevin Tickle, supported by well-versed chefs, kitchen gardeners and tweed-waistcoated front of house, creates plated poetry across two tasting menus (six or ten courses) in a thoroughly 21st-century country house hotel. Bouncy garlic crumpet with Baron Bigod cheese, ramson oil and a snowdrift of truffle sets the tasty tone, ditto a hot, fatty, gamey grey squirrel and pork 'critter fritter' with douglas fir mayo and lemony oxalis leaves. A curl of home-cured guanciale adds syrupy richness to asparagus, while the classic New York sandwich is translated into the softest spicy-smokey venison pastrami on slender rye with translucent pickled swede standing in for Gruyère. It's fun, tasty, inventive. The richness of sea trout, luxuriously butter-poached, is cut by radish and mustardy jack by the hedge picked from the hotel grounds, while a Jersey Royal purée with Morecambe Bay shrimps is as 'filthy' as the menu promises. Herdwick hogget loin and shoulder (from the owners' flock) comes with tangy ewe's milk curd and lovage oil, and sits pink and happy next to a tangle of charred spring onion, leeks and red ruble kale; in a separate bowl, crumbed sweetbread, tucked up with peppery leaves, is simple perfection, especially when scooped through smoked potato custard. Mugwort ice cream is an almost savoury bridge to the sweetness of aerated white chocolate infused with rowan and served with poached strawberries, clotted cream and freshening anise hyssop. Wine from a largely organic or biodynamic list starts at a punchy £40, leaving the flight (£55 or £85) the recommended option, although a Coravin system means a classy Gevrey-Chambertin could tempt by the £25 glass.

Chef/s: Kevin Tickle. **Closed:** Mon, Tue. **Meals:** tasting menu L £40 (4 courses) to £80 and D £80 (6 courses) to £105. **Details:** 40 seats. V menu. Bar. Wheelchairs. Parking. Music. Children over 8 yrs at D.

The Jumble Room

Cooking score: 1
International | £40
Langdale Road, Grasmere, LA22 9SU
Tel no: 015394 35188
thejumbleroom.co.uk

£5 OFF 🍴

For cooking packed with heart and soul – and stacked with generous eccentricity – head to this colourful jumble of a place that rings a welcome change from the predictable Grasmere diet of tea rooms and fellside picnics. The menu swerves erratically from fish and chips to Persian lamb with all the aubergine-pomegranate-harissa flavours you'd expect, and from spanking-fresh crab crostini to a Malaysian seafood curry plump with tiger prawns, coconut and chilli. A monster of a strawberry pavlova beat one diner; an Italian affogato was an altogether more refined option. Pick wines from a functional list that opens at £18.95.

Chef/s: Chrissy Hill and James O'Campo. **Closed:** Tue. **Meals:** main courses £15 to £28. **Details:** 50 seats. Music.

Background music

Prefer to eat in quiet surroundings? Check the details at the bottom of the review to see if the restaurant plays background music.

▌Houghton

★ NEW ENTRY ★

Lounge on the Green

Cooking score: 3
Modern British | £30
27 The Green, Houghton, CA3 0LF
Tel no: 01228 739452
loungeonthegreen.co.uk

£5 OFF £30 🍴

'Carlisle has long awaited a really good restaurant on its doorstep,' comments one appreciative local on this Houghton village newcomer. Chef James Hill's proposition is simple: stone and wood fittings reflect the Lakeland landscape, and set menus of British and European influence offer dinner and weekend lunches. 'Beautiful hors d'oeuvres' are praised as 'a perfect start to the meal'. Next up might be vibrant pea soup crowned with crab and bacon 'millefeuille' and lightly seared sea bass on sweet carrot purée with samphire and lemongrass. Highly rated Lakeland beef is cooked low (55°C), then pan-roasted and served pink. Vegetarians are well served, too – broccoli gets star status in a dish that sees the humble brassica roasted, pickled and puréed, then served with pine nuts and lemon thyme in a complex mix of flavours and textures. Desserts are carefully crafted as in a glossy dark chocolate ganache offset by sweet pickled cherries, almond soil and amaretto cream. A competent drinks list is unusually cognisant of drivers' options.

Chef/s: James Hill. **Closed:** Mon, Tue, Wed. **Meals:** set D £28 Thur to Sat (2 courses) to £34. Tasting menu Thur to Sat £50 (8 courses). Sat and Sun L £22 (2 courses) to £27. **Details:** 26 seats. Bar. Wheelchairs. Music.

▮ Pooley Bridge
★ NEW ENTRY ★
1863
Cooking score: 2
Modern British | £40
Elm House, High Street, Pooley Bridge,
CA10 2NH
Tel no: 017684 86334
1863ullswater.co.uk
£5 OFF 🍴

Pooley Bridge at the northern end of
Ullswater is home to this solid Cumbrian
townhouse that has done service as the village
blacksmith, post office and now a glitzy
restaurant with rooms. The bar and dining
room are a riot, with feature wallpaper,
mirrors, clocks, antlers and chandeliers. At
inspection, Phil Corrie's skill was illustrated in
a superb amuse-bouche of celeriac and truffle
custard, while Jersey Royals were enjoyed at
their seasonal best in a dish that added charred
spring onion and hen of the wood
mushrooms. Guinea fowl dusted with truffle
was accompanied by a crisp croquette of leg
meat, then garnished with pickled shallots and
morels. However, a starter of Dover sole
disappointed, having been re-formed into a
small sausage, although an accompanying
salad of fresh peas, broad beans and a chervil
liquor compensated. The kitchen got back on
track at dessert with a textbook treacle tart and
a contemporary take on ginger sponge, paired
with lemon curd and a brandy snap. Choose
from a good range of wines by the glass from a
serviceable list.
Chef/s: Phil Corrie. **Closed:** 2 to 16 Jan.
Meals: main courses £16 to £26. Tasting menu £65
(6 courses). **Details:** 32 seats. Bar. Wheelchairs.
Parking. Music. Children over 10 yrs after 8.30pm.
Deposit required for tasting menu.

▮ Sedbergh
★ NEW ENTRY ★
The Black Bull
Cooking score: 2
International | £33
44 Main Street, Sedbergh, LA10 5BL
Tel no: 015396 20264
theblackbullsedbergh.co.uk
£5 OFF 🍴

This 17th-century coaching inn was all but
derelict when Nina Matsunaga and James
Ratcliffe of Three Hares (see entry) took it on.
They've done an impressive job, creating 18
tasteful bedrooms and a restaurant stylishly
kitted out with planked walls, grey banquettes
and greenery in the form of Japanese-inspired
kokedama moss balls. An ambitious menu
from Matsunaga draws from the rich local
larder. Although a starter of cured tomatoes
with crab and buckwheat failed to make its
mark, mains fared better. Herdwick lamb
reared on the surrounding Howgill Fells came
with new potatoes, baby gem, anchovy and
thinly sliced radish. 'Coastal greens', aka
seaweed, provided a salty, iron-rich finish to a
pleasing dish of sea trout, artichoke purée and
asparagus. Liquorice carrots and well-crisped
hand-cut chips were successful sides. A
serviceable wine list, opening at £21, bolsters
a selection of handpumped ales and spirits
from small-batch producers.
Chef/s: Nina Matsunaga. **Meals:** main courses £15
to £66. Set L £16 (2 courses) to £19. Sun L £15.
Details: 60 seats. 30 seats outside. Bar. Music.

LOCAL GEM
Three Hares
British | £10
57 Main Street, Sedbergh, LA10 5AB
Tel no: 015396 21058
threeharescafe.co.uk
£30

Nut-brown sugary doughnuts, millionaire's
shortbread thick with caramel, cinnamon
swirls, Victoria sponge, pistachio cake and
fluffy fruit scones are the work of baker Nina

Matsunaga and husband James Ratcliffe, who run this cheerful bakery and café. Now that the couple have opened The Black Bull (see entry) opposite, they have scaled down the offering here to soup, sandwiches, fat sausage rolls and salads. However, with a tangy courgette and yuzu soup on offer and sandwiches made with Nina's crusty ciabatta rolls, that's no hardship. Choose from a short list of wines, soft drinks and good coffee.

Windermere

★ NEW ENTRY ★

Gilpin Spice
Cooking score: 3
Pan-Asian | £30
Gilpin Hotel & Lake House, Crook Road, Windermere, LA23 3NE
Tel no: 015394 88818
thegilpin.co.uk

Some restaurants make you happy simply stepping over the threshold. Such is the case here, where only the frostiest could fail to warm to its exuberant, madcap spin through pan-Asian food. Share knockout pani puri snacks, crisp shells filled with gently spiced chickpeas, the flavour freshened by a tamarind and mint sauce, then perhaps a gently aromatic moilee (coconut velouté) with a vegetable samosa, or seafood Thai red curry with plump tiger prawns in a starring role. Finish deliciously with kulfi, fudge-like in texture and heady with cardamom, pistachio and rum-steeped raisins, or trifle in which mango, ginger and black pepper transport the British classic to Asian shores. If the menu bewilders, relinquish all decision-making by choosing the tasting menu (vegetarian version available) – it might offer crumbed gilthead bream with a sweet-sour coconut broth, or biryani whose nutty-fruity-spicy fragrance is released when you break through the puff pastry topping. A short wine list opens at £25.

Chef/s: Hrishikesh Desai. Closed: 25 Dec. Meals: small plates £6 to £15. Large plates £12 to £18. Tasting menu £40 (4 courses). Details: 60 seats. 20 seats outside. V menu. Wheelchairs. Parking.

Hrishi at Gilpin Hotel & Lake House
Cooking score: 6
Modern British | £70
Crook Road, Windermere, LA23 3NE
Tel no: 015394 88818
thegilpin.co.uk

Drawing on his own global journey, Hrishikesh Desai's imaginative and elegantly styled dishes blend the contemporary and the traditional with the tastes of East and West. Under a less skilful hand, this might feel clumsy or forced but by bringing together exemplary classical skills, sublime local ingredients and an artist's eye for colour and craft, Desai succeeds in delivering 'perfection in every possible way – a magical experience of pleasure and flavours'. After appearing on 2019's *Great British Menu*, the chef's celebration of British pop history has become part of his tasting menu. Start with a vibrant ochre ceviche of scallop in a ginger, chilli, orange and sherry dressing on saffroned carrots as a nod to the golden oldies. Follow up with a tribute to the local Lakeland scene with tender Cartmel venison loin paired with a glazed venison kofta, jewel-like root vegetables, truffled potatoes and a boldly matched Cumbrian sloe gin and blackberry sauce. Winning desserts include a glossy dark chocolate délice with peanut butter semifreddo, banana bread, raspberry gel and milk sorbet. The luxurious surroundings of the Gilpin add an extra layer of occasion, as does the extensive wine list with its range of less common by-the-glass 'luxuries', thanks to a Coravin system.

Chef/s: Hrishikesh Desai. Meals: set L £38. Set D £70. Tasting menu £90 (7 courses). Sun L £38. Details: 52 seats. 30 seats outside. Vg menu. Bar. Wheelchairs. Parking. Music. Children over 7 yrs.

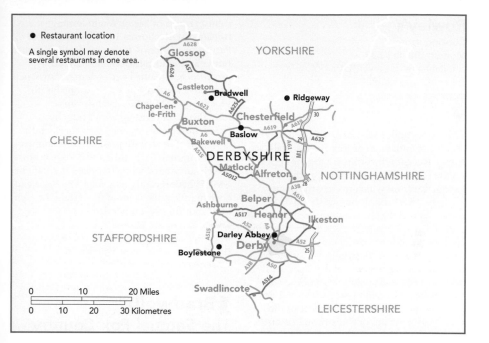

Baslow

Fischer's Baslow Hall

Cooking score: 6
Modern European | £79
Calver Road, Baslow, DE45 1RR
Tel no: 01246 583259
fischers-baslowhall.co.uk

Built in 1907 by a local family with a penchant for all things archaic, Baslow Hall can look a tad intimidating, but inside it's as warm and toasty as a family home. Some tasteful redecoration has lightened the mood in the high-ceilinged dining room, and there have been changes in the kitchen, too, with Rupert Rowley stepping down and sous-chef James Payne promoted to the top job. Judging by recent meals, the food remains as intriguing as ever – classically based, seasonal and impressively executed, with clever touches and trendy accents elevating every dish. Seafood is a strong suit, from beautifully sweet hand-dived scallops with a ham hock

'fritter', lentils and crunchy apple matchsticks to pan-fried mullet accompanied by an emulsion of green veg (from the hotel's productive kitchen garden), Jersey Royals and an unlikely but brilliantly effective smudge of malt extract. Meat is more robustly treated – witness loin of veal cooked three ways with rich jus, artichoke and a nest of deep-fried potato filled with 'utterly delicious' smoked potato purée. Opt for one of the tasting menus and you'll be confronted by three desserts, including a textbook soufflé served with a shot of something alcoholic. A weighty, all-embracing wine list offers plenty by the glass (including a generous Coravin selection), as well as big-ticket bottles from £24.

Chef/s: James Payne. **Closed:** Mon, 25 and 26 Dec.
Meals: set L £25. Set D £65 (2 courses) to £79.
Tasting menu £88 (8 courses). Sun L £38 (2 courses) to £45. **Details:** 72 seats. V menu. Bar. Parking.
Music. Children over 8 yrs.

Rowley's

Cooking score: 1
Modern British | £27
Church Lane, Baslow, DE45 1RY
Tel no: 01246 583880
rowleysrestaurant.co.uk
£30

This stone-built two-storey village pub is the humble attendant on nearby Baslow Hall (see entry). Recent refurbishment has brought a smarter air to the ground floor, with velour banquettes from which to view the open kitchen, where simple but satisfying dishes come together. Spicy sticky chicken wings and crisp-fried whitebait are a good intro to seared rainbow trout with parmentier potatoes and spring greens in wild garlic sauce, or the pièce de résistance, a ribeye cut of dry-aged local beef with triple-cooked chips and Café de Paris butter. At pudding stage, it's a case of duelling spoons all wanting a piece of the sticky toffee action, or rhubarb and custard bavarois with ginger ice cream. On-trend wines populate a short list that opens at £4.45 for a glass of blush-pink Grigio.
Chef/s: Matt Booth. **Meals:** main courses £12 to £25. Set L £20 Mon to Fri (2 courses) to £25. Sun L £16. **Details:** 130 seats. 18 seats outside. Bar. Wheelchairs. Parking. Music.

▮ Boylestone
The Lighthouse Restaurant

Cooking score: 5
Modern British | £60
New Road, Boylestone, DE6 5AA
Tel no: 01335 330658
the-lighthouse-restaurant.co.uk

'A lovely dining experience and the food is sublime' was the verdict of one visitor to this 'remote rural location'. Barn-like with its exposed brick and high rafters, the dining room is spacious and airy with most tables facing the open kitchen where Jon Hardy and his team produce some assured and innovative cooking. A summer tasting menu skips around the globe, from Asian snacks such as Cornish crab doughnut with satay sauce to a

robust risotto of Isle of Wight heritage tomatoes with chorizo and 18-month aged Parmesan. St Mawes turbot cooked in Cornish butter and wild garlic is handled with precision and teamed with warm tartare sauce, smoked eel and confit potato topped with vinegar powder, while local sirloin of longhorn beef turns up with a punchy chimichurri and a separate beef cheek chilli con carne. Finish with passion fruit 'tiramisu', coffee caramel, cocoa tuile and cookie mousse. A well-annotated wine list opens at £24. The owners have recently reopened The Rose and Crown pub at the front of the restaurant – an ideal spot for pre-dinner drinks.
Chef/s: Jon Hardy. **Closed:** Mon, Tue, Sun, first 2 weeks Jan. **Meals:** tasting menu £60 (8 courses). **Details:** 40 seats. V menu. Vg menu. Bar. Wheelchairs. Parking. Music.

▮ Bradwell
The Samuel Fox Country Inn

Cooking score: 4
Modern British | £32
Stretfield Road, Bradwell, S33 9JT
Tel no: 01433 621562
samuelfox.co.uk
£5 OFF

A few years ago this was just another pub in fine countryside. James Duckett has transformed it into a warmly welcoming inn with rooms, shifting the emphasis firmly to the food – dishes are rather more cutting edge than you might expect in this out-of-the-way Dales location. Local and regional suppliers play a role, their produce worked into a familiar run through the modern brasserie catalogue, whether on the good-value lunch or early dinner menu, carte or seven-course evening taster. A spring meal could bring cured scorched sea trout fillet with fennel and orange, a much-praised grilled feather blade of beef served pink and accompanied by a fricassée of mushrooms, shallots and green beans, a red wine sauce and a side of excellent chips, and finish with sticky toffee pudding with stout ice cream. To drink there are local ales and a reasonably priced wine list (from £17.50).

Chef/s: James Duckett. **Closed:** Mon, Tue, 2 to 16 Jan. **Meals:** main courses £15 to £26. Set early D £18 (2 courses) to £24. Tasting menu £55 (7 courses). Sun L £22 (2 courses) to £28. **Details:** 36 seats. 15 seats outside. V menu. Bar. Wheelchairs. Parking. Music.

▌Darley Abbey
Darleys

Cooking score: 3
Modern British | £45
Darley Abbey Mill, Haslams Lane, Darley Abbey, DE22 1DZ
Tel no: 01332 364987
darleys.com

With views of the river Derwent from its decked waterside terrace and the sightseeing attractions of a World Heritage Site all around, this converted cotton mill is a sure-fire crowd-puller, tailor-made for tourists and families on a day out. Whatever the occasion, Darleys has all bases covered: there are dedicated options for vegetarians and vegans, a fixed-price teatime menu and an ever-changing repertoire of modern dishes gleaned from the world larder. Anything goes, whether your taste is for seared scallops with seaweed 'salad cream' and cured egg yolk; shredded duck with vegetable slaw, lotus root crisp and pomegranate dressing; Chinese-style pork belly or a resounding dish of venison loin with blueberry crumble, Jerusalem artichoke purée, hogweed oil and winter squash. After all that globetrotting, desserts settle closer to home for, say, warm bread and butter pudding with apples or roast rhubarb with gingerbread crumb and crème fraîche ice cream. Then it's back round the world for wines that start below the £20 mark.

Chef/s: Jonathan Hobson. **Closed:** Mon, 24 Dec to 9 Jan, 7 to 14 Jul. **Meals:** main courses £25 to £28. Set L £20 (2 courses) to £25. Tasting menu £50 (7 courses). Sun L £30. **Details:** 60 seats. 50 seats outside. V menu. Vg menu. Bar. Wheelchairs. Parking. Music.

▌Ridgeway
The Old Vicarage

Cooking score: 6
Modern British | £70
Ridgeway Moor, Ridgeway, S12 3XW
Tel no: 0114 247 5814
theoldvicarage.co.uk
🍷

The sweeping driveway past copses and croquet lawns to a stone-built early Victorian house reminds us that old vicars once enjoyed a rather splendid time of it compared to the more make-do arrangements of today. Inside, oil portraits and floral pictures adorn a linened dining room where an atmosphere of decorous relaxation holds sway. Tessa Bramley is into her fourth decade at The Vicarage and time has been powerless to dim her diligence or enthusiasm in offering residents and diners the full country house experience. At the summit of her kitchen team's production is a seven-course Prestige Menu full of unimpeachable materials and exciting detail, embracing perhaps a lobster raviolo with asparagus in a wild garlic beurre blanc, and an ingenious mushroom wellington with puréed carrots, pine nuts and basil cream, building to the principal offering of dry-aged Yorkshire beef fillet, which is partnered by its braised nutmegged bone marrow, roasted grapes and hazelnuts. A pre-dessert paves the way for a finale of São Tomé bitter chocolate mousse with coffee parfait and pistachio sponge. The matching wine flight is not only chosen with delicate precision, but explained in illuminating detail by the sommelier as it is poured. If you care to roam unassisted through the wine collection, you'll discover strength in depth, stellar growers and outstanding vintages from a base price of £28.

Chef/s: Tessa Bramley, Nathan Smith and Terry Washington. **Closed:** Mon, Sun, 26 Dec to 7 Jan, 14 to 18 Apr, 5 and 26 May, 28 Jul to 10 Aug. **Meals:** tasting menu £70 (7 courses). **Details:** 44 seats. V menu. Bar. Wheelchairs. Parking. Children over 10 yrs at D.

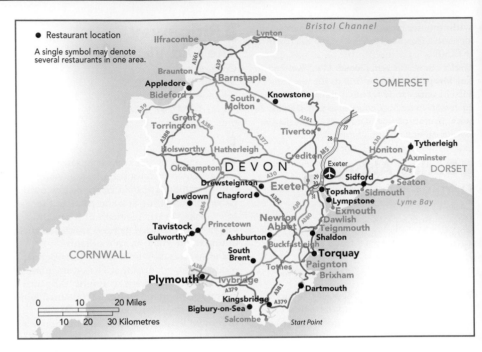

- ● Restaurant location

A single symbol may denote
several restaurants in one area.

Bristol Channel

Ilfracombe
Lynton
Braunton
Appledore
Bideford
Barnstaple
Knowstone
South Molton
SOMERSET
Great Torrington
Tiverton
27
28
Holsworthy
Hatherleigh
Crediton
Honiton
Tytherleigh
Okehampton
DEVON
Exeter
Axminster
DORSET
Drewsteignton
Exeter
29
30
Sidford
Seaton
Lewdown
Chagford
Topsham
Sidmouth
Lympstone
Lyme Bay
31
Exmouth
Tavistock
Princetown
Newton Abbot
Dawlish
Teignmouth
Gulworthy
Ashburton
Shaldon
CORNWALL
Buckfastleigh
South Brent
Torquay
Totnes
Paignton
Plymouth
Ivybridge
Brixham
Dartmouth
A379
Kingsbridge
Bigbury-on-Sea
Salcombe
Start Point

0   10   20 Miles
0 10 20   30 Kilometres

█ Appledore
The Royal George
Cooking score: 2
Modern British | £30
Irsha Street, Appledore, EX39 1RY
Tel no: 01237 424138
trgpub.co.uk

Recently refurbished having lain derelict for four years, this is now a 'fantastic family-friendly' dining pub offering real ales, well-made pub staples and a dining room with spectacular views across the Taw Torridge Estuary, from where much of the daily changing menu is sourced. After a starter of scallops, celeriac, pork belly and apple, or ham croquettes served under a blizzard of Cornish Kern cheese, expect a generous portion of crisp, beer-battered cod and chips with a pot of 'seriously scrumptious' homemade curry sauce, and more unusual offerings such as salt-baked celeriac with pickled mushroom, and an aubergine and potato rendang with tangy carrot salad and flatbreads. The ground-floor bar is relaxed and dog-friendly, while the first-floor dining room leads to a small roof terrace, hugely popular on sunny days. There's a compact wine list, all available by the glass, with bottles from £18.95.
Chef/s: Greg Martin. **Closed:** 6 to 12 Jan.
Meals: main courses £13 to £20. **Details:** 80 seats. 22 seats outside. Bar. Wheelchairs.

█ Ashburton
The Old Library
Cooking score: 3
Modern European | £38
North Street, Ashburton, TQ13 7QH
Tel no: 01364 652896
theoldlibraryrestaurant.co.uk
£5
OFF

The inhabitants of this stannary town on the south-east fringe of Dartmoor look kindly on Amy Mitchell and Joe Suttie's small modern eatery and it's easy to see why. Not only is there a notable lack of pretension and a genuine

Join us at thegoodfoodguide.co.uk

willingness to please – the menu is full of the kind of things everyone wants to eat – but there's also a feeling that the place 'runs on rails'. From the kitchen come confident, flavour-packed dishes, from a starter of crab tortelli with crispy seaweed and lemon emulsion to mains of prune-crusted pork loin with prune and Armagnac-glazed salsify, or hake with braised and charred leeks with exotic mushroom tea. Desserts push the right buttons, as in a pineapple and coconut soufflé decadently partnered by caramel sauce. There's a selection of local cheeses, plus breakfasts and brunches. A short, mainly European wine list opens at £17.
Chef/s: Amy Mitchell and Joe Suttie. **Closed:** Sun, 23 Dec to 15 Jan. **Meals:** main courses £16 to £27. Set D £20 (2 courses) to £25. **Details:** 25 seats. 8 seats outside. Wheelchairs. Parking. Music.

▌Bigbury-on-Sea

LOCAL GEM

The Oyster Shack

Seafood | £30
Milburn Orchard Farm, Stakes Hill, Bigbury-on-Sea, TQ7 4BE
Tel no: 01548 810876
oystershack.co.uk

£30

The Shack is a riot of summery colour, with a big orange awning to shelter the outdoor tables and an air of nautical jollity prevailing inside. Daily sourced oysters are offered hot or cold in a number of dressings, from Japanese to blue cheese and bacon, while the *ne plus ultra* is an 18-course tasting menu that offers an all-inclusive tour of the sea, from shrimp fritters and crab soup, via lobster, to a final affogato. The tidal wash of the Avon means that the road to the Shack might be submerged; check the timetable. Wines are £6.10 a standard glass, and there are groovy Devon gins.

▌Chagford
Gidleigh Park

new chef/no score
Modern European | £125
Chagford, TQ13 8HH
Tel no: 01647 432367
gidleigh.co.uk

Perched on its hill, looking out over 100 acres, including a kitchen garden and terraces, with the North Teign babbling by in the lower distance, Gidleigh Park is one of the treasures of Dartmoor. Its panelled interiors are patrolled by brigades of well-versed staff, making the whole experience several cuts above the country house norm. After a transitional few months, it was announced in 2019 that the new executive chef is to be Chris Eden, who will make the journey here after 12 years at Driftwood in Portscatho, Cornwall (see entry). His arrival came too late for an inspection this year, but we can confidently expect that he will maintain the style of gently inventive modern European cooking that Gidleigh has made its own, with a main carte supplemented by tasting menus in both omnivore and vegetarian guises. Whatever the new dishes will be, Gidleigh's wine list will assuredly remain a shining beacon of refined drinking, with Coravin glass selections, interesting rosés, outstanding producers in Germany, Austria and the southern hemisphere, and a run of Krug vintages for the lottery winners. Prices are stiff, though: ordinary glasses start at £13.
Chef/s: Chris Eden and Gareth Howarth. **Meals:** set L £65. Set D £125. Tasting menu £145 (8 courses). **Details:** 45 seats. V menu. Bar. Wheelchairs. Parking. Children over 8 yrs.

Closed

Where closures are listed, these are for full days only. Please check opening times with the restaurant before travelling.

Dartmouth
The Seahorse

Cooking score: 4
Seafood | £45
5 South Embankment, Dartmouth, TQ6 9BH
Tel no: 01803 835147
seahorserestaurant.co.uk

Mitch Tonks and Mat Prowse's pink-and-white-fronted quayside restaurant might be just a decade old, but the elegant dining room with its polished walnut tables, Art Deco lamps and comfortable button-back leather banquettes has the look and feel of a longer-established place. It deals in fish from nearby Brixham and local meat, often cooked without fuss and frills over charcoal. Start, perhaps, with veal brains classically served with brown butter, capers and parsley. John Dory cooked on the bone with garlic and lemon, or Barnsley chop with broad beans and mint might follow, and there's a chocolate nemesis with pouring cream to finish. Opening at £25, the Italian-heavy wine list is packed with carefully sourced small producers, and six different bottles from a special selection are opened each day and served by the glass, carafe or bottle. The duo also run the growing collection of informal and family-friendly Rockfish seafood restaurants, eight of which are dotted around the South West coastline, including one a few doors down in Dartmouth.
Chef/s: Jake Bridgwood. **Closed:** Mon, 25 and 26 Dec, 1 and 2 Jan. **Meals:** main courses £10 to £40. Set L and early D £20. **Details:** 45 seats. 6 seats outside. Bar. Wheelchairs. Music.

Average price

The figure given in bold denotes the average price of a three-course dinner without drinks.

Drewsteignton
The Old Inn

Cooking score: 4
Modern European | £55
Drewsteignton, EX6 6QR
Tel no: 01647 281276
old-inn.co.uk

This 17th-century former village inn to one side of Drewsteignton's little square, now a contemporary restaurant with three guest rooms, makes a fine bolthole for exploring the northern fringe of Dartmoor. Within its warm, low-ceilinged embrace, Duncan Walker offers concise menus of regionally supplied dishes that have a noticeable French leaning. Grilled mackerel fillet niçoise is full of sharp, classic flavours, or there may be veal sweetbreads sautéed in brown butter and balsamic to kick things off. Mains reliably feature the excellent Dexter beef sirloin in meaty array with braised oxtail and smoked bacon, as well as distinctly lighter grilled brill with mussels and samphire and the beguiling scent of saffron. Finish with densely rich chocolate marquise or chilled rice pudding and rhubarb glazed with Champagne sabayon. The well-chosen wine list is particularly strong in white Burgundies, but boasts impressive growers throughout. Bottles start at £23.
Chef/s: Duncan Walker. **Closed:** Mon, Tue, Sun, 3 weeks Jan, 1 week Jun. **Meals:** set D £48 (2 courses) to £55. **Details:** 16 seats. Children over 12 yrs.

Gulworthy
The Horn of Plenty

Cooking score: 3
Modern British | £53
Gulworthy, PL19 8JD
Tel no: 01822 832528
thehornofplenty.co.uk

The location of this long-running country hotel is quite something. It stands on a hill overlooking the rolling contours of

Dartmoor's fringe, with Cornwall to the left and Devon to the right. Although it would be easy for the dining room to rely on its magnificent views alone, Ashley Wright's quietly assured cooking has its eye on the regional larder and has garnered a strong local following; The Horn of Plenty is undoubtedly a highlight of the area. A winter opener might be a 'standout' monkfish ceviche with pork crackling and apple, or there may be Creedy Carver duck terrine with a slow-cooked egg and truffle. Local ingredients come into their own in a main course of Bocaddon Farm veal with salt-baked swede, shallots and sage, while a selection of Devon cheeses is an alternative to desserts such as lemon posset with rhubarb gel and meringue. The global wine list has good options by the glass.

Chef/s: Ashley Wright. **Meals:** set L £21 (2 courses) to £26. Set D £53. Tasting menu £70 (6 courses). Sun L £21 (2 courses) to £26. **Details:** 50 seats. 25 seats outside. Bar. Parking. Music.

∎ Kingsbridge

LOCAL GEM
Beachhouse
Seafood | £35
South Milton Sands, Kingsbridge, TQ7 3JY
Tel no: 01548 561144
beachhousedevon.com

£5 OFF

If only every beach had one. With its unencumbered sea view, this perpetually busy whitewashed shack is worth making a bee-line for in its own right. There's bench seating inside and out, plus a blackboard menu carried from table to table that offers a plethora of sharing dishes, local fish specials and seafood platters: there's no standing on ceremony here. Get cracking with dressed crab or local lobster, or go for seafood linguine with garlic and chilli. For early birds, there's the 'full monty' cooked breakfast, and sandwiches to take away come lunchtime. Approachable wines major on classic, fish-friendly whites. Open daytime all week, and evenings in the summer. It's worth booking ahead.

∎ Knowstone
The Masons Arms
Cooking score: 4
Modern British | £48
Knowstone, EX36 4RY
Tel no: 01398 341231
masonsarmsdevon.co.uk

Even in the context of Devon's byways, Knowstone takes a bit of unearthing, but persistence is rewarded in the shape of Mark Dodson's late medieval heavily beamed inn, where the low ceilings and the option of a rocking chair by the fire are offset by a clean-limbed modern dining room with views over the surrounding farmland. The kitchen works to a modern British-European template, with French and Italian influences discernible in dishes such as rabbit, bacon and leek terrine with puréed beans and celeriac and apple salad, or arancini with beetroot dressed in horseradish cream. Main-course fish is sensitively treated, as when potato-crusted brill is garlanded with pak choi and seaweed in a creamy cider sauce, but there could also be venison loin with a poached red wine pear and blue cheese potato gratin. Dessert treats aim to indulge by means of amaretto parfait with vanilla plum, or chocolate and raspberry mousse with raspberry sorbet. Wines by the glass from £4.50 lead off a Eurocentric list.

Chef/s: Mark Dodson. **Closed:** Mon, Sun, first week Jan, third week Feb, last week Aug. **Meals:** main courses £26 to £29. Set L £24 (2 courses) to £28. **Details:** 28 seats. 16 seats outside. V menu. Vg menu. Bar. Wheelchairs. Parking. Music. Children over 5 yrs at D.

Local Gem
These entries are brilliant neighbourhood venues, delivering good, freshly cooked food at great value for money.

Lewdown

Lewtrenchard Manor

Cooking score: 5
Modern British | £50
Lewdown, EX20 4PN
Tel no: 01566 783222
lewtrenchard.co.uk

Logged as a 'royal manor' in the Domesday
Book, restored during Jacobean times and
given a thoroughly Victorian gothic makeover
by the eccentric Gould family, this grey-stone
manor now shows its pedigree as a country
house retreat with gastronomic aspirations.
Horticulturalist Gertrude Jekyll's green-
fingered wisdom helped to create the
significant grounds, and much still depends
on seasonal bounty from Lewtrenchard's
kitchen garden when it comes to feeding
guests ensconced in the two dining rooms.
Former sous-chef Tom Browning has stepped
up to the top job and his team delivers a roster
of refined, intricate dishes in the modern
idiom – witness beef feather blade cooked
sous-vide with celeriac risotto and walnuts or
Loch Duart salmon (poached at 42 degrees)
with artichoke, hazelnut and truffle. Other
ideas strike a more robust note (a colourful
amalgam of molasses-glazed duck breast,
pistachios and cherries with a hash brown, for
example), while desserts are designed to show
off the kitchen's prowess – as in triple
chocolate délice or malted milk panna cotta
with hazelnut, 'gold chocolate' and Frangelico.
A dozen by-the-glass selections kick off the
wine list, which mixes vintage French classics
with more upbeat modern youngsters.
Chef/s: Tom Browning. **Meals:** main courses L £15
to £22 Mon to Sat. Set D £50. Tasting menu £49 (5
courses) to £74. Sun L £28. **Details:** 40 seats. 20
seats outside. V menu. Vg menu. Bar. Wheelchairs.
Parking. Children over 8 yrs at D.

Lympstone

Lympstone Manor

Cooking score: 6
Modern European | £135
Courtlands Lane, Lympstone, EX8 3NZ
Tel no: 01395 202040
lympstonemanor.co.uk

A meal here feels like an occasion. In fine
weather arrive early to wander the impressive
grounds of this Georgian manor and take in
the sweeping views over the Exe estuary. The
tasteful dining rooms, patrolled by staff
operating in stiffly formal mode, seem bland
by comparison with those vistas, so try to nab
a window table if you can. This is not a place to
come to be wowed by flash techniques or
challenging combinations, but do visit for the
deft touch of Michael Caines, who takes first-
rate ingredients and coaxes them into full
song. The fixed price à la carte and no-choice
tasting menus showcase the full-stretch
extravaganza of Caines' highly crafted dishes.
On the cheaper four-course lunch menu
enjoyed by one early summer diner, an
introductory appetiser of delicate smoked
salmon mousse with confit beetroot and
balsamic led confidently into a splendid
spinach and Parmesan raviolo with herb and
garlic purée, rosemary and braised celery. The
centrepiece was delicate butter-poached hake
perched on finely diced summer vegetables
mixed with clams and mussels and finished
with a rich basil-butter sauce. A definitive
caramelised lemon tart with confit lemon
sorbet brought up the rear. The wine list is a
roll call of fine vintages, with real depth in
France and plenty of exceptional bottles from
elsewhere. Do take advice from the
sommelier, who is equally helpful whether
you want a simple glass of red or something
colossally expensive.
Chef/s: Michael Caines MBE and Duncan Taylor.
Meals: set L £48 to £60. Set D £135. Tasting menu
£145 (7 courses) to £155. **Details:** 60 seats. Bar.
Wheelchairs. Parking. Music. Children over 5 yrs.

▌Plymouth
The Greedy Goose
Cooking score: 4
Modern British | £35
Prysten House, Finewell Street, Plymouth,
PL1 2AE
Tel no: 01752 252001
thegreedygoose.co.uk
£5
OFF

Occupying a suite of rooms in a late 15th-century merchant's house, The Greedy Goose takes a backdrop of roughcast stone walls and weathered panels – and scores of goose-themed decorative accoutrements – and carefully deposits a modern city restaurant in it. Run with smooth despatch, it's a well-supported place for modern British cooking that shows studious attention to detail. Clumps of crab and lemongrass mayonnaise with salmon roe adorn strips of spanking-fresh salmon cured in the city's ancestral gin for a prelude to main courses founded on the double protein principle – breast and leg of duck; cod and mussels; pork belly and sticky cheek. There's a Continental inflection to a pairing of mature lamb cutlets with braised mutton and aubergine, on a busy plate garnished with swipes of red pepper purée, cubes of creamy feta, stem broccoli and minty tzatziki. You could finish at the lighter end with rhubarb and custard parfait, but the signature chocolate mousse (actually dense ganache) with black cherry sorbet merits its canonical status. The set three-course menu at lunch and early dinner is superb value. A short wine list has standard glasses at £5.50.
Chef/s: Ben Palmer. **Closed:** Mon, Sun. **Meals:** main courses £16 to £31. Set L and early D £13. Tasting menu £60 (7 courses) to £90. **Details:** 70 seats. 40 seats outside. Bar. Wheelchairs. Music. Children over 4 yrs.

Rock Salt
Cooking score: 2
Modern British | £30
31 Stonehouse Street, Plymouth, PL1 3PE
Tel no: 01752 225522
rocksaltcafe.co.uk
£5 £30
OFF

This corner site has fared well since its transformation from boarded-up pub to modern-day café nearly a decade ago, despite being 'at the wrong end of Plymouth's alimentary canal'. But those who make it further than the gaggle of chains that dominate the city centre will be rewarded – there's a real feeling of something for everyone in David Jenkins' kitchen approach. Regular steak nights and pan-Asian nights lend lustre to the all-day breakfast and lunchtime sandwiches, and you can hardly jibe at the prices – a two-course lunch of curried and cured salmon with coriander, lime yoghurt and pickled carrot, then Dartmoor lamb rump with celeriac, charred shallot and cavolo nero is a positive bargain at £16. Evening brings sticky beef brisket buns with mushroom, cauliflower and beef gravy ahead of crispy red gurnard with warm tartare sauce, sardine ketchup and crispy potatoes, and there could be honey panna cotta to finish. A wide-ranging wine list starts at £14.95.
Chef/s: David Jenkins. **Closed:** 24, 26 Dec. **Meals:** main courses £14 to £26. Set L and D £16 (2 courses) to £18. Tasting menu £50 (7 courses). Sun L £16. **Details:** 60 seats. Vg menu. Music.

Send us your review
Your feedback informs the content of the *GFG* and will be used to compile next year's entries. To register your opinion about any restaurant listed in the Guide, or a restaurant that you wish to bring to our attention, visit: thegoodfoodguide.co.uk/feedback.

Shaldon

★ NEW ENTRY ★

Ode True Food

Cooking score: 1
Modern British | £20
Ness Drive, Shaldon, TQ14 0HP
Tel no: 01626 873427
odetruefood.com
£30

Tim Bouget's ever-transmuting Ode operation is now domiciled in converted stables above the Shaldon waterfront, with the river estuary flowing by in the middle distance. Paper pompoms and lanterns hang above foursquare wood tables and an unadorned rough floor, and the place has breezy informality in its genes. A café with outdoor tables during the day, it transforms into a restaurant on Friday and Saturday evenings, centring on a fixed main course (fish fritto misto and venison steak in béarnaise, respectively, as we go to press), with a few outliers fore and aft. Our fritto was great, comprising battered cod and squid and panko-crumbed plaice with sweet-sour and tartare dips and a monster heap of skinny chips. Beforehand, there may be sole goujons or chunky smoked haddock arancini, with nutty chocolate mousse or ginger pudding and butterscotch sauce to bring up the rear. Prosecco in squash glasses gives an indication of just how many of your airs and graces you had better leave at home.
Chef/s: Tim Bouget. **Closed:** 25 Dec. **Meals:** main courses £7 to £15. **Details:** 50 seats. 120 seats outside. Wheelchairs. Parking. Music.

£5 voucher

£5 OFF Restaurants showing this symbol are participating in our £5 voucher scheme, redeemable against a meal for two or more. Vouchers can be found at the back of this book.

Sidford
The Salty Monk

Cooking score: 2
Modern British | £40
Church Street, Sidford, EX10 9QP
Tel no: 01395 513174
saltymonk.co.uk
£5 OFF

On the main road through Sidford, this distinctive cream-coloured building housed monastic supplies of salt centuries ago, but is these days a comfortable and well-run restaurant with rooms that's strong on hospitality. One of the two dining rooms, furnished with chunky tables, looks out on to the back garden. Andy Witheridge cooks in homely modern British bistro style, opening with a classic take on seared scallops and black pudding with a garnish of celeriac purée, before mains bring on hake fillet marinated in lemongrass and chilli with couscous and red pepper salsa, or a loin-girding duo of roast venison with more meat in the shapes of a faggot and a suet-crusted wine-rich pie, and a portion of mash to temper it all. Finish with chocolate torte served with coffee ice cream and chocolate sauce. The wine list is arranged by style and chock-full of information, with bottles starting at £22.50.
Chef/s: Andy Witheridge and Stephen Foster.
Meals: main courses £18 to £32. Tasting menu £65 (7 courses). **Details:** 28 seats. 24 seats outside. Vg menu. Bar. Wheelchairs. Parking. Music.

South Brent
Glazebrook House

Cooking score: 4
Modern British | £45
Wrangaton Road, South Brent, TQ10 9JE
Tel no: 01364 73322
glazebrookhouse.com
£5 OFF

Glazebrook's pastoral surroundings might suggest a sleepy version of country house cooking, but sights have always been trained higher than that – a point of view that extends to the interior. With its unusual fit-out (a designer mix of retro, vintage and just plain quirky), Glazebrook has been reinvented as a modern-day restaurant with rooms. Josh Ackland continues to head the kitchen and his 'excellent value and very enjoyable' set lunches, à la carte and tasting menus put the emphasis on seasonality and local producers. Starters might include Devon dressed crab teamed with sea buckthorn and carrot, or blue cheese and beetroot tart with pickled red onion. To follow, gin-rubbed guinea fowl comes with pork belly, braised red cabbage and potato fondant. After that a Tunisian orange cake 'Claudia Roden would have applauded' vies with the likes of dark chocolate fondant with caramel sauce and coffee ice cream. Service comes in for praise and there are some pleasing wines to set things off.

Chef/s: Josh Ackland. **Meals:** main courses £16 to £36. Set L £16 (2 courses) to £20. Tasting menu £50 (6 courses) to £64. Sun L £26. **Details:** 45 seats. 24 seats outside. Bar. Wheelchairs. Parking. Music.

▌Tavistock
The Cornish Arms

Cooking score: 3
Modern British | £30
15-16 West Street, Tavistock, PL19 8AN
Tel no: 01822 612145
thecornisharmstavistock.co.uk

£5 OFF 🛏 £30

The pride of Tavistock is John and Emma Hooker's converted pub on one of the central shopping streets. A series of four spaces unfurls along its width, with the emphasis very much on dining. Admirably coordinated staff ensure it runs seamlessly, and the lengthy menus of modern British brasserie food are full of obvious appeal. Duck liver pâté is richly creamy, cunningly served with candied hazelnuts under a gratinated top like a crème brûlée, with light shallot chutney to balance, or there may be a smoked haddock omelette enriched with aged Parmesan. Daringly meaty treatments for fish come into their own when a fillet of sea bream appears napped with chicken stock and mushroom butter sauce

alongside cep purée, while a delve into meats themselves might turn up saddleback pork belly with puréed roasted cauliflower, raisins and capers. The more populist route through would take in Scotch egg, sausages and mash in onion gravy, and perhaps a finisher of raspberry trifle. Our early-summer inspection lunch closed with a properly tangy lemon posset with honeycomb and strawberry sorbet. A short wine list opens at £4.95 a glass.

Chef/s: John Hooker. **Meals:** main courses £14 to £29. **Details:** 75 seats. 75 seats outside. Vg menu. Bar. Wheelchairs. Parking. Music.

▌Topsham
Salutation Inn

Cooking score: 5
Modern British | £45
68 Fore Street, Topsham, EX3 0HL
Tel no: 01392 873060
salutationtopsham.co.uk

🛏

The handsome portico entrance advances over its narrow bit of pavement to show that even little Topsham was once worthy of a Georgian coaching inn with aspirations to grandeur. Today's more obviously boutique feel suits it well, and extends to a modestly proportioned linened dining room with oblique views of the garden. Tom Williams-Hawkes is firing on all burners here; immaculately sourced ingredients come together in unfashionably complex dishes of French-inflected modern British cooking, and even though there is a lot going on, it all hangs together. A spring dinner opened with an appetiser of new asparagus in watercress velouté, and proceeded to a bouillabaisse-themed starter, with a deep brown crustacean sauce surrounding a piece of cured sea trout, garnished with saffron rouille, tomatoes and croûtons. The main course was eloquently flavoured guinea fowl with a clump of hen of the woods mushrooms, romanesco, charred leeks and roast shallots, a couple of creamy purées offsetting a sparingly applied jus gras. To finish, a properly crisped crème brûlée flavoured with Earl Grey was teamed with exquisitely sharp lemon accompaniments – curd, sorbet and candied peel – as well as pecan praline. If the overall cost seems high, the attention to detail does a conscientious job of justifying it. Good choice by the glass, from £5.75, is a feature of a compact wine list that incorporates some stylish growers.

Chef/s: Tom Williams-Hawkes. **Meals:** set D £45 (4 courses) to £85. **Details:** 42 seats. V menu. Wheelchairs. Parking. Music.

▌Torquay
The Elephant by Simon Hulstone
Cooking score: 5
Modern British | £45
3-4 Beacon Terrace, Torquay, TQ1 2BH
Tel no: 01803 200044
elephantrestaurant.co.uk

Not far above secluded Beacon Quay, with boats bobbing in the middle distance, Simon Hulstone's welcoming seaside venue is a beacon in itself. Well supported by locals, it offers a dressed-down ambience of bare boards and animated chatter, and a kitchen, just visible through the narrow pass, turning out finely constructed renditions of modern, seasonal dishes. Openers can be as light as golden beetroot dressed in dukkah with burrata and elderflower vinegar, or as unexpectedly substantial as a thick, spiced crumpet, piled with duck leg confit and pumpkin chutney in sherry vinegar, a dish that resembled 'an ungarnished main course' for one spring diner. Mains – all attractively composed – might bring on the local catch as in Brixham hake with shellfish ravioli in lemongrass dressing and puréed fennel, or Devon meats and allotment veg: majestic guinea fowl breast, say, with a perfectly rendered glazed pithivier of wild mushroom mousse, roasted quince, parsnip purée and a delicately truffled jus. Desserts tend mostly to the chocolate and caramel end of the spectrum, but there could be something as refreshingly featherlight as citrus parfait with candied and gelled mandarin and raspberry

sorbet, garlanded in lemon verbena. The wine list seems overdue a thorough overhaul but, from £22, is fairly priced.

Chef/s: Simon Hulstone. **Closed:** Mon, Sun, 1 week Nov, 2 weeks Jan. **Meals:** main courses £15 to £28. Set L £22 (2 courses) to £25. Tasting menu £80 (7 courses). **Details:** 55 seats. Wheelchairs. Music.

▌Tytherleigh
The Tytherleigh Arms
Cooking score: 2
Modern British | £38
Tytherleigh, EX13 7BE
Tel no: 01460 220214
tytherleigharms.com

🛏

Sitting on the A358 at the point where east Devon yields to Dorset, The Tytherleigh is a 16th-century inn that wears its great age lightly in the form of some exposed stonework within, amid the gentle modernising job that has added mauve bar stools and light wood furniture. Chef Jack Luby is a veteran of England's cutting-edge South-east, and brings neat imaginative touches to a revivified menu here. Briefly seared and peppered yellowfin tuna is served with pickled kohlrabi, white asparagus and lotus root crisps, dressed in lightly wasabi-spiked mayonnaise to make a palate-piquing starter. Mains bring on sea bream with a tempura-battered oyster and braised hispi in nettle velouté, or three lamb preparations – herb-crusted rack, braised belly and crispy sweetbread – with pickled sprouting broccoli. Light lunch dishes are a nice idea, perhaps pork tenderloin with cumin-spiced carrots and salty kale in veal jus, but there is also a simpler offering of sandwiches and burgers. Finish with dark chocolate mousse and blood orange garnished with vanilla cream and mint gel. A good spread of wines within a fittingly modest compass offers genuine choice. Medium glasses start at £4.90.

Chef/s: Jack Luby. **Closed:** 25 and 26 Dec, 6 to 21 Jan. **Meals:** main courses £13 to £26. **Details:** 60 seats. Parking. Music. Children over 5 yrs.

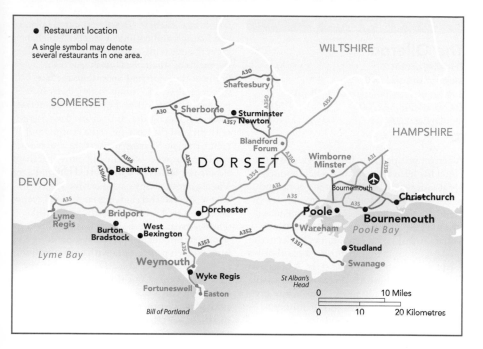

- Restaurant location

A single symbol may denote several restaurants in one area.

WILTSHIRE

SOMERSET

Shaftesbury

Sherborne

Sturminster Newton

HAMPSHIRE

Blandford Forum

DORSET

Wimborne Minster

Beaminster

DEVON

Bournemouth

Christchurch

Bridport

Dorchester

Poole

Bournemouth

Lyme Regis

Burton Bradstock

West Bexington

Wareham

Poole Bay

Lyme Bay

Studland

Weymouth

Swanage

Wyke Regis

St Alban's Head

Fortuneswell

Easton

0   10 Miles

Bill of Portland

0   10   20 Kilometres

◼ Beaminster

**★ LOCAL RESTAURANT AWARD ★
REGIONAL WINNER**

Brassica
Cooking score: 4
Modern British | £30
4 The Square, Beaminster, DT8 3AS
Tel no: 01308 538100
brassicarestaurant.co.uk
£30

Good design meets clever cooking in this handsome former toll house, where chef Cass Titcombe and expert trendwatcher Louise Chidgey set up shop in 2014. Bright textiles, whitewashed panelling and contemporary ceramics give an impeccably offbeat charm, and the menu seals the deal with fantastic local produce, fresh flavours and the odd Italian influence. Titcombe relishes a rummage through the best of the culinary archives for inspiration, pulling out starters of roast leeks with hazelnut and pickled celery or Berkshire porchetta tonnato, with partridge and red wine ragù with soft polenta and grilled treviso to follow. Occasional fixed suppers offer four-course snapshots of the seasonal kitchen; in late spring, a main course might be rolled organic lamb with roast new potatoes, land cress, pickled raisins, almonds and capers, with strawberry cheesecake pavlova for afters. Wine is from £22, and there's just space to drink it outside, if you're lucky.
Chef/s: Cass Titcombe. **Closed:** Mon, Tue, 25 Dec to 6 Jan. **Meals:** main courses £16 to £22. Set L £16 (2 courses) to £20. Sun L £23 (2 courses) to £28. **Details:** 40 seats. 6 seats outside. Music.

Anonymous

At *The Good Food Guide*, our inspectors dine anonymously and pay their bill in full. These impartial review meals, along with feedback from thousands of our readers, are what informs the content of the *GFG*. Only the best restaurants make the cut.

The Ollerod

Cooking score: 3
Modern British | £40
3 Prout Bridge, Beaminster, DT8 3AY
Tel no: 01308 862200
theollerod.co.uk

A perfect prospect, the former Bridge House Hotel has been reinvented as a neighbourly restaurant where boutique guest rooms and a well-stocked inglenooked bar are the comforting adjuncts to a culinary operation that suits this affluent town in a charming, casual kind of way. Chris Staines cooks in the modern idiom in both format – a small plates menu as well as a carte – and style. A meal here might open with Isle of Wight tomato salad with sesame, avocado purée, shiro white soy sauce, tomato dashi, basil and cucumber sorbet, which appears on both menus. It could continue with a substantial main-course fillet of fjord trout poached in olive oil and served with asparagus, broad beans and lemon verbena, and finish with an elderflower set custard dotted with raspberries, raspberry purée, lemon curd and elderflower beignets. To drink, there are cocktails and a decent wine list that keeps prices reasonable.
Chef/s: Chris Staines. **Meals:** main courses £20 to £25. Small plates £4 to £16. Set L £25 (2 courses) to £30. Sun L £35. **Details:** 50 seats. 30 seats outside. Vg menu. Bar. Wheelchairs. Parking. Music.

▐ Bournemouth

The Larderhouse

Cooking score: 2
Modern European | £35
4 Southbourne Grove, Bournemouth, BH6 3QZ
Tel no: 01202 424687
thelarderhouse.co.uk

A few miles east of Bournemouth's centre, the district of Southbourne is making quite the culinary name for itself, and on the main street is a singular place that has the air of a farmhouse kitchen. Chunky wood furniture and fittings, and copiously stocked bar shelves greet the eye with a cheering prospect, as does the menu of small plates and tapas dishes. Some of these are trad Spanish to the last splash of olive oil – boquerones, Padrón peppers – while others branch out into terra (relatively) incognita, as in charred mackerel with pickled rhubarb, morcilla crumbs and crème fraîche. Sharing platters are a huge hit, while mains wheel out the big guns – perhaps slow-roast ox cheek with braised red cabbage, Vichy carrots, crispy oats and Blue Vinny cheese, or crab and clam tagliatelle in a creamy sauce powered with wild garlic and paprika. The determination to please is still going strong at the conclusion, when something like butterscotch panna cotta with coffee praline and cocoa shortbread is an alternative to the excellent cheeses. The illustrated wine list is less perplexing than it might at first appear, with glasses from £5.50.
Chef/s: Bartek Wujczak. **Closed:** 24 to 26 Dec. **Meals:** main courses £16 to £23. Small plates £4 to £7. **Details:** 40 seats. 40 seats outside. Bar. Wheelchairs.

Roots

Cooking score: 4
Modern European | £50
141 Belle Vue Road, Bournemouth, BH6 3EN
Tel no: 01202 430005
restaurantroots.co.uk

The location in a parade of shops in Southbourne is the first counterintuitive aspect of Jan Bretschneider's highly personal venue. Inside, it looks like an all-day café, with a brick-walled bar and good-sized bare wood tables. As soon as the food starts arriving, though, the resemblance fades. Innovative, high-end modern dining comes in the form of a tasting menu, beginning with nibbles that take in a small cone of baba ganoush, all cumin and cinnamon, in crunchy puffed wild rice. Seaweed custard with crab salad in lemongrass dashi might follow, before a highly technical service of breads, which involves slicing the butter with a hot knife on a rotary cheese cutter. The fish dish could be butter-poached sea bass with Jerusalem artichoke in oat milk, while main-course meats have included venison haunch with squash, sauced in passion fruit and bitter chocolate. Desserts might pair almond parfait with poached apricot, garnished with apricot sorbet and – the only clanger of an otherwise successful evening – candied black olives. The wine pairings are pitch perfect, and you will become quite intimate with Geza, the Hungarian maître d' who leads the front of house with missionary zeal.

Chef/s: Jan Bretschneider. **Closed:** Mon, Tue, 15 Sept to 2 Oct, 23 Dec to 8 Jan. **Meals:** set L £35 Fri and Sat. Tasting menu £50 (5 courses) to £70. Sun L £31 (2 courses) to £36. **Details:** 16 seats. V menu. Music.

LOCAL GEM

West Beach
Seafood | £40
Pier Approach, Bournemouth, BH2 5AA
Tel no: 01202 587785
west-beach.co.uk

£5
OFF

A beachfront fixture for nigh on two decades, the warmth and chatter of this smart, light-filled dining room are familiar to its many loyal patrons, both locals and visitors, while the decked terrace is quite the place to be when the sun shines. The menu is an expectedly – although not exclusively – fishy affair. Scallops come teamed with crisp pork belly and Granny Smith purée, there are seafood platters, mussels every which way, and turbot fillet with colcannon fishcake and a periwinkle and mustard sauce. Wines from £19.

Seaside ingredients

The spoils of coastline foraging are turning up on menus nationwide

Samphire The sea plant you're most likely to see in the supermarket, marsh samphire has a salty pop and is an easy win with seafood cooked in lots of butter. Rock samphire is more likely to be served as a pickle, as it's a bit stinky when fresh.

Sea buckthorn The orange berries of this coastal plant have a mouth-puckering acidity, and are beloved of principled chefs who would rather use them over imported lemons in their desserts.

Carrageen Traditionally gathered on the rocky coasts of Scotland and Ireland, this seaweed gives a lovely soft set to milky puddings, and is a vegetarian alternative to gelatine.

Dulse Collected at low tide, the 'bacon of the sea' adds umami to snacks and body to broths. It works its salty magic in butter to slather on sourdough.

Nori Made using what Welsh, Scottish and Irish foragers would know as laver, these toasted seaweed sheets are the classic wrap for Japanese maki and handrolls. Dull on one side, shiny on the other – the latter should face outwards.

▌Burton Bradstock
Seaside Boarding House
Cooking score: 2
Modern British | £38
Cliff Road, Burton Bradstock, DT6 4RB
Tel no: 01308 897205
theseasideboardinghouse.com

If the name conjures for those of a certain generation a monochrome reverie of tinned soup, stodgy breakfasts and faded curtains, you can safely wake up. Burton Bradstock's finest occupies a plum position overlooking Chesil Beach, with an expansively wide, airy dining room and terrace to command it. Here, the emphasis is on modern British brasserie cooking with precision and personality to spare. Start with scallops and borlotti beans with a wodge of sage polenta, before rocking on with one of the substantial but well-balanced mains such as roast lamb leg in anchoïade with cavolo nero, or a hefty tranche of brill with leeks in chive butter. Sunday set lunches look like a very good excuse for a day out, when roast sirloin with Yorkshires and all the trimmings take centre stage, and desserts aim to send you fulfilled into the coastal breezes by means of rhubarb and custard tart or apple and Calvados crème brûlée. A compact but expertly constructed wine choice opens at £22.
Chef/s: Craig Whitty. **Meals:** main courses £14 to £22. Set L £15 (2 courses) to £18. Sun L £25 (2 courses) to £30. **Details:** 60 seats. 40 seats outside. Bar.

Hive Beach Café
Seafood | £30
Beach Road, Burton Bradstock, DT6 4RF
Tel no: 01308 897070
hivebeachcafe.co.uk

Much expanded since it opened in 1991, this has become the quintessential beachside seafood venue. A backdrop of wide-open views of the Jurassic Coast and Lyme Bay add to the allure of this no-bookings café, where you queue to order breakfast and lunch (or dinner from mid-June to the end of October). Seafood platters are piled high with local lobster, crab and crevettes, and handpicked crabmeat sandwiches are doorstep-thick. Alternatively, tuck into pan-fried skate with baby prawns, capers and gherkins. Drink house beers or wines from £4.75 a glass. The Club House in West Bexington (see entry) is from the same owners.

▌Christchurch
The Jetty
Cooking score: 1
Modern British | £50
Christchurch Harbour Hotel & Spa, 95 Mudeford, Christchurch, BH23 3NT
Tel no: 01202 400950
thejetty.co.uk

In an officially designated Area of Outstanding Natural Beauty, Alex Aitken's harbourside restaurant overlooks Mudeford Quay and Christchurch Harbour. Floor-to-ceiling glass provides magical water's edge views and sets the scene for a menu with a strong seafood bent, although seasonal game makes a dutiful appearance. Local fish, some caught in the waters directly in front of the restaurant, are handled sensitively, as in a main course of turbot cooked on the bone and served with caramelised celeriac, oyster fritter and brown shrimp butter. That dish might be preceded by slow-cooked pork belly teamed with seared prawns, lime syrup and ginger cream. Wines start at £18.95.
Chef/s: Alex Aitken. **Meals:** main courses £23 to £30. Set L and early D £23 (2 courses) to £26. Tasting menu £55 (7 courses). Sun L £35. **Details:** 70 seats. 20 seats outside. V menu. Vg menu. Bar. Wheelchairs. Parking. Music.

▌Dorchester

Sienna

Cooking score: 4
Modern British | £35
36 High West Street, Dorchester, DT1 1UP
Tel no: 01305 250022
siennadorchester.co.uk

First-time visitors may view the lurid frontage and position on a busy road next to a bus stop with a little concern, but once inside the tiny dining room, everything starts to make sense. Chef proprietor Marcus Wilcox serves a series of tasting menus of four, six or eight courses, plus a good-value set lunch (two choices per course) with deceptively terse menu descriptions underplaying the amount of work involved. The tiny kitchen doesn't seem to hamper ambition or creativity either. A starter of cured salmon with compressed cucumber, apple purée and dill has impressed with its combination of textures and forthright flavours, as has an impressively tender duck breast cooked sous-vide and topped with crushed pistachios and served with a silky celeriac purée, poached cherries and wilted chard, while a take on an éclair with pineapple, yeast and lychee is one of the arresting desserts on offer. The compact wine list opens at £20.
Chef/s: Marcus Wilcox. **Closed:** Mon, Sun.
Meals: set L £20 (2 courses) to £25. Tasting menu £35 (4 courses) to £70. **Details:** 14 seats. Music.

▌Poole

Guildhall Tavern

French | £40
15 Market Street, Poole, BH15 1NB
Tel no: 01202 671717
guildhalltavern.co.uk

Here, there are French-themed evenings with a prize quiz on Gallic matters and a live accordionist. Sitting proud in navy and white on a narrow corner in the Old Town, the Tavern specialises in seafood in a mood that leans to the opposite side of La Manche.

Expect rope-grown mussels in Muscadet marinière, hollandaised halibut wrapped in pancetta, or a whopping sea bass on the bone flambéed in Pernod, together with a couple of meat dishes. Finish with tarte tatin. Exclusively French wines from £19.95.

▌Studland

Pig on the Beach

Modern British | £40
Manor House, Manor Road, Studland, BH19 3AU
Tel no: 01929 450288
thepighotel.com

Like its boutique siblings, this branch of the burgeoning Pig hotel chain is fuelled by an (almost) self-sufficient green agenda that involves an impressive vegetable garden, foraging, home-curing and an awareness of 'food miles'. Housed within an elegant 18th-century villa overlooking Studland Bay, the greenhouse-style restaurant serves up home-grown and local produce in sprightly seasonal dishes ranging from Poole Bay mackerel tartare with pickled fennel, salad burnet and chilli oil to braised shoulder of home-reared Gloucester old spot pork on pappardelle with sea beets and Isle of Wight tomatoes. 'British bubbles' top the intriguing global wine list.

▌Sturminster Newton

Plumber Manor

Cooking score: 2
Anglo-French | £40
Sturminster Newton, DT10 2AF
Tel no: 01258 472507
plumbermanor.com

The Prideaux-Brune family, whose ancestral home this has been since Jacobean times, aim to provide the ultimate in home-from-home hospitality. Winter fires, comfortable sofas, classic cocktails and a resident black lab to welcome your own faithful friends are only

part of the story, with the surrounding bucolic acres of Hardy country supplying the remainder. Louis Haskell provides the nourishment in refined country house mode, that style of Anglo-French opulence that is fast becoming an endangered species in British catering. Dinner might open with wild mushroom millefeuille in a sauce of brandy, spinach and cream, before gliding into the realms of pheasant breast on apple and rosemary bubble and squeak, or brill with orange and chives. An array of puddings served from the trolley will make for agonies of indecision. The traditional approach to wine sees Bordeaux and Burgundy given star billing, and there are magnums on hand for larger parties. Pricing, from £18.50, is fair at all levels.
Chef/s: Louis Haskell. **Closed:** Feb. **Meals:** set D £33 (2 courses) to £40. Sun L £32. **Details:** 65 seats. Bar. Wheelchairs. Parking.

◼ West Bexington
The Club House
Cooking score: 2
Seafood | £42
Beach Road, West Bexington, DT2 9DG
Tel no: 01308 898302
theclubhousewestbexington.co.uk
£5
OFF

Steve Attrill from Hive Beach Café at Burton Bradstock (see entry) is the brains behind this enterprising eatery housed in a reconfigured Art Deco bungalow right on Chesil Beach. The look may suggest New England rather than the Jurassic Coast, but there's a real sense of localism to the food and drink on offer. Vegetables are supplied by the organic farm next door, and headlining seafood is hauled in by the south coast boats – witness unfussy dishes such as buttermilk-fried huss with shellfish mayo, grilled blue lobster or sand soles with brown shrimps and sea purslane. West Country game also gets a decent outing (perhaps Exmoor venison with elderberry and port sauce), while desserts such as honey-roast plums with bramble cream have an emphatic local flavour too. Bread comes from the

owners' own microbakery, they serve (bookable) breakfast from 10am, and there are some local names on the fish-friendly wine list.
Chef/s: Charlie Soole. **Closed:** Mon, Tue (Jan, Feb), 25 Dec, 13 and 14 Jan. **Meals:** main courses £17 to £50. Sun L £18 (2 courses) to £22. **Details:** 65 seats. 60 seats outside. Wheelchairs. Parking. Music.

◼ Wyke Regis
LOCAL GEM
Crab House Café
Seafood | £36
Ferryman's Way, Portland Road, Wyke Regis, DT4 9YU
Tel no: 01305 788867
crabhousecafe.co.uk

More shack than 'house', this wooden hut overlooks the pebbles of Chesil Beach and the oyster beds supplying the restaurant. Naturally, the freshest seafood is the main focus here, whether you sit inside near the crab and lobster tanks or grab a bench table outside under the frilly parasols. The menu changes depending on the day's catch but you might find a starter of razor clams, chorizo and broad bean crumb or a main course of pan-fried grey mullet fillet with lime and coriander butter. Wine from £18.40.

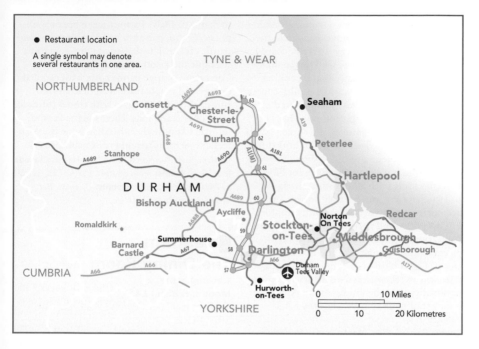

- Restaurant location

A single symbol may denote several restaurants in one area.

TYNE & WEAR

NORTHUMBERLAND

Consett
Chester-le-Street
Durham
Stanhope
Seaham
Peterlee
Hartlepool

D U R H A M

Bishop Auckland
Romaldkirk
Aycliffe
Barnard Castle
Summerhouse
Darlington
Stockton-on-Tees
Norton On Tees
Middlesbrough
Redcar
Guisborough

CUMBRIA
Durham Tees Valley
Hurworth-on-Tees

YORKSHIRE

0   10 Miles
0   10   20 Kilometres

◼ Hurworth-on-Tees

The Bay Horse

Cooking score: 3
Modern British | £40
45 The Green, Hurworth-on-Tees, DL2 2AA
Tel no: 01325 720663
thebayhorsehurworth.com

It's more than a decade since Jonathan Hall and Marcus Bennett took over this ancient inn; in that time, it has become a spirited foodie destination with dapper interiors to match – a pair of dark grey wood-panelled dining rooms, highly polished tables and comfortable chairs, plus a fire-warmed bar for drinkers. Visitors relish the fixed-price menus, which show real skill in getting the best out of cheaper ingredients: note a dish of confit lamb belly in a red wine jus with roast carrots, asparagus, new potatoes and petits pois à la française that so delighted one lunchtime diner. Elsewhere, the kitchen delivers elaborate assemblages, perhaps fried fillet of sea bream, cured red bream and battered baby squid rings with finely sliced fennel, dabs of saffron aïoli and dill. The dessert taster means you needn't choose between milk chocolate délice and caramelised rice pudding. You will drink well from the stylistically arranged wine list, service is welcoming and the outside terrace is a lovely spot.
Chef/s: Andy Simms. **Closed:** 25 Dec. **Meals:** main courses £12 to £32. Set L £17 (2 courses) to £21. Set D £23 (2 courses) to £28. Sun L £24 (2 courses) to £30. **Details:** 41 seats. 60 seats outside. V menu. Vg menu. Bar. Wheelchairs. Parking. Music.

The Orangery

Cooking score: 4
Modern European | £55
Rockliffe Hall, Hurworth-on-Tees, DL2 2DU
Tel no: 01325 729999
rockliffehall.com

£5 OFF 🛏

With its long approach, acres of garden, golf course, spa treatments and so forth, this lavishly modernised country house is quite the tonic for the urban escapee. Drinks are taken in the bar before guests move through to the striking Victorian orangery where Richard Allen continues to oversee the kitchen, his highly detailed, technically sound cooking offered via a fixed-price carte or multi-course tasting menu. Allen takes his cue from the seasons and, in spring, promises the likes of chalk stream trout – smoked and cured – with cucumber, dill and dashi, ahead of Yorkshire lamb with a 'bolognaise' of the shoulder given oomph from olives and anchovies, or North Sea lemon sole with langoustine, marigold and a rich rarebit sauce. Fancy desserts bring a deconstructed apple pressing with crumble, English toffee and toasted rice or a lovely confection of gariguette strawberries with pieces of mint sponge cake and Brillat-Savarin cream. The cooking is certainly ambitious, while the excellent service delivers a lot more personality than the dining room. As for the wine list, it helps to have a healthy bank balance.

Chef/s: Richard Allen. **Meals:** set D £55. Tasting menu £65 (6 courses). **Details:** 48 seats. V menu. Vg menu. Bar. Wheelchairs. Parking. Music. Children over 7 yrs.

▌Norton-On-Tees
Café Lilli
Cooking score: 2
International | £28
83 High Street, Norton-On-Tees, TS20 1AE
Tel no: 01642 554422
lillicafe.co.uk
£5 OFF £30

For many readers there's no doubt that Roberto Pittalis's restaurant defines a good local eatery, the warmly jumbled decor and ambition to provide great food and drink without breaking the bank finding much approval. The kitchen majors in broad-shouldered seasonal dishes with overtones from Italy and the Mediterranean. Passion for quality runs through every dish, from pan-fried cod cheeks with chorizo jam and cauliflower salad or ham hock and pistachio terrine with black pudding and brown sauce

to mains of Hall's Farm chicken breast with potato gratin, pancetta, wild mushrooms and truffle cream. The daily pasta dish remains a strength and risotto is also pitch perfect. Carrot and orange panna cotta with candied orange and maple tuille is a good way to finish, although affogato with cinder toffee ice cream has many fans. There's praise for the service, likewise the all-Italian wine list with its flexible measures and reasonable prices.

Chef/s: Josh Harrison and Andrew Hayes. **Closed:** Mon, Sun. **Meals:** main courses £12 to £25. Set D £17 (2 courses) to £22. **Details:** 70 seats. Bar. Wheelchairs. Parking. Music.

▌Seaham
The Dining Room
Cooking score: 2
Modern British | £45
Seaham Hall, Lord Byron's Walk, Seaham, SR7 7AG
Tel no: 0191 516 1400
seaham-hall.co.uk

This impressive Georgian house has been amply extended and is now a palatial edifice complete with spa, wedding packages and acres of grounds all in close proximity to the North Sea. A meal here is designed to feel like an occasion, a feeling reinforced by the grand proportions of the dining room with its cream, brown and gold colour scheme and pair of statement chandeliers. Dinner is the main event and the cooking continues to ply a modernised country house line, with pressed slow-cooked Goosnargh chicken terrine served with crisp chicken skin topped with smoked cod's roe and thin slices of carrot, followed by fillet of North Sea hake with braised peas, lettuce and wild garlic. British artisan cheeses with fruit loaf and oatcakes, or the likes of caramel apple with cider mousse, marigold ice cream and crunchy hazelnuts, close the show. Unclothed tables and cheerfully willing service help you forget you're in a hotel dining room. Wines start at £24.

Chef/s: Damian Broom. **Meals:** main courses £20 to £32. Sun L £29 (2 courses) to £35. **Details:** 42 seats. Bar. Wheelchairs. Parking. Music.

▌Summerhouse

★ TOP 50 ★

The Raby Hunt

Cooking score: 8
Modern British | £140
Summerhouse, DL2 3UD
Tel no: 01325 374237
rabyhuntrestaurant.co.uk

🍶 🛏

Single-mindedness and a fiery determination to produce the best define James Close's food, the soaring sophistication of his razor-edge cooking seemingly at odds with the rural setting: on the outside a stone-built, creeper-clad former village pub; within a modern, minimalist space with a state-of-the-art kitchen. Forever breaking new ground, Close is known for his freewheeling palate and instinct for building nuanced contrasts, and his 17-course tasting menu is a thrilling amalgam of flavours and textures. One minute, Close will do the non-interventionist thing more typical of a Japanese chef, sending out exquisite nigiri or a sweet raw scallop given a hint of acidity and heat by simple accompaniments of lime, jalapeño and radish; the next there'll be dinky tacos topped with nuggets of crab and salsa verde or suckling pig with avocado salsa. Later, beef tartare, brought into focus by smoked eel cream and caviar, is followed by a bitesize, richly flavoured pastrami burger, a delicate spring salad of unimpeachable freshness and a kuzu crisp topped with an intense lamb ragù, before a more conventional dish of pink herdwick lamb loin with winter greens and a dab of anchovy. A warm, slightly molten chocolate mousse with a black olive crisp dotted with toffee and a sheep's yoghurt ice cream is the perfect curtain-raiser for a mango and yuzu tart filled with a Brillat-Savarin mousse. Front of house is top-drawer, dismantling the formalities and putting people at ease while staying vigilant. And wine? It's an authoritative list with many desirable bottles and interesting producers, but with prices from £45 it's worth thinking about a matching flight or giving the sommelier a budget to get the best out of it.
Chef/s: James Close. **Closed:** Mon, Tue, Sun, 2 weeks Dec to Jan. **Meals:** tasting menu £140 (17 courses). **Details:** 24 seats. Wheelchairs. Parking. Children over 8 yrs.

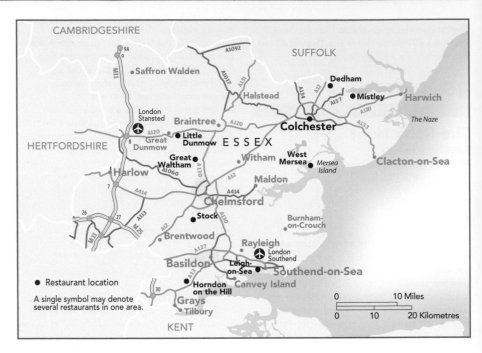

▮ Colchester

Church Street Tavern

Cooking score: 2
Modern British | £29
3 Church Street, Colchester, CO1 1NF
Tel no: 01206 564325
churchstreettavern.co.uk

£5 OFF ▮ £30

Old banks across the country are finding new
lives as places to eat and drink, and this
offshoot of the Sun Inn in Dedham (see entry)
is no exception. Carefully decorated in
modern style with warm colours and
comfortable furnishings, the spacious rooms
(ground-floor bar, first-floor dining room)
are civilised spots for both drinkers and diners.
If you're in for a glass or two but working up
an appetite, then bar snacks – rare breed beef
burger, loaded fries with pulled pork – should
do the trick. Otherwise, a menu of up-to-date
pub cooking draws European influences into
its British ambit, marrying fillet of cod and
crab velouté with leeks, bacon crumb and

parsley sauce, or adding caper and anchovy
sauce to lamb cutlets and sprouting broccoli.
Among desserts, there could be rose water
parfait with coconut ice, pistachio and Turkish
delight. An intelligently composed wine list is
arranged by style with eloquent tasting notes
and demonstrably fair prices.
Chef/s: Ewan Naylon. **Closed:** Mon, Tue, 1 week
Jan, 25 and 26 Dec. **Meals:** main courses £13 to
£25. Set L and early D £16 (2 courses) to £21. Sun L
£22 (2 courses) to £28. **Details:** 85 seats. 25 seats
outside. Vg menu. Bar. Wheelchairs. Music.

Wine list

▮ Restaurants showing this symbol
have a wine list that our experts
consider to be outstanding, either for
its in-depth focus on a particular region,
attractive margins on fine wines, or strong
selection by the glass.

Grain

Cooking score: 3
Modern European | £32
11a North Hill, Colchester, CO1 1DZ
Tel no: 01206 570005
grain-colchester.co.uk

Whether you eat outside – in a pleasant central courtyard – or inside, settled in sturdy wicker chairs at reclaimed tables, this unusual weatherboard, brick and glass building hard by a multi-storey car park is quite a find. The bare wood and neutral tones fit the laid-back style of inspired small plates, a kind of 'build your own tasting menu' with four options each from the Garden, Water and Land sections. Great flavour combinations have been put together with skill in a dish of artfully piled-up carrots, salt-baked and pickled, layered with a glossy basil pesto, houmous, pine nuts and a vibrant carrot purée. Cured mackerel teamed with a salty salad of fennel, samphire and gooseberry purée cranks things up a notch but the star of the show is brown shrimp with courgette (roasted and barbecued) in a rich brown butter sauce. Finish with a dense and creamy blackcurrant mousse with shards of juniper meringue, crushed hazelnuts and vanilla ice cream. The brief wine list offers interesting drinking at reasonable prices.
Chef/s: Paul Wendholt and Jordan Sidwell. **Closed:** Mon, Sun, 22 Dec to 13 Jan, 1 week Aug.
Meals: small plates £6 to £12. Set L £18 (2 courses) to £21. **Details:** 48 seats. 16 seats outside. V menu. Vg menu. Bar. Wheelchairs. Music.

▌Dedham
The Sun Inn

Cooking score: 3
Modern British | £29
High Street, Dedham, CO7 6DF
Tel no: 01206 323351
thesuninndedham.com
£5 OFF 🍷 ⬜ £30

Piers Baker's sunset-yellow hostelry sits squarely on Dedham's handsome Georgian high street. With a proper (non-bookable) bar

area serving locally brewed ales, and a two-tiered restaurant with low beams and dark wood tables, it's utterly charming, with a distinctly pubby charm rather than being 'a fancy restaurant masquerading as a pub'. And the menu? It has a keen eye for the seasons and an obvious Italian flavour – as in celeriac carpaccio with a fabulous fritter of Wigmore cheese and blobs of tapenade-style pickled walnut or a really tender fillet of flamed mackerel with a tangle of agretti, winter tomatoes and shallots in a tangy dressing. Elsewhere, spot-on whole plaice is teamed with two puffed-up zesty ricotta gnudi and given oomph by a chicken butter sauce, while Mersca Island lamb rump is perfectly pink and nicely seasoned. Round off with espresso tart, burnt meringue, vanilla ice cream and praline. The wide-ranging wine list is a corker, with quirky categories including 'desert island cellared wines', 'broody', and 'touch of earth', and good choices by the glass. Not all staff know their way around the wine list 'so you'll need to find one who does if you want advice'.
Chef/s: Jack Levine. **Closed:** 25 and 26 Dec.
Meals: main courses £13 to £25. Set L and early D £18 (2 courses) to £23. **Details:** 75 seats. 100 seats outside. Vg menu. Bar. Parking. Music.

Le Talbooth

Cooking score: 3
Modern British | £58
Gun Hill, Dedham, CO7 6HP
Tel no: 01206 323150
milsomhotels.com
£5 OFF 🍷

Once a toll booth for horse-drawn traffic crossing the river Stour, this entrancing medieval beamed building has been the Milsom family's domain and Essex showpiece since 1952. As a discreetly welcoming retreat, it promises special-occasion dining – whether you're ensconced in the elegantly appointed restaurant or eating outside on the canopied terrace. The kitchen works to a broad remit, pleasing traditionalists with Mersea crab mayonnaise and Dedham Vale beef Rossini, while also satisfying those with more adventurous palates. Confit pavé of cod with crisp lobster cannelloni, cauliflower, almond and curry velouté is a typically intricate and forward-thinking fish dish, while seasonal game might yield roast local partridge or saddle of Thetford Forest venison with black pudding, dark chocolate, crosnes and blackberries. For afters, perhaps try passion fruit soufflé with coconut ice cream and coriander jelly. Set lunches are a perennial hit, and the commendable wine list promises fairly priced drinking from £21.25 a bottle.

Chef/s: Andrew Hirst. **Meals:** main courses £23 to £34. Set L £29 (2 courses) to £36. Sun L £43. **Details:** 80 seats. 60 seats outside. V menu. Bar. Wheelchairs. Parking. Music.

▌Great Waltham

★ NEW ENTRY ★

Galvin Green Man

Cooking score: 3
Modern British | £30
3 Main Road, Howe Street, Great Waltham, CM3 1BG
Tel no: 01245 408820
galvingreenman.com
£30

If ever two brothers have demonstrated a Midas touch when it comes to running restaurants, it's the Galvins. Their pub restaurant on Essex home turf shines as brightly as any of their urban establishments and is as devoted to its immediate village community as it is to delivering fine dining for guests travelling to eat here. A bar menu offers smart classics – Gloucester old spot Scotch eggs with pickles, or magnificent burgers with provolone cheese and smoked tomato mayo – while the restaurant, with its precisely plated but robustly delicious food, is where chefs spread creative wings. A subtly seasoned chilled cucumber velouté is given substance from a finger of toast with horseradish cream and pieces of plump, salty anchovy. Follow with a towering vol-au-vent filled with smoked chicken and confit leek, or the tenderest of pork fillets, tea-smoked and

served with sweet peach and sharp kalamansi lime purée that cuts laser-like through the glossiest gravy. A lip-smacking lemon tart and raspberry sorbet keeps dessert classic. There are house wines on tap and bottles on the sensible one-page list start at £26.

Chef/s: Daniel Lee. **Meals:** main courses £15 to £18. Set D £17 (2 courses) to £21. Sun L £25 (2 courses) to £32. **Details:** 104 seats. 48 seats outside. V menu. Vg menu. Bar. Wheelchairs. Parking. Music.

▌Horndon on the Hill

The Bell Inn

Cooking score: 3
Modern British | £37
High Road, Horndon on the Hill, SS17 8LD
Tel no: 01375 642463
bell-inn.co.uk

With six centuries of history etched into its timber frame, heavy beams and panelled walls, this is a proper inn – warmly welcoming and restorative, complete with real ales, real fires and pub classics in the bar (beer-battered whiting with gherkin mayo, say, or pork and leek sausages with crispy onion rings). Move on through, however, and you'll find a pleasing restaurant where the food is several notches above the pub norm with a menu promising the likes of roast pigeon breast with sweet potato purée, venison cottage pie, cranberry gel and confit shallot jus. Elaborate starters, including charred monkfish marinated in curry oil with pink grapefruit, orange curd and a herb crust also speak of an ambitious, creative kitchen, as do desserts such as hazelnut crème brûlée with mascarpone chantilly, vanilla tuile and a warm baby apple. Australian house wine is £17.95.

Chef/s: Stephen Treadwell. **Closed:** 25 and 26 Dec. **Meals:** main courses £14 to £30. **Details:** 80 seats. 40 seats outside. Bar. Wheelchairs. Parking.

Leigh-on-Sea

★ NEW ENTRY ★

Food by John Lawson

Cooking score: 3
British | £48
92 Leigh Road, Leigh-on-Sea, SS9 1BU
Tel no: 01702 667226
foodbyjohnlawson.com

John Lawson's no-menu restaurant in this up-and-coming part of Essex is worth tracking down. With its grey walls and chunky crockery, the vibe is part Scandi-cool and part ebullient warmth from a first-rate front of house. The vibe is also health – read Lawson's powerful story on the website – but there's nothing holier-than-thou about the organic or foraged produce, the vegan or free-from dishes, or grass-fed meat: they are quite simply delicious. A four-course spring meal opens with snacks – a spear of asparagus to dip into cashew nut cream, and a delicate bowl of fresh celeriac and almond rémoulade – a prelude to more asparagus, young peas in their pods, foraged herbs and a mint dressing. Wild garlic, some wilted, some puréed, adds heft to sweet, flaking skate, while memorable Aberdeen Angus feather blade, cooked to pink perfection, comes with the smokey sweetness of roasted cauliflower and cauliflower-cashew purée. Enjoy the play of textures, temperatures and flavours in a triumphant finale of rhubarb compôte and ice cream, coconut yoghurt, ginger granita and toasted buckwheat. A short but interesting wine list includes a sparky Kentish white from the organic Davenport vineyard (£13 a glass) and a jammy Morgon Côte du Py Beaujolais (£15).
Chef/s: John Lawson and Liam Lingwood. **Closed:** Mon, Tue, Wed, 1 to 17 Jan. **Meals:** set L £38. Tasting menu £48 (4 courses). Sun L £38. **Details:** 26 seats. No children at D.

Little Dunmow

Tim Allen's Flitch of Bacon

Cooking score: 4
Modern British | £58
The Street, Little Dunmow, CM6 3HT
Tel no: 01371 821660
flitchofbacon.co.uk

🛏

'On a Thursday lunchtime, the car park was already full,' observed one visitor to this ambitious – and clearly popular – operation in a postcard setting in a little Essex village. The Flitch delivers welcoming warmth alongside a repertoire of inventive, lively European-inflected British dishes. At the heart of the operation is a seven-course tasting menu that wears its local roots on its sleeve and might embrace a set of variations on heritage carrots, garnished with wing and skin of chicken, goat's curd and pesto. A Scottish scallop lies among English peas with a foaming spicy vadouvan sauce. Bacon from the titular glazed flitch adorns a spring dish of asparagus and sautéed red prawns, while the main business might be herdwick lamb, salt aged and served two ways in Provençal array, including fragrant ratatouille. Both pre-dessert and dessert itself incline to lightness, the latter perhaps incorporating strawberries, lemon verbena sorbet and strawberry gel. Glasses in three sizes lead into a confident wine list that gives equal shakes to European vineyards and those beyond.
Chef/s: Tim Allen. **Closed:** Mon, Tue. **Meals:** set L £25 (2 courses) to £32. Set D £58. Tasting menu £70 (7 courses). **Details:** 42 seats. Bar. Wheelchairs. Parking. Music.

Get social

Follow us on social media for the latest news, chef interviews and more.
Twitter @GoodFoodGuideUK
Facebook TheGoodFoodGuide

Mistley
The Mistley Thorn
Cooking score: 2
Modern British | £26
High Street, Mistley, CO11 1HE
Tel no: 01206 392821
mistleythorn.co.uk
£5 OFF ⊨ £30

Established as a coaching inn around 1723, this one-time hostelry now functions as a casual restaurant with rooms known for its dedication to top-drawer seafood (much of it from the Essex boats). Beamed ceilings, terracotta-tiled floors and bentwood chairs set the scene for some carefully executed cooking and a mixed bag of lively, eclectic ideas drawn from 'land' and 'sea'. The former might yield wood-grilled Suffolk beef or chicken breast with celeriac purée, curly kale and Madeira cream sauce; the latter could bring crab arancini with saffron aïoli followed by a bonanza of grilled local fish or a daily special such as seared sea bream fillet with seaweed crushed potatoes, wilted chard and shellfish sauce. Thursday night means 'moules madness', while puddings always include owner Sherri Singleton's 'mom's cheesecake' with toffee sauce, plus a tart of the day. The wine list features a generous selection by the glass or carafe, with bottles from £18.
Chef/s: Karl Burnside. **Meals:** main courses £12 to £26. Set L and early D £16 (2 courses) to £18. Sun L £18 (2 courses) to £20. **Details:** 80 seats. 12 seats outside. V menu. Vg menu. Bar. Wheelchairs. Parking. Music.

Stock
The Oak Room at the Hoop
Cooking score: 1
Modern British | £40
21 High Street, Stock, CM4 9BD
Tel no: 01277 841137
thehoop.co.uk

Originally converted from a cluster of medieval weavers' cottages, this Essex watering hole has been supplying locals and travellers with draught ales and victuals for more than 450 years. You can enjoy a pint and some pub classics in the bar (a haggis Scotch egg, pie and mash or calf's liver and bacon, perhaps), although the kitchen saves its best efforts for the bookable Oak Room restaurant on the first floor. Come here for whipped chicken liver parfait, or chickpea fritters with mango yoghurt followed by grilled skate with caper and parsley butter, or slow-braised beef cheek with black cabbage and celeriac. Wines include a few representatives from the New Hall Vineyard in Purleigh.
Chef/s: Phil Utz. **Closed:** Mon, 25 Dec to 3 Jan, 20 May to 7 Jun. **Meals:** main courses £13 to £32. Sun L £25. **Details:** 40 seats. Music.

West Mersea
LOCAL GEM
West Mersea Oyster Bar
Seafood | £25
Coast Road, West Mersea, CO5 8LT
Tel no: 01206 381600
westmerseaoysterbar.co.uk
£30

Mersea Island's renowned rock oysters and Colchester natives find their way into top kitchens worldwide, but nothing beats slurping them just a stroll from their beds on the Blackwater Estuary. This weather-boarded shack gets packed to the gunwales, so be prepared to queue if you're after a takeaway or haven't booked in advance. Plates of minerally *Ostrea edulis* are the big attraction, but the short menu also promises everything from crab chowder to battered skate, grilled lobster or Cajun-style salmon – plus piled-high seafood platters. Drink wine, beer or a cheering cuppa.

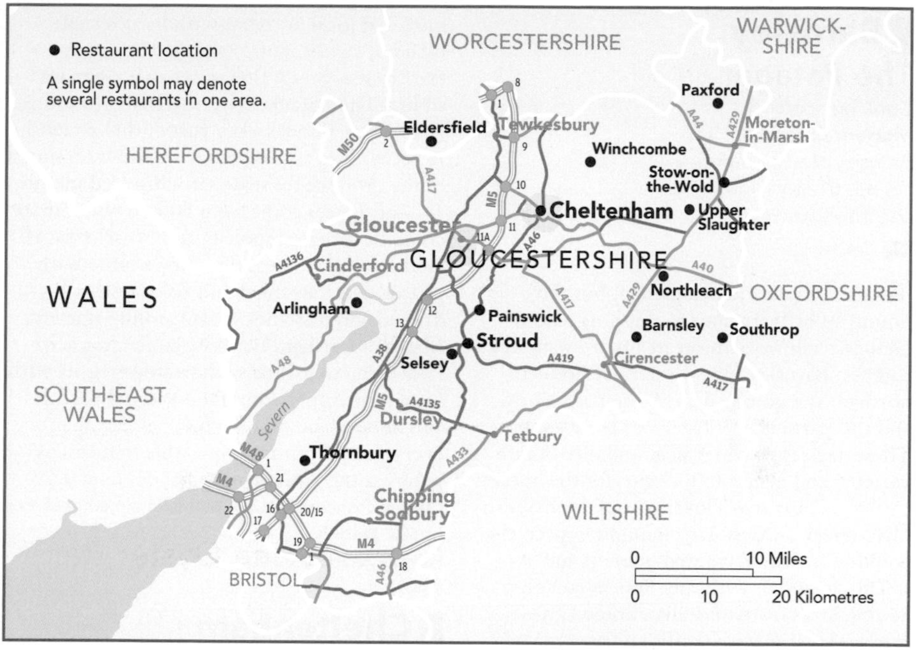

Arlingham
The Old Passage

Cooking score: 2
Seafood | £50

Passage Road, Arlingham, GL2 7JR
Tel no: 01452 740547
theoldpassage.com

£5 OFF

While not too far from the M5, The Old Passage still feels wonderfully remote, cupped in its oxbow bend, with the tidal Severn alternating between full bore and exposed mudflats. A converted whitewashed pub with bright blue shutters, it nails its colours to the seafood mast with a saltwater tank in which lobsters drift unsuspectingly. Crabmeat in both colours, the white in a salad, the brown in mayonnaise, is served with assertive pickled veg. Red mullet and brown shrimps join forces in a buttery risotto with plenty of acidulating lemon, and monkfish with a crisp-fried mussel, curried crab cannelloni and beetroot indicate the broad-minded approach taken here. Not everything is a total success, and those in need of a sugar fix should prepare themselves for a tasting menu that doesn't come with a dessert. They do have some, though – perhaps sticky toffee pudding with stout ice cream. Glasses of wine open at £5.60 for the nearby Three Choirs Vineyards rosé.

Chef/s: Lewis Dixon. **Closed:** Mon. **Meals:** main courses £20 to £35. Set L £19 (2 courses) to £22. Tasting menu £68 (7 courses). **Details:** 40 seats. 20 seats outside. Wheelchairs. Parking. Music. No children at D.

Send us your review

Your feedback informs the content of the *GFG* and will be used to compile next year's entries. To register your opinion about any restaurant listed in the Guide, or a restaurant that you wish to bring to our attention, visit: thegoodfoodguide.co.uk/feedback.

Barnsley

The Potager

Cooking score: 3
Modern European | £45
Barnsley House, Barnsley, GL7 5EE
Tel no: 01285 740000
barnsleyhouse.com

'Potager' means kitchen garden, but the bountiful beds attached to this gorgeous Gloucestershire mansion are no ordinary veg patches: Barnsley House was once home to horticultural grande dame Rosemary Verey, and this particular potager was her passion. These days, it provides an abundance of rare varieties and generous pickings for the hotel's titular restaurant – a lovely room done out in olive-green shades. As you might expect, the cooking is clear-flavoured, vibrant and strictly seasonal, with chef Francesco Volgo adding ideas from his Italian homeland – celeriac lasagne with truffle and apple salad is typical, or you might begin with hand-dived scallops, parsnip purée, speck and radicchio. There's also room for some glorious classics such as ham hock terrine with homemade piccalilli or beef fillet with carrot purée, sprouting broccoli and peppercorn sauce, while puddings of vanilla custard cream or banana cake with honeycomb ice cream stay in the comfort zone. Cutely categorised wines ('old school', 'curve ball', etc) start at £24.
Chef/s: Francesco Volgo. **Meals:** main courses £16 to £32. Set L £29 (2 courses) to £32. **Details:** 40 seats. 20 seats outside. Bar. Parking. Music.

The Village Pub

Cooking score: 2
Modern British | £35
Barnsley, GL7 5EF
Tel no: 01285 740421
thevillagepub.co.uk

Standing proud at the heart of the village, this stone-built inn is a place everyone seems to fall in love with. The very image of a lovingly nurtured local hostelry, with its agreeable blend of rusticity and creature comforts, it's the dressed-down alternative to grown-up sibling The Potager at nearby Barnsley House (see entry). Food is a key part of the operation. A network of trusted suppliers provides much of the produce for seasonally inspired menus, and influences come from far and wide: there could be tomato caponata and bruschetta, as well as jellied ham and parsley terrine with piccalilli or a steamed bun filled with a soy-dressed shredded duck salad among starters. Mains range from Barnsley lamb chop with salsa verde to grilled salmon atop fregola with brown shrimp, bacon, Tenderstem broccoli and hollandaise sauce, while desserts span everything from apple crumble to hibiscus panna cotta. A short wine list opens at £23.
Chef/s: Francesco Volgo. **Meals:** main courses £16 to £22. **Details:** 65 seats. 42 seats outside. Bar. Parking. Music.

Cheltenham

★ TOP 50 ★

Le Champignon Sauvage

Cooking score: 8
Modern French | £70
24-26 Suffolk Road, Cheltenham, GL50 2AQ
Tel no: 01242 573449
lechampignonsauvage.co.uk

It's more than three decades since David and Helen Everitt-Matthias opened a neighbourhood restaurant in the Montpellier Quarter, and the continuing press of business speaks for itself. Bypass the compact bar in favour of the dining room, with its well-spaced white-clad tables and colourful artworks. Cooking is French in the modern manner – scrupulously seasonal, meticulously sourced and offered on a carte that gives little away. 'Fillet of Cornish mackerel, kohlrabi, avocado purée, caviar' may tell you the ingredients, but nothing about how the dish is put together. But the prosaic descriptions only add to the sense of adventure and that dish, as well as Dexter beef tartare with corned beef,

wasabi mayonnaise and pickled shimeji, has proven to be a punchy, exciting start. Visitors have also spoken well of a rich and flavoursome venison dish, served with parsnip purée, black pudding and a deep, bitter chocolate sauce, and of lamb (loin and sweetbreads) teamed with alliums and sheep's yoghurt. Desserts play on interesting combinations, as in mango and Thai-spiced cream with Thai green curry sorbet. Ancillaries – appetisers, petits fours, bread, the cheeseboard and so on – are determinedly good, lunch is considered a bargain and service is 'friendly and non-intrusive'. The wine list, notably strong in France, opens at £24.
Chef/s: David Everitt-Matthias. **Closed:** Mon, Tue, Sun, 2 weeks Dec to Jan, 3 weeks Jun. **Meals:** set L £28 (2 courses) to £70. Set D £55 (2 courses) to £70. **Details:** 38 seats.

Koj

Cooking score: 2
Japanese | £30
3 Regent Street, Cheltenham, GL50 1HE
Tel no: 01242 580455
kojcheltenham.co.uk
£30

Koj is what Andrew Kojima's closest friends get to call him, unless of course, you're referring to his small Japanese grazing room in the centre of town. The menu forsakes sushi and sashimi for more speculative takes on Japanese formats, with shiitake okonomiyaki, a bubble-and-squeak pancake lashed with sriracha mayonnaise and bonito flakes; aubergine glazed with spicy peanut miso; and donburi rice bowls topped with spicy pork mince, tofu and pickled greens. The traditional Japanese buns prove popular, and include a daring ox heart burger with tonkatsu mustard and mushrooms, while the bento sets make for much happy mixing and matching. Umami-rich miso finds its persistent way into the desserts, too, from the signature burnt white chocolate ice cream to sticky toffee pudding with miso butterscotch. Exciting cocktails should not be missed – the Okinawa

variant of an old fashioned brings in Evan Williams bourbon, PX sherry, shiso vinegar and bitters – and there are sakes and Japanese whiskies, as well as a functional wine selection from £5 a glass.
Chef/s: Andrew Kojima and Robin Stock. **Closed:** Mon, Sun. **Meals:** main courses £10 to £14. Bento £20. **Details:** 36 seats. Bar. Music.

Lumière

Cooking score: 5
Modern British | £70
Clarence Parade, Cheltenham, GL50 3PA
Tel no: 01242 222200
lumiere.cc
£5
OFF

Jon and Helen Howe's well-established restaurant wears its fine-dining credentials lightly. Cloths are white, crockery is immaculate and staff 'excellent, informed and professional'. Jon Howe's compact fixed-price menus bristle with modern ideas and between-course action, from snacks (including a very good kedgeree arancino with egg yolk and coriander) via home-baked breads to a pre-dessert of deconstructed carrot cake. One diner was underwhelmed by a dish of Orkney diver-caught scallops in which thinly sliced ox tongue didn't show enough contrasting texture or flavour, though celeriac crisp and cep jus compensated. Praise was poured on a meaty fillet of Newlyn dayboat cod, the sweetness of the fish accurately balanced by 'deliciously umami' cauliflower, salami, sea kale, fennel and black garlic. Cotswold woodland venison with crapaudine beetroot, Stilton, port and chervil tuber makes another superb main, while among desserts the soufflé – say damson with yoghurt, almond, muscovado and meadowsweet – is a favourite pick. The wine list offers plenty of well-chosen bottles from £18.
Chef/s: Jon Howe. **Closed:** Mon, Tue, Sun, 2 weeks Christmas, 2 weeks summer. **Meals:** set L £35. Set D £70. Tasting menu L £70 (6 courses) and D £90 (9 courses). **Details:** 24 seats. V menu. Music. Children over 8 yrs.

Set menus

If a set lunch (L) or dinner (D) is offered, this is indicated under 'Meals'. Prices are for a standard three-course meal unless otherwise specified.

Purslane

Cooking score: 5
Modern British | £41
16 Rodney Road, Cheltenham, GL50 1JJ
Tel no: 01242 321639
purslane-restaurant.co.uk

Since setting up shop in 2012, Gareth and Helena Fulford have proved that it's possible to create a genuinely classy neighbourhood restaurant without resorting to gimmicks or PR hype. Purslane is the best sort of local, a straightforward proposition offering comfort without overkill, keen service and a soundtrack reflecting the owners' personalities. As for the food, Gareth commits to local and regional produce – although his first love is seafood, which arrives in landlocked Cheltenham from Cornwall and elsewhere. The result is a roster of dishes that are precise, full-flavoured and harmonious but never over-fancy – perhaps hand-dived Orkney scallops with suckling pig belly, cauliflower and black pudding or a much-praised amalgam of monkfish, chervil root, sprouts, almonds and curry sauce. You'd also expect the titular (sea) purslane to put in an appearance, and sure enough it garlands a starter of Twisting Spirits gin-cured brill, monk's beard and sea kale. There's also room for land-based specialities such as a triumphant wintry combination of Cotswold hare, hay-baked celeriac, trompettes and chestnuts, while desserts such as Yorkshire rhubarb with yoghurt sorbet also follow the seasonal theme. A selection of around 50 global wines start at £22.

Chef/s: Gareth Fulford. **Closed:** Mon, Sun, last 2 weeks Jan, last 2 weeks Aug, 24 to 26 Dec. **Meals:** main courses £22. Set L £17 (2 courses) to £20. Set D £32 (2 courses) to £41. Tasting menu £60 (5 courses). **Details:** 34 seats. 4 seats outside. Music.

Eldersfield
The Butchers Arms

Cooking score: 4
Modern British | £41
Lime Street, Eldersfield, GL19 4NX
Tel no: 01452 840381
thebutchersarms.net

Mark and Jo-Anne Block are making 'a pretty good fist of things' since taking over this brick-and-tile 16th-century pub in the borderlands between Gloucestershire and Worcestershire. Their predecessors ran The Butchers Arms as a proper village local that just happened to serve fine food, and that's not about to change – so expect real ales and chatter in the beamed bar, plus 'confident and very assured cooking' along the lines of venison loin and croquette with red cabbage, celeriac purée and griottine cherries or line-caught Cornish cod and St Austell mussels accompanied by saffron sauce and sprouting broccoli. After that, the succinct daily menu offers up comforting desserts such as parkin cake with blood oranges, ice cream and warm spices. The introduction of 'incredibly good-value' midweek deals has also given the place a boost – judging by the high praise heaped on dishes such as baked sea bream with new potatoes, samphire and gooseberry compôte. The 'reasonably priced' wine list promises decent drinking from £23.50.

Chef/s: Mark Block. **Closed:** Mon, Tues, 26 Dec to 6 Jan. **Meals:** main courses £17 to £30. Set D Wed and Thu £21 (2 courses) to £25. **Details:** 30 seats. Bar. Wheelchairs. Parking. Children over 10 yrs.

Northleach
The Wheatsheaf Inn
Cooking score: 2
Modern British | £35
West End, Northleach, GL54 3EZ
Tel no: 01451 860244
theluckyonion.com

This stone-built former coaching inn has it all: country-chic good looks, well-chosen artwork, smouldering winter log fires, a fabulous terraced garden for summer drinks, all set in a one-time Cotswold wool town. With the accompanying laid-back vibe there's no wonder it draws a loyal crowd. Equally appealing is the modern repertoire of dishes to be found on seasonal menus that showcase the best local and regional ingredients. A meal in spring could bring classic devilled kidneys on toast or the signature twice-baked Cheddar soufflé with spinach and grain mustard. Next could be lemon sole with samphire, capers and beurre noisette or spiced lamb shoulder teamed with stewed chickpeas and mint yoghurt, with lemon posset, lemon curd and shortbread to finish. Other pluses are pizzas in the garden in summer and a vegan menu. The well-annotated wine list offers some impeccable choices, with 11 by the glass.
Chef/s: Peter McAllister. **Meals:** main courses £15 to £26. **Details:** 100 seats. 80 seats outside. Vg menu. Bar. Wheelchairs. Parking. Music.

Painswick
The Painswick
Cooking score: 4
Modern European | £40
Kemps Lane, Painswick, GL6 6YB
Tel no: 01452 813688
thepainswick.co.uk

A Palladian mansion that started life in the 18th century as Prospect House is, like many of the Cotswold stone-built homes in Painswick, built on wool money. Surrounded by Italianate gardens and with sweeping views, it's now a contemporary country house hotel with a well-appointed dining room – think parquet flooring, vibrant artwork on the walls, teal-blue leather chairs – and an appropriately elegant setting for chef Jamie McCallum's modern European cooking. The chef combines popular staples such as ribeye steak and triple-cooked chips with enticing seasonal dishes along the lines of a starter of Cornish crab teamed with avocado, blood orange, kohlrabi and brown crabmeat toast. To follow, try breast and faggot of Creedy Carver duck with chicory and January king cabbage, or beef wellington, dauphinois potatoes and buttered greens, before rounding off with lemon curd, greek yoghurt sorbet and meringue. Vegetarians and vegans are well catered for and the compact wine list opens at £25.
Chef/s: Jamie McCallum. **Meals:** main courses £7 to £28. Set L £21 (2 courses) to £25. Sun L £25.
Details: 60 seats. 25 seats outside. V menu. Vq menu. Bar. Parking. Music.

Paxford
The Churchill Arms
Cooking score: 2
British | £35
Paxford, GL55 6XH
Tel no: 01386 593159
churchillarms.co

'It was so gratifying on this pleasant Friday evening to see a mix of local drinkers, diners, kids out in the beer garden – it is the archetypal country pub.' So ran the notes of one visitor to Nick Deverell-Smith's 17th-century Cotswold stone inn. It stands opposite a church on the main road through the village and manages the mix of ancient and modern inside rather well: open plan with clean plastered walls, a bit of unadorned stonework, a flagstoned bar with a large, log-filled inglenook and wood-burner. Menus offer an eclectic mix of British traditional favourites (fish and chips, plus full-on Sunday lunch) with some global gatherings. Cornish sea trout with tom kha gai, pak choi and clams, and chicken kiev with purple sprouting broccoli and wild garlic show seasonal ingredients and flavour combinations that work. Or you could share a beef wellington with truffle mash. Apple pie and vanilla ice cream is a good way to finish. Drink regional ales or a glass from the global wine list (bottles from £19.50).

Chef/s: Nick Deverell-Smith. **Meals:** main courses £15 to £33. Sun L £25 (2 courses) to £30. **Details:** 60 seats. 45 seats outside. Bar. Wheelchairs. Music.

Selsley
The Bell Inn
Cooking score: 1
Modern British | £30
Bell Lane, Selsley, GL5 5JY
Tel no: 01453 753801
thebellinnselsley.com

This tastefully refurbished old stone inn sits high above the Woodchester Valley right in the heart of the Cotswolds. Here chef patron Mark Payne makes as much as he can in-house, from the bread to the ice cream, and although pub classics like beef burgers, and steak and triple-cooked chips please all-comers, it's the seasonal dishes that appeal most. A typical meal could open with venison Scotch egg served with chanterelles and pancetta crisp, and go on to slow-cooked pig's cheek with mustard mash and spinach. For dessert, try star anise pear tarte tatin with cinnamon ice cream. A kindly priced wine list opens at £17.

Chef/s: Mark Payne and Jack Dowdswell. **Meals:** main courses £13 to £19. **Details:** 55 seats. 40 seats outside. Bar. Wheelchairs. Parking. Music.

Local Gem
These entries are brilliant neighbourhood venues, delivering good, freshly cooked food at great value for money.

Southrop
The Swan at Southrop
Cooking score: 2
Modern British | £40
Southrop, GL7 3NU
Tel no: 01367 850205
theswanatsouthrop.co.uk

Back in the 17th century, this was a local watering hole for villagers and workers on the Southrop Farm Estate, but now The Swan is part of an 'English country destination' called Thyme, a complete hospitality package that includes a cookery school and spa, as well as accommodation spread across various cottages, outbuildings and converted barns. Casual eating and drinking take place in the rustic 'old bar', while more formal meals are served in a rustic-chic dining room with cosy corners, sofas, open fires and farmhouse furnishings. Produce and pickings from the 150-acre farm dictate a seasonal menu that's big on sustainability and 'slow food', from pheasant rillettes with sourdough to chalk stream trout accompanied by leek mash, spinach and dill cream. Italian flavours are also added to the mix in specialities such as crisp polenta with salt-baked turnip or rack of Cotswold lamb with cavolo nero and anchovy dressing. A short list of Old World wines starts at £20.

Chef/s: Matt Wardman. **Meals:** main courses £15 to £22. **Details:** 60 seats. 40 seats outside.

Stow-on-the-Wold
LOCAL GEM
The Old Butchers
British | £40
7 Park Street, Stow-on-the-Wold, GL54 1AQ
Tel no: 01451 831700
theoldbutchers.com

A stylish restaurant in a former butcher's shop seems an appropriate setting for Peter Robinson's seasonal nose-to-tail cooking, although seafood is given equal billing. Against a backdrop of retro prints and posters, choices run from Cornish oysters or Scottish langoustines to brasserie favourites of escalope of veal, capers, fried egg and hand-cut chips or local Todenham Manor Farm steaks cooked over charcoal. Service, led by Louise Robinson, is spot-on and there is a carefully curated wine list from £19.75.

▌Stroud

LOCAL GEM
The Woolpack Inn
British | £34
Slad Road, Stroud, GL6 7QA
Tel no: 01452 813429
thewoolpackslad.com

Artist Daniel Chadwick has brought a bohemian feel to Cotswold author Laurie Lee's favourite watering hole overlooking the bucolic Slad Valley. Enjoy a pint of local Clavell & Hind ale on the terrace in summer or settle into one of the three unspoilt rooms for no-frills seasonal dishes like devilled lamb's kidneys on toast, followed by Tamworth pork chop and Puy lentils or dhal, fried potatoes, green beans and yoghurt. Leave space for custard tart, rhubarb and clotted cream. Good by-the-glass wine selections supplement the well-kept beers and ciders.

▌Thornbury
Ronnie's of Thornbury
Cooking score: 2
Modern European | £45
11 St Mary Street, Thornbury, BS35 2AB
Tel no: 01454 411137
ronnies-restaurant.co.uk

Don't let the somewhat bleak pedestrianised shopping-precinct setting of this one-time schoolhouse dampen expectations – it's actually rather charming, and the cooking of chef owner Ron Faulkner modern and seasonal. The interior combines old and new to good effect with rustic stone walls and contemporary fittings, while the kitchen deals in classic European and British ideas with an eye to 21st-century tastes. Opening courses

run to slow-roasted pork belly with sticky maple sauce, or wild mushroom risotto enriched with Champagne and truffle oil. Among the enticing mains, Badminton Estate venison is matched with spiced pear and pickled parsnips, and sea bass with crab dumplings and seafood cream. There's a brace of tasting menus (with optional wine flights) and a keenly priced set lunch. Finish with vanilla panna cotta, pistachio crumb and blood orange. Half a dozen English fizzes add sparkle to the global wine list, with one available by the glass.
Chef/s: Ron Faulkner. **Closed:** Mon, Tue, 25 and 26 Dec, 1 to 12 Jan. **Meals:** main courses £20 to £27. Set L £18 (2 courses) to £23. Tasting menu L £29 (5 courses) and D £55 (6 courses). Sun L £25 (2 courses) to £29. **Details:** 72 seats. Wheelchairs. Music.

▌Upper Slaughter
The Atrium
Cooking score: 6
Modern British | £95
Lords of the Manor, Upper Slaughter, GL54 2JD
Tel no: 01451 820243
lordsofthemanor.com

A pristine oasis set in exceptional gardens, this former rectory wears its history lightly, teasing visitors with lush lawns and light-toned chic interiors before playing its trump card – two dining rooms. The headline act is The Atrium, where Charles Smith cooks in the present tense via an eight-course tasting menu. Dish descriptions are terse – perhaps 'marinated Orkney scallop, cider, apple, lime' – but there's no arguing with the technique or the commitment to harmonious seasonal pairings. English rose veal carpaccio is invigorated by anchovy, horseradish and crème fraîche; a dish of silky, deeply flavoured red mullet arrives topped with a thin layer of Espelette brioche and set in a bouillabaisse dotted with saffron-rich rouille and liver tapenade, while a single chop of herdwick lamb keeps company with spring greens, ewe's curd and confit pearl potatoes. To finish, an alliance of grapefruit, jasmine tea, lavender honey and bee pollen is a 'lovely balance', while Eton mess is reworked with white, wild and red strawberries, a meringue-coated basil sorbet with vanilla-rich chantilly cream and a strawberry and white balsamic syrup. The wine list puts the emphasis on pricey Bordeaux and Burgundy but has 15 wines by the glass from £10. The second restaurant, The Dining Room, offers a bistro-style à la carte every evening and at weekend lunchtimes. **Chef/s:** Charles Smith. **Closed:** Mon, Tue. **Meals:** tasting menu £95 (8 courses). **Details:** 14 seats. Bar. Wheelchairs. Parking. No children.

▋ Winchcombe

5 North Street

Cooking score: 5
Modern British | £54
5 North Street, Winchcombe, GL54 5LH
Tel no: 01242 604566
5northstreetrestaurant.co.uk

The gnarled beams and little bay windows of the façade fit the Ashenfords' high street restaurant snugly into its historical era, an impression reinforced when you step into the low-ceilinged, restricted but comfortable interior. It's been around since 2003, copiously supplied with local custom for the warmth of the approach and the fine-tuned modern British cooking at which Marcus Ashenford excels. Dishes may not always look the prettiest, but the resonant impact of their main ingredients booms through, hardly more so than in a starter plate of roasted ox tongue with celeriac, field mushrooms and braised onion in an umami-rich brown sauce. Salcombe crab offers a lighter intro, in a salad with mango jelly and lemongrass foam, before mains such as spiced monkfish with cheesy leeks, crisp capers and a red wine sauce, or rib and belly of old spot pork with a grilled fig and caramelised chicory in Madeira reduction. There's a nifty banoffee to finish, or else a more Med-influenced polenta and olive oil cake with pistachios and lemon meringue,

albeit partnered with flapjack ice cream. The wine list is a pleasing international miscellany at prices that don't stray out of double figures. **Chef/s:** Marcus Ashenford. **Closed:** Mon, 1 week Jan, 1 week Jun. **Meals:** set L £27 Wed to Sat (2 courses) to £32. Set D £55 Tue to Sat. Tasting menu £75 (7 courses). Sun L £38. **Details:** 26 seats. V menu. Music.

Wesley House

Cooking score: 1
Modern European | £30
High Street, Winchcombe, GL54 5LJ
Tel no: 01242 602366
wesleyhouse.co.uk
£5 OFF 🍴 £30 🍷

The setting may be a crooked-looking 15th-century merchant's house stuffed with ancient timbers, rugged stonework, mullioned windows and mighty inglenooks, but all is smart and cosy in the dining room of this personally run restaurant with rooms (named after Methodist minister and former guest John Wesley). Come here for accessible and dependable cooking in the European mould, from ham hock terrine with celeriac rémoulade to chargrilled chicken suprême on mushroom tagliatelle or pan-fried fillet of salmon with crushed new potatoes, baby leeks and dill cream sauce. Tuesday night is steak night, set menus are terrific value and the international wine list promises fairly priced drinking from £21 (£5.50 a glass). **Chef/s:** Cedrik Rullier. **Closed:** Mon, 26 Dec. **Meals:** main courses £16 to £35. Set L £15 Tue to Fri (2 courses) to £20. Set D £24 Tue to Fri (2 courses) to £28. **Details:** 60 seats. V menu. Vg menu. Bar. Music.

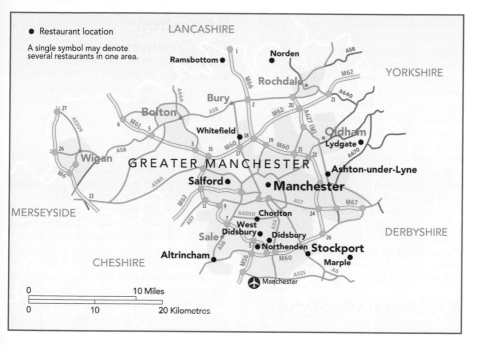

Altrincham

Porta

Cooking score: 2
Spanish | £22
50 Greenwood Street, Altrincham, WA14 1RZ
Tel no: 0161 465 6225
portatapas.co.uk
£30

Once a neglected town centre, Altrincham is now a lively destination, centred around a revived market. Food businesses like Porta are a powerful draw, and nimble service, laid-back environs and a pared-down list of good tapas dishes mean this one continues to thrive. Easy ways in include a plate of Zamorano sheep's milk cheese with quince, air-dried beef with pickled chillies or croquetas of the day. Follow with bavette steak, pickled walnuts, fennel seeds and chilli, or charred purple sprouting broccoli with almonds and a breathily rich romesco sauce. There are also king prawns cooked on the plancha, or happily messy chicken wings pimentón. To drink, you're looking at Spain; three whites, three reds and a rosé make a virtue of having a short, manageable list. As at its sister restaurants in Chester and Salford (see entries), no reservations are taken; when the market is buzzing, get in here quick.
Chef/s: Joaquim Nunes. **Closed:** Mon. **Meals:** tapas £3 to £10. **Details:** 60 seats. 24 seats outside. Music. No reservations.

Sugo Pasta Kitchen

Cooking score: 3
Italian | £29
22 Shaw's Road, Altrincham, WA14 1QU
Tel no: 0161 929 7706
sugopastakitchen.co.uk
£30

When nothing but pasta will do, the clatter of spoons and big busy tables lead inexorably to Sugo. The Altrincham original is a merry crush; the second branch, in Ancoats (46 Blossom Street, Manchester M4 6BF), is bigger but just as lively. The same menu is offered in both, anchored by fresh cavatelli, strozzapreti and orecchiette made in Puglia and dressed with bold, often chilli-spiked sauces. The house beef and pork ragù is a banker, and shell-on seafood combos like the cavatelli with mussels, baby squid and king prawns are messily satisfying. Authenticity may be a troubled concept, but Sugo's pasta certainly tastes like the real deal. The bits on the side have evolved since the early days, and pesto-stuffed arancini or mussels with bottarga are a good way to start. Salads like Sicilian fennel with orange, chicory, black olives and mint hit the spot, while dessert might be treacle tart or panna cotta with rhubarb. Limited Italian wines start at £13.50 by the carafe.

Chef/s: Anthony Slater. **Closed:** Mon, Sun. **Meals:** main courses £9 to £17. **Details:** 25 seats. 12 seats outside. No cash.

Ashton-under-Lyne

LOCAL GEM
Lily's Vegetarian Indian Cuisine
Indian vegetarian | £12
1 Dean Street, Ashton-under-Lyne, OL6 7DY
Tel no: 0161 339 4774
lilys-indian-vegetarian-cusine.business.site

£5 OFF £30

The move across the road has seen what was a pretty basic environment turn into a smart, contemporary restaurant, one with comfortable seating, vibrant colours and hand-painted murals. There's no shortage of choice for plant-based eaters, the long menu ranges from farsan, samosas, spicy lentil kachori or minted fried paneer to an array of filled dosas or uttapam, curries and sizzler plates. Flavours are vibrant, and accompaniments of coconut chutneys and mint yoghurts fresh and homemade. Few make it to dessert (a long list), so take out for later. It's now licensed so pair it all with wine or beer but you may prefer a mango lassi.

Chorlton
The Creameries
Cooking score: 2
British | £20
406 Wilbraham Road, Chorlton, M21 0UF
Tel no: 0161 312 8328
thecreameries.co.uk
£30

This former dairy now feels more like the kids' wing of an art gallery: plain walls and communal tables, greenery galore, and a huge blackboard with menu up top, childlike scribble below. In the kitchen, day-to-day duties have passed from Mary-Ellen McTague to Hannah Whelan but the ethos remains the same. Food is wholesome in the old-fashioned sense, with emphasis on the baker's oven and the cheesemaker's craft. Food isn't wasted, and you're never far from a ferment. By day, nourishment comes via split pea chips with mustard ketchup or goat's cheese with a beetroot fritter, pickled leek and duck egg, and an evening menu might add ricotta dumplings with broad beans and herb oil, mussels with cider, burnt butter and the house focaccia, or a big hot cheese to share. Simple, careful bakes like custard tart with seasonal fruit or flourless chocolate cake with fennel cream and fermented strawberry round things off. To drink, think cocktails or cordial.
Chef/s: Mary-Ellen McTague and Hannah Whelan. **Closed:** Mon. **Meals:** small plates £3 to £8. Large plates £14 to £16. **Details:** 40 seats. 20 seats outside. Bar. Wheelchairs. Music. No reservations.

Didsbury
Hispi
Cooking score: 3
Modern British | £50
1c School Lane, Didsbury, M20 6RD
Tel no: 0161 445 3996
hispi.net

Gary Usher's crowdfunding business model means that many customers come ready to love places like his Didsbury joint; after all, they helped to get it off the ground. But you don't have to be overly invested to appreciate a solid bistro in the suburbs, and with some 'dead clever' touches, that's what Hispi is. Readers report high satisfaction levels for dishes like a winter starter of stuffed, rolled lamb breast with baked swede or 'perfectly cooked' plaice with a light butter and caper sauce; for all the easy-going vibes, there's nothing slapdash about the cooking. The considered approach continues in dishes like roast lamb neck with a glazed Roscoff onion tart, courgette and mustard leaf pesto, and the house speciality is always a meaty braise with truffled chips. Puddings include a hard-to-beat custard tart, and the wine list is easy to like, from £22.

Chef/s: Gary Usher and Matt Fearnley. **Meals:** main courses £15 to £30. Set L £17 (2 courses) to £19. Set D £18 (2 courses) to £21. Sun L £25 (2 courses) to £29. **Details:** 84 seats. V menu. Vg menu. Wheelchairs. Parking. Music.

◼ Lydgate
The White Hart
Cooking score: 4
Modern British | £35
51 Stockport Road, Lydgate, OI4 4JJ
Tel no: 01457 872566
thewhitehart.co.uk
£5 OFF 🛏

Hugely popular hereabouts, this long-standing hostelry with stunning Pennine views suits all manner of occasions, from casual lunches to celebratory dinners. Mike Shaw's kitchen is bang on the money, offering an admirable mix of pub classics (calf's liver, smoked bacon, crispy onions and Cumberland sauce) alongside clever ideas for more inquisitive palates. Our meal in the cosy brasserie – log burner, bare tables, pale heritage green colours – celebrated seasonal British produce, from Wye Valley asparagus with a Parmesan-infused mayo-cum-hollandaise emulsion and (best dish of the meal) seared scallops with cubes of roast pork belly in an apple caramel XO sauce, to perfectly timed wild sea bass served with sweet mussels in a white wine velouté, wilted

spinach and Jersey Royals. Lemon posset with poached blueberries and creamy blueberry sorbet was a fitting finale. It's all backed up by really pleasant service. Drinks – including well-kept ales and a wide-ranging wine list – do their best to keep up with the food.
Chef/s: Michael Shaw. **Closed:** 26 Dec, 1 Jan. **Meals:** main courses £15 to £30. Set L £20 (2 courses) to £23. Sun L £28. **Details:** 95 seats. Wheelchairs. Parking. Music.

◼ Manchester
20 Stories
Cooking score: 3
Modern British | £55
No.1 Spinningfields, 1 Hardman Square, Manchester, M3 3EB
Tel no: 0161 204 3333
20stories.co.uk

As the city below carries on as usual, there have been changes at Manchester's swaggering restaurant in the sky. Aiden Byrne has departed to Restaurant MCR (see entry), chef-with-chops Brian Hughson has arrived and the grill has been subsumed into the restaurant. Diners now have the run of the glamorous indoor space, with better views as a result, and the menu encompasses grill, restaurant and 'homely classic' dishes. It's possible to get in and out for the price of a beef and onion pie (£14 and mighty) or to dally over well-conceived restaurant dishes with a nod to the seasons. Hughson puts asparagus on truffled brioche toast and serves it with Parma ham and a soft duck egg; wild garlic mayo may be a textural step too far, but the thinking is sound. Shetland cod with a sticky caper and raisin purée is showered (somewhat heavily, perhaps) with crisp pickled cauliflower. For pudding, head for dishes with an element of baking; thyme shortbread with a strawberry crème brûlée is very good indeed. The wine list, from £26, is all about bubbles, large formats and showing off.
Chef/s: Brian Hughson. **Meals:** main courses £12 to £55. Set L and early D £23 (2 courses) to £28. **Details:** 200 seats. 50 seats outside. Bar. Wheelchairs. Music.

Adam Reid at The French

Cooking score: 8
Modern British | £65
The Midland, 16 Peter Street, Manchester,
M60 2DS
Tel no: 0161 235 4780
the-french.co.uk

£5 OFF

Whatever praise you've heard of Adam Reid's glitzy city-centre restaurant, readers say, 'it really is that good'. It occupies an 'iconic room in an iconic Manchester building' – stories abound about the old days of both hotel and dining room, where Becks once took Posh. But under the stewardship of Reid and restaurant manager Kamilla Plonska's warm, capable front of house team, The French has evolved into a contemporary and stealthily luxurious space, dedicated to all the fun of good eating. Over four, six or nine courses, Reid demonstrates refined technique and a distinctive northern sensibility. Snacks such as whipped cod's roe on a squid ink cracker, dusted with paprika, are 'very convincing', while one of Reid's signatures, a take on beef tartare with tiny root veg dice and mushroom ketchup, served with beer bread and beefed-up butter, is 'entirely successful'. There's no arguing with the appeal of larger courses like smoked Gigha halibut with a seaweed butter sauce pinging with the acidity of baby capers, or Goosnargh duck with lentils and beetroot, the earthiness of the accompaniments balanced by sour cherry. The accomplished approach continues through cheese (perhaps Baron Bigod with walnut biscuit) to dessert; Reid has a sure hand here, with fruit a speciality in his own version of rhubarb and custard, or a delicate sugar 'easy peeler' shell containing white chocolate and sea buckthorn. The wine list, divided by grape, has plenty of interest, although some readers wish there were more half bottles.
Chef/s: Adam Reid. **Closed:** Mon, Sun, 1 week Dec, 2 weeks Aug. **Meals:** set L and D £65 (4 courses) to £90. **Details:** 48 seats. V menu. Bar. Wheelchairs. Music. Children over 8 yrs.

The Allotment

Cooking score: 2
Vegan | £30
18-22 Lloyd Street, Manchester, M2 5WA
Tel no: 0161 478 1331
allotmentvegan.co.uk

£30

By moving from Stockport to the heart of the city centre, the owners of this lower-ground-floor restaurant have brought its imaginative and beautifully presented plant-based dishes to a wider audience. The Allotment's five- and ten-course tasting menus provide a broad introduction to the style and ambition here, with weekday menus and sharing plates also on offer in the warehouse-style space. An inspection meal opened with a salad of delicate sweet, charred watermelon with cucumber dipped in sesame and pistachio paste, and cauliflower 'hot wings' coated in gram flour and paprika, deep-fried and served with a hot-sour chipotle and apple sauce. Next came thick-cut aubergine steaks with potato wedges and a creamy papaya corn sauce, and a celebration of mushrooms: charred king oyster, pan-fried shiitake and battered enoki. Service is knowledgeable and the short wine list offers some interesting bottles.
Chef/s: Adam Leavy. **Closed:** 25 and 26 Dec, 1 Jan. **Meals:** main courses £15. Set L £10 (2 courses) to £20. Set D £20. Tasting menu £40 (5 courses) to £65. Sun L £25. **Details:** 70 seats. V menu. Vg menu.

Dishoom

Cooking score: 2
Indian | £30
32 Bridge Street, Manchester, M3 3BT
Tel no: 0161 537 3737
dishoom.com

£30

In December 2018, the cavalcade of flavour, fragrance and informality that characterises Dishoom clattered joyously into trendy Spinningfields. A gracious former freemason's hall, customised with quirky references to 19th-century Irani Mumbai, provides the backdrop to extensive all-day street-food menus – designed for sharing. Couples, work colleagues and groups of friends reach across tables dipping warm buttered brioche into the mashed vegetable delights of pau bhaji or picking at crispy prawn koliwada and blackened ginger lamb chops. Service is amiable, and eating out here is more exuberant than elegant. A bracing salad of mint, broccoli, dates, chilli and lime perfectly balances hot, sweet and sharp, while creamy murgh malai renders chicken thighs rich from overnight spicing. Desserts offer alleged Indian twists on Eton mess or chocolate pud, although the kala khatta gola ice is a more intriguing chilli-salt take on fruit granita. On-theme cocktails, lassis and traditional sodas complement an accessible wine list. **Chef/s:** Naved Nasir. **Closed:** 25 and 26 Dec, 1 and 2 Jan. **Meals:** main courses £8 to £17. **Details:** 98 seats. 25 seats outside. Bar. Wheelchairs. Music.

El Gato Negro
Cooking score: 2
Spanish | £30
52 King Street, Manchester, M2 4LY
Tel no: 0161 694 8585
elgatonegrotapas.com
£30

It may not be the only tapas place in town, or even on King Street, but it sure beats the competition for buzz. That's partly because there are bars both downstairs and up, and partly due to the lively sense of appetite kindled by little dishes crossing the open kitchen counter. Owner Simon Shaw has continued his Iberian adventure by opening Portuguese restaurant Canto across the city in Ancoats, but the black cat is all about his take on Spain. Reliable charcuterie and cheeses (perhaps paired in a toasted, truffled 'bikini' sandwich) might kick things off, supplemented by salt cod croquetas with piquillo pepper purée and alioli, or hake with tomato, sherry and garlic sauce. Inventive veg dishes include smoked potatoes with caper,

shallot and parsley butter; roast cauliflower with fried chickpeas and shabu shabu dressing shows a gentle outside influence. Doughnuts with hot chocolate sauce are a favourite pud, and there's no shortage of Spanish wine. **Chef/s:** Antony Shirley. **Meals:** small plates £5 to £13. Set L £15. **Details:** 110 seats. 16 seats outside. Bar. Wheelchairs. Music.

Hawksmoor
Cooking score: 4
British | £60
184-186 Deansgate, Manchester, M3 3WB
Tel no: 0161 836 6980
thehawksmoor.com

A rare bird, one that combines complete and utter reliability with the frisson of a real treat. A clubby dining room nods heavily to the steakhouses of the past, especially at lunch, but there's no mistaking the modern approach to ingredients, sourcing and the seasons here. Oysters, Doddington Caesar salad or even old spot ribs are feasible starters, but the stars will always be classic cuts of steak, sold by weight, charred by highly skilled chefs and served with luxurious sides such as Stichelton hollandaise or macaroni cheese. A salted caramel Rolo, the filling balanced by a complex, fruity chocolate shell, is a great finish, or you can take a box away. Service here continues to be widely commended, and there's something special about being looked after by a team that, seemingly, really wants to be at work. Drinking starts in the bar, and the wine list is great fun even when, as can happen with the eminently appealing menu, readers end up going higher than planned. **Chef/s:** Szymon Szymczak. **Closed:** 25 and 26 Dec, 1 Jan. **Meals:** main courses £14 to £57. Set L and early/late D £26 (2 courses) to £29. **Details:** 137 seats. Bar. Wheelchairs. Music.

Indian Tiffin Room

Cooking score: 3
Indian | £23
2 Isabella Banks Street, Manchester, M15 4RL
Tel no: 0161 228 1000
indiantiffinroom.com
£5 OFF £30

Occupying a large contemporary space –
think exposed ducting meets spicy Indian
colours – this Deansgate eatery can generate
quite a hubbub when busy (which it usually
is). The street foods of southern India are the
mainstays of a menu that might entice you to
graze and share, but there's also plenty of
opportunity to keep a full-flavoured curry to
yourself. A host of dosas include masala and
chilli cheese versions, while more traditional
snacks of, say, idli vada stand alongside the
more outré chicken lollipops on the broad
menu. A platter of zingy puris is a good way to
start. Among the curries, methi mattar malai
is a veggie number fragrant with fenugreek,
and a fiery Rajastani-style lamb laal maas flies
the flag for India's north. A few noodle
options feature, thanks to the Chinese
influence in Kolkata. Drink appropriately
spicy cocktails, draught beers or lassis. There
are branches in Leeds and Cheadle.
Chef/s: Selvan Arulmozhi. **Closed:** 25 Dec, 1 Jan.
Meals: main courses £8 to £15. **Details:** 100 seats.
Vg menu. Bar. Wheelchairs. Parking. Music.

★ NEW ENTRY ★

Kala

Cooking score: 3
Modern British | £30
55 King Street, Manchester, M2 4LQ
Tel no: 0161 839 3030
kalabistro.co.uk
£30

In what used to be a branch of upmarket
clothing store Whistles, the sixth Gary Usher
bistro wears its sharpest city togs. The
crowdfunding king of the North West has
done it again, this time with a little chic; forest
green banquettes and an open kitchen frame a

pared-back mezzanine dining room with bar
below. Fans can seek and find signature
flavours – chicken liver parfait or feather blade
with truffle and Parmesan chips. But there's
room, too, for Brit bar snacks and punchy
openers like a plate of pickles or cauliflower
soup laced cleverly with shallots and lemon
oil. A generous hand (sometimes too
generous, at least with the salt) is at work in a
kitchen that turns out a series of good ideas;
pan-roast chicken with spices, onions and a
bracing lime pickle purée, or bream with roast
mussel cream and a tangle of fennel. Puddings
like parkin with butterscotch or a banoffee
choux bun kindle joyful abandon. Wine starts
at £2.50 for a lunch-hour-friendly 75ml
pour; reckon on £35 for plenty of choice by
the bottle.
Chef/s: Gary Usher and Jack Huxley. **Closed:** 25
and 26 Dec. **Meals:** main courses £15 to £30. Set L
and early D £20 (2 courses) to £23. **Details:** 90
seats. Vg menu. Bar. Wheelchairs. Music.

Lunya

Cooking score: 1
Spanish | £25
Barton Arcade, Deansgate, Manchester,
M3 2BB
Tel no: 0161 413 3317
lunya.co.uk
£5 OFF £30

Born of a genuine and unwavering love of
Spain, Peter and Elaine Kinsella's Catalan-
skewing tapas business sits above their
Deansgate deli wonderland. Meat, fish and
salads, perhaps a quartet of anchovies (for that
really deep dive into preserved fish), escalivada
or country pâté make their way up to the
dining room. From the kitchen, try deep-
fried aubergines with saffron yoghurt and
pickled chillies, chargrilled octopus with
potatoes, smoked paprika and sea salt, or the
signature Catalan hotpot. Feasty feelings are
catered for generously with paellas, suckling
pig (order ahead) and grilled meat platters.
The Spanish wine selection is extensive.

Chef/s: Jon Daley. **Closed:** 25 Dec, 1 Jan.
Meals: tapas £5 to £23. Set L £11 (2 courses) to £15.
Set D £15 (2 courses) to £22. **Details:** 142 seats. 20
seats outside. V menu. Bar. Wheelchairs. Music.

★ NEW ENTRY ★

Mana
Cooking score: 5
Modern British | £105
42 Blossom Street, Manchester, M4 6BF
Tel no: 0161 392 7294
manarestaurant.co.uk

Compelled by a devotion to the natural and
the Nordic, Simon Martin's complex food is
served in the unlikely environs of a spanking-
new Ancoats block. The centre of a spare (some
might say sterile) modern dining room is the
exposed island kitchen, from which chefs
deliver a quickfire menu of earthy trompe
l'oeil snacks and produce-forward bigger
dishes. Texture is masterfully balanced, with
hits including melting yakitori eel with
roasted yeast, and a cabbage-wrapped oyster
with miso fudge. It's rather an earnest
endeavour, but the violent-looking steak
knife offered with a plate of barbecued greens
(rubbed with – what else? – dehydrated
scallops and beeswax) raises a smile as well as
pointing out that this clever dish packs a meaty
punch. In winter, the headline dessert is
reindeer moss coated in mulled wine
chocolate with a pool of whisky eggnog for
dipping; fans of crispy chocolate nests will be
in their element. It is, frankly, a tough ask for
any drinks list to keep up; try dipping in and
out of the wine or beer pairings instead.
Chef/s: Simon Martin. **Closed:** Mon, Tue, Sun.
Meals: tasting menu L £50 (7 courses) and D £105
(10 courses). **Details:** 32 seats. V menu. Bar.
Wheelchairs. Music.

Refuge by Volta
Cooking score: 2
International | £30
Oxford Street, Manchester, M60 7HA
Tel no: 0161 233 5151
refugemcr.co.uk

🛏 💷30

A doozy as hotel restaurants go: fabulously
turned out, undemanding of its customers and
absolutely of its place. In a proud city, this
refurbed insurance building is a proud
achievement, no tiling is left unpolished, no
grand architectural gesture unacknowledged.
Putting two relatively untested Mancs – the
owners of West Didsbury's Volta (see entry) –
in charge of the dinners was a bold move that
has, broadly, paid off. Entered through the bar,
adjoining games room or gorgeous winter
garden, the dining room plays host to a small
plates menu buzzing with global influences.
Meaty 'voltini' might be the much-loved
spiced lamb flatbread with pomegranate and
mint, slow-cooked beef short rib with red
wine or tamarind-glazed chicken wings, but
lighter options abound. Try fattoush with
beetroot, cucumber and sumac, perhaps.
Desserts include knickerbocker glory and a
chocolate fondue to share. A simple wine list
covers most bases, and customers looking for
an off-list cocktail are urged to 'Speak to us. We
are nice.'
Chef/s: Ian Worley. **Meals:** small plates £6 to £11.
Details: 120 seats. V menu. Vg menu. Bar.
Wheelchairs. Music.

Restaurant MCR
Cooking score: 5
Modern British | £50
Tower 12, 18-22 Bridge Street, Manchester,
M3 3BZ
Tel no: 0161 835 2557
restaurantmcr.com

A high-stakes game of musical tower blocks
recently saw Aiden Byrne depart what was
Manchester House to launch nearby 20
Stories; now he's back in this, his former gaff,
rechristened Restaurant MCR. Readers think

Byrne's return 'feels right', especially as he's serving dishes that are 'belting', 'interesting' and 'clever'. Service has been gently formalised, and tasting menus rule, with the three-course lunch lifted from the longer versions. There might be a warm salad of Jerusalem artichokes and mushrooms, a likeable exercise in sweet, sour and earthiness with a punchy broth poured at the table. Meatier intent comes from braised beef short rib with tartare, draped with a slice of fatty, farmyardy cured secreto, bold in its lack of greens. To finish, an elegant apple pithivier with layers of frangipane and custard is a successful new dish. Drinkers will note that the old Manchester House bar, with its swaggering views, has not been reinstated. The wine list, from £26 with a few surprises, is served at the expansive tables.
Chef/s: Aiden Byrne. **Closed:** Mon, Sun. **Meals:** set L £35. Tasting menu £50 (6 courses) to £75. **Details:** 82 seats. V menu. Bar. Wheelchairs. Music.

★ NEW ENTRY ★

The Spärrows
Cooking score: 3
Central European | £15
Unit 3 Mirabel Street, Manchester, M3 1PJ
Tel no: 07711 300116
thesparrows.me
£30

Named after the birdlike shapes formed when spätzle batter hits hot water, this charming endeavour is fittingly small and delicately white. It's tucked away on a street that would be unremarkable without the presence of Umezushi (see entry) in the arches opposite, whose owners recently refurbed the kitchen here. Sake supplier Kasia Hitchcock and chef Franco Concli took it on, and the rest is spätzle – and pierogi, pelmeni, freshly cut pasta and chunks of pillowy focaccia. Mix and match sauces go with gnocchi or the light but uniquely comforting 'sparrows'. Chorizo with tomatoes, spinach and cream is salty and silky, but the trad option is 'käse', with Emmental, Gruyère and braised onion. Handmade pierogi with a potato and cheese filling, pan-

hot, fluffy and scattered with buttery onions are testament to the kitchen's dumpling-producing abilities. The dessert list is short, but an Earl Grey panna cotta with marmalade syrup is an elegant way to finish – alongside excellent sake or high-end Japanese tea.
Chef/s: Franco Concli. **Closed:** Mon. **Meals:** main courses £6 to £18. **Details:** 12 seats.

★ NEW ENTRY ★

Tast
Cooking score: 3
Spanish | £40
20-22 King Street, Manchester, M2 6AG
Tel no: 0161 806 0547
tastcatala.com

Football finance doesn't always bode well for restaurants, but between them City manager Pep Guardiola and much-admired chef Paco Pérez have created a Catalan restaurant with purity of vision and great tomato bread. Two chic but rather spare spaces (ground-floor bar kitchen with window tables, and a dining room above) form this King Street temple to small bite 'tramuntanades' and larger 'tastets'. While there's a tendency for dishes to sound more thrillingly avant-garde than they are, there's undeniable skill, and the crockery (formed into hollowed-out aubergines and outlandish octopi) is rather wonderful. Textbook croquetas might combine hot oil wizardry with the comfort of roast chicken, while cauliflower comes glazed with funky Bauma cheese, and octopus with a riot of red and green mojo sauces and tiny, crisply wrinkled potatoes. Trays of Catalan rice, perhaps with prawns, squid and seaweed mayo, are an appealing centrepiece, but wildly overpriced. We're hearing good early reports about the elaborate Enxaneta tasting menu served upstairs, and if you like regional Spanish wine, you're in the right place.
Chef/s: Miguel Villacrosa. **Closed:** Mon, 25 and 26 Dec, 1 and 2 Jan. **Meals:** main courses £19 to £49. Set L £18. Tasting menu £42 (6 courses) to £60. **Details:** 120 seats. 10 seats outside. Bar. Wheelchairs. Music.

Umezushi

Cooking score: 4
Japanese | £40
4 Mirabel Street, Manchester, M3 1PJ
Tel no: 0161 832 1852
umezushi.co.uk

In a city with its fair share of fancy, fiddly and fashionable sushi, this under-the-arches gem is where readers go for the good stuff. Its more unconventional characteristics – the modest location, an executive chef who's not Japanese – belie solid knife skills, a consistent focus on quality and a menu that can hardly fail to please. Beautifully cut sashimi, fat temaki, super-safe veggie hosomaki and traditional nigiri are joined by a blackboard of hot specials – hamachi head or tuna and chickpea curry, perhaps. Among the rice bowls, high rollers could do a lot worse than the special kaisen-don, loaded with fish and seafood. Worthwhile sides include a rainbow pickle platter, steaming, silky chawan mushi and plain old miso soup. It's all delivered by a warm, laid-back front of house team. With just 18 seats, capacity is limited, booking essential and dinner a rare treat (although you can also take away for lunch Wednesday to Friday). Celebrate scoring a seat with fish-friendly wine or sake.
Chef/s: Omar Rodriguez Marrero. **Closed:** Mon, Tue, 23 to 30 Dec, 29 Jun to 25 Jul. **Meals:** sushi £4 to £12. Sushi platters £16 to £60. Tasting menu £64 (6 courses). **Details:** 18 seats. Wheelchairs. Deposit required.

★ NEW ENTRY ★

Wood

Cooking score: 3
Modern British | £48
Jack Rosenthal Street, Manchester, M15 4RA
Tel no: 0161 236 5211
woodmanchester.com
£5
OFF

Urban but cosy, big but friendly, Simon Wood's restaurant is all about putting fine dining in the city and doing it at scale. An open kitchen lines one wall, comfortable booths take up the other, and with readers reporting 'service excellent', it's an easy place to be. At its best, Wood's food is flavour-forward and packed with interest, as in a mushroom raviolo plated on a hearty mushroom stew, or a main course of just-right Anjou squab with the bird's tiny heart at the centre and salty bacon butty bread sauce to bring it together. Diners 'really do wonder' about value for money on main-course dishes that top out at £35, although little touches – Pollen Bakery bread and a couple of intensely savoury snacks – go some way to compensate. Puddings like a mirror-shiny take on tiramisu or moulded white chocolate 'honeycrisp' apple taste more straightforward than they look. Wines are strongest in the medium range, but start at £25.
Chef/s: Simon Wood. **Closed:** Mon, Sun, 25 Dec. **Meals:** main courses £18 to £35. Set L and early D £23 (2 courses) to £28. Tasting menu £49 (5 courses) to £99. **Details:** 80 seats. Bar. Wheelchairs. Music.

Yuzu

Cooking score: 2
Japanese | £21
39 Faulkner Street, Manchester, M1 4EE
Tel no: 0161 236 4159
yuzumanchester.co.uk
£30

Innovation is great, but have you tried the chicken karaage at Yuzu? This Japanese stalwart of Manchester's Chinatown was changing guard in the kitchen when we went to press, but there's not much that needs fixing. Wooden benches and tables are ranged around a semi-open kitchen. Edged with a battalion of empty sake bottles (if you want booze here, it's mainly sake), it produces a comfortable range of compellingly fried starters, soups, katsu, sashimi and tempura, with the odd special – try tuna tataki – on the blackboard. A starter of agedashi tofu is subtle with its thin transparent jacket and inch of broth; yakitori chicken is juicy and properly charred, the blackened spring onion just as good as the meat. Mains might be tempura kishimen, flat wheat noodles in a delicate broth with prawn and vegetable tempura on the side and scraps of batter floating crunchily in the soup. Service is brisk without being relentless, and the soundtrack is of ever-rolling jazz.

Chef/s: Yui Nagami. **Closed:** Mon, Sun, 2 weeks Christmas, 2 weeks Aug. **Meals:** main courses £8 to £20. **Details:** 26 seats. Music.

Albert Square Chop House
British | £30
The Memorial Hall, Albert Square, Manchester, M2 5PF
Tel no: 0161 834 1866
albertsquarechophouse.com

£5 OFF 🍷 £30

Lodged in the confines of the Victorian Memorial Hall at the pulsing heart of the city, the Chop House offers all-day brasserie dining to a smart city crowd. Sharing roasts of beef rib, rump cap and whole Goosnargh chicken hark back to the restauration of centuries past, and you can top and tail them with plates of smoked salmon or chicken liver pâté with quince jam, and an excursion into the British pudding repertoire such as steamed marmalade sponge with proper custard. To cap it all off is an exemplary wine list arranged by style. Covering the major regions of western Europe, the southern hemisphere and the Americas, it is a generous choice in both scope and pricing. A selection by the glass comes in three sizes, the standard measure starting at £5 for a roast-friendly Australian Shiraz.

The Pasta Factory
Italian | £24
77 Shudehill Street, Manchester, M4 4AN
Tel no: 0161 222 9250
pastafactory.co.uk

£30

Resolutely unfancy and none the worse for it, this carby haven on the fringes of the Northern Quarter is driven by a

straightforward love of Italian food. The pasta specialism doesn't feel like a narrowing of options. Choices like the one between spaghetti with saffron, courgettes and scamorza or black bucatini with broccoli, anchovy and fried mussels can seem agonising. Vegans do well with Sicilian chickpea fritters and truffled mushroom ravioli, while a quartet of Italian cocktails offers fortification for £7 and under.

TNQ
Modern British | £33
108 High Street, Manchester, M4 1HQ
Tel no: 0161 832 7115
tnq.co.uk

£5 OFF

Occupying the ground floor of a typically Mancunian red-brick corner plot opposite the historic old fish market and with floor-to-ceiling windows, this stalwart of the famed Northern Quarter has a pared-back, utilitarian look in keeping with its location. A warm welcome, wide-ranging menus and genuine good value are what to expect here. Coastal cheddar and onion soup with chive oil, cheese crisp and burnt onion powder might begin a meal that continues with a stew of market fish and shellfish with langoustine bisque, wilted greens and aïoli, and ends with lemon and almond polenta cake with lemon sorbet and lemon posset. Wines from £18.

Wine list
🍾 Restaurants showing this symbol have a wine list that our experts consider to be outstanding, either for its in-depth focus on a particular region, attractive margins on fine wines, or strong selection by the glass.

▌Marple

LOCAL GEM

Chaat Cart

Indian | £27

13-15 Derby Way, Marple, SK6 7AH
Tel no: 0161 427 8234
chaatcart.co.uk

£30

Readers speak highly of this 'unique offering' in a small town a few miles from Stockport. It's warm and welcoming, with a vibrant yet cosy interior and tasteful nods to the owner's Indian heritage, the menu built around south Indian street food – bold, vibrant small plates of bhel puri, maach masala, slow-cooked goat, and pork uttapam. There's praise for Keralan sea bream baked whole with a tamarind, chilli and lime sauce, onion and kale bhajia, roasted bone marrow roti and 'fantastic' service. Drink cocktails or spice-friendly wines.

▌Norden

Nutters

Cooking score: 2
Modern British | £40
Edenfield Road, Norden, OL12 7TT
Tel no: 01706 650167
nuttersrestaurant.com

Set in peaceful grounds in the hills just outside Rochdale, this converted manor house has been home to a hospitality dynasty since 1993. Chef patron Andrew Nutter, who now runs the eponymous restaurant with his mother, Jean, is a flamboyant local hero whose services to the community go beyond simply feeding them generously. But feed them he does, with the good stuff: Lancashire cheese, Goosnargh duck and Eden Valley beef. Menus have an unashamed retro streak – a starter of melon with Champagne granita is not unheard of – but an understanding of produce and flavour is evident in dishes like lamb loin with rhubarb chutney and goat's curd, or beef feather blade with onion and pancetta fricassée and crispy kale. To finish, carefully chosen

cheese comes with a warm Eccles cake, or try crème brûlée with a poached pear. The bar and lounge keep evolving, but the hefty wine list is a lasting tribute to the vinous passions of the late Rodney Nutter.

Chef/s: Andrew Nutter. **Closed:** Mon, 25 to 27 Dec, 1 and 2 Jan. **Meals:** main courses £25 to £27. Set L £20 (2 courses) to £23. Tasting menu £48 (6 courses), Sun L £28. **Details:** 160 seats. V menu. Bar. Wheelchairs. Parking. Music.

▌Northenden

LOCAL GEM

Mi & Pho

Vietnamese | £25

384 Palatine Road, Northenden, M22 4FZ
Tel no: 0161 312 3290
miandpho.com

£5 OFF £30

Hung with paper lanterns, this no-nonsense café is brisk and buzzy by day, cosier by night. It serves an enviable range of Vietnamese classics – fat summer rolls, noodles and salads – in which freshness marries with comfort, plus specials like a hunk of pork belly in a light but flavourful broth of coconut water and pandan leaf. Locals love getting plenty of banh mi for their buck, with portions generous, prices low and corkage modest.

▌Ramsbottom

Baratxuri

Cooking score: 2
Spanish | £35
1 Smithy Street, Ramsbottom, BL0 9AT
Tel no: 01706 559090
levanterfinefoods.co.uk

A convincing slice of northern Spain with counter seating and cramped tables, this tiny, deeply endearing offspring of Levanter (see entry) attracts hordes of ravenous fans – booking is essential. Opening proceedings are simple, to-the-point pintxos, listed on a blackboard or displayed on the counter, delivering punchy flavours. It's hard to choose from exemplary renditions of gambas a la plancha, fideuá negra (paella-style pasta with squid ink), Ibérico pig's cheek cooked in red wine and sherry, or patatas with salsa verde. But it's the wood-fired oven that forms the nerve centre, and much is made of the standout roasted lemon sole, the whole salt-baked sea bass, or new season's Segovian suckling spring lamb – all for two to share. Finish with baked cheesecake with Pedro Ximénez-soaked raisins or dark chocolate and rosemary mousse. A likeable Spanish wine list opens at £19.

Chef/s: Rachel Stockley. **Closed:** Mon, Tue.
Meals: small plates £4 to £29. Sharing plates £26 to £50. **Details:** 24 seats. Bar. Wheelchairs. Music.

Levanter

Cooking score: 3
Spanish | £30
10 Square Street, Ramsbottom, BL0 9BE
Tel no: 01706 551530
levanterfinefoods.co.uk
£30

This split-level spot may lack elbow room, but the food certainly packs a punch, for pocket-sized Levanter is dedicated to 'consistently excellent and innovative tapas'. Sharing platters of hand-carved Ibérico ham, croquetas of salt cod, and chorizo cooked with tomatoes in honey and sherry vinegar should charge up the appetite for the likes of chilindrón – a roasted red pepper stew with pheasant, partridge, mallard and rabbit – or Ibérico pig's cheeks cooked in Rioja and served with butter bean mash. Frito Mallorquín (diced lamb's liver with fried peppers and onions) has impressed, as have chickpeas with spinach, egg, garlic and cumin seeds. The fish plates are no less enticing – plump whole gambas cooked on the plancha, say, or sea bass fillet with salsa verde, and a classic pulpo a la Gallega. Drinks are fun, too, from glasses of sherry, sangría or Spanish artisan beers to reliable Spanish wines from £18.

Chef/s: Yvonne Lumb. **Closed:** Mon, Tue.
Meals: tapas £5 to £16. **Details:** 24 seats. Wheelchairs. Music.

▌Salford

★ NEW ENTRY ★

Porta

Cooking score: 2
Spanish | £25
216 Chapel Street, Salford, M3 6BY
Tel no: 0161 459 7854
portatapas.co.uk
£30

First Chester, then Altrincham (see entries), now Salford; the Porta model – good tapas, just enough vermouth, minimum of fuss – can certainly travel. On the Costa del Salford, a mere five minutes from Manchester, there's more space to spread out – in an old bank with its parquet floor and wood panelling still intact. If the parliamentary green scheme looks dour and rather hastily done, the double-height space (eat downstairs or up on the mezzanine), echoing to the sound of The Smiths, has its own quiet drama. The menu is pretty much word for word across the group, so settle in for some acknowledged hits, including wonderfully assertive Picos de Europa blue drenched in honey, airy croquetas (perhaps flavoured with sobrasada) in a crisp, friable shell, great bread and good plain tortilla, oozing even when just a shade too cold. Don't walk away from the modest-looking chocolate mousse, topped with a good inch of golden honeycomb crumb. Sip iced vermouth or crisp manzanilla from an all-Spanish drinks list that takes in a clutch of wines, beers and spirits.

Chef/s: Mihai Dan Muzas. **Closed:** 25 Dec to 1 Jan.
Meals: tapas £4 to £10. **Details:** 60 seats. 30 seats outside. Bar. Music. No reservations.

▌Stockport

★ TOP 50 ★

Where The Light Gets In
Cooking score: 7
British | £90
7 Rostron Brow, Stockport, SK1 1JY
Tel no: 0161 477 5744
wtlgi.co

Ambition doesn't always taste good. Since opening in 2017, Sam Buckley's ex-warehouse destination has edged closer to that sweet spot where a kitchen's esoteric adventures produce food that sparks joy. This year, the team has comprehensively cracked it. It's a good job really since dinner can run to 17 no-choice courses, payment is in advance and accessibility is not a strong suit – so there's a need for goodwill. It's conjured through a carefully timed tumult of bright seasonal veg, brilliant ideas, bang-on technique and a sense of real possibility. Produce from WTLGI farm stars on many plates, including a palate-resetting first course of very baby vegetables with a shallow pool of nutty farm honey, complete with kombucha to sip through a sweet cicely straw. Technique quickly gathers pace as the menu rolls through toasty potato poppadoms with blood orange and rhubarb chutney; a loose, silky take on chawan mushi with scallop, soy and crunchy asparagus; and a steamed Carlingford oyster with cherry mead and leek oil. Subtle greenery (a sorrel soup, or kefir curd with more asparagus and herbs) contrasts with big-hitting courses, which include DIY lettuce wraps with pig's head, pickles, fish sauce and 'old bread' miso dressing, or heritage potatoes cooked in crab stock with a gorgeously ruddy crab soup. Bread and desserts are pitch perfect, with aged butter adding a savoury flake to the pastry in a Bakewell pudding. Sour-sweet, long-caramelised whey is drizzled over sheep's milk frozen yoghurt, served, in a rare moment of knowing pretension, from the churn. Juice and wine pairings are available alongside a short selection of natural-skewing wines with an in-built element of zesty challenge.

Chef/s: Samuel Buckley and Joseph Otway. **Closed:** Mon, Tue, Sun, 2 weeks Sept. **Meals:** Sat L £65 (8 courses). tasting menu £90 (12 courses). **Details:** 30 seats. Music. No children. Pre-payment required.

LOCAL GEM
Bombay to Mumbai
Indian | £25
10 Fir Road, Bramhall, Stockport, SK7 2NP
Tel no: 0161 439 0055
bombaytomumbai.co.uk
£5 OFF £30

'Everything you want from a neighbourhood restaurant,' notes a reader who loves everything about this hospitable, reasonably priced Indian. At weekends, you can lunch on Mumbai-style 'breakfast' snacks such as medu vada (spiced lentil doughnuts), but there are ample riches on the main menu too: textbook bhel puris, Indo-Chinese chilli chicken and lai bhari (a mild, creamy dish of lamb or chicken pointed up with peanuts, tamarind and jaggery), plus sweet delights including a well-matched combo of kulfi and falooda. Drink bottled Bombay Bicycle Ale.

▌West Didsbury
Indique
Cooking score: 2
Indian | £25
110-112 Burton Road, West Didsbury, M20 1LP
Tel no: 0161 438 0241
indiquerestaurant.co.uk
£5 OFF £30

Despite the arrival of a new head chef as the Guide went to press, Indique retains a strong sense of purpose – to lead the field of local Indian restaurants and to do it with elegance. At the table, slates and cloches are part of the deal, but slightly fussy presentation does 'nothing to detract' from the quality of regional dishes. Readers rate the precisely cut Indo-Chinese chilli paneer with green chilli and soy, or crisp bhel puri with a polite (but effective) tamarind sauce. To follow,

Hyderabadi lamb dalcha with lentils is 'rich yet earthy, absolutely bang on', while the tomato sauce that turns lamb chops into laal maas is tweaked to suit each customer's taste. A dessert of mango and pistachio kulfi is 'another success'. Overall, readers have 'such a nice time' here that they can't resist telling us about it.
Chef/s: N Singh. **Meals:** main courses £7 to £17. **Details:** 92 seats. 12 seats outside. Wheelchairs.

The Lime Tree

Cooking score: 3
Modern British | £32
8 Lapwing Lane, West Didsbury, M20 2WS
Tel no: 0161 445 1217
thelimetreerestaurant.co.uk

'We keep coming back here because it ticks all the boxes as a local restaurant', notes a regular who appreciates everything about this long-running West Didsbury trouper. Staff are always 'friendly and efficient', value for money is never in doubt (especially if you opt for one of the set menus) and the kitchen puts its faith in local and seasonal ingredients – the owners even have a 20-acre smallholding that yields supplies of rare breed pork, lamb and other good things. Flavoursome well-aged steaks are 'accurately cooked as requested', hake is given 'butch' Spanish treatment with roasted peppers, aïoli, patatas bravas and chorizo, while Goosnargh duck breast keeps company with Yorkshire rhubarb, wilted kale and rösti. More nibbles and vegetarian dishes have been added to the repertoire and the sweet-toothed are well served – thick, creamy rice pudding with Armagnac-steeped prunes, for instance. The savvy wine list picks up inspired selections from small producers and big names worldwide, creates interest with its 'monthly highlights' and offers tremendous value across the board; house selections start at £18.
Chef/s: Jason Parker and David Hey. **Closed:** Mon, 25 and 26 Dec, first week Jan. **Meals:** main courses £15 to £20. Set L £15 (2 courses) to £18. Set D £19 Tue to Thur (2 courses) to £22. Sun L £19 (2 courses) to £22. **Details:** 70 seats. 30 seats outside. Bar. Wheelchairs. Music.

Menu? What menu?

You'd think a menu was a given but some chefs are chucking out the rulebook and keeping their dishes under wraps until they reach the table

At **Food by John Lawson** in Leigh-on-Sea, the titular chef creates four courses that reflect what's best that day. A delightful spring meal included asparagus, young peas and foraged wild garlic combined into thoughtful, tasty dishes. It's the same for Sam Buckley at Stockport's much-fêted **Where The Light Gets In,** who says he wants to connect with 'weather patterns, sea conditions and the earth's response' when compiling his 12-course no-choice taster.

'If you don't like surprises, then this is not the place for you' says the chef patron of **Menu Gordon Jones** of his idiosyncratic Bath restaurant where artistic plates of food stream from the kitchen unfettered by a menu, but with plenty of excitement – maybe haddock with chorizo crisps or Muscat grape parfait partnered by Tokaji jelly. At **Winteringham Fields** in Lincolnshire, it's all about the unexpected: Colin McGurran selects tiptop produce from his smallholding to create an eight-course Surprise Menu that changes pretty much daily. Take a dive into the delicious unknown.

LOCAL GEM

Volta
International | £30
167 Burton Road, West Didsbury, M20 2LN
Tel no: 0161 448 8887
voltafoodanddrink.co.uk

£30

Established in 2013 and still effortlessly cool, this is the small suburban spot that spawned city restaurant Refuge (see entry). Out in West Didsbury, the small plates keep spinning, and globetrotting dishes that can never leave the menu include deep-fried Monte Enebro goat's cheese with honey; smoked feta with beetroot, hazelnut and dill; and lamb shawarma with yoghurt and harissa. The wine list is as flexible as the menu; finish the carafe on the lively pavement terrace.

Sweet indulgences include raspberry and white chocolate cheesecake in raspberry coulis. Glasses of wine start at £4.50.
Chef/s: David Gale. **Closed:** 26 to 28 Dec, 1 and 2 Jan. **Meals:** main courses £16 to £18. **Details:** 75 seats. 20 seats outside. Bar. Wheelchairs. Parking. Music.

■ Whitefield

One Eighty Eight
Cooking score: 2
Modern British | £30
188 Bury New Road, Whitefield, M45 6QF
Tel no: 0161 280 0524
one88whitefield.co.uk

£5 OFF   £30

'Been to many parties upstairs in the function room,' sighs a reader in tales-I-could-tell mode, who has also enjoyed everything from brunch to dinner at David Gale's invaluable local suburban resource. A clean wood-lined interior makes a relaxed setting for unbuttoned brasserie food with unabashed populist instincts. Chicken and bacon Caesar salad or a spiced grilled vegetable wrap with curried mayo are among the salad and sandwich options, if you're not minded to head straight into the main menu of roasted scallops with black pudding and chorizo, followed perhaps by a majestic preparation of sea bass with shaved fennel, crushed new potatoes, samphire and salsa verde, or one of the plethora of steak possibilities. Get there early for Sunday roasts, which are provided on a WIGIG (when it's gone, it's gone) basis.

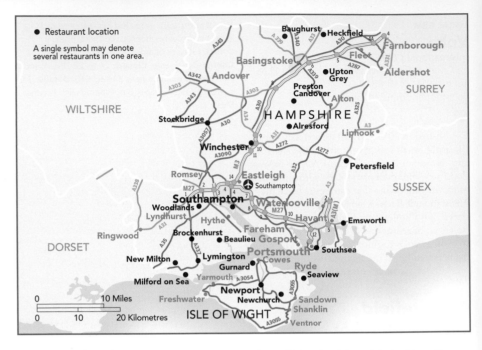

- Restaurant location

A single symbol may denote several restaurants in one area.

WILTSHIRE

Baughurst
Heckfield
Farnborough
Basingstoke
Fleet
Aldershot
Andover
Upton Grey
Preston Candover
SURREY
Alton
HAMPSHIRE
Stockbridge
Alresford
Liphook
Winchester
Romsey
Petersfield
Eastleigh
Southampton
SUSSEX
Southampton
Waterlooville
Woodlands
Lyndhurst
Havant
Hythe
Emsworth
Ringwood
Brockenhurst
Fareham
Beaulieu
Gosport
DORSET
Portsmouth
Southsea
New Milton
Lymington
Cowes
Gurnard
Ryde
Yarmouth
Seaview
Milford on Sea
Newport
0   10 Miles
Freshwater
Newchurch
Sandown
0   10   20 Kilometres
ISLE OF WIGHT
Shanklin
Ventnor

▌Alresford

Pulpo Negro

Cooking score: 4
Spanish | £30
28 Broad Street, Alresford, SO24 9AQ
Tel no: 01962 732262
pulponegro.co.uk

£5 OFF   £30

It was the tail end of 2014 when Andres and Marie-Lou Alemany opened on this pretty Georgian shopping street, and if there was any doubt about the locals' desire for tapas, they soon evaporated. And word has spread. It's a 'slice of urban cool' in a period building, with a kitchen (open, naturally) that takes both traditional and modern approaches to superb ingredients. Get off the mark with 'picoteo', or nibbles, such as the classic Catalan tomato bread and Majorero cheese with Canarian palm sugar, and expect everything from charcuterie (chorizo Ibérico) to creative vegetable dishes (barbecued carrots with pistachios) to deliver full-on flavours. The chargrill does its thing with the likes of chicken thighs, served with almonds and capers. Classic tortilla and Padrón peppers recall Spanish holidays, while the signature pulpo negro is a deeply savoury dish worthy of the name. Finish with crema catalana. Stimulating selections of gins and sherries support the Spanish-driven wine list.
Chef/s: Andres Alemany. **Closed:** Mon, Sun, bank hols, 25 and 26 Dec, 1 Jan. **Meals:** small plates £3 to £18. **Details:** 60 seats. 12 seats outside. Bar. Wheelchairs. Music.

Anonymous

At *The Good Food Guide*, our inspectors dine anonymously and pay their bill in full. These impartial review meals, along with feedback from thousands of our readers, are what informs the content of the *GFG*. Only the best restaurants make the cut.

£5 voucher

£5 OFF Restaurants showing this symbol are participating in our £5 voucher scheme, redeemable against a meal for two or more. Vouchers can be found at the back of this book.

Baughurst
The Wellington Arms

Cooking score: 4
Modern British | £35
Baughurst Road, Baughurst, RG26 5LP
Tel no: 0118 982 0110
thewellingtonarms.com

This whitewashed country inn of modest dimensions is also a fun place to stay, with rooms in the barn and the hayloft. Organic own-grown produce and local supplies form the backbone of an ecologically conscientious operation in which recycling and composting play their parts. An air of relaxed civility reigns in the quarry-tiled dining room, where the menu is chalked on a board and the free range eggs at breakfast were laid within the previous 24 hours. The cooking has a pleasingly domestic feel, with seasonal simplicity the watchword. Expect a soup of roasted home-grown pumpkin swirled with sour cream, or crab and avocado salad with garden leaves, to precede hearty main dishes like chargrilled pork chop on sticky red cabbage with parsnip crisps and mash, or a Brixham skate wing classically doused in capers and brown butter. A proper Eton mess is made with strawberries from the Wellington plot in a storm of whipped cream and shattered meringue. Wines made by organic and biodynamic methods inspire confidence through a stylistically classified list that comes at rational prices. Glasses start at £6.50.
Chef/s: Jason King and Helen Slater. **Meals:** main courses £12 to £25. Set L £18 (2 courses) to £20. **Details:** 30 seats. 20 seats outside. Wheelchairs. Parking. Music.

Beaulieu
The Terrace at The Montagu Arms

Cooking score: 4
Modern British | £70
Palace Lane, Beaulieu, SO42 7ZL
Tel no: 01590 612324
montaguarmshotel.co.uk
£5 OFF

Luminaries of the arts and politics have passed through the Montagu's portals since its ascent to grandeur in the late Victorian era, and The Terrace restaurant, with its sober panelling and soothing views over the gardens, is very much in keeping. Matthew Whitfield took up the culinary reins at the start of 2019, and looks set to maintain the pace for well-constructed modern British dishes of evident panache. A doorstop slab of beef brisket terrine with hazelnuts and pickled carrots makes a bold opener, where more delicate appetites might plump for chilled and minted pea velouté. There is an assured touch in balancing components of main dishes, perhaps honey-glazed chicken breast with braised gem lettuce and spring onions, or cod fillet with samphire, poached artichoke and butter-laden mash. Pick of the desserts is salt caramel fondant with chocolate crémeux and vanilla ice cream. The sensational wine list is curated by a knowledgeable and personable sommelier, as much at home with his Welsh Pinot Noir as with anything more southerly. Biodynamics add class. House selections are £7.50 a glass.
Chef/s: Matthew Whitfield. **Closed:** Mon, Tue. **Meals:** main courses £22 to £38. Set L £25 (2 courses) to £30. Tasting menu £80 (5 courses) to £90. **Details:** 100 seats. 30 seats outside. V menu. Bar. Wheelchairs. Parking. Children over 12 yrs.

Brockenhurst

LOCAL GEM

The Pig

Modern British | £40
Beaulieu Road, Brockenhurst, SO42 7QL
Tel no: 01590 622354
thepighotel.com

This, the original Pig (there are now five more in the litter), is a New Forest retreat with beds, treatment rooms and a kitchen garden that supplies the glasshouse restaurant. The aim is to ensure that other ingredients come from within 25 miles. It's an ethos that makes good eating, from starters of smoked pork belly with pickled clams and oregano crème fraîche to mains of Poole Bay silver mullet with tomato dressing and marsh samphire. Simple preparations of veg are a highlight that match the setting. There's Hampshire fizz from Hambledon Vineyard on the well-compiled wine list.

Emsworth
36 on the Quay

Cooking score: 4
Modern European | £58
47 South Street, Emsworth, PO10 7EG
Tel no: 01243 375592
36onthequay.co.uk

Ramon and Karen Farthing have now passed the mantle wholly over to Gary and Martyna Pearce, and regulars report that it's business as usual: 'The food — both quality and style — is exemplary.' The kitchen's output feels current and fresh, with the likes of torched mackerel with cucumber, passion fruit mouli and yoghurt crisp, and poached hake fillet with katsu curry potato terrine, Cornish crab, spiced cauliflower and coconut dashi. If some have felt there is a little over-gilding of the lily at times, that's hardly the case in a refreshingly direct opener of Welsh waygu tartare served with pickled onions, garlic and mustard mayonnaise, nor in the roast chicken breast

with lemon-thyme-glazed swede, winter greens and chicken jus from the good-value lunch menu. Intriguing desserts include baked apple with malt brioche, oat crumb and Emsworth ale ice cream with apple caramel. Service is 'attentive without being over formal', and wines are priced for deep pockets. **Chef/s:** Gary Pearce. **Closed:** Mon, Sun, 1 week Oct, 24 to 27 Dec, 2 weeks Jan, 1 week May. **Meals:** set L £24 (2 courses) to £29. Set D £48 (2 courses) to £58. Tasting menu L £45 (5 courses) and D £70 (8 courses). **Details:** 50 seats. 10 seats outside. Bar. Wheelchairs. Music.

Heckfield

★ NEW ENTRY ★

Marle

Cooking score: 4
British | £60
Heckfield Place, Heckfield, RG27 0LD
Tel no: 0118 932 6868
heckfieldplace.com

It's not often that luxury and sustainability come together in glorious harmony but that's precisely what's happened at the newly opened Heckfield Place. This grand house and park have been impeccably restored and Skye Gyngell, a chef known for searching out the best local ingredients and making them shine, has been involved from the start. Her menus combine produce grown on the estate with that from partner farm Fern Verrow, in Herefordshire. Marle, one of two restaurants here overseen by Gyngell, is housed in a beautiful modern extension with fantastic views over the grounds and a huge terrace for when the weather is kind. You don't have to be a hotel guest to get a taste of what all the fuss is about, from freshly made tagliolini with a buttery cream and sage sauce, to beautifully balanced sweet-sour lobster tamarind curry, decorated with shavings of roasted fresh coconut. A rich and creamy lemon posset is a fitting finale, whatever the season. The wine list is full of interest for the curious, and big names for those who have an urge to splash out, but there are enough choices by the glass and carafe for ordinary folk. What the staff lack in experience, they make up for in charm and enthusiasm.

Chef/s: Skye Gyngell. **Meals:** main courses £23 to £34. Set L £28 (2 courses) to £32. **Details:** 85 seats. 50 seats outside. Bar. Wheelchairs. Parking. Music.

▌Isle of Wight

★ LOCAL RESTAURANT AWARD ★
OVERALL WINNER

The Little Gloster

Cooking score: 4
Modern European | £35
31 Marsh Road, Gurnard, Isle of Wight,
PO31 8JQ
Tel no: 01983 298776
thelittlegloster.com

This Scandi-looking restaurant with rooms on the north coast, near Cowes, enjoys sweeping views of the Solent from a light-flooded room of pale wood. Hanging sailcloth and lifebelts emphasise the maritime location, as does a goodly proportion of islander Ben Cooke's menu (wife Holly ably runs front of house). Rabbit, chicken and chorizo fritters come with Swedish mustard for daubing, and a plate of house-cured Hampshire trout gravadlax with croûtons of sprouted spelt and dill crème fraîche is lifted by a hit of fresh horseradish. Sail on into mains with dayboat hake fillets with oyster velouté, caramelised onion purée, kale and parsley or fresh Uffa pasta – named after the couple's son and the basis of the hugely popular Pasta Thursdays. If you're more inclined to meat, look to a confit duck leg with oyster mushrooms, cornichons, pancetta and tarragon. 'Miss the truffle and Parmesan frites at your peril,' warned one visitor. Desserts come in irresistible layers, as in a subtly tropical piña colada baked Alaska. A vigorous modern miscellany of wines opens at £19.95, and there are pedigree listings of Scotch and rum to ponder.

Chef/s: Ben Cooke. **Closed:** Mon, Tue, 4 to 20 Nov, 23 to 26 Dec, 30 Dec to 13 Feb. **Meals:** main courses £15 to £22. Set L and D £17 (2 courses) to £20. **Details:** 70 seats. 60 seats outside. Wheelchairs. Parking. Music.

★ NEW ENTRY ★

The Seaview Hotel

Cooking score: 2
Modern European | £28
High Street, Seaview, Isle of Wight, PO34 5EX
Tel no: 01983 612711
seaviewhotel.co.uk

The sea view is more notional than actual from this relaxed hotel, but the place constitutes a major part of the action in a small community of the same name at the north-east corner of the island. There are tables for drinkers on an outdoor terrace, while the dining room itself is a slightly drab linened affair. Fortunately, colour comes in the form of Tom Bull's modern bistro food, which engages plenty of forthright flavours at cracking value. A Scotch egg of smoked salmon comes with bright yellow curried mayo, or there could be a slab of marbled chicken terrine with shallot jam and brioche. For main, a piece of hake looks and tastes the part in the seaside circumstances, accompanied by Jersey Royals and samphire in caper butter, while rump and belly of lamb come with spring veg and salsa verde. Finish with a textbook crème brûlée and shortbread, or sumptuous pistachio soufflé. House wines are £4.35 a glass on a list with plenty below £30.

Chef/s: Tom Bull. **Meals:** main courses £11 to £23. Set L £18 (2 courses) to £22. Set D £28. **Details:** 100 seats. 30 seats outside. Bar. Wheelchairs. Parking.

Thompson's

Cooking score: 6
Modern European | £55
11 Town Lane, Newport, Isle of Wight,
PO30 1JU
Tel no: 01983 526118
robertthompson.co.uk

£5
OFF

Deserving of its reputation as the best food on
the island, Thompson's shouldn't be kept for
high days and holidays – especially given that
three courses of precise, flavour-forward
cooking is available at lunch for under £30.
An advocate of the local larder, boss Robert
Thompson makes the most of dayboat fish,
local game and Isle of Wight mushrooms; the
end result, says one reader, is 'wholly
enjoyable'. Sent out from an open kitchen,
starters might be a take on pigeon pie with
boudin noir, apple and caramelised
cauliflower, sharpened with red wine and
cider jus, or tagliatelle of Cornish cuttlefish
with charred purple sprouting broccoli and a
Japanese-inspired dressing. To follow,
confident technique sees monkfish roasted on
the bone with coronation coleslaw, and a
delicate raviolo filled with duck egg yolk and
truffled potato. To finish, there's a beachy feel
to barbecued pineapple with spiced rum or a
chilli-spiked chocolate tart with lime and
mascarpone sorbet. Wines include both
organic and staunchly conventional bottles,
from £19.
Chef/s: Robert Thompson. **Closed:** Mon, Tue, Sun
(Oct to May), 2 weeks Nov, 1 week Dec, 2 weeks Feb
to Mar. **Meals:** set L £24 (2 courses) to £29. Set D
£47 (2 courses) to £55. Tasting menu £65 (7
courses). **Details:** 48 seats. Bar. Wheelchairs. Music.

LOCAL GEM

The Garlic Farm Restaurant

Modern British | £25
Mersley Lane, Newchurch, Isle of Wight,
PO36 0NR
Tel no: 01983 867333
thegarlicfarm.co.uk

£5 🛏 £30
OFF

The owners of this renowned farm not only
grow innumerable obscure varieties of *Allium
sativum*, but also allow visitors to sample the
stuff in their restaurant. Its pungent aromas
permeate everything from the breakfast
sausages and meze platters to the profiteroles
and ice cream – although there's also plenty
for those who prefer to steer clear. Starters of
potted beef or broccoli fritters could precede
smoked pork loin with bubble and squeak,
while garlic-free desserts might include date
and apple pudding. There's even bottle-
fermented black garlic beer to drink, plus
wine from £16.95.

▌Lymington
The Elderflower

Cooking score: 4
British | £45
4-5 Quay Street, Lymington, SO41 3AS
Tel no: 01590 676908
elderflowerrestaurant.co.uk

If the cobbled street out front and quaint bow
windows bring out feelings of nostalgia, a
glance at Andrew Du Bourg's menu – where
line-caught sea bass tartare keeps company
with plankton mayonnaise, pickled seaweed
and essence of anise – should bring you back
to the 21st century. Equally, the dining room
matches old beams with some contemporary
touches, but gently so, and the pervading
mood is soothingly decorous. Tasting menus
of four, five or seven courses show the way, so
pick a number, sit back and wait to see what
arrives. British- and French-inspired ideas
reveal the chef's evident creative instincts:
beetroot and blood orange temper the
glorious meatiness of grilled duck heart, while

mackerel might be partnered by smoked oyster and pickled mushrooms. Finish with lemon posset or New Forest gâteau, a lighter riff on the Black Forest original. A Simple Pleasures menu – think fish and chips or chargrilled hot dog – is a more workaday alternative on all but Saturday nights. The wine list majors in France.

Chef/s: Andrew Du Bourg. **Closed:** Mon, Tue. **Meals:** main courses £9 to £27. Tasting menu £45 (4 courses) to £65. **Details:** 36 seats. Music. Children over 12 yrs at Fri and Sat D.

▌ Milford on Sea
La Perle
Cooking score: 2
British | £40
60 High Street, Milford on Sea, SO41 0QD
Tel no: 01590 643557
laperle.co.uk
£5 OFF

Sam Hughes' restaurant on the high street of this attractive seaside village serves up both seafood and seasonal produce from the surrounding countryside with gusto. The chef's time working with Raymond Blanc is evident in classical preparations: Lymington lobster ravioli, fillet of sea bass with a pungent lobster bisque, and chateaubriand. A vegetarian option might be goat's cheese and spinach tortellini. If you find yourself in the vicinity during the day, the set lunch menu is an act of benign generosity delivering, say, Provençal fish soup, confit pork belly, and apple and rhubarb crumble. Desserts such as chocolate fondant that was, for one couple, simply 'superb', and passion fruit and mandarin crème brûlée are shown just as much care and attention as everything else, including the sourdough bread. The concise wine list includes appealing options by the glass and carafe.

Chef/s: Sam Hughes. **Closed:** Mon, Sun, first week Jan. **Meals:** main courses £17 to £25. Set L £12 (2 courses) to £15. **Details:** 30 seats. V menu. Music.

Verveine
Cooking score: 4
Seafood | £44
98 High Street, Milford on Sea, SO41 0QE
Tel no: 01590 642176
verveine.co.uk
£5 OFF

Tucked at the back of a fishmonger's in a sleepy seaside town, David Wykes' fish restaurant punches way above its weight. The split-level room is overseen by an open kitchen, and looks out on to a homely garden complete with shed. From the moment a crisp waffle loaded with Comté arrives, it's clear that Wykes has ambition to mix with the modern British gang. His tasting menus are bold and inspired, perhaps encompassing sweet prawns with orange peel purée, and punchy salmon tail with ras el hanout cauliflower and smoked walnut pesto, among earlier courses. The main business might be a majestic piece of wild sea bass, accompanied by a heap of silky fettuccine with salami and shaved egg (a kind of reimagined carbonara) and San Marzano tomatoes in truffle butter. Dessert keeps things relatively light: perhaps hazelnut sponge garnished with strawberries and their sorbet, shards of honey caramel and lemon cream. A European-led list of largely white wines opens with standard glasses from £5.75.

Chef/s: David Wykes. **Closed:** Mon, Sun, 24 Dec to 14 Jan, 1 week Jul. **Meals:** set L £17 (2 courses) to £33. Tasting menu £44 to £90. **Details:** 32 seats. Wheelchairs. Children over 8 yrs.

Send us your review
Your feedback informs the content of the *GFG* and will be used to compile next year's entries. To register your opinion about any restaurant listed in the Guide, or a restaurant that you wish to bring to our attention, visit: thegoodfoodguide.co.uk/feedback.

■ New Milton
Chewton Glen, The Dining Room
Cooking score: 4
Modern British | £62
Chewton Glen Hotel, Christchurch Road, New Milton, BH25 6QS
Tel no: 01425 275341
chewtonglen.com

This elegant Georgian house looks a treat when viewed in summer sun from the rolling acreage of the croquet lawn. It's that sort of place – grandiose but managed with welcoming ease of emphasis on the proprieties, the garden-viewed dining room a restful setting for Simon Addison's considered country house cooking. Classical French leanings are evident in pressed duck liver terrine dressed in Sauternes and served with brioche for a luxe starter, or else a twice-baked soufflé of potently rich Emmental. Main courses bring on regional meats such as Quantock duck with sweet potato, plum and pak choi, or Wiltshire venison loin and choucroute, but there are lighter options too, in the shape of cod on truffled beluga lentils with accompaniments of cauliflower and almond. Add a side of mashed Bintjes (potato) and what more do you want? Apart from apple crumble and tonka ice cream, perhaps, or a regally attired pineapple and black pepper tarte tatin for two. Wine is taken very seriously on a list distinguished by little essays, viticultural maps of Bordeaux and parades of bobby-dazzlers. If you've £50 to spend on a bottle, there's plenty of room for manoeuvre.
Chef/s: Simon Addison. **Meals:** main courses £22 to £45. Set L £25 (2 courses) to £32. Sun L £40. Tasting menu £70 (6 courses). **Details:** 180 seats. 40 seats outside. Bar. Wheelchairs. Parking. Music. Children over 8 yrs after 8pm.

■ Petersfield
Annie Jones
Cooking score: 3
Spanish | £35
10 Lavant Street, Petersfield, GU32 3EW
Tel no: 01730 262728
anniejones.co.uk
£5 OFF

An indispensable neighbourhood resource that seemingly has all bases covered, from party spreads and paella to a patisserie selling whole cakes, all packed into apparently modest premises on a provincial shopping street. At the heart of the operation, the principal menu now deals in tapas plates for sharing and combining. Off-piste proposals include Peruvian-style fish ceviche with tomato, lime and chipotle chilli, quince-glazed Basque-style pork belly in sherry vinegar, and poached duck egg with potato foam, Ibérico ham and Parmesan. It's all served in an atmosphere of bubbly bonhomie, the tapas room with its high tables supplemented by a glassed-in garden bar and courtyard. On Sundays, traditional roast lunches come into play, the beef topped by gigantic Yorkshires, while weekend brunches are the best way of taking a very late breakfast, perhaps of chorizo, bacon and cauliflower hash, crowned with a poached egg. Wines start at £15.
Chef/s: Andrew Parker. **Closed:** Mon, 25 and 26 Dec. **Meals:** tapas £5 to £9. Sun L £16 (1 course). **Details:** 46 seats. 60 seats outside. Bar. Music.

■ Preston Candover
LOCAL GEM
The Purefoy Arms
Modern British | £33
Preston Candover, RG25 2EJ
Tel no: 01256 389514
thepurefoyarms.co.uk

'Once again a very impressive lunch from a chef punching above his weight': local readers are certainly enamoured of chef patron Gordon Stott's easy-going pub on the outskirts of this quiet village. There's still space for drinking at the bar, although most people favour the adjoining dining rooms. Beef fillet topped with chestnut crumb and matched with 'really tasty' creamed potatoes, spinach and red wine jus remains a favourite on the menu, but other ideas also show undoubted skill and creativity, including sea bass with a lobster emulsion, and desserts such as dark chocolate délice. Drink local ales or a good selection of wines by the glass and bottle.

▌Southampton

LOCAL GEM

The Dancing Man Brewery
Modern British | £30
1 Bugle Street, Southampton, SO14 2AR
Tel no: 023 8083 6666
dancingmanbrewery.co.uk
£5 £30
OFF

A godsend for travellers using the Red Funnel ferry terminal, this freestanding medieval wool house is now home to a go-getting brewery: sample its beers in the downstairs bar before heading up to the maritime-themed restaurant for some quirkily named seasonal dishes with British overtones. Kick off with a smoked haddock Scotch egg and curried mayo before tackling The Duke (pork wellington with black pudding and Swiss chard) or Rosemary's Baaaaby (herb-crusted lamb rump). Vegetarians, vegans, kids and dogs do well, and there are wines (from £17.95) for those who don't fancy a pint of Jesus Hairdo.

▌Southsea

Restaurant 27
Cooking score: 4
Modern European | £59
27a South Parade, Southsea, PO5 2JF
Tel no: 023 9287 6272
restaurant27.com

Kevin and Sophie Bingham run their fine-dining restaurant as a proper family business: they live 'above the shop' and maintain a personal approach to hospitality, gently tweaking their offer from time to time. The carpeted dining room suggests quiet restraint (dark red drapes, upholstered seats, bare tables), but the food is what matters here, and Kevin stakes everything on high-end tasting menus showcasing his self-styled brand of 'global French' cooking – a fusion of locally sourced ingredients, cutting-edge technique and detailed presentation. Dinner might begin with a soupçon of Isle of Wight garlic velouté, then comes home-baked charcoal bread (with Marmite butter) and a compendium of meat and fish courses – perhaps glazed beef cheek with celeriac and apple or roast sea bass accompanied by artichoke and caviar. There's always cheese, too, before a selection of mini desserts is brought to the table on a huge ceramic platter. To drink, pick some appropriate by-the-glass options from the 60-bin global list.
Chef/s: Kevin Bingham. **Closed:** Mon, Tue, 25 to 27 Dec, 1 to 3 Jan. **Meals:** tasting menu £49 (5 courses) to £59. Sun L £35. Sun tasting menu £49 (6 courses). **Details:** 36 seats. V menu. Bar. Music.

▌Stockbridge

The Greyhound on the Test
Cooking score: 2
Modern British | £38
31 High Street, Stockbridge, SO20 6EY
Tel no: 01264 810833
thegreyhoundonthetest.co.uk

This high street inn, painted a head-turning shade of pale lemon, features an enticing beer garden that stretches down to the river Test, with a fishing hut to take advantage of The Greyhound's angling rights in Hampshire's finest chalk stream. Inside, bare boards, low beams and a brick-built inglenook set the scene for an extensive range of lively modern pub food. Sharing boards of charcuterie or fish (including tempura monkfish cheeks and smoked Test trout) are an agreeable way to work up an appetite for one of the fully loaded main plates. How about tender guinea fowl breast with roast butternut, chestnuts and blackberries, alongside vinaigrette-dressed savoy cabbage, or fried pollock in seaweed

butter with girolles, cauliflower, kale and fennel fondue? The boldness of these combinations mostly pays off, right through to desserts such as peanut butter parfait with blood orange jam, frosted zest, peanut sponge pudding and meringue. Friday fish and chips is a strong draw. Glasses start at £6.75 on a commendable international wine list.
Chef/s: Chris Heather. **Closed:** 25 and 26 Dec. **Meals:** main courses £14 to £30. Set L £16 (2 courses) to £20. Sun L £26 (2 courses). **Details:** 68 seats. 30 seats outside. Parking. Music.

▌Upton Grey
The Hoddington Arms
Cooking score: 2
British | £30
Bidden Road, Upton Grey, RG25 2RL
Tel no: 01256 862371
hoddingtonarms.co.uk
£5 OFF £30

'Our only regret is that we don't live nearer,' is one of the more plaintive notes in reader reports, but it's earnestly meant by the four who make their monthly pilgrimage here. What they look forward to is a thoroughly homely village inn that's all crooked beams and roughcast brick with sofas for lounging and a menu of locally sourced, smartly turned out pub cooking. Gratinated scallops in garlic and breadcrumbs, or grilled crottin with salt-baked and pickled beetroots in truffled hazelnut dressing are the lead-in to substantial mains like venison pot pie, salmon on crushed potatoes in chorizo brown butter, or well-wrought standards such as steaks and beer-battered haddock, perhaps with hard-to-resist dripping chips. Sweet treats might embrace lemon curd tart with blood orange sorbet or crème brûlée with rum and raisins. A relaxed atmosphere and welcoming staff complete the picture. The appealing short wine list opens at £5.20 a glass.
Chef/s: Chris Barnes and Tom Wilson. **Closed:** 1 Jan. **Meals:** main courses £14 to £25. Set L £22 (2 courses) to £27. Sun L £22 (2 courses) to £27. **Details:** 60 seats. 40 seats outside. Wheelchairs. Parking. Music.

How to eat oysters

Lusted after by the Romans but considered poor man's food in the 18th century, these briny, slurpy shellfish bring celebratory sparkle to a meal. In the UK, wild natives are in season from September to April, while farmed Pacific or rock oysters are harvested year-round. Typically served raw on ice, they need nothing more than a mignonette dressing (diced shallots, vinegar and pepper), a dash of Tabasco or squeeze of lemon to bring out their flavour.

Not sure about eating them raw? Dinner at Paul Ainsworth's Padstow restaurant, **No. 6**, starts with a lightly crumbed Porthilly rock, quickly deep-fried; or head to **The Unruly Pig** near Woodbridge for an oyster velouté, a delicious way to enjoy the flavour if a raw oyster is too much. Otherwise, try:

Rockefeller This New Orleans recipe has many variations, but most involve topping the oyster with onion cooked in butter, spinach, parsley and breadcrumbs before grilling.

Kilpatrick (or Kirkpatrick) Oysters are topped with a sauce of tomato, diced bacon and Worcestershire sauce, then crumbed and grilled.

Angels on horseback Oysters, removed from the shell, are wrapped in bacon and baked.

◼ Winchester

The Black Rat

Cooking score: 3
Modern British | £60
88 Chesil Street, Winchester, SO23 0HX
Tel no: 01962 844465
theblackrat.co.uk

Among David Nicholson's portfolio of enterprises spread across the city – including a quirky B&B, pub and wine bar – this former 18th-century tavern stands out as a culinary hot spot. The ancient bones of the building give character, the decor is atmospheric, and at the stoves Jon Marsden-Jones turns out complex contemporary dishes built around seasonal ingredients, some grown in the restaurant's own kitchen garden, others foraged gleanings delivered to the door. It all adds up to a creative output that packs celeriac, wild mushrooms and damsons kimchi into dumplings (served with shaved root vegetables and dashi) and adds a seed crumble to a dish of squab pigeon breast, crispy leg and offal. Halibut arrives with mussels, squid ink and sea vegetables, and non-meat offerings are no less inventive judging by a plate of salt-baked celeriac and spelt barley. Finish with buttermilk crémeux with medjool dates and gorse flower. Well-chosen wines start at £28.

Chef/s: Jon Marsden-Jones. **Closed:** 24 Dec to 10 Jan. **Meals:** main courses £22 to £34. Set L £29 weekends (2 courses) to £34. Tasting menu £60 (6 courses). **Details:** 36 seats. 16 seats outside. Bar. Music. Children over 12 yrs at D.

The Chesil Rectory

Cooking score: 4
Modern British | £36
1 Chesil Street, Winchester, SO23 0HU
Tel no: 01962 851555
chesilrectory.co.uk

The half-timbered rectory dates from around 1450, yet picture-perfect medieval as it is, the interior has a sophisticated contemporary feel. Sure, there are ancient boards, beams and fireplaces, but intelligent use of colour and design suits present-day tastes. There's a stylish lounge bar on the first floor, and an enticing courtyard garden replete with shrubs, herbs and flowers. Co-owner and chef Damian Brown cooks with classical good sense and measured invention, so rhubarb purée and spiced granola partner ham hock ballotine, and haddock and leek risotto arrives with prawn beignets and lime beurre blanc. Main courses are similarly well grounded: fillet of hake, say, with blood orange and chive butter sauce, or roasted rump of lamb with pickled carrots and hotpot potatoes. A local tasting menu shows where the kitchen's heart lies, and a Coravin system ensures enticing vintages are available by the glass.

Chef/s: Damian Brown. **Closed:** 25 Dec, 1 Jan. **Meals:** main courses £14 to £22. Set L and early D £18 (2 courses) to £22. Tasting menu £55 (5 courses). Sun L £25 (2 courses) to £29. **Details:** 75 seats. 40 seats outside. V menu. Bar. Music. Children over 10 yrs at D.

◼ Woodlands

LOCAL GEM

Spot in the Woods

British | £15
174 Woodlands Road, Woodlands, SO40 7GL
Tel no: 023 8029 3784
spotinthewoods.co.uk

Tucked away in the New Forest, surrounded by soaring trees, this daytime café, deli and boutique B&B is a delightful spot indeed. The bedrooms are spacious and smart (it used to operate as Hotel TerraVina), while the Kitchen Café serves up everything from breakfast of eggs florentine to sandwiches and wraps (local sausages, say, or crayfish with lemon mayonnaise), afternoon tea and hearty lunches of pea and mint risotto, fish and chips, or imaginative salads and platters. A few wines and bottled beers cover the boozy bases.

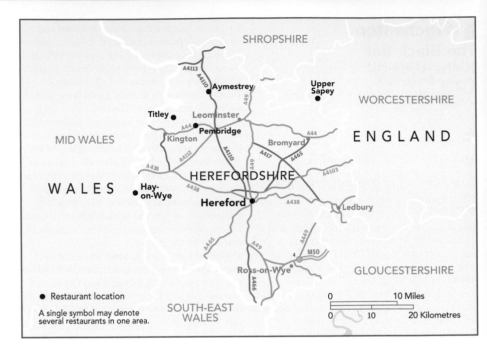

■ Aymestrey
The Riverside at Aymestrey

Cooking score: 3
Modern British | £30
Aymestrey, HR6 9ST
Tel no: 01568 708440
riversideaymestrey.co.uk

A steep hillside looms behind this pub, a 16th-century half-timbered building that stands by the banks of the river Lugg. Outside, there's a stunning one-acre kitchen garden and three bedroom cabins; inside a heavily beamed warren of rooms with wonky wooden floors, open fires and simple furnishings, as well as a striking barn-like dining area with glass walls overlooking an inner courtyard. Although it's still very much a pub, Andy Link's modern seasonal menus draw diners from afar for dishes that showcase fresh pickings from the garden and produce from local farms and artisan suppliers: sustainability, ethical sourcing and food miles are taken very seriously here. A typical meal could take in cured river Lugg trout with hazelnut mayonnaise, followed by Weobley Ash mutton with asparagus, wild garlic and ewe's milk curd or hake with thyme cream sauce, then honey and walnut tart with ginger and spiced apple compôte. The wine list offers interest and good value with 14 selections by the glass.
Chef/s: Andy Link. **Meals:** main courses £11 to £26. Sun L £22. **Details:** 70 seats. 30 seats outside. Bar. Parking. Music.

Symbols

🛏 Accommodation is available
£30 Three courses for £30 or less
£5 OFF £5 off voucher scheme
🍷 Notable wine list

▋ Hay-on-Wye

LOCAL GEM
Richard Booth's Bookshop Café
Modern British | £18
44 Lion Street, Hay-on-Wye, HR3 5AA
Tel no: 01497 820322
boothbooks.co.uk

£30

With a cinema next door and a yoga studio in the eaves, Richard Booth's Bookshop is the unofficial cultural hub of Hay-on-Wye – a year-round asset that really starts rocking during the town's celebrated literary festival. The stone-walled in-store café does a sterling job, serving up daytime sustenance for bibliophiles and tourists alike – so tuck into buttermilk pancakes and bacon butties for breakfast or drop by later for smoked haddock and crayfish chowder, or kale Caesar salad with a glass of wine. Those wanting something sweet can opt for warm scones or lemon polenta cake with rhubarb jam.

▋ Hereford
★ NEW ENTRY ★
The Bookshop
Cooking score: 1
British | £40
Aubrey Street, Hereford, HR4 0BU
Tel no: 01432 343443
aruleoftum.com

£5
OFF

Part of a small restaurant group that runs burger joints in Hereford and Worcester, this town centre restaurant has been lovingly restored, creating a cosy space with warm lighting and industrial fittings. The concept is a simple one: choose your cut of meat from the blackboard (sirloin, fillet, côte de boeuf, say) and add your desired sauces and sides (at additional cost), perhaps roasted heritage carrots with coriander and tahini or Jerusalem artichokes with pear and smoked hazelnuts. In addition, readers are fulsome in their praise for

the triple cooked chips, traditional Sunday lunches of rump of beef, pork belly and Welsh lamb, as well as sticky toffee pudding. There's a short list of good-value wines.
Chef/s: Katie Lane. **Closed:** Mon, Tue, 25 Dec. **Meals:** main courses £13 to £27. **Details:** 44 seats. Music.

LOCAL GEM
Madam & Adam
Modern British | £29
23 Bridge Street, Hereford, HR4 9DG
Tel no: 01432 639964
madamadamhereford.co.uk

£30

Perched on the northern end of the old bridge spanning the river Wye, Swav Lewandowski's tiny restaurant has quickly established itself as a local favourite in this cathedral city. Intelligently curated small plates are what's on offer and the cooking is built on sound technical skills and bold flavours, as demonstrated by whipped goat's cheese paired with boozy umeboshi plums, red cabbage, green tomato salsa, walnuts and nasturtiums, or Breton-style butterbean cassoulet with Gruyère scone, kabanos sausage and micro greens. Wines from £20.

▋ Pembridge

LOCAL GEM
The Cider Barn
Modern British | £34
Dunkertons Cider Mill, Pembridge, HR6 9ED
Tel no: 01544 388161
the-cider-barn.co.uk

Visitors to Dunkerton's pioneering organic cider mill will be delighted to discover this café bar and restaurant housed in a Grade II-listed converted barn close to the action. At lunchtime, you can graze on small plates but it pays to trade up to dinner in the pleasingly informal restaurant, where sharply tuned eclectic food is the deal. Kick off with soy-marinated cod, proceed to duck breast and leg with hay-baked carrots, pistachio crumble and cherry sauce, then finish with honey panna cotta, blood orange salsa and rapeseed jelly. Wines from £18.95.

Titley
The Stagg Inn
Cooking score: 4
British | £40
Titley, HR5 3RL
Tel no: 01544 230221
thestagg.co.uk

Over the past 20 years Steve and Nicola Reynolds have built up and maintained their pub's reputation as one of Herefordshire's best dining spots. Unchanged inside, with a rustic bar draped with hops and the usual pub paraphernalia (there's also a smart dining room), it's a soft spot in many a regular's heart. Service is gregarious but relaxed, reflected also in cooking that doesn't try too hard yet nods to Steve's classical background. Try not to peak too early – not only are the nibbles tempting, they are also delicious (barbecue pork bonbons were a huge hit at inspection), but snacks such as homemade flatbread and wild garlic pesto are irresistible. The menu bears the fruits of the surrounding countryside, featuring seasonal, local produce such as asparagus and salted egg, lamb rump with Jerusalem artichokes and spring cabbage or Herefordshire beef fillet. Elsewhere there's cod fillet with fennel, shrimp, lemon, parsley and parmentier potatoes, and lemon tart and black cassis sorbet. On a sunny day, sit outside to soak up the silence in the immaculate garden. The compendious and reasonably priced wine list includes some fabulous half bottles, useful notes and plenty below £30, although of course there are local ciders, perries and even gins to tempt.
Chef/s: Steve Reynolds. **Closed:** Mon, Tue, 2 weeks Nov, 25 to 27 Dec, 1 week Jan to Feb. **Meals:** main courses £18 to £26. Sun L £23. **Details:** 70 seats. 16 seats outside. V menu. Vg menu. Parking.

Upper Sapey
The Baiting House
Cooking score: 1
Modern British | £35
Upper Sapey, WR6 6XT
Tel no: 01886 853201
baitinghouse.co.uk
£5 OFF

A stone-built inn surrounded by green fields was once the haunt of drovers, but now serves as a destination spot for well-executed modern pub food. Salmon pink walls and foursquare furniture form the backdrop for such popular strokes as a smoked haddock rarebit tart with caramelised onion, followed by rack and shoulder of local lamb in its own jus with turnip dauphinois and broccoli, or cod with charred leeks, celeriac and spinach in crab bisque. The triple-cooked chips are hard to swerve, and desserts have equally nefarious ways of tempting in the form of Turkish delight cheesecake with granola and chocolate sorbet. A commendably broad-minded short wine list starts at £5.50 a glass.
Chef/s: Charles Bradley. **Closed:** Mon, Jan. **Meals:** main courses £14 to £24. Set L £20 (2 courses) to £25. Sun L £20 (2 courses) to £25. **Details:** 50 seats. 30 seats outside. Bar. Wheelchairs. Parking. Music.

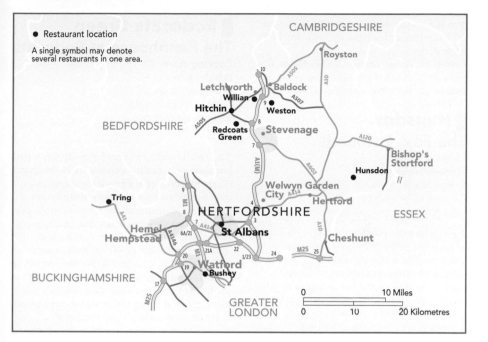

- ● Restaurant location

A single symbol may denote
several restaurants in one area.

CAMBRIDGESHIRE

Royston

Letchworth   Baldock
Willian
Hitchin   Weston

BEDFORDSHIRE   Redcoats   Stevenage
Green

Bishop's
Stortford
Hunsdon

Welwyn Garden
City   Hertford

Tring   HERTFORDSHIRE   ESSEX

Hemel
Hempstead   St Albans   Cheshunt

Watford
Bushey

BUCKINGHAMSHIRE

0   10 Miles
GREATER
LONDON   0   10   20 Kilometres

▌Bushey

LOCAL GEM
St James
International | £45
30 High Street, Bushey, WD23 3HL
Tel no: 020 8950 2480
stjamesrestaurant.co.uk
£5
OFF

'This was a fine lunch, very good value, in a
relaxed atmosphere, and we shall be very
pleased to continue coming,' summed up a pair
of regulars to this long-established restaurant.
The menu fits the bill, listing the kind of food
everyone likes to eat, whether twice-baked
cheese soufflé gratin, grilled calf's liver and
bacon (with creamy mash, red onion jam and
red wine jus) and a well-made chocolate and
orange tart with vanilla ice cream. Service is
excellent. Wines from £17.50, with a basic
selection by the glass.

▌Hitchin

Hermitage Rd
Cooking score: 1
Modern British | £30
20-21 Hermitage Road, Hitchin, SG5 1BT
Tel no: 01462 433603
hermitagerd.co.uk
£5 £30
OFF

This expansive first-floor pub and restaurant is
based in a former ballroom. The industrial-
chic interior is striking, but it's the sweeping
grandeur of the arched windows that really
commands attention. The menu features pub
classics alongside dishes from further afield.
Cooking is competent – a precisely roasted
cod loin is well matched with crushed
hazelnuts and browned butter, while a
generous helping of crisp-fried Szechuan
squid is let down only by the absence of any
punchy spice. Family favourites in the form of
burgers, fish and chips, and meaty grills are
popular at lunch, and sweet treats such as
fudgy brownies and strawberry ice cream

provide a comforting conclusion. The wine list has vegan and organic options, and kicks off at £21.

Chef/s: Joe Walker. **Closed:** 25 Dec. **Meals:** main courses £14 to £26. Sun L £22 (2 courses) to £17. **Details:** 150 seats. Bar. Wheelchairs. Music.

▍Hunsdon
The Fox & Hounds

Cooking score: 2
Modern British | £35
2 High Street, Hunsdon, SG12 8NH
Tel no: 01279 843999
foxandhounds-hunsdon.co.uk

This captivating pub is now firmly established as a relaxed neighbourhood eatery, the attractive blue and white façade giving out an air of sophistication that draws you in. The locals seem well aware of what a gem they have on their doorstep, judging by the happy throng. James Rix is a passionate chef, delivering a seasonal repertoire with carefully sourced produce and no little refinement. Start with lightly curried lamb's sweetbreads with spinach and toasted almonds, or pappardelle with a rich game ragoût, before a veal loin chop from the Josper oven or a five-hour-cooked shoulder of salt marsh lamb served with gratin dauphinois. Among desserts, apple cake with custard, caramel sauce and hazelnut ice cream has comfort writ large, or go for lemon posset served with raspberries and shortbread. Set lunches and dinners are terrific value, and the reasonably priced wine list opens at £22.50.

Chef/s: James Rix. **Closed:** Mon. **Meals:** main courses £14 to £39. Set L and D £19 (2 courses) to £24. Sun L £26 (2 courses) to £33. **Details:** 80 seats. 50 seats outside. Parking.

Visit us online

For the most up-to-date information about *The Good Food Guide*, go to thegoodfoodguide.co.uk.

▍Redcoats Green
The Farmhouse at Redcoats

Cooking score: 2
British | £36
Redcoats Green, SG4 7JR
Tel no: 01438 729500
farmhouseatredcoats.co.uk

🛏

This small rural hotel may be newly renovated but parts of it date back to the 1400s. Inside, there's plenty of character, with open fires, a cosy bar, an airy conservatory and a lovely private dining room in the former farmhouse kitchen. The kitchen nods to the pubby roots of its owner, Anglian Country Inns, with steak and chips, slow-braised mutton suet pudding and Sunday roasts, but the rest of the menu is cosmopolitan brasserie fare with a confident European slant. Pick through the menu and you might find wild mushroom and tarragon risotto with goat's curd and gremolata crumb, ahead of stone bass with saffron, mussel and root vegetable chowder and parmentier potatoes. After that, caramelised apple and ginger custard with rhubarb compôte and spiced doughnuts is a sound bet. Real ales and a clutch of good-value wines keep drinkers happy.

Chef/s: Sherwin Jacobs. **Meals:** main courses £16 to £28. Sun L £18. **Details:** 70 seats. 30 seats outside. Bar. Wheelchairs. Parking. Music.

▍St Albans
Loft

Cooking score: 4
Modern British | £40
23b George Street, St Albans, AL3 4ES
Tel no: 01727 865568
loftstalbans.com

£5
OFF

Nick and Louise Male have been calling the city's picturesque Cathedral Quarter home since 2015, and their contemporary restaurant in a medieval building is pitch perfect. At the end of a cobbled street, an iron staircase takes you up to the 15th-century dining room, replete with carved beams (although if the weather's playing ball, the courtyard's an option, too). A seasonal menu that dashes across continents, from French onion soup to charred cauliflower with onion bhajia, then to a 'beautifully cooked' sea bass with squid, might give some the jitters, but all the dishes deserve their place and epitomise Nick Male's astute blend of culinary innovation and classicism. As a finale, indulge in treacle tart with orange sorbet and gingerbread crumb. Visitors commend the family-friendly ethos, especially on a Sunday for the Family Feast roasts. Global wines offer plenty of interest for all budgets, and special selections for fine-wine lovers.

Chef/s: Nick Male. **Closed:** Mon, 25 Dec, 1 Jan. **Meals:** main courses £16 to £32. Set L and D £20 (2 courses) to £24. Sun L £29. **Details:** 62 seats. 24 seats outside. Bar. Music.

Thompson St Albans

Cooking score: 5
Modern British | £55
2-8 Hatfield Road, St Albans, AL1 3RP
Tel no. 01727 730777
thompsonstalbans.co.uk

The first-floor dining room of this cottage conversion may be decorated in a sombre all-grey palette but there's nothing dull about chef patron Phil Thompson's modern British cooking, for which one diner was happy to make a 140-mile round trip. Highlights are many and could include silken chicken and duck liver parfait, lavished with butter and cream, and countered with orange segments and crunchy granola. Main courses also excel, notably a magnificent chunk of suckling pig belly, topped with crisp crackling and partnered with the pungency of a tiny salt-baked turnip, while vegetarian dishes include pastel-hued wild garlic garganelli, studded with earthy morels and cloaked in a sauce rich with butter and savoury mushroom flavour. Desserts are exceptional, especially the custardy chocolate crémeux served with banana ice cream. A decent selection of global wines includes many by the glass. There's a

lovely relaxed vibe throughout, although the airy, conservatory-style ground-floor dining room is the space to aim for.

Chef/s: Phil Thompson. **Closed:** Mon. **Meals:** main courses £25 to £32. Set L £19 (2 courses) to £23. Set D £21 (2 courses) to £25. Tasting menu £55 (5 courses) to £69. **Details:** 90 seats. 18 seats outside. V menu. Bar. Wheelchairs. Music.

LOCAL GEM
The Foragers
Modern British | £24
The Verulam Arms, 41 Lower Dagnall Street, St Albans, AL3 4QE
Tel no: 01727 836004
the-foragers.com
£30

As the HQ for a pair of wild-food enthusiasts, this pub with an offbeat proposition showcases the foraged bounty of Hertfordshire. Tommy Forrester's kitchen goes all in, with robust pub dishes given flavours often found in more tweezered, high-end surrounds: carrot soup with hogweed, or campfire pork goulash with home-smoked peppers, wild fennel and carrot seed and spiced potato and onion bread. The preserver's art is on show in ketchups, pickles and jams, not to mention hedgerow fizz made with a liqueur of rhubarb, mulberry and Japanese knotweed.

▌Tring

★ NEW ENTRY ★

Crockers
Cooking score: 6
Modern British | £48
74 High Street, Tring, HP23 4AF
Tel no: 01442 828971
crockerstring.co.uk
£5
OFF

While diners are welcomed into a modern bar and attached dining area, the real action happens at the top of two flights of retro-styled carpeted stairs. Here, in a light-filled room with blue-grey and copper walls, 15

diners sit on orange leather stools around a horseshoe-shaped counter – the chef's table – giving a ringside view of the open kitchen as Scott Barnard (a 2015 finalist in *MasterChef: The Professionals*) showcases his fine-dining skills. Teaser bites might include crisp cones filled with musky truffle-infused goat's curd, or rabbit and duck liver terrine accompanied by an impressive entourage of pearl-like turnip droplets, translucent apple wisps and crunchy hazelnut granola. A recent visitor was much taken with succulent pork belly, wild garlic pesto and silken pea purée and even the crusty bread made with Tring Brewery beer is 'splendid'. The good news continues with a modern version of lemon meringue pie: a dab of fennel compôte, then a pastry disc and dome of creamy lemon curd, and finally a magnificent cloak of torched meringue. Service, like the cooking, doesn't miss a beat. The three-course set lunch and excellent wine pairings are more affordable than the indulgent, but pricier, evening offering.
Chef/s: Scott Barnard. **Closed:** Mon, Sun, 24 Dec to 4 Jan, 14 to 18 Apr, 18 to 29 Aug. **Meals:** set L £35. Set D £48. Tasting menu £90 (7 courses). **Details:** 15 seats. Bar. Music.

▌Weston

LOCAL GEM
The Cricketers
Modern British | £25
Damask Green Road, Weston, SG4 7DA
Tel no: 01462 790273
thecricketersweston.co.uk
£30

The test of a good pub is whether you would like it at the end of your road. And as far as this sympathetically extended 19th-century village hostelry is concerned, the answer is a resounding 'yes please'. Open all day for *de rigueur* steaks and burgers, the kitchen also turns out modern ideas such as soy, ginger and chilli sticky pork belly, followed by Goan cod, prawn and coconut curry with cardamom granola. A wood-fired oven supplies pizza to

eat in or take away, the beer is from Brancaster Brewery, and a short, global wine list starts at £19.50.

▌Willian
The Fox
Cooking score: 2
Modern British | £30
Willian, SG6 2AE
Tel no: 01462 480233
foxatwillian.co.uk
£30

A sterling local asset and a godsend for travellers wanting a welcome break from the A1, this rebooted 18th-century pub with rooms is a hostelry of two halves. Keep it casual by staking your claim in the refurbished open-plan bar with one of the regularly rotated guest ales and a plate of lamb sausages with BBQ sauce, say, or ham hock hash with broccoli and wild mushroom risotto, or upgrade to the atrium-style dining room for more ambitious modern dishes. The owners also run The White Horse, Brancaster Staithe (see entry), so expect regular supplies of fish, bivalves and crustacea from the north Norfolk coast alongside the likes of honey-glazed duck breast with fennel purée, balsamic-macerated fig and red wine jus or pan-fried pork belly and pig's cheek croquette with pea purée and pickle-roasted onion. Seasonal puds might include strawberry Eton mess or peach and vanilla cheesecake with peach schnapps jelly. The well-annotated wine list includes good glass and half-bottle selections.
Chef/s: Aron Griffiths. **Meals:** main courses £17 to £24. Sun L £24 (2 courses) to £29. **Details:** 100 seats. 80 seats outside. Bar. Wheelchairs. Parking. Music.

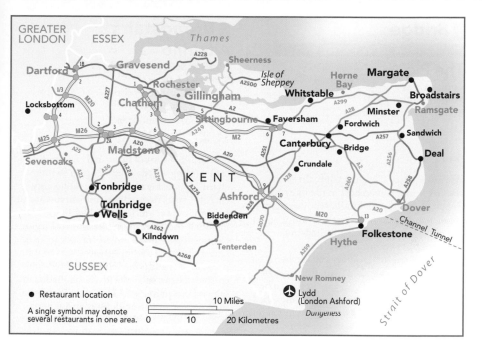

GREATER LONDON | ESSEX | Thames
Dartford · Gravesend · Sheerness · Isle of Sheppey · Herne Bay · Margate
Locksbottom · Rochester · Gillingham · Whitstable · Broadstairs
Chatham · Sittingbourne · Faversham · Minster · Ramsgate
Maidstone · Canterbury · Fordwich · Sandwich · Bridge · Deal
Sevenoaks · Crundale
KENT
Tonbridge · Ashford · Dover
Tunbridge Wells · Biddenden · Channel Tunnel · Folkestone
Kilndown · Tenterden · Hythe
SUSSEX
New Romney
Lydd (London Ashford) · Dungeness
Strait of Dover

• Restaurant location
A single symbol may denote several restaurants in one area.
0   10 Miles
0   10   20 Kilometres

Biddenden
The West House
Cooking score: 5
Modern European | £48
28 High Street, Biddenden, TN27 8AH
Tel no: 01580 291341
thewesthouserestaurant.co.uk

Graham Garrett's restaurant with rooms
occupies a rather lovely weaver's cottage with
beamed ceilings and roughcast timbered walls
in the heart of a well-heeled village. But
banish all thoughts of rusticity – this is a
venue for serious contemporary cooking
offered via a series of fixed-price menus and a
six-course taster (including a vegetarian
option). Combinations make sense and
everything hangs together nicely. Warm oak-
smoked haddock and quail's egg gets a flourish
from bacon dressing, and grilled fillet of hake
is a main course enriched by cep ragoût, pine
nuts, winter greens and a button mushroom
velouté. Salt marsh lamb confirms the passion

for regional ingredients, teamed with confit
turnip, cavolo nero, smoked paprika ketchup,
feta and rosemary sauce, while desserts such as
blood orange rum baba served with a
buttermilk ice cream maintain the artistry to
the end. Wine-wise, glasses from £6 lead the
charge on an authoritative list stuffed with
classy names and curious discoveries.
Chef/s: Graham Garrett and Tony Parkin. **Closed:**
Mon, Tue, 1 week Dec, 2 weeks summer. **Meals:** set
L £25 (2 courses) to £29. Set D £38 (2 courses) to
£48. Tasting menu £65 (6 courses). Sun L £38.
Details: 35 seats. V menu. Wheelchairs. Parking.
Music.

Wine list
Restaurants showing this symbol
have a wine list that our experts
consider to be outstanding, either for
its in-depth focus on a particular region,
attractive margins on fine wines, or strong
selection by the glass.

Bridge

★ NEW ENTRY ★

The Pig

Cooking score: 2
Modern British | £40
Bourne Park Road, Bridge, CT4 5BH
Tel no: 0345 225 9494
thepighotel.com

As Bridge Place Country Club, this 17th-century house played host to the likes of Led Zeppelin, but the strikingly renovated Grade I listed manor is now the sixth iteration of The Pig group of hotels. The polished-but-cluttered posh country house decor, beautifully tended grounds and kitchen garden could be plucked from the pages of a glossy magazine, and everyone seems to be having a jolly good time in the potting-shed-inspired dining room. No wonder, given that simple dishes coming from the open-plan kitchen offer superior seasonal produce – home-grown or sourced within 25 miles – and service is warm and welcoming. Begin, perhaps, with a snack of brown crab paste soldiers before starters of charred cuttlefish with crispy chorizo and sauce vierge or tomato and smoked pork loin salad with cubes of Sister Sarah goat's cheese. A pie of tender rosemary-infused lamb with buttery mash and a little jug of proper green liquor, and a chocolate mousse with apple-brandy-soaked prunes both went down a storm at inspection. There's a Kentish cheeseboard and the county's wines feature on a well-curated list.
Chef/s: Kamil Oseka. **Meals:** main courses £14 to £32. **Details:** 80 seats. 30 seats outside. Bar. Parking.

Get social

Follow us on social media for the latest news, chef interviews and more.
Twitter @GoodFoodGuideUK
Facebook TheGoodFoodGuide

Broadstairs

Albariño

Cooking score: 2
Spanish | £30
29 Albion Street, Broadstairs, CT10 1LX
Tel no: 01843 600991
albarinorestaurant.co.uk
£5 OFF £30

Steven Dray should be heartily congratulated for bringing a little taste of Spain to this charming seaside town. Dishes at his tiny, cheerful tapas restaurant demonstrate careful sourcing: charcuterie (including Ibérico bellota lomo and jamón serrano) and regional cheeses appear beside chistorra sausage (a fine-textured chorizo from Navarra) served with patatas fritas and romesco sauce. Tried-and-trusted classics such as a textbook tortilla or salt cod croquetas with lemon and tarragon mayonnaise give way to more inventive combinations: tender octopus with potatoes and sweet smoked paprika, say, or moreish chickpea and fennel chips with aïoli, spinach, sultanas, soft goat's cheese and honey on toast. Round off with comforting crema catalana or churros with chocolate sauce. The sound all-Spanish wine list, which opens with a selection of sherries, majors in Albariño and is as accessibly priced as the food.
Chef/s: Steven Dray. **Closed:** Sun, 19 Dec to 2 Jan. **Meals:** tapas £3 to £22. Table sharing menu £27. **Details:** 26 seats. Bar. Wheelchairs. Music.

Stark

Cooking score: 5
Modern European | £60
1 Oscar Road, Broadstairs, CT10 1QJ
Tel no: 01843 579786
starkfood.co.uk

Once Thanet's best-kept secret and now most definitely on the map, Ben and Sophie Crittenden's tasting-menu-only restaurant in this truly tiny wood-panelled space (a former sandwich bar) has been open since 2017. The proposition is simple: Ben cooks, Sophie hosts, and you get what you're given. 'Good

food laid bare' is the maxim, a modest one given the calibre of Ben's cooking, a deftly orchestrated procession of six seasonal courses – each plate a painterly, technically astute combination of three core ingredients: 'beef, mushroom, wild asparagus' equates to far more than the sum of its parts, anchored by an intensely savoury jus, and 'mackerel, carrot, yolk' is an innovative delight in form, taste and texture. The sweet courses, including goat's curd with strawberries and pistachio, share the clarity of flavour and ingenuity that characterises Ben's food. The menu changes weekly, and symbiotic wine pairings are worth the extra £30, although there's a snappy list of bottles starting at £17.
Chef/s: Ben Crittenden. **Closed:** Mon, Tue, Sun. **Meals:** tasting menu £60 (6 courses). **Details:** 10 seats. Music.

Wyatt & Jones

Cooking score: 4
Seafood | £36
23-27 Harbour Street, Broadstairs, CT10 1EU
Tel no: 01843 865126
wyattandjones.co.uk
£5 OFF

Moored on the steep incline of Harbour Street leading down to the sea, Wyatt & Jones's long stepped dining room is an inviting prospect, particularly on the lower floor next to the open kitchen, where you can take in views of Viking Bay. It's an all-day operation and new chef Joe Hill's fish cookery brings sea to table with style and consummate skill. To find out what lies in store, direct your glance to the blackboard, and don't skip the appetisers, where sourdough comes with seaweed-flecked butter or smoked cod's roe. Moving on, impeccably baked scallops with salsify and Sauternes sauce or monkfish scampi with squid ink batter speak volumes of the kitchen's intention to feed you well. Meat and fish marry cleverly in mains of pearlescent baked pollock with rich pork and fennel sauce or John Dory with chicken butter (there's ribeye steak and fries for fish refuseniks). Finish on a (sugar) high with white chocolate brioche and

butter pudding. The single-page wine list, accessibly priced and with interesting producers, starts at £24.
Chef/s: Joe Hill. **Closed:** 25 and 26 Dec. **Meals:** main courses £15 to £24. **Details:** 54 seats. Bar. Music.

▌Canterbury
The Goods Shed

Cooking score: 3
Modern British | £37
Station Road West, Canterbury, CT2 8AN
Tel no: 01227 459153
thegoodsshed.co.uk

If there's one thing better than a good farmers' market, then it's a good farmers' market that does the cooking for you. This former railway shed next to Canterbury West station is just that – alongside the stalls selling local fruit and veg, meat, cheese, fish and more, there's a sit-down restaurant with a simple, bare-brick fit-out, amiable service and exactly the right take on seasonality. The result is a roster of up-to-the-minute dishes that might offer simple snacks of fresh radishes and grilled chicken hearts with prunes, followed perhaps by starters of cured trout teamed with cucumber and a dollop of crème fraîche, or pork terrine with a punchy piccalilli and excellent sourdough bread. Diners generate a lively buzz and there's praise for a host of things, from lamb shoulder with aubergine caponata and new potatoes or local cod with charred sprouting broccoli and a warm tartare sauce to the British cheeseboard and a rhubarb frangipane tart. To drink there are locals ales, ciders and English sparkling wines; house French is £20.
Chef/s: Rafael Lopez. **Closed:** Mon. **Meals:** main courses £17 to £20. **Details:** 60 seats. Parking.

Crundale
The Compasses Inn
Cooking score: 5
Modern British | £35
Sole Street, Crundale, CT4 7ES
Tel no: 01227 700300
thecompassescrundale.co.uk
£5
OFF

With thick walls, low beams, open fires and plain wooden tables, this ancient hostelry suits its remote rural location to a T, although the food tells a different story. Chef Robert Taylor cooks to a traditional template, so dishes are based on first-class seasonal, frequently local, ingredients but with the addition of modern touches. It's a style that's eloquently demonstrated in a dish of rump cap, a woefully underused cut of beef, aged for 40 days and served with breaded brisket, gratin potatoes, confit Roscoff onion, cavolo nero and horseradish cream. Before that might come salt-baked celeriac with goat's curd, hazelnut granola and walnut ketchup or roast skate with pickled mussels and stout syrup. Sticky toffee pudding with caramelised banana and vanilla ice cream is a dessert not to be missed, even if you have filled up on the wonderful bread and addictive Marmite cream cheese. Drink Shepherd Neame ales or wine from £17.
Chef/s: Robert Taylor. **Closed:** Mon, Tue, bank hols.
Meals: main courses £19 to £24. Set L £19 (2 courses) to £23. **Details:** 47 seats. Bar. Parking. Music.

Deal
Frog and Scot
Cooking score: 2
Anglo-French | £35
86 High Street, Deal, CT14 6EG
Tel no: 01304 379444
frogandscot.co.uk
£5
OFF

Benoit and Sarah Dezecot (the eponymous 'frog' and 'Scot') opened their bistro in the heart of this seaside town with more than its fair share of bohemian charm in 2016. Their formula of modern, unshowy Franco-centric food, in a convivial room of tightly packed mismatched furniture, fits right in. The blackboard menu is a market-driven affair: a meal might begin with oysters with cucumber jelly and dill cream, or wild mushroom croquettes, moving on to a beautifully roasted cod loin with black pudding, Jerusalem artichoke purée and carrot top pesto, or roast chicken leg with a sumptuous truffle cream sauce. There's classic steak, chips and salad – top-notch meat comes from the local Black Pig butcher. Lemon and lime posset makes a lovely finish. The eclectic French-focused wine list features a robust selection of natural, organic and biodynamic wines from £22 (the Dezecots have a wine bar and shop a few doors down the street).
Chef/s: Bruce Stratford. **Closed:** Mon, Tue.
Meals: main courses £17 to £30. Set L £15 (2 courses) to £18. Set D £24 (2 courses) to £27.
Details: 55 seats. 12 seats outside. Bar. Wheelchairs. Music.

★ NEW ENTRY ★

Whits of Walmer
Cooking score: 2
Seafood | £45
61 The Strand, Walmer, Deal, CT14 7DP
Tel no: 01304 368881
whits.co.uk

Devoted regulars and first-timers rub shoulders in this small seafront dining room that exudes personable civility. Steve Whitney's quietly assured cooking of fish and shellfish is a beguiling proposition with classical combinations and a good amount of regional produce. Expect pretty restaurant-style dishes with modern accents, from local lobster ravioli with spinach and lobster sauce to an excellent millefeuille of tuna with local crab, mango, apple and a light curry vinaigrette. Occasionally, plates get too cluttered, as in a main of roast fillet of halibut with crab and Parmesan crust, squid ink spaghetti, scallops and saffron garlic sauce, although a classic combination of skate wing, capers, brown shrimp and beurre noisette served with buttery mashed potato gets things back on track. There's a return to form with dessert, which might offer up a perfectly risen banana soufflé with banana ice cream and honeycomb Eton mess. The food is backed by well-chosen wines.

Chef/s: Steve Whitney. **Closed:** Mon, Tue, Wed. **Meals:** main courses £17 to £28. Tasting menu £36 (5 courses). Sun L £25. **Details:** 32 seats. 25 seats outside. Music.

Faversham
Read's
Cooking score: 6
Modern British | £60
Macknade Manor, Canterbury Road, Faversham, ME13 8XE
Tel no: 01795 535344
reads.com
🍷 🛏

Suggesting a rare level of reliability and consistency, this welcoming restaurant has been ably run by David and Rona Pitchford since 1977, relocating to a splendid Georgian manor in 2002. It continues to attract a trail of well-deserved reviews, not least for its fresh and modern cooking, which successfully fuses diverse ideas. A salmon fillet is served, for example, with curried cauliflower, Bombay potatoes, almonds and lemongrass sauce, while a more traditional confit duck comes together with savoy cabbage, fondant potato and Grand Marnier sauce. Local supply lines furnish the menus, from Stour Valley game to Kentish lamb (robustly flavoured with smoked potato purée, haggis and lovage tart, roasted onion and lamb sauce), while the garden delivers vegetables (salt-baked celeriac with green apple, mushroom ketchup, pickled celery and autumn truffle) and the cheeseboard is British. Finish with a soufflé – the blackberry has been highly praised. There's praise for the good-value set lunch menu, which offers four dishes at each course. The lovingly compiled wine list champions quality producers from across the globe, with

the French leading the pack; a condensed list of best buys is a user-friendly way into the extensive collection.

Chef/s: David Pitchford. **Closed:** Mon, Sun, 2 weeks Jan, 2 weeks Sept, 25 and 26 Dec. **Meals:** set L £32. Set D £60. Tasting menu £40 (5 courses) to £65. **Details:** 50 seats. 25 seats outside. Bar. Wheelchairs. Parking.

Folkestone
The Folkestone Wine Company
Cooking score: 4
Modern French | £32
5 Church Street, Folkestone, CT20 1SE
Tel no: 01303 249952
folkestonewine.com

This is what is meant by a good local restaurant: a convivial, friendly place that has a firm regular following. Rather like the decor, the cooking is stripped to its essentials, but Dave Hart understands balance, seasons deftly and every dish contributes to creating a delightfully coherent meal. The short blackboard menu changes daily according to market availability, but can be relied upon to offer initial bites along the lines of rock oysters, a simple dish of Bayonne ham with celeriac and mustard, wild garlic soup with crème fraîche, or Parmesan gnocchi with basil pesto. Mains run to free range chicken breast teamed with morels, given serious class by a rich, silky sherry cream sauce and a perfectly timed cod fillet that comes garnished with pink fir potatoes, leeks and aïoli. Sign off with a choux bun filled with praline cream and almonds. Polly Pleasence ensures seamless service and back-up comes from an appealing wine list with good by-the-glass selection.

Chef/s: David Hart. **Closed:** Mon, Tue, Sun (Jun, Jul, Aug), 25 and 26 Dec, 1 Jan. **Meals:** main courses £15 to £23. Set L £18 (2 courses) to £22. **Details:** 26 seats. 8 seats outside. Music.

Fordwich

The Fordwich Arms

Cooking score: 6
Modern British | £55
King Street, Fordwich, CT2 0DB
Tel no: 01227 710444
fordwicharms.co.uk

You could be forgiven for thinking this brick-built Arts and Crafts hostelry is just a pub for food. One mouthful of the Fordwich's near-peerless cooking and 'my goodness you are soon disavowed of that'. Sourcing ingredients is a serious business, whether it's game from nearby shoots, Gloucester old spot pork, Whitstable oysters or local crab, or produce from further afield such as Orkney scallops and Scottish langoustines. Options include a short à la carte or a four- or seven-course tasting menu, with good-value set lunches boosting the bid for accessibility. And readers' opinions on the food? 'Beautifully crafted and presented, and the flavours were quite superb.' Highlights this year have included duck liver parfait with clementine, Sauternes and warm doughnuts, and roast rump of Hereford beef with new season's peas, glazed salsify and smoked bone marrow. Fish cookery – as in line-caught turbot with morels, white asparagus, monk's beard and wild garlic – is just as you'd hope. As for dessert, dark chocolate mousse with Valpolicella-poached spiced pear and a dinky financier is highly recommended. Bread – sourdough and Irish soda – deserves special mention, as does the accompanying whipped pork fat with Marmite and crisp smoked bacon crumbs. An enjoyably diverse wine list unrolls across both hemispheres; bottles start at £25.
Chef/s: Daniel and Natasha Smith. **Closed:** Mon, 25 Dec. **Meals:** main courses £26 to £29. Set L £35. Tasting menu £65 (4 courses) to £85. **Details:** 45 seats. 38 seats outside. V menu. Bar. Wheelchairs. Parking. Music.

Kilndown

★ CHEF TO WATCH ★

The Small Holding

Cooking score: 4
Modern British | £30
Ranters Lane, Kilndown, TN17 2SG
Tel no: 01892 890105
thesmallholding.restaurant
£5 OFF £30

Striding confidently into its second year, Will Devlin's restaurant shows no sign of slowing down – 'a truly sensational experience' is one fan's heartfelt comment. The splendidly rural former pub comes with simple, rustic decor, an intimate dining room and broad outdoor terrace – it's a beautiful spot and a lot of effort has gone into creating a warm, unpretentious atmosphere. Fiercely seasonal five- or ten-course tasting menus are what to expect, although there's a good-value set lunch too. The level of ingenuity generated by a kitchen on turbo drive, fuelled by its own smallholding, hen coop and piggery, is prodigious, the opening statement of intent laid out in nibbles of beetroot macaroon and mushroom gyoza. There's a feel for proper flavour in thoughtful assemblages of halibut with a classic beurre blanc sauce, Dexter beef tartare perfectly balanced with a slow-cooked duck egg, and in virtuoso desserts such as a strawberry and basil tartlet or a pear and miso combo. The whole show is fleshed out with brilliant bread, engaging service and a wine list that is gleaned from hands-on organic producers.
Chef/s: William Devlin. **Closed:** Mon, Tue. **Meals:** set L £20. Tasting menu £30 (5 courses) to £50. **Details:** 26 seats. 20 seats outside. V menu. Vg menu. Bar. Wheelchairs. Parking. Music.

Locksbottom

Chapter One

Cooking score: 6
Modern European | £43
Farnborough Common, Locksbottom,
BR6 8NF
Tel no: 01689 854848
chapteronerestaurant.co.uk

'Excellent food as always, never had a bad meal', is praise indeed for this well-established restaurant, taken over in 2017 by its long-standing chef Andrew McLeish. Recent renovations have only increased support for this 'busy and buzzy' local venue that does the old-fashioned things supremely well. There are Sunday roasts that include sirloin of beef and crispy pork belly, and McLeish supplements a three-stage menu du jour with a carte and a tasting menu. The cooking has overtones of the modern European style with intelligent classical underpinnings, extending perhaps to gin-cured chalk stream trout with compressed cucumber and dill and yoghurt dressing, followed by feuilleté of rabbit with white asparagus, pea pureé and Gewürztraminer sauce or baked hake with pistachio and hazelnut crust with roasted cauliflower and cauliflower couscous. Alluring desserts embrace Valrhona dark chocolate marquise with griottine cherries and cherry sorbet. As for wine, there are lots of accessible, familiar options at fair prices, but plenty of interest, too, on a wide-ranging, well-curated list that opens at £25.
Chef/s: Andrew McLeish and Dean Ferguson. **Closed:** 6 to 8 Jan. **Meals:** set L £20 (2 courses) to £43. Set D £38 (2 courses) to £43. Tasting menu £65 (6 courses). Sun L £30. **Details:** 160 seats. 20 seats outside. V menu. Bar. Wheelchairs. Parking. Music.

Margate

Angela's of Margate

Cooking score: 5
Seafood | £35
21 The Parade, Margate, CT9 1EX
Tel no: 01843 319978
angelasofmargate.com

Since opening in 2017, this tiny seafood restaurant has made a big impression. Bordering the Old Town, close to the beach, its formula of sustainability and simple, exemplary fish cookery has won a devoted following. Lee Coad and Charlotte Forsdike's environmental manifesto influences all aspects of the operation, from fuel to ingredients and food waste, but there's nothing po-faced about the place: it's all about good food, good wine and good times. The set lunch and à la carte are built around the morning's catch. After succulent ray knobs (aka the tender cheeks, so often discarded) served with aïoli, or local whelks in garlic butter, opt for turbot on the bone, or a Dover sole with cockles, served with locally grown vegetables, and finish with trifle, or junket with honeycomb. Expect English wines from forward-thinking small producers. Dory's, Angela's seafront sibling, is a no-reservations all-day seafood bar and shop that shares the same ethos (see entry).
Chef/s: Rob Cooper. **Closed:** Mon, Tue, Christmas, New Year. **Meals:** main courses £14 to £22. Set L £15 Wed to Fri (2 courses) to £18. **Details:** 28 seats.

Bottega Caruso

Cooking score: 3
Italian | £29
2-4 Broad Street, Margate, CT9 1EW
Tel no: 01843 297142
bottegacaruso.com
£30

Firmly stamped with the individuality of its owners, this one-off Italian in the heart of the old town has a loyal band of regulars who praise its atmosphere, service and great food. A fair amount of the kitchen's supplies come

direct from family sources in Italy, the rest provided by a carefully nurtured network of local suppliers, while the cooking is an expansive mix of big flavours and hearty dishes from southern Italy. The focus is on excellent pasta, made fresh each morning, perhaps served with a ragù of pork and beef, or wild sea bass enlivened by preserved lemon and cured mullet roe. Another sure-fire success has been organic chicken leg boned and stuffed with pancetta and chestnuts and cooked in red wine. Creamy mozzarella with spicy wild black pig sausage is a favourite starter, while a 'marvellous light' tiramisu and 'best doughnut ever – filled with copious vanilla cream' make fitting finales. The concise, all-Italian wine list (from £19.75) bursts with low intervention and artisan gems.
Chef/s: Simona Di Dio and Harry Ryder. **Closed:** Mon, Tue, Wed. **Meals:** main courses £13 to £18. **Details:** 28 seats. Music.

Hantverk & Found
Cooking score: 2
Seafood | £30
18 King Street, Margate, CT9 1DA
Tel no: 01843 280454
hantverk-found.co.uk
£5 OFF £30

The philosophy is simple: chef proprietor Kate de Syllas serves what she loves to cook. Following expansion into the shop next door, she now runs a two-pronged operation: a seafood restaurant with a basement art gallery, and an evening-only natural wine and tapas bar. The restaurant, with bare wood tables, remains as tiny as ever, but don't expect a diminutive attitude when it comes to the food – majoring in punchy, fresh flavours, the menu focuses on Kate's affection for Japanese, Spanish and North African cuisines. Oysters with yuzu ponzu and toasted nori share the billing with meticulously cooked roast mackerel with chermoula, warm salad of Jersey Royals, tomatoes and olives, and hake with summer vegetable ragoût and clams. Popular house-smoked prawns and creative vegetarian dishes are mainstays, and there

might be chocolate brownie or affogato to finish. Expect plenty of European wines, with quite a few offbeat, new-wave bottles.
Chef/s: Kate de Syllas. **Closed:** Mon, Tue, Wed, 2 weeks Dec to Jan. **Meals:** main courses £13 to £22. Seasonal sharing menu £30. **Details:** 26 seats. 15 seats outside. Bar. Music.

LOCAL GEM
Dory's of Margate
Seafood | £10
24 High Street, Margate, CT9 1DS
Tel no: 01843 319978
angelasofmargate.com
£30

For the many fans of nearby Angela's (see entry), the opening of this seafront café deli from the same owners has proved a boon – an all-day, no-reservations hangout that satisfies the urge for a bottle of wine and something simple to eat when you don't have a booking elsewhere. It continues the laudable formula of impeccable sourcing and minimal waste, with the day's selections of keenly priced small plates chalked up on a blackboard. Expect the likes of Whitstable rock oysters, smoked prawns with aïoli, cod brandade, seafood tart stuffed with lobster and crab, BBQ mackerel fillet, salads and a cheese plate. English wines feature on a list that opens at £19.50.

LOCAL GEM
GB Pizza Co.
Italian | £17
14a Marine Drive, Margate, CT9 1DH
Tel no: 01843 297700
greatbritishpizza.com
£30

Catch one of the town's famous sunsets from this bright and cheerful place on the seafront. Most of the thin, crisp, wood-fired pizzas are topped with locally sourced ingredients, and 'interesting flavour choices' might include peppers, Kentish goat's curd and basil, or pear and British blue cheese on a ricotta base. Gluten-free versions and vegan cheese mean no one's left out. Choose from Kentish cider or beer, fizz, or help-yourself wine straight from a tap. There's a second branch in Didsbury, Greater Manchester, M20 6UR.

The Kentish Pantry
British | £20
1 Duke Street, Margate, CT9 1EP
Tel no: 01843 231150
thekentishpantry.co.uk

£5 OFF £30

There's a lot of competition in the old town these days, but this friendly and welcoming little café cheerfully holds its own, drawing visitors back with fresh and tasty cooking. Dishes deliver simple pairings of good raw ingredients, whether you've just popped in for a poached egg (local and free range, of course) served on toast with roasted tomato and buttered sprouting broccoli or a classic boeuf bourguignon with tartiflette potatoes. The daily changing 'real proper pie' is a good pick, and there's baked rice pudding brûlée, too. Wines from £15.

▌Minster
The Corner House
Cooking score: 1
British | £30
42 Station Road, Minster, CT12 4BZ
Tel no: 01843 823000
cornerhouserestaurants.co.uk

£5 OFF £30

In the heart of a quiet village not far from Canterbury, this restaurant with rooms is the kind of place you would love to have as your local, with nurturing food, friendly service and a lively buzz. The kitchen focuses on local suppliers and crowd-pleasing recipes, delivered with aplomb. Chicken liver parfait with port jelly might be followed by Stour Valley duck breast with mash, carrots and an orange and star anise sauce. Slow-braised shoulder of lamb (for two or four people) gets the thumbs-up, as does pear upside-down

cake with tonka bean ice cream. Drink Kentish ales or global wines from £17. There is another branch at 1 Dover Street, Canterbury, CT1 3HD.
Chef/s: Predrag Kostic. **Meals:** main courses £16 to £24. Set L £16 (2 courses) to £20. Sun L £20 (2 courses) to £24. **Details:** 40 seats. 20 seats outside. Vg menu. Bar. Wheelchairs. Parking. Music.

▌Sandwich
The Salutation
Cooking score: 4
Modern European | £55
Knightrider Street, Sandwich, CT13 9EW
Tel no: 01304 619919
the-salutation.com

£5 OFF

Sir Edwin Lutyens built this house for a family of lawyers and bankers just before the Great War, its sumptuous gardens laid out as a series of discrete spaces. Now a boutique hotel, the place comes equipped with an ambitious dining room in the hands of Shane Hughes. His style is precise and thoughtful, with smart presentations emphasising the ingenuity of the dishes. Smoked monkfish tail stars with pink grapefruit in shellfish and sorrel consommé infused with lemongrass and lime leaf. The multi-layered nature of the dishes works to highlight their main ingredients, as when seared turbot is partnered with crab, fermented carrot and fennel, a chilli and coriander beignet and laverbread sauce. Gressingham duck two ways comes with butternut squash and blue cheese terrine, and wild mushrooms in five-spiced and honeyed jus. Chocolate indulgence comes via a tiered construction of ganache, mousseline and brownie, with hazelnut crémeux and mango sorbet. A diagrammatic cocktail selection is one of the features of a drinks list offering refinement and panache, with quality-conscious wines in the hands of a Master of Wine. Glasses start at £6.
Chef/s: Shane Hughes. **Meals:** main courses £25 to £32. Tasting menu £55 (4 courses) to £75. Sun L £30. **Details:** 60 seats. 30 seats outside. V menu. Vg menu. Bar. Wheelchairs. Parking. Music.

Tonbridge

The Poet at Matfield

Cooking score: 2
Modern British | £45
Maidstone Road, Matfield, Tonbridge,
TN12 7JH
Tel no: 01892 722416
thepoetatmatfield.co.uk

A quintessential Kentish brick and tile-hung village hostelry, this popular roadside destination still has its quota of beams and open fires (plus a portrait of Matfield's poetic son Siegfried Sassoon in the bar), although most people come for the food served in the rustic flower-festooned dining room. South African chef Petrus Madutlela is a man on a mission, tackling a host of ambitious global dishes such as tuna tataki with nashi pear, hazelnut crumb and miso mayonnaise, as well as delivering more traditional satisfaction – perhaps a trio of lamb (braised shoulder, cutlet and sweetbread) with Tenderstem broccoli and pommes Anna. There's well-aged beef from Surrey farms too, while desserts might run to mango and cardamom soufflé or tarte tatin with malt ice cream – all helpfully paired with unusual wine suggestions. Additional midweek attractions include a Tuesday 'steak and Malbec' night and an eight-course tasting dinner (for two) Wednesdays and Thursdays.
Chef/s: Petrus Madutlela. **Closed:** Mon.
Meals: main courses £21 to £36. Set L and Tue to Thur D £20 (2 courses) to £24. Sun L £25 (2 courses) to £29. **Details:** 50 seats. 100 seats outside. Bar. Parking. Music.

Tunbridge Wells

Thackeray's

Cooking score: 4
Modern European | £55
85 London Road, Tunbridge Wells, TN1 1EA
Tel no: 01892 511921
thackerays-restaurant.co.uk

Behind the ancient weatherboarded exterior, polished wood floors, white linen and well-spaced tables promise 'relaxed fine dining'.

Head chef Patrick Hill focuses on provenance, with excellent meat and fish locally sourced and modern flavour combinations evident in dishes such as cauliflower kimchi with Melba toast, sweetcorn salsa, goat's curd and kaffir lime balanced with a good kick of chilli, or a well-judged brill fillet with carrot, ginger and poached raisins. However, at a late June meal more was made of Orkney scallops and Scottish lobster than local seasonal produce, and the promised Groombridge asparagus in a well-executed main course of pea and mint arancini with braised Puy lentils was replaced by leeks with no warning. Desserts feature complex combinations such as roast apricot with chamomile and tonka bean flapjack or a hot banana soufflé. The comprehensive wine list means business with well-chosen bottles clearly described and an interesting selection of wines by the glass, courtesy of the Coravin system. Despite some assured cooking, inconsistency and inattentive service are an ongoing concern; as a recent diner suggested, 'maybe Thackeray's needs some competition in Tunbridge Wells'.
Chef/s: Patrick Hill. **Closed:** Mon. **Meals:** set L £18 (2 courses) to £20. Set D £55. Tasting menu £78 (7 courses). **Details:** 68 seats. 30 seats outside. V menu. Vg menu. Bar. Music.

Whitstable

Harbour Street Tapas

Cooking score: 4
Spanish | £26
48 Harbour Street, Whitstable, CT5 1AQ
Tel no: 01227 273373
harbourstreettapas.com
£5 OFF   £30

Welcoming, cheerful, light and bright, this diminutive restaurant is unassuming and easy-going, with simplicity and honest freshness the hallmarks of a meal here. Tim Wilson's zingy, confident take on classic tapas has drawn appreciative crowds since opening in 2016. If you can tear yourself away from jamón croquetas, patatas bravas and fried squid with anchovy aïoli, there is spatchcocked quail served with excellent romesco sauce,

monkfish and jamón pinchito teamed with spiced cauliflower purée, and lamb cutlets accompanied by merguez sausage and winter tabbouleh. The menu changes frequently, but white beans with spinach, pine nuts and raisins is a particular favourite among regulars, as is roast squash houmous with flatbread. Baked yoghurt with rhubarb and ginger makes a great finish. The compact, all-Spanish wine list comes by the glass (from £4) or bottle (£18) and it is good to note that bookings are now taken.
Chef/s: Tim Wilson. **Closed:** Mon, Tue. **Meals:** tapas £6 to £18. **Details:** 44 seats.

JoJo's

Cooking score: 4
Mediterranean | £30
2 Herne Bay Road, Tankerton, Whitstable, CT5 2LQ
Tel no: 01227 274591
jojosrestaurant.co.uk
£30

Whatever the weather, Nikki Billington's seafront restaurant has a sunny disposition that is matched by the cooking. The bare wooden tables and floor, and light, bright dining room set the tone for fuss-free tapas that are Mediterranean in style but anchored by impeccably sourced ingredients including the freshest fish. Kicking off with a vegetarian or charcuterie-based sharing platter is a must for most visitors, and mutton and feta koftas or patatas bravas are menu mainstays. There's also chargrilled mackerel fillet with a seasonal dip, or marinated bavette steak, but expect to see imaginative tapas getting their moment of glory on the specials board. Reserve a table (phone bookings are taken up to two weeks in advance) or pop in for a drink with 'dips and bits' in the first-come-first-served cocktail bar. The sea and sunset make for a pretty irresistible vista from the dining room or little terrace, and wines start at a very reasonable £4.50 a glass.

Chef/s: Nikki Billington, Buddy Rowden, Carmen Canet and Artis Kafiskins. **Closed:** Mon, Tue, Wed. **Meals:** small plates £5 to £9. Large plates £8 to £12. **Details:** 60 seats. 20 seats outside. Bar. Wheelchairs. Music.

Samphire

Cooking score: 2
Modern British | £35
4 High Street, Whitstable, CT5 1BQ
Tel no: 01227 770075
samphirewhitstable.co.uk
£5 OFF

By day this is a relaxed venue for breakfast or lunch, by night it's a proper restaurant with charm and prices that keep locals coming back. The high street location, a pebble's throw from the beach, suits the light and casual interior, with wood floors and tables, and an open kitchen that plunders the local area to create an appealing modern menu. At a late-spring lunch, pork belly croquette with wild garlic pesto and slaw proved to be a winner, followed by a huge bowl of mussels in Biddenden cider with onion, garlic and thyme. But the kitchen can summon up big meaty flavours, too, perhaps in an evening dish of braised short rib with boulangère potatoes, broccoli and onion ketchup. The British cheese selection is well worth exploring, as are traditional desserts such as lemon posset or poached rhubarb with an excellent chewy vanilla-cream pavlova. Everyone is put at ease by the relaxed, personable service, and the wide-ranging wine list is as kindly priced as the food.
Chef/s: Billy Stock. **Closed:** 25 and 26 Dec. **Meals:** main courses £15 to £21. Set L £17 (2 courses) to £20. **Details:** 38 seats. Music.

★ TOP 50 ★

The Sportsman

Cooking score: 7
Modern British | £45
Faversham Road, Seasalter, Whitstable,
CT5 4BP
Tel no: 01227 273370
thesportsmanseasalter.co.uk

Taking its easy tempo from the coastal marsh
setting, the Harris brothers' sturdy white-
painted pub shows no sign of resting on its
laurels, even after 20 years. Its dedication is
appreciated by readers, as is the lack of
pretension – evident in the paper napkins,
bare wooden tables and the requirement to
place your order at the bar. In the kitchen Dan
Flavell interprets Steve Harris's produce-first
approach brilliantly in a repertoire that
integrates local ideas and ingredients with
some up-to-date flourishes and a good
measure of comfort. He's right at home
putting together an ingenious – and almost
legendary – tiny mushroom and celeriac tart
with a runny egg yolk at its heart, cooking a
pink, succulent roast saddle of Kentish lamb
or a perfect plate of turbot with smoked pork.
These are dishes from the tasting menu (which
should be preordered on booking), although
the blackboard à la carte has its own pleasures:
mussel and bacon chowder, steamed cod with
local leeks and a chorizo and cream sauce, and
slow-cooked rib of beef with creamy mash
and greens in a horseradish sauce. For the final
act, a glossy dark chocolate and salted caramel
tart with clotted cream, or raspberry soufflé
with raspberry ripple ice cream are heartily
endorsed. There's excellent bread, too,
especially the focaccia, and service is serene
and calm. The short, reasonably priced wine
list opens at £18.95 for a Languedoc Viognier.
Chef/s: Stephen Harris and Dan Flavell. **Closed:**
Mon, 25 to 27 Dec, 1 Jan. **Meals:** main courses £16
to £29. Tasting menu £55 (5 courses) to £70.
Details: 50 seats. Wheelchairs. Parking. Music. No
children at D.

Wheelers Oyster Bar

Cooking score: 4
Seafood | £38
8 High Street, Whitstable, CT5 1BQ
Tel no: 01227 273311
wheelersoysterbar.com

'Great fish dishes in a tiny, cosy parlour, BYO',
was how one reader neatly summed up this
landmark restaurant, now well into its second
century. The fabulously old-fashioned oyster
bar and original parlour, and its more recent
light-filled dining room extension, are
dedicated to the delivery of respectfully
treated seafood, which Mark Stubbs handles
with dexterity. His influences are wide, as seen
in a stunning crispy cod BLG toastie (with
bacon jam, lettuce and Gruyère rarebit), blowtorched mackerel or BBQ-smoked eel, served
with an apple, grape, celery and watercress
salad, blini and a side of beetroot soup.
Substantial mains are very much on point:
poached hake in an intense Asian-style
mushroom consommé arrives with
outstanding prawn and kimchi dumplings.
The kitchen rarely puts a foot wrong and that
goes for desserts, too – pistachio soufflé and
bitter chocolate ice cream being a high point at
one spring meal. The place is run with bundles
of personable charm, but remember to pick up
a chilled bottle of wine from the offie across
the road, and bring cash.
Chef/s: Mark Stubbs. **Closed:** Wed, 2 weeks Jan.
Meals: main courses £21 to £24. **Details:** 32 seats.
Wheelchairs. Cash only.

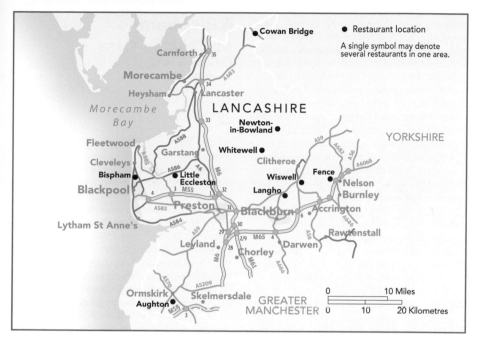

Map legend:
● Cowan Bridge   ● Restaurant location
A single symbol may denote several restaurants in one area.

Carnforth 35
Morecambe
Heysham 34 Lancaster
Morecambe Bay 33 LANCASHIRE
Newton-in-Bowland ●
Fleetwood Whitewell ● YORKSHIRE
Cleveleys Garstang ● Clitheroe
Bispham ● Little Eccleston ● Wiswell ● Fence ●
Blackpool Langho ● Nelson Burnley
Preston Blackburn Accrington
Lytham St Anne's
Leyland ● Chorley Darwen Rawtenstall
Ormskirk
Aughton ● Skelmersdale GREATER MANCHESTER

0   10 Miles
0   10   20 Kilometres

▌Aughton
The Barn
Cooking score: 4
Modern British | £38
Moor Hall, Prescot Road, Aughton, L39 6RT
Tel no: 01695 572511
moorhall.com

The British brasserie offspring of Mark Birchall's Moor Hall (see entry) shows another side to the chef's vision. Sited in an old barn adjacent to the main house, the ground floor is given over to a dairy, bakery, microbrewery, and meat ageing and curing room. The magnificently beamed and airy first-floor dining room makes an ideal casual dining spot. A menu of exemplary dishes with a strong seasonal accent is bang on the money. Evergreens such as traditional Sunday roasts are way above the norm and diehards can feast on various steaks with a choice of peppercorn or béarnaise sauce, but king oyster mushroom with black garlic, shiitake parfait and Stilton,

and slow-cooked veal cheek with organic carrot and parsley pesto are more typical of the kitchen's flexible approach. To finish, spiced pear with honey parfait, almond and thyme succeeds at every step. The wine list opens at £25 and there's a pretty garden terrace for sunny days.
Chef/s: Mark Birchall and Nathan Cornwell. **Closed:** Mon, Tue, Jan. **Meals:** main courses £15 to £42. Sun L £28 (2 courses) to £35. **Details:** 65 seats. 24 seats outside. V menu. Bar. Wheelchairs. Parking. Music.

★ TOP 10 ★
Moor Hall
Cooking score: 9
Modern British | £70
Prescot Road, Aughton, L39 6RT
Tel no: 01695 572511
moorhall.com

Without doubt the hottest restaurant in Lancashire by a country mile; many readers are in agreement that 'from the moment you walk in... everything is simply perfect'. Staff are young, enthusiastic yet professional and add to the impression that this is very much a restaurant in its prime. Indeed, from the moment the gone-in-a-mouthful snacks arrive – among them a colourful flower-topped disc of smoked eel, layered with thin crisps of potato and fermented garlic, and a single oyster with cured ham, dill and buttermilk adding a delicate sweet-sourness – it is clear that this is a place for serious dining. And Mark Birchall's food excels. Look no further than his astonishing signature dish of Holstein Friesian beef tartare, where barbecued celeriac, mustard and shallot add piquancy to the well-aged meat; or the tantalising combination of velvety crabmeat topping thinly sliced raw turnip with its hint of anise hyssop and a broth that manages to get 'more deliciousness out of a turnip than you would have thought possible'. Two hits from the recent past give an idea of the style of the four- or eight-course tasting menus: a single Scottish langoustine, the cooking judged to a second, perfectly complemented by slivers of kohlrabi, sorrel and asparagus; and spot-on roasted herdwick lamb loin served with smoked broccoli, artichoke and anchovy, its accompanying bowl of lamb ragoût sinfully rich but with enough edge to allow the next mouthful to be approached with glee. To finish, perfect green strawberries with sweet cicely and cream cheese (one of three desserts) is a light treat (a visit to the tiny cheese room is another). Alex Freguin is a premier league sommelier who provides verbal notes for a wine list that ticks the boxes for remarkable breadth and quality.

Chef/s: Mark Birchall. **Closed:** Mon, Tue, 2 weeks Jan, 2 weeks Aug. **Meals:** tasting menu £65 (4 courses) to £125. **Details:** 52 seats. V menu. Vg menu. Bar. Wheelchairs. Parking. Music.

▌Bispham
Mi Casa Su Casa

Cooking score: 2
Spanish | £30
117 Red Bank Road, Bispham, FY2 9HZ
Tel no: 01253 351993

£30

A voluble sense of hospitality animates this classic Spanish tapas venue just off the seafront tram route, where everybody is greeted as though they were long-lost relatives. A laminated menu is supplemented by little blackboards inscribed with the specials, and the food, which emerges from behind a counter at the back, combines honest simplicity with strong, true flavours. Start with fried shrimps on toast or fresh sardines, before moving on to big protein hits from chicken, lamb or swordfish sautéed in oil, offset perhaps with the crispness of a tomato and spring onion side salad. Chips are good, and the desserts are given the full ice cream and cream treatment, maybe for a wedge of lemon tart that has all the expected zing. There are only a few wines, but no need to stray from the well-chosen Spanish house selections.

Chef/s: Liz Cooper. **Closed:** Wed, Sun.
Meals: tapas £3 to £8

▌Cowan Bridge
Hipping Hall

Cooking score: 5
Modern British | £70
Ingleton Road, Cowan Bridge, LA6 2JJ
Tel no: 01524 271187
hippinghall.com

Chef Oli Martin is a proud Lancastrian, but not too proud to look beyond the red rose county for inspiration – especially as the restaurant sits between two national parks, inside Lancashire but close enough to Cumbria and Yorkshire to take advantage of their larders. Goosnargh duck, Kirkham's Lancashire, Yorkshire rhubarb and Cumbrian beef make regular appearances on multi-course menus that offer a 'wonderful balance of ingredients, taste, textures and surprises'. Visually, an opener of butter pie bears scant resemblance to those scoffed hungrily on the football terraces, although the crisp little pillow hits all the right nostalgic notes. Culinary borrowings from the Scandinavian school are germane: smoked salsify and elderberries with aged duck; buttermilk and roe with chalk stream trout reflect the environment from which they come. The 'spaghetti bolognese' dessert (as seen on *MasterChef: The Professionals*) is a calling card. Service has 'just the right balance of chat and attention' and the wine list, from £26, has natural and biodynamic inclinations with plenty of offbeat selections from small producers.

Chef/s: Oli Martin. **Closed:** Mon, Tue. **Meals:** tasting menu L £30 Thur to Sun (4 courses) to £45 and D £70 Wed to Sun (10 courses). **Details:** 32 seats. Bar. Wheelchairs. Parking. Music.

Ellel

READERS RECOMMEND

The Bay Horse

Bay Horse Lane, Ellel, LA2 0HR
Tel no: 01524 791204
bayhorseinn.com

'Melt in the mouth lamb followed by orange and almond sponge, my favourite dessert. Great wine selection, too. Staff very attentive and friendly without being intrusive and nothing is too much trouble. Lovely surroundings. Not the first time I've eaten there and definitely won't be the last.'

Fence

The White Swan

Cooking score: 6
Modern British | £35
300 Wheatley Lane Road, Fence, BB12 9QA
Tel no: 01282 611773
whiteswanatfence.co.uk

Sitting on the edge of a trim village (named in honour of the enclosure that once penned in Henry VII's deer), Tom Parker's smart pub offers an appealing balance of old and new. The front rooms, adorned with gilt-framed mirrors and landscape etchings, are dedicated to dining, a bar room sits to the rear. Menus arrive in buttoned wood cases and offer an energetic version of British country cooking, with forthright flavours and seasonal freshness much in evidence. An expressive tomato consommé is poured over a heap of cherry tomatoes, black olives and basil, with a little slab of goat's cheese gnocchi for good measure, while another starter sees a prickly-sharp wasabi buttermilk decanted on to a fillet of cured salmon on diced apple, garnished with tart apple gel and flowering dill. At main, a hunk of Whitby cod is greened up with tender young asparagus and new peas, or there could be crackled suckling pig with garden courgette, morels and nasturtium leaves. Triple-cooked chips make a side that's hard to swerve, but leave room for refreshing desserts such as gariguette strawberries with peanut butter ice cream, strawberry jelly and honeycomb. Cheeses from The Courtyard Dairy are served with Périgord truffle honey. The short wine list falls a little short of the context, although there is a comprehensive range of Timothy Taylor ales.

Chef/s: Tom Parker. **Closed:** Mon, 26 Dec, 1 to 8 Jan. **Meals:** main courses £18 to £36. Set L and D £27 (2 courses) to £35. Tasting menu £60 (5 courses). Sun L £27 (2 courses) to £35. **Details:** 40 seats. Wheelchairs. Parking. Music.

Langho

Northcote

Cooking score: 6
Modern British | £70
Northcote Road, Langho, BB6 8BE
Tel no: 01254 240555
northcote.com

£5 OFF 🍷 🛏

A recent change of ownership hasn't dulled the glow many readers get from a visit to Northcote. Lisa Goodwin-Allen's food remains the ultimate in country refinement and the wines aren't bad either. Readers warmly and consistently recommend an evening in Northcote's cosseting, fulsomely appointed dining room, although at inspection the staff's friendly approach had to make up for service that was rather less than pin-sharp. Founding chef Nigel Haworth made northern produce the star here, and it remains so on menus that take home-cooked flavours and run all the way with them. The six-course tasting menu feels like good value, and might go from Norfolk quail ballotine with liver slice, orchard apple and a prune purée, through a 'really wonderful' creamy veal sweetbread with onions and thyme, to the eye of Cumbrian mutton with confit carrot and fat mutton sausage. An interactive, spoonable coconut dessert rules the room at pudding time. It's luxurious in all the right places – a description that also fits the wine list, which demands (and repays) careful attention.

Chef/s: Lisa Goodwin-Allen. **Meals:** main courses £23 to £52. Set L £29 (2 courses) to £36. Tasting menu £70 (4 courses) to £90. Sun L £36 to £43. **Details:** 70 seats. Bar. Wheelchairs. Parking. Music.

▌ Little Eccleston
The Cartford Inn

Cooking score: 2
Modern British | £30
Cartford Lane, Little Eccleston, PR3 0YP
Tel no: 01995 670166
thecartfordinn.co.uk
£5 OFF 🍽 £30

A landmark in these parts as much for its sprawling footprint as its enviable location by the river Wyre, The Cartford can be whatever you want it to be: pub, riverside restaurant, hotel, deli, terrace, child-friendly space or adults-only zone. If service must race on occasion to meet everyone's needs, the menu is always odds-on for success. There's a playful Lancastrian streak in à la carte dishes such as onion churros, corned beef terrine with pickled turnip, or pan-fried ray nobs, while main courses might be confit Goosnargh (where else?) duck leg with blood orange and borlotti bean cassoulet and smoked bacon, or pork belly cut through with the bitterness of a chicory tartlet. Pub-sized appetites are catered

for with classics including a winter suet pudding of oxtail, beef skirt and real ale, or the house fish pie. To finish, a cheeseboard in this location is never a bad idea, while the drinks list is worth lingering over.

Chef/s: Chris Bury. **Closed:** 25 Dec. **Meals:** main courses £14 to £25. **Details:** 70 seats. 16 seats outside. Bar. Wheelchairs. Parking. Music.

▌ Newton-in-Bowland
Parkers Arms

Cooking score: 3
Modern British | £35
Hallgate Hill, Newton-in-Bowland, BB7 3DY
Tel no: 01200 446236
parkersarms.co.uk
£5 OFF 🍽

Heading north from Clitheroe, you'll notice the landscape emptying of trees as you head into The Trough, Lancashire's peaty moorland, exposed to the elements way above sea level and ravishing with it. The Parkers is a renovated inn on a road bend in a slip of a village, bare-boarded and slated inside. Stosie Madi cooks in unrestrained Lancashire style, turning local produce into robust, hearty dishes that deliver wallops of flavour. Her pies are legendary, hulking brutes in roughly crimped hot-water pastry jackets, filled with beef brisket, liver and kidney, or gently curried hogget of estimable tenderness. Fish of the day takes a lighter approach, as in a fillet of immaculately timed cod on wilted greens, and there are mounds of creamy mash, or bundles of thrice-cooked chips, to accompany. Top and tail it with something like beetroot-cured salmon or an earthy terrine of pheasant, pork and pistachio, with perhaps Basque-style cheesecake and poached rhubarb to finish, and the job's a good'un. A short wine list has a fair few by the glass, from £3.60.

Chef/s: Stosie Madi. **Closed:** Mon, Tue, first 2 weeks Nov. **Meals:** main courses £16 to £29. Set L and D £28. Sun L £30. **Details:** 100 seats. 150 seats outside. Wheelchairs. Parking.

Whitewell
The Inn at Whitewell
Cooking score: 1
British | £34
Forest of Bowland, Whitewell, BB7 3AT
Tel no: 01200 448222
innatwhitewell.com

Quite the institution in these parts, this ancient inn features all that is Old English: roaring fires, real ales, rugs and flag floors, polished antique furniture, with the bonus of a summer terrace facing the river Hodder. The menu offers generous portions of traditional pub food along the lines of fish and chips, Cumberland bangers and champ, or the hugely popular simply grilled Norfolk kipper, with more contemporary offerings running to a salad of mulled figs with goat's cheese and walnuts or confit Goosnargh duck legs with sweet potato purée. Save room for sticky toffee pudding or excellent British and Irish cheeses. The wine list is a great read, offering quality drinking arranged helpfully by style with lots of options by the glass.
Chef/s: Jamie Cadman. **Meals:** main courses £16 to £27. **Details:** 180 seats. 16 seats outside. Bar. Wheelchairs.

creatures, hunting prints and an ambience of panelled cosiness. Amiable staff deliver plates of exciting food that are all about the distilled essence of flavour. Even during the spring renovation period, while a simpler menu was being offered, there was a superlative velouté of Jersey Royals with sour cream, caviar and chives, as warmly embracing a welcome as you'll find anywhere, and the Wellgate Smokehouse's excellent salmon, garnished with capers, cucumber, herb oil and a homemade crumpet. Main-course meats might include a tender Barnsley chop slathered with wild garlic pesto and served with truffled Parmesan fries, with a side perhaps of leek fondue and chopped hazelnuts. The sticky toffee pudding is as good as it gets, made with medjool dates and crowned with clotted cream, or there might be a trifled-up version of Eton mess, with a vanilla custard layer and a topping of coconut ice cream. Wines are taken very seriously, from the serving of honey-rich Billecart-Salmon as house Champagne to the pedigree dessert wines. Standard glasses start at £5.50.
Chef/s: Steven Smith. **Closed:** Mon, Tue.
Meals: main courses £24 to £38. Set L and D £20 (2 courses) to £25. Tasting menu £75 (6 courses) to £100. Sun L £35. **Details:** 70 seats. 20 seats outside. V menu. Bar. Wheelchairs. Music.

Wiswell
Freemasons at Wiswell
Cooking score: 7
British | £48
8 Vicarage Fold, Wiswell, BB7 9DF
Tel no: 01254 822218
freemasonswiswell.co.uk
£5 OFF

It takes some doing to hide in a hamlet as tiny as Wiswell, but the Freemasons looks as though it has sidled bashfully in between the cottages. That said, nothing else about Steven Smith's village inn is about the hiding of lights under bushels. Indeed, 2019 has seen new guest bedrooms and a chef's table installed. The core of the venue is an old country pub, replete with the mounted heads of stuffed

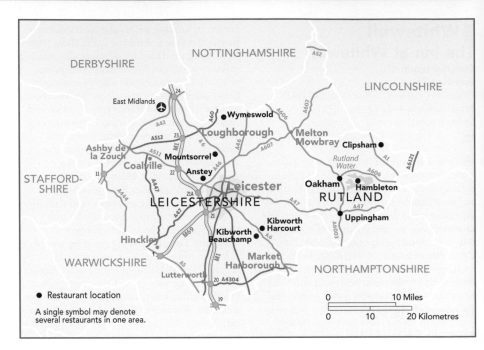

East Midlands

Restaurant location

A single symbol may denote several restaurants in one area.

0   10 Miles
0   10   20 Kilometres

▮ Anstey
Sapori
Cooking score: 1
Italian | £35
40 Stadon Road, Anstey, LE7 7AY
Tel no: 0116 236 8900
sapori-restaurant.co.uk

It may be marooned in a north Leicester suburb, but this cute and charming trattoria and pizza place is 'a cut above your average high street Italian' – no wonder it's enduringly popular with local families. The pizzas come with unusual toppings, while the kitchen shows its ambitions with a repertoire that spans everything from lasagne and aubergine Parmigiana to seven-hour sous-vide rock octopus with 'pancotto' of broccoli or 'utterly delicious' oxtail ravioli (a special served with Parmesan and lemon crumble, confit cherry tomatoes and black truffle). Antipasti plates are loaded with top artisan ingredients, while

desserts move from tiramisu and torta della nonna to an elaborate confection entitled 'chocolate texture'. Wines from £18.50.
Chef/s: Andrea Scarpati. **Closed:** Mon, Sun, first 2 weeks Jan. **Meals:** main courses £14 to £25. Tasting menu £60 (7 courses). **Details:** 60 seats. Bar. Wheelchairs. Music.

▮ Clipsham
The Olive Branch
Cooking score: 2
Modern British | £38
Main Street, Clipsham, LE15 7SH
Tel no: 01780 410355
theolivebranchpub.com

Gifted to Clipsham by a local squire in 1890 and rescued from extinction by three friends in 1999, this handsome stone pub is a fully fledged success story – a popular pit stop not far from the A1 and heaven-sent for locals who revel in its appealing menus and community-focused spirit. It was an early adopter of local

sourcing and still trumpets its wares with a map of suppliers on the back of each menu – consult the cartography to discover where your dishes came from. All preferences are accommodated here, whether your taste is for fillet steak with 'pub chips' or pan-fried turbot with cockle risotto, parsley oil and coriander. In between, there might be cider-cured trout, caramelised onion tarte tatin or roast chicken with tarragon gnocchi and Madeira sauce, while desserts embrace everything from glazed lemon tart to chocolate délice with toffee popcorn. Drinks also score highly, thanks to top-notch regional ales and an ever-changing list of good-value wines.
Chef/s: Sean Hope and Chris Ansell. **Closed:** 31 Dec, 1 Jan. **Meals:** main courses £11 to £28. Set L £19 (2 courses) to £23. Tasting menu £40 (5 courses). Sun L £30. **Details:** 45 seats. 20 seats outside. Bar. Wheelchairs. Parking. Music.

▮ Hambleton
Hambleton Hall
Cooking score: 7
Modern British | £78
Ketton Road, Hambleton, LE15 8TH
Tel no: 01572 756991
hambletonhall.com
🍷 🍴

'One hopes that the owners and chef can keep going for a few more years yet,' was the fervent wish of one regular, noting that Tim and Stefa Hart have been custodians of this stunningly located aristocratic hotel for nearly four decades; chef Aaron Patterson is well into his third. Indeed, for many the whole experience is 'perfect'. A couple who took advantage of a winter 'lunch for less' offer – foaming mushroom pasta, lamb shank and apple crumble soufflé – considered their meal 'faultless and worth the money'. For Patterson, seasonality is king (he's built up a network of trusted suppliers over the years) and fresh flavours are evident at every turn. His classic techniques allow him to pull off dishes that still manage to feel contemporary and relevant. Thus a meal in February could open with Cornish crab teamed with radish and

ginger caviar, and go on to roast fillet of cod with mussels, cauliflower, cumin and coriander sauce, or presa Ibérico with caramelised fennel, apple and crackling, before finishing with a taste of Yorkshire rhubarb. The personable front of house approach is delightful, and the wine list a true masterpiece – expertly curated, trustworthy and allowing you to drink well without breaking the bank.
Chef/s: Aaron Patterson. **Meals:** set L £32 Mon to Fri (2 courses) to £40. Set L and D £78 to £98 (4 courses). Tasting menu £95 (6 courses). Sun L £60. **Details:** 60 seats. V menu. Bar. Parking. Children over 5 yrs.

▮ Kibworth Beauchamp
The Lighthouse
Cooking score: 2
Modern European | £28
9 Station Street, Kibworth Beauchamp, LE8 0LN
Tel no: 0116 279 6260
lighthousekibworth.co.uk
£5 £30
OFF

The people of Kibworth Beauchamp are lucky to have this convivial neighbourhood restaurant right in their midst. It may be just about as far as it's possible to get from the coast, but that doesn't deter chef patron Lino Poli from turning out a confident seafood menu that champions familiar dishes with flair. Start with a creamy chowder or a clattering pile of moules marinière, or perhaps the much-loved potted shrimps with sourdough toast, before pan-fried halibut with lobster bisque and wilted pak choi, or whole gilthead bream given an Asian spin with a stuffing of lemongrass, ginger and lime leaves. Meat eaters aren't left out – there's venison chilli, tender loin of lamb with celeriac purée and root vegetables, or a puff pastry turkey pie. If you simply can't decide, pull up a seat at the Captain's Table, explain your likes and dislikes, and let the kitchen suggest five delicious courses. Choose an Italian-leaning dessert –

affogato, sgroppino or panna cotta – unless an utterly British fruit crumble and custard is more your thing. Wine from £18.75.
Chef/s: Lino Poli and Tom Wilde. **Closed:** Mon, Sun, 25 and 26 Dec, 1 Jan. **Meals:** main courses £9 to £22. Set D £17 Tue to Thu (2 courses) to £20. Tasting menu £40 (5 courses). **Details:** 60 seats. Wheelchairs. Music.

▊ Kibworth Harcourt

LOCAL GEM
Boboli
Italian | £29
88 Main Street, Kibworth Harcourt, LE8 0NQ
Tel no: 0116 279 3303
bobolirestaurant.co.uk

£5 OFF   £30

A handsome village cottage is filled with la dolce vita from morning (damn fine coffee and cake) until night (pasta, pizza and more). A family-friendly attitude pervades and those pizzas – buffalo mozzarella with anchovies, say – have broad appeal. Bring an appetite for rich pasta dishes including tagliatelle with veal ragù. Exuberant secondi run to roast rabbit with olives and pine nuts, and lamb shank with onion risotto. Desserts are of the Italy's-greatest-hits variety (tiramisu, affogato, gelati) and the same goes for the wine list, from £18.75.

▊ Mountsorrel
John's House
Cooking score: 6
Modern British | £55
Stonehurst Farm, 139-141 Loughborough Road, Mountsorrel, LE12 7AR
Tel no: 01509 415569
johnshouse.co.uk

£5 OFF

The creeper-covered frontage in a row of brick buildings echoes the foursquare concept of John Duffin's place. It is very much his house, situated next to the family farm that his brother runs. Inside, there is a bare-board floor, naked brick walls and tables got up in

their best whites. Informed by his passage through the kitchens of Claude Bosi and Simon Rogan, Duffin works in the contemporary vein, bringing excitement and intensity to the humblest ingredients, and imagination to their combinations. Start with oxtail in a risotto of toasted grains, the richness accentuated with Comté, artichoke and truffle, or perhaps with horseradish-fired chilled crab cream. Pedigree meats and impeccable fish line up together for mains such as old spot piglet with leeks, smoked eel and mint, or lightly salted cod fillet with brawn, aubergine and passion fruit, all scented with curry spices. Artisan cheeses are the alternative (or addition) to idiosyncratic desserts like parsnip sorbet with yoghurt, liquorice and mint, or Williams pears poached in muscovado and thyme with sweet cheese. Wines are articulately described on a list that spans the globe with glass selections from £7, extending to choice Coravin picks.
Chef/s: John Duffin. **Closed:** Mon, Sun, 2 weeks Christmas, 2 weeks Aug. **Meals:** set L £26 (2 courses) to £30. Set D £48 (2 courses) to £55. Tasting menu £79 (7 courses). **Details:** 30 seats. V menu. Parking. Music.

▊ Oakham
★ NEW ENTRY ★
Hitchen's Barn
Cooking score: 3
Modern British | £32
12 Burley Road, Oakham, LE15 6DH
Tel no: 01572 722255
hitchensbarn.co.uk

At the beginning of 2019, Neil and Louise Hitchen upped sticks from their old billet at The Berkeley Arms in Wymondham and headed for this old stone-built barn conversion in a market town 10 miles or so further south. Kitchen utensils are on display in the beamed and bare-boarded dining room, where mismatched side plates and fresh flowers give a homely impression, reinforced by Louise's friendly front of house approach. Local produce is the mainstay of Neil's menus, which retain the Wymondham formula for robust dishes that exert strong popular appeal. Heirloom tomatoes bursting with sweet ripeness, served with goat's curd and pesto, or cured sea trout with blood orange in hazelnut dressing, are simple fresh intros to mains such as halibut on the bone with asparagus and brown shrimps, or perhaps a sturdy meat dish like salty-skinned duck breast on hispi cabbage with potato gratin in a thyme-scented red wine jus. Finish with passion fruit cheesecake, or a sundae glass of rhubarb and orange trifle garlanded with herb leaves and almonds. Wines from a European-focused list start at £4.85 for a small glass.

Chef/s: Neil Hitchen. **Closed:** Mon, Tue, first 2 weeks Jan, 2 weeks summer. **Meals:** main courses £15 to £25. Set L £19 (2 courses) to £23. **Details:** 43 seats. 2 seats outside. Bar. Wheelchairs.

▌Uppingham
The Lake Isle
Cooking score: 1
Modern British | £35
16 High Street East, Uppingham, LE15 9PZ
Tel no: 01572 822951
lakeisle.co.uk
£5 OFF

There's lots of love for this little high street restaurant and its menu that roams far and wide for inspiration. Parsnip and apple bhajias could precede classic moules-frites on a winter menu, or you could conjure up some Greek sunshine with a spring dish of baked feta and salsa of cucumber, olives and dried tomatoes, before braised pork belly, pak choi and Korean barbecue dip whisks you east. A Belgian chocolate and Cointreau truffle with satsuma ripple ice cream will finish the gastronomic tour off deliciously. Wine from £18.50.

Chef/s: Stuart Mead. **Closed:** 27 to 29 Dec. **Meals:** main courses £16 to £30. Sun L £29. **Details:** 35 seats. 20 seats outside. Bar. Music.

▌Wymeswold
The Hammer & Pincers
Cooking score: 2
Modern European | £45
5 East Road, Wymeswold, LE12 6ST
Tel no: 01509 880735
hammerandpincers.co.uk

Over the years Daniel and Sandra Jimminson's village pub has evolved into the well-bred hostelry it is today, with food top of the agenda. The menu is rooted in great British ingredients and the kitchen goes about its work with dexterity. A dish of Brixham crab layered with lime, chilli, coriander and mint mayo, salted cucumber and compressed watermelon, served with a watermelon and ginger sorbet and a toasted peanut and sesame tuile added up to 'a great combination of flavours'. Seared scallops with a light celeriac 'risotto', apple caramel, compressed Granny Smith, lovage purée and shaved summer truffle was another winning composition. For mains, smoked pork fillet arrives with a crispy pig's cheek croquette and morcilla, accompanied by cavolo nero, white bean and garlic purée, fennel poached in white Rioja and parsley butter beans. There's praise, too, for 'really great bread' and an apple tarte tatin with Calvados VSOP ice cream and hot toffee sauce. House vin de pays is £18.95.

Chef/s: Daniel Jimminson. **Closed:** Mon, 25 Dec. **Meals:** main courses £26 to £30. Set L and D £24 (2 courses) to £29. Tasting menu £60 (10 courses). **Details:** 42 seats. 30 seats outside. Bar. Parking. Music.

Send us your review
Your feedback informs the content of the GFG and will be used to compile next year's entries. To register your opinion about any restaurant listed in the Guide, or a restaurant that you wish to bring to our attention, visit:
thegoodfoodguide.co.uk/feedback.

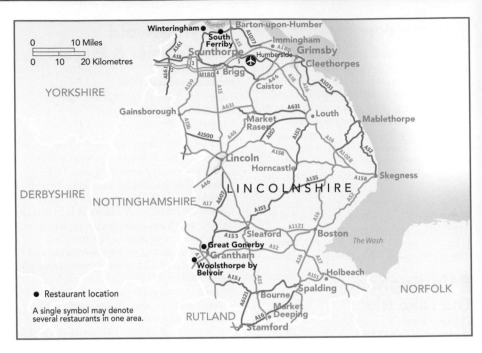

Great Gonerby
Harry's Place
Cooking score: 4
Modern French | £68
17 High Street, Great Gonerby, NG31 8JS
Tel no: 01476 561780

£5
OFF

For the past three decades, Harry and Caroline
Hallam have been welcoming guests – just 10
at a time – for a meal in their front room.
Eating out doesn't get more intimate than this,
with close-set candlelit tables surrounded by
the knick-knackery of family life the setting
for Harry's ultra-classic cooking. You can't
check out the handwritten, daily changing
menu beforehand for this is a resolutely
website-free operation, but suffice to say there
are two choices at each course from a
comfortable repertoire. The evening might
start with fresh tomato soup with a punchy
provençale pistou, or chicken livers in sherry
aspic, before moving on to wild bass in a
Sauternes sauce or fillet of Lincoln red beef

with a horseradish mayonnaise. There's praise
for the prune and Armagnac ice cream, and a
dark chocolate mousse served with a spoonful
of mascarpone, plump blackberries and a
dusting of icing sugar hits the spot for many, as
does the carefully composed cheeseboard. A
short wine list opens at £28 or £8.50 a glass.
Chef/s: Harry Hallam. **Closed:** Mon, Sun, bank hols,
2 weeks Aug, 25 and 26 Dec. **Meals:** main courses
£40. **Details:** 10 seats. Parking. Children over 5 yrs.

Anonymous

At *The Good Food Guide*, our inspectors
dine anonymously and pay their bill in full
every time.These impartial review meals,
along with feedback from thousands of
our readers, are what informs the content
of the *GFG*. Only the best restaurants
make the cut.

South Ferriby

★ NEW ENTRY ★

Hope & Anchor

Cooking score: 2
British | £33
Sluice Road, South Ferriby, DN18 6JQ
Tel no: 01652 635334
thehopeandanchorpub.co.uk
£5 OFF

You might easily drive past this rambling ale house opposite the cement works without giving it a second glance, but Slawomir Mikolajczyk (Slawek for short), former head chef at the much-garlanded Winteringham Fields (see entry) now operates this commendable food pub on the south bank of the Humber, complete with splendid views across the reed beds to the river and the majestic bridge. A homely interior and a menu that is largely meat-based – with a plant-based menu on request – offers lamb, venison, fillet steak and ribeye cooked over charcoal on the Josper with showstoppers like chateaubriand for two plus onion rings, triple-cooked chips, béarnaise sauce and salad. It's not all meat; expect Lindisfarne oysters, mussels, cod brandade with fermented cabbage and nori dressing, and beautifully presented white crabmeat with brown crab butter and spiced mango ketchup. It's mostly excellent. Desserts include a textbook custard tart and a similarly admirable crème brûlée. Wines start at £21.
Chef/s: Ryan Cook. **Closed:** Mon, 30 Dec to 2 Jan. **Meals:** mains £13 to £31. Set L £21 (2 courses) to £25. **Details:** 99 seats. 78 seats outside. V menu. Vg menu. Bar. Wheelchairs. Parking. Music.

Scoring explained

Local Gems, scores 1 and 2
Scoring a 1 or a 2 in The Good Food Guide, or being awarded Local Gem status, is a huge achievement. We list the very best restaurants in the UK; for the reader, this means that these restaurants are well worth visiting if you're in the area – and you're extremely lucky if they are on your doorstep.

Scores 3 to 6
Further up the scale, scores 3 to 6 range from up-and-coming restaurants to places to watch; there will be real talent in the kitchen. These are the places that are well worth seeking out.

Scores 7 to 9
A score of 7 and above means entering the big league, with high expectations of the chef. In other words, these are destination restaurants, the places you'll long to talk about - if you're lucky enough to get a booking.

Score 10
This score is extremely rare, with chefs expected to achieve faultless technique at every service. In total, only eight restaurants have achieved 10 out of 10 for cooking since the scoring system was introduced in 1998.

See page 13 for an in-depth breakdown of The Good Food Guide's scoring system.

Winteringham

★ TOP 50 ★

Winteringham Fields

Cooking score: 7
Modern European | £55
1 Silver Street, Winteringham, DN15 9ND
Tel no: 01724 733096
winteringhamfields.co.uk

£5 OFF 🍴

Who says you have to schlep to a city to find
contemporary cooking of the highest order?
Head to Winteringham, the quiet village
where fertile north Lincolnshire slips
verdantly into the Humber, and where Colin
McGurran and his talented brigade get on –
unruffled by urban frazzle – with the business
of cooking remarkable food. His eight-course
'surprise' evening menu (it's six courses or à la
carte at lunch) is an ingredient-led delight. A
cushioning salon – it's overwhelmingly so for
some – in the warren-like old building is
where aperitifs and snacks such as Lincolnshire
poacher mousse with smoked eel (punching
well above its frangible tuile weight) are taken.
There follows a sequence of plates that sing in
harmonious tune from the very opening notes
of gin-cured sea trout with pops of ponzu gel
and salty roe, through to the extravagant
chocolate soufflé finale. There are highlights
aplenty in between: a slow-cooked egg (90
minutes at 63 degrees, for McGurran's
cooking is the stuff of precision if not pomp)
with celeriac purée, wild rice crumb and
morteau sausage is a triumph of flavour and
texture; wonderfully butter-rich mash comes
alongside deep-fried chicken thighs in a case
of the ordinary made extraordinary; and
crisp-skinned, pristine-white cod flakes
chunkily, a mussel velouté giving savouriness,
fennel adding playful pep. Coconut and crème
fraîche sorbet under a meringue igloo is a
perky preamble to a jauntily angled,
dissolvingly light chocolate soufflé and sunny
mango sorbet. The wine flight (£75) is
expertly presented, but go your own way if
you wish from £30 a bottle.

Chef/s: Colin McGurran. **Closed:** Mon, Sun, 22 Dec
to 3 Jan. **Meals:** main courses £16 to £34. Tasting
menu £65 (6 courses) to £89. **Details:** 60 seats. Bar.
Wheelchairs. Parking. Music.

Woolsthorpe by Belvoir

Chequers Inn

Cooking score: 1
Modern British | £29
Main Street, Woolsthorpe by Belvoir,
NG32 1LU
Tel no: 01476 870701
chequersinn.net

£5 OFF 🍴 £30

As bucolic settings go, the Vale of Belvoir is
hard to beat, and this tastefully restored 17th-
century coaching inn, with its rural charm and
warm hospitality, fits in perfectly. Take your
pick of dining areas, two with log fires (and
there's warm-weather seating outside) and
expect food that has broad appeal, from a
'Chequers classic' of sausages, mash and gravy
to a more inventive main of fillet of rainbow
trout with baby fondant potatoes, spinach,
tomato and dill beurre blanc. To drink, there
are traditional ales and a global list of wines
helpfully organised by style.
Chef/s: Keith Martin. **Meals:** main courses £13 to
£26. Sun L £17 (2 courses). **Details:** 120 seats. 80
seats outside. Bar. Wheelchairs. Parking. Music.

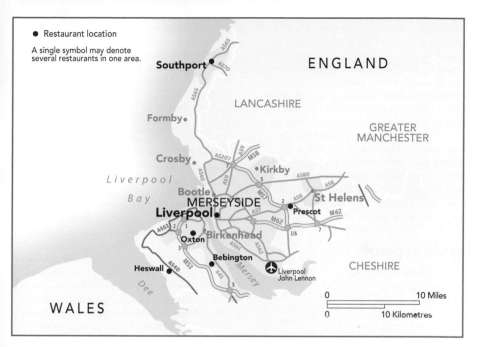

Restaurant location

A single symbol may denote several restaurants in one area.

ENGLAND

LANCASHIRE

GREATER MANCHESTER

Southport

Formby

Crosby

Kirkby

Liverpool Bay

Bootle

MERSEYSIDE

Liverpool

St Helens

Prescot

Oxton

Birkenhead

Bebington

Heswall

Liverpool John Lennon

CHESHIRE

WALES

Dee

Mersey

0   10 Miles

0   10 Kilometres

▌Bebington

LOCAL GEM

Claremont Farm Café

British | £18
Old Clatterbridge Road, Bebington,
CH63 4JB
Tel no: 0151 334 1133
claremontfarm.co.uk

£30

'Fresh, local and seasonal' is the message
chalked up behind the counter at this easy-
going farm shop and café overlooking the
Wirral countryside. Home-grown produce
always figures prominently on the menu,
whether you're here for a 'pick your own'
cooked breakfast, a freshly assembled salad or a
sturdy lunch – perhaps chicken, leek and
mushroom pie, kedgeree or a veggie curry.
Cakes and sweet treats are served throughout
the day, and the owners also run cookery
workshops. To drink, check out the selection
of craft beers on tap upstairs.

▌Heswall

Burnt Truffle

Cooking score: 3
Modern British | £30
106 Telegraph Road, Heswall, CH60 0AQ
Tel no: 0151 342 1111
burnttruffle.net

£30

In an upmarket corner of the Wirral, the
second link in Gary Usher's fast-growing
chain of crowdfunded neighbourhood bistros
oozes informality. Occupying a sandstone
cottage set back from the town's main
thoroughfare, it features an open kitchen on
the ground floor – a useful distraction should
your date prove less than scintillating – and a
whitewashed first-floor dining room.
Straightforward cooking of globally inspired
dishes at sensible prices is the mantra here,
with the early evening set menu particularly
appealing at £19 for two courses. Add a side
order of Usher's signature truffle and
Parmesan chips, or the exceptional sourdough

and truffle butter, and the final bill can soon mount, however. Pig's head croquette with barbecue sauce and apple is one way to start, followed by sea bass fillet with cider and mustard sauce, hispi cabbage and dill, or spring lamb rump with honey-roast carrots, savoy cabbage and caramelised cauliflower. Italian house selections open the wine list at £19.50, although there are oddballs and underdogs for the vinously curious.

Chef/s: Gary Usher and Thomas Keegan. **Closed:** Mon, 25 and 26 Dec. **Meals:** main courses £16 to £30. Set L and early D £19 (2 courses) to £22. Tasting menu £70 (6 courses). Sun L £26. **Details:** 56 seats. 26 seats outside. Music.

■ Liverpool
The Art School

Cooking score: 5
Modern European | £75
1 Sugnall Street, Liverpool, L7 7EB
Tel no: 0151 230 8600
theartschoolrestaurant.co.uk

Sitting adjacent to the Philharmonic Hall in one of Liverpool's cultural quarters, Paul Askew's place aims to impress. Under its expansive skylight the dining room, with well-spaced linened tables and a window into the kitchen, has the feel of a stage set on which something dramatic is about to happen. As indeed it is. At the heart of proceedings is a series of Menu Excellence variations – omni, fish, veggie and vegan – replete with considered dishes characterised by finely judged richness and intensity. Grilled red mullet is garnished with langoustines on saffron potato risotto in a sauce of pastis for that Riviera touch, as a possible preamble to a trio of cuts of Hebridean hogget (loin, shoulder and belly) with charred leek and confit carrot in a deeply savoury jus, or perhaps a pithivier of savoy cabbage, walnuts, wild mushrooms and butternut squash, alongside roast parsnips and balsamic-laced beetroot purée in black truffle butter. A peanut butter jelly sandwich with peanut parfait, beurre noisette crémeux and raspberry and cinnamon toast will fill any remaining

gaps. The globalised wine list exudes confidence, with small glasses from £5.25 for a snappy Hungarian Grüner Veltliner.

Chef/s: Paul Askew. **Closed:** Mon, Sun, 1 week Jan, 1 week Aug. **Meals:** set L and early D £27 (2 courses) to £34. Set D £75. Tasting menu £95 (8 courses). **Details:** 48 seats. V menu. Vg menu. Children at L and early D only.

Belzan

Cooking score: 2
Modern European | £25
371 Smithdown Road, Liverpool, L15 3JJ
Tel no: 0151 733 8595
belzan.co.uk
£5 OFF **£30**

'Not a single false note in the entire evening and delightful service,' noted one visitor to this 'busy place', part of an exciting new wave of restaurants opening across the city. White-painted brick walls, bentwood bistro chairs and an abundance of pot plants give this neighbourhood bistro and bar a strong Scandi feel but the food emerging from the open-plan kitchen is global in outlook. The small plates offering featured 'amazing' baked celeriac, Tunworth cheese, thyme and crispy shallots. Other noteworthy dishes have included butter beans with beetroot miso, garlic and cavolo nero, and charcoal-braised beef shin with polenta and Parmesan. Keep an eye on the blackboards for daily fish dishes and also the six-quid 'staff dinner' – perhaps pork belly ramen. As a finale, an intriguing but delicious olive oil ice cream with sea salt and lemon has been singled out for particular praise. The compact wine list starts at £19 (carafes from £13).

Chef/s: Sam Grainger. **Closed:** 25 Dec, 1 Jan. **Meals:** small plates £6 to £14. **Details:** 28 seats. V menu. Vg menu. Wheelchairs. Music.

Delifonseca Dockside

Cooking score: 1
Modern European | £28
Brunswick Way, Liverpool, L3 4BN
Tel no: 0151 255 0808
delifonseca.co.uk
£5 OFF £30

Combining the virtues of a cosmopolitan deli and a casual big-city eatery, this recently expanded branch of Delifonseca by Liverpool's dockside is a boon for foodie shoppers and those who simply want to embark on some global grazing. Come here for plates of Spanish charcuterie and tapas, Middle Eastern meze, Thai salads, croques, proper handmade raised pies and even some US diner classics (pastrami on rye, New Orleans po' boys). Also check the blackboard for daily specials covering even more territory (ricotta croquettes with beetroot rémoulade followed by harissa-spiced lamb rump, for example). Repair to the new bar area for world beers and international wines (from £19).
Chef/s: Martin Cooper. **Closed:** 25 and 26 Dec, 1 Jan. **Meals:** main courses £12 to £32. **Details:** 150 seats. 50 seats outside. Bar. Wheelchairs. Parking. Music.

The London Carriage Works

Cooking score: 2
Modern British | £44
Hope Street Hotel, 40 Hope Street, Liverpool, L1 9DA
Tel no: 0151 705 2222
thelondoncarriageworks.co.uk
🛏

A contemporary dining space within a grand old hotel on one of the city centre's happening streets, the Carriage Works' stripped wood flooring, unclothed tables and bare brick walls with full-length windows speak of a breezy urban setting. The kitchen matches the mood with dishes that mobilise the on-trend elements of piquancy and pungency with fine prime ingredients, perhaps in a starter of red mullet in consommé with strawberries, black pepper and basil before mains of loin and shoulder of venison in bitter chocolate with barbecued cauliflower and raisins, or a marine array of halibut, clams and mussels in buttermilk with spinach and nasturtiums. Sharing platters in three versions – fish, cured meats and veggie – as well as tempting side dishes help to expand the three-course format, but desserts such as baked Alaska with Earl Grey and matcha show no loss of imaginative energy. Fine cheeses are articulately described on the menu. An extensive wine list offers plenty of inspired choice.
Chef/s: Mike Kenyon. **Meals:** main courses £18 to £30. Set L and D £24 (2 courses) to £29. **Details:** 100 seats. Bar. Wheelchairs. Music.

Lunya

Cooking score: 1
Spanish | £22
55 Hanover Street, Liverpool, L1 3DN
Tel no: 0151 706 9770
lunya.co.uk
£5 OFF £30

Like its younger sibling in Manchester (see entry), Peter and Elaine Kinsella's colourful venue is part Catalonian restaurant/tapas bar, part international deli. Occupying a vast rough-walled warehouse on Hanover Street, it feeds famished Liverpudlians with all manner of Spanish delights ranging from butifarra breakfast rolls to a Catalan take on traditional 'scouse' stew involving chorizo and morcilla. The menu also embraces cured meats, cheeses and creative plates such as sea bass sliders, lamb neck on Navarran lentils or crispy parsnips with zaatar and pomegranate molasses. To drink, there's a terrific list of G&Ts, beers, sherries and all-Spanish regional wines from £18.95. The Kinsellas have also opened a sister venue, Lunyalita, on Liverpool's Albert Dock.
Chef/s: Jon Daley. **Closed:** 25 Dec, 1 Jan. **Meals:** tapas £5 to £23. Set L £11 (2 courses) to £15. Set D £15 (2 courses) to £22. Tasting menu £27 (5 courses) to £37. **Details:** 135 seats. 15 seats outside. V menu. Vg menu. Bar. Wheelchairs. Parking. Music.

Maray

Cooking score: 1
Middle Eastern | £26
91 Bold Street, Liverpool, l 1 4HF
Tel no: 0151 709 5820
maray.co.uk
£30

The name references Le Marais, the Parisian
arrondissement known for its falafel shops,
but this funky all-day canteen ups the ante
with a menu that mixes authentic Middle
Eastern flavours with lots of off-piste cross-
cultural interventions. Visitors can now sip
fashionable drinks in the basement bar before
decamping to the no-frills dining room for a
live-wire assortment of small plates ranging
from shakshuka and lamb kofta to halloumi
with tamarind caramel, buttermilk fried
chicken with pickled onions and veggie
assemblies such as sprouts, kimchi, rose
harissa, coconut milk and peanuts. Cocktails
are the headline drinks, but there are some
decent-value wines, too. Maray has an
offshoot at 57 Allerton Road, L18 2DA.
Chef/s: Jonathan Kelly. **Meals:** small plates £4 to
£12. Set L £13. **Details:** 47 seats. Vg menu. Bar.
Wheelchairs. Parking. Music.

Röski

Cooking score: 6
British | £55
16 Rodney Street, Liverpool, L1 2TE
Tel no: 0151 708 8698
roskirestaurant.com
£5
OFF

'Refreshingly unpretentious with a sense of
humour and place,' was how one reader
summed up Anton Piotrowski's Georgian
Quarter restaurant. He may hail from Devon
but Piotrowski has made Merseyside his home
and he doffs his hat to the city's multicultural
history by embracing global flavours
throughout his contemporary repertoire.
Whether or not you go for the seven-course
tasting menu, a meal will inevitably begin
with 'snacks' inspired by a childhood 'chippy
tea'. This might include a single triple-cooked
chip filled with strong Lincolnshire Poacher
cheese and dribbled with insanely rich wagyu
beef gravy or a 100-day aged beef nugget with
'chip shop' curry sauce. Liverpool's long-
established Chinese community is honoured
with a starter of chilli ginger squab pigeon and
black garlic purée, perhaps followed by
turbot, Devon crab, sea aster and langoustine
sauce. To finish, a deconstructed dessert
inspired by a piña colada cocktail includes a
white chocolate shell coated with desiccated
coconut filled with a set cream made from
coconut milk, pistachio sponge, popping
candy and a bracing lime sorbet. International
wines from £23.
Chef/s: Anton Piotrowski. **Closed:** Mon, Sun.
Meals: set L £25. Set D £55. Tasting menu £55 (5
courses). **Details:** 28 seats.

Wreckfish

Cooking score: 2
Modern British | £35
60 Seel Street, Liverpool, L1 4BE
Tel no: 0151 707 1960
wreckfish.co

Fuelled by bouts of crowdfunding, Gary
Usher is rolling out a series of idiosyncratic
restaurants across the North West, and this
handsome, important-looking grey-stone
building on Liverpool's Seel Street is another
success story. Like his other venues, such as
Sticky Walnut in Chester (see entry),
Wreckfish is in the business of delivering
'terrific value' via a menu of cleverly contrived
contemporary dishes – from perfectly
textured 'flamed' sea bream with fennel, a
jammy baked plum and crunchy, peppery
togarashi spicing to a delicate main course of
steamed whole plaice with ratte potatoes,
capers and watercress. Meat dishes are given
similarly eclectic treatment (rolled lamb breast
with ras el hanout, pine nuts, wood sorrel and
goat's yoghurt, for example), while dessert
might bring tonka bean crème brûlée or a
delightfully light marmalade sponge with
chantilly cream. Staff are 'really engaged', the
whole place is intelligently run, and the wine
list offers interesting drinking from £19.

Chef/s: Gary Usher and Ryan Howarth. **Meals:** main courses £14 to £28. Set L and early D £19 (2 courses) to £22. Sun L £25. **Details:** 95 seats. Bar. Wheelchairs. Music.

Etsu
Japanese | £29
25 The Strand (off Brunswick Street),
Liverpool, L2 0XJ
Tel no: 0151 236 7530
etsu-restaurant.co.uk

£30

Tucked away in a corner of the glassy modern Beetham Plaza (a 'mixed-use development' to use the architectural vernacular), this is a sleek contemporary space where Japanese minimalism reigns and welcoming staff dish up a menu of classic sushi, noodles and donburi boxes. Kick off with plump niku gyoza or crisp prawn tempura, before sparklingly fresh sushi (spicy tuna maki, say) and a donburi box of grilled eel (unagi) or kitsune udon noodles with deep-fried tofu. Chilled and warm sake hit the spot.

▌Oxton

★ TOP 50 ★

Fraiche
Cooking score: 8
Modern European | £90
11 Rose Mount, Oxton, CH43 5SG
Tel no: 0151 652 2914
restaurantfraiche.com

The local press was abuzz with 'news' that Fraiche was to shut at the end of 2018. Perish the thought: the good ship sails on dauntless. Its resolutely blank exterior is the colour of a Dreadnought submarine, the better to wow you on entry to the cocoon-like dining rooms. Lucky Wirrallers are of the opinion that Marc Wilkinson has just got better and better over his decade and a half here, and there is a strong feeling of inventive impetus to the menu conceptions, not least their exquisite

presentations. The evening drill is an eight-course tasting menu that draws on natural flavours, unusual textures and strong counterpointing seasonings to bring the best out of impeccable produce. For one couple, opening nibbles included a raspberry and verbena shot that proved Wilkinson had 'lost none of his touch', and a smoked eel sandwich that was 'perhaps the best of the lot'. Next up could be a serving of sublimely succulent Nordic smoked salmon dressed in bergamot and pineapple. Carrot textures offset the natural sweetness of the root with smoked yoghurt, while fish such as Cornish turbot is accorded the umami treatment with dashi broth and spinach. An earthy approach to main meat sees black pudding and beetroot supporting Loire quail, or an 'intricate preparation of Cumbrian lamb', before a pre-dessert heralds a pair of sweet things. An early summer visit brought on 'exceptionally flavoured gariguette strawberries', fresh, marinated and gelled and served with a coconut meringue crisp described as 'the best course of the evening'. Wine matches from an exemplary list are chosen with both care and imagination to complete a thoroughly high-class operation.
Chef/s: Marc Wilkinson. **Closed:** Mon, Tue, 24 Dec to 10 Jan, 2 weeks Jul. **Meals:** tasting menu £90 Wed to Sat (8 courses). Sun L £48 (4 courses). **Details:** 12 seats. 4 seats outside. Bar. Wheelchairs. Music. Children over 10 yrs at D. Pre-payment required.

▌Prescot

★ NEW ENTRY ★

Pinion
Cooking score: 2
Modern British | £31
39 Eccleston St, Prescot, L34 5QA
Tel no: 0151 493 0660
pinionbistro.com

Once at the heart of the UK's watchmaking industry, this small town, a short train ride from Liverpool, feels like it could be on the way back up, thanks in part to the arrival of Gary Usher's smart bistro. Sandwiched

between a travel agent and an amusement arcade in a main street of Georgian buildings, this former shop has been stripped back to its bare brickwork and kitted out with aubergine-coloured leather banquettes, bistro chairs and dark wood floors. One wall has six framed lists of the people who helped with the restaurant crowdfunding campaign. Although by no means a facsimile of his other restaurants, the concise menu is recognisably Usher, right down to the famed truffle and Parmesan chips. Begin with smokey, tender ox heart served with roast beetroot, swede and smoked corn, continue with sea bream fillet, Isle of Wight tomatoes, ricotta and red onions, and finish with banana cake teamed with honeycomb semifreddo and toasted peanuts. Drink Pinion Pale, or choose from the one-page wine list starting at a wallet-friendly £19.
Chef/s: Gary Usher and James Connolly. **Closed:** Mon, Tue, 25 and 26 Dec. **Meals:** main courses £12 to £23. Set L £15 (2 courses) to £23. Early D £16 (2 courses) to £19. Sun L £20 (2 courses). **Details:** 65 seats. 10 seats outside. Wheelchairs. Music.

▮ Southport
Bistro 21
Cooking score: 3
Modern European | £32
21 Stanley Street, Southport, PR9 0BS
Tel no: 01704 501414
bistro21.co.uk

Done out in contemporary style with elegantly laid tables, suede-covered chairs, cream-coloured walls and modern lighting, this affluent town-centre bistro is a local asset offering good value as well as quality. The kitchen deals in mainstream European fare with the occasional oriental intrusion, so expect anything from crab and prawn beignets with lobster bisque dip or beef salad dressed with ginger, soy and garlic to cod fillet with lettuce, peas, bacon and mash or crispy-skinned chicken breast accompanied by truffled cannellini beans and chorizo. To finish, it's familiarity all the way – from sticky toffee pudding with salted caramel ice cream

to warm chocolate brownie with cherry rum syrup. There's a tasting menu for those who want to sample a few more dishes, while the table d'hôte offers simpler pleasures in the shape of mushroom risotto, 'open' steak pie, buttermilk chicken or fish and chips. Thirty workmanlike wines start at a very reasonable £16.95 (£4.25 a glass).
Chef/s: Michael Glayzer. **Closed:** Mon, Sun, 25 and 26 Dec, 1 Jan. **Meals:** main courses £17 to £27. Set L £13 (2 courses). Set D £17 Tue to Thur (2 courses). Tasting menu L £20 (5 courses) and D £25 (5 courses). **Details:** 28 seats. V menu. Vg menu. Wheelchairs. Music.

Bistrot Vérité
Cooking score: 3
French | £32
7 Liverpool Road, Southport, PR8 4AR
Tel no: 01704 564199
bistrotverite.co.uk

Marc Vérité cooks while his wife Michaela oversees front of house at this polished Gallic bistro in well-to-do Birkdale – famed for its championship golf course and sandy beaches. Bare tables, low lights and pale green wood panelling set the scene for capable cooking of French classics – as in a salad of Roquefort, pears, chicory and hazelnuts, beef bourguignon or garlicky thyme-roasted rump of lamb with woodland mushrooms. Marc rings the changes on his seasonal menu, although you can always be sure of steaks from the chargrill, as well as numerous signature fish dishes – hake suprême with langoustine velouté or grilled sea bass fillet with seared scallops, basil, Parmesan and pine nuts, for example. Lunches offer top value across the board, while desserts are prettily adorned French fancies such as rhubarb and ginger crème brûlée or chocolate mousse with popcorn and salted caramel. Easy-drinking wines from France and beyond start at £19.
Chef/s: Marc Vérité. **Closed:** Mon, Sun, 1 week Feb, 1 week Aug. **Meals:** main courses £14 to £29. Set L £20 (2 courses) to £27. **Details:** 45 seats. 16 seats outside. V menu. Music.

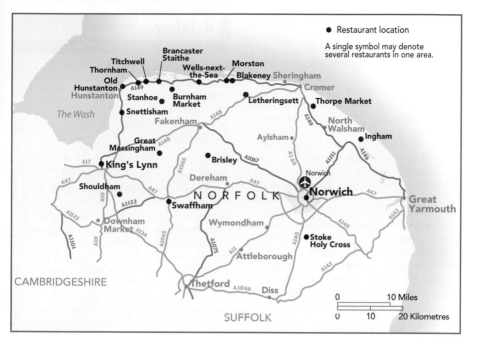

Blakeney
The Moorings

Cooking score: 2
Modern British | £32
High Street, Blakeney, NR25 7NA
Tel no: 01263 740054
blakeney-moorings.co.uk

'This is a friendly spot,' enthused one regular; 'another Norfolk favourite,' noted another. With golden-yellow walls and a please-all menu, it's not surprising that Richard and Angela Long's compact high street restaurant is frequently busy. People come, hot-foot from beach walks, for sandwiches, cakes, teas and coffees, but surprisingly accomplished meals, too. 'Beautifully cooked' seafood is a strength, perhaps spicy crab cake with chilli, lime and coriander salsa, ahead of sea bass with brown shrimp risotto and salsa verde. Among substantial meat dishes there could be locally shot roast partridge, teamed with pancetta, squash, rosemary and wild plum compôte, or pork tenderloin accompanied by sage, Parma ham, savoy cabbage and sauce soubise. Vast cakes are on display to tempt; otherwise there are a few traditional puddings listed on the specials board, perhaps sticky toffee pudding or treacle sponge. There's a good selection under £20 on the compact but wide-ranging wine list.
Chef/s: Richard and Angela Long. **Closed:** Mon, Dec, Jan, Mon to Thur (Nov, Feb, Mar). **Meals:** main courses £16 to £24. Sun L £19. **Details:** 50 seats. Music.

Brancaster Staithe
The White Horse

Cooking score: 2
Modern British | £35
Main Road, Brancaster Staithe, PE31 8BY
Tel no: 01485 210262
whitehorsebrancaster.co.uk

The lyrical waxing about the view from the contemporary, light-filled dining room at this roadside pub is entirely justified – think East

Anglian skies, creeks, little boats that are stuck in time (and marshy mud, too, at low tide). Bypass Instagram for a moment, though, to focus on the tempting menu. There's a strong 'when in Brancaster' case for choosing the exceptional mussels, or half a dozen local oysters served classically or tempura, or gently smoked cod from tiny Staithe Smokehouse, served with spinach, a poached egg and cockle hollandaise. For meatier appetites – and in preparation for that brisk coastal walk – a red poll sirloin with all the sides you'd expect, or a bowl of no-nonsense chilli and rice from the chalkboard bar specials, will set you up well, especially if followed by a bitter chocolate fondant and salted caramel sauce, or a plate of first-rate cheeses from Mrs Temple's nearby dairy. Wine from £19.50.

Chef/s: Fran Hartshorne. **Meals:** main courses £15 to £26. Sun L £16 (1 course). **Details:** 100 seats. 100 seats outside. Bar. Wheelchairs. Parking. Music.

LOCAL GEM

The Jolly Sailors
British | £23
Brancaster Staithe, PE31 8BJ
Tel no: 01485 210314
jollysailorsbrancaster.co.uk

£30

The menu at this roadside spot may doff its hat to the immediate area year-round, but don't expect airs and graces. Sure, the predictable is available (brie wedges, breaded king prawns, plenty for smaller appetites) but when in Brancaster... Lift the lid on a rattling, steaming pan of the freshest Brancaster mussels in winter; come summer, sweet dressed crab with a perky salad and butter-glossed, salt-flecked new potatoes sing of seasonality and location. There's love for crisp-edged stone-baked pizzas, and few can resist the sticky toffee pudding. On foot? A suitably jolly rum list is worthy of investigation and there are wines from £18.50.

Brisley

The Brisley Bell
Cooking score: 2
Modern British | £35
The Green, Brisley, NR20 5DW
Tel no: 01362 705024
thebrisleybell.co.uk

Marcus Seamen and Amelia Nicholson rang the changes here in 2017, refurbishing, extending and reopening this comely 17th-century pub with rooms overlooking the common. There are now three dining spaces (including a conservatory) alongside a bar where local ales hold sway. Dark green walls, bare brick and a hunting theme – look for the circular artwork made from pheasant feathers – fit with the 'traditional with a twist' schtick. Likewise, Norfolk produce is highlighted in a menu where creamy razor clam thermidor in a herb crust could precede tender soy-braised short rib of beef with horseradish mash and spanking fresh spring greens, or a whole lemon sole cooked to fall-off-the-bone perfection. Prompt, friendly service can be very chatty. A gelatinous vanilla and mascarpone cheesecake needed more oomph at inspection, but the concise, good-value wine list (sourced by local vintner Peter Graham and starting at £18.50) holds interest aplenty. Ding dong!

Chef/s: Hervé Stouvenel. **Closed:** Mon, 25 and 26 Dec, 1 Jan. **Meals:** main courses £14 to £25. Set L £20 (2 courses) to £25. Sun L £16 (2 courses) to £27. **Details:** 92 seats. 28 seats outside. Bar. Wheelchairs. Parking.

▌Burnham Market

North Street Bistro

Cooking score: 2
Modern European | £30
20 North Street, Burnham Market, PE31 8HG
Tel no: 01328 730330
20northstreet.co.uk
£5 OFF £30

Diminutive this restaurant may be, but that doesn't stop chef patron Dan Fancett packing punch after punch into an appealing menu that nods to France and Italy but celebrates local, or his partner Holly Minns delivering pitch perfect hospitality. North Street Bistro has fast built a reputation for diners coming (and coming back) because the food is precisely what they want to eat. Start local, perhaps, with a Brancaster mussel and tomato soup with saffron aïoli, or choose a whipped chicken liver parfait and toasted brioche, the sweetness cut with pickled walnut ketchup, fresh celery and radish. Lose yourself in the hug-in-a-bowl administered by a stew of the softest Holkham lamb shoulder with Parmesan gnocchi, any richness offset by spoonfuls of caper and mint dressing, or keep it light with skrei cod served with white beans, chorizo and more of those local mussels. To finish? The lightness of a buttermilk panna cotta with rhubarb and honeycomb made one diner happy, but a chocolate-loving companion declared undying love for a superlative fondant with vanilla ice cream. Wine from £19.

Chef/s: Dan Fancett. **Closed:** Mon, 14 to 30 Jan. **Meals:** main courses £13 to £22. **Details:** 26 seats. 8 seats outside. Music.

LOCAL GEM

Socius

Modern British | £25
11 Foundry Place, Burnham Market, PE31 8LG
Tel no: 01328 738307
sociusnorfolk.co.uk
£5 OFF £30

This friendly spot in an airy brick and flint building hits the mark with its daily changing line-up of modern British tapas: mild, creamy burrata with wild garlic pesto; broccoli purée, peas and almonds; arancini with Binham Blue cheese; king oyster mushrooms with garlic butter, artichoke and capers. Choose a few to share over a cocktail and 'drinking snacks' – crisp pickled mushrooms and aïoli, or king prawns in a sticky chilli glaze, say. Heartier fare might come in the shape of crisp chicken, chorizo, potatoes and chimichurri. Finish with a rich, glossy chocolate bar with salted caramel gelato, or mango and passion fruit Alaska. Wine from £19.50.

▌Great Massingham

The Dabbling Duck

Cooking score: 2
British | £26
11 Abbey Road, Great Massingham, PE32 2HN
Tel no: 01485 520827
thedabblingduck.co.uk
🛏 £30

It's not hard to understand the appeal of this pretty pub. It has the village green location (complete with ducks) and rustic, comfortable interiors, the space for children to play, and the space just to have a drink. The menu appeals widely, too. Come for a Dexter burger with everything you'd expect, game harvested in season from the owners' land, or rump steak with a classic béarnaise, but look out, too, for dishes with global punch such as bhuna curries, bang-bang cauliflower with peanut sriracha, tuna steak or seared scallops with kimchi. Non-meat eaters are well looked after, and a seitan steak is an option for vegans, while pizza and street food served outside in the summer months satisfy another need. Finish with the pure comfort of sticky banoffee pudding with banana ice cream, or sweet pumpkin pie with flavours of maple, pecan and s'mores. Wine from £17.95. **Chef/s:** Dale Smith. **Meals:** main courses £14 to £25. **Details:** 100 seats. 30 seats outside. Wheelchairs. Parking. Music.

▉ Ingham
The Ingham Swan
Cooking score: 4
Modern British | £35
Sea Palling Road, Ingham, NR12 9AB
Tel no: 01692 581099
theinghamswan.co.uk

From the ugly devastation of fire, in spring 2019 a beautiful Swan emerged, feathered, fabulous and with much of its character intact. Getting to this corner of north-east Norfolk is a trip for most, but the cooking of Daniel Smith and Alex Clare is worth every winding mile. Notes of cider and a touch of cream, a spoonful of salsa verde, crunch of buckwheat and hint of leek ash turn an onion velouté amuse-bouche into so much more than mere onion soup. Follow with tomatoes in all their jewel box glory, seasoned gently with black olive crumb, goat's cheese mousse giving a tangy dimension. Careful cooking is respectful of ingredients, evident in a dish of roasted stone bass with vivid young samphire and globe artichoke, and in the heft of Swannington ribeye, chimichurri and beef dripping potatoes. To finish? Smith's 'modern peach Melba' with its silky-smooth raspberry cream, and crème fraîche ice cream rippled with raspberries, is the sharp and sweet, flighty and substantial one to choose. Wine, from a list with plenty by the glass, from £23. **Chef/s:** Daniel Smith and Alex Clare. **Closed:** 25 and 26 Dec. **Meals:** main courses £17 to £28. Set L £20 (2 courses) to £25. Set D £24 (2 courses) to £28. Tasting menu £58 (7 courses). Sun L £28. **Details:** 52 seats. 16 seats outside. V menu. Bar. Wheelchairs. Parking. Music.

▉ King's Lynn
Market Bistro
Cooking score: 3
Modern British | £40
11 Saturday Market Place, King's Lynn, PE30 5DQ
Tel no: 01553 771483
marketbistro.co.uk
£5 OFF

If you find yourself in west Norfolk with a yen for good food cooked with a whole lot of love and understanding, wriggle through old King's Lynn to this gem of a neighbourhood restaurant. The compact, ever-changing menu promises (and delivers) a vivacity of flavour that belies the simplicity of the ingredients – a spirited heritage tomato starter with tomato carpaccio, thyme crumb, pickled cucumber, goat's curd and mint balances texture, flavour and temperature faultlessly, and there's praise for 'unusual, creative' Rosary Ash goat's cheese cannelloni with fresh and emulsified peas. Delicately flavoured cod, pan-roasted until it flakes satisfyingly, is lifted by a broccoli salsa verde, hints of smoked garlic, a crunchy scatter of almonds, and sweet apple, while pork belly, smoked beetroot and celeriac rémoulade left another diner content. Chocolate lovers will delight in a crémeux with praline and peanuts, but for something fresher, try the lemon curd with lavender crumble, pear sorbet and blackberry. Consider the thoughtful wine pairings, or choose from an accessible list that opens at £21. **Chef/s:** Richard Golding. **Closed:** Mon, Sun, first 2 weeks Jan. **Meals:** main courses £15 to £26. Set L £17 (2 courses) to £22. Tasting menu £45 (5 courses). **Details:** 42 seats. Bar. Wheelchairs. Music.

Marriott's Warehouse

Modern European | £26
South Quay, King's Lynn, PE30 5DT
Tel no: 01553 818500
marriottswarehouse.co.uk

£30

This quayside warehouse – hauled up to 21st-century standards, of course – flourishes now much as it no doubt did during King's Lynn's 16th-century Hanseatic prime. Today it's about quick bites rather than trading corn or salt, guests choosing from an easy-going menu that includes the likes of a packed seafood crumble, rich venison stew with mash or a towering burger. The place buzzes brightly morning, noon and night, with Sunday roasts, delivered family-style to carve yourself, a particular weekend draw, perhaps followed by a bowl of Marriott's apple crumble and custard. Wine from a chirpy £17.

Letheringsett

The Kings Head

Modern British | £28
Holt Road, Letheringsett, NR25 7AR
Tel no: 01263 712691
kingsheadnorfolk.co.uk

£30

If ever you need convincing of the scope of East Anglian produce, book a table at this handsome pub in a village just outside handsome Holt. The menu scours the region hungrily for the best ingredients to be had – heck, even the flour for loaves baked daily on site is milled in Letheringsett. Smoked salmon from Brancaster Staithe with capers and pickled cucumbers could precede locally shot pheasant pot-roasted with squash gnocchi and a cider and sage cream. In season, don't miss Sharrington berries, perhaps topping a pavlova or served alongside a chocolate délice or vanilla cheesecake. Wines from £18.50.

Morston

Morston Hall

Cooking score: 7
Modern European | £90
The Street, Morston, NR25 7AA
Tel no: 01263 741041
morstonhall.com

'Classy, special, delicious,' noted one diner after eating at this intimate country house hotel. You could file Morston Hall in the 'decorous grande dame' category, because for over 25 years it has welcomed guests into its comfortable flint-and-brick arms with levels of food, wine and service that don't miss a beat. But what's remarkable is that the food continues to evolve within its classic ambit, exciting diners afresh at every visit. Start the seven-course dinner (after a civilised 7.15pm apéritif) with the smoothest of butternut squash veloutés scattered with King's Lynn brown shrimps and cubes of roasted squash, a prelude perhaps to an exceptional lobster raviolo or delicate bass from Stiffkey with a whey butter sauce. Simple menu descriptions indicate key components, because here it's the ingredient, carefully sourced and prepped, that's more important than any technical fandango behind the (unquestionably Instagrammable) dishes. Nor is this kitchen shackled wearily to the local: it roams hungrily in search of the best. The ice cream alongside a blackcurrant délice may be made with raw milk from Suffolk's Fen Farm Dairy, but plump langoustines are from Scotland, crisp-skinned suckling pig is from the Wye Valley, and the cheeseboard is a celebration of Europe's finest. Tasting notes on the 'ever-evolving labour of love' that is the wine list are informative, whether you choose the £28 Chilean Sauvignon Blanc opener, or are tempted to sink four figures into a complex, velvety 1982 Saint-Émilion grand cru, surely as memorable as the restaurant in which it is being poured.

Chef/s: Greg Anderson. **Closed:** 1 to 24 Jan.
Meals: tasting menu £90 (7 courses). Sun L £45.
Details: 55 seats. Bar. Wheelchairs. Parking.

Symbols

🛏 Accommodation is available
£30 Three courses for £30 or less
£5 OFF £5 off voucher scheme
🍷 Notable wine list

▊ Norwich

Benedicts

Cooking score: 6
Modern British | £39
9 St Benedict's Street, Norwich, NR2 4PE
Tel no: 01603 926080
restaurantbenedicts.com

Regulars remain firm in their copious enthusiasm for one of Norfolk's finest: a pleasingly low-key shop conversion on an attractive old city-centre street. The cooking is thoroughgoing British modernism, carefully considered, unerringly consistent. Richard Bainbridge's menus – whether three-course prix fixe or multi-course tasting – are seasonally influenced. Most ingredients come from the region, delivering much gratification for one March diner in the form of succulent Blickling Hall Estate confit lamb, teamed with potato, salted turnip and mint, then perfectly timed skrei cod with parsnip, roasted onions and shellfish bisque. Elsewhere, Tim Allen's South Creake pork loin and confit belly has been described as 'so beautiful and soft' and desserts draw plenty of enthusiasm, the high point being the ever-popular Nanny Bush's trifle with milk jam, but there's praise, too, for rhubarb and duck egg tart. Service is described as 'the best side of helpful and attentive'. The wine pairings are an enticing option with the tasting menus, or go it alone with a bottle from £19.
Chef/s: Richard Bainbridge. **Closed:** Mon, Sun, 23 Dec to 8 Jan. **Meals:** set L £18 (2 courses) to £22. Set D £31 (2 courses) to £39. Tasting menu £50 (6 courses) to £62. **Details:** 36 seats. V menu. Vg menu. Music.

Roger Hickman's

Cooking score: 5
Modern British | £48
79 Upper St Giles Street, Norwich, NR2 1AB
Tel no: 01603 633522
rogerhickmansrestaurant.com
£5 OFF

'Flavour is the word that predominates at this delightfully small restaurant,' noted one reader who enjoyed the full works at this discreet Norwich bolthole. The dining room isn't actually that petite, but the mood is civilised, intimate and congenial – helped along by service that is 'slick and knowledgeable' without overgilding the lily. Proceedings begin with drinks and 'mini bites' (perhaps goat's cheese on Parmesan shortbread, tiny bacon muffins and a weeny portion of pea velouté), while dishes from the fixed-price menu are 'cooked to perfection' and always 'pleasing on the eye': exactly timed scallops with apple purée, ginger, fennel and toasted hazelnut crumb; halibut with 'textures of parsnip', pear, curry and mussels; duck breast and leg dressed with cherry, turnip, a dollop of mash and hazelnuts. Knowledgeably sourced local and seasonal ingredients are treated with the respect they deserve (be it smoked venison or wild sea bass), and Hickman's pursuit of forthright flavour extends to reworked dessert classics such as tiramisu or lemon meringue with Calvados and apple. A private dining room upstairs has its own kitchen, while the thoughtfully assembled wine list is peppered with impressive growers and classy vintages.
Chef/s: Roger Hickman. **Closed:** Mon, Sun, 31 Dec to 11 Jan. **Meals:** set L £21 (2 courses) to £26. Set D £39 (2 courses) to £48. Tasting menu £41 (5 courses) to £70. **Details:** 45 seats. V menu.

Shiki

Cooking score: 3
Japanese | £30
6 Tombland, Norwich, NR3 1HE
Tel no: 01603 619262
shikirestaurant.co.uk
£30

Set in the city's attractive old heart, Shunsuke Tomii's 16-year-old townhouse restaurant sports an authentically minimalist interior, with bare wooden benches, tables and flooring. Vibrant Japanese paintings add colour, as do plates of skilfully presented creations from the informal, izakaya-style menu. Come for an inexpensive bento lunch of salmon teriyaki, perhaps, or a warming bowlful of beef udon noodle soup. The delicate batter of the vegetable tempura shows the kitchen's lightness of touch. The good value continues at dinner, especially for the popular Tuesday sushi nights when, during a two-hour slot, diners have the run of a 35-strong menu ranging from fish-egg nigiri via pork tonkatsu to handsome California rolls. Otherwise, peruse the à la carte nigiri where turbot and surf clam lie in wait. Japanese students flock here, served by brisk, purposeful staff. To drink, choose from tea, sake, Norfolk cider, Japanese beers or wine (from £21).
Chef/s: Shunsuke Tomii. **Closed:** Mon, Sun, Jan. **Meals:** small plates £3 to £20. Set L £14 (2 courses). Set D £22 (2 courses) to £65. Tasting menu £45 (8 courses) to £65. **Details:** 80 seats. 50 seats outside. Wheelchairs. Parking. Music.

Wild Thyme

Cooking score: 2
Vegetarian | £28
The Old Fire Station Stables, Labour in Vain Yard, Norwich, NR2 1JD
Tel no: 01603 765562
wildthymenorwich.co.uk
£30

Sprouting anew after smoke damage in 2018, this well-loved provider of vegetarian treats (from breakfasts to dinners) is sited above a wholefood store, with additional tables on a quaint courtyard near Norwich's Guildhall. Inside, it's attractive, spacious and woody, with bare brick walls and arched windows. Staff are young, efficient and, like the food, anything but dour. Bright colours, carefully matched textures, a global array of flavours and expert presentation characterise the likes of tangy spiced beetroot with lentils, goat's cheese, preserved lemon and rosemary salad. Follow this, perhaps, with hearty white bean and tomato stew, or an enticing assembly of sticky aubergine steak, bulgur wheat and tzatziki with coriander and cashew salsa. Micro-leaf garnishes come via the restaurant's own hydroponic growing system. Not every advertised ingredient was discernible at inspection, but puddings such as chocolate orange and coconut cheesecake are a vegan delight. The brief wine list (organic, vegan) starts at £18.
Chef/s: Linde Rose. **Closed:** Sun. **Meals:** main courses £10 to £11. **Details:** 53 seats. 16 seats outside. V menu. Vg menu.

★ LOCAL RESTAURANT AWARD ★
REGIONAL WINNER

Woolf & Social

Cooking score: 3
International | £25
21-23 Nelson Street, Norwich, NR2 4DW
Tel no: 01603 443658
woolfandsocial.co.uk
£5 OFF £30

The simple no-frills decor (plank floor, plain tables, unforgiving chairs) has the look of many a contemporary restaurant. But there's an authenticity here, a passion for simple things done well. It's the sort of no-nonsense place you'd love on a corner in your neighbourhood and it's clearly popular with a local crowd who come here for generous sharing plates offering a mix of home-grown and global flavours. Ingredients are of the highest quality and 'both the cooking and presentation worthy of a far fancier place'. Although meat and fish get a fair look in – the fried buttermilk chicken is something of a signature, while mackerel with 'sproutkraut' and sorrel, and pork with quince hoisin and onion are sure-fire hits – the kitchen ushers vegetables into the spotlight with the likes of broccoli with miso and chilli or Jerusalem artichoke with black garlic and pine nuts. For drinkers there are craft ales or a brief selection of wines from £19.

Chef/s: Francis Woolf. **Closed:** Mon, 25 Dec. **Meals:** small plates £5 to £15. **Details:** 30 seats. 28 seats outside. Bar. Wheelchairs. Music.

▊ Old Hunstanton
The Neptune
Cooking score: 5
Modern European | £62
85 Old Hunstanton Road, Old Hunstanton, PE36 6HZ
Tel no: 01485 532122
theneptune.co.uk

In its Georgian youth, this restaurant with rooms was used as a store for contraband goods seized on the north Norfolk coast, which adds a novelistic thrill to the experience of staying at Kevin and Jacqueline Mangeolles' elegantly converted place. Light grey tones and a wood floor maintain a breezy feel in the dining room, where Kevin's artfully composed modern European dishes rule the roost. He is skilled at emphasising the principal components with ingenious but discreet accompaniments, as when a slice of truffled quail terrine and brioche are garnished with pickled grapes and fried sprout leaves. But he's also content to leave well alone, adding only a little apple and dried cherry tomato to salty-rich smoked haddock brandade. Local seafood shows up well in a pairing of lemon sole and Brancaster mussels with polonaise dressing, pink firs and kale, while Goosnargh duck breast is partnered with red cabbage, butternut purée and dauphinoise. Inviting combinations of texture and temperature, such as sticky toffee pudding with peanut butter ice cream and pineapple,

lift desserts out of the ordinary. A commendable wine selection includes some half bottles, as well as glasses in two sizes. **Chef/s:** Kevin Mangeolles. **Closed:** Mon, 10 to 17 Nov, 26 Dec, 3 weeks Jan, 1 week May. **Meals:** set D £47 (2 courses) to £62. Tasting menu £78 (9 courses). Sun L £32 (2 courses) to £40. **Details:** 20 seats. Bar. Parking. Music. Children over 10 yrs.

▊ Reepham
READERS RECOMMEND
The Dial House
Reepham, NR10 4JJ
Tel no: 01603 879900
thedialhouse.org.uk
'We had a lovely stay, it's a really quirky place because everything is for sale. The food is very flavourful – I loved my BBQ carrots with quinoa and baba ganoush.'

▊ Shouldham
LOCAL GEM
King's Arms
British | £22
28 The Green, Shouldham, PE33 0BY
Tel no: 01366 347410
kingsarmsshouldham.co.uk

£30

Winter fires: tick; summer beer garden: tick; hearty home-cooked food: big tick. Drop into this community-owned village pub to be fed, watered and welcomed, whether you're after a salad of Norfolk-made Binham Blue cheese and roasted walnuts, a plate of (local) ham, (free range) egg and (ace) chips, or a crisp-pastried asparagus, brie and mushroom pie. Roast cod with lemon and caper butter, or a scallop and smoked haddock gratin will please seafood lovers, and who can honestly say no to sticky toffee pudding? Wines from £16.50.

▌Snettisham
The Old Bank
Cooking score: 3
Modern British | £38
10 Lynn Road, Snettisham, PE31 7LP
Tel no: 01485 544080
theoldbankbistro.co.uk
£5
OFF

'Blown away by the whole experience,' one happy visitor felt moved to report, after dinner at this delightful bistro. Opening salvos from the compact, creative menu, rich with carefully chosen ingredients, might be Norfolk beef tartare with punchy anchovy-caper mayonnaise and roasted Jerusalem artichokes, or raw milk Baron Bigod cheese from over the border in Suffolk with salt-baked beetroot and sweet raisin jam. Local asparagus, served simply with a 'divine' sauce and flutter of Parmesan kicked things off perfectly for one diner. Follow with a hearty plate of Sandringham venison, the comfort of roasted cod with Brancaster mussels and chive mash, or superbly plump Cornish scallops with heart-stoppingly delicious pork belly. To finish? Coconut and lime rice pudding is a fresh take on a classic, but you'd be forgiven if an almond brownie with white chocolate mousse and raspberry sorbet diverts your attention. 'Attentive and knowledgeable' service hits just the right solicitous note, and there's wide appreciation for the good-value lunch offer, the tasting menu and wine list, which opens with a classic Spanish Verdejo for a reasonable £19.
Chef/s: Lewis King. **Closed:** Mon, Tue, 1 week Nov, 2 weeks Jan, 1 week May. **Meals:** main courses £15 to £24. Set L £18 (2 courses) to £22. Tasting menu £55 (7 courses). **Details:** 24 seats. 12 seats outside. Wheelchairs. Music.

LOCAL GEM
The Rose & Crown
Modern British | £28
Old Church Road, Snettisham, PE31 7LX
Tel no: 01485 541382
roseandcrownsnettisham.co.uk
£5 🛏 £30
OFF

This long-popular and much-extended pub with rooms now seems firmly back on track; early grumbles following the arrival of a new chef can be put down to teething trouble. An inspection dinner from the all-day wide-ranging menu produced a generous portion of juicy pork belly with tangy apple purée, followed by a succulent chunk of hake with seafood velouté. There's praise, too, for the luxurious chocolate 'bomb'. True, service can be slow, but the cosy old bar (with Norfolk ales) and attractive beer garden keep crowds returning. Wine from £18.

▌Stanhoe
The Duck Inn
Cooking score: 3
British | £35
Burnham Road, Stanhoe, PE31 8QD
Tel no: 01485 518330
duckinn.co.uk
£5 🛏
OFF

If there's one thing that visitors, locals and Guide inspectors agree on, it's the pleasure to be had from a meal at The Duck. A combination of superlative local ingredients in the hands of confident but ego-free chefs, relaxed service and a comfortable setting elevate it beyond the ordinary. Come hungry, for the portions are as generous as the flavours are muscular. A classic steak tartare arrives gold-topped with a confit egg yolk, the flavours sharpened by pickled mushrooms; haggis is fried until crisp and served with rare-roasted pigeon and sweet carrot purée. Follow with ox cheeks, braised long and slow in red wine and served with truffle mash and asparagus, or go lighter with butter-poached chalk stream trout, clams and miso sauce.

Chocolate torte is irresistibly laden with candied walnuts, and a crisp polenta shortbread 'jammy dodger' is filled thickly with clotted cream and strawberries. A carefully composed wine list offers the usual suspects at around £20 but some intrigue if you're prepared to spend a little more.
Chef/s: Shaun Ireson. **Closed:** 25 Dec. **Meals:** main courses £9 to £29. **Details:** 100 seats. 90 seats outside. V menu. Vg menu. Bar. Wheelchairs. Parking. Music.

▌Stoke Holy Cross
Stoke Mill
Cooking score: 4
Modern British | £40
Mill Road, Stoke Holy Cross, NR14 8PA
Tel no: 01508 493337
stokemill.co.uk

The white weatherboarded walls could tell a story or two about the industrial heritage of this part of East Anglia. They would tell of mustard milling and how the caring Jeremiah Colman (of mustard fame) would ensure his workforce had a daily hot meal of meat, vegetable stew and a pint of coffee. Scroll forward some 200 years and the elegant, airily refurbished mill is still in the business of food, although the meat is more likely to be a prettily composed, expertly balanced plate of pork loin, belly and cheek, the vegetable not a stew but colourful beetroot (grown on site), artichoke and broad bean risotto, and the coffee a punchy espresso rather than a pint. The contemporary menu flits around Europe for inspiration, finding ratatouille to go with pan-fried bass and crisp crab cakes, and the mussels, prawns, squid and chorizo of a Spanish paella to accompany halibut. Finish by sharing an apple tarte tatin with butterscotch sauce and vanilla ice cream, which reassuringly requires a 20-minute wait. Wine from £22.
Chef/s: Andrew Rudd. **Closed:** Mon, Tue, first week Jan. **Meals:** main courses £16 to £27. Set L £16 (2 courses) to £20. Set D £20 (2 courses) to £26. Tasting menu £45 (5 courses) to £55. Sun L £28. **Details:** 65 seats. Bar. Wheelchairs. Parking. Music.

The Wildebeest
Cooking score: 3
Modern British | £40
82-86 Norwich Road, Stoke Holy Cross, NR14 8QJ
Tel no: 01508 492497
thewildebeest.co.uk
🛏

This former country pub may keep things informal with its bare boards and comfortable leather chairs but there's nothing restrained about the ambitious food emerging from the open kitchen. Norfolk produce dominates the menus, whether you opt for the carte or the kindly priced 'dinner du jour'. In an age when menu descriptions seem to get more truncated, the dishes read like recipes themselves, as in glazed Swannington pig's cheeks with spiced pear, salt-baked celeriac, Parma ham crisp, burnt conference pear purée, pork puff and braising liquor. An equally elaborate main might follow, say pan-seared stone bass fillet with crab risotto, crispy fishcake, chargrilled baby leeks, broccoli, walnuts and chervil velouté. After that, toffee apple and cinnamon soufflé with burnt butter and toasted almond ice cream brings things to a satisfying conclusion. Opening at £21, the extensively annotated wine list includes some cracking bottles from New and Old Worlds.
Chef/s: Charlie Wilson. **Closed:** 25 and 26 Dec. **Meals:** main courses £17 to £28. Set L £18 (2 courses) to £23. Set D £24 (2 courses) to £28. Sun L £28. Tasting menu £45 (6 courses). **Details:** 60 seats. 24 seats outside. Wheelchairs. Parking. Music.

▌Swaffham
Strattons Hotel
Cooking score: 2
Modern British | £30
4 Ash Close, Swaffham, PE37 7NH
Tel no: 01760 723845
strattonshotel.com

Take the steps down to this quirky hotel restaurant just off the market square to find a menu that flies the flag energetically (and with a long-standing commitment to sustainability) for Norfolk, and in particular the restaurant's immediate Breckland surroundings. Start with soup made using produce brought in by local gardeners, or Cromer crab with basil mayo and pickled samphire. Look out for Brancaster mussels on a main course of grilled hake and sautéed artichokes; quail from nearby Fakenham, roasted and served with caramelised cauliflower, black garlic and roasted onions; or Ellingham goat's cheese from Fielding Cottage near Norwich, part of a vegetarian dish of griddled purple sprouting broccoli, roast new potatoes, salsa verde and hazelnuts. Don't overlook the kitchen's pastry skills – choose a dark chocolate ganache with poached rhubarb, pistachio meringue and crème fraîche ice cream, or come another day for her themed afternoon tea spreads. The wine list opens at £20 and is arranged helpfully by flavour profile, a key indicating ideal food pairings.
Chef/s: Jules Hetherton and Dan Freear. **Closed:** 1 week Christmas. **Meals:** main courses £16 to £20. **Details:** 40 seats. 20 seats outside. Bar. Music.

Local Gem
These entries are brilliant neighbourhood venues, delivering good, freshly cooked food at great value for money.

▌Thornham
LOCAL GEM
The Yurt
Global | £30
Drove Orchards, Thornham, PE36 6LS
Tel no: 01485 525889
£5 OFF £30

'Awesome food served in a tent' is what this easy-going north Norfolk spot (formerly Shuck's) promises – and delivers – all day long and with genuine heart and soul. There's lots to share on Phil Milner's flavour-fuelled menu: punchy beef brisket nachos, meze boards or a seafood mixed grill loaded with tempura red mullet, squid, seared king scallops (and the rest), for example. Confit Gressingham duck with chorizo and butter bean cassoulet, and katsu chicken burger with kimchi continue the riot of taste bouncing off these (rounded) walls. Homemade cakes and bakes displayed on the counter could finish a meal sweetly. Wine from £16.

▌Thorpe Market
The Gunton Arms
Cooking score: 2
British | £35
Cromer Road, Thorpe Market, NR11 8TZ
Tel no: 01263 832010
theguntonarms.co.uk

Crank your appetite up to the max before visiting this eccentric pub restaurant on the Gunton Estate a few miles inland from Cromer. Standing in a thousand acres of solitude on parkland grazed by fallow deer, it is a place to revel in venison. Venison sausages come with mash and onion gravy, a mixed venison grill is as robust in flavour as it is light in food miles, and all the offal is used of course – a starter of devilled venison liver on toast could have been more devilish, but the rich meat was butter-soft and smooth. Blythburgh pork chops, 10oz sirloin steaks or a sharing rib of beef are all cooked under the gaze of diners on the magnificent Elk Room fire, while a conventional kitchen turns out the likes of pollock with spring peas and broad beans or the owner's favourite crab pasta with chilli and coriander. A tangy buttermilk panna cotta that judders just as it should comes with local raspberries, or you could go all out with chocolate truffle torte and griottine cherries. Wine from £21.

Chef/s: Stuart Tattersall. **Closed:** 25 Dec.
Meals: main courses £12 to £65. **Details:** 100 seats. 40 seats outside. Bar. Wheelchairs. Parking. Music.

■ Titchwell
Titchwell Manor
Cooking score: 4
Modern European | £42
Titchwell, PE31 8BB
Tel no: 01485 210221
titchwellmanor.com

£5 OFF 🛏

Covering all bases for visitors to the north Norfolk coast, this boutique hotel-restaurant-café-bar looks as vibrant as ever with its striking furnishings and bold colour scheme, while the food continues to evolve. Florid multi-course tasting menus have been abandoned in favour of a more conventional carte, but the owners' dedication to regional British ingredients and fish from the Norfolk boats is as strong as ever. The house style is typified by starter plates of chilled mussels and razor clams with smoked yoghurt and bread crisp, although the broad repertoire spans everything from a duo of wild sea bass and Dorset snails partnered by artichokes à la grecque, crosnes, black garlic and salted gooseberries to Creedy Carver duck 'roasted on the crown' with confit leg and astute accompaniments including orange sauce, golden beetroot and thyme. A separate 'classics' menu deals in homespun favourites such as mushroom soup, fish pie and treacle tart, while coffee comes with a 'chocolate tasting'. The global wine list is broken down by style and opens with 20 house selections from £22.

Chef/s: Chris Mann. **Meals:** main courses £18 to £24. Sun L £25 (2 courses) to £30. **Details:** 80 seats. 30 seats outside. Bar. Wheelchairs. Parking. Music.

■ Wells-next-the-Sea
LOCAL GEM
Wells Crab House
Seafood | £30
38-40 Freeman Street, Wells-next-the-Sea, NR23 1BA
Tel no: 01328 710456
wellscrabhouse.co.uk

£5 OFF £30 ♥

It looks every inch the seafood restaurant, from its ship's wheel mirrors and wooden fish sculptures to crabs scuttling up the wall and anchors on cushions. As for the menu, 'if you choose carefully I think this place is a gem' seems to be the consensus. Dishes can be over-complicated, so keep it simple and choose one of the vast platters (large enough for two) centred around locally caught crab or lobster and accompanied by cockles, king prawns, crayfish and the like. Alternatively, there's dressed crab or garlic-buttered lobster with fries. A serviceable wine list starts at £18.

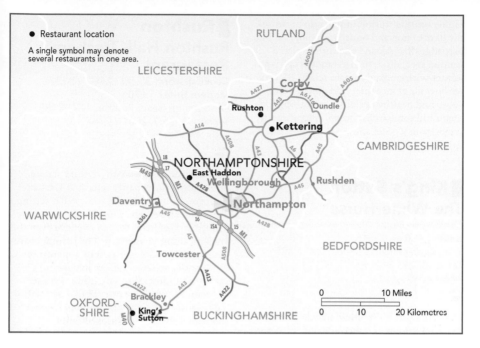

Restaurant location

A single symbol may denote several restaurants in one area.

East Haddon
The Red Lion
Cooking score: 2
Modern British | £30
Main Street, East Haddon, NN6 8BU
Tel no: 01604 770223
redlioneasthaddon.co.uk

East Haddon's crowning glory makes quite a statement with its immaculate thatched roof, honey-stone walls and pretty garden overlooking glorious countryside. You can eat (and drink) in the slate-floored bar, although the recently refurbished 'library' dining room offers something more atmospheric with its bookcases and vaulted ceiling. The menu has its share of fail-safes, from chicken liver parfait with 'the sweetest fruit chutney ever' to 28-day aged steaks cooked exactly as requested, but there are also more enterprising ideas to tease the palate. Teriyaki-glazed pork belly 'bites' are great for nibbling, while mains might run from salmon fishcakes with courgette 'noodles' and shellfish sauce to a baked choux bun filled with spinach, mushrooms and Stilton. To finish, try the vanilla panna cotta partnered by a fruity jelly spiked with locally distilled rhubarb gin. The succinct wine list includes a dozen selections by the glass.

Chef/s: Chloe Haycock. **Closed:** 25 Dec.
Meals: main courses £11 to £28. **Details:** 90 seats. 70 seats outside. Wheelchairs. Parking. Music.

Kettering
LOCAL GEM
Exotic Dining
Indian | £28
1st Floor, 3-5 Newland Street, Kettering, NN16 8JH
Tel no: 01536 411176
dineexotic.co.uk

You could order a 'golden oldie' (lamb pasanda, chicken tikka masala, rogan josh), but why play safe when the menu at this highly unusual 'fusion Indian' also promises the likes of hot-and-sour 'moja moja' rabbit, partridge dhansak and exquisitely plated seafood specialities such as tandoori piri-piri lobster with smoked tomato relish? It's easy to see how it got its name. Add gluten-free, vegan and healthy options, a promising kids' menu and some well-chosen, spice-friendly wines from £13.95 and you'll understand the appeal.

King's Sutton
The White Horse

Cooking score: 2
British | £30
2 The Square, King's Sutton, OX17 3RF
Tel no: 01295 812440
whitehorseks.co.uk
£30

Hendrik Dutson-Steinfeld may not be the first chef to want to reinvigorate British pub classics, but he's made a cracking job of it at the mellow stone hostelry he runs with his wife, Julie. Done out with a confident rustic sparsity – think a handsome oak bar and roaring fires in winter – it's a proper pub. But on the food front, a Scotch egg is reinterpreted as a smoked mackerel version, with burnt onion soubise, while Newbottle venison loin might be teamed with salt-baked artichoke and a nutty potato hotpot, with every plate at its Instagrammable best. Oxford Blue cheesecake (with pickled celery and walnut dressing) shows the kitchen's passion for regional ingredients, as does the hay-baked local duck for two to share, served with crispy leg and smoked breast. Fish includes classic fish and chips (chef's style), and gilthead bream with bacon and mussel chowder. Finish with chocolate fondant, orange purée and chocolate sorbet. To drink, real ales and reasonably priced wines await.
Chef/s: Hendrik Dutson-Steinfeld. **Closed:** Mon, 25 Dec. **Meals:** main courses £14 to £27. Set L £17 (2 courses) to £19. Sun L £20 (2 courses) to £24. Tasting menu £55 (7 courses). **Details:** 70 seats. 16 seats outside. Bar. Wheelchairs. Parking. Music.

Rushton
Rushton Hall, Tresham Restaurant

Cooking score: 3
Modern British | £70
Desborough Road, Rushton, NN14 1RR
Tel no: 01536 713001
rushtonhall.com

Set within a glorious 16th-century stately home hotel, the recently relocated Tresham trades on its undoubtedly spectacular setting. Tapestries and extravagant chandeliers create a hushed atmosphere that can overawe even the well-meaning young staff. The baronial oak-panelled bar and 1593 Brasserie (opened in 2018, with a relatively affordable menu) are still more august. Set-price dinners at the Tresham are reliable, rather than daredevil, haute cuisine affairs. After amuse-bouche (perhaps a cornetto of smoked salmon mousse), evenings could begin with a beautifully presented trio of smoked, cured and poached trout with Exmoor caviar, although the accompanying celery sorbet proved too sweet for the timidly flavoured fish. Follow with precisely cooked beef fillet with sweetbread and punchy gravy, where excellent ingredients are allowed to shine. Puddings are equally well turned out – try the luscious mango crémeux with coconut sorbet and little discs of meringue. Occasionally, seasoning is meek and combinations off kilter, but the wine list is solidly Old World-centric – if pricey (from £29).
Chef/s: Adrian Coulthard. **Closed:** Mon, Sun, 24 to 26 and 31 Dec. **Meals:** set D £70. **Details:** 24 seats. Bar. Wheelchairs. Parking. Music. Children over 12 yrs.

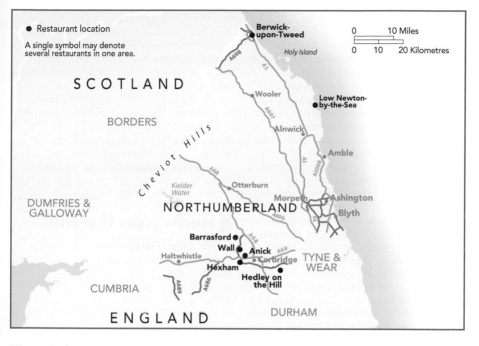

Anick
The Rat Inn
Cooking score: 2
British | £27
Anick, NE46 4LN
Tel no: 01434 602814
theratinn.com
£5 OFF £30

Described as the 'perfect country pub' and a 'must visit' destination, readers return time and again for the 'perfectly cooked' local beef ribs from named farms that are served by weight and cooked to order, as well as the local Lindisfarne oysters simply paired with shallot vinaigrette. This solid stone building with its endearing cottage garden and splendid views offers a distillation of rural Northumberland through local produce, great cask ales and warm hospitality. The seasonal menu is supplemented by daily chalkboard specials that might include pheasant breast with confit leg hash, parsnip and cider sauce or delightfully caramelised pan-fried coley with

wild mushroom risotto. The care that goes into the moreish home-baked bread extends to desserts, including a zesty lemon tart with elderflower strawberries showing a delicate touch suited to the season. Wines have been personally selected to complement the menus, with some interesting occasional bin ends.
Chef/s: Phil Mason and Kevin MacLean. **Closed:** 25 Dec, 1 Jan. **Meals:** main courses £11 to £27. Set L and early D £18 (2 courses) to £20. **Details:** 70 seats. 70 seats outside. Bar. Parking. Music.

Barrasford
The Barrasford Arms
Cooking score: 2
Modern British | £32
Barrasford, NE48 4AA
Tel no: 01434 681237
barrasfordarms.co.uk
£5 OFF

Michael and Victoria Eames swapped working in large hotels to take over this former Victorian coaching inn three years ago, and

quickly adapted to running a rural establishment popular with cyclists and walkers from nearby Hadrian's Wall. They offer traditional country hospitality and well-made, generous pub and bistro classics utilising the best of Northumberland produce. The restaurant is cosy and there's a terrace overlooking the wooded river valley for warmer days. Meals might open with confit pork belly terrine, served with spiced apple chutney and pea shoots, then move on to seared lamb's liver with streaky bacon, pomme purée and crispy onion rings, or even homemade steak pie with creamed mash and braised red cabbage. If you still have room, there's vanilla mascarpone rice pudding and lemon curd or a trio of cheeses with biscuits, caramelised onion and cranberry chutney. Corney & Barrow-supplied wines start at £17.95 or drink locally brewed ales.
Chef/s: Michael Eames. **Closed:** Mon. **Meals:** main courses £14 to £22. Set L £16 (2 courses) to £20. Sun L £17 (2 courses) to £20. **Details:** 60 seats. 30 seats outside. Bar. Parking. Music.

∎ Berwick-upon-Tweed
Audela

Cooking score: 2
Modern British | £35
64-66 Bridge Street, Berwick-upon-Tweed, TD15 1AQ
Tel no: 01289 308827
audela.co.uk

£5
OFF

Handy for the town's two art centres – The Maltings and The Granary – and run with personal charm and good humour, this tiny restaurant is an upbeat place that knows how to win friends. Readers love the way it strikes the right note between traditional and contemporary, and applaud the cooking from a 'very talented chef with the ability to blend and mix good flavours'. The focus is the produce of this bountiful part of the country, so a meal can open with a roast Scottish partridge, served with a tangle of assorted greens, Puy lentils and creamy garlic mash, all pulled together by a 'superbly flavoured jus',

and end with panna cotta topped with forced Yorkshire rhubarb. In between there could be fillet of Eyemouth halibut with potato terrine, fermented salsify, samphire and a mussel and parsley sauce, or an almost-never-off-the-menu twice-baked Northumberland cheese and leek soufflé with apple and rocket salad. Wines are a global, affordable selection starting at £17.25.
Chef/s: Craig Pearson. **Closed:** Tue, Wed. **Meals:** main courses £14 to £21. Sun L £19 (2 courses) to £24. **Details:** 28 seats. Wheelchairs. Music.

∎ Hedley on the Hill
The Feathers Inn

Cooking score: 3
British | £27
Main Street, Hedley on the Hill, NE43 7SW
Tel no: 01661 843607
thefeathers.net

£5   £30
OFF

The consensus on Rhian Cradock and Helen Greer's beguiling village pub is that it 'does food and hospitality far beyond the normal standard'. Inside may be unashamedly old-fashioned (beams, log burners) but there's an inventive streak in the kitchen with fiercely seasonal cooking making a virtue of simplicity and economy. In spring, there could be a comforting dish of baked duck egg with morels, wild garlic and cream, or home-cured Dexter ox tongue pastrami with potato salad and pickled beets. Roast mallard teamed with marmalade, Cointreau, celeriac purée and grilled radicchio di Treviso may be offered alongside an upbeat pub classic of homemade mangalitza pork and leek sausage with mash and ale gravy. Sticky toffee pudding with toffee sauce and toffee ripple ice cream makes a rich finish. Local cask ales get support from homemade liqueurs, infused gins and a brief list of well-chosen wines at sensible prices.
Chef/s: Rhian Cradock. **Closed:** Mon, Tue, first 2 weeks Jan. **Meals:** main courses £12 to £25. Sun L £17 (1 course) to £26. **Details:** 34 seats. 10 seats outside. Parking.

▌Hexham
Bouchon Bistrot
Cooking score: 4
French | £29
4-6 Gilesgate, Hexham, NE46 3NJ
Tel no: 01434 609943
bouchonbistrot.co.uk
£5 OFF **£30**

This local institution ticks all the right boxes when it comes to the French bistro experience – a thoroughly sympathique atmosphere backed up by knowledgeable, enthusiastic staff and the kind of food whose quality speaks for itself. The menu is built around established standards and it's this consistency that brings diners back time and again. Escargots in parsley butter; chicken liver parfait; tartiflette with Reblochon cheese and bacon are all present and correct, and mains are equally classic in style. Look out for steamed lemon sole paupiette with carrot moussceline and clam velouté; crisp duck confit, or rabbit saddle with oyster mushrooms and fresh tagliatelle with sauce moutarde à l'ancienne. A plate of well-kept cheeses might lead the way to equally Gallic desserts of griottine clafoutis or apple tarte tatin comme il faut. The predominantly French wine list opens with house Duboeuf at £17.50.
Chef/s: Nicolas Kleist. **Closed:** Sun. **Meals:** main courses £13 to £22. Set L £17 (2 courses) to £18. Set early D £18 (2 courses) to £19. **Details:** 145 seats. 20 seats outside. Bar. Wheelchairs. Music.

The whey forward

In the 'waste not, want not' spirit, today's environmentally aware chefs are rediscovering whey, a byproduct of the cheesemaking process.

Time was, whey – the liquid left when milk curds are drained to make cheese – would go straight into food processing or animal feed. We've found some far more delicious uses.

Delica pumpkin and whey are combined in a broth at James Lowe's Shoreditch restaurant **Lyle's**.

At near self-sufficient **Coombeshead Farm** in Cornwall, whey is put to multiple uses including in the Miss Muffet-esque curd dumplings with whey.

Whey crops up in desserts too: try whey caramel with fermented apple sorbet at Robin Gill's **The Dairy** in Clapham or carbonated yoghurt whey at Scott Smith's **Fhior** in Edinburgh.

At ever-pioneering Stockport restaurant **Where The Light Gets In**, Sam Buckley reduces 40 litres of whey down to just one for a treacle-like consistency that's perfect in a tiny petit four tart.

Low Newton-by-the-Sea

LOCAL GEM

The Ship Inn

British | £25

Newton Square, Low Newton-by-the-Sea, NE66 3EL

Tel no: 01665 576262

shipinnewton.co.uk

£30

Home-brewed ales with names like Squid Ink are one of the prime attractions at this low-ceilinged, whitewashed pub just 50 bracing yards from the North Sea. They have occasional live music and film nights, as well as laying on some very decent sustenance based largely on Northumbrian produce. Lunch means kipper pâté on toast, hand-picked crab stotties, pies and ploughman's with cheeses from the region, while evening meals move up a notch for the likes of roast cod with crispy pancetta and pea mash. Wines from £18.25.

Wall

★ NEW ENTRY ★

Hjem

Cooking score: 5

Scandinavian | £45

Hadrian Hotel, Front Street, Wall, NE46 4EE

Tel no: 01434 681232

restauranthjem.co.uk

Alex Nietosvuori worked in a number of high-profile restaurants in his native Sweden and in Denmark, as did his partner, Northumbrian Ally Thompson – returning to her roots for their first joint venture. Locals can still enjoy a pint and pub staples in the front bar of this small village hotel. The light and minimalist Hjem (pronounced 'yem' and meaning 'home') occupies a room at the back overlooking the verdant hills of the Tyne Valley. A fully open kitchen within the restaurant means diners get a close-up of Alex

preparing Scandi-influenced 'surprise' tasting menus conjured from local and foraged produce. 'Tacos' of hispi cabbage leaf topped with mussels, lemon balm and nasturtium flowers could be followed by lightly baked cod, broad bean shoots and bacon broth. A toffee-like apple caramel with horseradish ice cream makes an impressive finale. Dishes are expertly paired by sommelier Anna Frost, who used to work at L'Enclume in Cumbria and Brawn in London (see entries), with glass selections from £6.

Chef/s: Alexander Nietosvuori. **Closed:** Mon, Tue, Sun, 22 Dec to 1 Jan. **Meals:** tasting menu £45 (6 courses) to £75. **Details:** 24 seats. Bar. Wheelchairs. Parking. Music.

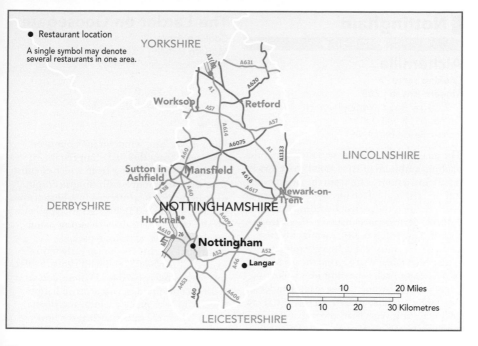

- Restaurant location
A single symbol may denote several restaurants in one area.

YORKSHIRE

Worksop   Retford

LINCOLNSHIRE

Sutton in Ashfield   Mansfield

Newark-on-Trent

DERBYSHIRE   NOTTINGHAMSHIRE

Hucknall

26   • Nottingham

• Langar

LEICESTERSHIRE

0   10   20 Miles
0   10   20   30 Kilometres

■ Langar
Langar Hall
Cooking score: 4
Modern British | £45
Church Lane, Langar, NG13 9HG
Tel no: 01949 860559
langarhall.com

Langar Hall was built in the late 17th century after the depredations of the plague year had forced the abandonment of its predecessor. In its present family ownership for more than 30 years, it has become a country retreat of singular gentility, wearing its eccentricities lightly and combining tradition and modernity in both decorative style and culinary approach. Ross Jeffrey cooks a prix fixe that develops as the week draws on, the highlights including a much-praised main-course assiette of Langar lamb with goat's curd, baby turnips and beer mustard sauce. The style mixes elements of country house tradition, from twice-baked cheese soufflé or lobster ravioli in its own rich bisque, to more obviously contemporary dishes such as charred pork fillet with smoked ham hock, a seared scallop, hispi cabbage and black apple. The closing note could be as startling as smoked orange parfait with yuzu and toasted sourdough ice cream, or as indelibly English as local strawberries with almond milk and elderflower sorbet. Wines by the glass come at a mostly uniform price of £7.75.

Chef/s: Gary Booth and Ross Jeffrey. **Meals:** set L £25 (2 courses) to £33. Set D £55. Sun L £40. **Details:** 70 seats. 20 seats outside. Bar. Wheelchairs. Parking. Music.

Anonymous

At *The Good Food Guide*, our inspectors dine anonymously and pay their bill in full. These impartial review meals, along with feedback from thousands of our readers, are what informs the content of the *GFG*. Only the best restaurants make the cut.

▌Nottingham

★ TOP 50 ★

Alchemilla
Cooking score: 7
Modern British | £65
192 Derby Road, Nottingham, NG7 1NF
Tel no: 0115 941 3515
alchemillarestaurant.uk

The unassuming frontage says little about the vaulting ambition of Alex Bond's bare-brick restaurant, a short walk from the city centre, but the strikingly stark interior of this former coach house is the perfect backdrop for a culinary performance that takes flight from the off. The drill is tasting menus only; five, seven or ten courses of culinary exploration with dishes taken way beyond the meat-and-two-veg approach ('the most mind-blowing experience' according to one reader). Indeed, vegetables often play a starring role and there are interesting vegetarian and vegan choices for those swerving meat entirely. Three bite-sized snacks open proceedings and then the menus take off into their tersely worded repertoire. Fresh, concentrated flavours and pinpoint seasoning characterise the cooking, and textures and temperatures are thoroughly investigated for the depth they can bring. Lots of rich fat – cured pork fat, say, draped over powerful umami-laden BBQ shiitake or celeriac cooked in goat's butter with black garlic purée and beurre noisette – is a signal of the kitchen's confidence with flavour. A magnificent, full-flavoured dish of Moroccan lamb is a judicious coalition of spice, aubergine and tomato. Details such as the unmissable home-baked bread and clever desserts also create good vibrations. As for drink, ferments and cocktails flow, and the wine list is properly tailored to the demands of the food.
Chef/s: Alex Bond. **Closed:** Mon, Sun, 21 Dec to 7 Jan. **Meals:** tasting menu £65 (5 courses) to £90. **Details:** 56 seats. V menu. Vg menu. Bar. Wheelchairs. Music.

The Larder on Goosegate
Cooking score: 2
Modern British | £30
16-22 Goosegate, Hockley, Nottingham, NG1 1FF
Tel no: 0115 950 0111
thelarderongoosegate.co.uk
£5 OFF **£30** ▼

Floor-to-ceiling windows look out over Goosegate from this first-floor restaurant in a Grade II-listed building from which chemist Jesse Boot set about establishing an empire back in the 1880s (as attested by a blue plaque outside, and an old Boots sign and apothecary bottles within). The daily changing menu revels in the sort of flavour-packed combinations that encourage early return – grilled Cornish mackerel with rhubarb salsa, ox cheek, slow cooked for 14 hours and served with suet dumplings, and Scottish halibut perked up with pickled lemon and ricotta gnudi. There are steaks, such as the 10oz hanger, while meatless options might run to acorn squash roasted with ras el hanout, chickpeas and hits of mint and chilli. Spices get a look-in at dessert too, with nutmeg ice cream partnering egg custard tart. Regional beers compete for your attention alongside a compact wine list arranged by style.
Chef/s: Ewan McFarlane. **Closed:** Mon, Sun, 1 to 5 Jan. **Meals:** main courses £12 to £23. Set L and D £17 (2 courses) to £20. **Details:** 65 seats. Music.

£5 voucher
£5 OFF Restaurants showing this symbol are participating in our £5 voucher scheme, redeemable against a meal for two or more. Vouchers can be found at the back of this book.

Restaurant Sat Bains

Cooking score: 9
Modern British | £110
Lenton Lane, Nottingham, NG7 2SA
Tel no: 0115 986 6566
restaurantsatbains.com

To ensure that 10 courses flow, as one captivated diner put it, 'like a well-written novel' is quite an achievement. But Sat Bains, John Freeman and the team pull it off, service after service, nailing the combination of artistry, invention, balance, pace and – of course – taste that confirms the international bestseller status of this unshowy Nottingham restaurant. For lucky regulars, there are flashes of familiarity to the story: a pungent horseradish ice cream, served at a late-spring dinner with an exceptional lovage velouté and sourdough tuile, is deemed 'as good as ever'; the warm treacle loaves still irresistible; and the Anish Kapoor-inspired beef tartare with its blood-red cloak of beetroot gel is as dramatic, glossy and flavour-packed as on a previous visit. Sat's cooking is muscular, uncompromising. There's no questioning the authority of umami in a dish of smoked eel, black truffle and turnip, or the embarras de richesse in a main course of butter-poached Loch Duart salmon with sharp pickled cucumber, sweet glazed pork belly, wasabi mayo, daikon and mushroom purée. A small bowlful of delicate béarnaise-infused dashi provides respite with fresh pear, mellow salt-baked turnip and sweet-salty bellota ham. Lenton Lane is the sort of dessert chocolate lovers live for, the wisp of tobacco through the fairy-light Aero-like confection giving the faintest grassy notes, a superb chocolate sorbet bringing icy contrast and bitterness, and nitro-frozen chocolate scattered over at the table a dose of theatre. It was the subsequent dessert of coconut ice cream, delicate perilla jelly and nub of cherry – simple, clean perfection – that left this guest wanting more, however. The wine list (bottles from £33) is as big and bold as the menu, but the ready advice of superb sommeliers makes choosing a sip a relaxed, fun exercise.
Chef/s: Sat Bains and John Freeman. **Closed:** Mon, Tue, Sun. **Meals:** tasting menu £105 (7 courses) to £120. **Details:** 44 seats. 14 seats outside. Bar. Wheelchairs. Parking. Music. Children over 8 yrs.

LOCAL GEM

Delilah Fine Foods

Modern European | £20
12 Victoria Street, Nottingham, NG1 2EX
Tel no: 0115 948 4461
delilahfinefoods.co.uk
£30

A Nottingham favourite for 15 years, Delilah occupies a former bank within earshot of the clattering trams of Market Square. These days, shoppers come to make withdrawals of fragrant cheeses, charcuterie and wine in the well-stocked aisles of the deli. On the mezzanine, diners can choose from a brief but dependable menu of platters, frittatas, salads, soups and tapas – polenta chips with smoked garlic mayo, perhaps, or honey and balsamic-glazed chorizo. An Old-World focused wine list starts at £15 – or opt for a Delilah Pale Ale from the local Magpie Brewery.

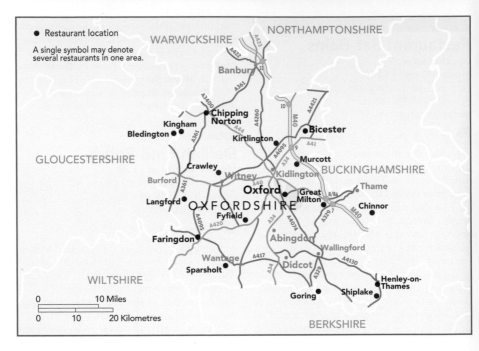

Restaurant location

A single symbol may denote
several restaurants in one area.

█ Bicester

Delhish

Indian | £16
7 Church Street, Bicester, OX26 6AY
Tel no: 01869 388070
delhish.com

£30

Opened in December 2018 in the oldest part
of Bicester, Delhish is a cosy family-run
vegetarian spot with genuine Gujarati
cooking and Mumbai street food that's a
Subcontinent away from the Oxfordshire
norm. Try the savoury dhokla steamed cake or
the bargain lunch deals, but for dinner don't
miss the wide breadth of flavours in the thali.
Jaya, the charming chef owner, might well
talk you through her enticing list of daily
specials: spiced jackfruit wrap, say. Service is
keen (if occasionally green) and wine starts at
£20 a bottle.

█ Bledington

★ NEW ENTRY ★

The King's Head

Cooking score: 1
British | £32
The Green, Bledington, OX7 6XQ
Tel no: 01608 658365
thekingsheadinn.net

Overlooking a timeless village green bisected
by a trickling stream, this 16th-century stone-
built country pub is in a perfect location for
visitors looking for that quintessential
Cotswold experience. It's still frequented by
muddy-booted farmers knocking back pints
of local ale, but diners can grab a wobbly table
and wooden settle by the inglenook fireplace
or head to the restaurant for straightforward
dishes like Cotswold lamb's kidneys on toast
with devilled sauce, and whole plaice with
new potatoes, green beans, black olives and
rainbow chard. Finish with sticky date

pudding and butterscotch sauce or British cheeses. There are global wines by the glass, carafe or bottle (from £20.50).

Chef/s: Calvin Mallows. **Closed:** 25 and 26 Dec. **Meals:** main courses £14 to £17. **Details:** 85 seats. 54 seats outside. Bar. Parking. Music.

▮ Chinnor
The Sir Charles Napier
Cooking score: 5
Modern British | £49
Sprigg's Alley, Chinnor, OX39 4BX
Tel no: 01494 483011
sircharlesnapier.co.uk

🍾

Julie Griffiths has been at the helm of this hidden away flint-built Chilterns pub since the 1970s. Surrounded by beech woods, high on Bledlow Ridge, this long-serving Guide entry is full of character, with a comfortably well-worn bar, a couple of cottagey dining rooms and a pergola-covered terrace with views of the sculpture-filled garden. The kitchen sticks rigidly to the seasons, and impeccably sourced ingredients are cooked 'with restrained creativity'. At inspection, a generous piece of lightly roasted veal sweetbread arrived with super-fine slices of sweet-sour pickled white beetroot and a candied walnut crumb, to be followed by a juicy rump and salt-baked shoulder of lamb teamed with shallot purée and a well-flavoured lovage pesto. Dark chocolate, salted caramel and peanut terrine with caramelised banana ice cream was hailed a 'wonderfully precise, tasty and indulgent' dessert. A list of Old and New World wines, including some big names, starts at £21.50, with glasses from £6.50, and there's an impressive selection of half bottles and magnums.

Chef/s: Liam Leech. **Closed:** Mon, 25 and 26 Dec, 2 weeks Jan. **Meals:** main courses £25 to £35. Set L and D £22 Tue to Fri (2 courses) to £27. **Details:** 70 seats. 70 seats outside. V menu. Bar. Wheelchairs. Parking. Music. Children over 6 yrs at D.

▮ Chipping Norton
Wild Thyme
Cooking score: 2
Modern British | £40
10 New Street, Chipping Norton, OX7 5LJ
Tel no: 01608 645060
wildthymerestaurant.co.uk

£5 OFF 🛏

Nicholas and Sally Pullen's unpretentious restaurant with rooms has been a good food beacon in these parts for 12 years. A devoted commitment to seasonality and local sourcing permeates the cooking, which is rooted in the classics but wide-eyed enough to embrace contemporary techniques and flavours. In winter, dressed Cornish crabmeat on a toasted crumpet with pink grapefruit, fried quail's egg and watercress is a typical starter and might be followed by pan-roasted loin and braised haunch of local venison with crushed potatoes, winter greens, butternut squash, Piccolo parsnips, chanterelles and blackberry port wine jus. Braised beef carbonnade with melting onions, pomme purée, greens and glazed carrots might feature on the well-priced set lunch menu, perhaps finishing with apple, lemongrass and ginger crumble topped with vanilla ice cream or a plate of three carefully selected local cheeses. A thoroughly annotated wine list opens at £19 and offers plenty of choice by the glass.

Chef/s: Nicholas Pullen. **Closed:** Mon, Sun, 1 week winter, 1 week summer. **Meals:** set L £20 (2 courses) to £25. Set D £32 (2 courses) to £40. **Details:** 35 seats.

Wine list

🍾 Restaurants showing this symbol have a wine list that our experts consider to be outstanding, either for its in-depth focus on a particular region, attractive margins on fine wines, or strong selection by the glass.

Crawley

★ NEW ENTRY ★

The Lamb

Cooking score: 3
Modern British | £32
Steep Hill, Crawley, OX29 9TP
Tel no: 01993 708792
lambpub.co.uk

'An affordable, pretty and characterful local that serves good beer and a varied menu of enjoyable, generously plated food' is how one local summed up Sebastian and Lana Snow's latest venture. The style is similar to The Five Alls (the Snows' former place), with bare stone, ancient beams and pristine wood panelling offset by antique wood tables and chairs, cushion-loaded wooden banquettes, and an array of ornaments, vases and paintings hung with style. There's a foundation of solid simplicity in dishes such as warm salad of trout with pig bits, sautéed potatoes and a poached egg, and fillet of plaice in a buttery sauce with asparagus and cucumber, while a rich steak and kidney pie arrives with a crisp dripping-based shortcrust. Hard to fault, too, is a trifle of Champagne-poached rhubarb in a jelly made from the poaching liquor with chopped stem ginger. The short wine list is price-conscious (from £20) with some 16 by-the-glass options

Chef/s: George Tauchman. **Closed:** Mon.
Meals: main courses £13 to £23. **Details:** Bar.

Faringdon

★ NEW ENTRY ★

The Eagle Tavern

Cooking score: 4
Modern European | £26
Little Coxwell, Faringdon, SN7 7LW
Tel no: 01367 241879
eagletavern.co.uk
£5 OFF 🛏 £30

Originally a watering hole for thirsty local farm hands, this sturdy late Victorian boozer is still the hub of the village, although it now attracts workers – and less industrious types – from further afield. Self-taught Slovakian-born chef and owner Marcel Nerpas channels his creative energies into a small, well-crafted menu with 'unthinkably low' prices but bags of refinement and care. The must-have starter (and a worthy signature dish) is Oxford Blue – a cross between a panna cotta and a savoury brûlée involving the namesake cheese dressed with palate-cleansing apple sorbet and walnuts. After that, there might be deboned buttermilk fried quail with Padrón peppers, braised local brisket with quinoa crunch or slow-roast shoulder of chalk downs lamb accompanied by asparagus spears and a silky cauliflower and wet garlic purée. Desserts always include a cake, but don't miss the 'remarkable' Amedei chocolate délice with a dulce de leche centre and a dollop of sorbet-like coffee ice cream. Beers are well kept and there are some impressive bottles on the short, price-conscious wine list.
Chef/s: Marcel Nerpas. **Meals:** set L and D £21 (2 courses) to £26. **Details:** 38 seats. 12 seats outside. Bar. Wheelchairs. Music.

Fyfield

The White Hart

Cooking score: 3
Modern British | £36
Main Road, Fyfield, OX13 5LW
Tel no: 01865 390585
whitehart-fyfield.com
£5 OFF

The 15th-century bones of this ancient hostelry are very much in evidence in the great hall, complete with minstrels' gallery and lofty ceiling. In this historic setting, Mark and Kay Chandler have introduced the 21st century with some divertingly up-to-date cooking. A vegetable garden helps to fuel the kitchen, and local ingredients keep the carbon footprint down, as seen in an inspired spring vegetable salad with goat's milk purée, quail's egg and wild garlic mousse. Follow with slow-roasted belly of Kelmscott pork with apple, carrots, celeriac purée, crackling and cider jus. This may be landlocked Oxfordshire, but seafood dishes come up trumps from a subtly spicy shellfish masala to pan-fried sea bream with samphire and crab bisque. Beautifully presented desserts, perhaps triple chocolate délice or rhubarb and ginger cheesecake, are a strong suit. Engaging, down-to-earth staff keep things running smoothly, as does an astute wine list with diverse options by the glass. Refurbishment is planned as we go to press.

Chef/s: Mark Chandler. **Closed:** Mon (exc bank hols). **Meals:** main courses £15 to £25. Set L £20 (2 courses) to £23. Sun L £26 (2 courses) to £29. **Details:** 90 seats. 40 seats outside. Wheelchairs. Parking. Music.

Goring
The Miller of Mansfield
Cooking score: 4
Modern British | £45
High Street, Goring, RG8 9AW
Tel no: 01491 872829
millerofmansfield.com

This ivy-clad red-brick Georgian pub is all Home Counties charm, although it has its eye on boutique guest room custom and aspirational dining these days. Mary Galer runs a tight ship out front in the bare-boarded dining room, while husband Nick produces well-considered contemporary dishes that are all about working with the grain of English tradition. There's a version of seafood cocktail to start, complete with tomatoey marie rose sauce, or an excellent rendition of duck liver parfait with sweet-sour fruity chutney and toasted brioche. The main item might be a substantial fillet of plaice in chicken-stock sauce with confit beef tomato and pickled cucumber, or perhaps roast cannon of lamb with broad beans, sheep's yoghurt and burnt rosemary. Sides of triple-cooked chips are worth the extra. Finish with featherlight banana cake with matching ice cream, salt caramel sauce and dots of orange zest purée. A nine-course tasting menu is available to preorder. Wines in all three colours start at £5.40 a glass.

Chef/s: Nick Galer. **Closed:** 6 to 13 Jan. **Meals:** main courses £18 to £30. Tasting menu £65 (9 courses). **Details:** 68 seats. 40 seats outside. Bar. Music.

Great Milton
Belmond Le Manoir aux Quat'Saisons
Cooking score: 7
Modern French | £175
Church Road, Great Milton, OX44 7PD
Tel no: 01844 278881
belmond.com

'A true delight... so complete in every aspect', concluded one happy couple after a visit to Raymond Blanc's Oxfordshire retreat – with the bonus of showpiece organic gardens and a kitchen that is still tuned in to its French master's voice. Meals proceed at a leisurely pace and nothing is ever rushed, from Champagne and 'delicate yet savoury' canapés in the drawing room to the main event in the 'wonderfully light and airy' conservatory-style restaurant. Seasonal flavours and ingredients from the garden dictate much of the culinary repertoire, and the results are creative, intelligent, balanced and immensely satisfying, whether you are eating a five-course lunch or wending your way through 'les spécialités du moment'. Fish dishes currently top the list of readers' recommendations, from a thick cut of Cornish turbot decorated with oysters, segments of cucumber, dots of caviar and wasabi to a 'very fine' fillet of Dover sole on cauliflower purée with a 'just-set' scallop and a superb savoury jus. Elsewhere, crisp veal sweetbreads are perfectly enhanced by Scottish girolles, watercress and toasted hazelnuts, while divine patisserie is the hallmark of desserts such as pear almondine with caramel croustillant and a beautifully 'restrained' ginger sauce. Generally speaking, service is everything you could wish for ('smart, organised, helpful and discreetly attentive'), although occasional mishaps are not unknown. Of course, prices are through the roof (especially if you launch into the heavyweight French-led wine list) but for most of us, this is a special-occasion one-off and no place for penny-pinching. **Chef/s:** Raymond Blanc and Gary Jones. **Meals:** set L and D £175. Tasting menu L £105 (5 courses) Thur and Fri to £145 Thur to Sun and D £190 (7 courses). Sun L £145 (7 courses). **Details:** 80 seats. V menu. Vg menu. Bar. Wheelchairs. Parking. Music.

▌Henley-on-Thames
Shaun Dickens at the Boathouse

Cooking score: 6
Modern British | £49
Station Road, Henley-on-Thames, RG9 1AZ
Tel no: 01491 577937
shaundickens.co.uk

A spot on the upper reaches of the Thames with an outdoor terrace to enjoy the riverside view is a cinch in summer, but autumn squalls and winter nip might spoil the fun. No longer. Shaun Dickens now has a set of heated 'igloos' for inclement months. His food reflects the seasons, too, as is only fitting for a former farm manager. Deftly executed by head chef James Walshaw, these are platefuls of vibrant colour, often breathtakingly pretty, with intricate flavours and textures woven through them. A serving of charred broccoli with preserved lemon, toasted almonds, pickled stems and roast garlic velouté makes a strong opening statement, or there may be red-wined shallots, herb granita and green chilli with a platter of Porthilly oysters. Imaginative treatment of meat and fish lifts main dishes into another class entirely, when confit cauliflower, cime di rapa and green tapenade accompany Cornish stone bass, or venison haunch comes with butternut and patty pan squashes, chestnuts, crispy kale and barley. Tatin for two with vanilla ice cream is a dream-date dessert, or there's shortbread with lemon curd, meringue and yoghurt sorbet. A good spread of wines by the glass opens a brisk list.

Chef/s: James Walshaw. **Closed:** Mon, Tue. **Meals:** main courses £22 to £26. Set L £26 (2 courses) to £30. Tasting menu £63 (6 courses) to £75. Sun L £30. **Details:** 45 seats. 25 seats outside. Bar. Wheelchairs. Music.

▌Kingham
The Wild Rabbit

Cooking score: 4
Modern British | £49
Church Street, Kingham, OX7 6YA
Tel no: 01608 658389
thewildrabbit.co.uk

Owned by Lady Carole Bamford (of Daylesford Organics), this decidedly upmarket pub-restaurant is manna for trend-conscious foodies who like a slice of Cotswold rustic-chic with their dinner. Pitched somewhere between a vast farmhouse kitchen and a medieval hall, the dining room comes with a full quota of pale wood, stone floors, open fires and artsy design features. Nathan Eades remains at the stoves, fashioning assured food with strong seasonal overtones and a bias towards free range and organic produce (some of it from the family's Gloucestershire farm). Jerusalem artichokes appear in company with scallops, sunflower seeds and parsley, while rump and belly of Cotswold lamb might be paired with asparagus, woodland mushrooms and sheep's yoghurt. Daylesford's daisy-fresh salad leaves pop up here, there and everywhere, before accomplished desserts such as blood orange soufflé or Wye Valley rhubarb with almond frangipane and rhubarb sorbet close the show. Regional ales and Daylesford cider are boozy alternatives to the smart, well-spread wine list.

Chef/s: Nathan Eades. **Closed:** Mon, Tue. **Meals:** main courses £23 to £32. Tasting menu £65 (7 courses). **Details:** 40 seats. 50 seats outside. V menu. Bar. Wheelchairs. Parking. Music.

▮ Kirtlington

LOCAL GEM

The Oxford Arms

Modern British | £33
Troy Lane, Kirtlington, OX5 3HA
Tel no: 01869 350208
oxford-arms.co.uk

£5
OFF

This is precisely the kind of cosy, welcoming inn you'd hope to find in the heart of a quintessential English village: exposed beams, rough stone walls, evening candles and a log fire to crank up the traditional charm. And there's serious foodic intent from chef proprietor Bryn Jones. Fine seasonal, home-grown and regional ingredients form the backbone of a menu that deals in clear-headed, straightforward combinations, from wild mushroom, spinach and chestnut tart to warm game salad with Ramsay black pudding and blueberries. It's all good value, including wines from £19.50.

▮ Langford

★ NEW ENTRY ★

The Bell Inn

Cooking score: 2
Modern British | £30
Langford, GL7 3LF
Tel no: 01367 860249
thebelllangford.com

🛏 £30

At first glance, this whitewashed village hostelry is a 'convincingly ancient', beautifully restored boozer with rooms, where steak nights and happy hours are a boon for lucky locals and the Oxfordshire-brewed ales are kept in good order. While the buzzy, characterful Bell does a good line in pub food, pleasing the diehards with double cheeseburgers, pies, battered fish and generously topped artisan pizzas with 'burnished crusts', it also entices those with more adventurous palates. Tersely worded 'bites' might include peas in their pods or lamb 'scrumpets' with ketchup, and the full line-up is peppered with good things – from a fun dish entitled 'Cotswold IPA rarebit with soldiers and pickles' (actually a fondue-like dip with fingers of toasted sourdough) to chicken milanese, lamb chops or nicely gamey venison meatballs in rich tomato sauce with soft polenta and Parmesan. Desserts such as rhubarb jelly with custard make less of an impact but the good-value wine list (bottles from £20) amply compensates.
Chef/s: Tom Noest. **Closed:** 25 Dec. **Meals:** main courses £10 to £23. **Details:** 44 seats. 50 seats outside. Bar. Parking. Music.

▮ Murcott

The Nut Tree Inn

Cooking score: 5
Modern British | £52
Main Street, Murcott, OX5 2RE
Tel no: 01865 331253
nuttreeinn.co.uk

£5
OFF

Pristine inside and out, this 15th-century thatched building is still run as a proper pub (albeit with smart dining rooms), delivering bags of charm in the form of a log burner, Chesterfield sofas and exposed stonework. Run by the North family, with Mike joined by his sister Mary in the kitchen, the menus play to the crowds with a handful of pub classics such as fish and chips or steak frites, but for the most part the focus is on more ambitious cooking. Cornish crab could be teamed with citrus fruits, yoghurt, mint, coriander and chilli, for example, while best end and braised shoulder of lamb en crépinette comes with herb aïoli and braising juices. There's more than a hint of luxury to proceedings, and that runs through to desserts such as Valrhona Guanaja chocolate ganache with rum raisins and banana ice cream. In addition, there's a separate bar and garden menu offering the likes of soup, deli plates and smoked salmon and scrambled eggs on toasted brioche. Wine-wise, there is a strong focus on France and Europe and plenty of choice by the glass.

Chef/s: Mike and Mary North. **Closed:** Mon, 27 Dec to 10 Jan. **Meals:** main courses £15 to £38. Tasting menu £75 (8 courses). **Details:** 60 seats. 30 seats outside. V menu. Vg menu. Bar. Parking. Music.

▌Oxford

Arbequina

Cooking score: 3
Spanish | £25
74 Cowley Road, Oxford, OX4 1JB
Tel no: 01865 792777
arbequina.co.uk
£30

Lurking at the city end of the Cowley Road, the sister restaurant to Oli's Thai (see entry) deals in textbook Spanish tapas with some more creative frills to supplement the ever-popular classics. As the chatter rises and tabletops fill chaotically with plates of spicy, fatty loveliness, the satisfaction levels are palpable, none more so perhaps than of those sitting at the bar in true Iberian fashion. Expect marinated boquerones, onion tortilla, lomo Ibérico and Padrón peppers as standard, but don't neglect to explore the more adventurous likes of beetroot borani dip with feta and walnuts, aubergine with molasses and pomegranate, or courgettes in romesco. Robust cocido (stew) or a fillet of sea bass with piquillo peppers and fennel salad fill their starring roles admirably. Finish with almondy Santiago tart, or vanilla ice cream lashed with treacle-dense Pedro Ximénez. Iberian wines, as well as sherries in all styles from Fernando de Castilla, form the backbone of a serviceable drinks list.
Chef/s: Ben Whyles and Norberto Peña Nuñez. **Closed:** Sun, 20 Dec to 3 Jan. **Meals:** tapas £3 to £9. **Details:** 65 seats. Bar. Music. No children under 12 yrs after 7pm.

Branca

Cooking score: 2
Modern European | £28
111 Walton Street, Oxford, OX2 6AJ
Tel no: 01865 556111
branca.co.uk
£5 OFF £30

With its sparkling new extension and deli, Jericho's versatile all-day eatery, which celebrates 20 years in 2020, has been declared 'even better than usual'. Customers remain a loyal bunch, drawn back time and again for the likes of 'fiery gazpacho and deep-flavoured grilled sea bream'. There's no going wrong with Moroccan-spiced lamb kebabs with winter slaw, harissa-spiced flatbread and houmous either, or the stone-baked pizzas, risottos and pasta dishes that are the mainstay of the please-all menu. And if the weather is fine and you are able to bag a table on the outside terrace, then the cooking can conjure up 'something like a Mediterranean feel in the wondrous sunshine'. Attentive, friendly and unhurried service, reasonable prices and a 30-bin wine list (from £20), with most offered by the glass, carafe or bottle, means this is 'still a top recommendation'.
Chef/s: Edwin Blandes. **Meals:** main courses £11 to £25. Set L and D £16. **Details:** 120 seats. 60 seats outside. Bar. Wheelchairs. Music.

Cherwell Boathouse

Cooking score: 2
Modern British | £30
50 Bardwell Road, Oxford, OX2 6ST
Tel no: 01865 552746
cherwellboathouse.co.uk
£5 OFF £30

Few restaurants in Oxfordshire can match the sheer seductive pulling power of this converted Victorian boathouse with its punts for hire, superlative wine list and covetable decked terrace overlooking the river Cherwell. But that's not all. Emphatic English and French accents invigorate the seasonal menu, which offers creative but understated ideas ranging from brown shrimp fritters brightened up with carrot and caraway purée or chicken and mushroom tarte tatin with cannellini beans to skrei cod with wilted greens and Cornish clam chowder. To finish, sticky toffee pudding is given an unexpectedly intricate uplift with milk sorbet, caramelised banana and caramel sauce – or you could nibble on some Oxford Blue cheese. Prices are fair for the locality, although set lunch and evening deals offer the best value. Gentle pricing and realistic markups also apply to the wines: start by cruising through the house selections on the 'shortlist' (from £19.75 a bottle, £5 a glass), before considering the vintage Mersaults from Domaine des Comtes Lafon, the fabulous German Rieslings and other vinous treasures.

Chef/s: Paul Bell. **Closed:** 25 to 30 Dec. **Meals:** main courses £18 to £22. Set L £15 (2 courses) to £19. Set D £24 (2 courses) to £30. Tasting menu £40 (6 courses). **Details:** 65 seats. 45 seats outside. Wheelchairs. Parking.

Gee's
Cooking score: 2
Mediterranean | £45
61a Banbury Road, Oxford, OX2 6PE
Tel no: 01865 553540
gees-restaurant.co.uk

The prospect of eating in a capacious late Victorian glasshouse is quite a lure – this former florist's shop is now a purveyor of zesty Mediterranean food in a verdant smart-rustic space festooned with greenery and olive trees. Blue metal lamps, dangling light bulbs, chequered floors and comfy leather banquettes set the scene, while the kitchen focuses its efforts on big-flavoured sunny dishes ranging from chilli-spiked seafood linguine with fennel or fillet of cod on chorizo risotto to wood-fired specialities or three-bone rack of lamb with roasted beetroot and cavolo nero. There are pizzetti, salt cod croquettes and tapas-style antipasti to start, while desserts might run from hazelnut and white chocolate semifreddo to crema catalana or even pear and apple crumble. Brunch is a good call locally and it's also worth sipping a

racy cocktail or two at the striking marble bar. Well-chosen wines from Italy and beyond start at £24.

Chef/s: Russell Heeley. **Meals:** main courses £16 to £30. Set L £15 (2 courses) to £18. **Details:** 72 seats. 36 seats outside. Bar. Wheelchairs. Music.

The Magdalen Arms
Cooking score: 3
Modern British | £35
243 Iffley Road, Oxford, OX4 1SJ
Tel no: 01865 243159
magdalenarms.co.uk

More town than gown, this local hostelry on one of Oxford's busiest thoroughfares feels stripped back and streetwise with its bare tables, auction-room furniture, moody colour schemes and rough-and-ready back terrace. There are real ales on the handpumps and the food measures up when it comes to delivering big-boned, no-nonsense hits such as provençale fish soup or slow-cooked lamb shoulder with gratin dauphinois (one of the pub's renowned sharing dishes). It's easy to spot other European influences too, from leafy cavolo nero served with Hereford beef wellington to the Tuscan-style wood pigeon ragù piled on tagliatelle or pan-fried skate wing with butter beans, rocket and gremolata. There's no shame in starting off with a 'sharpener' (perhaps pear and Prosecco fizz or homemade cherry lemonade), while desserts promise sunny comfort in the shape of panna cotta with rhubarb or vin santo with cantuccini. House vin de pays is £21.50, with options by the glass or carafe.

Chef/s: Tony Abarno. **Closed:** 24 to 26 Dec, 2 Jan. **Meals:** main courses £13 to £28. **Details:** 100 seats. 100 seats outside.

Oli's Thai

Cooking score: 3
Thai | £25
38 Magdalen Road, Oxford, OX4 1RB
Tel no: 01865 790223
olisthai.com
£30

Did we say 'book weeks in advance' last year? Make that 'months'. Or if you can't, haunt the door before noon, when about five of the unbooked are accommodated at the little bar counter. From there, you can see Ladd Thurston busying herself untiringly in the diminutive kitchen, producing dishes from the Malay Peninsula that leap forth with energetic hugs of happy flavour. Textbook bouncy-textured fishcakes with vividly colourful nam jim dipping sauce, and chickpea salad with onion threads in splashes of chilli dressing prime the palate for the bravura main dishes. The duck panang is famous for miles around, crisp and succulent in its red curry sauce with green beans and coconut milk, but there is also stunning deep-fried sea bream in ecstatically pungent nam pla with quills of screaming-hot chilli and spring onions. Soothe that afterburn with a puffed custard tart, or perhaps a huge meringue coated in cream and ladled with passion fruit. The succinct wine list means business, with glasses and carafes of such on-trend styles as minerally Picpoul, scented South African Gewürz and sinewy volcanic País from Chile, with glasses from £6.
Chef/s: Ladd Thurston. **Closed:** Mon, Sun, 2 weeks Christmas. **Meals:** main courses £13 to £29.
Details: 22 seats. 4 seats outside. Wheelchairs. Music. Children over 10 yrs.

The Oxford Kitchen

Cooking score: 5
Modern British | £45
215 Banbury Road, Oxford, OX2 7HQ
Tel no: 01865 511149
theoxfordkitchen.co.uk
£5 OFF

Six years in, and this relaxed modern restaurant has become a firmly established fixture on the Summertown dining scene, very much worth the journey from the city centre. Pavement seating and a pared-back atmosphere of unclothed tables and bare brick walls indicate the informality of the approach, but there is nothing laidback about a kitchen knocking out an exhaustive gamut of menus, from Market and Chef's tasters to lunchtime cartes that change as the working week eases into Saturday. Paul Welburn enjoys the alchemy conjured by bringing together surprising marriages of ingredients: scallop with passion fruit, pork and caviar; halibut in apple dashi with chicken and kohlrabi; baked celeriac in buttermilk with blood orange and radish. Other dishes work with the familiar grain, yet still manage to produce revelations. Gin-cured trout with cucumber, dill, lemon, tonic and a lick of treacle is an agreeable sock in the taste buds, while beef sirloin in black garlic crumb laced with blueberry ketchup delivers up its riches most beguilingly. The finisher might be a lime ice cream sandwich with chocolate shortbread and cherry sorbet. Wines are categorised by style, with helpful notes throughout, starting at £28 for a gently oaked Languedoc Carignan.
Chef/s: Paul Welburn. **Closed:** Mon, Sun, 1 to 16 Jan. **Meals:** main courses £33 to £39. Set L £23 (2 courses) to £29. Tasting menu £45 (4 courses) to £75. **Details:** 74 seats. 12 seats outside. V menu. Wheelchairs. Music.

Pompette

Cooking score: 3
Modern European | £42
7 South Parade, Oxford, OX2 7JL
Tel no: 01865 311166
pompetterestaurant.co.uk

£5
OFF

At the heart of Summertown, Pompette (the name is French argot for 'a little tiddly') offers bistro food of undiminished heritage appeal in an expansive brick-walled room, with lots of pictures to peruse. Friendly, on-the-ball staff are ready with recommendations, which might be for something as unabashedly Gallic as globe artichoke en vinaigrette, but could venture into neighbouring territory for sharing boards of salumi, or hake on saffron fennel with olives. Crab mayonnaise is a generous heap of lemoned-up white meat under a bundle of naked agretti, and might be followed on the fish trail by halibut with pink fir potatoes and spinach in beurre blanc. Then again, resist if you dare the gargantuan chop of old spot pork, baby-pink and yielding, served with a slew of chickpeas and cime di rapa in a surprisingly shy liquor that promises anchovy, garlic and chilli. At the end, a substantial wedge of almond frangipane arrives with chopped strawberries and crème fraîche, or there may be shivering crème caramel in its mahogany-hued syrup. A decent wine list opens at £4 a glass.
Chef/s: Pascal Wiedemann. **Closed:** Mon, 24 to 28 Dec. **Meals:** main courses £16 to £36. Set L and D £17 Mon to Fri (2 courses) to £20. **Details:** 59 seats. 16 seats outside. Bar. Wheelchairs. Parking.

Turl Street Kitchen

Modern British | £27
16-17 Turl Street, Oxford, OX1 3DH
Tel no: 01865 264171
turlstreetkitchen.co.uk

🛏 **£30**

Sitting at one end of three-colleged Turl Street, the Kitchen is the catering arm of the Oxford Hub social charity, which mobilises students to do voluntary community work. In a bubbly, informal atmosphere that suits the student ethos, a menu of sustainably sourced, eco-friendly food deals in the likes of lime-dressed trout with pickled veg, lamb kofta with harissa yoghurt and couscous scented with pomegranate, mint and coriander, and glazed figs in whipped ricotta with a trickle of vanilla syrup. Wines from £5.60 a glass, and the Oxford gins are worth a whirl. Or get there early for breakfast.

▌Shiplake

Orwells

Cooking score: 7
Modern British | £65
Shiplake Row, Shiplake, RG9 4DP
Tel no: 01189 403673
orwellsrestaurant.co.uk

🍸

For 'inventive, top-class modern cuisine', readers have come to rely on Ryan and Liam Simpson-Trotman's whitewashed restaurant near Henley. Although the couple take hospitality seriously, the food has a distinct sense of humour. It's seen early on the tasting menu in a 'cheeky and very light' take on the Cheddar ploughman's, and continues with dishes that are 'full of welcome surprises'. A la carte choices are no less nimble: try a starter of Cornish cod with kohlrabi, dulse and a 'lovely' bacon broth, or Bajan-spiced Orkney scallop with carrot from the restaurant's nearby smallholding. The links with the garden ensure that main courses are rich with seasonal

veg – perhaps Jersey Royals, purple sprouting broccoli, wild garlic and hen of the woods mushrooms with a barbecued cauliflower steak, or hispi cabbage and crapaudine beetroot with muntjac venison. Desserts, grounded in total mastery of technique, are more intricate than they first appear, as in lemon tart with rhubarb and caramelised white chocolate, or Mill Lane honey sponge with salted caramel, honeycomb and strawberries. The whole experience is 'totally rewarding', as is the wine list, put together with genuine care and a sense of European adventure at the pocket-friendly end.
Chef/s: Ryan Simpson-Trotman. **Closed:** Mon, Tue, first 2 weeks Jan, last 2 weeks Aug. **Meals:** main courses £26 to £38. Set L £30 (2 courses) to £35. Set D £35 (2 courses) to £40. Sun L £35 (2 courses) to £40. Tasting menu £65 (5 courses) to £90. **Details:** 35 seats. 30 seats outside. V menu. Bar. Wheelchairs. Parking.

with dark chocolate financiers with salted caramel sauce and banana sorbet. Lunch is very good value and service is 'friendly and accommodating'. Wines from £19.
Chef/s: Matt Williams. **Meals:** main courses £15 to £22. Set L £20 (2 courses) to £23. **Details:** 70 seats. 40 seats outside. Bar. Parking. Music.

▉ Sparsholt
The Star Inn
Cooking score: 2
Modern British | £32
Watery Lane, Sparsholt, OX12 9PL
Tel no: 01235 751873
thestarsparsholt.co.uk
£5 OFF

Bags of rustic personality – flagstoned floors, ancient beams, plain wooden tables and chairs, a winter fire and a summer garden – signal that The Star is a comfortable country inn with all the necessary attributes, although most visitors come for the food. The kitchen is bang on the money, the menu offering appealing ideas that take in everything from burgers and steaks to British heritage cooking with a global feel. Cured and seared salmon, for example, could be teamed with Asian fishcake, peanut and soy dressing and a lime crème fraîche, or Westcombe Cheddar and mustard croquettes served with Roscoff onions, pesto and hazelnuts. A main-course roast guinea fowl breast and glazed thigh might arrive with chantenay carrots, truffled cauliflower cheese and potato terrine. Finish

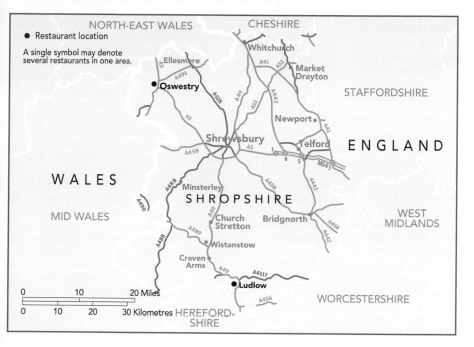

Restaurant location

A single symbol may denote several restaurants in one area.

Ludlow
Forelles at Fishmore Hall

Cooking score: 1
Modern British | £55
Fishmore Road, Ludlow, SY8 3DP
Tel no: 01584 875148
fishmorehall.co.uk

£5 OFF

Overlooking Ludlow and the Shropshire hills, this sympathetically restored Georgian mansion does duty as a boutique hotel with spa facilities in the garden, and a light-filled, white-walled conservatory dining room. Expect ultra-formal service and an ambitious contemporary menu based largely on produce gleaned from a 30-mile radius of the hotel – perhaps squab with broccoli, pumpkin, apple and blackberry. This is landlocked Shropshire, so fish comes from further afield (red mullet with mussel raviolo, kohlrabi, peas, saffron and tomato, for example), while desserts might see tarte tatin with elderflower, toffee doughnut, Calvados and vanilla ice cream. A modest international wine list starts at £25. **Chef/s:** Joe Gould. **Closed:** Sun, 2 to 13 Jan. **Meals:** set L £29 (2 courses) to £35. Set D £43 (2 courses) to £55. Tasting menu £79 (9 courses). Sun L £35. **Details:** 36 seats. V menu. Bar. Wheelchairs. Parking. Music.

Send us your review

Your feedback informs the content of the *GFG* and will be used to compile next year's entries. To register your opinion about any restaurant listed in the Guide, or a restaurant that you wish to bring to our attention, visit: thegoodfoodguide.co.uk/feedback.

Mortimers

Cooking score: 3
Modern British | £53
17 Corve Street, Ludlow, SY8 1DA
Tel no: 01584 872325
mortimersludlow.co.uk

In a town with an abundance of attractive, half-timbered medieval houses, this listed building with its fine original oak panelling ticks all the right aesthetic boxes. A hostelry in a former life, it's the place where Claude Bosi made his name with Hibiscus. Indeed, chef Wayne Smith and co-owner Andrew Brookes cut their hospitality teeth here and have returned to run the place under its current guise. With its thick carpet and neutral colours, the dining room makes a smart setting for the three-course set menu or the seven-course tasting menu. Smith's cooking balances classic haute cuisine with more contemporary ideas, as seen in an opener of rabbit paired with carrot, coriander and cep. Elsewhere, Hereford beef turns up with a more classical combination of baby leeks and roast shallots. Finish with a refreshing lemon parfait served with lemon curd and raspberry sorbet. The well-balanced wine list opens at £25.
Chef/s: Wayne Smith. **Closed:** Mon, Sun. **Meals:** set L £25 (2 courses) to £28. Set D £53. Tasting menu £65 (7 courses). **Details:** 30 seats. V menu. Parking. Music.

Old Downton Lodge

Cooking score: 2
Modern British | £50
Downton on the Rock, Ludlow, SY8 2HU
Tel no: 01568 771826
olddowntonlodge.com

£5 OFF 🚗

Readers don't hold back in their praise of the food at this extravagantly reconfigured medieval farmhouse, complete with cider mill and rambling outbuildings surrounded by courtyards, gardens and green acres deep in the Shropshire countryside. 'A visit here feels like an experience,' noted one happy guest. The stone-walled dining room looks like a cross between a feasting hall and a chapel, although Karl Martin's innovative food is of the moment, 'delicately but not too fussily presented on beautiful plates'. Tasting menus are the order of the day, with highlights ranging from a pairing of monkfish and octopus or rose veal with miso, celeriac, cabbage and truffle to a delectable dessert involving Welsh honey with yoghurt, chamomile and fennel. Service from a bevy of young staff in white gloves is 'attentive without being servile', while the wine list (from Tanners of Shrewsbury) has impressive global pickings on every page. Prices start at £30.
Chef/s: Karl Martin. **Closed:** Mon, Sun, 25 Dec, last 2 weeks Feb. **Meals:** set L £30 Thur to Sat (2 courses) to £40. Set D £40 (2 courses) to £50. Tasting menu £65 (6 courses) to £80. **Details:** 20 seats. 8 seats outside. Bar. Parking. Music.

LOCAL GEM

CSONS at The Green Café

Modern British | £25
Mill on the Green, Ludlow, SY8 1EG
Tel no: 01584 879872
thegreencafe.co.uk

£30 🍷

With equal capacity inside and out, this charming riverside favourite makes the most of its location and is now named after the four Crouch sons – geddit? – who run things. Small plates, 'proper lunches' and good bakes are kitchen mainstays; try Jerusalem artichoke with tahini and walnut salsa, pheasant curry or pork belly cassoulet, with puddings such as the family matriarch's 'lemon yum'. A similar menu runs on Friday and Saturday evenings, when it opens for supper, and there are themed events including celebrations of the art of the pie. Bottled beers and ciders join a dozen wines opening at £5.20 a glass.

The soft option

Teetotallers and designated drivers deserve better than sugary sodas and mass-market drinks when eating out. Happily, plenty of restaurants have come up with more creative ways to quench their customers' thirsts

At **Etch** in Brighton, you'll find a page of soft drinks of every stripe. Keep it local with Wobblegate juices and Regency tonic from Sussex.

The bartenders at **Charlotte's Bistro** in Chiswick make all their own purées, cordials and infusions. Seasonal delights might Include rhubarb iced tea or Kew punch made with homemade eucalyptus syrup.

There's a choice of two alcohol-free drinks flights available with Isaac McHale's multi-course tasting menus at **The Clove Club** in east London. Choose either juices or ambient teas including microlots of rooibos and pu'er from small estates.

Nationwide group **Hawksmoor's** ace bartenders do not overlook non-drinkers. Earl Grey iced tea, Steady Pete's Ginger Brew and the addictive cornflake milkshake are just some of the options.

Timberyard in Edinburgh keeps its foragers busy with a drinks list that includes sea buckthorn, pickled elderflower and rhubarb and pickled larch.

Oswestry
Sebastians
Cooking score: 2
French | £48
45 Willow Street, Oswestry, SY11 1AQ
Tel no: 01691 655444
sebastians-hotel.com

This wonky-walled, timber-beamed 17th-century building with wood-panelled walls and low ceilings has been home to Mark and Michelle Sebastian Fisher's restaurant with rooms for some 30 years. It's a firm local favourite, luring back loyal regulars with its faultless service and dependably good food – think classical French cooking with a twist and everything made from scratch, right down to the breads. A dainty tray of nibbles opens the monthly changing five-course set menu, which could go on to mackerel, mussels and asparagus in a lemon vinaigrette. Excellent local produce is a given, perhaps loin and shoulder of Welsh lamb, which could be served with Jersey Royals, mint sauce, date purée and a saffron jus. Finish perhaps with a red pepper sorbet enlivening a raspberry and goat's milk panna cotta (teamed with pistachio purée and a lovely brittle caramelised pistachio tuile). The wine list is mainly French.
Chef/s: Mark Sebastian Fisher. **Closed:** Mon, Tue, Sun, bank hols, 25 and 26 Dec, 1 Jan. **Meals:** set D £48 (5 courses). **Details:** 45 seats. 12 seats outside. V menu. Bar. Parking. Music. Children over 8 yrs.

Shrewsbury
READERS RECOMMEND
The Walrus
5 Roushill, Shrewsbury, SY1 1PQ
Tel no: 01743 240005
the-walrus.co.uk
'Eaten here three times. All uniformly good. The three-course dinner for £35 is excellent value. The poached breast of chicken with crispy leg, mushroom fricassée, roast garlic and lemon was simply the best I've eaten.'

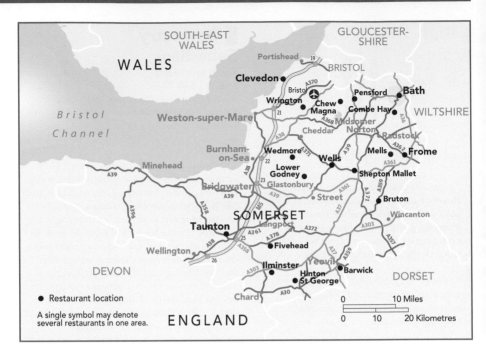

Restaurant location

A single symbol may denote several restaurants in one area.

ENGLAND

0   10 Miles

0   10   20 Kilometres

█ Barwick
Little Barwick House
Cooking score: 5
Modern British | £55
Rexes Hollow Lane, Barwick, BA22 9TD
Tel no: 01935 423902
littlebarwick.co.uk

🍷 ✴ 🛏

It's nigh on 20 years since Tim and Emma Ford became custodians of this handsome white Georgian dower house, which they run as a charming restaurant with rooms. Set in three acres, with garden views from the understated but elegant dining room, it's considered a special place that still attracts plenty of repeat custom — regulars returning for Tim's confident seasonal cooking of local meat and seafood from the nearby coast. Treatments are straightforward, ingredients allowed to speak for themselves rather than masked by foams and froths. Thus, grilled fillet of Cornish red mullet will be teamed with fennel and orange escabeche, a blue cheese soufflé turns up with a classic pear, walnut and watercress salad, and roasted rump of lamb is served with pea purée, rosemary sauce and aubergine caviar. Impressively crafted desserts include Breton shortbread with caramelised apple layer and Agen prune mousse. Grouped by style and opening at £25.95, the wine list includes plentiful half bottles and several options by the glass.
Chef/s: Tim Ford. **Closed:** Mon, Sun, first 3 weeks Jan. **Meals:** set L £29 (2 courses) to £32. Set D £50 Tue to Thu (2 courses) to £55 Tue to Sat. **Details:** 40 seats. 12 seats outside. Bar. Parking. Children over 5 yrs.

Anonymous
At *The Good Food Guide*, our inspectors dine anonymously and pay their bill in full. These impartial review meals, along with feedback from thousands of our readers, are what informs the content of the *GFG*. Only the best restaurants make the cut.

▌Bath

Acorn

Cooking score: 3
Vegan | £40
2 North Parade Passage, Bath, BA1 1NX
Tel no: 01225 446059
acornvegetariankitchen.co.uk
£5
OFF

At an address long associated with good vegetarian food, chef owner Richard Buckley has made a subtle shift: Acorn is now fully vegan. The panelled Georgian dining room, with its view of the abbey, could barely be more Bath, and dishes are just as labour intensive and complex as the literary feasts of the period. To start, for example, an 'old donkey carrot' is slow cooked, charred and served with parsley, seeded spelt and pickles, and beetroot might be presented with fine herbs and cultured cashew purée. The continuing pride of the main course section is a whole cauliflower cooked multiple ways and served with almond milk croqueta, spelt and a smoked almond emulsion. With dishes like these there is little possibility of boredom, but much of delight, and the inventiveness continues in puddings of, say, forced rhubarb with olive oil parfait, fennel carpaccio and Scots pine. The wine list is compiled to cope with these complex, vegetal flavours, but further guidance is always on hand.
Chef/s: Jamie Taylor and Richard Buckley.
Meals: set L £21 (2 courses) to £27. Set D £30 (2 courses) to £40. **Details:** 34 seats. Vg menu. Music.

The Bath Priory

Cooking score: 5
Modern French | £85
Weston Road, Bath, BA1 2XT
Tel no: 01225 331922
thebathpriory.co.uk
🛏

As peaceful a pile as one could hope to find anywhere, and a special treat after the tourist-raddled streets in the city centre, the four acres of lawns and gardens are an enduring part of this hotel's appeal, and tables looking over them much in demand. A setting like this demands at least a little formality, but the service team delivers it with a light hand. Chef Michael Nizzero populates his menus with clean, elegant treatments of premium ingredients, skewing mainly French. Expect Cornish crab with celery and lovage, or a little-seen pheasant egg with mushrooms and asparagus to start, followed by pigeon breast with cabbage and a modern touch of lime, or a more conservative fillet of beef with red wine and tarragon sauce. Dessert allows trad technique room to breathe; there's often a soufflé, perhaps blackcurrant with a matching sorbet. Wine starts at around £30, moving swiftly into reassuringly expensive territory.
Chef/s: Michael Nizzero. **Meals:** set L £30 (2 courses) to £55. Set D £85. Tasting menu £98 (7 courses). Sun L £34 (2 courses) to £39. **Details:** 50 seats. V menu. Vg menu. Wheelchairs. Parking. Music. Children over 12 yrs.

Chez Dominique

Cooking score: 2
French | £32
15 Argyle Street, Bath, BA2 4BQ
Tel no: 01225 463482
chezdominique.co.uk
£5
OFF

In a restored Georgian building hard by Pulteney Bridge, this 'worthy eatery' is well placed for passing trade. Inside, alcoves, bare floorboards and fireplaces blend happily with contemporary touches – an elegant but 'nicely informal' backdrop for food with a strong French accent underpinning its broader influences. To start, there might be wood pigeon with truffled potato purée and celeriac rémoulade or a salad of smoked eel with chicory and apple, while mains are mostly updated classics – sirloin steak with Café de Paris butter, rabbit leg with mustard sauce, sea bass fillet with fennel salad and saffron aïoli. Other dishes suggest a more broad-minded approach, as in charred ricotta with pickled pears and purple sprouting broccoli or a dessert of banana panna cotta with dulce de

leche – although cheeses are staunchly Gallic. Prix fixe menus are aimed at the city's theatre crowd, while French wines take pole position on the fairly priced 30-bin wine list.
Chef/s: Chris Tabbitt. **Closed:** 25 and 26 Dec. **Meals:** main courses £14 to £24. Set L and early D £15 (2 courses) to £18. Sun L £18. **Details:** 40 seats. 4 seats outside. Music.

The Circus
Cooking score: 2
Modern European | £30
34 Brock Street, Bath, BA1 2LN
Tel no: 01225 466020
thecircusrestaurant.co.uk
£30

'This place manages to feel really special without being overly formal,' said one enthusiastic visitor to the narrow, aubergine-fronted restaurant in the heart of Georgian Bath. A light-filled ambience of cream walls hung with small pictures brightens the interior, and the kitchen turns out an exuberant repertoire of well-wrought modern European dishes that have won it a band of firm local devotees. The warmest of welcomes helps things no end. Honey-glazed Creedy Carver duck breast ('succulent, tender and full of flavour') with five-spice and soy on a bed of soba noodles with stir-fried pak choi has its champions, and might be preceded by octopus Galician-style with chorizo, peppers, onions, sweet paprika, saffron and garlic. Main-course fish from the Newlyn dayboats or Start Bay are ringingly fresh. Warming desserts on the winter menu might take in cardamom and pistachio rice pudding with figs glazed in honey and garam masala. On the extensively annotated wine list, glasses start at £4.90.
Chef/s: Tom Bally and Ash Saman. **Closed:** Sun, 2 weeks Christmas. **Meals:** main courses £17 to £21. **Details:** 50 seats. 8 seats outside. V menu. Children over 7 yrs.

Corkage
Cooking score: 2
British | £25
132a Walcot Street, Bath, BA1 5BG
Tel no: 01225 422577
corkagebath.com
£30

The original manifestation of Corkage is an engaging tiny space with a wine shop counter and a kitchen at the back. Although wine is the driver, there is no printed list, and the food is chalked in single headwords on a board that does the rounds, the small dishes elaborated verbally. The little-plates-and-glasses ethos comes into its own here, with carefully worked cooking offering plenty for the wines to grapple with. Chopped prawns sautéed with bone marrow on sourdough toast, a south-east Asian salad of celeriac, radish and peanuts in a sharp Thai dressing, and a glorious take on cauliflower cheese, in which the cauli is baked under a gratinating rarebit layer, were all racing certainties for a pair of hungry lunchers. A lighter dessert option might be ginger panna cotta with popcorn-like almond brittle and anise-scented rhubarb. The wines are poured with garrulous aplomb and feature some inspired choices.
Chef/s: Tamas Albrecht. **Closed:** Mon, Sun, 24 to 26 Dec, 29 Dec to 8 Jan. **Meals:** small plates £7 to £14. Large plates £12 to £18. Set L and early D £15 (2 courses) to £19. **Details:** 42 seats. Bar. Wheelchairs. Music.

The Dower House
Cooking score: 4
Modern European | £70
Royal Crescent Hotel, 16 Royal Crescent, Bath, BA1 2LS
Tel no: 01225 823333
royalcrescent.co.uk

Overlooking the landscaped gardens of one of Bath's most prestigious addresses, this elegant hotel restaurant has genuine wow factor. In summer, you can dine outside on the terrace, or bag a linen-covered table inside next to the

French windows. Either way, the setting is as refined and luxurious as David Campbell's finely tuned classic cooking. Solid technical skill and flawless presentation are the cornerstones of the kitchen, with high-quality ingredients seen in a starter of BBQ and tartare of Cornish mackerel with baked potato, caviar, smoked roe cream and black garlic emulsion, and a main course of local organic Lacock pork loin and belly teamed with quinoa, apple sauce, roasted onion and pork skin crumb. After that, try honey-baked custard with poached pear, blackberry sorbet and candied walnut. The treasure trove of a wine list is true to its setting, opening at £30 and rising steeply with minimum effort.

Chef/s: David Campbell. **Meals:** set D £50 (2 courses) to £68. Tasting menu £78 (6 courses). **Details:** 42 seats. V menu. Vg menu. Bar. Wheelchairs. Parking. Music.

Henry's
Cooking score: 3
Modern British | £45
4 Saville Row, Bath, BA1 2QP
Tel no: 01225 780055
henrysrestaurantbath.com

'Definitely a place to go back to' was the verdict from one happy first-time visitor to this townhouse opposite the Assembly Rooms. Owner chef Henry Scott previously worked at nearby Bath Priory (see entry) and at the late Hibiscus in London with Claude Bosi and he was clearly paying attention. The no-frills dining room is as stripped back and minimalist as the menu – a trio of choices per course – although there is a four-course 'surprise' menu option. When it comes to influences, Henry takes a broad view – a starter of crispy squid with wasabi dressing, raw vegetable salad and basil cress may have an Asian bent but might lead on to a more classic partridge breast with black pudding, Puy lentils, polenta, roast salsify and herb purée. The sound level of skill continues through to a closing peanut and banana parfait with caramel sauce, fresh banana and peanut tuiles. Praiseworthy global wines from £22.50.

Chef/s: Henry Scott. **Closed:** Mon, Sun, 1 to 20 Jan. **Meals:** main courses £15 to £28. Tasting menu £50 (4 courses). **Details:** 60 seats. 15 seats outside. V menu. Music.

Menu Gordon Jones
Cooking score: 5
Modern British | £55
2 Wellsway, Bath, BA2 3AQ
Tel no: 01225 480871
menugordonjones.co.uk

The first rule of Menu Gordon Jones is that there is no menu at Menu Gordon Jones. Except in the mind of – you guessed it – Gordon Jones. Readers who enter wholeheartedly into the spirit of things – small dining room, surprise menu, eccentricities agogo – love it more often than not. Jones is a chef who, although he might like to surprise his guests, has no intention of disappointing them. Menus supplied after the event often feel less complex than the dishes in situ; either way, dinner is likely to start with bread and test tubes, perhaps with panzanella espuma, fennel sausage and Gentleman's Relish butter, and take in some top-notch British ingredients. Jones's Scottish upbringing might show itself in a dish of herring, cured and fried, with pickled raspberries and oats, and there are Indian notes, too, in a tea masala panna cotta with alphonso mango sorbet. Outside the wine flight it's tricky to match drinks, but a short, mostly European list is designed not to cause any major upsets.

Chef/s: Gordon Jones. **Closed:** Mon, Sun. **Meals:** tasting menu £55 (6 courses) to £60. **Details:** 22 seats. V menu. Vg menu. Children over 12 yrs.

The Olive Tree

Cooking score: 5
Modern British | £68
The Queensberry Hotel, 4-7 Russel Street, Bath, BA1 2QF
Tel no: 01225 447928
olivetreebath.co.uk

It may occupy the lower ground floor of a Georgian townhouse built for the Marquis of Queensberry, but there's nothing below par about the cooking at this smart hotel restaurant. The simple neutral look and feel of the pair of dining rooms still divides opinion: some find them 'nicely tucked away in a quiet place'; others think they present a 'rather plain' front. However, in the kitchen, Chris Cleghorn delivers some creative, big-impact dishes, from the delicacy of raw Orkney scallop, its sweetness countered by horseradish, pink grapefruit and dill, via the umami hit of tagliatelle with white truffle and 38-month aged Parmesan, to incredibly fresh stone bass with onion, artichoke, lardo and mushroom tea – the standouts from an autumn lunch. Others have praised the fallow deer served with BBQ cauliflower, golden raisins, sprout and bitter chocolate. On the downside, misfires are not unknown (an uninspired confection of blueberry, mascarpone, lemon balm and meringue, for example) and front of house service would benefit from tighter management. The intelligent, broadly based wine list starts with house selections from £28.

Chef/s: Chris Cleghorn. **Closed:** Mon, 1 week Nov, 1 week Jan, 1 week Apr, 1 week Aug. **Meals:** set L £26 Fri to Sun (2 courses) to £33. Tasting menu £68 (5 courses) to £85. **Details:** 50 seats. V menu. Vg menu. Bar. Music.

LOCAL GEM

Yak Yeti Yak

Nepalese | £25
12 Pierrepont Street, Bath, BA1 1LA
Tel no: 01225 442299
yakyetiyak.co.uk
£30

Cheaper than an air ticket to Kathmandu and less arduous than a gap-year trek, a meal in this cheery, multi-roomed basement brings genuine Nepalese home cooking in a setting of ethnic artefacts, prints and floor cushions. As a sampler, try the lamb tamar with bamboo shoots and black-eyed beans or marinated pork bhutuwa, but don't ignore the intriguing roster of vegetable-based dishes – aloo dum (potato and sesame salad) or bakula banda (stir-fried broad beans and white cabbage), for instance. Drink fresh limeade, saffron lassi, Khukuri beer or house wine.

Bruton

Roth Bar & Grill

Cooking score: 3
Modern British | £29
Durslade Farm, Dropping Lane, Bruton, BA10 0NL
Tel no: 01749 814700
rothbarandgrill.co.uk
£30

'A much anticipated return visit to this unique venue,' noted one couple, who found this magnificent 'art gallery/art installation/cocktail bar/café/restaurant' on a 1,000-acre working farm filled with returning customers 'like us'. Ingredients are given centre stage in dish after dish trumpeting freshness and flavour, perhaps in a plate of house charcuterie or Aberdeen Angus steaks dry-aged for 41 days in a glass-sided salt room that, given the location, 'you might be forgiven for mistaking for a Damien Hirst installation'. And there's a kaleidoscope of world ingredients in dishes such as 'lovely and spicy' homemade merguez sausage with white beans and harissa mayonnaise, lamb saddle with lentils, cavolo nero and aïoli, and Castlemead Farm chicken with chimichurri and Caesar salad. For a finale, lemon curd trifle won't disappoint. The short, global wine list, starting at £24, jostles for attention with regional artisan beers and inventive cocktails.

Chef/s: Steve Horrell. **Closed:** Mon, 25 and 26 Dec. **Meals:** main courses £12 to £30. **Details:** 80 seats. 80 seats outside. Bar. Wheelchairs. Parking. Music.

▌Chew Magna
The Pony & Trap

Cooking score: 4
Modern British | £45
Moorledge Road, Chew Magna, BS40 8TQ
Tel no: 01275 332627
theponyandtrap.co.uk

Don't take the name at face value. This rather plain-looking roadside hostelry has moved resolutely with the times and now does duty as a restaurant, complete with tasting menus and reservations strongly recommended. You can eat in the front bar but it's the simple dining room that capitalises on the ravishing view over the Chew Valley. Josh Eggleton's succinct seasonal menus come with a feel for proper flavour, his dishes revealing a commitment to local and regional suppliers, backed up by his own garden produce. Seafood is a leading suit, sweet, perfectly timed Cornish plaice served on the bone and piled with brown shrimp in a pool of light buttermilk sauce a sure-fire bet from the evening carte. There are also local meats such as Ston Easton lamb rack served with lovage, peas, sherry and anchovy. Finish lightly with an elderflower jelly with gooseberry purée, a cucumber and yoghurt ice cream and a green peppercorn tuile that perfectly evokes the flavours of early summer. Traditionalists are kept happy with classic ribeye with Café de Paris sauce and Sunday lunches, and to drink there are real ales and cocktails, with a well-annotated modern wine list bursting with organic and natural options.

Chef/s: Josh Eggleton. **Closed:** Mon, 25 and 26 Dec. **Meals:** main courses £14 to £29. Tasting menu £50 (6 courses) to £65. Sun L £35. **Details:** 65 seats. 20 seats outside. V menu. Bar. Parking. Music.

Local Gem

These entries are brilliant neighbourhood venues, delivering good, freshly cooked food at great value for money.

▌Clevedon

LOCAL GEM
Murrays
Italian | £25
91 Hill Road, Clevedon, BS21 7PN
Tel no: 01275 341222
murraysofclevedon.co.uk
£30

For three decades the Murray family has been delivering impeccably sourced Italian goods to locals in this genteel, unspoilt seaside town. In the unfussy and informal restaurant within a delicatessen, bakery and wine shop, the flexible menu rolls out through the day, with breakfast making way for sandwiches, pizzas and even a full à la carte at lunch, when a starter of cured Tuscan beef carpaccio with salted ricotta and pickled turnip could lead on to linguine with prawns in a tomato, lemon, saffron and chilli sauce. Decent regional Italian wines from £19.95.

▌Combe Hay
The Wheatsheaf

Cooking score: 3
Modern British | £36
Combe Hay, BA2 7EG
Tel no: 01225 833504
wheatsheafcombehay.com

You would be unlikely to stumble upon this secluded inn, even though it's just four miles from Bath; those in the know consider it well worth the journey along narrow lanes. Decked out in the vernacular style, with original features, heritage colours, cosy corners, log fires and a splendid suntrap terrace, it has the look of a country pub for our times. Similarly,

the culinary output includes traditional and contemporary flavours in feel-good combinations. Whether you are tucking into creamed wild mushrooms on charred focaccia with Old Winchester cheese or fillet of Dorset hake with Cornish crab risotto and asparagus, there's much to enjoy. There's a solid simplicity in wood-fired dishes such as pork and chorizo lasagne, and classily rendered classics include local sausages and creamy mash with red onion gravy and Butcombe beer-battered fish and chips. Pleasant, chatty staff lift the mood, children and dogs are made very welcome, and a love of Burgundy and Bordeaux dominates a European wine list pitched well above the pub norm.
Chef/s: Eddy Rains. **Closed:** Mon. **Meals:** main courses £15 to £28. Set L £24 (2 courses) to £30. Set D £20 (2 courses) to £26. Sun L £24 (2 courses) to £30. **Details:** 55 seats. 80 seats outside. V menu. Parking. Music.

Fivehead

The Langford
Cooking score: 4
Modern British | £45
Langford Fivehead, Lower Swell, Fivehead, TA3 6PH
Tel no: 01460 282020
langfordfivehead.co.uk

£5 OFF

As slices of English countryside go, this 15th-century golden stone manor in lovely grounds is nigh-on perfect. The rear courtyard looking on to the garden is a hidden gem when the weather is kind, and inside there are sitting rooms, a pair of dining rooms and real fires – the whole setting seems to mandate a sense of occasion. There's a sense of seasonality, too, in Olly Jackson's menus, which start from the kitchen garden and build upwards. The classy but accessible cooking delivers substance as well as style, and this year readers have praised a May meal that opened with New Cross farm asparagus teamed with slow-cooked egg, savoury granola and capers, went on to local lamb (roasted breast, croquette of shoulder, slow-cooked belly) partnered by carrot purée

and a garlic leaf pesto, and finished with dark chocolate délice with salted caramel ice cream and honeycomb. The French-focused wine list does the job, too.
Chef/s: Olly Jackson. **Closed:** Mon, Sun. **Meals:** set L £30 (2 courses) to £35. Set D £38 (2 courses) to £45. Tasting menu £60 (5 courses). **Details:** 24 seats. Wheelchairs. Parking. Music. Children over 8 yrs.

Frome
★ NEW ENTRY ★

Bistro Lotte
Cooking score: 1
French | £26
23 Catherine Street, Frome, BA11 1DB
Tel no: 01373 300646
bistrolottefrome.co.uk

£30

Relatively new to the town's cobbled streets, this dapper bistro with rooms has been warmly embraced by the community – so much so that an accompanying wine bar will open a few doors down in late 2019. Summer sees the windows thrown open to reveal all the welcoming bistro tropes – tiled floor, bentwood chairs and dried hops aplenty. Lunch brings croque monsieur or galettes, while dinner might start with a textbook French onion soup topped with a melting Gruyère croûton, or woodsy sautéed mushrooms with crispy polenta-coated artichoke hearts. A main course of gigot of lamb in a tarragon and red wine jus, and desserts of profiteroles or French apple tart, continue in the Gallic mode. Low-intervention wines are available by the carafe.
Chef/s: Jean-Pierre and Voy. **Meals:** main courses £14 to £22. **Details:** 130 seats. 4 seats outside.

The Garden Café

British | £15

16 Stony Street, Frome, BA11 1BU
Tel no: 01373 454178
gardencafefrome.co.uk

£30

The main draw of this daytime-only vegetarian café is – surprise, surprise – its verdant courtyard garden. Meals taken under the pergola might include a gooey courgette, halloumi and caramelised onion flan accompanied by a generous heap of the house salads – perhaps an apple and fennel slaw, or edamame with fresh herbs. Locals heap praise on the breakfasts, while staples such as a pie of the day and a Thai veggie burger feature on the main menu. A toasted cheese scone with a glass from the short list of organic wines is an indulgent afternoon treat. A dozen tables inside cater for the British weather.

Hinton St George
The Lord Poulett Arms

Cooking score: 2
British | £30

High Street, Hinton St George, TA17 8SE
Tel no: 01460 73149
lordpoulettarms.com

£5 OFF 🛏 £30

This stylish thatched 17th-century pub was taken over in the summer of 2018 by Charlie Luxton, Dan Brod and Matt Greenlees, better known as the team behind successful South West establishments The Beckford Arms and Talbot Inn (see entries). As well as undertaking a major refurbishment, they have added a courtyard terrace and created an exposed wine cellar in the inglenook fireplace. Keen to keep locals from this pretty village happy, they have also introduced bar snacks, a steak night and monthly 'pub suppers'. The menu covers all modern pub bases with sandwiches, cider-battered haddock and chips, and a decent burger, all of which sit happily alongside the likes of pan-seared sea

bream with houmous, roast romanesco, tomato and olive dressing or butter-roasted spring chicken, peas, chorizo and Jersey Royals. There is a notable English cheese platter, if the likes of warm skillet chocolate cookie and vanilla ice cream don't tempt you. As you'd expect, there's a commendable wine list starting at £20.

Chef/s: Phil Verden. **Meals:** main courses £15 to £20. **Details:** 50 seats. 50 seats outside. Bar. Wheelchairs. Music.

Ilminster

★ NEW ENTRY ★

Todays Menu

Cooking score: 2
Modern British | £35

1 North Street, Ilminster, TA19 0DG
Tel no: 01460 54054
todaysmenu.co.uk

£5 OFF

Alex Nutt last appeared in the Guide in 2017, at the Exmoor Beastro. He's now settled into this casual market town gaff, the welcome as friendly for passing tourists as it is for the many loyal locals. The please-all menu is perfect for the surrounds – a line-up taking in lunchtime sandwiches (fillet steak, say, with salad leaves and homemade tarragon mayonnaise) and small plates, with fancier ideas at dinner. Zealous local sourcing is key to the kitchen's efforts, as seen in dishes that positively bloom with freshness, perhaps a simple assembly of New Cross Farm asparagus and Fenton Farm fried egg topped with hazelnuts. Dinner might begin with smoked duck teamed with spring onions, lentils and house chilli sauce, ahead of mains of Asturian morcilla and Ibérico pork, served with sautéed potatoes, olives, almonds and Littlemore salad leaves, or spaghetti with herb pesto and almonds. A faultless tiramisu makes a fitting finale. Lovers of organic and boutique producers are in for a treat from a confidently chosen all-Italian wine list that, like the food, is kindly priced.

Chef/s: Alexander Nutt and Patrizia Ferrara. **Closed:** Mon, Tue, Sun, 10 days Dec to Jan. **Meals:** main courses £11 to £17. Set L £12 (2 courses) to £24. Set D £22 (2 courses) to £33. **Details:** 40 seats. Bar. Music.

Set menus

If a set lunch (L) or dinner (D) is offered, this is indicated under 'Meals'. Prices are for a standard three-course meal unless otherwise specified.

█ Lower Godney
The Sheppey

Cooking score: 2
Modern British | £28
Lower Godney, BA5 1RZ
Tel no: 01458 831594
thesheppey.co.uk

The low horizons and whispering fields of the Somerset Levels have their own special magic, and sitting out on the deck of this roadside inn overlooking the river, with a starling murmuration overhead, is one of the very best places to experience it. Inside, it's a proper pub with an arty, rustic edge – twinkling lights, dark, cosy corners, reclaimed retro furniture, modern artwork. The kitchen cooks everything from scratch – no mean feat with menus this long – and the food has an international flavour. Mussels with harissa, lemon, coriander and crusty bread, or lamb rump with chorizo, cannellini beans and tomato appear alongside appealing vegetarian and vegan options: perhaps fennel and kohlrabi soup with toasted almonds, or Puy lentil burger with baba ganoush, Wedmore cheese, pickled cucumber and lemon mayonnaise. Round off with apple cake anointed with salted caramel sauce and clotted cream. On the drinks front, there's an excellent selection of draught beers and ciders, and a clutch of organic and biodynamic wines.
Chef/s: Keiron Ash. **Meals:** main courses £11 to £23. Sun L £23 (2 courses). **Details:** 100 seats. 60 seats outside. Bar. Music.

█ Mells
Talbot Inn

Cooking score: 3
Modern British | £32
Selwood Street, Mells, BA11 3PN
Tel no: 01373 812254
talbotinn.com

This easy-going former coaching inn set in a collection of honey-stone buildings is a real charmer. Inside it's all exposed beams, uneven walls and quarry-tiled floors, the rambling sequence of rooms decked out in a modern-rustic style. There's been a change of chef since the last edition of the Guide, but the food is still a winning mix of updated pub classics (crispy chicken, guacamole and bacon bap with chips; ploughman's with Westcombe Cheddar) and more inventive dishes built around prime local ingredients. Charred pigeon breast with celeriac, crispy kale, roasted baby onions and red wine jus is a winning combination, and there's praise for cider-cured sea trout with sea vegetables, crab sauce, fregola and crispy seaweed. Desserts focus on the traditional – apple and cinnamon crumble, rice pudding with berry compôte and almonds, and sticky toffee pudding with butterscotch sauce. It's a laid-back place, but there's no corner cutting, and the attention to detail extends to an interesting wine list weighted towards the Old World, with much by the glass or carafe.
Chef/s: Dave Waine. **Closed:** 25 Dec. **Meals:** main courses £14 to £24. **Details:** 45 seats. 40 seats outside. Bar. Parking. Music.

Pensford

LOCAL GEM
The Pig
Modern British | £40
Hunstrete House, Pensford, BS39 4NS
Tel no: 01761 490490
thepighotel.com

The litter of Pig boutique country hotels is spreading quickly around the UK, each with a restaurant inspired by its location and the produce grown in the kitchen garden. The potting-shed-style dining room in this Georgian pile near Bath follows the same 'field to fork' mantra, with a roll call of local suppliers on the menu. Langley Chase lamb belly with rhubarb and tinkerbell chilli might be followed by broad bean and pea risotto, Westcombe ricotta, lemon and parsley crumb. There are plenty of gems on the wine list that opens at £22.

Shepton Mallet

LOCAL GEM
Blostin's
Anglo-French | £28
29 Waterloo Road, Shepton Mallet, BA4 5HH
Tel no: 01749 343648
blostins.co.uk

The inhabitants of Shepton Mallet have been supporting Blostin's since its inception in 1985 – and, in return, owners Nick and Lynne Reed have provided them with an inviting home-from-home noted for its cosiness and bonhomie. Nick's excellent-value fixed-price menus are based on sound principles: a solid foundation of classical cooking skills, clear attention to seasonality and reliable sourcing; typically French onion soup, chicken breast with mushrooms and tarragon sauce, iced ginger meringue parfait. Individually priced seasonal specials keep things interesting, and the modest wine list is wallet-friendly.

Taunton

Augustus
Cooking score: 3
Modern British | £30
3 The Courtyard, St James Street, Taunton, TA1 1JR
Tel no: 01823 324354
augustustaunton.co.uk

Hiding in a small courtyard not far from Taunton's landmark Castle Hotel, this laid-back restaurant continues to attract locals and visitors with its straightforward, rustic French cooking. High-quality, seasonal raw materials are very much to the fore in the finely tuned bistro classics. From the carte, seared Brixham scallops are embellished with crisp pancetta, a creamy cauliflower purée and beurre noisette. A full-flavoured braised shoulder of lamb with gratin potatoes, greens, apple and mint jelly is equally accomplished, but if fish is your thing, there's turbot with potato galette, purple sprouting broccoli and mussel butter sauce. Comforting desserts like steamed marmalade pudding with Grand Marnier custard close the show, unless you are tempted to explore the cheeses, displayed on a perambulating butcher's block. A functional, fairly priced wine list opens at £18 and offers plenty of fine options by the glass and carafe.
Chef/s: Richard Guest. **Closed:** Mon, Sun, 24 Dec to 2 Jan. **Meals:** main courses £14 to £26. **Details:** 40 seats.

Brazz
Cooking score: 1
British | £30
Castle Bow, Taunton, TA1 1NF
Tel no: 01823 252000
brazz.co.uk

Next door's Castle Bow (see entry) may be the jewel in the crown of The Castle Hotel but this modern all-day brasserie shows that the Chapman family, after seven decades at the helm, still knows a thing or two about classy

informality. Brazz shares the same kitchen as its more formal stablemate, so expect seasonality and provenance to shine out on the menu, whether it's lunchtime sandwiches, steaks, fish and chips or confidently executed dishes such as fishcake with slow-cooked leeks, white wine cream and chive sauce or confit duck leg with crushed carrots, sugar snap peas, rhubarb compôte and red wine gravy. Wines from £19.
Chef/s: Liam Finnegan. **Closed:** 25 Dec. **Meals:** main courses £13 to £16. Set L and early D £12 (2 courses). **Details:** 60 seats. 8 seats outside. Bar. Wheelchairs. Parking. Music.

Castle Bow
Cooking score: 6
Modern British | £45
Castle Green, Taunton, TA1 1NF
Tel no: 01823 328328
castlebow.com

Run by the Chapman family since 1950, the hotel's kitchens have launched the careers of notable chefs including Gary Rhodes and Phil Vickery. It is considered quite an institution, luxuriating in 1,000 years of history and with an Art Deco-inspired dining room providing a calm and elegant setting for Liam Finnegan, the latest chef to make a name for himself at the stoves. Finnegan's imaginative and modern British cooking is underpinned by classic technique, and he keeps a keen eye on the region's seasonal produce. A typical meal could open with cured Stream Farm organic trout teamed with fennel, cucumber, horseradish and Exmoor caviar, while Exmoor venison arrives partnered with red cabbage, Jerusalem artichoke and kale, or Lyme Bay cod with broccoli, hazelnuts, lemon and grilled octopus. There's a suberb selection of British cheeses, but there's also baked egg custard tart with forced rhubarb and nutmeg ice cream, one of the chef's signature desserts. The well-considered wine list opens at £23.

Chef/s: Liam Finnegan. **Closed:** Mon, Tue, Sun, 25 Dec, Jan. **Meals:** main courses £19 to £25. Tasting menu £64 (7 courses). **Details:** 32 seats. V menu. Bar. Parking. Music. Children over 5 yrs.

▌Wedmore
The Swan
Cooking score: 3
Modern British | £28
Cheddar Road, Wedmore, BS28 4EQ
Tel no: 01934 710337
theswanwedmore.com

This beautifully styled white Georgian coaching inn is serious about food, but still functions as a proper village pub. You can dine in the bar, where pale heritage colours, big mirrors and vintage furniture create a striking backdrop, or in the restaurant – a light, modern room with views on to the pretty terrace. Tom Blake hails from the River Cottage and his cooking reflects his time there: unpretentious, local and fresh, in a style that straddles tradition and invention. Smoked ham hock terrine with apple and gherkin salsa points the way, while mains run from gently spiced flat iron tikka chicken with raita and potato bhajia to a Med-influenced dish of Cornish mackerel stuffed with crab, capers and lemon and served with potatoes, squash, harissa and mussels. Puds – perhaps salted caramel and chocolate tart with cherry sorbet – vie for attention with local cheeses. The wine list pits classics against lesser-known finds, with a focus on mid-priced options.
Chef/s: Tom Blake. **Meals:** main courses £14 to £24. **Details:** 80 seats. 80 seats outside. Bar. Wheelchairs. Parking. Music.

Wells
Goodfellows

Cooking score: 3
Modern European | £36
5 Sadler Street, Wells, BA5 2RR
Tel no: 01749 673866
goodfellowswells.co.uk
£5 OFF

Not far from the cathedral you'll find this smart venue, one that neatly balances relaxation with a sense of occasion. There are two dining rooms, one sporting dramatic shades of slate blue and aubergine, the other dominated by an open kitchen. Either way, expect smooth service and a sense that you are far removed from the street outside. Adam Fellows' cooking is broadly European, as seen in a starter of warm goat's cheese and grilled aubergine with tomato and chilli sauce, and a main of rump of lamb with sautéed Mediterranean vegetables, spicy chorizo and a punchy lick of rouille. Seafood is a particular strength, perhaps pairing brandade of cod with focaccia and tapenade, or fillet of sea bass with squid ink linguine, saffron and shellfish sauce. An apricot, cherry and walnut frangipane tart keeps things on theme, while the wine list balances classics with interesting finds, although its heart is in France.
Chef/s: Adam Fellows. **Closed:** bank hols.
Meals: main courses £15 to £25. Set L £24 (2 courses) to £28. Tasting menu £50 (5 courses).
Details: 50 seats. 15 seats outside. Music.

Wrington
The Ethicurean

Cooking score: 4
Modern British | £45
Barley Wood Walled Garden, Long Lane, Wrington, BS40 5SA
Tel no: 01934 863713
theethicurean.com

Over the years, Iain and Matthew Pennington have banged the drum for ethical and garden-grown ingredients to an increasingly appreciative audience. This is where local means local and seasons are prolonged through pickling, fermenting, curing and bottling. You approach the restaurant (an extended Victorian glasshouse) through the walled garden and orchards that supply the kitchen. Diversion from the basic dining room comes from the spectacular views over the Mendip Valley, but your gaze is soon drawn to the creative cooking, much of it centred on an open charcoal grill. A late springtime visit sees rustic dishes piling on diverse flavours with brio, from small plates of oh-so-simple baked onion with beetroot and apple molasses and mace crumb to a main course of buttermilk chicken thighs served atop a carrot and star anise purée. Cast-iron cookie with an intense orange marmalade and salted caramel ice cream made a filling, indulgent finish. This is home-grown gastronomy with devotion, delivering excellent own-baked bread, enthusiastic service, experimental cocktails and a wine list that focuses on natural, low-intervention bottles at refreshing prices.
Chef/s: Iain and Matthew Pennington and Simon Miller. **Closed:** Mon, 2 weeks Jan. **Meals:** small plates £4. Large plates £7 to £14. Tasting menu £50 (7 courses). **Details:** 60 seats. 60 seats outside. V menu. Bar. Wheelchairs. Music.

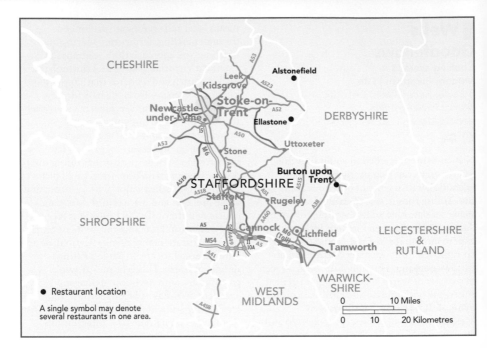

▌Alstonefield
The George
Cooking score: 3
Modern British | £38
Church Lane, Alstonefield, DE6 2FX
Tel no: 01335 310205
thegeorgeatalstonefield.com

'The atmosphere is welcoming, the decor meticulous, service exemplary and the food truly wonderful' – just one glowing verdict on this Peak District favourite 'twixt Ashbourne and Bakewell. Beams and rustic furniture may make you think of pies and pints, but the kitchen has higher ambitions: 'venison done three ways' or a much-praised dish of Derbyshire beef fillet and braised oxtail with truffled pomme purée and bone marrow crumb. Other recent hits have ranged from a pairing of king scallop, sweet potato, chicken wing, chicory and aubergine to locally reared lamb rump accompanied by sweetbreads, potato terrine, heritage beetroot and pickled blackberries. The excellent home-baked breads and cultured butter come with a hefty price tag and desserts, such as dark chocolate délice with white chocolate crémeux, fleur de sel and pine ice cream show serious intent. A dozen picks by the glass or carafe top the well-spread wine list.
Chef/s: Kelvin Guest. **Closed:** 25 Dec , Mon and Tue (Jan to Mar). **Meals:** main courses £17 to £24. Tasting menu £65 (6 courses) to £85. **Details:** 42 seats. 30 seats outside. Bar. Children over 12 yrs.

▌Burton upon Trent
99 Station Street
Cooking score: 1
Modern British | £30
99 Station Street, Burton upon Trent, DE14 1BT
Tel no: 01283 516859
99stationstreet.com

£5 OFF £30

Now into its second decade as a sterling local asset, this understated family-run venue has stuck to its guns, serving affordably priced food based on shrewdly sourced ingredients, with just enough pizzazz to keep everyone interested. Menus chime with the seasons where possible, so expect anything from sautéed mushrooms and baby onions with wild herbs on grilled chive polenta to parsley-crusted Packington pork with pea and mint purée, tempura cauliflower and asparagus tips. Well-aged steaks are tossed on to the grill, while desserts might feature homely treats such as warm rhubarb and crystallised ginger sponge cake with creamy custard. Wines from £15.45.

Chef/s: Daniel Pilkington. **Closed:** Mon, Tue.
Meals: main courses £15 to £24. Set L £15 (2 courses) to £17. Sun L £17 (2 courses) to £19.
Details: 40 seats. Bar. Wheelchairs. Music.

▌Ellastone

LOCAL GEM

The Duncombe Arms
British | £36
Main Road, Ellastone, DE6 2GZ
Tel no: 01335 324275
duncombearms.co.uk
£5 OFF 🛏

Roaring fires, studded leather and the odd beam make this pub with rooms an infinitely appealing prospect to the south of the Peak District. Readers commend food that helps it 'really stand out' in its detail and execution, perhaps watercress soup with pickled shallot and Granny Smith to start, followed by Derbyshire lamb rump with spiced belly, smoked yoghurt and dukkah. Add interesting wines (including large formats at Christmas) and the house ale for a formula that is 'justfiably popular'.

Going solo

Sharing is all the rage, from Sunday roasts served family-style to desserts we split because we're too full to order our own. But eating alone is increasingly common, whether through choice or necessity. Here are some tips from people who do it a lot

Go at lunchtime – it can feel less of an obviously social occasion.

Take something to read, write, or your phone to play Scrabble on or scroll through Instagram. Thoughtful staff (like the ones at the **Salutation Inn**, Topsham) might even bring you magazines.

Sit at the counter if there is one – there's kitchen action to watch and it's easier to strike up conversation if you wish. Try London's **Barrafina** tapas restaurants, take a high seat at **64 Degrees**, Brighton, or the central bar at **The Seafood Restaurant**, Padstow.

Busy pubs or brasseries may make it easier to blend in, but don't rule out fine dining places. Hats off to **Gauthier Soho**, where one solo diner found 'just the right level of chat from the sommelier to make you feel you're interacting with people'.

Don't assume that everyone's watching you – most likely, they're busy with their own meal or conversation.

Enjoy the experience! People-watch, reflect on life, read (or write?) that novel – without having to share even one crumb.

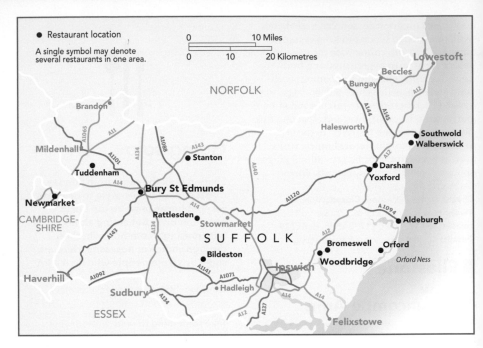

▊Aldeburgh

LOCAL GEM

The Aldeburgh Market

Seafood | £21

170-172 High Street, Aldeburgh, IP15 5AQ
Tel no: 01728 452520
thealdeburghmarket.co.uk

£5 £30
OFF

Locals are full of praise for the 'skilled fishmonger' at this 'brilliantly put together' deli, but its tiny café restaurant is considered a treat too, pulling in punters from further afield. Pavement tables under the scarlet awning are the first to go on a sunny day. Potted shrimps, fish soup or smoked haddock chowder, a simple fish pie or beer-battered fish and chips are the dishes to order, and there's vanilla crème brûlée or fruit crumble to finish. Wine from £15.95.

▊Bildeston

The Bildeston Crown

Cooking score: 5
Modern British | £35

104 High Street, Bildeston, IP7 7EB
Tel no: 01449 740510
thebildestoncrown.com

£5
OFF

Some chefs — thankfully — stick to their kitchen guns. Undistracted by the notion of small plates, outré ingredients or pared-back presentation, Chris Lee remains unwaveringly focused on what he does best: robustly classic cooking using the finest produce to create beautiful, generous dishes. Come hungry and start in the bar with substantial 'retro nibbles' such as truffle Welsh rarebit, or deep-fried Camembert with Cumberland sauce, before a starter of lobster Caesar salad or ragù of Suffolk rabbit with orecchiette pasta and pecorino. Mains pack punch after flavoursome punch, too, particularly when it comes to meat and game — locally shot venison, tender as you like, might come with parsnip, cavolo nero and hazelnuts. Push the boat out with whole lobster, or hail the king of fish with a fillet of turbot, snails, spring vegetables and herb sauce. A 'stunningly gorgeous' maple crémeux with stout, pear and chocolate was, for one enraptured guest, 'a whole different level of dessert', while others heap praise on a tropical passion fruit and mango baked Alaska with piña colada sauce. The well-annotated wine list kicks off below £18.

Chef/s: Chris Lee. **Meals:** main courses £18 to £25. Set L £16 (2 courses) to £22. Tasting menu £80 (7 courses). Sun L £16. **Details:** 80 seats. 20 seats outside. Bar. Wheelchairs. Parking. Music.

◼ Bromeswell
The Unruly Pig
Cooking score: 4
Modern European | £33
Orford Road, Bromeswell, IP12 2PU
Tel no: 01394 460310
theunrulypig.co.uk
£5
OFF

'We didn't want the experience to end,' sighed one visitor, reluctant to leave the unforced hospitality and accomplished, broadly Anglo-Italian cooking at this contemporary-meets-traditional pub restaurant. By all means come for burgers (in brioche buns with Roquefort and onion jam), steak (40-day aged ribeye with sweet-salty bone marrow) or a special Saturday brunch, but look out, too, for flavour-packed rabbit terrine, or braised Umbrian lentils with poached egg and cime di rapa from the separate vegetarian menu (there are also vegan and free-from menus), or perfectly pink lamb rack with stuffed saddle, a little shepherd's pie and blanched wild garlic. An exemplary custard tart whose smooth creaminess is offset by segments of blood orange and nubs of pistachio, or a 'stunning' amaretto panna cotta with port-drenched cherries, make fitting finales. The wine list is packed with interest from £17.50, while the 'wine of the week' encourages exploration beyond the obvious.

Chef/s: Dave Wall. **Meals:** main courses £12 to £25. Set L and D £16 (2 courses) to £20. **Details:** 90 seats. 40 seats outside. V menu. Vg menu. Bar. Wheelchairs. Parking. Music.

◼ Bury St Edmunds
1921 Angel Hill
Cooking score: 4
Modern British | £41
19-21 Angel Hill, Bury St Edmunds, IP33 1UZ
Tel no: 01284 704870
nineteen-twentyone.co.uk

This classy restaurant just off historic Angel Hill is just as good as ever. One diner's effusive report of 'a 168-mile round trip without fault' is echoed in spirit by others, such is the ability and creativity poured into the food and service by chef patron Zack Deakins. An artistic line-up of canapés sets the tone: a puck of cured cod, avocado and wasabi is a sparky mouthful, a cheese gougère as puffily light as it should be. Look out for a 'sensational' rabbit and trompette mushroom terrine, the slender slice en croûte lined up next to caramelised fig, pomegranate and a few flighty leaves. Follow with a 'stunningly beautiful' Anjou pigeon – claw and all – with flavours of sweetcorn and salt and vinegar potatoes, or stone bass whose gentle sweetness is deftly balanced by confit chicken, carrots, cockles and tarragon. Dishes remain elaborate, multi-layered creations to the end, a dessert of lemon curd parfait with delicate Earl Grey tea sorbet, crème fraîche and mint granita finding particularly enthusiastic fans. Exceptional front of house staff will advise knowledgeably on wine pairings from a list that opens at £20.50.

Chef/s: Zack Deakins. **Closed:** Mon, Sun, 24 Dec to 5 Jan. **Meals:** main courses £17 to £27. Set L £18 (2 courses) to £21. Tasting menu £75 (7 courses). **Details:** 50 seats. Bar. Wheelchairs. Music.

Drinking vinegars make a comeback

We are drinking less. A clear-headed 20% of the UK's adult population now actively chooses not to drink alcohol, says the Office for National Statistics, and restaurants and bars have responded accordingly. With guests expecting more than a lime and soda, enter shrubs, or drinking vinegars.

Or should that be re-enter? There's nothing new about this sweet-sour combination of ripe fruit and vinegar with its refreshing acidity and depth of flavour. Their history stretches back to the Babylonians who added date vinegar to water to make it safe to drink; the word comes from the Arabic 'sharab' meaning 'drink'. Later popularised by the Romans, Ottoman sultans, Victorians and America's temperance movement, today you'll find them on the best alcohol-free lists.

At **The Hand & Flowers**, Buckinghamshire, the Oopsy Daisy is made with Seedlip Garden 108, homemade raspberry shrub and lemonade. A blackcurrant and juniper Nonsuch shrub is served at **The Unruly Pig**, Suffolk. In Notting Hill, **The Ledbury** mixes Mother Root Ginger Switchel (a sweetened vinegar-based drink) with sparkling water and at **Rovi** in Fitzrovia, sip a plum and sorrel drinking vinegar.

Maison Bleue

Cooking score: 5
Modern French | £55
30-31 Churchgate Street, Bury St Edmunds, IP33 1RG
Tel no: 01284 760623
maisonbleue.co.uk

In this graceful town-centre restaurant service glides with an ease that is at once liquid-smooth and perfectly precise. As it does, it creates an elegant backdrop for Pascal Canevet's modern interpretation of classic French cuisine to offer, as one visitor put it, a 'really lovely dining experience'. There's seasonal vitality – and a lot of beauty – in an early summer meal of local asparagus with Café de Paris butter, perhaps followed by a pristine piece of Gigha halibut with plump clams, fresh peas and a shellfish sauce; ditto in winter, when a saddle of venison, cooked pink and perfect, is absolutely of the moment alongside savoy cabbage, a blackcurrant sauce and nutty crosnes. Cheese lovers will be seduced by the aromatic trolley, laden with some 30 cheeses at peak ripeness, but don't miss out on the prettiest desserts that could, time of year depending, celebrate Yorkshire rhubarb – poached, sorbet and mousse – or English strawberries, served with white chocolate and a dreamily light basil sponge biscuit. The wine list guides you through some of France's top vineyards, picking bottles for a list that opens at £17.95.
Chef/s: Pascal Canevet. **Closed:** Mon, Sun, first 2 weeks Sept, 23 Dec to 16 Jan. **Meals:** main courses £23 to £29. Set L £20 (2 courses) to £27. Set D £37. **Details:** 55 seats. Wheelchairs. Music.

Pea Porridge

Cooking score: 4
Modern British | £45
28-29 Cannon Street, Bury St Edmunds,
IP33 1JR
Tel no: 01284 700200
peaporridge.co.uk

In a restaurant world awash with menus for which 'please-all' and 'safe' are apt descriptors, comes – thank goodness – Pea Porridge. Bluff Scot Justin Sharp likes cooking the bits that make other chefs anxious, and regulars love him for that, so choose 'amazing as always' curried sweetbreads or duck hearts, snails sautéed with bacon and served with bone marrow, or confit lamb's tongue 'tonnato'. Less challenging but no less flavour-packed is a spring plate of courgettes with super-fresh raw milk curd from Suffolk's White Wood Dairy, generous glugs of olive oil, herbs and lemon and a crunchy scatter of roasted hazelnuts. Follow with an outstanding Barnsley lamb chop with chorizo, confit wet garlic, aubergine caponata and salsa verde, or share a whole fish baked with clams, samphire, tomatoes and onions. The 'out of this world' Italian-leaning wine list (from £20.95) suits the food with its line-up of natural, skin-contact, organic and biodynamic gems among more conventional styles. Bread lovers will be in focaccia heaven, and Justin's wife, Jurga, deserves recognition for being 'the epitome of front of house'.

Chef/s: Justin Sharp. **Closed:** Mon, Sun, 2 weeks Sept, 2 weeks Dec to Jan. **Meals:** main courses £15 to £20. Set L and D £15 Tue to Thur (2 courses) to £20. **Details:** 46 seats. Wheelchairs. Music. No children at D

LOCAL GEM

Ben's

Modern British | £30
43-45 Churchgate Street, Bury St Edmunds,
IP33 1RG
Tel no: 01284 762119
bensrestaurant.co.uk
£30

From Norfolk black pudding to Suffolk honey and Baron Bigod cheese (made in Bungay), East Anglian produce is at the heart of Ben Hutton's amiable local restaurant – although the jokey livestock motifs dotted around the cheerily decorated dining room are a reminder that Ben also rears his own Oxford sandy pigs and Jacob sheep. Dishes ranging from keema lamb Scotch eggs to wild rabbit tagliatelle with asparagus, or pulled pork, leek and bacon pie show the kitchen's versatility, while the drinks list celebrates the region's local heroes. Wines from £18.

■ Darsham

Darsham Nurseries

Cooking score: 3
Modern British | £25
Main Road, Darsham, IP17 3PW
Tel no: 01728 667022
darshamnurseries.co.uk
£30

It's a case of from potager to fork at this rustic nursery café, where tables spill on to a terrace beside raised beds. Open for lunches and brunches, there's also dinner on Fridays and Saturdays, the former a fixed-price affair. Vegetables lead the charge on a menu that flirts with global flavours, and what isn't home-grown is sourced with due diligence. The small plate format suits grazing and sharing, and choosing what *not* to have is a challenge. Sautéed potatoes with gremolata and confit garlic aïoli make an addictive trio, or what about grilled leeks with romesco, Graceburn cheese and mint? Roast cauliflower with vadouvan butter, herb yoghurt and pistachio dukkah is right on the contemporary nose, while tempting meat and fish options run to lamb chops with salsa verde, and cod with brown shrimps and sea vegetables. High House Farm rhubarb and custard tart is one of a clutch of appealing desserts. Local Adnams beers, cool cocktails and a concise wine list make for good drinking.

Chef/s: Nicola Hordern. **Closed:** 25 and 26 Dec. **Meals:** small plates £5 to £15. **Details:** 40 seats. 30 seats outside. Wheelchairs. Parking. Music.

Dunwich

READERS RECOMMEND

The Ship at Dunwich

St James Street, Dunwich, IP17 3DT
Tel no: 01728 648219
shipatdunwich.co.uk

'Love, love, love this place because it's everything a pub should be – really friendly and cosy with homely food done well. My fish pie the other week was incredible, my boyfriend had the burger, and the chips are the best I've had in ages.'

Haughley

READERS RECOMMEND

The Kings Arms

3 Old Street, Haughley, IP14 3NT
Tel no: 01449 257120
thekingsarmshaughley.co.uk

'This pub restaurant has come a long way in the last year. What a surprise when the food arrived... an egg deep fried in panko crumbs on beautifully cooked asparagus with homemade mayonnaise was a joy to see. Absolutely delicious!'

Readers recommend

These entries are genuine quotes from a report sent in by one of our readers. Please get in touch via our website if you agree with their recommendation.

Newmarket

★ **NEW ENTRY** ★

Montaz

Cooking score: 1
Indian | £30
30 Old Station Road, Newmarket, CB8 8DN
Tel no: 01638 665888
montaz.co.uk

£5 £30
OFF

Friday night Indian takeaway? The chefs in this family-run restaurant will happily pack you up a korma to go, but next time book a table, the better to explore the contemporary, seasonal, pan-Indian food they do so well. A tumbler of crisp kale and potato chaat, or pan-fried mackerel with a vivacious Goan masala are strong openers, and there's much love for ox cheek, braised for 12 melting hours, and a robust goat curry redolent with the flavours of the owners' Bangladeshi heritage. The notes of coconut, kaffir lime and coriander in a vivid Nilgiri sauce, poured over a superb piece of monkfish, sing lustily of southern India. Pick of the sips from a short wine list (bottles from £17) is a fresh Chenin Blanc from the Sula Vineyards north of Mumbai.

Chef/s: Golam Mobin. **Closed:** 25 and 26 Dec. **Meals:** main courses £11 to £18. Tasting menu £45 (5 courses). **Details:** 52 seats. Music.

Orford

The Crown and Castle

Cooking score: 3
British/Italian | £37
Market Hill, Orford, IP12 2LJ
Tel no: 01394 450205
crownandcastle.co.uk

In this hurly-burly world, it's sometimes good when things remain just as you remember and love them. So it is with The Crown and Castle and its Italy-meets-Suffolk menu, quirky Italophile wine list (bottles from £20) and appealing mix of contemporary style and coastal comfort. Come for bar snacks (cicchetti) that include Tuscan finocchiona, pecorino and glossy olives, then look to local producers for slow-roast Dingley Dell pork belly, or oak-smoked salmon from Pinney's just around the corner, served with Orford-baked Pump Street sourdough. A 'proper' shortcrust steak and kidney pie will – reassuringly – take 25 minutes, or you may be tempted by flavour-packed homemade paccheri with rich beef shin ragù, or calf's liver with Umbrian lentils and their familiar plate-fellows pancetta, sage and balsamic vinegar. Carefully considered menus for vegetarians and vegans might tempt with cime di rapa and a chilli and garlic risotto, or griddled radicchio with borlotti beans and salsa verde. Finish with a warm loganberry jam and frangipane tart, or dark treacle tart, both served with milk ice cream.

Chef/s: Rob Walpole. **Closed:** 25, 26 and 31 Dec. **Meals:** main courses £16 to £21. Set L £16 (2 courses) to £20. **Details:** 50 seats. 25 seats outside. V menu. Vg menu. Bar. Wheelchairs. Parking. Children over 8 yrs at D.

▌Rattlesden

★ NEW ENTRY ★

The Brewers

Cooking score: 3
British | £40
Lower Road, Rattlesden, IP30 0RJ
Tel no: 01449 736377
thebrewersrattlesden.co.uk

'A must', noted one reader after a spring dinner that danced exuberantly to the tunes of the season at this refurbished village pub. A slow-cooked duck egg with young asparagus, shaved truffle, Manchego and wild garlic oil was a 'sublime' prelude to sophisticated 'surf and turf' (plump lobster tail alongside braised-to-melting pig's cheeks glazed with soy and honey), before a sparkling finale courtesy of a set strawberry consommé with strawberry-basil salad, Champagne sorbet and the laciest of tuiles. Look out for exemplary wellingtons: there's one every evening, maybe made with local venison, free range pork or beef fillet, the latter carved at the table to share.

Leave room for Dan Russell's stop-you-in-your-tracks puddings, if not the strawberries then perhaps the creamiest of lemon possets with caramelised blueberries and sharp-edged marmalade ice cream, or rhubarb parfait with poached rhubarb, a chantilly-filled brandy snap, and flirty little meringue kisses. A knowledgeable front of house team will happily recommend wines (bottles from £18) with a Coravin system enabling some interesting by-the-glass sips.

Chef/s: Dan Russell. **Closed:** Mon, Tue. **Meals:** main courses £17 to £32. Tasting menu £50 (5 courses) to £70. **Details:** 55 seats. 20 seats outside. Bar. Wheelchairs. Parking. Music.

▌Southwold

Sole Bay Fish Company

Cooking score: 2
Seafood | £20
Shed 22e, Blackshore, Southwold, IP18 6ND
Tel no: 01502 724241
solebayfishco.co.uk

£30

You'll need to trudge on foot, navigate the winding road out of Southwold or take the ferry across the water from Walberswick to reach the harbour at Blackshore – home to weather-beaten fishing sheds, wooden jetties, working boats and this terrific lunch-only restaurant (with a fishmonger's attached). Inside, it's an ad hoc shack of a place stuffed with maritime paraphernalia and blackboards advertising the day's catch, home-smoked fish and a briny-fresh bare-bones menu. Specials such as beer-battered Colchester oysters are scrawled on a fish tank, although the kitchen's top calls are seafood platters, lobsters, crabs and battered fish (trendily served with chips in an enamel mug and mushy peas in a matching pie dish). There are hunks of artisan baguette for ballast, but no puds at all – it sounds almost ridiculously simple, but there's no arguing with the quality or freshness. This being fashionable Southwold, the drinks list includes fizz and some decent wines.

Chef/s: Nikol Hanzalová. **Meals:** main courses £4 to £21

Stanton
The Leaping Hare

Cooking score: 3
Modern British | £32
Wyken Vineyards, Wyken Road, Stanton,
IP31 2DW
Tel no: 01359 250287
wykenvineyards.co.uk

£5 OFF

Housed in a vast, stylishly converted barn with the white-clothed tables of the restaurant at one end, a busy cafe ('eggs benedict are ace') at the other, this rural eatery is part of a food-led enterprise created by Carla Carlisle – an unstinting champion of local and field-to-fork eating. Simon Woodrow heads the kitchen and he rises to the challenge, sourcing and cooking ingredients with unquestioning care and piling on diverse flavours with brio, serving Wyken Estate partridge breast with celeriac rémoulade, capers and raisins, or tempura plaice with charred lemon and warm tartare sauce. Mains cover everything from Creedy Carver duck breast and faggot with kale, smoked mash and burnt onion to cod fillet with leeks, sweet potato bhajia and curry sauce. Among desserts, the vanilla parfait with poached rhubarb, blood orange and pistachio has been highly rated. Wines from Wyken Vineyards head a short, carefully chosen list, which opens at £23.
Chef/s: Simon Woodrow. **Closed:** 25 Dec to 4 Jan. **Meals:** main courses £15 to £26. **Details:** 48 seats. 20 seats outside. Wheelchairs. Parking.

Tuddenham
Tuddenham Mill

Cooking score: 6
Modern British | £45
High Street, Tuddenham, IP28 6SQ
Tel no: 01638 713552
tuddenhammill.co.uk

£5 OFF

When a speck and honey bun bounces from oven to table, warm, sweet and salty, and an oyster cracker with Berkswell cheese snaps,

crackles and pops in one delicious mouthful, you're probably in the hands of chefs cooking at full confident tilt. This is confirmed with the vivid flavours in a starter of eel, its gently smoked meatiness providing a punchy backdrop to a consommé of crystalline clarity that captures the very essence of tomato, and again with rare duck breast that has simply been shown a hot pan, rested, sliced and seasoned with flourish. It is pared-back, thoughtful cooking – witness the simple broad bean tartare with the eel, or the young tomatoes whose warmed skinless flesh slips into the consommé when pressed, or the sprigs of sea herbs picked from Norfolk marshes. Everything has a contribution to make, from the bitter notes of chicory, and the ruby-red sweetness of English cherries and meadowsweet with the duck, to the flat white ice cream served with sun-kissed Fenland strawberries that have been allowed simply to steep in syrup fragrant with their own leaves and wild chamomile. The lengthy global wine list rises steadily from its £21 base.
Chef/s: Lee Bye. **Meals:** main courses £21 to £32. Set L £23 (2 courses) to £28. Early D £23. Tasting menu £70 (6 courses). Sun L £28 (2 courses) to £32. **Details:** 56 seats. 25 seats outside. V menu. Vg menu. Bar. Wheelchairs. Parking. Music.

Walberswick
The Anchor

Cooking score: 2
Modern British | £29
The Street, Walberswick, IP18 6UA
Tel no: 01502 722112
anchoratwalberswick.com

£30

Outside tables to the front and rear may hint at brisk business in fair weather, but step inside this handsome pub a short stroll from the beach and you quickly realise just how personally run it is, with a real commitment to the community and 'to doing things that bit better'. Freshly baked loaves sit on the bar, there are made-to-order wood-fired pizzas to take away, barbecues at the weekend and fish smoked in-house. Ingredients are well sourced

and well handled, whether in a pub classic – fish and chips, ploughman's, steak – or a daily changing special, say pigeon breast with bacon, mushrooms and spinach on toast, sea bass with samphire and beurre blanc or a whole roasted partridge with hasselback potatoes. To finish, the selection of English cheeses is highly rated or there could be a textbook apple crumble and custard, sticky toffee pudding or a selection of Suffolk Meadow ice creams. Easy-drinking wines are arranged by style with plenty of choice under £40.
Chef/s: Sophie Dorber. **Closed:** Fri, Sat, Sun, 25 Dec. **Meals:** main courses £13 to £23. **Details:** 75 seats. 200 seats outside. Bar. Wheelchairs. Parking.

▌Woodbridge

LOCAL GEM
The Table
Global | £27
3 Quay Street, Woodbridge, IP12 1BX
Tel no: 01394 382428
thetablewoodbridge.co.uk
£5 OFF £30

With coffee and cake in the morning, one-plate deals at lunchtime (chargrilled minute steak and fries, perhaps) and candles on tables in the evening, this unpretentious town-centre brasserie is all things to all people. The menu globetrots, trekking from crispy calamari with sriracha mayo or sweet potato fritters with cucumber raita to smoked haddock soufflé and Moroccan vegetable tagine – although curries are the kitchen's speciality (perhaps meatballs and paneer in a Sri Lankan-spiced sauce). Finish with lemon meringue pie or cheese on toast. Wines from £21.

▌Yoxford
Main's
Cooking score: 1
Modern European | £32
High Street, Yoxford, IP17 3EU
Tel no: 01728 668882
mainsrestaurant.co.uk

Husband and wife Jason Vincent and Nancy Main's restaurant in a one-time draper's shop is open for seasonally focused dinners three evenings a week and for Saturday brunch. They make everything on the premises (which even extends to Nancy's pottery) and serve up a broadly European-accented menu with regional ingredients to the fore. Saffron labneh with salad of radicchio, fennel and blood orange is a healthy boost, or go for the slightly more indulgent spinach baked custard with Parmesan mornay sauce. Follow on with roast leg of salt marsh lamb with wild samphire and thyme gravy, then round off with saffron rice pudding. Keenly priced wines open at £15.
Chef/s: Jason Vincent. **Closed:** Mon, Tue, Wed, Sun. **Meals:** main courses £13 to £22. **Details:** 30 seats. Wheelchairs.

Local Gem
These entries are brilliant neighbourhood venues, delivering good, freshly cooked food at great value for money.

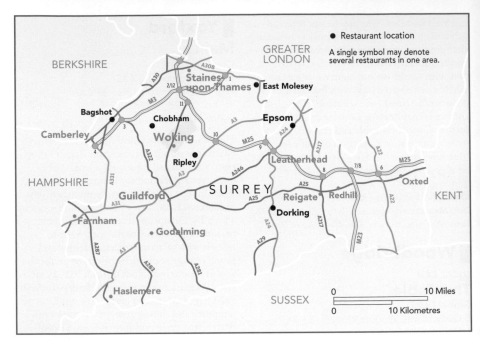

Restaurant location

A single symbol may denote
several restaurants in one area.

Bagshot

★ TOP 50 ★

Matt Worswick at the Latymer
Cooking score: 7
Modern British | £69
Pennyhill Park Hotel, London Road, Bagshot,
GU19 5EU
Tel no: 01276 486156
pennyhillpark.co.uk

Based in the oldest and most elegant part of a sprawling hotel and spa complex, this plush beamed and rather old-fashioned dining room indulges visitors in a full-on cosseting experience, which one recent guest considered 'decidedly out of tune with the lightness and modernity of the cuisine'. There's no doubt that Matt Worswick's confident, inventive and playful dishes are designed to impress. As an opener to the five-course tasting lunch, oyster emulsion, layered with diced cured sea trout and topped with sorrel granita, has just the right kick to jolt a dozy palate before the hits of umami in a modern take on wild mushroom risotto. But there's respect for the classic ways too, when a simple seared scallop is presented on a heap of spiced white crabmeat alongside a rich, intense sauce américaine. The star of the show is undoubtedly a triumphant Goosnargh duck breast with its just-seared liver, wholegrain mustard jus and contrasting mini Waldorf salad. And in a winning finale, a light rum baba arrives with alphonso mango and a marigold-dusted passion fruit sorbet. Details such as the unmissable sourdough bread and the cheese selection also create good vibrations, while professionalism and ease

£5 voucher

£5 OFF Restaurants showing this symbol are participating in our £5 voucher scheme, redeemable against a meal for two or more. Vouchers can be found at the back of this book.

define the service. The wine list is everything you would expect from a restaurant of this standing, plundering France and beyond for big-hitting treasure.

Chef/s: Matt Worswick. **Closed:** Mon, Tue, 2 to 16 Jan. **Meals:** tasting menu L £49 (5 courses) and D £69 Wed to Fri and Sun (5 courses) to £105. Sun L £59 (5 courses). **Details:** 55 seats. V menu. Vg menu. Bar. Wheelchairs. Parking. Children over 12 yrs.

■ Chobham
Stovell's
Cooking score: 4
Modern European | £48
125 Windsor Road, Chobham, GU24 8QS
Tel no: 01276 858000
stovells.com

£5
OFF

The setting is Chobham at its most chocolate box, an endearing red-roofed Tudor farmhouse on the B383, a place to cheer the heart on a dark night or summer lunchtime. The kitchen's intention to bring a Mexican sensibility to an essentially modern European repertoire produces some intriguing dishes. Some work better than others: an umami-rich broth of young leaves, herbs, flowers and smoked eel, presented in a lidded clay pot, and quail roasted on an open fire, served with roasted and pickled corn and shiitake mushrooms come in for praise. When attention wanders, the energy drains out of dishes, leaving turbot with clams and pickled pear purée oddly underpowered, and a vegetarian main course of ricotta gnocchi is a technical calamity. For dessert, smash open a vibrant piñata to get at the chocolate nougat and brazils within, or go for the signature carrot cake with confit baby carrots and smoked sour cream. Small glasses from £6 lead a list that does France proud, and features a modest spread of good South Americans.

Chef/s: Lukasz Krzysiek. **Closed:** Mon, 1 week Aug. **Meals:** set L £24 (2 courses) to £28. Set D £37 (2 courses) to £48. Tasting menu £60 (7 courses) to £75. Sun L £32. **Details:** 60 seats. 20 seats outside. V menu. Bar. Parking. Music.

■ Dorking
Sorrel
Cooking score: 6
Modern British | £65
77 South Street, Dorking, RH4 2JU
Tel no: 01306 889414
sorrelrestaurant.co.uk

Offering refuge from the busy thoroughfare running past its door, this striking local restaurant has no shortage of vocal support. Decor is agreeable (wonky beams, standing timbers, creaky floorboards galore), seating comfortable and tables well spaced, although they've increased capacity since the last edition of the Guide. There is evident skill combined with enthusiasm in the state-of-the-art kitchen. By starting with high-quality seasonal ingredients, Steve Drake ensures his cooking stands out from the crowd. His style is at once classical and contemporary, as seen in a beautifully composed venison tartare teamed with chicory marmalade, Cornish Gouda cheese and truffle toast, or an exquisitely presented dish of scallop with curried oat granola, cucumber and smoked cauliflower. Earthier notes surface in a main course of beef rib with yeast and celeriac, parsley gremolata and Kalamata olives, while desserts do deconstructive things with the likes of pear, hibiscus, goat's yoghurt and cardamom. The tasting menu of five or nine courses is the best way to hit the highlights, but there is a fixed-price carte and a good-value set lunch, too. The personable front of house approach makes this a pleasurable experience, as does the expertly curated wine list, which opens with a useful small-glass selection and offers quality and value across Europe and beyond.

Chef/s: Steve Drake. **Closed:** Mon, Sun, 21 Dec to 5 Jan, 6 to 10 Aug. **Meals:** set L £45. Set D £65. Tasting menu £65 (5 courses) to £95. **Details:** 40 seats. Parking.

Anonymous

At *The Good Food Guide*, our inspectors dine anonymously and pay their bill in full. These impartial review meals, along with feedback from thousands of our readers, are what informs the content of the *GFG*.

▌East Molesey

Petriti's

Cooking score: 3
Modern European | £40
98 Walton Road, East Molesey, KT8 0DL
Tel no: 020 8979 5577
petritisrestaurant.co.uk

£5
OFF

The modest brick and wood frontage is nothing to write home about, but all is posh and polished inside Sokol and Nargisa Petriti's suburban favourite. Well-spaced tables, comfortable chairs, a pastel colour scheme and pretty floral displays create a mood of low-key sophistication that's just the ticket for diners who come for elaborately plated dishes based on sound, carefully sourced ingredients. Menus are fixed-price, value for money is commendable and the kitchen proves its worth with canny seasonal creations such as duck with endive, parsnip, damson jus and sorrel or venison fillet accompanied by chestnut, kale, hen of the woods and winter berries. If you're in the mood for seafood, there might be monkfish with Puy lentils, sweetcorn custard, broccoli and chorizo oil, while a chocolate sphere with salted caramel, strawberries and tonka bean ice cream is typical of Petriti's sure-footed desserts. The wide-ranging wine list kicks off with 11 by-the-glass selections.
Chef/s: Sokol Petriti. **Closed:** Mon, 27 Dec to 15 Jan. **Meals:** set L £20 (2 courses) to £28. Set D £30 (2 courses) to £40. Tasting menu £40 (6 courses) to £55. Sun L £20 (2 courses). **Details:** 60 seats. V menu. Wheelchairs. Music. Children over 6 yrs.

▌Epsom

Dastaan

Cooking score: 4
Indian | £30
447 Kingston Road, Epsom, KT19 0DB
Tel no: 020 8786 8999
dastaan.co.uk

£30

Dastaan brings a splash of vivid colour to sedate Epsom, firstly in a room done in fairground pink and yellow, but also in the form of a vibrant approach to classic Indian cooking. There are samosas, vindaloo and rogan josh for traditionalists, but explore the interstices of the menu and you will find beetroot tikki dressed in yoghurt flamed with tempered whole spices, guinea fowl and chicken kebabs with apple preserve, and vegetable biryani made with Jerusalem artichokes, asparagus and peas. All the richness and generosity of long-simmered sauces and thoroughly infused spice mixtures exudes from the dishes, and the place seems to radiate a sense of enjoyment. With parathas and naans on the side, there's no excuse to come away hungry, and desserts such as kulfi, or a mango and fig version of kheer (rice pudding), are appropriately light on the digestion. A short wine list starts at £17.50, or there are Cobra and Kingfisher beers to wet your whistle.
Chef/s: Nand Kishor Semwak. **Closed:** Mon. **Meals:** main courses £8 to £14. **Details:** 52 seats. Wheelchairs. Music.

▌Guildford

READERS RECOMMEND

De Nada

12a Market Street, Guildford, GU1 4LB
Tel no: 01483 303479
denadatapas.co.uk
'Hidden away, with a quirky, laid-back feel, this is a great place for classic tapas done really well. There are interesting wines and specials, as well as live music occasionally. We love it just as much for a quick lunch as for a lingering evening of indulgence.'

■ Ripley
The Anchor
Cooking score: 3
Modern British | £40
High Street, Ripley, GU23 6AE
Tel no: 01483 211866
ripleyanchor.co.uk
£5 OFF

'I like it here,' declared a devotee of this high street hostelry, a lovely old building dating from the 16th century. It's pitched as a modern British pub and expectations are high, partly on account of owner Steve Drake's culinary reputation in these parts – he also owns Sorrel in Dorking (see entry) – and evident commitment to high quality. Michael Wall-Palmer is responsible for the day-to-day running of the kitchen and he treats food seriously yet without pretension, as in a starter of cumin-braised mutton accompanied by nothing more than lemon houmous and flatbread. Main courses are given extra shine by pedigree components, as in a dish of roast guinea fowl breast teamed with charred hispi cabbage and sarladaise potatoes. To conclude, there might be a sticky beer cake and spiced apple ice cream. 'Simple food but with a touch of class,' was one diner's summary. It's all backed up by local ales and a wine list that offers good drinking from £19.
Chef/s: Michael Wall-Palmer. **Closed:** 25 and 26 Dec, 1 Jan. **Meals:** main courses £16 to £26. Set L and early D £22 (2 courses) to £28. Sun L £26 (2 courses) to £32. **Details:** 45 seats. 20 seats outside. Vg menu. Bar. Wheelchairs. Parking. Music. No children after 7.30pm.

The Clock House
Cooking score: 5
Modern British | £70
High Street, Ripley, GU23 6AQ
Tel no: 01483 224777
theclockhouserestaurant.co.uk

Occupying a handsome brick building with a big old timepiece above the door, this elegantly appointed dining room is overseen by attentive staff who 'really care' about their work, while the kitchen shows its mettle via a series of fixed-priced menus that show off the chef's innovative contemporary style – it's 'overall a great experience'. Lunchtime hits have included a clever pairing of smoked eel, Isle of Wight tomatoes and nasturtiums, as well as a superior dish of plaice accompanied by courgettes, basil and fregola. They also do a 'sensational' hanger steak (perhaps served with beetroot and Roscoff onion). Dinner promises a few more elaborate ideas ranging from lamb with aubergine, shiso and ewe's curd to turbot with Admiral Collingwood cheese, sea kale and shrimps. Desserts, meanwhile, are 'absolutely perfect' confections such as fruit panna cotta or a colourfully exotic amalgam of white chocolate, pineapple, chamomile and pistachio. The pretty walled garden is ideal for pre-prandial drinks on warm days, and the well-spread global wine list offers plenty of appetising bottles from £28.
Chef/s: Fred Clapperton. **Closed:** Mon, Tue, Sun. **Meals:** set L £40 to £55. Set D £70. Tasting menu £90 (7 courses). **Details:** 40 seats. V menu. Bar. Music.

Get social
Follow us on social media for the latest news, chef interviews and more.
Twitter @GoodFoodGuideUK
Facebook TheGoodFoodGuide

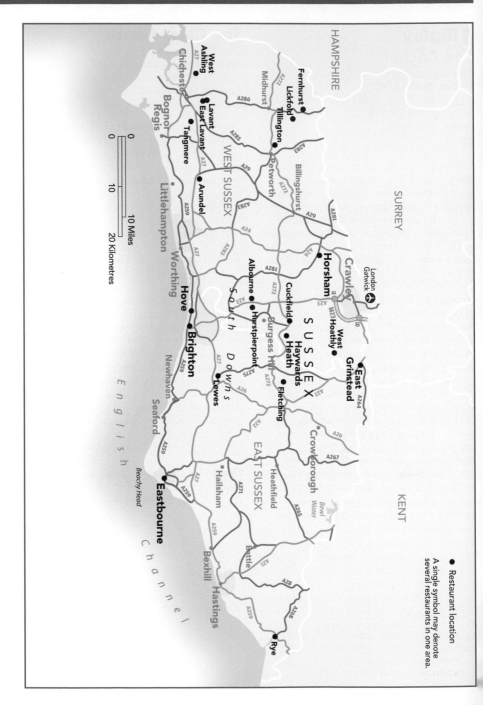

Join us at thegoodfoodguide.co.uk

■ Albourne
The Ginger Fox

Cooking score: 3
Modern British | £36
Muddleswood Road, Albourne, BN6 9EA
Tel no: 01273 857888
thegingerfox.com

Fetching views of the South Downs add to the pulling power of this bullishly revitalised Sussex hostelry – a family-friendly set-up with a dedicated children's play area in its expansive beer garden and even bike racks for passing cyclists. From the outside it looks picture-book folksy with an effigy of a fox chasing a pheasant crowning its intricately thatched roof, but the interior oozes cosmopolitan style – as you'd expect from a pub owned by the Brighton-based Gingerman restaurant group. Local ingredients figure prominently, but influences are garnered from further afield – as in a Golden Cross goat's cheese mousse with caper and raisin dressing or hoisin-glazed duck with confit potatoes, charred leeks, pickled cucumber and sesame purée. Seasonal vegetables are grown in the pub's own raised beds, while locally picked fruit shows up in desserts such as rhubarb panna cotta with rhubarb jelly, ginger crumble and honey ice cream. The well-rounded wine list includes some Sussex sparklers from the Ridgeview Wine Estate in nearby Ditchling.
Chef/s: Ben McKellar and Mark Bradley. **Closed:** 25 Dec. **Meals:** main courses £15 to £24. Set L £20 (2 courses). **Details:** 62 seats. 70 seats outside. Bar. Parking. Music.

■ Arundel
The Parsons Table

Cooking score: 3
Modern European | £38
2 & 8 Castle Mews, Tarrant Street, Arundel, BN18 9DG
Tel no: 01903 883477
theparsonstable.co.uk
£5 OFF

Not far from the castle, this personally run neighbourhood restaurant serves up assured modern food against a light, airy backdrop of blond wood tables and local prints on sky blue walls. Chef and co-owner Lee Parsons is a veteran of some big kitchens, including Belmond Le Manoir aux Quat'Saisons (see entry), and he proves his worth via a repertoire of precise, confident dishes – from a ballotine of grain-fed chicken with leeks, chanterelles and fennel emulsion to rack of South Downs lamb accompanied by a bonbon of braised shoulder, baby gem, pea purée and fondant potato. The day's catch from the Sussex boats also gets an outing, either 'simply prepared' or in more fancy garb (grilled mackerel with Jersey Royals, confit peppers and basil pesto, say). To conclude, Parsons' classically refined technique is highlighted in desserts such as a poached rhubarb and Champagne trifle incorporating chiffon sponge, set vanilla custard and rhubarb gel. Around 30 reasonably priced wines start at £21.50 (£5.50 a glass).
Chef/s: Lee Parsons. **Closed:** Mon, Sun, 24 to 26 Dec, 1 Jan, 1 week Feb, last week Aug. **Meals:** main courses £16 to £27. Set L £19 (2 courses) to £27. Tasting menu £85 (7 courses). **Details:** 36 seats. 20 seats outside. Music.

The Town House

Cooking score: 2
Modern British | £38
65 High Street, Arundel, BN18 9AJ
Tel no: 01903 883847
thetownhouse.co.uk
£5 OFF 🛏

First off, the splendiferous ceiling in the dining room of Lee and Katie Williams' Georgian restaurant with rooms opposite the castle walls warrants explanation: it's a 16th-century Florentine original, shipped over to Sussex, and a sight to behold. Luckily for your neck, distraction comes in the form of gilded mirrors and vibrant prints, as well as in Lee's seasonally inspired cooking. There's classical good sense on show in a menu that might take you from seared diver-caught scallops with the safe-as-houses combination of pea purée and crispy Parma ham, via pan-fried skrei cod with a rich lentil and bacon sauce, or fillet of South Downs venison with wild mushrooms, to desserts of chocolate and cherry marquise or caramelised pineapple tart. Vegetarian and set lunch menus broaden its appeal. The mostly European-focused wine list includes decent options by the glass and carafe.
Chef/s: Lee Williams. **Closed:** Mon, Tue, Sun, 2 weeks Nov, 25 and 26 Dec, 2 weeks Mar. **Meals:** main courses £19 to £26. Set L £19 (2 courses) to £23. **Details:** 28 seats. V menu. Music.

▉ Brighton

64 Degrees

Cooking score: 5
Modern British | £40
53 Meeting House Lane, Brighton, BN1 1HB
Tel no: 01273 770115
64degrees.co.uk
£5 OFF

Tucked in at the end of one of the Lanes, Michael Bremner's original Brighton venue (see also Murmur) has the kind of unhassled cosiness you expect from a backstreet joint in Lisbon, with low ceilings and a small counter around a busy kitchen adding to the infectious intimacy of it all. The small(ish) plates menu divides neatly into plant, marine and meat items, and there's hardly a dish that isn't bursting with clever counterpoints of intensity. Agnolotti pasta filled with potato and creamy Baron Bigod cheese come dressed in Parmesan and olive oil, with shavings of black truffle adding an umami punch, while a bowl of squid with nobbles of glorious chorizo and chickpeas is full of arresting richness. Even the lighter dishes – monkfish ceviche with pink grapefruit and marcona almonds, say – register strong and true, while tacos of short rib rolled with mushroom ketchup and beetroot salsa signal the kitchen's inventive flair. Finish with a bar of gold-dusted chocolate ganache on crumbled hazelnuts with malt ice cream. Wines by the small glass from £4.60 have been expertly chosen to accompany the food.
Chef/s: Michael Bremner. **Closed:** 24 to 26 Dec, 1 Jan. **Meals:** small plates £6 to £15. **Details:** 20 seats. Music. No children after 9pm.

Bincho Yakitori

Cooking score: 2
Japanese | £20
63 Preston Street, Brighton, BN1 2HE
Tel no: 01273 779021
binchoyakitori.com
£30
🍢

David Miney has really captured the clamorous earthiness of a Japanese izakaya on Brighton's Preston Street. Bincho's tightly packed tables, energetic soundtrack and laid-back attitude bring in the crowds, but it is the yakitori skewers that ensure they come back. The grill burns away behind a counter (where a few tables provide ringside seats) and blackboards reveal daily specials such as sea bream tempura. Pork belly yakitori is as soft and yielding as can be, likewise the chicken thigh and squid, and vegetarians can order a shiitake mushroom version. Non-meat eaters fare very well indeed, with aubergine and miso providing a glorious umami hit, and chunky cauliflower florets covered in a sticky Korean-style sauce. The food arrives as and when, the small plates designed for sharing. Japanese beers and sake are joined by a few wines from both hemispheres.

Chef/s: Tomo Ishii. **Closed:** Mon, 2 weeks Christmas. **Meals:** small plates £3 to £9. **Details:** 35 seats. V menu. Music.

The Chilli Pickle

Cooking score: 2
Indian | £28
17 Jubilee Street, Brighton, BN1 1GE
Tel no: 01273 900383
thechillipickle.com
£30

Bursts of vivid pinks, blues and yellows at Alun and Dawn Sperring's eatery (shared with Myhotel and a coffee shop) recall the vibrancy of Holi, the Hindu festival of colours, which celebrates the victory of good over evil. Good has certainly won out here, where regional Indian dishes are elevated to a higher plain by distinct spicing. Street-food favourite pani puri stands alongside new creations such as king prawn and squid pakoras, while a lunchtime thali is a real treat. Everything from 'addictively divine' garlic and aubergine pickle to curries including fragrant coconut cod and cockle moilee and the smokey South Indian chicken kolhapuri, have a fidelity that puts many a curry house to shame. The sigri charcoal grill fires up for whole sea bream and meaty mixed grill. Service is upbeat and informed. A slate of craft beers includes the house branded Thieving Monkey amber ale, with wines opening at £19.

Chef/s: Alun Sperring. **Closed:** 24 and 25 Dec. **Meals:** main courses £13 to £19. Set D £24 (2 courses) to £28. **Details:** 140 seats. 24 seats outside. Wheelchairs. Music.

Cin Cin

Cooking score: 2
Italian | £26
13-16 Vine Street, Brighton, BN1 4AG
Tel no: 01273 698813
cincin.co.uk
£5 OFF   £30

Fresh pasta is made a couple of times a day in the tiny open kitchen at this, the original Cin Cin – there's a second branch in Hove (see entry). And it's some pasta, ranging from cappelletti with smoked haddock, celeriac and capers to ceps fazzoletti (that's handkerchiefs to you and me), rich with wild duck and pickled mushrooms. The 21-seat counter makes for an intimate dining setting, but happily bar stools are sensitively carved for maximum comfort. The team dole out small plates and boards to share – daily selections of first-rate Italian salumi and cheeses, and zippy combinations such as whipped sheep's ricotta with glazed beetroot and blood orange, or crostini alla bolognese. To finish, banoffee pie panna cotta is a successful merger. A rhubarb Bellini is one of several aperitivi worth checking out, as is the collection of vermouths and concise list of Italian wines.

Chef/s: Jamie Halsall. **Closed:** Mon, Sun, 25 to 27 Dec, 1 Jan. **Meals:** small plates £7 to £14. Set L £20. **Details:** 21 seats. Music.

★ NEW ENTRY ★

Flint House

Cooking score: 1
Modern British | £30
13 Hannington Lane, Brighton, BN1 1GS
Tel no: 01273 916333
flinthousebrighton.com
£30

Lovers of small plates and tapas take note: Brighton's home-grown Gingerman restaurant group has entered the fray. Pull up a stool at the kitchen counter in the dapper ground-floor dining room or head upstairs to the first-floor cocktail bar with an outside terrace for sunnier days. The broad menu runs to classic ham croquettes and cured meats alongside 'wonderfully tender' braised squid with 'nduja, and miso mackerel with fennel and pomegranate, and if not all creative ideas hit the mark, there's plenty to commend. Just about everything on the canny wine list is available by the glass and 375ml carafe.

Chef/s: Tom Wright. **Closed:** 25 Dec. **Meals:** tapas £4 to £10. **Details:** 80 seats. 30 seats outside. V menu. Bar. Wheelchairs. Music. No reservations.

The Gingerman

Cooking score: 3
Modern European | £45
21a Norfolk Square, Brighton, BN1 2PD
Tel no: 01273 326688
gingermanrestaurants.com

He's known as 'the ginger chef', so it was only natural that Ben McKellar should name his flagship restaurant (and his Brighton-based mini-empire) after himself. Gingerman's bijou dining room looks and feels more casual than it did when it opened in 1998, but the food has lost none of its impact. You can drop by for just one course at lunchtime, although it pays to invest in the full works if you want to explore the kitchen's impressive repertoire. Seafood from the south coast boats is always a good call (perhaps monkfish with parsley purée and caper-studded dauphinois), but uncomplicated worldly wise ideas come thick and fast – from an Anglo-Asian mix of cauliflower bhajia, roasted cauliflower purée, cashews and coriander oil to a classically Gallic dish of duck breast and crispy leg with stuffed cabbage, Roscoff onion and fondant potato. For afters, coffee crème brûlée and white chocolate délice await. The appealing drinks list roams from Sussex fizz to reasonably priced European wines to swanky Coravin selections and classic cocktails.

Chef/s: Ben McKellar and Mark Charker. **Closed:** Mon, first 2 weeks Jan. **Meals:** set L £17 (2 courses) to £20. Set D £35 (2 courses) to £45. Tasting menu £60 (5 courses). Sun L £30. **Details:** 34 seats. Music.

Isaac At

Cooking score: 3
Modern British | £40
2 Gloucester Street, Brighton, BN1 4EW
Tel no: 07765 934740
isaac-at.com

On one of the quieter residential streets of the city's most self-consciously boho district, Isaac Bartlett-Copeland's venue is done in soberly neutral hue, both without and within. The approach is very much in the now, with Sussex produce transformed into a four- or seven-course tasting menu, with a pre-theatre deal and vegetarian and vegan offerings too. There is a pleasing informality to the presentations, the fashionable thrown-together look benefiting tripartite dishes such as celeriac, egg yolk and apple, haddock, cauliflower and parsley, or lamb, Brussels sprouts and shallots. Fresh, concentrated flavours and pinpoint seasonings characterise the cooking, with pear, cobnut and lemon thyme to close the show. A commendable all-British drinks list extends to local ales and ciders, wines embracing the crown jewels of the Sussex fizz scene, as well as regional Pinots and biodynamic blends, and a shrewd pick of English gins.

Chef/s: Isaac Bartlett-Copeland. **Closed:** Mon, Sun, 23 Dec to 14 Jan, 1 to 12 Aug. **Meals:** early D £35 (4 courses). Tasting menu £40 (4 courses) to £53. **Details:** 24 seats. V menu. Vg menu. Music. Children over 12 yrs. Pre-payment required.

Murmur

Cooking score: 3
Modern British | £30
91-96 King's Road Arches, Brighton, BN1 2FN
Tel no: 01273 711900
murmur-restaurant.co.uk
£5 OFF £30

From its prime location in revamped arches opposite the i360, diners can witness a murmuration of starlings – the inspiration for this all-day eatery's name – above the relic of the West Pier at dusk. Michael Bremner's second restaurant after 64 Degrees (see entry)

is 'clearly a class act'. It's casual and contemporary in looks and outlook, with a heated terrace and a kitchen that hitchhikes around the globe for ideas, picking up everything from grilled squid with kimchi and black sesame seeds to jerk squash (with coconut labneh, black bean curry, crispy shallots and puffed rice). Elsewhere, a starter of fish soup stuffed with the locally landed catch might be followed by cod fillet with a rosemary and butter bean casserole, fennel cream and smoked paprika crumb. If it's meat you're after, slow-roast pork belly with crispy skin, anise carrots and charred purple sprouting broccoli is a sure-fire winner. Apple millefeuille with Calvados crème fraîche is one of several satisfying desserts. Wines from £20.
Chef/s: Liam Brennan. **Closed:** 24 to 26 Dec. **Meals:** main courses £14 to £20. Set L £15 (2 courses) to £20. **Details:** 34 seats. 40 seats outside. Wheelchairs. Music.

Plateau
Cooking score: 1
Modern European | £25
1 Bartholowmews, Brighton, BN1 1HG
Tel no: 01273 733085
plateaubrighton.co.uk

Just a few minutes' stroll from the seafront, Plateau is positively buoyant for much of the time, helped along by a lively playlist. The kitchen shows European leanings with sharing plates of 'viandes' and 'poissons' the order of the day – perhaps a charcoal-roasted Boston butt (shoulder of pork) from Garlic Wood Butchery in West Sussex, served with squash gratin and house pickles. Small plates run to Hereford beef tartare, and bigger ones to coal-roasted plaice with spiced lentils, and roast cauliflower with hazelnuts and scarlet kale. The natural, organic and biodynamic wine list majors on France, but makes forays into the rest of Europe and beyond.

Chef/s: James Mcilveen. **Closed:** 25 and 26 Dec. **Meals:** main courses £14 to £18. Set L and D £16 (2 courses) to £20. **Details:** 78 seats. 8 seats outside. Bar.

The Salt Room
Cooking score: 3
Seafood | £45
106 King's Road, Brighton, BN1 2FN
Tel no: 01273 929488
saltroom-restaurant.co.uk

One of the more universally admired additions to the city's seafront, The Salt Room is a handsome devil, with its terrace attached limpet-like to one side of the Hilton Metropole Hotel. Its dapper interior, with exposed brickwork and echoes of Art Deco sophistication, is watched over by a well-drilled team. Seafood is the mainstay of the modern menu, with the blackboard revealing the market fish of the day: hake, sea bass, halibut, say, all cooked over charcoal, for two to share. Opening salvos such as 'sweet, soft octopus' in a rich ragoût with white beans and seaweed gremolata, and pollock ceviche with passion fruit and chilli impress with their attention to detail. Mains could include roast monkfish spiced up with cumin, joined by a few red meat and vegetarian alternatives (coal-roasted aubergine pastilla, perhaps). Finish with jazzed-up versions of peach Melba or Arctic roll. A persuasive list of wines by the glass encourages exploration, and cool cocktails seem just the thing in this setting.
Chef/s: Dave Mothersill. **Meals:** main courses £13 to £28. Set L and early D £18 (2 courses) to £20. Tasting menu £45 (5 courses). **Details:** 90 seats. 55 seats outside. Bar. Wheelchairs. Music.

Semolina

Cooking score: 2
Modern European | £28
15 Baker Street, Brighton, BN1 4JN
Tel no: 01273 697259
semolinabrighton.co.uk

£5 OFF £30

Given its position some way off the tourist
trail, this 'gem of a place' must rely on the
loyalty of its local following. It's all down to
the husband-and-wife partnership of Orson
and Linda Whitfield. He cooks with
confidence, and she is a smiling, efficient
presence out front, which is just what you
want in a neighbourhood restaurant. Regional
ingredients get a good showing in the broadly
European output, so seared mackerel is
matched with Sussex tomatoes, fennel and
horseradish, and pan-fried squid arrives with
chickpeas and gremolata and a hit of chilli.
Among main courses, roast rabbit is a
welcome sight, with broad beans, bacon and
herb beignets, and rump of lamb gets a North
African/Middle Eastern spin with harissa,
mint labneh and dukkah. Creative desserts run
to roasted apricots with frozen sheep's yoghurt
and almond crumb. The concise wine list
includes local Ridgeview fizz.
Chef/s: Orson Whitfield. **Closed:** Mon, Sun, 2 weeks
Christmas, 2 weeks spring, last 2 weeks Aug.
Meals: main courses £13 to £17. **Details:** 28 seats.
Music.

The Set

Cooking score: 3
Modern British | £28
Artist Residence, 33 Regency Square,
Brighton, BN1 2GG
Tel no: 01273 324302
thesetrestaurant.com

£5 OFF £30

Having recently embraced the flexibility of an
à la carte format, The Set is no longer a slave to
the set menu (but don't worry, there is still a
10-course 'chef's table' option for keenos).
They've also incorporated a rudderless area at
the front of the building, effectively doubling

the size of the restaurant. Counter stools
provide ringside seats at the tiny open kitchen,
while the interior remains sublimely
bohemian. The backbone of the menu is local
ingredients, and they arrive in inspired
combinations. Wee snacks include a brik
pastry with salsify and harissa, before starters
proper such as herring pickled in rhubarb with
lettuce emulsion, or Marmite-glazed ox
tongue atop a crumpet (with pickled cockles
and turnip). Then feast on pork with smoked
trotter samosa or two can share a whole
lobster. An inspired vegetarian main course
might be gnudi with hispi bolognese. Finish
with rhubarb and custard éclair. The wine list
opens at £21, and the cocktail bar, The Fix, is
worth a pre- or post-prandial visit (or both).
Chef/s: Marcin Miasik. **Meals:** main courses £13 to
£19. Tasting menu £65 (10 courses). **Details:** 40
seats. 10 seats outside. Bar. Music.

Terre à Terre

Cooking score: 3
Vegetarian | £40
71 East Street, Brighton, BN1 1HQ
Tel no: 01273 729051
terreaterre.co.uk

£5 OFF

'Fancy onigiri dairy'; 'rösti revisited'; 'snap,
crackle & choc' − just some of the dish names
that are typical of this free-spirited vegetarian
outfit on Brighton's East Street, a boho bastion
of the city's multicultural dining scene since
1993. It's less of a maverick these days, but Terre
à Terre still deals in global assemblages: how
about soft buttermilk-soaked halloumi
dipped in chip-shop batter, with vodka-
spiked preserved tomatoes, a 'sea salad tartare'
and lemony Yemeni relish? Elsewhere, their
take on KFC involves sesame-coated Korean-
fried cauliflower, kimchi and umeboshi
chestnut purée, while 'how's your vada' is a
twisted reboot of the Indian street-food snack
zhuzhed-up with paneer tikka, mango purée,
cavolo nero, fennel-seed coconut butter and
carrot-top pesto. Desserts don't let the side
down − try the boozy 'rum tum' tarte tatin
with tamarind and sticky date ice cream. To

drink, organic and biodynamic wines, vegan beers, nectars and zany cocktails tick all the boxes.

Chef/s: David Marrow. **Closed:** 25 and 26 Dec. **Meals:** main courses £17. Set L and D £35. **Details:** 110 seats. 17 seats outside. V menu. Vg menu. Wheelchairs. Music.

LOCAL GEM

The Coal Shed
Modern British | £45

8 Boyces Street, Brighton, BN1 1AN
Tel no: 01273 322998
coalshed-restaurant.co.uk

Tucked into the bustling heart of the city centre, The Coal Shed is a sibling of seafront The Salt Room (see entry), a place consecrated to the flame-grilling of cuts of pedigree beef sold by weight and sauced with béarnaise, chimichurri or what have you. These are the place's undeniable chief selling point, although the fire-roasting extends to a whole sea bream. Around the edges there are alluring peripherals such as seaweed-cured salmon with grapefruit, fennel and dill, and tempting finishers include lemon tart or strawberry trifle with mango sorbet. Cocktails and 'softails' prime you for the broadly based wine list, with glasses from £5.50.

LOCAL GEM

Curry Leaf Cafe
Indian | £28

60 Ship Street, Brighton, BN1 1AE
Tel no: 01273 207070
curryleafcafe.com

£30

A marriage of Indian street food, craft beers, gins and fermented soft drinks in jam-packed, newly spruced-up premises just a stroll from Brighton beach – that's the Curry Leaf Café in a (betel) nutshell. Daytime dosas, samosas, spinach pakoras and lunchtime thalis are quick options, or you can linger in the evening over forcefully spiced plates of Amritsari fish fry, Goan pork vindaloo or chicken chettinad.

Offbeat spice-friendly wines start at £20. There's also a kiosk at Brighton railway station and another outlet in Kemptown.

█ Cuckfield
Ockenden Manor
Cooking score: 3
Modern French | £65

Ockenden Lane, Cuckfield, RH17 5LD
Tel no: 01444 416111
hshotels.co.uk

£5 OFF 🛏

Hidden away at the end of a lane in the middle of the village, this 16th-century manor's rural aspect isn't fully appreciated until you enter the dining room and see the South Downs stretched before you. Stephen Crane's French-inspired cooking feels right at home in this formally attired space, but regional produce helps to provide a sense of place. A fixed-price carte is supported by tasting menus and a keenly priced lunch option, and vegetarians fare very well indeed. English asparagus soup, served with a waft of truffle oil, might start things off, while home-smoked salmon with squid tempura is the chef's signature dish. Newhaven cod arrives with a frothy velouté, fresh peas and a dinky mussel kiev, and meat is handled equally well judging by pork four ways (with cauliflower three ways and apple twice). Dark chocolate délice is a fine finale. The wine list majors in regional France and takes note of the rest of the world.

Chef/s: Stephen Crane. **Meals:** set L £23 (2 courses) to £30. Set D £55 (2 courses) to £65. Tasting menu £50 (5 courses) to £90. Sun L £40. **Details:** 70 seats. V menu. Bar. Wheelchairs. Parking. Music.

East Grinstead
Gravetye Manor
Cooking score: 4
Modern British | £80
Vowels Lane, East Grinstead, RH19 4LJ
Tel no: 01342 810567
gravetyemanor.co.uk

If you were circling the grounds of this illustrious Elizabethan manor by helicopter, you'd spot not only meadows and orchards, but also a peach house, polytunnels and a round kitchen garden originally designed by William Robinson, the Victorian godfather of natural gardening. Meanwhile, Gravetye's interior reveals even more treasures and treats, including a pleasing dining room where guests can sample the work of young chef George Blogg. Top billing goes to the 'Time and Place' tasting menu, a culinary tour that takes diners from the 'walled garden' (vegetables, yolks and flowers) via the 'chalk stream' to the 'forcing pots' (rhubarb and mint). Home-grown, local and seasonal produce also inform the monthly carte, which might run from a tartare of Jurassic Coast rose veal with red chicory, preserved lemon and sage to Trenchmore Farm beef accompanied by kohlrabi, nasturtium and horseradish. Everything looks exceedingly pretty, right down to the rosehip and ruby chocolate cream with lemon mint posset, leaf crisps and rosehip gel. Gravetye's aristocratic global wine list is all about good breeding and glorious drinking, whether your taste is for a vintage Burgundy or a sprightly New World stripling. Bottles start at £29.
Chef/s: George Blogg. **Meals:** set L £48. Set D £80. Tasting menu £70 (5 courses) to £95. Sun L £55. **Details:** 60 seats. V menu. Vg menu. Bar. Wheelchairs. Parking. Children over 7 yrs.

East Lavant
The Royal Oak Inn
Cooking score: 2
Modern British | £35
Pook Lane, East Lavant, PO18 0AX
Tel no: 01243 527434
royaloakeastlavant.co.uk

Goodwood is just a few minutes' drive (and canter) from this proper village inn, where photos and pictures recall days of glory on both the motor and racing tracks. There are fires, two terraces, beams and cask ales (and room to stand and sup if you wish), but most of the place is laid up for dining. The kitchen plays the populist card with classy versions of fish and chips and burgers (beef or vegetarian), but the modern British repertoire is given much more of a workout. Chargrilled local asparagus arrives with nettle pesto and wild garlic houmous, the source ingredients shouting loudly. The daily blackboard offers up fish from the south coast ('wonderfully fresh' hake, say, with herb crust and cheesy risotto) but there are 30-day aged steaks or an assiette of cauliflower with nut butter. Finish with raspberry Eton mess with almond butter. A racy wine list opens at £20.
Chef/s: Jamie Bailey. **Meals:** main courses £16 to £30. Tasting menu £70 (6 courses). **Details:** 50 seats. 50 seats outside. Parking. Music.

Eastbourne
The Mirabelle
Cooking score: 3
Modern European | £46
The Grand Hotel, King Edward's Parade, Eastbourne, BN21 4EQ
Tel no: 01323 412345
grandeastbourne.com

'Grand, *adjective*: magnificent and imposing in appearance, size or style.' Fair enough then, for this hotel is the grandest address on the town's seafront, with its lustrous Victorian façade facing out to the Channel. The hotel's fine-dining Mirabelle has its own entrance and, please note, a dress code (jacket or collared shirt required; no T-shirts). The room doesn't lack for grandeur with its giant French doors and the sort of plush furnishings you don't see too often these days, and the 'terribly civilised' formal service suits the setting. Head chef Stephanie Malvoisin's fixed-price menus deal in classic European ideas with modern additions, to varying degrees of success. To start, seared mackerel and cod's cheek get support from fennel compôte, and rainbow radishes add colour to a plate of pig's head terrine. Move on to pink lamb rump with mint salsa verde, or mushroom ricotta cannelloni, and finish with a chilled chocolate fondant. The wine list is a big beast with scary prices.

Chef/s: Stephanie Malvoisin. **Closed:** Mon, Sun, 2 to 16 Jan. **Meals:** set L £23 (2 courses) to £28. Set D £39 (2 courses) to £46. Tasting menu £67 (7 courses). **Details:** 50 seats. Bar. Wheelchairs. Parking. Music.

▮ Fernhurst
The Duke of Cumberland Arms

Cooking score: 3
Modern British | £37
Henley Hill, Fernhurst, GU27 3HQ
Tel no: 01428 652280
dukeofcumberland.com

A pubby prospect to savour, this spruce Sussex hostelry charms visitors with its ponds, herb beds and tiered landscaped gardens overlooking the South Downs National Park – but that's just the beginning. Step inside and you'll find real ales drawn straight from the cask, log fires and gnarled beams aplenty in the bar, plus a smart rustic dining room housed in an extension – it's the best of both worlds. You can eat anywhere you like from a menu that pleases the lunchtime crowds while offering something more enterprising for those who come for dinner. Sourdough baguettes, fishcakes, bangers, beer-battered haddock and charcuterie boards keep those daytime hunger pangs at bay, while evening

meals move into the realms of steak tartare with truffle mayo, Moroccan lamb rump with couscous or south coast sea bass fillets with vegetable fricassée and sauce vierge. To finish, keep it homespun with apple and rhubarb crumble or change it up with a cleansing pineapple carpaccio. Well-chosen wines from £19.50.

Chef/s: Simon Goodman. **Closed:** 25 and 26 Dec. **Meals:** main courses £16 to £30. **Details:** 82 seats. 100 seats outside. Bar. Wheelchairs. Parking.

▮ Fletching

LOCAL GEM
The Griffin Inn

Modern European | £35
High Street, Fletching, TN22 3SS
Tel no: 01825 722890
thegriffininn.co.uk

£5 OFF 🛏

The 16th-century Griffin is a heady mix of characterful indoor spaces and expansive verdant garden (with peachy pastoral views), all underpinned by a sincere enthusiasm for food and drink. It's the real deal, whether you want just a pint of local ale by the fire, lunch in the garden or dinner in the dressed-up dining room. The kitchen shows mostly European leanings with the likes of crab and chive tortellini, gambas crostini and côtes de boeuf. The comprehensive wine list includes ample options by the glass.

▮ Haywards Heath
Jeremy's

Cooking score: 5
Modern European | £45
Borde Hill Garden, Balcombe Road, Haywards Heath, RH16 1XP
Tel no: 01444 441102
jeremysrestaurant.co.uk

£5 OFF

Whether you're gazing from the windows of the sunnily appointed dining room or eating outside surrounded by plants and greenery, the verdant delights of Borde Hill Garden are a huge bonus for visitors to Jeremy Ashpool's captivating restaurant. Overseen by head chef Jimmy Gray, the kitchen takes its cue from the seasons and makes full use of pickings from the Victorian walled garden, as well as tapping into the Sussex food network for South Downs lamb, south coast fish and local game. Expect bright, lively flavours and striking presentation from veal sweetbreads with ricotta and watercress verde to sea bream and Selsey crab accompanied by gnocchi, spinach and onion salsa. There's always something interesting for vegetarians (farro with mushrooms, chicory and caper salsa, for example), while desserts point up the odd creative surprise such as rhubarb semifreddo with beetroot and borage. A special tasting menu is served on the first Tuesday of each month, accompanied by astute wine pairings from a wide-ranging list that also includes some locally produced fizz.

Chef/s: Jimmy Gray. **Closed:** Mon. **Meals:** main courses £16 to £27. Set L and D £24 Tue to Thur (2 courses) to £29. Tasting menu £45 (5 courses). Sun L £37. **Details:** 52 seats. 40 seats outside. Bar. Wheelchairs. Parking. Music.

▌Horsham

Restaurant Tristan
Cooking score: 6
Modern British | £50
3 Stans Way, East Street, Horsham, RH12 1HU
Tel no: 01403 255688
restauranttristan.co.uk

A dozen years since opening his town-centre restaurant, Tristan Mason continues to enjoy strong local support. Found on the first floor of a 16th-century building, the impressively timbered and sensitively modernised dining room provides a stylish backdrop for Mason's bold, assured cooking. Loyal diners come back time and again for the likes of richly flavoured duck egg yolk and pork belly with smoked eel and leek, or brilliantly executed turbot with beef daube, allium and truffle. Concertedly seasonal set menus include pescatarian, vegetarian and vegan versions, with familiar

ideas typically forming the backbone. A winter dinner began with a beautifully presented scallop with Braeburn apple and salt-baked celeriac, then venison tartare with smoked beetroot and fermented red cabbage, before main-course suckling pig with pickled rhubarb and January king cabbage, rounding off with plum soufflé, caramel and fromage frais. The fixed-price format means there are no surprises when the bill comes and even markups on the up-to-the-minute wine list are gentle. Broken down by category, there's good choice by the glass and bottle (from £25).

Chef/s: Tristan Mason. **Closed:** Mon, Sun, 25 and 26 Dec, 1 Jan. **Meals:** set L £30 to £35. Set D £44 to £50. Tasting menu £70 (6 courses) to £90. **Details:** 34 seats. V menu. Vg menu. Bar. Music. Children over 10 yrs.

▌Hove

Chard
Cooking score: 2
Modern British | £32
31a Western Road, Hove, BN3 1AF
Tel no: 01273 027147
chardbrighton.co.uk
£5 OFF

Secreted on the first floor of a stylish homes boutique, this one-time nomadic pop-up has put down roots. Entering via the shop at night feels like accessing an illicit dining den, and the pared-back simplicity of the space and disarmingly engaging service add to the sense of intrigue. Local and seasonal produce is the kitchen's passion, with a café vibe for elevenses and lunch, and some pretty darn good cooking in the evening. Flavours are not shy, presentation is rustic and there are good ideas in abundance. An opening salvo of octopus is perfectly tender, fired up with red chillies and fennel, gurnard with blood orange and purple sprouting broccoli keeps things light and zingy, while maximum flavour is extracted from a rabbit leg with tarragon sauce and pancetta dumplings. Desserts such as

chocolate honey pie show real technical savvy. The concise wine list opens at £21 and stays reassuringly low.
Chef/s: Benny Sullivan. **Closed:** Mon, Tue, Sun, 24 Dec to 10 Feb, 2 weeks Aug. **Meals:** main courses £15 to £18. **Details:** 30 seats. Music.

Cin Cin
Cooking score: 2
Italian | £30
60 Western Road, Hove, BN3 1JD
Tel no: 01273 726047
cincin.co.uk

 £5 OFF £30

The second Cin Cin is a little larger than its sibling in Brighton's North Laine (see entry), but it has the same spirit, an open kitchen and equally impressive handmade pasta. Perch at the counter or at high tables and tuck into a selection of Italian salumi or small plates of lardo, honey and truffle pizzetta before heftier portions of pasta – buckwheat pizzoccheri with January king cabbage, fontina and Roscoff onion, say. The grill is fired up in the evening for the likes of gurnard with Jerusalem artichoke caponata, or game sausage with Castelluccio lentils, while weekend brunches bring on Tuscan pecorino with tomato conserve and pane carasau, although it's worth keeping an eye on the daily specials, too. Among desserts, muscovado zabaglione arrives with a bombolone doughnut. Regional Italian wines, creative aperitivi and some in-vogue vermouths go down a treat.
Chef/s: Jamie Halsall. **Closed:** Mon, 25 and 26 Dec, 1 Jan. **Meals:** main courses £11 to £14. **Details:** 38 seats. 20 seats outside. Music.

Etch
Cooking score: 5
Modern British | £55
216 Church Road, Hove, BN3 2DJ
Tel no: 01273 227485
etchfood.co.uk

Head to the western end of Church Road for Steven Edwards' pace-setting corner-site restaurant, formerly a bank, where globe

lighting, a smart bar and views into the kitchen from a dozen tables establish a smooth contemporary tone. The drill is monthly changing tasting menus only, of five, seven or nine courses of culinary exploration. Yeasty bread with seaweed butter opens proceedings on the right rustic note, then the menus take off into their tersely worded repertoires. Dishes look original, even startling, with strange shapes and vivid colours abounding, each founded, however, on the defiant simplicity of a partnering of two essential components – turbot and lettuce, scallop and cucumber, veal and turnip. Textures and temperatures are thoroughly investigated for the depth they can bring, and even a juxtaposition like manjari chocolate with pearl barley at dessert makes sense in the eating. There is a vegetarian version, too. Plenty of wines by the small glass, from £6, are worth a cheer, as well as an honour-roll listing of Sussex sparklers, but the wine pairings with the menus are undoubtedly the best way to go.
Chef/s: Steven Edwards and George Boa. **Closed:** Mon, Tue, Sun, 25 to 27 Dec, 1 to 3 Jan.
Meals: tasting menu £55 (5 courses) to £75.
Details: 32 seats. V menu. Music.

★ NEW ENTRY ★

Fourth & Church
Cooking score: 2
Modern European | £25
84 Church Road, Hove, BN3 2EB
Tel no: 01273 724709
fourthandchurch.co.uk

£5 OFF £30

In case you were wondering, that's Fourth & Church American style – you'll find it where Church Road meets Fourth Avenue. It's a casual space covering a lot of bases, even serving lunchtime sandwiches to savvy local workers, but it's better known as a bottle shop and tapas restaurant. Racks of wines and spirits make for a tempting display, and a switched-on team delivers small plates made from first-rate ingredients. Inspiration comes from all over, with a decidedly sunny

Mediterranean warmth to creamy burrata with smokey almonds, beetroot and braised endive, and Indian spicing in an inspired cauliflower construction. European charcuterie and British cheeses confirm the tapas status, while a trendy crispy hake taco includes 'gloriously addictive' chorizo jam and roasted jalapeño purée. Finish with an intriguing chocolate marquise with beetroot meringue and hibiscus jelly. The drinks list is as energised as the food, with cocktails, sherries, beers and wines chosen on merit.
Chef/s: Sam Pryor. **Meals:** tapas £8 to £15.
Details: 32 seats. 8 seats outside. Music.

The Ginger Pig
Cooking score: 3
Modern British | £35
3 Hove Street, Hove, BN3 2TR
Tel no: 01273 736123
gingermanrestaurants.com

It's now a pig of generous proportions: the savvy addition of 11 en suite bedrooms and a revamp of the bar and dining area have porked up Ben McKellar's seaside pub and brought a dose of boutique swagger to west Hove. Its leather banquettes and fashionably dark tones make for a suitably cognisant setting for some cracking contemporary food. A focus on European ideas sees smoked almond croquettes arriving in full-flavoured partnership with pickled pear and Cashel Blue, while some broader Asian and Middle Eastern flavours pop up too: the titular pig's head, nicely crisped, might come with peanut crackling, carrot, gochujang and golden raisin purée, or fillet of bream with couscous, confit fennel and crab bisque – all done with style in the delivery. A top-drawer burger and a souped-up pie – chicken and chorizo with smoked chilli gravy, say – are crowd-pleasing favourites. Finish with honey and almond cake with yoghurt parfait. Classic cocktails support the well-chosen wine list.
Chef/s: Robin Koehorst. **Meals:** main courses £13 to £40. Set L £16 (2 courses) to £18. **Details:** 80 seats. V menu. Bar. Music.

The Little Fish Market
Cooking score: 5
Seafood | £69
10 Upper Market Street, Hove, BN3 1AS
Tel no: 01273 722213
thelittlefishmarket.co.uk
£5 OFF

With its bold artworks, red quarry tiles, Ikea chairs and enamel light shades, this remarkable little restaurant trades on dressed-down simplicity. It's open for dinner only and there's a no-choice six-course tasting menu – but who cares when you can savour the finest local seafood cooked with real passion? Chef Duncan Ray works fastidiously in the tiny basement kitchen, while Rob Smith takes care of the 20-cover dining room. Blackboard menus are dictated by the catch and they're intended as a showcase for different cooking techniques (rather like a Japanese kaiseki banquet): 'raw' might mean mackerel with rhubarb, cucumber and mustard, 'grilled' could be sea bream in bouillabaisse, and the 'pan-fried' option could see cod matched with lardo, prawns and parsnip. Most dishes are innately straightforward – but make no mistake, this is seriously refined food notable for its clarity, freshness and balance. Occasionally there's a bit of meat, too, while dessert might be chocolate and cherry vacherin. The short, modern wine list naturally majors in fish-friendly whites, mostly from the Old World.
Chef/s: Duncan Ray. **Closed:** Mon, Sun, 2 weeks Sept, 1 week Dec to Jan, 1 week Apr. **Meals:** tasting menu £69 (6 courses). **Details:** 20 seats. Music.

The Urchin
Cooking score: 2
Seafood | £30
15-17 Belfast Street, Hove, BN3 3YS
Tel no: 01273 241881
urchinpub.co.uk
£30

This one-time backstreet boozer was revitalised in 2015. It's still very much a pub, but with a seafood-only menu and a focus on craft beers: it even has its own brewery, Larrikin, in the basement. The dining area, with its scrubbed wooden tables, on-point colours and rope light fittings, is full much of the time (the adjacent bar is frequently rammed, too), so book ahead if you can. The menu is backed up by blackboard specials, and when it comes to culinary inspiration, the world is seemingly their oyster: crab could be potted, the crispy soft-shelled variety given oomph by spicy rémoulade or served whole with butter, or in the gloriously messy Singapore style. Scallops, moules marinière, Malaysian prawns – there's no doubt that shellfish rules. Vegetarians get a couple of choices, but the only place you'll find meat is in a chorizo-studded prawn jambalaya. The solo dessert might be spiced poached pear. The wines list majors in whites, with plenty of options by the glass.

Chef/s: Sean Brailsford. **Closed:** Mon. **Meals:** main courses £11 to £35. **Details:** 40 seats. 40 seats outside. Bar. Music.

Wild Flor

Cooking score: 3
Modern European | £30
42 Church Road, Hove, BN3 2FN
Tel no: 01273 329111
wildflor.com
£30

The antithesis of style over substance, this newcomer on Hove's main drag has dodged passing bandwagons to deliver a repertoire inspired by the classics that's set to go the distance. The room is pleasant enough, with its neutral colour scheme and pub-style tables and chairs. If the menu isn't exactly a racy read, it sure delivers on flavour. A blackboard lists daily specials such as rack of lamb, served properly pink with earthy girolles, and a pretty much perfect lemon tart. The best bistro traditions of France combine with British and Spanish influences to deliver the likes of roasted quail with cherry purée and Ibérico pig's cheek to start, followed by gloriously fatty glazed beef brisket or fillet of brill with a

spider crab bisque that is punchy enough to stand on its own. The canny wine list includes sherries, cellar selections and sterling options by the glass and carafe.

Chef/s: Oliver Darby. **Closed:** Tue, Wed, 25 Dec. **Meals:** main courses £14 to £20. Set L £18 (2 courses) to £22. Sun L £28 (2 courses) to £33. **Details:** 38 seats. Music.

◼ Hurstpierpoint

LOCAL GEM

The Fig Tree

Modern British | £35
120 High Street, Hurstpierpoint, BN6 9PX
Tel no: 01273 832183
figtreerestaurant.co.uk

With the South Downs on its doorstep, it's only right that James and Jodie Dearden's charming village restaurant puts the region's bountiful produce front and centre on its appealing menus. There's refinement in the execution of the classically inspired dishes, with langoustine and Dover sole folded into agnolotti, and sirloin and cheek of beef served with beef dripping potato and onion fondants. Fish gets a good outing in a main of butter-poached turbot fillet, partnered by wild mushrooms, chargrilled Jerusalem artichoke and a wild mushroom velouté and, to finish, how about caramelised custard tart with baked apple sorbet? There's a tasting menu, and local wines get deserved attention.

◼ Lavant

The Earl of March

Cooking score: 2
Modern British | £35
Lavant Road, Lavant, PO18 0BQ
Tel no: 01243 533993
theearlofmarch.com

Locals are doubtless aware of how lucky they are to have a village inn that services both pub and restaurant requirements. Displays of silk flowers and Champagne bottles make clear the intent in the dining room – after all, The Earl is owned by a former executive chef of The

Ritz. Start with steamed mussels flavoured with cider, parsley and cream, roasted butternut squash arancini, or a still-bubbling baked Camembert infused with thyme. Well-presented main courses run to pot-roasted guinea fowl with creamy cep velouté, or dressed Selsey crab, with a classy version of beer-battered cod and chips ever present, while Sussex beef is the star of Sunday lunch. Among desserts, triple chocolate brownie with raspberry sorbet is 'oh so right'. The 'epic' view – as one first-time visitor had it – from the rear garden is of a glorious expanse of South Downs countryside across to Goodwood, perfect for a stroll either before or after. Sussex sparklers join mostly French wines on the well-judged list, which starts at £21.50.

Chef/s: Craig Lashly. **Closed:** 25 Dec. **Meals:** main courses £18 to £30. Set L and D £25 (2 courses) to £28. **Details:** 70 seats. 60 seats outside. Wheelchairs. Music.

◼ Lewes
Limetree Kitchen
Cooking score: 3
Modern British | £30
14 Station Street, Lewes, BN7 2DA
Tel no: 01273 478636
limetreekitchen.co.uk
🍴 £30

Housed in a converted tea room close to Lewes station, this unobtrusive little bistro looks just the ticket with its sun-bleached floorboards and wooden wall panels. Food-wise, it's all about small plates, with plenty of local and seasonal produce on show, whether your appetite is for vegetables, seafood or meat. A typical plant-based option is roasted green beans with okra, purple potatoes, samphire and chilli, while fish fans might prefer tempura of Devon hake with tartare sauce and pea shoots. The blackboard menu also lists platters of Sardinian salami and cured meats to share, although possibilities also extend to dry-aged Sussex steaks with bone marrow butter or a mini take on Chinese crispy duck involving confit leg, a bao bun, hoisin sauce,

cucumber and spring onions. Finish with homemade ice creams or opt for an assiette of chocolate. Wines are reasonably priced, but don't ignore the self-styled 'gin kitchen' with its bespoke small-batch sips.

Chef/s: Alex Von Riebech. **Closed:** Mon, Tue. **Meals:** small plates £7 to £17. **Details:** V menu.

◼ Lickfold
The Lickfold Inn
Cooking score: 4
Modern British | £48
Highstead Lane, Lickfold, GU28 9EY
Tel no: 01789 532535
thelickfoldinn.co.uk
£5 OFF

If the old bones of the 15th-century Lickfold Inn suggest a traditional pub experience, a glance at the bar snacks will put you right – chicken skin, yoghurt and pine is not something you'd have seen down the Dog & Duck. Executive chef Tom Sellers is the man behind south London's Restaurant Story (see entry), which has received its fair share of column inches since opening in 2013. Here in leafy Sussex, head chef Graham Squire ably interprets Sellers' vision, turning top-class regional ingredients into creative plates served in the rustic first-floor restaurant with its air of contemporary refinement. A strongly seasonal evening carte might see a starter of Cornish crab, with tapioca and radishes its modish accompaniments. Mains of sea bream with stuffed courgette flower or guinea fowl with potato and artichoke for two to share are less unexpected. Finish with raspberry macaroon with bitter chocolate and rose. While local ales add support to a classy wine list and lunch sees the carte joined by an appealing fixed-price option, the presence of a six-course tasting menu at dinner leaves you in no doubt that this isn't your average village boozer.

Chef/s: Tom Sellers and Graham Squire. **Closed:** Mon, Tue, Sun. **Meals:** main courses £24 to £30. Set L £24 (2 courses) to £30. Tasting menu £65 (6 courses). Sun L £30 (2 courses) to £40. **Details:** 38 seats. 30 seats outside. Bar. Wheelchairs. Parking. Music.

▌Rye
Landgate Bistro
Cooking score: 2
British | £34
5-6 Landgate, Rye, TN31 7LH
Tel no: 01797 222829
landgatebistro.co.uk
£5 OFF

Striding confidently into its 15th year, Martin Peacock and Nella Westin's cottage restaurant shows no signs of slowing down − 'a gem of a find' is one first-time visitor's heartfelt comment. The appealing menu will never shock or startle, but the food rings with a confident sense of place and season. Start with onion and Kentish cider soup (with Welsh rarebit), locally shot pigeon breast teamed with spiced breadcrumbs and hazelnuts or Rye Bay scallops with pork belly and a 'perfectly balanced' cauliflower panna cotta. As a main course, various cuts and treatments of salt marsh lamb arrive with carrot purée, wild leeks and potato gratin or there could be roast fillet of locally caught cod served with cod fritters, beach vegetables and chickpeas. To finish, prune and Armagnac crème brûlée makes for an impressive finish, that's if you've not been tempted by the selection of well-kept British cheeses. 'Weekend set lunch menus are good value', as is the sharp list of global wines.
Chef/s: Martin Peacock. **Closed:** Mon, Tue, 25 and 26 Dec, 31 Dec to 1 Jan, 1 week Jun. **Meals:** main courses £15 to £21. Set L £20 weekends (2 courses) to £24. Set D Wed and Thur £22 (2 courses) to £26. **Details:** 32 seats. Bar. Music.

▌Tangmere
Cassons
Cooking score: 3
Modern British | £43
Arundel Road, Tangmere, PO18 0DU
Tel no: 01243 773294
cassonsrestaurant.co.uk

A couple of converted 18th-century cottages beside the A27 (access is from the westbound carriageway) have been home to Viv and 'Cass' Casson's exemplary restaurant since 2003. She (Viv) cooks and he presides over front of house, a successful formula that has garnered a loyal local following. The dining areas are homely, traditional spaces, which makes the pin-sharp contemporary cooking all the more of a revelation. Making use of regional ingredients, New Zealander Viv turns out attractive plates with intelligent flavour combinations: egg yolk ravioli, say, with shaved truffle and frothy cep cappuccino, or how about Asian-inspired confit salmon, kohlrabi salad and puffed Thai rice? Iberian pork pluma might come dressed with a quince glaze, while fish and fowl are winningly united in a dish of halibut with confit chicken wings, chicken butter and caper sauce. Finish with lemon curd parfait, ginger cake and clementine gel. The helpful wine list covers most bases, opening at £24.
Chef/s: Vivian Casson. **Closed:** Mon, Tue, 24 to 30 Dec. **Meals:** set D £34 (2 courses) to £43. Sun L £24 (2 courses) to £30. **Details:** 36 seats. 12 seats outside.

▌Tillington
The Horse Guards Inn
Cooking score: 3
Modern British | £34
Upperton Road, Tillington, GU28 9AF
Tel no: 01798 342332
thehorseguardsinn.co.uk
£5 OFF 🛏

The seasons ring the changes at the 350-year-old Horse Guards, with the wonderful garden coming alive in warmer months (complete

with striped deck chairs, hammocks and roaming chickens), while chillier times bring the glow of log fires to the spruce rustic interior. It's a gem of a place, whenever you visit, and the changing seasons are reflected in the food, much of it local. Things can be as satisfyingly simple as Rother Valley organic beef sandwich with dill pickle and fries, or as refined as ravioli of native lobster. There are top-notch organic steaks, hung for 35 days, and rack of lamb with sweetbreads, smoked garlic and mint croquette. Wild mushroom trenne pasta with blue cheese velouté is an umami-powered delight. Among equally enticing desserts, rhubarb and custard Arctic roll is a winning mash-up. Drink Sussex beers or global wines from £19.50, then walk it all off in neighbouring Petworth Park.
Chef/s: Lee Cowan. **Closed:** 25 and 26 Dec. **Meals:** main courses £14 to £25. **Details:** 50 seats. 50 seats outside. Bar. Music.

■ West Ashling
The Richmond Arms
Cooking score: 4
Modern British | £34
Mill Road, West Ashling, PO18 8EA
Tel no: 01243 572046
therichmondarms.co.uk
£5 OFF 🛏

In a village some five miles north-west of Chichester, where a mill pond is guarded by seven soaring willow trees, William and Emma Jack's pub and restaurant is a thriving bastion of contemporary food. It's more restaurant than pub these days, but a couple of cask ales and a few stools at the bar do the job (or grab one of the tables out front), and an old Citroën van adds wood-fired pizzas to the mix on Friday and Saturday evenings. The main restaurant snakes around the main bar, and is the setting for William's compelling modern menu, executed with bravura. Start with hot Selsey crab perched atop a crumpet, or warm and runny chorizo Scotch egg. Flavours are robust and true – crispy aromatic guinea fowl, say, with refreshing green mango salad and 'blooming lovely' macadamia nut satay. Steaks

and fresh fish are cooked over fire and, to finish, a deep-fried custard dessert is 'just divine'. Natural wines pepper the list.
Chef/s: William Jack. **Closed:** Mon, Tue, 21 to 29 Oct, 23 Dec to 15 Jan. **Meals:** main courses £16 to £27. Set L £17 (2 courses) to £20. **Details:** 40 seats. 40 seats outside. V menu. Vg menu. Bar. Wheelchairs. Parking. Music.

■ West Hoathly
The Cat Inn
Cooking score: 1
Modern British | £28
North Lane, West Hoathly, RH19 4PP
Tel no: 01342 810369
catinn.co.uk
£5 OFF 🛏 £30

A hilltop village high on a spur of the Sussex Weald provides the backdrop for this 16th-century tile-hung pub – a proper rural hostelry complete with an inglenook fireplace, gnarled beams and local ales on draught. You can eat in the bar, although most people head to the sizeable dining area at the back – especially on fine days, when the doors are flung open and the terrace comes into its own. Either way, expect a mix of sturdy pub classics alongside rustic dishes with eclectic overtones. Tapas boards and venison Scotch eggs with celeriac rémoulade could give way to cod with Toulouse sausage and butter bean cassoulet. After that, take comfort from blackberry trifle or raspberry Bakewell tart. Decently priced wines include an impressive choice by the glass or carafe.
Chef/s: Alex Jacquemin. **Meals:** main courses £14 to £26. **Details:** 80 seats. 45 seats outside. Wheelchairs. Parking. Children over 7 yrs.

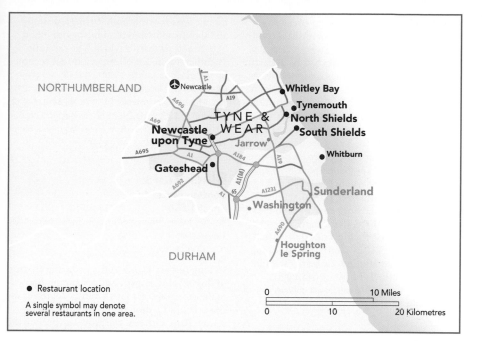

NORTHUMBERLAND

Newcastle

Whitley Bay
Tynemouth
North Shields
South Shields

Newcastle upon Tyne

TYNE & WEAR

Jarrow

Whitburn

Gateshead

Sunderland

Washington

DURHAM

Houghton le Spring

● Restaurant location

A single symbol may denote several restaurants in one area.

0 — 10 Miles

0 — 10 — 20 Kilometres

Gateshead
Eslington Villa

Cooking score: 2
Modern British | £32
8 Station Road, Low Fell, Gateshead, NE9 6DR
Tel no: 0191 487 6017
eslingtonvilla.co.uk

Beautifully secluded, this substantial suburban Victorian villa feels a world away from the bustle of Newcastle and Gateshead. Now a long-established hotel and restaurant, it is enjoying new life under new owners, although Jamie Walsh still heads up the kitchen. The smart conservatory dining room overlooks attractive sloped gardens, and makes for a pleasant spot for lunch when the good-value set menu might include chicken escalope with lyonnaise potatoes, curly kale and tarragon. At dinner, lamb spring roll partnered by mint, cauliflower, mooli and sesame seeds might be followed by braised beef cheeks with creamed potatoes, savoy cabbage and onion sauce or sea trout and olive oil crushed potatoes with cauliflower purée. Vanilla and ginger cheesecake with rhubarb compôte and ice cream is one way to finish, or look to the French and English cheeses, served with apple, red wine jelly and crackers. Wines from £19.95.
Chef/s: Jamie Walsh. **Meals:** main courses £16 to £24. Set L and early D £17 (2 courses) to £20.
Details: 100 seats. 30 seats outside. Bar. Wheelchairs. Parking. Music.

★ NEW ENTRY ★

Träkol

Cooking score: 3
Modern British | £30
Hillgate Quays, Gateshead, NE8 2BH
Tel no: 0191 737 1120
bytheriverbrew.co

In a cluster of rusty shipping units beneath the Tyne Bridge, this 'open fire' restaurant is part of a growing container community that includes a brewery and bustling street-food market. Träkol (charcoal in Swedish) is run by hip By The River Brew Co., whose craft ales form a large part of the drinks list. As befits the name, the philosophy brings robust outdoor cooking indoors – diners are separated from the kitchen by a protective glass wall through which they can watch the chefs cook prime cuts of British rare breed meat over the flames and smouldering coals. What are described as small plates turn out to be generous portions of such good things as grilled pork jowl and XO slaw, although signature feasting dishes to share – perhaps a 1kg beef T-bone with wild mushrooms, smoked bone marrow and fries – could easily feed three, if not four. Sea trout with cider-pickled cockles and coal-roasted leeks is a winning fishy alternative. Bookings one of the prized window tables to catch the sun setting on the Tyne. Wine from £17.

Chef/s: Tony Renwick. **Meals:** main courses £11 to £26. **Details:** 58 seats. Bar. Wheelchairs. Music.

▌ Newcastle upon Tyne

21

Cooking score: 3
Modern British | £38
Trinity Gardens, Quayside, Newcastle upon Tyne, NE1 2HH
Tel no: 0191 222 0755
21newcastle.co.uk

Terry Laybourne's flagship bistro has occupied its spacious home on Trinity Gardens ('not the easiest spot to find') for three decades and is still one of the top performers in Newcastle's lively Quayside quarter ('no pretence of scenic views'). Diners enjoy the buzz of the place, the sleek surrounds and the highly polished approach, but the real attraction is Chris Dobson's big-city food – a clever amalgam of local flavours and ingredients combined with ideas from further afield. Lindisfarne oysters are served with spicy sausages, Northumbrian game is transformed into a terrine, and Craster kippers appear in a warm salad with ratte potatoes and a poached egg. To follow, there are cuts of Himalayan salt-aged beef, monkfish osso buco or roasted hake with caramelised roots, brown shrimps, scallops and shellfish vinaigrette. Finish with blood orange and rhubarb pavlova. The carefully assembled wine list offers an admirable choice by the glass or carafe.

Chef/s: Chris Dobson. **Closed:** 25 and 26 Dec, 1 Jan. **Meals:** main courses £17 to £38. Set L £20 (2 courses) to £25. Early D £21 (2 courses) to £26. Sun L £27. **Details:** 120 seats. V menu. Vg menu. Bar. Wheelchairs. Music.

Blackfriars

Cooking score: 1
British | £50
Friars Street, Newcastle upon Tyne, NE1 4XN
Tel no: 0191 261 5945
blackfriarsrestaurant.co.uk

Its long history is one of the enduring charms of this 'absolutely brilliant' restaurant, housed in the refectory of a 13th-century Dominican friary behind a shopping centre in the city centre. Run with real warmth – it's been in the same hands since 2001 – loyal fans come as much for the hospitality as for the impeccably seasonal cooking. Winning dishes might include charred local mackerel with poached egg, crisp brown shrimps and dill or rare breed pork chop with caramelised onion, smoked potato mash and wild garlic. Desserts such as rhubarb soufflé crumble continue the theme, while drinks run from local beers to an affordable list of well-chosen wines.

Chef/s: Christopher Wardale. **Closed:** bank hols. **Meals:** main courses £15 to £34. Set L £15 (2 courses) to £18. Early D £18 (2 courses) to £21. Sun L £21. **Details:** 85 seats. 16 seats outside. Bar.

The Broad Chare

Cooking score: 4
Modern British | £35
25 Broad Chare, Newcastle upon Tyne, NE1 3DQ
Tel no: 0191 211 2144
thebroadchare.co.uk

With a ground-floor bar dispensing real ales, a Dickensian-style chophouse dining room above, this converted 18th-century warehouse certainly lives up to owner Terry Laybourne's description of 'proper pub, proper beer, proper food'. It's to be found in a quiet side street next to the city's quayside law courts and certainly has broad appeal, with its nose-to-tail treatment of impeccable local ingredients. A daily dish of the day – from Monday's mince and dumplings right through to Sunday's roast beef – is supplemented by specials such as devilled lamb's kidneys on toast and game pie for two to share. Elsewhere, a small plate of crispy pig's head and sauce gribiche might give way to steamed Shetland mussels with wheat beer and smoked bacon. Desserts are of the comforting variety, perhaps egg custard tart with Yorkshire rhubarb or ginger sponge with milk ice cream and butterscotch. If you can resist the excellent beer list, wines start at £19.

Chef/s: Dan Warren. **Closed:** 25 and 26 Dec, 1 Jan. **Meals:** main courses £11 to £25. **Details:** 74 seats.

Cal's Own

Cooking score: 1
Italian | £20
1-2 Holly Avenue West, Newcastle upon Tyne, NE2 2AR
Tel no: 0191 281 5522
calsown.co.uk
£30

With accreditation from the auspicious Associazione Verace Pizza Napoletana under his belt, joiner-turned-cook Cal Kitchin is now starting to push the pizza envelope – using techniques old and new, importing provisions from Campania, deploying local produce and blasting his pizzas at 260°C in a hand-built Stefano Ferrara oven from Naples. Cal's Own calzone obviously makes an appearance, while those wanting something 'not pizza' might graze on small plates such as spicy pig's cheeks or baked clams with bacon. After that, how about tiramisu or peanut butter pie? Drink Italian regional wine by the glass or craft beer by the bottle.

Chef/s: Calvin Kitchin. **Closed:** Mon, Tue. **Meals:** main courses £8 to £15. **Details:** 50 seats. 12 seats outside. Wheelchairs. Parking. Music.

Cook House

Cooking score: 2
Modern British | £30
Foundry Lane, Newcastle upon Tyne, NE6 1LH
Tel no: 07990 972009
cookhouse.org
£5 OFF   £30

What started life as a supper club run from two shipping containers has grown into one of the city's most talked about restaurants. Local food blogger Anna Hedworth has moved the operation to a two-storey bricks and mortar site around the corner and the transition has been seamless. Hedworth no longer cooks solo, having swapped her domestic oven for a professional kitchen including a barbecue and a team of chefs, and there's no doubt the food is more creative than before. Korean BBQ chicken skewers with black sesame and gochujang aïoli could lead on to braised octopus and butter beans in romesco sauce with sourdough toast, or BBQ lamb chops served with fermented carrot yoghurt, Israeli couscous, charred greens and salsa verde. Finish with spiced poached pear in red wine with toasted hazelnuts, crème fraîche and mint. A concise wine list opens at £18.

Chef/s: Anna Hedworth. **Closed:** Mon,1 week Jan, 1 week Aug. **Meals:** main courses £14 to £18. **Details:** 60 seats. 30 seats outside. Bar. Wheelchairs. Music.

House of Tides

Cooking score: 5
Modern British | £65
28-30 The Close, Newcastle upon Tyne, NE1 3RF
Tel no: 0191 230 3720
houseoftides.co.uk

Chef Kenny Atkinson returned to his Geordie roots when he took over this Grade II-listed merchant's house on Newcastle's Quayside, and he has managed to retain the building's historic aura while serving food that feels totally in tune with our times. Kick off in style with a cocktail in the ground-floor bar (all flagstone floors and mullioned windows),

before ascending to the main dining room – a mix of contemporary chic and urban heritage tones. Multi-course tasting menus are the only way to go, with high levels of creativity, modish presentation and a devotion to seasonal North Country produce typifying every plate. Dish descriptions don't give much away ('scallop, pork belly, sweetcorn and lardo', 'mussels, leek, sea purslane and caviar' etc), but the results are eye-opening, complex and harmonious. Servings of fermented rye bread follow a sequence of appetisers (Parmesan churro with onion and truffle or a tiny smoked cod's roe tart), while desserts such as a combo of apple, almond and marigold make an appearance as the culinary compass turns towards sweetness. The well-travelled wine list is full of possibilities from £30 up.
Chef/s: Kenny Atkinson. **Closed:** Mon, Sun, last week Dec, first week Jan. **Meals:** tasting menu L £55 (5 courses) to £80 and D £65 (5 courses) to £90. **Details:** 50 seats. Bar. Wheelchairs. Parking. Music. Children over 9 yrs.

The Patricia
Cooking score: 3
Modern European | £35
139 Jesmond Road, Newcastle upon Tyne, NE2 1JY
Tel no: 0191 281 4443
the-patricia.com
£5 OFF

Although it's hard by traffic-clogged Jesmond Road, the interior of this candlelit neighbourhood bistro immediately whisks you abroad with its dark floorboards and Gallic posters on aubergine-toned walls. Durham-born chef proprietor Nick Grieves named the place after his grandmother, and his ingredient-led cooking reflects time spent in high-profile kitchens such as The River Café (see entry) – hence Italian-accented dishes such as pappardelle with fennel sausage ragù or Cornish cod with lardo, Castelluccio lentils and January king cabbage. Elsewhere, tuna crudo comes dressed with roasted peppers and sudachi ponzu, while guinea fowl is cooked 'au Riesling' with wild mushrooms and ratte

potatoes. To start, nibble on Cantabrian anchovies or soft sopressa all'Amarone salame; to finish, try the unusual cherry pavlova with goat's curd and kombucha or stay with the Italian theme by ordering tiramisu. The enterprising wine list focuses on low-intervention and small-batch producers (mostly from Europe), with prices from £21.50 (£5 a glass).
Chef/s: Nick Grieves. **Closed:** Mon, Tue. **Meals:** main courses £16 to £24. Set D £20 (2 courses) to £25. Tasting menu £50 (8 courses). **Details:** 32 seats. Music.

Peace & Loaf
Cooking score: 4
Modern British | £60
217 Jesmond Road, Newcastle upon Tyne, NE2 1LA
Tel no: 0191 281 5222
peaceandloaf.co.uk
£5 OFF

The peripheral location and idiosyncratic approach to contemporary decor make this restaurant a surprising find but chef owner David Coulson has made it work well for the past seven years. Relaxed, on-point service is matched by the refined, innovative cooking of this former finalist in *MasterChef: The Professionals*, and bold seasonal flavours come to the fore whether you order from the carte, tasting menu or prix fixe. While key ingredients might be regional, the influence is global, as in a starter of Japanese rice pudding, shimeji mushrooms, sunflower seeds and chestnut, an Asian theme that continues with a main course of char siu-style Ibérico pork, cheek, belly and bao scallop. Lamb, artichoke, tongue, brown shrimp and purslane followed by Dover sole, French onion, baby gem and oyster is another route to follow. Either way, a closing rhubarb and custard puff pastry scented with star anise is a standout dessert. A lively wine list opens at £19.
Chef/s: David Coulson. **Closed:** Sun. **Meals:** main courses £22 to £28. Set L and early D £25 to £30. Tasting menu £80 (10 courses). **Details:** 60 seats. Bar. Wheelchairs. Parking. Music.

Route

Cooking score: 3
Modern British | £28
35 Side, Newcastle upon Tyne, NE1 3JE
Tel no: 0191 222 0973
routenewcastle.co.uk
£5 OFF £30

Close to the Tyne Bridge in the lively Quayside area, this modern bistro opened in May 2018 and has quickly made its mark on the city's dining scene, particularly with lawyers and office workers from the courts and chambers around the corner. It's a narrow, deep room with a relaxed, urban vibe and whitewashed brick walls, concrete floor and bistro furniture. Chef owner John Calton splits his time between here and his North Shields pub, The Staith House (see entry) and the concept is seasonal small plates in the modern European style showcasing local fish and nose-to-tail meat. The set menu offers notable value, although staff are happy for diners to mix and match with the main carte. Lamb sweetbreads might make an appearance with salt-baked turnip, mint and pickled carrot before a main of wild North Sea turbot, white asparagus, brown butter hollandaise and almonds. Finish with salted caramel chocolate mousse, honeycomb and fresh cherries. An interesting global wine list arranged by style opens at £19.50.
Chef/s: John Calton. **Closed:** Tue, first 2 weeks Jan, second and third weeks Jun. **Meals:** main courses £12 to £25. Set D £15 Mon to Fri. Sun L £28. **Details:** 35 seats. Music. No children after 6.30pm.

£5 voucher
£5 OFF Restaurants showing this symbol are participating in our £5 voucher scheme, redeemable against a meal for two or more. Vouchers can be found at the back of this book.

Bistro Forty Six

Modern British | £34
46 Brentwood Avenue, Newcastle upon Tyne, NE2 3DH
Tel no: 0191 281 8081
bistrofortysix.co.uk

In a row of suburban shops and bars close to the West Jesmond Metro station, Max and Ben Gott's no-frills bistro continues to widen its appeal. Game shot by the chefs themselves on newly acquired land indicates a kitchen that has become increasingly self-sufficient, with locally foraged ingredients popping up on the concise seasonal menu, too. Pheasant bonbon, celeriac and crispy onions could be followed by lamb rump, braised leeks, creamed potato and jus. Puddings include beetroot and chocolate brownie. A concise European wine list starts at £16.95.

Dobson & Parnell

Modern British | £39
21 Queen Street, Newcastle upon Tyne, NE1 3UG
Tel no: 0191 221 0904
dobsonandparnell.co.uk

'A great blend of fine dining in casual surroundings' was the verdict of one visitor to this spacious brasserie standing in the shadows of the Tyne Bridge close to Newcastle's quayside. Named after the two Victorian architects who designed the original building, this tile-clad dining room with its leather banquettes and dark wood floorboards keeps the cooking simple via North Sea fishcakes, roast cauliflower risotto, chargrilled steaks and comforting puddings such as sticky toffee pudding, salt caramel and vanilla ice cream. Global wines from £22.50 (£5 a glass).

READERS RECOMMEND

READERS RECOMMEND
Harissa Kitchen
31-33 Starbeck Avenue, Newcastle upon Tyne, NE2 1RJ
Tel no: 0191 261 5501
harissakitchen.co.uk

'Harissa is an absolute gem! Everything is carefully crafted and the food is local where possible. A small plate of cured sardines with crispy aubergine was delicious as was the lamb shawarma. We finished with a zingy grapefruit posset and some handmade chocolates. Service was relaxed but efficient. Can't fault it.'

◼ North Shields
The Staith House
Cooking score: 2
Modern British | £30
57 Low Lights, Fish Quay, North Shields, NE30 1JA
Tel no: 0191 270 8441
thestaithhouse.co.uk

On the less beachy side of Shields, a former fisherman's pub is now a beacon for good food on the quays. Boozier days are honoured with well-kept beers and a polished pubby interior (tasteful maritime knick-knacks a house speciality), and Sunday lunch is a draw. Chefs and co-owners John Calton and James Laffan focus on robust dishes that favour local seafood without letting it dominate. Snacks might be a corned beef fritter with grain mustard or a couple of Lindisfarne oysters. Grilled langoustines with chilli butter or seared ox tongue with heritage tomatoes and horseradish yoghurt are a good way to start proceedings proper, and mains offer the opportunity to give the kitchen a workout, perhaps with turbot with cauliflower and a black pudding and prawn fritter, or keep it simple with fish and chips. Desserts, including lemon posset, are straightforward and none the worse for it, while wine starts at £18.

Chef/s: John Calton and James Laffan. **Closed:** 25 and 26 Dec. **Meals:** main courses £13 to £26. Tasting menu £70 (9 courses). Sun L £26. **Details:** 45 seats. 40 seats outside. Wheelchairs. Parking. Music. No children after 7.30pm.

◼ South Shields
LOCAL GEM
Colmans
Seafood | £20
182-186 Ocean Road, South Shields, NE33 2JQ
Tel no: 0191 456 1202
colmansfishandchips.co.uk

£30

A South Shields institution, this family-run fish restaurant (since 1926) is a real crowd-puller – filled with regulars who appreciate the prompt and courteous service, and the fact that it stays true to its chippy origins. The fish is fresh, cooked to order and comes in generous servings: cod, plaice, hake, lemon sole or haddock fried in the lightest of batters or simply grilled with fresh herb butter. Finish with treacle sponge and custard – if you have room. Wines from £15.95.

◼ Tynemouth
Riley's Fish Shack
Cooking score: 2
Seafood | £25
King Edward's Bay, Tynemouth, NE30 4BY
Tel no: 0191 257 1371
rileysfishshack.com

£30

Although famous locally for curating street food and live music events, the owners of this glass-fronted shipping container facing the North Sea have attracted nationwide acclaim for their simple seasonal seafood. The day's dishes (and service times) often depend on the catch, and the blackboard menu is a rapidly depleted movable feast taking in everything from Lindisfarne oysters Rockefeller, bang-bang monkfish kebabs and pan-roasted whole plaice to the house speciality – seasonal chargrilled fish wraps in wood-fired flatbread. The food is conveniently served in cardboard cartons and wines are poured into plastic tumblers, so it's easy to take your lunch on to the tarpaulin-covered terrace or even trek down to the beach.

Chef/s: James Shaw. **Meals:** main courses £14 to £42. **Details:** 15 seats. 50 seats outside. Music. No reservations.

■ Whitburn

LOCAL GEM

Latimer's Seafood

Seafood | £25
Shell Hill, Bents Road, Whitburn, SR6 7NT
Tel no: 0191 529 2200
latimers.com

£30

With no bookings, it's first come, first served at ex-fisherman Robert Latimer's popular beachside café (which comes with its own wet-fish counter). Early birds bag the decked terrace with its wonderful views. Start with garlic king prawns or crab and whisky soup, while for mains, share one of the seafood platters or indulge in a pile of local langoustines bathed in melted butter. The day's catch is chalked up on the board outside and cooked 'naked' en papillote. House wines start at £16.50.

■ Whitley Bay

The Roxburgh

Cooking score: 2
British | £30
4 Roxburgh House, Park Avenue, Whitley Bay, NE26 1DQ
Tel no: 0191 253 1661

£30

Only its architect could love the red-brick block that The Roxburgh calls home, but that matters not a jot when you cross the threshold and enter Gary Dall's sanctum of nose-to-tail dining. There's a speakeasy vibe, a boho feel and a blackboard menu showing what you'll be feasting on that day. This is soul-nourishing

stuff, where bone marrow arrives with green sauce, parsley salad and toast (yours for a fiver), and local Lindisfarne oysters get fired up with black vinegar and chilli salt. Hake with mussels and creamed leeks is simple stuff done so well, and the same goes for pork belly partnered with white beans, egg yolk and croque-señor. Finish with The Stoner's Delight Vol. 3, a moreish chocolate and honeycomb confection, or the less mysterious cheeseboard served with lavash. They have a full licence now and a new bar, with wines kicking off at £17.

Chef/s: Gary Dall. **Closed:** Mon, Tue, Wed, 1 to 26 Jan. **Meals:** main courses £15 to £21. **Details:** 24 seats. Music.

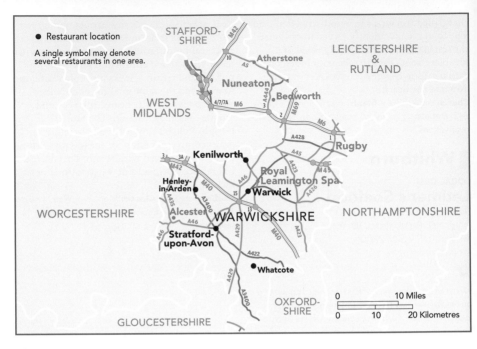

■ Henley-in-Arden
Cheal's of Henley
Cooking score: 5
Modern British | £45
64 High Street, Henley-in-Arden, B95 5BX
Tel no: 01564 793856
chealsofhenley.co.uk

£5
OFF

The ancient black and white timbered building on the main street of an equally ancient well-heeled market town is both relaxed enough for a lingering lunch and formal enough to make an evening here an occasion. Matt Cheal's careful, craftsmanlike cooking matches the compact set of comfortable beamed and timbered rooms. You'll find a good balance of flavours in a dish of guinea fowl served with intense smoked beetroot, toasted barley, cauliflower and tarragon with a slick of rich, sticky jus. Cotswold venison loin, cooked perfectly pink, is accompanied by a delicious humble pie flaunting exemplary pastry and served with yeasted pomme purée, cabbage and Madeira sauce. Our January lunch opened with whipped chicken livers topped with tiny diced pineapple, pomegranate, chicory and paper-thin slices of red onion, and a thyme-flavoured 'hobnob' biscuit on the side; it finished with a beautifully risen kaffir lime soufflé with coconut sorbet. An excellent wine list spreads its wings confidently, with good choice under £40.

Chef/s: Matt Cheal. **Closed:** Mon, Tue, 25 and 26 Dec, 1 to 17 Jan, 1 week Easter. **Meals:** set L £25 (2 courses) to £33. Set D £36 (2 courses) to £55. Tasting menu £77 (6 courses). Sun L £33. **Details:** 45 seats. V menu. Music.

Vegetarian and vegan
While many restaurants offer dishes suitable for non-meat eaters, those marked 'V menu' (vegetarian) and 'Vg menu' (vegan) offer separate menus.

▌Kenilworth

The Cross at Kenilworth

Cooking score: 6
Modern British | £55
16 New Street, Kenilworth, CV8 2EZ
Tel no: 01926 853840
thecrosskenilworth.co.uk
£5 OFF

'Everything was right, from the quality of the ingredients, to the presentation, to the orchestration of flavours,' observed one visitor to this undeniably upmarket pub restaurant. The interior – exposed stonework, leather banquettes, rich red walls – feels inviting, informal and closer to a pub than the cooking, the latter frequently summed up in readers' dispatches as 'superb'. Adam Bennett is adept at elevating classic and traditional dishes, note tartare of Cornish lamb enlivened with pickled mushrooms, anchovy mayonnaise, crispy quinoa, peppery leaves and spelt crackers, and a main of slow-cooked pork belly teamed with smoked pineapple, purple sprouting broccoli, chilli, sweet potato and tamarind. There are separate vegetarian and vegan menus (think artichoke soup with pear and hazelnuts, then roast king oyster mushroom with lentils, celeriac, baby onions and shallot vinaigrette) and for dessert Yorkshire rhubarb crumble soufflé with stem ginger ice cream and rhubarb sauce, or a floating island with caramel ice cream, almonds and vanilla sauce. Care and skill has been lavished on a wine list that delivers a good mix of classics and lesser-known finds, including organic and biodynamic options.
Chef/s: Adam Bennett. **Closed:** Mon, bank hols, 25 and 26 Dec, 1 Jan. **Meals:** main courses £27 to £34. Set L £33. Tasting menu £45 (6 courses) to £75. Sun L £30. **Details:** 83 seats. V menu. Vg menu. Bar. Wheelchairs. Parking. Music.

▌Shipston-on-Stour

READERS RECOMMEND

El Cafe

Spanish
6 New Street, Shipston-on-Stour, Warwickshire
Tel no: 01608 238494
elcafe.co.uk
'One of the best tapas bars we have eaten at and we go to Spain a lot. Don't miss the slow-roasted Ibérico ribs and the cheese croquetas. The courtyard is perfect on sunny days.'

▌Stratford-upon-Avon

No. 9 Church St

Cooking score: 2
British | £35
9 Church Street, Stratford-upon-Avon, CV37 6HB
Tel no: 01789 415522
no9churchst.com

'Faultless experience… can't beat it,' notes a visitor to Wayne Thomson's little restaurant in the heart of town. It takes up the first and second floors of a 400-year-old listed building decked out in rich shades of brown, gold and burgundy, with exposed oak beams and an ancient brick fireplace. Thomson prides himself on creating seasonal British dishes: one lunch, which took in cod cheeks in katsu sauce, navarin of lamb and a deconstructed lemon cheesecake, was declared great value. There's an early evening set menu, too, ideal for pre-theatre dinner. Things shift up a gear later on with the likes of hot game pie with pickled rhubarb, chicory and walnuts, and Cornish lamb noisette with salt-baked celeriac, sweetbreads, sticky chestnuts, wild mushrooms and red cabbage. Desserts such as vanilla-poached rhubarb with a custard slice and blood orange ice cream put a fun spin on a classic, while the wine list focuses on artisan finds at reasonable prices.
Chef/s: Wayne Thomson. **Closed:** Mon, Sun, 25 to 27 Dec. **Meals:** main courses £15 to £23. Set L and early D £16 (2 courses) to £21. Tasting menu £43 (5 courses) to £65. **Details:** 30 seats. Vg menu. Bar. Music.

Salt

Cooking score: 6
Modern British | £50
8 Church Street, Stratford-upon-Avon,
CV37 6HB
Tel no: 01789 263566
salt-restaurant.co.uk
£5
OFF

Paul Foster's pace-setting venue sits in the heart of this heritage-laden town, not far from the school where its most famous scion learned his grammar. The menus have been retooled into a brace of tasting menus (five courses or eight) and a short carte limited to two choices at each stage. Artfully presented dishes on bespoke crockery look intriguing, and their exploratory approaches mobilise today's preferences for curing and pickling, with umami-rich seasonings and saucing to emphasise rather than compete. Cured John Dory and cucumber are cooked in dashi and served with a Douglas fir emulsion, prior to Goosnargh duck with a purée of Roscoff onions and flavours of malt loaf, or roast cod and mussels with cauliflower and brandade. Textures and temperatures work in carefully considered balance, through to one of the famous rhubarb desserts, perhaps with buttermilk parfait, thyme meringue and almonds, or the innovative chocolate sorbet with caramelised white chocolate and goat's milk jelly. Cocktails bring youthful appeal to a drinks list that progresses to a small collection of wines that cover the major production regions, with glasses from £6.
Chef/s: Paul Foster. **Closed:** Mon, Tue, 23 Dec to 8 Jan, 1 week Apr. **Meals:** set L £23 (2 courses) to £28. Set D £43 (2 courses) to £50. Tasting menu L £50 (6 courses) and D £58 (5 courses) to £75. Sun L £30 (2 courses) to £35. **Details:** 34 seats. V menu. Music.

★ BEST NEW ENTRY, UK ★

The Woodsman

Cooking score: 4
British | £40
4 Chapel Street, Stratford-upon-Avon,
CV37 6HA
Tel no: 01789 331535
thewoodsmanrestaurant.co.uk

Shakespeare's birthplace counts on many places to eat, but they are geared towards day-tripping tourists, so Mike Robinson's collaboration with Hotel Indigo is a welcome beacon of hospitality. The co-owner of London's Harwood Arms (see entry) has created a smart-casual place with an urban vibe that suits this ancient building with its impressive timbered frontage dating from the 17th century. Venture into the stylish modern extension to see the wood-fired oven that is at the heart of the operation. Passion for quality runs through every aspect, from the focaccia and sourdough that open a meal, via a delicate crab tart piled with brown shrimps, cubes of cucumber and apple and a dab of mayonnaise to wood-roasted hake served with sweet pipérade, aïoli and a tangle of shaved kohlrabi and grilled squid. Wood-roasted venison and beef are strengths, perhaps pavé of 40-day aged Hereford beef, its superb flavour and texture nicely offset by a richly meaty faggot, with a 'dirty mash' heavy with butter and gravy the perfect accompaniment. Round off with a delicately flavoured strawberry mousse with crumbled pistachio cake and elderflower sorbet. As for drinks, it's hard to say no to the cocktail trolley, although wines, arranged by style, have a global reach with plenty by the glass (from £4.50).
Chef/s: Mike Robinson and Jon Coates.
Meals: main courses £17 to £23. **Details:** Bar.

◼ Warwick
Tailors
Cooking score: 3
Modern British | £35
22 Market Place, Warwick, CV34 4SL
Tel no: 01926 410590
tailorsrestaurant.co.uk

'From the moment we walked in, the service was fun, relaxed, impeccable... the food was incredible, brilliantly balanced, well thought out and exceptionally executed.' Praise indeed for this intimate, well-established town-centre restaurant. Mark Fry and Dan Cavell's cooking combines modern British ideas with obvious panache, featuring dishes such as quail (breast and confit leg) with celeriac, apple and vanilla chutney, and smoked haddock with pearl barley risotto on the good-value lunch menu. It's a six-course tasting menu in the evening, when mushroom, Parmesan and truffle quiche might be followed by sea trout served in a Thai green emulsion with coconut and sweet-and-sour chilli before venison haunch and ragù with neeps and tatties. Bargain no-choice three-course dinners are worth clearing Wednesday and Thursday diary space for. There's homemade soda bread and butter, too, and desserts such as vanilla cheesecake adorned with rhubarb and pistachios. Wines start at £19.95.
Chef/s: Dan Cavell and Mark Fry. **Closed:** Mon, Sun, 23 to 31 Dec. **Meals:** set L £18 (2 courses) to £22. Set D £35 Wed and Thur. Tasting menu £40 (6 courses) to £55. **Details:** 30 seats. V menu. Music. Children over 10 yrs.

◼ Whatcote
The Royal Oak
Cooking score: 5
British | £45
2 Upper Farm Barn, Whatcote, CV36 5EF
Tel no: 01295 688100
theroyaloakwhatcote.co.uk

When it comes to box-ticking country pub attributes, this ancient hostelry seems to have them all: gnarled beams, a drinkers' bar with

craft beers and real ales, pub quizzes and music nights. But when it comes to food, The Oak may 'sound like a pub but it's not', the airy modern dining room creating a setting that's more serious restaurant than local boozer. A relaxed professionalism helps to set the tone for Richard Craven's highly innovative, highly seasonal food. It is presented with a light touch and Craven obviously enjoys layering dishes with contrasting textures and carefully nuanced flavours – say pigeon raviolo with celeriac enriched by a pigeon and Armagnac consommé. Or for main course, when fish and shellfish from Cornwall – pollack and mussels – are teamed with cauliflower and monk's beard in a curried dressing. Otherwise, there could be hay-smoked hogget with wild garlic, stuffed morel and ewe's milk cheese. Breads include fantastic wholemeal with farmhouse butter and pork dripping, while a dark chocolate and caramel shortbread with peanut ice cream makes a perfect finale. A brief wine list (from £22) offers good choice by the glass.
Chef/s: Richard Craven. **Closed:** Mon, Tue. **Meals:** main courses £20 to £26. Set L and D £24 (2 courses) to £29. Tasting menu £55 (5 courses). Sun L £29 (2 courses) to £35. **Details:** 35 seats. Bar. Wheelchairs. Parking. Music.

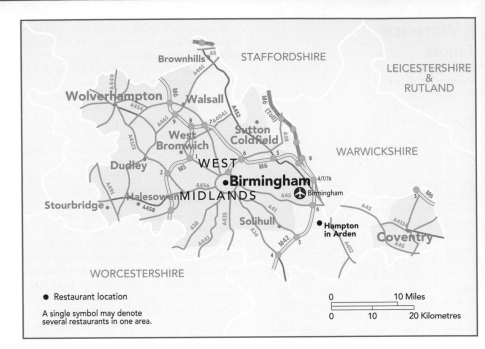

Birmingham

★ TOP 50 ★

Adam's

Cooking score: 7
Modern British | £65
New Oxford House, 16 Waterloo Street,
Birmingham, B2 5UG
Tel no: 0121 643 3745
adamsrestaurant.co.uk
£5 OFF

Providing welcome respite from the press of folk on the streets around New Street station, this urbane offering from Adam Stokes has become a reliable favourite. With neutral tones and well-spaced, unclothed tables, the dining room lays out its stall clearly – a light space devoted to the service of food. Menus, either a fixed-price carte or seven- or nine-course taster, with midweek set lunches to boost the bid for accessibility, are seasonally responsive, with Adam Stokes sourcing from end to end of the British Isles for materials that are treated with respect and a certain haute cuisine classicism. But there are imaginative strokes aplenty. The food is presented with a light touch and Stokes enjoys layering dishes with contrasts of texture and carefully worked nuances of flavour, as when a dollop of concentrated horseradish ice cream adds sharp focus to a rich gazpacho of red sorrel and red cabbage, or when cumin, date, carrot and dukkah are teamed with squab pigeon breast. And when a perfectly cooked tranche of wild turbot is partnered with asparagus, langoustine, morels, a generous blob of caviar and enriched by a verjus sauce, you know this is cooking designed to comfort and reassure. Similar contentment is to be found among desserts of white peach soufflé or gariguette strawberries with clotted cream, Thai basil and white balsamic. An assiduous approach to wine results in a French-led list that gathers the pick of each region and beyond, with Coravin glasses allowing modest entry. Bottles from £28.

Chef/s: Adam Stokes and Tom Shepherd. **Closed:** Mon, Sun, 2 weeks Dec to Jan, 1 week Easter, 2 weeks summer. **Meals:** set L £40 Tue to Thur to £65. Set D £65 Tue to Thur. Tasting menu £95 (7 courses) to £120. **Details:** 50 seats. V menu. Bar. Wheelchairs. Music.

Carters of Moseley
Cooking score: 6
Modern British | £65
2c St Mary's Row, Wake Green Road, Moseley, Birmingham, B13 9EZ
Tel no: 0121 449 8885
cartersofmoseley.co.uk

£5
OFF

Set amid a little parade of shops in the peaceful suburb of Moseley, Carters looks like the kind of venue that might once have been a decent neighbourhood bistro. This being 21st-century Britain, it's instead a hotbed of dynamically creative contemporary cooking based on sustainably sourced materials, rare breed meats, foraged plants and a keen historical sense for unjustly forgotten aspects of our culinary culture. Brad Carter's skills are manifested in the form of an eight-course tasting menu, preceded by outriders of inventive canapés (including a Porthilly oyster cooked in beef fat) and fabulous rustic bread. Memorable dishes from the winter offering included razor clams in pepper dulse with a strong hit of Old Winchester cheese, Gigha halibut with its smoked roe in buttermilk, and a dual serving of eloquently flavoured hogget – a dumpling in mint sauce, followed by the meat itself in a welter of marine flora and seaweeds. Counterbalancing those coastal notes, the earthiness that permeates many a dish continues through to a finisher of barley pudding with Yorkshire rhubarb, which comes after a taste of kelp-scented black rice. Presentations on rough and ready crockery look the part, and the drinks pairings are particularly inspired. Craft beers and ciders flesh out an authoritative listing of modern wines and sakes, ensuring an adventurous journey throughout.

Chef/s: Brad Carter. **Closed:** Mon, Sun, 1 to 16 Jan, 1 week Apr, 1 week Aug. **Meals:** set L £50 (4 courses) to £70. Set D £50 Tue to Thur (4 courses) to £70. Tasting menu (9 courses) £90. **Details:** 32 seats. V menu. Wheelchairs. Music. Children over 8 yrs.

Folium
Cooking score: 4
Modern British | £55
8 Caroline Street, Birmingham, B3 1TR
Tel no: 0121 638 0100
restaurantfolium.com

Inside the sombre grey frontage just off St Paul's Square is Ben Tesh's laid-back, light-filled dining room. A parquet floor and café-style tables keep things simple indoors, while Tesh's food is firmly in the vein of natural and wild flavours brought out with plenty of Japanese-inspired umami. Five or seven courses are the state of play on the tasting menu, which takes in finely honed seafood and fish dishes such as cured mackerel with an oyster in English wasabi, and turbot in dashi stock with hay butter. Meat could be rose-pink lamb with artichokes and seaweed, following which a pre-dessert such as spruce-scented sheep's yoghurt and lemon thyme heralds the finishing flourish of chocolate with cobnuts and burnt cream. Rough earthenware plates with speckled patterns offset the presentations most attractively. A slate of flavour-led wines by the small glass, from £6, leads into a compact, thoughtfully selected list.

Chef/s: Ben Tesh. **Closed:** Mon, Tue, 22 Dec to 8 Jan, 12 to 22 Apr, 26 Jul to 12 Aug. **Meals:** set L £28 (2 courses) to £33. Tasting menu £55 (5 courses) to £70. **Details:** 30 seats. V menu. Wheelchairs. Music.

Average price
The figure given in bold denotes the average price of a three-course dinner without drinks.

Harborne Kitchen

Cooking score: 6
Modern British | £60
175-179 High Street, Harborne, Birmingham, B17 9QE
Tel no: 0121 439 9150
harbornekitchen.com

Bare halogen bulbs hang above a room that looks as though it could double as an exhibition space, with monochrome walls and simple table accoutrements. Jamie Desogus's venue in a parade of shops is all about culinary display, to which end his kitchen is on view and his food is bright with eye-catching originality. He characterises his approach as 'playful', and the lightness of tone is enhanced by a willingness to offer contemporary cooking at something less than the stratospheric prices commanded elsewhere. Six- or eight-course tasting menus constitute the Chosen offering, but there is a Choice (aka carte) format too. A spring experience with the six-courser reconfirmed the ambrosial quality of the chicken liver parfait we noted last year, with succeeding courses including mi-cuit salmon with Arënkha smoked herring, Himalayan salt-aged Goosnargh duck with sand carrots and sesame, then a brace of desserts – refreshing roasted lime with yoghurt, coriander and mint and a rich chocolate creation with passion fruit and popcorn. It's a tribute to consistency when a reader's report never wavers in its enthusiasm through multiple dishes. Much careful consideration has been invested in the wine selection, which features plenty of interest, with standard glasses from £4.90.

Chef/s: Jamie Desogus. **Closed:** Mon, Sun.
Meals: set L £35 Thur to Sat. Set D £33 Tue to Thur. Tasting menu £60 (6 courses) to £80. **Details:** 50 seats. V menu. Bar. Wheelchairs. Music.

Lasan

Cooking score: 3
Indian | £35
3-4 Dakota Buildings, James Street, St Paul's Square, Birmingham, B3 1SD
Tel no: 0121 212 3664
lasan.co.uk
£5
OFF

Given that it's located in the now-fashionable Jewellery Quarter rather than the suburban fringes of the 'balti triangle', it's hardly surprising that Jabbar Khan's smart restaurant is a style-conscious kind of place. Featuring an ultra-modern, clean-lined dining room with bare tables, mirrored walls, decorative panelling, prints and ceiling fans, it deals in contemporary Indian cuisine – a clever blend of traditional ideas, regional recipes and influences from Western kitchens, with the emphasis on complex flavours, pinpoint spicing and intricate presentation. The tandoor can always be relied on to deliver some unusual stuff, from marinated king prawns with grapefruit and orange sirka (vinegar) to pineapple-infused paneer tikka enlivened with textures of beetroot and pineapple chutney. Meanwhile, other skills are put to telling use in dum-style biryanis (including a version with slow-cooked goat) and a Keralan beef chilli fry with curry leaves. Lasan's bartenders specialise in cocktails, while the wine list features plenty of spice-friendly bottles from £20.

Chef/s: Khalid Khan. **Closed:** 25 Dec, 1 Jan.
Meals: main courses £15 to £23. **Details:** 80 seats. Bar. Wheelchairs. Music.

★ NEW ENTRY ★

Opheem

Cooking score: 4
Indian | £40
48 Summer Row, Birmingham, B3 1JJ
Tel no: 0121 201 3377
opheem.com
£5
OFF

Aktar Islam, ex-Lasan (see entry), has moved to a corner site on the opposite side of the canal to the Jewellery Quarter. The interior is all twilit glamour, the dining room very softly illuminated by a spectacular light cluster, with a glass-fronted kitchen to distract the wandering eye. There is a seven-course tasting menu, but à la carte diners receive so many little incidentals that nobody will feel deprived. A regional approach to Indian food presented voguishly on piles of stones and hay is what Opheem is about, beginning with nibbles of smoked potato tartlets and curried lamb pâté. Starters of asparagus in green chilli and cardamom with ground raw mango and crispy duck egg post notice of the elegant intent. A main dish of beautifully pink beef fillet and 72-hour short rib comes with kohlrabi and cime di rapa, but it's the version of Hyderabadi biryani made with tender goat that knocks spots off everything around it. Finish with aam – an assembly of mango tapioca, lychee sorbet and mango mousse. The elegant spice-friendly wine list aims high, with glasses from £5.10.

Chef/s: Aktar Islam. **Closed:** Mon. **Meals:** main courses £19 to £24. Tasting menu £70 (7 courses). **Details:** 70 seats. Bar. Wheelchairs. Music.

Opus

Cooking score: 2
Modern British | £38
54 Cornwall Street, Birmingham, B3 2DE
Tel no: 0121 200 2323
opusrestaurant.co.uk
£5
OFF

A useful spot, well within walking distance of New Street, Snow Hill and the Bullring, this vast, good-looking restaurant favours clean lines and handsome trappings – olive leather upholstery, undressed tables, sleek wood floor – and has a clubby-looking bar at the rear. Service is well judged, if relatively formal, and the cooking is modern British brasserie with just the right take on seasonality. In winter that could mean game terrine wrapped in smoked bacon with poached winter fruits and quince jelly, and roasted breast of Merrifield Farm duck with fondant potato, roasted parsnips and buttered seasonal greens, while spring could bring an enjoyable pan-seared fillet of wild halibut served with asparagus, sweetly perfumed pickled chicory, roasted garlic croquette and a deep, meaty red wine jus. Finish up classically with a beautifully creamy and subtle vanilla crème brûlée served with an almond shortbread biscuit. Wines are a well-chosen and reasonably priced global selection starting at £25.

Chef/s: Ben Ternent. **Closed:** Sun, 24 Dec to 3 Jan. **Meals:** set L and D £33 (2 courses) to £38. Tasting menu £45 (5 courses). **Details:** 85 seats. V menu. Bar. Wheelchairs. Music.

★ NEW ENTRY ★

The Oyster Club

Cooking score: 4
Seafood | £55
43 Temple Street, Birmingham, B2 5DP
Tel no: 0121 643 6070
the-oyster-club.co.uk

With its light, modern decor, mix of counter and table seating, welcoming informality and a menu that encourages grazing, Adam and Natasha Stokes' second venue after Adam's (see entry) is an impressive newcomer in an area

filled with bars and restaurants. Focusing almost solely on seafood, the restaurant also offers nibbles and small plates to have with drinks, say half a dozen oysters (what else?), smoked cod's roe and oatcakes, sea bass ceviche with mooli, lime yoghurt and ginger vinaigrette, or mussels with a Prosecco and smoked caviar sauce. Otherwise, tuck into grilled salmon teriyaki with pak choi and sesame seeds or whole roasted Dover sole with beurre noisette and brown shrimps. There's also a fish pie (with or without lobster) topped with Old Winchester Cheddar mash, and a couple of token meat offerings – maybe wagyu burger and chips or roast chicken breast – and caramelised lemon tart with poached rhubarb and rhubarb sorbet to finish. Fish-friendly wines start at £6 a glass.
Chef/s: Adam Stokes and Rosanna Moseley. **Meals:** small plates £5 to £19. Large plates £16 to £33. **Details:** 54 seats. Vg menu. Bar.

Purnell's

Cooking score: 6
Modern British | £68
55 Cornwall Street, Birmingham, B3 2DH
Tel no: 0121 212 9799
purnellsrestaurant.com

£5 OFF

Glynn Purnell has been one of the prime movers in the culinary reinvention of Birmingham over the past decade and more. In a handsome Victorian red-brick building just off the city centre, comfortingly removed from the hubbub of the Bullring, a diverting space has been created, with fractals, stripes and filigree light globes positively designed to divide opinion. What tends to unite it, though, is the food, which retains a commitment to restless experimentation and development, rather than relying on a core repertoire of old favourites. A tasting menu headed There and Back Again – 2007-2019 is thus more than just a flick through the old photo album, for all that it opens with the witty take on haddock and eggs with cornflakes that *Great British Menu* fans will treasure. Monkfish of surpassing succulence

goes into an Indian-inspired masala with red lentils, coconut and coriander, before slow-cooked neck of Wiltshire Downlands lamb appears with Jerusalem artichoke and passe-crassane pear in a riot of sea herbs and black garlic. A tart made with Valrhona Biskélia milk chocolate has textural heft from pecans and a scoop of rum and raisin ice cream for the final touch of luxe. The wine list is styled as a Book of Wine, and they're not joking. Growers' Champagnes, sumptuous Rhônes, a brace of Otago Pinots, a Crimean sweet pink Muscat (at £110) support a superlative glass selection, from £7.50.
Chef/s: Glynn Purnell. **Closed:** Mon, Sun, 22 Dec to 2 Jan, 12 to 20 Apr. **Meals:** set L £35 Wed and Thur to £55. Set D Tue to Thur £68. Tasting menu £75 (6 courses) to £95. **Details:** 50 seats. Bar. Wheelchairs. Music.

Purnell's Bistro

Cooking score: 2
Modern British | £35
11 Newhall Street, Birmingham, B3 3NY
Tel no: 0121 200 1588
purnellsbistro-gingers.com

Not far from the flagship restaurant (see entry), Glynn Purnell's second venue takes a more informal approach in surroundings that are nonetheless supremely stylish, incorporating a spacious bar, Ginger's, that has a hint of luxury liner about it, and a monochrome-toned spotlit dining room run by switched-on staff. Here, on-trend modern brasserie dishes keep diners returning for lightly smoked salmon fishcake in chive cream, perhaps followed by a bowl of tagliatelle with sundried tomatoes and black olives, dressed in pesto and Grana Padano, or teriyaki beef with egg noodles and pak choi. Dry-aged beef fillet comes with a Marmite-glazed mushroom for ultimate populist appeal. Prix-fixe menus for lunch and early dinner are top value, perhaps concluding with sumptuous coconut cheesecake and mango sorbet. A concise list of fairly priced wines accompanies, if you can tear yourself away from the cocktail list, where 'molecular masterpieces' are among the attractions.

Chef/s: Glynn Purnell. **Closed:** 25 Dec to 1 Jan. **Meals:** main courses £15 to £21. Set L and D £16 (2 courses) to £20. Sun L £20 (2 courses) to £22. **Details:** 70 seats. Bar. Wheelchairs. Music.

Simpsons

Cooking score: 6
Modern British | £60
20 Highfield Road, Edgbaston, Birmingham, B15 3DU
Tel no: 0121 454 3434
simpsonsrestaurant.co.uk

This extended, modernised Georgian mansion, a couple of miles from the city centre, lures diners with comfortably appointed surroundings tailored to conversational get-togethers and special occasions. All is smiles and relaxed bonhomie in the airy, inviting dining room where the food, bang up to date, is something quite special. A passion for good ingredients underpins the whole enterprise, but it's a measure of the kitchen's finesse that while the cooking has unexpected twists it always retains a sense of balance. Luke Tipping oversees fiercely seasonal menus with plenty of attention-grabbing ideas. This certainly the case with a winter lunch of Roscoff onion broth with onion mayonnaise, croûtons, chickweed and Colston Bassett Stilton and a winning combination of fillet of sea bream (with skin crisp enough to eat – quite a rare thing) teamed with hispi cabbage, Avruga caviar, seaweed and tapioca. Desserts are hard to fault, whether a soufflé (raspberry has been praised) or chocolate crémeux with malted peanuts and peanut ice cream. The global wine list includes some big names from France and Italy with expense account price tags to match, although bottles start at £35.

Chef/s: Luke Tipping. **Closed:** Mon, 25 and 26 Dec. **Meals:** set L £45. Set D £60. Tasting menu £75 (6 courses) to £90. **Details:** 70 seats. 20 seats outside. V menu. Vg menu. Bar. Wheelchairs. Parking. Music.

▮ Hampton in Arden

★ NEW ENTRY ★

Peel's Restaurant

Cooking score: 5
Modern British | £75
Hampton Manor, Shadowbrook Lane, Hampton in Arden, B92 0DQ
Tel no: 01675 446080
hamptonmanor.com
£5 OFF

Reached via a tree-lined drive, the dark-stone former home of Victorian prime minister Sir Robert Peel has formal yet comfortable rooms. The dining room is particularly beguiling in the evening, its walls half panelled and hung with dramatic wallpaper, while soft lighting creates an elegance that sits well at the special-occasion end of the spectrum. Rob Palmer's cooking rises fully to the grandeur of the setting: his menus appreciably follow the seasons and are full of the scent of herbs from the manor's own kitchen garden – perhaps chive oil with potato velouté and tiny potato puffs, or marjoram pointing up flavour in a magnificent dish of pink, tender lamb with peas and lettuce. The accent is on well-judged flavours, such as a hugely successful opener of ripe tomato with dabs of cod's roe and rye, or perfectly timed turbot with creamy lentils and a tiny heap of crisp, battered onion rings. Meals come with lots of extras in the way of nibbles, appetisers and a pre-dessert, and own-baked bread is good, too. Service, which tends towards the formal despite the casual staff uniform, could be sharpened up. An unexpectedly resourceful wine list mixes classics and new-wave oenology with an extensive by-the-glass selection to encourage experimentation. Bottles from £26.

Chef/s: Rob Palmer. **Closed:** Mon. **Meals:** set D £75 (4 courses). Tasting menu £95 (7 courses). **Details:** 36 seats. Bar. Wheelchairs. Parking. Music. Children over 12 yrs.

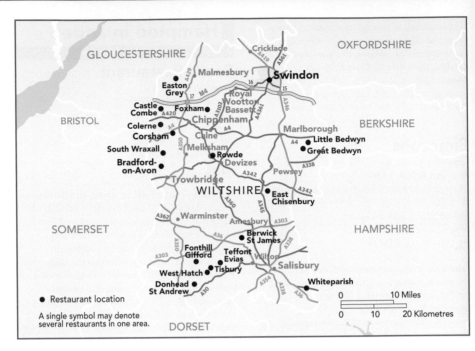

▌ Berwick St James

LOCAL GEM

The Boot Inn

British | £26
High Street, Berwick St James, SP3 4TN
Tel no: 01722 790243
theboot.pub

Homely and traditional, with a winter fire and summer garden, this small country pub feels English to a T. Its unpretentious approach is matched by a menu that doesn't try to punch above its weight, offering a straightforward run through the modern pub repertoire. Few seem to be able to resist the braised short rib of beef, and there's been praise for the cep risotto and fish pie with Cheddar mash. Finish with hot chocolate fondant pudding or a couple of scoops of 'proper' homemade ice cream. Drink Wadworth beers or wines from £19.75.

▌ Bradford-on-Avon

★ NEW ENTRY ★

The Bunch of Grapes

Cooking score: 2
Modern British | £35
14 Silver Street, Bradford-on-Avon, BA15 1JY
Tel no: 01225 938088
thebunchofgrapes.com

The summer of 2018 saw a new team take over the town's oldest pub. Cosmetically, little has changed – the informal ground-floor bar remains and the first-floor dining room retains its bare floorboards and teal paintwork. Chef Tony Casey has moved away from his predecessor's Anglo-French bistro cooking, embracing a more global outlook via prime ingredients that are sourced as locally as possible. At inspection, asparagus came dressed with white crab, chilli, brown crab mayonnaise and pickled mooli – a delicate and full-flavoured treatment – while breast of duck from nearby Woolley Park Farm delivered Asian flavours via sesame seeds, pak choi, hoisin sauce and a crisp spring roll of confit duck leg meat. A finale of strawberries, teamed with yoghurt, miso ice cream, meringue and honeycomb, pressed all the right flavour and texture buttons. A well-annotated wine list opens at £20 with plenty of quality drinking under £30. Well-kept local ales are also served.

Chef/s: Tony Casey. **Closed:** Mon. **Meals:** main courses £17 to £25. Tasting menu £40 (5 courses) to £50. Sun L £20 (2 courses) to £23. **Details:** 80 seats. Bar. Music.

▮ Castle Combe
The Bybrook
Cooking score: 6
Modern European | £75
The Manor House Hotel, Castle Combe, SN14 7HX
Tel no: 01249 782206
exclusive.co.uk

Cloaked in luxuriant greenery, and with a river running through its 365 acres of parkland, this imposing medieval manor sets out to impress from the off. Further delights await visitors to the hotel's restaurant, an intriguing mix of old and new with a stained-glass family crest, chandeliers, exposed stonework, leaf-themed artworks and purple-backed leather chairs. By contrast, chef Robert Potter's food is relentlessly contemporary, absorbing ideas and trends from the big wide world and fashioning complex multi-layered dishes from top-tier ingredients. An autumn salad of quail, confit egg yolk, mushrooms à la grecque, salsify and Wiltshire truffle sets the tone, while mains might run from a modish assemblage of Cornish cod with crushed new season Jerusalem artichokes, roast ceps, crosnes and chicken jus to a more classical take on roast partridge involving heritage potatoes, celeriac purée and savoy cabbage. On the home run, look for ambitious, highly worked desserts such as chocolate and praline millefeuille with apple caramel and hazelnut ice cream. Around 15 prestigious wines by the glass kick off a list

that moves from Taittinger Champagnes to intriguing sweet 'stickies'; bottle prices start at £26.50.
Chef/s: Robert Potter. **Meals:** set D £75. Tasting menu £95 (7 courses). Sun L £39. **Details:** 60 seats. Vg menu. Bar. Wheelchairs. Parking. Music. Children over 11 yrs.

▮ Colerne
Restaurant Hywel Jones by Lucknam Park
Cooking score: 5
Modern British | £87
Colerne, SN14 8AZ
Tel no: 01225 742777
lucknampark.co.uk

As a full-dress country-house experience, Lucknam Park has everything – a dramatic mile-long driveway to ramp up the sense of anticipation, a spa, an equestrian centre and 500 acres of parkland surrounding a Palladian mansion of lordly proportions. At the heart of things is the main restaurant – an opulent space with gold silk drapes, crystal chandeliers and an exquisite hand-painted ceiling testifying to its former life as a ballroom. It's an aptly luxurious setting for Hywel Jones' highly worked version of contemporary British cuisine, an approach that might yield anything from dressed Cornish crab with Exmoor caviar, lemongrass jelly, sesame and yuzu to pot-roast Yorkshire pigeon accompanied by creamed Brussels sprouts and chestnuts, ceps and blackberries. Seasonal flavours and indigenous ingredients are to the fore, as in Brecon lamb two ways, slow-cooked Roundway Hill pork belly or a dessert of vanilla crème brûlée with Wye Valley rhubarb and stem ginger doughnuts. The international wine list brings serious names and covetable vintages to the table, with prices from £30 (£8 a glass).
Chef/s: Hywel Jones. **Closed:** Mon, Tue. **Meals:** set D £87. Tasting menu £110 (7 courses). Sun L £39. **Details:** 64 seats. V menu. Wheelchairs. Parking. Children over 5 yrs.

Dynamic pricing

As consumers, we are no strangers to dynamic pricing – the term used to explain why the cost of hotel rooms and flights fluctuates depending on demand, dates or times. Now a number of restaurants have followed suit, charging different amounts for the same dining experience to encourage people to book when demand is typically lower.

Soho restaurant **Bob Bob Ricard** has a peak and off-peak system which means it's around 20% cheaper to eat at lunch time, as well as at dinner on Sundays and Mondays, than at other times. **The Lighthouse** in Derbyshire increases prices as the weekend approaches. Eat there on a Wednesday or Thursday and the tasting menu is £55 but that goes up to £60 on Friday and Saturday.

The Man Behind The Curtain in Leeds charges £55 for its six-course lunch menu on Fridays, rising to £65 on Saturdays. Book for dinner Tuesday to Thursday and pay £75 for 10 courses; later in the week you'll pay an extra £15 or £25.

Like finding a good hotel rate or a cheap flight, when it comes to dining, it may pay to shop around and keep your dates flexible.

■ Corsham

★ NEW ENTRY ★

The Methuen Arms

Cooking score: 3
Modern British | £39
2 High Street, Corsham, SN13 0HB
Tel no: 01249 717060
themethuenarms.com

This carefully styled three-storey Cotswold stone inn is the result of serious investment that has paid off in spades. The comfortable contemporary interior is nicely balanced by original features and antique touches, the welcome as warm towards locals here for a drink as it is to diners coming for Leigh Evans' accomplished cooking. Whether you're after pub classics such as beef burger with smoked bacon and Red Leicester cheese or Butcombe beer-battered haddock with hand-cut chips, mushy peas and tartare sauce, or upping the ante with more ambitious dishes, there's much to enjoy. Start, perhaps, with seared scallops with crisp prawn, Parma ham, apple, cauliflower and watercress, followed by two generous cubes of sirloin beef cooked pink and served with bolognese ravioli, beef dripping potatoes, celeriac and horseradish. Crème caramel with pear – poached and sorbeted – and a quenelle of white chocolate crémeux gave a glimpse of the kitchen's full capability. The wine list is a modest single-page affair starting at £18 and peaking at £60.
Chef/s: Leigh Evans. **Meals:** main courses £17 to £27. **Details:** 100 seats. 75 seats outside. Bar. Wheelchairs. Parking. Music.

Donhead St Andrew
The Forester
Cooking score: 2
Modern British | £32
Lower Street, Donhead St Andrew, SP7 9EE
Tel no: 01747 828038
theforesterdonheadstandrew.co.uk

Found down narrow country lanes, this ancient hostelry has everything you might expect: beams, exposed stone walls, real ales, real fires and a lovely garden for when the sun shines. There's an air of no-nonsense simplicity and, with hospitable service, it makes a convivial oasis. The cooking is appealing, too – basic ingredients are well sourced (many locally) and execution is generally on the money. Much of the menu runs along familiar lines, taking in excellent lamb's kidneys on toast with wholegrain mustard dressing or beetroot risotto with Parmesan and watercress. Follow with a cracking main course of slow-roast belly of Wiltshire pork with chorizo sauté potatoes, leeks and Jerusalem artichokes, or well-timed lemon sole, cooked on the bone, with new potatoes, wilted greens and lemon butter. And there's no diffidence about serving pub stalwarts such as fish and chips or hearty desserts, say brioche bread and butter pudding. Wines from £20.
Chef/s: Andrew Kilburn. **Closed:** Mon. **Meals:** main courses £15 to £29. **Details:** 60 seats. 35 seats outside. V menu. Bar. Parking.

East Chisenbury
The Red Lion Freehouse
Cooking score: 5
Modern British | £46
East Chisenbury, SN9 6AQ
Tel no: 01980 671124
redlionfreehouse.com

The name tag 'Freehouse' might suggest a real ale stronghold and there's no denying that this remote but snugly informal pub fulfils its duties as a busy, buzzy local with off-the-beaten-track beers on tap and plenty of garrulous chatter at the bar. However, Guy Manning is first and foremost a chef, and the food he produces is serious stuff, full of vibrant contemporary accents and seasonal detailing. His 'produce-first' approach shows up brilliantly in a salad involving five types of heritage tomato, each prepared differently and assembled as distinct components alongside Wiltshire burrata and basil oil. He's also right at home cooking a glorious chateaubriand of the very best Wiltshire beef ('juicy, fatty and loaded with beefy, gamey flavour') or putting together a 'perfect plate' of steamed John Dory, buttery new potatoes and foaming cream sauce with shrimps, spinach and wild asparagus. These are dishes from the seasonal tasting menu, although the carte has its own pleasures, from deep-fried calf's brains with sauce gribiche to desserts such as cocoa pound cake served with luscious chocolate sauce and fragrant orange blossom ice cream. If wine is your tipple, the 'nicely structured' list has plenty to offer.
Chef/s: Guy Manning. **Closed:** Mon, Tue. **Meals:** main courses £20 to £28. Set L and D £24 (2 courses) to £28. Tasting menu £65 (5 courses) to £75. **Details:** 48 seats. 34 seats outside. Parking. Music.

Easton Grey
Grey's Brasserie
Cooking score: 4
Modern British | £35
Whatley Manor, Easton Grey, SN16 0RB
Tel no: 01666 822888
whatleymanor.com

There may be a gated entrance and a long, winding driveway leading to this imposing Cotswold stone manor, but the whole operation is far from stuffy. Refreshingly free from pomp, the secluded hotel is run with precision and a lightness of touch, with this strikingly modern, comfortable brasserie the more relaxed of the hotel's two restaurants. It shares the same state-of-the-art kitchen and supply chain as The Dining Room (see entry), but here dishes are simpler, although no less imaginative, and there's a high level of technical skill displayed. Starters such as salmon sashimi cured in kombu and teamed with yuzu and aged soy, say, could lead on to loin of Wiltshire venison with confit Jerusalem artichokes, lemon and thyme, or skate wing with mashed potato, brown butter croûtons, parsley and capers. For a deliciously no-frills finale, try the treacle tart with bergamot ice cream. The accessible wine list opens at £29 with plenty of decent options by the glass.

Chef/s: Niall Keating. **Meals:** main courses £17 to £34. Set L £20 (2 courses) to £25. Sun L £36.

Details: 64 seats. 25 seats outside. Bar. Wheelchairs. Parking. Music.

★ TOP 50 ★

Whatley Manor, The Dining Room

Cooking score: 7
Modern British | £95
Whatley Manor, Easton Grey, SN16 0RB
Tel no: 01666 822888
whatleymanor.com

The Dining Room at Whatley Manor reopened after a brief closure at the start of 2019 with a shiny new kitchen worthy of an A-list talent. Young star Niall Keating has seized the occasion and is beginning to dazzle, his 12-course menu displaying the adventurousness of a new generation. After drinks and own-cured charcuterie in one of the many sitting rooms, the chef welcomes guests for snacks at a trio of high tables by the kitchen pass, before they take their places in the relaxed, cream-hued dining room. These snacks jump-start the palate with an interplay of sweet, salt and tart that couldn't be more finely orchestrated: a shot of chilled melon 'fresca' with caviar oil, a wedge of tamarind-glazed mango, and a smokey-sweet, friable parcel of eel, citrus and aigre-doux. Then it's on to the rest of the menu where Keating's Japanese chawan mushi-style savoury king crab custard with a

dab of caviar is 'sensational', as is the yeast beurre blanc accompanying perfectly timed salmon. His signatures have been fine-tuned to the nth degree: firstly, an intense sushi rice risotto, with raw Scottish scallop, kimchi glaze and a spicy XO-inspired chorizo vinaigrette, then a dramatic lardo-draped black tortellino with a 'divine' pork belly farce. Sourdough bread with a burnt leek and yeast ash butter 'rose' will probably join their number. And as a finale, a cube of chocolate topped with a dab of extra-virgin olive oil ice cream is beautifully realised, at once silky and dense. Finish with 'treats' such as dinky matcha-dusted choux buns. Service is warm and approachable. The wine list takes a global attitude, with bottles from England, Israel, Slovenia and beyond. Champagne is a focus.

Chef/s: Niall Keating. **Closed:** Mon, Tue, Wed.

Meals: tasting menu £95 (8 courses) to £110.

Details: 46 seats. V menu. Vg menu. Bar. Wheelchairs. Parking. Music. Children over 12 yrs.

▌Fonthill Gifford

The Beckford Arms

Cooking score: 3
Modern British | £30
Hindon Lane, Fonthill Gifford, SP3 6PX
Tel no: 01747 870385
beckfordarms.com
£5 OFF · £30

This creeper-clad 18th-century coaching inn on the edge of the 9,000-acre Fonthill Estate is owned by the team behind The Lord Poulett Arms at Hinton St George and the Talbot Inn at Mells, both in neighbouring Somerset (see entries). With its open fires and mature garden, this comfortably gentrified pub with rooms has year-round appeal as a weekending and dining destination but, with real ales and a cosy bar, it's popular with local drinkers too. The kitchen keeps a close eye on the seasons, matching pub classics – steaks, burgers, ploughman's and fish and chips – with the likes of lamb and mint croquette with cumin yoghurt, pickled red cabbage and anchovies, and Newlyn hake teamed with quinoa, samphire, roasted red pepper, avocado purée and herring roe. Rhubarb parfait, custard and gingerbread crumb provides a sweet finish. Eat in the more formal dining room or the bar. The short, well-priced wine list opens at £21 and offers plenty of interesting options by the glass and carafe.

Chef/s: Richie Peacocke. **Meals:** main courses £14 to £26. Set D £30 (2 courses) to £35. **Details:** 76 seats. 44 seats outside. Bar. Parking. Music.

▌Foxham
The Foxham Inn
Cooking score: 1
Modern British | £30
Foxham, SN15 4NQ
Tel no: 01249 740665
thefoxhaminn.co.uk
£5 OFF 🛏 £30 ♨

The setting is charming and simple, but don't let the bare bricks and plain wood furniture fool you — nowadays, this family-run pub with rooms is known as an eating place with no little ambition. Neil Cooper's unpretentious approach and strong relationship with local suppliers are shown to good advantage in dishes such as creamy garlic-spiked mixed Marlborough mushrooms with spätzle, and loin of venison with dauphinois potatoes, although there's beer-battered haddock or honey and mustard smoked ham and egg with chips for the pub traditionalists. The selection of homemade ice creams comes in for praise, and the short global wine list opens below £19.

Chef/s: Neil Cooper. **Closed:** Mon, 2 to 15 Jan. **Meals:** main courses £14 to £23. **Details:** 60 seats. 40 seats outside. Wheelchairs. Parking. Music.

Wine list ·
🍾 Restaurants showing this symbol have a wine list that our experts consider to be outstanding, either for its in-depth focus on a particular region, attractive margins on fine wines, or strong selection by the glass.

▌Great Bedwyn
The Three Tuns
Cooking score: 2
British | £27
1 High Street, Great Bedwyn, SN8 3NU
Tel no: 01672 870280
tunsfreehouse.com
£5 OFF £30 ♨

The owners of this delightful village pub close to the Kennet and Avon Canal have stamped it firmly with their personalities, offering shoot lunches, beer festivals and quiz nights, and making it very much the hub of the village. The menu takes all that into account: pub staples rub shoulders with more contemporary dishes, all delivered without fuss or posturing. After nibbles of rosemary- and olive-oil-fried almonds and perhaps a glass of Otter bitter at the bar, a typical meal could kick off with half a pint of prawns with aïoli and grilled focaccia, continue with confit chicken leg served with buttered mash, spinach, mushrooms, smoked bacon and pearl onions, and finish with a tangy lemon posset with rhubarb and almonds. An interesting wine lists opens at £20 and there's a blackboard of keenly priced weekly bin ends by the bottle and glass.

Chef/s: James Wilsey. **Closed:** Mon. **Meals:** main courses £14 to £22. Sun L £23 (2 courses) to £28. **Details:** 48 seats. Parking. Music. No children after 8pm.

▌Little Bedwyn
The Harrow at Little Bedwyn
Cooking score: 6
Modern British | £60
High Street, Little Bedwyn, SN8 3JP
Tel no: 01672 870871
theharrowatlittlebedwyn.com
🍾

Once the local pub in this out-of-the-way village on the Kennet and Avon Canal, and now a well-established restaurant, the Harrow has been run with serious commitment by

Roger and Sue Jones for the past 20 years. Divided by a central fireplace, the elegant pair of intimate dining rooms are relaxed spaces with informed but not over-formal service, the perfect setting for dishes built around impeccably sourced ingredients cooked with considerable skill and lightness of touch. From a trio of set menus of five, six or eight courses, standout dishes have included a light, fragrant shellfish salad of crab, lobster and shrimp dumpling in a Thai broth, and a simple fillet of local venison flavoured with Indian spices, as well as Cornish line-caught cod with a Champagne beurre blanc and Siberian caviar. From an extensive and lovingly curated wine list of around 1,000 bins, house bottles start at £28 and there is plenty of serious drinking to be had by the glass.
Chef/s: Roger Jones. **Closed:** Mon, Tue, Sun, 23 Dec to 7 Jan. **Meals:** set L £40 (5 courses). Tasting menu £60 (6 courses) to £85. **Details:** 34 seats. 30 seats outside. V menu. Vg menu. Wheelchairs. Music.

▉ Rowde
The George & Dragon
Cooking score: 3
Modern British | £32
High Street, Rowde, SN10 2PN
Tel no: 01380 723053
thegeorgeanddragonrowde.co.uk

🖂

With original beams and open fireplaces, this 16th-century roadside coaching inn could easily deliver a menu of pub classics but has long held a reputation for fish and seafood delivered daily from Cornwall. In the bar, locals congregate to enjoy real ales while diners study the printed menu and blackboard specials to see how the day's catch has inspired the kitchen. Dishes are uncomplicated but flavourful, a typical meal perhaps starting with moules marinière with cream, garlic and bay leaf or a salad of butterflied mackerel with new potatoes. Main courses might bring crisp crumbed Dover sole with chips and hollandaise sauce or monkfish wrapped in Parma ham with wild mushroom sauce. There

are a few meat dishes, perhaps devilled lamb's kidneys with a grainy mustard cream sauce. Desserts are traditional and comforting, Eton mess in summer, say, and ginger pudding on colder days. A concise list of seafood-friendly wines opens at £18.50.
Chef/s: Chippy Day and Thomas Bryant. **Meals:** main courses £14 to £32. Set L and D £18 (2 courses) to £23. Sun L £23. **Details:** 40 seats. 40 seats outside. Bar. Wheelchairs. Parking. Music.

▉ South Wraxall
The Longs Arms
Cooking score: 3
Modern British | £35
South Wraxall, BA15 2SB
Tel no: 01225 864450
thelongsarms.com

There is still a real village feel to this stone-built pub, which also doubles as the local shop (with neighbour Bob's eggs sold over the bar). Indeed, since buying the freehold three years ago, Rob and Liz Allcock have made significant improvements, notably with a refurbishment of the restaurant, while drinkers can hold court over a pint of Gritchie English Lore ale at the new bar, fashioned from a piece of local elm. Rob's gutsy British cooking continues to attract diners from all over, and local suppliers form a long list on the back of the daily changing menu. So expect West Country ingredients throughout, whether in a starter of citrus-cured monkfish with yoghurt, smoked almonds, ginger, sesame and radish or a main course of pork belly with crisp crackling, black pudding, wild garlic mash and spring greens. Strawberry choc ice with honeycomb, strawberries and yoghurt is a happy dessert choice. A good-value wine list starts at £19.
Chef/s: Rob Allcock. **Closed:** Mon, Tue, 2 weeks Sept, 3 weeks Jan. **Meals:** main courses £14 to £32. **Details:** 46 seats. 30 seats outside. Wheelchairs. Parking. Music.

Swindon

Helen Browning's Chop House

Cooking score: 2
Modern British | £29
19-21 Wood Street, Swindon, SN1 4AN
Tel no: 01793 527082
helenbrowningsorganics.co.uk
£5 OFF £30

As CEO of the Soil Association and owner of pioneering Eastbrook Farm in Bishopstone, Helen Browning OBE is one of the organic movement's key players – and she shows off her locally grown produce at this former shop in Old Swindon. It's naturally big on home-reared meats, ranging from burgers to ribs, chops, steaks and sharing boards: check out the slow-roast saddleback pork belly with mash, greens, apple sauce and gravy or piri-piri organic roast chicken served on the bone. There are fish boards and bowls of mussels, too, plus a separate selection tailored to vegetarians and vegans (caramelised onion and polenta cake with harissa sauce, say). To finish, try a chocolate brownie or one of the organic ice creams made by Ray's shop round the corner. Drinks also stay with the programme – Luscombe's juices, Dunkertons cider, craft beers and a dozen organic wines from £21.
Chef/s: Manfred Neder. **Closed:** 31 Dec, 1 and 2 Jan. **Meals:** main courses £10 to £27. **Details:** 34 seats. V menu. Vg menu. Wheelchairs. Music.

Teffont Evias

Howard's House Hotel

Cooking score: 3
Modern British | £47
Teffont Evias, SP3 5RJ
Tel no: 01722 716392
howardshousehotel.co.uk
£5 OFF

Set in a lush, beautiful garden in an immaculate village, this former dower house is instantly appealing, living up to most people's idea of a perfect country hotel. The dining room, with its white linen, floral curtains and fresh flowers, is tranquil and old school in the best possible sense, while Andrew Britton's sure-footed, satisfying food is clearly attracting return visitors. The fixed-price lunch and evening menu takes its cue from West Country produce – perhaps rustic game terrine or Lyme Bay scallops with cauliflower purée and chorizo soil. Loin of local roe deer could appear with celeriac purée, haggis bonbon, glazed beetroot and red wine jus, or there could be a smoked haddock fish stew with white wine cream sauce, mussels, clams and baby leeks. To finish, there are sweet hits from blood orange soufflé with clementine fruit sorbet, to a classic vanilla crème brûlée. The global wine list starts at a wallet-friendly £20.
Chef/s: Andrew Britton. **Closed:** 23 to 26 Dec. **Meals:** set L and D £28 (2 courses) to £47. Tasting menu £80 (8 courses). **Details:** 30 seats. 20 seats outside. Bar. Wheelchairs. Parking. Music.

Tisbury

The Compasses Inn

Cooking score: 2
Modern British | £28
Lower Chicksgrove, Tisbury, SP3 6NB
Tel no: 01722 714318
thecompassesinn.com
£30

Dating from the 14th century and tucked away in one of the many folds of the Wiltshire countryside, there's nothing more than a modest hanging sign to distinguish this hostelry from the other thatched buildings in this bucolic idyll. With tiny windows set in thick stone walls and candles on the antique tables, this low-ceilinged pub with rooms draws villagers to its welcoming bar. Local ales, a decent ploughman's and sandwiches keep walkers happy, while the daily changing lunch and dinner menus pull diners from further afield. The kitchen makes use of the abundant local larder but the inspiration has an international focus. Start in Italy with buffalo mozzarella, peperonata, basil and

grilled sourdough, before crossing to Morocco for spiced roast chicken, chips, smoked chipotle mayonaise and salad. Pork and apple sausages with mash, bacon-flecked savoy cabbage and red wine gravy is a more traditional choice. There's plenty by the glass and carafe on the helpful wine list, with bottles from £22.50.
Chef/s: Patrick Davy. **Meals:** main courses £10 to £20. **Details:** Bar.

▌West Hatch

LOCAL GEM
Pythouse Kitchen Garden
British | £30
West Hatch, SP3 6PA
Tel no: 01747 870444
pythousekitchengarden.co.uk

🛏 £30

This former potting shed in a picturesque Victorian walled garden provides much of the fruit and vegetables for the kitchen, and it's certainly not your average café. Pass dressers laden with homemade cakes, pickles and preserves and grab a table in the long glasshouse – all flagstone floors and exposed bricks. The menu changes daily but might feature cauliflower and local Blue Vinny soup, followed by slow-cooked shoulder of Wiltshire lamb with smashed root vegetables and wilted chard, rounding off with lemon verbena posset. Drink locally brewed beers and ciders or choose from the kindly priced wine list.

▌Whiteparish

★ NEW ENTRY ★
Betony by Matthew Tomkinson
Cooking score: 4
British | £40
The King's Head, The Street, Whiteparish, SP5 2SG
Tel no: 01794 884004
thekingshead.co.uk

🛏

Saved from the wrong kind of development, the whitewashed King's Head pub on the main road through this small village at the northern end of the New Forest has been equitably divided between a smartened-up bar with decent hand-cranked ales and, on the left, a rather swish restaurant. Betony is in the hands of Matthew Tomkinson, who produces a 'careful, assured and unpretentious' repertoire of modern British dishes to suit the circumstances. First up at inspection was a satin-smooth truffled velouté of Jerusalem artichoke, together with a hollowed globe artichoke filled with its diced flesh topped with crunchy hazelnuts – an absolute belter. Next was a pairing of duck confit croquette with a piece of beautifully fatted duck breast, cut by pickled pear and puréed celeriac. Butter-roasted cod was rather intimidated by its chaperones, black pudding and unyielding sprouting broccoli, but faith was restored by a serving of Creedy Carver chicken breast, its skin glass-brittle, with puffy gnocchi and brandy-lashed wild mushrooms. A dessert of warm chocolate mousse fell short of convincing, but the cheeses are superb. Wines, from £19.95, will do for the time being, but the cooking deserves a broader vinous spread.
Chef/s: Matthew Tomkinson. **Closed:** Mon, Tue, Sun. **Meals:** main courses £17 to £23. Tasting menu £55 (6 courses). **Details:** 50 seats. Bar. Parking.

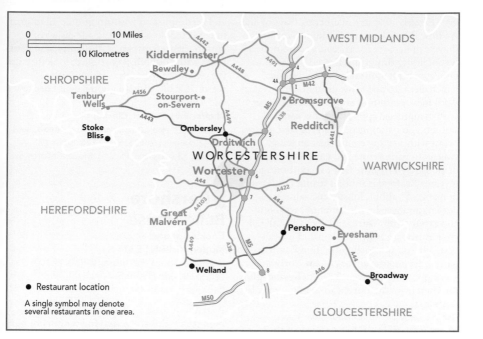

Broadway

The Lygon Arms

Cooking score: 2
Modern British | £45
High Street, Broadway, WR12 7DU
Tel no: 01386 852255
lygonarmshotel.co.uk

The quintessential Cotswold hostelry in a
quintessential Cotswold village has been
standing proud for more than 600 years –
although the current owners have done a good
job of blowing away the dusty old cobwebs.
The vast barrel-vaulted dining hall with its
minstrels' gallery, antler chandeliers and
massive stone inglenook has been rebranded as
Lygon Bar & Grill in an attempt to lighten the
mood, and 'enormously likeable' young staff
are now casually dressed in denim – although
service can lack professionalism. Similarly, the
menu now offers a more user-friendly
selection of brasserie-style dishes with British
overtones, from rabbit and ham hock terrine

with rhubarb to battered cod or herb-crusted
lamb with wild garlic, radish and spinach.
Local meats are sizzled on the grill and there
are salads, too, plus a roster of familiar desserts
including fruit crumble or iced honeycomb
parfait. Sunday lunch always features Scotch
beef wellington, while the wine list opens
with house selections from £16 a carafe.
Chef/s: Ales Maurer. **Meals:** main courses £17 to
£29. **Details:** 46 seats. Vg menu. Bar. Parking.

Russell's of Broadway

Cooking score: 3
Modern British | £40
20 High Street, Broadway, WR12 7DT
Tel no: 01386 853555
russellsofbroadway.co.uk

Named after the design pioneer Sir Gordon
Russell, whose showroom this once was, and
now a well-established modern restaurant
with rooms, a hugely popular terrace and a
loyal following, Russell's is run in a

marvellously unstuffy manner by Gaynor and Andrew Riley. Head chef is Jorge Santos who shows a preference for a broadly contemporary way of doing things; his fiercely seasonal dishes are built around key local produce, which seems to please the great majority. At an April meal, starters of truffled goat's cheese with compressed apple, kohlrabi, candied walnuts and balsamic gel, and smoked pigeon breast with a crispy confit chicken wing, sweetcorn panna cotta and parsley sponge demonstrated Santos's flair for combining textures. Seafood is another strong suit, as seen in mains of halibut, lobster and salmon cannelloni served with samphire, asparagus and caviar cream sauce, and sea bass with pak choi, Parmesan gnocchi, clam and mussel bouillabaisse and garlic aïoli. Finish with a passion fruit extravaganza of tart, sorbet, meringue and macaron. A decent by-the-glass selection from the European-leaning wine list starts at £6.

Chef/s: Jorge Santos. **Closed:** Mon, 1 Jan. **Meals:** main courses £15 to £32. Set L £20 (2 courses) to £24. Set D £23 (2 courses) to £27. Sun L £30. **Details:** 60 seats. 20 seats outside. Bar. Wheelchairs. Music.

◼ Ombersley
The Venture In

Cooking score: 2
Modern European | £45
Main Road, Ombersley, WR9 0EW
Tel no: 01905 620552
theventurein.co.uk

From the high street, step back in time through an almost concealed door into a low-beamed restaurant with some splendid original features. The menu majors in rich, classical dishes such as terrines and soufflés or asparagus with hollandaise sauce and a crispy hen's egg, followed perhaps by slow-cooked short rib of beef with sautéed wild mushrooms, red wine jus and creamed potato, and there are plenty of daily changing market fish specials – a particular passion of chef proprietor Toby Fletcher, developed during his time in Australia. His cooking is confident

and accomplished with attention paid to small unexpected details, such as side dishes of cumin-crusted carrots and parsnips, and petits fours with your bill. Take time to look through the extensive wine list – it's not only reasonable but offers a good balance of New and Old World styles.

Chef/s: Toby Fletcher. **Closed:** Mon, 1 week Dec, 1 week Mar, 1 week Jun, 2 weeks Aug. **Meals:** set L £31 (2 courses) to £35. Set D £45. Sun L £35. **Details:** 32 seats. Bar. Parking. Music. Children over 10 yrs.

◼ Pershore
Belle House

Cooking score: 3
Modern British | £37
5 Bridge Street, Pershore, WR10 1AJ
Tel no: 01386 555055
belle-house.co.uk

A standout feature on Pershore's handsome high street, this converted fire station not only houses a spacious modern restaurant, but also a traiteur and deli selling dishes made in the Belle House kitchen. Head chef and proprietor Steve Waites serves quality, classical ingredients and flavour combinations in a beautifully presented and modern way. The highlights on our visit were a Mediterranean-influenced dish of seared scallops with crab bisque, tomato and fennel, breast of guinea fowl with pistachio mousse, asparagus and mushrooms and rump of beef with roasted pickled shallots and pommes Anna. Dessert is not to be missed: the passion fruit posset is a delightfully refreshing way to end a meal, or there's a decadent chocolate and Guinness cake with malt ice cream. Can't decide? Order the assiette and cover all bases. A comprehensive wine list is well priced, and fine glassware and plates add to the upmarket feel.

Chef/s: Steve Waites. **Closed:** Mon, Tue, Sun, first 2 weeks Jan. **Meals:** set L £18 (2 courses) to £27. Set D £29 (2 courses) to £37. Tasting menu £45 (6 courses). **Details:** 75 seats. Bar. Wheelchairs. Music.

▌Stoke Bliss

★ NEW ENTRY ★

Pensons

Cooking score: 6
British | £60
Pensons Yard, Stoke Bliss, WR15 8RT
Tel no: 01885 410333
pensons.co.uk

The latest venture of Lee Westcott (formerly of London's Typing Room) is tucked away on the fringes of the historic Netherwood Estate, now a lifestyle hub comprising holiday lets, an interiors shop and weaving mill. Here Lee and his team forage and farm their own ingredients. The restaurant sits within a set of lovingly restored 15th-century barns, and although the architecture is modern – the interior feels Scandinavian, lit by floor to ceiling windows and featuring jars of ferments and minimalist furniture throughout – it preserves its agricultural past. The menu is short and showcases seasonal produce such as wild garlic, nettles, rhubarb and asparagus – encapsulating Lee's 'estate to plate' mantra. Of particular note at inspection was an umami-powered beef tartare with black garlic and cep crackers, while another starter of scallop with yeast, kale and apple delivered wonderful freshness and balance. A main of chalk stream trout with heritage tomatoes, chicory and smoked roe sauce led the way for a seasonal finale of gariguette strawberries teamed with Szechuan pepper and rapeseed oil. The food is exceptional value, the wine list rather limited, and the service confident, warm and unpretentious.
Chef/s: Lee Westcott. **Closed:** Mon, Tue, 25 Dec to 1 Jan, 1 week Aug. **Meals:** set L £27 (2 courses) to £32. Set D £50 Wed and Thur. Tasting menu £60 (5 courses) to £75. Sun L £27 (2 courses). **Details:** 50 seats. 20 seats outside. V menu. Bar. Wheelchairs. Parking. Music. No children at D.

Anonymous

At *The Good Food Guide*, our inspectors dine anonymously and pay their bill in full every time. These impartial review meals, along with feedback from thousands of our readers, are what informs the content of the *GFG*, the UK's number one selling restaurant guide. Only the best restaurants make the cut.

▌Welland

The Inn at Welland

Cooking score: 1
Modern British | £35
Hook Bank, Drake Street, Welland, WR13 6LN
Tel no: 01684 592317
theinnatwelland.co.uk
£5 OFF

Not an inn but a homely and welcoming restaurant with a substantial terraced garden and modern dining room where flamboyant hostess Gillian Pinchbeck runs a tight ship, ensuring everything goes smoothly. The menu offers time-honoured pub dishes, along the lines of beetroot and goat's cheese, scallops with cauliflower textures or cheese soufflé, plus burgers, sharing boards and twists on hearty dishes such as beef bourguignon. Of particular note is the selection of local cheeses, an extensive selection of wines by the glass, and a dessert wine list that includes a pear ice wine from Herefordshire, the recommended partner to a classic apple and rhubarb crumble.
Chef/s: Hanjo Veenstra. **Closed:** Mon. **Meals:** main courses £15 to £26. Sun L £23 (2 courses) to £27. **Details:** 80 seats. 40 seats outside. V menu. Wheelchairs. Parking. Music.

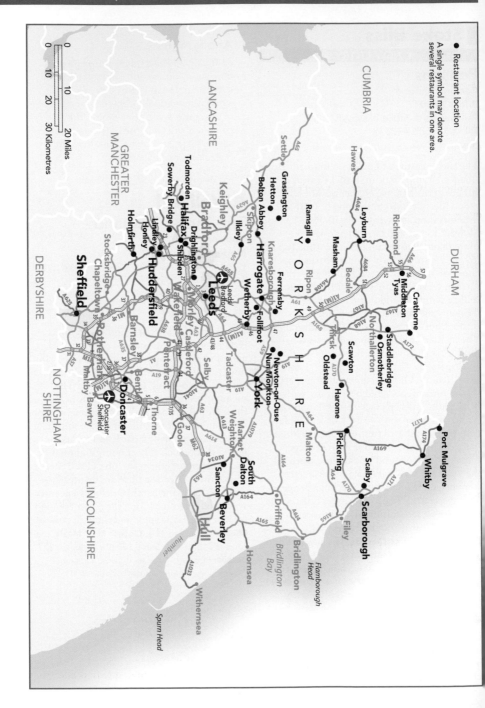

Beverley
Whites Restaurant

Cooking score: 5
Modern British | £58
12a North Bar Without, Beverley, HU17 7AB
Tel no: 01482 866121
whitesrestaurant.co.uk

Overlooking the medieval gate and town walls, John Robinson's intimate, down-to-earth restaurant occupies a three-storey townhouse with a newly created roof terrace. Unfussy decor and a lack of a printed menu – dishes on the tasting menus are verbalised – put the emphasis on the food emerging from the partially open kitchen. Our inspection meal opened with the freshest, sweetest Whitby crab paired with a fiery horseradish cream and dill oil – a standout dish, as was a light Yorkshire asparagus mousse served with raw asparagus and smoked eel. Then rich and sticky slow-cooked ox cheek and crisp ox tongue nuggets were served with a deconstructed Caesar salad spiked with herbs from the chef's allotment. To finish, a delicate slice of chocolate gâteau opera arrived with baked chocolate fondant, Yorkshire rhubarb, oats, coffee mascarpone and a fruity six-year-old homemade Seville orange marmalade. Drink wines from a dependable list with plenty of options by the glass.
Chef/s: John Robinson. **Closed:** Mon, Sun, 1 week Christmas, 1 week Aug. **Meals:** tasting menu D £30 Tue to Thur (4 courses) to £58 (9 courses). **Details:** 20 seats. Bar. Wheelchairs. Music.

LOCAL GEM

The Pig & Whistle

Modern European | £28
5 Sow Hill Road, Beverley, HU17 8BG
Tel no: 01482 874083
pigandwhistlebeverley.co.uk
£30

It's easy to walk past James Allcock's clever little bistro but it's well worth seeking out for French- and Spanish-inspired small plates (charred octopus and chorizo, potted mallard with rémoulade) and sharing boards of charcuterie and cheese. For one fan it is an 'ideal spot, whether just for a quick drink, snack or full dining experience'. Those in search of a proper meal can go on to boeuf bourguignon or tartiflette au Reblochon, and finish with churros with warm chocolate dipping sauce. Wines from £19.50.

Bolton Abbey
The Burlington

Cooking score: 6
Modern British | £75
The Devonshire Arms, Bolton Abbey, BD23 6AJ
Tel no: 01756 718100
burlingtonrestaurant.co.uk

Part of the Duke of Devonshire's fiefdom since 1753, The Devonshire Arms is a gilt-edged hospitality package with unimpeachable pedigree – a picture of aristocratic solidity cocooned within 30,000 acres of prime Yorkshire real estate. Given such auspicious surroundings, you might expect the flagship Burlington restaurant to be a stiff, starchy 'temple of gastronomy' but the reality is very different. There's a lighter touch and a more relaxed feel to the place these days (especially if you're seated in the delightful conservatory extension), although the cooking is as complex, technically ambitious and highly detailed as ever. Chef Paul Leonard understands his home turf and is eager to pinpoint the provenance of his raw materials, whether it's heritage carrots (paired with smoked eel, curds and spiced seeds), Yorkshire hogget (partnered by turnip, chard and mustard) or fish from the east coast boats (John Dory with dulse butter sauce, for example). There's roe deer from the estate, too (perhaps served as a tartare), while the garden and orchard contribute to deconstructed fruity desserts such as 'apple, sage and pumpkin' or 'bilberry, crème fraîche and clementine leaf'. The food is bolstered by an epic global wine list bulging with peerless vintages and great names from the world of viticulture – although you'll be hard-pressed to find much below £30.

Chef/s: Paul Leonard. **Closed:** Mon. **Meals:** set D £75. Tasting menu £85 (7 courses). **Details:** 40 seats. Bar. Wheelchairs. Parking.

The Devonshire Brasserie

Cooking score: 3
Modern British | £35
The Devonshire Arms, Bolton Abbey,
BD23 6AJ
Tel no: 01756 718100
thedevonshirearms.co.uk

Stepping into this casual brasserie and bar can be an eye-opening culture shock, given the venue's green and pleasant Dales location and its links to the aristocratic Devonshire Arms hospitality complex. Instead of pastoral shades, the interior is bright and cheery, all vivid clashing colours, patterned fabrics, painted chairs and kooky artworks – although those dreamy views of Wharfedale provide some quiet reassurance. With steak and fish nights added to the mix, the food is unashamedly populist, but there's no shirking when it comes to sourcing prime local ingredients. Grills and seafood platters are built for hearty appetites, while the rest of the menu speaks of assured brasserie cooking – from small plates of crab arancini or Yorkshire asparagus with truffled hollandaise to larger servings of garden pea and mint risotto, home-reared pork with champ, or monkfish accompanied by Parma ham, cockles, samphire and lobster bisque. The value-added wine list is a cherry-picked selection from The Devonshire Arms' world-class cellar.

Chef/s: Sean Pleasants. **Meals:** main courses £14 to £33. Set L and D £19 (2 courses) to £22. Sun L £26 (2 courses) to £30. **Details:** 55 seats. 30 seats outside. Bar. Wheelchairs. Parking. Music.

Symbols

🛏 Accommodation is available
£30 Three courses for £30 or less
£5 OFF £5 off voucher scheme
🍷 Notable wine list

▌Crathorne
Crathorne Arms

Cooking score: 2
Modern British | £35
Crathorne Village, Crathorne, TS15 0BA
Tel no: 01642 961402
thecrathornearms.co.uk

Readers who remember the McCoy brothers in their prime at the Cleveland Tontine (see entry) won't be surprised by the Crathorne Arms – a roadside pub reconfigured in typically eccentric style by Eugene and Barbara McCoy. Inside, it's a cleverly contrived hotchpotch of mirrors, antiques and personal memorabilia – cookbooks, tin lanterns, sherry barrels, even an old canoe. Appropriately, the menu revives many Tontine classics – the seafood pancakes, the boudin noir (here served with spiced beetroot purée and golden beetroot rémoulade), the cheese and onion soufflé, and the charcoal-grilled steaks. Also expect some newly minted ideas, ranging from cod cheek 'scampi' with piri-piri sauce to carrot cake with carrot sorbet and spiced pineapple. The Crathorne still trades as a proper pub with real ales, real fires and sandwiches in the bar, plus added inducements including Sunday roasts and live music nights. Around 50 carefully selected wines start at £24.70.

Chef/s: David Henry. **Closed:** Mon, 25 and 26 Dec 1 to 3 Jan. **Meals:** main courses £16 to £32. Set L £15. Set D £20 (2 courses) to £25. Sun L £27. **Details:** 66 seats. 22 seats outside. Bar. Wheelchairs. Parking. Music.

Doncaster

Clam & Cork

Cooking score: 1
Seafood | £19
Fish Market, Doncaster, DN1 1NJ
Tel no: 07830 124906
clam-cork.business.site

£30

Ex-miner turned fishmonger Michael Berry did his research in Porto; in Doncaster, it's an overcoat colder, but his stall in the fish market serves up fresh, Mediterranean-inspired plates. Seared scallops come with a vibrant mint, coriander and lime dressing, and tempura monkfish with slaw spiked with tamarind. Sea bass, white crab salad and brown crab mayo is deceptively simple, with something salty-sweet and hot setting off fireworks. Curried basa resembles your Friday night takeaway but there the similarity ends. Perch on high stools around three sides of the stall and watch fat prawns being thrown on the grill before being given the piri piri treatment; the regularly changing menu is typed on a sheet of brown paper, but look out for the specials, which might involve pork belly and cod. A glass of Prosecco keeps things lively; it's the best fun you can have with your hat and scarf on.
Closed: Mon, Sun. **Meals:** small plates £7 to £11. Large plates £9 to £12. **Details:** 12 seats. No reservations. L only.

Drighlington

Prashad

Cooking score: 2
Indian vegetarian | £26
137 Whitehall Road, Drighlington, BD11 1AT
Tel no: 0113 285 2037
prashad.co.uk

£5 OFF £30

The Patels have been at the forefront of the local Indian vegetarian scene for nigh on three decades, first as owners of a deli-cum-chaat house, and as custodians of this proper licensed restaurant since 2012. Occupying what was a cavernous three-storey roadside pub, Prashad's high-ceilinged rooms provide the perfect setting for specialities from the owners' native Gujarat – plus a few more generic dishes. Minal Patel has been running the kitchen since 2004 and her subtly spiced street snacks and intriguing curries continue to wow the crowds who pack the place. To start, try paneer tikka, kopra pethis (garlic-infused coconut balls) or perhaps a selection of puris with sauces and chutneys, before tackling a masala dosa, the famous chole (a complex chickpea curry with cinnamon and star anise) or a saffron-infused vegetable biryani. There are special mini thalis for 'junior curry lovers', while wines include a smattering of organic and biodynamic labels.
Chef/s: Minal Patel. **Closed:** Mon, 25 Dec. **Meals:** main courses £9 to £23. Tasting menu £39 (5 courses) to £48. **Details:** 75 seats. V menu. Vg menu. Wheelchairs. Parking. Music.

Ferrensby

The General Tarleton

Cooking score: 4
Modern British | £32
Boroughbridge Road, Ferrensby, HG5 0PZ
Tel no: 01423 340284
generaltarleton.co.uk

With all the bare brick, low beams, wood fires and stuffed sofas the enthusiast could wish for, The General Tarleton wrote the book on posh Yorkshire inns. It's also the secret weapon of drivers for whom a journey on the nearby A1 is not complete without a smart but generous feed. Starters such as popcorn king prawns with sriracha and tomato mayo, or Padrón peppers with burrata and romesco sauce, have a global outlook, but mains bring things closer to home. Here there's good Northern meat with rootsy garnishes, perhaps Cumbrian suckling pig with celeriac rémoulade, black pudding and pear, or Goosnargh duck with fondant potato, carrots and orange. Vegans get a look-in even at

popular Sunday lunch, when there's roast cauliflower steak served with mushrooms, nuts and a touch of truffle. The dessert section aims to please: you'll never be far from a sticky toffee pudding or chocolate fondant. Know your regions to get the best from a straightforward wine list, from £18.
Chef/s: John Topham. **Meals:** main courses £15 to £24. **Details:** 120 seats. 45 seats outside. Bar. Parking. Music.

▊ Follifoot

Horto

new chef/no score
Modern British | £40
Rudding Park Hotel, Follifoot, HG3 1JH
Tel no: 01423 871350
ruddingpark.co.uk

Rudding Park Hotel's spa promises pampering of the highest order, while your palate can be indulged at the horticulturally inspired restaurant. The cool white space with its colourful modern artworks provides a fresh backdrop for the inspired cuisine, which takes its cue from produce grown by Rudding's head gardener, Adrian Reeve – seasonality and freshness are a given. As we went to press, chef Murrray Wilson announced his departure and his replacement was yet to be named. The kitchen works its creative magic on ingredients that include obscure varieties you'd be hard-pressed to identify. There's some crossover between the evening carte and the seven-course tasting menu, from scallop with potato and caviar to 'mini milk' with damsons and honeycomb. In between, a neat chunk of Cornish turbot might be surrounded by a ring of morels, artichokes and dabs of seaweed sauce, while Nidderdale mallard could be paired with beetroot and pears. Everything on the well-chosen wine list is available by the glass, with bottles from £36.
Closed: Mon, Tue. **Meals:** main courses £27 to £35. Tasting menu £69 (7 courses). **Details:** 46 seats. V menu. Vg menu. Bar. Wheelchairs. Parking.

▊ Grassington

Grassington House

Cooking score: 3
Modern British | £40
5 The Square, Grassington, BD23 5AQ
Tel no: 01756 752406
grassingtonhouse.co.uk
£5
OFF

As Dales villages go, Grassington is more bustling than sleepy, with a grand cobbled square at its centre, over which the Ruddens' restaurant with rooms casts its benevolent gaze. Catering to both pub and dining constituencies, it's a valued neighbourhood resource, the latter crowd accommodated in an elegant biscuit-coloured room that extends out front into a conservatory space. John Rudden makes a capable fist of contemporary bistro cooking that deals in confidently executed dishes with broad appeal. A seared king scallop with glazed pork belly, crackling and apple might lead into main dishes like Thirsk lamb rump with roasted red pepper and aubergine in olive jus, or the day's beer-battered fish with minted peas and triple-cooked chips. Pre-dinner nibbles are tempting, including duck and chicken spring rolls, while desserts run to classic lemon meringue pie, or rhubarb – Yorkshire's finest – poached and served with custard panna cotta and crumble ice cream. Great care has been taken over the wine descriptions on a comprehensive list, with standard glasses from £5.25.
Chef/s: John Rudden. **Closed:** 25 Dec. **Meals:** main courses £14 to £25. Set L and D £18 Tue to Thur (2 courses) to £20. Sun L £21 (2 courses) to £24. **Details:** 58 seats. Bar. Wheelchairs. Parking. Music.

Halifax

Elder
British | £23
Unit 17, Piece Hall, Halifax, HX1 1RE
Tel no: 01422 414445
thisiselder.com

£30

On a good day, sit outside on the terrace of this small but light-filled café bar and bistro in a corner of the magnificently renovated Georgian Piece Hall and imagine yourself in an Italian palazzo. Alongside cheese and charcuterie boards (expect Dorset coppa, Suffolk chorizo and truffle-infused lardo) might be small plates of roasted cauliflower with a spiky lemon and tarragon dressing or larger sharing plates of braised beef brisket, pea fritters or lamb breast with romesco sauce. A blackboard flags up a handful of 'when they're gone, they're gone' specials. Finish with rhubarb and lemon posset with tarragon shortbread. Ales from Saltaire join gins and well-priced wines on the drinks list.

Harome
The Pheasant Hotel
Cooking score: 4
Modern British | £50
Mill Street, Harome, YO62 5JG
Tel no: 01439 771241
thepheasanthotel.com

It's hard to imagine that this elegant country hotel was once Harome's village smithy and a motley collection of barns, but it is now a destination for all seasons – complete with a snug bar, conservatory and smart dining room. Chef and co-owner Peter Neville cooks with confidence and technical brio, offering blissfully simple dishes such as rabbit pie with a fricassée of spring vegetables and tarragon butter, as well as weaving together more complex ideas – perhaps wild sea bass accompanied by celeriac and goat's cheese, garlic pasta and lovage velouté. Shellfish

platters come piled high, beef is aged for 60 days and desserts include a combo of tarte tatin with Richard III Wensleydale cheese. A simpler bar and lounge menu delivers pubby stalwarts, vegetarians are well served and readers also commend the 'interesting and varied' Sunday lunch offer. The ever-evolving wine list is a bespoke collection of choice vintages from around the globe: in particular, look for the Assyrtiko Wild Ferment (a Greek beauty), bottles from the Saint Clair Family Estate in New Zealand and Argentinian tipples from Bodega Norton. There's also a fine selection by the glass or carafe.
Chef/s: Peter Neville. **Meals:** main courses £20 to £35. Tasting menu £75 (7 courses). Sun L £34. **Details:** 60 seats. 30 seats outside. V menu. Vg menu. Bar. Wheelchairs. Parking. Music.

The Star Inn
Cooking score: 6
Modern British | £50
High Street, Harome, YO62 5JE
Tel no: 01439 770397
thestaratharome.co.uk

Located in a lovely part of bucolic North Yorkshire, this 14th-century part-thatched hostelry was a mould-breaker when it opened in 1996. Reports indicate that it is 'still as good as ever', still operating as a proper pub as well as a restaurant. Andrew Pern's cooking is serious and ingredients are seldom less than exceptional. Besides using local suppliers, Pern has established a kitchen garden and his finely honed dishes pay their dues to 'modern Yorkshire'. The menu moves confidently from a gutsy raviolo of locally shot hare to the subtler delights of North Sea turbot with white asparagus, given oomph by smoked eel, pink fir potato salad, 'green rice' and scorched horseradish cream. Barley-aged veal loin with hay-baked celeriac, roasted yeast, pale ale, Henderson's relish, morels and buttered spinach is a particularly winning combination. The cheese course is highly rated and puddings might include sherried fig frangipane with caramel notes coming from a trio of ice cream, quince and Pedro Ximénez syrup. The wine list is lovingly compiled, with plenty by the glass and real effort made to provide excellent choice under £35.

Chef/s: Andrew Pern and Stephen Smith. **Meals:** main courses £19 to £32. Set L and D £20 (2 courses) to £25. **Details:** 80 seats. 60 seats outside. V menu. Bar. Wheelchairs. Parking. Music.

▮ Harrogate
Orchid

Cooking score: 2
Pan-Asian | £35
Studley Hotel, 28 Swan Road, Harrogate, HG1 2SE
Tel no: 01423 560425
orchidrestaurant.co.uk

£5 OFF 🚊

The basement of the sober-looking Studley Hotel may not seem the obvious setting for pan-Asian cooking of note, but this has been a go-to address in Harrogate for close on two decades. It's been a happy partnership, with the restaurant delivering the flavours of the Orient in a calm space furnished in dark wood that manages to avoid cultural clichés. There are set menus if required, a Sunday lunchtime buffet, and a long à la carte that might take you from siu yuk (Hong Kong-style roasted pork belly with yellow bean and honey dip), via pad thai noodles to Malaysian curry with tiger prawns, scallops, squid and mussels. There are familiar options such as Vietnamese spring rolls, sweet-and-sour prawns and Thai green curry, but equally you might go for venison fired up with cumin, ginger and chilli. The wine list has handy tasting notes, or go for Thai, Japanese and Chinese lagers, or Yorkshire ale.

Chef/s: Kenneth Poon. **Closed:** 25 and 26 Dec. **Meals:** main courses £6 to £22. set L £25 (2 courses) to £20. Set D £34 to £40. **Details:** 78 seats. 24 seats outside. Bar. Parking. Music.

Stuzzi

Cooking score: 2
Italian | £25
46b Kings Road, Harrogate, HG1 5JW
Tel no: 01423 705852

£5 OFF £30

As good for locals as for delegates at the nearby Conference Centre, this lively Italian has cornered the market in relaxed dining. It's so popular that they've added a tented extension out front to fit in more tables. It's not a thing of beauty, but they've jazzed it up with flags and greenery, and the restaurant maintains a young, spirited vibe with knowledgeable staff and food that pleases. A dozen small plates feature arancini: deep-fried rice balls with veal marrow and 'nduja. Sardinian flatbread is layered with artichoke and mint pesto and smoked ricotta, and tagliatelle with mussels and tomatoes is given a creamy crab bisque. For freshness there's a raw salad of fennel, red onion, walnut and blue cheese. Tempting desserts include Sicilian cannoli filled with sweet ricotta, or warm zeppole doused in cinnamon and lemon sugar. A substantial Italian wine list starts at £24.50. A second Stuzzi in Leeds opened this year (see entry).

Chef/s: Brett Domendziak. **Closed:** Mon, Tue, 25 and 26 Dec, 1 Jan. **Meals:** small plates £4 to £12. **Details:** 40 seats. 20 seats outside. Bar. Music.

▮ Hetton
The Angel Inn

Cooking score: 5
Modern British | £45
Hetton, BD23 6LT
Tel no: 01756 730263
angelhetton.co.uk

£5 OFF 🚊

It's been a national treasure since 1983, when Denis Watkins began serving provençal fish soup and seafood-filled filo 'moneybags' and redefined British pub food forever. When he died in 2004 the mantle was taken up by his son, Pascal, and if The Angel lost some of the Watkins dynamism on the way, it has remained a much-loved institution. So when Michael Wignall, star chef of fine dining at Gidleigh Park, took it on last year there were fears he might meddle with a much-loved friend. In stripping away the clutter and giving the interior a fresh, pared-down look, he's created a restaurant that reflects his own lightness of touch. A spring menu brings expertly torched mackerel with cucumber and taramasalata. Soothing salt-baked celeriac comes with smoked ricotta and winter truffle. Delicate skrei cod is beautifully matched with a mini cassoulet of sea vegetables and haricots blancs. The wine list starts at a reasonable £20 and rises steeply. Soften the blow with a rum-soaked baba. The former wine cave across the road is being remodelled for fine dining, but for now, Wignall is cooking like an angel. The legacy is intact.

Chef/s: Michael Wignall. **Closed:** 2 weeks Jan, Tue and Wed (Jan to Mar). **Meals:** main courses £23 to £32. Tasting menu £65 (6 courses). **Details:** 72 seats. 15 seats outside. V menu. Parking.

■ Holmfirth

★ NEW ENTRY ★

Devour at The Dyehouse

Cooking score: 1
Italian | £25
Luke Lane, Thongsbridge, Holmfirth, HD9 7TB
Tel no: 01484 684793
devour.co.uk
£5 OFF £30

Marche-born Olivia Robinson's dream of bringing traditional Italian food to the area came true when she found a derelict mill in the Holme Valley. A sensitive renovation (stripped roof trusses, blasted stone walls) has resulted in a stylish, light-filled space that's backed up by a good-looking menu delivering such classics as fritto misto with a zingy lemon mayo and sweet baby roast tomatoes, fresh burrata on smokey prosciutto, and textbook arancini, light and moreish, flecked through with mozzarella. There's a decent range of homemade pasta dishes and a huge wood-fired pizza oven spitting out the likes of

Taleggio and salsiccia, and super-sized calzone. Start in the cool lounge with cicchetti and a negroni or a glass of Fiano; the all-Italian wine list matches the food nicely. On the way out, stop by the deli counter and take home house-made Altamura-style bread, pasticcini and cannoli.

Chef/s: Carl Frost. **Closed:** Mon, Tue. **Meals:** main courses £10 to £25. Set L and D £25 (2 courses) to £30. **Details:** 80 seats. 60 seats outside. Bar. Wheelchairs. Parking.

LOCAL GEM

Philomena Foggs

British | £10
Unit 11 Albion Mills, Miry Lane, Thongsbridge, Holmfirth, HD9 7HP
Tel no: 01484 683444
philomenafoggs.co.uk
£5 OFF £30

'Great food, great atmosphere,' notes one reader. 'Extremely friendly and efficient service', praises another. It's worth getting lost trying to find this characterful former mill tucked away in a slightly scruffy yard in the Holme Valley. The rewards of this quirky café are many: good choices on the breakfast menu, and lunch brings homely comforts in the shape of shepherd's pie, burgers, goat's cheese tart or smoked haddock chowder. Cakes and breads are homemade, the coffee's excellent and there are three cabinets of gin. Terrific value, too.

■ Honley
Mustard & Punch

Cooking score: 2
Modern British | £30
6 Westgate, Honley, HD9 6AA
Tel no: 01484 662066
mustardandpunch.co.uk
£30

An industrious and ebullient local favourite that has been doing sterling service in Honley since the turn of the millennium, this is a pure-bred bistro – right down to its comfy banquettes, Champagne posters, racks of wine and deep red walls. The cooking follows suit, although this is the eclectic modern world of confit pork shoulder with peppered squid, spice-cured salmon with Bombay potato salad and treacle-braised ox cheek with Jerusalem artichokes. Bigger plates also celebrate Whitby fish and Yorkshire meats – perhaps a trio of locally reared beef, saddleback pork, or pheasant from Upperwood Estate (served with caramelised red onion tarte tatin, heritage carrots and game sauce). To finish, mini desserts ('little treats') are always worth a nibble, or you could splash out on Yorkshire parkin with vanilla-poached rhubarb and liquorice ice cream. Tuesday night is steak night, Sunday lunch brings a thumping roast, and there's plenty for vegetarians and vegans too. Easy-drinking international wines start at £18 (£4.50 a glass).

Chef/s: Will Orme. **Closed:** Mon, Tue, 1 to 3 Jan. **Meals:** main courses £16 to £26. Set L £14 (2 courses) to £18. Set early D £20 Wed to Sat (2 courses) to £25. Sun L £19 (2 courses) to £23. **Details:** 55 seats. V menu. Music.

LOCAL GEM

Punch Bar & Tapas

Spanish | £26
11 Westgate, Honley, HD9 6AA
Tel no: 01484 662359
punchhonley.co.uk

£30

Never ones to let the grass grow under their feet, Richard Dunn and Wayne Roddis have expanded their empire in cobbled Honley to include a craft beer bar, an Italian bistro and this fun tapas joint. Some dishes might not be what you'd expect to find in Spain (although albondigas and croquetas are in the line-up) but that's no bad thing: gin-and-beetroot-cured salmon packs a punch, as does smoked haddock rarebit, while pig's cheeks and onglet are worth seeking out. The vibe is jolly, service is sweet and prices are reasonable, especially for house wines (from £15); there are draught beers and cocktails, too.

■ Huddersfield
Epicure Bar & Kitchen

Cooking score: 2
Modern British | £35
37-39 Queensgate, Huddersfield, HD1 2RD
Tel no: 01484 961587
epicurebarandkitchen.co.uk

There are a number of reasons to head for this unpretentious café and bistro, not least the splendidly varied breakfast, brunch and lunch menus, with the likes of homemade beans on sourdough or pulled pork with Manchego and pickled radish on house flatbread. But it all goes up a couple of notches on Friday and Saturday evening, when chef Lewis Myzak is given free rein. Expect flavour-packed combos such as black pudding and cave-aged Cheddar dumpling with chicken stock and pickled onions or a stunning wood-fired chicken breast with bacon fat potato purée, cherry ketchup and soused cabbage. Myzak has a fondness for unusual pairings, so don't be surprised to find a spicy samphire bhajia with poached haddock or Tabasco beetroot with crispy lamb belly; he has a novel way with bubble and squeak too. There's a good beer offer and the wine list is short but well thought through.

Chef/s: Lewis Myzak. **Closed:** Mon. **Meals:** small plates £7 to £18. **Details:** 45 seats. Bar. Music.

■ Ilkley
The Box Tree

Cooking score: 5
International | £70
35-37 Church Street, Ilkley, LS29 9DR
Tel no: 01943 608484
theboxtree.co.uk

🍷

It's now 15 years since Rena and Simon Gueller brought some much-needed stability to this renowned Ilkley restaurant. In 2019, Simon was joined in the kitchen by Michael Carr and together they apply classic techniques and an instinctive feel for tastes and textures to a menu that explores an extensive larder exemplified by a terrine of duck with chicory, enoki mushrooms and dashi. Plant-based dishes impressed, with a beetroot sorbet accompanied by candied beetroot, cream cheese and nasturtium leaves, followed by baked celeriac, hen of the wood mushrooms and melted burrata served in a miniature copper pan. Passion fruit soufflé with a mango and lime sauce poured at the table is a Gueller classic, and deservedly so. Service is formal but approachable as one regular diner reports: 'This restaurant cannot be beaten for service.' The expertly managed wine list roams the globe; sommelier Didier Da Costa's picks are usefully highlighted for those who feel overwhelmed by choice and there are one-off bin ends for the vinously adventurous.

Chef/s: Simon Gueller and Michael Carr. **Closed:** Mon, Tue, 26 to 31 Dec, 1 to 8 Jan. **Meals:** set L £35 (2 courses) to £45. Set D £70. Tasting menu £85 (6 courses). Sun L £45. **Details:** 50 seats. Bar. Music. Children over 5 yrs at L, over 10 yrs at D.

★ NEW ENTRY ★

Host

Cooking score: 3
Modern British | £30
60 The Grove, Ilkley, LS29 9PA
Tel no: 01943 605337
hostilkley.co.uk
£5 OFF £30

'Genuinely overwelmed with this delightful new restaurant,' says a recent visitor to the quietly stylish addition to the Ilkley food scene. Host has an airy, cool whiff of Scandi, with good art on muted walls. Chef owner Joel Monkman's distinguished food heritage is deployed effectively in a short but appealing menu featuring the likes of smoked cheese and onion gougères, hogget scrumpet – totally neckable lamby, breadcrumbed cubes on a vivid, minty puddle – and simple but effective cured sea trout, beetroot, apple and horseradish. Cauliflower is roasted with confit garlic and sits on a house-made flatbread with Kashmiri spiced butter sauce; you'll also find monkfish fritters in featherlight tempura. Of the three dessert choices, the moist, spiced

parkin with Yorkshire forced rhubarb sorbet and whipped thyme custard is a winner. The grown-up wine list offers matches with each course, and to finish who could resist a wicked espresso martini with the dark chocolate and walnut millefeuille?

Chef/s: Joel Monkman. **Closed:** Mon, Tue. **Meals:** small plates £6 to £22. Set L £12 (2 courses). **Details:** 44 seats. 16 seats outside. Bar. Music.

■ Leeds

Home

Cooking score: 5
Modern European | £55
16-17 Kirkgate, Leeds, LS1 6BY
Tel no: 0113 430 0161
homeleeds.co.uk

For a masterclass in thoughtful, ingredient-led cooking, push through a blink-and-you'll-miss-it doorway on Kirkgate, climb the dark, winding staircase and emerge into a spacious bar and dining room with an open kitchen at one end. The chefs here have glossy pedigrees and they go about their business with gusto, offering a monthly changing tasting menu of five or ten courses. Based on a zealous enthusiasm for entirely fresh ingredients, the food is a reworking of classic European dishes and flavours, with aged oxtail, roast langoustine, roast turbot and saddle of red deer all coming in for praise at a November meal. March could bring rare breed pork beignets with rhubarb jam, lavender-smoked duck with a pistachio-flecked pâté of the bird and slices of blood orange, or smoked salmon with stuffed artichokes, caviar and lemon. A selection of snacks, good brioche with a mix of butter and meat juices, and desserts, including the kitchen's take on lemon meringue pie, are much appreciated. Service is smooth and the wine pairings spot-on, while the list itself is well constructed, with good choice by the glass.

Chef/s: Elizabeth Cottam and Mark Owens. **Closed:** Mon, Tue, 25 Dec to 9 Jan, 27 Jul to 13 Aug. **Meals:** tasting menu £55 (5 courses) to £75. Sun L £55 (7 courses). **Details:** 42 seats. V menu. Bar. Music. Pre-payment required.

Issho

Cooking score: 3
Japanese | £40
Victoria Gate, Leeds, LS2 7AU
Tel no: 0113 426 5000
issho-restaurant.com

Tucked away in a corner of the glossy Victoria Gate shopping centre, a lift silently swooshes you up to the Kori rooftop bar where decking and low-slung sofas are set on a leafy terrace. If the roofscape is nothing to shout about, then the sake, cocktails and Japanese snacks will make up for it. The large restaurant, all neutral tones and natural materials, serves dinner, lunch, Sunday brunch and Japanese afternoon tea taking in sushi, sashimi, maki rolls, hot and cold dishes and the ever popular pork or chicken stuffed bao buns. Sweet potato with smoked lime and coconut butter comes off the robata grill or go for broke with the terrific miso black cod. Teams of waiting staff are on hand to advise or, if it's all too daunting, opt for the Gourmet or Emperor set menus. To drink, choose from a short wine list and a long list of sakes.
Chef/s: Joe Grant. **Closed:** 25 Dec, 1 Jan.
Meals: small plates £4 to £14. Large plates £18 to £34. Set L £15. Early D £25 (4 courses). Tasting menu £45 (6 courses) to £65. **Details:** 114 seats. 24 seats outside. Vg menu. Bar. Wheelchairs. Music.

★ TOP 50 ★

The Man Behind The Curtain

Cooking score: 7
Modern British | £85
68-78 Vicar Lane, Leeds, LS1 7JH
Tel no: 0113 243 2376
themanbehindthecurtain.co.uk

Since relocating to this marble-clad monochrome basement in 2017, Michael O'Hare has really hit his stride – this is quite the bucket list restaurant now. The luxuriantly coiffeured O'Hare and his leather-aproned, black T-shirt-wearing team deliver a series of snacks and small dishes to the sound of Lou Reed, The Killers, Roxy Music and New

Order floating from impressive wall speakers. An evening here is pure theatre with a blast of rock 'n' roll: 'one of the most exciting meals I've had in ages,' enthused one visitor. There's no actual menu so you just have to sit back and see where the journey takes you. Snacks, say crisp tuna belly nigiri teamed with wasabi, freeze-dried blackcurrant and Fishermen's Friend cough sweets, and a char siu octopus hot dog, lead into the meal proper. Highlights of our visit included incredibly fresh Dénia red prawn topped with thermidor sauce, a deeply flavoured tartare of 160-day aged Hereford beef and a fragrant, spicy dish of sweetbread in XO with tuna belly tartare, garlic purée, Exmoor caviar, fermented iceberg and a generous shaving of black truffle. The famed 'Emancipation' is a tongue-in-cheek take on traditional fish and chips, with snow-white cod loin offset by Jackson Pollock-style splashes of black squid ink and vinegar powder, and crisp shards of black fried potatoes. Another stunning combo is squab pigeon breast with rhubarb and hoisin sauce, enoki mushrooms, crispy pigeon legs and wasabi. Desserts include a Lilliputian cupcake with an edible case and one inspired by Drumstick lollies. As for drinks, match dishes with house beers or wines from a compact list.
Chef/s: Michael O'Hare. **Closed:** Mon, Sun.
Meals: tasting menu L £55 (6 courses) to £65 and D £75 (10 courses) to £125. **Details:** 42 seats. V menu. Wheelchairs. Music. Pre-payment required.

★ NEW ENTRY ★

Matt Healy x The Foundry

Cooking score: 2
Modern European | £35
1 Saw Mill Yard, Leeds, LS11 5WH
Tel no: 0113 245 0390
mhfoundry.co.uk

Holbeck (now South Bank for those of us who didn't get the memo from the council) was a part of town you didn't venture into after hours. But the dark satanic mills have had a facelift and the 2016 *Masterchef: The Professionals* finalist Matt Healy's post-industrial venue is the business: all exposed brick, filament bulbs, lofted arches and a polished concrete floor. The open kitchen, above which is the neon-lit legend 'Food to swear by', is populated by a young crew putting together a series of (mostly) small plates. There's careful balance at play – the vibe might be bold but the food is subtle and delicate – along the lines of torched mackerel offset with tart apple and a scatter of Instagrammable purple viola, exemplary beef tartare topped with an egg yolk and with a blue cheese and onion toastie side, or a vivacious sea bass ceviche. To finish, there's smooth-as-silk lemon posset with tiny meringues and a sprinkle of sherbet, and a textbook chocolate and hazelnut fondant with sharp raspberry sorbet and praline rubble. The considered wine list roams the world.

Chef/s: Matt Healy. **Closed:** Mon, 24 Dec to 2 Jan. **Meals:** small plates £6 to £12. Large plates £18 to £31. Set L £15 (2 courses). **Details:** 44 seats. 24 seats outside. Bar. Wheelchairs. Music. No children at D.

Ox Club
Cooking score: 3
Modern British | £32
Headrow House, The Headrow, Leeds, LS1 6PU
Tel no: 07470 359961
oxclub.co.uk

Headrow House, a converted textile mill, is rammed with opportunities to have a good time. But the beer halls and roof terraces can wait: the smart money is on starting at Ox Club, where good old-fashioned fire is at the heart of the kitchen. There's a new chef, Andy Castle, in charge of the unwieldy wood-fired grill, but its searing heat is still being used to fine effect – if an ingredient can be grilled, it will be, including a starter salad of purple sprouting broccoli with Cheddar sauce and chive oil. Mains might be ox cheek with smoked mash and chestnut gremolata or grilled sea trout with shiso butter and 'Tokyo frites', a clump of rustling shredded potato with a little Japanese spice. Finish with rye parfait with amaretto and chocolate mousse,

or marmalade-accented bread and butter pudding. A short Europe-skewed wine list can handle all that smoke, from £19.

Chef/s: Andy Castle. **Closed:** Mon, 24 to 26 Dec, 1 Jan. **Meals:** main courses £14 to £28. Early D £20 (2 courses) to £23. **Details:** 38 seats. Bar. Wheelchairs.

The Reliance
Cooking score: 3
Modern British | £29
76-78 North Street, Leeds, LS2 7PN
Tel no: 0113 295 6060
the-reliance.co.uk
£30

At this former Victorian cloth mill (now a bar, restaurant and cinema), there's a proud industriousness to the kitchen. For a start, the owners make their own home-cured charcuterie, bread and pickles, which form part of the sharing boards, and all meat is reared in Yorkshire. Combined with a welcome informality and the fact that prices are so keen (given the generous portions and quality of the raw ingredients), it means this has become a popular foodie hub. The open kitchen in the high-ceilinged first floor dining room keeps things simple with a range of big-flavoured small plates, say duck livers with ras el hanout, fennel, radicchio and pomegranate molasses, or queen scallops teamed with golden sultanas and cauliflower, which could precede a large plate of lamb shoulder with turnips and salsa verde, or cod served with romesco, spring onions and roast tomato. Drink local beers and global wines from £18.

Chef/s: Tom Hunter. **Closed:** bank hols. **Meals:** main courses £12 to £16. **Details:** 80 seats. 4 seats outside. Bar. Wheelchairs. Music.

Visit us online
For the most up-to-date information about *The Good Food Guide*, go to thegoodfoodguide.co.uk.

Salvo's

Cooking score: 2
Italian | £28
115 Otley Road, Headingley, Leeds, LS6 3PX
Tel no: 0113 275 5017
salvos.co.uk
£5 OFF £30

Salvatore Dammone opened this big, brash and noisy fixture of the Headingley scene back in 1976 – and it's still in the family. Old-timers will remember when queuing was obligatory, but crowds still pack the place for some of the finest pizzas and pastas in town, all served in a buzzy revamped space with bare tables, leather-backed chairs and family photos on the walls. The flame-blistered pizzas come with all sorts of toppings, from quattro formaggi and calabrese (with 'nduja and ricotta) to Kiev (a folded variant stuffed with pulled chicken, Yorkshire ham and garlic butter). Alternatively, begin with some antipasti (perhaps mushroom arancini or fritto misto) before tackling a generous secondo such as lamb rump with cannellini bean purée and charred broccoli. Salvo's aims to please all-comers, from families and students to vegans and those on gluten-free diets, while the all-Italian drinks list runs from regional wines and obscure craft beers to gins and cocktails.
Chef/s: Gip Dammone and Oliver Edwards.
Closed: 25 and 26 Dec, 1 Jan. **Meals:** main courses £11 to £29. Set L £12 (2 courses). Set D £15 (2 courses) to £19. Sun L £19 (2 courses) to £23.
Details: 85 seats. 20 seats outside. Vg menu. Bar. Wheelchairs. Music.

★ NEW ENTRY ★

Stuzzi

Cooking score: 3
Italian | £25
7 Merrion Street, Leeds, LS1 6PQ
Tel no: 0113 245 5323
£30

Don't be put off by the entrance in dowdy Merrion Street. The blacked-out windows and gold lettering make it look more like a nightclub than an Italian-inspired small plates eatery, but if you make it up the stairs to the sunlit attic, the daily changing menu of a dozen sharing dishes will be your reward. This attractive room with its skylight, feature arched window and contemporary bentwood furniture is the work of the four enthusiastic lads who created Stuzzi, Harrogate (see entry) five years ago, bringing the same good-natured zeal to this, their second branch. Our inspection visit revealed deep-fried courgette flower stuffed with lemon ricotta; orecchiette with shavings of juicy, sticky ham hock, and outstanding porchetta stuffed with Neapolitan sausage flavoured with fennel and chilli then roasted with balsamic onions and potatoes soaked in porky juices. An expansive and prestigious Italian wine list starts at £20.50 and rises to dizzy heights.
Chef/s: Brett Domendziak. **Meals:** small plates £7 to £17. **Details:** 80 seats. Bar.

The Swine that Dines

Cooking score: 4
Modern British | £25
58 North Street, Leeds, LS2 7PN
Tel no: 0113 2440387
swinethatdines.co.uk
£5 OFF £30

A casual visitor would never imagine that this informal little dining room with its Duralex glasses and wipe-clean tables is serving some of the best food in Leeds. It may have had a recent freshen-up with new signage and a lick of paint, but it remains Stuart and Jo Myers' clever operation, where for a bargain £50 for two, Stuart prepares a beautifully balanced evening menu of seven original and well-paced dishes to share. The line-up changes monthly but might feature sweetcorn cobs with smoked sage butter, heritage tomatoes with labneh and dill, seaweed cured salmon with asparagus and buttermilk and, the first week of the month, the popular Roots to Shoots vegetarian menu. In a new departure there's a small plates menu on Friday and Saturday lunchtimes and, twice a month, Pie Sunday brings a choice of exquisite pies,

maybe venison suet pudding, pork, shallot and lardo roll or chickpea, leek and mint with a puff pastry lid. Terrific ice creams and BYO drink with no corkage are added bonuses.
Chef/s: Stuart Myers. **Closed:** Mon, Tue, alternate Sun, last 2 weeks Aug. **Meals:** small plates £5 to £9 Fri and Sat. Tasting menu for 2 £50 (7 courses). Sun L £18 (2 courses) to £23. **Details:** 16 seats. V menu. Music.

Tharavadu

Cooking score: 2
Indian | £30
7-8 Mill Hill, Leeds, LS1 5DQ
Tel no: 0113 244 0500
tharavadurestaurants.com
£5 OFF £30

The name translates as 'ancestral home', and it is the culinary traditions and aromatic flavours of Kerala that are explored at this Mill Hill eatery. The expansive dining room is adorned with natural wood and regional artefacts while the kitchen is very much at home when it comes to vegetarian and seafood cooking. Classic dosas, puris and idli come with pungent and aromatic accompaniments, and king fish arrives in a fragrant Alleppey sauce. Lamb is a regional treat, too; adu cheera mappas is a classic curry usually eaten at Easter, while an everyday favourite is kohzi curry (chicken with roasted coconut with distinctive spicing). Those with a sweet tooth will enjoy vattayapam fudge cake and jaggery dosa. The helpfully annotated wine list is focused on varietals that can cope with the spicing, and Yorkshire fares well on the list of craft beers.
Chef/s: Ajith Nair. **Closed:** Sun, 23 to 26 Dec. **Meals:** main courses £12 to £20. **Details:** 138 seats. V menu. Vg menu. Wheelchairs. Music.

Local Gem

These entries are brilliant neighbourhood venues, delivering good, freshly cooked food at great value for money.

Zucco

Italian | £28
603 Meanwood Road, Leeds, LS6 4AY
Tel no: 0113 224 9679
zucco.co.uk
£30

More Lazio than Leeds, this main-road neighbourhood venue takes its inspiration from a backstreet Italian bacaro, right down to the tiled walls and copper-panel ceiling. The Leggiero brothers – Rosario cooks, Michael charms diners – are hands-on owners and their personalities are stamped all over the wedge-shaped dining room. Sharing dishes range from spaghetti with clams, pancetta, chilli and garlic, and saffron risotto with Taleggio to braised beef pappardelle with Grana Padano, and pheasant with mixed mushrooms and blueberry jus. A thoughtful Italian wine list opens at £17.40.

■ Leyburn
The Sandpiper Inn

Cooking score: 2
Modern British | £34
Market Place, Leyburn, DL8 5AT
Tel no: 01969 622206
sandpiperinn.co.uk

Over the past 20 years Jonathan and Janine Harrison have done a grand job of maintaining this characterful stone-built inn with rooms. It still operates as a traditional watering hole with the cosy bar dispensing real ales, but the emphasis is on things culinary. Menus foreshadow Jonathan Harrison's direct style, which acknowledges current trends as well as offering tried-and-true pub dishes. So whether you are in the mood for a classic ham hock terrine or grilled rib burger with streaky bacon and smoked Cheddar or something more ambitious – fillet of cod with wilted greens, potato gnocchi and a caviar sauce or lemon-roasted chicken breast on a leek and porcini risotto –

you won't put the kitchen off its stroke. Don't miss tempting desserts such as blackcurrant and white chocolate bread and butter pudding or crème brûlée with shortbread. Wines start at £18.

Chef/s: Jonathan Harrison. **Closed:** Mon, Tue (winter only), 2 weeks Jan, 2 weeks May. **Meals:** main courses £14 to £19. **Details:** 56 seats. 20 seats outside. V menu. Vg menu. Bar. Parking. Music.

READERS RECOMMEND

Thirteen

13 Railway Street, Leyburn, DL8 5BB
Tel no: 01969 622951
thirteenatleyburn.co.uk

'It's all about flavour here. Perfectly cooked hake fillet came with a delicious black olive crust and a rich, savoury crab risotto that sang of the sea. Warm almond cake, gooey with fruit syrup, was topped with poached peaches and raspberries.'

▌Lindley

Eric's

Cooking score: 3
Modern British | £45
73-75 Lidget Street, Lindley, HD3 3JP
Tel no: 01484 646416
ericsrestaurant.co.uk

On a suburban shopping street in handsome Lindley, a couple of clicks from the centre of Huddersfield, Eric Paxman has been flying the flag for contemporary fine dining for the past decade. There is evidence of Paxman's experience in kitchens across the globe in menus that show creative flair, but Yorkshire produce is at the heart of things. The smart modern space matches the ambition of the food, with a changing landscape of local art on the walls. Things get off to a colourful start when sea bass is matched with pomegranate, and Asian mango and soy dressing, while a more European-inspired alternative might be seared calf's liver with pulled ox cheek risotto and puffed potato. Roasted bream sees more of those Eastern leanings, this time paired

with ginger, chilli and miso broth, while tender pigeon breast might be complemented by pumpkin and wild mushroom ravioli. Fixed-price lunches are a steal. For pudding, how about sticky treacle and pecan tart? The clued-up wine list opens at £21.

Chef/s: James Thompson and Chris Kelly. **Closed:** Mon. **Meals:** main courses £22 to £30. Set L and early D £20 (2 courses) to £25. Sun L £20 (2 courses) to £25. **Details:** 70 seats. V menu. Vg menu. Bar. Wheelchairs. Music.

▌Masham

Samuel's

Cooking score: 3
Modern British | £60
Swinton Park, Masham, HG4 4JH
Tel no: 01765 680900
swintonestate.com

There's a lot going on at this stately castellated pile set in 20,000 acres in the heart of Lower Wensleydale: glamorous bedrooms, a cookery school, a state-of-the-art spa and, at its heart, a formal restaurant. This is opulent dining of the highest order, with linen-dressed tables, heavy drapes and a gold-leaf ceiling. Expect a modern menu in which chef James Cooper makes use of Swinton's kitchen garden and game, rabbit and venison from the estate. Cooper serves smoked trout from the river Ure, venison loin with honey and lavender glazed turnips. Poached pear, bitter chocolate mousse and lemon custard with rhubarb sorbet all feature at dessert. A bountiful wine list provides a generous selection by the glass. The spa's Terrace restaurant offers more informal dining with Josper grilled skate wing in brown butter, slow-roast pork belly, pasta, risotto, salads and small dishes to share.

Chef/s: James Cooper. **Closed:** Mon, Tue. **Meals:** set D £60. Tasting menu £75 (7 courses). Sun L £28. **Details:** 70 seats. Bar. Wheelchairs. Parking. Music. Children over 8 yrs.

▊ Middleton Tyas
The Forge
Cooking score: 4
Modern British | £75
Middleton Lodge, Kneeton Lane, Middleton
Tyas, DL10 6NJ
Tel no: 01325 377977
middletonlodge.co.uk

This glorious 18th-century estate, just two
miles from the A1 at Scotch Corner, continues
to develop. We previously reported on The
Coach House, but this has now been refigured
as an all-day casual dining venue, and chef
Gareth Rayner has transferred his considerable
skills to The Forge, housed in an adjacent
building. It's an attractive suite of rooms of
exposed beams, honeyed stone and
candlelight, offering a no-choice tasting
menu which makes the best use of the estate's
walled garden. Memorable dishes at
inspection included a delicate plate of
broccoli, artichoke and Parmesan with a touch
of sweetness from pickled broccoli stalks.
Local outdoor-reared pork belly, pig's cheek
and crisp jowl also impressed, as did the finale,
a fusion of cherry sorbet, poached cherries,
almond and chocolate. Expect charming
service from a predominantly local team.
Choose from the hefty wine list or the menu
pairings (£40 and £45) or the signature
pairing at a punchy £90.
Chef/s: Gareth Rayner. **Closed:** Mon, Tue, Sun.
Meals: tasting menu £75 (9 courses). **Details:** 40
seats. V menu. Vg menu. Bar. Wheelchairs. Parking.
Music.

Tommy Banks
The Black Swan, Oldstead & Roots, York

**What do you enjoy most about being
a chef?**
The people. I'm privileged to work with so
many fantastic, like-minded individuals.

**What is the most unusual cooking or
preparation technique you use?**
I think the secret to our success is
applying classic cooking techniques to
unusual ingredients, rather than the other
way around.

**If you could ban one thing from your
kitchen, what would it be?**
I already have. It's chewing gum. Why
would a chef want a mouthful of artificial
mint flavour when they're supposed to be
tasting for a living?

**When you get home at the end of a long
day, what do you like to eat?**
I rarely eat late at night. I've noticed a real
change in chefs' eating habits over the
years. A lot of young chefs I know are as
likely to have a protein shake as they are
a beer at the end of the evening.

**And finally... tell us something about
yourself that will surprise your diners.**
When I go to the cinema I don't eat
popcorn but I do take a little cheese,
some cured meats and a few olives!

▋ Newton-on-Ouse
The Dawnay Arms

Cooking score: 3
Modern British | £30
Moor Lane, Newton-on-Ouse, YO30 2BR
Tel no: 01347 848345
thedawnayatnewton.co.uk
£30

It secured its prime position by the river Ouse way back in 1779, and the view down the garden and across the water from this handsome inn has changed little. An abundance of original features within adds to the timeless atmosphere, while the standards of hospitality and the quality of the food are aimed firmly at contemporary appetites. A sandwich by the river is a summertime treat (local pork sausages with onion chutney, say, and surely a pint of Black Sheep). Seasoned chef Martel Smith runs a kitchen that displays adroit technical ability and delivers rollicking flavours. Get off the mark with caramelised chicory tart with Wensleydale Blue salad, or ham hock ballotine with black pudding Scotch egg and a pineapple pickle to cut through all that meaty gorgeousness. The ribeye steak comes with triple-cooked chips and a choice of sauces, or go for a veggie cottage pie with spiced red cabbage. Finish with cherry and almond tart. Drink regional ales or wines from £15.
Chef/s: Martel Smith. **Closed:** Mon, 1 week Jan. **Meals:** main courses £14 to £28. Set L and D £15 (2 courses) to £18. Sun L £18 (2 courses) to £22. **Details:** 65 seats. 50 seats outside. Bar. Wheelchairs. Parking. Music.

▋ Nun Monkton

★ NEW ENTRY ★

The Alice Hawthorn

Cooking score: 3
Modern British | £36
The Green, Nun Monkton, YO26 8EW
Tel no: 01423 330303
thealicehawthorn.com
£5
OFF

Named after a famous racehorse, this handsome pub of mellow brick is set in an archetypal English village complete with duck pond and green. Inside, it's neat and trim with a restful blue-grey palette, flagged floors and winged armchairs of soft Yorkshire tartan (12 bedrooms will be added this year). The food is equally polished. Dinner might begin with a soup of cauliflower and Harrogate blue cheese or a salad of soused mackerel with fennel, orange, beetroot and pink peppercorns. Mains could be venison haunch or, from the daily fish board, halibut with asparagus or curried monkfish, all with well-considered accompaniments: the chargrilled Ibérico pork comes with dauphinois potatoes, roast beetroot, poached pear, cauliflower purée and spinach. Desserts feature crumble, sticky toffee pudding and an elegant Yorkshire rhubarb mousse wrapped in a paper-thin tuile and, alongside, poached rhubarb, jelly, compôte and rhubarb crisp. There are plenty of wines by the glass from a list that opens with a bottle of Pays d'Oc at £18.
Chef/s: Simon Ball. **Closed:** Mon, Tue. **Meals:** main courses £15 to £29. **Details:** 70 seats. 20 seats outside. Bar. Wheelchairs. Parking. Music.

Oldstead

★ TOP 50 ★

The Black Swan

Cooking score: 7
Modern British | £98
Main Street, Oldstead, YO61 4BL
Tel no: 01347 868387
blackswanoldstead.co.uk

Is it a country pub? You may enter via a flagstoned bar with log fire but the Banks family's ancient hostelry has been reinvented for the 21st century as a stand-out dining destination. The food is hard-wired to the Yorkshire soil, much of it grown in the 20-acre kitchen garden next door, and is all about nudging boundaries, broadening culinary perceptions. It's also about the sheer pleasure of fine food in all its diversity – a light-hearted, conversational place where no one feels out of their depth, thanks to superb management and confident staff who know how to demystify the details without losing their sense of humour. Tommy Banks' extraordinary 12-course menu evokes flavours that are strikingly vivid, as these highlights from a spring menu reveal: the hint of lemon in layers of whipped buttermilk, crab and asparagus; the minerally tang of raw diced venison richly combined with garlic mayo, smokey butter and aromatic sorrel leaves; a gorgeously fresh scallop, its sweetness offset by the gentle acidity in a sauce of onion, smoked butter, rhubarb, finely chopped samphire and diced razor clams. And when it comes to orthodox cooking, Banks can cut it with the best – note roasted monkfish on a bed of trompette mushrooms in a fermented celeriac and mushroom stock sauce, beurre noisette spooned at table adding rich nutty notes. Even the sourdough bread is in a class of its own. You can slip in an extra course from the cheese trolley or move on to desserts proper – perhaps a rhubarb and clotted cream ice cream sandwich or the heady confection of crisp chicory root crumble and silky mousse topped with a charlotte potato custard and a

syrup of chicory and salted caramel. The fold-out drinks list is less daunting than it first appears – alongside house-infused cocktails, wines are arranged by style to encourage experimentation, with every bottle offered by the glass.
Chef/s: Tommy Banks and Will Lockwood.
Meals: tasting menu £98 (12 courses) to £125.
Details: 50 seats. V menu. Bar. Parking. Music. Children over 10 yrs. Pre-payment required.

Osmotherley
Golden Lion

Cooking score: 2
International | £35
6 West End, Osmotherley, DL6 3AA
Tel no: 01609 883526
goldenlionosmotherley.co.uk

'Very simple pub food in a handsome setting' is how one diner summed up a visit to this enchanting stone-built hostelry with its dark, polished wood furniture, blazing fire and evening candles. It remains a highly accessible place to eat and drink with straightforward cooking and a loyal following. From the busy kitchen might come sweet apple spare ribs or ham hock terrine, followed by main-course pub classics of beef burgers or salmon fishcakes, as well as coq au vin with roasted garlic and thyme mash, or monkfish wrapped in Parma ham with creamed leeks. Puddings bring on hazelnut and raspberry Bakewell tart or sloe gin jelly with blackcurrant sorbet and cinder toffee. Real ales keep the bar ticking over and there is a short list of reasonably priced wines – from £17.95 for a Sicilian red.
Chef/s: Michael Dalton. **Closed:** 25 Dec.
Meals: main courses £12 to £25. **Details:** 67 seats. 16 seats outside. Wheelchairs. Music.

Cheesy does it

As chefs look to support local producers, we're seeing more and more British cheeses on menus around the country

Graceburn

Made from raw cow's milk to a Persian feta recipe by Blackwoods Cheese Company in Kent. Find it in a rib eye sandwich with watercress and anchovy hollandaise at branches of **Hawksmoor**.

Elmhirst

A luxurious unpasteurised triple cream cheese produced by Sharpham Dairy in Devon. Find it in truffled form on the near-legendary cheeseboard at Wandsworth's **Chez Bruce**.

Doddington

A hard, unpasteurised cow's milk cheese named after the Northumberland village where it is produced. Find it in Mark Birchall's signature baked carrot dish at **Moor Hall** in Lancashire.

Cardo

A raw goat's milk washed-rind cheese created by the late, great Mary Holbrook at Sleight Farm in Somerset. It's part of the not-to-be-missed cheese course at **Lyle's** in east London.

▮ Pickering
The White Swan Inn

Cooking score: 1
British | £36
Market Place, Pickering, YO18 7AA
Tel no: 01751 472288
white-swan.co.uk

This old creeper-covered inn has been run by the same family for a quarter of a century, although its history dates back to the 16th century. Darren Clemmitt has manned the stoves for two decades and it's this consistency that has kept visitors coming back. A charcoal grill is the mainstay of the kitchen, so steaks with classic accompaniments and whole Dover sole with clams and local watercress sauce are a good bet. Among opening salvos, devilled whitebait comes with lime mayonnaise, and Shetland mussels are flavoured with Ampleforth Abbey cider and lardons. Classic fish and chips complete the picture. Drink regional ales or wines from £21.95.
Chef/s: Darren Clemmitt. **Meals:** main courses £14 to £36. Sun L £20 (2 courses) to £25. **Details:** 50 seats. 20 seats outside. Bar. Wheelchairs. Parking.

▮ Port Mulgrave
★ NEW ENTRY ★
Restaurant Number 20

Cooking score: 4
Modern British | £45
20 Rosedale Lane, Port Mulgrave, TS13 5JZ
Tel no: 01947 459647
restaurantnumber20.com

Readers responded with dismay when Sue and Jason Davies closed their little Fox & Hounds restaurant on a blustery clifftop near Whitby. Happily they are back with a new restaurant in a new location but the same ethos of sourcing top-quality ingredients and cooking them beautifully and simply. The one-room restaurant is modest and cheerful, with rough wooden tables, a wood-burning stove and an open kitchen where Jason Davies works his magic. The short menu might feature aged Galician blond beef seared on the Josper grill, perfectly seasoned and served with Parmesan, wild rocket and a thyme salmoriglio or fillet steak with Italian accompaniments of polenta, grilled radicchio and salsa verde. Spider crab, turbot, monkfish and locally caught wild sea trout feature among the fish dishes. A short and well-managed wine list is selected by Sue Davies, who keeps everything in hand front of house.

Chef/s: Jason Davies. **Closed:** Mon, Tue, Sun. **Meals:** main courses £18 to £34. **Details:** 24 seats.

▌ Ramsgill
The Yorke Arms

Cooking score: 6
British | £53
Ramsgill, HG3 5RL
Tel no: 01423 755243
theyorkearms.co.uk

Buried deep amid meadows in the North Yorkshire Dales, at the head of the Gouthwaite Reservoir, The Yorke is a Georgian coaching house that looks as pretty as a picture in summer and beckons you to a comfy old sofa by the fireside when the chill descends. Frances Atkins sailed confidently into her third decade here following a change of ownership in 2018, and the culinary approach now sees five- and eight-course tasting menus in the main dining room, with a three-course carte in its smaller neighbour. A precise balancing act between modern thinking and classical technique creates an assured, high-gloss feeling to most dishes, resulting in main courses such as pearly grilled turbot with leeks and caviar, or tender sirloin of Nidderdale beef with portobello mushroom and tomato. The tasters break into the realms of pickled butternut with pressed morels, and winter-spiced mutton loin with smoked tongue. A pair of summer lunchers pronounced everything 'excellent', through to their desserts of chocolate mousse cake, and strawberry and rose meringue with matching sorbet and clotted cream. There are plenty of interesting discoveries throughout a wine list that opens at £7 a small glass.

Chef/s: Frances Atkins. **Meals:** main courses £25 to £27. Tasting menu £75 (5 courses) to £105. Sun L £35 (2 courses) to £50. **Details:** 40 seats. 20 seats outside. Bar. Wheelchairs. Parking. Music.

▌ Sancton
The Star Inn

Cooking score: 4
British | £40
King Street, Sancton, YO43 4QP
Tel no: 01430 827269
thestaratsancton.co.uk

'This is not your average village local' is how one visitor viewed this fully grown pub success story. Run with well-honed professionalism and attracting local drinkers to the fire-warmed, stone-flagged bar, The Star is primarily a destination for people who care about food. Ben Cox's cooking stands out from the crowd not least because he starts with high-quality, often local ingredients. He's a straight-talking chef, too, dealing in big, beefy flavours. He pulls ideas from the British tradition, his filled Yorkshire puddings (braised oxtail, caramelised onion and red wine jus, say) are a hit, and he keeps the home crowd happy with chicken and black pudding terrine teamed with piccalilli and a Yorkshire blue cheese beignet, and fennel and thyme braised pork belly with a smoked bacon and chickpea cassoulet and a potato terrine. Desserts include a nicely nostalgic Yorkshire tea loaf with Wensleydale. Value is fair throughout (especially at lunch) and also applies to the wide-ranging wine list which is full of interesting selections helpfully annotated with useful descriptions.

Chef/s: Ben Cox. **Closed:** Mon, 1 week Jan. **Meals:** main courses £18 to £33. Set L £18 (2 courses) to £20. **Details:** 80 seats. 32 seats outside. Vg menu. Bar. Wheelchairs. Parking. Music.

Cheesy does it continued...

Rollright
A pasteurised cow's milk washed-rind soft cheese made in the alpine style in the village of Little Rollright in Oxfordshire. Find it on the Franco-British cheeseboard at **Roux at the Landau**.

Baron Bigod
A British take on classic French brie from Fen Farm in Suffolk. Find it at nearby **Darsham Nurseries** with quince jelly, walnuts and oatcakes. At **64 Degrees** in Brighton, they use it alongside potato to stuff agnolotti.

St James
A soft ewe's milk cheese with thrilling flavour produced at Holker Farm Dairy in Cumbria. Find it on the all-British cheeseboard at **Forest Side** in Grasmere.

Cornish Gouda
Produced by a Dutch family based near Looe in Cornwall using milk from their pedigree herd. Find it on truffle toast served with venison tartare and chicory marmalade at **Sorrel** in Dorking.

▌Scalby

LOCAL GEM

The Plough Inn
Modern British | £34
21–23 High Street, Scalby, YO13 0PT
Tel no: 01723 362622
theploughscalby.co.uk

£5 OFF

Revitalised in 2015, this warm and inviting hostelry stands in a pretty village on the edge of the North York Moors, just a short drive from Scarborough. It's a proper local with drinkers at the bar and Yorkshire ales on tap. From the short seasonal carte and daily blackboard, choose tapas – say potted local crab with kohlrabi slaw, and pork, apple and black pudding sausage roll – followed by pheasant and thyme pie with mustard gravy or a pub classic such as fish and chips, and finish with a chocolate and raspberry tart. Sunday roasts are hugely popular. Wines from £18.

▌Scarborough

Lanterna
Cooking score: 3
Italian | £35
33 Queen Street, Scarborough, YO11 1HQ
Tel no: 01723 363616
lanterna-ristorante.co.uk

£5 OFF

'How we love the Lanterna with its 1970s decor, old-fashioned table service and pictures of famous faces who have eaten here', notes a reader who dreads the day when the owners decide to retire. Since taking over this Scarborough landmark in 1997, Giorgio and Rachel Alessio have shunned trattoria clichés in favour of reinterpreted regional classics, spankingly fresh fish from the Scarborough boats and princely Piedmontese truffles (their arrival every November is eagerly awaited and handsomely celebrated). Aside from some daily market specials, the menu 'rarely changes from year to year', but rock-solid consistency is guaranteed – whether you opt for an 'old-style' chickpea

stew with oxtail followed by 'sublime' halibut in lemon sauce or pears baked in red wine with a Gorgonzola sauce ahead of pasta (venison ravioli or agnolotti with black pudding and English mustard sauce, perhaps). To finish, regulars praise the semifreddo with blue cheese, honey and walnuts and the 'fabulous' zabaglione. The Alessios also select and import wines direct from Italian regional producers.
Chef/s: Giorgio Alessio. **Closed:** Mon, Sun, last 2 weeks Oct, 25 and 26 Dec, 1 Jan. **Meals:** main courses £16 to £50. **Details:** 34 seats. Wheelchairs. Music.

LOCAL GEM

Eat Me Café and Social
International | £18
2 Hanover Road, Scarborough, YO11 1LS
Tel no: 07445 475328
eatmecafe.com
£5 £30
OFF

There's something very democratic about this cracking little café next to the Stephen Joseph Theatre (and across the road from the train station). You'll find all ages and types here, plus kids and dogs — sometimes even sharing a table, for which there may be a short wait. Pass the time appreciating the quirky decor and scanning the multicultural menu, which includes the likes of meatballs, Thai curries, tin-plate lunches and ramen noodle bowls, which are generous and packed with flavour. Non-meat eaters do well here, too. You can't put a price on the vibe, but the bill is so ungrasping as to be unreal.

◼ Scawton
The Hare Inn
Cooking score: 6
Modern British | £60
Scawton, YO7 2HG
Tel no: 01845 597769
thehare-inn.com
£5
OFF

In a beautiful but very remote corner of North Yorkshire, this rural restaurant, housed in a centuries-old inn, opens just four nights a week, and booking is essential for what many readers agree is a thoroughly memorable experience. Paul Jackson's terse tasting menus of six or eight courses allow him to flex his muscles and show his talent for brilliantly executed modern cooking. It's creative, confident stuff, full of twists, turns and assured technique, with a strong sense of freshness, flavour and balance. Snacks set the bar high, and standout dishes this year have included a delicate, perfectly cooked piece of crisp-skinned bass with artichoke and sorrel, venison with beetroot and preserved elderberries, and Japanese-inflected mackerel served in two courses. It's a mightily impressive package, topped off by fabulously ripe cheeses, a near-legendary milk and honey pre-dessert, and a satisfying combination of chocolate, salted caramel and hazelnut delivering the final hit. The restaurant itself is relaxed and welcoming, run with considerable panache by Liz Jackson. Wines do a good job too, whether you plump for the wine pairings or order a bottle from the brief, global list.
Chef/s: Paul Jackson. **Closed:** Mon, Tue, Sun, 1 week Nov, Jan, 1 week Jul. **Meals:** tasting menu £60 (6 courses) to £80. **Details:** 16 seats. V menu. Bar. Wheelchairs. Parking.

Wheelchairs

We only indicate that a restaurant is wheelchair accessible if this includes access to toilets.

▪ Sheffield

Jöro

Cooking score: 5
New Nordic | £50
Krynkl, 294 Shalesmoor, Sheffield, S3 8US
Tel no: 0114 299 1539
jororestaurant.co.uk

£5
OFF

Kelham Island was originally the beating heart of the city's heavy industry, but the old warehouses, steelworks and factories are now home to modern apartments, art galleries, microbreweries and restaurants. Jöro ('earth' in old Norse) is housed in interconnecting shipping containers on a busy road circling the island, a seemingly unlikely venue for such cutting-edge Nordic cooking. But it all makes sense when you see Luke Sherwood-French and his team at work with such verve and ambition in the open kitchen, deploying contemporary techniques and hyper-local produce, much of it foraged, to produce fiercely seasonal small plates. Presentation may be impeccable, but it's the flavours that sing – in raw line-caught Scottish mackerel with English wasabi and yuzu, or Gloucester old spot pork belly with katsu ketchup. Bramley apples with rice, English kaffir lime and frozen quince tea kombucha makes for an assertive finish. A lively and interesting wine list opens at £22.50, and a newly built cocktail and wine bar at the rear makes for a great bolthole for pre-dinner drinks.
Chef/s: Luke Sherwood-French. **Closed:** Mon, Tue, Sun, 30 Sept to 9 Oct, 22 Dec to 27 Dec.
Meals: small plates £6 to £20. Set L £24 (2 courses) to £30. Tasting menu £50 (9 courses) to £65.
Details: 38 seats. Bar. Wheelchairs. Music.

No Name

Cooking score: 2
Modern British | £35
253 Crookes, Sheffield, S10 1TF
Tel no: 0114 266 1520

This compact restaurant occupies a converted shop in the Crookes district, a click away from the city centre. Decor-wise, it looks a lot like a secondhand shop, with a bare concrete floor, random bric-a-brac, antiques and fairy lights. With a menu handwritten on a large roll of brown paper, BYO wine policy and no card payments, this is quite a quirky dining experience. Thomas Samworth cooks alone in the tiny kitchen – separated from diners by a drape – with just two basic induction hobs, but his seasonal cooking is not lacking finesse or ambition. Start with smokey duck leg sausage with wild garlic risotto, spring onions and Parmesan. A precisely timed pan-fried sea bass fillet might follow, teamed with braised leek, toasted hazelnuts and romesco sauce. Desserts could feature honeycomb crème brûlée with fresh honeycomb and honey beer ice cream. Bookings are essential for the two nightly sittings.
Chef/s: Thomas Samworth. **Closed:** Mon, Tue, Sun, 21 Dec to 4 Jan. **Meals:** main courses £16 to £20.
Details: 20 seats. Music. Cash only.

Rafters

Cooking score: 4
Modern British | £50
220 Oakbrook Road, Nether Green, Sheffield, S11 7ED
Tel no: 0114 230 4819
raftersrestaurant.co.uk

£5
OFF

In the Ranmoor district, 10 minutes out of the city centre, Rafters disguises itself from casual view by hiding above shop premises on a busy junction. It's a well-appointed room with smart grey upholstery and exposed brickwork. Tom Lawson is on fine form, offering a wad of fixed-price menus, from a classic three-courser to Experience Two, a multi-stage taster. All the stops are pulled out

for dishes that achieve high impact, often through surprising economy of means. A version of steak tartare made with impeccably aged beef dressed in three-year-old Parmesan and gherkin ketchup has plenty to say for itself, and might be followed by opalescent Cornish cod with langoustine and purple sprouting broccoli. The principal meat could be majestic salt-aged Goosnargh duck with January king cabbage and carrot textures, with a pair of desserts to close the show – perhaps yoghurt panna cotta with blood orange, then single origin 72% chocolate crémeux with flavours of passion fruit, banana and tonka. A compact wine list changes seasonally in accord with the cooking, starting at £24.
Chef/s: Tom Lawson. **Closed:** Mon, Sun, 21 to 30 Dec, 24 to 30 Aug. **Meals:** set D £50. Early D £30 Tue to Thur and Sat. Tasting menu £80 (8 courses). **Details:** 34 seats. Bar. Music.

■ Shibden
Shibden Mill Inn
Cooking score: 3
Modern British | £35
Shibden Mill Fold, Shibden, HX3 7UL
Tel no: 01422 365840
shibdenmillinn.com

£5 🛏
OFF

The cobbled lane leading to the bottom of Shibden Valley doesn't get any less steep but the rewards are plenty. In summer, the flagged terrace of this handsome wisteria-clad 17th-century inn is the perfect place for lunch, or head inside to the deeply traditional, deeply cosy bar and dining room, where in colder months open fires warm. They've had an unsteady time, chef-wise, but there's new blood in the kitchen in the guise of Will Webster, and readers have been quick to praise his cooking: 'an amazing meal full of flavours and demonstrating a very high level of detail to all dishes... lamb hogget was exceptional!' Find the likes of pigeon Rossini – packed with flavour – and cured chalk stream trout with fennel pollen crème fraîche, beetroot and treacle dressing. Halibut loin with chicken fat rösti and smoked garlic sauce delivers, too,

while Webster's take on a Magnum ice cream is huge fun. There's plenty of choice for vegans, who are also well served by the descriptive wine list, with good selections by the glass (from £3.50) and carafe.
Chef/s: Will Webster. **Meals:** main courses £14 to £30. Set L £17 (2 courses) to £21. **Details:** 80 seats. 60 seats outside. Vg menu. Parking. Music.

■ South Dalton
The Pipe & Glass
Cooking score: 5
Modern British | £50
West End, South Dalton, HU17 7PN
Tel no: 01430 810246
pipeandglass.co.uk

🍷🛏

James and Kate Mackenzie took over the former 17th-century gatehouse to Dalton Park in 2006 and set about realising their vision of an informal country inn serving some of the best modern British dishes, an aim of which they've never lost sight. A seat by the fire in the bar is the spot for quality sandwiches or a menu (the same in both bar and restaurant) that makes the best of local and seasonal produce, invariably with an added dose of Mackenzie creativity. The restaurant proper is more spacious and a little more formal, including a long conservatory table for large parties. Expect a wide-ranging repertoire that extends from pub classics of fish pie topped with Cheddar and parsley mash through to an elegant roast pheasant with pheasant and chestnut sausage roll and pickled blackberries, or blackboard specials of North Sea mackerel with curried mussels. There could be sticky toffee pudding with stout ice cream or a pistachio and Yorkshire rhubarb baked Alaska for Afters. The exhaustive wine list has been organised to match the food with a huge range by the glass and distinctly ungreedy markups with house selections from £20.
Chef/s: James Mackenzie. **Closed:** Mon, 2 weeks Jan. **Meals:** main courses £13 to £33. **Details:** 100 seats. 70 seats outside. V menu. Vg menu. Bar. Wheelchairs. Parking. Music.

◼ Sowerby Bridge

Gimbals

Cooking score: 4
International | £35
76 Wharf Street, Sowerby Bridge, HX6 2AF
Tel no: 01422 839329
gimbals.co.uk
£5 OFF

Colourful and gloriously eclectic, the Bakers' restaurant sports a hodgepodge of vintage finds. Front of house is run with great warmth and energy by Janet, while Simon turns out commendable food based on fresh ingredients, the style more comforting than assertive. Twice-baked pecorino soufflé with balsamic figs and shallots, medlar syrup-dressed endive and rosemary-roasted pine nuts points the way for an opener as eclectic as the surroundings. Elsewhere, pork fillet wrapped in serrano ham is paired with braised pork cheek, boudin noir croquette and a sweet onion and pink lady apple purée, or from a generous vegan menu might come harissa roast butternut squash and tofu with preserved lemon-stewed white beans, vadouvan onions and salsa mojo. Sticky toffee pudding always gets the thumbs-up from readers and the wine list offers plenty of good-value finds from around the world.
Chef/s: Simon Baker. **Closed:** Mon, Sun.
Meals: main courses £18 to £29. Set L and D £20 Mon to Fri (2 courses) to £24. Tasting menu £29 (5 courses). **Details:** 56 seats. Vg menu. Bar. Wheelchairs. Music.

The Moorcock Inn

Cooking score: 5
British | £35
Moorbottom Lane, Sowerby Bridge, HX6 3RP
Tel no: 01422 832103
themoorcock.co.uk

'Ingredient-led cooking' is an overused phrase but has real meaning at this isolated, no-frills pub 'set on a windy escarpment'. Alisdair Brooke-Taylor and his team make full use of their two-acre garden alongside goodies foraged from hereabouts, or sourced from the region. Any produce that isn't used immediately is preserved, so ingredients in their cured, pickled or fermented guises feature frequently on the regularly changing tasting menus of five to eight courses. Expect challenges, surprises and a fair bit of creativity. The sourdough bread is as popular as ever, but reported highlights this year have included snacks of Brussels sprouts in rosehip and tomato, cured trout with 'bushels of delicate little herbs' and a dollop of cured cream for dipping, wood-roast pear with onion and sea herbs, and Hebridean mutton with feta and green tomato – although one visitor thought the potato tart that preceded the meat would have made a better accompaniment. A simple sponge cake cooked in a skillet with goose egg ice cream makes a fitting finale. If you find the pared-back look austere, it's partly mitigated by amiable staff whose attentive, clued-up approach is a great asset. With drinks ranging from local ales to uncompromising natural wines, it seems to have the balance between travelling foodies and local drinkers nailed.
Chef/s: Alisdair Brooke-Taylor. **Closed:** Mon, Tue, 1 to 17 Sept. **Meals:** tasting menu £35 (5 courses) to £45. **Details:** 50 seats. 30 seats outside. Bar. Parking. Music.

◼ Staddlebridge

The Cleveland Tontine

Cooking score: 4
Modern British | £30
Staddlebridge, DL6 3JB
Tel no: 01609 882671
theclevelandtontine.com
£5 OFF   £30

Considered quite an institution hereabouts, this former coaching inn, now a small hotel, is a hugely enjoyable place where everyone feels at home. It's something of an all-rounder, with a choice of smart public rooms and a quirky basement restaurant – 'a lovely room of starched tablecloths, glowing silver and glassware, where the fire is invariably lit' – offering down-to-earth bistro cooking with good-value set lunch and dinner options.

Here, starters might take in game terrine or a taste of seafood (including crab, langoustine and scallop), while mains could assemble halibut with clams, pak choi, lotus root and a gently spiced curry sauce or prime fillet of chateaubriand (for two) with twice-cooked chips, confit tomato and a choice of béarnaise or au poivre sauce. Indulgent puds are reassuringly familiar, perhaps sticky toffee pudding with butterscotch sauce, although a trio of chocolate desserts with iced cherry and pistachio allows for gentle experimentation. There is good drinking to be had by the glass or bottle on a well-annotated global list.
Chef/s: Luke Taylor. **Meals:** main courses £15 to £33. Set L £17 (2 courses) to £19. Set D £22 (2 courses) to £25. Sun L £22 (2 courses) to £27. **Details:** 144 seats. 20 seats outside. Bar. Parking. Music.

Todmorden
The White Rabbit
Cooking score: 2
Modern British | £35
1 White Hart Fold, Todmorden, OL14 7BD
Tel no: 01706 817828
whiterabbittodmorden.com
£5 OFF

David and Roybn Gledhill certainly pull some lovely things from their culinary hats at their restaurant in this Pennines market town, just 20 or so miles from Manchester. In the cosy dining room with its hand-painted Alice in Wonderland wall murals, it's a tasting menu-only affair, with a choice of five or eight courses that change monthly, and vegetarian menus, too. Seasonal dishes combine poise with playfulness: start with carrot with whipped goat's cheese, puffed seed granola and Calderdale honey, perhaps, moving on to sticky Porcus pork belly bao bun with noodle fries, and a fish course of roast salmon with tomato consommé, basil and lemon, if you go all out for eight. Finish on a high with chocolate and hazelnut tart. Forget the chaos of a Mad Hatter's Tea Party – the service is

'magically imperceptible' – and put yourself in capable hands with matching wine flights, or steer your own vinous course.
Chef/s: David and Robyn Gledhill. **Closed:** Mon, Tue, Sun, 25 Dec to 1 Jan. **Meals:** tasting menu £35 (5 courses) to £55. **Details:** 22 seats. V menu. Children over 12 yrs.

Wetherby
LOCAL GEM
Mango
Indian vegetarian | £25
12-14 Bank Street, Wetherby, LS22 6NQ
Tel no: 01937 585755
mangovegetarian.com
£5 OFF £30

Rekha Sonigra opened her veggie restaurant in two old cottages back in 2008 and continues to bring a taste of the Gujarat and southern India to this admired market town. Starter platters include flavour-packed pani puri and delicately spiced dhokla, before classic dosas or a chana curry made with white and black chickpeas. A good deal of the output is vegan and gluten-free. For dessert, try the classic mango and pistachio kulfi. Wines start at £15.95.

Whitby
Bridge Cottage Bistro
Cooking score: 3
Modern British | £30
East Row, Sandsend, Whitby, YO21 3SU
Tel no: 01947 893438
bridgecottagebistro.com
£5 OFF £30

The inviting simplicity of the interior, charming rusticity of the outdoor eating area and proximity to the beach would make this an asset to any coastal village. Add the cooking of chef owner Alex Perkins to the equation and Sandsend is the envy of many a community. There's a lack of pretension to the kitchen's output with dishes, chalked on the wall, loyal to local and regional produce and reflective of the seasons. Potted shrimps or crab and goose egg tart could be an intro to main dishes of slow-cooked pork belly with salt-baked celeriac, or Black Sheep ale-battered fish with chips and smashed peas, and twice-baked Ribblesdale soufflé with spring vegetables. Sticky toffee pudding remains a popular dessert, but there's been praise for a custard tart with rhubarb compôte. Homemade cakes and afternoon tea fill in the gaps, and there's a small, eclectic group of wines from £19. **Chef/s:** Alex Perkins. **Closed:** Mon. **Meals:** main courses £12 to £30. Tasting menu £40 (9 courses). Sun L £17 (2 courses). **Details:** 26 seats. 20 seats outside. Wheelchairs. Music.

LOCAL GEM

Mademoiselles
French | £33
1 Skinner Street, Whitby, YO21 3AH
Tel no: 01947 602970
mademoiselles.co.uk

Tucked up a side street, this Georgian building is the last word in glamour, full of finds by owners Sue Duck and Richard Hutton: chaises longues, antique dressers, rococo mirrors, gleaming glassware and chandeliers galore. Expect classic French dishes along the lines of huge fat prawns with sweetly roasted garlic cloves and a deep, richly truffled mayo, suprême de volaille with grapes, chestnuts and a sublime tarragon butter, and a 'totally indulgent' take on bread and butter pudding made with brioche, white chocolate and raspberry coulis. At lunchtime there could be moules marinière or a Gruyère tartine. Drink well-priced wines or Whitby gin.

LOCAL GEM

The Magpie Café
Seafood | £30
14 Pier Road, Whitby, YO21 3PU
Tel no: 01947 602058
magpiecafe.co.uk

£5 OFF £30

Synonymous with fish and chips, family holidays and proper old-fashioned Britishness, this redoubtable whitewashed café overlooking Whitby harbourside is as good-natured and irrepressible as ever. Join the queue and be prepared to wait (even in foul weather), but pass the time by dreaming about mighty portions of crisply battered skin-on haddock (or hake, or woof etc). Blackboard specials promise everything from crab bisque to prawn katsu curry, and there's a huge choice of homemade puddings, from knickerbocker glory to jam roly poly, to finish you off. As for liquid refreshment, seafood-friendly wines, a beer or a cuppa usually hit the spot.

York

★ NEW ENTRY ★

Cave du Cochon
Cooking score: 3
Modern European | £28
19 Walmgate, York, YO1 9TX
Tel no: 01904 633669
caveducochon.uk

£5 OFF £30

This estimable wine bar, the younger sibling to Josh Overington's ambitious Cochon Aveugle (see entry), presents top-quality sharing boards of meat and cheese served with dark crusted, tangy sourdough that one visitor described as 'utterly outstanding'. Since installing a kitchen, the repertoire has been expanded with an expansive blackboard menu that takes in slip sole meunière and buttermilk fried chicken. They also reprise some of the standout dishes from Cochon Aveugle's menu: Kumamoto oysters topped with a vin jaune granita or their stellar sweet-savoury signature, boudin noir macarons. The turnip soup with smoked eel cream is remembered as 'a glorious confection. Quite astonishing.' Bare floorboards, rough wooden tables and candles in bottles set the mood, with additional seating on the first floor and a secret courtyard garden at the back. As you might expect, there is a strong list of natural, organic and classic wines from a highly individual list. **Chef/s:** Josh Overington. **Closed:** 25 and 26 Dec. **Meals:** main courses £10 to £22. **Details:** 45 seats. 10 seats outside. Music.

Chopping Block at Walmgate Ale House

Cooking score: 2
Modern British | £30
25 Walmgate, York, YO1 9TX
Tel no: 01904 629222
walmgateale.co.uk
£30

Michael and Lucy Hjort's flagship Melton's restaurant (see entry) has been a Guide regular since the early 90s. Walmgate Ale House came 10 years later, a cheerful bistro housed in a rambling 17th-century workshop of a former saddle maker and ropery. The first-floor restaurant was renamed in 2018, although it looks much as before – with exposed brick, rough wood floors and a relaxed informality. Yet now Michael Hjort himself is heading the kitchen, and the signs are that the Chopping Block is moving up a gear. It still offers well-priced, satisfying bistro fare like steak and chips, but there's also seafood gratin with scallops and king prawns, lamb-stuffed aubergine with pomegranate, and pancakes with ratatouille, labneh and pesto. Desserts include stalwarts such as sticky toffee pudding and panna cotta. Watch out for good-value offers such as half-price fizz on Friday and kids eat free early Saturday. The wine list is well constructed and fairly priced.
Chef/s: Michael Hjort. **Closed:** Mon, 25 and 26 Dec, 1 Jan. **Meals:** main courses £14 to £21. Set L and D £16 (2 courses) to £18. Sun L £18 (2 courses). **Details:** 120 seats. Bar. Wheelchairs. Music.

Le Cochon Aveugle

Cooking score: 4
French | £85
37 Walmgate, York, YO1 9TX
Tel no: 01904 640222
lecochonaveugle.uk

It began as Michael O'Hare's cheeky little French bistro with Josh Overington as head chef. When O'Hare went off to create the garlanded Man Behind the Curtain (see entry), Josh and his wife, Victoria – sommelier and front of house – took over and transformed the bistro into something way more refined. Five years on they present a 'blind' six- or eight-course dinner with wine pairings – a little bit French in technique and taste but very much their own take on modern European food. Beef tartare with Tunworth cheese and artichoke, scallops in sea urchin butter and guinea fowl with aged Parmesan have all made appearances alongside Overington's chewy sourdough bread served with his own sea-salted butter. Another regular is his trademark boudin noir macaron, which marries sweet macaron with savoury black pudding to brilliant effect. This year a complete kitchen and dining room makeover has given this little pig a home that now matches the food. A wide-ranging collection of wines comes by the glass, carafe or bottle.
Chef/s: Joshua Overington. **Closed:** Mon, Tue, Sun, 25 and 26 Dec, 5 to 21 Jan. **Meals:** tasting menu Sat L £55 (5 courses) and D £70 Wed and Thur (12 courses) to £85 Fri and Sat. **Details:** 20 seats. V menu. Music. Children over 10 yrs.

Melton's

Cooking score: 5
Modern British | £45
7 Scarcroft Road, York, YO23 1ND
Tel no: 01904 634341
meltonsrestaurant.co.uk
£5 OFF

Founded by Michael and Lucy Hjort in 1990, and still a force to be reckoned with amid York's increasingly diverse restaurant scene, Melton's occupies unassuming premises in a Victorian terrace temptingly close to York racecourse. The hospitable dining room is overseen by Lucy – although Michael has handed over responsibility for the kitchen to his culinary lieutenant Calvin Miller. Dressed-up British flavours and fastidiously sourced North Country ingredients dominate the menu, from East Coast cod with a shopping list of accompaniments including smoked cream, mussels, apples, dates, raisins and fennel pollen to Yorkshire duck with potato and confit leg terrine, turnip, endive and burnt citrus purée or Holme Farm venison in company with bitter chocolate, pear, panisse and parsley root. There's a lot going on here, but flavours are precisely judged and all those different components gel cohesively on the plate. Desserts generally include a trademark soufflé (perhaps hot prune and brandy) alongside fancy confections such as Bramley apple mousse and thyme parfait with hazelnut brittle and cream cheese ice cream. The personally compiled wine list kicks off with house selections at £21.50.

Chef/s: Calvin Miller. **Closed:** Mon, Sun, 2 weeks Dec. **Meals:** set L and early D £30 (2 courses) to £35. Set D £35 (2 courses) to £45. Tasting menu £60 (6 courses) to £65. **Details:** 42 seats. Music.

Partisan

Cooking score: 4
Modern British | £40
112 Micklegate, York, YO1 6JX
Tel no: 01904 629866
partisanuk.com

£5
OFF

'This has become a York favourite with a laid-back, bohemian feel and imaginative cooking': praise indeed for this unassuming, easy-going café. Decor is vintage – scrubbed tables, mismatched chairs, rusty lamps – and it has few pretensions beyond providing fresh, interesting dishes whether for brunch, lunch or the occasional evening (Thursday to Saturday). Shakshuka or Mexican eggs (with spicy refried beans, avocado, lime, sour cream, grated Cheddar, fresh salsa and coriander) may start the day, with lunch bringing aubergine Parmigiana or a chicken Zanzibar curry with star anise, jasmine rice, cucumber and poppy seed salsa. And there is plenty of interest at dinner, too, when chef James Gilroy might conjure up cod, chilli and oregano empanadas, or cider-glazed sea trout with spätzle, crispy turnip leaf and crab mayonnaise. It's all washed down with craft ales, cocktails and a short, modern wine list with bottles from £17.

Chef/s: James Gilroy. **Meals:** main courses £17 to £25. **Details:** 50 seats. 25 seats outside. Wheelchairs. Music.

The Rattle Owl

Cooking score: 4
Modern British | £36
104 Micklegate, York, YO1 6JX
Tel no: 01904 658658
rattleowl.co.uk

There's a welcome glow that comes from the big, bold brass letters on the wall, the polished wood floors, the shiny black panelling, the brass light fittings, the candles and the flowers – the work of owner Clarrie O'Callaghan and her vision for a relaxed restaurant that is as much about place as food. Head chef Tom Heywood shares that insight with dishes that are both original and interesting, without delving into the dainty or try-hard. For starters Heywood cleverly contrasts a soothing duck liver parfait with pink grapefruit sorbet, while curried granola turns out to be an inspired match for devilled crab. A main of mutton with wild garlic, roast hispi cabbage and goat's curd is pleasing, but the real tour de force is salmon with roast aubergine, a relish of olive and miso and a wonderfully inspired sweet fennel jam, disparate elements that somehow work harmoniously together. A rhubarb and date pavlova complete an impressive meal. Service is spot-on and a well-curated organic wine list opens at £24.

Chef/s: Tom Heywood. **Closed:** Mon, Tue, 1 week Jan. **Meals:** main courses £18 to £19. Sun L £21 (2 courses) to £26. **Details:** 42 seats. Bar. Wheelchairs. Music.

★ NEW ENTRY ★

Roots

Cooking score: 5
Modern British | £55
68 Marygate, York, YO30 7BH
rootsyork.com

A short stroll from the railway station, what was once known as The Bay Horse has been conjured into a serious restaurant by the Banks

family of Black Swan at Oldstead fame (see entry). This late Victorian former boozer is attracting a very different crowd now, lured by the prospect of Tommy Banks' astonishing food. His flagship restaurant has accrued sackfuls of cred for self-sufficiency, growing its own food and supporting local producers, an ethos that has extended to this stellar destination, where small and large sharing plates show ingredients at their dazzling best. Take your pick from lamb and fermented turnip bao, a textbook interplay of fatty, sweet and astringent notes, or a riff on carrots with crunchy hazelnuts, fennel and goat's curd deftly accentuating the sweetness of the roots. This is pin-sharp cooking defined by natural-born flavours, from a sizeable cut of perfectly cooked Thornback ray wing given heft with a chunky, acidic tartare sauce, to salt beef topped with a generous grating of Old Winchester cheese and offset by sharp dabs of mustard and gherkin purée. Among highly original desserts, a sensational 'Angel Delight', a creamy amalgamation of Jerusalem artichoke and chicory is a fine balance of texture and flavour. This is a relaxed, comfortable place where cheery, chatty staff match the convivial mood. The reasonably priced modern wine list does its best to keep up, with everything offered by the glass, carafe or bottle, and cocktails are appropriately inventive.
Chef/s: Tommy Banks and Joel Foulds. **Closed:** Tue. **Meals:** small plates £6 to £11. Large plates £18 to £24. Tasting menu £55 (11 courses). **Details:** 71 seats. V menu. Bar. Wheelchairs. Music. Children over 5 yrs at L, over 10 yrs at D.

Skosh

Cooking score: 4
Modern British | £25
98 Micklegate, York, YO1 6JX
Tel no: 01904 634849
skoshyork.co.uk
£30

With its open-to-view kitchen, contemporary good looks and a menu of potent Asian-inspired plates for sharing (or not), Skosh – a diminutive of the Japanese for

small – is one of the most vital addresses in the city. Neil Bentinck makes use of the region's best produce and draws inspiration from far and wide. The glorious Lindisfarne oyster gets dressed up with pickled ginger granita, the humble cauliflower is fired up Manchurian-style, and pork loin 'hoisin' is a clever combination of flavours, with rhubarb, Szechuan chilli and peanuts. The plates vary in size from wee to rather more burly. If you fancy a cheese course, 'stunning' Yorkshire fresh pecorino with beetroot, rhubarb and lovage is an inspired choice. Among sweet courses, gingerbread parfait gets good notices, while the Skosh 'sphere' will melt the heart of any chocolate lover. Drink seasonal cocktails, British and Asian craft beers, and well-chosen wines by the glass, carafe or bottle.
Chef/s: Neil Bentinck. **Closed:** Mon, Tue, 2 weeks Sept, 1 week Jan, 1 week May. **Meals:** small plates £3 to £16. **Details:** 40 seats. Music.

The Star Inn the City

Cooking score: 2
Modern British | £38
Museum Street, York, YO1 7DR
Tel no: 01904 619208
starinnthecity.co.uk

To be hit by a kitchen fire in the run-up to Christmas must be a restaurateur's worst nightmare, but Andrew Pern took it in his stride, moving all bookings to his other York venue and getting on with repairs. This modern two-storey restaurant reopened in late winter 2018 with a simpler and more coherent menu and on much better form. The Star's strapline, 'a taste of the countryside in the city', is evident in dishes such as treacle-braised pork belly, roast lamb with a little shepherd's pie or, quite simply, Yorkshire pudding with ale and onion gravy. There are daily changing specials, a sensible children's menu and terrific breakfasts, all taken in the lovely Garden Room with an outlook across the river. The River Room – dominated by a copper barrel of Pilsner Urquell – and terrace can get uncomfortably crowded on race days and sunny weekends, but that's because The

Star has arguably the best riverside location in the city. Seasonal cocktails join global wines (from £23) on the extensive drinks list.
Chef/s: Monty Kanev. **Closed:** 25 and 26 Dec, 1 Jan. **Meals:** main courses £14 to £25. **Details:** 150 seats. 80 seats outside. Bar. Wheelchairs. Music.

The Greenhouse Tearoom
British | £15
Vertigrow, Lawnswood House, Malton Rd, York, YO32 9TL
Tel no: 01904 400082

£30

A plant lovers' paradise on the city's rural outskirts is home to a recently revamped conservatory tea room that exceeds the classic something-warm-with-a-bit-of-cake expectations. If the weather is cooperating, take a seat outside on the terrace to fully appreciate the verdant and tranquil setting, and expect lunch that goes that extra mile. Yes, there are sandwiches, Yorkshire rarebit on homemade sourdough, or scones and cream for afternoon tea, but there's also smoked haddock and king prawn fishcake with curried mayonnaise and salad. And plenty of standout freshly baked cakes. Unlicensed.

Los Moros
North African | £26
15-17 Grape Lane, York, YO1 7HU
Tel no: 01904 636834
losmorosyork.co.uk

£30

'A brilliant place for a relaxed feast with friends,' this casual eatery is the bricks-and-mortar cousin of the Los Moros street-food stall on the Shambles Market. Spicily aromatic North African cuisine is the deal, and there are treats galore on the short menu, from whipped feta with smokey Urfa pepper oil to homemade merguez sausages with butterbeans and yoghurt – all mopped up with copious quantities of pitta bread. Follow

with raspberry and rose cheesecake with 'pearls' of Turkish delight. Brew York beer and Hebden herbal teas feature on the drinks list.

Mannion & Co
Modern European | £20
1 Blake Street, York, YO1 8QJ
Tel no: 01904 631030
mannionandco.co.uk

£30

An enticing daytime mix of deli, café and bistro, Mannion & Co can send you home laden with superb artisan breads, cakes and provisions, but grab a seat if you can (they don't take bookings). Cheese and charcuterie boards are piled high, or explore the blackboard where daily specials of bresaola with goat's cheese and pickled walnuts might sit alongside Moroccan-style chicken with pea and feta fritters, courgette and labneh. Wines by the glass open at £4.50. Another branch is at 5 Castlegate, Helmsley, YO62 5AB.

SCOTLAND

South Scotland, West Scotland & Glasgow,
Central & Lothian, Mid-Scotland & Fife,
North East Scotland, Highlands & Islands

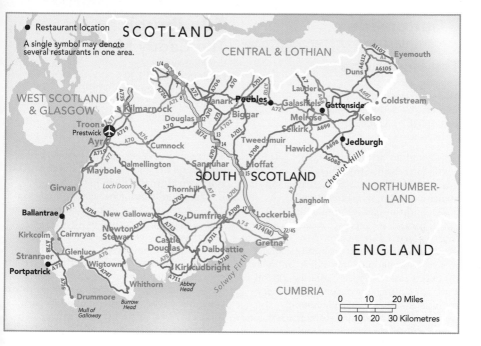

Restaurant location

A single symbol may denote several restaurants in one area.

SCOTLAND

CENTRAL & LOTHIAN

WEST SCOTLAND & GLASGOW

SOUTH SCOTLAND

NORTHUMBER-LAND

ENGLAND

CUMBRIA

■ Ballantrae
Glenapp Castle

Cooking score: 4
Modern British | £53
Ballantrae, KA26 0NZ
Tel no: 01465 831212
glenappcastle.com
£5 OFF

No one could come upon this Victorian castle by accident. From the gated entrance and long wooded drive to the elegant drawing room, everything is carefully considered. To be cosseted in the grand style – met at the door, fed from monogrammed plates – is an unusual and old-fashioned pleasure, accomplished without extraneous stuffiness. Served in two dining rooms, big on silverware and candlelight, the best of David Alexander's food is almost defiantly simple. Over six courses, dishes include a little salad of tenderest quail, apple, hazelnut and punchily acid beetroot; buttery fillet of Luce Bay turbot

with a warm tartare sauce; and salmon with new potatoes, crisp new season asparagus and a herb hollandaise. The bridge to pudding might be an impeccable lemon posset with a single fat raspberry, followed by passion fruit soufflé with matching sorbet. The wine list looks mostly to France at big-city prices, with service that's both watchful and hospitable. **Chef/s:** David Alexander. **Meals:** set L £40. Set D £53. Tasting menu £73 (6 courses). Sun L £40. **Details:** 40 seats. Bar. Wheelchairs. Parking.

Send us your review

Your feedback informs the content of the *GFG* and will be used to compile next year's entries. To register your opinion about any restaurant listed in the Guide, or a restaurant that you wish to bring to our attention, visit: thegoodfoodguide.co.uk/feedback.

Gattonside

★ NEW ENTRY ★

The Hoebridge

Cooking score: 3
Modern European | £35
Hoebridge Road East, Gattonside, TD6 9LZ
Tel no: 01896 823082
thehoebridge.com

Chef Hamish Carruthers left Gattonside in his youth, but returned from New York in 2015 to buy this old village pub with partner and co-owner Kyle Tidd, who offers artful transatlantic hospitality front of house. A clever, pared-back approach to design extends from the airy transformation of the old byre to the short but imaginative monthly seasonal menus. Without doubt it is stylish, but not at the expense of substance – offering a blend of authentic Scottish provenance with a hefty sprinkle of cosmopolitan glamour. A springtime starter of crispy baby artichoke and lemon with charred asparagus and ricotta is aptly followed by chicken with wild garlic and pine kernels on butter-braised fennel. Prime Angus beef from Hardiesmill comes with outrageously slender frites – worth the visit alone. Finish with decadent chocolate tart, perfectly balanced with raspberry ganache, bitter cacao nibs and mint ice cream redolent of Arabic teahouses. Kyle curates an imaginative wine list that positively encourages affordable oenological adventures. It's a perfect 10-minute evening stroll from Melrose via the pedestrian suspension bridge over the Tweed.
Chef/s: Hamish Carruthers. **Closed:** Mon, Tue, Sun. **Meals:** main courses £16 to £24. **Details:** 50 seats. Bar. Parking. Music.

Jedburgh
The Caddy Mann

Cooking score: 2
Modern British | £30
Mounthooly, Jedburgh, TD8 6TJ
Tel no: 01835 850787
caddymann.com
£30

The welcome is personal and homely and the decor is on the traditional side, but then Ross and Lynn Horrocks' focus in this long-standing family business is clearly on the food. This is fine with loyal regulars and passers-by, who are perhaps surprised to discover such quality cooking in simple surroundings. The daily changing menu is an eclectic and extensive collection of dishes reflecting seasonal availability and the chef's fancy. Slow-roasted pig's head terrine with crispy ear crackling, preserved apple and quince, haggis Melba toast and piccalilli oil dressing illustrates the unapologetically hearty style – although Ross's clear culinary pedigree ensures it retains finesse. Pan-seared pigeon with red wine spelt risotto, truffle and homemade game ravioli is rooted in its local context and the produce of neighbouring estates. Vegetarians are generously served in the same bold style. Desserts might include rich baked cheesecake or sumptuous home baking. An extensive gin range and simple wine choices should meet the needs of those not needing to drive.
Chef/s: Ross Horrocks. **Closed:** Mon. **Meals:** main courses £14 to £22. **Details:** 50 seats. 20 seats outside. V menu. Wheelchairs. Parking.

Symbols

🛏 Accommodation is available
£30 Three courses for £30 or less
£5 OFF £5 off voucher scheme
🍾 Notable wine list

▮ Peebles

Osso

Cooking score: 2
British | £35
Innerleithen Road, Peebles, EH45 8BA
Tel no: 01721 724477
ossorestaurant.com

Ally McGrath must be a born people-pleaser. From his modest premises at the Innerleithen end of the town's main street, he manages to juggle and satisfy the culinary needs and expectations of his diverse customer base. By day, the extensive menu of this café and tea room ensures the coffee, brunch, lunch and cake desires of locals and tourists are well met. By night, dimmer lighting creates a more upscale feel, while the competent cooking and local, seasonal ingredients go up a notch. Crispy monkfish cheek scampi arrives plump with a tangy warm tartare, St Bride's Farm guinea fowl set on a bed of cabbage and bacon might be complemented by earthy mushroom and Madeira flavours, while hazelnut gnocchi gets a twist with goat's curd and spruce. Boldly flavoured desserts include a tonka bean panna cotta with brown butter ice cream or stem ginger parfait with lemon curd and aerated white chocolate. A short, global wine list will suit both palates and pockets.
Chef/s: Ally McGrath and Craig Turner. **Closed:** 25 Dec, 1 Jan. **Meals:** main courses £17 to £20. Set D £22 (2 courses) to £28. **Details:** 38 seats. 4 seats outside. Wheelchairs. Music.

▮ Portpatrick

Knockinaam Lodge

Cooking score: 4
Modern British | £70
Portpatrick, DG9 9AD
Tel no: 01776 810471
knockinaamlodge.com
£5 OFF 🍾 🛏

With wooded glens, wind-ravaged trees and rocky shorelines as a backdrop – and even a craggy cove all its own – this Victorian hunting lodge revels in splendid Scottish isolation; surrounded by 30 acres of grounds, it feels a world away from the madding crowds. Dutiful staff and traditional interiors ensure that guests are suitably coddled. As for the food, Tony Pierce continues to dole out a refined but reassuring daily menu. Top-notch ingredients are given respectful treatment in a succession of just-so dishes ranging from a delicate chicken and confit leg sausage with crispy pancetta and Madeira emulsion to grilled fillet of 'native' salmon accompanied by cauliflower purée, pak choi, micro fries and a red wine reduction infused with star anise. A soup always features in the line-up (perhaps a cappuccino of celeriac and truffle), while dessert is usually an elaborate confection such as double vanilla panna cotta with poached rhubarb, white chocolate macaroon and ginger caramel. Owner David Ibbotson's lovingly curated and endlessly fascinating wine list is an authoritative global compendium with impeccable pedigree, informative tasting notes and a dozen house selections from £26.
Chef/s: Tony Pierce. **Meals:** set L £25 (2 courses) to £40. Set D £70 (6 courses). Sun L £33 (4 courses). **Details:** 20 seats. Bar. Wheelchairs. Parking. Music. Children over 12 yrs at D.

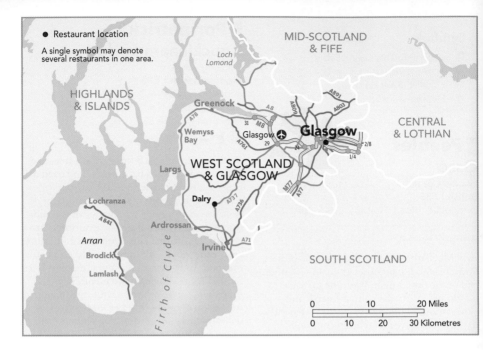

▮ Dalry
Braidwoods

Cooking score: 5
Modern British | £50
Drumastle Mill Cottage, Dalry, KA24 4LN
Tel no: 01294 833544
braidwoods.co.uk

There's no pretending that Nicola and Keith Braidwood's long-standing restaurant isn't in the middle of a field – but it's a nice field, with a hedge full of feeding birds, and an easy tootle from Glasgow. The restaurant may have occupied its whitewashed mill cottages for nigh on a quarter century, but the hospitality feels fresh and genuine, and the cooking is blessedly guest-centred. Both are likely reasons for its continued success, and for the need to book ahead. The kitchen shows off a real eye for colour, as in a blue cheese panna cotta with all the colours of beetroot and a prosciutto wafer, or a plate of grilled hand-dived Wester Ross scallops on beurre blanc with vivid herb oil and a mound of asparagus

and wild garlic risotto. To finish there's often a generous slice of parfait. The pecan and espresso version comes with nutty praline rubble, blood orange and amber caramel; it's food you absolutely want to eat. There's a balanced wine list, with plenty in the house selection for under £30, and rewards above.
Chef/s: Keith Braidwood. **Closed:** Mon, Tue, first 2 weeks Sept, 25 Dec to 1 Feb. **Meals:** set L £29 (2 courses) to £35. Set D £50 to £55. Sun L £35.
Details: 24 seats. Parking. Children over 12 yrs at D.

Get social

Follow us on social media for the latest news, chef interviews and more.
Twitter @GoodFoodGuideUK
Facebook TheGoodFoodGuide

■ Glasgow

111 by Nico

Cooking score: 2

Modern European | £28

111 Cleveden Road, Glasgow, G12 0JU

Tel no: 0141 334 0111

111bynico.co.uk

£30

Diners are asked to trust the kitchen and leave most of the decision-making to chef Modou Diagne and his team at this idiosyncratic neighbourhood restaurant in Kelvinside. As an 'immersive dining experience', eating here is amazingly good value for a seasonally changing six-course line-up using tiptop Scottish ingredients. Following an amuse-bouche of, say, salmon gravadlax, guests are offered a choice of two core ingredients per course – perhaps yellowfin tuna or confit duck, Arbroath smokie or Scottish lamb belly, Scrabster coley or Ayrshire pork, which arrive suitably embellished, garnished and refashioned in up-to-the-minute style. Vegetarians have their own options (aubergine, BBQ sprouting broccoli), while dessert could involve anything from forced rhubarb to sweet potato. There's an easy-going buzzy vibe and drinks are also great fun in their own right, whether you're after a gin-based cocktail, a Scottish craft beer (Stewart Brewing Ka Pai, say) or a bottle from the gently priced wine list.

Chef/s: Nico Simeone and Modou Diagne. **Closed:** Mon, 25 and 26 Dec, 1 Jan. **Meals:** tasting menu £28 (6 courses). Sun L £20 (5 courses). **Details:** 47 seats. V menu. Wheelchairs. Music. No children.

Alchemilla

Cooking score: 3

Middle Eastern | £35

1126 Argyle Street, Glasgow, G3 8TD

Tel no: 0141 337 6060

thisisalchemilla.com

Finnieston is flush with bistros and brasseries, but there is only one Alchemilla. As cool as it is crowded, this modestly stylish spot has become a magnet for eaters (including local chefs) who don't need the dishes, or the experience, to be deluxe. Its reputation, developed under its former chef, Rosie Healey, is rather for lively, instinctive combinations in the loosest of Mediterranean directions. Thankfully for its many regulars, this approach, which throws up some gems, has survived Healey's departure. A flexible menu accommodates companionable sharing or eyes-on-the-prize focus; either way, snacks of 'nduja with honey and thyme or excellent bread are fine statements of intent and there's seasonal veg aplenty, perhaps marinated violet artichokes or fennel with lentils, mint, chilli and lemon. Meatier plates include Swaledale chicken leg with potatoes, smoked lardo and sage, and to finish a simple Italian-inspired pudding might be chocolate cremoso with sea salt and olive oil. Wine is often natural or unfiltered, from £4 a glass.

Chef/s: Craig Grozier. **Meals:** small plates £7 to £14. **Details:** 54 seats.

Brian Maule at Chardon d'Or

Cooking score: 4

French | £51

176 West Regent Street, Glasgow, G2 4RL

Tel no: 0141 248 3801

brianmaule.com

From Lyon to Le Gavroche, Brian Maule's training was classically French. So too is his restaurant, yet a love of good ingredients sometimes takes dishes further afield. The dining room is governed by an appreciation of tradition and restraint; look elsewhere for funky ferments and waiters in trainers, come here for something rather more grown-up. Tried-and-true winter combinations might be, at starter stage, lamb sweetbreads with creamed wild mushrooms and crisp puff pastry, or goat's cheese with celery, walnut and apple crunch and a sesame biscuit – a little nod to the cheeseboard, which is, of course, replete with both Scottish and French selections. Main courses might be roast stone bass with Puy lentils, salsify and charred shallot, or duck fillet with cumin chickpeas and roast Jerusalem artichokes. Tarte tatin is the favoured finish, although a dalliance with the chocolate and coffee mousse with biscotti is understandable. Wines are easy to navigate, and chosen to flatter the classics.

Chef/s: Brian Maule. **Closed:** Mon, Sun, 25 and 26 Dec, 1 and 2 Jan. **Meals:** main courses £23 to £33. Set L and early D £23 (2 courses) to £26. Tasting menu £60 (6 courses). **Details:** 160 seats. V menu. Vg menu. Bar. Music. No children after 8pm.

★ TOP 50 ★

Cail Bruich

Cooking score: 7
Modern British | £45
725 Great Western Road, Glasgow, G12 8QX
Tel no: 0141 334 6265
cailbruich.co.uk

£5
OFF

Opposite Glasgow's Botanic Gardens, this compact, informal restaurant brings the outside in via a window full of ferns, a giant mossy artwork and some of the best produce available in Scotland and beyond. But it's what you do with it that counts, and from neat snacks (a crisp tube of Arbroath smokie and preserved lemon) to barbecued potato bread with truffled Tunworth cheese, Chris Charalambous's team is doing all the right things. Attention to detail is one of the strengths of a kitchen that produces both six-course tasting menus and neat two-course lunches, cooked at the back of a contemporary room with an eat-over bar, sage banquettes and the barest suggestion of tweed. Three courses might start (after excellent pickles and otherworldly bread) with loin and belly of Loch Etive sea trout, the distinct texture of each cut emphasised by a confit treatment and the kiss of the barbecue, served with a pale sauce studded with caviar, rhubarb and cucumber. Goosnargh duck is plated with a generous hand, and a show made of the duck offal topped with an assembly of sweet, sour, crisp and fried beetroot; the subtle grip of walnut in a soy-based jus brings it all together. The urge to subvert expectations shows in a

dessert of lemon tart with white asparagus, but a cheese course of Crottin de Chavignol served with a tiny pissaladière and thyme-scattered caramelised pear more than earns its place. The good-humoured service style extends to wine, which embraces the quirky in both delivery and its selection of unusual European finds.

Chef/s: Chris Charalambous. **Closed:** 1 week Jan. **Meals:** set L £24 (2 courses) to £30. Set D £50. Tasting menu £45 Mon to Thur (5 courses) to £76. Sun L £30. **Details:** 48 seats. V menu. Vg menu. Bar. Parking. Music. Children over 8 yrs.

Crabshakk

Cooking score: 2
Seafood | £40
1114 Argyle Street, Glasgow, G3 8TD
Tel no: 0141 334 6127
crabshakk.com

Crabshakk celebrates a decade of claw-cracking, finger-licking, oyster-shucking popularity. Despite the Finnieston area's ever-expanding dining repertoire, regulars and newcomers still crowd in to enjoy simply treated fish and shellfish. 'It's small, cramped and a bit noisy but we love it for what it is,' sums up the convivial buzz. An informal menu enables simple grazing or more traditional three-course approaches. Whether perching at the bar with a dozen briny bivalves and a glass of white or booking one of the tiny tables to tackle a show-stopping platter of fruits de mer, sweet whole crab or a daily special such as halibut with Arbroath smokie mash, this is a celebration of the sea. Those of a carnivorous or vegetarian persuasion get a token nod but essentially seafood lovers rule and the weighted white wine list supports that. Simple desserts such as panna cotta or chocolate cake offer a sweet ending but are not the main attraction.

Chef/s: David Scott. **Closed:** 25 and 26 Dec, 1 and 2 Jan. **Meals:** main courses £8 to £18. **Details:** 50 seats. 8 seats outside. Bar. Wheelchairs. Music.

Eusebi Deli

Cooking score: 2
Italian | £29
152 Park Road, Glasgow, G4 9HB
Tel no: 0141 648 9999
eusebideli.com
£5 OFF £30

Giovanna Eusebi's Italian-Scottish success story is a delicious one, starting with the family deli in the East End and a selective approach to bringing artisan produce from the old country. This handsome red and white corner site is the product of these traditions, continuing them in approachable style across a heaving ground-floor deli and café with restaurant below. The scale makes Eusebi a versatile spot for weekend brunch (think eggs Benedict with slow-cooked beef shin replacing ham, or the soothing blanket of bianca pizza with pancetta and pecorino), coffee and a snack or a companionable evening downstairs. Dinner might be game and pistachio terrine with preserved plums, or a plate of truffled meat and cheeses with Eusebi fig jam and honeycomb, followed by pasta produced daily in the in-house 'laboratory' – perhaps the rarely seen chickpea flour macaroni with tomato and beans. Alongside beer from the Veneto and Italian cocktails, wines are exactly as you'd expect.
Chef/s: Sebastian Wereski. **Closed:** 25 to 27 Dec, 1 to 3 Jan. **Meals:** main courses £12 to £24. **Details:** 65 seats. 18 seats outside. Wheelchairs. Music.

Gamba

Cooking score: 3
Seafood | £35
225a West George Street, Glasgow, G2 2ND
Tel no: 0141 572 0899
gamba.co.uk

Derek Marshall's well-established fish emporium has nurtured the pescatarian predilections of loyal regulars and Glasgow newbies for more than 20 years. Narrow steps lead down to a tranquil haven that achieves elegance without stuffiness. The extensive menu tends to classic French treatments of seasonal seafood, with the occasional Asian twist to mix things up, and while the repertoire is not the most contemporary in terms of cooking style, flavours are good and well balanced and there is enough interest in even quite simple combinations, such as a starter of pickled herring, beetroot, mangetout and horseradish, to meet diner expectations. Lindisfarne oysters, delicate tuna sashimi, or the famed fish soup, piquant with crab, ginger, coriander and tiny prawn dumplings, could be followed by turbot fillet with prawns, samphire and capers, or a crisp fried sea bream, with Greek salad, pine kernels and sesame. Desserts offer comfort over complexity as this is not where the chef's focus lies, but a warm brownie sandwich with milk sorbet and salted caramel reflects the local sweet tooth.
Chef/s: Derek Marshall. **Meals:** main courses £11 to £30. Market menu £35. **Details:** 65 seats. Bar. Music.

The Gannet

Cooking score: 3
Modern British | £32
1155 Argyle Street, Glasgow, G3 8TB
Tel no: 0141 204 2081
thegannetgla.com
£5 OFF

Visitors to this modish Finnieston restaurant and bar are enamoured of its seasonal take on the Scottish larder and championing of local suppliers. Against the informality of exposed brick, Ivan Stein and Peter McKenna lay bare their passion for contemporary Scottish food. Their quirky Flora Caledonia cocktail list unearths hedgerow ingredients in sweet cicely sour or rowan fizz to accompany aperitif snacks of chicken parfait cornetto and pork belly dumpling. The subsequent seasonal tasting menu might open with shorthorn beef carpaccio with tiny pickled and fried shallot rings and an eclectic nigella seed granola. Barbecued Scrabster monkfish is arguably a little heavy on the searing for its delicate bisque, while Borders lamb two ways (rare loin and slow shoulder) with kidney fat sauce is a more harmonious, if rather traditional, collation. Wild rose bavarois with strawberry sorbet, meadowsweet ice cream and meringue is the epitome of summer. Matched wines lean heavily on natural producers although the list offers a wider range grouped accessibly by style not geography.

Chef/s: Peter McKenna. **Closed:** Mon, 25 and 26 Dec, 1 and 2 Jan. **Meals:** Tasting menu £32 (4 courses) to £45. **Details:** 60 seats. V menu. Wheelchairs. Music.

★ LOCAL RESTAURANT AWARD ★
REGIONAL WINNER

Number 16
Cooking score: 1
Modern British | £35
16 Byres Road, Glasgow, G11 5JY
Tel no: 0141 339 2544
number16.co.uk

£5
OFF

Celebrating 10 years in 2019, Joel Pomfret and Gerry Mulholland's bijou bistro continues to please its local Glaswegian constituency, offering chummy service and sharp cooking in a wee space that encourages socialising. The food is always fresh and innovative, with enough surprises to keep the regulars interested: breast of wood pigeon comes with cauliflower and yeast purée; crispy lamb belly is partnered by pearl barley and green sauce; fillet of halibut gets a topping of chicken and parsley crumb. To finish, there's Turkish delight with pistachio parfait, rose water marshmallow and blood orange jelly. 'Cooking of this quality, very reasonably priced, with exceptionally good service just made me smile all the way home,' enthused one recent visitor. Wines from £15.75.

Chef/s: Sean Currie. **Meals:** main courses £16 to £22. Set L £18 (2 courses) to £22. **Details:** 35 seats. Wheelchairs. Music.

Turn it up

Choosing the right music for a restaurant needn't mean buying in a readymade playlist of easy listening and predictable classical. The coolest places are compiling soundtracks that are as exciting as their food

At **Ynyshir**, Gareth Ward's restaurant with rooms near Snowdonia, the music selection is far from sedate: prepare for anything from 90s hip hop to the Rolling Stones.

Guests staying at **Inver** on the shores of Loch Fyne can unwind in their bothy with a selection of vinyl, while in the restaurant, there might be contemporary Scottish folk on the turntable.

Hip Hackney newcomer **Peg** appeals to diners with its on-trend offering of natural wines, Japanese-inspired small plates and great tunes on vinyl.

Leroy brought its record collection in the move from Hackney to Shoreditch. The team eschews bland, curated playlists in favour of back-to-back classic albums.

'Wine, beats & bites' is the tagline at **Plateau** in Brighton. Expect electronica, dub and everything in between.

Six by Nico

Cooking score: 2
International | £28
1132 Argyle Street, Glasgow, G3 8TD
Tel no: 0141 334 5661
sixbynico.co.uk
£30

Chef patron Nico Simeone has made quite an impact on Glasgow, encouraging expansion to Edinburgh, Belfast and soon Manchester. His concept is simple: a six-course menu that changes every six weeks, at a fixed, wallet-friendly price. Menus are loosely arranged around 'stories' that may be geographic (New York, Catalonia), whimsical (Picnics, Childhood) or more esoteric (Forest, Illusion). From Catalonia, heirloom tomato exudes Mediterranean sunshine in its pretty arrangement of olive textures, goat's curd, and dried tomatoes bathed in grassy oil and silky gazpacho. Follow on with paella blanca, the bomba rice paired with violet artichokes, fino sherry and aged Manchego. Barbecued coley comes with coriander-laden mojo verde and anchovy tempura, while braised pig's check is matched with morcilla and sobrasada. Crema catalana masterfully assembles Valencian orange with almond biscuit, pollen and Italian meringue. A slightly formulaic approach overall? Maybe, and some menus work better than others, but when they're delivered so enthusiastically, it is crowd-pleasing stuff that makes advance booking essential. Matched wines, an affordable list and extensive gin selections complement a lively experience.
Chef/s: Nico Simeone and Stephen Crawford.
Closed: Mon, 25 and 26 Dec, 1 Jan. **Meals:** tasting menu £28 (6 courses). **Details:** 38 seats. V menu. Wheelchairs. Music.

Stravaigin

Cooking score: 2
Global | £32
28 Gibson Street, Glasgow, G12 8NX
Tel no: 0141 334 2665
stravaigin.co.uk

From brunch to dinner, this community stalwart has met the eclectic tastes of its cosmopolitan clientele for nearly 25 years. The arrival of a chef from sister establishment Ubiquitous Chip in 2018 (see entry) has upped the ante in the kitchen. By popular demand, favourites like homemade haggis, neeps and tatties or curry of the moment are never off the menu, but expanded daily specials – four variants on Argyll venison perhaps, indicative of a day's successful stalking – demonstrate the kitchen's inherent class. It's proudly Scottish produce given an unashamedly global slant. Expect big flavours, bold combinations and healthy disregard for established rules: perfectly cooked rustic bavette steak teamed with Indonesian acar awak pickles, fiery sambal and a poached egg, or a toothsome freekeh risotto with smoked aubergine and labneh for a Middle East-Milanese mash-up. The accessible drinks list includes 'love them or hate them' orange wines, while cocktails and craft beers flow at the lively bar.
Chef/s: James MacRae. **Closed:** 25 Dec, 1 Jan.
Meals: main courses £18 to £28. **Details:** 62 seats. 12 seats outside. Bar. Wheelchairs. Music. No children after 10pm.

Ubiquitous Chip

Cooking score: 5
Modern British | £40
12 Ashton Lane, Glasgow, G12 8SJ
Tel no: 0141 334 5007
ubiquitouschip.co.uk

Hanging baskets and potted plants soften the exterior view at the legendary Chip, where a repurposed stable-block courtyard down a cobbled lane has been home to some quality drinking, and not a little serious eating, since the year of decimalisation. The brasserie half of the operation deals in big brunches, Shetland mussels in wine and cream, and Angus steaks in garlic butter, but the restaurant arm takes a more innovative tack with its sterling Scottish produce. Poached cod with its smoked roe, pickled fennel and blood orange might lead the way to guinea fowl breast with medjool dates and harissa, or stone bass with wild garlic gnocchi in oyster velouté. Dishes are thoughtfully arranged on the plate, and first-timers are advised not to miss the famous Caledonian (pralined oatmeal) ice cream with poached plums and honeyed oats. One glance at the wine list will demonstrate why the place is so famous for its cellar; a longer browse will ferret out treats such as Australian Petit Manseng, mature Bandol and biodynamic crémant d'Alsace. Wines by the glass start at £5.95.

Chef/s: Andrew Mitchell. **Closed:** 25 Dec, 1 Jan. **Meals:** main courses £20 to £35. Set L and early D £20 (2 courses) to £24. Sun L £24. **Details:** 115 seats. 20 seats outside. V menu. Vg menu. Bar. Wheelchairs.

LOCAL GEM
The Finnieston
Seafood | £35
1125 Argyle Street, Glasgow, G3 8ND
Tel no: 0141 222 2884
thefinniestonbar.com

Some 200 years ago, this diminutive blue-fronted building was a rakish local tavern; now it's a hip destination serving sustainable seafood to the residents of trendy Finnieston and beyond. Low ceilings, stained-glass panels and close-packed booths set the scene for a menu that runs from steamed Shetland mussels in Thai broth or poached cod with sobrasada, spinach, pine nuts and pimentón oil to flat iron steaks and vegetarian salads. The Finnieston also features a gin bar, with more than 60 brands on show, alongside creative cocktails and some very decent wines.

LOCAL GEM
Ox and Finch
International | £30
920 Sauchiehall Street, Glasgow, G3 7TF
Tel no: 0141 339 8627
oxandfinch.com

£30

There's a familiar stripped-down look to this contemporary spot, with extraction pipes tracking above a space that gets pretty lively when the evening session is motoring. The drill is a series of globally inspired sharing plates that emerges from the open kitchen as and when. Robust combinations take in lime leaf and lemongrass fishcakes with green nam jim, baked pastrami with Jerusalem artichoke, pine nuts, capers and cornichons, and braised lamb neck alongside smoked potato and wild garlic salsa verde. Finish with dark chocolate crémeux. Wines from £20.

LOCAL GEM
Saramago
Vegetarian | £20
Centre for Contemporary Arts, 350 Sauchiehall Street, Glasgow, G2 3JD
Tel no: 0141 352 4920
cca-glasgow.com

£30

Organic breads baked in-house are just one of the worthy treats on offer at this vegetarian café and bar in the atrium of Glasgow's Centre for Contemporary Arts (CCA). The kitchen scours the globe for inspiration, serving everything from sweet potato and pinto bean fritters to Sri Lankan jackfruit curry, udon noodle bowls, pizzas and meze platters. Sandwiches include a mock Reuben made with tempeh 'rashers', sauerkraut and mustard, while the house cheesecake is baked with a hazelnut and oat base. Affordable wines start at £17.50 (£4.55 a glass).

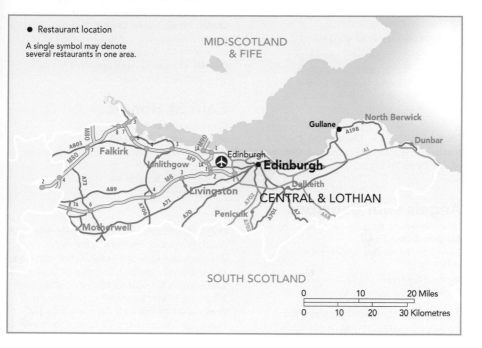

- ● Restaurant location

A single symbol may denote several restaurants in one area.

MID-SCOTLAND & FIFE

North Berwick

Gullane

Dunbar

Falkirk

Edinburgh

Edinburgh

Livingston

Dalkeith

CENTRAL & LOTHIAN

Penicuik

Motherwell

SOUTH SCOTLAND

| 0 | | 10 | | 20 Miles |
| 0 | 10 | | 20 | 30 Kilometres |

▮ Edinburgh

Aizle

Cooking score: 6
Modern British | £70
107-109 St Leonard's Street, Edinburgh,
EH8 9QY
Tel no: 0131 662 9349
aizle.co.uk

'This is what eating out should be all about,' enthused one visitor to Stuart Ralston's neo-bistro not far from The Meadows in the city's university area. Ralston shows a keen understanding of the art of combining flavours and textures to create 'something a bit different'. Provenance is absolutely key, so expect a glorious array of produce from Scotland and beyond (a subtle nod to Ralston's kitchen experience across the world) used to memorable effect across a six-course no-choice tasting menu. A trio of gone-in-a-mouthful 'snacks' might lead to a bridging dish of sheep's milk agnolotti with wild leek and whey sauce, followed by delightful cod with celeriac, grapes and a smoked mussel sauce, and then hogget with spring greens, peas, pink fir potato and charred onions. Everything is on point, from a glorious confit chicken sourdough brioche bun to a stunning pre-dessert of Amalfi Coast lemon sorbet with lemon cream and a poppy seed crumb, and then Yorkshire rhubarb with oats and hibiscus gratings. Service is really engaged. As befits the food, inventive cocktails and soft drinks are offered alongside a concise modern wine list (from £27).

Anonymous

At *The Good Food Guide*, our inspectors dine anonymously and pay their bill in full. These impartial review meals, along with feedback from thousands of our readers, are what informs the content of the *GFG*. Only the best restaurants make the cut.

Vegetarian and vegan

While many restaurants offer dishes suitable for non-meat eaters, those marked 'V menu' (vegetarian) and 'Vg menu' (vegan) offer separate menus.

Chef/s: Stuart Ralston. **Closed:** Mon, Tue, Sun. **Meals:** tasting menu £70 (6 courses). **Details:** 36 seats. V menu. Wheelchairs. Music. No children after 10pm.

Angels with Bagpipes

Cooking score: 4
Modern British | £40
343 High Street, Royal Mile, Edinburgh, EH1 1PW
Tel no: 0131 220 1111
angelswithbagpipes.co.uk

The original 'angel with bagpipes' is a beautiful historic carving in nearby St Giles' Cathedral, and there's a similar figure above the staircase in this cosmopolitan brasserie. Spread over two floors with an upper room (Halo) lit by winged angels bearing candles, it offers a menu of contemporary Scottish-inspired dishes with modern European nuances and a refreshing lack of touristy clichés. Apart from the occasional steak with pepper sauce or 'black' haggis with neeps and tatties, the menu speaks of modish creativity, with most items taking their cue from seasonal native produce – as in monkfish cheeks with smoked roe and pickled sea herbs, celeriac with quinoa, hen of the woods and shimeji mushrooms, or venison paired with kale, plums and parsnips. When it comes to pudding, the kitchen likes to play new tricks with old favourites – witness rhubarb with duck egg custard, tonka bean and yoghurt. Scottish ales and uptown cocktails are tempting alternatives to the modest but appealing wine list.

Chef/s: Alistair Munro. **Closed:** 2 weeks Jan. **Meals:** main courses £17 to £34. Set L £18 (2 courses) to £22. Tasting menu £45 (4 courses). **Details:** 62 seats. 16 seats outside. V menu. Vg menu. Wheelchairs. Music.

Café St Honoré

Cooking score: 4
Modern European | £40
34 North West Thistle Street Lane, Edinburgh, EH2 1EA
Tel no: 0131 226 2211
cafesthonore.com
£5 OFF

France and Scotland have been famously cordial since the first days of the Auld Alliance, and Café St Honoré is testament to this – a 'lovely, relaxed, friendly little place' in Edinburgh's New Town that's a dead ringer for a Parisian bistro. Inside are chequerboard floors and vast mirrors that nod to the Left Bank and Montmartre. The menu, however, is another matter. Sure there are starters like classic French onion soup, but the stars of the show are the ingredients from Caledonia's pantry – such as Belhaven smoked organic salmon, crafted into a terrine with pickled cucumbers and toasted rye bread. Sound sourcing shows, too, in mains like Peterhead John Dory with Shetland musssels, leeks and bacon; or a warming pork belly with Arran mustard mash, studded with Stornoway black pudding, perfect for a blustery night. Both nations come together in indulgent desserts such as crème brûlée with homemade shortbread, while expertly curated Scottish craft beers vie for attention with organic bottles on a French–dominated wine list.

Chef/s: Joe Simpson and Neil Forbes. **Closed:** 24 to 26 Dec, 1 Jan. **Meals:** main courses £17 to £28. Set L £17 Mon to Fri (2 courses) to £21. Set D £22 (2 courses) to £28. Sun L £28. **Details:** 45 seats. Music.

Cannonball

Cooking score: 2

Modern British | £35

Cannonball House, 356 Castlehill, Edinburgh, EH1 2NE

Tel no: 0131 225 1550

contini.com

Two million people visit Edinburgh Castle every year. Some of them, alongside appreciative regulars, are sensible enough to stop at the Contini family's restaurant and whisky bar next door on the way past. The titular ammunition (lodged high in the wall) is just one of the building's historical features. Provenance is more than just a buzzword for the Contini family, and the menu is rich in Scottish treasure, paired with flavours that flatter. To start, that might mean Burnside Farm pigeon breast with honey-glazed plums, lardons and sprout leaves, or Lanark Blue cheese soufflé with confit leek cream and candied walnuts – or haggis cannonballs, if the mood strikes. Dinner might progress with approachable dishes of cullen skink or lobster mac and cheese, or gussied-up roasts like Ayrshire pork belly with crackling and spiced pear jam. Knickerbocker glory or Contini ice creams enlivened with a nip of booze strike a note of pure joy at pudding. Wines are from £24, but there's whisky galore in the ground-floor bar downstairs.

Chef/s: Marcin Medrygal. **Closed:** Mon, Sun, 25 and 26 Dec. **Meals:** main courses £16 to £55. Set L and early D £15. Tasting menu £45 (5 courses). **Details:** 66 seats. V menu. Vg menu. Bar. Wheelchairs. Music.

Budget

£30 At restaurants showing this symbol, it is possible to eat three courses (excluding drinks) for £30 or less.

★ TOP 50 ★

Castle Terrace

Cooking score: 7

Modern French | £75

33-35 Castle Terrace, Edinburgh, EH1 2EL

Tel no: 0131 229 1222

castleterracerestaurant.com

Dominic Jack trained assiduously in some of Paris's most covetable kitchens, and his connections to Edinburgh's own Kitchin (see entry) provide the inspiration here at this Georgian townhouse restaurant. There is naturally a commitment to fine Scottish produce, from Orkney scallops and Stobo venison to herbs from the chef's own garden. Presentations look relatively simple, the better to emphasise the depth and clarity of their principal ingredients. The famous Eden Valley organic spelt risotto is intensely savoury and tender, with sautéed squid in the starring role. For a meatier start, look to warm ballotine of Perthshire mallard served in its own clear consommé with a bouquet of pickled vegetables. Both ends of monkfish – tail and jaw – are enterprisingly offered with confit Brussels sprouts and pumpkin for a memorable seafood dish, while confirmed landlubbers might turn to the comprehensive trio of beef brisket, ox tongue and sweetbreads with roasted salsify and spinach. A trolley of prime French and British cheeses is worth dithering over as a course in itself, but the desserts are also full of allure, as in the refreshing citrus tones of a ruby grapefruit and clementine tart with crème fraîche and a juniper tuile. Markups will have you swallowing hard, but the wine list is an undeniably fine collection of modern and classical oenology, whether you're tempted by a barrique-aged Greek Roditis or an old posho from the Haut-Médoc. Wines by the glass, from £8.50, are wonderful.

Chef/s: Dominic Jack and Phil Blackburne. **Closed:** Mon, Sun, 24 Dec to 13 Jan, 9 to 13 Apr. **Meals:** set L £35. Set D £75. Tasting menu £85 (6 courses). **Details:** 60 seats. Bar. Wheelchairs. Music. Children over 5 yrs.

Contini

Cooking score: 1
Italian | £33
103 George Street, Edinburgh, EH2 3ES
Tel no: 0131 225 1550
contini.com

Described as a 'ridiculously lovely, OTT place to be', this former banking hall is an absolute riot of elaborate rococo flourishes – Romanesque mosaic floors, Renaissance frescoes, high arched windows, towering columns and much more besides. Owned by the locally renowned Contini clan, it offers family-friendly comfort and all-day sustenance for hordes of Edinburgh locals, tourists and theatre-goers who love the ornate setting and are happy to take advantage of some 'nicely done' Italian staples. Pizza and classic pasta dishes such as spinach and ricotta ravioli are the mainstays, bolstered by salads, bruschette, grills and seafood. Special diets are admirably accommodated and there are even some vegan wines on the all-Italian list.
Chef/s: Carina Contini. **Closed:** 25 and 26 Dec.
Meals: main courses £16 to £23. Set L and early D £17 (2 courses) to £20. Tasting menu £45 (5 courses). **Details:** 120 seats. 30 seats outside. V menu. Vg menu. Bar. Wheelchairs. Music.

Dishoom

Cooking score: 2
Indian | £30
3a St Andrew Square, Edinburgh, EH2 2BD
Tel no: 0131 202 6406
dishoom.com
£30

This branch of the seven-strong restaurant group, with sites in London and Manchester, occupies three floors of a handsome Art Deco building on the south side of St Andrew Square. It's a grand address for this clever vintage concept based on the Irani cafés of old Mumbai, where all were welcome. Something of that inclusive spirit lives on here, as students, tourists and families gather together for anything from breakfast of tea and bacon naan rolls to a celebratory spread of curries and cocktails. The house special, salli boti, a Parsi lamb curry garnished with crispy straw potatoes, is available in half portions, the better for fitting in such temptations as paneer pineapple tikka, buttery keema pau, 24-hour black dhal and sides of fried green chillies. All manner of Indian tipples are served including Thums Up soda, lassis, chai, Kingfisher beer and racy cocktails in the Permit Room basement bar.
Chef/s: Naved Nasir. **Closed:** 25 and 26 Dec, 1 and 2 Jan. **Meals:** main courses £7 to £17. **Details:** 98 seats. 25 seats outside. Bar. Wheelchairs. Music. No reservations. Bookings after 5.45pm for groups of 6 or more only.

★ NEW ENTRY ★

Fhior

Cooking score: 4
Modern British | £40
36 Broughton Street, Edinburgh, EH1 3SB
Tel no: 0131 477 5000
fhior.com
£5
OFF

Meaning 'true' in Gaelic, this labyrinthine venue aims for authenticity. Certainly, the clean and minimal design doesn't overwhelm the diner with artifice, while the fixed four- or seven-course dinner menus, and a broader lunchtime selection, reinforce localism and reflect the trend for ingredient listing. At inspection, a pinwheel of wafer-thin cured pork brought as a pre-starter was notable for its rich fat, giving advance notice of the kitchen's confidence with flavour; a smoked yoghurt velouté with toasted pumpkin seeds offered a similar punch. Asparagus, pine, sorrel and egg brought together simple ingredients in a complex arrangement: verdant roasted spears with spruce three ways – as sweet jam, pungent dust and tiny flower-like scatterings – topped with shavings of confit yolk. Hogget, perfectly rare, needed little but a wild garlic emulsion to accompany it, and rhubarb, served three ways (what else?), was partnered by brown butter and candied foraged alexanders. The small bar proposes some signature mixed drinks along with a predominantly modern European wine selection including matched flights.

Chef/s: Scott Smith. **Closed:** Mon, Tue, Sun, 16 to 19 Oct, 1 to 14 Jan. **Meals:** small plates L £5 to £13. Tasting menu D £40 (4 courses) to £65. **Details:** 32 seats. V menu. Vg menu. Bar. Music.

Field

Cooking score: 2

Modern British | £29

41 West Nicolson Street, Edinburgh, EH8 9DB
Tel no: 0131 667 7010
fieldrestaurant.co.uk

£30

Tucked in between a bookshop and an Indian restaurant in the student quarter, Rachel and Richard Conway's eatery looks the dressed-down part, but the focus is where it matters in a menu of modern rustic, seasonal food. Strong savoury seasonings illuminate starters such as smoked duck with pickled plum, Asian mushrooms, peanuts and mizuna, or seared scallops with pork crackling, pork rillettes ravioli and artichoke purée. 'Gutsy' is a word that visitors reach for, and might as easily characterise a main course of fried bream with caponata and basil oil as a preparation of pheasant breast with dates and blue cheese, accompanied by caramelised onion purée and a Scotch egg. Students may be tickled by the appearance of Weetabix parfait with a blueberry tuile among desserts, although the chocolate and hazelnut s'more with beetroot marshmallow will also tempt. The lunch and pre-theatre menu is a steal, and there's an unexpectedly extensive wine list from £19.

Chef/s: David Louwrens. **Closed:** Mon, Sun, 25 and 26 Dec. **Meals:** main courses £13 to £20. Set L and early D £15 (2 courses) to £18. **Details:** 22 seats. Music.

Fishers Leith

Cooking score: 1

Seafood | £30

1 The Shore, Leith, Edinburgh, EH6 6QW
Tel no: 0131 554 5666
fishersrestaurantgroup.co.uk

£30

Something of an old stager amid the restaurant hubbub on Leith's waterfront, this compact seafood eatery knows its business well. Staff are described as 'friendly' and 'great with small children' while the 'hospitality felt [is] genuine'. The sea is both the decorative and culinary theme, and the kitchen wends its way from grilled Anstruther langoustine tails with garlic butter via 'cooked to perfection' hake with potato, tomato and olive tagine and chermoula to fillet of turbot with cockles, clams, ham hock, cavolo nero and samphire. Meat isn't ignored, nor are vegetarians and vegans, and the weekday set menu is considered 'superb value'. Old-school desserts include bread and butter pudding. Wines from £19.50.

Chef/s: Andrew Bird. **Meals:** main courses £14 to £27. Set L £15 Mon to Fri (2 courses) to £18. **Details:** 36 seats. 16 seats outside. V menu. Vg menu. Bar. Music.

Forage & Chatter

Cooking score: 4

Modern British | £34

1a Alva Street, Edinburgh, EH2 4PH
Tel no: 0131 225 4599
forageandchatter.com

Amid the Georgian terraces of the West End, this intriguingly named basement venue is done in hard-edged contemporary style, with tartan-backed banquette and booth seating overlaid with a minty green theme. It's well run and deservedly popular. If you provide the chatter, the kitchen most definitely does the foraging, with wild ingredients in abundance on the modern Scottish menus, now under the careful stewardship of Giorgio Alexiou. An early dinner after he took over featured a novel approach to the ubiquitous beetroot, teaming it with potato gnocchi and ginger, with sturdy, flavour-driven main dishes of lamb rump with turnips, sprouts and salsify, and sea bass with broccoli, walnuts and spelt. Imaginative combining at dessert stage might see chocolate mousse arrive with a poached pear, and pear and lime sorbet, while a dairy-rich blow-out adds ricotta and dulce de leche to caramel parfait. Cosmopolitan wines by the glass, from £5.65, lead a list that combines quality and concision.

Chef/s: Georgiou Alexiou. **Closed:** Mon, Sun. **Meals:** main courses £16 to £24. Set L £15 (2 courses) to £18. **Details:** 44 seats. Bar. Music.

The Gardener's Cottage

Cooking score: 2
Modern British | £45
1 Royal Terrace Gardens, London Road, Edinburgh, EH7 5DX
Tel no: 0131 558 1221
thegardenerscottage.co

This former horticultural hideaway literally leads you up the garden path to a dining experience centred on growing and sharing. Seated communally and often very cosily at one of three large refectory tables, diners can expect a convivial, quirky experience in simple surroundings with honest, gutsy cooking from the open kitchen. Lunch offers various choices while dinner is a tasting menu that invites you to simply accept 'the best from that day's harvest, catch or shoot'. This might start with a salad of sweet crab, crisp radish and apple followed by scallop, razor clam and brown shrimp in summery sauce vierge. Depending on the season, a prime cut of native roe deer or local spring lamb might come next, with dessert perhaps a quirky fusion of dark chocolate and sea buckthorn with granola and sorbet. The owners' Quay Commons bakery furnishes excellent sourdough while house cocktails and a selection of craft beers and spirits support a Spanish-led wine list. On Calton Hill above is new venture The Lookout (see entry), sharing much of the same ethos from its loftier perch.

Chef/s: Dale Mailley. **Closed:** 25 to 27 Dec. **Meals:** main courses £10 to £18. Tasting menu £60 (5 courses). **Details:** 30 seats. 8 seats outside. V menu. Vg menu. Music.

★ NEW ENTRY ★

Grazing by Mark Greenaway

Cooking score: 5
Modern British | £40
Waldorf Astoria, Rutland Street, Edinburgh, EH1 2AB
Tel no: 0131 222 8857
markgreenaway.com

With dark wood, leather and tartan providing more than a hint of gentleman's club, the august surroundings of the Waldorf Astoria may not seem the natural environment for relaxed, chef-led dining. In contrast, enthusiastic staff in aprons and denim shirts inject an informality that suits the 'grazing' concept of Mark Greenaway's latest venture. The menu features modern reimaginings of British classics such as shepherd's pie for sharing, lighter Japanese-inspired specialities – barbecued shiitake mushrooms, say – and international hotel favourites, presumably in an attempt to please all-comers. Individual dishes, elevated by dramatic crockery, demonstrate the high levels of culinary skill, attention to detail and elements of surprise that are the chef's signature. Dark, beery treacle bread with duck-fat butter sets early expectations high. Perfectly seasoned beef tartare with honeycombed dehydrated egg-yolk-and-garlic oil-infused Melba toast is served with grated frozen Parmesan, creating delightful texture, temperature and flavour hits. Soft-shell crab tempura – as light and crisp as you'd hope – is offset by a foamed creamy tartare sauce spiked with nonpareille capers. Classy desserts such as the summery strawberry pavlova are colourful masterpieces, and even petits fours with coffee nestle in their own cacao pod. The wine list offers a range and prices geared towards a hotel clientele.

Chef/s: Mark Greenaway and Andrew Logie.
Meals: small plates £9. Large plates £14 to £43.
Details: 160 seats. Bar.

Hawksmoor

Cooking score: 4
British | £60
23 West Register Street, Edinburgh, EH2 2AA
Tel no: 0131 526 4790
thehawksmoor.com

The steady march north of this London-based steakhouse group continues, and its first Scottish outpost is bang on the money. Set in a former banking hall, it's a grand space, furnished in luxe-vintage fashion: parquet flooring salvaged from a Blackpool ballroom, coffered ceiling. The single-page menu opens with oysters, followed by Scottish seafood-leaning starters – the signature scallops roasted with white port and garlic are as good as ever. The main event is steak, of course: native charcoal-grilled beef, available as larger cuts to share (or not), priced per 100g, or individual portions sold a-piece. The beef's deep, mineral tang and complex flavour speaks of a classy pedigree, and it's complemented by sides such as bone marrow with onions, and spinach with lemon, but there's plenty for those in the mood for fish. Desserts include peanut butter shortbread with salted caramel ice cream. Exploring the carte can be costly, but the lunch specials and set menus are a great-value way in. A steak-friendly Hawksmoor-blend Malbec is a safe bet on the global wine list, and there are cocktails for all moods.
Chef/s: David Howard-Smith. **Closed:** 25 and 26 Dec. **Meals:** main courses £14 to £34. Set L and early/late D £25 (2 courses) to £28. **Details:** 185 seats. Bar. Wheelchairs. Music.

The Kitchin

Cooking score: 7
Scottish French | £80
78 Commercial Quay, Leith, Edinburgh, EH6 6LX
Tel no: 0131 555 1755
thekitchin.com

One of the reference points for Edinburgh's dining scene over the past decade and more, Tom Kitchin's converted whisky warehouse on the Leith waterfront is done up in an appealing mixture of natural colours and materials. Service has always hit the right balance of properly knowledgeable and genuinely welcoming, making a visit as much of a treat as the utterly distinctive cooking demands. Styled boldly as 'Scottish French', Kitchin's food takes the produce of national land and waters and gives it the highly polished treatments of classical cuisine, a tendency fully in evidence on the top-value lunch menus. A vol-au-vent of sautéed lamb sweetbreads with sprouting broccoli, followed by seared North Sea hake in a slew of shellfish with gnocchi and wild garlic, and then a lemon soufflé with Knockraich Farm yoghurt ice cream, is the kind of lunch you'll be talking about for a fair while. It's that ringing freshness and unarguable pedigree that speaks all through the carte, too, as when Orkney scallops baked in the shells are given a dressing of white wine, vermouth and herbs, or the dual serving of Highland wagyu is spiked with lardons in a deeply savoury bone marrow sauce. Nothing feels forced, but all ingredients are allowed their moment in the spotlight. A crystal-clear jelly and sorbet of rhubarb accompany frozen whisky mousse rolled in toasted oats for the heritage finish. A wine list of undeniable class is particularly strong in France, with distinctive bottles from vanguard producers throughout, albeit at pretty tough markups.

Chef/s: Tom Kitchin. **Closed:** Mon, Sun, 15 to 19 Oct, 24 Dec to 11 Jan, 2 to 6 Apr, 16 to 20 Jul. **Meals:** set L £35. Set D £80. Tasting menu £90 (6 courses) to £140. **Details:** 75 seats. V menu. Bar. Wheelchairs. Parking. Music. Children over 5 yrs.

The Little Chartroom

Cooking score: 4
Modern European | £40
30-31 Albert Place, Edinburgh, EH7 5HN
Tel no: 0131 556 6600
thelittlechartroom.com

Unarguably diminutive in stature (booking is essential), this popular newcomer compensates with massive helpings of personal passion and culinary ambition from owners Roberta Hall and Shaun McCarron. From kitchen and front of house respectively, they bring a quality pedigree to their daily changing seasonal menu, where delicate portions are ably supported by excellent gnarly homemade breads. A Portuguese octopus starter is meltingly tender, with vibrant heirloom tomatoes and the bitter bite of bur chervil. Next up, pancetta-wrapped loin of rabbit with a leg meat croquette is confidently garnished with the sweetest kidney and baby carrots, freshly podded peas and lightly braised little gem. To close, a chocolate and raspberry délice has a well-judged touch of salt in the crumb and properly tart Scottish raspberry sorbet to ensure indulgence that doesn't overwhelm. A simple but considered selection of small-batch spirits, local beers and a flexible wine list should meet most needs. Good food doesn't come cheap, although the set lunch is an affordable entry. **Chef/s:** Roberta Hall. **Closed:** Mon, Tue, 1 to 10 Sept, 1 to 14 Jan. **Meals:** main courses £17 to £24. Set L £16 (2 courses) to £19. **Details:** 18 seats. Music.

The Lookout by Gardener's Cottage

Cooking score: 5
British | £45
Calton Hill, Edinburgh, EH7 5AA
Tel no: 0131 322 1246
thelookoutedinburgh.co

A partnership between the well-established Gardener's Cottage (see entry) and contemporary arts venue Collective, this stunningly located cantilevered glass cube at the top of Calton Hill offers arguably the finest views in Edinburgh. This gives the food plenty to live up to, and with chefs working in front of diners, there are no hiding places. Happily, culinary competence, impeccable ingredients and no shortage of ambition mean the menus are every bit as impressive as the setting, with dishes achieving a perfect balance of rusticity and finesse. An egg yolk raviolo, cosseted in a silken Tunworth cheese and crow garlic eiderdown, is crowned with a tumble of slender, salty game chips. Follow with soft, sinuous skate, its inherent sweetness offset by lightly pickled razor clam and burnt lemon, or perhaps a caramelised potato terrine with morels that is as richly satisfying as the ingot of rare sirloin it accompanies. Confit swede and piquant gathered greens are the breakthrough stars of the tempting side dishes, while a simple-sounding salted caramel, clotted cream and chocolate dessert provides a platter of happy surprises. The short but thoughtfully curated drinks list offers good variety and there are matched wines with the tasting menu – just don't forget you've got to get back down the hill. **Chef/s:** Dale Mailley. **Meals:** main courses £27 to £33. Tasting menu £75 (5 courses). **Details:** 42 seats. 18 seats outside. V menu. Vg menu. Wheelchairs. Music.

Number One

Cooking score: 6
Modern European | £90
The Balmoral, 1 Princes Street, Edinburgh,
EH2 2EQ
Tel no: 0131 557 6727
roccofortehotels.com

A venerable station hotel since 1902, The
Balmoral dominates the Princes Street skyline,
with a clock tower that runs three minutes fast
to ensure tardy passengers catch their trains.
Those with a few idle hours spare should make
their way to the subterranean red-lacquered
dining space that is Number One – the hotel's
flagship restaurant and 'a place for big occasion
dining'. Here a formidable kitchen team,
including recent appointee Mark Donald, is
kept on track by long-standing exec chef Jeff
Bland with a menu finely tuned to the Scottish
seasons. The clarity of the Highland seas shines
through in a starter of Dingwall scallop with
cured pork, redcurrant and black garlic
ketchup, or in roast langoustine accompanied
by squash, wakame and pumpkin seeds.
Intricate mains involve clever constructions:
venture to the Lowlands with Borders
partridge, braised lentils, game chips and
pancetta, or tender Tweed Valley beef
alongside beetroot and bone marrow. The
biggest swoons are reserved for dessert,
notably the flamboyant chocolate millefeuille
with bergamot and caramel ice cream. The
wine list centres on aristocratic French
vintages. Prices here might hit you like a first-
class ticket to Penzance, although based on our
inspection, it's a ride worth taking. In
addition, readers this year have praised the
classic bistro dishes and reasonable bill at The
Balmoral's second restaurant Brasserie Prince,
overseen by Alain Roux of The Waterside Inn.
Chef/s: Jeff Bland and Mark Donald. **Closed:** 2
weeks Jan. **Meals:** set D £90. Tasting menu £105 (7
courses). **Details:** 60 seats. Bar. Wheelchairs. Music.
Children over 5 yrs.

Ondine

Cooking score: 3
Seafood | £40
2 George IV Bridge, Edinburgh, EH1 1AD
Tel no: 0131 226 1888
ondinerestaurant.co.uk

Roy Brett's loyal fan base keeps his polished
monochrome seafood restaurant perched
above the Royal Mile enduringly popular – it
celebrated its 10th anniversary in 2019. The set
lunch and early dinner is startlingly good
value and ingredients are carefully sourced,
too: grilled Loch Fyne oysters with chipotle
butter, ahead of haddock goujons with tartare
sauce and chips, say. The big selling point is
plainly served seafood – whole boiled brown
crab with shellfish mayonnaise, perhaps;
grilled half-shell scallops with garlic butter
and bacon jam; or whole lemon sole with
brown shrimps, lemon, parsley and capers.
The grand platters of fruits de mer are very
popular, too. Tempura squid with Vietnamese
dipping sauce and crispy chillies makes a good
start, praline and coffee profiteroles a sweet
finish. Despite the odd gripe about service,
this is an address worth knowing, especially
for its list of accessible food-friendly wines
from £25.
Chef/s: Roy Brett. **Closed:** Sun. **Meals:** main
courses £15 to £75. Set L and early D £23 (2
courses) to £29. **Details:** 88 seats. Wheelchairs.
Music.

Purslane

Cooking score: 2
Modern British | £35
33a St Stephen Street, Edinburgh, EH3 5AH
Tel no: 0131 226 3500
purslanerestaurant.co.uk
£5
OFF

Located in well-heeled Stockbridge, this
compact restaurant may be below the
pavement but Paul Gunning's cooking aims
high. Close-packed tables and a tiny corner
bar create a refreshingly casual setting,
although some would call it cramped. Top-
quality raw materials are allowed to star in

contemporary dishes that are precise and competitively priced. A typical starter centres on scallops cooked a la plancha and teamed with Provençal vegetables, romesco sauce and toasted pine nuts, while mains take in elegant presentations of baked hake with smoked haddock, confit potatoes, baby spinach and leeks, or Perthshire venison with roasted root vegetables, dauphinois potatoes, kale and juniper jus. For dessert, look out for chocolate crème brûlée with bourbon ice cream and vanilla and bourbon foam, or a selection of cheeses from nearby Iain Mellis. Wines start at £22, with plenty by the glass.

Chef/s: Paul Gunning. **Closed:** Mon. **Meals:** set L £15 (2 courses) to £18. Set D £30 (2 courses) to £35. Tasting menu £50 (5 courses) to £60. **Details:** 20 seats. Music.

★ TOP 50 ★

Restaurant Martin Wishart

Cooking score: 7
Modern French | £90
54 The Shore, Leith, Edinburgh, EH6 6RA
Tel no: 0131 553 3557
martin-wishart.co.uk

On Leith's regenerated waterfront strip, Martin Wishart's sophisticated but approachable flagship is an immediately inviting space, naturally lit during the day, gently subdued in the evening. The style is clean-lined and contemporary, with light wood panelling, nods to 1960s style and views across the water from its windows – an understated counterpoint to Wishart's masterly and highly individual take on modern French cuisine. Scottish ingredients stand proud on the menu as the building blocks for some gently adventurous dishes that make an impact without descending into madcap alchemy or showboating: Gigha halibut is fashioned as a ceviche with mango and passion fruit, while Kilbrannan langoustines are paired with parsnip, verjus and smoked butter. Moving on, there might be ravioli of snails served with mussels, baby leeks and white onion velouté or a plate of flat

iron steak cut from black Angus beef, embellished with asparagus, a broad bean croquette, black garlic and a soupçon of roasted onion sauce. Each dish is properly thought through, as the kitchen reels off a succession of intense, vividly flavoured mini masterpieces. If you're looking for a dazzling sweet finale, consider the Calvados ganache matched with fragrant dill parfait or the equally daring white chocolate meringue with parsnip mousse and lapsang souchong ice cream. The superlative wine list offers oenophiles a world tour, turning up rare treats from lesser-known countries alongside international big hitters priced from £28 upwards; half bottles are in good supply, as are superior house selections by the glass.

Chef/s: Martin Wishart and Joe Taggart. **Closed:** Mon, Sun, 22 to 26 Dec, 31 Dec to 17 Jan. **Meals:** set L £35 Tue to Fri. Set D £90 (4 courses). Tasting menu £85 (6 courses) to £120. **Details:** 50 seats. V menu. Wheelchairs. Music. Children over 7 yrs.

Le Roi Fou

Cooking score: 4
French | £45
1 Forth Street, Edinburgh, EH1 3JX
Tel no: 0131 557 9346
leroifou.com

£5 OFF

Since opening in the New Town two years ago, Jérôme Henry's self-described 'salon' has swiftly become a key player in the city's lively food scene. It's an elegant yet diminutive place with a wine bar up front and dining room out back. With his Haute-Savoie roots and a CV including a seven-year stint as head chef at London's Mosimann's, Henry's food attests to his classical culinary background, but there's nothing's fanciful just for the sake of it – clean flavours are his hallmark. From the extensive carte, expect whatever's at peak season: Wye Valley asparagus with horseradish, nettle and wild garlic aïoli, perhaps, followed by signature hand-cut beef tartare with frites or fricassée of new season vegetables with polenta and roasted pepper pipérade. And don't miss the Orkney scallops if they are on. For an easier-on-the-pocket bill, there are lunch and early bird deals. The well-rounded Europhile wine list opens at £5.50 a glass.

Chef/s: Jérôme Henry. **Closed:** Mon, Sun. **Meals:** main courses £15 to £32. Set L and early D £21 (2 courses) to £26. Tasting menu £55 (6 courses). **Details:** 50 seats. Bar. Music.

The Scran & Scallie
Cooking score: 3
British | £35
1 Comely Bank Road, Edinburgh, EH4 1DT
Tel no: 0131 332 6281
scranandscallie.com

For those south of Hadrian's Wall, 'scran and scallie' means 'food and scallywags' – and this being a pub owned by local foodie aristocracy Tom Kitchin and Dominic Jack, the emphasis definitely lands on 'scran'. Dining tables take priority over bar stools in a room that blends Nordic sparseness with teal and tartan surfaces – as well as tall windows overlooking the leafy streets of Stockbridge. 'Sit ye doon yer welcome', proclaims the menu. Also written in Scots, Yer Starters might include dressed Newhaven crab and toast, or half a dozen Loch Fyne oysters. Meanwhile, Yer Mains see familiar pub staples recast – ham, egg and chips is deconstructed into tender ham hock, served with pineapple, capers and a piping-hot pan of runny eggs, while moreish smoked haddock rarebit is slumped atop pink fir potato and spinach. Round off with vanilla cheesecake and poached pear from Yer Puddins, or launch into a whisky flight from the bar, with single malts arranged by region. Some bemoan the distinctly unpub-like prices, although weekday set lunches are available.

Chef/s: Tom Kitchin, Jamie Knox and Dominic Jack. **Closed:** 25 Dec. **Meals:** main courses £13 to £26. Set L £19 Mon to Fri. **Details:** 75 seats. Bar. Wheelchairs.

★ NEW ENTRY ★

Six by Nico
Cooking score: 2
International | £28
97 Hanover Street, Edinburgh, EH2 1DJ
Tel no: 0131 225 5050
sixbynico.co.uk
£30

Nico Simeone's Glasgow original of the same name (see entry) has spawned a pair of extra outlets in Belfast and here, just off Queen Street, where a narrow mauve frontage leads to a stripped-down interior with buttoned banquettes and bentwood chairs. They work to the same formula of a six-course taster that changes every six weeks, with themes this year including Catalan and Orient Express nights.

Chef/s: Nico Simeone and John Peter Ferguson. **Closed:** Mon, 25 and 26 Dec, 1 Jan. **Meals:** tasting menu £28 (6 courses). **Details:** 57 seats. V menu. Wheelchairs. Music.

★ NEW ENTRY ★

Southside Scran
Cooking score: 3
Modern European | £35
14-17 Bruntsfield Place, Edinburgh, EH10 4HN
Tel no: 0131 342 3333
southsidescran.com

To anyone who's eaten at Tom Kitchin's other places, his 'From Nature to Plate' ethos, writ large over his menus and in his innovative Scottish cookery, will be familiar. At his latest Edinburgh venture, French culinary tradition and local ingredients coalesce in seamless yet casual fashion. The slick bistro dining room – tailored, it seems, for the well-to-do of leafy Bruntsfield – has a clubbish feel, all moody greens, brass and wood. An open rôtisserie grill is at the heart of the operation, turning out petite plates of pricey yet delectable chicken or Ayrshire pork leg and pan-fried fillet with pineapple salsa. There's generous battered haddock with tartare sauce and chips. Sides and salads are made for sharing: try leek vinaigrette, macaroni cheese or warm French beans with hazelnuts and shallots. Unbidden appetisers and petits fours are a delight, as is a chocolate tart with milk ice cream – hats off to the pastry chef. The list of some 100 wines swiftly heads skyward, but thankfully over half are available by the glass.

Chef/s: Tom Kitchin and Craig McKenzie. **Closed:** 25 Dec. **Meals:** main courses £11 to £32. Set L £22 (2 courses) to £30. Sun L £27. **Details:** 65 seats. Bar. Wheelchairs. Music.

Taisteal
Cooking score: 2
International | £30
1-3 Raeburn Place, Edinburgh, EH4 1HU
Tel no: 0131 332 9977
taisteal.co.uk
£30

Take one look at the globetrotting portfolio of foodie pictures lining the walls of Gordon Craig's compact Stockbridge restaurant and you know you're in for a meal whose influences will come from far and wide. The rolling menu marries Scottish seasonal produce with diverse culinary inspiration – perhaps pig's cheek tortellini in Asian broth or pan-fried scallops matched with chicken satay sauce, black pudding and pomegranate. Elsewhere, dishes such as game pithivier, coq au vin and pan-fried hake with smoked mussels, Champagne and caviar sauce are firmly in the European mainstream, while veggie haggis bonbons cater to the meat-averse. Desserts such as raspberry crémeux with olive oil cake, salted hazelnuts and raspberry sorbet are mostly in the Western tradition too, although a yuzu meringue pie is an exotic twist on the classic. Keenly priced wines, beers and cocktails chime with the overriding international theme.

Chef/s: Gordon Craig. **Closed:** Mon, Sun, 2 weeks Sept, 1 week Jan. **Meals:** main courses £14 to £19. Set L and early D £13 (2 courses) to £16. Tasting menu £40 (5 courses) to £50. **Details:** 44 seats. Music.

Timberyard
Cooking score: 5
Modern British | £56
10 Lady Lawson Street, Edinburgh, EH3 9DS
Tel no: 0131 221 1222
timberyard.co

'An impressive space, a massive room, candles everywhere, lots of rustic wood and log-burning stoves, courtyard outside for warm days, blankets supplied.' So ran the notes of one visitor to the Radford family's converted Victorian warehouse. Things are equally upbeat in the kitchen, where chef Ben Radford's commitment to the seasons extends to foraged pickings, and big-hearted flavours are stuffed into lively menus – small plates at lunch, four-, six- or eight-course tasters at dinner (including vegetarian and vegan options). Typically accomplished dishes might run to BBQ langoustines with celeriac and watercress, salt cod with leeks, mussels, ramsons and parsley, or glazed lamb with smoked curd, turnip and daikon. Rhubarb with yoghurt, almond and woodruff is one of the striking desserts. Service is unforced and engaged, and as for drinks, there are cool cocktails and small-batch beers alongside an up-to-the-minute list of low-intervention wines from European vineyards.

Chef/s: Ben Radford. **Closed:** Mon, Sun, 1 week Oct, 25 and 26 Dec, 1 week Jan, 1 week Apr. **Meals:** small plates L and early D Tue to Thur £7 to £15. Tasting menu L £40 (5 courses) and D £57 (4 courses) to £79. **Details:** 65 seats. 35 seats outside. V menu. Vg menu. Bar. Wheelchairs. Music. Children over 10 yrs at D.

Valvona & Crolla
Cooking score: 2
Italian | £26
19 Elm Row, Edinburgh, EH7 4AA
Tel no: 0131 556 6066
valvonacrolla.co.uk
£5 OFF £30

This temple of Italian produce was established in 1934, providing tinned tomatoes, olives and dried herbs for expat Italians looking for a taste of home. The stock has expanded enormously since then but V&C remains the go-to shop for Italian ingredients and an eye-boggling selection of wines. Pick up a bottle to match a meal in the caffè bar at the back – they add just £4 corkage across the range. The comprehensive menu covers well-loved favourites such as pork and beef meatballs in tomato sauce, Tuscan sausage and red peppers, pork milanese, frittata and flat iron steak and tomato salad, along with pizzas and pasta dishes, perhaps Sicilian penne with peas, cream and artichoke. Can't manage a whole bottle? Glass selections from the Italian-heavy wine list start at £4.10. Evening openings have been extended to five nights a week and there are regular wine tastings, talks, music events and more.

Chef/s: Mary Contini. **Closed:** 25 and 26 Dec, 1 and 2 Jan. **Meals:** main courses £10 to £18. Set L and D £16 (2 courses) to £19. **Details:** 74 seats. V menu. Music.

The Wee Restaurant

Cooking score: 3
Modern British | £37
61 Frederick Street, Edinburgh, EH2 1LH
Tel no: 0131 225 7983
theweerestaurant.co.uk

Craig Wood's wee second iteration, after an original in North Queensferry in neighbouring Fife (see entry), sits snugly in a sweeping Georgian terrace in New Town. Tables are generously spaced, given the limited dimensions, and padded chairs add to the comfort of a sparsely adorned room. Prime beef from the Black Isle, Ross and Cromarty is at the heart of the operation: ribeyes, sirloins and fillets are aged for four weeks, then chargrilled and sauced in Café de Paris butter, with a choice of chips or dauphinois potatoes. There could be panko-crumbed goat's cheese with beetroot vinaigrette, or classic moules marinière to kick off, followed by pancetta-wrapped cod on Puy lentils and spinach in truffle oil dressing. Desserts offer a spin on bread and butter pudding, and a pineapple version of tatin with coconut ice cream, or

there are Iain Mellis cheeses. A couple eating in late winter found much to enjoy on the plate, but encountered leaderless service resulting in tedious waits. Wines are a classy international collection with useful notes and small glasses from £4.25.

Chef/s: Craig Wood. **Closed:** Mon, Sun, 24 to 27 Dec, 1 and 2 Jan. **Meals:** set L £16 (2 courses) to £21. Set D £29 (2 courses) to £37. **Details:** 40 seats. Music.

LOCAL GEM

Baba

Middle Eastern | £25
130 George Street, Edinburgh, EH2 4JZ
Tel no: 0131 527 4999
baba.restaurant

£30

The western end of George Street and the area around Saint Andrew's Square are full of casual dining possibilities – but this all-day eatery operated by the team behind Glasgow's Ox and Finch (see entry) stands out. The flavour is Middle Eastern and small sharing plates are the thing here, so start with meze of labneh and yellow muhammara with chopped walnuts or baba ganoush before kofta of beef, lamb and bone marrow with sumac onions and smoked tomato salmorejo. Cauliflower shawarma with ras el hanout, pomegranate and mint stands out among the side dishes. Interesting cocktails and a good-value wine list add to the appeal.

LOCAL GEM

Bia Bistrot

European | £30
19 Colinton Road, Edinburgh, EH10 5DP
Tel no: 0131 452 8453
biabistrot.co.uk

£30

This well-established neighbourhood eatery is tucked away in the Morningside area and, as befits a 'bistrot', the atmosphere is relaxed and informal, with rustic wooden floors, purple walls and high-backed leather chairs at bare tables. Bia's owners – it means 'food' in Gaelic – hail from Ireland and France, so expect to see influences from both countries on their short seasonal menus. Start perhaps with mackerel fillet with samphire, spring onions and romesco sauce, follow with lamb rump with pea purée, layered potato cake and mint, before rounding off with chocolate terrine. The simple set lunch is very good value. Wines from £19.50.

Harajuku Kitchen
Japanese
10 Gillespie Place, Edinburgh, EH10 4HS
Tel no: 0131 281 0526
harajukukitchen.co.uk
'The sushi is fresh, delicious and beautifully presented. The prawn tempura large, crispy and succulent and the pork gyoza are unbeatable! Lovely staff; a warm welcome in a relaxed, cosy little restaurant.'

▌Gullane
★ NEW ENTRY ★

The Bonnie Badger
Cooking score: 2
Modern European | £36
Main Street, Gullane, EH31 2AB
Tel no: 01620 621111
bonniebadger.com

Tom Kitchin's expanding portfolio embraced this sister venue to Edinburgh's Scran & Scallie (see entry) in late 2018. No expense has been spared in creating a succession of linked but differently targeted spaces, including a properly pubby bar area and a classy dining room, The Stables, with a more formal feel and service style. The all-day menu is available in all areas (with additional snacks offered in the bar). None of it is complicated: crispy pig's ear turns out to be the best pork scratching; ham, egg and chips may have a retro pineapple garnish but gets a contemporary makeover elevating its status significantly; steak and

bone marrow pie is pastry perfection with pearled jellies of marrow in a bone funnel. Elsewhere, daily specials such as tender lamb sweetbreads with peas step just beyond the otherwise pub classics repertoire, while homely desserts include an excellent treacle tart with clotted cream. There are craft beers and cocktails plus an extensive wine list covering all bases from affordable to blow-the-budget – clearly targeting visitors attracted by top-class local golf.
Chef/s: Tom Kitchin, Dominic Jack and Matthew Budge. **Meals:** main courses £13 to £22. Set L £19. **Details:** 120 seats. 25 seats outside. Bar. Wheelchairs. Parking. Music.

La Potinière
Cooking score: 4
Modern British | £39
34 Main Street, Gullane, EH31 2AA
Tel no: 01620 843214
lapotiniere.co.uk

Gullane's main street leads golfing pilgrims to Muirfield and a host of other courses that hug the coast a few miles east of Edinburgh. It is also where you'll find La Potinière, which has been part of Scotland's culinary heritage for a generation or more and, since the early noughties, in the capable hands of Mary Runciman and Keith Marley. It's a traditional sort of place where formality is upheld and the region's ingredients get their due. The fixed-price format includes a couple of choices at each course, plus optional intermediary soup and cheese plate. Twice-baked goat's cheese soufflé is richly comforting, teamed with red onion marmalade, followed perhaps by seared monkfish with creamy mash and a medley of local seafood. Scotch beef is handled with skill and, among sweet courses, apple gets a full workout in a parfait, compôte, coulis and sorbet. There's a decent selection of half bottles on a wine list that opens at a modest £17 (£3.50 a small glass).
Chef/s: Mary Runciman and Keith Marley. **Closed:** Mon, Tue, bank hols, Jan. **Meals:** set L £23 (2 courses) to £29. Set D £39 to £47 (4 courses). **Details:** 24 seats. Wheelchairs. Parking.

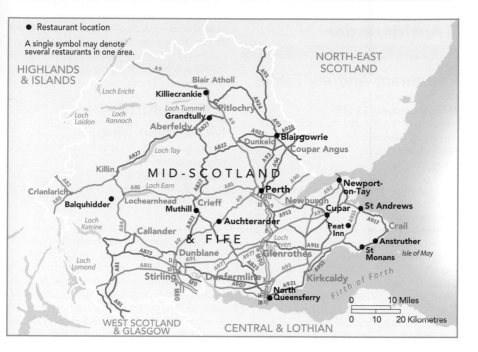

Restaurant location

A single symbol may denote several restaurants in one area.

▮ Anstruther
The Cellar

Cooking score: 6
Modern British | £70
24 East Green, Anstruther, KY10 3AA
Tel no: 01333 310378
thecellaranstruther.co.uk

A decades-old restaurant, The Cellar continues to thrive under chef proprietor Billy Boyter. He's a local lad called back from Edinburgh by the possibilities of the East Neuk. Anstruther might be a village, but here Boyter's culinary horizons seem expanded, rather than contained, over a six-course tasting menu at lunch and eight at dinner. Substantial but relaxed, the dining room is softened by natural textures and personable service. Neat early mouthfuls might include a smoked mussel with dabberlocks seaweed and lemon. Dishes, composed with an eater's appreciation of colour, reveal themselves in pleasing layers, as in a signature bowl of caramelised ox tongue with aged Parmesan

velouté and truffle. As the menu progresses, North Sea halibut with razor clam and onion broth is a little homage to the labours of the coast, while a dessert of koji rice with black banana, finger lime and chocolate brings a more exotic mood. The wine flight, £55 for six glasses, is the favoured option for drinks. **Chef/s:** Billy Boyter. **Closed:** Mon, Tue, 2 weeks Sept, 2 weeks Jan, 1 week May. **Meals:** set L £40 (6 courses). Set D £70 (8 courses). **Details:** 26 seats. Bar. Music. Children over 12 yrs.

Send us your review

Your feedback informs the content of the *GFG* and will be used to compile next year's entries. To register your opinion about any restaurant listed in the Guide, or a restaurant that you wish to bring to our attention, visit: thegoodfoodguide.co.uk/feedback.

▌Auchterarder

★ TOP 50 ★

Restaurant Andrew Fairlie

Cooking score: 8
Modern European | £110
Gleneagles Hotel, Auchterarder, PH3 1NF
Tel no: 01764 694267
andrewfairlie.co.uk

£5 OFF 🛏

Established by one of hospitality's very good guys, Restaurant Andrew Fairlie now continues in the chef's honour after his death in early 2019. As one would expect at the heart of the Gleneagles resort, the dining room speaks the language of international luxe, all low-lit comfort, high ceilings and heavy drapes, with spotlit art instead of windows. In the gloaming, a talented service team works hard to give every diner a memorable experience, making once-in-a-lifetime customers feel like regulars. The chat is easy, but the knowledge of each French-Scottish dish is brilliantly sharp, all the better to match the kitchen's classical technique. Four à la carte courses might blend a foray into international modernity, as in notes of yuzu with white crab and a pan-fried langoustine tail, with the generous application of luxury (caviar in this case, and plenty of of it). Or there's the vanishingly rare treat of mountain hare chou farci, with a transparent Chinese cabbage leaf containing a fat pillow of gently gamey hare matched with silky carrot purée and sharper vinaigrette. Balance is the watchword in main dishes, too; perhaps monkfish capped with a layer of caramelised chicken mousse and surrounded by gently acidulated white asparagus and artichoke hearts. Dessert might feel a little overrefined, but citrus flavours are layered effectively in a pecan parfait with blood orange crémeux and a pitch perfect mandarin sorbet. No detail – from butter patted into golf balls to melting whisky truffles – is added in vain. A wine list dominated by the Old World is deftly handled, and although the sky's the upward limit, £60 is a decent baseline.

Chef/s: Stephen McLaughlin. **Closed:** Sun, 25 and 26 Dec, 3 weeks Jan. **Meals:** Set D £110. Tasting menu £155 (7 courses). **Details:** 50 seats. V menu. Vg menu. Wheelchairs. Parking. Music. Children over 5 yrs.

▌Balquhidder

Monachyle Mhor

Cooking score: 5
Modern British | £65
Balquhidder, FK19 8PQ
Tel no: 01877 384622
mhor.net

🛏

It may have started as an exercise in grow-your-own self-sufficiency, but this remote whitewashed hotel deep in The Trossachs is now the flagship for a family empire that also includes a bakery, roadside motel, chippy and catering service. Tom Lewis has been the driving force since 1983, and he is king of his own backyard when it comes to seasonal produce, overseeing the smallholding and livestock pastures as well as tapping into the Scottish regional network. Meanwhile, the kitchen applies global grace notes to all those top-notch ingredients, adding just enough refinement to satisfy those who have travelled hundreds of miles to eat here – from an inspired opening salvo of home-reared Tamworth pork belly with chicory and barley to Monachyle's own blackface lamb paired with Jerusalem artichoke, wild garlic and kimchi. Roe deer from the Balquhidder hills is appropriately dressed with bramble vinaigrette, while fish could be Scrabster pollock with rainbow chard and lightly curried smoked haddock broth. Innovation also extends to Scottish-themed desserts such as crowdie cheesecake with honeycomb, oat praline and caramel ice cream. The wine list mixes superior by-the-glass selections with big-name global classics and 'oddballs' from obscure growers.

Chef/s: Marysia Paszkowska and Graham Kerr.
Meals: set L £24 (2 courses) to £30. Set D £65.
Tasting menu £85 (7 courses). Sun L £35. **Details:** 40
seats. 20 seats outside. Bar. Wheelchairs. Parking.
Music.

LOCAL GEM

Mhor 84

Modern British | £30
Balquhidder, FK19 8NY
Tel no: 01877 384646
mhor.net

For sheer oomph, this laid-back offshoot of
Monachyle Mhor (see entry) knocks spots off
catering at most all-day cafés. With an honest,
simple approach to food (built around fierce
seasonality and produce from the Lewis
family's farm and bakery), it's no wonder
there's glowing support from locals and
tourists. Breakfast is a top deal, at lunch the
emphasis shifts to sandwiches, burgers and
steaks, and for dinner there could be shoulder
of lamb with wild garlic potato gratin and
salsa verde. There are cakes all day, and a well-
stocked bar and interesting wine list.

■ Blairgowrie

Kinloch House

Cooking score: 4
Modern British | £55
Dunkeld Road, Blairgowrie, PH10 6SG
Tel no: 01250 884237
kinlochhouse.com

Boasting all the essentials of a Scottish country
house hotel, plus an antique Tibetan moon
bear for good measure, the atmosphere at
Kinloch House is 'serene and genteel'. A series
of spotless panelled lounges lead to an airy
dining room ornamented by china cabinets
and chandeliers, where service is friendly but
bounded by tradition. Given these luxuries, a
lesser kitchen may coast a little; not at
Kinloch, which, reports one diner, 'does
everything well'. A starter of gently spiced

langoustine and hake is matched with a
superlatively light aubergine purée, heady
with garlic and cumin, while breast of guinea
fowl is served with a wild mushroom 'sausage'
with subtle truffled notes. To finish, there
might be citrus sorbets, a cinnamon and
almond cake, or a generous slice of salted
caramel parfait with warm caramel cake and a
crisp wafer of honeycomb. Wine is predictably
French, from £28, and willingly decanted.
Chef/s: Steve MacCallum. **Closed:** 15 to 29 Dec.
Meals: set L £28. Set D £45 (2 courses) to £55. Sun L
£30. **Details:** 30 seats. Wheelchairs. Parking.
Children over 6 yrs at D.

Little's

Cooking score: 2
Seafood | £35
Riverside Road, Blairgowrie, PH10 7GA
Tel no: 01250 875358
littlesrestaurant.com

'The ambience of Willie Little's newish place
is lovely,' notes a fan of this 'fantastic' bijou fish
restaurant, now happily ensconced within a
gorgeous-looking converted church across the
river Ericht. Simple, honest seafood cookery is
Little's forte, from a 'cluster of fat, juicy
mussels' with bacon, garlic and creamy white
wine sauce to cod fillet with smoked salmon
risotto or lemon sole fillet exotically paired
with banana, mango chutney and straw chips.
Also look out for the daily roster of
blackboard specials, which deliver 'huge
pieces of delicious well-cooked fish' ranging
from smoked haddock with a poached duck
egg and mash to herb-crusted halibut with
rösti and vegetables. There are steaks in various
guises, too, and even a few pizzas on offer for
those who want something completely
different. After that, pick an ultra-traditional
dessert such as rice pudding with stewed
apples or the decadent Baileys chocolate
cheesecake with orange sorbet. Wines
from £20.95.
Chef/s: Willie Little. **Closed:** Mon. **Meals:** main
courses £15 to £28. Set L and D £24 (2 courses). Sun
L £18. **Details:** 80 seats. 16 seats outside. Bar.
Wheelchairs. Parking. Music.

Cupar
Ostlers Close
Cooking score: 4
Modern British | £50
25 Bonnygate, Cupar, KY15 4BU
Tel no: 01334 655574
ostlersclose.co.uk

A treasured fixture of the Scottish regional scene for nigh on four decades, Jimmy and Amanda Graham's neighbourly restaurant occupies what was once the scullery of a temperance hotel. These days, an air of cheery hospitality wafts through the bijou dining room with its country pine furniture, freshly picked flowers and rich colour schemes. Menus are neatly handwritten each day, and Jimmy's painstaking cooking is all about extracting the maximum flavour from top-drawer ingredients – some of which are grown in his weather-protected polytunnel. To start, there might be wild mushroom tarte tatin (Jimmy is a keen forager) or roast pheasant breast on a herb potato scone with pardina lentils and sweet chorizo sauce, while mains could range from a bounteous assortment of local seafood with boulangère potatoes and langoustine bisque sauce to various cuts of meat and game with classic stock reductions. Finish in Caledonian style with some toasted oat meringues. Reasonably priced hand-picked wines start at £22.
Chef/s: Jimmy Graham. **Closed:** Mon, Tue, Sun. **Meals:** main courses £25 to £30. **Details:** 26 seats. V menu. Children over 6 yrs.

Grandtully
Ballintaggart Farm
Cooking score: 4
Modern British | £45
Grandtully, PH9 0PX
Tel no: 01887 447000
ballintaggart.com
£5 OFF 🛏

'Like a second honeymoon'; 'food for the soul'; 'utter dedication and pure passion': clearly there's a lot of love for Chris and Rachel Rowley's farmhouse B&B in deepest Perthshire. Chris stages mini masterclasses as a warm-up for dinner, which finds guests seated around a big mahogany table in the lovely cookbook-lined dining room. Seasonal Scottish produce is at the heart of things and it provides the inspiration for some truly innovative cooking: artisan sharing boards supply the opening salvo, while the garden might yield purple sprouting broccoli with beetroot, dill, confit garlic and crème fraîche. After that, expect anything from hot-smoked scallop with Brussels sprouts, hazelnuts, lemon aïoli and dulse to juniper and caraway-cured Gartmorn duck with pickled kohlrabi, Pedro Ximénez and mizuna – plus desserts such as blood orange and thyme financier with almond cream. Out front, Rachel's attention to detail makes for a 'truly fulfilling experience', further enhanced by some cannily chosen wines. Note: the Rowleys have taken charge of Ballintaggart's reinvigorated Grandtully Hotel (see entry).
Chef/s: Chris Rowley. **Closed:** 23 Dec to 7 Jan. **Meals:** set L £18 (2 courses) to £25. Set D £45. Tasting menu £65 (6 courses). Sun L £25. **Details:** 45 seats. 12 seats outside. Bar. Parking. Music. No children at D.

★ NEW ENTRY ★

The Grandtully Hotel
Cooking score: 4
Modern British | £32
Grandtully, PH9 0PL
Tel no: 01887 447000
ballintaggart.com
🛏

From the team behind nearby Ballintaggart Farm (see entry) comes another 'great example of what country dining can be like'. This 'absolutely beautiful hotel' has been renovated with a strictly modern aesthetic. Like its location by the rushing Tay, it's gorgeous, but Scottish enough not to show off about it. Eat in the saloon, with its teal bar and graphic detailing, or in the shuttered, candlelit dining room. The menu, big on local produce, features snacks (a single pork croquette with piquant smoked ketchup), then small and large plates and a welcome *plat du jour* for a tenner. Salt and pepper squid, fresh, firm and almost creamy, with a pungently hot-sour sauce, is a huge hit. There's classic technique on show, too in a langoustine bisque served with Scrabster hake, the suggested bowl of purple sprouting with chilli and shallots the perfect match. Pudding might be lemon and thyme meringue pie, the filling refreshingly chilled, pastry super-thin and meringue suitably perky. Drinks, rather than just wine, are a serious endeavour; make time to finish a carafe of something interestingly European in the book-lined whisky lounge.

Chef/s: Chris Rowley. **Closed:** Mon (Oct to Apr). **Meals:** small plates £5 to £8. Large plates £10 to £24. **Details:** 30 seats. 30 seats outside. Bar. Wheelchairs. Parking. Music.

Killiecrankie
Killiecrankie Hotel
Cooking score: 1
Modern British | £45
Killiecrankie, PH16 5LG
Tel no: 01796 473220
killiecrankiehotel.co.uk

£5 OFF

Occupying a really special spot, with gorgeous gardens and the Pass of Killiecrankie beyond, this well-appointed hotel is a nailed-on favourite for lunch with a view in the conservatory, or a fancier dinner in the small, elegant dining room. A bowl of butternut, coconut and chilli soup, or roe-on scallops with beetroot and horseradish might make lunch. A daily changing dinner menu could feature guinea fowl with apple and walnut mousse, with steamed orange and raspberry pudding to follow. Chocolates are homemade, wines are matched and the owner presides over friendly service.

Chef/s: Mark Easton. **Closed:** 3 Jan to 20 Mar. **Meals:** set D £45 (4 courses). **Details:** 35 seats. V menu. Bar. Wheelchairs. Parking. Music.

Muthill
Barley Bree
Cooking score: 3
Anglo-French | £45
6 Willoughby Street, Muthill, PH5 2AB
Tel no: 01764 681451
barleybree.com

£5 OFF

Hugely welcoming in brisk (or indeed any) conditions, this former coaching inn is worth a diversion from nearby Crieff. When the wood stove's crackling, all feels right with the world. Fabrice and Alison Bouteloup have earned a solid local reputation for French cooking with international leanings, and it's the simple dishes that really shine. Oak-smoked salmon might come with crystal-clear lemon gel, sharp as you like, and the deep savoury crunch of toasted kombu. Local venison finds its way into a Scotch pie with mustardy cabbage slaw, or there's pheasant breast with Stornoway black pudding, black truffle emulsion and green tomato chutney. Apple tarte tatin is rich with glossy caramel, the pastry flaky and light, and such a hit it makes appearances at lunch (a steal) as well as dinner. There's plenty of drinking under £30 in a neat list that allows for drivers' measures.

Chef/s: Fabrice Bouteloup. **Closed:** Mon, Tue, 24 to 26 Dec. **Meals:** main courses £12 to £26. Set L £18 (2 courses) to £22. **Details:** 48 seats. 12 seats outside. V menu. Bar. Parking.

Newport-on-Tay
The Newport
Cooking score: 5
Modern British | £50
1 High Street, Newport-on-Tay, DD6 8AB
Tel no: 01382 541449
thenewportrestaurant.co.uk

Could Dundee's best restaurant be in Fife? Just across the Tay Bridge, with expansive views over the estuary and the hills beyond, the Newport is an ex-pub with a thriving bar. Diners head upstairs to one of two sparse yet

chic rooms where chef Jamie Scott cuts a distinctly northern dash. In a procession of well-judged dishes, humble potatoes and onions have equal billing with asparagus and spanking-fresh fish. Rich local dairy is a highlight, whether in cultured butter served with ale and treacle bread, whipped cream through which a Jersey Royal should be dragged with abandon, or smoked goat's cream paired with asparagus and sweet pickled shallots. The main event might be indecently sticky mutton breast with slices of loin, tarragon emulsion and a king oyster mushroom. Puddings such as a take on tiramisu, with a coffee jelly shrouded in chocolate and served with buttermilk sorbet and whipped crowdie, are calibrated to bring the fun without compromising the spare elegance of the tasting menu. Wine is a wide-ranging selection, full of interest, from £26.
Chef/s: Jamie Scott and Anastasios Neofitos.
Closed: Mon, 24 to 26 Dec, 1 to 8 Jan. **Meals:** main courses £21 to £29. Tasting menu £55 (6 courses). Sun L £35. **Details:** 60 seats. 12 seats outside. V menu. Vg menu. Bar. Wheelchairs. Parking. Music.

■ North Queensferry
The Wee Restaurant
Cooking score: 3
Modern British | £37
17 Main Street, North Queensferry, KY11 1JG
Tel no: 01383 616263
theweerestaurant.co.uk

Not as 'wee' as the name suggests, Craig and Vikki Wood's restaurant is nevertheless a cosy and convivial retreat – hidden away in a stone-clad building beneath the Forth Bridge. In the kitchen, the emphasis is on constructing accomplished brasserie-style dishes from seasonal Scottish ingredients in their prime – in summer, crab with herb mayonnaise, say, chilled gazpacho or sakura cress and walnut toast; come winter, smoked pork and mustard rillettes with piccalilli. Main courses always feature chargrilled Scottish beef (from the Black Isle) as well as more fashionably eclectic plates such as roast cod fillet in pancetta, or confit duck leg and spiced chorizo salad with

crispy artichokes and fried duck egg. For afters, there are cheeses from Iain Mellis, alongside classic European desserts such as île flottante with crème anglaise or cherry and almond clafoutis. A well-spread international wine list offers dependable drinking from £21. There's an offshoot in Edinburgh's New Town (see entry).
Chef/s: Sam Dorey. **Closed:** Mon, Sun, 24 to 26 Dec, 1 and 2 Jan. **Meals:** set L £16 (2 courses) to £21. Set D £29 (2 courses) to £37. **Details:** 40 seats. Music.

■ Peat Inn
★ TOP 50 ★
The Peat Inn
Cooking score: 8
Modern British | £65
Main Street, Peat Inn, KY15 5LH
Tel no: 01334 840206
thepeatinn.co.uk
£5 OFF

'So good they named the village after it' might have been the marketing slogan for the original hostelry, here since the mid-1700s. Against such historical pedigree, the Smeddles' careful 13-year stewardship has earned them a wholly deserved reputation for elegant hospitality and thoughtful, imaginative cuisine that places The Peat Inn at the very heart of the Scottish culinary firmament. From the welcoming lounge through the three interconnected dining rooms, contemporary styling in beige and blue is punctuated with traditional accents of wood, stone and leather, resulting in a modern, calming atmosphere that nonetheless feels firmly rooted in Scotland. This ethos carries through to the food – confidently grounded in classical French technique – with Geoffrey Smeddle and his head chef Nick Briggs adding a contemporary alchemy to assertively seasonal local ingredients. A classic tartare is enhanced with smoked Cairngorm venison, confit yolk in a crisp potato crust, earthy pickled horse mushrooms and sweet parsnip chips. Following on might be a gently

roasted breast of Goosnargh duck, traditionally accompanied by Puy lentils, shallot tarte tatin and zesty bigarade sauce, lifted further with pink grapefruit and wild sea leeks. Desserts are visual delights and a wonderfully friable millefeuille of lemon posset and raspberries with lemongrass, chilli and ginger sorbet is equally impactful on the palate. A classy wine list offers the deep-pocketed enthusiast a surfeit of choice, particularly in Burgundy, while still giving entry-level value.
Chef/s: Geoffrey Smeddle and Nick Briggs. **Closed:** Mon, Sun, 23 to 29 Dec, 1 to 9 Jan. **Meals:** main courses £26 to £35. Set L £25. Set D £58. Tasting menu £78 (6 courses). **Details:** 50 seats. V menu. Vg menu. Bar. Wheelchairs. Parking. Music.

▌Perth

Deans
Cooking score: 3
Modern British | £40
77-79 Kinnoull Street, Perth, PH3 1LU
Tel no: 01738 643377
letseatperth.co.uk

The perennial indie every city needs, this family-run restaurant is well supported even by those who mean to branch out – dining room chatter includes such praise as, 'I always mean to try somewhere different, but this is so good'. The individual streak is there in the lipstick-red upholstery and Scots brasserie vibes, alongside a menu that aims to please all-comers. This is especially so at a (lively) lunch, when tempura-crisp fish and chips fairly fly off the pass, but house favourites also include oozy twice-baked soufflés, perhaps as a special with Arbroath smokie and smoked salmon, gratinated under a rich cheese sauce. Mains might be Orkney beef fillet with robust accompaniments of whisky sauce, mushrooms and a hefty potato and black pudding crush. Delicacy appears at pudding stage, where a slice of crème brûlée tart is plated beautifully with crushed lemon shortbread and raspberries galore. The wine list needs a polish, but prices start at 'why not?'.

Chef/s: Jamie Deans. **Closed:** Mon, Tue, 1 week Nov, 1 Jan, 2 weeks Jan. **Meals:** main courses £16 to £29. Set L £15 (2 courses) to £20. Set D £19 (2 courses) to £24. Sun L £25. **Details:** 70 seats. Bar. Wheelchairs. Music.

The North Port
Cooking score: 3
Modern British | £32
8 North Port, Perth, PH1 5LU
Tel no: 01738 580867
thenorthport.co.uk
£5
OFF

Handily placed behind Perth's Horsecross Theatre & Concert Hall, this family-run bistro inhabits a sturdy stone-clad 18th-century building that has been sympathetically restored in traditional style. Step into the dining room and you can almost feel the antiquity, with dark panelled walls and ceilings, boarded floors and bare tables (all glossily varnished) adding to the cosseting atmosphere. However, the kitchen lives firmly in the present, sourcing its seasonal Scottish ingredients with care and deploying them for a repertoire of impressive modern dishes ranging from North Sea hake with cauliflower, spinach and west coast langoustine to rump and rib of Black Isle lamb with parsnip, red cabbage and gravy laced with Windswept Weizen wheat beer. Elsewhere, Perthshire pigeon gets a boozy Dalrannoch stout dressing, Scrabster plaice is partnered by seaweed mayo, and inspired desserts promise the likes of Knockraich crowdie cheese mousse with almonds and raisin purée. Thirty wines offer sound drinking from £17.95.
Chef/s: Andrew Moss. **Closed:** Mon, Sun, 24 Dec to 7 Jan. **Meals:** main courses £15 to £25. Set L £15 (2 courses) to £18. Early D £18 (2 courses) to £21. **Details:** 35 seats. V menu. Vg menu. Music.

▌St Andrews
The Seafood Ristorante

Cooking score: 3

Seafood | £52

The Scores, Bruce Embankment, St Andrews, KY16 9AB

Tel no: 01334 479475

theseafoodristorante.com

£5 OFF 🍷

Quite a sight on the famous West Sands, this dramatic glass pavilion was originally called the Seafood Restaurant before a new team arrived in 2017 and rebranded it as a Ristorante. The kitchen still takes its cue from supplies of fresh Scottish fish, but the resulting flavours now have a decidedly Mediterranean bias – from a soup of red mullet with East Neuk crab tortellini or Scrabster monkfish with Orkney scallop, truffle gnocchi and sweetcorn to a showpiece main course of whole sea bream baked in salt with ratte potatoes, fennel, green beans and anchovy salad. Other ideas are more mainstream (wild halibut with Cumbrae oyster, cauliflower and black truffle), while meat dishes might include Scottish blackface lamb with asparagus, morels and Bonnet goat's cheese. There are cicchetti to start, plus some very Italian dolci to finish. As you'd expect, the wine list features a strong contingent of Super Tuscans and the like, but it also touts a fine selection of serious vintages from growers in France, Spain, South Africa and beyond. There's an impressive selection by the glass or carafe, with bottles starting at £24.

Chef/s: David Aspin. **Closed:** 24 to 26 Dec, 1 Jan, 6 to 16 Jan. **Meals:** main courses £26 to £34. Set L £25 (2 courses) to £30. Sun L (winter only) £30 (2 courses) to £35. **Details:** 65 seats. 25 seats outside. V menu. Vg menu. Bar. Wheelchairs. Parking. Music.

▌St Monans
Craig Millar at 16 West End

Cooking score: 3

Modern British | £45

16 West End, St Monans, KY10 2BX

Tel no: 01333 730327

16westend.com

Forged from a 400-year-old fisherman's cottage overlooking the harbour, Craig Millar's restaurant is famous for two things – its stupendous views and its sharply focused contemporary cooking. In the evening, there are two menus (Land and Sea), although, given the location, the freshest fish is generally the bigger draw. If you're taking that route, be sure to order the signature 'sea-reared' trout (cooked at 44 degrees) with miso caramel and oyster sauce, and follow, perhaps, with halibut, cavolo nero, mushrooms, caramelised cauliflower purée and a hand-dived scallop. If meat is your preference, consider duck liver parfait dressed with orange, cardamom and vanilla reduction ahead of slow-cooked pig's cheek partnered by a langoustine, pickled kohlrabi and parsley root purée. There are vegetarian options too, while dessert might be brown butter and chocolate ganache with apricot sorbet. Lunch is a hotchpotch of dishes from both camps, and the wide-ranging wine list includes an egalitarian mix of whites and reds with bottles from £26.

Chef/s: Craig Millar. **Closed:** Mon, Tue, 1 week Oct, 2 weeks Jan. **Meals:** set L £22 (2 courses) to £34. Set D £45 to £65 (5 courses). **Details:** 42 seats. 22 seats outside. Bar. Wheelchairs. Parking. Music. Children over 5 yrs at L, over 12 yrs at D.

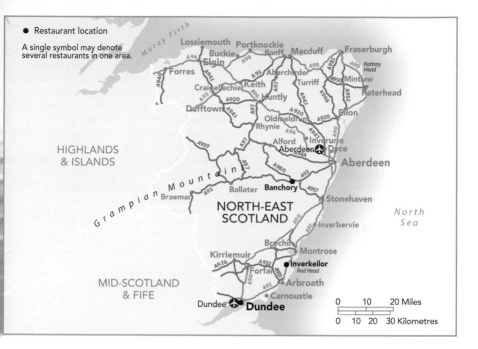

- Restaurant location

A single symbol may denote several restaurants in one area.

HIGHLANDS & ISLANDS

Grampian Mountains

NORTH-EAST SCOTLAND

North Sea

MID-SCOTLAND & FIFE

Banchory

LOCAL GEM
The Cowshed
British | £30
Raemoir Road, Banchory, AB31 5QB
Tel no: 01330 820813
cowshedrestaurantbanchory.co.uk

£30

Now less a shed, more a clutch of comfortable spaces overseen by a statuary of Highland cattle, Graham and Joy Buchan's restaurant aims at simplicity and welcome. They do both well. In these parts there's a lot to be said for the cosy embrace of a gratin of Peterhead smoked haddock or a spiced-up Scotch lamb shepherd's pie, followed by a white chocolate panna cotta with butter shortbread. Fish and chips are a house speciality, although the lovely views are more green than sea. The short wine list opens at £20 (£3.75 a glass).

Banff

READERS RECOMMEND
The Old Kirk Cafe & Bistro
Church Street, Fordyce, Banff, AB45 2SL
Tel no: 01261 843410
'We came across this bistro quite by chance. It appears to be an out of the way gem of a restaurant and is well worth recommending. A snack lunch of crab and langoustine risotto tasted absolutely delicious.'

Dundee
Castlehill
Cooking score: 3
Modern British | £38
22-26 Exchange Street, Dundee, DD1 3DL
Tel no: 01382 220008
castlehillrestaurant.co.uk

There's been a change of guard in the kitchen at Castlehill, but as befits its location on one of Dundee's many historic streets, the dining room is still comfortably Scottish. Think red leather, Burns quotes on the walls and backlit beauty shots of magnificent deer. Satisfying takes on classic combinations pervade the à la carte, with enough flourishes to keep things interesting. To start, there might be a slow-cooked pig's cheek with paper-thin shards of bacon, black garlic purée and white onion cream, followed by Scrabster hake with generous amounts of cockle butter and the kind of creamy leeks too luxurious to count as a vegetable. Pudding isn't a dead cert – on our visit, a citrus panna cotta with a lively fromage frais sorbet was overset – but Scottish cheeses with quince and chicory make a good diversion. Service is prompt and amiable, and wines start from £21 for organic Murcian red or white.

Chef/s: Adam Newth and Lewis Donegan. **Closed:** Mon, Sun. **Meals:** set L and early D £18 (2 courses) to £22. Set D £29 (2 courses) to £38. **Details:** 40 seats. Wheelchairs.

▌ Inverkeilor
Gordon's
Cooking score: 5
Modern British | £65
Main Street, Inverkeilor, DD11 5RN
Tel no: 01241 830364
gordonsrestaurant.co.uk

An end-of-terrace property on the main road through a peaceful Angus village near Lunan Bay, this restaurant with rooms has been the Watson family's labour of love since the mid-1980s. It's gradually acquired a rather smart boutique feel and there's praise for the 'friendly and unhurried atmosphere'. The format is five courses, with a pair of alternatives at all but second stage, when a rich velouté of spiced parsnip with Arbroath smokie and crab dumplings might intervene. 'All the dishes showed Garry Watson's skill and flair in the kitchen,' a reader reports. 'The attention to detail is marked and the balance of flavours and eye-provoking plating are truly amazing.' The signature venison tartare with pickled shimeji, hazelnut aïoli, apple and confit egg

yolk makes a powerful overture, while mains might offer a choice of halibut in a ragoût of sea kale with chorizo and fennel cream, or breast and confit leg of Goosnargh duck with baby turnips in a rich honey jus. The finishing tape is reached with a luxurious Valrhona crémeux and brownie with crystallised sesame and tahini ice cream. Standard glasses from £6 lead the charge on a well-annotated wine list arranged by style.

Chef/s: Garry Watson. **Closed:** Mon, Jan. **Meals:** set D £65 (5 courses). **Details:** 24 seats. Bar. Wheelchairs. Parking. Music. Children over 12 yrs.

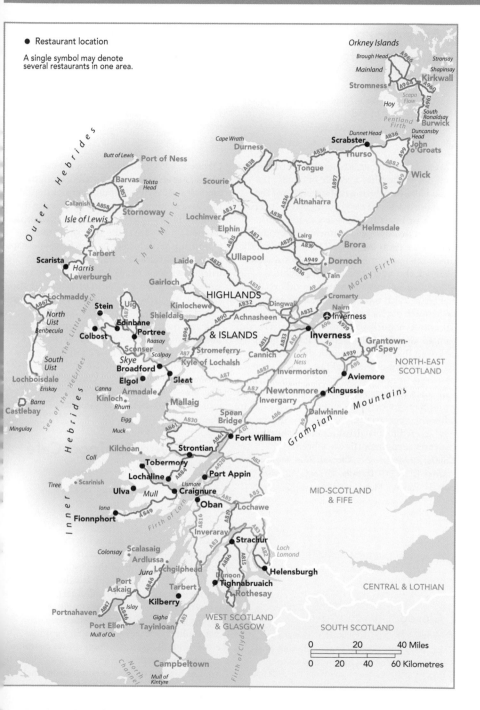

● Restaurant location

A single symbol may denote
several restaurants in one area.

Orkney Islands

Brough Head · A966 · *Stronsay*
Mainland · *Shapinsay*
Stromness · A964 · **Kirkwall** · A960
Hoy · *Scapa Flow* · *South Ronaldsay* · **Burwick**
Pentland Firth

Cape Wrath · **Durness** · Dunnet Head · **Scrabster** · Duncansby Head · John o'Groats
Butt of Lewis · **Port of Ness** · **Thurso** · A836 · A99 · **Wick**
Barvas · Tolsta Head · **Tongue** · A882
Callanish · A858 · **Stornoway** · *Scourie* · A897 · A9
Isle of Lewis · *The Minch* · **Altnaharra**
Scarista · **Tarbert** · *Lochinver* · A837 · A838 · **Helmsdale**
Harris · **Elphin** · A835 · Lairg · **Brora**
Leverburgh · *Laide* · **Ullapool** · A837 · A839 · **Dornoch**
Gairloch · A835 · A949 · *Tain*
Lochmaddy · **HIGHLANDS** · *Dingwall* · **Cromarty** · *Moray Firth*
Stein · *Uig* · Kinlochewe · A832 · **Nairn** · **Inverness**
North Uist · **Edinbane** · *Shieldaig* · **Achnasheen** · A96 · A939
Benbecula · **Portree** · A896 · **& ISLANDS** · A832 · **Inverness** · **Grantown-on-Spey**
Colbost · *Raasay* · A833 · *Cannich* · A9 · A939 · **NORTH-EAST SCOTLAND**
Sconser · *Scalpay* · **Stromferry** · *Loch Ness* · A95
South Uist · *Skye* · **Kyle of Lochalsh** · **Invermoriston** · **Aviemore**
Lochboisdale · **Broadford** · A87 · A887 · **Kingussie**
Eriskay · *Canna* · **Elgol** · **Sleat** · **Newtonmore** · A87
Barra · *Rhum* · *Armadale* · **Invergarry** · *Grampian Mountains*
Castlebay · **Kinloch** · **Mallaig** · *Dalwhinnie*
Mingulay · *Eigg* · *Spean Bridge* · A830
Muck · A861 · **Fort William**
Coll · **Strontian** · A82
Kilchoan · A861
Tiree · *Scarinish* · **Tobermory** · A884 · **Port Appin**
Lochaline · *Lismore* · A85
Ulva · *Mull* · **Craignure** · A85
Iona · A849 · **Oban** · *Lochawe*
Fionnphort · *Firth of Lorn* · **Inveraray** · **MID-SCOTLAND & FIFE**
Colonsay · **Scalasaig** · A819
Ardlussa · *Loch Lomond*
Jura · **Lochgilphead** · **Strachur**
Helensburgh
Port Askaig · **Tarbert** · **Dunoon** · A82 · **CENTRAL & LOTHIAN**
Kilberry · **Tighnabruaich** · *Rothesay*
Portnahaven · *Islay* · *Gigha*
Port Ellen · **Tayinloan** · **WEST SCOTLAND & GLASGOW** · **SOUTH SCOTLAND**
Mull of Oa
North Channel · **Campbeltown** · *Firth of Clyde*
Mull of Kintyre

0 · 20 · 40 Miles
0 · 20 · 40 · 60 Kilometres

▌Aviemore
Mountain Café
Cooking score: 1
International | £24
111 Grampian Road, Aviemore, PH22 1RH
Tel no: 01479 812473
mountaincafe-aviemore.co.uk
£30

This splendid pine-clad café above a mountain equipment shop has a couple of tables on a small balcony offering distant views of the Cairngorms. It's an easy-going place, cheering visitors by providing unfussy food from breakfast through to late lunch, and so popular you must expect to queue. The menu cleverly mixes the familiar – soup (perhaps smoked haddock chowder served with a savoury scone), sandwiches made with good bread and burgers – with more Mediterranean-inspired dishes such as chicken and chorizo salad or Tuscan-style pork and fennel meatballs in a tomato sauce with a jewelled salad of pearl couscous in a lime and honey dressing. Everyone praises the breakfast fry-up, there's a vast array of homemade cakes, ranging from brownies, flapjacks and three types of scone to millionaire's shortbread and red velvet cake. In addition, vegetarians, vegans and children are well catered for. To drink, there's a short wine list and Cairngorm Brewery beers.
Chef/s: Kirsten Gilmour. **Closed:** Wed. **Meals:** main courses £8 to £15. **Details:** 40 seats. 12 seats outside. Parking. Music.

Closed
Where closures are listed, these are for full days only. Please check opening times with the restaurant before travelling.

▌Fort William
Crannog
Cooking score: 1
Seafood | £34
Town Pier, Fort William, PH33 6DB
Tel no: 01397 705589
crannog.net
£5 OFF

Opened in 1989 on the back of a successful smokehouse business in Fort William, this pierside seafood restaurant overlooking Loch Linnhe is a long-serving local favourite. Fairy lights, chunky bistro interiors and maritime-themed artworks set the scene for a menu brimming with locally landed fish – perhaps salmon en croûte or Parmesan-crumbed plaice fillet on a mixed bean cassoulet. Smoked items and crustacea are always on offer and it's also worth consulting the rapidly depleted specials board for highlights from the day's catch. Vegetarians get a nominal look-in, as do meat dishes, while luscious puds might bring raspberry trifle or chocolate tart with gin sorbet. Wines start at £19.75.
Chef/s: Stewart MacLachlan. **Closed:** 1 week Nov to Dec. **Meals:** main courses £17 to £25. Set L £17 (2 courses) to £20. **Details:** 55 seats. Wheelchairs. Music.

Lochleven Seafood Café
Cooking score: 2
Seafood | £43
Onich, Fort William, PH33 6SA
Tel no: 01855 821048
lochlevenseafoodcafe.co.uk

Many venture up the lochside road towards Kinlochleven between March and October on the promise of some of the best and freshest seafood in Britain, and this bustling water-to-waiter operation certainly delivers. It may have grown over the years from simple shack to proper restaurant, but still retains a café atmosphere – bare tables, paper napkins, close-set tables. The kitchen shows restraint and delicacy, whether in surf or razor clams by weight, or plump langoustines from the loch outside, and nothing upstages the fresh seafood. For a pair of visitors not partial to raw oysters, 'the cooked ones here were a revelation – just lightly steamed with a little butter'. The signature hot roasted shellfish platter for two is a mountainous masterpiece and blackboard specials might take in turbot with wild mushroom orzo. Well-conceived vegetarian and meat alternatives suit those hijacked by pescatarian pals and Earl Grey panna cotta with lemon crumb is a refreshing finish. A largely Iberian wine list is full of affordable, seafood-friendly choices.

Chef/s: Katie MacFarlane Slack. **Closed:** 31 Oct to 15 Mar. **Meals:** main courses £8 to £43. **Details:** 50 seats. 16 seats outside. Wheelchairs. Parking.

Helensburgh
Sugar Boat
Cooking score: 2
Modern Scottish | £28
30 Colquhoun Square, Helensburgh,
G84 8AQ
Tel no: 01436 647522
sugarboat.co.uk

£5 £30
OFF

Restaurateur Will Smith's egalitarian eatery is 'very accessible', a multi-pronged operation that's part café, part bistro and wine shop, where you can have breakfast, soup and a sandwich, coffee and cake or something 'a tad more posh'. It may be modern in style, with fantastic city influences' reflecting Will's time as co-owner of London's Wild Honey, but the kitchen sticks to the classics. The lunch and dinner menus are fairly priced and rely on top-drawer produce, running from country terrines, grilled sardines with shallot dressing, and black pudding with bacon and fried egg to a pie of the day and burgers. Wider influences can be seen in main courses of cod with potato rösti, shrimps and baby gem salad, or whole roast lemon and garlic spatchcock chicken. Clafoutis with salted caramel ice cream is one way to finish; a selection of farmhouse and artisan cheeses from acclaimed

cheesemonger George Mewes is another. A thoughtfully assembled choice of wines opens at £20.

Chef/s: Scott Smith. **Closed:** 1 Jan. **Meals:** main courses £11 to £18. Sun L £13. **Details:** 65 seats. Bar. Wheelchairs. Music.

Inverness
Chez Roux at Rocpool Reserve
Cooking score: 3
French | £40
14 Culduthel Road, Inverness, IV2 4AG
Tel no: 01463 240089
rocpool.com

The modest exterior, notwithstanding its pedimented portico entrance, belies an elegant boutique hotel, in which it comes as a pleasant surprise to find a northerly outpost of the Roux empire, this one testament to Albert Roux Snr's determination to offer classical French cooking at a manageable outlay. In a dining room whose slight air of all-white sterility is relieved by the kind of carpet pattern you won't quickly unsee, Lee Pattie provides a deft touch with a mixture of ancestral dishes, like the famous soufflé suissesse or truffled Jerusalem artichoke velouté with mushroom duxelles, and more obviously contemporary productions. Rarebit-crusted hake with white bean ragoût in mussel and leek sauce is a covetable main dish, competing with the likes of Speyside hogget with its sweetbread and an onion tarte fine in rosemary-fragrant jus, while dessert brings things to a conclusion with Maître Albert's reference-book lemon tart, its piquant filling matched by mango sorbet and blood orange, and offset by caramelised white chocolate. A global wine list opens with glasses from £9.50.

Chef/s: Lee Pattie. **Closed:** Mon, Tue (Nov, Jan, Feb). **Meals:** main courses £19 to £28. Set L £30 (2 courses) to £40. Set D £32 (2 courses) to £42. **Details:** 40 seats. Bar. Wheelchairs. Parking. Music.

Rocpool

Cooking score: 2
Modern European | £42
1 Ness Walk, Inverness, IV3 5NE
Tel no: 01463 717274
rocpoolrestaurant.com

Opposite the castle in the heart of Inverness, this family-run restaurant has become a landmark of a more modest and accessible kind; a constant for customers who hanker after Scottish produce with an international brasserie spin. Settle into a banquette and start with, say, spiced crab and sweetcorn soup with mussels, scallops and prawns, given some zip with coconut, chilli and coriander, or pappardelle with beef ragù. Main courses include rump of lamb with pearl barley and spicy salami served with roast tomatoes with chilli, olives and baby leeks or, at lunch, Shetland salmon with kedgeree. Dishes might be overloaded on occasion, but relative simplicity reigns at pudding time, when there's a lemon meringue pie still warm from the oven, and rhubarb sorbet with vanilla cream and fresh brioche. The wine list is characterfully annotated, making navigation fun. Choose from easy-drinking Italian house bottles (£19.95) through to Old and New World special reserves.
Chef/s: George Sleet. **Closed:** Sun, 24 to 26 Dec, 1 to 3 Jan. **Meals:** main courses £14 to £26. Set L £18 (2 courses). Early set D £21 (2 courses). **Details:** 55 seats. Wheelchairs. Music.

Isle of Harris
Scarista House

Cooking score: 2
Modern British | £50
Scarista, Isle of Harris, HS3 3HX
Tel no: 01859 550238
scaristahouse.com

Blue waters, yellow sands and shifting skies form the backdrop to this charming Scottish manse – considered one of the most remote places to dine in the UK. Tim and Patricia Martin have been at the helm for over two decades, and have created a blissfully homely interior with the emphasis on comfort and relaxation. Scott McKenzie's cooking makes the most of local and home-grown produce: from porcini risotto with Argyll smoked ham and grilled quail to veal and pork terrine with pickled garden vegetables and Cumberland jelly. Or you might fancy langoustine ravioli with langoustine butter sauce, ahead of local scallops teamed with vanilla vinaigrette, tomato confit, cauliflower purée, new potatoes and wilted spinach. To finish, look to the comforts of tarte tatin, or bread and butter pudding with demerara rum sauce. The interesting wine list favours France, with plenty by the glass.
Chef/s: Scott McKenzie. **Closed:** 18 Oct to 6 Apr. **Meals:** set D £50. **Details:** 20 seats. Bar. Parking. Children over 8 yrs.

Isle of Mull
Café Fish

Cooking score: 3
Seafood | £35
The Pier, Main Street, Tobermory, Isle of Mull, PA75 6NU
Tel no: 01688 301253
thecafefish.com

£5 OFF

When the owners of this seafood restaurant declare that 'the only things frozen are our fishermen', they really mean it. Their own boat (*The Highlander*) works out of nearby Tobermory harbour and the rest of the catch is wholly dependent on the seasons and the weather: there's no corner-cutting here. Sustainability is the watchword and freshness is the key as the kitchen delivers a succession of clear-flavoured dishes ranging from creel-caught Mull langoustines doused in garlicky herb butter to miso-glazed scallops with a crunchy Asian salad and miso and ginger vinaigrette. You can get simply grilled items too, along with Croig oysters, cracked crab claws, fish stew and seafood platters (hot or cold), while ribeye steaks and spicy chicken shawarma satisfy those with more carnivorous tendencies. Sandwiches and salads are on hand

for quick lunchtime fill-ups, and there's always something enticingly sweet to finish – perhaps a chocolate and red berry sundae or warm Belgian waffles. Fish-friendly wines from £18.50.
Chef/s: Liz McGougan. **Closed:** Nov to Feb. **Meals:** main courses £13 to £38. **Details:** 32 seats. 60 seats outside. Music.

Ninth Wave

Cooking score: 5
Modern British | £48
Bruach Mhor, Fionnphort, Isle of Mull, PA66 6BL
Tel no: 01681 700757
ninthwaverestaurant.co.uk
£5 OFF

At the western extremity of the long southern arm of Mull, Ninth Wave is, in its own way, very much a neighbourhood restaurant, if you bear in mind the neighbourhood is one where your hosts catch their own fish and seafood in the waters of the Sound, and have it on the table for you that evening. Carla Lamont draws on influences from the Mediterranean to the Pacific Rim for energetic dishes that preserve the integrity of their main ingredients. Oysters in herb sabayon with Argyll smoked ham and a 'caviar' of green apple might preface an intermediate course of creamily dressed octopus salad with salsa verde made of own-grown perilla. The main attraction could be wrasse in caper gremolata with mussels and samphire, or gurnard given the Persian treatment with garlic yoghurt, golpar-seeded walnuts, rose petals and barberry couscous. All the fragrance and freshness of the preceding courses is sustained in a dessert of lemon custard cream in almond pastry with kaffir lime meringues, and lemon balm and borage jelly. Scottish cheeses are hard to pass up for those with the capacity. A concise list of well-described wines comes at manageable prices, from £24.
Chef/s: Carla Lamont. **Closed:** Mon, Tue, mid-Oct to end Apr. **Meals:** set D £48 to £68 (5 courses). **Details:** 18 seats. Wheelchairs. Parking. Children over 12 yrs.

Pennygate Lodge

Cooking score: 3
Modern British | £40
Craignure, Isle of Mull, PA65 6AY
Tel no: 01680 812333
pennygatelodge.scot
£5 OFF

Located just a pebble's throw from Craignure Pier, where monies were once collected from passengers disembarking the ferry (hence the name), this Georgian manse is now a smart, personally run B&B that serves lunch and dinner to guests and non-residents. There are entrancing views of Craignure Bay from the windows of the handsome dining room (all heritage colours and hand-picked antiques), and the food strikes a refined, modern note with Scottish ingredients taking centre stage. Dish descriptions may be fashionably terse ('partridge – caramelised cauliflower – pickled pear', for example), but the results have real substance and impact: loin and slow-cooked neck of Lochbuie hogget are paired with salsify, celeriac and onion, while a mixed seafood grill is served with herb crushed potatoes, beetroot and kale. To finish, Isle of Mull cheeses vie for attention alongside a couple of desserts such as chocolate brownie with white chocolate sorbet. A dozen wines start at £19.
Chef/s: Jordan Clark. **Closed:** Mon, Tue, Nov to Mar. **Meals:** main courses £18 to £30. Set L £20 (2 courses) to £25. Set D £30 (2 courses) to £35. Tasting menu £40 (5 courses) to £60. Sun L £25. **Details:** 26 seats. 10 seats outside. Parking. Music.

■ Isle of Skye
Coruisk House

Cooking score: 2
Modern European | £47
26 Elgol, Isle of Skye, IV49 9BL
Tel no: 01471 866330
coruiskhouse.com

Legend has it that Bonnie Prince Charlie holed up in a now-famous cave by the sea at Elgol, but this most remote of Skye hideaways also boasts a much comfier retreat in the shape of this converted croft, run with style and grace by ex-London lawyers Clare Winskill and Iain Roden (she oversees front of house, he cooks). Occupying an extension at the front of the building, the 12-cover dining room provides a suitably intimate setting for Iain's fixed-price dinner menus – a showcase for Scottish seafood, meat and game in various imaginative guises. Fish might mean 'double-dived' Sconser scallop with wild mushrooms and apple-mint beurre blanc, while carnivorous options could include Orbost 'Iron Age' pork four ways with caramelised apples and almond sauce. Vegetarians aren't neglected, nor are sweet-toothed diners with a penchant for, say, chocolate bavarois and sea-salted caramel ice cream. The 'regular' wine list is bolstered by special finds from the owners' seasonal travels to Europe.
Chef/s: Iain Roden. **Closed:** 1 Nov to 29 Feb. **Meals:** set D £39 (2 courses) to £47. **Details:** 12 seats. V menu. Bar. Wheelchairs. Parking.

Creelers of Skye

Cooking score: 1
French | £31
Lower Harrapool, Broadford, Isle of Skye, IV49 9AE
Tel no: 01471 822281
skye-seafood-restaurant.co.uk

£5
OFF

Fish cookery with a French accent is the main attraction at this roadside shack overlooking the waters of Broadford Bay, although there's a tendency to slather all that fresh Scottish seafood in rich, cream-heavy sauces (sautéed Skye scallops with a vermouth reduction, fillet of red mullet with a sauce of carrageen seaweed, for example). Simpler items such as hot-smoked salmon with saffron and dill aïoli work well, bouillabaisse gets a starring role, and wee buckets of skin-on chips are excellent. The menu also touts a few international crowd-pleasers for fish-averse visitors (chicken milanese, vegetable tikka masala etc), while puddings are traditional standbys such as tarte au citron. Wines from £19.50.
Chef/s: David Wilson. **Closed:** Sun, 1 Nov to 1 Mar. **Meals:** main courses £18 to £22. **Details:** 30 seats. 8 seats outside. Wheelchairs. Parking. Music.

Dulse & Brose

Cooking score: 3
Modern British | £35
9-11 Bosville Terrace, Portree, Isle of Skye, IV51 9DG
Tel no: 01478 612846
bosvillehotel.co.uk

In a town of culinary mixed fortunes, it is worth knowing about the 'good solid eating experience' to be had at this agreeable restaurant comfortably located in the Bosville Hotel. The kitchen sources quality local produce, and seasonality makes a big impact on the menu, which might see Atlantic cod paired with new season's potatoes and white wine sauce, or mussels with samphire. A selection of Scottish seafood in a rich tomato and fennel stew makes a satisfying starter, while cured trout with smoked trout rillettes is a lighter alternative. There are pedigree meats, too: slow-cooked lamb shoulder with toasted shallots, kale and pearl barley jus, for example, or a crossover dish of Sconser scallops served with pork belly, celeriac and apple rémoulade and BBQ sauce. A selection of Scottish cheeses is an alternative to desserts such as baked cheesecake with stem ginger ice cream and honeycomb. To drink, there are local beers from the island's craft brewery and the wine list is commendably good value, opening at £22.

Chef/s: Darryl Macintosh. **Meals:** main courses £18 to £23. **Details:** 48 seats. Bar. Music.

Kinloch Lodge

Cooking score: 4
Modern British | £80
Sleat, Isle of Skye, IV43 8QY
Tel no: 01471 833214
kinloch-lodge.co.uk

The setting on the shores of Loch na Dal is ravishing, wild and natural, while within all is civilised formality and comfort – log fires, family portraits and elegant furnishings. Isabella Macdonald was brought up here, and the takeover from her food writer mother, and her father, the 34th chief of the Macdonald clan, has been seamless. It helps that chef Marcello Tully, who has been here since 2007, continues to deliver such skill and refinement, his dishes built around the abundant regional larder, perhaps seared west coast scallops teamed with 'Marcello's miso' or Wester Ross salmon balanced by fragrant lime and coconut. Black Isle lamb is a favourite, too, or go for Fort Augustus venison with red wine and balsamic jus. Apple and salted caramel make for a harmonious finish. The wine list is a mighty tome with considered descriptions; prices start gently but rise sharply.

Chef/s: Marcello Tully. **Meals:** set L £40 (2 courses) to £45. Set D £80 (5 courses) to £95. Tasting menu £95. Sun L £40 (2 courses) to £45. **Details:** 45 seats. Bar. Wheelchairs. Parking. Music.

Loch Bay

Cooking score: 4
Seafood | £44
1-2 Macleod's Terrace, Stein, Isle of Skye, IV55 8GA
Tel no: 01470 592235
lochbay-restaurant.co.uk

The sight of this converted 18th-century fisherman's cottage overlooking the Waternish peninsula may pander to your inner romantic, but there's nothing dewy-eyed about Michael Smith's exact and finely tuned contemporary cooking. Top billing goes to his Skye Fruits de Mer tasting menu, a fitting showcase for the island's stunning seafood. The seasonal haul might yield 'twice-dived' Sconser scallops (served with citrus fruits, hazelnut and sorrel), a duo of turbot and oyster with velvet crab sauce or a pot au feu loaded with lobster and prawns, while bookends are provided by a 'soup and sandwich' starter and desserts such as Smith's signature clootie dumpling soufflé. Eat from the lunch menu or the evening carte and you might find brill and crab with fennel and local cress, short rib and onglet of beef with carrots and parsley relish or squash and crowdie cheese cannelloni. To drink, a modest list of mostly French wines vies with Scottish beers and numerous wee drams.

Chef/s: Michael Smith. **Closed:** Mon, Jan, Feb, first week Aug. **Meals:** set L £30 (2 courses) to £34. Set D £44. Tasting menu £70 (5 courses). Sun L £44. **Details:** 22 seats. V menu. Parking. Music.

Scorrybreac

Cooking score: 3
British | £48
7 Bosville Terrace, Portree, Isle of Skye, IV51 9DG
Tel no: 01478 612069
scorrybreac.com

As teeny as it is delightful, Scorrybreac ticks boxes that other restaurants can only dream of – idyllic island location, fabulous local larder, Portree Harbour views and a fresh sensibility that makes for contemporary dishes with a strong sense of heritage and place. All this

means it's in demand, so book early and be prepared for your table to be turned. The rewards are handsome: vibrant dishes such as a starter of monkfish with beetroot, orange and crème fraîche, or slow-cooked beef, perhaps short rib or oxtail, with truffle, toast and a pool of something luxurious. Seasons have a huge impact here, and are reflected in dishes such as lamb rump with sweetbreads, alexanders, Jerusalem artichoke and wild garlic. Pudding might be rhubarb, meringue and almond, and wine starts at £22, with pairings available. Keep an eye out for experiments with tasting menus and seasonal opening hours.
Chef/s: Calum Munro. **Closed:** Mon, Tue, Nov, Dec. **Meals:** set D £48. **Details:** 20 seats.

The Three Chimneys

Cooking score: 7
Modern British | £69
Colbost, Isle of Skye, IV55 8ZT
Tel no: 01470 511258
threechimneys.co.uk

In April 2019, The Three Chimneys changed hands, when it was acquired by Gordon Campbell Gray, who is building a portfolio of Scottish hotels and restaurants. It was a smooth transition, with previous co-owner Shirley Spear advising during the handover, and continuity importantly maintained in the kitchen with the retention of Scott Davies. The place itself hasn't budged an inch from its glorious isolation on the western shore of Loch Dunvegan, the calm waters hauntingly glimpsed at eventide through little cottage windows in the dining room. Highland produce bolsters the menus, with scorched langoustines from the loch outside turning up alongside pickled beetroot, oyster mousse and puffed wild rice, while fire-roasted local red deer is partnered with a richly savoury faggot, creamed potato and salsify. Japanese seasonings are a favourite trope, so that even the Land and Sea menu that offers a premium tour of Skye brings in roasted monkfish in dashi and seaweed, as well as Orbost rose beef

with miso and mushroom in a sauce of Tarasgeir craft beer. Innovative desserts are inspiring – brie cheesecake and poached rhubarb, or a meringue pie of sea buckthorn with rosemary and olive oil. A page of Softs on the drinks list makes for much creative spirit-matching at aperitif time, and wines are an intelligent selection of hot-button producers from many of the emergent regions. Small glasses from £8.
Chef/s: Scott Davies. **Closed:** 16 Dec to 16 Jan. **Meals:** set L £30 (2 courses) to £42. Set D £57 (2 courses) to £69. Tasting menu L £65 (6 courses) and D £98 (10 courses). **Details:** 40 seats. V menu. Bar. Wheelchairs. Parking. Music. Children over 8 yrs to D.

LOCAL GEM

Edinbane Lodge

Modern British | £65
Old Dunvegan Road, Edinbane, Isle of Skye, IV51 9PW
Tel no: 01470 582217
edinbanelodge.com

There's a true sense of dedication about this ancient former hunting lodge, now a carefully refurbished restaurant with rooms. It offers just the sort of hospitality that both travellers and locals appreciate, delivering attentive service and a 'fantastic dining experience' that puts provenance at the very heart of the menu. This means that on the evening taster menu you can expect Scrabster-landed wild halibut with lemon verbena, cucumber and smoked herring roe, as well as dark chocolate crémeux with Angus strawberries and Auchentullich Farm milk sorbet.

∎ Isle of Ulva

LOCAL GEM
The Boathouse

Seafood | £15
Dervaig, Isle of Ulva
Tel no: 01688 500241
theboathouseulva.co.uk

£30

'Just delightful,' enthused one summer visitor who made the five-minute ferry crossing from Mull to this sparsely inhabited island and its simple bistro. The kitchen is run by cousins Emma McKie and Rebecca Munro, who bake excellent bread and cakes – once again we recommend the chocolate fudge cake. Soup and generously filled rolls (including Ulva venison steak) are served alongside local oysters, langoustines (just cooked and still warm from the pan) and crab (potted, with bread and salad). Blackboards list the daily catch, including a much-praised seafood platter. There's wine and bottled beer, too.

∎ Kilberry
The Kilberry Inn

Cooking score: 3
Modern British | £35
Kilberry Road, Kilberry, PA29 6YD
Tel no: 01880 770223
kilberryinn.com

£5
OFF

At the end of a long single-track road overlooking the islands of Gigha, Islay and Jura, this erstwhile croft has kept its vintage looks, with exposed stone, aged beams, log fires, and a red tin roof reinforcing the building's history. These days, it fulfils an equally vital purpose as a lovingly upgraded restaurant with rooms. Clare Johnson's cooking matches the setting, with incredibly fresh seafood a strong point, from a crab and radicchio gratin or Loch Fyne queenie scallops toasted with garlic and white port, to a majestic main course of Isle of Gigha halibut with griddled fennel and shellfish sauce. Meatier offerings also make bold statements,

as when a winter serving of roasted pheasant is teamed with root vegetable mash and red wine shallots, or roast rump of lamb is marinated in honey and coriander, and served with cucumber, mint and yoghurt, toasted almonds and bulgur wheat. Sticky toffee pudding with tonka bean ice cream is a fittingly sweet finale. The thoughtful wine list (from £22) demonstrates personal insight from co-owner David Wilson.

Chef/s: Clare Johnson. **Closed:** Mon, 1 Jan to mid-Mar. **Meals:** main courses £14 to £25. **Details:** 20 seats. 10 seats outside. Bar. Parking. Music.

∎ Kingussie
The Cross

Cooking score: 4
Modern British | £55
Tweed Mill Brae, Ardbroilach Road, Kingussie, PH21 1LB
Tel no: 01540 661166
thecross.co.uk

If you're not immediately seduced by the four acres of riverside gardens, the red squirrels leaping from tree to tree or the sturdy exterior of this converted Victorian tweed mill, then a visit to its dining room should seal the deal. Original beams and rough stone walls point up the pastoral theme, although the artwork is contemporary and the cooking keeps its focus firmly planted in the present. Fillets of John Dory are seared and partnered by roast langoustine, confit tomato, onion purée and shellfish foam, while stone bass is luxuriously matched with sweet potato fondant, cep dumpling and truffle jus. Confident technique and intricate flourishes are hallmarks of David Skiggs' cooking, and he also pays his dues when it comes to local produce – as in loin of Donald Gilmour's lamb with cannelloni of shoulder, artichokes, broccoli, glazed onions and jus gras, or raspberry soufflé with lemon sorbet and glazed raspberries. The wine list is a treasure, with lots of natural and organic labels, a broad global reach and a decent selection of half bottles at accommodating prices; also check out the fascinating whisky flights.

Chef/s: David Skiggs. **Closed:** Mon, Sun, Dec, Jan (exc Hogmanay). **Meals:** set L £30. Set D £55. Tasting menu £65 (6 courses). **Details:** 26 seats. 12 seats outside. V menu. Vg menu. Bar. Wheelchairs. Parking.

Lochaline
The Whitehouse

Cooking score: 5
Modern British | £45
Lochaline, PA80 5XT
Tel no: 01967 421777
thewhitehouserestaurant.co.uk

There are no airs and graces at this roughcast white block of a building overlooking the Sound of Mull. Inside, it could be a library tea room with its foursquare wooden furniture and grotto walls, but then Mike Burgoyne's food starts arriving and you could be somewhere distinctly uptown. It's a family affair, everybody pitching in to look after the hens, gather in the greens and forage for seasonal gleanings. Greet the spring with treacle-brined Ardshealach smoked salmon, pickled radish relish and dill apple. Fish dishes are generally astonishing, as witness the haddock double act of Hebridean kippered finnie (cold smoked haddock) and Tobermory smoked haddie in saffron-scented seawater crema with blood orange and shoreline botanicals, but meats are of unarguable quality too, including blackface lamb roasted in goose fat, with buckwheat groats, confit beetroot and fermented plums. If you haven't gone entirely Highland native by this stage, Scottish cheeses with Benbecula oatcakes should seal it, or consider a dessert of rose and vanilla sheep's yoghurt with rhubarb, Turkish delight and pistachio granola. Wines start at £6.50 a glass.

Chef/s: Mike Burgoyne. **Closed:** Mon, Sun, Nov to Easter. **Meals:** set L and D £30 (2 courses) to £45. Tasting menu £75 (6 courses). **Details:** 26 seats. 8 seats outside. V menu. Vg menu. Wheelchairs.

Oban
Ee-Usk

Cooking score: 1
Seafood | £29
North Pier, Oban, PA34 5QD
Tel no: 01631 565666
eeusk.com

£30

Oban and seafood go hand in hand, and this glass-fronted waterside restaurant is as close to the action as possible. Watch the fishing boats go about their business while eating the result – Loch Creran oysters to start, say, and then a selection of halibut, sea bass and a fish of the day, all oven-baked in parsley sauce and served with vegetables and potato croquettes. Other treats include butterflied langoustines with garlic butter, Thai fishcakes and seared king scallops with potato gratin, vegetables and mornay sauce. The substantial wine list features plenty of favourites, plus some lesser-known finds, and don't miss the superb malt whisky list to finish.

Chef/s: David Kariuki. **Closed:** 24 and 25 Dec, 1 Jan, 3 weeks Jan. **Meals:** main courses £11 to £24. Set L and D £16. **Details:** 100 seats. 36 seats outside. Wheelchairs. Music. Children over 12 yrs at D

Port Appin
Airds Hotel

Cooking score: 4
Scottish | £58
Port Appin, PA38 4DF
Tel no: 01631 730236
airds-hotel.com

This small luxury country house, with an eye to an international clientele via its Relais & Châteaux membership, may offer a dining room and style of service that feels a little old-fashioned, but the experience is greatly enhanced by the stunning seascapes outside, positive vibes from fellow guests and efficient service. Chris Stanley's kitchen offers classical treatments of quality ingredients, perhaps a

deeply flavoured yet crystal-clear chicken consommé enriched with a pasta pillow of intense oxtail and a punchy sorrel sauce, ahead of a local lamb cannon paired with braised neck, ingots of crispy polenta and wild garlic from the local hedgerows. Desserts are well crafted and surprisingly light: coconut panna cotta exudes tropical energy with its passion fruit coulis, lemongrass ice cream and pleasing palate punctuations of black pepper and fresh chilli sugar shards. The wine list is extensive but perhaps leans a little towards safety for those of more modern vinous disposition.
Chef/s: Chris Stanley. **Meals:** set D £58 (5 courses). Tasting menu £81 (7 courses). Sun L £25. **Details:** 34 seats. 20 seats outside. V menu. Bar. Parking. Children over 8 yrs.

▇ Scrabster
The Captain's Galley
Cooking score: 4
Seafood | £56
The Harbour, Scrabster, KW14 7UJ
Tel no: 01847 894999
captainsgalley.co.uk

Jim and Mary Cowie's restaurant, fashioned out of a barrel-vaulted former ice house and salmon bothy, is a guiding light – one of the country's most compelling addresses for world-class seafood. The couple proudly fly the flag for seasonality and sustainability, with local boats providing the daily haul and the kitchen doing the rest. Ideas may come from all over, but there's always respect for the ingredients, whether in a lobster bisque with a spicy hit from kimchi in a full-flavoured first course, or in pan-roasted scallop teamed with braised pig's cheek and crispy croquette. Among main courses, chargrilled gurnard with a seafood-loaded paella, and roast cod with roast peppers and beans are spot-on. A meat option might include wild sika venison, and hot chocolate pudding is a crowd-pleasing dessert. Head to the adjacent Scrabster Seafood Bar for fish and chips and the like, and check out the set lunch menu. The succinct wine list opens at £17.95.

Chef/s: Jim Cowie. **Closed:** Mon, 25, 26 and 31 Dec, 1 and 2 Jan. **Meals:** set D £56. **Details:** 30 seats. 25 seats outside. Wheelchairs. Parking. Music.

▇ Strachur
★ TOP 50 ★
★ CHEF OF THE YEAR ★
Inver
Cooking score: 7
Modern Scottish | £35
Strathlachlan, Strachur, PA27 8BU
Tel no: 01369 860537
inverrestaurant.co.uk

Inver is rooted as solidly in the ethos of quality cooking and hospitality as it is in the spectacular landscape on its doorstep. One visitor to the whitewashed cottage with its elegantly simple decor observed 'the whole atmosphere is superb from the beautiful setting to the pitch perfect service – however, the food remains the star of the show, pulsating with pops of flavour and pristine natural ingredients'. An envy-inducing culinary library greets guests – wearing a patina of personal love and use that affirms the technical foundations, creativity and care within each and every dish. Although perfectly attuned to the Scottish context and natural larder on her doorstep, chef Pam Brunton is adept at weaving in wider geographic or historic influences with a high level of ambition and individuality. A sublime starter of creamy heritage potato ice cream with caviar and pepper dulse might reflect recent travels in Japan, while a dessert of whipkull, burnt honey and Seville orange re-animates a long-forgotten syllabub-like festive custard from the Shetlands. Supplies come from within 20 miles: Shellfield Farm lamb cooked with the lightest of touches grazes on nearby salt marshes while langoustines from the loch lapping the garden need only the addictive homemade butter and sourdough to make them stars. Vegetarians are equally indulged. Front of house, Rob creates bespoke mixed drinks, sources an intriguing selection of predominantly natural wines and curates an artful playlist on the gramophone. Stylish eco-bothies provide welcome overnight accommodation in this remote spot. You might never leave.

Chef/s: Pam Brunton. **Closed:** Mon, Tue, 16 to 28 Dec, 2 Jan to 19 Mar. **Meals:** main courses £13 to £24. Tasting menu D £55 (4 courses). **Details:** 40 seats. 20 seats outside. Bar. Wheelchairs. Parking. Music.

■ Strontian
The Kilcamb Restaurant & Brasserie

Cooking score: 3
Modern British | £50
Strontian, PH36 4HY
Tel no: 01967 402257
kilcamblodge.co.uk

Sandwiched between the shores of Loch Sunart and a backdrop of soaring trees, there's no doubt you're in the Highlands. In this majestic setting, chef Gary Phillips presides over a kitchen that makes the most of the region's larder. Whether you opt for the informal Driftwood Brasserie or the dressed-up restaurant, expect cooking with a strong sense of place. In the latter, locally foraged mushrooms might find their way into a risotto enriched with truffles, while hot-smoked Ardshealach salmon is served with a salad of chicory, Kintyre Blue, pear and grilled chorizo. Follow with braised feather blade of Highland beef with herb mash and crispy haggis cannelloni, or a taste of west coast seafood (including a salt cod soufflé, tempura langoustine and hand-dived scallop). Finish with pear and toffee almond crumble tart, or Scottish artisan cheeses. Afternoon tea is a real treat, especially if the weather is kind and you can head to the suntrap terrace. The wine list, arranged by style, opens at £25.

Chef/s: Gary Phillips. **Meals:** main courses £18 to £30. Set L £28 (2 courses) to £35. Set D £28 (2 courses) to £65. Tasting menu £78 (7 courses). Sun L £25. **Details:** 40 seats. 20 seats outside. Bar. Parking. Music.

■ Tighnabruaich
LOCAL GEM
Botanica at the Barn

British | £20
Millcroft, Millhouse, Tighnabruaich, PA21 2BW
Tel no: 01700 811186
botanicafood.co.uk

£30

Enjoying the good life on Argyll's isolated secret coast, the well-established Botanica in Tighnabruaich has moved up the road to become Botanica at the Barn. More space for organic produce, outdoor cooking and even goats, pigs and chickens, sees this family-friendly food spot offer everything from artisan coffee and cakes to hearty lunches and regular evening pop-ups. Locally reared and foraged ingredients might become nettle and leek tortilla with aged Manchego, sweet-cured pig's cheeks or rich seafood stew with mussels and langoustine. A perfect stop-off before the ferry to Kintyre. Unlicensed.

WALES

Mid-Wales, North-East Wales,
North-West Wales, South-East Wales,
South-West Wales

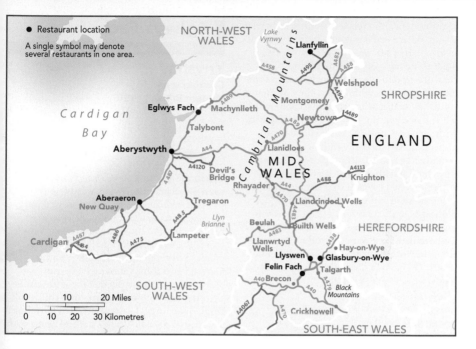

Restaurant location
A single symbol may denote several restaurants in one area.

Aberaeron
Harbourmaster
Cooking score: 2
Modern British | £35
Pen Cei, Aberaeron, SA46 0BT
Tel no: 01545 570755
harbour-master.com

Right on the harbour's edge, this long-established venue is surely one of Wales's prettiest dining spots, popular with locals and visitors alike. It combines a modern, lively bar with a more refined restaurant (in the original harbourmaster's house), where sea-blue walls and harbour views make the most of the waterside setting. Daytime food runs from appealing snacks such as potato bhajia or houmous and homemade bread through to starters of properly mustardy Welsh rarebit or plump salmon fishcakes with a tangy lemon mayonnaise. Follow this, perhaps, with fresh sea bass, thyme-roasted courgettes, tomato, prawn and a crunchy hazelnut butter or, in the evening, a more ambitious dish of rare breed pork belly with apricot and bacon lentils. For dessert, an impressively rich sticky toffee pudding will hit the spot, while the wine list has broad appeal.
Chef/s: Ludovic Dieumegard. **Closed:** 25 and 26 Dec. **Meals:** main courses £11 to £28. Set D £28 (2 courses) to £35. Sun L £19 (2 courses) to £25. **Details:** 100 seats. 15 seats outside. Bar. Wheelchairs.

Aberystwyth
Ultracomida
Cooking score: 2
Spanish | £20
31 Pier Street, Aberystwyth, SY23 2LN
Tel no: 01970 630686
ultracomida.co.uk
£30

A couple of recent visitors were delighted with a 'pilgrimage to this outpost of Spain', making a beeline through the 'excellent deli' to the restaurant at the rear and finding 'a good buzz of enjoyment'. It's a relaxed, slightly utilitarian set-up, where you'll potentially find yourself sharing large, bare wood tables with other diners. The tapas-style menu features charcuterie, delicate white anchovies and the likes of houmous with warm, juicy, aromatic lamb. Salt cod appears in a rich tomato sauce, while a smokey, slow-cooked bowl of lentils with serrano ham and chorizo dazzled on inspection. Wonderfully fluffy churros shouldn't be missed, although battered apple rings served with cream deserve attention. Alternatively, a barraquito – coffee with Licor 43, condensed and steamed milk – is a gloriously spicy dessert in a glass. Service is 'welcoming, helpful, easy yet swift' and there's a superb drinks offering, including 36 wines alongside lots of vermouth, gin and cocktails. **Chef/s:** Cheryl Price. **Closed:** 25 and 26 Dec, 1 Jan. **Meals:** tapas £4 to £11. **Details:** 32 seats. Vg menu. Wheelchairs. Music.

LOCAL GEM

Pysgoty
Seafood | £32
The Harbour, South Promenade, Aberystwyth, SY23 1JY
Tel no: 01970 624611
pysgoty.co.uk

'What a treat!' exclaimed one reader after a visit to this amiable harbourside eatery where fish and seafood take centre stage. Cardigan Bay is perfectly framed through the first-floor windows, and it looks even better from the outside terrace. The menu takes 'the freshest local produce' on a global tour, so you might go from tempura monkfish cheeks with citrus aïoli, or slow-braised octopus with chorizo and butter beans, to coconut fish curry, or sea bass with wild mushroom and laverbread risotto. Drink craft beers or wines from £16.

▮ Eglwys Fach
★ TOP 10 ★

Ynyshir
Cooking score: 9
Modern British | £150
Eglwys Fach, SY20 8TA
Tel no: 01654 781209
ynyshir.co.uk

£5 OFF ▮ ▭

When the opening shot is 'not French onion soup' – a clear, crunchy, seaweedy-sour broth of a palate cleanser – and a tiny wagyu burger, all crisp outer and soft inner, delivers a robustly umami hit, you know you are in the hands of an unconventional chef, one who creates a dining experience like no other. Gareth Ward thinks about flavour, not in a classic three-course way, but through a full-throttle series of punchy bites that you won't forget in a hurry. This is confirmed with the vivacity of pork belly char siu, and again with Aylesbury duck from Fishguard that plays on the sweet notes of a superior crispy Peking duck in just a few glorious mouthfuls. Everything on the 20-course tasting menu has a contribution to make, from superb sourdough bread, which arrives with miso-flavoured cultured butter and Welsh wagyu beef dripping, to the balanced acidity of the elder vinegar that cuts the richness of a just-seared scallop winningly paired with aged wagyu fat. Equally deft is the beautifully aged Welsh lamb, which arrives in two parts: a tiny rib, rich with crisply rendered fat, and then a nugget of meltingly tender loin, all minty, sweet and salty. Among desserts, sharp, intense rhubarb is offset by a rich egg custard, and a dish that has fast become a signature eclipses any tiramisu you've ever had. There's an unfussy mood in the understated dining room, which is dominated by the open kitchen, plus genuinely committed service, mainly from chefs. Masterly wine advice is on hand, too, whether you want help to guide you through the list, or pointers on matching a series of glasses.

Chef/s: Gareth Ward. **Closed:** Mon, Tue, Sun, 1 week Dec to Jan, 1 week Apr, 2 weeks Aug to Sept. **Meals:** tasting menu £150 (20 courses) to £180. **Details:** 22 seats. Bar. Wheelchairs. Parking. Music. Pre-payment required.

∎ Felin Fach
The Felin Fach Griffin
Cooking score: 3
Modern British | £35
Felin Fach, LD3 0UB
Tel no: 01874 620111
felinfachgriffin.co.uk
£5 OFF 🛏

One of a trio of revitalised British pubs owned by Charles and Edmund Inkin, this Welsh outpost remains on good form, turning out interesting and assured modern British dishes reflecting the kitchen garden and the surrounding countryside. The interior is a study in country style – bare floorboards, modern artwork, capacious sofas, a blazing fire and plenty of cosy nooks and side rooms, and service is prompt and efficient. Typical dishes include smoked duck with feta and pickled garden berries, and lamb belly with peas, courgette and fondant potato. Meat-free dishes are handled well, with a couple of appealing options at each course – maybe heritage tomatoes with smoked mascarpone and hazelnut, or farro risotto with sweet potato and truffle. There's a good range of ales but the international wine list also means business, offering meticulously sourced selections, many by the carafe or glass, plus local delights from Monmouth's Ancre Hill.
Chef/s: Ben Porritt. **Closed:** 25 Dec, 4 days Jan. **Meals:** main courses £18 to £24. Set L £19 (2 courses) to £24. Set D £24 (2 courses) to £29. Sun L £28. **Details:** 55 seats. 30 seats outside. Bar. Wheelchairs. Parking. Music.

Local Gem
These entries are brilliant neighbourhood venues, delivering good, freshly cooked food at great value for money.

∎ Glasbury-on-Wye
LOCAL GEM
The River Café
Anglo-European | £25
Glasbury Bridge, Glasbury-on-Wye, HR3 5NP
Tel no: 01497 847007
wyevalleycanoes.co.uk
🛏 £30

It may share its name with the legendary Hammersmith institution but this riverside café bar restaurant is housed within the more modest confines of the Wye Valley Canoe Centre. It's popular with walkers and tourists, as well as those hiring boats, the vibrant cooking a major draw. Open for breakfast and light lunches with coffee and cakes to fill the gaps, the menu moves up a gear at dinner with the likes of broccoli and Perl Las blue cheese soup, followed by pan-fried hake fillet, Welsh rarebit gratin, peperonata and gnocchi. Wines join Wye Valley ales, Ty Gwyn ciders and Chase spirits on the drinks list.

∎ Llanfyllin
Seeds
Cooking score: 1
Modern British | £30
5 Penybryn Cottages, High Street, Llanfyllin, SY22 5AP
Tel no: 01691 648604
£30

Celebrating 19 years in 2020, Mark and Felicity Seager's family-run village restaurant has local feeling on its side. Found in a delightful, simply furnished 15th-century cottage, it's run with old-fashioned charm, with classic modern British dishes the drill. Baked tomato and Stilton pastry with a rich

tomato sauce, then roast rack of Welsh lamb with a Dijon and herb crust, or cod with roasted Mediterranean vegetables may all appear on the good-value fixed-price evening carte (lunch brings lighter choices and sharing platters). Finish with a lemon posset with a mixed berry sauce. Wines from £16.95.
Chef/s: Mark Seager. **Closed:** Mon, Tue, Sun, 2 weeks Oct, 2 weeks Jan. Limited opening in winter (telephone in advance). **Meals:** main courses £13 to £22. Set D £27 (2 courses) to £30. **Details:** 20 seats. 6 seats outside.

■ Llyswen
Llangoed Hall
Cooking score: 5
Modern British | £50
Llyswen, LD3 0YP
Tel no: 01874 754525
llangoedhall.co.uk

£5 OFF 🛏

Visitors have written enthusiastically about this grand country house: from the extensive grounds and kitchen gardens to the elegance, comfort and quiet confidence of the interior, it's considered a classy rural package. The food, by Nick Brodie, meets with similar approval, the chef gathering seasonal ingredients from the garden, region and beyond for tersely worded menus of three, six and nine courses, all packed with appetising modern ideas. Dishes are impressive in their emphatic precision, from duck with fermented garlic and a sweet magnolia glaze to the mini brioche toastie with Black Bomber Cheddar that precedes a dessert of rhubarb with passion fruit, yoghurt and ginger. For diners, details lingering passionately in their memories include a dynamic suckling pig with choi sum (Chinese greens), cuttlefish and pineapple, and the excellent house sourdough served with smoked butter. This bold, carefully considered cooking is matched by a wine list with excellent by-the-glass selections and some fine drinking from reputable names.

Chef/s: Nick Brodie. **Meals:** set L £35. Set D £50. Tasting menu £60 (6 courses) to £90. Sun L £25. **Details:** 38 seats. V menu. Vg menu. Bar. Wheelchairs. Parking. Music.

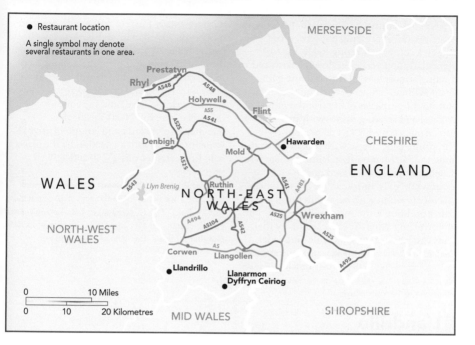

Restaurant location

A single symbol may denote several restaurants in one area.

■ Hawarden
The Glynne Arms

Cooking score: 1
International | £28
3 Glynne Way, The Highway, Hawarden, CH5 3NS
Tel no: 01244 569988
theglynnearms.co.uk
£5 OFF £30

This 200-year-old former coaching inn is owned by descendants of William Gladstone, the Victorian prime minister whose Sunday alcohol ban lasted in Welsh pubs for a century. There are no such restrictions now, with local ales and cocktails dispensed in the bar or served in the eclectically styled dining room, where mounted antlers oversee Victorian jelly moulds on the mantelpiece. The Gladstones also run the farm shop on the Hawarden Estate, which means a steady supply of produce grown on the doorstep. Welsh faggot with pot-roast vegetables might be followed by sea bass served with cockles, asparagus,

pommes Anna and wild garlic butter. Desserts are a run-through of 'all the classics', including a homemade sticky toffee pudding, and are served all day, every day.
Chef/s: Adam Stanley. **Meals:** main courses £12 to £26. Sun L £14 (1 course). **Details:** 70 seats. 36 seats outside. Bar. Wheelchairs. Parking. Music.

■ Llanarmon Dyffryn Ceiriog
The West Arms

Cooking score: 2
Modern British | £35
Llanarmon Dyffryn Ceiriog, LL20 7LD
Tel no: 01691 600665
thewestarms.com
🛏

Surrounded by steep hills and twisty country lanes, this 15th-century inn with rooms feels delightfully remote. Nicky and Mark Williamson took over in early 2018 and have overseen renovations over the past year;

exposed oak beams, inglenook fireplaces with cosy fires and a recurring pheasant motif suggest a country shooting lodge. Visitors particularly appreciate the 'lovely warm and relaxing atmosphere' of this 'absolute gem'. Grant Williams continues to head the kitchen, putting the emphasis on local and regional produce and creating dishes with 'imaginative flair', from a crumbly tart of creamy Shropshire Blue cheese with poached pear to a 'must try' Welsh mountain lamb, perhaps with dauphinois potatoes, glazed carrots and parsnip purée. To finish, a slate of local cheeses vies for attention with bara brith bread and butter pudding with buttermilk custard. The globetrotting wine list is backed up by the pub's vast array of gins, local ales and ciders.

Chef/s: Grant Williams. **Meals:** main courses £17 to £20. Tasting menu £75 (5 courses). **Details:** 70 seats. 65 seats outside. V menu. Vg menu. Bar. Wheelchairs. Parking. Music.

with no overly forceful statements, nowhere more typically than in sea bass with laverbread beurre blanc and Jersey Royals. Desserts run the classical rule over prune and almond tart, or poach a pear in red wine and match it with Stilton ice cream and candied walnuts (a sweet spin on a classic salad) and the cheeses themselves are top Neal's Yard Dairy merchandise. A classy and comprehensive wine list opens with a selection by the glass or half-litre carafe, from £7.50 and £19 respectively.

Chef/s: Bryan Webb. **Closed:** Mon, Tue, 1 week Nov, last 2 weeks Jan. **Meals:** set L £32 (2 courses) to £39. Set D £58 (2 courses) to £70. Tasting menu £85 (6 courses) to £95. Sun L £32 (2 courses) to £39. **Details:** 40 seats. Bar. Wheelchairs. Parking.

▮ Llandrillo
Tyddyn Llan Restaurant
Cooking score: 6
French | £70
Llandrillo, LL21 0ST
Tel no: 01490 440264
tyddynllan.co.uk

🍷 🛏

To a converted shooters' lodge in the rolling tranquillity of the Dee Valley is where Bryan and Susan Webb lit out when they left London a generation ago, and the roots they have put down here are deep and extensive. In an atmosphere of comforting refinement, with swagged curtains, oak furniture and windows all around a dining room in cornflower blue, the heart of the operation is thoroughbred Welsh produce. Tasting menu options of six or eight courses supplement a broadly based carte, which might open on Welsh black bresaola with rocket and Parmesan, or a grilled half lobster doused in a spicy butter of ginger, lime and coriander. Mains might look to local lamb, the rib and breast, with a light stew of artichokes, broad beans, peas and mint. Everything is defined by precision and clarity,

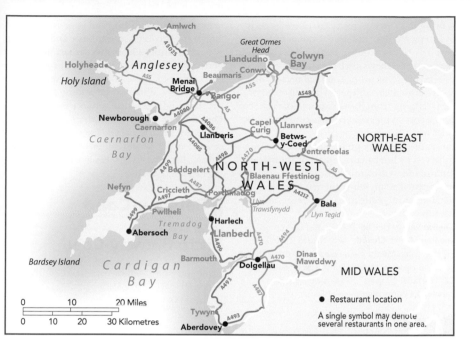

◼ Aberdovey
Seabreeze
Cooking score: 1
Modern European | £30
6 Bodfor Terrace, Aberdovey, LL35 0EA
Tel no: 01654 767449
seabreeze-aberdovey.co.uk

Wood floors, exposed brickwork and deep blue walls create an attractive, homely backdrop for some big-hearted cooking that visitors applaud for being great value. An easy-going menu could include generous bowls of plump Welsh mussels in a green Thai broth of ginger, garlic, lemongrass and coconut milk, followed by half a grilled Cardigan Bay lobster with chilli, ginger and garlic butter served with hand-cut chips. Confit pork belly appears with cauliflower purée, caramelised apple, fondant potato and red wine jus, while a crunchy iced-banana parfait with salted caramel, dark chocolate crumb and a crisp cinnamon tuile is a good way to round things off. Drinks-wise, there's a substantial international selection of wines at very reasonable prices.
Chef/s: Henry Severn. **Closed:** 25 and 26 Dec.
Meals: main courses £11 to £23. **Details:** 40 seats.
10 seats outside. Wheelchairs. Music.

◼ Abersoch
Porth Tocyn
Cooking score: 2
Modern British | £49
Bwlch Tocyn, Abersoch, LL53 7BU
Tel no: 01758 713303
porthtocynhotel.co.uk

'We have eaten here for over 30 years and it still delivers on every level,' notes a reader who has nothing but praise for the Fletcher-Brewers' hotel overlooking Cardigan Bay (a Guide stalwart for more than six decades). The current incumbents are fostering Porth Tocyn's reputation for warm, personable hospitality, with younger family members waiting in the wings ready to follow in their footsteps. Meals in the stone-walled restaurant have a distinctive 'dinner party' vibe, although the kitchen eschews clichés in favour of eclectic modern cuisine founded on seasonal Welsh ingredients. Expect a broad spread of ideas ranging from Pant-Ysgawn goat's cheese panna cotta with sweet pepper coulis to pork fillet with Parmentier potatoes, salt-baked pineapple and black pudding bonbons, followed by hot banana soufflé or rhubarb semifreddo with candied pistachios. Lunch is a more casual affair, while the wine list is notable for its gentle markups – especially at the top end.

Chef/s: Louise Fletcher-Brewer and Darren Shenton-Morris. **Closed:** early Nov to 2 weeks before Easter. **Meals:** main courses L £15 to £28. Set D £42 (2 courses) to £49. Sun L £22 (2 courses) to £27. **Details:** 50 seats. 50 seats outside. Bar. Parking. Children over 6 yrs at D.

■ Bala

Palé Hall

Cooking score: 5
Modern European | £60
Palé Estate, Llandderfel, Bala, LL23 7PS
Tel no: 01678 530285
palehall.co.uk

A prime slice of Victorian architectural pastiche on the edge of Snowdonia, Palé Hall stands resplendent amid woodland gardens that unfurl gently down to the river Dee. Inside, it has been done in grand country interiors style, with a pair of adjacent dining rooms to choose from, both enjoying lush views over the valley. Staff flit about with conscientious efficiency, and the cooking ploughs a productive furrow between classic fine dining and gentle Welsh modernism. Smoked haddock on a crumpet with a poached egg in tomatoey Choron sauce might be the lead-in to a whole roast poussin with chou farci and game chips with bread sauce. The tasting menus, of six or ten courses, bring on roast halibut with celeriac, truffle and glazed onion, and Norfolk quail with

beetroot, black pudding and Jerez sauce. A lemon study comprising mousse and preserved lemon sorbet hits the tart notes to perfection, or there may be coconut panna cotta with pineapple, mango and Nepalese timur berries. Wines are very fairly priced for the surroundings, with bottles from £28.

Chef/s: Gareth Stevenson. **Meals:** main courses £22 to £35. Set L £25 to £32. Tasting menu £70 (6 courses) to £90. **Details:** 50 seats. 10 seats outside. V menu. Bar. Wheelchairs. Parking. Music. No children after 6.30pm.

■ Betws-y-Coed

LOCAL GEM
Bistro Betws-y-Coed

British | £35
Holyhead Road, Betws-y-Coed, LL24 0AY
Tel no: 01690 710328
bistrobetws-y-coed.co.uk

£5 OFF

Thoroughly rooted amid the bustle of this mountain tourist village, Gerwyn Williams' down-to-earth bistro is warm and inviting whatever the season. The cooking is a fine compromise between local and regional ingredients with a style alert to the wider world. Dinner is the main event – lunch is served only at weekends – with good-value plates of chicken, Madeira and Welsh whisky paté with caramelised onion relish and port syrup, say, and slow-cooked beef cheek with potato gratin and red cabbage. Wines from £15.50.

■ Brynsiencyn

READERS RECOMMEND
Tide at Halen Môn

Ty Halen, Brynsiencyn, LL61 6TQ
Tel no: 01248 430871
halenmon.com
'Amazing outdoor café and restaurant with an unparalleled view and delicious, ingredient-led food. Ate Welsh rarebit, dressed crab and grilled veg flatbread with brilliant coffee and cinnamon buns.'

◼ Dolgellau
Mawddach
Cooking score: 2
Modern European | £33
Llanelltyd, Dolgellau, LL40 2TA
Tel no: 01341 421752
mawddach.com

The outlook over the mountains of the Cader Idris range and the Mawddach estuary is confirmation, if confirmation were needed, of the beauty of North Wales. The family farm within Snowdonia National Park is home to Ifan and Will Dunn's restaurant, the glorious landscape reflected in the materials used in the sleek, contemporary barn conversion, and in the ingredients that find their way on to Ifan's menus. There's a broader European influence, though, with local beef prepared carpaccio style with salsa verde and Parmesan, and whey risotto served with Swiss chard and cavolo nero. Welsh lamb appears as slow-cooked shoulder, say, with a stew of cannellini beans and aubergines. Among sweet courses, orange and almond cake with mascarpone cream encourages recollections of sunnier climes, while Welsh cheeses bring you right back to base. The wine list includes Welsh fizz from Monmouthshire's own Ancre Hill Vineyard.
Chef/s: Ifan Dunn. **Closed:** Mon, Tue, Wed, Nov, Jan. **Meals:** main courses £12 to £22. Sun L £25. **Details:** 40 seats. 40 seats outside. Bar. Wheelchairs. Parking. Children over 5 yrs.

◼ Harlech
Castle Cottage
Cooking score: 2
Modern British | £42
Y Llech, Harlech, LL46 2YL
Tel no: 01766 780479
castlecottageharlech.co.uk

Located in the shadow of Harlech Castle, a stone's throw from the sea, this low-beamed 16th-century cottage has been house and home to Glyn and Jacqueline Roberts since 1989 – making it one of the Guide's longest-serving restaurants. Castle Cottage is also something of a labour of love, a bistro with rooms promising warmth, congeniality and generous cooking with international overtones but a dedication to Welsh seasonal produce. Glyn's fixed-price menus always begin with home-baked bread and Welsh butter, before – say – cream of local gammon and pea soup or local game terrine with date and apple chutney. After that, Welsh lamb, local steaks and pheasant appear regularly alongside the odd seafood dish – perhaps grilled monkfish and king prawns with paprika, baby spinach, chorizo and a ragoût of white beans. Flavours are straight and true, right down to puds such as winter Eton mess or a trio of chocolate desserts. A serviceable 70-bin wine list starts at £18.
Chef/s: Glyn Roberts. **Closed:** Mon, Tue, Sun, 3 weeks Nov, Jan. **Meals:** set D £39 (2 courses) to £42. Tasting menu £45 (5 courses). **Details:** 30 seats. Bar. Music.

◼ Llanberis
LOCAL GEM
The Peak
Modern British | £30
86 High Street, Llanberis, LL55 4SU
Tel no: 01286 872777
peakrestaurant.co.uk

Snuggled away in the foothills of Snowdonia, this gem of a place attracts walkers, climbers and tourists with hearty outdoor appetites. Step forward Angela Dwyer, a chef who knows how to keep things simple but colourful, while putting big flavours on the plate. Her concise menu mixes local produce with lively global ideas – perhaps toasted goat's cheese salad or Thai fishcakes followed by poached hake with coconut dhal, or rump of Welsh lamb dressed with roasted shallots and garlic cream. Two dozen wines start at £15.95.

▌Menai Bridge
Freckled Angel

Cooking score: 3
Modern British | £25
49 High Street, Menai Bridge, LL59 5EF
Tel no: 01248 209952
freckled-angel-fine-catering.co.uk
£30

Menai Bridge has taken to small plate dining as though to the manner born, and Michael Jones's double-fronted high street venue feels just the right setting for it. These plates are on the generous side of small, be it noted, and laden with potent and compelling flavours, making them hard to resist. Reporters sing in unison of the twice-baked Perl Las blue cheese soufflé moated with balsamic grapes, while other notable successes have included roast and salt cod with pickled shallots, roast pork fillet with celeriac ragoût and burnt apple, and enticing accompaniments such as potato, creamed leeks and smoked bacon. It's comfort food with an inventive flourish, engagingly served by family staff who are good with recommendations. Leave room for lemon and thyme posset with peppered shortbread, or caramel lava cake with banoffee ice cream, to round things off in style. Barely more than a dozen wines, from £18.50, do their best to keep up.

Chef/s: Michael Jones. **Closed:** 1 week Oct, 25 to 31 Dec. **Meals:** small plates £6 to £7. **Details:** 26 seats. Music.

Anonymous

At *The Good Food Guide*, our inspectors dine anonymously and pay their bill in full. These impartial review meals, along with feedback from thousands of our readers, are what informs the content of the *GFG*. Only the best restaurants make the cut.

★ TOP 50 ★
Sosban & The Old Butcher's

Cooking score: 7
Modern British | £94
Trinity House, 1 High Street, Menai Bridge, LL59 5EE
Tel no: 01248 208131
sosbanandtheoldbutchers.com

'Is it a celebration tonight?' asked Bethan Stevens as she greeted the couple on the next table. 'Er, no, it's just a celebration that we finally have a table!' came the tongue-in-cheek reply. With limited opening times and just 12 seats, the Stevens' converted butcher's shop has always been booked up months in advance, and a recent refurbishment has even moved the original front entrance to an easy-to-miss 'secret' side door. Even so, such a modest room and small operation in an Anglesey town doesn't quite prepare you for the level of skill and creativity: there's no printed menu and no choice, the genial Bethan describing each dish in detail, with husband Stephen staying focused in the open kitchen. The seasonal, locally sourced dishes are finely tuned, ingredient driven and firmly in the vanguard of contemporary Welsh cooking, seen in the likes of an intensely flavoured mushroom soup, thickened with a fermented egg yolk and topped with crisp, locally foraged moss, or a deep-flavoured confit of lamb's tail (almost like mutton), teamed with a delicate, grassy lettuce purée, Anglesey new potatoes, sea kale, and yoghurt seasoned with shrimp. Elsewhere, cod cooked sous-vide turns up with rich Anglesey brown crabmeat, asparagus and crumbled chicken skin, while cured Highland wagyu beef sirloin (looking like Parma ham) is flanked by Isle of Wight tomatoes, wild garlic and subtly flavoured charcoal. A chocolate-coated lemon ice cream lolly is the finale to a trio of desserts – dusted with chopped Kalamata olives, the salty, briny flavour is a fascinating complement to the dark chocolate and sharpness of the lemon. A snappy global wine list opens at £23.

Chef/s: Stephen Owen Stevens. **Closed:** Mon to Wed, Sun, 25 Dec to end Jan. **Meals:** tasting menu D £94 (8 courses). Sat L £50. **Details:** 12 seats. Wheelchairs. Deposit required. Children over 12 yrs.

▮ Newborough
The Marram Grass
Cooking score: 4
Modern British | £60
White Lodge, Penlon, Newborough, LL61 6RS
Tel no: 01248 440077
themarramgrass.com

Sometimes great food can be found in the most incongruous of settings. Repurposing a run-down caff on their parents' campsite, enterprising Liverpudlian brothers Liam and Ellis Barrie have created a place of culinary pilgrimage – it goes without saying that booking is essential. The corrugated iron roof remains (the place is no looker) and the homely wood interior hardly shouts haute cuisine, but Ellis's 'inventive' approach to seasonal cooking results in some special food. What the brothers nurture in their kitchen garden, rear on the fields or what naturally thrives in their vicinity dictates the menu, perhaps delicate fish tartare with kohlrabi, cucumber, apple, horseradish–buttermilk and dill oil, followed by pork with torched cauliflower, cauliflower mornay purée, mashed potato and savoury raisins. Conclude with a 'memorable' Mon Las blue cheese, iced fruit and salted blackberry malt almond tart. There are wine flights for those looking to experience the full spectrum of Ellis's inquisitive, technically astute approach, while the brief list is helpfully arranged by style.
Chef/s: Ellis Barrie. **Closed:** Mon, Tue, Wed. **Meals:** set L and D £60. Tasting menu £50 (5 courses) to £75. **Details:** 40 seats. 10 seats outside. Parking. Music.

All the trimmings

Some of the country's best-known chefs are cutting down on food waste by getting creative with leftovers. Here are some restaurants with a conscience that have caught the eye of our inspectors

Scraps from the kitchen at Nottingham's **Restaurant Sat Bains** are 'cooked' in a composter to provide food for the on-site garden which fulfils 40% of the restaurant's produce needs. Day-old sourdough gets a delicious outing the following evening in the form of a tuile served with a stunning lovage velouté.

Roots, stems, flowers, leaves; at **L'Enclume** in Cumbria, there's a use for everything and chefs are encouraged to be creative with the whole plant, or the entire animal. For instance, the trim from the morels and the guinea hen in two separate dishes is combined to create a deeply flavourful ragout served in another of the 15 courses.

Plants are the focus of the menu at Yotam Ottolenghi's most recent opening, **Rovi** in Fitzrovia. Ingredients come from a biodynamic farm in Sussex and an organic co-operative in east London. Much of what isn't used goes into creating drinking vinegars for the cocktail menu or rich stocks.

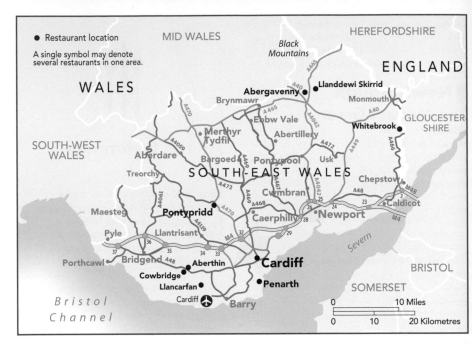

■ Abergavenny
1861
Cooking score: 4
Modern British | £40
Cross Ash, Abergavenny, NP7 8PB
Tel no: 01873 821297
18-61.co.uk

£5
OFF

A winding drive through lush countryside
brings you to this pretty roadside building,
named after the date of its construction. The
simple interior sees dark beams and stonework
offset by fresh white walls. It's a family affair:
Simon King is in the kitchen, wife Kate a
warm and welcoming front of house. Simon
favours refined classics built on locally sourced
ingredients. A gratin of leeks with confit
pheasant chimes nicely with the country
setting; seasonal game features prominently
among the mains, too – maybe as a trio of
roast partridge, venison cannelloni and
pheasant faggot. Elsewhere, there could be
hake with Champagne and chive cream or

fricassée of wild mushrooms in a puff pastry
case. Desserts add interest to the familiar:
acorn panna cotta with iced pumpkin parfait,
for example. Most bottles on the global wine
list are under £30 and there's plenty of choice
by the glass.
Chef/s: Simon King. **Closed:** Mon, Tue, first 2 weeks
Jan. **Meals:** main courses £22 to £26. Set L £25 (2
courses) to £30. Set D £40. Tasting menu £70 (7
courses). Sun L £30. **Details:** 35 seats. Bar. Parking.
Music.

★ NEW ENTRY ★

The Gaff
Cooking score: 2
Global | £50
No. 4 The Courtyard, Lion Street,
Abergavenny, NP7 5PE
Tel no: 01873 739310
thegaffrestaurant.co.uk

Meaning 'home' in Irish, this welcoming
restaurant occupies three previously derelict
and crumbling sheds in a quiet courtyard close

to the market in the town centre. A light and minimal space with high, beamed ceilings and an open kitchen at one end, it's a first venture for Danielle Phillips (front of house) and chef Dan Saunders, who both spent several years working for Shaun Hill at the famed Walnut Tree (see entry). Seasonal local ingredients drive the menu, which follows the trend for small plates, but many are generous enough to be main-course size. However, the cooking takes a global view, with Sri Lankan spiced potato, vada, sambal and pickles rubbing shoulders with middle white pork chilli, mushroom rice and salsa. Elsewhere, there's turbot with sweetcorn, brown shrimps and bacon, or duck (pink breast and dark, sticky braised leg) with smoked sausage and spring onion. A pud of buttery milk cake with raspberry sorbet and lemon curd brings this closer to home. Drink Welsh beers and wines from £25.

Chef/s: Daniel Saunders. **Closed:** Tue, Wed, 26 Dec to 1 Jan, 14 to 30 Jan. **Meals:** small plates £10 to £15. Set L £18 (2 courses) to £22. Tasting menu £50 (6 courses). Sun L £24 (2 courses) to £27. **Details:** 36 seats. 17 seats outside. Wheelchairs. Music.

The Hardwick
Cooking score: 3
Modern British | £35
Old Raglan Road, Abergavenny, NP7 9AA
Tel no: 01873 854220
thehardwick.co.uk

Is it really 15 years since Stephen Terry left a life cooking in some of London's top kitchens for the relative peace of rural Wales? Over time, the chef has transformed this former roadside pub into a smart, cosmopolitan restaurant with rooms. A short drive from Abergavenny and set against the spectacular backdrop of the Black Mountains, it delivers an appealing blend of relaxed rusticity and high-quality eating, although some prices may now be aimed more at visitors than locals. The cooking is bold and interesting, with carefully sourced raw ingredients turning up in dishes of global influence. A starter of deep-

fried pork belly and black pudding with pickled white cabbage, apple and mustard sauce is a typically gutsy opener. It might be followed by roast hake and braised octopus with a white bean, pea and chorizo fabada, saffron mayonnaise and tomato sauce. Finish with vanilla panna cotta and Sicilian blood orange in honey and Aperol. A well-spread international wine list starts at £19.

Chef/s: Stephen Terry. **Meals:** main courses £17 to £30. **Details:** 100 seats. 25 seats outside. V menu. Vg menu. Bar. Parking. Music.

■ Aberthin
Hare & Hounds
Cooking score: 3
Modern British | £30
Maendy Road, Aberthin, CF71 7LG
Tel no: 01446 774892
hareandhoundsaberthin.com
£30

'An absolutely brilliant place', enthused one visitor to this proper village pub with dried hops above the bar, an open fire, ales and photos of local teams. However, step into the dining room and the stark white walls and open kitchen give notice that something special is happening here. Chef Tom Watts-Jones follows a no-nonsense philosophy, his modern British dishes assembled with a zealous insistence on seasonality. In winter, the short evening carte might yield marinated lamb's heart with cavolo nero, celeriac and pickled walnut, or mussels with laverbread, cockles, purple sprouting broccoli and smoked butter. Mains could be something as big-flavoured and traditional as roast woodcock, or brill with Jerusalem artichoke, salsify, chestnuts and chicken butter, and then it's on to desserts such as buttermilk pudding with honeycomb and Bramley apple, soufflé (rhubarb or plum, say) or lemon sponge pudding. A well-annotated European wine list opens at £17.95.

Chef/s: Tom Watts-Jones. **Closed:** Mon, Tue. **Meals:** main courses £12 to £24. Set L £18 (2 courses) to £22. Tasting menu £55. **Details:** 50 seats. 25 seats outside. Bar. Wheelchairs. Parking. Music.

■ Cardiff
Asador 44

Cooking score: 2
Spanish | £35
14-15 Quay Street, Cardiff, CF10 1EA
Tel no: 029 2002 0039
asador44.co.uk

£5
OFF

Dry-ageing cabinets and a bespoke wood-fired grill are clear signals of the ethos of this good-looking offshoot of the Bar 44 group of tapas restaurants, which includes the Cowbridge original (see entry). Welsh and Spanish meats take centre stage, aged in-house and cooked over charcoal – local 40-day aged rump cap (aka picanha), say, or 60-day aged rubia Gallega chuletón (bone-in rib) from Galicia. Openers include the likes of rabbit and game terrine with burnt apple and pickled mushrooms, or mackerel with smokey ajo blanco. Check the blackboard for the whole wild fish, which also gets the flame-grilled treatment. To finish, Iberian cheeses compete with Spanish-inspired desserts such as a burnt Basque cheesecake with Tempranillo blueberries and crisp tejas de tolosa. The regional wine list stays true to the theme (Spanish, not Welsh), supported by some feisty cocktails and sherries.
Chef/s: Ian Wood. **Closed:** Sun, 25 and 26 Dec, 1 Jan. **Meals:** main courses £11 to £28. Set L £15 (2 courses) to £20. **Details:** 90 seats. Wheelchairs. Music.

Bully's

Cooking score: 2
Modern French | £40
5 Romilly Crescent, Cardiff, CF11 9NP
Tel no: 029 2022 1905
bullysrestaurant.co.uk

There's a feeling of Gallic neighbourhood bonhomie about Russell Bullimore's long-established bistro, and it chimes agreeably with the locals in this part of Cardiff. The kitchen looks to France for most of its culinary inspiration, albeit with more than a nod to native British ingredients, a theme that is picked up in the decor: French background music sets the tone in a colourful dining room crammed with antiques and curios, an idiosyncratic mix of Parisian parlour and English junk shop. Come here for grilled lemon sole with sauce véronique, followed by a Welsh dry-aged fillet steak with Madeira sauce, or free range Pembrokeshire duck breast with confit leg, potato terrine, braised chicory, roasted shallots and spiced plum sauce. To finish it has to be an apple tarte tatin, unless you fancy warm sticky toffee pudding with toffee sauce and vanilla ice cream. A well-annotated wine list roams the globe, starting with a good selection of French house wines by the glass, carafe or bottle.
Chef/s: Christie Matthews. **Closed:** Mon, Tue, 24 to 26 Dec, 1 Jan. **Meals:** main courses £17 to £29. Sun L £25. **Details:** 40 seats. Bar. Music.

Casanova

Cooking score: 1
Italian | £35
13 Quay Street, Cardiff, CF10 1EA
Tel no: 029 2034 4044
casanovacardiff.com

£5
OFF

The unpretentious interior, 'welcoming and helpful' proprietor and upbeat vibe wouldn't count for much if the cooking wasn't up to snuff, but at Antonio Cersosimo's restaurant close to the Principality Stadium, the flavours and aromas of Italy hit home. Venetian sweet-and-sour sardines on toasted focaccia is a simple enough proposition, but the short, regularly changing menu can also pack a punch with ragù of goat, slow cooked with tomatoes and red wine and served with filei (Calabrian pasta), or a Milanese stew of pork, pork sausage and savoy cabbage braised in white wine. Reasonable pricing extends to the all-Italian wine list.
Chef/s: Antonio Cersosimo. **Closed:** Sun, bank hols, 24 to 26 Dec, 1 Jan. **Meals:** main courses £15 to £21. Set L £16 (2 courses) to £20. **Details:** 34 seats.

Heaneys

Cooking score: 4
Modern British | £43
6-10 Romilly Crescent, Cardiff, CF11 9NR
Tel no: 029 2034 1264
heaneyscardiff.co.uk

Crowdfunding raised £40,000 for *Great British Menu* chef Tommy Heaney to open this suave and airy restaurant in one of the city's upmarket suburbs. There's certainly much to please the crowds, but don't expect predictable dishes: Heaney's cooking smacks of originality and flair. The surroundings provide a smart and neutral backdrop, dominated by shades of palest dove grey, but the plates burst with colour and flavour. From a selection of small sharing dishes, favourites have included a fat Porthilly oyster topped with yoghurt granita and dill oil, sourdough bread with Marmite butter, and a main of Wye Valley asparagus with tender lobster, pepper dulse, hollandaise and a deeply savoury bisque. This cooking puts a spin on the ordinary, without veering out of control – a dessert of salted caramel parfait with frozen yoghurt and honeycomb emphasised the chef's ability to make sensible choices with a broadly British palate. The wine list is the product of a partnership with Berkmann Wine Cellars, and offers a pleasing mix of classics and off-the-beaten-track options.
Chef/s: Tommy Heaney. **Closed:** Mon. **Meals:** main courses £9 to £15. Set L £16 (2 courses) to £21. Tasting menu £43 (10 courses). Sun L £25 (2 courses) to £30. **Details:** 60 seats. 30 seats outside. V menu. Bar. Wheelchairs. Parking. Music.

Budget

£30 At restaurants showing this symbol, it is possible to eat three courses (excluding drinks) for £30 or less.

Purple Poppadom

Cooking score: 1
Indian | £32
Upper Floor, 185a Cowbridge Road East, Cardiff, CF11 9AJ
Tel no: 029 2022 0026
purplepoppadom.com

£5 OFF

Tucked up a flight of stairs on busy Cowbridge Road East, the restaurant is suitably purple inside, from lighting to walls. The menu covers the expected Indian favourites and a few lesser-known creations, all freshly cooked and bursting with flavour. You could start with a seekh kebab, after which the thali-style platters are a good way to go (the vegetarian option comes highly recommended, with dishes running from tarka dhal to paneer makhani). For dessert, look out for the signature chocolate samosa. The nicely annotated wine list covers 20 affordable options.
Chef/s: Anand George. **Closed:** Mon, 25 and 26 Dec, 1 Jan. **Meals:** main courses £14 to £20. Tasting menu £48 (7 courses). Sun L £28. **Details:** 70 seats. Music.

LOCAL GEM

Canna Deli

British | £15
2 Pontcanna Mews, 200 Kings Road, Cardiff, CF11 9DF
Tel no: 07767 726902

£30

Set on a quiet courtyard in the leafy suburb of Pontcanna, this bright daytime-only deli café majors in unpretentious dishes made with ingredients stocked in the shop. Run by a family of Anglesey cheesemakers, the food here is intentionally simple, allowing beautiful ingredients to shine – it's a good place to sample their renowned output. Offerings include Welsh beef cawl, sandwiches and traditional brunch options (scrambled egg on toast with smoked salmon, for example). Drinks run from milkshakes to a minimalist selection of wines.

▌Cowbridge

LOCAL GEM
Bar 44
Spanish | £25
44c High Street, Cowbridge, CF71 7AG
Tel no: 0333 344 4049
bar44.co.uk

£5 OFF £30

Head through the mosaic-tiled doorway and up to the first-floor dining room of this straightforward tapas restaurant, part of a small, local chain. Spanish charcuterie and cheeses, patatas bravas, tortilla, boquerones straight out of Cádiz, and chicken livers fired up with smoked pancetta and Pedro Ximénez are the order of the day. And to drink? A glass of crisp sherry or a bottle from the all-Spanish wine list. Sister Bar 44s can be found in Bristol, Penarth and Cardiff, where Asador 44 (see entry) is also part of the family.

▌Llancarfan

★ NEW ENTRY ★

The Fox and Hounds
Cooking score: 1
British | £28
Llancarfan, CF62 3AD
Tel no: 01446 781287
fandhllancarfan.co.uk

£30

'A lovely country pub with roaring fires in the winter and a sunny beer garden in the warmer months,' notes a regular to this peaceful spot in the Vale of Glamorgan. Jim Dobson's 'excellent' cooking is unpretentious but successfully ambitious, making impressive use of local ingredients. Expect considered, sophisticated food: Hendrick's gin-cured salmon with pickled cucumber, fennel and crème fraîche is a delight, as is the 'delicious, beautifully cooked' roast cod with mussels and a potato and celeriac broth, while the sticky toffee pudding has many fans. Wines are taken seriously with a substantial list favouring European finds from £18.

Chef/s: Jim Dobson. **Meals:** main courses £11 to £17. **Details:** Bar. Parking. Music.

▌Llanddewi Skirrid
The Walnut Tree
Cooking score: 5
Modern British | £50
Llanddewi Skirrid, NP7 8AW
Tel no: 01873 852797
thewalnuttreeinn.com

'It couldn't have been better,' notes one happy diner of a 'lovely evening' at this famed inn. The setting is delightful, all country-chic with a rustic edge, and chimes well with cooking that manages to be unpretentious yet deeply skilled. The commitment of Shaun Hill is hugely appreciated, and the chef is very much in evidence in the kitchen, his classical sensibilities dictating a menu that takes in the likes of lobster omelette Victoria, squab pigeon with petits pois à la française, black truffle and Parmesan risotto, and globe artichoke with quail's egg, morels and hollandaise. This is cooking rooted in culinary tradition, yet it feels totally of the moment. Main courses might include rabbit fricassée, fillet of beef with shin bourguignon, or cod with cauliflower and hazelnut dressing. Game makes a good showing and fig tart with honey and ricotta ice cream, or baked cheesecake with blood orange and popcorn, are a fine finale. The wine list favours small and artisan makers, with house Champagnes from Billecart-Salmon.

Chef/s: Shaun Hill. **Closed:** Mon, Sun, 1 week Christmas. **Meals:** main courses £18 to £36. Set L £25 (2 courses) to £30. **Details:** 50 seats. 12 seats outside. Bar. Wheelchairs. Parking.

■ Penarth

★ TOP 50 ★

Restaurant James Sommerin

Cooking score: 7
Modern British | £50
The Esplanade, Penarth, CF64 3AU
Tel no: 029 2070 6559
jamessommerinrestaurant.co.uk

🛏

Visitors to this 'stunning' restaurant on The Esplanade, with its views of the Bristol Channel and an Edwardian pleasure pier, all agree that this is one of Wales's finest restaurants. It offers a pleasant ambience, well-spaced tables and a busy, open-to-view kitchen where James Sommerin's precise balancing act between modern thinking and classical technique results in undeniably first-class workmanship. Although breaking new ground is not Sommerin's game, his cooking really stands out from the crowd – not least because he starts with high-quality raw materials and takes seasonality seriously. Dishes are impressive in their willingness to mix natural flavours with unusual textures – fresh creamy burrata with heritage carrot, basil and seeds, for example. Others evoke flavours that are strikingly vivid, as in a signature pea ravioli, its sweetness offset by sage and Parmesan foam with serrano ham adding welcome saltiness, or a triumphant Welsh lamb fillet and confit of shoulder, with butternut squash purée, Jerusalem artichoke, pak choi and a cumin and lamb sauce. A 'stupendous raspberry soufflé into which was poured a hot raspberry sauce at the table' makes a winning finale. There are extra treats thrown in, of course, and a sommelier providing advice on a wine list that ticks the boxes for serious intent, quality and reasonable choice under £45.
Chef/s: James Sommerin. **Closed:** Mon, Tue, 26 Dec, 1 Jan. **Meals:** main courses £20 to £32. Tasting menu £65 (6 courses) to £95. Surprise menu £75 (6 courses) to £95. **Details:** 60 seats. Wheelchairs. Music. Pre-payment required.

Ferments explained

Out for dinner but want to feel like you're doing your microbiome a favour? Chefs are playing with the funky flavours of ferments while honouring food traditions of the past

Kefir This fermented milk-based drink with a gentle fizz gets its probiotic life from 'grains' of culture. It provides a novel way for chefs to introduce a clean-but-complex, slightly sour note to desserts.

Kimchi The prince of pickles is part of everyday life in Korea, where it's traditionally made by packing huge jars full of cabbage, salt, garlic, chilli and shrimp. The fermentation produces a pungently addictive hot spicy relish.

Miso A reliable way to add savour, this Japanese paste is made by fermenting steamed soya beans with salt and a starter called koji. Traditionally used as a base for soup, this year we've seen miso in fudge and in a sauce for drizzling over pork tacos.

Sourdough Made using a flour and water starter which gets its active properties from naturally occurring bacteria, sourdough bread and pizza bases have a cracking crust and a distinctive tangy flavour.

Kombucha This refreshing drink is based on tea and lightly fermented with a scoby – a symbiotic culture of bacteria and yeast. It makes for a refreshing palate reset before long tasting menus.

▌Pontypridd

Bunch of Grapes

Cooking score: 3
Modern British | £30
Ynysangharad Road, Pontypridd, CF37 4DA
Tel no: 01443 402934
bunchofgrapes.org.uk
£5 OFF £30

Sitting beside a disused canal, this former labourers' watering hole takes some finding, despite being close to the heart of Pontypridd. Do persevere, though, and you'll be rewarded with a stunning selection of beers and a menu that far outstrips standard pub offerings. Chef proprietor Nick Otley used to be a fashion photographer and his bold style can be seen in the deep blue walls, wood panelling and modish lighting. Lunch brings cracking upmarket sandwiches (pork and beef meatballs with basil pesto, rocket and Monterey Jack, say) and comforting pubby mains. In the evening, try pan-fried cockles with leeks, laverbread and pancetta, perhaps followed by slow-braised ox cheek with potato and celeriac terrine, oyster fritter and cavolo nero. Homely desserts include tiramisu and sticky toffee pudding. Those beers are matched by an impressive global wine list.
Chef/s: Nick Otley and Matthew Traylor.
Meals: main courses £12 to £23. Sun L £16 (2 courses). **Details:** 60 seats. 20 seats outside. Bar. Parking. Music.

▌Whitebrook

★ TOP 50 ★

The Whitebrook

Cooking score: 7
British | £85
Whitebrook, NP25 4TX
Tel no: 01600 860254
thewhitebrook.co.uk
£5 OFF

'Certainly tucked away,' noted one visitor to this remote restaurant with rooms perched on a steep hillside high above the river Wye,

where 'you could probably spend days without a mobile signal'. Oak floors and a wood burner in the old fireplace of this former village pub add a cabin feel but linen-clad tables in the dining room channel a stylishly minimalist aesthetic. A former protégé of Raymond Blanc (and a winner of *Great British Menu*), Chris Harrod has made a name for himself as a chef who relies heavily on the locally foraged ingredients growing within walking distance of his kitchen. Harrod combines finely tuned classical techniques with some genuinely exciting flavour combinations. Dishes feature so many foraged ingredients that menu descriptions are often reminiscent of captions in antiquarian wildflower books. A late spring inspection meal opened with Wye Valley asparagus teamed with crisp hogweed leaves, maritime pine, hedgerow clippings and foam flavoured with mead made in nearby Tintern. Then a piece of mackerel fillet, cured in meadowsweet and accompanied by discs of crisp, sharp compressed apple, fruity meadowsweet pickle, bitter red amaranth leaves and rock samphire, while Cornish plaice turned up with sautéed violet artichokes, sweet brown shrimps, hop shoots and garlicky jack by the hedge leaves. Hereford strawberries, paired with a bracing, lemony sorrel ice cream, wood sorrel leaves, honeyed oats, almonds and white chocolate was a fitting finale. An interesting wine list that embraces all things natural, organic and biodynamic opens at £29 and is helpfully broken down by category.
Chef/s: Chris Harrod. **Closed:** Mon, Tue, 2 weeks Jan. **Meals:** set L £42. Tasting menu L £55 (5 courses) and D £85 (7 courses). **Details:** 26 seats. V menu. Parking. Music. Children over 12 yrs at D.

Anonymous

At *The Good Food Guide*, our inspectors dine anonymously and pay their bill in full. These impartial review meals, along with feedback from thousands of our readers, are what informs the content of the *GFG*. Only the best restaurants make the cut.

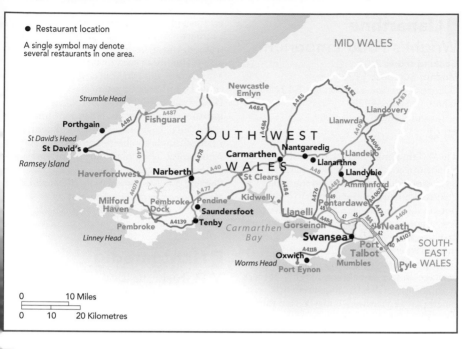

Restaurant location

A single symbol may denote
several restaurants in one area.

Carmarthen

The Warren

Cooking score: 2
British | £29
11 Mansel Street, Carmarthen, SA31 1PX
Tel no: 01267 236079
warrenmanselst.co.uk
£30

Launched after a crowdfunding campaign,
this fetching restaurant is suitably
labyrinthine, rambling through several rooms
lit by candles and fairy lights. Founder and
chef Deri Reed cut his teeth on the festival
food scene, and his cooking is as free-spirited
and wholesome as those origins suggest.
Everything is made on site and there's a long
list of local suppliers, so Welsh mussels might
come in a Welsh cider and bacon cream with
soft, seeded homemade bread, and the beef
will be from Carmarthenshire, perhaps
Himalayan-salt-aged rump steak. An
excellent carrot burger is teamed with avocado
and pickled red cabbage in a fluffy home-
baked bun and comes with crisp wedges and
spiky aïoli, while a dessert of apple and
rhubarb crumble baked in a pastry case
delights with its deceptive simplicity. A
relatively brief, crowd-pleasing international
wine list offers plenty of options by the glass.
Chef/s: Deri Reid and Danut Lonascu. **Closed:** Mon.
Meals: main courses £15 to £20. **Details:** 70 seats.
Bar.

Get social

Follow us on social media for the latest
news, chef interviews and more.
Twitter @GoodFoodGuideUK
Facebook TheGoodFoodGuide

▌Llanarthne
Wright's Food Emporium
Cooking score: 2
Modern European | £22
Golden Grove Arms, Llanarthne, SA32 8JU
Tel no: 01558 668929
wrightsfood.co.uk

The Wright family's stylish roadside food emporium combines the rustic charm of a farm shop with the sharp-eyed sourcing of a deli. You can buy food and drink to take home, but you'd be missing a treat if you didn't take a seat in one of the lovely vintage-styled rooms and pick a few dishes from the blackboard menu. Expect 'really excellent ingredients and intelligent, interesting combinations with a heritage flavour, but also thoroughly modern sensibilities' – salt beef croquettes with sauerkraut and anchovies, maybe, and then big, fall-apart-tender short ribs with melt-in-the-mouth carlin peas and lardons, and bread and butter pudding with cranberries and white chocolate, described as 'the best I've ever tasted'. Drinks are another strength: Wright's own lager goes down beautifully with the food, while the French wine list, with wines imported directly from small suppliers, is full of interest and offers much by the glass.
Chef/s: Aled Evans. **Closed:** Tue, 25 to 28 Dec, 1 and 2 Jan. **Meals:** main courses £7 to £14.
Details: 80 seats. 20 seats outside. Wheelchairs. Parking. Music.

▌Llandybie
Valans
Cooking score: 1
British | £25
29 High Street, Llandybie, SA18 3HX
Tel no: 01269 851288
valans.co.uk

Smart, but with a simple decor that lets the cooking do the talking, Dave and Remy Vale's unassuming little restaurant has been keeping regulars happy since 2005. This is a great area

for fresh ingredients, from Gower lamb to Carmarthenshire beef and plentiful fish and seafood, and all of these make a good showing on a menu full of comforting classics. Mushrooms and Perl Wen cheese on a crostini could be followed by crumbed confit of Gower salt marsh lamb with creamy garlic potatoes, fennel, carrots, redcurrant and lamb-stock sauce. To finish, expect the likes of tiramisu, apple and berry crumble and vanilla panna cotta. The global wine list offers good value for money.
Chef/s: Dave Vale. **Closed:** Mon, 20 Dec to 13 Jan.
Meals: main courses £18. Set L and D £16 (2 courses) to £28. Sun L £19. **Details:** 36 seats. Wheelchairs. Music.

▌Nantgaredig
Y Polyn
Cooking score: 3
Modern European | £40
Capel Dewi, Nantgaredig, SA32 7LH
Tel no: 01267 290000
ypolyn.co.uk

There's a storybook magic to this roadside tollhouse-turned-restaurant. Set snug to a winding road with trees all around and a stream tumbling almost underneath, it's a perfect waypoint on a country jaunt. Old meets new inside, with the warmth of original features paired with a bold, glass-sided extension – the result is homely yet forward-looking. The same could be said of the menu, which gives a modern twist to traditional European favourites – oxtail ragù with pappardelle, Parmesan and pangrattato, for example, then slow-cooked pork belly with roast cauliflower purée, a crispy pork bonbon, pickled red cabbage, buttered mash and crackling. The dauphinois is appropriately billed as 'legendary'. The puddings, meanwhile, are as comforting as the word suggests: try rhubarb and custard knickerbocker glory, or warm pear and frangipane tart with stem ginger ice cream. The meaty wine list offers a good global spread and something for all pockets, with plenty under £30.

Chef/s: Susan Manson. **Closed:** Mon. **Meals:** main courses £18 to £28. Set L £17 (2 courses) to £21. Set D £30 (2 courses) to £40. Sun L £24 (2 courses) to £29. **Details:** 100 seats. 15 seats outside. Bar. Wheelchairs. Parking. Music.

▌Narberth
The Fernery at The Grove
Cooking score: 5
Modern British | £69
Molleston, Narberth, SA67 8BX
Tel no: 01834 860915
thegrove-narberth.co.uk
£5 OFF 🛏

'Excellent ingredients, precise cooking and an enjoyable element of originality' is how one visitor summed up Douglas Balish's cooking at this gracious country house. It's reached via a long, gated driveway amid lush countryside, and neogothic, Jacobean and Arts and Crafts influences jostle pleasantly inside and out, with the decor referencing Wales at every turn (a coffee tabletop made from coal; a slate bar; charming wool blankets). The more refined dining option – and Balish's domain – is The Fernery, a classically styled room with real ferns on the tables and walls. Local ingredients underpin dishes with a modern British flavour: steamed kohlrabi in nettle velouté topped with olive oil sorbet and a nettle crisp made a fresh and lively late spring opener, while roast scallop chimed nicely with black truffle, a shallot reduction, garden chives and a bright zing of lime. A main of lamb loin, neck and belly showcased impeccable, tender meat with wild garlic, morels and a rich jus. This is delightfully sure-footed fare, right through to desserts such as a Breton biscuit prettily topped with poached rhubarb, honeycomb, rhubarb sorbet and a tonka bean cream – fruity, tart, creamy and sweet. A wine list of grand proportions is supported by an excellent sommelier, with much available by the glass.
Chef/s: Douglas Balish. **Meals:** set D £69. Tasting menu £79 (6 courses) to £94. **Details:** 28 seats. Bar. Wheelchairs. Parking. Music. Children over 12 yrs.

LOCAL GEM
Artisan Rooms
Modern British | £40
The Grove, Molleston, Narberth, SA67 8BX
Tel no: 01834 860 915
thegrove-narberth.co.uk
🛏

This 'wonderful rural retreat' continues to develop. A recent remodelling to form more relaxed dining areas as an alternative to dinner-only The Fernery (see entry) has drawn fulsome praise from readers. Spacious, light and cleverly decorated in modern country style, it's a relaxing setting for popular brasserie dishes that are several cuts above the norm. Typical dishes might run to smoked haddock fishcake with pickled cucumber and dill mayo, perfectly pink slices of rump of roast lamb, and cod with greens, creamed potatoes, cod's roe and a mild curry sauce. Finish with bara brith pudding and coffee ice cream. There's good choice by the glass on the short wine list.

▌Oxwich
Beach House
Cooking score: 5
Modern British | £52
Oxwich Beach, Oxwich, SA3 1LS
Tel no: 01792 390965
beachhouseoxwich.co.uk
£5 OFF

'I cannot think of a better place to spend a warm afternoon listening to the sea and being treated and fed so well,' writes a visitor to this expansive raftered dining room overlooking the bay on the Gower Peninsula. Hywel Griffith and his team are justly proud of what they do, to the extent of describing dishes in meticulous detail as they are served, and pointing out the fishing boat moored at the water's edge in which the kitchen's catch is landed. Seafood is naturally a leading card, perhaps cod in Ibérico ham with salsify, rösti and brown butter, steamed hake in Indian guise with curried butter sauce, yoghurt, lentils and an onion bhajia, or the incomparable local lobster. Elsewhere, it might be ox cheek cannelloni with beetroot, apple, parsnip and kale for a compendious prelude to roast Welsh beef fillet and slow-cooked shoulder with hen of the woods, carrot and celeriac in a ragoût of Gower Gold ale. Happiness is complete when pwdin (the menu is in both languages) turns up bara brith soufflé with tea ice cream, or poached rhubarb tart, this time with blood orange ice cream. Welsh cheeses should not be shunned, and the wine list takes a cosmopolitan tack, hauling in German Riesling, Indian Sangiovese and even Turkish rosé in its capacious net. Small glasses start at £7.

Chef/s: Hywel Griffith. **Closed:** Mon, Tue, 2 weeks Jan. **Meals:** main courses £23 to £32. Set L £30. Tasting menu £58 (5 courses) to £78. **Details:** 48 seats. 20 seats outside. V menu. Vg menu. Bar. Wheelchairs. Parking. Music.

■ Porthgain
The Shed
Cooking score: 1
Seafood | £29
Porthgain, SA62 5BN
Tel no: 01348 831518
theshedporthgain.co.uk
£30

Billed as a 'fish and chip bistro', this harbourside spot occupies one of several buildings that hark back to Porthgain's days as a slate quarry. Informal inside, it sports red and white chequered tablecloths, whitewashed walls and local artwork, and offers two menus: one for classic fish and chips (which they do admirably), the other detailing more ambitious dishes made with dayboat deliveries. Recent hits include a classic fish soup with a big aïoli-slathered rustic croûton, and very fresh hake with a creamy leek and smoked bacon sauce. Service is charming, there's a decent selection of reasonably priced, seafood-friendly wines, and desserts such as homemade apple strudel deliver satisfaction.

Chef/s: Brian Mullins. **Meals:** main courses £13 to £19. **Details:** 70 seats. 30 seats outside. Wheelchairs. Music.

■ St David's
Cwtch
Cooking score: 2
Modern British | £38
22 High Street, St David's, SA62 6SD
Tel no: 01437 720491
cwtchrestaurant.co.uk
£5 OFF

The Welsh word for 'cuddle' can also mean a small, cosy room and this charming little restaurant certainly lives up to its name – it's comforting and enveloping. The interior makes a feature of whitewashed stonework and exposed beams, and the simple wooden furniture chimes well with the rustic vibe. Chef Richard Guy pitches his menu neatly between classics (Caesar salad, steak and chips) and less common dishes such as rolled rabbit haunch stuffed with black pudding and rabbit, served with a cider jus, braised red cabbage and garlicky dauphinois potatoes. On inspection, this latter dish was bookended by a generous jar of dill-spiked potted crab with Melba toast and a dessert of hot cross bun and butter pudding with butterscotch sauce and cinnamon and raisin ice cream. Drinks-wise, a decent international wine selection is bolstered by an impressive range of cocktails.

Chef/s: Richard Guy. **Closed:** 1 Jan to 5 Feb. **Meals:** main courses £19 to £27. Sun L £20 (2 courses) to £24. **Details:** 50 seats. Wheelchairs. Music.

Vegetarian and vegan

While many restaurants offer dishes suitable for non-meat eaters, those marked 'V menu' (vegetarian) and 'Vg menu' (vegan) offer separate menus.

◼ Saundersfoot

Coast

Cooking score: 4
Modern British | £42
Coppet Hall Beach, Saundersfoot, SA69 9AJ
Tel no: 01834 810800
coastsaundersfoot.co.uk

A hit with locals and tourists for the past six years, this contemporary cedar-clad building occupies an unbeatable location overlooking Coppet Hall Beach and Carmarthen Bay. The curved suntrap terrace offers spectacular views of the bay, the source of much of the menu's seafood. Since stepping up as head chef at the end of 2017, Tom Hine has stamped his personality firmly on the concise, very seasonal menu, offering a refined assemblage of prime ingredients in appetisers of, say, Galician octopus with avocado and sweet chilli, and starters such as salmon ballotine with dill, lemon and cured keta caviar. These might lead on to an on-point tranche of cod teamed with cauliflower, grapes, almond and vermouth sauce or Ryeland hogget with sweet potato, baby gem and salsa verde. Perfectly executed desserts could include a light and fluffy mango mousse served with coconut tuile and coconut sorbet. To drink, there are carefully curated international wines from £24.
Chef/s: Tom Hine. **Closed:** Mon, Tue, 5 to 22 Jan. **Meals:** main courses £24 to £28. Set L £29. Tasting menu £55 (5 courses). **Details:** 56 seats. 20 seats outside. V menu. Vg menu. Bar. Wheelchairs. Parking. Music.

◼ Swansea

Hanson at the Chelsea

Cooking score: 2
Modern European | £38
17 St Mary Street, Swansea, SA1 3LH
Tel no: 01792 464068
hansonatthechelsea.co.uk
£5 OFF

Andrew Hanson's compact bistro has all the old-school trappings you'd hope to find: bare floorboards and tables, cheery yellow walls and a bustling, chatty atmosphere. It's the place to enjoy a good-value lunch or linger over a more extensive evening offer, the whole repertoire a user-friendly mix of updated classics and more eclectic ideas. To start, try pork rillettes with apple jelly and toasted sourdough, or fishcakes with dill and mustard mayonnaise, before tackling slow-cooked veal rump with Madeira velouté or grilled halibut teamed with ginger-chilli marinated tiger prawns accompanied by peanut pad thai rice noodles. To finish, warm chocolate brownie with honeycomb ice cream has been well received, or you might fancy brioche bread and butter pudding with honey and whisky. House Chilean is £15.95, or £4.75 a glass.
Chef/s: Andrew Hanson. **Closed:** Sun. **Meals:** main courses £14 to £25. Set L £17 (2 courses) to £22. Tasting menu £40 (7 courses). **Details:** 42 seats. Music.

Slice

Cooking score: 4
Modern European | £42
73-75 Eversley Road, Swansea, SA2 9DE
Tel no: 01792 290929
sliceswansea.co.uk

This tiny, wedge-shaped building in an upmarket suburb is home to a well-respected restaurant offering inventive cooking at reasonable prices. Its quirky layout sees the chefs cooking on the ground floor, fully visible through a shop window, while diners head upstairs to be seated in an understated first-floor dining room of stripped wood floors, white walls and simple furnishings. Chef proprietors Chris Harris and Adam Bannister champion local ingredients in dishes that lend a modern twist to European classics, such as a wellington (a pigeon and pistachio version with textures of beetroot and sherry vinegar sauce) or apple tarte tatin with brown sugar egg custard and vanilla ice cream. In between might be halibut, barbecued and served with Jerusalem artichokes, charred leeks and cockle beurre blanc, or venison loin with boulangère potatoes, salsify and cavolo nero. There's much to love here – including the matching wines that are recommended at each course. The full list offers good global reach at reasonable prices.

Chef/s: Chris Harris and Adam Bannister. **Closed:** Mon, Tue, Wed, 2 weeks Oct, 1 week Dec, 1 week Apr, 1 week Jul. **Meals:** set L £29 (2 courses) to £32. Set D £42. Tasting menu L £48 (6 courses) and D £55. **Details:** 16 seats. V menu. Music.

■ Tenby
The Salt Cellar
Cooking score: 3
Modern British | £39
The Esplanade, Tenby, SA70 7DU
Tel no: 01834 844005
thesaltcellartenby.co.uk
£5
OFF

Don't be dismayed by the fact that this seaside restaurant is squirrelled away below stairs in the rather anonymous Atlantic Hotel, because it really is quite a find. Run with enthusiasm and passion by four friends, it comprises a casual bar and over-the-road terrace for sunnier days, as well as a calming dining room with bare tables, coastal pictures and a menu of up-to-the-minute flavours allied to generous helpings of seasonal Welsh produce. Fish from the Pembrokeshire coast receives typically modish treatment, from torched mackerel with Jersey Royal sag aloo to fillet of 'market fish' partnered by Carmarthen Bay mussel and bacon chowder, smoked leeks and herb oil. Elsewhere, smoked breast and confit leg of local chicken appear in a terrine, while slow-cooked belly and faggot of Welsh pedigree

pork are accompanied by salt-baked swede, bubble and squeak and pickled dates. For afters, try the Tenby ale cake laced with Black Flag rum porter. There's a small selection of wines by the glass on the good-value list which starts at £18 and includes a white blend from nearby Monnow Valley.

Chef/s: Duncan Barham and Matt Flowers. **Meals:** main courses £19 to £26. Set L £19 (2 courses) to £23. Sun L £20 (2 courses) to £25. **Details:** 45 seats. 20 seats outside. Bar. Music.

CHANNEL
ISLANDS

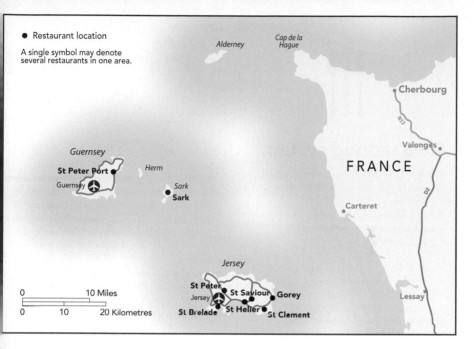

● Restaurant location

A single symbol may denote
several restaurants in one area.

Alderney

Cap de la Hague

Cherbourg

FRANCE

Valongès

Guernsey

St Peter Port ●

Guernsey

Herm

Sark
Sark

Carteret

Lessay

Jersey

0   10 Miles
0   10   20 Kilometres

St Peter
Jersey
St Brelade

St Saviour   **Gorey**
St Helier ●
St Clement

■ Guernsey
La Frégate
Cooking score: 3
Modern British | £50
Beauregard Lane, Les Cotils, St Peter Port,
Guernsey, GY1 1UT
Tel no: 01481 724624
lafregatehotel.com

Expansive harbour views and tantalising
glimpses of ancient Castle Cornet come with
the territory at this sympathetically extended
18th-century manor house that now functions
as a stylish hotel and restaurant. The kitchen
works to a conventional, French-inspired
menu that takes full advantage of fish from
local boats: Herm Island oysters in different
guises, scallops, brill and 'local water' sea bass
(served with Guernsey crabmeat, crushed new
potatoes, buttered samphire and Champagne
sauce), for example. Irish beef and English
lamb also feature, while Creedy Carver duck
might appear intricately plated with fondant

potato, parsnip and vanilla purée, broccoli,
Armagnac and griottine cherry jus. Staff relish
the old ways, dutifully preparing steak tartare
tableside, flambéeing crêpes Suzette with
theatrical splendour and presenting
chateaubriand with all the necessary
accoutrements. Wines from France dominate a
weighty list that offers up some welcome
bargains among its more prestigious vintages;
bottles start at £22.
Chef/s: Tony Leck. **Meals:** main courses £19 to £26.
Set L £20 (2 courses) to £25. Sun L £25. **Details:** 60
seats. Vg menu. Bar. Parking. Music.

Send us your review
Your feedback informs the content of
the *GFG* and will be used to compile
next year's entries. To register your
opinion about any restaurant listed in the
Guide, or a restaurant that you wish to
bring to our attention, visit:
thegoodfoodguide.co.uk/feedback.

GFG scoring system

Score 1: Capable cooking with simple food combinations and clear flavours.

Score 2: Decent cooking, displaying good technical skills and interesting combinations and flavours.

Score 3: Good cooking, showing sound technical skills and using quality ingredients.

Score 4: Dedicated, focused approach to cooking; good classical skills and high-quality ingredients.

Score 5: Exact cooking techniques and a degree of ambition; showing balance and depth of flavour in dishes.

Score 6: Exemplary cooking skills, innovative ideas, impeccable ingredients and an element of excitement.

Score 7: High level of ambition and individuality, attention to the smallest detail, accurate and vibrant dishes.

Score 8: A kitchen cooking close to or at the top of its game. Highly individual with impressive artistry.

Score 9: Cooking that has reached a pinnacle of achievement, making it a hugely memorable experience.

Score 10: Just perfect dishes, showing faultless technique at every service; extremely rare and the highest accolade.

LOCAL GEM

Da Nello
Italian | £40
46 Lower Pollet, St Peter Port, Guernsey, GY1 1WF
Tel no: 01481 721552
danello.gg

£5
OFF

The determinedly old-fashioned ambience of Manuel Teixeira's restaurant is one of its enduring charms. It's something of a local hot spot, where warm service and good cooking meld happily. Focusing on bright, sunny Mediterranean flavours, the kitchen sends out generous plates of fettuccine with crab, calf's liver and bacon or saltimbocca alla romana. Guernsey lobster is a speciality, Dover sole is served chargrilled or meunière, and there are local sea scallops with balsamic syrup, crispy bacon and buttered spinach. The mainly Italian wine list opens at £23.95.

LOCAL GEM

Octopus
Seafood | £35
Havelet Bay, St Peter Port, Guernsey, GY1 1AX
Tel no: 01481 722400
octopusgsy.co.uk

If slurping local oysters by the sea with a morning pick-me-up is your idea of breakfast heaven, then Octopus should fit the bill admirably. From the outside it may look like a bloated garden shed, but this is a smart, glass-fronted set-up with an all-day menu touting everything from fish and chips to tofu ramen. Fresh seafood (including the titular cephalopod) is the headline act, but also expect steaks, burgers, flatbreads, veggie salads and much more besides, with plenty of good stuff for the little ones, and beers, cocktails and wines for the drinkers.

Jersey

★ TOP 50 ★

Bohemia

Cooking score: 8
Modern European | £55
The Club Hotel & Spa, Green Street, St Helier,
Jersey, JE2 4UH
Tel no: 01534 880500
bohemiajersey.com
£5 OFF 🛏

Embedded within a luxury hotel, this
sophisticated dining room inspired by the
clean geometric simplicity of Art Deco style
brings the added appeal of a paved roof terrace
and bar and a very commodious chef's table
banquette. It's in many ways peak St Helier,
and Steve Smith's restless creative intelligence
plays no small part in that. Sourcing primarily
from Jersey's abundance, his menus explore
the possibilities of a recognisable modern
European idiom, but with unsuspected
intensities of flavour and curiosities of texture
popping up throughout. A plumply tender
scallop is partnered with apple and smoked
eel, as well as the earthier notes of truffled
celeriac, for a high-impact opener. Then
might come venison with cherries and
nasturtiums in bitter chocolate jus with
almonded cauliflower, or the dynamic duo of
John Dory and octopus with braised fennel in
a smouldering Espelette butter sauce. The
drivers of the kitchen's production are the set
menus, which come in pescatarian, vegetable
and everything versions, with a Prestige Menu
at the summit, that last delivering Jersey Royal
velouté and ice cream with sorrel, veal tartare
with lentils and jellied broth, and Cumbrian
lamb with Jerusalem artichoke, goat's cheese,
morels and wild garlic. Top-notch chocolate
forms the base of some of the most memorable
desserts, although blood orange tart with
buttermilk and olive oil, or rhubarb and
hibiscus mess with vanilla custard are
admirable contenders. Wines are classy, but the
firmly French emphasis tends to fire prices
into the blue Channel Islands sky. Glasses start
at £5.50.

Chef/s: Steve Smith. **Closed:** Sun, 24 to 30 Dec.
Meals: main courses £19 to £38. Set L £27 (2
courses) to £35. Set D £55 (2 courses) to £69. Tasting
menu £89 (8 courses) to £105. **Details:** 60 seats. V
menu. Bar. Wheelchairs. Parking. Music.

Green Island Restaurant

Cooking score: 1
International | £40
Green Island, St Clement, Jersey, JE2 6LS
Tel no: 01534 857787
greenisland.je

Billed as 'the most southerly restaurant in the
British Isles', this seafront eatery and beach hut
makes the most of its location. There are
glorious views from its sought-after alfresco
tables, while the menu is peppered with
seafood from the local boats — perhaps brill
with Parmesan polenta or lemon sole fillets
with cockle and mussel marinière, crushed
Jersey Royals and samphire. Otherwise, the
kitchen casts its net far and wide, offering
anything from vine leaves with lamb kofta and
houmous to an assiette of pork with savoy
cabbage and cider jus or Thai green lentil and
chickpea curry. Wines from £19.75.
Chef/s: Daniel Teesdale. **Closed:** Mon, Christmas,
New Year, Jan. **Meals:** main courses £19 to £29. Set
L £20 (2 courses) to £23. **Details:** 35 seats. 25 seats
outside. Wheelchairs. Parking. Music.

The Green Olive

Cooking score: 3
Mediterranean | £30
1 Anley Street, St Helier, Jersey, JE2 3QE
Tel no: 01534 728198
greenoliverestaurant.co.uk
£5 OFF £30

The eye-catching aesthetic at Paul Le Brocq's
first-floor restaurant runs right through from
a clever use of natural wood, original artworks
and Scandi-style furniture to the pretty and
colourful presentation of the food.
Contemporary techniques and a measured
passion for fusion flavours result in some
satisfying combinations, with the island's
produce at the heart of it all. Among opening

salvos, local hand-dived scallops might be teamed with tender pork belly and piccalilli purée, and chicken liver parfait with a spiced fruit chutney, pickled carrot and brioche. There are spices on a main course cod, too, served up with curried cauliflower and mango, while spring lamb loin is prepped in a more European manner with peas and mint, and roast pan juices. Keen, informed service complete the picture. The concise wine list manages to cover the globe, opening at £18.95 for Argentinian Malbec or Chardonnay.
Chef/s: Paul Le Brocq. **Closed:** Mon, Sun, Jan. **Meals:** main courses £15 to £23. **Details:** 45 seats. Music.

Longueville Manor
Cooking score: 6
Modern French | £70
Longueville Road, St Saviour, Jersey, JE2 7WF
Tel no: 01534 725501
longuevillemanor.com

Pass through Longueville's venerable stone entrance and you'll feel like a returning pilgrim, staff are so hospitable. Parts of the building hark back to the reign of Edward III, when itinerant justices heard local cases here. Andrew Baird hasn't been here quite that long, but his fourth decade looms. The cooking remains as energetic and satisfying as ever, informed by an essentially modern French discipline and thoroughbred island produce. Asian seasonings bring yuzu mayonnaise to both seared yellowfin with foraged greens and crab with watermelon, while main dishes take a more traditional approach, adding tartiflette and béarnaise to a line-up of Angus fillet, sticky rib and oxtail bonbon. A fish main course might be turbot with vanilla-poached langoustine and chicken confit; dessert brings on lemon mousse with ginger sablé biscuits and gin and tonic sorbet. Local artisan cheeses are among the highlights of a double-decker trolley fashioned from vintage oak. Vegetarian and vegan menus aim for true inclusivity rather than lip service, and when it comes to wine, Longueville – and its fine sommeliers –

have it nailed. A state-of-the-art cellar embraces everything from Alsace to the USA, with deep-pocketed Francophiles especially well served. A Veneto Pinot Grigio at £8 leads the glass selection.
Chef/s: Andrew Baird. **Meals:** set L £28. Set D £58 (2 courses) to £70. Tasting menu £92 (7 courses). Sun L £45 (4 courses). **Details:** 90 seats. 35 seats outside. V menu. Vg menu. Bar. Wheelchairs. Parking. Music.

Mark Jordan at the Beach
Cooking score: 3
Modern British | £50
La Plage, La Route de la Haule, St Peter, Jersey, JE3 7YD
Tel no: 01534 780180
markjordanatthebeach.com

Midway between St Brelade and St Helier, Mark Jordan's seafront venue is well positioned to show the principal Channel Island off at its sparkling maritime best. If weather permits, head for the covered terrace, or nab one of the foursquare wooden tables by the window for bay views. Seafood specialities are an obvious draw, from oysters in various liveries to mackerel escabèche or pressed smoked salmon with guacamole, crab mayonnaise and a buttery sauce of sun-dried tomatoes and tarragon. Not everything seems quite in harmony, according to one reader who felt that scallops, pulled pork and celeriac espuma weren't doing much for each other. Mains run to classic lobster thermidor with Jersey Royals, baked aubergine with ratatouille and goat's cheese, or Gressingham duck roasted in honey and five-spice with apple gel and vanilla jus. Finish with an accomplished raspberry soufflé. Wines by the glass start at £6.50 for an Italian Chardonnay, leading on to a lively international miscellany and some fine bottles.
Chef/s: Mark Jordan and Alex Zotter. **Meals:** main courses £17 to £27. Set L £23 (2 courses) to £28. Set L £28. **Details:** 50 seats. 30 seats outside.

No 10 Restaurant & Bar

Cooking score: 6
Modern British | £50
10 Bond Street, St Helier, Jersey, JE2 3NP
Tel no: 01534 733 223
number10jersey.com

£5
OFF

Joe Baker's town-centre spot opposite the parish church is a magnet for those in the know, which includes anybody who saw him lighting up *Great British Menu*. The two-tiered operation comprises a basement cocktail bar and a wood-floored dining room in battleship grey at ground level, overseen by smartly clued-up staff. Baker works with the grain of seasonal contemporary cooking, letting island produce shine, the starters doubling as small plates, in a style of cooking that is unostentatious yet ringing with exciting flavours and combinations. A knockout starter of luscious pork belly comes on a heap of samphire in a subtly fiery Asian broth of preserved lemon, coriander and chilli, all topped with a smoked anchovy, or there might be an inspired composition of octopus with Ossau-Iraty cheese, 'nduja and confit tamarillo. Lamb (saddle and breast) might be juxtaposed with maritime notes from brown shrimps and sea beet, as well as violet artichokes and strained yoghurt, while fish itself might be lightly browned cod in oyster and horseradish velouté, with astringently peppery broccoli purée and buttered almonds. Finish with a copious bowl of baked hay custard topped with blanched rhubarb and its jelly, with strips of torn basil adding heavenly aromatics. A short wine list needs more inspired choices by the glass, which start at £5.50, but prices are agreeably restrained.
Chef/s: Joe Baker. **Closed:** Mon, Sun. **Meals:** main courses £18 to £25. Set L and D £25 Tue to Thur (2 courses) to £30. **Details:** 50 seats. Bar. Music.

Ocean Restaurant

Cooking score: 4
Modern British | £55
Atlantic Hotel, Le Mont de la Pulente, St Brelade, Jersey, JE3 8HE
Tel no: 01534 744101
theatlantichotel.com

Enveloped among gardens in Jersey's tranquil south-west corner, the Atlantic Hotel feels like a proper island retreat. There's a faintly colonial-era air to the pristine dining room with its ceiling fans and ocean views through louvred windows. Layers of linen and solicitous service set the tone for an old-school approach that Will Holland's menus throw into gentle relief. At the more speculative edge, a trio of toasted scallops are teamed with air-dried ham and a strip of leek gratinated under Parmesan and truffle, with roast hazelnuts for textural contrast, or there could be pig's head terrine with soused mushrooms, Thai shallots and powdered cep. The main-course pairing of roast loin and braised shoulder of island lamb, the latter wrapped into a rösti potato bonbon, didn't quite achieve the lift-off expected at inspection, but fish dishes take up the slack: John Dory comes with lobster tagliatelle, tarragon purée and truffled lobster cream. Desserts include a deconstruction job on lemon meringue pie that comes with lemongrass jelly, toasted marshmallow and lemonade granita. Long and short tasting menus, and a concise Market Menu, broaden the options, but pricing is fairly ambitious throughout, with wines inevitably contributing to the outlay.
Chef/s: Will Holland. **Closed:** Jan. **Meals:** main courses: £30 to £38. Set L £23 (2 courses) to £28. Set D £55. Tasting menu £55 (4 courses) to £85. Sun L £33. **Details:** 60 seats. V menu. Vg menu. Bar. Parking. Music.

Oyster Box

Cooking score: 3
Modern British | £38
Route de la Baie, St Brelade, Jersey, JE3 8EF
Tel no: 01534 850888
oysterbox.co.uk

Descend the steps from the coast road at St Brelade's Bay in south-west Jersey for an enviably located beachside seafood restaurant. Marine blue seating, and light fittings like giant bubbles are features of the newly refurbished dining room, where the views over the briny help no end in the enjoyment of a fine fish and shellfish repertoire. Local oysters naturally receive star billing, Champagne-buttered or Gruyèred and Worcestered, before the main menu starts in with copiously garnished crab salads and seared tuna with sesame, pickled ginger, wasabi and chilli. Fish takes a traditional approach for battered haddock, monkfish 'scampi' with chips and tartare sauce, and smoked haddock risotto. Meat dishes, far from being afterthoughts, involve a full range of steaks, as well as pancetta-wrapped pork or duck breast in red wine. Lighter desserts, say white chocolate mousse and raspberry panna cotta, set you up for a post-prandial seaside stroll. French varietals in all three colours at £22 head up a usefully varied list.
Chef/s: Tony Dorris. **Closed:** 25 Dec, 1 Jan. **Meals:** main courses £13 to £26. **Details:** 100 seats. 40 seats outside. Wheelchairs. Music.

Samphire

Cooking score: 5
Modern European | £55
7-11 Don Street, St Helier, Jersey, JE2 4TQ
Tel no: 01534 725100
samphire.je
£5 OFF

On the site of the former Ormer, this urbane brasserie complete with luxe trimmings, dusky blue banquettes, assorted prints and flamboyant chandeliers has been in fine fettle since opening its doors in 2018. Oysters from Jersey's Royal Bay are served three ways as an opener (perhaps tempura with Vietnamese dressing) and other local seafood is given a typically modish workout: scallop with katsu curry, pickled onion and a rice cracker or monkfish with carrot, lemongrass, vadouvan sauce and Bombay mix, for example. Meat eaters can feast on côte de boeuf or ribeye with chips and béarnaise sauce, while the sweet-toothed might drool over the raspberry pavlova with lavender cream and clotted cream ice cream. You can also come here for breakfast, brunch and afternoon tea – and they even offer a special menu for dining at home. The wide-ranging and knowledgeably curated wine list starts at £25 with plenty of impressive drinking by the glass, including an elite Coravin selection.
Chef/s: Lee Smith. **Closed:** Sun, bank hols, 25 and 26 Dec, 1 Jan. **Meals:** main courses £16 to £38. Set L and D £29. **Details:** 55 seats. 35 seats outside. V menu. Vg menu. Bar. Wheelchairs. Music.

Sumas

Cooking score: 2
Modern British | £40
Gorey Hill, St Martin, Gorey, Jersey, JE3 6ET
Tel no: 01534 853291
sumasrestaurant.com
£5 OFF

You may not be as lucky with the weather as the reader who got to eat on the terrace in March, but the seafood on offer ('some of the best I've eaten') is available come rain or shine. And thanks to generous glazing, the views over the harbour and Mont Orgueil can be enjoyed all year. The kitchen turns out spirited contemporary plates with ingredients from land and sea, so among first courses, slow-braised oxtail risotto with aged Parmesan and smoked bone marrow stands alongside treacle-cured salmon, fennel and blood orange. Move on to lemon sole served on the bone, local brill with crab tortelloni and bisque, or Dingley Dell pork belly in a creative surf and turf combination with line-caught squid and a croquette made with barbecued shoulder meat. Finish with orange and frangipane tart with yoghurt ice cream. The wine list has a global spread and decent options by the glass.

Chef/s: Dany Lancaster. **Closed:** 21 Dec to 18 Jan. **Meals:** main courses £17 to £30. Set L and D £22 (2 courses) to £27. **Details:** 35 seats. 20 seats outside. Vg menu. Bar. Wheelchairs. Music.

Tassili

Cooking score: 5
Modern European | £45
Grand Jersey Hotel, The Esplanade, St Helier, Jersey, JE2 3QA
Tel no: 01534 722301
handpickedhotels.co.uk

Ensconced within the Grand Jersey Hotel, which must have looked distinctly avant-garde when it went up in the late Victorian era, the dining room makes a virtue of busy patterning, on walls and floor alike. Nonetheless, professional service ensures a restful ambience in which to appreciate Nicolas Valmagna's modern Jersey cooking, which fuses French technique with outstanding island produce. Tasting menus include Land and Sea or Garden (vegetarian) themes, as well as the flagship version, and there is a small plates offering for the grazers. Main dishes might encompass John Dory on saffron risotto with mussels, rock samphire and caviar, or a dish of pork three ways comprising belly, cheek and black pudding with compressed apple and spring truffle. Preliminary dishes are all about piquing the taste buds, perhaps with crab, lime and yuzu gel, while dessert might involve a treatment of local pear with Touraine-style dried fruit, Williams pear sorbet and Piedmont hazelnuts. The considered wine list opens at £23 and there are good-value selections from some of France's best-known regions.

Chef/s: Nicolas Valmagna. **Closed:** Mon, Sun, Jan. **Meals:** set D £45. Tasting menu £62 (5 courses) to £75. **Details:** 24 seats. V menu. Bar. Wheelchairs. Parking. Children over 12 yrs.

Decode the wine list

Biodynamics A viticultural system inspired by the theories of Rudolf Steiner in which soil treatments are intended to respect the land and planting schedules are determined by the astrological calendar. Producers say the practice enhances clarity and staying power.

Natural wines Made without non-biological intervention, these wines are generally not treated with sulphur dioxide, nor are they clarified or filtered, so that the whites in particular may look hazy and off-coloured. The term has no legal definition, so producers can set their own parameters.

Orange wine An ancient method of making wine by leaving the fermenting juice of white grapes in contact with the skins, thereby acquiring deeper colour, more complex flavours and some tannins. Orange wines can taste heavier and coarser than white wines that have had the skins removed at pressing.

Pét-nat Short for pétillant naturel, these wines have their fermentation interrupted so that a slight fizz is left in them, as well as some natural sugar.

Coravin A preservation tool invented in 2011 that allows wine to be poured from a bottle without removing the cork. It's used by many restaurants for serving more exalted wines by the glass.

■ Sark
La Sablonnerie
Cooking score: 2
French | £45
Little Sark, Sark, GY10 1SD
Tel no: 01481 832061
sablonneriesark.com

Guests who arrive at Sark harbour en route to this roadside gem can be taken to their destination by vintage horse-drawn carriage. It's just one of the services provided by the owners of this 400-year-old farmhouse hotel – a dream-ticket hideaway complete with a suntrap 'tea garden', a croquet lawn and sub-tropical foliage all around. Dining here is a resolutely old-school experience in wonderful time-warp surroundings, where the wine list touts Piesporter and the laminated menu advertises a 'water ice' between courses. 'Classique' French cuisine looms large across the board, from a terrine of monkfish and salmon with brunoise of vegetables or best end of lamb filled with a purée of veal and tarragon served on a gâteau of spinach with a light garlic sauce to lemon chiffon tart or warm chocolate mousse. It may sound archaic, but this is serious stuff founded on top-notch local ingredients and executed with a degree of aplomb. Wines offer value and variety from £16.50 a bottle.
Chef/s: Colin Day. **Closed:** end Oct to late Apr. **Meals:** main courses £20 to £40. **Details:** 39 seats. 36 seats outside. Bar. Music.

dining room makes an atmospheric setting for dishes of lobster and cauliflower bisque with curried crab, two cuts of island lamb with sea vegetables and creamed potato in red wine jus, or perhaps pistachio-crusted brill fillet in beurre noisette. Finish with lemon tart served with poached rhubarb and matching sorbet. More casual dining is provided in the poolside bistro and bar. Wines are mostly brought in directly from France, with house selections at £6.25 a glass.

LOCAL GEM
Stocks
British | £40
Le Grand Dixcart, Sark, GY10 1SD
Tel no: 01481 832001
stockshotel.com

This handsome grey-stone building is tranquil car-free Sark's main hotel, an 18th-century house that became a hotel in late Victorian times. A candlelit oak-panelled

NORTHERN IRELAND

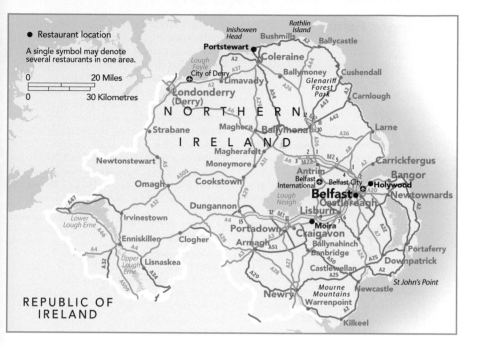

- Restaurant location

A single symbol may denote several restaurants in one area.

0   20 Miles

0   30 Kilometres

▌Belfast, Co Antrim
Deanes Eipic

Cooking score: 5

Modern European | £70
28-40 Howard Street, Belfast, Co Antrim, BT1 6PF
Tel no: 028 9033 1134
deaneseipic.com

Michael Deane has been a major player on the Belfast restaurant scene for more than two decades, but his most recent venture, established in 2014, is his most ambitious – a three-pronged gastro-multiplex not far from City Hall. Inside you'll find Love Fish and Meat Locker as well as Eipic, a high-achieving dining room serving tasting menus in a dimly lit, grey-walled setting, pointed up with white leather upholstery, silver-framed mirrors and a trio of suspended silver-foil 'moons'. In the kitchen, head chef Alex Greene and his brigade fashion intricate of-the-moment creations from quality ingredients: venison carpaccio offset by kohlrabi, mushrooms and almonds; halibut with artichoke, bone sauce and sea purslane; a slab of Glenarm shorthorn beef given more classical treatment with boulangère potatoes, carrots, cavolo nero and lovage. Desserts such as rhubarb with caramelised white chocolate and ginger are in a similar vein, while meals are bookended by a cavalcade of savoury and sweet 'snacks' designed to show off the kitchen's virtuosity. A giant vertical wine 'cave' dominates the centre of the room, and it's worth seeking guidance from the sommelier if you're looking for by-the-glass recommendations from the global list.

Chef/s: Alex Greene. **Closed:** Mon, Tue, Sun, 25 to 26 Dec, first 2 weeks Jan, 15 to 21 Apr, first 2 weeks Jul. **Meals:** set L £30. Tasting menu L £45 Wed and Thur (7 courses) to £70. **Details:** 30 seats. V menu. Bar. Wheelchairs. Music. No children after 9pm.

Bar

Where 'bar' is specified, it means there is a separate area available to have drinks.

The Ginger Bistro

Cooking score: 1
Modern British | £35
68-72 Great Victoria Street, Belfast, Co Antrim,
BT2 7AF
Tel no: 028 9024 4421
gingerbistro.com

For nigh on two decades, Simon McCance's
affable bistro has been serving contented locals
who still value the place for its cheery vibe,
decent prices and cosmopolitan food. The
kitchen merrily mixes influences and ideas
from around the globe, moving easily from
French onion soup or steak and chips to tea-
smoked duck breast salad with wilted carrots
and sesame seeds or sea bass fillet accompanied
by orzo pasta, fennel cream, leeks and crab
claws – although Ginger's 'squid with dips' is
the perennial bestseller. For afters, perhaps try
crème brûlée with raspberry compôte.
Draught ales from Whitewater Brewery,
County Down, are alternatives to the
workmanlike wine list.
Chef/s: Tim Moffet and Conor Mcgreeve. **Closed:**
Mon, Sun, 24 to 26 Dec, Easter Mon and Tue.
Meals: main courses £16 to £25. **Details:** 104 seats.
V menu. Bar. Wheelchairs.

Hadskis

Cooking score: 3
Modern European | £28
33 Donegall Street, Belfast, Co Antrim,
BT1 2NB
Tel no: 028 9032 5444
jamesstandco.com
£30

Named after the family which once forged
iron pots and pans on this site, this slick bistro
makes the most of its location down a cobbled
alleyway in Belfast's Cathedral Quarter. Run
by Niall McKenna of James St (see entry), the
dining room sports a pared-back look with
muted colours, bare tables and counter stools
facing the open kitchen, while the menu is a
mix of fashionable small plates, grills and
brasserie-style dishes with strong
Mediterranean overtones. Start with a

seasonal taster of cured mackerel and pickled
rhubarb or a bright salad of fennel, quinoa and
blood orange before a slab of beef from
County Tyrone or a combo of veal rump, red
wine and radicchio with a Taleggio risotto and
gremolata. Daily specials are worth noting,
and you could finish with a fruit tart or
coconut rice pudding with sherry prunes.
Weekend brunch, frisky cocktails and a savvy
global wine list complete the offer.
Chef/s: Alan Doyle. **Closed:** 25 and 26 Dec, 1 Jan,
Easter Sun, 12 and 13 Jul. **Meals:** main courses £13
to £24. Early D £19 (2 courses) to £23. **Details:** 80
seats. 10 seats outside. Bar. Wheelchairs. Music.

Il Pirata

Cooking score: 3
Italian | £20
279-281 Upper Newtownards Road,
Ballyhackamore, Belfast, Co Antrim, BT4 3JF
Tel no: 028 9067 3421
ilpiratabelfast.com
£5 OFF £30

Main road premises in the Ballyhackamore
district of Belfast may not look the loveliest
from outside, but readers love the quirky
interior with its tiled walls, kitchen counter
and soft spotlights. Rustic Italian cooking is
the focus of the menus, with simple dishes of
big-hearted flavour. That goes as much for
cicchetti of truffle-oiled and black-peppered
burrata, and nibbles of sourdough bruschetta
topped with 'nduja, cannellini beans and basil,
as it does for main-course showstoppers such
as duck in red wine ragù with gnocchi and
spinach. Those in the market for nothing more
than a plate of pasta won't be disappointed by
pappardelle with traditional meaty bolognese,
its beef and pork braised good and slow, the
whole thing showered with Parmesan. If
you've not quite had enough truffle elsewhere,
it's also in the polenta fritters that make an
irresistible side. Desserts include affogato and
tiramisu but, like the little wine slate, which
opens at £19, aren't exclusively Italian.
Chef/s: Marc Herron. **Closed:** 25 and 26 Dec.
Meals: main courses £9 to £25. **Details:** 84 seats. Vg
menu. Wheelchairs. Parking. Music.

James St

Cooking score: 4

Modern European | £35

21 James Street South, Belfast, Co Antrim,
BT2 7GA

Tel no: 028 9043 4310

jamesstandco.com

Time doesn't stand still even at one of the city's
most established foodie addresses. On James
Street South, Niall McKenna has mixed
things up – those things being his estimable
restaurant James Street South and the adjacent
bar and grill. The rejuvenated James St has
kept the neon artwork and crisp bistro appeal,
and opens all day, keeping pace with city
customers who never know when they might
need a chunk of something local and a glass of
good wine. Although the offering is more
accessible, the kitchen hasn't shaken off the
habit of immaculate sourcing or careful
cooking; from the à la carte, try goat's curd
with broad beans, pearl barley and sorrel,
corn-fed chicken with wild mushrooms and
salt-baked celeriac, or fish cooked simply on
the bone with prawn butter. Powerfully
grilled meat is another speciality, while
desserts such as sticky toffee sundae go straight
for the pleasure points. Wine is listed by style,
favouring France.
Chef/s: David Gillmore. **Closed:** 25 and 26 Dec, 1
Jan, 12 Apr, 12 and 13 Jul. **Meals:** main courses £13
to £34. Early D £20 (2 courses) to £24. Sun L £20 (2
courses) to £25. **Details:** 110 seats. Bar.
Wheelchairs. Music.

Mourne Seafood Bar

Cooking score: 2

Seafood | £30

34-36 Bank Street, Belfast, Co Antrim, BT1 1HL

Tel no: 028 9024 8544

mourneseafood.com

£30

Despite the name, there's no bar at this casual
seafood joint – a younger sibling of the
Seafood Bar in Dundrum Bay. Enter, via a
wet-fish counter that opens on to the street,
into a room with no soft surfaces to absorb the
sound of raucous diners – yet it still manages
to lift the spirits. With all-day opening and a
strong following, Mourne specialises in very
fresh fish with pretty much any taste and
degree of appetite. Crustacea are a given and
there are daily market specials, but the menu
also wends its way from crab croquettes and
seafood chowder with wheaten bread via spicy
fried cod with fries and Thai mayo to a fillet of
hake with butternut squash, chickpea curry
and tempura green beans. Finish with classic
desserts such as sticky toffee pud or chocolate
fondant. In addition, there are risottos and
pasta, and lengthy queues for weekend
lunches. A well-rounded serviceable wine list
starts at £19.75.
Chef/s: Andy Rea. **Closed:** 24 to 26 Dec, 1 Jan, 12
Jul. **Meals:** main courses £12 to £28. **Details:** 80
seats. Music.

The Muddlers Club

Cooking score: 3

Modern European | £55

Warehouse Lane, Belfast, Co Antrim, BT1 2DX

Tel no: 028 9031 3199

themuddlersclubbelfast.com

The atmosphere of bare brickwork, metal
ducting, caged bottle shelves and open kitchen
are very much the new Belfast, and Gareth
McCaughcy's Cathedral Quarter venue
attracts a correspondingly in-the-know crowd
of city diners. Seasonal tasting menus with
wine pairings, available in vegetarian and
vegan guises, are the backbone of the
operation, with a short carte for those who like
to choose. Vibrant combinations abound, as in
Caesar-dressed trout with broccoli, almonds
and roe, or beef tartare with oyster mayo, gem
lettuce and beetroot. Main-course ingredients
are of demonstrable quality, whether you're in
the market for the day's fish catch or miso-
spiked Mourne lamb with artichokes. Round
things off with a dessert composed of flavours
such as lemon, blackberry and white
chocolate, or rhubarb, blood orange and apple.
Cocktails are fun (try the chilli-rimmed spin
on Margarita), and there's a short list of hot-

button wines from Picpoul to Malbec, via biodynamic blush Grigio from the Abruzzi. Glasses from £5.50.

Chef/s: Gareth McCaughey. **Closed:** Mon, Sun, 24 to 26 Dec, 1 to 6 Jan, 14 to 18 Apr, 7 to 20 Jul. **Meals:** main courses £15 to £30. Tasting menu £45 (4 courses) to £55. **Details:** 45 seats. V menu. Vg menu. Bar. Wheelchairs. Music. No children after 9pm.

Ox

Cooking score: 6
Modern European | £50
1 Oxford Street, Belfast, Co Antrim, BT1 3LA
Tel no: 028 9031 4121
oxbelfast.com

£5
OFF

Stephen Toman's place occupies snug but stylish premises overlooking the river Lagan, with Andy Scott's *Beacon of Hope* sculpture just outside. A little creative redesign has exposed the kitchen to public view, but otherwise Ox is in a powerfully steady state, producing seasonally informed, imaginative tasting menus that concentrate on seducing the palate as well as the eye. Here, seasons aren't defined as quarterly but weekly, emphasising the care that goes into sourcing. A February menu opened with truffled and lovaged celeriac broth with chicken skin, before moving to Wicklow venison with turnip in verjus. Fish cookery is rich and compelling, with dulse and sea lettuce pointing up the freshness of turbot in red wine. Tincture of Earl Grey gave Skeaghanore (County Cork) duck with salsify and figs an aromatic presence. Desserts take seemingly disparate elements and make them lifelong friends – rhubarb, white chocolate, almonds and jasmine. Wine pairings are bold but make consummate sense, such as a sturdy Madiran with the duck and luscious Muscat de Rivesaltes with the rhubarb. If you're going your own way with wine, bottles start at £29.

Chef/s: Stephen Toman. **Closed:** Mon, Sun, 23 Dec to 2 Jan, 13 to 21 Apr. **Meals:** set L £22 (2 courses) to £28. Tasting menu £50 Tue to Thur (4 courses) to £60. **Details:** 40 seats. V menu. Vg menu. Bar. Wheelchairs. Music.

Shu

Cooking score: 4
Modern European | £42
253 Lisburn Road, Belfast, Co Antrim, BT9 7EN
Tel no: 028 9038 1655
shu-restaurant.com

Despite the Chinese-sounding name, this smart restaurant set in a Victorian terrace not far from the Windsor Park football stadium is named in honour of the Egyptian god of the air and wind, while the culinary repertoire is modern Irish, with influences from all over Europe. There are cocktails in the basement and private dining on the first floor, with a modern ground-floor dining room and open kitchen in between. Here, a smoked haddock croquette with spring onion aïoli could be the preamble to properly slow-cooked beef bourguignon with roast red onion and mash, or roast cod, which comes in its own red wine sauce with parsley risotto. Main dishes have more obviously the air of classics than do the official Classics, which include wood pigeon in lapsang souchong with celeriac purée and beetroot or caramelised pork belly with cider-soaked raisins, but it's as well not to get hung up on definitions. Finish, classically or otherwise, with blood orange sponge, honey ice cream and citrus curd. Wines start at £6.25 a glass.

Chef/s: Brian McCann. **Closed:** Sun, 24 to 26 Dec, 1 Jan, 12 and 13 Jul. **Meals:** main courses £12 to £32. Set L £15 (2 courses) to £20. Set D £18 (2 courses) to £24. **Details:** 85 seats. 12 seats outside. Bar. Wheelchairs. Music. No children in bar area after 9pm.

Anonymous

At *The Good Food Guide*, our inspectors dine anonymously and pay their bill in full. These impartial review meals, along with feedback from thousands of our readers, are what informs the content of the *GFG*. Only the best restaurants make the cut.

Six by Nico

Cooking score: 2

International | £28

23-31 Waring Street, Belfast, Co Antrim,
BT1 2DX

Tel no: 028 9032 9467

sixbynico.co.uk

£30

From the Glasgow original of the same name
(see entry), Nico Simeone's enterprising
formula of a six-course tasting menu that
changes every six weeks has spawned two
offshoots, in Edinburgh and here in the heart
of the Cathedral Quarter. Small café tables on
a parquet floor, with an open kitchen
overseeing proceedings, form the setting for
themes such as Childhood or The Chippie (the
latter running from chips and cheese to – gulp
– a deep-fried Mars bar).
Chef/s: Nico Simeone and John Wright. **Closed:**
Mon, 25 and 26 Dec, 1 Jan. **Meals:** tasting menu
£28 (6 courses). **Details:** 78 seats. V menu.
Wheelchairs. Music.

Yūgo

Cooking score: 4

Pan-Asian | £30

3 Wellington Street, Belfast, Co Antrim,
BT1 6HT

Tel no: 028 9031 9715

yugobelfast.com

£5 OFF £30

Dangling light shades hover overhead like a
herd (thank you, Google) of sea urchins, leafy
green plants soften the sleekly minimalist
urban space and a long counter overlooks the
chefs at work. If the presentation brings Asia
to mind, the menu duly delivers in the form of
enticing, flavour-packed plates large and
small. Steamed pork dumplings come under
the heading Snacks, while Smalls sees lamb
cutlets matched with potato dumpling and
cumin curry sauce. Bigs might be a hunky
beef short-rib massaman for two, while bao
buns arrive with prawns and wasabi kewpie

(mayo), or hoisin duck with pickled ginger.
Among Sides, hand-cut chips come with
togarashi seasoning, and wok-fried green
beans with spicy pork mince. Lunchtime sushi
includes soft-shell crab futomaki, and
blowtorched scallop with prawn nigiri and
yuzu kosho. A concise wine list and Asian
beers go down a treat with the food.
Chef/s: Gerard Mcfarlane. **Closed:** Sun.
Meals: small plates £5 to £12. Large plates £18 to
£19. **Details:** 40 seats. Wheelchairs. Music.

■ Holywood, Co Down

LOCAL GEM

The Bay Tree

Modern British | £25

118 High Street, Holywood, Co Down,
BT18 9HW

Tel no: 028 9042 1419

baytreeholywood.co.uk

£5 OFF £30

Doors open at 8am and the people they do
come. This all-day café has been serving the
community for 30 years, but has moved with
the times. Smoothies and oats supplement the
morning fry-up, while lunchtime specials
extend to port-glazed chicken livers or an
open sandwich of Cajun-spiced wild Atlantic
prawns. A bistro vibe descends for Friday-
night dinner, when Kilkeel crab rémoulade
with shaved fennel and watercress, and slow-
braised brisket of beef with roasted garlic
mash and red wine and juniper sauce could be
served. Wines start at £16.95.

■ Moira, Co Armagh

Wine & Brine

Cooking score: 4

Modern British | £35

59 Main Street, Moira, Co Armagh, BT67 0LQ

Tel no: 028 9261 0500

wineandbrine.co.uk

£5 OFF

Behind its pristine white exterior, the
McGowans' understandably popular local
venue fairly packs them in. The bare-boarded

floor and open-to-view kitchen feed into the modern-dining aesthetic, and Chris McGowan, a veteran of the *Great British Menu*, has a firm grasp of the contemporary approach. Sourced from estimable regional growers and producers, his menus deal in the likes of cured and torched mackerel with sea lettuce in dashi dressing, with rump and pressed shoulder of glorious Mourne lamb and smoked aubergine to follow. Don't miss the nibbles, though, which set the tone with combinations such as 'nduja and brandade or warm crab brioche roll. Game season delivers a majestic pie featuring woodcock, and desserts could hardly be more comforting than when spice cake comes warm with blood orange curd and mascarpone. The vegetarian repertoire centres on main dishes such as salt-baked carrot, peanuts and smoked yoghurt. A concise wine list extends to a listing of Fine Wines, but prices are agreeably restrained in general, with bottles from £20.

Chef/s: Chris McGowan. **Closed:** Mon, Tue, first 2 weeks Jan, 2 weeks Jul. **Meals:** main courses £17 to £28. Sun L £28. **Details:** 80 seats. V menu. Bar. Wheelchairs. Music.

Portstewart, Londonderry
Harry's Shack
Cooking score: 2
Seafood | £28
116 Strand Road, Portstewart, Londonderry, BT55 7PG
Tel no: 028 7083 1783
£30

The upcycled surf-shed vibe – mismatched wooden furniture and bare boards, the ceiling strung with bulbs, picnic benches outside – suits the gutsy bistro cooking that focuses on the fish and seafood of the abundant surrounding waters. Huge windows ensure you're not denied views of the natural, unspoilt splendour of Portstewart Strand, with its sweeping two-mile stretch of sandy beach (a boon in winter months, when the wood burner's fired up and the coast bears the might of the Atlantic). The brief menu speaks of comfort and sustenance, and you can be sure the fish hasn't travelled far. Haddock coated in a crisp, light buttermilk batter is a popular choice; there's spiced whitebait, bowlfuls of Mulroy Bay mussels, Kilkeel hake given oomph by a tomato and chorizo stew, and burgers if fish doesn't float your boat. Finish with the signature chocolate pot. Drink the house Shacked IPA or choose from the short wine list.

Chef/s: Ian Malcolm. **Meals:** main courses £10 to £13. **Details:** 65 seats. 30 seats outside.

ATLAS MAPS

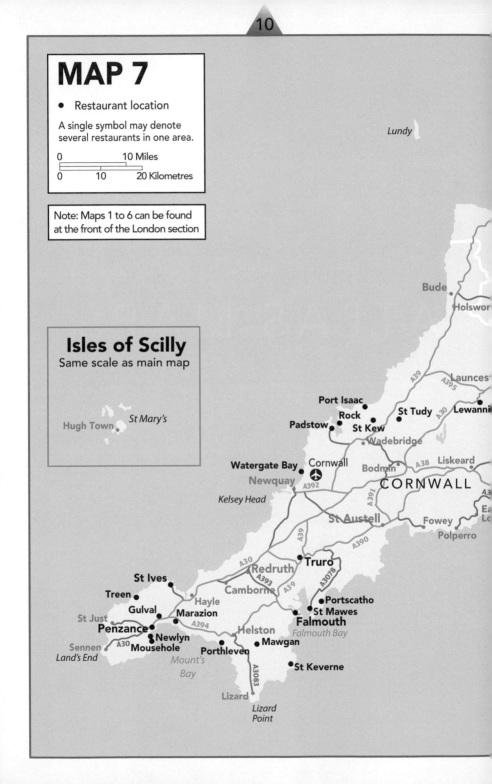

MAP 7

- Restaurant location

A single symbol may denote several restaurants in one area.

0   10 Miles

0 10 20 Kilometres

Note: Maps 1 to 6 can be found at the front of the London section

Isles of Scilly
Same scale as main map

Hugh Town St Mary's

Lundy

Bude
Holswor

Launces
A39 A395

Port Isaac
Rock St Tudy Lewanni
Padstow St Kew A30
Wadebridge

Watergate Bay Cornwall Bodmin A38 Liskeard
Newquay A392 CORNWALL
Kelsey Head A391

St Austell Fowey Ea
  A390 Polperro

A30 Redruth Truro
St Ives A393
Treen Camborne A39
Gulval Hayle Portscatho
St Just Marazion St Mawes
Penzance A394 Falmouth
Sennen A30 Newlyn Helston *Falmouth Bay*
Land's End Mouseholе Porthleven Mawgan
 Mount's Bay St Keverne
 A3083
Lizard
Lizard Point

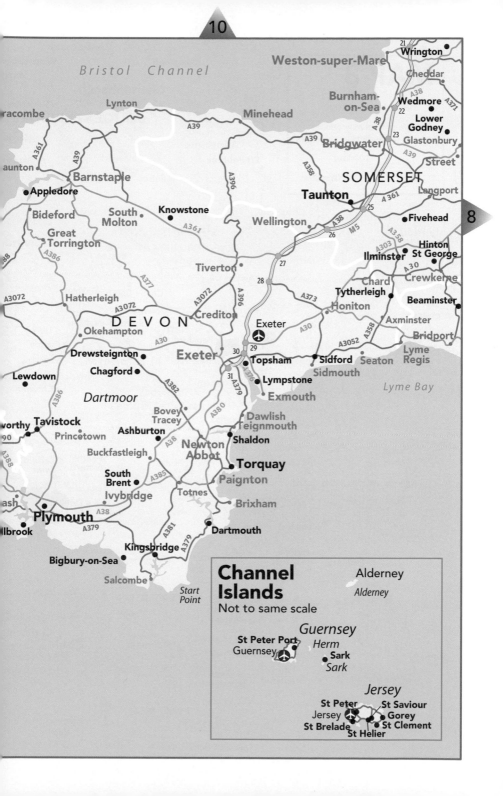

Bristol   Channel

Weston-super-Mare
Wrington
21
Cheddar
Burnham-on-Sea
Wedmore
22
A38
A371
Lower
Godney
23
Glastonbury
Minehead
Lynton
racombe
A39
A361
A39
A39
Bridgwater
Street
A39
aunton
Barnstaple
SOMERSET
Langport
Appledore
A396
Taunton
A361
Knowstone
25
Fivehead
Bideford
South
Molton
A361
Wellington
M5
Great
Torrington
A386
26
A358
Hinton
St George
A303
Ilminster
A30
Crewkerne
Tiverton
27
A3072
A3072
Chard
Tytherleigh
Beaminster
Hatherleigh
A377
A3072
28
A396
A373
Honiton
A3072
Crediton
DEVON
Axminster
A30
Bridport
Okehampton
Exeter
A358
Lyme
Regis
A30
A3052
Drewsteignton
Exeter
30
29
Topsham
Sidford
Seaton
Lewdown
A382
31
Lympstone
Sidmouth
Chagford
A30
A379
A386
Dartmoor
Exmouth
Lyme Bay
vorthy
Tavistock
Bovey
Tracey
Dawlish
Teignmouth
90
Princetown
Ashburton
A38
Shaldon
A388
Buckfastleigh
Newton
Abbot
A380
Torquay
South
Brent
A385
Paignton
ash
Ivybridge
Totnes
Brixham
Plymouth
A38
A381
A379
Dartmouth
lbrook
A379
Kingsbridge
Bigbury-on-Sea
Salcombe
Start
Point

8

Channel Islands
Not to same scale

Alderney
Alderney

Guernsey
St Peter Port
Guernsey
Herm
Sark
Sark

Jersey
St Peter
St Saviour
Jersey
Gorey
St Brelade
St Clement
St Helier

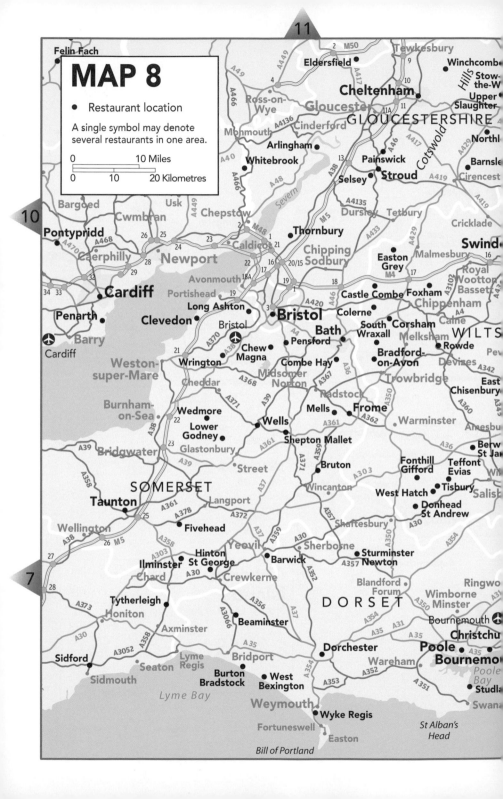

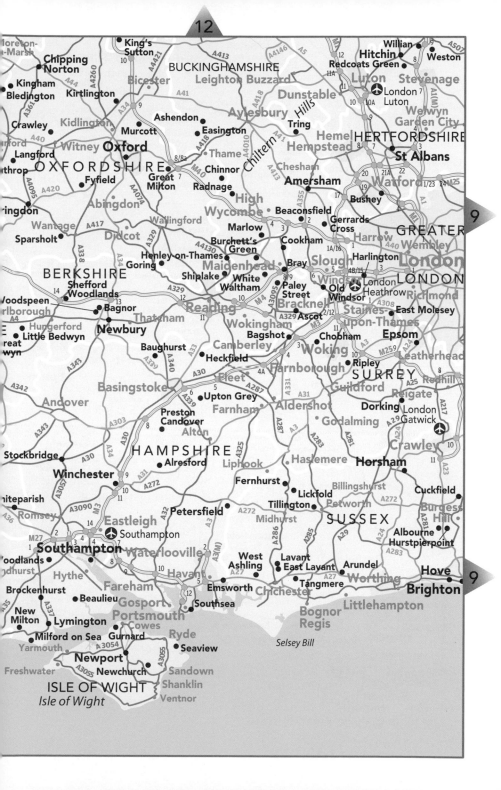

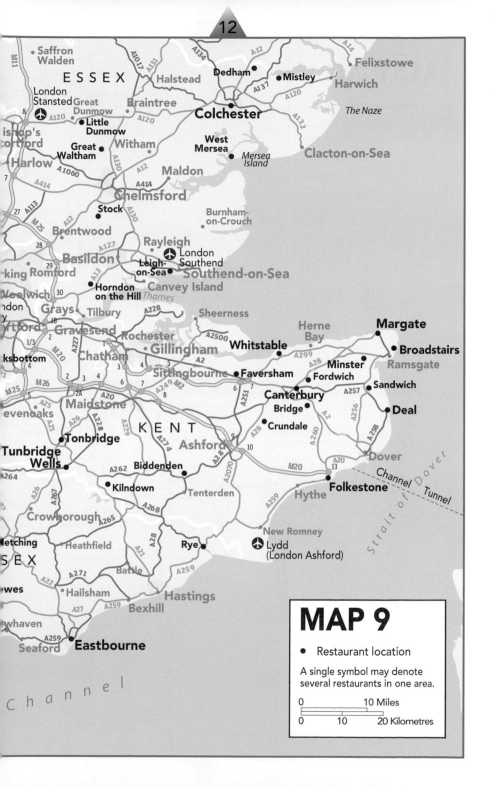

MAP 9

● Restaurant location

A single symbol may denote
several restaurants in one area.

0   10 Miles

0   10   20 Kilometres

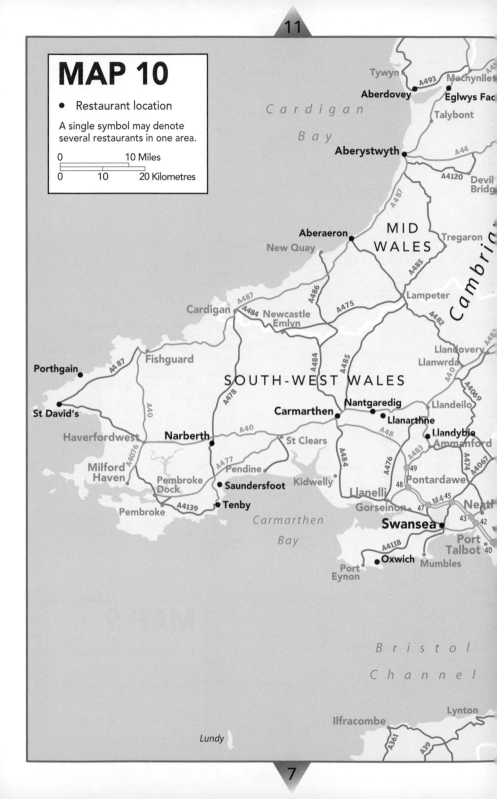

MAP 10

- Restaurant location

A single symbol may denote
several restaurants in one area.

0   10 Miles

0   10   20 Kilometres

Cardigan

Bay

Tywyn
A493
Machynlleth
Aberdovey
Eglwys Fach
Talybont

Aberystwyth
A44
A4120
Devil's
Bridge

A487

Aberaeron
New Quay

MID
WALES
Tregaron

Cambria

A485

Lampeter

Cardigan
A484
A487
Newcastle
Emlyn
A475
A482

A486

Fishguard

A487

Porthgain

St David's

Haverfordwest

Milford
Haven

A4076

Pembroke
Dock

Pembroke

A4139

A478

A40

Narberth

A477
Pendine

Saundersfoot

Tenby

Llandovery
Llanwrda

A40

A40

A4069

SOUTH-WEST WALES

A484

A485

Nantgaredig
Llanarthne

Carmarthen

Llandeilo

Llandybie
Ammanford

A474
A4067

St Clears

Kidwelly

A48

A484

A416

A483
49

48
Pontardawe

A474

Llanelli
Gorseinon
47
M4
45

Neath

Swansea
43
42

Port
Talbot
40

Carmarthen

Bay

A4118
Oxwich
Mumbles

Port
Eynon

Bristol

Channel

Lundy

Ilfracombe
Lynton

A361
A39

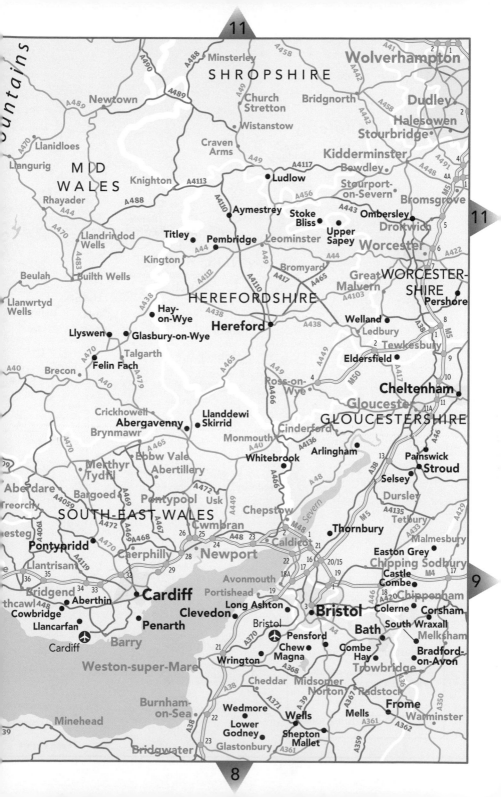

SHROPSHIRE

Minsterley
Wistanstow
Church Stretton
Bridgnorth

Wolverhampton

Dudley
Halesowen
Stourbridge

Newtown

Craven Arms

Kidderminster
Bewdley

Llanidloes
Llangurig

MID WALES

Knighton

Ludlow

Stourport-on-Severn

Bromsgrove

Rhayader

Aymestrey
Stoke Bliss
Ombersley

Droitwich

Titley
Pembridge
Leominster
Upper Sapey
Worcester

Llandrindod Wells

Kington

Bromyard

WORCESTER-SHIRE

Beulah
Builth Wells

HEREFORDSHIRE

Great Malvern

Llanwrtyd Wells

Hay-on-Wye

Pershore

Welland
Ledbury

Llyswen
Glasbury-on-Wye
Hereford
Tewkesbury

Talgarth
Eldersfield

Brecon
Felin Fach

Ross-on-Wye

Cheltenham

Gloucester

Crickhowell
Abergavenny
Llanddewi Skirrid

GLOUCESTERSHIRE

Brynmawr
Monmouth
Cinderford

Aberdare
Treorchy

Ebbw Vale
Abertillery

Whitebrook

Arlingham

Painswick
Stroud

Merthyr Tydfil

Selsey

Bargoed
Pontypool
Usk

Dursley

Pontypridd

SOUTH-EAST WALES

Chepstow
Tetbury

Llantrisant

Caerphilly

Cwmbran
Newport

Thornbury

Malmesbury

Easton Grey
Chipping Sodbury

Bridgend
thcawl

Caldicot

Castle Combe

Aberthin
Avonmouth

Chippenham

Cowbridge
Cardiff
Clevedon
Portishead

Long Ashton
Bristol
Colerne
Corsham

Llancarfan
Penarth
Bristol
Bath
South Wraxall
Melksham

Cardiff
Barry
Pensford
Combe Hay
Bradford-on-Avon

Weston-super-Mare

Chew Magna
Wrington
Trowbridge

Cheddar
Midsomer Norton
Radstock

Burnham-on-Sea
Wedmore
Wells
Mells
Frome
Warminster

Minehead
Lower Godney
Shepton Mallet

Bridgwater
Glastonbury

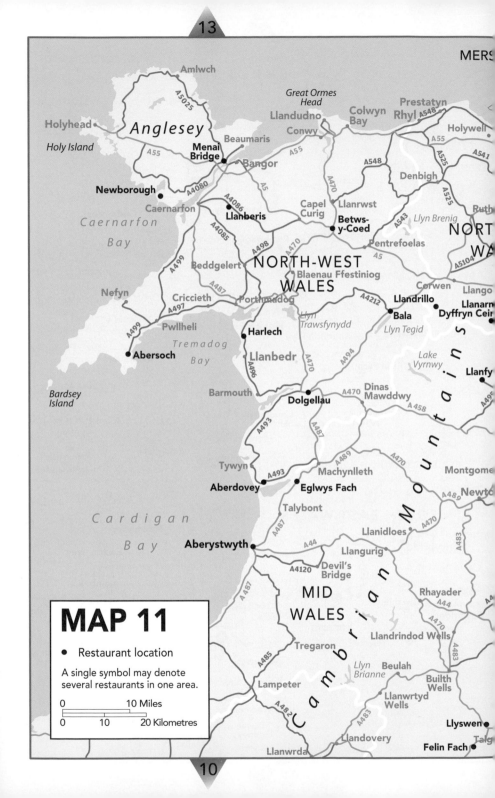

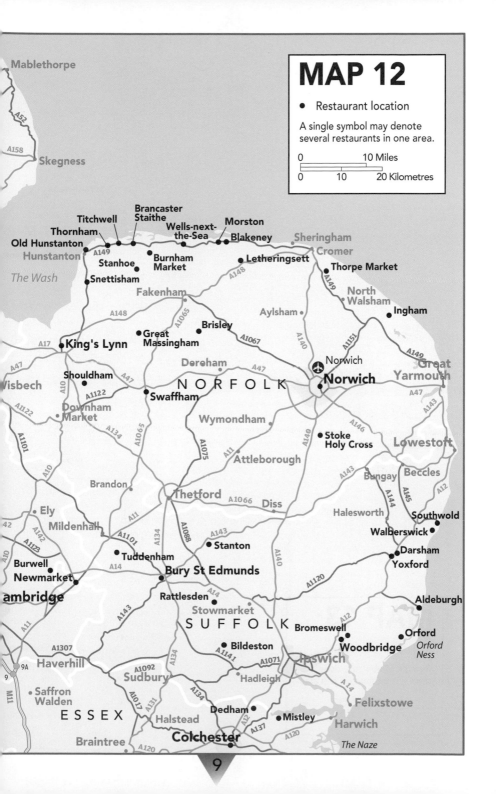

MAP 12

- Restaurant location

A single symbol may denote several restaurants in one area.

0 _____ 10 Miles
0 ____ 10 ____ 20 Kilometres

Mablethorpe

A52

A158

Skegness

The Wash

Old Hunstanton
Hunstanton
A149

Thornham
Titchwell
Brancaster
Staithe
Wells-next-the-Sea
Morston
Blakeney
Sheringham
Cromer

Stanhoe
Burnham Market
Letheringsett
Thorpe Market
Snettisham

Fakenham

A148

North Walsham

Ingham

A148

A1065

Brisley

Aylsham

A149

Great Massingham

A1067

A140

A1151

King's Lynn

A17

Dereham

A47

Norwich

A149

Great Yarmouth

Shouldham

A47

Wisbech

A10

A1122

N O R F O L K

Norwich

A47

A143

Downham Market

Swaffham

Wymondham

A146

Lowestoft

A1122

A134

A1065

A1075

A11

A140

Stoke Holy Cross

A1101

A10

Brandon

Thetford

A1066

Diss

A143

Bungay

Beccles

A12

Ely

Mildenhall

A11

A1101

A134

A1088

A143

Halesworth

Southwold

A144

A145

42

A142

A1123

Burwell

Newmarket

Tuddenham

A14

Stanton

A140

Walberswick
Darsham
Yoxford

Cambridge

Bury St Edmunds

A1120

Aldeburgh

Rattlesden

A14

A143

Stowmarket

S U F F O L K

Bromeswell

A12

Orford
Orford Ness

A11

A1307

Haverhill

Bildeston

A1141

Woodbridge

9A

A1092

Sudbury

A134

A1071

Ipswich

9

Saffron Walden

A1017

A131

A134

Hadleigh

A14

Felixstowe

M11

Dedham

Mistley

Harwich

E S S E X

Halstead

A2

A137

A120

Braintree

A120

Colchester

The Naze

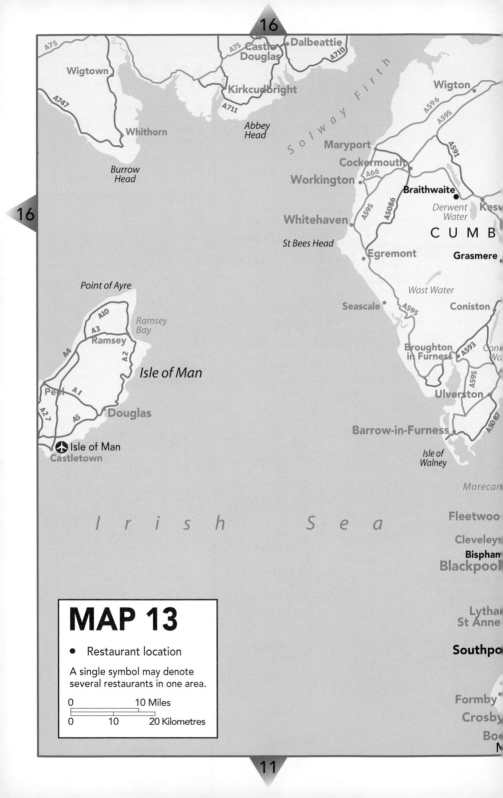

A75
Wigtown

A75 Castle Douglas • Dalbeattie
A710

A747

Kirkcudbright
A711

Whithorn

Abbey Head

Solway Firth

Wigton

A596

A595

Maryport

Cockermouth

Workington
A66

A595 A5086

Braithwaite •

Derwent Water Kes

C U M B

A591

Burrow Head

Whitehaven

St Bees Head

Egremont

Grasmere

Wast Water

Point of Ayre

Ramsey Bay

A10
A3
Ramsey
A2

A4

Isle of Man

Seascale •
A595

Coniston

Broughton in Furness •
A593 Con Wa

A595

Peel A1

A27 A5

Douglas

Ulverston
A590 87

Barrow-in-Furness

Isle of Walney

✈ Isle of Man
Castletown

Morecam

I r i s h   S e a

Fleetwoo

Cleveleys

Bispham

Blackpool

MAP 13

• Restaurant location

A single symbol may denote
several restaurants in one area.

Lytha
St Anne

Southpo

0 ————————— 10 Miles
0 ——— 10 ——— 20 Kilometres

Formby •

Crosby

Bo
N

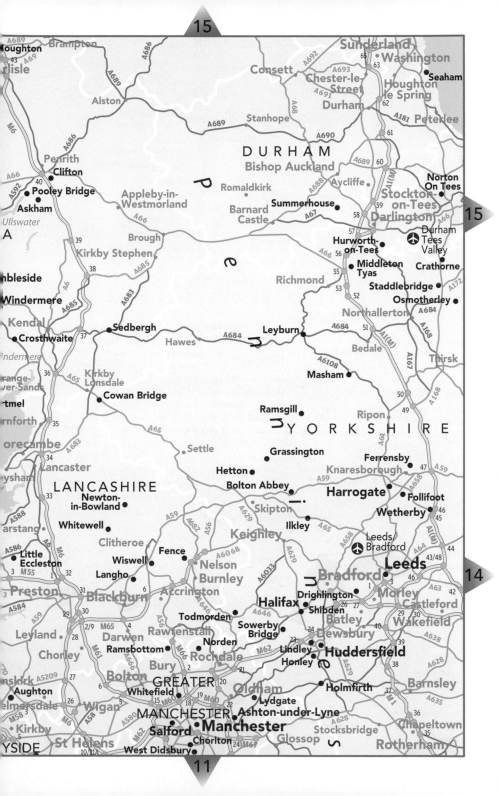

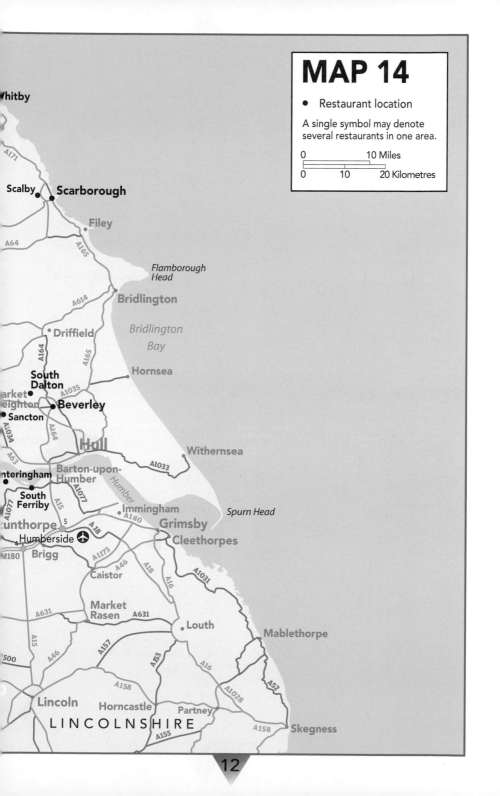

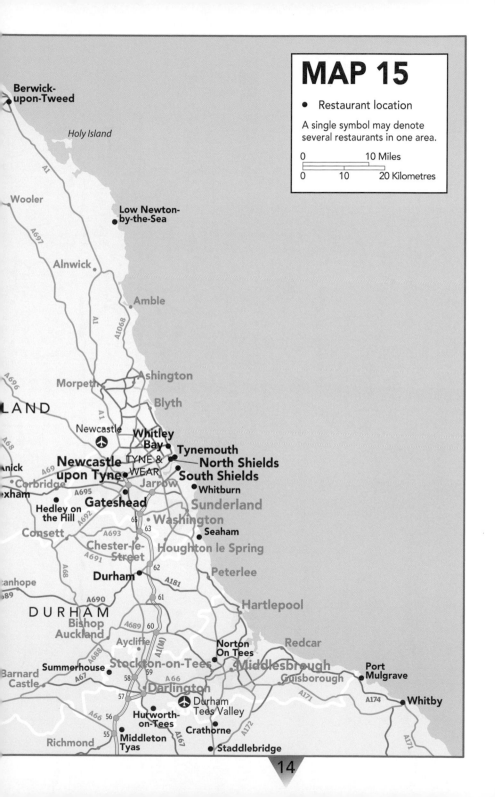

MAP 15

- Restaurant location

A single symbol may denote several restaurants in one area.

0   10 Miles

0   10   20 Kilometres

Berwick-upon-Tweed

Holy Island

Wooler

Low Newton-by-the-Sea

Alnwick

Amble

A696

Morpeth

Ashington

LAND

Blyth

A68

Newcastle

Whitley Bay

Tynemouth

nick

Newcastle upon Tyne

TYNE & WEAR

North Shields

South Shields

Corbridge

Jarrow

Whitburn

xham

A695

Hedley on the Hill

Gateshead

Sunderland

Consett

A693

Washington

Seaham

Chester-le-Street

Houghton le Spring

anhope

Durham

Peterlee

89

A690

61

DURHAM

Hartlepool

Bishop Auckland

A689   60

Aycliffe

Norton On Tees

Redcar

Barnard Castle

Summerhouse

Stockton-on-Tees

Middlesbrough

Guisborough

Port Mulgrave

A67

58   59

Darlington

A171

A174

Whitby

57

Durham Tees Valley

A66   56

Hurworth-on-Tees

Crathorne

Richmond

55

Middleton Tyas

A167

Staddlebridge

14

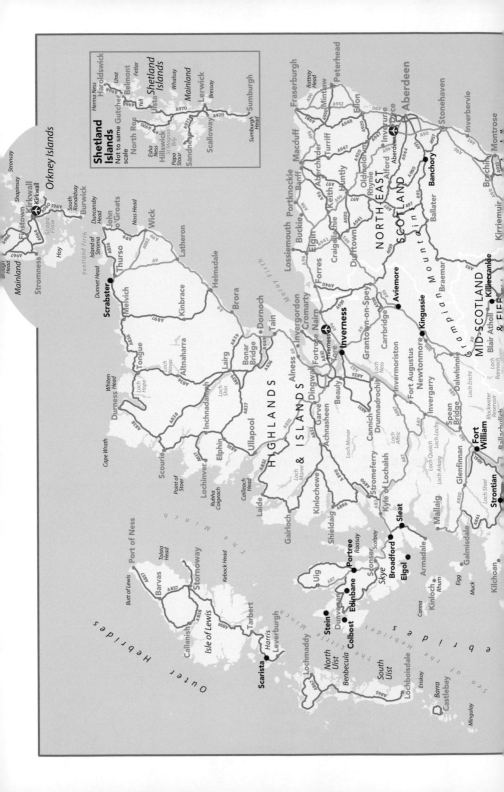

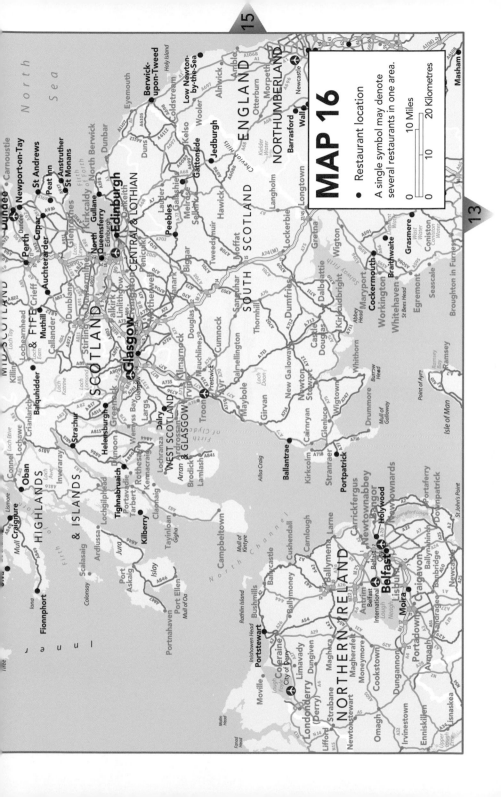

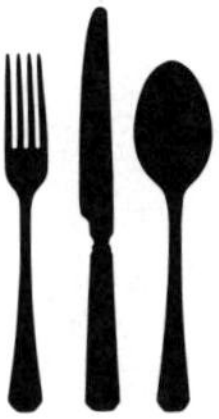

INDEX

Note: The INDEX BY TOWN does not include London entries.

Join us at thegoodfoodguide.co.uk

Join us at thegoodfoodguide.co.uk

Join us at thegoodfoodguide.co.uk

RESTAURANT | INDEX

Thank you

This book couldn't have happened without a cast of thousands.
This is just a sample of the many contributors to whom thanks are due.

Kaz Abbassi
Alex Abbott
Andrew Abbott
Elizabeth Acaster
Alasdair Adam
Judith Adam
John Adams
Karen Adams
Sue Adams
Tom Adams
Beatrice Adamson
Martin Adcock
Clare Addison
Lesley Agutter
Danielle Ahmed
Mohammed Ahmed
John Aird
Dave Airston
Paul Aiston
John Aitken
Mishal Akbar
Jay Alam
Hannah Albone
Kaylee Alden
Lisa Alekna
Anthony Alexander
Dayana Alfred
Akthar Ali
Ismail Ali
Naser Ali
David Allan
Pat Allan
David Allen
Ian Allen
Rosie Allen-Roach
Tessa Allingham
Hatty Almond
Maya Ambrosi
Simon Amey
Denise Anderson
Ian Anderson
Peter Anderson
Rebecca Anderson
Lily Andrews
Martin Andrews
Stephen Andrews
Sebastian Anstey
Anna Anthony
Wendy Anthony
Andrew Appleby
Robert Appleby
Saho Arakawa
Haylea Archer
Luciano Arcuri
Neil Arkley
David Armstrong
Hilary Armstrong

Matthew Armstrong
Ashleigh Arnott
Paul Arthur
Xanthe Arvanitakis
Rachel Ashby
Robin Ashley
Rebecca Ashman
Jane Ashton
Helen Ashwell
Andrew Aspden
Rose Aspinall
Michael Asquith
Chris Astley
Viv Astling
Peter Aston
Margaret Atherton
Nina Athey
Helen Atkins
Joanne Atkins
Paul Atkins
James Attard
Frank Attwood
Helen Aubrey
Nicola Aubrey
Terresa Aubrey
John Aust
Edward Auterii
Sue Axtell
Melanie Ayling
Sue Ayre
Robert Babb
Chris Bacon
Claire Badcock
Andrew Baddeley
Carole Baguley
Jack Bailey
Kathy Bailey
Susan Bailey
James Baird
Emma Baker
Peter Baker
Robyn Baker
Yoanna Baker
Victoria Balduin
Bob Bales
Mandy Ballett
Sandra Balmforth
Filipa Baltazar
Rosemary Banner
Jackie Bannister
Emma Barker
Iain Barker
Sharon Barnea
Mary Barnes
Nicholas Barnes
Steven Barnes
Paul Baron

Alger Barrington
Lisa Barrington-Kay
William Barritt
Barbara Barrow
Ezel Barrow
Ann Barry
Sarah Barry
Emily Bartle
Sally Bartlett
Elizabeth Bartram
Stuart Bartram
Lorraine Bate
Nicolas Bateman
Andrea Batey
Terry Batten
Tim Battle
Jacqueline Baxendale
Megan Baxter
Eddie Bayfield
Nicola Bayliss
Lesley Beach
Charlotte Beadle
Sue Beadle
Russell Beale
Jessica Beard
Peter Beard
Paula Beardsley
Christine Beatty
Stephen Beaumont
Anita Beechey
Chris Beer
Georgina Beetham
Ellie Beggs
Hena Begum
Seema Begum
Jennifer Bell
Nevena Belovodska
Jayne Belton
Tom Bemand
Stephanie Bendall
Johb Bendelow
Emily Bennett
Alexandra Bennigsen
John Bennigsen
Gemma Bentley
Richard Bergson
Rosie Bergson
Sam Berry
Emily Best
Peter Best
W J Best
Simon Bettany
Mike Bevans
Georg Bikritsky
Henrik Bill
Holly Bilous-Jones
Angela Bird

James Bird
Sylvia Bird
Roger Bishop
Susan Bishton
Sally Bisset
Harry Bistock
John Bistock
Diane Black
Heather Blackley
Deborah Blagg
Lesley Blanchard
Charmaine Blatchford
Rebecca Bler
Tracy Blinkhorn
Steven Bliss
Jane Bloomfield
Melanie Board
Kim Bodman
Jacques Boissevain
Peter Bolton
Yasmeen Bond
Joanne Bone
Merlin Bonning
Justin Boorman
Jay Boot
Kim Booth
Vicki Bordewich
Dean Borgazzi
Ken Bourne-Turner
Mary Bowden
George Bowen
Andrea Bowey
Nicholas Bowlby
Douglas Boyle
Matt Boyles
Gill Bracey
Helen Bracher
Anthony Bradbury
Nicholas Bradbury
Ray Bradnock
Charlotte Bradshaw
Martin Brady
Keely Brassington
Michelle Bray
Fiona Braybrook
Lisa Brazil
Alexander Breach
Anne Breese
Karen Brett
Anthony Brewer
Belinda Brewin
Jane Brick
Geoffrey Bridge
Abigail Briggs
Glenn Briggs
Harrison Briggs
Mark Briggs

Morgan Briggs
Katie Brigstock
Julie Briscoe
Caroline Broadley
Caroline Brock
Helen Broderick
Trudy Brolly
Amanda Brooke
Jane Brooke
Karen Brookes
Emma Brooks
Margaret Brooks
Duncan Brooksbank
Marion Brooksbank
Moragh Brooksbank
Sandra Broome
William Broome
Sarah Broomfield
Adrian Brown
Dina Brown
Hannah Brown
Karen Brown
Mandy Brown
Michael Brown
Olivia Brown
Paul Brown
Ray Brown
Stephen Brown
Dayni Browne
Stephen Browne
George Browning
Ann Brownless
Ceri Brugeilles
Elaine Bruton
David Bryant
John Bryant
Val Buckingham
Vivienne Buckland
Laura Buckley
Ian Buckner
Tom Bucks
Richard Bugg
Todd Bullen
Samantha Bullivant
Michael Bunbury
Jennifer Bunn
William Burke
Caroline Burnett
Sam Burnett
Alex Burrow
Helen Burrows
Samuel Burt
Nicholas Busbridge
Ashley Bush
Deborah Bush
Lea Butcher
Georgie Butler

Megan Butler
Robert Butler
Haydn Buxton
Natalie Byrne
Peter Cabara
Kenneth Cairns
Julie Cakebread
Daniel Callus
Marcus Calvani
Stuart Calver
Liz Calvert
Nebibe Cambaz
Lee Cameron
Victoria Cameron
Claire Campbell
Victor Campbell
Philippa Camps
Sarah Canfer
Gemma Canham
Michael Canham
Steve Cann
Julie Cannon
Shonna Cardello
David Carmichael
Hayley Carr
Naomi Carr
Rob Carr
Susan Carr
Mo Carroll
David Carruthers
Louise Carruthers
Victoria Carruthers
David Carter
Andrew Cartwright
Rachael Cartwright
Patrizia Caruana Pisani
Jackie Carubia
Ana Casapu
Giles Casey
Enfys Cashmore
Aernout Casier
Marie Cassidy
Andy Cast
Eirian Castellini
Jose Castillo-Bernaus
Antonio Casula
Harriet Cater
Deniseellen Caton
Lois Caughey
Vicki Cavanagh
Judy Cave
Olivier Certain
Joseph Cesare
Sophie Chadd
Kai Chakartash
Lyn Challis
Rebecca Challis
David Chalu
Jodie Chamberlain
Annie Chan
Stephanie Chan
Danielle Chapman
Elizabeth Chapman
Gill Chapman
Heidi Chapman
Laura Chapman
Karen Charlwood
Heather Charman
Kirsty Cheetham
Michael Cheetham
Sue Chesterman
Alex Cheung
Susan Chilton
Linda Chilvers
John Chittock
Mark Chown
Adam Christie
Richard Christopher
Lore Chumbley
Mauro Ciaccio

Francesco Cinotti
Andreea Ciobanu
Margaret Clancy
Jack Clark
Martin Clark
Gabrielle Clarke
Kathryn Clarke
Mollie Clarke
Samantha Clarke
Stacey Clarke
Stephen Clarke
David Clasper
Pauline Clasper
Daniel Claughton
Elizabeth Clayton
Jo Clayton
Robert Clayton
Mel Clegg
Caroline Clelland
David Clelland
Olivia Clemence
John Clements
Vanessa Clifford
Rachel Clinton
Adam Coates
Emma Cockerham
Roger Cockhill
Richard Code
Paul Codman
Ann Coffey
Emma Coleman
Sarah Coles
Katie Collard
Pip Colledge
Darren Collett
Fabienne Collett
Alison Collins
David Collins
Duncan Collins
Robert Collins
William Collins
Victor Collinson
Angela Colston
Jane Colston
Rebecca Compton
David Congreave
Lisa Coniry
Hilary Coogan
Ben Cook
Christopher Cook
Helene Cook
Phil Cook
Theresa Cooke
Philippa Cookson
Rachel Coombe
Ruth Coombs
Janice Cooney
John Cooney
Cynthia Cooper
Jacqueline Cooper
Kate Cooper-Owen
Rachel Coquard
Amanda Corn
Sonia Costa
Carole Costin
Christopher Cottam
Andrew Cotterill
Tracy Cottingham
Peter Couch
Alex Coulcher
Louise Couzens
Nigel Coverdale
John Cowell
Jim Cownie
Caroline Cox
Victoria Cox
Ann Coxhead
Joanna Craft
Carson Crandall
Gill Crawley

Angie Cresswell
David Crisp
Arron Croad
Helen Crofts
Neville Croker
Emma Crook
Jacqui Crook
Wave Crookes
Rebecca Cross
Joanna Crossley
Emma Crouch
Roger Crow
David Crowshaw
Luke Crowther
David Crozier
David Crutchley
Mae Cumming
Amy Cundal
Martin Cundey
Terence Cunnane
Maggie Currie
Emma Curry
Diane Curtis
Sian Curtis
Wendy Cussens
Rachel Cutting
Wendy Dadd
Craig Dainton
Helen Dallison
Alexander Daniel
Paul Daniel
Jemma Daniels
Lynda Daniels
Samantha Dare
Roben Das Gupta
Lynne Davenport
Joanna Davey
Sarah Davidson
Alun Davies
Barbara Davies
Julie Davies
Lisa Davies
Oliver Davies
Richard Davies
Shella Davies
Danny Davis
Gill Davis
Kara Davis
Rupert Davis
Sean Davis
Gerald Davison
Helen Davitt
Angela Dawson
Kimberley Dawson
Sally Dawson
Tom Dawson
Matt Day
Sheila Day
Roz Deacon
Pascal Deacor
Rosie Deakin
Andrew Dean
Gemma Debono
Jonathan Decker
Bruno Declynsen
Terri Deeney
John Deer
Miranda Deer
Mason Deevey-Ryan
Theresa Deevey-Ryan
Lucy Delap
Joel Delhopital
Nicholas Dellanno
Vincenzo Dellapietra
Anthea Delmar
Lisa Demetriou
Kim Denholm
Clare Denison-Pender
Pippa Dequincey
Aurelia Destrez

Thomas Devries
Carolynn Dewaal
Punam Dhakal
Allan Dickie
Luca Dickie
Andrea Dickinson
James Dickinson
Matthew Dickinson
Katie Dickson
Sarah Dilley
Angela Dilnot Smith
Nicholas Dimmock
Erato Dimopoulou
Brian Dive
Elizabeth Diver
Claire Dixon
Dawn Dixon
Paul Dixon
Helen Dobb
Martin Dodd
George Dodsworth
Peter Dolan
Natalie Donald Trinh
Hannah Donbavand
David Donoghue
Jodie Donoghue
Lisa Donoghue
Ingrida Dornbrook
Steven Dow
Chris Dowling
Suzanne Dowling
Julia Downer
Carol Downes
Gerald Doyle
Paul Drabble
Zoe Draper
Michaela Drosten
Celia Drummond
Derek Dryden
Bridget Dudgeon
Chris Dudley
Linda Duffin
Beryl Duffus
Ian Duke
Deo Duncan
Julie Dunlevy
Annette Dunster
Clive Dutson
Lin Dutton
John Dyer
James Easley
Mary Easterbrook
Lindsay Easton
Sara Eastwood
Michelle Eccles
Gary Eckersall
Claire Eden
Gail Edensor
Susan Edge
Andrew Edmiston
Judith Edwards
Karin Edwards
Kim Edwards
Liz Edwards
Malcolm Edwards
Millie Edwards
Pete Edwards
Roy Edwards
Stephanie Edwards
Steve Edwards
Sue Edwards
Susan Edwards
Brian Edye
Elisabeth Egelund
Tony Elckmbe
Myra Elderfield
Ray Elderfield
Johnathan Eliot
Paul Eliott
Cara Elkin

Jameica Ellaway
Jude Eller
Jennifer Elliot
Catherine Elliott
Louis Elliott
Neil Elliott
Jade Ellis
Joanna Ellis
Maria Ellis
Rupert Ellwood
Jacob Emerson
Marie Endean
Matt England
Sandra England
Jane English
Jasmine Entwistle
Francesco Errico
Ellen Evans
Ian Evans
Jon Evans
Josephine Evans
Julie Evans
Kate Evans
Margaret Evans
Nathan Evans
Toni Evans
Claire Evennett
Joanna Ewing
Norma Fabri
Tom Fahey
Neil Fairbrother
Jacqueline Faller
Deborah Fanning
Andrew Farkas
Adam Farley
Gill Farrow
Harry Farrow
Penny Farrow
Gill Faulding
Samantha Faull
Danielle Fear
Richard Fegen
Alan Fellows
David Fenn
Gordon Fenn
Greg Fenn
Ian Fenn
James Fentiman
Peter Ferguson
Robin Fern
Carrie Ferris
Debbie Figgis
Neville Filar
Elizabeth Finlay
Brenda Finn
Paul Finnegan
Diane Firby
Jason Fisher
Joanne Fisher
Mandy Fisher
Paul Fisher
Esther Fishwick
Laura Fitz-Costa
Ben Fitzgerald
Sheila Fitzgerald
Wendy Fitzgerald
Gary Fleming
Joanne Fleming
Chris Fletcher
Jane Fletcher
Lisa Flude
Jenny Foden
Gillian Fogg
Angela Folwell
Ian Forbes
Nicholas Ford
Genhary Forscourt
Peter Fosker
Ann Foster
Mandy Foster

Natasha Foster
Rebecca Foulkes
Alison Fountain
Lizzy Fowle
Robert Fowler
Christine Fox
Josephine Fox
Sian Fox
Ella Francis
Emily Francis
John Francis
Nick Francis
Simon Francis
Alan Franck
Silvana Franco
Tara Franklin
Jane Fraser
Jeffrey Freedman
Jacky Frere
Susan Friswell
Derek Frost
Innogen Fryer
Catherine Fuell
Vicki Furphy
Sam Gallagher
Wendy Galloway
Roman Ganenko
Anthony Gannon
David Ganz
John Garden
Lou Gardner-Thomas
Nicola Garland
Mary Garner
Peter Garner
Gareth Gates
Felicity Gathe
Anthony Gatrell
Stefan Gatti
Michael Gaylor
Paul Geary
Andrew Geeves
Jamieson Gellatly
Richard Gelling
Martin George
Melinda Gerard
David Gerrard
Kieran Gibbons
Hilary Gibbs
Karen Gibson
Kevin Gibson
Susan Gilbert
Pauline Gilchrist
Wendy Gill
Courtney Gillibrand
Ray Gilliland
Alison Gillings
Paul Gillyon
Denise Giorgi
Chris Glass
Linda Glass
Lucy Glass
Margaret Glasspoole
Eric Gledhill
Houghton Gledhill
James Glennie
Poppy Glossop Hillam
Eleanor Glover
Toni Gockel
Martin Goddard
Polly Godden
Angela Godsall
Clare Goff
Laura Gomez
Simon Good
Amy Goodfellow
Joel Goodlet
Grant Goodman
Jonathan Goodwin
Mary Goodwin
Mike Goolden

Lucien Gordon
Paul Gordon-Saker
Alun Gorgon Adamson
Amanda Gracey
Liz Grady
Donald Graham
Georgia Graham
Matthew Grainge
David Grant
Dale Grassby
Alison Gratton
Thomas Graves
David Gray
Lawrence Greasley
Josh Greatrix
Kim Greaves
Victoria Grech
Allen Green
Andy Green
Brett Green
Caroline Green
Denis Green
Howard Green
Keith Green
Martin Green
Rosie Green
Scott Green
Tony Green
Fraser Greenhill
Michael Greenwood
Tracey Greenwood
Lynne Gregory
Nicky Gregory
Val Grey
Jackie Grice
Trevor Grice
Richard Griffith
Sheila Griffiths
Jim Grimes
Steve Grimsley
Alan Grimwade
Eleanor Groves
Steve Groves
Susan Groves
Dominika Grund
Annice Grundy
Ian Grundy
Roopa Gulati
Jessica Gunn
Ian Gunning
Francesca Guppy
Pranaya Gurung
Rod Gutteridge
Mary Gwynn
Pauline Gysbers
Laura Hadland
Brian Hagger
Sam Haine
Ally Hales
Sarah Halford
Daniel Hall
Glyn Hall
Kris Hall
Lucy Hall
Rachael Hall
Sarah Hall
Julian Hallett
Cara Halling
Christine Halliwell
David Hallowell
Danny Hamilton
Douglas Hamilton
Gordon Hamilton
Martine Hamilton
Penny Hammond
Sharon Hammond
Tracy Hammond
Albert Hampson
David Hancock
George Hannison

Sarah Harbour
Jennifer Hardington
Matthew Hardman
Angela Hardwick
Tom Hardy
David Haresign
John Hargress
Sarah Harland
Rachel Harries
Adrienne Harris
Aimee Harris
Alan Harris
John Harris
Charlotte Harrison
David Harrison
Holly Harrison
Phil Harris
Roger Harrop
John Hartley
Barry Hartshorne
Dawn Harvey
Louise Harvey
Samantha Harwood
Craig Hasson
Elizabethm Hawksworth
Jill Hayes
Donald Haywood
Barbara Hearn
Alan Heason
Angela Heath
Ann Heath
Peter Heath
Matthew Heaton
Elliot Hedley
Julian Hedley
Lucy Hedley
Joseph Hedworth
Tarn Heeks
Katy Hemmings
Anne Hemsley
David Hemy
Nigel Henderson
Cameron Hendey
Mat Henning
Dan Herbert
Sarah Herriman
Barbara Hervas
Ramperez
Shelley Heseltine
James Heslegrave
Michael Hession
Francesca Hetherington
Clive Hewgill
Anne-Marie Hewitt
Deborah Hewitt
Spencer Hewitt
John Hicks
Bethany Hill
Nicola Hill
Sally Hill
Ross Hilliard
Susan Hills
Barbara Hilton
Danielle Hilton
Kay Hinde
Martha Hine
Rachel Hine
Katie Hitchen
Mandy Hobbs
Peter Hobson
Michelle Hodder
Miriam Hodge
Annie Hodges
Hayley Hodgkinson
Karen Hodgson
Philip Hodgson
Robert Hodgson
Brent Hofman
Claire Hogarth
Katherine Holbrook

Nicola Holcombe
Christine Holdcroft
James Holden
John Holland
Sam Hollick
Jeff Hollingworth
Jordan Hollingworth-Bickle
Mike Hollis
John Holloway
Peter Holloway
Alison Holt
Meryl Homer
Robert Hoolahan
Sarah Hopcroft
Richard Hopkinson
Karen Hopwood
Nick Hopwood
Fiona Horigan
Rachel Horigan
Steve Horigan
Angie Horney
Amy Horrigan
Joyce Horwood
Claire Houchell
Michelle Houkes
Carmel Howard
Philippa Howell
Tim Howland
Michael Howlin
Adam Howse
Amanda Hoyle
David Hoyle
Gillian Hoyle
Kay Hoyle
Diane Hubbard
Maria Hucker
Susan Hucker
Joanne Hudson
Kerim Hudson
Michael Hudson
Claire Hughes
Doreen Hughes
Gina Hughes
Kirstie Hughes
Rebecca Hughes
Tracy Hughes
Will Hughes
William Hughes
Amy Hughes-Tiley
Nathan Hui
Rachael Humphrey
Nigel Humphries
David Hunt
Helen Hunt
Karen Hunt
Natasha Hunt
Angela Huntley
Reginald Hurrell
Tom Hurrell
Sopna Hussain
Marie Hussey
Ruben Hussey
Debbie Hutchinson
Jeanette Hutchinson
Philip Hyde
Veronica Ierston
Eluned Ikin
Nick Ikin
Clare Inglesham
Jane Inglis
Dan Ingram
Rosanna Innes
Sajid Iqbal
Greta Iredale
Charlie Irvine
Robert Isaac
Stephen Isaac
Tatum Isaacs
Salun Issa

Annabel Jackson
Gilly Jackson
India Jackson
Kirsty Jackson
Esther Jackson-Taylor
Nicola Jago
Alistair James
Bruce James
Jeremy James
Mark James
Sandra Jameson
Lauren Jameson
Nigel Jamieson
Robert Jamieson
Angelika Jarecka
Alison Jarvis
Ian Jarvis
Katie Jefferson
Craig Jeffery
Sue Jefferys
Haydn Jeffreys
Samantha Jenkins
Steven Jenkins
Victoria Jenkins
Andrew Jenner
Susan Jennings
Emma Jennings-Frisby
Alex Jessop
Androula Joannou
Edward John
Steve Johns
Christine Johnson
Lindsey Johnson
Nicola Johnson
Sadie Johnson
Jamal Johnston
Julie Johnston
Beverley Johnstone
John Johnstone
Abigail Jones
Adam Jones
Amanda Jones
Bradley Jones
Christine Jones
Christopher Jones
Damian Jones
Daniel Jones
David Jones
Edwin Jones
Evan Jones
Gail Jones
Gavin Jones
Gemma Jones
Gillian Jones
Heather Jones
Helen Jones
Hilary Jones
Ian Jones
Julie Jones
Kath Jones
Kaye Jones
Llio Jones
Marian Jones
Matt Jones
Nell Jones
Rachel Jones
Richard Jones
Teresa Jones
Vanessa Jones
Samara Jones-Hall
Carl Jordan
Alan Josey
Chloe Judd
Suki Kainth
George Kane
Maurice Kane
Momoko Kashiwabara
David Kaye
Charmian Kayes
Sally Keane

Wendy Keeble
Stephen Keeley
Sarah Keir
Tina Kekoe
Jane Kellett
Catherine Kelly
Helen Kelly
Beth Kennedy
Stuart Kennedy
Patricia Kenny
Richard Kenyon
Samuel Keong
Mante Kerbelyte
Andrew Kerr
Celia Kerr-Patton
Catherine Kershaw
David Kershaw
Marian Ketchin
Jilly Key
Mohammmes Khan
Cath King
Rebecca King
Sebastian King
Michael Kingerlee
Beckie Kingsnorth
Katie Kininmonth
Sarah Kipping
Michelle Kirby
Holly Kiri
Amanda Kirk
Ed Kirk
Mark Kirkbride
Barbara Kirton
Robin Kirton
Susanne Knapp
Ryan Knapton
Ben Knight
Chris Knight
Jamie Knight
Piers Knight
Penny Kokkali
Jozsef Kondas
Fabian Korner
Dawn Kossick-Plumpton
Karoliina Kreem
Rosemary Kroiter
Gary Krost
Natallia Kunets
Ryota Kurose
Jason Kurtini
Adrian Lacatus
Bex Laird
Michael Laird
Rachel Lake
Ryan Lake
Eileen Laker
Simon Lamb
Ewen Lamont
Annie Lancaster
Daniel Lancaster
Anna Land
Kay Land
Tony Landau
Julian Landy
Sharon Lane
Mark Langley
Ramani Langley
Rhea Langley
John Lansgton
Lee Larking
Richard Latter
George Lavery
Caroline Law
Jessicamae Lawton
Heather Lay
Paul Leadbeater
Gordon Leah
Vanessa Leak
Alan Leaman
Geoffrey Lear

Shane Leavesley
Rhiannon Lebeau
Bansuri Lee
John Lee
Jonny Lee
Seonaid Lee
Steven Lee
Winnie Lee
Laura Leedham
Pam Lees
Ava Lefton
Ricky Leigh
John Lemaire
Denita Lenane
Ian Lennox
Angie Leonard
Emma Leonard
Graham Lever
Viv Lever
Michael Levy
Sarah Lewington
Edward Lewis
Eric Lewis
Jonathan Lewis
Martyn Lewis
Toni Lewis
Jennifer Liggins
Estella Lightfoot
Cathy Limbrick
Roy Lindop
Richard Linnell
Lord Lipsey
June Lister
Michala Little
Karen Littlechild
Stephen Littlechild
Abbey Littler
Charlie Lloyd
Rob Lloyd
Sylvie Lloydfox
Jessica Lobendhan
Allan Lockett
Daniel Loftus
Elaine Loftus
Caroline Lo-Giudice
Kaia Logue
Monica Logue
Rachel Lomas
Tanna Lonergan
Graham Long
John Long
Lesley Long
Mel Long
Matthew Longworth
Barbara Lopez
Jane Lord
Luisa Loughlin
Sarah Louise
Ben Lovell
David Lowe
Diane Lowe
Gillian Lucas
Helen Lucas
Heidi Luck
Amanda Luckett
Magdalena Ludl
Karen Luke
Chloe Lumb
Anna Lupton
Aine Lynch
Spence Lyon
Irene Lysons
David Mabey
Jean Macdonald
Joe Macdonald
Morna Macdonald
Cathy Mackenzie
Katie Mackenzie-Doyle
Peter Mackenzie-
Williams

Clare Mackie
Fiona Mackinnon
Andrew Mackrill
Richard Maclaverty
Gillian Maclellan
Susan Macleod
Michael Maddocks
M Madi
Andi Magill
Bruno Magnani
Alice Maguire
Alan Maine
Amit Maisuria
Annabel Makan
Besmir Malaj
Karolina Malecka
Tomasz Maliszewski
Alison Mallett
Elaine Malone
Hayley Malone
Ovidiu Manaila
Allan Manham
Emily Mann
Juliet Mann
Raynor Manuel
Lara Marks
Charles Markus
Gavin Markwick
Keith Marriott
Ian Marris
Alan Marsh
Alice Marsh
John Marsh
Thomas Marsh
Tomas Marsh
Ian Marshall
Paul Marshall
Sian Marston
St.John Marston
Stjohn Marston
Basil Martin
Graham Martin
Ian Martin
John Martin
Judith Martin
Karen Martin
Leah Martin
Leonie Martin
Lily Martin
Michelle Martin
Nigel Martin
Valerie Martin
Meredith Martinek
Ian Martini
Rita Martins
Cheryl Mason
Helen Mason
Emma Masters
Sarah Matarazzo
Elliot Mates
Geoff Mather
Simon Mather
Midhuna Mathew
Roy Mathias
Paul Mathieu
Louise Matthers
Dominic Matthews
Dorothy Matthews
Laura Matthews
Robert Matthews
Warwick Mattick
Alexandria Maunder
Veronica Maxey
Jonathan Maxfield
Sam May
Kerrie Mayes
June Mayo
Annaick Mazou
Hayley McAllister
Jessica McArdle

Adam McArthur
John McAuley
Sophie McAuley
David McBrien
Scott McCall
Stuarr McCandlish
Sharon McCarney
Kate McConnell
Janet McCook
Kate McCree
Marie McDonald
Clare McDougall
Ruth McElvenney
Kadin McElwain
Erin McEnaney
Tony McEvoy
Tracy McGahey
Natasha McGganity
Mark McGlashan
Tracy McGlone
James McGlynn
Gemma McGoldrick
Barrie McGreevy
Richard McGregor-Johnson
Naouele McHugh
Martha McIntosh
Christine McKay
John McKennall
Michelle McLaughlin
Joan McLeod
Tracy McLoughlin
Gemma McMullan
Ian McPherson
Rachael McSherry
Jonathan Mears
Sarah Mcharg
David Melzack
Shelagh Meredith
Gemma Merot
Deb Merrony
Debbie Merry
Nick Metcalfe
Dafydd Meurig
Amanda Mewins
Kamal Miah
Shahnaz Miah
Jodi Michell
Alastair Michie
Amanda Middleditch
Kasia Mijas-Galloway
Jake Milburn
Corinne Mildiner
Lilly Miles
Christina Millard
Angela Miller
Ann Miller
Barry Miller
David Miller
Edward Miller
Peony Miller
Steve Miller
Alexandra Mills
Lisa Mills
William Mills
Dennis Millward
Rebecca Mill-Wilson
Elaine Milner
Gina Milsom
Chris Minchin
Gillian Mindham-Walker
Robert Mintern
Nikos Mishelakis
Nisha Mistry
Denise Mitchell
Karen Mitchell
Nicki Mitchell
Simon Mitchell
Ciprian Mitrea
David Moffatt

Nailah Mohamed
Adam Moliver
Carrie Molloy
Juan Moncayo
Nigel Montgomery
Caron Morey
Arabella Morgan
Beth Morgan
Charlotte Morgan
Claire Morgan
John Morgan
Keith Morgan
Natalie Morgan
Richard Morgan
Colin Morison
Ruth Morley
Alan Morris
Ann Morris
Caroline Morris
Joshua Morris
Julie Morris
Lucy Morris
Steve Morris
Teresa Morris
Nadine Morriss
Simon Morriss
Terry Morrow
Kelly Morson
Marina Morton
Stacey Morton
Ned Moseley-Turner
Adele Moss
Shirley Moss
Mariam Motamedi
Laura Mottram
Gary Mountford
Jonathan Moyse
Rebecca Muller
Laura Mulligan
Paul Mulligan
Steve Munro
Colette Murphy
Grainne Murphy
Mariel Murphy
Rhys Murphy
Cath Murray
Susan Murton
Chris Myddleton
Jean-Mary Myers
Gillian Nairn
Dominic Nancekievill
Lisa Nash
Barry Natton
Tatiana Nazarova
Helen Neal
Stehen Neale
Bridget Neame
Rachel Neame
Ricky Negus
Ashiqun Nehar
Karen Neil
How Nesbitt
Sarah Nesfield
Ian Neville
Rod Newbery
Katie Newham
Carol Newman
Dawn Newman
Jamie Newman
Mary Newman
Paul Newman
Alison Newton
Jeffrey Ng
Tien Ngo
Sophie Nguyen
Corinne Niccoli
Angela Nicholls
Maggie Nicholls
John Nicholson
Sue Nicholson

Gary Nichol-Velt
Laura Nickoll
Alison Niddrie
Hamoudi Niff
Fred Nilsen
Samantha Nirthcote
Dan Nobu
Peter Noke
Anita Norman
Charlie Norman
Victoria Norris
Karl North
Kerry North
Letas Novichok
Gillian Nowell
Patricia Nugent
Mandy Nutt
Jane Nuttall
Danielle Oakford
Jim O'Brien
Talis O'Brien
Billie O'Connor
Maeve O'Driscoll
Nicky Oehl
Edna Ogden
Matt Ohalloran
Joanne O'Hare
Patricia Oldcorn
Charlotte Olivares
Jemma Oliver
Susan Olliver
Terry Olpin
Adele Onder
Christine Openshaw
Andrei Orange
Janet Orchard
Dave Ord
Kayley O'Riordan
Marc Orme
Michelle Orme
Mark Ormrod
Anna Orton
Carol Osborn
Mark Osborne
Richard Osborne
Gaynor Osborne-Leeds
Kieran O'Shea
Jonathon Ostick
Olivia O'Sullivan
Karen Outhwaite
Beverley Owen
Deborah Owen
Helen Owen
Nicholas Owen
Alex Pace
Stephen Page
David Pallier
Ben Palmer
Cathy Palmer
Desmond Palmer
Dinah Palmer
Hilary Palmer
Richard Palmer
Valerie Palmer
Chung Pamela
Audrey Pantelis
Natalie Papworth
Vicki Park
Charlotte Parker
Gail Parker
John Parker
Laura Parker
Maggie Parker
Sue Parker
Paul Parnell
Jeffrey Parrott
Lee Parry
Graeme Partridge
Katrina Partridge
Derek Paterson

Marios Patsalis
Nick Patton
Becky Paull
Ian Pawley
Daniel Pay
Emma Payne
James Payne
Magdalena Payne
Francesca Payton
Diana Peace
Abigail Pearce
David Pearce
Theresa Pearce
Alun Pearson
Ruth Pearson
Stuart Pearson
Zekai Pekri
Janet Pender-Cudlip
Michael Pender-Cudlip
Mike Pendleton
Angela Penfold
Giles Pepler
Annette Perfect
Ross Perfect
Charles Perkins
Silvia Perruzza
Alan Pettitt
Catrin Petty
Tracey Pheby
Matthew Philip
Teresa Philip
Amy Phillips
David Phillips
Julie Phillips
Mandy Phillips
Jayne Pickston
David Pickup
Calvin Pillay
Susan Pilling
Mezcal Pinto
Stephen Pitfield
Shaun Pitt
Rhea Platt
Robert Platt
Ian Platten-Higgins
Jeannie Pleban
Maureen Plumpton
Patrick Polome
Philippe Ponton
Gill Poore
Annette Pope
Michele Pope
Octavian Popovici
Matteo Porpora
David Porter
Jamie Porter
Nadia Porter
Mark Porterfield
James Portway
Sarah Possingham
Kostas Postica
Ian Potter
Howard Potts
Michael Power
Mette Poynton
John Pratt
Mark Presney-Archer
Rosemarie Prest
Johannes Pretorius
Anne Price
Catherine Price
Maria Price
Michael Price
Nigel Price
Sandra Price
Margaret Pritchard
Barry Probert
Severine Proctor
Sue Proctor
Steve Prower

Norman Pryce
Charlotte Pugh
Claire Pullinger-Murray
Terri Puplett
Derek Purnell
Helen Pye
Rosaline Quinlivan
Anna Quinn
Nancy Race
Navi Rahman
Alan Rainford
Aditya Raja
Nadine Ramsay
Nicholas Ramsbottom
Mark Randall
Ronald Rankine
Malcolm Ranson
Lauren Rastall
Peter Ratzer
Tim Rawlings
Sharon Rawsterne
Jenna Rayner
Ian Rayney
Chris Read
Paul Reading
Sophie Reap
Daniel Redfern
Jack Redfern
Philip Redmond
Margaret Reed
Mike Reed
Amy Reeves
Susan Reeves
Amanda Reid
Meena Reid
Steve Rencontre
Brian Restall
Claire Reuben
Patrick Reubinson
Jenny Revell
Jane Reynolds
Jennifer Reynolds
Emma Rhoden
David Rhodes
Luke Rhodes
Lucy Rhys-Williams
Kathleen Ribeiro
Gillian Richards
Peter Richards
Geoff Richardson
Glenn Richardson
John Richer
Jasmine Ricketts
Joanne Riding
Johngerrie Ridley
Norman Rigby
Richard Rigby
Florence Riley
Martin Riley
Rebecca Riley
Sarah Riley
Zach Riley
Cynthia Riordan
Kim Rivers
James Robbins
Richard Robbins
Adrienne Roberts
Evelyn Roberts
Hannah Roberts
Jeenie-Leigh Roberts
John Roberts
Kate Roberts
Katy Roberts
Marsha Roberts
Paul Roberts
Gemma Robertson
Jim Robertson
Robert Robertson
Hayley Robinson
Iain Robinson

Maria Robinson
Paul Robinson
Polly Robinson
Roderick Robinson
Karen Robson
Cristina Rodriguez
Maria Rodriguez
Peter Roe
Chrissie Rogers
Claire Rogers
Daniel Rogers
Jasmine Rogers
Louise Rogers
Rosemary Rogers
Susan Rogers
Tim Rogers
Sarah Rogerson
Louis Rohl
Jack Rooke
Rosie Roots
Hollie Roper
Ed Rosa
Kim Rose
Rob Rose
Siggi Rosen-Rawlings
Michael Rosenthal
Catherine Ross
Stuart Ross
Tamzine Rosser
Joe Rossiter
Rebecca Rossiter
Lin Rothwell
Alison Rouse
Glenda Rousseau
Emma Roustoby
Colin Rowe
Rosalind Rowett
Benjamin Rowland
Anne Rowlands
Cadi Rowlands
Louisa Rowlandsds
Anne-Marie Rowley
Chris Rowley
Bibi Roy
Elaine Rudge
Frederic Rufin
Pran Rughani
Marta Ruiz
Jean Rundle
Jan Rush
Celene Rushbrook
Annette Russell
George Russell
Jonathan Russell
Ashley Rustage
Teresa Ruszala
Arvis Ruters
Sandra Rutman
Bruce Ryan
Susan Ryan
John Ryde
Jeff Rymer
Sarah Sabatini
Moira Sabin
Colin Sales
Sallyann Salmon
Keith Salway
Joy Sandbrook
Caroline Sanders
Redland Sanders
Caroline Sandford
Andrew Sangster
Angeli Santos
Lloyd Satchwell
Nailah Sattar
Claire Saunders
Plum Savill
Stephanie Saville
Claire Sawyer
Lorna Sawyer

Lucy Sawyer
Tracy Saxton
Andrew Sayer
Andrew Sayers
Edward Scarf
Jonathan Scarfe
Adelie Schadegg
Simon Schiff
Gill Schlangen
Andy Schofield
Peter Schreiber
Nick Schumann
Thomas Scorer
Hugh Scorgie
Angela Scott
Heather Scott
Kirsty Scott
Mark Scott
Stephanie Scott
Mike Scott-Baumann
Laurie Scott-Nicol
Nancy Sculco
David Sefton
Clara Segon
Clare Selby
Abdul Selemani
Geoffrey Senior
Clare Serginson
David Seth
Dilys Severs
Gareth Severs
Jennette Seviour-Martin
Andy Sewell
Jess Sewell
Wendy Sewell
Mathias Sexton
Gary Shacklady
Dawn Shaefer
Mayur Shah
Paul Shanahan
Peter Shanklin
Margaret Shannon
Sapna Sharma
Annie Shaughnessy
Dawn Shaw
Michael Shaw
Robert Shaw
Laura Sheffield
Janey Sheldon
Anthony Shephard
Nick Sheridan
Brod Sherwood
Margaret Shilling
Gilbert Short
Lee Shorten
Sheila Sillick
Carlos Silvas
Andy Simpson
Christopher Simpson
Edward Simpson
Kaori Simpson
Keith Simpson
Michaela Simpson
Jackie Singleton
Debbie Skelson
Rebecca Slater
Urmita Slater
Andrew Smerdon
Robert Smethurst
Barry Smith
Betty Smith
Brian Smith
Emily Smith
Frances Smith
Gillian Smith
Ian Smith
Kate Smith
Malcolm Smith
Martyn Smith

Mary Smith
Molly Smith
Oliver Smith
Paul Smith
Paula Smith
Peter Smith
Ria Smith
Richard Smith
Robert Smith
Sean Smith
Steve Smith
Trev Smith
Valerie Smith
Richard Smithson
David Snart
Martin Snazell
David Snell
Jude Sockett
Peter Solloway
WeiChieh Soon
Aravind Sopinti
Georgia Southam
Louise Spackman
William Spaight
Matt Spearing
Sinead Spearing
John Speller
Amanda Spence
Claire Spencer
Gordon Spencer
Linda Spencer
Claire Spicer
Louise Spicer
Peter Spindley
Louise Spurdle
Jill Stagg
Georgie Standen
Christine Standeven
Janine Stansell
James Stanton
Daniel Starling
Christopher Stean
Karen Stears
Catriona Steedman
Russell Steedman
Catharine Steele-Kroon
Sue Stephenson
Dick Sterne
Geoff Stevens
Ann Marie Stevenson
Sam Steventon
Jane Stewart
John Stewart
Pam Steyn
Ben Still
David Stimpson
Adam Stockton
Adrian Stokes
Kate Stokes
Camille Stonehill
Andrew Storm
Sophie Stout
Gillian Stowell
Mandi Street
Derek Stride
Trudy Stripp
Craig Stroud
Michael Strzelecki
Neil Stuart
Irene Stubbs
Emma Sturgess
Joanne Sullivan
Sathees Sun
Tony Sunman
Am Supawan
Daishi Suzuki
Annette Swan
Karen Swan
Sarah Sweetland
Jacob Swift

Kirsty Swift
Graeme Swinburne
Kathryn Sword
Paul Sykes
Jane Symonds
Alison Szafranski
Paul Szomoru
Pawel Szweda
Linda Szymanska
David Taberner
Keith Tadhunter
Neil Taggart
Andre Tajchmab
Dave Tappy
Gareth Tartt
Sue Tarvit
Steven Tatworth
Peter Tautz
Elizabeth Tayler
Andrew Taylor
Bryan Taylor
Charlotte Taylor
Ed Taylor
Hazel Taylor
Jane Taylor
Jean Taylor
Jonathan Taylor
Kev Taylor
Lucy Taylor
Margaret Taylor
Mark Taylor
Robert Taylor
Ross Taylor
Ryan Taylor
Sharon Taylor
Steven Taylor
Katherine Taysom
Carys Tecwyn
Brian Telfer
Kaz Terkselsen
Alice Tester
Graham Tester
Michael Tetternborn
Siobhan Thacker
Bryan Thal
Charlotte Thind
Oliver Thind
Ellen Thomas
Glan Thomas
Judith Thomas
Kara Thomas
Michael Thomas
Richard Thomas
Sarah Thomas
Brenda Thompson
David Thompson
Jason Thompson
Lauren Thompson
Fiona Thomson
Helen Thomson
Matthew Thomson
Natalie Thorne
Jonathan Thorne-May
Elizabeth Threlfall
Laura Thumwood
Robert Thurlow
John Tibbells
Seres Tibor
Jane Tierney
Adam Tiffany
Benjamin Tilley
David Tilley
David Tilly
Charlotte Timmins
Teerapong
Tiyaboonchai
Paul Tock
Richard Tomalin
Tara Tomes
Claire Tomkinson

Adam Tomlinson
Carole Tomlinson
Richard Tomlinson
Sian Tomos
Charlie Tonkiss
Selina Toor
Bram Tout
Lesley Townend
Martin Townend
Lottie Towning
Ian Townsend
Chris Traxson
Frank Treeby
David Tregaskes
Angela Trenchard
Beryl Trippick
Reem Trivedi
Byam Trotter
John Trow
Ling Tsang
Theodosis Tsiolas
Carla Turner
Cindy Turner
James Turner
Kathryn Turner
Keith Turner
Louise Turner
Sarah Turner
Gillian Turpin
Jill Turton
Andrew Turvil
Emma Tussaud
Elspeth Twist
Lynn Twitchen
Andrew Tye
Kirsty Tyler
Peter Ugle
Lisa Unsworth
Elizabeth Usher
Ian Usher
Dara Vakili
Sue Vakilzadeh
Colette Vandeberg
Gidy Vangaans
Ettienne Vanstaden
Shane Vant
Cornelis VanWoerkom
Nicole VanWymeersch
Kirsty Varaty
Jonathan Varey
Denise Varley
Debbie Vaughan
John Vaughan
Philip Veal
Allan Venables
Rochelle Venables
Rina Vergano
Sunita Verma
Rob Verrion
Jes Verwey
Max Verwey
Tim Verwey
Ana Viazovskiene
Alexandru Vladulescu
David Voller
Malgorzata Wadas
Richard Wadman
Nick Wagner
Simon Wagstaff
Stuart Wake
Mark Walden
Heather Waldron
Adrian Walker
Barbara Walker
Dominique Walker
Lee Walker
Polly Walker
Sarah Walker
Trevor Walker
Paula Walkling

Donna Wallbank
Susan Wallis
Mike Walsh
Carol Walters
Nigel Walters
Steven Walters
Tania Walters
David Walton
Philippa Walton
Stuart Walton
Jackie Wand-Tetley
Craig Wanless
Nicki Warboys
Becky Ward
Lesley Ward
Martin Ward
Diana Wardley
Vivien Ware
John Warren
Joanne Waterworth
Matt Watkins
Aubrey Watson
Janie Watson
Keith Watson
Tina Watts
Martin Wearne
Gordon Webb
Jonathan Webb
William Webb
Geoffrey Webber
Terry Webber
Annabel Webster
Andrew Welch
Claire Welch
Sophie Wellan
Sarah Weller
Steve Weller
Wendy Weller
Ralph Wellock
Trudi Wells
Pippa Welsh
Sarah Wenden
David Wentworth
Jane West
Richard Westaway
Kathryn Western
Jane Weston
Poppy Wetherill
Spencer Wharton
Hazel Wheeler
Mark Wheeler
Maria Whelan
Abigail Whipp
Elizabeth Whitaker
Joanne Whitcombe
Charles White
Jenny White
Linda White
Richard White
Shane White
Colin Whitehead
Nicola Whitehead
Susan Whitehead
Lisa Whitehouse
Becky Whiteman
Paul Whitfield
Elaine Whitney
Melanie Whittaker
Peter Whittle
Caroline Whyatt
Nigel Wicks
Gill Wight
Chris Wightman
Emma Wilcox
Tony Wilcox
Nigel Wild
Rosie Wild
Barry Wiling
Adam Wilkinson
Rob William

Bethan Williams
Blanche Williams
Caroline Williams
Charlotte Williams
Chelsey Williams
Davis Williams
Ingrid Williams
Jo Williams
Lloyd Williams
Rebecca Williams
Robert Williams
Sara Williams
Sarah Williams
Elizabeth Williamson
Nigel Willimer
Steve Willis
Glenda Willmot
Jill Willmott
Angie Wilson
Jane Wilson
Kay Wilson
Keith Wilson
Lauren Wilson
Ralph Wilson
Ralphg Wilson
Robert Wilson
Sarah Wilson
Barry Winfield
Howard Winik
Chris Winnick
Lacey Winspear
Daniel Winstanley
Josh Winter
Anna Wise
Faye Wolley
Georgie Wood
Huxley Wood
Inez Wood
Jaimie Wood
Matthew Wood
Natasha Wood
Sean Wood
Martyn Woodhouse
Simon Woodroffe
Ken Woodruff
Kate Woods
Mark Woods
Ben Woodward
Emily Woodward
Malcolm Woodward
Steve Wooldridge
Karen Woolerton
Emma Woolfenden
Phil Woollen
Karen Woolton
Katherine Worton
Amanda Wragg
Zara Wrathall
Julie Wray
Philip Wray
Chloe Wright
Elizabeth Wright
Howard Wright
Kelly Wright
Lucy Wright
Melanie Wright
Melanje Wright
Natalie Wright
Peter Wright
Catherine Wrighy
Gosia Wrzeszcz
James Wwd
Louise Yandell
Jennifer Yarnall
Helen Yates
Kevin Yates
Denise Young
Jacqueline Young
Julie Young
Klaudia Zaluszniewska

Longest serving

The Good Food Guide was founded in 1951. The following restaurants have appeared consistently since their first entry in the guide.

The Connaught, London, 67 years

Gravetye Manor, West Sussex, 63 years

Porth Tocyn Hotel, Gwynedd, 63 years

Le Gavroche, London, 50 years

Ubiquitous Chip, Glasgow, 48 years

Plumber Manor, Dorset, 47 years

The Waterside Inn, Berkshire, 47 years

Airds Hotel, Argyll & Bute, 44 years

Hambleton Hall, Rutland, 41 years

The Seafood Restaurant, Cornwall, 39 years

The Sir Charles Napier, Oxfordshire, 39 years

Little Barwick House, Somerset, 38 years

Ostlers Close, Fife, 37 years

Paris House, Bedfordshire, 37 years

The Angel Inn, Yorkshire, 36 years

Brilliant, London, 35 years

Clarke's, London, 35 years

Le Manoir aux Quat'Saisons, Oxfordshire, 35 years

Blostin's, Somerset, 34 years

The Castle at Taunton, Somerset, 34 years

Launceston Place, London, 34 years

Read's, Kent, 34 years

The Three Chimneys, Isle of Skye, 34 years

Tyddyn Llan, Denbighshire, 34 years

Wilton's, London, 34 years

The Lime Tree, Greater Manchester, 33 years

Northcote, Lancashire, 33 years

Cherwell Boathouse, Oxford, 32 years

The Old Vicarage, Derbyshire, 32 years

Le Champignon Sauvage, Gloucestershire, 31 years

Bibendum, London, 30 years

The Chester Grosvenor, Chester, 30 years

Crannog, Highlands, 30 years

Harry's Place, Lincolnshire, 30 years

Ynyshir, Powys, 30 years

Eslington Villa, Gateshead, 29 years

Horn of Plenty, Devon, 29 years

Melton's, York, 29 years

Castle Cottage, Gwynedd, 28 years

Kilcamb Lodge, Highlands, 27 years